Praise for *Truman*

"Perhaps the highest tribute one can pay a biographer is to say that through him one comes to know his subject almost as though in person. In fostering the reader's acquaintance with Harry Truman, not once does McCullough get in the way. This is in every respect a splendid work."

—Myron A. Marty, *St. Louis Post-Dispatch*

"Since I've been in national politics, whenever I've been asked who my favorite political leader of the century is, I have always said Harry Truman. . . . David McCullough has always been a favorite of mine. The Truman biography is outstanding."

—Jimmy Carter, *The Boston Phoenix*

"Exemplary and riveting. . . . The book is like a comfortable Victorian three-decker novel. There are two plots, a hero and heroine, and a glittering cast of characters ranging from Dean Acheson, Churchill and General Marshall to the Pendergasts and General MacArthur, as well as a splendid collection of Shakespearean clowns. . . . McCullough's book will stand for a long time as the outstanding analysis of an extremely important subject: the greatness of Truman, and its role as an exogenous 'cause' in the history of his time."

—Eugene V. Rostow, *Times Literary Supplement,* London

"An impressive and valuable study of Truman, worthy of its subject."

—C. Vann Woodward, *The New York Review*

"Truman is biography as good as it gets, as absorbing and readable as it is voluminous. McCullough writes like a novelist, digs like a zealous reporter and puts things in perspective like the superb historian he is."

—Lorenzo Carcaterra, *People* magazine

"This is the biography of President Harry S. Truman against which not only all other Truman biographies but probably all other presidential biographies will be measured. It is comprehensive, well reasoned, insightful and yet elegantly simple. It is written with a love for the subject that is contagious."

—Steve Weinberg, *The Kansas City Star*

"McCullough takes us on a beautifully guided tour of recent history—a journey that is as much a celebration of American experience as it is a captivating portrait of the ordinary 'man from Missouri' who became an extraordinary figure in the Cold War world. Keeping Truman himself always vividly in the foreground, Mr. McCullough has written a stirring, masterly, thoroughly absorbing book."

—Jean Strouse, author of *Alice James: A Biography*

"We are always at Truman's side, at poker and bourbon and at his high moments. Coverage is complete and fascinating. . . . Now we know Truman in all his candor, courage, straightforwardness, determination and his occasional blunder. . . . This long, penetrating book is biography at its best."

—W. A. Swanberg, *Chicago Sun-Times*

"Sweeping and vivid. . . . As a comprehensive and highly readable account of one of the most American of Americans, this is a distinctive and distinguished volume."

—Hoyt Purvis, *The Dallas Morning News*

"An enthralling and fluidly told surprise-success story. . . . A book that handles an enormous amount of material with deftness, taste, and an acute understanding of Truman's world and the men who made it."

—Rhoda Koenig, *New York* magazine

"Superbly researched and carried forward by McCullough's narrative drive, *Truman* is endlessly readable. The Harry we were all wild about is re-created exactly as Harry was—feisty, preposterous, decisive, tireless, outrageous, but always honorable, always courageous, always guided by his inner gyroscope of conscience and character."

—William Manchester, author of
William Spencer Churchill: The Last Lion

"David McCullough brings Truman vividly to life in this masterpiece of American biography. It's a superb political study and human story."

—Steve Neal, *The Philadelphia Inquirer*

"Splendid . . . an elegantly written, even moving work . . . deserves a wide audience—if nothing else to remind us of what we were and what we had."

—Stanley I. Kutler, *Chicago Tribune*

"Surefooted, highly satisfying biography.... an impressive tribute to a man whose brisk cheerfulness and self-confidence were combined with a God-fearing humility."

—*Publishers Weekly*

"Not only outstanding biography but a great American story as well—by a master of the art. It is about how modern America was made. It is also about character and leadership in a time that needed both."

—Daniel Yergin, author of *The Prize*

"Harry Truman has found his biographer. David McCullough's monumental *Truman* perfectly mirrors its subject—vivid, straightforward, fast moving, intensely human, never boring for a moment. Truman himself once asserted the right to be both a president and a human being; it is McCullough's great achievement as a biographer that he has managed to pin both Trumans to paper."

—Geoffrey C. Ward, author of
The Civil War: An Illustrated History

"David McCullough has a rare gift for combining scholarship with storytelling. His *Truman* ranks with William Manchester's *American Caesar* and Edmund Morris's *The Rise of Theodore Roosevelt* among the finest biographies of our time. To call *Truman* definitive is an understatement. For what Mr. McCullough has created is a vast panorama of American life and politics, from the stagecoach to the space capsule, all swirling around a seemingly ordinary protagonist whose extraordinary qualities make Truman's life a stirring confirmation of democracy at its finest."

—Richard Norton Smith, Director, Herbert Hoover Library

"A fresh, wonderful new biography . . . My only complaint about this marvelous book is how much it makes me miss the old guy with the snappy bow tie."

—Daniel Schorr, *USA Today*

"Plain wonderful."

—Justin Kaplan

"Masterful.... Everyone seems to be reading *Truman*. Those who are sixty years of age or more, and therefore old enough to have adult memories of the man himself, recognize the loving accuracy of McCullough's account. Professional historians of any age will acknowledge that McCullough has done the hard work necessary for good history and has added zest and imagination—qualities often absent from academic writing."

—Gaddis Smith, *The Yale Review*

David McCullough

TRUMAN

SIMON & SCHUSTER PAPERBACKS

New York   London   Toronto   Sydney

SIMON & SCHUSTER PAPERBACKS
Rockefeller Center
1230 Avenue of the Americas
New York, New York 10020

For information about special discounts for bulk purchases,
please contact Simon & Schuster Special Sales:
1-800-456-6798 or business@simonandschuster.com
Designed by Eve Metz
Manufactured in the United States of America

43 45 47 49 50 48 46 44

Library of Congress Cataloging-in-Publication Data
McCullough, David G.
Truman/David McCullough.
p.   cm.
Includes bibliographical references and index.
1. Truman, Harry S., 1884–1972.
2. Presidents—United States—Biography.
I. Title.
E814.M26   1992
973.918'092—dc20   [B]   92-5245   CIP

ISBN 0-671-45654-7
ISBN 0-671-86920-5 (pbk)

FOR DORIE KANE MCCULLOUGH

CONTENTS

CONTENTS

PART FIVE—WEIGHT OF THE WORLD

PART SIX—BACK HOME

We can never tell what is in store for us.
—Harry S. Truman

PART ONE

SON OF THE MIDDLE BORDER

1

Blue River Country

*As an agricultural region, Missouri is not surpassed by any
state in the Union. It is indeed the farmer's kingdom....*

— The History of Jackson County, Missouri, 1881

I

In the spring of 1841, when John Tyler was President, a Kentucky farmer
named Solomon Young and his red-haired wife, Harriet Louisa Young,
packed their belongings and with two small children started for the Far
West. They had decided to stake their future on new land in the unseen,
unfamiliar reaches of westernmost Missouri, which was then the "extreme frontier" of the United States.

They were part of a large migration out of Kentucky that had begun
nearly twenty years before, inspired by accounts of a "New Eden" in
farthest Missouri—by reports sent back by Daniel Morgan Boone, the son
of Daniel Boone—and by the fact that in 1821 Missouri had come into
the Union as a slave state. The earliest settlers included families named
Boggs, Dailey, and Adair, McCoy, McClelland, Chiles, Pitcher, and Gregg,
and by 1827 they had founded a courthouse town called Independence,
pleasantly situated on high ground in Jackson County, in what was often
spoken of as the Blue River country. Those who came afterward, at the
time of Solomon and Harriet Louisa Young, were named Hickman,
Holmes, and Ford, Davenport, McPherson, Mann, Noland, and Nolan,
Freeman, Truman, Peacock, Shank, Wallace, and Whitset, and they numbered in the hundreds.

Nearly all were farmers, plain-mannered and plain-spoken, people with
little formal education. Many of them were unlettered, even illiterate.
They were not, however, poor or downtrodden, as sometimes pictured

15

—only by the material standards of later times could they be considered wanting—and though none were wealthy, some, like red-haired Harriet Louisa, came from families of substantial means. She had said goodbye to a spacious Greek Revival house with wallpaper and milled woodwork, the Kentucky home of her elder brother and guardian, William Gregg, who owned numerous slaves and landholdings running to many hundreds of acres.

The great majority of these people were of Scotch-Irish descent. They were Baptists and they were Democrats, and like Thomas Jefferson they believed that those who labored in the earth were the chosen people of God. They saw themselves as the true Americans. Their idol was Andrew Jackson, Old Hickory of Tennessee, "One-man-with-courage-makes-a-majority" Jackson, the first President from west of the Alleghenies, who was of their own Scotch-Irish stock. It was for him that Jackson County had been named, and like him they could be tough, courageous, blunt, touchy, narrow-minded, intolerant, and quarrelsome. And obstinate. "Lord, grant that I may always be right, for Thou knowest I am hard to turn," was a line from an old Scotch-Irish prayer.

With their Bibles, farm tools, and rifles, their potent corn whiskey, their black slaves, they brought from Kentucky a hidebound loathing for taxes, Roman Catholics, and eastern ways. Their trust was in the Lord and common sense. That they and their forebears had survived at all in backwoods Kentucky—or earlier in upland Virginia and the Carolinas—was due primarily to "good, hard sense," as they said, and no end of hard work.

They were workers and they were loners, fiercely independent, fiercely loyal to their kind. And they were proudly prolific. David Dailey, recorded as the first man to break the prairie sod in Jackson County, came west with a wife and twelve sons, while Christopher Mann, who outlived everybody of that generation, had already produced with his Betsie seventeen sons and daughters and with a second marriage fathered eight more. (Years afterward, at age eighty-seven, this memorable Jackson County pioneer could claim he had never lost a tooth from decay and could still hold his breath for a minute and a half.) They believed in big families, they came from big families. Children were wealth for a farmer, as for a nation. President Tyler himself had eight children, and in another few years, at age fifty-four, following the death of his first wife, he would remarry and have seven more children, making a total of fifteen, a presidential record.

Solomon Young, who was one of eleven children, and his wife Harriet Louisa, one of thirteen, were from Shelby County, Kentucky, east of Louisville. And so was Nancy Tyler Holmes, a widow with ten children, who made the journey west to Missouri three or four years later, about 1845, once her sons had established themselves in Jackson County. Carrying a sack of tea cakes and her late husband's beaver hat in a large leather hatbox, she traveled in the company of several slaves and her two youngest daughters, one of whom, Mary Jane Holmes, was secretly pining for a young man back in Shelby County named Anderson Truman. He was one of twelve children.

If Solomon and Harriet Louisa Young were acquainted with any of the Holmes or Truman families by this time, there is no record of it.

Nearly everyone made the expedition the same way, traveling the wilderness not by wagon or horseback but by steamboat. The route was down the winding Ohio River from Louisville, past Henderson and Paducah, to the confluence of the Mississippi at Cairo, then up the Mississippi to St. Louis. Changing boats at St. Louis, they headed west on the Missouri, the "Big Muddy," fighting the current for 457 miles, as far as the river's sudden, dramatic bend. There they went ashore at either of two miserable, mudbound little river settlements, Wayne City or Westport, which put them within a few miles of Independence, still the only town of consequence on the frontier.

With the "terrible current" against them, the trip on the Missouri took a week. The shallow-draft boats were loaded so deep the water broke over the gunwales. Wagons and freight jammed the deck, cordwood for the engines, mules, horses, piles of saddles and harness, leaving passengers little room. (One side-wheel steamer of the era that sank in the river and was only recovered more than a century later, carried cargo that included everything from ax handles and rifles to school slates, doorknobs, whale oil lanterns, beeswax candles, 2,500 boots and shoes, and thousands of bright-colored beads and buttons intended for the Indian trade.) Day after day, the heavy, shadowed forest passed slowly by, broken only now and then by an open meadow or tiny settlement where a few lone figures stood waving from among the tree stumps. Some trees towering over the river banks measured six feet through. On summer mornings the early filtered light on the water could be magical.

These were the years of the great Missouri River paintings by George Caleb Bingham. The river Bingham portrayed was the settlers' path. The distant steamer appearing through the sun-filled morning haze in his *Boatmen on the Missouri,* as an example, could be the *Radnor,* the *Henry Bry* or *Winona,* any of twenty-odd river packets that carried the Kentucky people.

The only notable sign of civilization west of St. Louis was the state capitol on a bluff at Jefferson City, a white limestone affair, "very substantial in execution," within which was displayed a full-length portrait of Senator Thomas Hart Benton, Missouri's own thundering voice of westward expansion. The painting was said to have cost the unheard-of sum of $1,000.

Besides those from Kentucky, the migration included families from Virginia, the Carolinas, and Tennessee, who, with the Kentuckians, made it a predominantly southern movement and so one of numerous slaveholders other than Nancy Tyler Holmes. Possibly, Solomon Young, too, brought slaves. In later years, it is known, he owned three or four—a cook, a nursemaid, one or two farmhands—which was about the usual number for those bound for Jackson County. They were farmers, not cotton planters, and for many, a slave was a mark of prosperity and social station. Still, the accumulative number of black men, women, and children traveling to the frontier was substantial. Incredibly, one Jabez Smith, a Virginia slave trader who set up business near Independence, is on record as having transported more than two hundred slaves.

White, black, young and old, they crowded the upbound steamers in the company of hellfire preachers and cardsharps, or an occasional pallid easterner traveling west for his health. Old journals speak, too, of uniformed soldiers on their way to Fort Leavenworth, blanketed Kaw (or Kansas) Indians, French fur traders and mountainmen with their long hair and conspicuous buckskins—a seemingly endless, infinitely colorful variety of humankind and costume. Nancy Tyler Holmes is said to have worn a white lace cap that concealed an ugly scar. As a child in Kentucky, during a Shawnee uprising, she allegedly saved herself by pretending to be dead, never moving or making a sound as she was being scalped. True or not, the story served long among her descendants as a measure of family grit.

The feeling in surviving accounts is of noisy good company and wild scenery and of "history" as an immediate and entirely human experience. Lieutenant John Charles Frémont, the celèbrated Path Finder, came up the river in 1842, on his first exploring expedition to the Rockies. (One traveler described Frémont's party as "healthy and full of fun and elasticity . . . by no means a choir of Psalm-singers, nor Quakers. They ate, drank, talked, sang, played cards and smoked cigars when they pleased and as much as they pleased.") The following year, 1843, came John James Audubon. In the summer of 1846 a young historian from Boston, Francis Parkman, stood at the rail of the *Radnor* marveling at the immense brown sweep of the river, its treacherous snags and shifting sandbars. "The Missouri is constantly changing its course," Parkman was to write in *The*

California and Oregon Trail, his classic account of the journey, "wearing away its banks on one side, while it forms new ones on the other. Its channel is continually shifting. Islands are formed, and then washed away, and while the old forests on one side are undermined and swept off, a young growth springs up from the new soil upon the other." It was "frightful," he noted, "to see the dead and broken trees, thick-set as a military abattis, firmly imbedded in the sand, and all pointing downstream, ready to impale any unhappy steamboat that at high water should pass over them." The landing near Independence was described approvingly as a "wild and enterprising region."

It was also in that summer of 1846 that Anderson Truman came on from Kentucky, and, for some unexplained reason, on horseback, which was one of the few exceptional things ever recorded about Anderson Truman. Possibly he couldn't afford boat passage.

Of this first Truman to reach Jackson County, there is not a great deal to be said. His full name was Anderson Shipp (or Shippe) Truman. His people were English and Scotch-Irish and farmers as far back as anyone knew. His father, William Truman, had come into Kentucky from Virginia about 1800 and reportedly served in the War of 1812. Andy, as he was called, grew up on the Truman farm near the tiny crossroads village of Christianburg, Kentucky. He was slight, gentle, soft-spoken, thirty years old, and without prospects. Nonetheless, Mary Jane Holmes, who was five years younger, had seen enough in him to defy her mother and marry him. On the pretext of visiting a married sister, she had returned to Kentucky earlier that summer and once there, announced her intentions.

Her mother, the redoubtable Nancy Tyler Holmes, was horrified, as she let Mary Jane know in a letter from Missouri dated July 24, 1846—a letter dictated to another of her daughters, which suggests that Nancy Tyler Holmes may have been illiterate. Since hearing the news she had been unable to sleep or eat. "Mary are you the first daughter I have that has refused to take my advice?" What made Anderson Truman so unacceptable is unclear. An explanation given later was that Mother Holmes thought Mary Jane was "marrying down," since the Trumans had no slaves.

The wedding took place in Kentucky in mid-August at the home of the married sister, a handsome red-brick house with white trim that still stands. Then Mary Jane's "Mr. Truman," as she would always refer to him, set off by horse for "the wild country" of Missouri, intending to stay only long enough to secure the blessing of his new mother-in-law.

His first letter from Missouri reached Mary Jane a month later. To his amazement, he had been welcomed with open arms, her mother and sisters all hugging and kissing him, everybody laughing and crying at once. He was urged to stay and take up the frontier life. He could be happy anywhere, even in Missouri, he wrote to Mary Jane, if only she were with him. "As for myself I believed that I would be satisfied if you was out here . . . I believe I can live here if you are willing."

She arrived by steamboat, and with her mother's blessing and the wedding gift of a Holmes slave named Hannah and her child, the young couple settled on a rented farm belonging to a prominent local figure, Johnston Lykins, a Baptist missionary (preacher and physician) who had come to the frontier originally to bring salvation to the Indians, but had lately turned to land speculation. He and others were in the throes of founding a new town on the Missouri's great bend, at the juncture of the Kansas River and the Missouri, this to be ambitiously named Kansas City. To such men the future was in towns and trade. They talked of geographic advantages plain to anyone who looked at a map. Here was the Missouri, the great "natural highway" downstream to St. Louis, and so to New Orleans, Louisville, or Pittsburgh. There, upstream, beyond the great bend, stretched all the Northwest and its immeasurable opportunities.

Here also, importantly, began the overland trails to Santa Fe, California, and Oregon. Jackson County was the threshold, the jumping-off point, to an entire second America of dry grasslands reaching clear to the Rockies. In a newly published guidebook to the Santa Fe Trail called *Commerce of the Prairies* (1844), the author, Josiah Gregg of Jackson County, portrayed Independence as *the* port of embarkation for the "grand prairie ocean."

In fact, Independence, "Queen City of the Trails," was the country's first western boomtown, and to newly arrived settlers, after long days on the river, it seemed a metropolis of stores, blacksmith sheds, wagon shops, of crowded streets and unceasing commotion. The crack of bullwhips split the air like rifle fire as wagon trains made up for Oregon. Mexican caravans from Santa Fe rolled in with still more wagons, pack mules, and hundreds of thousands of dollars in Mexican gold to be spent on American trade goods. The spring Solomon Young and his family arrived, one Santa Fe caravan of twenty-two wagons is reported to have brought $200,000 in gold specie. Like a seaport town Independence had a customshouse.

"Mules, horses, and wagons at every corner," observed Francis Parkman. "Groups of hardy-looking men about the stores, and Santa Fe emigrant wagons standing in the fields around. . . . Some of these ox-wagons contained large families of children, peeping under the covering."

The permanent population of Independence by the 1840s was perhaps only seven hundred people, but on any spring day two or three thousand would be congregated in or about Jackson Square, at the center of which stood a trim red-brick courthouse with a fanlight over the door. Of the several public houses around the Square, the largest and best known, the two-story, brick Noland House, was acclaimed the westernmost hotel in America, offering accommodations for four hundred guests, provided no one minded sleeping two or three to a bed. The nearby wagon shops were the shipyards of the "prairie ocean" and no wagons supposedly were better suited for the rigors of a prairie crossing than those built by a free black man named Hiram Young, an enterprising manufacturer who, like nearly everyone involved with the feeding, housing, or outfitting of emigrants, was prospering handsomely.

But it was land that the Kentucky people came for, the high, rolling, fertile open country of Jackson County, with its clear springs and two "considerable" rivers, the Little Blue and the Blue, both flowing out of Kansas Territory. Every essential was at hand—limestone quarries, splendid blue-grass pastures very like those of Kentucky, and ample timber where the creeks and rivers ran. "To live in a region devoid of the familiar sight of timber seemed unendurable," reads one old chronicle, "and the average Kentuckian could not entertain the idea of founding a home away from the familiar forest trees." They counted hickory, ash, elm, sycamore, willow, poplar, cottonwood, and oak in three or four varieties. Walnut, the most prized, was the most abundant. Entire barns and houses were to be built of walnut.

It was land beautiful to see, rising and falling in broad swells and giving way to long horizons. Prairie grass was "high and green." Wildflowers, wild herbs—meadow rose, turtlehead, snakeroot, wolfberry, thimbleweed—grew in fragrant profusion everywhere the prairie remained unbroken, and starting about ten miles south of Independence the country was nearly all still prairie.

To cut through the sod with a plow took six to eight yoke of oxen. Horses wouldn't do. But beneath the crust, the dark prairie loam could be two to six feet deep. In places along the river bottoms, it was 20 feet deep. Josiah Gregg, the guidebook author, having seen all the country from the Missouri to the Rio Grande, declared that the "rich and beautiful uplands in the vicinity of Independence might well be denominated the 'garden spot' of the Far West."

Much of the best land, it happens, was already under cultivation. Moreover, it had been violently contested when, a decade earlier, the "garden spot" had been the setting for what were politely referred to as the

Mormon Difficulties. In 1831, only a few years after the founding of Independence, a small, advance party of the Church of Jesus Christ of Latter-Day Saints arrived on the scene and were at first regarded by the local citizenry as little more than harmless fanatics. But more followed. They bought land, founded a settlement and a ferry crossing on Blue River, opened their own general store in Independence, and established the town's first newspaper. Some began speaking out against slavery. In little time, seen as a threat, they were decried as "the very dregs" of the East, vicious, immoral, and in education "little above the condition of our blacks." That they referred to the Indians across the border in Kansas Territory as their fellow tribes of Israel struck many hard-bitten old pioneers as close to insane.

More ominous was their announced intention to become proprietors of the entire region. Joseph Smith, their prophet and leader, proclaimed Jackson County holy land and commanded that Independence become their City of Zion. By the summer of 1833, with the Saints in the county numbering more than a thousand, or roughly a third of the population, it appeared they might control the fall elections. A mass meeting was called at the courthouse. Angry speeches were made and a proclamation issued declaring Mormons no longer welcome.

Violence quickly followed. A mob smashed the Mormon printing press, a Mormon bishop was tarred and feathered. On Halloween night armed riders, "without other warrant than their own judgment of the requirements of the situation," attacked the Mormon settlement on Blue River, driving women and children from their homes. Crops and barns went up in flame, men were dragged into the fields and flogged. Jackson County was in a state of "dreadful fermentation." In another clash three men were killed.

When, on the night of November 12, the skies ignited in a spectacular meteor shower like none ever seen on the Missouri frontier, many took it as a sign to rid the land of Mormons once and for all. More than a thousand people were forced from their homes and driven across the Missouri River into less settled territory to the north, where their persecutions only grew worse, but with the difference now that they fought back. The governor of Missouri, an Independence storekeeper named Lilburn W. Boggs, called out the militia and declared that for the public good all Mormons must leave the state or be "exterminated." A religious war was under way, Missouri's first civil war, and ended only when the Mormons departed for Illinois in 1839.

Such events were past history by the time Solomon Young and his small family arrived in 1841. Yet only a year later, in 1842, a lone assassin, a Mormon presumably, crept to a window in Independence and shot Lilburn W. Boggs, all but killing him. As favored by nature as the Blue River country may have been, it was no peaceable kingdom.

Nor was nature ever entirely benign in Missouri, as the new settlers learned soon enough. Winters could be severe, or marked by weeks of raw gloom when the whole country looked as grim and hard as iron. The cold cut to the bone. The diary of one farmer, though written years later, speaks for generations of Jackson County people:

> Awful cold; I did not work today, too cold; Colder than it has been this year; I slept cold; Cloudy and wind blowing; I am chilly; Tremendous windy and cold; Cold, blue cold this morning...too cold to work; Awful cold, all of us housed up, nobody stirring; I got very cold....

It was a climate of great extremes, even in the span of a day. Temperatures could rise or drop 50 degrees in a matter of hours. Summers turned too dry or too wet and either way were nearly always broiling hot. The year 1844 brought the worst floods on record, followed by a tornado that tore up trees and fences and killed a number of people.

But then no one came to the frontier expecting things to go easily, least of all a farmer.

Solomon and Harriet Louisa Young made their start on a farm known as the Parrish place, not far from the Missouri River and well within the projected outlines of Kansas City. Then, shortly afterward, in 1844, possibly because of the flood, they made a first claim to public land on high ground back from the Blue River approximately sixteen miles south of Independence, near the settlement of Hickman's Mills, on what was called Blue Ridge. It was high, fertile, well-drained ground, ideal grazing country, good for corn and wheat, as high and fine as any land in the county, with distant views miles into Kansas Territory.

This first Blue Ridge claim comprised just 80 acres, the minimum purchase required by the Land Act, and Solomon Young paid $1.25 an acre, the minimum price for public land. To gain title he was also obliged to occupy the land for a time, and consequently stories were passed down of how he and Harriet Louisa came there with "a gun and an axe and two babies and a blanket." Grandchildren would listen to Harriet Louisa tell how Solomon rode off to file his claim at the land office at Clinton, seventy miles distant, and describe the nights she spent in a shelter of fence rails and brush, alone with the two children, Susan Mary and William, who, if not exactly babies any longer, were still quite small.

The family expanded and so did Solomon's holdings. Six more children were born—Sarah Ann, Harrison, Elizabeth, Laura Jane, Martha Ellen, and Ada—as ever larger parcels of land were acquired. A house and barn went up. Blue Ridge became the homeplace. Solomon's financial setbacks were frequent and might have crushed a less resilient spirit, but by reputation he was one of the best farmers and stockmen in the county and in the long run he prospered. He had an eye for horses, he knew mules, he knew land, and he bought and sold either at every opportunity. In time he established a trans-prairie freighting enterprise and amassed landholdings that, for Jackson County, amounted to a small empire. Indeed, by all accounts, Solomon Young was a remarkable man, and considerably more is known about him and Harriet Louisa than about Anderson or Mary Jane Truman.

He was born in Shelby County, Kentucky, near the town of Simpsonville, in 1815, the year of Andrew Jackson's triumph at the Battle of New Orleans, which made him twenty-six when he came to Missouri. His father, Jacob Young, was a Revolutionary War veteran from North Carolina. His mother, Rachael Goodnight Young, died when he was twelve. When his father remarried and moved on, Solomon was left to fend for himself, earning his keep weighing hogs and trading livestock. Full grown he was tall, powerful, self-reliant, bounding with energy, and a world-beating talker. Talk was nourishment for Solomon, as it never was for Harriet Louisa.

Unlike so many who came out from Kentucky, he was neither Scotch-Irish nor a Baptist, but of German descent (the name had been spelled Jung in North Carolina) and only a nominal Methodist. Skeptical of preachers or anyone who made too much show of religion, he liked to say that whenever he heard a man praying loudly, his first instinct was to go home and lock the smokehouse. Politics interested him not at all.

Solomon had married Harriet Louisa Gregg in the second week of January 1838. She was Scotch-Irish, her people ardent members of Kentucky's first and largest Baptist congregation, the Long Run Baptist Church at Simpsonville, which had been built on land once owned by Abraham Lincoln's grandfather, Captain Abraham Lincoln. Her first child was born in 1839, her second two years following, the same spring she and Solomon started west, which means she must have been nursing the baby on the boat trip up the Missouri. Remembered for her imperturbable disposition, no less than her abundant red hair, Harriet Louisa was not known to have complained or lost heart then or at any time afterward, whatever happened. "She was a strong woman . . . and there wasn't a thing in the world that ever scared her," it would be said. Her last pregnancy was in 1856, but the baby did not survive. Nearly forty, she was well past middle age by the standards of the day, yet still short of midpoint in what was to be an extremely long, eventful life.

Exactly when Solomon went west on the first of his wagon-train expeditions, leaving Harriet Louisa in charge of everything, is not clear. It is known only that he went several times prior to the Civil War, beginning as early perhaps as 1846, the momentous year of the Mexican War and the trek of the Mormons out of Illinois to the Great Salt Lake (not to mention the year of Anderson Truman's arrival in Independence). Such undertakings were epic in scale, in any event. The customary overland train was made up of forty to eighty giant canvas-covered freight wagons, each requiring six yoke of oxen or mules and two drivers. A single wagon and team stretched 90 to 100 feet. And since the practice under way was to keep the wagons about 100 feet apart, some trains would be strung across the prairie for as far as three miles. To keep his bearings, Solomon carried a brass telescope, like a sea captain.

The goods hauled could be worth a fortune, $30,000 or more, and the profits, if all went as planned, could be correspondingly large. Solomon, who at census time now listed himself as a freighter, appears to have done quite well. In 1850, his recorded wealth was $5,000. Ten years later, he was worth ten times that. At age thirty-five he could count himself a wealthy man, with land and property valued at nearly $50,000. He is said to have owned as much as 5,000 acres, fancy, blooded horses, and there was real silver on the table.

Because the Santa Fe Trail first headed south out of Independence, before swinging west across the Blue River, it passed within only a few miles of the Young farm. Solomon would depart in the spring. Large and full-bearded, wearing a wide-brimmed hat, he must have been something to see as he pushed off, as his family saw him and remembered him—a man "who could do pretty much anything he set his mind to." Once, he started for California with a herd of fifteen hundred cattle. It took him a year and he lost five hundred cattle on the way, but he made it, through every kind of weather and hardship, across half the continent. At Sacramento he traded the surviving herd for a ranch of 40,000 acres. But this, as the story goes, he was forced to sell to cover the debts of a partner. A man made good on his debts, a man stood by his friends. And a world-beating talker had a tale to tell his children, and they theirs.

Another year, 1860, Solomon took forty wagons to Utah, with goods and salt pork for the Army, and his arrival at Salt Lake caused a stir:

The wagons were coupled together in pairs [noted the August 16, 1860, edition of the Deseret News], one behind the other, each pair having on board about sixty hundred pounds and drawn by six pairs of oxen.

25

... Mr. Young is of the opinion that the couple of two wagons together in that manner is the most economical way of freighting to this Territory. . . . Mr. Young's cattle look remarkably well, and, as we are informed, he did not lose a single ox by accident or otherwise during the trip.

When the officer in charge at Salt Lake refused for some reason to receive the goods, Solomon met with Brigham Young, who, though no relation, was a fellow Mason and agreed to take the whole shipment if Solomon would extend him credit. The bargain worked out to the satisfaction of both.

Meantime, Solomon also did a thriving trade in outfitting and advising emigrants bound for Oregon or Santa Fe, who now, every year, numbered in the thousands. But by 1849 and 1850, the years of the California Gold Rush and the greatest traffic through Independence, the little town's time in the sun was nearly over. For the same human tide brought virulent cholera. In the spring of 1849 ten people died at the Noland House within a single day. In 1851 cholera struck again. In 1854, with no rain from June to November, crops failed all over the county. Scarlet fever, pneumonia, and cholera were epidemic the next several years. In the spring of 1857 the Youngs themselves lost a child, nine-year-old Elizabeth, who died of causes unrecorded.

And all the while across the line in Kansas, the old issue of slavery was building to a terrible storm that was to affect the lives and outlook of nearly everyone in Jackson County for a very long time to come.

II

To many in western Missouri the Civil War commenced not in 1861 with the attack on Fort Sumter in South Carolina, but in 1854, when Congress passed the fateful Kansas-Nebraska Act, leaving to the residents of the territories of Kansas and Nebraska the decision of whether to allow slavery. Missouri had come into the Union as a slave state following the famous Missouri Compromise of 1820–21, another congressional inspiration that admitted Maine, a free state, at the same time and prohibited slavery north of Missouri's southern border, latitude 36°30'. Now the old Missouri Compromise line was gone. The new bill, designed to ease tension, had exactly the opposite effect.

What compounded the problem was the disproportionate size of the slave population along Missouri's western border—where possibly fifty thousand slaves were held, which was nearly half the slaves in all Missouri. In Jackson County alone there were more than three thousand, and their owners, whatever their feeling for the Union, dreaded the prospect of free territory so close, to which a slave might escape, or from which could come armed bands of slave liberators. For the owner, his slave was very often his most valuable possession, in addition to being vital to his livelihood, and as the chances of war increased, the monetary value of every slave increased steadily, to the point where a male in good health was worth $3,000, as much as 500 acres of prime land.

Elsewhere in the nation Kansas was seen as the issue that would settle things. "Come on then, gentlemen of the Slave States," said Senator William H. Seward of New York in a speech in Washington, "... We will engage in competition for the virgin soil of Kansas, and God give the victory to the side that is stronger in numbers as it is in right." As if in answer, several thousand pro-slavery Missourians—"enough to kill every God-damned abolitionist in the Territory," as one of their leaders expressed it—stormed over the border with guns and whiskey to help Kansas elect a pro-slavery legislature.

In response, more Free-Soilers poured in from the East, a new kind of emigrant traffic from which struggling little Kansas City began to benefit. When armed pro-slavery ruffians, later to be known as "bushwhackers," tried to close passage on the Missouri by terrorizing the riverboats, the Free-Soilers merely crossed overland through Iowa.

Time obviously was running out.

On May 22, 1856, hard-riding Missouri "Border Ruffians" shot up the town of Lawrence, Kansas, an abolitionist stronghold. Two days afterward, a strange, wild-looking old man named John Brown, a new Kansas settler, decided the moment had come to "regulate matters." Armed with broadswords honed to razor sharpness, Brown and his sons descended after dark on three isolated cabins on little Pottawatomie Creek. There they took five pro-slavery Kansas men and boys, none of whom had anything to do with the raid on Lawrence, and chopped them to pieces—"as declared by Almighty God," said John Brown.

No sooner had the Free-Soilers gained control in Kansas in the next round of elections than Kansas riders came charging over the line into Missouri to take their turn at murder and arson. For years before the Civil War began in the East, this terrible Border War—civil war in every dreadful sense of the term—raged all up and down the Missouri-Kansas line and continued until the surrender at Appomattox. It was like some horrible chapter out of the Middle Ages, with gangs of brigand horsemen roaming the land. They could appear out of nowhere any time, led often by men who were no better than young thugs, some possibly deranged, like the bantam-sized "Doc" Jennison, whose outlaw Kansans were called Jayhawkers or Red Legs (for their red leather leggings), or the Missouri guerrilla "Bloody Bill" Anderson, who liked to mutilate his victims. It was a war of plunder, ambush, and unceasing revenge. Nobody was safe. Defenseless towns were burned. Osceola, Missouri, and Shawneetown, Kansas, were all but wiped from the map.

Neither then nor later did the rest of the country realize the extent of the horrors. Nor was it ever generally understood that most Missourians remained loyal to the Union—including slaveholders like Solomon Young and Anderson Truman—or that most Missourians bore no resemblance to the infamous bushwhackers. The popular picture of all western Missourians as gun-slinging, whiskey-swilling riffraff was grossly inaccurate—as inaccurate as the idea that every Kansan was a transplanted, upright New England abolitionist. Atrocities were committed on both sides, and it was innocent civilians who suffered most. As one Kansan later said, "The Devil came to the border, liked it, and decided to stay awhile."

Jackson County became "the burnt country." Judge Henry Younger of Lee's Summit saw his farm destroyed during Jayhawker "Doc" Jennison's first sweep through the county, and Judge Younger was a Union man. Later, he was brutally murdered, which led his hot-blooded son Coleman, or Cole, to join up with the celebrated Missouri guerrilla chief, William Quantrill.

A Jackson County physician named Lee was gunned down in cold blood because his sons had joined the Confederate Army. John Hagan, a farmer, was stopped by Union cavalry while out for a Sunday drive with his family. Ordered to get down from the wagon, he was led into the woods and shot through the head for no known reason. Christopher Mann, the prolific old Kentucky pioneer who had the ability of holding his breath for a minute and a half, was made to stand by at gunpoint and watch his farm burned by Missouri guerrillas. "They asked me if I was not a black abolitionist, and when I told them, 'I am a Union man, sir!' one of the bushwackers struck me with his revolver and broke out two of my teeth."

A first battle of Independence was fought before dawn the morning of August 11, 1862, when Quantrill and his ragtag band came screaming into the Square and a uniformed Confederate force overran a sleeping Union camp. In a second battle two years later, another Confederate victory, fierce block-to-block fighting raged back and forth across town for two days.

The worst atrocity, the unpardonable Lawrence Massacre, was committed by Quantrill, a brave, ingenious, wretched man who was continuously in and out of Jackson County, hiding in the heavy brush of the winding Blue River bottoms. To most slaveholders Quantrill was a hero and in memory, in after years in Jackson County, he would acquire a romantic glow, an aura like that of no other figure of the war, as if he had been the very soul of Old South gallantry in service of the Cause. In reality, he came from Ohio. Nor had he ever shown any southern sympathies or convictions, until the killing began.

At first light the morning of August 21, 1863, with a force of nearly 500 men riding under a black silk flag, Quantrill struck Lawrence, Kansas. Most of the town was still asleep. His orders were to kill every man big enough to carry a gun and to burn the town. When it was over, at least 150 men and boys had been murdered. The day was clear and still and smoke from the inferno, rising in tremendous black columns, could be seen from miles away.

Like many others in Jackson County, Solomon and Harriet Louisa had a personal tie to the bushwackers. Their third child, Sarah Ann, had married a man named James J. Chiles, a highly unsavory character known as Jim Crow Chiles. He was the dark side of frontier life, a future skeleton for the Young-Truman family closet.

Jim Crow, whose nickname was said to have been bestowed in boyhood for his exuberant performance of a popular dance called the "Jim Crow Set," belonged to one of the original pioneer families in the county, and large landholders, which initially stood him well with the Youngs. But in 1857, Jim Crow had killed a man in the bar at the Noland House, a stranger who had done no more than remark on his table manners. (Another man who traveled with Jim Crow to Santa Fe shortly afterward remembered him as often good-natured, even jovial, "but subject to violent fits of anger, and when angry, a very dangerous man.") Tried for murder at the Independence Courthouse in 1859, he got off, the standing of the Chiles family weighing heavily in the jury's decision, and it was almost immediately afterward that he and Sarah Ann, or Sallie, were married. She was sixteen. Jim Crow, a "dashing fellow," was notable for his dark eyes and "powerful, symmetrical build."

At the onset of the war, Jim Crow took off with Quantrill and Bloody Bill Anderson, and quickly demonstrated that like them he enjoyed killing, "always exhibiting the traits of the most inhuman savage," as a Kansas City paper would write at the time of his death. He was an active participant, for example, in the capture of Union Captain Daniel H. David on the Little Blue, when Captain David and his men were hacked to death John Brown style.

In this pitiless onrush of history, the Youngs, too, were caught in the middle no less than anyone along the border, and their stories of what happened, of all that was taken and destroyed, would be told repeatedly, some events merging in memory with others as time passed, some details being dropped or made a touch more vivid than the truth perhaps, depending on who was telling the story to whom and when. Whether, for example, the fanatical "Grim Chieftain of Kansas," Jim Lane, struck the Young farm the summer of 1861, two years before the Lawrence Massacre, as Lane headed through Missouri to burn Osceola, or whether it was earlier, just after the war officially began in the spring of 1861, is a matter of some confusion. But there is no doubt that he came or that Solomon was somewhere far afield on one of his expeditions. (Solomon may have reasoned that since he was an avowed Union man his family would be safe.) Will Young, the oldest son, was also absent—Will had joined the Confederate Army—which left Harriet Louisa alone with the children.

In a theater of war characterized by strange, terrifying human apparitions, James Henry Lane may have been the strangest, most terrifying of all. Tall, gaunt, always wildly disheveled even in uniform, he had a sallow hatchet face, atrociously bad teeth, and a voice with a raspy, unearthly sound. He was also a brilliant orator and a rampant political opportunist. As an overnight, fire-eating Republican he had been elected as one of the first two senators from the new state of Kansas. Arriving in Washington on the eve of the war, he organized a Frontier Guard to protect Abraham Lincoln and for a few nights he and his men actually bivouacked in the East Room of the Executive Mansion. In Missouri he was known as a "freedom" soldier, meaning he would free you of anything he could lay his hands on—food, forage, money, silk dresses, the family silver, even a piano on occasion. Everybody knew about Jim Lane. He was as feared and reviled on the Missouri side of the line as was Quantrill in Kansas. For Harriet Louisa there could have been no mistaking who it was in Union blue riding up the road.

In the formal claim she filed in 1902, more than thirty-five years after the war, it is recorded that Union forces under five different officers came to the farm on five different occasions, beginning with General Lane in May 1861. All that they took or destroyed is itemized. If the record is accurate, then Lane was accountable only for fifteen mules and thirteen horses valued at $4,525. But by Harriet Louisa's own recollection on numerous occasions before and after the report was filed, as well as the stories repeated by those of her children who were witness to the same events, this is what happened:

Lane and his Kansans proceeded to shoot four hundred Hampshire hogs, then cut out only the hams, leaving the rest to rot. Harriet Louisa was ordered to bake biscuits, which she did "until her hands blistered." Some of the soldiers passed the time playing cards in the yard, sitting in the mud on her best hand-sewn quilt. Others, "out of sheer cussedness," blasted away at her hens.

Whether Lane knew of the family's connection to Jim Crow Chiles or the fact that Will Young had joined the Confederates is not known. But, to determine the whereabouts of Solomon Young, the Kansans took the "man of the place," fifteen-year-old Harrison, looped a rope about his neck, threw the other end over a tree, and said they would hang him if he didn't tell where his father was hiding. Harrison, according to the story, told the truth, saying Solomon had gone west with a wagon train. They tightened the rope, "stretching his neck," and asked again. Harrison answered as before. Then, suddenly, bored with their game, the men let him go. Hay barns were set ablaze. Lane and the rest rode off, taking the hams, biscuits, feather beds, and the family silver.

According to Harriet Louisa's formal claim, however, it was a Colonel Burris, not Lane, who made off with 1,200 pounds of bacon in October of 1862, as well as 65 tons of hay, 500 bushels of corn, 44 head of hogs, 2 horses (one with bridle and saddle), 1 "lot of beds and bedding," 7 wagons, and 30,000 fence rails. A General Sturgis was also responsible for taking 150 head of cattle and a Captain Axaline for 13,000 fence rails, 1,000 bushels of corn, and 6,000 "rations." The total value of everything confiscated came to $21,442, the equivalent in present-day money of a quarter of a million dollars.

Interestingly, no family silver is listed. Nor is there any reference to buildings destroyed. Yet the theft of the family silver by Old Jim Lane would be talked of repeatedly in after years, and Martha Ellen Young, who was nine at the time, would one day describe for a *New York Times* writer how she and her mother, their faces blackened with the soot and ash that rained down from the burning barns, stood in the yard watching the hated blue soldiers ride away.

Though possibly no silver ever was taken, certainly it might have been, and if no buildings were actually destroyed on the Young farm, the little girl may well have been witness to other farms going up in flames in "the burnt country." The resulting hatred was the same in any event. The stories were what mattered as they were passed along, not the formal claim. From such times and memories, as was said, a family "got solid" in its feelings.

But nothing that happened in western Missouri during the course of the war left such a legacy of bitterness as the infamous Union measure known as General Order No. 11. Estimating that two thirds of the outlying Missouri populace were either "kin to the guerrillas" (like the Youngs) or "actively and heartily engaged in feeding, clothing, and sustaining them" (like the Slaughter family, near neighbors of the Youngs on Blue Ridge), the Union commander at Kansas City, Brigadier General Thomas Ewing, decided to deny the guerrillas their base of supply by depopulating the entire area.

The order was issued August 25, 1863. All civilians in Jackson, Cass, and Bates counties, except those living within a mile of Union posts at Kansas City, Independence, Hickman's Mills, Pleasant Hill, and Harrisonville, were to "remove from their present places of residence" within fifteen days. If they could prove their loyalty to the Union to the satisfaction of the post commander, they could remain in those towns or cross over into Kansas. If not, they must leave Missouri. All grain and hay found in the district after the deadline was to be destroyed.

Twenty thousand people were driven from their homes. The country was depopulated in a matter of weeks, as Union cavalry helped themselves to whatever of value was left behind, then put a torch to buildings and crops. "It is heartsickening to see what I have seen," wrote a Union officer to his wife. ". . . A desolated country and men and women and children, some of them almost naked. Some on foot and some in old wagons. Oh God." Another Union officer appalled by the suffering he witnessed firsthand was the artist George Caleb Bingham, whose outrage would take form after the war, when, settling in Independence, he painted *Order No. 11,* in which General Ewing himself would be seen driving a family from their home.

At the Young farm, the policy appears to have been carried out to the letter, despite the fact that Solomon had signed a loyalty oath more than a year before. The family was permitted to take away one wagonload of possessions. Little Martha Ellen would remember trudging northward on a hot, dusty road behind the swaying wagon, headed for "bitter exile" in Kansas City.

Anderson Truman, meantime, had fared far better. He too had signed a loyalty oath. He wanted only "the Union as it was," like the rest of the Trumans back in Kentucky. ("I hope you have not turned against this glorious Union," wrote his brother John Truman from Shelby County, where, as in Missouri, families and neighbors were sharply divided.) But earlier Anderson and his family had moved across the Missouri to Platte County, which, close as it was, the war hardly touched. An increasingly religious man, he wished no part in violence. He hated Catholics, but little else apparently, and he kept to his land and labors, living simply and almost without incident. Once, after dark, the slave Hannah heard screams and a commotion of horses at the adjoining farm. Everyone assumed the Red Legs had arrived and Grandmother Holmes, then in her eighties, fled with the youngest Truman children to hide in a cornfield. The Red Legs proved to be a detachment of Confederate cavalry who had come to press a neighbor's sons into service. This was as close as the war ever came to the Trumans.

The children numbered five, three girls, Margaret, Emma, and Mary, and two boys, William and John, neither of whom was old enough to fight in the war.

When it was all over in April 1865, Anderson loaded his five slaves—Hannah, Marge, and their three daughters—into a big farm wagon with a month's supply of food and drove them to Leavenworth, Kansas, the place they had chosen to begin their freedom. When he returned to Leavenworth some years later to learn what had become of them, nobody knew.

"They never bought one, they never sold one," a keeper of the family annals would later conclude, speaking somewhat defensively of the Anderson Trumans and their slaves.

The wounds of nearly nine years of war in Missouri were a long time healing. While most veterans of the defeated Confederate Army took up life as best they could, married, and settled down, others found it impossible to return to anything like the old ways. Cole Younger turned desperado and with his brothers joined forces with two more who had fought with Quantrill, Frank and Jesse James. The gang held up its first bank on the main square of little Liberty, Missouri, about ten miles from Independence as the crow flies, in February 1866. Later they hit upon the novel idea of robbing trains.

Closer to home was the case of Jim Crow Chiles, who for years conducted his own one-man reign of terror, using a notorious gambling hall in Kansas City called Headquarters as a base of operations. Having made himself leader of the toughest element in that now wide-open town, he swaggered about armed with two heavy dragoon revolvers, two pocket Derringers, and a black snake whip that became his trademark. His home was in Independence, where he owned a livery stable and kept a pack of bloodhounds that bayed half the night, but that nobody ever dared complain about. He was "universally hated," the kind of town bully who figured in children's nightmares. To black people he was a living terror. On drinking sprees, he would mount a horse and hunt them down with his whip. It is recorded that he killed two black men in cold blood on

33

two different occasions in Independence, shot them "to see them jump." Reportedly, he had killed nine men altogether and was under indictment for three murders by the time a deputy marshal named James Peacock decided to stand up to him as no one ever had.

Both men were heavily armed and both accompanied by a young son, also armed, the morning of the confrontation on the west side of the courthouse square. September 21, 1873, was a Sunday and a number of people on hand witnessed everything.

Advancing on Peacock, Jim Crow challenged him to fight, then hit him in the face. Peacock struck back and at once they tore into each other with fists and pistols, pellmell in the dust of the street, the two boys plunging in. Jim Crow's son, Elijah, had eyesight so poor he was nearly blind, yet he never hesitated. Shots were fired. Jim Crow was hit in the shoulder, Peacock in the back. Elijah, too, was hit. Then Peacock fired point blank into Jim Crow's face, killing him instantly.

Jim Crow's body was carried to the Noland House, to the same barroom where he had killed his first man. The boy Elijah died the next night. Peacock, however, survived, a bullet lodged in his spine, and as the sheriff who killed Jim Crow Chiles, he became a county legend and unbeatable at election time, the Chiles family, meanwhile, having publicly exonerated him from any blame.

For the Youngs, as for the Chileses, it was a tragedy of terrible proportions and one they refused to discuss, then or later, though it is said Solomon Young cursed his daughter Sallie and that Martha Ellen, her father's pet, burned a portrait of Jim Crow. Sallie, a widow at thirty, was expecting another child. Her son Elijah had been all of thirteen.

III

For Martha Ellen Young—Matt or Mattie, as she was known—life had picked up again three years after the war, in 1868, the year she turned seventeen and the family resettled on Blue Ridge in a new, more spacious house. Harriet Louisa had chosen the spot. The new house faced west at the end of a straight quarter-mile drive lined with double rows of elm trees that Mattie helped her father plant. The house, wood frame and painted white with green shutters, had a wide front veranda and two large square front parlors off a central hall. Dining room and kitchen were in a wing to the rear, this enclosed by more porches. Beyond, to the rear, past the orchard, stood a huge red barn built entirely of heavy walnut planks and beams taken from the old, original mill at Hickman's Mills.

The immediate farm comprised 600 acres, with fields bound by squarely built limestone walls—rock fences, as they were known. Whatever his losses from the war, Solomon appears to have taken hold again. Matt had her pick of several fine saddle horses and would spend some of the happiest days of her life riding sidesaddle over the high, open land. If she never learned to milk a cow, her father advised, she would never have to milk a cow. So she never learned.

She did learn to bake and sew and to use a rifle as well as a man. If she swept the veranda, she made the broom fly. "Lively" is the adjective that turns up in old correspondence to describe Mattie Young. Presently, she was sent away to the Lexington Baptist Female College, in sedate, tree-shaded Lexington, Missouri, where for two years she learned to sketch, play the piano, and acquired a lifelong love of books and the poetry of Alexander Pope.

Of above average height—about 5 foot 6—she was a slender young woman with dark hair, a round bright face, and a way of looking directly at people with her clear, gray-blue eyes. Like her father, whom she adored, she was inclined also to speak her mind.

Life on the farm, meantime, had returned to the old rhythms of seasons and crops and work. Talk at the dinner table was of hog prices and taxes; of the Mormons who had begun returning to the county from Utah, convinced still that Independence was their City of Zion; and of the new Hannibal Bridge at Kansas City, the first railroad bridge over the Missouri, which promised to change everything.

Kansas City was growing beyond anyone's dreams. The bridge was finished in 1869, the year of the opening of the transcontinental railroad. By 1872, just three years later, there were seven railroad lines in and out of Kansas City. The days of steamboats and wagon trains were all but vanished. Missouri—"Muzoorah," as one was supposed to pronounce it—was no longer the Far West, but the Great Center of the country.

In the summer of 1874 grasshoppers came in black clouds that shut out the sky. When they were gone, the land was as bare as if scorched by fire. The following year they came again, as if to mock the progress people talked about.

The social occasions Mattie Young loved best were the dances at home in the front parlors, or at neighboring farms. She was a spirited dancer, a "light-foot Baptist." One winter, after a blizzard, there was a dance every night for a week. Neighbors would dance most of the night, then spend the following day riding in big box sleighs cross-country to the next house.

Possibly it was on such a night that she first met John Truman, who

35

since the end of the war had returned with his family to Jackson County and taken up farming nearby. In any event, they seem to have known one another for some while before announcing their plans to marry in 1881, by which time Mattie was twenty-nine.

John Anderson Truman, who was a year older, had had no education beyond a rural school, and except for the night during the war when he fled with Grandmother Holmes into the cornfield, he had had no known adventures. Nor had he any special skills or money. None of the Trumans had ever had money. Still he was ambitious—he aspired to be a stock trader like Solomon Young—and he was a hard worker, cheerful, eager to please. He loved to sing while Mattie played the piano. He also had a violent temper, though thus far this had landed him in no trouble. Overall he made a good impression. In a thick new *History of Jackson County, Missouri* published the year he and Matt were married, it was said of John A. Truman that "he resides with his father and manages the farm; he is an industrious and energetic young man, and one that bids fair to make a success in life."

His mother, Mary Jane Truman, had died two years before in 1879. The indomitable Nancy Tyler Holmes was also in her grave by this time, having lived to age ninety-four.

Appearances would always matter greatly to John Truman. For his wedding photograph taken in Kansas City, he wore a white string tie, kid gloves, and a black frock coat. His boots were gleaming, his thin reddish-brown hair clipped and plastered to perfection. He also chose to be seated for the picture, it is said, because he was sensitive about his height. At 5 foot 4, he was two inches shorter than Mattie. She stood beside him in brocaded satins and a wide lace collar, her hair parted in the middle and brushed smoothly back, in the current fashion, her left hand resting on his shoulder, her eyes, like his, directly on the camera.

As a wedding gift, Solomon gave her a three-drawer burl walnut dresser, with a marble top and a mirror with small, side shelves. She was never to own another piece of furniture quite so fine.

The ceremony took place at the homeplace three days after Christmas, December 28, 1881. The couple's own first home was in Lamar, Missouri, a dusty, wind-blown market town and county seat (Barton County), ninety miles due south. For $685 John became the proud owner of a corner lot and a white frame house measuring all of 20 by 28 feet, which was hardly more than the dimensions of the Youngs' kitchen. It had six tiny rooms, no basement, no running water, and no plumbing. But it was new, snug and sunny, with a casement window in the parlor on the southern side.

For another $200 John bought a barn diagonally across the street and there he opened for business, his announcement in the Lamar *Democrat* reading as follows:

> Mules bought and sold. I will keep for sale at the White Barn on Kentucky Avenue a lot of good mules. Anyone wanting teams will do well to call on J. A. Truman.

A spinster sister, Mary Martha Truman, who, like John's father, came for an extended stay, considered Lamar the end of the world. The place made her miserable, yet Mattie, she observed, remained "lively as ever."

Mattie's first child, a boy, was stillborn the couple's first autumn in Lamar. A year and a half later a second child, a boy, was born in a bedroom off the parlor so small there was barely space for the bed. The attending physician, Dr. W. L. Griffin, received a fee of $15, and to celebrate the occasion the new father planted a seedling pine in the front yard. A story that John Truman also nailed a mule shoe over the front door for luck is apocryphal.

The date was May 8, 1884.

Two days later, a Baptist circuit rider took the baby out into the spring air, and holding him up in the sunshine, remarked what a sturdy boy he was.

Not for a month afterward, however, did Dr. Griffin bother to register the birth at the county clerk's office up the street, and even then, the child was entered nameless. In a quandary over a middle name, Mattie and John were undecided whether to honor her father or his. In the end they compromised with the letter S. It could be taken to stand for Solomon or Shipp, but actually stood for nothing, a practice not unknown among the Scotch-Irish, even for first names. The baby's first name was Harry, after his Uncle Harrison.

Harry S. Truman he would be.

The child would have no memory of Lamar or the house where he was born, for shortly afterward John Truman sold out and moved everybody north again, to a farm near Harrisonville, only seven miles from the Young place. The earliest written description of Harry Truman is in a letter from Harrisonville dated April 7, 1885, when he was still less than a year old. "Baby is real sick now," wrote John's sister Mary Martha, "he is so cross we can't do anything."

The mule business at Lamar had been disappointing. And so, apparently, was the Harrisonville farm, for the Trumans remained there even less time, only two years, during which a second son was born, John

37

Vivian Truman—named for his father and a popular Confederate cavalry officer, John Vivian—who was to be known henceforth as Vivian.

Of these Harrisonville years little Harry would remember just two incidents. His earliest memory, interestingly, was of laughter. He was chasing a frog around the yard, laughing every time it jumped. To Grandmother Young, who had observed so many children, so splendid a sense of humor in a two-year-old was quite remarkable. The second memory was of his mother, for fun, dropping him from an upstairs window into the outstretched arms of his very large Uncle Harry, who was to be a particular favorite from then on.

Solomon Young, by now in his seventies and among the most respected men in the county, was still fit and active. It seemed nothing could touch him, not wars or epidemics or advancing years. But in 1887, the John Truman family moved back to the Young farm and John became Solomon's partner. To what extent John's two false starts influenced the decision, or how much say Mattie had, can only be imagined.

Thus it was to be the Young homeplace where small Harry S. Truman made most of his earliest observations of the world, beginning at age three. Grandfather Anderson Truman also moved in—he was given a room of his own upstairs—and a place was found for one of the fatherless Chiles grandchildren, Cousin Sol. Counting everybody—Harrison, who remained a bachelor, sister Ada, a hired girl, several hired hands, and nearly always a visiting relative or stray neighbor child—this made a household of seldom less than fourteen or fifteen people spanning three generations, all under one roof on the same Blue Ridge where Solomon and Harriet Louisa had made their claim so many years before.

2

Model Boy

Now Harry, you be good.

—MARTHA ELLEN TRUMAN

I

Harry Truman liked to say in later years that he had the happiest childhood imaginable. Grandpa Young took him riding over the country-side in a high-wheeled cart behind a strawberry roan trotting horse. Grandpa adored him, the boy knew. One summer, every day for a week, they drove six miles to the Belton Fair and sat together in the judges' stand watching the races and eating striped candy. It was "the best time a kid ever had." Grandpa was "quite a man, a great big man" with a flowing white beard and strong hands.

Until Mamma gave birth to a third child, the boy's only competition for attention was little Vivian, who still wore his hair in curls. On a day nearly as memorable as those at the Belton Fair, Grandpa and he conspired to give Vivian a haircut, sitting him up in a highchair on the south porch. Mamma was furious when she discovered what they had done, but amaz-ingly she said nothing, so unassailable was Grandpa's authority.

The porch where the haircut took place overlooked a broad bluegrass pasture with a creek where the boys were allowed to explore on their own, accompanied by a black-and-tan dog of uncertain ancestry called Tandy and a cat named Bob. Harry would also remember a swing under an old elm close to the house and another swing indoors in the front hall for rainy days. The long porch on the north side of the house made a perfect race track for their red express wagon.

They went hunting for bird nests and gathered wild strawberries in prairie grass as tall as they. The farm was "a wonderful place." These were "wonderful days and great adventures." The Young land seemed to go on and on. A few miles beyond the immediate farm with its 600 acres was a second farm owned by Grandpa, this with nearly a 1,000 acres. There were herds of cattle, saddle horses, draft horses, mules, sheep, hogs, chickens, ducks, and geese. Harry's father presented him with a black Shetland pony and a new saddle. With the pony on a lead, he let the boy ride beside him as he made his rounds. "I became familiar with every sort of animal on the farm," Harry wrote long afterward, "and watched the wheat harvest, the threshing and the corn shucking, mowing and stacking hay, and every evening at suppertime heard my father tell a dozen farmhands what to do. . . ."

It was a time of self-contained security and plenty, such as the Trumans were not to know again.

Most marvelous in memory for Harry was the abundance of food— dried apples, peaches, candy and nuts of all kinds, "wonderful cookies," pies, corn pudding, roasting ears in summer. "There were peach butter, apple butter, grape butter, jellies and preserves," he would write, all produced in a big crowded kitchen by Grandma Young and a German hired girl. Following the late autumn freeze and hog-killing time came homemade sausages, souse, pickled pigs' feet, and lard rendered in a tremendous iron kettle said to have been too heavy for Old Jim Lane to carry away.

From his Aunt Ada, the boy learned to play euchre. Uncle Harry told amusing stories and taught him a card game called cooncan, a form of gin rummy then more popular than poker. Though Uncle Harry, the bachelor uncle, had forsaken farming for the "bedazzlements" of Kansas City, he returned often, bringing candy and toys. Like Grandpa Young, he was a big man, over six feet tall, "strong as a wrestler," good-humored, handsome, and like Grandpa Young, he made Harry feel he was some-body particular, because he was named for him. "When he came it was just like Christmas."

The child liked everybody, to judge by his later recollections. Cousin Sol Chiles, then in his teens and often surly and difficult, would be re-membered as somebody who "really made life pleasant." Sol's mother, Aunt Sallie, was a "lovely person." Aunt Laura, another frequent visitor from Kansas City, was "somebody we always enjoyed."

Yet life had its troubles and woes. On the summer day when his Grand-father Truman died, three-year-old Harry had rushed to the bed to pull at the old man's beard, trying desperately to wake him. Climbing on a chair sometime afterward, in an attempt to comb his hair in front of a mirror, he toppled over backward and broke his collarbone. Another time he would have choked to death on a peach stone had his mother not responded in a flash and decisively, pushing the stone down his throat with her finger, instead of trying to pull it out. Later, when Grandpa Young lay sick in bed and the little boy approached cautiously to inquire how he was feeling, the old pioneer, fixing him with a wintry stare, said, "How are you feeling? You're the one I'm worried about."

It was Mamma, Harry decided, who understood him best. She was brighter than anyone, he thought, and cared most about his well-being. Holding him in her lap while explaining the large print in the family Bible, she taught him to read before he was five. Then the summer of 1889, following his fifth birthday, Mamma surprised him with a baby sister, of whom nothing had been said in advance. From the sound of crying upstairs he and Vivian thought a new pet had arrived. The baby was named Mary Jane, after John Truman's mother, the grandmother they had never known, and to Harry she was a miracle. He adored her.

It was Mamma also, a year later, who hustled him off to Kansas City for expensive eyeglasses. Though he had been badly handicapped by poor eyesight all along—"blind as a mole," in his words—no one seems to have noticed until the night of a July Fourth fireworks when Matt saw him responding more to the sound of the skyrockets than to the spectacle overhead. The Kansas City optometrist diagnosed a rare malformation called "flat eyeballs" (hypermetropia, which means the boy was far-sighted) and Matt agreed to a pair of double-strength, wire-rimmed spectacles at a cost of $10.

All at once the world was transformed for him, as if by magic. And as quickly he became a curiosity, small boys with eyeglasses being almost unknown in rural Missouri.

Her heart went out to him, Matt later said, but she was determined not to pamper. While Grandma Young gave every youngster free rein, Mamma taught that punishment followed transgression. She had a switch and she would use it. When Harry led Vivian and another child on an expedition to a water hole in the south pasture, to spend a glorious afternoon plastering each other with mud, she punished Harry severely, and Harry alone, for being the ringleader.

But more painful by far were Papa's occasional outbursts, for though John Truman never spanked, never laid a hand in anger on any of his children, which seems remarkable for a man of such known temper, his scoldings were enough to "burn the hide off." One incident was never forgotten. His father had been leading him on the pony when Harry fell off, only to be told that any boy who could not stay on a pony at a walk must walk himself. Harry cried all the way back to the house, where Mamma let it be known she thought he had been unjustly treated.

Still more change followed in the summer of 1890, the summer of the

41

eyeglasses, when Mamma announced they were leaving the farm, moving to Independence, so that Harry could receive proper schooling. With money inherited from his father, John Truman acquired a house and several lots on South Crysler Avenue, close to the Missouri Pacific railroad tracks. At age forty, having attained nothing like the success forecast in the Jackson County *History,* John had decided to try again as a stock trader. He paid $1,000 down for house and land, and took out a mortgage for $3,000, certain he had driven a good bargain with the owner, Samuel Blitz, one of the few Jews in town.

For Harry, whose world, through the new eyeglasses, had only just come into focus, the next few years were to be a time of great adjustment.

In 1892, Solomon Young died at age seventy-seven. Less than a year later, a black servant girl trying to light a coal-oil lamp accidentally ignited a fire that burned the Young house to the ground. Practically nothing was saved, and though a small house, intended as a temporary replacement, was put up on the same spot for Grandma Young, and Uncle Harrison returned to help manage things, the old way of life at the homeplace was over. The one personal possession of Grandpa Young's to survive the disaster was the brass telescope from his days on the plains, which he had given to Matt sometime before.

Nine-year-old Harry's feelings at the time of his Grandfather Young's death went unrecorded. But in later years he would talk often of the "big man" in his background who had made his own way in the world, on nerve and will, who had seen the Great West when it was still wild, who played a part in history, and who—of course—came home always to Missouri. With such a grandfather a boy could hardly imagine himself a nobody.

He appears to have liked school from the start. He liked his first-grade teacher, Miss Mira Ewin. He liked his second-grade teacher, Miss Minnie Ward. He liked *all* his teachers, by his later account—"I do not remember a bad teacher in all my experience," he would reflect—and learned quickly how to make them like him. In this he felt he had quite a knack. He made a study of people, he remembered. "When I was growing up it occurred to me to watch the people around me to find out what they thought and what pleased them most. . . . I used to watch my father and mother closely to learn what I could do to please them, just as I did with my schoolteachers and playmates." It was thus, by getting along with people, he discovered, that he could nearly always get what he wanted.

By all surviving evidence he was an exceptionally alert, good little boy of sunny disposition who, with the glasses that so greatly magnified his blue eyes, looked as bright and interested as could be. Mira Ewin, the first-grade teacher, remembered never having to reprimand him. "He just smiled his way along," she said. A report card for second grade shows him consistently in the 90's in spelling, reading, and deportment. His lowest grade for the first marking period was an 86 in writing—naturally left-handed, he was being taught to use his right hand—but by the third marking period he had brought that up to a 90, while for both language and arithmetic he received a perfect 100 percent.

The fourth marking period is missing because in midwinter, early in 1894, both he and Vivian came down with diphtheria, and though Vivian recovered quickly, Harry took a dramatic turn for the worse. He became paralyzed in his legs and arms and could only lie helplessly. For months Matt wheeled him about in a baby carriage, until abruptly, miraculously he recovered, and from that point on was seldom sick again.

When it was suggested to Vivian years later that his mother had to have been terribly frightened by the crisis, he said she "didn't scare easy."

Tutored through the summer, Harry made such progress that he was allowed to skip third grade and go directly into fourth. By now also he was reading "everything I could get my hands on—histories and encyclopedias and everything else." For his tenth birthday, in the spring of 1894, his mother presented him with a set of large illustrated volumes grandly titled in gold leaf *Great Men and Famous Women*. He would later count the moment as one of life's turning points.

There were four volumes: *Soldiers and Sailors, Statesmen and Sages, Workmen and Heroes,* and *Artists and Authors*. They were not books for children, but anthologies of essays from *Harper's* and other leading American and English magazines. The subjects, numbering in the hundreds, ranged from Moses to Grover Cleveland. The authors included Edward Everett Hale on Goethe, Lord Macaulay on Samuel Johnson, H. Rider Haggard on Cortéz, and young Theodore Roosevelt on Winfield Scott. Harry would eventually plow his way through all of them, *Soldiers and Sailors* appealing especially. He dreamed of becoming a great general. He loved best the story of Hannibal, who had only one eye. "There is not in all history [he read] so wonderful an example of what a single man of genius may achieve against tremendous odds. . . ." Of the American heroes, his favorites, not surprisingly, were Andrew Jackson and Robert E. Lee, who was his mother's idol. It was to be worthy of her, he would one day confide to a friend, that he studied the careers of "great men."

Included in the Lee biography was a letter from Lee to his son written in 1860. Though she could never have found the words, it was what Matt herself might have written to the boy as the new century approached:

You must be frank with the world; frankness is the child of honesty and courage. Say just what you mean to do on every occasion, and take it for granted you mean to do right. . . . Never do anything wrong to make a friend or keep one; the man who requires you to do so, is dearly purchased at a sacrifice. Deal kindly, but firmly with all your classmates; you will find it the policy which wears best. Above all do not appear to others what you are not.

Matt and John Truman both wanted books in the house. John kept loose change in a tray from an old steamer trunk, to save for a set of Shakespeare. Harry would never recall being bored, "not once," he said, because "we had a houseful of books." He read the Bible (twice through by the time he was twelve, he later claimed), "pored over" *Plutarch's Lives,* a gift from his father, and in time to come, read all of the new set of Shakespeare. The reading was not something you talked about outside the house, he explained. "It was just something you did."

Home now was a white clapboard, carpenter's-planbook house not unlike a number of others in Independence, except for a cupola with a gilded rooster weathervane. Sloping away at the back was an unusually deep lot of several acres, where John Truman, an avid gardener, grew strawberries and vegetables, and kept cows, horses, and whatever live-stock he happened to be trading at the moment, which could be a surprising number. For a time there were no fewer than five hundred goats quartered on the property. Trying to sink a well, he hit natural gas, with which he heated both his house and that of a neighbor. It was a rare piece of good luck for John Truman.

Beyond the back fence, about 150 yards or so distant, was the Missouri Pacific depot, while on the north side of the house the main tracks ran so close the trains would rattle the kitchen dishes. The soot and noise were something for Matt to contend with, not to say the smell of five hundred goats.

Harry was fascinated by trains, and daily a total of twenty-three went by. He would sit alone on the roof of the coal shed behind the house counting freight cars, or, on winter nights, awake in his bed, listen for the eastbound Kansas-Nebraska Limited, which made no stop at Independence and began shrieking its warning whistle miles beyond town.

"Harry, do you remember how much you loved the trains?" his cousin Ethel Noland would ask years afterward.

"I still do," he said.

First and second grade were at the Noland School on South Liberty Street, which was a long walk, but when the new eight-room Columbian School opened on South River Boulevard, he had only to go three blocks.

He kept to himself more than most boys his age and in later years he would speak feelingly of the isolation of childhood. "It's a very lonely thing being a child." He seldom played games. He was afraid of the rough-and-tumble of the schoolyard and because of his glasses, felt incapable of any sport that involved a moving ball. He much preferred being at home.

To help with the cooking and washing, the family now employed a woman named Caroline Simpson, who was "black as your hat," and who, with her husband, "Letch," and four children, lived with the Trumans. Caroline Simpson taught Harry to cook on the big wood stove and talked to him by the hour. He liked the warmth and chatter of the kitchen, liked to look after his little sister. He would sit with her in a rocking chair for hours at a time, braiding her hair or singing her to sleep. No one was ever so nice to her as her brother Harry, Mary Jane would say in later years. Outside in the yard he never took his eyes off her, afraid she might hurt herself, as he once had. The cellar door had slammed on his foot and cut off the end of his big toe. Mamma had rushed to the rescue, found the severed piece, and held it in place until the doctor arrived to secure it with a coating of crystalline iodoform and a bandage.

For a small boy he was also abnormally neat and clean. John Truman was the kind of father who wanted everything looking just so—grass clipped around fence posts, horses "slicked up," and his children turned out in like fashion. But in a photograph of Harry made in Kansas City when he was thirteen and about to enter high school, he looks not just spotless, every detail in order, but like a boy who will stay that way.

He was never popular like other boys, never one of the fighters as he called them. Reminiscing long afterward, he spoke of the teasing he endured because of his glasses. "To tell the truth, I was kind of a sissy," he would say, using the hated word. He ran from fights, he admitted. Yet his brother Vivian had no memory of Harry being teased about his glasses, and to judge by the recollections of several boyhood friends he wasn't considered a sissy exactly, only different, "serious," as one recalled:

> They wanted to call him a sissy, but they just didn't do it because they had a lot of respect for him. I remember one time we were playing . . . Jesse James or robbers and we were the Dalton brothers out in Kansas . . . and we were arguing about them . . . we got the history mixed up . . . but Harry came in and straightened it out, just who were the Dalton brothers and how many got killed. Things like that the boys had a lot of respect for. They didn't call him sissy.

45

With girls of his own age he was so shy he could barely speak. His initial brush with other children in Independence was at Sunday School when the family first moved to town. Matt had sent him to the big, new red-brick First Presbyterian Church on Lexington Street, rather than to one of the Baptist churches, because the Presbyterian minister had been especially welcoming to her. At the Presbyterian Sunday School Harry met a blond-haired, blue-eyed little girl named Elizabeth Wallace and decided she was the most entrancing creature he had ever seen. But it was five years before he dared say a word to her. The only girls with whom he felt at ease were his cousins Ethel and Nellie Noland, the daughters of his father's sister Ella and her husband, Joseph Noland.

His days passed largely in the company of women—Mamma, Caroline Simpson, his teachers, or Grandma Young, who came often to visit. He was surrounded by "women folk" and he got along with them splendidly, kidding and telling stories. His mother liked to say he was "intended for a girl" anyway, an observation he seems to have taken always in good spirit.

II

John Truman was getting on in the world. There was money now for servants, books, for studio photographs. As a surprise for the children he bought a pair of matched red goats, with custom-made harness, and a miniature farm wagon. The little rig became the talk of the neighborhood.

John was an early riser, an all-day striver, and thought to be "pretty ingenious" besides—because of his backyard gas well and various inventive ideas. He patented a staple puller for use on barbed-wire fences. For an automatic railroad switch that he devised, the Missouri Pacific reportedly offered an annual royalty of $2,000. When the Chicago & Alton topped that with an offer of $2,500, four times what most American families had to live on in a year, John asked for double the amount, with the result that both railroads turned him down and adopted another version of the same thing—pirated his idea apparently—and he wound up with nothing. It was a story told usually to show just how stubborn John Truman could be.

As a livestock trader, he stood well in the community. He had "a good eye." He could determine the age of mules or horses at a glance, seldom needing to examine their teeth, and though a quiet man, he had perfected a nice "line of trade talk." More important, John Truman's word was good. "A mighty good trader, John Truman," recalled a neighbor, ". . . very stubborn, but on the square."

Because of Harry's obvious affection for his mother, his eagerness to please her, and the enjoyment he took from her company as time went on, much would be said later of her influence, the extent to which he was "his mother's son." But as time would also tell, he and his father had much in common, more indeed than either of them realized through much of Harry's boyhood, and the influence of the father on the son would never be discounted by those who knew John Truman, or by anyone in the family, including Harry himself.

Small and compact, like a jockey, John had a weathered, sunburned face and crow's-feet that gave a hint of a smile around the eyes. The grin, when it came, was the kind people warmed to and remembered, as they remembered the temper. Touchy about his size, his honor, he would explode at the least affront, "fight like a buzz saw," as Harry would say. Once, at the courthouse, when a lawyer accused him of lying, John took after the man with his fists, chasing him out the door and into the street. On election day John Truman was nearly always in a fight. One boyhood friend of Harry's, Mize Peters, who was also the son of a horse trader, remembered a man coming into his father's place, his head covered with blood, saying he had had an argument with John Truman, who hit him with a whip.

To the town, such ferocity seemed a remarkable thing in someone so unprepossessing physically and so good-natured ordinarily. "A fiery fellow," it would be said. "But a man of John Truman's integrity and industry . . . you excuse a whole lot of things."

Like many men of the time, John had a strong, sentimental veneration of women. "No one could make remarks about my aunts or my mother in my father's presence without getting into serious trouble," Harry recalled. Of the three children, Mary Jane was John's favorite. Papa, it seems, was as partial to Mary Jane as Mamma was to Harry. That Harry spent so much time watching over Mary Jane was in part because he knew how much it would please Papa.

Unlike his own father, John was considered a "liberal" in religion. He professed great faith in God, but faith also in what could be accomplished through courage and determination. "He had no use for a coward," according to a niece named Grace Summer. "He raised his children to have faith in themselves and their potentialities. . . ."

Assisted by the black hired man, Letch Simpson, John did a little farming still on rented land south of town, and occasionally he dabbled in real estate. Possibly, too, by this time he had begun speculating in grain futures in Kansas City. He was looking always for the main chance, wanting desperately to get rich. Meanwhile, as Harry said, he would trade nearly anything he owned.

In 1895, when the boy was eleven, John traded their house for another several blocks to the north, receiving some $5,400 in the bargain. Though the new house had less property than the one on Crysler Avenue, it stood on a corner lot at Waldo Street and River Boulevard, a more fashionable neighborhood and within easy walking distance of the courthouse square. Crysler Avenue had never been the wrong side of the tracks, but for an ambitious man, 909 Waldo was unquestionably progress in the right direction.

A down payment was made on a new piano for Matt, who would be remembered playing for her own "amusement and amazement." When Harry showed signs of interest, she first tried teaching him herself, then arranged for regular lessons with a young woman next door, Florence Burrus.

A piano in the parlor had become part of the good life in America, a sign of prosperity and wholesome home entertainment, and the Trumans had an upright Kimball, the most popular piano of the day, priced at about $200. ("Music for the multitudes" was the Kimball company's slogan.) Customarily, piano lessons were for the young women of a household, but Harry took to it wholeheartedly, pleased by his progress and by the approval of both parents.

For Harry, no less than for his father, life was picking up. The new neighborhood was filled with children of his own age. He was making friends as never before. The Waldo Street years would be remembered, like those on the farm, as nothing but "wonderful times."

He had a "gang" now. "Our house became headquarters for all the boys and girls around. . . . There was a wonderful barn with stalls for horses and cows, a corn crib and a hayloft in which all the kids met and cooked up plans for all sorts of adventures. . . ." Mamma remained "very patient," whatever went on.

As he started high school, the friendships meant even more. Paul Bryant lived on the other side of Waldo at little Woodland College for Women, where his father was president. Across the back alley was Fielding Houchens, the Baptist minister's son. Elmer Twyman was the son of the Truman family doctor who had seen Harry through the siege of diphtheria and restored the severed tip of his toe. There was Tasker Taylor, who could draw better than anyone, and tall, shy Charlie Ross, who never missed a day of school and who, like Harry, read everything in sight.

Yet, as much as he liked them all, Harry had no best pal among the boys. His only close friends remained his girl cousins Ethel and Nellie

Noland, who were as good-natured and well read as he, interested in everything, not at all vain (or pretty), and, importantly, devoted to him. Harry once calculated that he had a grand total of thirty-nine cousins, but Ethel and Nellie were the favorites and they would remain so all of his life. Ethel in particular would understand him as almost no one else ever did.

Just six months older than Harry, Ethel was a year ahead in school. Nellie, who was four years older, was very like a big sister to him. As a threesome they spent hours together after school and in the evenings, usually at the Noland house on Maple Avenue. In summer the girls were regular visitors at the farm on Blue Ridge. Harry was always considerate, always companionable, Ethel remembered. "Harry was always fun." They read Shakespeare aloud, taking parts. After doing *Hamlet,* Ethel began calling him Horatio, brave Horatio, the staunch friend.

The Noland sisters knew, too, how much he still secretly cared for Elizabeth Wallace, who had been in his class from the time he switched to the Columbian School in fourth grade, and who, year after year, because of the alphabetical seating arrangement, occupied the desk immediately behind him.

Bessie, as everyone called her, lived on North Delaware Street, two and a half blocks from the Trumans, in a tall frame house, number 608, with a bur oak shading the front lawn. "If I succeeded in carrying her books to school and back home for her I had a big day," he would later say, appraising how far he had advanced in overcoming his shyness.

She was his "ideal." She was popular. She stood out in class, always dressed in the latest thing. A natural all-round athlete, she played baseball as well as a boy (as third baseman she had no trouble with the long throw to first). She could run faster than her brothers and beat them in tennis. She was better at tennis than almost anyone her age, as Harry knew from watching her on the courts at Woodland College. In winter he would stand and watch her race off on skates across the college pond. She could skate, she could dance, she could do so much that he could not, that he had never learned. She could even whistle through her teeth, as almost no girl ever could.

Her street, North Delaware, with its ample houses and sidewalks of hexagonal flagstone, was considered the finest street in Independence, the houses lending an air of dignity to the whole neighborhood west of the Square. The tall gray residence of her wealthy grandfather, George Porterfield Gates, up the street on North Delaware, was one of the showplaces of town. Grandmother Gates was English. At Christmas, Bessie gave gifts to her friends wrapped in fancy paper and wore silk dresses to formal parties and dances of the kind to which Harry was never invited.

Besides, Bessie was a Presbyterian, which socially put her at "the top of the pole." (Since the war, the Baptists had slipped to perhaps third or fourth place, below the Campbellites and the Northern Methodists and Southern Methodists, but were still ahead of the Lutherans, the Catholics, and the Reorganized Latter-Day Saints, those Mormons who had come back from Utah.) Asked long afterward whether she remembered Harry Truman hanging about the Wallace house in the years they were all growing up, Bessie's close friend and next-door neighbor, Mary Paxton, responded emphatically, "No! No! Harry was a Baptist."

III

It was, as people said, the kind of town where everybody knew everybody and everybody's business. The population was six thousand and growing, but only slowly. Compared to Kansas City it was a sleepy backwater, churchgoing, conservative, rooted to the past, exactly as most residents preferred. Kansas City was a brassy Yankee town, "money-wise" and full of "new people." Independence was southern in both spirit and pace—really more southern than midwestern—and very set in its ways.

There had been considerable building since the war. The coming of the railroads, the pellmell growth of Kansas City, the rise of several new local enterprises had had an effect. North Delaware Street, which ran north-south, four blocks west of the Square, was a perfect example of the changed look. The large Bullene house, the Sawyer house with its Tiffany glass windows, the big Gates place were all new since the war, like the money that built them. The Bullenes belonged to the family that founded Kansas City's most popular dry goods firm, Emery, Bird, Thayer. Aaron Sawyer was head of the Bank of Independence, which had been organized since the war. George Porterfield Gates was partner in the Waggoner-Gates Milling Company of Independence, founded in 1866, which hit a bonanza with "Queen of the Pantry Flour," a product known throughout the Midwest.

Gates himself was part of a postwar Yankee influx. He had come from Vermont by way of Illinois, joined William Waggoner in the milling business in 1883, and two years later greatly remodeled and expanded his relatively modest house at the corner of North Delaware and Blue Avenue, spending in all, according to the Independence *Sentinel,* a fabulous $8,000. Painted gray with black trim at the windows, the finished clapboard "mansion" had fourteen rooms, verandas front and rear, fancy fretwork, tinted ("flashed") glass in the front bay windows, slate roof, gas illumination, and hot and cold running water.

Gates's partner, William Waggoner, lived in even grander style, across from the mill on Pacific Street, in the house George Caleb Bingham once occupied, but that Waggoner had done over sparing no expense. It sat on a knoll, in a leafy, parklike setting of 20 acres.

The Swope place on South Pleasant Street had a ballroom on the top floor. (The Swope fortune came from land in Kansas City.) The Vaile house on North Liberty, the showiest house in Independence, was a towering stone-trimmed, red-brick Victorian wedding cake, with thirty-one rooms and Carrara marble fireplaces. The Vaile stable had mahogany-paneled stalls. There was a greenhouse and four full-time gardeners. If Harvey Vaile, who made his money in "pure water" and contract mail delivery, was not the richest man in town, he certainly lived as though he were.

Overall it was quite a handsome community. The primary streets were paved, clean, and shaded by large old elms and cottonwoods. People took pride in their gardens. On summer evenings, after dark, families sat visiting on front porches, their voices part of the night for anybody crossing the lawns between houses.

National holidays and politics provided what little excitement occurred from one year to another. Most memorable for young Harry Truman was the day of Grover Cleveland's second victory, in 1892, when the family was still in the house on Crysler Avenue. John Truman had scrambled to the top of the roof to tie a flag to the gilded weathervane, and that night, looking extremely proud, he rode a gray horse in a torchlight parade. Bessie Wallace's friend Mary Paxton, a latter-day chronicler of town life, remembered how the men with their blazing torches came swinging down North Delaware leaving a trail of light under the dark trees. She, Harry, all their generation would remember it as a night of nights, since twenty years went by before Democrats, with the election of Wilson, could celebrate another presidential victory.

In lots of ways it was a country town still. Roosters crowed at dawn. Dinner remained a midday meal in many households. The standard Sunday dinner after church was fried chicken, buttered peas, mashed potatoes, cream gravy, and beaten biscuits, which, being made of Queen of the Pantry Flour, a "soft wheat" flour, were understood to be the world's best. Mud-spattered buggies and farm wagons clogged the Square on Saturday nights when the farmers came to town for haircuts and supplies. Town boys grew up with farmer's chores as part of the daily routine.

Harry and Vivian had cows to milk, horses to curry, water, and feed, wood to split for the kitchen stove.

On clear winter nights, with the trees bare and the soft glow of gas and oil lamps still the only light in the windows of town, stars in the black sky overhead blazed with a clarity that residents of a later, "electrified" era would never experience.

Local boosters insisted on calling it a city and bragged about the new electric plant under construction at a cost of $30,000, or the new high school, which had cost still more. Local merchants were described as unexcelled "in regard to integrity, uprightness and faithfulness in business affairs and cordiality and good nature in social life."

Yet for all this there was an air of great understated gentility, even sophistication. There were those in town, among the old moneyed families, who talked of travels in Europe, or summers in Colorado Springs. "Study groups" met to discuss literature and poetry, and with a degree of appreciation and vitality that could take visitors by surprise.

The teaching in the schools Harry attended was superb. In addition to Woodland College for Women, there was Presbyterian College, also for women, and St. Mary's Academy for girls. These, to be sure, were only tiny, struggling institutions—the usual graduating class at Woodland numbered just a dozen or so—but they were well regarded and cause for much local pride. Independence, remembered Ethel Noland years later, "stood for culture," a claim easy for outsiders to scoff at, she knew, but that she and others like her took very much to heart.

"There was conversation," she said. "I mean by that talk about what was going on in the world, talk about ideas."

The town supported two bookstores and most of the leading families took the Kansas City papers, in addition to the *Sentinel* or the Jackson *Examiner*. Kansas City, furthermore, was only a ten-mile ride by trolley or on the new train known as the Airline. So there was little sense of being cut off from the wide world, if the wide world was what you wished.

And with so much history attached to the town, no one with a feeling for the past could find it uninteresting. "No town in the west is richer in historical interest than the beautiful city of Independence," declared a new guide to Independence. At the point south of town where the wagon trains had crossed Blue River, crevices worn by their wheels were still plainly evident. George Caleb Bingham had painted his *Order No. 11* in one of the old outbuildings at the Waggoner estate. The brick walls of the Chrisman-Sawyer Bank, on the northwest corner of the courthouse square, showed the scars still of Civil War battles, and on pleasant mornings in the years of Harry Truman's boyhood, old Marshal Peacock could often be seen walking stiffly about town, a spare, erect figure with a white beard and cane, who, as everyone knew, still carried the bullet fired by Jim Crow Chiles lodged in his spine.

George Porterfield Gates, Bessie Wallace's grandfather, liked to frighten and delight Bessie and her friends with his tale of a late-night drive home in a buggy from a long-ago country wedding. A mysterious rider had appeared out of the dark, put a gun to Gates's neck, and held it there all the way into town. It was Jim Crow Chiles, who, Gates was sure, had only murder in his heart. But, as they turned down North Delaware Street, Jim Crow "laughed his fiendish laugh" and vanished in the night, as suddenly as he had appeared.

The atmosphere remained pervadingly southern—antebellum Old South, unreconstructed. Handkerchiefs were waved whenever the band played "Dixie." The United Daughters of the Confederacy thrived, and such formal parties as attended by genteel young folk like Bessie Wallace and her friends were hardly different from those put on in Macon or Tuscaloosa, from the floral decorations entwining stair rails to the refreshments of chicken salad and charlotte russe. The biggest memorial in Woodland Cemetery was the Confederate monument. Portraits of Lee and Jackson were displayed prominently in many front parlors, and in summer Quantrill's "boys"—grizzled, tobacco-chewing, Border War veterans dressed as if for church—gathered for daylong outdoor reunions, a portrait of Quantrill draped in crepe as their centerpiece. Often Jesse James's brother Frank appeared for such occasions, causing great excitement.

At school, one of Harry's favorite teachers, Ardelia Hardin, who taught Latin, would describe for the class how her father had been hit three times during Pickett's Charge at Gettysburg and left for dead until discovered by Catholic sisters and taken to a Baltimore hospital, where, once recovered, he refused to swear allegiance to the United States and for this was imprisoned for the remainder of the war. "Harry always wanted to know about that," Miss Hardin would remember half a century later, very pleased.

Virtually the entire town was American-born, though nearly every black resident past the age of forty had been born in slavery. Immigrant Irish, Italians, Croatians, and other foreign, impoverished people of the kind crowding into the vile West Bottoms of Kansas City were rarely ever seen in Independence.

Black residents lived in what was called "Nigger Neck," a cluster of makeshift houses and shacks in a persimmon grove northwest of the Square. Blacks were unwelcome at most stores and were denied use of

53

the town library. Black children went to a separate school—the Young School, named for the free-black wagonmaker of pioneer days, Hiram Young—and while white families like the Trumans might feel great, life-long affection for their own black servants, words like "nigger" and "coon" were used as a matter of course in so-called "polite society." And below the surface always lay a threat of violence, should any blacks forget their "place." News of lynchings in the South were given lurid play by both local papers, invariably in the spirit that the victim only got what he had coming to him. The summer of 1901, the year Harry finished high school, the Jackson *Examiner* declared on its editorial page:

> The community at large need not be especially surprised if there is a Negro lynching in Independence. The conditions are favorable at this time. There are a lot of worthless young Negro men in town who do nothing. They do not pretend to work and stand around on the streets and swear and make remarks about ladies and others who may pass by. They crowd into the electric cars and become offensive....

There were also in town, the editors were careful to add, many law-abiding Negroes "who are good citizens and who understand the truth of what we say as well as anyone."

Certain precepts and bywords were articles of faith in such a place, in such times, and nearly everybody growing up there was imbued with them, in principle at least:

Honesty was the best policy. It saved time and worry, because if you always told the truth you never had to keep track of what you said.

Make yourself useful.

Anything worthwhile required effort.

If at first you don't succeed, try try again. "Never, never give up," Harry's father would say.

Children were a reflection of their parents. "Now Harry, you be good," his mother would tell him time after time as he went out the door.

He appears never to have questioned such dictates, any more than he questioned the established inequality of black people. "In those days," he would remember, "right was right and wrong was wrong, and you didn't have to *talk* about it."

Many of the most familiar guidelines came directly from the Bible: "Honor thy father and mother." "A good name is rather to be chosen than great riches." "Seest thou a man diligent in his business? He shall stand before kings." "Be of good cheer."

From Sunday School and his own reading of the Bible, Harry knew many passages by heart—particularly Matthew 5, 6, and 7, the Sermon on the Mount. "Ye are the salt of the earth. . . . Let your light so shine before men, that they may see your good works. . . ."

He memorized a prayer, one he would say through much of his life:

Oh! Almighty and Everlasting God, Creator of Heaven, Earth and the Universe:

Help me to be, to think, to act what is right, because it is right; make me truthful, honest and honorable in all things; make me intellectually honest for the sake of right and honor and without thought of reward to me. Give me the ability to be charitable, forgiving and patient with my fellowmen—help me to understand their motives and their short-comings—even as Thou understandest mine!

Amen, Amen, Amen.

Say what you mean, mean what you say, he was taught at home. Keep your word. Never get too big for your britches. Never forget a friend.

They were more than words-to-the-wise, they were bedrock, as clearly established, as integral to the way of life, it seemed, as were the very landmarks of the community, its schools, church steeples, and court-house. Not everyone lived up to them, of course, but to Harry it seemed everyone ought to try.

The Square was the center of the world if the town was the limit of your experience and at age fourteen, while still in high school, Harry went to work on the Square at J. H. Clinton's drugstore. It was his first paying job.

Clinton's drugstore stood at the northeast corner of the Square. Propri-etor Clinton lived upstairs. Harry's job was to come in each weekday morning at 6:30 to open up the place, sweep the sidewalk, mop the floor, wipe the counters, and do as much overall dusting and cleaning as pos-sible before seven o'clock when Mr. Clinton came down and it was time for Harry to leave for school. More than half a century later, he could remember it all in detail:

There must have been a thousand bottles to dust and yards and yards of patent-medicine cases and shelves to clean. At least it seemed that way, because I never finished the bottles and shelves by schooltime and had to start the next morning where I'd left off the day before. By the time I got around them all, it was time to start over.

Two large glass vases in the front windows had to be cleaned and dusted, as well as a surrounding display of patent medicines. The win-dows were to be washed once a week, the prescription cases dusted "very, very carefully." Saturdays and Sundays the boy worked from four in the afternoon until ten at night by the courthouse clock, when Mr. Clinton would lock up and Harry would head off in the dark, the lights in other shop windows along the Square going out one by one. Hurrying, he could make it home in twelve minutes.

J. H. Clinton advertised "Cigars, Smokers Supplies & Tobaccos, Perfumes, Toilet Articles, Soaps & Stationery, Prescriptions Carefully Compounded Day or Night." But the store accommodated the town in yet another way, as Harry soon discovered, and it was this apparently that awakened him for the first time to the hypocrisies of certain prominent citizens known for their moral rectitude, the "high hats," as he called them.

In a little closet under the prescription case, which faced the front and shut off the view of the back end of the store, was an assortment of whiskey bottles. Early in the morning, sometimes before Mr. Clinton arrived, the good church members and Anti-Saloon Leaguers would come in for their early morning drink behind the prescription case at ten cents an ounce. They would wipe their mouths, peep through the observation hole in front of the case, and depart. This procedure gave a fourteen-year-old boy quite a viewpoint on the public front of leading citizens and "amen-corner-praying" churchmen.

He would set the bottle on the counter and wait. "They'd put their dimes on the counter, and I'd leave all those dimes there until Mr. Clinton came in, and he'd put them in the cash register." It was because these customers were such "counterfeits" that he hated having any part in the transaction. Far better, he thought, were the "tough old birds" around town who bought a proper drink in a real saloon whenever they wished, regardless of appearances.

The drugstore was one of several shops and stores fashioned out of what had once been the old Noland House, the frontier hotel and saloon where the body of Harry's infamous uncle, Jim Crow Chiles, had been laid out after the shooting, a point of history Harry surely knew all about but never spoke of. The store was at the corner of Maple and Main, which with Lexington and Liberty, framed the Square. A jewelry store, a bookshop, two groceries, the Hotel Metropolitan, H. W. Rummel's harness and saddle shop, a dry goods store, and the Courthouse Exchange Saloon were in the same block on Maple. Elsewhere around the Square, all facing the courthouse, were three more drugstores, two more saloons, A. J. Bundschu's Department Store ("Once a patron, always a patron"), two barbershops, a tobacco shop, a shoe store, a theater, an opera house, a hardware store, a bakery, and an ice cream parlor. Three banks—the First National, the Bank of Independence, and the old, brick Chrisman-Sawyer—stood prominently at three different corners, while upstairs over several of the stores were various law and dental offices and Miss Dunlap's dancing classes. A lumberyard, the Western Union offices, a barbershop for blacks, two livery stables, a feed store, the post office, the town jail, and the Airline railroad station were just off the Square, which meant that most of life's necessities were all extremely handy, including the Ott-Mitchell Undertaking Parlor, which stood catty-cornered to J. H. Clinton's drugstore.

But for size and impressiveness, nothing approached the courthouse, rising from its shaded lawn at the center of the Square. The simple, dignified little building of old with its fanlight over the door had long since disappeared, swallowed up by a great red-brick renovation in the high-Victorian mode with a mansard-roofed clocktower five stories tall. The courthouse was the focal point of Independence—the clocktower could be seen for miles jutting above the trees—and the courthouse, of course, was Democratic, for though Republicans were not unknown in Independence, the town remained solidly Democratic. People were born and raised Democrats as they were born and raised Baptists or Catholics. It was not something you questioned. As one said, "You were a Democrat come hell or high water. Or you were a Republican."

In the warm months, on wooden benches in the dappled light of the courthouse lawn, the town loafers and "philosophers" congregated. Courthouse politicians, tradesmen, out-of-town salesmen, store clerks and bank presidents, mothers in long skirts shopping with their daughters—a good part of the town—passed up and down the sidewalks, stopping frequently to "visit." The dark green Kansas City streetcar arrived and departed, making its cautious turn at Liberty and Lexington with bell clanging and a screech of wheels. In full summer, farm wagons laden with fresh produce lined the curbstones. Some summers, to keep the dust down, the town water wagon had to circle the Square several times daily.

To go up to the Square each morning to a regular job was for a boy to be very like a man. It was to be known, to be spoken to, and spoken well of if one were a brisk, cheerful, dependable boy like Harry Truman—and however disillusioned he may have been by some of the clientele at the drugstore, he was clearly enjoying himself and probably would have stayed on had his father not intervened. His first week's wages of three silver dollars were, in memory, "the biggest thing that ever happened to me." He bought a present for his mother and tried to give what money was left to his father, who said kindly that he should keep it for himself.

After three months, John Truman told the boy he had done enough. Better that he concentrate on his studies.

IV

He grew dutifully, conspicuously studious, spending long afternoons in the town library, watched over by a white plaster bust of Ben Franklin. Housed in two rooms adjacent to the high school, the library contained perhaps two thousand volumes. Harry and Charlie Ross vowed to read all of them, encyclopedias included, and both later claimed to have succeeded. Harry liked Mark Twain and Franklin's *Autobiography*. He read Sir Walter Scott because Scott was Bessie Wallace's favorite author. The fact that the town librarian, Carrie Wallace, was a cousin to Bessie may also have influenced the boy's show of scholarly dedication.

"I don't know anybody in the world that ever read as much or as constantly as he did," remembered Ethel Noland. "He was what you call a 'book worm.' "

History became a passion, as he worked his way through a shelf of standard works on ancient Egypt, Greece, and Rome. "He had a real feeling for history," Ethel said, "that it wasn't something in a book, that it was part of life—a section of life or a former time, that it was of interest because it had to do with people." He himself later said it was "true facts" that he wanted. "Reading history, to me, was far more than a romantic adventure. It was solid instruction and wise teaching which I somehow felt that I wanted and needed." He decided, he said, that men make history, otherwise there would be no history. History did not make the man, he was quite certain.

His list of heroes advanced. To Andrew Jackson, Hannibal, and Robert E. Lee were added Cincinnatus, Scipio, Cyrus the Great, and Gustavus Adolphus, the seventeenth-century Swedish king. No Jeffersons or Lincolns or Leonardos were part of his pantheon as yet. Whatever it was that made other boys of turn-of-the-century America venerate Andrew Carnegie or Thomas Edison, he had none of it. The Great Men by his lights were still the great generals.

Few boys in town ever went to high school. The great majority went to work. High school, like piano lessons, was primarily for girls. In Harry's class, largest yet at the new high school, there were thirty girls and just eleven boys.

Harry was good in Latin, "very good" in math, poor in spelling, and greatly influenced by his teachers who were all women except for "Professor" W. L. C. Palmer, the principal, who taught science, the one subject Harry didn't care for. The women were spinsters, as required by the school system. (When his Latin teacher, Ardelia Hardin—she with the Pickett's Charge grandfather—became the wife of Professor Palmer, she had to give up teaching.) Known by everybody, they comprised a kind of town institution unto themselves, as upholders of standards. They were "the salt of the earth," Harry would say. "They gave us our high ideals, and they hardly ever received more than forty dollars a month." They taught the old rooted values—loyalty, love of home, unquestioning patriotism—no less than Latin, history, or Shakespeare. She could never enter the classroom, said Miss Tillie Brown, without hearing the admonition to "put off thy shoes from thy feet, for the spot on which thou standest is holy ground." And while some may have snickered at her manner, none doubted her sincerity.

The influence of his teachers on his life, Harry later said, was second only to that of his mother, and when crediting a Tillie Brown or a Margaret Phelps for all they had done for him, he did so with the assumption that everybody of his generation had a Tillie Brown or Margaret Phelps in their background and could therefore understand how he felt.

The panorama of history, as taught by Margaret Phelps, began with Adam and Eve. Tall, slender, her upswept hair always in place, she was an exacting person and somewhat frightening to most of her pupils until they got to know her. Harry liked her best of all his teachers and it was in history that he did best. There was no more important field of study, Margaret Phelps affirmed in a memorable statement of faith: "It cultivates every faculty of the mind, enlarges sympathies, liberalizes thought and feeling, furnishes and approves the highest standards of character."

Tillie Brown, Matilda D. Brown, the English teacher, was hardly less impressive—"a genius at making us appreciate good literature"—and two of Harry's composition books done under her guidance would survive, one from 1899, the other dated 1900–1901, his senior year. His focus was on people and moral ideals. He responded strongly to the stamp of patriotism on an author or a character. He abhorred sham. Courage counted above all, to judge by what he wrote. At times, when writing of the corrupting influences of money and of what he called "the passions," the boy seemed wise beyond his years. How much of what he wrote was his own, how much the outlook of Tillie Brown is impossible to know, but as one who, by his own account, knew how to please a teacher, he may well have been giving her as much Brown as Truman in his value judgments.

Of James Fenimore Cooper he wrote in 1899:

> The name Cooper suggests to me stories of Indians, the sea and the Revolution, in which we go through a great many adventures and narrow escapes. It also makes me think of a man who upheld his country and who would not step out of his way because it was hard or because he had to meet a quarrel. He was a man who would not let another "run over him." He would support an argument to the last.

"Cooper's books," he also observed, "are interesting and famous but his sentences are too long."

Under the heading "Courage," he wrote in a strong, clear, straightaway hand, "The virtue I call courage is not in always facing the foe but in taking care of those at home. . . . A true heart, a strong mind and a great deal of courage and I think a man will get through the world." In an essay on *The Merchant of Venice,* in the composition book from senior year, writing on Antonio, he said that though ideal men were few, his ideal man "should in the first place be brave; then he should fear his God . . . he must not be cold, haughty, or hypocritical; but he must have a warm heart and love someone (a woman is preferable)."

Shylock interested him primarily because Shylock was a strong man. Shylock's failing was that he let his passions rule him. "When a man loses control of his passions he is gone," wrote sixteen-year-old Harry Truman. Further along, he had this to say about Bassanio:

> This world is made up of all sorts of conditions of men, from the best one could wish to the basest one could imagine. There are men who love money who will do anything for money, who will sell their souls for money. Then there are men who love money for the good that is in it, who like to use it to make others happy. There are men who love everything worldly, love wine women and a good time; then there are those who are so religious they have no time to think of anyone or anything. These men are extremists who run the thing into the ground. I like a man who has enough worldly wisdom to take care of himself; but I like him to have time to love both his God and those around him.

But it was the boy's "steadfastness" that most impressed his teachers, said Ardelia Hardin. When called on to speak in class, he would stand clear of his desk and square his shoulders before saying a word.

What his grades were remains unknown, since the school's records were later destroyed in a fire.

Measured by the time and effort expended, the most important activity in his life was the piano. Having progressed beyond the abilities of Miss Burrus, who taught by a numbers system, he began going twice weekly to Kansas City for lessons with Mrs. E. C. White, a gifted teacher who had studied under Fannie Bloomfield Zeisler, one of the leading American pianists of the era, and with Theodore Leschetizky, who had been a teacher of Paderewski. Harry grew extremely fond of Grace White. (He was fond of most older people, as his cousin Ethel observed. "He was brought up to be fond of them.") She opened a new world for him and his response was to work with exceptional determination, practicing two hours a day without fail, beginning at five o'clock every morning. As a grown man he would often speak lightly of "tickling the ivories," as if it were only something he had happened to pick up along the way. But the slender, straight-backed youth with the round eyeglasses who sat at the keyboard in the half-light of dawn every morning was in dead earnest. He thought he had the makings of a concert pianist. And apparently so did Mrs. White.

He was willing not only to do the work, but to face whatever ridicule might come. His friend Charlie Ross would remember Harry going up the street with a music roll under his arm hurrying to catch the trolley for Kansas City. "Mothers held him up as a model, so he took a lot of kidding. It required a lot of courage for a kid to take music lessons in a town like Independence." Another friend, Henry Bundschu, said Harry was the sort of boy who "seemed to do whatever his mother told him."

He also loved music; he genuinely adored the great classical works Mrs. White guided him through and insisted he learn. On a big Steinway in her old-fashioned house on Brooklyn Street in Kansas City she drilled him in Bach, Beethoven, Mendelssohn's "Songs Without Words," pieces by Weber and Grieg. He learned the new "Woodland Sketches" by the contemporary American composer Edward MacDowell. For the rest of his life he could play Paderewski's Minuet in G and several Chopin waltzes by heart. He was moved by "sad music," Beethoven's Sonata Pathétique and Chopin's Funeral March. Von Weber, he thought, wrote "beautiful things"—the Rondo Brillante, the Polka Brillante. But he liked still more the Chopin waltzes and polonaises. Mozart he loved most of all and with Mrs. White's help eventually mastered the Ninth Sonata.

He was playing serious music with utmost seriousness and going to concerts at every opportunity. Many of the concert greats of the day came to Kansas City. Twice when Fannie Bloomfield Zeisler performed, first at the Lyceum, later at Pepper Hall, Harry was in the audience. He heard her play Scarlatti's Pastorale and Capriccio, and Beethoven's Sonata, Opus 111, which a reviewer in the Kansas City *Journal* called her "most profoundly developed offering." This was in 1898, the year he worked in the drugstore, when he was fourteen. Later he heard Josef Lhévinne, who was "the best on the globe," he thought. In 1900, when Paderewski came to Kansas City on tour, Mrs. White arranged a meeting backstage with "the great man," who treated Harry to a private demonstration of how to play his Minuet in G.

As a boy brimming with such musical aspiration, his head filled with Shakespeare and noble Romans, as one who had taken teasing in a town where appearances were vital, and where every youngster bore the constant scrutiny of innumerable aunts, uncles, teachers, shopkeepers, and neighbors, he might well have burned to rebel. He might have longed for escape, as had Willa Cather growing up in Red Cloud, Nebraska, or to strike back somehow against the kind of small-town minds and souls that Sinclair Lewis would remember from boyhood in Sauk Centre, Minnesota. But nowhere in all that Harry Truman wrote and said about his youth, or in the lengthy recollections of him by friends and family, is there even a hint of anger or hurt or frustration over his surroundings. Clearly he liked Independence, Missouri, and its people. He liked being Harry Truman.

He had thinned out, stretched out, to perhaps 5 foot 7, which was not as tall as he would be, but above average and already several inches taller than his father. Neat, clean, cheerful, he had still the gift for getting along with almost anyone. People knew who he was and people liked him, and partly because of the music roll and the eyeglasses. He had no enemies, he held no grudges. He had done no wrong, nor anything yet to be ashamed of, so far as is known. Importantly, his father approved of him, for all their seemingly different interests. Harry was "all right," John Truman said. "He knew Harry had ability," Vivian remembered. "He liked the way he never had an idle moment. . . ."

Vivian, in contrast to his girlish-sounding name, was a sturdy, man's kind of boy, who was good at games and wished no part of books or piano lessons. Already Vivian had shown such a knack for horse trading that John Truman gave him a checkbook and set him up as a "partner" at the age of twelve. Harry, try as he might, had no heart for trade. As he would later explain to Bessie Wallace, "When I buy a cow for $30 and then sell her to someone for $50 it always seems to me that I am really robbing that person of $20."

Where Harry and his father found common ground was in the sociability and excitement of politics. Among the happiest of all Harry's boyhood memories would be the big Democratic picnics every August at Lone Jack. John Truman would have everyone up early. He and the boys would hitch two of the best mules to a spring wagon, and with everything ready, the whole family would set out for the five-mile drive, the wagon filled with fried chicken, cakes, and pies. By noon at Lone Jack there would be thousands of people spreading food on tablecloths on the grass, and visiting back and forth. Then, about two, the speaking would begin. Harry liked particularly a candidate known as Colonel Crisp, "a colonel by agreement," who ran for Congress time after time but never won and was famous for his annual picnic oration on the Battle of Lone Jack during the Civil War. Challenged once on his accuracy by a veteran who had been in the battle, Crisp responded, "Goddamn an eyewitness anyway. He always spoils a good story." Another speaker, Congressman William S. Cowherd from Lee's Summit, told a story that Harry would take pleasure in retelling the rest of his life. Speaking of certain provisions in a pending tariff bill that he found unpalatable, the congressman was reminded of a farmer on a visit to New York, having his first experience in a fancy hotel dining room. First he was served celery, which he ate, then a bowl of consommé, which he drank. But when the waiter placed a lobster before him, the farmer looked up indignantly and said, "I ate your bouquet. I drank your dishwater. But I'll be darned if I'll eat your bug."

Now, in the summer of 1900, Harry went with his father to Kansas City to attend the Democratic National Convention that renominated the Great Commoner, William Jennings Bryan, to run a second time against William McKinley. John Truman sat in a box seat, as the guest of one of Kansas City's most up-and-coming citizens, William T. Kemper, a friend in "the grain business" and a national committeeman. Harry was consigned to the balcony or ran errands for Kemper, and hugely enjoyed himself. He remembered the immense sweep of the great hall and a crowd of seventeen thousand people, nearly three times the population of Independence, all under one roof. The nominating speech for Bryan touched off a demonstration that lasted half an hour.

Harry and his father declared themselves thorough "Bryan men," and though Bryan and his running mate, Adlai Stevenson of Illinois, went down to defeat in November to McKinley and Theodore Roosevelt, Bryan remained an idol for Harry, as the voice of the common man.

The Democrats made imperialism the issue in the election of 1900, but it was McKinley prosperity that carried the country, the Republicans campaigning on the theme of the "Full Dinner Pail." How aware the boy may have been of his own family's unprecedented prosperity at the moment is unknown. But by speculating in grain futures, through such contacts as he had established with "insiders" like William T. Kemper, John Truman was moving rapidly toward his dream of riches.

With his senior year under way that same fall, Harry found himself busier than ever. He, Charlie Ross, Tasker Taylor, and several others launched a first yearbook for the school. Charlie named it *The Gleam,* after Tennyson's poem "Merlin and the Gleam." Tasker did the illustrations. As part of their Latin studies, Harry and Charlie worked on translations of Cicero —*Salus populi suprema est lex,* "The people's good is the highest law." Charlie, who was class president as well as editor of *The Gleam,* was also first in scholarship.

With Elmer Twyman, Harry spent weeks building a wooden model of Caesar's bridge over the Rhine, as described in Caesar's *Commentaries,* and met regularly with his cousin Nellie Noland, who was a "whiz" at Latin. The Noland family by this time had moved to 216 North Delaware, a small frame house opposite the Gates mansion. Best of all, Bessie Wallace was now part of the group there.

She was "over a good deal," Cousin Ethel would remember. "I don't know whether they got much Latin read or not because there was a lot of fun going on." Harry had taken up fencing. "He had two foils, or rapiers, or whatever you call them; and so we would sometimes practice fencing, which we knew absolutely nothing about, but it was fun to try, and we had the porch . . . room here to play and have fun . . . which we did, with a little Latin intermingled."

Progress and the new century were popular topics. " 'Progress' is the cry on every hand," wrote Elmer Twyman in *The Gleam;* "and invention, reform, and improvement is everywhere—in weapons, heat, light, food, medicine, building, transportation. Truly we are wizards performing miracles. We lack nothing but the airship and the philosopher's stone, or, perhaps, the 'fountain of youth.' " Harry copied down and saved the lines of a favorite poem by Tennyson, "Locksley Hall," describing all the wonders to come, including airships and air warfare and universal law:

> *For I dipt into the future, far as human eye could see,*
> *Saw the Vision of the world, and all the wonder that would be;*
>
> *Saw the heavens fill with commerce, argosies of magic sails,*
> *Pilots of the purple twilight, dropping down with costly bales;*
>
> *Heard the heavens fill with shouting, and there rain'd a ghastly dew*
> *From the nations' airy navies grappling in the central blue;*

Far along the world-wide whisper of the south-wind rushing warm,
With the standards of the peoples plunging thro' the thunder storm;

Till the war-drum throbb'd no longer, and the battle flags were furl'd
In the Parliament of Man, the Federation of the World.

There the common sense of most shall hold a fretful realm in awe,
And the kindly earth shall slumber, lapt in universal law.

For the class picture taken outside the school's main entrance, Harry stood by himself in back of the back row. Elmer Twyman, who stood nearby, proudly holding a man's hat, had decided to become a doctor like his father. Charlie Ross, who sat on the ground at the near end of the front row, his long legs drawn up so that his socks were showing, was headed for the University of Missouri and a career in journalism. Harry had removed his glasses for the picture. He was not smiling, only paying attention to the photographer, his right hand resting on the shoulder of the slight, wistful-looking boy in front, Will Garrett, the class poet. Harry had decided to try for West Point. He and Fielding Houchens, who wanted to go to Annapolis, were preparing for the examinations by taking extra hours in history with Miss Phelps. Bookish Harry, who fenced with girls, who had never been in a fight in his life and was admittedly afraid of guns, thought he might make a general, if not a concert pianist.

Intentionally or not, his position in the picture put him about as distant as possible from Bessie Wallace, who sat smiling at the far end of the second row.

The night of graduation, it seemed half the town was packed into the high school auditorium. The girls were in white, the boys in dark suits and stiff collars. According to the Jackson *Examiner,* no finer-looking set had ever gathered on a single platform. Harry was not one of the student speakers, he received no awards or honors. The date was May 30, 1901, Memorial Day—Decoration Day as it was more commonly called—and so there had been band music and flags flying since morning. Harry was seventeen.

3

The Way of the Farmer

Experentia does it—as Papa used to say.

—CHARLES DICKENS, *David Copperfield*

I

Within a year of Harry's graduation from Independence High School, calamity struck the Truman family, changing the course of their lives in ways none of them could have anticipated. For Harry it was as if a curtain suddenly descended, marking the end of boyhood and the small-town life he loved and that had seemed so secure and suited to him.

John Truman's run of luck on wheat futures had ended. He began losing heavily that same summer of 1901, and to recover his losses kept risking more and more until he had gambled away nearly everything he and Matt owned—as much as $40,000 in cash, stocks, and personal property, including 160 acres of prime land on Blue Ridge given to Matt by her father.

The situation could not have been much worse. At age fifty-one, John Truman was wiped out. The Waldo Avenue house had to be sold. For a while the family lived in another part of town, trying to keep up appearances, but eventually they had to pack and leave Independence altogether. They moved to a modest neighborhood in Kansas City, where John took a job for wages, something no Truman had done before. He went to work as a night watchman at a grain elevator. It was the best job he could find, at pay comparable to that of a farmhand. For a man of such fierce pride, and for those who loved him, it could only have been a painful time.

But there were no complaints. The Trumans were never a complaining people. It was not nice to tell your troubles, one must always be cheerful,

Ethel Noland would remember. If asked how you were, you were always to respond, "I'm fine. And you?" Keep your troubles to yourself. She knew from experience, for her own father, having "plunged" in railroads, went "very flat indeed."

Of his father's catastrophe, Harry would only say in later years, "He got the notion he could get rich. Instead he lost everything at one fell swoop and went completely broke."

Harry had tried a little gambling himself the summer after graduation, while traveling east by train to visit his favorite Aunt Ada, Matt's younger sister, in southern Illinois. It was his first time away from home alone, and on the return trip, stopping in St. Louis to see still more of Matt's people, a great-aunt named Hettie Powell and her family, he was taken to a horse race and urged by a cousin and three other young men to put in one of the five dollars they bet on a long shot called Claude. As Harry learned afterward, Claude was a well-known "mud horse"—the worse the track, the better he ran. Just as the race was to start, rain came in torrents. Not only did Claude finish first, he paid 25 to 1. Harry had never felt so rich in his life, but he was not to bet on a horse again for another forty years.

West Point had turned him down because of his eyes. Now, with his father's financial troubles, college of any kind was out of the question. Back from St. Louis he signed up for an accounting course at little Spaulding's Commercial College in downtown Kansas City, but even that had to be abandoned as too costly. To help the family, he went to work in the mailroom at the Kansas City *Star*. Then, in late summer, after the tragic death of a school friend, a better job came available. Tasker Taylor, the artist of the class, had been working as a construction timekeeper on the Santa Fe Railroad. On a hot evening in August, he was drowned while swimming in the Missouri River just upstream from the Independence pumping station. At John Truman's urging, Harry took the job, which, for a boy who had seen so little of life, proved a rough initiation.

The Santa Fe was doubling its tracks into Kansas City. Harry worked ten-hour days, six days a week for $30 a month, plus board, which meant living with the labor gangs in their tent camps along the river, eating greasy food, and listening to their talk. On an hourly basis the pay was not much better than at Clinton's drugstore. The talk included profanity and raw observations on life of a kind he had never imagined.

He kept tabs on everybody's time—mule drivers, blacksmiths, and the common laborers who were mostly hoboes, four hundred men in total —and saw that they were paid off every two weeks, a transaction customarily performed on Saturday nights in a saloon, so the men would drink up their earnings and thereby guarantee a return to work Monday morning, a strategy that, Harry observed sadly, nearly always worked.

Much about the job he found highly enjoyable. He liked particularly traveling up and down the line from camp to camp, spinning along alone in a handcar. And the longer he was with them, the more he liked the men—"A very down-to-earth education," he would call it—and they liked him. When the work was completed six months later, and the time came to say goodbye, a foreman, wishing him well, announced to all within earshot that Harry Truman was an "all right" fellow. "He's all right from his asshole out in every direction."

It was Harry's first public commendation.

On Friday, April 24, 1903, looking scrubbed and spruce in a dark suit and high starched collar, every bit the perfect candidate for a bank clerk, he walked up Walnut Street in Kansas City and applied for a job at the stately National Bank of Commerce.

"Are you good at figures?" he was asked on a two-page employment application form. "Fair," he wrote. Had he ever been fired? No. Did he smoke? Did he use intoxicating spirits? Had he any debts? No to all three, he answered, moving steadily down the page, using a swift dash line to indicate ditto. "Have you ever gambled or played cards for money?" No, again. "Have you ever 'played the races' or speculated in any way?"

To what extent the memory of Claude came rushing back can only be guessed, but here he hesitated, as is evident in the surviving document. He began to write something—there is the start of the down stroke of a letter—but thinking better of it apparently, he quickly repeated his ditto line. The answer was no once more, and it is the earliest known sign in his own hand that he was capable of telling less than the truth if the occasion warranted, capable of being quite human.

Asked if he had any extravagant tastes or habits, he answered that he didn't think so. "In what forms of recreation or amusement do you find pleasure?" Theaters and reading, he wrote. "Where do you spend your evenings and Sundays?" At home. All true.

He had a letter from Dr. Twyman describing him as a "model young man." Possibly, too, he had help from William T. Kemper, John Truman's friend from better days, who was a director of the bank. In any event, he was hired as a clerk in the vault starting at $20 a month, which was about what his father was making at his night watchman's job, and there he stayed for two years. In the view of his employers, his performance was outstanding. His immediate superior, a man named A. D. Flintom, could hardly say enough for him. "He is an exceptionally bright young man and is keeping the work up in the vault better than it has ever been kept," Flintom wrote in a first report on young Harry Truman.

He is a willing worker, almost always here and tries hard to please everybody. We never had a boy in the vault like him before. He watches everything very closely and by his watchfulness, detects many errors which a careless boy would let slip through. His appearance is good and his habits and character are of the best.

In a later report, "Trueman," as Flintom spelled it, was again praised for his "excellent character and good habits." He was accurate. He was "always at his post of duty," his work was "always up." Further, he was "very ambitious." "I do not know of a better young man in the bank than Trueman," wrote Flintom to vice-president Charles H. Moore. Nor was Flintom one to lavish praise indiscriminately, as is clear from what he said of Vivian Truman, who had also come to work at the bank by this time. Vivian, though "nice appearing," was "possessed of very little ability," thought Flintom. "He is a very different boy from his brother. . . ."

The vault where Harry spent his days—"the zoo," as the clerks called it—was below street level, downstairs from the bank's cavernous main lobby with its Corinthian columns and brass spittoons. He cleared checks drawn on country banks, sometimes handling as much as a million dollars a day, while keeping all notations in longhand. It was not work calling for much initiative or imagination or that he especially cared for; and Charles H. Moore, the vice-president, appears to have been the first person Harry actually disliked. Moore, said Harry Truman years later, was "never so happy as when he would call some poor inoffensive little clerk up before him in the grand lobby of the biggest bank west of the Mississippi and tell him how dumb and inefficient he was. . . ." Harry continued to do his best, however, and his pay advanced steadily. In time he was earning $40 a month, which made him the family's number one breadwinner.

His years at the National Bank of Commerce were 1903 to 1905. Two months after he went to work came the stunning news that Bessie Wallace's father, David Wallace, one of the best-known men in Independence, had committed suicide. The story was in the papers. At first light the morning of June 17, while his family still slept, he had gotten up from bed, taking care not to disturb his wife, dressed fully, took a revolver from a dresser, and walked down the hall to the bathroom where, standing in the middle of the floor, he placed the muzzle of the gun behind his left ear and fired. He was forty-three years old and had, in the words of the Jackson *Examiner,* "an attractiveness about him that was natural and spontaneous." In addition to his wife, Madge Gates Wallace, and Bessie, age eighteen, he was survived by three sons, ranging in age from sixteen to three. He left no note.

"Why should such a man take his own life?" asked the *Examiner.* "It is a question we who loved him are unable to answer. . . ." Included also in the story was the gruesome detail that the bullet had passed through his head and landed in the bathtub.

Older friends and neighbors in Independence remembered the wedding of Madge Gates to David Wallace twenty years earlier as one of the most elegant occasions in the town's history. It had been a brilliant moonlit night, the lawn at the Gates mansion ablaze with Chinese lanterns. Wedding presents in the parlor included oil paintings and an after-dinner coffee service in silver and china. David Wallace was the son of one of the old settlers from Kentucky, but until his marriage had had no wealth or social standing to speak of. He was a courthouse politician. Yet the importance of the Gates family more than compensated and David Wallace, many believed, was the handsomest man in Independence. He was like the elegant small-town figure in Edwin Arlington Robinson's poem "Richard Cory," who "fluttered pulses" with his good looks and who also "one calm summer night, / Went home and put a bullet through his head."

What the *Examiner* did not mention, but that everyone knew, was that David Wallace had a drinking problem—often he had to be carried home by friends—and most efforts to fathom the tragedy came back to that. Or to gossip about money troubles, the view being he was badly in debt "and didn't see any way out."

If the Trumans had known shame during John's financial downfall, it was little compared to what the family of a suicide would experience. The Trumans had moved away. Madge Gates, with Bessie and the younger children, left for Colorado Springs, not to return for a year. No one close to the family would ever discuss the subject except in strictest confidence. It was not something "decent people" wished to talk about. Sixty years had to go by before Bessie's friend Mary Paxton described how her father had awakened her early that morning and told her to go next door at once to be with Bessie, because Mr. Wallace had killed himself. "[Bessie] was walking up and down back of the house with clenched fists, I remember. She wasn't crying. There wasn't anything I could say, but I just walked up and down with her. . . ." Harry Truman is not known ever to have said a word on the subject outside the family.

He had seen nothing of Bessie in the time since the Trumans left town. Nor did he now. Even after she was back from Colorado Springs and began commuting to the Barstow School, Kansas City's finishing school for wealthy young women, they kept to their separate lives. With her grief-stricken mother and her brothers, Bessie moved in permanently with Grandfather and Grandmother Gates at 219 North Delaware. So at a time when the Truman family's "circumstances" were so greatly reduced, Bessie had become the "family princess" of the Gates mansion. What news Harry had of her came from the Noland sisters, who from their observation post across the street knew as much as anyone.

Since starting at the bank, Harry had been living at home, or what for the time being passed for home in Kansas City, spending little more than car-fare and lunch money, which, according to the pocket account book he kept, came to about 50 cents a day. Once, throwing economies to the wind, he spent $11 for "Ties Collar Cuffs Pins, etc." Later $10 went for "Music," piano lessons with Mrs. White, which he soon had to drop. He would sometimes say later that he quit because playing the piano was "sissy." The truth was the lessons had become more than he could afford.

His one indulgence was the theater, which he loved and for which he was willing to splurge, sometimes as much as two dollars. He went to vaudeville at the Orpheum and the Grand. For a while he worked as an usher on Saturday afternoons at the Orpheum, just to see the show for free. He saw the Four Cohans and Sarah Bernhardt. He went to concerts and the opera at Convention Hall. A note from "Horatio" dashed off on National Bank of Commerce stationery, telling his cousins Ethel and Nel-lie where to meet him for their theater date, ends: "I understand that Mr. Beresford is exceedingly good so don't fail to come. I've already got the seats. . . ." A performance by Richard Mansfield in *Dr. Jekyll and Mr. Hyde* left Harry so shaken he was afraid to go home alone.

With a population of 200,000, Kansas City was still a cow town and a grain town. St. Louis was by contrast old metropolitan and old money. St. Louis looked eastward, Kansas City faced west. They were two entirely different cities. But Kansas City was growing by leaps and bounds and prided itself in offering the latest and best of everything. There was hardly a city in America where an observant youth could have had a better day-to-day sense of the country's robust energy and confidence at the start of the new century. To Harry it was a place of "things doing." Once, with the other clerks, he rushed out of the bank and down 10th Street to see President Theodore Roosevelt speak from the back of a railroad car. It was his first chance to see a President, and though a Republican who spoke with a piping voice and who seemed surprisingly short, Roosevelt gave a good speech, Harry thought. The crowd was delighted. "They wanted to see him grin and show his teeth, which he did."

In May of 1905, Harry signed up with a new National Guard unit. "I was twenty-one years old in May of that year," he remembered, "and could do as I pleased." It was a far cry from the dream of West Point, but Private Truman began drilling with Missouri's Light Artillery, Battery B, First Brigade. ("They needed recruits," he also said later, in explanation of how, with his poor eyesight, he passed the physical exam.) His first encampment that summer was at Cape Girardeau, in the far-off southeastern corner of Missouri. He went by train as far as St. Louis, then down the Mississippi by steamboat, "quite an experience." He came home a corporal—"the biggest promotion I ever received"—and for a weekend visit to the Young farm put on his new dark blue dress uniform with its beautiful red piping on the sleeves, expecting to impress his grandmother. But as he stepped through the door, she could think only of Union soldiers. He was never to wear it again in her presence, she said.

Largely he was on his own by now. John Truman, fed up with city life, miserable in his job, had decided to try still another new start. He rented a small farm at Clinton, Missouri, about seventy miles southeast, on Grand River in prosperous farm country. Again Matt had to pack and move, and Harry began boarding out with John's sister Emma, Mrs. Rochester Colgan, in Kansas City.

It was a wide-open town still, more than living up to its reputation. Sporting houses and saloons far outnumbered churches. "When a bachelor or stale old codger was in sore need of easing himself [with a woman], he looked for a sign in the window which said: *Transient Rooms* or *Light Housekeeping,*" remembered the writer Edward Dahlberg, whose mother was proprietor of the Star Lady Barbershop on 8th Street. To Dahlberg, in memory, nearly everything about the Kansas City of 1905, the city of his boyhood, was redolent of sex and temptation. To him it was a "wild, concupiscent city." Another contemporary, Virgil Thomson, who was to become a foremost composer, wrote of whole blocks where there were nothing but saloons, this in happy contrast, he said, to dry, "moralistic" Kansas across the line. "And just as Memphis and St. Louis had their Blues, we had our *Twelfth Street Rag* proclaiming joyous low life." But with such joyous low life Harry appears to have had little or no experience. Long afterward, joking with friends about his music lessons, he would reflect that had things gone differently he might have wound up playing the piano in a whorehouse, but there is no evidence he ever set foot in such a place, or that he "carried on" in Kansas City in any fashion.

After several months with Aunt Emma, he moved to an altogether respectable boardinghouse kept by a Mrs. Trow on Troost Avenue where, for room and board (breakfast and dinner), he paid five dollars a week.

Another young boarder was a messenger at the Bank of Commerce named Arthur Eisenhower from Abilene, Kansas. (Arthur's younger brother, Dwight David, was still at home in high school.) "Harry and I had only a dollar a week left over for riotous living," Arthur would recall.

Refused another raise at the Bank of Commerce, Harry quit and went to work for the Union National Bank at 9th and Baltimore, in Kansas City's famous ten-story New York Life Building, with its giant bronze eagle over the main entrance. The pay was better—$75 a month—and the Union National a pleasanter place to work. As an assistant teller, he was soon making $100 a month, truly, as he said, a magnificent salary.

With the new job, the big paycheck, his new friends, his drill sessions with the National Guard, Harry was as busy and happy as he had ever been. Had he gone to college four years earlier, he would only now be looking for his first job. He bought a Panama hat. He had his photograph taken. At the lavish new Willis Wood Hall, he saw Sir Henry Irving and Ellen Terry in *The Merchant of Venice*.

But any thoughts he may have entertained about a career in banking were shortlived. Beset by more misfortune—his entire corn crop was lost to floods at Clinton—John Truman had agreed to move in with Grandma Young and run the Blue Ridge farm. Uncle Harrison, who had been in charge until now, had found the work more than he could handle and wanted to move to the city. The farm was large and good help ever harder to find.

The new arrangement appeared to suit everybody, and in October 1905 all the Trumans but Harry moved back to Blue Ridge. The problem was John also found the work too much, even with Vivian to help. So some four or five months later, Harry was told to quit his job and come home. The family came first. If Harry harbored any regrets or resentment, he never let on. His friends were sure he wouldn't last as a farmer.

II

The change from his life in Kansas City was stunning. For five years, until he rediscovered Bessie Wallace, his preoccupations were to be almost exclusively those determined by crops, seasons, weeds, insects, rain and sunshine, livestock, farm machinery, bank loans, and the dictates of an energetic, opinionated father who was determined to succeed at last.

Everything now revolved about the farm. It was the focus of the whole family's life, its livelihood, its constant responsibility, its sole source of income. Everyone worked, "and woe to the loafer," as Harry remembered.

"Well, if you don't work, you don't make it," was the common philosophy as expressed by a neighbor. "You may do a lot of work and not make it, too, but you've got to do it or you won't make it."

"The simple life was not always so simple," remembered another. "It was a hard life . . . a life which demanded perseverance. . . . It demanded first things first."

The day began for Harry with his father's call from the bottom of the stairs at five in the morning when it was still dark and cold outside. (That spring of 1906, Harry's first on the farm, happened to be one of abnormal cold in Jackson County, of mud and heavy rains.) And it was his father who kept at him through the day, showing him what to do, working as hard as two men, and warning Harry time after time not to hurt himself, not to try to lift anything too heavy. A building up of both the farm and the owlish-looking bank clerk was apparently much on John Truman's mind.

Harry learned to drive an Emerson gang plow, two plows on a three-wheeled frame pulled by four horses. The trick was to see that each horse pulled his part of the load. With an early start, he found, he could do five acres in a ten-hour day. Some mornings, to keep warm, he walked instead of riding. Some mornings, he remembered, not even a sweater, two coats, and an overcoat were enough to keep out the cold.

As spring moved on, he took instructions in driving the corn planter and wheat drill. John Truman would tolerate no crooked rows in the corn, no skipped places in the wheat, the money crop. If bare spots appeared in the corn or wheat, Harry would hear about it all summer. "My father told me to adjust the planter before starting, have the horses well in hand and under control, pick out an object on the other side of the field usually a quarter or a half mile away, point the tongue of the planter at that object and keep it there, letting the horses step out at a lively gait." It was how Harry would conduct much of his life.

Some of the wheat fields were immense. One horse made such trouble that Harry found himself yelling at him in his sleep.

With its nearly 600 acres, the farm was among the largest in the county, more than four times the size of the average Missouri farm, and required the full-time efforts of John, Harry, Vivian, and several hired men. For John Truman, Harry observed, everything about the life seemed second nature. The small, weatherbeaten man could not understand why anybody would wish to sleep past 5:00 A.M. Nothing about the work daunted him. Harry disliked milking cows, particularly when they flipped their manure-soaked tails in his face. Raking hay was a "cussin' job." He hated the whole business of putting rings in hogs' noses and thought husking corn, with the dirt and dust flying about, was work devised by Satan. Yet

John Truman was happier than his children had seen him in years. He would never have left the farm in the first place, he told them, had it not been for their education. Mary Jane would remember knowing where he was almost any time of day because she could hear him singing at his work.

He knew how to make them all "step lively," but was also quick to single out good work when he saw it. "Yes, and if you did a good job, he would compliment you," said Gaylon Babcock, a neighbor who from boyhood helped at threshing time. "He made you want to do a good job." Another man recalled seeing the Trumans planting a cornfield with three teams of horses working at once. A few days later he saw the same three teams cultivating the corn before it was up, to get a head start on the weeds.

Every day was work, never-ending work, and Harry did "everything there was to do"—hoeing corn and potatoes in the burning heat of summer, haying, doctoring horses, repairing equipment, sharpening hoes and scythes, mending fences. Some things he did better than others. Using an ax or saw left-handed, he took a lot of kidding for work that looked left-handed. He learned the song of the meadowlark (it said, "Pretty boy go to work," according to local tradition) and that wind from the northwest meant rain. By paying attention to what his father had to teach, he became highly knowledgeable about livestock, as proficient nearly as Vivian. They raised registered short-horn cows and bulls, sheep, mules, thoroughbred horses, and Hampshire hogs. John won prizes for his horses. Harry's "real love" was the hogs, which he gave such names as "Mud," "Rats," and "Carrie Nation." Harry also kept the books, listing which crops were sold to whom and for how much:

Potatoes, Oct. 1906

Ben Vest	2 bu[shels] @ 7 p.	Paid	1.40
Mrs. Allen	1/2 bu	Paid	.35
H. M. Dyer	5 bu	Paid	3.50

Hogs and Cattle

Aug 23	9 hogs to K.C.		74.38
24	1 " " "		15.93
Oct 18	1 cow " "		32.85
Nov 4	Difference on horse trade		3.00

Miscellaneous

Oct 18	Phillips 8 bu Apples	Paid	2.00
Nov 2	Jno. Sweeten 6 1/2 bu on a/c		1.65
Sept 16	5/4 bu green beans		6.80
Nov 4	12 bu turnips Mr. Brown		3.00

Boundary lines for the farm were the same rock fences from Solomon Young's time, and two of his big square limestone gateposts marked the main entrance from the rock road. The elm trees along the front drive had grown huge by now, so that the whole distance from the road to the house was in deep shade. Beyond the house still, through the orchard, was the old walnut barn, solid as ever and still painted red.

The only neighbors in view were the Slaughters, to the north, with whom the Trumans shared a common boundary of nearly a mile. A large family of eight children, the Slaughters were the most prosperous farmers in the vicinity. O. V. Slaughter and his wife Elizabeth had known Matt since childhood. Theirs were the only lights to be seen after dark. Everything else in view was cropland, trees, and sky.

The big change in community life in the years the Trumans had been away from Blue Ridge was the growth of Grandview, a mile to the south. The little town was the creation of two railroads that cut through corners of the farm, the Kansas City Southern and the St. Louis & San Francisco, or "Frisco," both built shortly before Solomon Young's death. Post office, bank, grocery, feed, and hardware stores and the two railroad depots were now only a ten-minute ride down the rock road. On Sunday mornings the bells of Grandview Baptist Church carried clearly.

The whole farm belonged still to Grandma Young. The small, frame farmhouse built for her after the fire was well kept but crowded now with the five Trumans. Painted plain white with dark green trim, it had seven rooms, all very small—kitchen, dining room, front parlor, sitting room, and two bedrooms at the top of the front stairs. Harry and Vivian slept under the eaves over the dining room, in a tiny room with two tiny windows down at floor level, reachable only by a narrow back stairway.

The house was without electricity. There was no running water or plumbing. Matt cooked on a coal stove. In winter, the hand pump often froze solid. In summer, Harry and Vivian's room under the eaves became a furnace. Except for Matt's walnut dresser, the furnishings were of the plainest kind. The single modern convenience was a telephone, which hung on the wall beside the front door.

Neighbors remembered the house being scrupulously neat and clean. No one took such pleasure in creating a disturbance with a broom as did his mother, Harry observed. "The coldest day in winter she'll raise all the windows, get a broom and a dust rag, and just be perfectly blissful while the rest of us freeze," he wrote. "Whenever the dog and cat see her coming they at once begin hunting means of exit."

It was all rich land still, some of the most valuable in the state. Harry was satisfied it was the "finest land you'd find anywhere." To his astonishment, he was taking great interest in "the creation of things that come out of the ground." He read Cato's *De agri cultura* with its advice on planting beans, sowing clover, making compost, curing hams, and the medicinal value of cabbage. He pored through *Wallace's Farmer* and, for scientific ideas, reports from the agricultural colleges. In advance of most farmers in the area, the Trumans began rotating crops and some years the results were impressive—from yields of 13 bushels of wheat an acre to 19 bushels. To hold back erosion, Harry dumped bales of spoiled straw into gullies. Once soil had washed over the straw, he sowed timothy seed. It was an idea no one around Grandview had tried before.

Ed Young, the local veterinarian, described Harry as "always bustling around getting things done." If John Truman was a stickler for doing jobs just so, Harry was, too, the more time passed. Brownie Huber, one of the hired men, recalled that Harry was the only man he ever worked for who had him take all the buckles off the harness before oiling so the oil would get under the buckles.

Harry also had two further attributes, according to Brownie Huber, who was with the Trumans for six years. Harry could "stir up as good a batch of biscuits as any woman" and he could admit a mistake. Thirty years later Huber recalled an incident that occurred one fall when he was plowing for winter wheat:

> The ground was terribly hard so I was having to stop every round to let a three-year-old colt rest. Somebody in the family must have mentioned that I was stopping a lot because about the second day Harry came out and said, "Brownie, I'd keep them going pretty steady." I was on my third round without stopping when the colt suddenly tumbled over. I called Harry and he came running out very much upset. We got the horse unhitched, into the shade and cooled out, after which Harry turned to me and said, "Brownie, from now on use your own judgment." And those orders were never changed as long as I worked for Harry.

To more than a few people Harry seemed somehow different. One Grandview resident considered him so neat and polite he was sure Harry must be a preacher. Another, a young woman, remembered how easy he was to talk to. "He was so down-to-earth, yet he was something else, too, even then," she said.

At threshing time, when neighboring farmers came to help the Trumans, as part of the season's usual exchange of labor, Harry would work through the morning, but then, just before the big midday meal, while the other men were relaxing, he would clean up quickly and go to the kitchen to help his mother and sister. Stephen Slaughter, youngest of the Slaughter children, would remark that he never saw Harry wearing bib overalls like every other farmer, which seemed to distinguish him. "He always looked neat—not dressed up, but he looked neat. No, no, no, he never wore bib overalls." Stephen's first glimpse of Harry was on the morning of a threshing day at the Slaughter farm when Stephen was a small boy. Harry had come swinging into the yard driving one of the wagons, only Harry drove standing up and wore a Panama hat.

His circle was enlarging. After three years on the farm, he joined the Masons. Both grandfathers had been Masons and John Truman, though he never joined, said he always meant to. Harry was elected to receive degrees at the Belton Lodge on January 30, 1909. By March, having become "letter perfect" in the ritual, he passed to Master Mason. He greatly enjoyed the fellowship and took the ritual and spiritual teachings of Freemasonry with extreme seriousness. He felt uplifted by brotherhood in an order claiming great antiquity and to which both Mozart and Andrew Jackson had belonged, as had so many presidents, including Theodore Roosevelt and his recent successor, William Howard Taft. As every Mason knew, George Washington took the oath of office on a Masonic Bible and laid the cornerstone of the Capitol with a Masonic trowel.

In the autumn of 1909, Harry Truman was appointed a deacon. The following year he organized a new lodge at Grandview, in a room over a store on Main Street. By age twenty-six, he was already a figure of importance in the community. "Harry was a very good lodge man," recalled Gaylon Babcock, a brother Mason, who happened not to be as impressed as were others by Harry's abilities as a farmer, or by Harry's personality. To Babcock, Harry seemed more of a "utility man" around the Truman place. Babcock, further, was bothered by the fact that Harry, a grown man, played the piano and still called his mother "Mamma." Babcock much preferred Vivian or John Truman. Nonetheless, he thought Harry did "a good job in the lodge work—excellent."

The man primarily responsible for Harry's involvement in the Masons was Frank Blair, a clerk in the bank at Belton. "Frank Blair got Harry interested . . . and Harry was, as a bright fellow, ambitious," Stephen Slaughter remembered. "And he [Harry] had ideas . . . I'm sure he had ideas . . . that he might even go into politics." Stephen's father, O. V. Slaughter, was president of the Jackson County Farm Bureau, which Harry also joined.

• • •

In December of 1909, shortly after her ninety-first birthday, Grandma Young died. Harry, who had been devoted to her, tried to imagine all she had seen in her life. She had been born in 1818. She had once told him of a time when Solomon was away and a band of Indians came to the door saying they wanted honey and hung about sharpening their knives on the grindstone until she turned a big dog loose and sent them flying. In recent years she liked to sit silently in the sunshine in a rocker smoking a corncob pipe. Her death was the first to touch Harry directly. That Christmas without her, he said, was the saddest he had ever known.

By the will of Harriet Louisa Young the farm went to Matt and Harrison, her five other children sharing none of it on the grounds that they had played no part in the work and should consider the money gifts they received over the years as fair compensation. Not surprisingly a storm broke over the will.

Meantime, Harry delighted in the increasingly frequent visits of Uncle Harrison, who came out from Kansas City full of funny stories and eager to beat Harry in a game of double dummy bridge. Uncle Harrison, as Harry came to appreciate, was a "character," a huge, talkative, profane, generous-spirited man, a kind of Missouri Falstaff who had a splendid time doing—or talking about doing—most of the things one wasn't supposed to. Certainly he was not like anyone in Grandview. Six feet tall and extremely stout—Harry estimated he weighed 240 pounds—he wore good three-piece suits, a gold watch chain, and always carried lots of cash. He prized the time he spent loafing, loved vaudeville, gambling, and Kansas City women, and thought it time Harry learned a new dance step called the "Pigeon Wing." He also drank considerably, and asleep on the couch, he could, as Harry noted, set a record for snoring.

All Trumans, Harry decided, were worriers by nature, but Uncle Harrison said he let others do his worrying for him. Uncle Harry was part of Harry's education, as they both appreciated.

He was filling out, becoming much stronger physically. The time with his father had also brought an important change. Working together in all seasons, they had grown closer than either ever supposed they might. Indeed, John Truman had come to depend on Harry and to respect his judgment. When a horse pulled a beam over on John in the barn, breaking his leg, Harry took charge and ran things for three months, until April of 1911. Then a calf knocked Harry down and broke his left leg below the knee. The attention and kindness showered on him by both parents through the next weeks took him by surprise. "Papa buys me candy and fruit as if I were a two-year-old," he wrote, "and Mamma spends half her time making me comfortable and making my favorite pies. You really don't know how much you're thought of until you get knocked out. I shall try to keep my head though."

Later in the year, when Vivian was married to Luella Campbell, the daughter of a nearby farmer, and moved off the homeplace, John made Harry a full partner, as once Solomon Young had done for him. If, in a good year, the farm cleared $4,000, then Harry might make as much as $2,000, or twice what he had earned at the bank. But by the same agreement Harry also assumed equal responsibility for John Truman's debts, which were substantial.

They had new stationery printed for "J. A. Truman and Son, Farmers." By the standards of the family's time-honored way of life, not to say the viewpoint of the surrounding community, Harry Truman had arrived. "To be a good farmer in Missouri—that's tops. That's the finest thing you can say about a man," Vivian would declare emphatically a lifetime later. Harry himself, writing in October 1911, summed up generations of bedrock faith in the old Jeffersonian dream of a nation of farmers:

> You know as long as a country is one of that kind, people are more independent and make better citizens. When it is made up of factories and large cities it soon becomes depressed and makes classes among people. Every farmer thinks he's as good as the President or perhaps a little bit better.

This was in a letter, one of many, designed to inform and influence Bessie Wallace of Independence, who knew nothing of farms or farming. For by now Harry was head over heels in love.

III

"Well, I saw her," he is said to have exclaimed with a grin to the Noland sisters one summer night in 1910.

Ethel and Nellie Noland, who had both become schoolteachers, were still living in the family house on North Delaware Street. According to Ethel, keeper of family history, Harry had stopped for a visit when someone mentioned a cake plate that should be returned to Mrs. Wallace and Harry volunteered "with something approaching the speed of light." He crossed the street, went up the walk to the Gates house, up four steps and onto the porch, cranked the bell of the tall, double-leafed front door, then stood waiting. "And Bess came to the door," remembered Ethel, who must have been watching from her own porch, "and of course nothing could have been a bigger occasion than that, to see her again and talk to her." He didn't return for two hours.

From the farm to North Delaware Street was only sixteen miles, but a long ride by horse and buggy—four hours or more round trip—even assuming John Truman would make the horse and buggy available when Harry wished. Nor was going by train much faster or easier. Harry had to walk into Grandview and catch the Frisco to Kansas City, then change to an Independence train. Relatively few trains stopped at Grandview, however, and connections were poor, with long delays even if everything went right. The one other possibility was to hitch a ride by buggy to a point called Dodson on Blue River, where he could take the interurban, the electric streetcar, into Kansas City, then transfer to another streetcar to Independence. Whichever way he chose seemed designed to make life difficult. Yet he made the trip at every opportunity, often spending the night on a couch at the Nolands'. Old friends and relatives in town were greatly impressed by such ardor. To people in Independence, Grandview was "the sticks."

He was invited to Sunday dinner and sat politely with Bessie and her very formal mother, her brothers, and Grandmother and Grandfather Gates, as a black servant passed dishes. In the parlor afterward he played the piano for them. Bessie also accepted his invitations to concerts and the theater in Kansas City and went with him to meet his former piano teacher, Mrs. White. Harry was sure they would like one another. ("Isn't she a caution?" he said later of Mrs. White.) Yet Bessie, as others noticed, did not go out to the farm to meet his family.

But it was in letter after letter—hundreds of letters as time passed—that he poured himself out to her, saying what he found he never could in her presence, writing more than he ever had in his life and discovering how much satisfaction there was in writing. He also longed desperately for her to write him, which, as he told her, was the main reason he wrote so often and at such length. Phone calls on a party line were out of the question, with the neighbors listening. He didn't like the telephone under any circumstances. "I'm always rattled and can never say what I want to," he explained to her.

What she wrote to him, what tone her correspondence took, can only be imagined, or deduced from what he said in response, since none of her letters from this period has survived.

It was a cheerful, often funny, consistently interesting, extremely alert, straightforward, and irrepressible young man that she came to know in this outpouring of mail from Grandview. And she possessed many of the same qualities. Her vitality and good humor, in particular, had made her quite popular in her own circles. Several young men had found her attractive well before she was rediscovered by Harry Truman. Chrisman Swope, son of one of the wealthiest families in Independence, had come calling frequently. There was a Mr. Young, a Mr. Harris, and a "romance" apparently with a young man named Julian Harvey from Kansas City. As Harry understood from the start, she was used to attention.

He could not spell very well, as he was aware. ("Say, it sure is a grand thing that I have a high school dictionary handy," he wrote. "I had to look on the back to see how to spell the book itself.") And clearly he delighted in talking about himself. He was his own favorite subject, yet nearly always with a sense of proportion and a sense of humor. She had never received letters anything like them—and very fortunately she saved them.

It is necessary to sit about half a mile or so from the horses when you drive an old binder [he explained in one] and it's yell or stand still. My whip is just too short. If I make it longer it grinds up in the machinery and causes a disaster not only to the insides of the binder but to my record in the Book of Justice. It's cheaper to cuss the team.

"This morning I was helping to dig a grave," he reported in another letter, attempting to illustrate that farmers "get all kinds of experience in lots of things. . . ."

It is not nearly such a sad proceeding as you'd think. There were six or seven of us, and we'd take turns digging. Those who weren't digging would sit around and tell lies about the holes they'd dug and the hogs they'd raised. We spent a very pleasant forenoon and then went to the funeral.

They were hardly love letters, no "nonsense or bosh." He told her about Uncle Harry, about the hired men, and while he bragged occasionally of how hard he worked, he in no way romanticized life on the farm for her benefit. If anything, he went to the other extreme. "I have been to the lot and put about a hundred rings in half as many hogs' noses. You really haven't any idea what a soul stirring job it is, especially on a day when the mud is knee deep. . . ." He described being stuck in the eye by a blade of corn, and how his face had burned to the color of raw beef after hauling hay all day.

He had strong opinions and no small share of bigotry, though she never saw it that way, never found his use of expressions like "coon," "nigger," "bohunk," "Dago," or "Chink" objectionable, or she would have let him know and that would have been the end of it, since as he said, "I'm horribly anxious for you to suffer from an excessively good opinion of me!"

In his way he could also become quite philosophical, a word he didn't like.

"You know when people can get excited over the ordinary things in life, they live," he said at one point.

"You've no idea how experience teaches sympathy," he observed in another letter, soon after breaking his leg.

Of his religious convictions, a matter he knew to be of great importance to her mother, he said that while he remembered well their Presbyterian Sunday School days together and though he had since joined the Baptist Church, he was only a reasonably good Baptist as the term was understood in Grandview. "I am by religion like everything else. I think there's more in acting than in talking." Bessie had invited him to attend an Episcopal service in Independence. (The Wallaces, too, had abandoned the Presbyterian Church.) It was his first time at an Episcopal service, he told her. He knew nothing of "Lent and such things." Once, on a Sunday in Kansas City, he confessed, "I made a start for church and landed at the Shubert."

They exchanged views on writers. Mark Twain was his patron saint in literature, Harry said. The year before, as he did not tell her, he had spent $25 of his own money for a twenty-five-volume set of Twain's works. She urged him to read the longer novels of Dickens and in a letter written in May 1911, after his accident, he told her that to his surprise he was greatly enjoying *David Copperfield*:

> I have been reading *David Copperfield* and have really found out that I couldn't appreciate Dickens before. I have only read *Oliver Twist* and *Tale of Two Cities*. They didn't make much of an impression on me and I never read anything else. A neighbor sent me *Dombey & Son* and *David C.,* and I am glad for it has awakened a new interest. It is almost a reconciliation to having my leg broken to contemplate the amount of reading I am going to do this summer. I am getting better fast and I am afraid I'll get well so soon I won't get to read enough. . . . I do think Mr. Micawber is the killingest person I have run across in any book anywhere. He is exactly true to life. I know a half-dozen of him right here in Grandview. They are always waiting for something to turn up. . . .

Then, out of the blue, that June, he proposed to her by mail, mixing affection with a little self-deprecation and caution, fearful she might laugh at him.

You know, were I an Italian or a poet I would commence and use all the luscious language of two continents. I am not either but only a kind of good-for-nothing American farmer. I've always had a sneakin' notion that some day maybe I'd amount to something. I doubt it now though like everything. It is a family failing of ours to be poor financiers. I am blest that way. Still that doesn't keep me from having always thought that you were all that a girl could be possibly and impossibly. You may not have guessed it but I've been crazy about you ever since we went to Sunday school together. But I never had the nerve to think you'd even look at me. . . . You said you were tired of these kind of stories in books so I am trying one from real life. I guess it sounds funny to you, but you must bear in mind that this is my first experience in this line and also it is very real to me.

Three weeks passed without a word from her. He waited, agonizing, then wrote to ask if he had said anything to offend her. She responded by turning him down, and apparently over the phone. That same day he wrote as follows:

Grandview, Mo.
July 12, 1911

Dear Bessie:

You know that you turned me down so easy that I am almost happy anyway. I never was fool enough to think that a girl like you could ever care for a fellow like me but I couldn't help telling you how I felt. I have always wanted you to have some fine, rich-looking man, but I know that if ever I got the chance I'd tell you how I felt even if I didn't even get to say another word to you. What makes me feel good is that you were good enough to answer me seriously and not make fun of me anyway. You know when a fellow tells a girl all his heart and she makes a joke of it I suppose it would be the awfullest feeling in the world. You see I never had any desire to say such things to anyone else. All my girlfriends think I am a cheerful idiot and a confirmed old bach. They really don't know the reason nor ever will. I have been so afraid you were not even going to let me be your good friend. To be even in that class is something.

You may think I'll get over it as all boys do. I guess I am something of a freak myself. I really never had any desire to make love to a girl just for the fun of it, and you have always been the reason. I have never met a girl in my life that you were not the first to be compared with her, to see wherein she was lacking and she always was.

84

Please don't think I am talking nonsense or bosh, for if ever I told the truth I am telling it now and I'll never tell such things to anyone else or bother you with them again. I have always been more idealist than practical anyway, so I really never expected any reward for loving you. I shall always hope though. . . .

Then, promising to put on no hangdog airs when next he saw her, he changed the subject. Did she know of any way to make it rain?

They exchanged photographs and Harry had a standing invitation to Sunday dinner at the Gates house. Week after week, with no success, he tried to get her to come to Grandview. In August, he announced he was building a grass tennis court for her on a level place near the house. She could bring her friends, make a day of it. At Montgomery Ward in Kansas City he bought a heavy roller. Since neither he nor anyone else on the farm, or anyone in Grandview, played tennis or knew the requirements for a court, he had her send directions. He hoped to have everything ready by Labor Day. Mamma would cook a chicken dinner, he promised. "Not town dinner but midday meal, see? So be sure and come. . . . Now be sure and come out on Labor Day."

In the flurry of excitement, seeing how intent on success he was, Matt decided to have several rooms papered. With only three days to go, Harry sent Bessie a map with directions. The Sunday before Labor Day he worked the day through on the court and by nightfall had everything ready, including a supply of watermelons.

But she didn't come. She sent word it was raining in Independence. He wrote at once of his "disappointment" and asked if she could make it another time, adding that Mamma would still like her to come for dinner and that the weather in Grandview on Labor Day had been fine. When she did at last appear, for an impromptu visit some weeks later, the court was found to be insufficiently level for a proper game.

Yet, he would not be discouraged. He kept at courtship as he had kept to his piano lessons, with cheerful, willing determination. He told her of his progress in the Masons, he sent her books, commented on stories in his favorite magazines, *Everybody's, Life,* and *Adventure.* "I was reading Plato's *Republic* this morning," he also informed her at one point, "and Socrates was discoursing on the ideal Republic. . . . You see, I sometimes read something besides *Adventure.*"

He knew he had a gift for conversation. He had found he could get most anything he wanted if he could only talk to people. The letters were his way to talk to her as he never could face to face.

That he particularly liked cake, pie, Mozart, Chopin, and Verdi became clear. She learned also how much there was he did not like: dentists, guns, snobs, hypocrisy in any form, prizefighters, divorce, the Kansas City *Star* (for its Republican bias), lawyers (now that his grandmother's will was being contested), and Richard Wagner, who he thought must have been "in cahoots with Pluto." He regretted much about his looks. He wrote of his "girl mouth" and the fact that he blushed like a girl. He confessed to such other ladylike traits as yelling when he had a tooth pulled and an "inordinate desire to look nice" when having his picture taken. Coming home alone in the dark, he could get "scared to an icicle," he told her. He was afraid of getting knocked on the head by the hoboes who hung about at the point where he changed trains at Kansas City, fearful of both ghosts and hoboes as he made his way home on foot from the Grandview depot on nights when there was no moon.

Once approaching the house in the pitch dark, groping his way to the kitchen door, he walked headlong into the pump. The next day, he painted the pump white.

One man was as good as another, he thought, "so long as he's honest and decent and not a nigger or a Chinaman." His Uncle Will Young, the Confederate veteran, had a theory that "the Lord made a white man of dust, a nigger from mud, then threw up what was left and it came down a Chinaman." Apparently Harry thought this would amuse her. "He does hate Chinks and Japs. So do I," he continued. "It is race prejudice I guess. But I am strongly of the opinion that negroes ought to be in Africa, yellow men in Asia, and white men in Europe and America."

But on an evening when Mary Jane was practicing a Mozart sonata at the piano, he wrote, "Did you ever sit and listen to an orchestra play a fine overture, and imagine that things were as they ought to be and not as they are? Music that I can understand always makes me feel that way." Had Bessie been the girl in a stage musical of the kind he took her to see, she would have accepted him then and there.

The fact that he had no money and that he craved money came up repeatedly, more often and more obviously than probably he realized. In Grandview circles, financial wealth was something people seldom talked about or judged one another by. "We never rated a person by the amount of money he had," remembered Stephen Slaughter. "Always, first and foremost, it was his character, his integrity." No family, not even the Slaughters, had large bank accounts or costly possessions. Everybody, including the Slaughters, had debts. But Harry wanted more than what sufficed for Grandview; or, in any event, he clearly wanted Bessie Wallace to think he aimed higher.

He told her of his longing for an automobile. "Just imagine how often

I'd burn the pike from here to Independence." He saw a $75 overcoat in Kansas City that he wanted. If ever he were rich, he too would live in Independence. Writing one cold night before Christmas 1911, he told her also of the secret burden he carried with his father, the "hat-full of debts," asking only that she keep this to herself since no one knew. Later, he said he had two reasons for wanting to be rich. The first was to pay his debts and build his mother a fine house. The second was to win her.

If only she cared a little, he would double his efforts "to amount to something." Bessie replied saying that she and Mary Paxton had concluded that a woman should think seriously only of a man who could support her in style. Harry said he would take this as a sign of encouragement, whether she meant it that way or not.

He wanted so to live up to expectations, and his own most of all, but he didn't know what to do with his life, what in the world to be. Like David Copperfield, he longed to know if he would turn out to be the hero of his own story.

He was pleased to learn that her mother admired his piano playing. (Mrs. Wallace herself was considered an accomplished pianist. In her youth she had studied at the Cincinnati Conservatory.) "I really thought once I'd be an ivory tickler but I am glad my money ran out before I got too far," Harry told Bess honestly. He had dropped out of the National Guard. Military life, too, had lost its pull: "I am like Mark Twain. He says that if fame is to be obtained only by marching to the cannon's mouth, he's perfectly willing to go there provided the cannon is empty. . . ."

He had been offered a job running a small bank in the southern part of the county, but from what he had seen of bankers he had little heart for it. "You know a man has to be real stingy and save every one-cent stamp he can. Then sometimes he has to take advantage of adverse conditions and sell a good man out. That is one reason I like being a farmer. Even if you do have to work like a coon you know that you are not grinding the life out of someone else to live yourself."

He admitted he was thinking about politics. "Who knows, maybe I'll be like a Cincinnatus and be elected constable someday." Mostly, he was restless.

With two other men from Grandview he went by train to South Dakota to take part in an Indian land lottery. At stations along the way people on the returning trains had shouted at them, "Sucker! Sucker!" Nothing came of the trip, or of another after it, to look at land in New Mexico, though he traveled some "mighty pretty country." Approaching Santa Fe by train, up the valley of the Rio Grande, he saw a rainbow that held in the sky ahead for mile after mile. "I wanted to get off," he wrote to her, "and chase the end of it down, thinking perhaps it really might be on a gold mine out here."

She had lately told him Bessie was a name she no longer cared for. So his letters now began "Dear Bess," though they closed as always, "Sincerely, Harry," or sometimes, "Most sincerely, Harry."

IV

The years Harry Truman spent on the farm were to be known as the golden age of American agriculture, with farm prices climbing steadily. If ever there was a time to have been a farmer, this was it. Wheat, corn, hay, everything was going higher—wheat was up to 90 cents a bushel in 1912 —and for Harry and his father it meant continuously harder, longer days. Once in the summer of 1912 they spent twelve hours loading nearly three hundred bales of hay into a railroad car. It was the hottest work Harry had ever done. By sundown he was ready to collapse. But that night, seeing lightning on the horizon, his father insisted they go back out again and cover the hay that had still to be baled. They worked on in the dark, Harry handing 14-foot boards up to his father, who placed them on the top of the haystack—thirty-two 14-foot boards by Harry's count.

John Truman bought more cows, more than doubling their herd, from thirty to eighty-two. "I have been working like Sam Hill this morning sowing wheat," Harry informed Bess in a letter written in September 1913. "Papa has a fit every time I heave a one-hundred-pound sack of wheat. . . . Get to lay off the wheat this afternoon and pitch hay while they thresh." That year they had enough hay for six hundred bales, and his father talked of a wheat crop for the next year of four hundred acres, enough, if all went well, to put them "out of the woods." At night in the parlor, as Harry sat writing to Bess, his father would fall asleep in his chair.

It was a killing schedule Harry was keeping, with his work, his travels to Independence and Kansas City, his Lodge nights and letter writing. Though few sons were ever so dutiful, John accused him of losing interest in the farm and many mornings had trouble waking him. Once, when Harry missed his train and arrived home extremely late, he found his father still up and in a "terrible stew," certain that something awful had happened to him. "He was sure I had been knocked on the head or fallen in the creek. When I told him I'd missed the car he had another fit. . . ."

But Harry's main concern was his father, who, he was sure, was working too hard. When he learned that John, through friends at the Independence Courthouse, was going after the job of road overseer for the southern half of Washington Township, which included Grandview, Harry had immediate misgivings. The upkeep and repair of country roads was a task performed by local men with their own teams of horses, either for hire or as a way to work off a six-dollar school tax. The work was never-ending and the job of overseer, an appointed political post, was one that paid two dollars a day and that almost nobody wanted. It was his father's incurable love of politics that made him go after the job, Harry told Bess. "Politics is all he ever advises me to neglect the farm for." If Harry could have his way, his father would have no part of it.

When John Truman got the job of overseer, others in Grandview took it as a sign that the Trumans were "strapped" and needed the money. John was considered a good man and a good neighbor. As Stephen Slaughter would recall, "I don't think we would have traded him for anybody." But by contrast to the Slaughters, the Trumans always seemed hardpressed financially. The Slaughter farm was not as large as the Truman farm, their land no better than the Truman land, yet the Slaughters prospered. O. V. Slaughter sent all eight of his children to college. "I never understood," said Stephen years later. "They raised crops on that farm. We raised crops. They were always broke. We weren't broke."

Nonetheless, the improved quality of work on the roads under John Truman's supervision was soon apparent. And with his father determined to keep the roads, no less than the farm, in prime condition, Harry thought he'd best help with the roads too. But should his father, on the strength of this job, decide to run for any other political office, Harry told Bess, then he, Harry, would go out and make speeches against him.

The truth was, Harry went on, warming to his subject, he was torn by his own yearnings. He wanted money, yet he knew it to be a less than satisfactory measure of success, let alone personal value. He saw the seductions and the pitfalls of politics. He knew it to be a dirty business and he scorned the kind of posturing it produced in some men. Yet the fascination remained. It was a remarkable letter:

> Politics sure is the ruination of many a good man. Between hot air and graft he usually loses not only his head but his money and friends as well. Still, if I were real rich I'd just as soon spend my money buying votes and offices as yachts and autos. Success seems to me to be merely a point of view anyway. Some men have an idea that if they corner all the loose change they are self-made successful men. Makes no difference to them if they do eat beans off a knife or not know whether Napoleon was a man or a piece of silver.

Some others have a notion that if they can get high offices and hold up themselves as models of virtue to a gaping public in long-winded, high-sounding speeches that they have reached the highest pinnacle of success. It seems to me that the ability to hand out self-praise makes most men successes in their own minds anyway. Some of the world's greatest failures are really greater than some of the other kind. To succeed financially a man can't have any heart. To succeed politically he must be an egoist or a fool or a ward boss tool. To my notion, an ideal condition would be to have to work just enough so if you stopped you'd not go busted at once—but still you'd know if you didn't work you couldn't live. And then have your home and friends and pleasures regulated to your income, say a thousand a month. I am sure I'd be satisfied then to let vile ambition, political or monetary, starve at the gate.

When the newspaper in Belton called John Truman one of the "henchmen" of the Jackson County Court, John took off for Belton to "whip" the editor, but failed to find him, which Harry thought much for the best. "I told him that was a very mild remark and should be accepted as a compliment to a man who has a political job." It was the first sign of John's old temper in years and privately Harry appears to have been pleased.

He himself was known as the "mild-tempered" Truman. Through the furor over Grandma Young's will, in the crossfire of charges and counter-charges in court and out, Harry alone of the family seemed able to get along with everyone. He was the one person they could all talk to, the family peacemaker.

In September 1913 he made another try in an Indian land lottery, traveling this time farther from home than ever before, nearly to the Canadian border in northeastern Montana, in the company of a half-dozen other Grandview men, including his father. Harry loved these trips, but this one most of all. On a postcard to Ethel Noland mailed from Minneapolis, he said he was "feeling as good as an angel full of pie."

Then, at long last, on a Sunday in November 1913, as Harry sat speechless, Bess said that if ever she married anyone it would be him. She wrote a letter to confirm the promise. They agreed they were secretly engaged. Harry was beside himself, "all puffed up and hilarious and happy." She had made a confirmed optimist of him, he said. She called him an enigma. He said that sounded fine to him and especially coming from her, "for I always labored under the impression that it took smart people to be one."

On a date in Kansas City, he took her to see Julia Sanderson and Donald Brian starring in a new show, *The Girl from Utah,* and held her hand as the handsome dark-haired leading man sang the show's biggest hit, a song by Jerome Kern, "They'll Never Believe Me."

> *And when I tell them, and I'm certainly going to tell them,*
> *That I'm the man whose wife one day you'll be,*
> *They'll never believe me, they'll never believe me,*
> *That from this great big world you've chosen me.*

There were no bounds now to his horizons. "How does it feel to be engaged to a clodhopper who has ambitions to be Governor of Montana and Chief Executive of the U.S.?" he inquired, the expansive aspirations intended as humor only. To his surprise, she wrote at once to say how much she cared for him. "I know your last letter word for word and then I read it some forty times a day," he said. "Oh please send me another like it." He thought perhaps he should put it in a safe deposit vault to keep from wearing it out.

> You really didn't know I had so much softness and sentimentality in me, did you? I'm full of it. But I'd die if I had to talk it. I can tell you on paper how much I love you and what one grand woman I think you, but to tell it to you I can't. I'm always afraid I'd do it so clumsily you'd laugh. . . . I could die happy doing something for you. (Just imagine a guy with spectacles and a girl mouth doing the Sir Lancelot.) Since I can't rescue you from any monster or carry you from a burning building or save you from a sinking ship—simply because I'd be afraid of the monsters, couldn't carry you, and can't swim—I'll have to go to work and make money enough to pay my debts and then get you to take me for what I am: just a common everyday man whose instincts are to be ornery, who's anxious to be right. You'll not have any trouble getting along with me for I'm awful good. . . . Do you suppose your mother'll care for me well enough to have me in her family?

This last point was a large question indeed, for Madge Wallace remained, as would be said, a virtual "prisoner of shame" over her husband's suicide and clung to Bess as a figure of strength greater than her own. She needed Bess quite as much as John Truman needed Harry. As the only daughter of an important family, Bess would have been a guarded "prize" even under normal circumstances. The prospects for a debt-ridden, farm-boy suitor would have been extremely remote, however persistent or well mannered he might be.

"Mrs. Wallace wasn't a bit in favor of Harry," remembered one of the Noland family, all of whom were strongly on Harry's side. "And she says,

'You don't want to marry that farmer boy, he is not going to make it anywhere.' And so she didn't push it at all. She kind of tried to prevent it. . . ."

Every call Harry made at 219 North Delaware Street could only have been a reminder of what distances remained between his world and hers. The etched glass in the front door, the plum-colored Brussels carpets, the good china and heavy lace curtains at the long parlor windows, the accepted use of silver dessert forks, the absence of any sign that survival meant hard physical labor day in, day out, the whole air of privacy, of unruffled comfort and stability, reflected a way of life totally apart from anything in his experience. ("We have moved around quite a bit and always the best people are hardest to know," he once told Bess defensively.) Had he only to overcome the obvious differences in their station, he would have had an uphill haul, as he would have said. But the problem was greatly compounded by how Madge Wallace felt toward anyone or any cause that threatened to take Bess from her.

"Yes, it is true that Mrs. Wallace did not think Harry was good enough for Bess," a member of the Wallace circle would comment with a smile sixty years afterward, her memory of it all quite clear. "But then, don't you see, Mrs. Wallace didn't think *any* man was good enough for Bess."

In March 1914 his own mother suddenly took ill. The local doctor called in a specialist who decided that an operation for hernia must be performed and at once, there in the house. Harry had to stand beside her bed and hold a kerosene lamp while the doctor worked and "parts" were removed from his mother. It was, Harry said afterward, an experience he hoped he would never have to repeat.

Apologetically he told Bess he would be unable to leave home for several days. Mamma, as he had once written, was a person for whom there was no substitute. "I hope she lives to be a hundred and one."

How direct a connection there was between his steadfast performance during the operation and afterward and the event that followed is not certain. But it was only a few weeks later when Mamma gave him the money to buy an automobile. And it was to be no farmer's Model T Ford. If anyone had ever rewarded a son with one grand generous gesture, she had. Nothing could have pleased him more or made such an immediate difference in his life. He had never had anything of his own of such value or that drew such attention. He was to love automobiles all his life, but this was *the* automobile of his life.

It was a big, black, five-passenger 1911-model Stafford, hand-built in Kansas City by a man named Terry Stafford. Only three hundred of the cars were ever made. It had a four-cylinder engine, right-hand drive, a high brass-framed windshield, and Presto-Lite lamps nearly the size of the lamps on locomotives. On a good road, Harry soon demonstrated, it could do 60 miles an hour. It was a rich man's car. New, it sold for $2,350. Harry paid $650. The house needed paint; payments on loans and the cost of the lawsuit over his grandmother's will had stretched the family's finances to the limit. From all practical viewpoints such an automobile was a huge extravagance—$650 would have been more than enough to pay for two hired men for a year—but to Harry $650 for such an automobile was a "bargain." While not the first in Grandview, it was certainly the fanciest. In Independence, not even George Porterfield Gates had anything like it. With a little work on the engine, Harry found, he could go up Dodson Hill—considered the great test locally—so fast he had to shut off the power before reaching the crest.

He could come and go as he pleased now, and mostly it was go, on Blue Ridge Boulevard to Independence. Rolling through the shaded streets of Independence on a spring Sunday, wearing a sporty new cap, a fresh white shirt and proper Sunday necktie, the top down on the car, its brass all polished, he would never be taken for a hayseed. Bess and three or four others would pile into the "machine," off with him for an afternoon of fishing on Blue River or a picnic at the waterworks beside the Missouri at Sugar Creek. Or Harry would treat them to "a spin" in the country.

He had a gang again, as he had not since boyhood. Besides Bess and the Noland sisters, there were Bess's two brothers Frank and George and their best girls, Natalie Ott and May Southern. Harry and his car were the center of attention. They would all pose for pictures with the car, Harry at the wheel. Harry was always good company, said May Southern, who would soon marry Bess's brother George. Harry, she said a lifetime later, never complained about anything unless there were onions in the potato salad. "Harry didn't like onions."

Uncle Harrison also enjoyed "a spin" with the top down, in any weather. One expedition for his benefit was to Monegaw Springs, an old Missouri spa about eighty miles from Grandview. Mamma, too, had insisted on going along for the ride in Lizzie, as Harry was calling the car by this time.

I started for Monegaw Springs on Sunday [he began a memorable account for Bess]. Mamma went along and we almost reached the springs without an accident. We got within a half mile of them and ran over a stump. I spilled Uncle Harry over the front seat and threw

Mamma over my own head. Neither of them were hurt, except Uncle Harry renewed his profane vocabulary. I backed Lizzie off the stump and ran her into town with a badly bent axle. Mamma and I started for home at 6:00 A.M. on Monday. Got within seventy-five miles of it and it began to rain. Had the nicest slipping time you ever saw. What with a crooked axle and a bent steering wheel I could hardly stay in the road. Five miles south of Harrisonville Lizzie took a header for the ditch and got there, smashing a left front wheel into kindling. I phoned to Ferson and he sent me his front wheel. The accident happened within a half mile of a R.R. station, Lone Tree by name. Mamma and I sat there from 1:30 till 8:00 P.M. waiting for the wheel. It arrived all right and I couldn't get it on. Then it began to rain in real earnest. I got soaked. A good farmer came and took us up to his house and we stayed all night. Next morning he hitched his team to Lizzie and pulled her out of the ditch. (I had tried to put the wheel on wrong end to, the night before.) He would not have a cent for keeping me nor pulling the car out. We started for Harrisonville and got about five miles north of there when we ran through a puddle and got the mag wet. Had to phone back to Harrisonville and get a man to come and tear it up—cost a five-dollar bill. Another good farmer took us to dinner free. Finally got to Grand-view at 3:00 P.M. . . .

Mary Jane had spoken up, saying she wanted driving lessons—"I guess I'll have to do it, though," said Harry reluctantly, "since Mamma paid for the thing." When Mary Jane crashed into the front gate, Harry was thankful it was only the gate she hit and not the stone post.

In three months he drove 5,000 miles. Not since his first pair of eye-glasses had anything so changed his life, and again it was Mamma who made it happen. Her decision was also, of course, a way of telling him she approved of his reason for wishing to be on the road. If Bess Wallace was what he wanted, she would do what she could to see nothing stood in the way.

In time, Papa, too, declared himself "well pleased" with the purchase and by midsummer would "raise a rumpus" for Harry to drive him out to survey the roads. "Imagine working the roads in a machine," Harry wrote.

But by midsummer 1914, the summer the Great War began in Europe, it had become apparent that something was seriously the matter with John Truman. He had strained himself sometime earlier, exactly as he had so often warned Harry not to. Trying to move a boulder from one of the roads, the hard, stubborn little man had refused to give up and so had been done in by a stone in the path, like some figure in a parable.

Though the pain persisted, he refused to see the specialists, as Matt had, fearing an operation. By Labor Day an X-ray revealed that a severe hernia was causing an intestinal block. John was told he had to decide between surgery or the grave. He had already lost a great deal of weight and looked dreadful.

"If anyone asks him how he's feeling," wrote Harry, "he always says fine, even if he can't raise up his head." Fearing the worst, Harry urged the operation as the only choice left.

The automobile now became the means for getting his father to and from the doctor in Kansas City, who was a Chinese, the supposed family hatred of Orientals notwithstanding. Harry worried continually. He didn't see how he could ever get by without his father, he confessed to Bess. "You know he is sixty-three and an operation at that age is nearly always fatal."

Harry ran the farm, took over the road work, and drove John to the doctor as often as four times a week. He wondered if the fates were conspiring against him, he told Bess, but her "good letters" helped "put that backbone into me to accomplish what I've set out to do in spite of the devil and all his angels." Some evenings his father could hardly talk and Mamma, as she had never done before, asked Harry to forgo the trips to Independence. Meantime, it was essential that Harry "make things hum" and get in 200 acres of wheat.

The operation on John Truman was performed at the Swedish Hospital in Kansas City in October. Bess sent flowers, which greatly pleased Harry and his father, who refused to let the nurse throw them away until they were entirely gone. John returned home, but Harry knew he could not last long. Word of his condition spread and neighbors began to call.

"I remember the Sunday afternoon Father and Mother drove over to the Truman home to visit him," wrote Stephen Slaughter. "It was known at the time that Mr. Truman had only a short time to live. And I remember the sadness Father and Mother felt after the visit." Full of despair, John had said he was a failure in life. "Father had given him what comfort he could," Stephen remembered. John was told what a good neighbor he had been. He was reminded of the friends he had made, the useful work he had done, the fine family he had raised. Undoubtedly Harry was present as his father talked of his failure, for by this time Harry was rarely away from his father's side.

John Truman died the morning of Monday, November 2, 1914.

"I was with him," Harry said years later. "I had been sitting with him and watching a long time. I nodded off. When I woke up he was dead."

Brownie Huber, the hired man, who was also at the house, recalled:

"Harry and I often got up real early and very quietly so as not to awaken his mother and sister. He would make biscuits, cook oatmeal and fry eggs. That is the way it was the morning his father died. I was eating breakfast while Harry went in to stay with the old gentleman, when he appeared at the door and said, 'Dad just passed away.'"

The day of the funeral, schools were closed in Grandview. Friends came to the service at the house from everywhere in the county. Their buggies and horses and Model T's were drawn up all along the drive beneath the bare trees. A headline in the Independence *Examiner* reported the loss of "An Upright Citizen Whose Death Will Be a Blow to His Community." Burial was at the old Forest Hill Cemetery in Kansas City, at the brow of a slope beside the graves of Solomon and Harriet Louisa Young.

To Bess, Harry wrote: "I have quite a job on my hands now. . . . You know, I've been in the habit of running the farm for some time, but Papa always made it go."

V

If it was sure-enough war, wheat would go higher still, farmers had been saying all summer. And then it had come, in the first week of August, when sixty thousand German troops crossed into Belgium at Liège. The papers were filled with war news and as Willa Cather would write, even to "quiet wheat-growing people, the siege guns before Liège were a menace; not to their safety or their goods, but to their comfortable, established way of thinking. They introduced the greater-than-man force which afterward repeatedly brought into this war the effect of unforeseeable natural disaster. . . ." By September the German armies had swept through Belgium and into France as far as the Marne River, where the French were making a heroic stand.

To Harry, with his sense of history, his fascination with military heroes, his previous part in the National Guard, all this, presumably, should have been of greatest interest. But the letters he wrote said nothing of the war. Even after his worries and grief over his father had passed, the subject of the world at large received no mention. To judge by what he was writing to Bess Wallace, little beyond his own immediate life ever drew his attention or thoughts from the time he first began corresponding with her in 1910. The only exception was the presidential contest of 1912 that elected Woodrow Wilson, the first Democrat to win the presidency since Grover Cleveland, and to Harry, a great man. If he was at all concerned about what was happening in France, or perceived any connection between the war headlines in the papers and his own fate, he gave no sign of it except once, two years later, when he told Bess he had had a dream. He had fallen from a plane over France and wound up in a hospital crying because he couldn't see her.

As it was, he had plenty to think about. He felt the responsibility of the farm keenly and "gave it everything he had," as his sister later said. "I almost got done planting corn this evening.... I was in the field at six o'clock and quit at seven. Nearly a day's work," he informed Bess in April 1915. "... I've simply got to make things come across this year if I have to work night and day." He worried about the weather. He worried about his debts. He worried that the men would never work for him as they had for his father.

He kept on as road overseer for another six months, until a rival faction took over at the Independence Courthouse and he was out. From February to August he also served as postmaster in Grandview, though in name only, since he left the work to an assistant, a widow, who he thought needed the money more than he did.

He was up with the sun every morning, still, even with Papa gone. Early morning was the best time for "solid thinking," he liked to say. He was thirty years old. He had been on the farm eight years, or more than a quarter of his life. He had lost none of his devotion to the family, or his determination to win Bess Wallace, or his good humor. (She must send him another picture of herself soon, he said, so he could have one downstairs as well as up. "It's right unhandy to chase upstairs every day to see how you look.") Yet his restlessness was greater than ever. He hated his "slow progress" at home, even with the rise in farm prices. He had reached a point, in fact, where he might have gone off in any of several directions with his life, given the opportunity.

With Uncle Harry in tow, he traveled to Texas hoping to entice him into some land speculation. The trip, like his earlier ones, came to nothing. Involved next in a zinc mine in Oklahoma, he told Bess, "There's no one wants to win half so badly as I do." He pictured the two of them in an ideal country house and the thought made the delays nearly unbearable. "Then I wake up and see our old house going to wreck for want of paint and repairs because I must pay interest on a debt I had no hand in making and my dream has to keep waiting."

When the suit over his grandmother's will was settled at last, after six years, his mother wound up no better off than before. She won the case and kept the farm, but what money came of it was consumed in lawyers' fees. Even before John Truman's death she had been forced to put another mortgage on the land. To pay off doctors' bills and funeral expenses, Harry had to sell some Black Angus cattle he had only recently acquired. Now, along with Uncle Harry, his mother was advancing him money for his zinc-mine venture, which infuriated Vivian, who thought Harry had already been given quite enough and would be better off paying attention to the farm.

Vivian proved correct. The zinc mine was Harry's first big experience with failure of his own doing.

The mine was located at a point called Commerce in the northeast corner of Oklahoma, just over the Missouri line, and 192 miles from Grandview. If the weather was right, the roads passable, and provided he had no blowouts and succeeded in fording four river bottoms, he could make it in the Stafford, he claimed, in seven hours. More often he took the train.

"This place down here is certainly one beyond the limit," he wrote from Commerce early in 1916. "When it rains there is water six inches deep over everything. When it's dry the dust is as deep over everything." He was homesick, lonesome, yet expecting to be "on velvet" before long. Someday, he vowed, he would have a Pierce Arrow.

"I don't suppose I'd ever have been real pleased if I hadn't tried just once to get rich quickly," he would tell Bess before it was over.

He had put up several thousand dollars to go into partnership with two brother Masons, Thomas Hughes, a Grandview farmer, and a Kansas City promoter named Jerry Culbertson, neither of whom knew any more about mining than he did. They called themselves the T-H-C Mining Company and bought what was known as the Eureka Mine at Commerce, hoping to cover their start-up expenses with the waste ore that had been left lying about above ground by the previous owner. Their troubles began almost immediately. The superintendent they hired turned out to be a crook. A rival group shut off the water needed for processing the ore. Equipment failed. Meantime, Harry kept shunting back and forth to Grandview, often twice a week, trying to hold things together at both ends.

Jerry Culbertson had no interest in the day-to-day operations of the mine, and when lightning struck Tom Hughes's barn at Grandview, burning it to the ground, Hughes refused to give any more of his time, leaving the job to Harry, whose outlook swung from "blue-sky" confidence to abject gloom and back again. It was proving a liberal and expensive education, he observed during one of his high points. Of necessity he became a mechanic, mine superintendent, night watchman, and, above all, "official straightener" of mix-ups. He had never worked so hard or worried so much. And he refused to give up. "I can't possibly lose for-ever," he wrote plaintively to Bess. He had put Mary Jane in charge at home, but the hired men resented taking orders from a woman. When two of them quit, Harry had to catch the next train.

He saw his money vanishing. On May 19, 1916, feeling unusually sorry for himself after a trying day at Grandview, he wrote Bess a letter of a kind she had not seen before. He had begun to think his knack for failure was hereditary:

> The mine has gone by the board. I have lost out on it entirely. If Uncle Harry had not been sick I should have gone down there Tuesday evening. It is a setback from which I don't suppose I shall very soon recover. If I don't lose all the livestock I have, it will only be because I shall turn it over to Mamma. I shall join the class who can't sign checks of their own I suppose. It is a hard nut to crack but it had to be done. There was never one of our name who had sense enough to make money. I am no exception.
>
> I shall endeavor to make the farm go as usual but I'll have to stay on it. My finances are completely exhausted. . . . You would do better per-haps if you pitch me into the ash heap and pick someone with more sense and ability and not such a soft head.

Then, after a good night's sleep, his first in a long while, he assured her he was as hopeful as ever. He could "continue business as Harry Truman yet." Frank Blair at the Belton Bank had come to the rescue with a loan, after telling Harry what a mistake he had made ever getting in-volved with Culbertson. How would Bess like coming in as a partner and help run the mine, Harry wanted to know.

"It's about 110 degrees in the shade all the time down here," he wrote from Commerce in July. "We also have a very active brand of mosquitoes. They work all night every night. The flies work in daytime." It was the summer of the battles of Verdun and the Somme.

"Wish heavy for me to win," he told her. "Keep wishing me luck because it means everything to me," he urged again in August.

He wanted to buy an engagement ring but felt he must hold off because buying it with borrowed money would be bad luck. His luck, their luck, the will of the Fates, were all uppermost in his mind. He talked of open-ing a Ford agency in Commerce, certain now that that was the path to fortune.

The zinc mine closed that September of 1916. By November Harry was in the business of buying and selling oil leases, out of an office in Kansas

TRUMAN

City. Again he had gone in with Jerry Culbertson, despite Frank Blair's warning, despite what he must have known himself from the experience at Commerce. But he was after the main chance now, as much as ever John Truman had been. The third partner in this new venture, David Morgan, later said it was actually the gamble of the business—the "hazard"—that appealed to Harry. Morgan, an Oklahoma lawyer and oil man, also knew what he was doing, as Harry appreciated.

Harry put in $5,000—five notes for $1,000 due in ten months, these, according to the contract, to be "signed also by Martha E. Truman, the mother of said Harry S. Truman." She urged him to keep her father in mind, rather than his father. Grandpa Young, she said, had been wiped out three times that she knew of, but he "came up every time with something else." Grandpa Young, the family success, the strong, self-made man who had never given up trying, was the example to take heart from.

Morgan was the president of what became the Morgan Oil & Refining Company. Culbertson handled sales and promotion. Harry was treasurer and so listed on the firm's new stationery. However, a bookkeeper named Brelsford later said Harry's real specialty was seeing people. "Truman was surrounded by people, people, people. Salesmen, lease men, lease owners, scouts, and what-have-you. Morgan had his duties, but he shoved quite a burden of seeing people over to Mr. Truman."

Though he appears to have made no sales himself, Harry had become a boomer. "If this venture blows, I'll know I'm hoodooed," he told Bess, who was among those who bought stock.

If Harry had no premonitions about American involvement in the European war, Culbertson was banking on it. "In the event this country is unfortunately brought to war," said a newspaper advertisement written by Culbertson, "the absolute necessity of gasoline and other byproducts of crude petroleum are bound to come to such urgent demand that the price will soar beyond all expectations. . . ."

Morgan was convinced that fortunes were waiting beneath the farmlands of Kansas, Oklahoma, and Texas. The company leased thousands of acres in all three states and in Louisiana as well. But then in April 1917 Woodrow Wilson was calling on Congress for a declaration of war and the war, rather than bringing a bonanza to Morgan Oil & Refining, eventually finished it off. There was no manpower to pursue oil, investors disappeared, the company went out of business. Only later was it discovered that one of their leases in southeastern Kansas was part of the famous Teeter Pool, a supply of oil that would have made millions for the company and its officers had they just drilled deeper.

. . .

Bess, like other investors in the venture, lost all she had put in, while Harry seems to have come out even. How much he lost altogether in the zinc mine is unclear. He said $11,000 at the time, but later gave a figure of $7,500. Either way it was a lot of money and all of it borrowed money. If his part in his father's debts was $12,000—the figure he once confided to Bess—then possibly his total indebtedness by this time was $23,000. Perhaps not coincidentally, Matt put another mortgage of $25,000 on the farm in 1917.

Yet as bad as Harry felt about all this—and he could get extremely blue —the farm, mortgages and all, meant security as almost nothing else could have. Good years brought a clear income of maybe $4,000, at a time when the average working family earned less than $1,000. Exceptional years might mean $7,000, and apparently the Trumans had a few such years.

Further, the farm now belonged solely to the Trumans. The previous summer of 1916, Uncle Harrison had died, leaving all of his part to Matt and her children. In plain monetary terms they were sitting on a fortune. The price of wheat in 1916 hit a new high of $1.65 a bushel. Good land in Jackson County by 1917 was selling for $200 an acre. At the least the farm was worth $100,000, but it might have sold for twice that. Matt had no intention of selling any of it. Still, there it was if troubles came, and it was in prime shape still, since, as their neighbors so often said, the Trumans were good farmers.

Ethel Noland, who understood Harry as well as anyone, said she knew all along he was never meant for a farmer. And clearly he knew it, too. Yet he had held on for ten years, doing his share and more. He had also discovered in Commerce, Oklahoma, that between farming and zinc mining, he would take farming.

Much later he would remember the years on the farm as invaluable experience. He would talk of the drudgery, and he would call it the best time he ever had in his life. A farm gave a person time alone to himself, which he liked and needed, for all his enjoyment and need of people. "Riding one of these plows all day, day after day, gives one time to think," he would say, reminiscing long afterward. "I've settled all the ills of mankind in one way or other while riding along. . . ."

As would be said later in newspaper articles, he never lost the farm habits of early rising and hard work. His mother would say the farm was where Harry got his common sense. "It takes pride to run a farm same as anything else," he would tell her, sounding very like his father.

4

Soldier

It is the great adventure, and I am in it.

—CAPTAIN HARRY TRUMAN, AEF

I

The war in Europe that changed the world in such drastic fashion need hardly have concerned Harry Truman of Grandview, Missouri, much beyond what he might have read in the Kansas City papers or some of his favorite magazines. Had he chosen, he could have played no part in it, and nobody would have expected him to have done otherwise. He turned thirty-three the spring of 1917, which was two years beyond the age limit set by the new Selective Service Act. He had been out of the National Guard for nearly six years. His eyes were far below the standard requirements for any of the armed services. And he was the sole supporter of his mother and sister. As a farmer, furthermore, he was supposed to remain on the farm, as a patriotic duty. Upon the farmers of the country, said President Woodrow Wilson, rested the fate of the war and thus the fate of the nation and the world.

So Harry might have stayed where he was for any of several reasons. That he chose to go, almost from the moment of Wilson's call to Congress for a declaration of war in April 1917, was his own doing entirely and the turning point in his life. He left the responsibility for the farm and care of his mother to his sister Mary Jane, who, later, would say simply and dutifully, "We got through," but whose own life as a consequence was not to be the same.

She had grown into an attractive young woman with a bright smile and even disposition. Some people thought her the best looking and, overall, the most appealing of the Trumans. In a studio photograph made for

Harry to take with him to war, she posed in a big picture hat with an expression that seemed to combine both strength and gentleness. She was twenty-eight the summer he left for Camp Doniphan. She was still unmarried and without serious prospects for marriage, but popular. From that point on, she was to have little life of her own or any society much beyond Grandview. The worries and responsibilities that had weighed so heavily on Harry since their father's death were all now hers, and she would be more alone than ever he had been, a point he seems to have felt deeply after a time. "It was quite a blow to my mother and sister," he conceded years afterward. His idealism and "overzealous conduct" got him "into things" before he had a chance to realize what the consequences might be to others. Mary Jane, who adored him, also thought he had grown a bit self-preoccupied and conceited.

Bess Wallace's response to his decision was to say they should be married at once. Harry, almost unimaginably, said no. She must not tie herself to a man who could come home a cripple or not at all, he said. They would wait until he came home whole.

In an effort to explain why he went, he offered most of the reasons given by hundreds of thousands of American men in that emotionally charged time. He still disliked guns, he had never been in a fight of any kind or risked his life over anything. But it was "a job somebody had to do." It would make a man of him. He would not be a "slacker" no matter what, however old, blind, or untried he might be, and no one who understood him or cared for him should expect otherwise. Besides, he would say, there wasn't a German bullet made for him and the war would soon be over, once Americans were in the fight. He would remember feeling "we owed France something for Lafayette," and being "stirred heart and soul" by the war messages of Woodrow Wilson. Greatest of all was the sense of joining in a noble crusade across the sea, "over there" in old Europe.

Over there. Over there.
Send the word, send the word over there,
That the Yanks are coming . . .

He played it now on the piano, along with the other rousing and sentimental songs—"Good-bye Broadway, Hello France," "Keep the Home Fires Burning." Trying long afterward to describe the emotions of the time, he would stress that most Americans responded as he did, "stirred by the same flame that stirred me in those great days."

The hard truth was that human beings had never been slaughtered in such numbers or so rapidly as in this hideous war. Nor with less to show for it. The machine gun, automatic rifles, massed artillery, poison gas, flamethrowers, the airplane, and the tank made a mockery of old-style textbook stratagems and old-style battlefield heroics. In the previous year, 1916, there had been 2 million casualties on the Western Front, the line of battle that reached all the way from the North Sea to the Swiss border, 350 miles in length, and despite such appalling butchery the line had hardly moved either way. In just four months at the Battle of the Somme, between July and October 1916, the Germans alone lost more men than were killed in all four years of the American Civil War. That spring of 1917, as Harry Truman, feeling "all patriotic," helped organize a new Missouri artillery battery, a frontal assault by the British at Ypres gained 7,000 yards at a cost of 160,000 dead and wounded in five days.

Initially, the common view had been that the fighting wouldn't last long. It was a war that would be quickly over. But from the summer of 1914 the slaughter had continued year after year, consuming a whole generation of English, Scots, French, and Germans. "It is a fearful thing to lead this great peaceful people into war, into the most terrible and disastrous of all wars," Woodrow Wilson had said, stating the harsh reality, in his famous war message. Yet it was a war like the Civil War, the imagined pageantry of bright legions and banners flying, and such ringing words as Pétain's at Verdun, "They shall not pass," that stirred the souls of the young Americans signing up to "make the world safe for democracy," the noble phrase of Wilson's that people remembered above all.

Harry Truman felt, he later said, as if he were "Galahad after the Grail, and I'll never forget how my love cried on my shoulder when I told her I was going. That was worth a lifetime on this earth."

His convictions made him an effective recruiter. He painted the Stafford automobile bright red and went dashing about Kansas City in it wearing his new uniform. He lived in uniform. Nothing even remotely so exciting had ever happened to him before. Every day had focus now.

He had little trouble rejoining the National Guard and went immediately to work organizing a new artillery battery, Battery F, expecting to be made a sergeant. Instead, he was elected a first lieutenant, officers in the Guard then still being chosen by the men as in Civil War days. It was one of life's great moments. He had never been elected anything until now.

Drilling began in May in the streets of Kansas City across from Union Station and inside Convention Hall. When the 2nd Missouri Field Artillery, as they were known, became the 129th Field Artillery of the 60th Brigade attached to the 35th Division, Harry had to face a regular Army physical for the first time. He was stripped, weighed, measured, examined for hernia, gonorrhea, piles, fallen arches, and defects of vision. He managed to pass the eye examination, according to his brother Vivian, by memorizing the chart. (Harry, Vivian liked to say, couldn't see over the fence without his glasses.) The actual record of the examination shows that Harry had uncorrected vision of 20/50 in the right eye, 20/400 in the left eye, which theoretically meant he was blind in the left eye.

According to the same record he also stood 5 feet 8 inches tall and weighed 151 pounds, which made him 10 pounds heavier and an inch taller than the average recruit. His chest measured 33 inches "at expiration," 37 inches "at inspiration." All else was categorized "normal."

The first units of the American Expeditionary Forces were by now in France, under the command of General John J. Pershing, who as every true son of Missouri knew was Missouri born and raised. On July 4, 1917, when Harry turned up at Bess Wallace's house in full uniform, sporting silver spurs and a riding crop, American infantry of the 1st Division were parading through Paris to a tumultuous welcome.

In September Harry was on his way to Doniphan, a huge new tent encampment on a windswept plain adjacent to Fort Sill, at Lawton, Oklahoma, within the old Comanche Indian Reservation. There was not a tree, and Lawton, a prairie tank town, was twenty miles away. Except for some barren hills to the west, the hard country was as flat as a tabletop. Approaching trains could be seen for miles. The camp had been named for Alexander Doniphan, a Mexican War hero who had led a band of eight hundred Missouri volunteers on one of the longest marches in military history, more than 3,000 miles from Santa Fe to El Paso to Chihuahua to Buena Vista, while defeating several larger Mexican forces en route.

Reveille was at 5:45, breakfast at 6:30 A.M. Drill began at 7:30. Nights were surprisingly cold and the wind that blew almost constantly day or night was described in one formal account as "misery-producing." "It was sure enough cold and still is," Harry recorded early in October. Soon the dust storms struck. "A tent fifty yards away is invisible. Dust in my teeth, eyes, hair, nose, and down my neck." The men were saying they would give Oklahoma to the Germans and call it even. On the rare days when the wind didn't blow, Harry reported, "we are all very happy."

The truth was he was happy under nearly any conditions. Bess was not to worry for a minute. He was too busy to be down in spirits or getting into any "meanness," he told her, by which he seems to have meant troubles with women of the kind soldiers were known to be susceptible to. (In one letter he said she need not worry about him thinking of anyone but her, since there were only Indians in Lawton and "ugly ones at that," but then, thinking better of what he had written, he quickly added that it wouldn't matter if "all the Lillian Russells and Pauline Fredericks in this Republic were down here for I don't like but one style of beauty and that's yours.")

His duties with the men included instruction in the handling of horses —about which he knew more than most new officers—trench-digging exercises, and artillery training with 3-inch guns which were few in number. He tried to accustom himself to thinking and figuring in the metric system. Most artillery terms were already familiar from his earlier days in the Guard: *Defilade,* "Protection from view by an object in front, such as a hill, a wood or building. . . ." *Enfilade,* "To rake a line lengthwise from the side, by rifle or shell fire. . . ." *Field of fire,* "The area which is within range of a gun or battery and not protected by intervening obstructions or defilade." He stood inspection, played his part on the drill field. "I have been squads east and squads sideways, arms up and hands down until I can't open my mouth without telling someone to straighten up and get in step." He could march perfectly at the prescribed cadence of 120 steps a minute, 32 inches per stride. He was also acquiring an ability to curse like Captain Kidd, he said, and wondered if he might sometime have to face a high reckoning for it.

Each evening officers assembled for "school" on artillery fire and field service regulations, or to hear someone report on operations in France. "I learned how to say Verdun, Vosges, and Belgium, also camouflage," he wrote after a lecture from a French officer. Another night, having listened to an English colonel who had been on the Western Front, he wrote to Bess, "He made us feel we were fighting for you and mother earth and I am of the same belief. I wouldn't be left out of the greatest history-making epoch the world has ever seen for all there is to live for. . . ."

In a twenty-four-hour exercise under "actual battlefield conditions," he spent a night in the trenches and observed for the first time the famous rapid-firing French 75 in action. At special instructions on gas protection, he learned to put on a mask, then sat in a so-called "gas house" for ten minutes. When a rainstorm in January 1918 turned to snow to sleet to the worst blizzard he had ever seen, it made him think of Grandpa Young and all he had endured on the plains. For weeks the temperature stayed at zero or below. The bread froze and had to be cut with a saw. He was still living in a tent, heated by a Sibley stove of the kind used by the Army in the time of the Plains Indian wars.

After a day on horseback in February he decided he must be getting pretty tough, since he wasn't the least tired. To find he could also make men "toe the line" seems to have come as an even greater revelation.

In addition to his regular duties, he had been assigned to run the regimental canteen—a dispensary for candy, sodas, cigarettes, tobacco, shoelaces, writing paper—and it was this that soon made him known to nearly everyone in camp. (Virgil Thomson, the future composer, who had also enlisted in the 129th and was at Doniphan at the same time, would remember Lieutenant Truman years later as "one of our most effective officers.") To help make the operation a financial success (as most Army canteens were not) Harry took on a partner, Sergeant Edward Jacobson, a former clerk in a Kansas City clothing store. "I have a Jew in charge of the canteen by the name of Jacobson and he is a crackerjack," he told Bess, as if that were all the reason anyone would need to expect a profitable outcome. And it was indeed Jacobson who ran things, as Harry was always first to acknowledge.

They became fast friends. "Each day Harry would write a letter to his girl, Bess Wallace," Jacobson remembered, "and I would write one to my sweetheart Bluma Rosenbaum . . . and when I went into town [to replenish supplies], I would mail them." Harry had brought the Stafford to camp and had it stripped down to serve as a truck. The bright red car, with Truman at the wheel, Jacobson beside him, became a familiar sight rolling through camp, trailing a column of dust.

To finance the canteen every man in the regiment was assessed $2, which produced an instant capitalization of $2,200. In no time Truman and Jacobson had a "grand, rushing" business, taking in $500 to $900 a day. A barbershop and a tailor shop were added. After six months business was so successful overall that the canteen paid dividends of $10,000, which made Truman and Jacobson extremely popular and led them to conclude they were an unbeatable business combination. Some of the other officers began kidding Harry, calling him a "lucky Jew" and "Trumanheimer." "I guess I should be very proud of my Jewish ability," he said.

His one private worry was that he might somehow fail to measure up as an officer and be disqualified and disgraced. Rumors of an imminent departure for France had by now become commonplace. Faced with another physical exam and a doctor who twice refused to pass him because of his eyes, Harry simply kept talking until the doctor relented. He supposed he could put on a "real good conversation when circumstances demand it," he told Bess. But it had been a close call.

He missed her terribly. "Jacobson says he'd go into the guardhouse thirty days for one night on Twelfth Street. I'd go for forty days if I could see you thirty minutes." After a flying visit to Independence during which he was able to see her for little more than an hour, he wrote, "I didn't know how crazy I was about you until I went to leave." His letters, however, carried none of the old anguish over what he might make of himself in life. There was no more self-doubt, or self-pity over his supposedly bad Truman luck. Except for an attack of what he discreetly described as "indigestion," he remained in perfect health, and even the indigestion ended quickly when a young Catholic chaplain, Father L. Curtis Tiernan, came to the rescue with a bottle of whiskey.

Sergeant Jacobson and Father Tiernan were among the half dozen or so he counted now as his real pals. The others were fellow officers, including three from Independence, Edgar Hinde, Spencer Salisbury, and Roger Sermon. Another, James M. Pendergast, was the nephew of the Kansas City politician T. J. Pendergast. When Lieutenant Pendergast was called before a board of inquiry after the death of three of his men in the explosion of a live shell they had found on the reservation, it was Lieutenant Truman, as a member of the board, who did the most to defend him and to see that he was exonerated.

It was also at Harry's urging that two of his superior officers, Colonel Karl D. Klemm and Lieutenant Colonel Robert M. Danford, joined the Masons and this, too, he felt, helped greatly to expand his influence. Both Klemm and Danford were West Point graduates, Class of 1905, which would have been Harry's class had he been admitted to the Academy. Klemm, a Kansas City man, was efficient, humorless, and, like Harry, had been elected to his position. Considered a strict, "Prussian type" officer, he would, as time went on, cause Harry and others considerable grief. "We elected Klemm and then were sorry we had," Harry later admitted.

Danford, by striking contrast, had all the qualities in a leader that Harry most admired and hoped to cultivate in himself. Danford knew what he was talking about (he had helped write the artillery manual), and while an exacting disciplinarian, he knew also to treat those under him with kindness and understanding. Though Harry would serve under Danford but briefly, and only in training, he was never to forget him and the example he set. "He taught me more about handling men and the fundamentals of artillery fire in six weeks than I'd learned in the six months I'd been going over to the school of fire and attending the regimental schools." While other instructors seemed determined to make a dark mystery of the mathematics involved, Danford, who had taught military science at Yale, emphasized that the point was to make the projectile hit the target. That Danford was among the few officers who also wore eyeglasses must have provided still further reason to admire him.

The closest friend, however, was First Lieutenant Ted Marks, who was nothing like the rest of the Missouri men, but an Englishman with what seemed a natural military bearing, a pleasant, open face, and protruding ears. Two years older than Harry, Marks was a Kansas City tailor in civilian life whose beautiful custom-made suits sold for as much as $75. He had been born in Liverpool, ran away from home at age sixteen, and served three years in the Grenadier Guards before coming to America. He and Harry had first met more than ten years earlier, in 1906, when Marks walked into the National Guard offices to join up and found a bespectacled young corporal named Truman officiating behind the desk. As Marks would always remember, Harry had asked him how long he had been in the country. Marks said six months and Harry responded, "You speak pretty good English for the time you've been here," which led Marks to wonder what sort of a country he had come to after all.

On one of the bitterest of Camp Doniphan's bitter cold days, Marks, Truman, and another lieutenant, Newell Paterson, went for examination for promotion before General Lucian D. Berry, a hard-bitten old Army martinet who, with his big mustache, looked like a figure out of a Frederic Remington painting, and had a reputation for chewing up National Guard officers. By his lights, they were no better than "political officers," unworthy of rank or respect. Once, when Truman's captain, also a Guard officer, submitted an efficiency report full of praise for Harry Truman and recommending promotion, General Berry sent it back with the comment, "No man can be that good."

The three lieutenants stood in the numbing cold outside Berry's office waiting their turns. The temperature was near zero. When Lieutenant Paterson was called first, Marks and Truman remained standing for another hour and a half. When Harry's turn came, the general and three colonels took him "over the jumps" for more than an hour, Berry becoming so loud and rough that Harry had trouble remembering anything. If he had the right answer, it only made Berry more angry. If he was unable to answer at all, Berry would stalk up and down the room pulling on his mustache and shouting, "Ah, you don't know, do you?" or, "It would be a disaster to the country to let you command men!"

Harry came out flushed and angry and fearing the worst. Then, because it was nearly the lunch hour, Marks was kept only thirty minutes. As it turned out, all three lieutenants were passed, though Harry was not to learn of his promotion for another several months. He was told only that he and Paterson would be going overseas in advance of the others, as part of a select group of ten officers and one hundred men to be given further training in France, which he knew to be a high commendation.

"I suppose you will have to spend the rest of your life taking the conceit out of me," he wrote Bess. "Mary is fully convinced that I am overloaded with it, although I never thought so."

On the eve of departure, not knowing what else to do about his automobile, he sold it for $200.

The night of March 19, 1918, he was "moving out at last," by troop train, the ride so rough he could hardly complete his letter to Bess. "I'd give anything in the world to see you and Mamma and Mary before I go across," he wrote. ". . . You can write me Detachment 35th Division, 129th F.A., Camp Merritt, New Jersey, and I'll probably get it." When the train stopped briefly in the Kansas City yards, he was out of the car in an instant, running down the tracks in the dark looking for a telephone. A switchman in a shed told him to help himself. "The phone's yours," Harry would long remember the man saying. "But if she doesn't break the engagement at four o'clock in the morning, she really loves you."

On leave in New York before sailing, he and four other officers put up at the McAlpin Hotel on Broadway, and "did the town" as best they could in the little time available. They saw a vaudeville show at the Winter Garden, rode the subway, walked up Broadway after dark, up Fifth Avenue the next morning. By high-speed elevator they went to the top of the fifty-eight-story Woolworth Building, the world's tallest skyscraper. They crossed the Brooklyn Bridge, ate in a Chinese restaurant. Harry, who had expected to be overwhelmed with admiration for New York, found it all very much overrated. The show at the Winter Garden was a flat disappointment. The celebrated lights on Broadway looked no different to him than those on 12th Street in Kansas City. The McAlpin was no better than Kansas City's Muehlebach (which he spelled Muleback). And besides there were too many Jews. He called it a "Kike town" in a letter to Bess, and to the Nolands explained that in addition to the millions of "Israelitist extraction," there were millions of "wops" as well. As for pretty girls, Kansas City had twice as many.

Only the Woolworth Building lived up to expectations. The view from the top was well worth the 50-cent admission.

Shopping on Madison Avenue, he was touched by the patriotic feelings of an optometrist who charged him just $17.50 for two pairs of aluminum-framed glasses, much less than he would have had to pay at home. To be on the safe side Harry was going to France with six pairs of glasses, all pince-nez.

"I imagine his vision with glasses is 20–20, but without the glasses he couldn't recognize his brother twenty feet away," another officer named Harry Vaughan would later explain. They had become friends at Doniphan. "So, he always has had several pair on hand in case . . . he would be so helpless without them, and he was advised that he could not wear the ordinary glasses with the side pieces over the ears in action, because it would interfere with wearing your gas mask, you see. It would leave a hole on either side that you would be able to get gas through. So he brought . . . I believe he said, four or five of his lens prescriptions in pince-nez."

The *George Washington,* a confiscated German luxury liner with seven thousand troops aboard, sailed the night of March 29, 1918, Good Friday, nearly a year to the day since the President's declaration of war. "There we were watching New York's skyline diminish and wondering if we'd be heroes or corpses," Harry remembered. He and Lieutenant Paterson stood at the rail for some time talking about German submarines and "a lot of things ahead." Then they went below and, as Harry recalled, passed the rest of the night playing poker.

The weather was clear the whole way across, perfect submarine weather. The ship was part of a convoy, sailing a zigzag course once it reached the submarine zone. There were endless lifeboat drills and calisthenics on deck. Life preservers were worn at all times. At night, the ship was dark, smoking on deck forbidden. No one had much space. Officers were sleeping six to a cabin. As the time passed, Harry, who did not know how to swim and had never seen an ocean, wondered why anyone would ever want to be a sailor. He ached for home. The water was either blue or lead-colored, he noted, depending on whether the sun was out or in. The only variety in the panorama came at sunrise or sunset, and the sunsets weren't half as good as back home.

II

The *George Washington* steamed into the crowded harbor of Brest the morning of April 13. The day was warm and sunny, and First Lieutenant Truman thought the town looked "quite wonderful." It wasn't Paris, but if Paris was as much livelier as it was bigger, then Paris had to be "some town." Bands were playing, welcoming crowds lined the shore, thousands of people cheering and waving flags.

The American Expeditionary Forces (AEF) in France by this time numbered nearly a million men, a figure that would have been inconceivable a few years earlier. Only the summer before, on July 4, when the first American infantry unit marched through Paris, there had been just fourteen thousand American troops in all of France. Now, the seven thousand "doughboys" who came down the gangways from the *George Washington* were but a fraction of the monthly total. That April, 120,000 arrived. Soon there would be 250,000 landing every month until eventually there were 2 million American troops in France.

Four hundred miles away from the docks at Brest, to the northeast at the Belgian border, one of the most savage battles in history was raging. Field Marshal Erich Ludendorff had launched a massive frontal assault on the Allied lines along the River Lys, near Armentières. With Russia out of the war since December, after the fall of the czarist regime, the Germans were free to concentrate on one front, as they had wanted from the beginning, and this was intended to be their deciding offensive. The losses were appalling. Only the day before, April 12, the British commander, General Sir Douglas Haig, issued his famous order: "With our backs to the wall, and believing in the justice of our cause, each one of us must fight on to the end." The Battle of the Lys lasted three weeks until the Ludendorff offensive was stopped. Winston Churchill would consider it the critical struggle on the Western Front and, thus, of the war. Yet to Lieutenant Truman and the thousands arriving with him, none of this was apparent. What they saw their first days ashore and for weeks, even months to come, was the France that was not the war. As Harry wrote to the Noland sisters, he felt like Mark Twain in *Innocents Abroad,* as much a tourist as a soldier.

Being an officer in the AEF, he found, meant accommodations such as he had never known or expected. At the hotel in Brest he had a room to himself larger than any in the Gates mansion. There were double lace curtains at the window and a white marble mantelpiece with a seventeenth century Dutch clock under a glass case, a beautiful affair even if it didn't run. Chairs were upholstered in red plush, floors polished smooth as glass. He admired a crystal water decanter and a mahogany wardrobe with a full-length mirror in which he could also admire himself in his new overseas cap and Sam Browne belt.

For nearly two weeks he did little more than enjoy himself. If he had been disappointed by New York and the Atlantic Ocean, France more than made up for it. He enjoyed the food (the bread especially) and the wine. He admired gardens so well cultivated and cared for that there was hardly a weed to be seen. The whole surrounding countryside with its irregular patchwork of fields and hedgerows made him wish he were a painter, he told Bess. "The people generally treat us fine and seem very glad to accommodate us in any way they can." Later he wrote, "I'm for the French more and more. They are the bravest of the brave." They also knew how to build roads as smooth and solid as a billiard table, "and every twenty meters there are trees on each side." Nor could he get over the way audiences at the movies clapped and cheered during the love scenes. "They are the most sentimental people I ever saw," he noted approvingly. If ever he had to give up being a Missourian, he decided, he would be a citizen of France, though so far he hardly dared try the language other than to say, "*Je ne comprends pas.*"

Good food, wine, and cognac were all plentiful and an American soldier's pay went far. Harry calculated that his came to 1,100 francs a month, enough nearly "to retire on over here." A fine meal cost about 10 francs. Wine and cognac were a comparable bargain. Most of the 35th Division, having been too long in Oklahoma, seemed determined to drink France dry. But they were certain to fail, he also noted, the supply being "inexhaustible."

As he did not report to Bess, women, too, were plentiful. Temptation beckoned in Brest, as it would later in every interior city he went to in France. One American lieutenant wrote in his diary, "Wandering through dark streets. Ever-present women. So mysterious and seductive in the darkness. . . . A fellow's got to hang on to himself here. Not many do." But apparently Harry did.

"Personally, I think Harry is one of the cleanest fellows . . . the cleanest fellows morally that I ever saw, or know," First Lieutenant Edgar Hinde of Independence would remember. "I never saw him do anything out of the way that would be questionable in the way of a moral situation. He was clean all the way through. I always admired him for that quality and you know when a man's in the Army, why his morals get a pretty good test."

"Wish I could step in and see you this evening," Harry wrote to Bess the night of April 17, after five days in France. "Have only seen one good-looking French woman and she was married to some French general or admiral or something, anyway he had seven or eight yards of gold braid on him."

At the end of April he was assigned to an elite artillery school 500 miles to the east, near the hilltop town of Chaumont, in Lorraine, where Pershing had his headquarters. The first-class coach Harry traveled in was upholstered like a Pierce Arrow limousine, he reported happily to Ethel Noland. No wealthy civilian on tour ever had things better.

His new quarters were even more splendid than anything he had yet seen, a seventeenth-century gray stone château set in a lovely, walled park in the middle of a picture-book village called Montigny-sur-Aube, this in turn set in a gently sloping valley. There was a magnificent garden, a moat, stone walls six feet thick, tile floors, marble stairs, hand-carved woodwork, "everything you like to read about," he told Ethel. "You'd never think that a war was raging in this same land, it is so peaceable and quiet and pretty." Spring had arrived in full glory, with soft, fragrant air and trees along the brows of near fields all a delicate green. His one problem was the bells that kept him awake the first few nights. The church clock would strike eleven, "and then the clock on the Hotel de Ville would strike eleven five minutes later and then five minutes later some clock that I haven't been able to locate yet would strike eleven. By that time the church clock had started on eleven fifteen and it was one continual round of pleasure all night long."

Forbidden to give his location, he was able to say only that he was "somewhere in France."

The first week at the artillery school was the most difficult ordeal he had ever experienced. After that, the work got harder. He felt he was in over his head, having never been to college, and worried constantly that he would fail. The mathematics was all at the college level. He studied surveying and astronomy. There was no time for anything but work, from seven in the morning until ten at night. There was hardly time to get from one class to the next. He had no idea what was happening in the war and of the outside world, he said, he was as ignorant as if he were in Arkansas.

Training in the classroom and on the firing range centered on the French 75-millimeter gun, a small, rapid-fire, rifled cannon known for its mobility and phenomenal accuracy. It had been developed twenty years before, its technology guarded by the French as a military secret. The slim, 6-foot barrel was of nickel steel and other alloys that were kept classified. The breechblock, gun carriage, and hydropneumatic recoil system were all of special design. Because the gun recoiled on its carriage, it stayed in place with each shot, and thus no time was lost correcting its aim between shots, which was the secret of its rapid fire. It could get off twenty to thirty shots a minute and had an effective range of five miles. Being light in weight compared to most cannon, a little over a ton and a half, and maneuverable with its high-spoked wooden wheels, it was considered ideal for trench warfare. The fire from a battery of four was murderous.

It was called the marvel weapon. The French would later say it won the war for them. No American or British-made fieldpiece could compare and American units relied on it almost exclusively. (Virtually no American fieldpieces—or American airplanes or tanks—were used in the war, for all the troops supplied by the United States.) To the Germans, it was the "Devil Gun."

> I've studied more and worked harder in the last three weeks than I ever did before in my life [Harry wrote to Bess at the end of May] . . . right out of one class into another and then examinations and thunder if you don't pass.
>
> We had a maneuver yesterday and General Pershing himself was there. I was in command of a battalion of artillery and he did not even come around to see if I could fire that many guns. . . . My part was mostly play-like except the figures. I was supposed to have three batteries, which were represented by three second lieutenants. Had a second lieutenant for adjutant and a major for regimental commander. We had a good time and walked about six miles besides. There were Major Generals, Brigadiers, Colonels, Majors and more limousines than a January funeral. It was a very great pleasure to see a Major General click his heels together and nearly break his arm coming to a salute when The General came along. You don't often see Major Generals do that.

On Sundays he attended services at the Catholic church, where the air was chill and he was unable to understand a word. France was a grand place for Frenchmen, he had decided, and he didn't blame them for fighting for it; "and I'm for helping them, but give me America, Missouri and Jackson County for mine with the finest girl in the world at the county seat," he wrote on May 5, three days before his thirty-fourth birthday.

One of his examinations given on a Saturday in May would have driven the president of Yale University to distraction, he reported. The Sunday after, with little to do, he discovered volumes of music—Beethoven, Mozart, Schumann—and a "dandy" piano in a YMCA that had once been the home of a wealthy local family. He played at length while the other officers listened. "It sure was a rest after the week's work."

After five weeks, his ordeal over and feeling extremely lucky to have "slipped through," he was ordered to rejoin his old regiment, which by now had arrived in France and was stationed at Angers. Heading west again by train, he seldom took his eyes off the passing scenery. Like so many American soldiers, he was astonished not only at how beautiful the country was but how very old. A young officer traveling with him, Arthur Wilson, remembered being amazed at Harry's knowledge of French history. "He had maps and he knew where we were going. It didn't mean anything to me. . . ." During a wait at Orléans, Harry insisted they get out and see the city's famous cathedral and the equestrian bronze of Joan of Arc in the main square.

. . .

At Angers, to his total surprise, he learned he had been made a captain months earlier. No one had bothered to tell him. He only found out when he saw it reported in *The New York Times*.

As adjutant of the 2nd Battalion, he was assigned to teach the other officers what he had learned. "I just barely slipped through at the school, and now they've got me teaching trig and logarithms and surveying and engineering," he told Bess. Didn't she think it amusing that an "old rube" from Missouri was handing out such knowledge to the Harvard and Yale boys? In another letter, he said he had never known how valuable a university education was until now.

She wrote to him faithfully, as did Mamma, Mary Jane, and Ethel Noland. Their letters took a month or more to reach him and arrived usually in batches of six or seven. "Please keep writing," he told them. Knowing how they worried, he said nothing upsetting, never a word of discouragement or serious complaint. "No I haven't seen any girls that I'd care to look at twice. . . ." He was eating well, walking as much as fifteen miles a day. He never felt better, nor looked so good with his new captain's bars. "I look like Siam's King on a drunk when I get that little cockeyed cap stuck over one ear, a riding crop in my left hand, a whipcord suit and a strut that knocks 'em dead." ("That was one of the things about this war," Willa Cather would write, "it took a little fellow from a little town, gave him an air and a swagger. . . .") He had Arthur Wilson take his picture sitting on a horse. Like every good American soldier, Captain Harry Truman conceded, he had an "insane desire" to let the home folks know how he looked.

In the chest pockets of his tunic he carried three photographs. In the right pocket were Mamma and Mary Jane in her picture hat. In the left, over his heart, was a wistful portrait of Bess that he adored more than any ever taken of her. She had written on the back for him: "Dear Harry, May this photograph bring you safely home again from France."

The first week of July the 129th Regiment moved from Angers to what had once been Napoleon's artillery base, Camp Coëtquidan, near Rennes, for final training before going into action. Again to his enormous surprise, Captain Truman learned he was to be a battery commander. He was summoned before Colonel Karl D. Klemm and told to begin at once. It was his highest ambition come true and he was scared to death. He would have command of 4 guns and 194 men.

Thursday morning, July 11, 1918, shoulders back, head up, he walked out onto the parade field to face for the first time Battery D of the 2nd

Battalion, 129th Field Artillery, "Dizzy D," by reputation, most of them Irish Catholics from Kansas City. "They were a pretty wild bunch of Irish, I'll tell you that," remembered Lieutenant Hinde. "They had [had] one captain named Charlie Allen and they had two or three others there, none of them could handle them, and finally they assigned Truman to command the battery. He was a third degree Mason in a Catholic battery and we thought he was going to have a pretty rough go of it. . . ."

He was not at all what the men expected. One of them, recalling the scene, said he looked like "a sitting duck." Another remembered "a stirring among the fellows. . . . Although they were standing at attention, you could feel the Irish blood boiling—as much as to say, if this guy thinks he's going to take us over, he's mistaken." A private named Vere Leigh would recall "a rather short fellow, compact, serious face, wearing glasses. And we'd had all kinds of officers and this was just another one you know." To others Harry looked, with the pince-nez spectacles, like a store clerk or a professor and totally out of his element. "Yes," said Private Edward McKim, "you could see that he was scared to death."

Harry, who would remember the moment more vividly than anyone, said he had never been so terrified. He could feel all their eyes on him, feel them sizing him up. "I could just see my hide on the fence. . . . Never on the front or anywhere else have I been so nervous."

According to Private Albert Ridge, who later became a judge in Kansas City, the new captain said nothing for what seemed the longest time. He just stood looking everybody over, up and down the line slowly, several times. Because of their previous conduct, the men were expecting a tongue lashing. Captain Truman only studied them. As he was to confess long afterward, writing about himself in the third person, "He was so badly scared he couldn't say a word. . . ."

At last he called, "Dismissed!" As he turned and walked away, the men gave him a Bronx cheer. ("And then we gave Captain Truman the Bronx cheer, that's a fact," said Vere Leigh.) As the day wore on, they staged a sham stampede of their horses. After taps, a fight broke out in the barracks and several men wound up in the infirmary.

In the morning Captain Truman posted the names of the noncommissioned officers who were "busted" in rank. "He didn't hesitate at all," remembered Private Leigh. "The very next morning this was on the board. He must have sat up all night. . . . I think the First Sergeant was at the head of the list."

Harry called in the other noncommissioned officers and told them it was up to them to straighten things out. "I didn't come over here to get along with you," he said. "You've got to get along with me. And if there are any of you who can't, speak up right now and I'll bust you right back now." There was no mistaking his tone. No one doubted he meant exactly what he said. After that, as Harry remembered, "We got along." But a private named Floyd Ricketts also remembered the food improving noticeably and that Captain Truman took a personal interest in the men and would talk to them in a way most officers wouldn't.

He proved a model officer and extremely popular with "wild Irish" Battery D. "Well, I would say that his major characteristic was great friendliness, that he had such warmth and a liking for people," recalled Arthur Wilson. "He was not in any way the arrogant, bossy type, or Prussian type of officer. A lot of us youngsters, you know, when they put gold bars on our shoulders, why we thought that we sort of ruled the world. And he had, as an older man, a very quiet sort of a way of serving as a leader. . . . And he was a disciplinarian but he was very fair. I don't know, I can't describe what the personal magnetism was except that he had it."

"You soldier for me, and I'll soldier for you," Harry told the men. "Soldier, soldier all the time," his favorite colonel, Robert Danford, had said at Camp Doniphan.

For one month he drilled the men on the firing line, trying to teach them everything he knew about the French 75. They thought the weapon a wonder and, with practice, claimed, in Missouri style, that they could pick off a sparrow on a wire at 9,000 yards.

Working them hard, insisting on strict behavior, making them "walk the chalk," and driving himself no less, he found his satisfaction in the task, his pride in the men, as well as his own newfound sense of power, were like nothing he had ever known. "Talk about your infantryman," he boasted, "why he can only shoot one little old bullet at a time at the Hun. I can give one command to *my* battery and send 862 on the way at one round and as many every three seconds until I say stop." Whatever dislike or fear of guns he had known before appears to have vanished. He knew how much was riding on his judgment now. "You've no idea what an immense responsibility it is to take 194 men to the front," he told Bess. Were he to get them killed, he would never be able to look anyone in the face again.

How brave he might be once the high-explosive shells began flying weighed heavily on him. He kept thinking of a man Uncle Harrison once described who had the bravest kind of head but whose legs "wouldn't stand."

Enthusiasm in the camp was fueled now by daily dispatches of Americans in action at last. Through most of that spring, while Captain Truman was at Montigny-sur-Aube, the numerical superiority of the Germans on the Western Front had become clear. The great question was whether American forces would arrive in time and in sufficient strength to make the difference. By June the Germans were back again on the banks of the Marne, within cannon shot of Paris. The situation was grim. The leaders of France, Italy, and Great Britain warned Woodrow Wilson of the "great danger of the war being lost" unless American forces became available as rapidly as possible. Pershing had been bound and determined to commit his troops only as a separate American command, but because of the emergency more than 250,000 Americans were rushed to the front to support the French under the command of Marshal Ferdinand Foch. The Americans fought bravely at Château-Thierry and Belleau Wood. Then, on July 15, the Germans unleashed another huge offensive aimed at Paris, the Second Battle of the Marne, sending fifty-two divisions against thirty-four Allied divisions, nine of which were American. In three days, from July 15 to July 18, the tide of battle turned. To Ludendorff, American forces had been the "decisive" factor, and the German chancellor later confessed that "at the beginning of July 1918, I was convinced . . . that before the first of September our adversaries would send us peace proposals. . . . That was on the 15th. On the 18th even the most optimistic among us knew that all was lost. The history of the world was played out in three days."

But for the Americans, the worst was still ahead.

In the time allotted, Captain Truman had transformed what had been generally considered the worst battery in the regiment to what was clearly one of the best, as was demonstrated in conspicuous fashion the day of their departure for the front, on August 17. The 129th Field Artillery began moving out from a nearby railyard, one battery at a time. To a very large degree the war was fought with railroads. The movement of troops and equipment by rail was ever critical, hence great store was set on how well officers and men managed things when the time came to go. For artillerymen especially, "moving out" was a terrific undertaking. The trains for each of the batteries were comprised of some seventeen flatcars, thirty "dinky" French boxcars (these marked "40 Hommes, 8 Chevaux"), and a single passenger coach for officers. Everything needed had to go aboard—troops, guns, caissons, field kitchens, horses, harness, hay, feed, battery records, extra supplies of every sort—in the quickest time, with the least wasted motions possible.

As it was, each battery managed to get on board and under way in about an hour. The time for Battery D was 48 minutes, a record.

They were rolling by eight in the morning and the trip lasted two days, their train passing close enough to Paris that they could see the top of the Eiffel Tower. Beyond Paris, except for the scars of war, the rolling countryside might have been Missouri or eastern Kansas. Then they were beside the Marne, traveling past Château-Thierry, scene of a great American victory, then along a narrowing valley, past Epernay, in the heart of the champagne country. They turned southeast. For mile after mile, in a landscape of broken wooded hills, one small village after another looked much alike with their orange tile roofs and single church steeples.

They were heading for the beautiful Vosges Mountains, in Alsace, nearly to the Swiss border, which was the extreme eastern end of the front. Long the sleepiest sector of the war, it was, the American high command had decided, the ideal place for green troops to get some experience holding the lines, as a preliminary to an all-out American offensive. The first American battle casualties had been suffered in the Vosges, the autumn before, and in the time since one division after another had been moved in and out.

The end of the line, hours later in the dark, was the town of Saulxures, by a swift little river in a mountain valley. In mid-August, on the night Battery D arrived, the air outside the train was sweet with the smell of giant firs and patches of purple thyme along the river banks. Harry would remember, too, how good the local beer tasted.

The following morning, August 20, puffs of white smoke could be seen in the sky five or six miles to the east, and, in the middle, a moving speck. It was anti-aircraft shrapnel being fired at an enemy observation plane, and the first real sign of war. But by then Harry was already on his way into the mountains.

III

"It was just a quiet sector to give the boys a little indoctrination in trench warfare," recalled Sergeant Frederick Bowman, one of the small detachment that went with Captain Truman to locate a gun position. They traveled by truck at first, over twisting roads to a tiny, picturesque village called Kruth. Then, with horses and accompanied by a French officer who spoke no English, they began a hard, steady climb into the fir-clad mountains, up logging roads as steep as a roof. It was terrain such as the Missouri men had never seen, with rushing streams, beds of green moss inches deep, great granite boulders heaped on all sides, and everything heavily shadowed beneath the huge, shaggy trees. The enemy's batteries were on an opposite mountainside. As Sergeant Bowman said, the topography was "kind of a V-shaped affair," and so wild and rugged, it appeared, that either side might fire away endlessly and do no harm.

The sky was clear, the day warm and sunny, visibility excellent—not ordinary conditions in the Vosges—but the men and horses were well concealed under the trees. At one point only, when they came to an open ridge in plain view of the Germans, did the French officer have them go at intervals, one man at a time.

They found the spot they wanted at the edge of the trees at an elevation, Harry reckoned, of more than 2,000 feet above the valley. The men would remember making a meal of cold beans and beef, hardtack and a mess kit full of wild red raspberries picked en route, these topped off with champagne provided by the French officer.

Camping in the woods, they spent several days getting set up. Then the rest of the battery began the long, hard climb from below, hauling the guns. "It was surely some steep hill," Harry wrote. Once, a can of lard broke loose from a wagon and bounced the whole way to the bottom. Clouds had moved in on the mountain, meantime, shrouding the trees in mist. The chance of being seen was no longer a worry, but in the damp air now even the least sound carried. To muffle the wheels of the guns Harry had them wrapped in burlap, which struck some of the men as silly. And indeed, the whole struggle of hauling everything into place seemed doubly absurd when, after days of doing nothing in the clouds, then days of rain, the battery was told to pack and move on again.

Harry had been ordered to take up a position about a mile closer to the German lines and prepare to fire a gas barrage. So his first action would be to shell the enemy with poison gas.

The battery moved after nightfall, horses, guns, and men laboring up and down roads now slick with mud and rain. And it was raining still the next afternoon when they took their new position, everyone exhausted from no sleep but also extremely excited and eager to commence firing for real at last. The targets were some German batteries four miles distant. The barrage was to begin after dark and to be what in artillery parlance was called "fire for neutralization," to "suppress the activities of the enemy" without necessarily destroying his position.

When the command was given at precisely 8:00 P.M., August 29, four batteries of the 129th opened up. The piercing crash of the 75s went on for half an hour. Battery D fired five hundred rounds. "We were firing away and having a hell of a good time doing it," remembered Private Leigh, "until . . . [we] woke somebody up over there."

The barrage over, the night was suddenly still. There was only the sound of the rain. At this point the battery was supposed to move out with all speed, to take a new position before the Germans had time to return the fire. Horses were to be brought up at once from the rear, the guns hauled away. But the first sergeant in charge of the horses was nowhere to be found. The job of first sergeant was assigned on a rotating basis and the first sergeant that night was Glen Wooldridge, who didn't appear with the horses for nearly half an hour. Then, with everybody charging about in the dark rushing to make up for lost time, things became miserably scrambled. Fearing the Germans would retaliate with a gas barrage of their own, the men had their masks on. Some were struggling frantically to get masks on the horses.

When the first German shells came screaming over, Harry was up on a horse trying to see what was going on. A shell burst with a shattering roar not 15 feet from him. His horse was hit—or slipped—and went over into a shell hole and rolled on top of him, pinning him down helplessly. By the time he was pulled free by a big, heavy-shouldered lieutenant named Vic Housholder, his breath was nearly gone—Housholder remembered him "gasping like a catfish out of water." Meantime, half the horses and two of the guns had charged off in the dark, over a hill in the wrong direction to become hopelessly mired in the mud. Then all at once, the same unfortunate Sergeant Wooldridge, in panic, began yelling at the top of his voice for everyone to run, saying the Germans had a "bracket" on them.

Wooldridge himself took off. Others ran after him, though how many is uncertain. No one could see much of anything in the black night and pouring rain, and with such wild confusion all around. With their masks on, telling who was who was nearly impossible, even at close range. Private Walter Menefee said later there was only Captain Truman and maybe three or four others who didn't run. "I led the parade!" Menefee admitted. Vere Leigh thought hardly anyone took off except Wooldridge.

In any event, Captain Truman stood his ground, and once having recovered his breath, let fly with a blast of profanity that had stunning effect chiefly because it came from the officer who, heretofore, had seemed so proper and reserved. "I got up and called them everything I knew," was how Harry himself remembered the moment. He was livid and terrified.

For years afterward at reunions in Kansas City, with whiskey flowing, there would be much lighthearted banter and kidding over this first encounter with the enemy, Battery D's so-called "Battle of Who Run." But there was nothing the least comical about the situation at the time.

With his blistering verbal barrage and the vivid example of his own fierce courage under fire, Captain Truman succeeded finally in getting things in control. Two horses were dead, two others had to be shot. The guns, in mud to their axles, were impossible to move with manpower only. They could be rescued later, he decided, and marched the men back to base position through the dark and the continuing downpour.

At about four in the morning, after a hot meal, he went to his tent, collapsed, and slept for twelve hours.

He was worried sick, sure he was disgraced. But his superior, Major Marvin Gates, told him reassuringly that green troops often behaved badly their first time and to forget about it. Gates recommended only that Sergeant Wooldridge be court-martialed at once. Unable to bring himself to do that, Harry had Wooldridge broken to private and transferred to another battery, where, as it turned out, he later performed well and bravely.

In a letter to Bess, Harry said it had not been until the day after that terrible night that he figured out what had happened. "The men think I am not much afraid of shells but they don't know I was too scared to run and that is pretty scared."

Because no one had been killed in the melee, the men decided that Captain Truman—Captain Harry—besides being cool under fire, was good luck. When time came to go back for the abandoned guns, a potentially perilous mission, every man in the battery volunteered. Harry, deeply touched, did the job with only the necessary men and horses.

At first light, September 3, the regiment was on the move again and in full battle dress—helmets, gas masks at the ready, blanket rolls, and full packs that weighed as much as 70 pounds, or more than half the weight of some of the men. A sign on Grand Avenue, Kansas City, had said: "Join the Artillery and Ride." Now, to save the horses on the steep roads, everybody was on foot, officers included.

Harry was struck by the beauty of the mountain valleys. Hay and grain were being harvested, but by old people and children, the old women all in black. "It was literally true that the manhood of France was in the army," wrote a lieutenant named Jay Lee. "Only the very old and the crippled were exempt from the army, but not from the work."

At the village of Vagny two days later, the regiment boarded another train, this bound north. The next night, at Bayon on the Moselle River, a curious incident occurred that frightened Harry more than he let on. At the station a young lieutenant colonel from a Missouri infantry division told him to get his men off the train and find cover fast, before daylight. The whole area, he said, was under bombardment from German planes. In the dark Harry could make out the carcasses of two dead horses beside the platform. The colonel introduced himself. He was Bennett Clark, the son of Speaker of the House of Representatives Champ Clark of Missouri, who had been one of John Truman's favorite Democrats. Colonel Clark said he would hate to see Harry and his men suffer the same fate as the horses. "Well, I was scared green," Harry later wrote. "I was in command of the train and there was absolutely no one to pass the buck to. I simply had to unload that battery and find a place for it before daylight." Guns, horses, ammunition were off the train and into the pine woods in the least time possible, everybody moving with breakneck urgency. But as the morning passed and no German planes came, Harry walked back to the station, where he found Clark grinning. The joke was on Harry, Clark said. There had never been any German planes. When Harry asked about the dead horses, Clark said they had been shot by a veterinarian.

Harry appears to have taken this in good spirits, partly because his men had enjoyed a much-needed rest and a chance to bathe in the river. He and Bennett Clark were to have a great deal to do with one another in time to come, but for now neither had any reason to expect to see the other ever again.

By dusk the regiment was on its way on foot. They marched most of the night and the following day. In a pocket diary Harry marked their progress: "September 10. Leave Coyviller at dark. Rain . . . September 11. Leave Bosserville at 7:30 P.M. Rain Rain Rain Went through Nancy dark as hell."

"Who can ever forget the impression of those night marches!" Lieutenant Jay Lee would write after the war, in a privately published history of the 129th Regiment.

We sometimes went as far as 30 or 35 kilometers [18 to 20 miles] in a night, which wasn't so bad except when, as so often happened, obstruction or congestion in the road caused . . . fretful stops and starts. The wonderous fact of all these men over there made a vivid and solemn impression . . . the long line of horses, limbers, guns, caissons and men stringing out interminably before and behind . . . thousands of men, all alike in outward appearance of round helmets and army raincoats; all with common purpose and determination, but each occupied with his own thoughts. . . .

They were part of the first big American push, half a million men on their way to Saint-Mihiel, south of Verdun.

So slow was our progress that after six hours we had only advanced three or four miles [continued Lieutenant Lee, describing the night march through Nancy] when . . . the whole front to our north broke out in flame, and a tremendous, continuous and awe-inspiring roar of artillery began; while huge searchlights, interspersed with many-starred signal rockets, shot their shafts like the Northern Lights constantly across the sky. We had heard or seen nothing in our experience like it. . . .

"American drive begins," Harry scrawled in his diary on Thursday, September 12. "Heard first roar of American artillery."

They were held in reserve short of Saint-Mihiel for several days, horses harnessed, everything ready to move at a moment's notice. It was now that Harry felt himself in "the great adventure" at last. In long lines, thousands of bedraggled German prisoners marched past. "We are doing our best to finish the job and get home," he wrote to Bess, "but we can't leave until it's done. In fact, we don't want to leave until it's done."

Among those in his command he had come to depend on were Sergeant Edward Meisburger, who in the midst of the chaos at "Who Run" never flinched, and Sergeant Ralph Thacker, who, though only nineteen, had the judgment and staying quality of a much older man. Lee Heillman, the cook, Frank Spina, the barber, were the best in the Army. Harry Kelley, the instrument sergeant, was "very, very bright," an "excellent soldier," who could figure the firing data quite as well as Harry could.

The night of September 16, in bright moonlight, they began the forced march that none of them would forget. Orders had changed. Saint-Mihiel had been a sudden, resounding American victory. The Germans were overrun in two days. So the 129th was en route to the Argonne Forest.

"It was march all night and part of the day, grab a few hours sleep and march some more," Harry wrote.

The Supreme Command had decided on a colossal, all-out offensive to end the war. The attack, infinitely greater than any that had gone before, would extend along the entire Western Front from Verdun to the sea. The sector allotted to the American Army ran from the Meuse River, north of Verdun, to the Argonne Forest, a distance of twenty-four miles. The American objective was to cut the German rail lines at Sedan.

This great Meuse-Argonne offensive, as it would be known, was the largest action in American military history until then. No larger American army had ever been seen than the one now on the roads. Fifteen divisions were moving up—600,000 men, nearly 3,000 artillery pieces, trucks, tanks, supply wagons, more than 90,000 horses—a logistical problem of staggering proportions that had been worked out by an exceptionally able officer on Pershing's staff, Colonel George C. Marshall. Infantry and ammunition were carried by big, lumbering, chain-drive trucks, but because the horse-drawn artillery moved so much more slowly, the order of march was mixed, to keep solid columns. Discipline on the road was poor, congestion often a nightmare. Everything was moving up by just three roads and much of the time the traffic was two-way, with the French troops that were being relieved coming back from the front. Furthermore, to keep the Germans from knowing what was happening, nothing could go forward or back except under the cover of darkness. Officers in charge of the roads had often to brandish revolvers to keep traffic moving. And after the first moonlit night, a fine rain fell nearly all the while, turning the roads to rivers of mud. Many horses were in such poor shape by this time that they began dropping in their traces and had to be destroyed.

To lessen the burden on the horses, the artillerymen carried all they could. "And there was an order out," Private Floyd Ricketts remembered, "that we cannoneers who were walking and following the guns were not to hold onto any part of the gun or caissons so as not to put any more burden on the horses. But walking along almost dead on your feet, you could hardly resist grabbing a hold of the caisson to help you along."

Colonel Klemm, in a state such as the men had never seen, kept riding up and down the line shouting orders "like a crazy man" and at one point senselessly ordered an advance at double-time up a long hill. Had he not been wearing a yellow rain slicker, some of the men later speculated, he might have been shot in the back. But because Father Tiernan had on the same color coat no one would have risked making a mistake in the dark.

Harry took the men off the road to rest. Klemm found out and demanded to know what he was doing. "Carrying out orders, sir," Harry answered, after which, it is said, the men adored him as never before.

Later, Harry let a man with a twisted ankle, Sergeant Jim Doherty, ride his horse, which was against orders. Klemm, seeing Doherty, flew into a rage and ordered him down. Harry told Klemm that as long as he, Harry, was in command of the battery, Doherty would ride. Klemm, furious, turned and rode off, but not, apparently, before telling Harry what he thought of him.

"The Colonel insults me shamefully," Harry wrote in his diary. "No gentleman would say what he said. Damn him."

(Reminiscing about the march long afterward, some of the men would speculate that Klemm really had gone crazy for the moment, or was drunk. Klemm would remain a troubling memory for years. In 1925 in his Kansas City business office, he shot and killed himself.)

The march went on for a week. "The weather was bad, rainy, and we would sleep in the daytime in thickets or in woods and then take off at dusk and march all night," said Private Ricketts. They passed places called Ourches, Loisy, and Rembercourt, which were nothing but ruins. Sometimes Harry and Father Tiernan walked together at the head of the battery, talking about "the history of the world and I don't know what all," Harry remembered. If all priests were like him, he told Tiernan, there wouldn't be any Protestants.

The morning of September 22, they pulled off to sleep in a rain-soaked forest opposite Rarécourt, close to their final position. From here on they would travel light, free of their supply train, and as rapidly as possible, everybody riding.

Harry's diary entry for Monday, September 22, says only, "Wild ride to position tonight." Later, for Bess, he wrote this vivid account:

I stripped the battery for action. I knew I was in for it this time because I only took the firing battery and just enough men to run the guns and they for the first time were allowed to ride. I got stuck getting out of the woods. One caisson got pigheaded and I couldn't budge the cussed thing with either prayers or cuss words. I tried both. Finally hooked all the men onto it with ropes and got it out and then and there began the wildest ride I ever hope to have. It seemed as though every truck and battery in France was trying to get to the same front by the same road that I was going. I had twelve carriages in my column, four guns, six caissons and two fourgon wagons, one of them full of instruments and one full of grub. I don't know which I'd rather have lost. . . . Well I finally got my battery out on the main highway and headed for the front. The real front this time west of Verdun and just alongside the Argonne Forest. Those devilish trucks kept trying to cut me in two. It was necessary to keep the battery moving at a trot and a gallop nearly all the way and I had to ride the line to see that they stayed closed up. Every time I'd get a chance I'd cut in ahead of a row of trucks and sew 'em up until I got the whole battery by and every time a truck would get a chance he'd cut through the battery. They didn't get very many chances because when we got the right of the road I made it a point never to let 'em through. . . . I don't know if I told you but it was raining as usual and the road was as slick as glass.

It had been a forced march of nearly 100 miles and they arrived on time. Indeed, the whole massive move to the front had been a total success. Incredibly, not a single unit failed to reach its appointed place on schedule. The 129th Regiment's designated position was Hill 290, a gradual slope half a mile from a crossroads village called Neuvilly, which consisted mainly of a ruined stone church that would serve as a field hospital and where a much-published photograph would be taken of the wounded in stretchers crowded beneath a huge painting of the Ascension that had miraculously survived and still hung on the shattered wall above the altar.

Captain Truman and Battery D were assigned to a clump of saplings near a fair-sized wood across a field of mud. They arrived in pitch dark at 3:00 A.M., the rain still coming down, men and horses exhausted. Only by hitching twelve horses to each gun and having every man push were they able to get all four guns in place by daylight. In the distance, across an open No-Man's-Land, was the German strongpoint of Boureuilles.

The next three days were spent in preparation for "H-Hour." Trenches were dug, ammunition stacked, trees cleared for a field-of-fire. From time to time, German shells came screaming over. The second night several hit the exact spot where Harry had slept the first morning and would have made small pieces of him, as he said, had he not shifted locations. The evening of Wednesday, September 25, in Colonel Klemm's dugout, the battery commanders received their orders. The offensive was to begin in the morning, "H-Hour," at 5:30 A.M. Each battery was to fire 1,000 rounds an hour. This meant six rounds per gun per minute, since each gun would need ten minutes every hour for cooling off. The first hour, before the infantry moved out, would be "preparation" fire, to destroy barbed-wire entanglements. Afterward, at "H-Hour," would come a two-hour "rolling" barrage during which the range of fire would have to advance steadily, 100 meters every four minutes, over the heads of the advancing infantry. Thus even a small mistake by battery commanders or gun crews could bring down disaster on their own troops.

"Everything was now in readiness, with the quiet which precedes the storm," wrote Lieutenant Jay Lee in his formal history. "Late in the afternoon Captain Roger T. Sermon, Regimental Personnel Officer, paid the men, according to routine, a ceremony that never failed to arouse general interest, even on so eventful an occasion as this."

Harry, Lieutenant Housholder, and Sergeant Kelley were up all night going over their final computations.

At a different point along the line, a swashbuckling American tank commander, Lieutenant Colonel George Patton, impatient for morning, wrote to his wife, "Just a word to you before I leave to play a part in what promises to be the biggest battle of the war or world so far."

The bombardment began long before daylight when the air was chill, at 4:20 A.M., the morning of Thursday, September 26, 1918. Two thousand seven hundred guns opened fire all along the front with a roar such as had never been heard before. In three hours more ammunition was expended than during the entire Civil War—and at an estimated cost of a million dollars per minute. The American air ace Captain Eddie Rickenbacker, who took off in his plane before daybreak, said, "Through the darkness the whole western horizon was illumined with one mass of jagged flashes." From Hill 290 it looked as though the sky was on fire— "as though every gun in France was turned loose," said Harry.

At 5:30, "H-Hour," exactly on schedule, the rolling barrage opened up. "That gun squad worked just like clockwork," remembered Corporal Harry Murphy. "It was—it was a sight, they just were perfect. They just got those rounds off so fast that—unbelievable."

"My guns were so hot," wrote Harry, "that they would boil [the] wet gunnysacks we put on them to keep them cool."

When the barrage ended all was still except for distant machine-gun fire that sounded oddly, Harry thought, like a typewriter.

The infantry had pushed off into a charred, cratered landscape with no visible landmarks, then disappeared into a thick white fog. The first phase of the fighting, as George Marshall would write, was "confusing in the extreme." The Germans, though greatly outnumbered, were solidly dug in on high ground, ideal ground defensively, and a nightmare for those on the attack. Up the center ran a huge hogback, heavily wooded, with high points where the Germans had all the advantage, after four years of work on their defenses. Most of the American divisions being hurled at them had never had contact with an enemy before. Some troops had never handled a rifle until now.

The 129th Field Artillery was ordered forward, to follow the infantry. Captain Truman and Major Gates went out ahead trying to spot enemy gun emplacements and for a while were pinned down on a road by machine-gun fire. From where they had started to the sheltering woods on the other side of No-Man's-Land was only about a mile and a half, but hauling the guns through the shell-blasted muck, craters, and twisted barbed wire was a long day in hell. The crossing took twelve hours, the struggle lasting into the night. Men and horses pushed and hauled under nearly constant fire. The German shells came over with a sound like the scream of air brakes, then hit with a terrific explosion, throwing up dirt and pieces of iron in all directions. Yet so exhausted were the men as night wore on that some of them were falling asleep on their feet.

The next day, after some confusion in orders, they started forward again. They saw the dead now, scattered here and there, and nearly all were Americans, since the retreating Germans carried their dead and wounded back with them. At a crossroads near Cheppy, heaped in a pile, were seventeen American dead, infantrymen, while down the road a dozen more were lying "head to heel," all "shot in the back after they'd gone by," Harry surmised. He would remember how quiet his men became at the sight and the sergeant who spoke up, "Now you sons-of-bitches, you'll believe you're in a war."

West of Cheppy the battery moved into a peach orchard. Harry and one of his lieutenants, Leslie Zemer, Sergeant Kelley and Corporal William O'Hare went out ahead to establish an observation post, stringing a telephone line and advancing, unknowingly, several hundred yards beyond the infantry. About dusk, from the crest of a hill, Harry saw an American plane drop a flare off to the west, then turning his field glasses on the spot, saw a German battery pulling into position on the left flank, across a small river in front of the 28th Division, which was beyond his own assigned sector. Standing orders were to fire only at enemy batteries facing the 35th Division. Harry decided to disregard that.

"Truman didn't panic," remembered Private Leigh, "he let them [the Germans] take their horses away from the guns, which was exactly what he should have done. If it had been me I would have hollered for D Battery to start firing as soon as I saw them. He didn't do that, he let them get into position, get all set to fire, with their horses by this time a couple of miles away. Then he had his firing data exact. It's no good to have a man up there if he don't know what the hell he's doing. . . ."

"Truman sent back the data," Private McKim recalled. "We went into action and he said, 'Fire at will, fire as fast as you can,' and we just poured them in there."

The decision undoubtedly saved lives in the 28th Division, and though an outraged Colonel Klemm was on the phone almost at once, threatening Captain Truman with court-martial for violating orders, nothing came of it.

A German plane, meantime, had spotted the battery in the peach orchard—the pilot had actually flown in at about 300 feet and lobbed down a few German "potato-masher" hand grenades—so Harry, back with his battery, ordered everyone to pull out at once. German artillery fire, a "lot of heavy stuff," came soon after. "You know," said Vere Leigh, "when you're in the artillery they don't shoot at you with machine guns. You're back from the line, and they shoot at you with that heavy stuff. They wiped that peach orchard out."

This was on September 27. Later that same night, as the battery moved on, Harry was on horseback when he was hit in the face by a low-hanging branch and suddenly found himself without his glasses and unable to see.

The horse kept moving with the column. Harry turned frantically in the saddle to look behind, only to find the glasses sitting nicely on the horse's back.

In his diary he had time for the barest record:

> September 28: Moved to position on Cheppy-Varennes road Fire on Boche O.P. [Observation Post] . . . on Boche Bty moving out.
>
> September 29: Fired barrages
>
> September 30: Same as yesterday

One soldier wrote, "The artillery fire has been something awful for the past two days. Shells are screaming over our heads constantly. The Germans shell us quite often, and we are continually hugging the earth, making ourselves as thin as possible. I feel like a man of fifty. . . ."

On the afternoon of the 29th, reports came that the infantry was losing ground. American stragglers began streaming past. The Germans were about to counterattack. Harry's immediate superior was Major John Miles and as every man knew there were just two possible orders to give for a position about to be overrun. One was "direct fire"— point-blank fire into the advancing enemy—and then stand by the guns to die or be captured. The other was to abandon the guns and fall back. "Well, men," Miles said. "Get ready and we'll give them direct fire."

The German attack never came. Still, as Lieutenant Lee would write, "The coolness, the steady courage, the readiness to stand fast to the last, evidenced by Major Miles and his men on that anxious afternoon, were none the less inspiring that they were not pressed to the final sacrifice."

Casualties among the infantry were heavy—as high as 50 percent in the 35th Division. Litter cases at the dressing station at Cheppy numbered in the hundreds. Fourteen ambulances loaded with wounded had been sent to the rear from that one station in a single day. On September 30 thousands of men were being fed there, most of whom had been wounded or gassed. Father Tiernan was busy burying the dead under fire all afternoon. One ambulance company alone suffered more than fifty casualties.

The Meuse-Argonne offensive was to have been another swift, smashing American victory, like Saint-Mihiel, but it was not. Sedan was ultimately taken, but at appalling cost. The Meuse-Argonne was the battle that produced the so-called "Lost Battalion," an infantry unit that was trapped for five days and suffered casualties of nearly 70 percent, and also the most appealing American hero of the war, infantryman Alvin York from the hills of Tennessee, who single-handedly captured 132 Germans in one day. In all, in 47 days of fury, there were 117,000 American casualties. In the military cemetery on the Romagne Heights, at the center of the battle-field, 14,246 dead would be buried, making it the largest American military graveyard in Europe.

"It isn't as bad as I thought it would be but it's bad enough," Harry wrote Bess in the first week of October. The heroes, he added, are all in the infantry.

The regiment was pulled back for rest. His own men looked like scare-crows and their respect for him had never been greater. "He was the Captain, he was the head man," Vere Leigh said later, "and he was treated as such, we respected him, and he earned it. That's why we respected him, because he earned it. . . . He's not a dramatic type or anything like it. He's no Patton, you know. He might have been a better soldier than Patton, but he was not a showoff."

Harry had lost 20 pounds. He could hardly believe what he had been through. Terrible as it had been, it was also "the most terrific experience of my life." He couldn't help feeling proud. His men were alive and in one piece.

In mid-October, with the weather still cheerless and colder than be-fore, the regiment took up new positions on the bleak heights east of Verdun, above the Meuse River Valley, in preparation for what was to be the final drive. Days were spent laying telephone wires, digging new dugouts, and camouflaging. His battery was soon so perfectly concealed that Harry himself had trouble finding it after dark. His dugout, down the road, was a "palace," with stove, table and chair, a telephone beside his cot—"all the comforts of home except that I'll have such a habit of sleeping underground that I'll have to go to the cellar to sleep when I get home."

Lieutenant Harry Vaughan, who was in a different regiment and who had been out of touch with Harry since Camp Doniphan, was seeing more of him now and puzzled how, after weeks in the trenches, any man could look so consistently clean and dapper.

Before Battery D, in the distance, rising on the grim horizon like the hump of an evil subterranean monster, was the famous bastion of Douau-mont, once the showpiece of French defenses, the greatest fortress in the world. Harry thought it and the surrounding landscape comprised the most dreary prospect he had ever looked upon. Shattered dead trees stood like ghosts. The ground everywhere was a mass of shell craters. In Verdun itself not a building remained undamaged. The ancient city had caught the full force of the war. The civilian population had long since fled. Harry tried to imagine the same panorama before the war, with everything as cultivated and beautiful as the rest of France he had seen.

To stem the German tide in 1916, France had sent an unending column of men and artillery to Verdun. The fury and horror had been like nothing in history. The French, Harry was told, had put their 75s "hub-to-hub" for direct fire at the advancing enemy. The battle lasted ten months, the longest ever. Casualties on both sides came to 900,000 men. The ground everywhere was still a rubbish heap of weapons, shells, shreds of clothing, and no one knew how many dead. In a letter to the Noland sisters, he described a field a short distance to the west of his position "where every time a shell lights it blows up a piece of someone." In none of his letters did he complain. In none did he even begin to describe the truth of the horrors he had seen. Like nearly every man writing home, he tried to put a good face on things. Only now did he seem to waver somewhat. He couldn't shake the presence of the dead from his mind. "When the moon rises . . . ," he told Bess, "you can imagine that the ghosts of the half-million Frenchmen who were slaughtered here are holding a sorrowful parade over the ruins." He did not, however, mention the smell or the rats everywhere.

To Ethel Noland he sent a poppy he found among the rocks near his new observation post, close to the German lines, at the end of a four-mile, zigzag hike through the trenches. He had brought back two flowers, the other for Bess.

The men were kept busy working on their positions, gas-proofing dugouts, moving ammunition, standing guard. The shelling continued. Guns boomed somewhere, near or far, almost continuously.

The weather turned colder. There was more rain. A day with sunshine was an event worth noting in his diary. "Fine day," Harry wrote October 28. "Very fine day," reads the entry for October 29. Before dawn on November 1 came another "show" like the one at the Argonne, as every battery opened up on the German lines for five straight hours.

For weeks there had been rumors of peace. A German pilot shot down just behind Battery D said the war would be over in ten days. On November 7 a United Press correspondent, Roy Howard, sent a cable from Paris saying hostilities had ceased at two o'clock that afternoon. The news was false.

133

On November 9 the infantry went forward once more, after an hour-long barrage. Harry's friend Captain Ted Marks, and Battery C, were ordered forward in support of the infantry. The next day the drive and its artillery support continued. The morning of November 11, Battery D was firing again when, at about 8:30, Captain Truman was notified by headquarters that in exactly two and a half hours, at 11:00 A.M.—the eleventh hour of the eleventh day of the eleventh month—the Germans would sign an armistice agreement.

Sergeant Meisburger was called to Captain Truman's dugout, where he found the captain stretched on the ground eating a blueberry pie, a wide grin on his face. "He handed me a piece of flimsy and said between bites, 'Sergeant, you will take this back and read it to the members of the battery.' " What puzzled Meisburger was where Captain Truman had obtained the blueberry pie.

"My battery fired the assigned barrages at the times specified," Harry wrote. "The last one was toward a little village called Herméville. . . . My last shot was fired at 10:45."

> When the firing ceased all along the front line [he continued] it . . . was so quiet it made me feel as if I'd been suddenly deprived of my ability to hear.
>
> The men at the guns, the Captain, the Lieutenants, the sergeants and corporals looked at each other for some time and then a great cheer arose all along the line. We could hear the men in the infantry a thousand meters in front raising holy hell. The French battery behind our position were dancing, shouting and waving bottles of wine. . . . Celebration at the front went on the rest of the day and far into the night. Very pistols, rockets and whatever else was handy were fired.
>
> I went to bed about ten P.M. but the members of the French Battery insisted on marching around my cot and shaking hands. They'd shout "Vive le Capitaine Américain, vive le Président Wilson," take another swig from their wine bottles and do it over. It was 2 A.M. before I could sleep at all.

A lieutenant named Broaddus of Battery F had been up in a balloon directing artillery when the cease-fire came. Below him, he remembered, "people went so wild celebrating that they forgot to pull me down . . . and I sat there for two hours."

"You've no idea how happy we all were to have the war end," wrote Harry to Ethel Noland. "You know that the continual and promiscuous dropping of shells around you will eventually get on your nerves considerably and mine were pretty tightly strung by 11 o'clock November 11. It was the most agreeable sigh of relief I ever have [had] when word came to cease firing."

The Great War was over and to the victors it seemed a triumph for civilization. It was left now to the statesmen to make a lasting peace. In less than a month President Wilson was on his way to France on the *George Washington,* the ship that had brought Harry and so many thousands.

For the 129th Field Artillery the war had been the Meuse-Argonne offensive and it had cost the regiment 129 battlefield casualties. Battery D suffered only three men wounded, one of whom later died, but they had been on a special detail with an ammunition train at the time, not under Captain Truman's command. "We were just—well, part of it was luck and part of it was good leadership," said Private Vere Leigh. "Some of the other batteries didn't have that kind of leadership."

IV

Two weeks and two days after the Armistice, Captain Harry Truman was on leave in Paris dining at Maxim's. At a nearby table he saw the prettiest woman he had laid eyes on since coming to France and to his delight found she was an American with the Red Cross. After dinner he and several other officers went to the Folies-Bergère, where the "little ladies" clustered about them during the intermission. (Years later he would call the show "disgusting," but at the time he told Ethel Noland it was about "what you'd expect at the Gaiety only more so.") He saw Notre Dame and Napoleon's Tomb. At the Arc de Triomphe, his trench coat belted tight against the November air, he posed for a snapshot beside a captured German cannon. He rode a taxi the length of the Champs-Elysées, up the Rue Royale, down the Madeleine, back up the Rue de Rivoli, over the Seine by the ornate Alexander III Bridge. He visited the Luxembourg Palace, the Tuileries Gardens, the Louvre, strolled the Boulevard de l'Opéra, "and a lot of side streets besides." All in twenty-four hours.

From Paris they took the train to Nice. Paris, said Harry, was "as wild as any place I saw." Nice was "ideal," with the Mediterranean on one side, the foothills of the Alps on the other. His hotel, "a dandy place," overlooked the sea. "The view from my window is simply magnificent. . . . There is no blue like the Mediterranean blue," he told Bess, "and when it is backed by hills and a promontory with a lighthouse on it and a few little sailing ships it makes you think of Von Weber's 'Polacca Brillante,' which I am told was composed here." She was all that was needed to make the place heaven.

He saw his first palm trees, walked in the sunshine, ate like a king, and in the first days of December drove to Monte Carlo, where he was startled to see a real-life princess drinking beer. He and Major Gates hired a car and drove to the Italian border, returning to Nice by way of the Grande Corniche, "the most beautiful drive I ever had."

In Paris again, his leave about over, he and Major Gates went to the opera, to a performance of *Thaïs* by the French composer Massenet, which was then immensely popular in France. The Place de l'Opéra was ablaze with lights, as it had not been since 1914. After his days on the Riviera, with his longing for the woman he loved, the sensuous music stirred him deeply. It was "beautifully sung and the scenery [more palm trees] was everything that scenery can possibly be." This, he emphasized in his letters, was the "real" opera. He would have paid the admission if only to see the gilded glory of the building.

He returned to a division encampment near Verdun notable only, he said, for its copious mud. The wait to go home became endless. "To keep from going crazy we had an almost continuous poker game," remembered his friend from Independence, Captain Roger Sermon of Battery C. When news of the influenza epidemic at home reached camp, Harry became so alarmed he hardly knew how to contain himself. Bess and her brother Frank had both been down with the "Spanish flu," he learned, Mary Jane and Ethel Noland as well, all through the weeks he had been on leave, and though all four were on the mend he kept worrying. "Every day nearly someone of my outfit will hear that his mother, sister or sweetheart is dead," he wrote. "It is heartbreaking almost to think that we are so safe and so well over here and that the ones we'd like to protect more than all the world have been more exposed to death than we." By the time the epidemic ran its course, vanishing mysteriously early in 1919, the number of deaths in the United States reached 500,000, including 25,000 soldiers, or nearly half the number of American battlefield deaths in the war. At Camp Doniphan alone fifty-one had died.

When in late January Harry learned that his favorite battery clerk, Sergeant Keenan, had died in the base hospital of appendicitis, he wrote in his diary, "Would as leave lost a son."

General Pershing and the Prince of Wales came for a division review. Pershing shook Captain Truman's hand and told him he had a fine-looking bunch of men and to take them home as "clean morally and physically as they were when they came over. . . ." Harry took the order quite to heart.

It's some trick to keep 190 men out of devilment now [he wrote later to Ethel Noland]. I have to think up all sorts of tortures for delinquents. It's very, very lucky that we are far from wine, women and song or we'd have one h--- of a time. Sometimes I have to sock a man with extra duty that I sure hate to punish. You know justice is an awful tyrant and if I give one man a nice muddy wagon to wash on Sunday, because he went to Verdun without asking me if he could, why I've got to give another one the same duty if he does the same thing even if he has the most plausible excuse. I'm crazy about every one of 'em and I wouldn't trade my messiest buck private for anybody's top sergeant. It very nearly breaks my heart sometimes to have to be mean as the dickens to some nice boy who has been a model soldier on the front and whose mail I've probably censored and I know he's plum crazy about some nice girl at home but that makes no difference. I have to make 'em walk the chalk. You'd never recognize me when I'm acting Bty Commander.

He was thinking constantly of home and what was ahead for him. He wrote in his letters of returning to the farm, but he mentioned also the possibility of running for political office on his war record—for eastern judge in Jackson County, possibly even for Congress. After what he had seen of peacetime Army life, he said, he would give anything to be on the House Military Affairs Committee. Like a great many of his fellow reserve officers, he had acquired a decided bias against West Pointers. He thought most of them pompous, lazy, and overrated, and couldn't imagine himself living under such a system. "I can't see what on earth any man with initiative and a mind of his own wants to be in the army in peacetimes for," he wrote. "You've always got some fossil above you whose slightest whim is law and who generally hasn't a grain of horse sense." As a boy, he told Bess, he had "thirsted for a West Point education . . . only so you could be the leading lady of the palace or empire or whatever it was I wanted to build." All he knew now for certain was that he longed to get "back to God's country again," to "the green pastures of Grand Old Missouri"; that, in fact, he had no place to go but home; that he was broke, and in love—"I love you as madly as a man can"—and eager to be both out of the Army and married just as soon as possible. He dreamed of walking down North Delaware Street. He dreamed of owning a Ford and touring the country with her. "Maybe have a little politics and some nice little dinner parties occasionally just for good measure. How does it sound to you?"

"We'll be married anywhere you say at any time you mention," he wrote in another letter, "and if you want only one person or the whole town I don't care as long as you can make it quickly after my arrival."

"You may invite the entire 35th Division to your wedding if you want to," she wrote in response, in the earliest of her letters to have survived. "I guess it's going to be yours as well as mine." Her mother, she said, hoped they would move in with her at 219 North Delaware. "Just get yourself home and we won't worry about anything."

He hated the waiting. He wished "Woodie" (Woodrow Wilson) would quit his "gallivanting" in France and depart, so every American soldier could, too. Saving the world was of no concern any longer. "As far as we're concerned," he told Ethel Noland, "most of us don't give a whoop (to put it mildly) whether Russia has a Red Government or no Government and if the King of the Lollypops wants to slaughter his subjects or his Prime Minister it's all the same to us."

In March, the regiment moved south to Courcemont, near Le Mans, where the officers were again quartered in luxury at the Château la Chenay, once the home of Ferdinand de Lesseps, the great canal builder. Harry had one more chance at a flying visit to Paris, during which he saw Woodrow Wilson ride by and, in a shop on the Rue de la Paix, he bought a wedding ring. Then on April 9, 1919, with the 52 other officers and 1,274 men of the 129th Field Artillery, he sailed for New York on the former German liner *Zeppelin*.

On this homeward voyage, the last act of his great adventure, the returning hero was violently seasick nearly the whole way. For a time he wished he were back at the Argonne where he might die honorably. Yet he could bear any agony, he knew, given the direction they were heading.

PART TWO

POLITICIAN

5

Try, Try Again

I've had a few setbacks in my life, but I never gave up.

—HARRY TRUMAN

I

As his observant cousin Ethel Noland once remarked, Harry Truman was at heart a nineteenth-century man. He had been born when Chester A. Arthur was President and among the more pressing issues was whether the nation should continue building a wooden Navy. He was a grown man, thirty-three years old, middle-aged nearly, by the time of the Great War, the event which, more than any turn of the calendar, marked the end of the old century and the beginning of something altogether new. His outlook, tastes, his habits of thought had been shaped by a different world from the one that followed after 1918. As time would show, the Great War was among history's clearest dividing lines, and much that came later never appealed to Harry Truman, for all his native-born optimism and large faith in progress.

He had been more at home in the older era. He never learned to like the telephone, or daylight saving time, an innovation adopted during the war. He tried using a typewriter for a while, but gave it up. Mark Twain and Charles Dickens remained his favorite authors. Andrew Jackson and Robert E. Lee were to be his lifelong heroes. Until he met George C. Marshall, he wondered if the "modern" times were capable of producing a great man.

The kind of art that had burst upon the public with New York's Armory Show of 1913—the first big American exhibition of modern paintings, which included Marcel Duchamp's sensational *Nude Descending a Staircase*—had no appeal or meaning for Harry Truman. "Ham and eggs art,"

141

he called it. He liked the old masters. His taste in American art, not surprisingly, ran to the paintings of Missouri riverboatmen and Missouri politics by George Caleb Bingham, or the western scenes of Frederic Remington, who had once owned a saloon in Kansas City.

If Harry Truman had even a little interest in the theories of Einstein or Freud, he never said so. Words like "libido" or "id," so much in vogue after the war, were never part of his vocabulary. Indeed, he despaired over a great deal that became fashionable in manners and mores. He disliked cigarettes, gin, fad diets. He strongly disapproved of women smoking or drinking, even of men taking a drink if women were present. When after much debate Bess decided it was time she bobbed her hair, he consented only reluctantly. ("I want you to be happy regardless of what I think about it," he told her.) He disliked the very sound of the Jazz Age, including what became known as Kansas City jazz. Life in the Roaring Twenties as depicted in the novels of F. Scott Fitzgerald or John O'Hara was entirely foreign to his experience, as it was for so much of the country. He never learned to dance. He never learned to play golf or tennis, never belonged to a country club. Poker was his game, not bridge or mah-jongg. "It was characteristic of the Jazz Age that it had no interest in politics at all," insisted F. Scott Fitzgerald, but Harry Truman, in those years, discovered politics to be his life work.

As the war was a watershed time for the world, so it was in his life. "I have always wondered," he later wrote, "how things would have turned out in my life if the war had not come along just when it did." What it most obviously did was to take him from the farm, and he would not go back again, except as a visitor. That much was settled for him, as it was for tens of thousands of others who came home. ("How you gonna' keep 'em down on the farm / After they've seen Paree?" went the hit song of 1919.) More important, he was not the same man who left for France only the year before. The change was astounding. He had new confidence in himself. He had discovered he could lead men and that he liked that better than anything he had ever done before. He found he had courage —that he was no longer the boy who ran from fights—and, furthermore, that he could inspire courage in others.

He had come home with a following, his biggest, best "gang" ever, his battery "boys," who looked up to him as they would an older brother. He was the captain who brought so many sons of Jackson County home safe and sound. Alone in the dim light of his tent or dugout in France, late at night, he had spent hours answering letters from the mothers and fathers of men in his command, a consideration not commonplace among officers of the AEF, and one that would not soon be forgotten in Kansas City.

He had been a big success as a soldier. The war had made him a somebody in the eyes of all kinds of people, including, most importantly, Bess Wallace, who had only decided to marry him once she heard he was enlisting. By nice coincidence, the signing of the Peace Treaty at Versailles and their wedding took place on the same day.

Also because of the war he had met and befriended Eddie Jacobson and Jim Pendergast, who, with Bess, were to have so much to do with the new and different life that began the morning the 129th Field Artillery had its triumphal return.

"Well, I remember when he came back, what a day it was," said Ethel Noland. "We all went into the city and saw them parading through the streets. . . . Then we went to the Convention Hall and had a great reception."

The 129th marched uptown from Union Station in dazzling morning sunshine, under full packs, wearing their "tin derbies," as they had marched in France. Harry and the other officers were on horseback. Flags brightened buildings and lampposts. The crowds along both sides of Grand Avenue were fifty deep. At 11th Street stood a huge Welcome Arch. People were cheering, weeping, holding up children to see. One young woman, carrying a baby, walked parallel to her husband from the station all the way to the Convention Hall in high heels.

Three days later, May 6, at Camp Funston, Kansas, the men were given their final discharges, and seven weeks and four days after that Bess and Harry were married. But not before two important events took place.

On May 8, Harry's birthday and his second day home, he and Bess had their first and apparently their last heated argument. Possibly it was over the wedding plans, or possibly over her mother's insistence that they live with her. Whatever the cause, Harry would remember the day and its misery for the rest of his life. In a letter to Bess written thirty years later, he would refer to it as their "final" argument.

Then, a month in advance of the wedding, he and Eddie Jacobson took a lease on a store in downtown Kansas City. Though Jacobson had served with another battery in France, they had seen each other occasionally and Jacobson, too, had come home on the *Zeppelin*. They had decided to join forces again and open a men's furnishing store, a haberdashery, convinced their partnership at Camp Doniphan had been only a prelude to great merchandising success. It was a decision made quickly, even impulsively, and, on Harry's part, it would seem, one designed to impress Bess and her mother.

The wedding, on Saturday, June 28, 1919, took place at four in the afternoon in tiny Trinity Episcopal Church on North Liberty Street in

Independence, and the day was the kind Missouri summers are famous for. The church, full of family and friends, became so stifling hot that all the flowers began to wilt.

The bride wore a simple dress of white georgette crepe, a white picture hat, and carried a bouquet of roses. Her attendants, cousins Helen Wallace and Louise Wells, were dressed in organdy and they too carried roses. The groom had on a fine-checked, gray, three-piece business suit made especially for the occasion, on credit, by his best man, Ted Marks, who had returned to his old trade of gentleman's tailor. The groom also wore a pair of his Army pince-nez spectacles and appeared, as he stood at the front of the church, to have arrived directly from the barbershop.

Frank Wallace, the tall, prematurely balding brother of the bride, escorted her to the altar, where the Reverend J. P. Plunkett read the service.

Present at the reception afterward, on the lawn at the Gates house, were Mrs. Wallace and her mother, Mrs. Gates, Mr. and Mrs. Frank Wallace, Mr. and Mrs. George Wallace, and young Fred Wallace, while the "out-of-town" guests, as recorded in the papers, included Mrs. J. A. Truman, her daughter Miss Mary Jane Truman, and Mr. and Mrs. J. Vivian Truman. All the Nolands attended, of course, as did several of Harry's former brothers in arms. One who was unable to be there wrote to him, "I hope you have the same success in this new war as you had in the old."

Punch and ice cream were served. The wedding party posed for pictures, Harry looking extremely serious, Bess a bit bemused. Presently, bride and groom departed for the train in Kansas City, driven by Frank Wallace, with more cars following.

At the station, waiting on the platform, Ted Marks remarked to Harry's mother, "Well, Mrs. Truman, you've lost Harry."

"Indeed, I haven't," she replied.

Recalling the day years later, Mary Jane spoke more of what she had been through before she and Mamma ever reached the church. They had been harvesting wheat at the farm. Mary Jane had cooked noon dinner for twelve farmhands—meat, potatoes, fresh bread, homemade pies, "the usual," she said.

Ethel Noland remembered Harry's expression as he stood watching Bess come down the aisle. "You've just never seen such a radiant, happy look on a man's face."

It had been nine years since the night Harry returned the pie plate. He was now thirty-five; Bess was thirty-four.

The honeymoon couple stopped at Chicago, Detroit, and Port Huron, Michigan. In Chicago, they stayed at the Blackstone. At Port Huron, they were at the beaches of Lake Huron, where the weather was as perfect as their time together. So sublime were these days and nights beside the ice-cold lake that for Harry the very words "Port Huron" would forever mean the ultimate in happiness.

It was all too brief. Worried over her mother's health—Madge Wallace suffered from sciatica, among other real and imagined complaints—Bess felt they must return to Independence sooner than planned. As her mother wished, they moved into 219 North Delaware, taking Bess's room at the top of the stairs on the south side. The immediate household now consisted of Bess, Harry, Madge, Fred, who was a college student and his mother's pet, and the elderly Mrs. Gates, who had a room on the first floor off the front parlor. In back of the house, beyond the driveway, in what was formerly the garden, two small, one-story bungalows had been built, facing Van Horne Boulevard, one each for brothers Frank and George and their wives. Thus the whole family was together still in a "kind of complex," under the watchful eye of Mother Madge Wallace, a neat, straight little woman with a rather sweet expression, her hair done up in a knot, who still wore an old-fashioned velvet choker. Among the neighbors she was perceived as possibly the most perfect lady in town and "a very, very difficult person."

Bess considered the arrangement temporary. She and Harry would stay only long enough for her mother to become accustomed to the idea that she was married. Harry moved in with his clothes, a few books, and a trunk full of his Army things, which was nearly all he owned.

II

Truman & Jacobson was located at 104 West 12th Street, Kansas City, on the ground floor of the Glennon Hotel, catty-cornered from the larger Muehlebach Hotel, which made it a choice location. By agreement Harry was to keep the books; Eddie would do the buying. Between them they would take turns with the customers.

Jacobson, short, cheerful, and conscientious, was twenty-eight years old, but with his glasses and rapidly thinning hair looked perhaps thirty-five, and unlike Harry, he had had twelve years' experience in the retail clothing business. One of six children and known by everyone as "Eddie," never "Edward," he was the son of impoverished immigrant Jews from Lithuania who had settled first on New York's Lower East Side, where he was born, and later in Kansas City, where he went to work at age fourteen as a stock boy in a dry goods store. Eddie, too, was soon to be married—to Bluma Rosenbaum at B'nai Jehudah, Kansas City's oldest Reform temple, in December of that year—and so, like Harry, he had every reason to wish to succeed.

It was to be a "first-class operation," specializing in famous brands. They would sell no suits or coats, but a full line of "gents furnishings"—shirts, socks, ties, belts, underwear, hats. To get started, they combined their money and borrowed from the bank. The store was remodeled inside and out. The cost of their initial inventory came to $35,000.

Harry put in $15,000, most of which he obtained by selling off livestock and machinery from the Grandview farm. He had hoped the farm might continue as before and tried to persuade Mary Jane to keep it running, but she refused if he was unwilling to be there and do his part. Two years had been enough, she said. That fall they auctioned off horses, hogs, plows, seed drill, nearly everything, the proceeds going to Harry for the store, an arrangement that was hardly fair to Mary Jane, given all she had done, and that pleased no one in the family except Harry. The land would now be rented for someone else to farm.

The store opened for business in late November 1919, and would be remembered by friends and patrons as "right up to snuff," "a sharp place."

The name "Truman & Jacobson" was set in colored tiles at the street entrance, between two large plate-glass show windows filled with shirts in striped pastels, fifteen to twenty hats, and a hundred or more stiff, detachable collars, suspended by wire in vertical columns. The shirts and collars were all Ide brand, as proclaimed in formal lettering across the top of the storefront, above the plate-glass windows. Inside, long showcases were filled with shirts, leather gloves, belts, underwear, socks, collar pins, cuff links, while behind, on open shelves, were boxes of more shirts, more detachable collars—"Marwyn" collars by Ide, which, like those in the windows, featured "the smart roll-front." But what immediately caught the eye was a display of silk neckties, hundreds of ties in every color and pattern, strung from an overhead wire on the left that reached the length of the store.

It all looked fresh and clean. The tiled floor was kept shined. Glass countertops gleamed. There were big electric fans overhead, a glistening new cash register, and close by on one showcase, the store's proud conversation piece, a huge silver loving cup, four feet high, a gift to "Captain Harry" from the boys of Battery D. Above the hat shelves at the back of the store, arranged like a bouquet, were the five flags of the Allied nations.

With the loving cup and flags, the atmosphere was not unlike that of a college shop, the college in this instance having been the war. For anyone who liked clothes as Harry did, who had liked always to "look nice," the effect must have been very pleasing.

Yet it is hard to imagine the adjustment from battery commander to storekeeper as anything but difficult, hard to imagine him not finding it a painful comedown from such career aspirations as he had confided to Bess, or from parading with a victorious army up Grand Avenue. Nor does there appear to be an explanation, unless it was that he—and Bess also—wanted money quite as much as in the years before the war and saw the partnership as the opportunity, while at the same time keeping contact with his "boys," the city, and people of a kind who might do him good should politics ever become his "line." His only explanation later was, "I didn't know what I wanted to do."

He and Eddie opened their door regularly at eight every morning and remained open until nine at night. Times were prosperous. "Sporty" 12th Street—the 12th Street of *Twelfth Street Rag*—was "jumping." Conventioneers poured in and out of the Muehlebach. In the Dixon Hotel, across the street, were two gambling houses. Prostitutes worked the neighborhood. Day or night, salesmen, secretaries, shoppers from outlying towns, nearly everybody seemed to have money to spend. "Twelfth Street was in its heyday and our war buddies and the Twelfth Street boys and girls were our customers," Eddie Jacobson would recall with pleasure. "Silk underwear for men, and silk shirts, were the rage. We sold shirts at sixteen dollars. Our business was all cash. No credit." Shirts, the main stock in trade, were Eddie's specialty. Harry, who called it "the shirt store," would stand poised for business between two of the showcases, an elbow on one countertop, a hand on the other, his shoes shined, tie straight, the overhead lights glinting in his thick glasses. Like the store, he always looked fresh and clean.

As hoped, it became a rendezvous for their Army pals, a number of whom now looked to Harry as financial adviser, legal adviser, "and everything else," as Eddie said. "We'd all drop in there sometime during the day—it was the hangout," remembered Eddie McKim. Some evenings there was barely room for the real customers. "But Harry seemed glad to have us," said former Sergeant Meisburger. Even the policeman on the corner, Walter "Cushionfoot" Teasley, had been a first lieutenant with the battery at Camp Doniphan.

Harry returned the favor of their patronage as best he could. He bought his suits from Ted Marks, had his hair cut at Frank Spina's barbershop. They were just like his family, he would say. Bess objected to the haircuts. But Frank Spina was one of his boys, Harry would explain. "You can't quit them."

Others living elsewhere around the country wrote to wish Harry well.

"I see no reason," said one man, "why you, with your engaging personality and honest morals, should not be very successful in that business."

"Well, sir, don't forget me," wrote another, Eugene Donnelly, in a letter from a remote Texas oil field, "and when you see a keen young lady come out of the Muehlebach, just say to yourself gee I'd hate to be old Donnelly, living seven miles from a railroad, enjoying the company of two hundred men." Once, in France, after the Armistice, when Donnelly and several others from Battery D were due to go to Paris on furlough but had no money, Harry had found out about it and loaned them what they needed. "We'd have done anything for him then," Donnelly would say in an interview years afterward, "and nobody that I know has changed his mind."

Eddie's wife Bluma said later that her husband never worked as hard as he did that first year in the 12th Street store, nor Harry either, she supposed. There were no signed agreements between them, there was never a need for it. "They just felt that close to one another that they could trust each other, which they did all through their lives."

By the year's end they had sold $70,000 worth of goods, which meant a high return on their investment.

In his campaign for President in 1920, the handsome Republican candidate, Senator Warren G. Harding of Ohio—who had been picked in a famous "smoke-filled room" at the Blackstone Hotel in Chicago, just a year after Mr. and Mrs. Harry Truman stopped there—called for a return to "normalcy." The American people, Harding said, had had enough of heroism, and he and his running mate, former Massachusetts Governor Calvin Coolidge, defeated the Democratic ticket of James Cox and Franklin Roosevelt with a bigger majority than in any previous election. Normalcy seemed indeed to be what the country wanted, and in this respect Truman and Jacobson, restocking their shelves in Kansas City, waiting on customers, seemed in perfect step with the times. Harry joined the Kansas City Club, the Triangle Club (a businessmen's lunch group much like Rotary), and the Kansas City Athletic Club, where, with relentless determination, he taught himself to swim, using a strange, choppy, self-styled sidestroke, his head above water, so he could keep his glasses dry. With Ted Marks or Jim Pendergast, he ate regularly at the Savoy Grill, in the old Savoy Hotel on 9th Street, his favorite place for lunch. He dreamed also of a new car, to replace the second-hand, four-cylinder Dodge roadster he was driving to and from the city.

The one looming worry was that the farmers were hurting and the reasons were plain enough at the same Kansas City grain exchange where

John Truman had lost his money twenty years earlier. Prices were tumbling. Wheat that had sold for a record $2.15 a bushel in 1919 had dropped to $1.44 a bushel by the fall of 1920. Farm prices overall fell 40 percent and the farmers' plight began to spread. The Middle West was especially hard hit. By 1921 the silk shirt that had been such a symbol of the postwar boom became the shirt Truman & Jacobson could no longer sell. By mid-year their "flourishing business" had evaporated. With the country in a full-scale depression, Harry and Eddie Jacobson were in trouble. To keep their stock up to date, they were forced to borrow more money.

The same old friends kept dropping in, but no one was buying as before. Several now found the store a convenient place to borrow an extra five or ten dollars. It became a combination club and unemployment agency, and, because of Harry's generosity, small loan office. If they came in asking for "Captain Harry," Eddie Jacobson recalled, he knew it was for a touch. If they asked for "Captain Truman," he knew he had a sale.

It was Harry also who paid for the damages after a Battery D reunion on St. Patrick's Day, 1921, a dinner at the Kansas City Elks Club that turned into a brawl, with the "boys" hilariously "airlining" soup and dinner rolls at one another. There had been no shortage of whiskey for the evening, Prohibition notwithstanding, and things were finally so out of hand that the police had to be called. But then one of the police turned out to be a former Battery D sergeant, George Brice, who, to the delight of the other police, was unceremoniously relieved of his revolver and most of his clothes.

As the depression grew worse and the partners had less and less to do, Harry became increasingly restless. "He would get out and go to lunches and mix with people . . . and Eddie Jacobson would stay around and take care of business," said Ted Marks, who had not encouraged Harry to go into the retail line. Now they talked about anything and everything but Harry's troubles. "We all were having a hard time those days. . . . Rents were high and starting anew—it was pretty rough," Marks remembered.

Harry and Eddie had an ink blotter printed up as a flyer to hand out at the counter:

Dr. A. Gloom Chaser Says:
"It Takes 65 Muscles of the Face to Make a Frown
and 13 to Make a Smile—Why Work Overtime?"
Buy Your Men's Furnishings from Us at New Prices. YOU
Will Smile at the Great Reductions. WE will Smile at the
Increased Business. Then NONE of US Will be Overworked.

In the fall of 1921, when plans were announced for an American Legion convention in Kansas City, as part of ceremonies to dedicate the site for a colossal new war memorial, Harry at once volunteered his services. As chairman of the decorations committee, he raised money, ordered flags and bunting, and launched a campaign to have every downtown business, trade association, club, every household "show the flag" in what he promised would be the most patriotic gathering ever in the country and one certain to make Kansas City "the most talked about town in the world." He was brisk, enthusiastic, and effective. The big day was November 1. France sent Marshal Ferdinand Foch; Great Britain sent Admiral Earl David Beatty; Italy, General Armando Diaz; and Belgium, General Baron Jacques, a strapping figure with a pink face and huge cavalryman's mustache. General Pershing came to town—a thrill for Harry—and Eddie Rickenbacker and Vice President Coolidge, who, reportedly, looked and acted so effacingly vice-presidential that he had trouble gaining admittance to several gatherings. Eighty-five bands marched and sixty thousand men of the American Legion, including former Captain Harry Truman, who was chosen for the honor of presenting flags to the Allied commanders. Foch, whose presence on the reviewing stand electrified the crowds, said he had never seen such a display of feeling, such patient, "almost sacred," attention from so many people. More than a hundred thousand had turned out.

Later activities, however, were considerably different in spirit. "That," remembered Harry's friend and fellow legionnaire, Harry Vaughan, "was when we took the Hotel Baltimore to pieces." Somebody drove a Texas steer into the hotel lobby. A crap game in the street outside stopped traffic. Eddie McKim could not recall Harry taking part in any of the "high jinks . . . except he probably looked out of his haberdashery store door and would see some of the ladies' negligées floating down from the windows of the Muehlebach Hotel. They used to lodge in the trolley wires. . . ."

The goodwill and mutual respect between Harry and Eddie Jacobson, meantime, seemed not to suffer from the strain they were under, though it remained at heart a business friendship. Eddie's wife sensed a certain distance between the Trumans and the Jacobsons that she took to be a sign of anti-Semitism among Harry's in-laws. The Wallaces, she said, were considered aristocracy, and under the circumstances the Trumans could not afford to have Jews in their house. But then Harry seldom if ever brought any of his friends home to North Delaware Street. The privacy of Madge Wallace's world was one thing, the world without was another, and so it would remain.

. . .

Truman & Jacobson failed in 1922. After much discussion, the partners decided not to file for bankruptcy—and thereby wipe out their debts—but to try to pay off their creditors as best they could, little by little as time went on. The business was approximately $35,000 in the red. Eddie, who went on the road as a shirt salesman, did all he could to meet his part of the debt, but in three years, unable to keep up, was forced to declare himself bankrupt. Some time later, when the two friends met for lunch downtown, Harry, seeing Eddie's frayed suit, gave him some money and told him to buy some new clothes. Fifteen years after the store went under, Harry would still be paying off on the haberdashery, and as a consequence would be strapped for money for twenty years. But like his father, he never ever neglected appearances.

The store had been a dismal failure. Yet few thought it Harry's fault. He was the victim of circumstances, the times were against him. "It was a nice store, and he was just a victim of circumstances like all the rest of us," remembered former First Lieutenant Edgar Hinde, who was trying to sell Willys-Overland automobiles in Independence. "It was rough, I'll tell you, it was rough!" The price of wheat in 1922 was 88 cents a bushel.

An exception to this view was Harry's former Grandview neighbor and Lodge brother Gaylon Babcock, who remembered Harry's downfall coming as no surprise. To Babcock, whose father had put money in the store, it was just another case of "There goes Harry again."

Harry blamed the Republicans in Washington. The fault was neither in himself nor in his stars, but in the tight money policy of Secretary of the Treasury Andrew Mellon, he insisted. But it could also be said that the trouble began in 1920 when the Wilson administration suddenly cut government spending and raised taxes.

III

To his wife Bess, who regarded most of his Army friends as roughnecks, Harry once described Jimmy Pendergast as "a nice boy and as smart as the old man he's named for."

The old man in question, the original James Pendergast, was the legendary Alderman Jim, the first Pendergast in Kansas City politics and founding father of what became a famous, or infamous, depending on one's point of view, Kansas City dynasty. His was a familiar American story. The son of Irish Catholic immigrants who had settled and raised a numerous family in St. Joseph, upstream on the Missouri River, Alderman Jim had come to Kansas City in the centennial year of 1876, a young man with neither money nor connections and in desperate need of a job. He found work first in a slaughterhouse, then in an iron foundry, in the West Bottoms, a roaring industrial section that stretched across the muddy lowlands between the river's great bend and the bluffs of the city. Jim Pendergast was brawny and gregarious and with his sunny disposition made friends rapidly. He also saved his money and in 1881, after betting on a winning horse called Climax, he purchased a combination hotel and saloon which, in tribute to his lucky horse, he called the Climax. Other saloons were acquired as years passed, these, too, proving popular and profitable, especially with the added attraction of back-room gambling. In addition, Jim Pendergast moved into the wholesale liquor business.

His real love, however, was politics. He was of course a Democrat and a natural vote-getter. In time, with the hardworking, hard-drinking, steadily expanding populace of the West Bottoms, the First Ward, as his base of power, he built Kansas City's first political organization and made himself boss, a term he disliked. "I've got friends," he would say cheerfully. "And, by the way, that's all there is to this boss business—friends." In 1889, Jim brought three younger brothers, Michael, John, and Thomas, on from St. Joseph to help manage things. Three years later, in 1892, he ran for alderman from the First Ward. "There is no kinder hearted or more sympathetic man in Kansas City than Jim Pendergast," said one devoted Democrat introducing the candidate. It was a reputation not lightly earned.

> No deserving man, woman or child that appealed to Jim Pendergast went away empty-handed [remembered a contemporary], and this is saying a great deal, as he was continually giving aid and help to the poor and unfortunate. . . . There was never a winter in the last twenty years that he did not circulate among the poor of the West Bottoms, ascertaining their needs, and after his visit there were no empty larders. Grocers, butchers, bakers, and coal men had unlimited orders to see that there was no suffering among the poor of the West Bottoms, and to send the bills to Jim Pendergast.

He remained on the city council for eighteen years, never losing an election. He was "Big Jim," "King of the First," conspicuously, proudly Irish and Catholic, with a physical resemblance to the great Irish-American hero of the day, prizefighter John L. Sullivan, which did him no harm as a public personality. With his love of good food he had grown to well over 200 pounds. He had a thick, black handlebar mustache, wore small black bow ties and a heavy gold watch chain, and worked steadily for public improvements—parks, boulevards, buildings, all projects that meant work for his people. He fought for higher pay for firemen. He fought the anti-Catholic American Protective Association. He fought the reformers, kept the saloons open and purchased another on Main Street, a block from City Hall, which he made his headquarters. He had courage and a much-loved sense of humor. When a bill was put before the state legislature in Jefferson City that would have prohibited anyone who owned a saloon from holding elective office and reporters asked what he thought of it, Alderman Jim said probably the bill was intended as a way of improving the reputation of saloonkeepers.

With the city growing by leaps and bounds, he reached out more and more to constituencies other than the Irish—to blacks, Poles, Slavs, Croatian slaughterhouse workers, to every immigrant group, and particularly the largest, the Italians, whose stronghold lay beyond the First Ward in the teeming, crime-ridden North End. The peak of his power came after the turn of the century, at the time when the bankrupt Truman family had moved to Kansas City. By then he had picked his own mayor, James A. ("Fighting Jim") Reed, in addition to nearly every other key office at City Hall. Charges of vote fraud in the First Ward led to investigations that produced no evidence of wrongdoing. "I never needed a crooked vote," Jim enjoyed telling reporters. "All I want is a chance for my friends to get to the polls."

Following his death in 1911, a ten-foot bronze statue was erected in Mulkey Square, on the heights overlooking the West Bottoms, a commanding seated figure of Alderman Jim paid for by public subscription and inscribed "to the rugged character and splendid achievements of a man whose private and public life was the embodiment of truth and courage." Even the Kansas City *Star,* arch-opponent of machine politics, lamented his passing. His word had been his bond, said the paper. "His support of any man or measure never had a price in cash."

It was the Pendergast "organization," however, that stood as Big Jim's great legacy, and it was to his brother Tom, sixteen years his junior— young enough nearly to have been his son—that he passed the mantle of leadership. "Brother Tom will make a fine alderman, and he'll be good to the boys—just as I have been," an ailing Jim had reassured a gathering of patrons at his Main Street saloon. As bookkeeper for the saloons and precinct captain, young Tom had learned the business and politics from the ground up, rising to superintendent of streets, a job second only to mayor in the patronage it offered. At Jim's retirement, Tom was elected to Jim's old seat on the city council. But unlike Jim, Tom cared little for public office and retired from the council in 1915, not to run for anything ever again.

Tom—Thomas Joseph Pendergast, or T.J.—was no one to quarrel with. Though only 5 feet 9, he was a blond, ruddy-faced bull of a man, with a head so massive it looked oversized even on so large and powerful a body. His neck seemed part of his heavy shoulders, almost as though he had no neck, and it was well known that he could knock a man senseless with a single blow. Yet for all this, he had a kind of jauntiness, an appealing ease of manner. People spoke of the warmth, not menace, in his large, oddly protruding, pale blue eyes. It was the eyes, in combination with his "hugeness," according to a close observer named William Reddig, that made Tom look both formidable and engaging. To Reddig, a veteran reporter for the *Star,* Tom was one of the most arresting figures ever seen in Kansas City, and once seen, never forgotten.

Like his brother, Tom was a saloonkeeper who abhorred drunkenness and drank only an occasional glass of beer. He dutifully attended early mass every morning. He liked to say he had never spent a night away from his wife. Further, as Big Jim had long appreciated, Tom was acutely intelligent.

Though the Pendergast operations had never suffered from lack of money, and money, as often said, was nowhere more useful than in politics, Tom, the bookkeeper, perceived politics as a business opportunity to a degree Jim never had. He acquired more saloons. He expanded the wholesale liquor business. Brother Mike Pendergast, meantime, was made the liquor license inspector for all Jackson County, which gave him the power to say yes or no to the operations of more than six hundred saloons, this naturally depending in no small part on how willingly the proprietors did business with the Pendergasts.

Even more important, as time would tell, was the Ready-Mixed Concrete Company established by Tom, one of the first companies anywhere to mix concrete in a plant, then deliver it by truck to the construction site. With his love of public improvements, Jim had been known as a builder —all the Pendergasts were builders—but Tom, with the city growing as never before, saw no reason why others should profit from the work if the organization could. In addition to the Ready-Mixed Company, he eventually founded or had substantial interest in the W. A. Ross Construction Company, the Midwest Paving Company, the Midwest Precoat Company, the Kansas City Concrete Pipe Company, the Centropolis Crusher Company, a cigar company, an oil company, and something called the Public Service Pulverizing Company. To charges that he used his political power to control contracts and furnish material for public use, Tom would reply, "Yes. Why not? Aren't my products as good as any?" And, by and large, they were, often better.

Hundreds of people from all walks of life, every level of society, would later testify to the kindness, generosity, and fundamental decency of Tom Pendergast, not to say his impressiveness as a political leader. "He was a master! He had an analytical mind," said one loyal foot soldier in the organization, a street repair inspector. "He ran the organization for people. His first concern was *always* people. . . . He was a man of immense heart and imagination. . . . He was always courteous. He would always listen you out." To a young lawyer with no connection to the organization, a single face-to-face meeting with Tom was enough to convince him that "that fellow could probably talk anyone into anything."

"He did so much for poor people," it would be said again and again. "Oh, he was a wonderful man. To me he was a Robin Hood," said a woman for whom he had found a job in a hospital laundry, one of the thousands of jobs he had provided over the years. "No, I never had a sense of evil when I was with him," remembered a Catholic priest. "The man never exuded a sense of evil." Even the judge who later sent Pendergast to prison would concede afterward that had he known him, he, too, very likely would have been one of his friends.

Reticent by nature, Tom kept himself to himself, as would be said, and this supposedly was his "edge." But those associated with him in his long career, including Harry Truman, were to hear certain observations repeated many times:

The amateur failed in politics because politics was concerned with "things as they are." "Most people don't think for themselves. They lean on newspapers." "You can't make a man good by passing a law that he must be good. It's against human nature." Politics, as his brother Jim had so often professed, was primarily a business of friends. "We have the theory that if we do a man a favor he will do us one. That's human nature." Few people were ingrates. Ingratitude was a cardinal sin. "Let the river take its course."

To reporters, with whom he was invariably courteous, he would describe himself only as a realist and claim to know more about how the people felt than anyone in town, or any newspaper. "It's my business to know."

As his admirers also liked to point out, Tom Pendergast was not the kind to flaunt his power. He was never seen parading about the courthouse or City Hall. He preferred to run things quietly, keeping tabs on the precincts where the organization was in business 365 days a year.

"Politics is a business, an all-the-year-round competitive business. To the victor belong the spoils. I might as well be honest about it. It may be cynical but that's the fact. It's the same locally and nationally. Nobody gets a job on an appointment because he's a nice fellow. He must deserve it politically. It's the same as in any other business."

The pattern of the organization followed the pattern established by law for election purposes. There was a ward leader, a precinct captain for each precinct, and a block leader for every square block within the precinct. The precinct captain was the first person who called on newcomers to the neighborhood, who saw that their water was connected, gas and electricity turned on. Coal in winter, food, clothing, and medical attention were all provided by the organization to whoever was in need at no charge, and as those benefiting from such help would remember fondly, the system involved no paperwork, few delays, no stigma of the dole. "When a man's in need," T.J. would lecture, "we don't ask whether he's a Republican or Democrat. . . . We function as nearly as we can 100 percent by making people feel kindly toward us."

Politics was personal contact. When winter storms hit the city, trucks from the various Pendergast enterprises would arrive in the West Bottoms loaded with overcoats and other warm clothing to be handed out to the homeless, the drunken derelicts, to any and all who were suffering. At Christmas, Tom gave out three thousand free dinners. Many people would remember for the rest of their lives how at the height of the deadly influenza epidemic in 1918–19 and at great personal risk Tom Pendergast had made a personal survey, house to house, to see who needed help.

All that was expected in return was gratitude expressed at the polls on election day. And to most of his people this seemed little enough to ask and perfectly proper. Many, too, were happy to be "repeaters," those who voted "early and often" on election day. The woman who worked in the hospital laundry, as an example, started as a repeater at age eighteen, three years shy of the voting age, and enjoyed every moment. She and several others would dress up in different costumes for each new identity, as they were driven from polling place to polling place in a fine, big car. It was like play-acting, she remembered years later. She would vote at least four or five times before the day ended. "Oh, I knew it was illegal, but I certainly never thought it was wrong."

But for all his sway and subsequent notoriety as the machine overlord of Kansas City, Tom Pendergast was not without rivals. His power was as yet limited, even as late as the 1920s. In opposition was another Democratic faction led by another exceedingly adroit, popular Irish-Catholic politician named Joseph B. Shannon. In the parlance of Jackson County, Pendergast Democrats were the "Goats," whereas Shannon's people were the "Rabbits," and both sides proudly so. The names began, supposedly, because the poverty-stricken families aligned with Alderman Jim had kept goats on the bluffs above the West Bottoms, while the Shannon people occupied a territory overrun by rabbits. It was also said that once on a march to a political convention Alderman Jim had roared, "When we come over the hill like goats, they'll run like rabbits." In any event, Joe Shannon was nothing like a rabbit in temperament. He was smooth, well dressed, and handsome in much the way Warren G. Harding was handsome. He was also quite as fearless as any Pendergast and had both the pluck and personality to inspire a following. And since the Republicans rarely had support enough to carry a general election in the county, the real knockdown contests were always in the primaries, among Democrats, where the lines were sharply drawn. Every Democrat counted himself either a Goat or a Rabbit, whether in town or out in the country. John Truman in his time had been a Goat and it was his Goat friends at the Independence Courthouse who made him a road overseer. So in that sense John Truman had been a Pendergast man, as was Harry briefly when he replaced his father as overseer.

The difference in the two factions was mainly a matter of style. The Goats liked to win with strength, with big turnouts on election day. The Rabbits were known for their cleverness. But both sides could play rough —with money or by calling out the saloon bullies. Strong-arm tactics at the polls, ballot-stuffing, ballot-box theft, the buying of votes with whiskey or cash, bloody, headlong street brawls, all the odious stratagems that had made big-city machine politics notorious since the time of New York's Boss Tweed, had been brought to bear to determine which side within the party gained the upper hand. "Stealing elections had become a high art," wrote one man, "refined and streamlined by the constant factional battles...." And the prize at stake always was power—jobs, influence, money, "business," as Tom Pendergast would say. It was "the game" played by "the boys" with zest, and never over such issues of reform as inspired periodic Republican or independent citizens' crusades. That the Republicans so rarely ever triumphed was taken by Democrats, whether Rabbit or Goat, as proof that Republican bosses just weren't as smart as a Joe Shannon or a Tom Pendergast.

Years before, in the time of Alderman Jim, a landmark bargain had been struck, largely because Alderman Jim had at last concluded that the Rabbits were there to stay. He and Shannon reached what became known as the Fifty-Fifty Agreement, whereby the prize of patronage after every election was to be divided evenly, no matter which faction won, thereby guaranteeing that neither side could ever lose. But Goat and Rabbit loyalties remained strong all the same, the battles continued. Politics, after all, in the words of one Casimir Welch, a tough ward boss of "Rabbit persuasion," was "a game for fighters."

To every Goat Tom Pendergast was the Big Boss, while his brother Mike was the "enforcer of loyalty." Mike was hard and combative, yet a charmer when he wished, or at least an easier man to talk to than Tom. Mike, who ran the "Bloody Tenth" Ward, liked to get out and see people, in contrast to Tom, who preferred to stay in his cubbyhole office off the lobby of the somewhat disreputable Jefferson Hotel, another Pendergast enterprise. They were different in appearance as well. Mike stood six feet tall. He was broad-shouldered and slim, his hips so narrow that to keep his trousers in place he felt obliged to wear both belt and suspenders. Mike had a resolute, chiseled look, strong chin, and eyes of an even paler blue than Tom's. He was really quite a handsome man. His great flaw, as everyone knew, was his temper. He was a "tenacious fighting type of the old school," a hothead who hated double talk and compromise, which was why Alderman Jim had passed him over and put Tom at the head of the organization. There was never any halfway ground with Mike. As was said, you were either with him or against him. He detested all Rabbits and was credited with claiming their extinction as among his foremost ambitions. One Saturday he had walked alone into a saloon famous for being a Rabbit stronghold, and after inviting a half-dozen men to join him for a drink at the bar, for a toast to the spirit of Fifty-Fifty, he hurled his glass in their faces, only to be jumped and severely beaten. But it had all been worth it, Mike said afterward.

Because of his closeness to Tom, who called him "Michael," Mike's views were invariably taken as Tom's own, and this gave him a standing second to none except Tom. Also, besides the Tenth Ward, Mike had responsibility for what was called the country vote, the whole outlying eastern section of the county that included such towns as Grandview, Lee's Summit, and Independence. (For some reason, as Harry Truman would recall, Tom Pendergast had no interest in the country vote.) In addition, most importantly, Mike had produced the heir apparent. Tom had three children, but two were girls and his only son was still, in the early 1920s, a small child. Mike, however, had a daughter and six sons, the oldest of whom was being groomed to take over. He was Harry's friend Jim Pendergast, and it was pleasant-mannered, pleasant-looking Jim who one day brought his father around to the haberdashery on 12th Street to meet Harry Truman.

· · ·

The time of the meeting was probably the late fall or early winter of 1921, which was still several months before the final collapse of Truman & Jacobson but well past the point when Harry knew the business was doomed.

They wanted to know if Harry would like to run for eastern judge of Jackson County, a courthouse job in Independence, which under the Missouri system was not a judicial post but administrative, the equivalent of a county commissioner, and a prime spot politically, which Harry already understood. With three judges on the court—an eastern judge (for the outlying country), a western judge (for Kansas City), and a presiding judge—having one vote of the three was worth a great deal, if only for trading purposes. The judges had control of the county purse strings. They hired and controlled the road overseers, as well as road gangs, county clerks, and other employees numbering in the hundreds. They could also determine who was awarded county contracts, and for the county road system, such as it was, there seemed a never-ending need for maintenance and repairs.

According to Pendergast family tradition, the idea of running Harry was Jim's alone, and, interestingly, his father gave his consent even before meeting Harry because, in part, of what he knew of John Truman. If Captain Truman was all Jim said, and he was John Truman's son, then, providing he had no link to the Ku Klux Klan or any such anti-Catholic faction, Captain Truman was all right with Mike.

Harry accepted their offer at once, with no hesitation. To a friend he wrote, "They are trying to run me for Eastern Judge, out in Independence, and I guess they'll do it before they are through." This was in a letter dated February 4, 1922, suggesting the anonymous "they" already had things so well in hand there could be no turning back. At a meeting at Mike's Tenth Ward Democratic Club, Harry sat quietly as Mike, who disliked making speeches, got up and said, "Now, I'm going to tell you who you are going to be for, for county judge. It's Harry Truman. He's got a fine war record. He comes from a fine family. He'll make a fine judge."

Had he wished, Mike could also have stressed that Harry Truman was a Baptist and a Mason who could talk farming with farmers as no big-city Irish politician ever could, that Harry was of old pioneer stock, the son of an honest farmer and an honest road overseer, that Harry was a fresh face in county politics, and, not incidentally, known himself to be an honest and honorable man—strong attributes under any circumstances, but ideal for what the organization needed to win the country vote. Indeed, for the Pendergasts' purposes, Harry Truman was just about ideal, a dream candidate, which is what led some to observe then, as later, that he offered more to the Pendergasts than they to him.

"Old Tom Pendergast wanted to have some window-dressing," Harry's friend Harry Vaughan would later explain, "and Truman was really window-dressing for him because he could say, 'Well, there's my boy Truman. Nobody can ever say anything about Truman. Everybody thinks he's okay.' "

For Harry, the timing could not have been better. He badly needed rescuing. To some latter-day admirers and students of his career, the suggestion that he turned to politics in desperation, because of his business failure, would be unacceptable, a fiction devised to cast him in the worst possible light. It would be stressed that his interest in politics was longstanding, that the Pendergasts had come to him, not he to them, and that in any event their power then was by no means absolute, hardly enough to dictate a political destiny. And all this was true. Yet to Harry himself there was never much question about the actual state of his affairs or to whom he owed the greatest debt of gratitude.

"Went into business all enthusiastic. Lost all I had and all I could borrow," he would write in a private memoir. "Mike Pendergast picked me up and put me into politics and I've been lucky." Mike was nothing less than his "political mentor," continued Harry. "I loved him as I did my own daddy."

He remembered he had been standing behind the counter "feeling fairly blue" the day Mike and Jim came into the store. What he wished to make especially clear was not that the Pendergasts had played no part of consequence, or that he had little indebtedness to them, but that it was Mike, not Tom, the Big Boss, whose interest made the difference. Harry was not even to meet Tom Pendergast for some time to come.

The job of eastern judge paid $3,465 a year. If elected, Harry would serve two years.

His Army friends were nearly unanimous for the idea. Only a few tried to dissuade him. Eddie McKim, his former sergeant, told him he was crazy. When Harry sat down with Edgar Hinde, in Hinde's Willys-Overland garage in Independence, to explain what he was about to do—grinning, as Hinde recalled—Hinde told him he wasn't the political type, to which Harry responded, "Well, I've got to eat."

To sample opinion among those of the older generation who had influence in Independence, Harry called on Colonel William Southern, editor of the *Examiner*. Colonel Southern, whose rank was strictly honorary, was the father of May Southern Wallace, Bess's brother George's wife, which, in a manner of speaking, made him one of the family, as well as someone whose goodwill and backing could matter significantly. A short, pink-faced, cigar-chewing man with a goatee, who customarily wore his hat at his desk, the colonel listened patiently to Harry, then told him what a fool he would be to "mess up" his life with politics. "I told him all the bad effect a life of chronic campaigning could have on a man," he would later recount. "I told him how poor were its rewards . . . how undermining the constant need for popular approval could be to a man's character." Harry, smiling, only shook his head and said he had made up his mind.

What opinions Bess had, what her mother was saying privately, or Mamma Truman thought, are not recorded. Ethel Noland, it is known, strongly approved and would later explain Harry's willingness to take up with the Pendergasts as succinctly as anyone would: "They always like to pick winners, and they endorsed him. And, indeed, if he hadn't been endorsed by the machine he couldn't have run. He was very grateful to them. . . ."

IV

Candidate Truman opened his campaign two months short of his thirty-eighth birthday, March 8, 1922, at a rousing, foot-stamping rally of war veterans in an auditorium at Lee's Summit. About three hundred people turned out for speeches, free cigars, and music, and to see Harry Truman launched, ostensibly, as the American Legion candidate, an idea acclaimed as admirably new and progressive. ("If they [the veterans] want to mix in politics it is their right and when they take such matters into their hands they will settle affairs of state as they settled the Kaiser's in France," said the Lee's Summit *Journal.*) The Battery D "Irish bunch" were there in force, along with a "sprinkling" of Pendergast people. Harry, when introduced by former Colonel E. M. Stayton, another veteran of the Argonne, said he was willing to run and was only just able to say that, so "thoroughly rattled" was he by stage fright. "That first meeting was a flop for me," he would recall long years afterward. "I was scared worse than I was when I first came under fire in 1918." But his speech was all the crowd wanted. The highlight of the evening came when Ethel Lee Buxton of Kansas City, who had been a Red Cross entertainer in France, sang "When Irish Eyes Are Smiling," then closed with "Mother Machree."

Another evening Harry spoke at Grandview, another from a rough wooden platform in front of the Hickman's Mills church, and on neither occasion was he able to say much more than that he was in the race and welcomed the support of his friends. At Hickman's Mills the introduction was made by his old neighbor O. V. Slaughter, who had headed the Jackson County Red Cross during the war and was now president of the Grandview Bank, the kind of man who knew senators and governors, yet remained "strictly and primarily" a farmer. Gray-bearded, he looked like an old-style patriarch, and though seldom known to speak in public, he was considered highly persuasive when he did. One line only would be remembered from his remarks. "I knew Harry Truman before he was born," he said, and to others who had known John and Matt Truman, or who, like Slaughter, remembered Solomon and Harriet Louisa Young, no stronger endorsement could have been spoken. Reportedly there were only three votes in the precinct against Harry.

Four other Democrats were in the race—a farmer and road overseer named Thomas Parent; an Independence businessman, James V. Compton; another Independence man, George W. Shaw, who was a road contractor; and Emmett Montgomery, a banker from Blue Springs—and all were thought formidable opponents. Parent had the support of a former judge, a flashy politician named Miles Bulger, who was neither Rabbit nor Goat but a spoiler. Compton had served previously on the court and could stress the value of experience. Shaw was known to be honest, which, as Harry said, was considered unique in a contractor. But the man to beat was Emmett Montgomery, the Rabbit candidate.

Harry Truman stood for better roads and a return to sound management of county business. The most that could be said for his early speeches was that they were brief. One, at a night rally at Sugar Creek, an oil refinery town in the lowlands by the river just north of Independence, was remembered by Edgar Hinde as "the poorest effort of a speech I ever heard in my life. I suffered for him." But as the weeks wore on, and with the oncoming summer and the increased demands of a "hot race," the speeches improved somewhat. "If you're going to be in politics," Harry later reflected, "you have to learn to explain to people what you stand for, and to learn to stand up in front of a crowd and talk was just something I had to do, so I went ahead and did it."

Edgar Hinde, Eddie McKim, Tom Murphy, and Ted Marks worked steadily, knocking on doors, handing out leaflets, showing up wherever and whenever needed. "We'd do whatever was necessary to help Harry," remembered Tom Murphy, who had been a sergeant in Battery D. As the campaign went on, Murphy, McKim, and the others put out a flyer proclaiming Harry Truman "the best liked and the most beloved Captain, officer in France or elsewhere."

Frank and George Wallace lent a hand. Harry's former Latin teacher, Ardelia Hardin Palmer, organized a door-to-door canvass in Independence to bring out the women's vote, a new element in the political picture.

Harry spoke at White Oak, Raytown, Lone Jack, Englewood, and Blue Springs. He covered every township and precinct, driving himself in the old four-cylinder Dodge over roads so rough he had to put sacks of cement in the trunk for ballast, to keep the car from slamming him through the windshield.

The main event of the political summer took place in July, a picnic at Oak Grove attended by four thousand people, twice the number expected. Every Democratic candidate was scheduled to speak. As a way of giving Harry added attention, Eddie McKim arranged for him to arrive by airplane. Harry and the pilot, another war veteran named Clarence England, sailed over the crowd in the open cockpits of a two-seat Jenny of the kind flown in France. After circling several times, dropping leaflets, they landed in a pasture beside the picnic ground, stopping with difficulty just short of a barbed-wire fence. As the crowd rushed forward, the candidate climbed out, leaned over the fence, and became violently ill. Apparently it had been his first ride in a plane. He then proceeded to the rostrum.

It was by far the largest crowd he had ever faced and an opportunity, he knew, such as he had not been given before. He was the last to speak. "I am now going to tell you what I stand for and why you should vote for me," he began in a flat, rapid voice. "The time has arrived for some definite policy to be pursued in regard to our highways and our finances. They are so closely connected with our tax problem that if they are properly cared for the tax problem will care for itself. . . ."

Eddie McKim, remembering earlier appearances in the campaign, thought Harry had come a long way. A style was evolving. Having stated the problem, he proceeded to a solution joined to a fundamental philosophy plainly expressed.

"I want men for road overseers who know roads and who want work —men who will do a day's work for a day's pay, who will work for the county as they would for themselves. I would rather have 40 road men for overseers who are willing to work than to have 60 politicians who care nothing about work. I believe that honest work for the county is the best politics anyway."

Running the county into debt was bad business and bad politics, he said. He wanted it stopped.

Thus far in the campaign only one charge had been brought against him—that in an election in 1920 he had voted for a Republican, Major

John Miles, who had been his superior officer at the Argonne. It was the worst his opponents had been able to come up with, and given the spirit of Jackson County politics, it was a serious charge. He chose the moment now to explain himself.

"You have heard it said that I voted for John Miles as County Marshal. I'll plead guilty . . . along with 5,000 other ex-soldiers. I was closer to John Miles than a brother. I have seen him in places that would make hell look like a playground." His tone was flat no longer.

> I have seen him stick to his guns when Frenchmen were falling back. I have seen him hold the American line when only John Miles and his three batteries were between the Germans and a successful counterat- tack. He was of the right stuff and a man who didn't vote for his comrade under circumstances such as these would be untrue to him- self and to his country. My record has been searched and this is all my opponents can say about me and you knowing the facts can appreciate my position. I know that every soldier understands it. I have no apology to make for it. John Miles and my comrades in arms are closer than brothers to me. There is no way to describe the feeling. But my friend John is the only Republican I ever voted for and I don't think that counts against me.

At that moment, for many who were listening, the primary election for eastern judge was over, and Harry Truman had won.

No county election in years had aroused such interest, a phenomenon attributed by some to the novelty of the women's vote. Harry, however, was dwelling more and more on what the influence might be of the Ku Klux Klan, the growing strength of which was another sign of the times. Crosses had been burned near Lee's Summit. Klan membership was growing in Independence and two of his opponents, Parent and Shaw, had Klan support. Edgar Hinde urged Harry to sign up with the Klan, to join immediately, convinced it was "good politics." Hinde himself had already joined, "to see what was going on, you know," as he later ex- plained. A Klan organizer named "Jones" told him to bring Harry in any time, saying it was all Harry had to do to guarantee Klan backing.

Harry refused at first, but then gave Hinde $10 for membership. "Jones" insisted on meeting Harry privately at the Baltimore Hotel and Harry agreed. But when at the meeting "Jones" told him he would get no support unless he promised never to hire Catholics if elected, Harry ended the discussion. He had commanded a mostly Catholic battery in France, he said, and he would give jobs to whomever he saw fit. Appar- ently the $10 was returned.

It had been a grievous mistake ever to have said he would join in the first place. It was an act either of amazing naivete, or one revealing a side he had not shown before, a willingness under pressure to sacrifice principle for ambition. Either way the whole incident was shabby and out of character, and hardly good politics. How he thought Klan support might offset the devastating effect such an alliance would have on the Pendergasts—not to say the effect on his own beloved "Irish bunch"—is difficult to imagine.

In his defense later, it would be said that the Klan in 1922 seemed still a fairly harmless organization to which a good God-fearing patriot might naturally be attracted, that it offered a way for those who felt at odds with the changes sweeping the country to make known their views. Yet only the year before Harry had lent his support to a Masonic effort to suppress the Klan in St. Louis. He had to have known what the Klan was about. William Reddig of the *Star* would remember Jackson County Klansmen of the time as anything but good fellows. "They didn't just hate Catholics, Jews, and Negroes," Reddig wrote. "They hated everybody."

A rumor was now circulated by the Klan that Harry's grandfather, Solomon Young, was a Jew. At a Klan meeting in Independence just before the primary on August 1, a guest speaker from Atlanta said Harry Truman was less than 100 percent American—that is, not sufficiently opposed to Catholics and Jews. Edgar Hinde stood up and protested. There were shouts to throw him out. A friend of Harry's from Grandview named Toliver rose to say they could throw him out, too, which, as Hinde remembered, had a "cooling influence." But the Klan's previous indifference to the Truman candidacy had ended.

He said later it was the soldier vote plus "kinfolks in nearly every precinct" that put him over. He would talk of being "accidentally" elected and suggest that his failure with the haberdashery also had an important influence. "Most people were broke and they sympathized with a man in politics who admitted his financial condition." Others close to the campaign said the deciding factor was Harry Truman. People liked him—and largely because he so obviously liked them and being among them.

Privately, Harry was disappointed in the efforts of the Pendergast people in his behalf. He had expected more.

The campaign ended with a big Saturday night rally at the courthouse. On election day cars covered with placards were busy back and forth across town bringing people to the polls. "The smell of old 'alky, hooch, and 'good' whiskey is on the breath of many a man," wrote Colonel Southern, a teetotaler.

As the day wore on, the rough play began. At a polling place at Fairmont Junction, close to the Kansas City line, an armed gang of Shannon henchmen tried to make off with the ballot box before the Pendergast people could get to it, only to be confronted by two deputy marshals who had rushed to the scene on orders from Harry's Republican friend, Marshal John Miles. Guns were drawn, when suddenly Shannon himself materialized out of the shadows and with the barrel of Deputy John W. Gibson's 45-caliber automatic pressing on his ample stomach, announced it would be best if everybody quieted down and went home. Had Shannon's men succeeded in their mission, Harry would most likely have lost the election. As it was he defeated the Rabbit candidate, Emmett Montgomery, by a bare 279 votes out of a total (for all five in the race) of more than 11,000.

It was "the damn Republicans" who were to blame, Joe Shannon complained bitterly. If they had only kept out of things, Harry Truman would never have won. Probably that was so. Deputy Gibson, the man with the .45, was, like John Miles, a veteran of the 129th Field Artillery.

V

The fall election was a formality only—every Democrat won—and on New Year's Day, 1923, in a ceremony at the courthouse, the new county court was seated. The other two judges were Elihu Hayes and Henry McElroy. Hayes was the presiding judge, and though a Rabbit, "a fine old gentleman" in Harry's estimate. McElroy, the new western judge, was a through-and-through Goat and close associate of Tom Pendergast, a spare, bucktoothed, ambitious businessman commonly praised for his efficiency. The huge basket of red roses in the courtroom was the gift of McElroy admirers from Little Italy.

To be called "Judge" pleased Harry immensely. He enjoyed the prestige of the job and the way people greeted him as he walked briskly to and from the courthouse. He had rank again.

As presiding judge, Elihu Hayes should have been the dominant figure and leader of the court, and by the Fifty-Fifty Agreement his Rabbit friends looked forward to an equal share in county jobs and every other form of largess under the court's control. Things did not work out that way, however. It was Henry McElroy who took charge from the start and McElroy showed no desire to give anything to the Rabbits. With Judge Truman voting with him, there was not much to keep McElroy from having his way. ("He ran the court with my vote," Harry later said.) The roster of road overseers was filled with Goats only. Goats were named to county jobs large and small. Rabbits already on the payroll were always the first to be fired.

The old adage of Andrew Jackson, that to the victors belong the spoils, was gospel again in Jackson County, Missouri. The decision had come down from the Pendergasts. Fifty-Fifty was finished. And though in hindsight Harry would see the peril in this, at the time he did not. He was preoccupied with being businesslike, concentrating on cost cuts, improvements in services, determined to perform as promised.

He also knew what pleasure the plight of the Rabbits was bringing to his mentor, Mike Pendergast.

"We ran the county, but we ran it carefully and on an economic basis," Harry claimed later, and in truth the new court stood in striking contrast with what had gone on before under the renegade Miles Bulger. Under McElroy and Truman a county debt of more than a million dollars was cut in half. The county's credit rating improved. So did county services and, most notably, the quality of work on the roads. Harry Truman, as he later boasted, made himself "completely familiar with every road and bridge . . . visited every state institution in which the county had patients." Years of mismanagement and crooked contracts had produced roads so poorly constructed that they caved in like pie crusts. Bridges were inadequate or in sad repair. The improvements made now were impossible to ignore. Even the Kansas City *Star* had praise for what was happening under the crisp, efficient new county administration. And if Harry was taking McElroy's cue on matters political, McElroy appeared no less dependent on Harry on practical questions. "When a road project or a bridge application is brought before the county court, here is what happens," wrote one Republican. "Judge McElroy turns to Judge Truman and asks him what about it. Nine times out of ten Judge Truman already has been on the ground and knows all about the proposition. He explains it to the court. Judge McElroy then says, 'All right, if you say so I move the work be done,' and it is ordered."

At a Triangle Club lunch at the Muehlebach Hotel, Judges Hayes, McElroy, and Truman were given a standing ovation. It seemed a new era had dawned.

But the job, Harry discovered, wasn't enough to satisfy. To his surprise, he felt restless for more to do. He wanted other ways to make himself known, other associations beyond "the courthouse crowd." He grew increasingly active in the Masons and the Army reserve. He became Deputy Grand Master of the 59th Masonic District of Jackson County. The summer of 1923 he spent two weeks on active duty at Fort Leavenworth, Kansas, his first long separation from Bess since their wedding day. In September he enrolled in night courses at the Kansas City School of Law, where he studied hard (Blackstone, contracts, criminal law), keeping pages of notes. Only someone of extraordinary energy could have maintained the pace.

Meantime, life at home at 219 North Delaware—the Gates house, as Harry would always refer to it—went on quietly and privately. Bess had taken no part in his political campaign because, as known only within the family, she had suffered a second miscarriage. The first had occurred the spring of 1920, when prospects were still bright at the store, and nothing had been said then either. With friends Harry left no doubt that he and Bess wanted children but implied that if there was a problem it was with him. When a cousin, Ralph Truman, wrote from Springfield to say he had a new child, Harry responded, "I wish you would send me a pair of your old breeches to hang on the bed, maybe I can have some luck."

His devotion to Bess was unstinting as ever and because of their separation the summer of 1923, when he was at Fort Leavenworth and they were again corresponding, it is known how much she, too, cared for her "Old Sweetness."

"It is now 10:20 and I am in bed. There was a black bug on my bed when I turned the sheet down and I had to kill it myself —but that wasn't the first time I had wished for you," she wrote. "Lots and lots of good night kisses."

She would wait for hours by the front window watching for the postman. A night toward the end of the two weeks was "the worst night yet."

"You be a good girl and I'll be a good boy," he wrote. A week later he was saying he hoped he would never have to be away so long again. He was feeling "marvelous," he told her, ready to come home and "lick all the Rabbits."

As they both knew, she was already two months pregnant.

The arrival of the baby, in the midst of a snowstorm, Sunday, February 17, 1924, was, with the exception of his wedding day, the biggest event of Harry Truman's life thus far, and the one bright moment in what otherwise was to be a bad year for him.

He had urged Bess to go to a hospital. She and her mother insisted the baby be born at home. Out of superstition that too much advance fuss could again bring disappointment, there was not even a crib or cradle at hand. The baby would spend the first days of life on pillows in a bureau drawer.

About noon, Harry was told to call the doctor, Charles E. Krimminger, a big red-faced man remembered for his huge hands—"hands as big as a frying pan"—who came in covered with snow and went directly upstairs. A practical nurse, Edna Kinnaman, arrived soon after and would remember Mrs. Wallace and Harry waiting patiently through the afternoon in the upstairs hall, the very proper Mrs. Wallace seated on a cedar chest, Harry in a chair looking amazingly composed.

Bess, according to Nurse Kinnaman, "got along beautifully." It was a normal birth. The baby, a girl, weighed 7½ pounds. "We didn't have to announce it [when the baby arrived] . . . because they heard her cry and the grandmother and daddy came into the room." It was five o'clock. Harry called his mother and sister and told them the name would be Mary Margaret, after Mary Jane and Mrs. Wallace. The wife of a friend who saw him soon afterward said "his face just beamed."

There had not been a baby in the old house since Madge Wallace's own childhood. Now, for several months, until the death of Mrs. Gates that spring, there were four generations in residence. Little Margaret, as everybody was calling her, was more than just Bess and Harry's firstborn, she was the delight and center of attention for great-grandmother, grandmother, four Wallace aunts and uncles in the adjoining houses to the rear who remained childless, Uncle Fred, who was still part of the household, and the two Noland sisters across the street. Her arrival changed the entire atmosphere of the family. For Harry, on the verge of forty, life had new meaning. Nurse Kinnaman remembered his devotion to the child was both remarkable and instantaneous.

For Democrats everywhere it was a dismal time. At the national convention in New York's Madison Square Garden the delegates took a record 103 ballots to pick an unknown, unlikely Wall Street lawyer as their candidate for President, John W. Davis, who seemed destined to lose. A drive to nominate the colorful Catholic governor of New York, Al Smith, had failed, along with a resolution to denounce the Ku Klux Klan. When William Jennings Bryan tried to speak, he was rudely shouted down. To the Jackson County delegation it was a pathetic show. The single ray of hope was Franklin Roosevelt, who, though crippled with polio, made the nominating speech for Smith. Tom Pendergast was "carried away" by it and said Roosevelt would have been the choice of the convention had he been physically able to withstand the campaign. "He has the most magnetic personality of any individual I have ever met," Pendergast later declared.

The Republicans, to the surprise of no one, nominated Calvin Coolidge, who had assumed the presidency the year before, after the sudden death of Warren G. Harding. And though the Harding administration had left a trail of scandal, giving the Democrats a promising campaign issue, Coolidge, who sat out the campaign in the White House, was to win in November by a popular margin of nearly two to one.

If Judge Truman saw actual defeat in store when he began to campaign for reelection that spring, he never let on. As friends were to observe so many times in his life, Harry refused ever to look discouraged. The remedy of "Dr. A. Gloom Chaser" was not forgotten. "He kept his feelings to himself," remembered a young Pendergast worker named Tom Evans, "and he was always very, very cheerful. . . ."

The Shannon forces, bitter over how they had been treated, burning for revenge, lined up with the Ku Klux Klan to try to beat both McElroy and Truman in the primary—the fact that Joe Shannon was a Catholic, the fact that Shannon personally spoke out against the Klan at the national convention, all notwithstanding. When McElroy and Truman won in the primary, Shannon quietly decided to bolt the ticket in the fall and throw his support, with that of the Klan, to the Republicans.

That Harry Truman survived the primary, winning by more than 1,000 votes, was impressive under the circumstances, and due in good measure to all-out support from the Kansas City *Star.* Putting aside its distaste for Pendergast for the moment, the paper had declared candidates McElroy and Truman superior public servants. It seemed inconceivable, said the *Star,* that the Democrats could care more about "factional advantage" than efficiency in public office. "The record of the county court of Jackson County is refreshing. . . . Expenditures of the court last year were more than $640,000 less than those of the previous year. To date the deficit has been reduced nearly one half, and there is now a cash balance of more than a quarter of a million dollars." Harry Truman, said the Independence *Sentinel,* was the very model of a public man. "To even talk about throwing him out of office after two years of faithful service would be to destroy the incentive for a public official to make good," declared the paper, and the *Star* agreed, saying everyone who believed in good government should vote for Judge Harry Truman.

In the same issue of the *Star* the local head Klansman, Todd George, announced that his organization was "unalterably opposed" to Harry Truman. Later, Harry said the Klan had threatened to kill him. When the Klan staged a big outdoor, daylight rally at Lee's Summit, Harry decided to drive out and confront them. Perhaps a thousand people were gathered, many of whom he knew. "I poured it into them," he remembered. "Then I came down from the platform and walked through them to my car." On the way home, he met another car headed for the rally filled with "my gang" armed with shotguns and baseball bats. Had they come earlier, he knew, things might have become very unpleasant.

The Republican nominee for eastern judge was Henry Rummel, the Independence harnessmaker who, years before, had made the special equipage for the team of red goats to pull the Truman children in a miniature farm wagon. Harry, who liked "old man" Rummel and respected him, said nothing against him in the campaign.

Rummel won. Harry was out of a job again, and McElroy also. Harry showed no sign of bitterness. The morning after the election, on a corner near the square, seeing a friend, Henry Chiles, who had worked hard with the Rabbits for Rummel, he crossed the street to shake hands and say there should be no hard feelings. When Chiles expressed regret over the part he had played in defeating Harry, saying he felt ashamed of himself, Harry told him to put it out of his mind. "You did what your gang told you and I did what my gang told me." That was the way it was in politics.

Cousin Ralph Truman, in a letter of encouragement, said that were Harry to run again in two years he would win by a landslide, a conclusion Harry had already reached on his own.

In the intervening time, he became something of a man of affairs in Kansas City. From an office in the Board of Trade Building, he began selling memberships in the Kansas City Automobile Club, working on commission, which, after expenses, came to approximately five dollars for every new member he recruited. In a year he had sold more than a thousand memberships and cleared $5,000, which, with a family to support and debts to pay, he greatly needed. Roads, highways, the new age of the automobile had become his specialty. He was named president of the National Old Trails Association, a nonprofit group dedicated to building highways along the country's historic trails and to spreading the concept of history as a tourist attraction. (Writing from Kansas during one of many trips in behalf of the group, he told Bess, "This is almost like campaigning for President, except that the people are making promises to me instead of the other way around.") He kept up contacts with old friends, stayed active in the Masons and the Army reserve. Only his interest in law school seemed to suffer. After nearly two years of work there, he dropped out.

In times past, during the early days of the Morgan Oil Company, he had been described as constantly surrounded by people—"people, people, people." It was the same again now. Ted Marks would remember him everlastingly on the move. "If one thing did not work—he'd get into something else right away. He was never idle, always operating."

One thing he got into was another of his mistakes. With Colonel Stayton, Spencer Salisbury, and several others he took over a tottering little bank called the Citizens Security, in Englewood, adjacent to Independence. He and his partners soon discovered they had been lied to about its assets. Reporting the situation at once, they got out as quickly as possible, selling their interest to new management. No one made money in the transaction. There is no evidence of wrongdoing. But the bank failed soon afterward and its new president, B. M. Houchens, a brother of Harry's high school classmate Fielding Houchens, killed himself in his garage. To many people the whole episode seemed shadowy and left bad memories.

A further venture involved selling stock in the new Community Savings and Loan Association of Independence, and in this, too, Spencer Salisbury was in league—a sign, many were to say later, that Harry was not always the best judge of character when it came to his friends. Another of the Argonne brotherhood, Salisbury belonged to an old, well-to-do Independence family and was a lifelong operator, lively, talkative, and "smart," by reputation, though "a little slick." Tall and spare, he was known to those who knew him best as "Snake-eye" Salisbury. Even his own sister would remember him as "kind of a cold bird." Asked long afterward why Harry ever associated himself with the man, Edgar Hinde replied, "Anybody who's ever been a friend of his . . . they've got to hit him right in the face before he'll drop them. And I think that's one of Harry's big faults."

Salisbury was cheating him in the business, Harry concluded after a while, and so withdrew, saying nothing publicly. Only in private did he vent his anger, writing some years later that Salisbury "used me for his own ends, robbed me, got me into a position where I couldn't shoot him without hurting a lot of innocent bystanders, and laughed at me. It nearly makes me a pessimist." He had never had an enemy before.

Seeing Harry Truman go on to bigger and better things in later years, Salisbury would refer to him as "a no-good bastard." But Truman by then had used his influence in Washington to put federal investigators on to Salisbury's subsequent business activities in Independence, with the result that Salisbury spent fifteen months in Leavenworth prison. In turn, a few years after that, it was Salisbury, an avowed member of the Klan, who told reporters that Harry Truman had definitely joined the Klan, which was a lie and potent enough to carry far.

Between times, in the years 1925 and '26, Harry kept in close touch with Jim and Mike Pendergast. On pleasant evenings he would drive into town to sit and talk for hours on Mike's big front porch on Park Avenue. Mike thought Harry should run next time for county collector, an appealing prospect since the job offered an inordinately high salary of $10,000 plus allotted fees that could mean that much again. But then Mike took Harry to meet Tom, who said he had already promised the job to someone who had been with the organization longer than Harry. Tom thought that Harry, with his experience on the court, would be better suited for presiding judge, which had a salary of $6,000. Mike advised Harry to fight for the collector's job, if that was what he wanted, but Harry thought it better to do as Tom wished.

For Harry, this apparently was the first face-to-face encounter with the Big Boss. It took place early in 1926, in Tom's office at 1908 Main Street, the new headquarters for the Jackson Democratic Club, a nondescript two-story building of pale yellow brick that Tom had had put up beside the small Monroe Hotel, which he also owned. The neighborhood was one of drab little stores, cheap restaurants, and machine shops, anything but a center of power by appearances. The big banks, office towers, and department stores, all that visitors took as emblematic of Kansas City wealth and vitality, were six or seven blocks to the north. The club's meeting room and Tom's office were on the second floor, over a wholesale linen supply store. The aura of the narrow stairway, a flight of twenty wooden steps, was about that of the approach to a dance studio or tailor shop.

So it was settled. Harry would run for presiding judge, and since the Pendergasts and Joe Shannon had by now patched up their differences, there was never much doubt about the outcome. Harry ran in the primary unopposed. In November, he and the entire Democratic slate swept into office. Henry McElroy became the new city manager of Kansas City. As presiding judge, Harry Truman himself had real authority at last.

VI

The term of office was four years, rather than two, and he served two consecutive terms, eight years, from January 1927 to January 1935. His performance was outstanding, as judged by nearly everyone—civic leaders, business people (Republicans included), fellow politicians, the press, students of government (then and later) and, emphatically, by the electorate. In the 1926 election he won by 16,000 votes. When he ran again for presiding judge in 1930, his margin of victory was 58,000.

Something unusual had happened, said the Independence *Examiner* halfway through his first term: "No criticism or scandals of any importance have been brought with the county court as a center and no political charges of graft and corruption have been made against it." The *Star* praised him for his "enthusiastic devotion to county affairs." Harry Truman was efficient, known to be always informed. "Here was a man you could talk to that knew what was going on, and knew what ought to be done about it," said a representative of the Kansas City Civic Research Institute. At a conference on better state and local government sponsored by the University of Missouri at Columbia, an editor of the St. Louis *Star-Times* noted that Judge Truman was the only Missouri official present who could discuss administrative problems on an equal basis with visiting experts.

> Every subject of debate tended sooner or later to center in the views of a quiet-spoken man who sat across the table from me [wrote the editor]. It was with surprise amounting almost to incredulity that I observed this trend of affairs, for the quiet man whose opinions had so much respect in a gathering of reformers was the presiding judge of . . . Jackson County . . . home bailiwick of the notorious Pendergast machine.

More important and equally unexpected was the way in which he proved himself a leader. His first day in office he spoke to the point:

> We intend to operate the county government for the benefit of the taxpayers. While we were elected as Democrats, we were also elected as public servants. We will appoint all Democrats to jobs appointable, but we are going to see that every man does a full day's work for his pay. In other words we are going to conduct the county's affairs as efficiently and economically as possible.

The other new members of the court, Howard Vrooman and Robert Barr, were expected to follow his lead. Vrooman, the western judge, was an affable Kansas City real estate executive and a Rabbit. Barr, a gentleman farmer and graduate of West Point, had been Harry's own choice to fill his former position as eastern judge. For all intents and purposes, therefore, Presiding Judge Truman was the chief executive officer. Later in his political career it would be charged that he had had no executive experience. But in fact he was responsible now for an annual operating budget of $7 million, more than the budget of some states, and for seven hundred employees—county treasurer, sheriff, county councilor, road overseers, surveyors, highway engineer, health officials, parole officers, purchasing agents, a coroner, a collector (the job he had wanted), a recorder of deeds, superintendent of schools, liquor license inspector, election commissioners, and nine justices of the peace. He had overall responsibility for the county home for the aged, the county hospital, the McCune Home for (white) Boys, the Parental Home for (white) Girls, the Home for Negro Boys and Girls, and more than a thousand miles of county roads. He also had charge of two courthouses (with jails), since Kansas City, too, had a courthouse. He had the most say in apportioning the budget, and keeping the books was ultimately his responsibility. It was, theoretically, within his power now to award contracts, adjust tax rates, float bond issues, or determine what sums for the county would be borrowed from which banks and when. As the county's topmost official he was also expected to be its chief spokesman, to appear at business lunches, take part in conferences, spread the word of Jackson County progress and opportunities.

In theory, he had only the electorate to report to, and his constituency was no longer just the country vote, as before when he was eastern judge. It was the whole county now, including all Kansas City, which had a population of nearly 500,000. Theory apart, there was also Tom Pendergast, with whom he had had almost no prior contact. Mike Pendergast could be counted on to stand by him. Mike came calling frequently at the court, still the mentor, arriving in a dark green Peerless sedan with Jim driving and accompanied sometimes by Mike's youngest son Robert, a small boy who liked to take a turn spinning about in Judge Truman's swivel chair. But Mike was not Tom. Mike, furthermore, had suffered something like a nervous breakdown from the strain of political battles, and at the urging of his doctors and family, he had eventually to relinquish his place in the organization.

Instead of borrowing county funds from Kansas City banks at 6 percent interest, as had been the practice for years, Judge Truman went to Chicago and St. Louis and negotiated loans at 4 percent, then 2½ percent. Told by outraged Kansas City bankers that he was inflicting unjust punishment on their stockholders, he said he thought the taxpayers of the county had some rights in the matter, too.

When the Republican National Committee announced Kansas City as the choice for their national convention in 1928, then appeared to be reconsidering because of costs, Harry helped raise money locally for the Republicans, on the sensible ground that the Kansas City economy could only benefit. (It was in Kansas City's Convention Hall, on June 12, that the Republicans nominated Herbert Hoover.)

He hired Democrats only, as promised, both Goats and Rabbits, and apparently on an even basis. He also put his brother Vivian on the payroll, as purchasing agent for the county homes, and hired Fred Wallace, his youngest brother-in-law, as county architect, primarily to appease Bess and her mother. Fred, like his father, was a drinker and a worry, and still the apple of his mother's eye.

Roads, however, were the priority. Within days after taking office, Judge Truman named a bipartisan board of two civil engineers, Colonel (later General) E. M. Stayton and a Republican named N. T. Veatch, Jr., to appraise the roads of the entire county and draw up a plan, something that had never been done before. He also accompanied them on much of their survey, covering hundreds of miles in all. The report, issued three months later, described 350 miles of " 'pie crust' roads clearly inadequate to stand the demands of modern traffic," and stressed that the cost just to maintain them would exceed what might be raised by taxes. The plan was to build 224 miles of new concrete roads, in a system so designed that no farmer would be more than two miles from at least one of them. The cost was to be $6.5 million, this raised by a bond issue, which, again, was something that until now had not been done for roads in Jackson County. Bond issues of any kind had seldom fared well in years past. Harry, however, was convinced the people would support the program if guaranteed honest contracts and first-rate construction.

Great skepticism was expressed by the Kansas City *Star* and by Tom Pendergast, when Harry went for his approval. "You can't do it. They'll say I'm going to steal it," Harry would remember "the Big Boss" insisting. If he told the people what he meant to do, they would vote the bonds, Harry said. He could tell the voters anything he liked, Pendergast replied, which Harry took to mean he had an agreement.

It was as though all he had absorbed in his readings in the history of the Romans, the memory of the model of Caesar's bridge, the experience of countless misadventures by automobile since the days of the old Stafford, the memory of the roads he had seen in France, not to say his own experience with the farm roads in and about Grandview and the father who had literally died as a result of his determination to maintain them properly, converged now in one grand constructive vision. He would build the best roads in the state, if not the country, he vowed, and see they were built honestly.

He set off on another speaking tour, town to town. "I told the voters we would let the contracts to low bidders and build under the supervision of bipartisan engineers." It was early spring, the mud season, so no one needed reminding of the condition the roads were in. Every voter received a map showing where the improvements would come.

The bond issue was enlarged to include a new courthouse and jail for Kansas City, a new county hospital, and a home for retarded children. The courthouse, jail, and children's home were voted down. The roads and hospital carried, the vote taking place on Harry's forty-fourth birthday, May 8, 1928. It was a stunning victory—the vote in favor of the bond issue was three to one. Good as his word, he let a first contract of $400,000 to a construction firm from South Dakota. Other work soon went to other firms not usually chosen for public projects in Jackson County.

The roads were built, and extremely well. Five years later, in 1933, the *Examiner* could report:

> It is now generally recognized that every promise made at that time [1928] by the County Court . . . and by General E. M. Stayton and N. T. Veatch, Jr., the bipartisan board of engineers, selected to supervise the construction of the system of roads . . . has been carefully fulfilled. Every road proposed in the plans submitted has been built exactly as promised, and all well within the money voted and the estimates of the engineers.

Trees were planted along the sides, as Harry remembered from France, seven thousand seedling elms and poplars in all, though to his sorrow, Jackson County seemed as yet unready for the look of the Loire Valley. The farmers mowed them down.

He repeatedly stressed the practical in much of what he said, but he attempted the trees and, with the roads completed, he published a handsomely designed booklet, *Results of County Planning,* showing in more than a hundred pages of photographs what beauty there was in the landscape of the county to be enhanced, not destroyed, by progress, and for the benefit of everyone. "Here were hundreds of square miles . . . hundreds of thousands of people . . . *each dependent on the other* . . . and only a plan and a determined spirit needed to develop these opportunities and make each available to an understanding of the other!" In time, the report continued, would come "parks and recreation grounds at points easily available to all the county population—the healthful places of diversion that every large and growing population needs for its own pleasure and for the sake of coming generations." The pictures were of schools, farms, industry, main streets and the mushrooming Kansas City skyline, bridges over the Missouri, the Blue and Little Blue, and mile after mile of roads through rolling countryside, where so much pioneer history had taken place. The interest in history, felt so strongly by the presiding judge, was all through the book. A caption under a photograph of Raytown's main street read: "Raytown, once a favorite place for assembling teams for Santa Fe caravans, also had the distinction of a home nearby which was framed and cut in Kentucky and shipped here by water —the Jesse Barnes home, 2½ miles southwest of Raytown. A part of the house is still standing." Another photograph showed the path worn by the wagons where the Santa Fe Trail crossed the Big Blue. Under another, of a frame house set among old elms, the caption read: "Since 1867, Mrs. Martha E. Truman has lived on this farm on Blue Ridge Boulevard. She was born in Jackson County in 1852. She is the mother of Judge Harry S. Truman, presiding judge of the County Court."

"Oh! If I were only John D. Rockefeller or Mellon . . . I'd make this section (six counties) the world's real paradise," he wrote privately. As it was, the road system was completed on schedule and, almost unimaginably, for less than the original estimate.

Another bond issue was voted, for more roads, for the Kansas City Courthouse, and for a total remodeling of the Independence Courthouse. The new Kansas City Courthouse, to replace a Victorian firetrap with creaking elevator and oiled wood floors, would be the county's part in an extensive Ten-Year Plan that would include a new City Hall and civic auditorium. It was among the most ambitious city projects in the country and one championed vigorously by both the *Star* and Tom Pendergast, which meant it was certain to go forward.

Brisk about his business as always, seemingly tireless, Harry insisted that everything be done just so and concerned himself with details of a kind others would never have bothered with. Raised on the idea that appearances mattered, as an expression of self-respect, raised on the old premise that any job worth doing was worth doing well, ambitious for his community and for himself, he was determined to give the county a courthouse in Kansas City second to none.

Unsure of exactly what he wanted in the new building, he decided he wouldn't know until he had educated himself. Thus he set off by automobile—in his own car, at his own expense—on an amazing cross-country tour to look at public buildings of all kinds and to talk to their architects. He traveled thousands of miles—as far west as Denver and Houston, east all the way to Brooklyn, south as far as Baton Rouge—and took with him, for company and to help with the driving, a man named Fred Canfil, whose companionship he apparently enjoyed, but who to a great many people seemed to personify nearly everything odious about Kansas City politics. By appearance, manner, by reputation, Canfil was the typical Pendergast roughneck, "a loudmouthed, profane, vulgar, and uncouth person . . . a low ward heeler of the worst type," in the words of testimony that would be taken some years later by agents of the FBI. He was considered a bully, a braggart, "a big bag of wind," overbearing and crude. Six feet tall and built like a heavyweight wrestler, he had a dark, glowering expression nearly all of the time. He wore the brim of his hat low over his eyes and stood with his legs apart, feet firmly planted, as if braced to block a doorway. He was called peculiar and secretive, "a mystery man," and as time went on, because of his booming voice, "Whispering Fred." And it was whispered of "Whispering Fred" that he had a criminal record.

People who had worked with him for years had no idea where he lived or where he came from, whether even he was married. Earlier, before going to work for Judge Truman, Canfil had kept an office in the Board of Trade Building, but there had been no name on the door or telephone listed. He drove a good car, his suits were custom-tailored. Yet no one knew what he did for a living. One prominent Kansas City Democrat who was considering Canfil for a job tried in vain to find out more and finally asked him face to face, "What the hell do you do for a living?" Canfil only laughed and said lots of people would like to know. Refusing to give up, the man asked the police commissioner, as a favor, to put a tail on Canfil. But after several days the police could report only that Canfil had lunch regularly in a booth at the Savoy Grill with Harry Truman and Ted Marks. (Probably this was in 1925, when Harry was selling memberships for the Kansas City Automobile Club and had his own office in the Board of Trade Building, as did Ted Marks, who no doubt made the good suits Canfil wore.)

The facts about Canfil, as Harry Truman knew, were these:

He was Harry's own age and had grown up on a farm in Kansas. Unmarried, he lived with a sister in a small house on East 77 Terrace, Kansas City. Until the war, he had worked briefly as treasurer for a circus and for several years ran the service department of a Cadillac agency in Shreveport, Louisiana, his mother's hometown. At the time he had the office in the Board of Trade Building, Canfil was working as a rent collector for a Kansas City landlord. Contrary to rumor, he had no criminal record.

How long he had been involved with the Pendergast organization is not known, but, according to later testimony, it was his association with Judge Truman that had kept him in good graces with the organization and not the other way around.

Harry had met Canfil first in the Army. After being elected to the court, he hired Canfil as a tax investigator. Harry liked him, liked how he went about his work. "Fred's a little rough, but Fred's all right; he's as loyal as a bulldog," he would explain long afterward, recalling the years Canfil had been at his side. The loud mouth and crude language were largely a front. As a soldier Canfil had been superb, rising from sergeant to lieutenant by dint of his own merit, a point that counted greatly with Harry, and one that later investigators would find amply documented in Canfil's service record. "Character excellent right along and recommended as an unusually efficient officer," read one entry in the file at the War Department. "He generally worked twelve to fifteen hours a day," read another. "But I never saw him worn out or tired. He was ever full of enthusiasm and eager for the next task. . . ."

It was in Shreveport, Canfil's old place of business, that Harry saw a building that he admired more than any others on the tour, the massive new Caddo Parish Courthouse, and decided to hire its architect, Edward F. Neild, as a consultant. The building was in what would later be known as the Art Deco style. Though disdainful of the "modern" in painting, Harry was very definite in his admiration of Art Deco.

As he would have trees for his roads, so he determined now to have an equestrian bronze of Andrew Jackson for the front of the courthouse. In Charlottesville, Virginia, he saw one of Stonewall Jackson that he thought exceptional and at once commissioned its sculptor, Charles L. Keck of New York. Concerned about historical accuracy—and out of long affection for "Old Andy"—he drove to the Hermitage, Jackson's home in Tennessee, to make measurements of Jackson's clothing. He would have his hero's statue no larger or smaller than life. "I wanted a real man on a real horse."

The Kansas City *Times* declared the new road system "a distinct achievement that would be creditable to any county in the United States," which it was. The *Star* lauded the "extraordinary record" of Presiding Judge Truman. He was elected the president of the Greater Kansas City Plan Association, made the director of the National Conference of City Planning.

With his reputation fast growing he seemed to everyone who knew him still the cheery, optimistic "same old Harry," for whom work was a tonic. But it was not that way entirely. He had become so tense, so keyed up, as he wrote Bess from one of his journeys, "that I either had to run away or go on a big drunk." He loathed the sound of the telephone and at home or his office the telephone rang incessantly—"and every person I've ever had any association with since birth has wanted me to take pity on him and furnish him some county money without much return." He suffered from headaches, dizziness, and insomnia. As time went on and the stress of the job increased, the headaches grew more severe. The telephone and headaches were among the chief reasons he went away so often, on his cross-country surveys of public buildings or to Masonic meetings or to summer Army camp, where, interestingly, the Army doctors found him exceptionally fit. One said he was as physically sound as a twenty-four-year-old.

"I haven't had a headache since I came," he wrote to Bess three days after arriving at Camp Riley, Kansas, the summer of 1927. "This day has been successful. I have a letter from you, have been horseback riding, watched the Battery fire nine problems, had an hour swim, a good meal and am tired as I can be without any *headache*," he told her another day. Some of the other officers in the reserve, like Harry Vaughan, wondered at times why they bothered keeping up with it. "We didn't have any equipment," Vaughan would remember. "We didn't have any enlisted personnel, we had no materiel . . . we just didn't have anything." But for Harry the chance to be outdoors, the exercise, the companionship without the pressures of politics, were a godsend.

He had become a terrible worrier. He was anxious about little Margaret, who was too thin and pale, too often ill. He began taking medicine for his nerves. He worried about money. He worried about possible entrapment with women, an old device for destroying politicians. Once, responding to a call for a meeting in a room at the Baltimore Hotel, he asked Edgar Hinde to go along, just in case. When they knocked at the room, Hinde remembered, a blond woman in a negligée opened the door. Harry spun on his heels and ran back down the hall, disappearing around the corner. Hinde thought it was a fear verging on the abnormal.

I've been around Legion conventions with him. He'd have his room there, [and] naturally, everybody would kind of gravitate to his room. If some fellow brought a woman in there, or his wife even, I've seen him pick up his hat and coat and take off out of there and that would be the last you'd see of him until those women left. He just didn't want any women around his room in a hotel. . . . He had a phobia on it.

"Three things ruin a man," Harry would tell a reporter long afterward. "Power, money, and women.

"I never wanted power," he said. "I never had any money, and the only woman in my life is up at the house right now."

On April 30, 1929, after Harry had assigned something over $6 million in road contracts, a judgment by default for $8,944.78 was brought against him for his old haberdashery debts. His mother, meantime, had been forced to take another mortgage on the farm. Yet when one of his new roads cut 11 acres from her property, he felt he must deny her the usual reimbursement from the county, as a matter of principle, given his position. Had he not been the presiding judge, her payment would have been $1,000 an acre or $11,000.

He was scrupulous over money almost to a fault, but also over the range of small favors and shortcuts, the expedient little "arrangements" by which politicians traditionally benefited—so much so that stories about him would be told for years.

A young man from Independence named Yancey Wasson, who worked for his cousin at Guy Wasson's Fabric Company on Magee Trafficway in Kansas City, would remember Judge Truman coming in to buy seat covers for his car. The bill came to $32, but on instructions from his cousin, young Wasson said Judge Truman could forget the bill if he just arranged for the company to get some business on county cars and trucks. Harry gave him a look. "Son, I don't do business that way," he said, and paid the bill.

Sometime later, when Tom Pendergast ordered seat covers for his car that were to cost $65 and Yancey Wasson, calling at Pendergast's office, made a similar offer, Pendergast, leaning back in his chair, said, "I think we can do that."

"About two hours later," Wasson recalled, "I walked out of the police garage with an order for 200 quick-change seat covers for 100 cars on the police register and an order for 20 front rubber mats."

On September 2, 1929, seven weeks before the stock market crash, Mike Pendergast, whom Harry had "loved like a daddy," died of heart failure. With the onset of the Depression, the pressures on Judge Truman, as the county's chief executive, intensified dramatically, for the harder work was to find, the more farms and businesses failed, the more his county contracts and county employment mattered. Even the most insignificant jobs that he had to give out became plums. Friends and family were after him continually and at the very time he had to start cutting back on the payroll, since the county, too, was in trouble, as increasing numbers of people fell delinquent on taxes. At the end of the day when he had at last to fire two hundred county employees, he went home and became sick to his stomach.

With Nurse Kinnaman accompanying her, Bess had taken Margaret to Biloxi, Mississippi, on the Gulf, in the hope that a change of climate for a few weeks might restore the child's health. To find a little peace and quiet for himself, and a night's rest, Harry would drive to Grandview and sleep in his old bed over the kitchen, or arrange with the manager of a downtown hotel to give him a room without registering, "so no job holder who wants to stay on can see or phone me."

The afternoon of Monday, November 3, 1930, on the eve of election day, an attempt was made to kidnap six-year-old Margaret from her first-grade classroom at the Bryant School on River Boulevard, just four blocks from home.

According to her teacher, Madeline Etzenhouser, an unknown middle-aged man who kept his hat on appeared at the door of the room shortly before the afternoon recess, saying he had come to pick up Judge Truman's child, Mary Margaret. "I was a little curious about that," Miss Etzenhouser later said, "since we always called her Margaret, never Mary Margaret. I also was puzzled because either Mrs. Truman or one of Margaret's uncles always picked her up after school." Telling the man to wait, she hurried to the principal's office. When she returned, the man was gone. "In a few minutes Mrs. Truman came into the room. She was panicky. I believe she thought Margaret was not there, and she was extremely relieved to find her all right." Judge Truman and several deputy sheriffs arrived soon after. "It was quite a stir. . . ."

The following day, election day, while Harry was out in the county visiting the precinct polls, Margaret and her mother, accompanied by the deputy sheriffs, were taken to a hotel in town to spend the day under close security. To what extent the incident was connected with politics, Bess and Harry could only wonder. Nothing further was learned. But Margaret was to be closely watched thereafter and the tragedy of the Lindbergh kidnapping two years later was deeply felt by the Trumans.

As he never let on at the time, Harry was in terrible turmoil over what he had found politics to be in reality. He was suffering from disillusionment and pangs of conscience such as he had never before known, all of which may have had a great deal to do with his headaches.

"While it looks good from the sidelines to have control and get your name in both papers every day and pictures every other day, it's not a pleasant position," he confided to Bess. "Politics should make a thief, a roué, and a pessimist of anyone," he said in another letter, "but I don't believe I am any of them. . . ." But could he withstand the pressures?

Later would come a vivid, if fragmented, picture of what he was going through behind the scenes, described in occasional reminiscences, and in one long, extraordinary, private, undated memoir written on two or three different nights when he hid away alone in the Pickwick Hotel in downtown Kansas City, pouring himself out on paper, writing page after page for no one but himself.

VII

Trouble had come immediately after the road bond issue passed, as soon as Tom Pendergast discovered that Harry meant to keep his promise to the voters and refuse favoritism on contracts.

"The Boss wanted me to give a lot of crooked contractors the inside and I couldn't," he wrote. Pendergast became furious when Harry held his ground. The code of honor that meant so much to Harry, said T.J., was worth nothing in the real world. He dismissed the road plan as needless fuss that would serve only to give the engineers big reputations. Bids need merely be doctored so that the right people got the contracts, Pendergast told him. Harry held firm, arguing that his way was the best for the public and for the party, and it seems Pendergast realized for the first time the sort of man his brother Michael had brought into the organization. Possibly T.J. had been testing Harry. In any event, his anger appeared to pass. A meeting was called at his office, a confrontation that may have been arranged in part for T.J.'s own amusement, and one that Harry would enjoy recounting in later years.

The office at 1908 Main was so small, all of 12 by 14 feet, that it seemed overcrowded when T.J. sat there alone. Two windows with Venetian blinds overlooked the street. Furnishings were sparse—a rolltop desk against the wall, a few chairs and spittoons, a faded green rug, and over the desk, in a frame, the original drawing of an old cartoon from the *Star* showing an expansive Alderman Jim with a box of First Ward votes in his grip. The spittoons were an accommodation for guests, since T.J. smoked cigarettes only, using an elegant cigarette holder. Customarily he also kept his hat on while at his desk and sat well forward in his wooden swivel chair, as though about to leave on other business, a technique, he found, that helped keep conversations short. Stationed just outside the office was his massive, veteran secretary, or gatekeeper, Elijah Matheus, a former riverboat captain called "Cap," who was as large as T.J. himself.

Five were present for the meeting—Pendergast, Harry, and three road contractors who were old friends of the organization and all extremely upset over Harry's attitude, according to Harry's later account, which is the only one available. One man, Mike Ross, was not only head of Ross Construction, in which T.J. had part interest, but ward boss in Little Italy, which made him extremely important. Privately Harry considered Ross "a plain thief."

"These boys tell me that you won't give them contracts," Pendergast began.

"They can get them if they are low bidders," Harry answered, "but they won't get paid for them unless they come up to specifications."

"Didn't I tell you boys," said Pendergast. "He's the contrariest cuss in Missouri."

When the meeting ended and the three contractors left, Pendergast told Harry to go ahead and run things as he thought best, adding only that of course he, Pendergast, always had the two other judges to call on if he needed to vote Harry down.

From that point forward apparently Pendergast was as good as his word, never asking Harry to do anything dishonest. "And that's the God's truth. I did my job the way I thought it should be done," Harry said in an interview years afterward. "And he never interfered. . . ."

They were not close—there was never to be the kind of relationship Harry had with Mike—but they grew to respect one another. Pendergast recognized Harry's integrity as an asset. Harry, in the Pickwick Hotel memoir, written close to events, portrayed the Big Boss as a man of parts whose code, though very different from his own, he could not help but admire. Pendergast was no hypocrite, no "trimmer," however rough and sordid his background. "He, in times past, owned a bawdy house, a saloon and gambling establishment, was raised in that environment, but he's all man." He wondered, Harry wrote, who was worth more in the sight of the Lord, Tom Pendergast or the "sniveling church members who weep on Sunday, play with whores on Monday, drink on Tuesday, sell out to the Boss on Wednesday, repent about Friday and start over on Sunday?"

He felt he understood Tom Pendergast. At least he knew where he stood with him. It was Vrooman and Barr, the other two on the court, who dismayed and infuriated him. Any man who was dissolute with women, Truman believed, was not a man to be trusted entirely. He had discovered that Vrooman and Barr both "loved the ladies" and kept "telephone girls" on the payroll. ("I'll say this for the Big Boss," he wrote as an aside, "he has no feminine connections.") Vrooman, the western judge, though a "good fellow," seemed determined to make any profit possible from county transactions. Barr, the eastern judge and Harry's own choice for the job, was a total disappointment, and, to Harry, beyond understanding:

Since childhood at my mother's knee, I have believed in honor, ethics and right living as its own reward. I find a *very* small minority who agree with me on that premise. For instance, I picked a West Pointer, son of an honorable father, a man who should have had Washington, Lee, Jackson, Gustavus Adolphus for his ideals, to associate with me in carrying out a program and I got—a dud, a weakling, no ideals, no nothing. He'd use his office for his own enrichment, he's not true to his wife (and a man not honorable in his marital relations is not usually honorable in any other). He'd sell me or anyone else he's associated with out for his own gain. . . .

Worse than Barr's immorality, more troubling than anything for Harry, was a situation, only vaguely described in his account, in which he had found it necessary to do wrong himself in order to prevent a greater wrong. Barr, it appears, had been in on the theft of some $10,000, and Harry, who found out, felt he must let Barr get away with it to protect his bond issue and to keep Barr from stealing even more.

This sweet associate of mine, my friend, who was supposed to back me, had already made a deal with a former crooked contractor, a friend of the Boss's . . . I had to compromise in order to get the voted road system carried out . . . I had to let a former saloonkeeper and murderer, a friend of the Boss's, steal about $10,000 from the general revenues of the county to satisfy my ideal associate and keep the crooks from getting a million or more out of the bond issue. Was I right or did I compound a felony? I don't know. . . . Anyway I've got the $6,500,000 worth of roads on the ground and at a figure that makes the crooks tear their hair. The hospital is up at less cost than any similar institution in spite of my drunken brother-in-law [Fred Wallace], whom I'd had to employ on the job to keep peace in the family. I've had to run the hospital job myself and pay him for it. . . . Am I an administrator or not? Or am I just a crook to compromise in order to get the job done? You judge it, I can't.

This and more came pouring out of him in the hotel room. He went on for pages. He described how Vrooman and Barr would shoot crap while court was in session, crouching down behind the judge's bench as Harry tried to transact business. (He had actually found it easier to get things accomplished if they were so occupied.) He had always thought most men had a sense of honor. Now he wasn't at all sure. Pendergast, as if lecturing a slow student, had told him that very few men stayed honest if given opportunity to cheat and get away with it. What chance was there for a clean honest government, he wondered, when a bunch of vultures sat on the sidelines? "If we only had Tom to deal with, the public might have a chance, but Tom can't operate without Joe [Shannon] and Cass

[Welch]. Cass is a thug and a crook of the worst water, he should have been in the pen twenty years ago. Joe hasn't got an honest appointee on the payroll. . . ."

The more Harry wrote, the angrier he grew:

> I wonder if I did the right thing to put a lot of no account sons of bitches on the payroll and pay other sons of bitches more money for supplies than they were worth in order to satisfy the political powers and save $3,500,000. I believe I did do right. Anyway I'm not a partner of any of them and I'll go out poorer in every way than I came into office.

He reckoned he could already have pocketed $1.5 million, had he chosen, which, as future disclosures would make plain, was altogether realistic. As it was, "I haven't $150." He wondered if he might be better off if he quit and ran a filling station.

"All this," he added, "gives me headaches. . . ."

To little Sue Ogden, the big house where her playmate Margaret Truman lived was a magnificent sanctuary secure from the troubles of Depression times. Margaret's Grandmother Wallace was an elegant lady who wore her old-fashioned clothes with style. Margaret had a beautiful new bicycle. Margaret had a new swing set. Whenever Margaret's father came home from a trip, he brought her a present. "She had everything she wanted," Sue remembered. Judge Truman always looked dressed up and there was a black servant, Vietta Garr, who did the cooking and waited on the table.

Independence was hard hit by the Depression. In 1931, three banks closed within three weeks. Hundreds of families were suffering. According to the records, in the fiscal year 1931–32 more than 900 families in town, some 2,800 people, were receiving relief—food and clothing—from a half-dozen organizations, including the Community Welfare League, the Red Cross, the Kiwanis Club, and the Salvation Army. The Salvation Army had set up a soup kitchen on the Square. The Welfare League had taken over the old county jail as a distribution center and the lines there grew steadily longer. In 1932–33, families "comprising 4,347 individuals" received help, more than half again the number of the year before. Sue Ogden's father, a machinist, had trouble finding work of any kind and kept leaving town to look elsewhere. She would remember being hungry during the times her father took the family away with him to other towns. Margaret, she knew, was never hungry. To Sue and her family, Margaret Truman was a child of wealth and privilege.

Margaret would remember that because of the Depression her allowance had been cut from 50 cents a week to 25 cents. "And this was a disaster!"

Sue Ogden and her older sister Betty lived next door, across a narrow alley on the south side. Mrs. Truman encouraged Margaret to play with the two Ogden girls, who were tomboys, as Mrs. Truman had been once, and because they lived so close by. They were playmates "without risk," as Sue remembered, and since the kidnapping scare, the Trumans were "terribly fearful" about Margaret. "We kind of had to teach her how to play."

Judge Truman seemed always relaxed and friendly, "just a father." He "wasn't upset to be caught in his pajamas. He was just very calm about having us around the house. We played on his rowing machine in the bathroom and he didn't mind."

The two Ogdens were in and out of the house as if it were their own, or playing out back on the driveway, where Mrs. Truman or Vietta Garr could keep watch. The house was a "wonderful place" to play. A basement called "the dungeon" was big enough to ride Margaret's bicycle in. A "fine attic" was filled with old-fashioned clothes for dressing up. It was a household that seemed to run smoothly year after year, with never a sign of friction. "If there was ever any bad feeling, even an undercurrent of bad feeling, they certainly hid it well," Sue recalled. Vietta Garr, who had first come to work in 1927, said later, "I never heard a squabble the entire time I was with them. I have never seen Mr. Truman angry...." Her father had been groomsman for Grandfather Gates. "The whole family had good dispositions and were easy to work for," she remembered. "They liked things nice, and that is the way I liked them, so we got along fine."

For Bess, life was ordered, private, sociable within bounds. She belonged to a bridge club and served as secretary of the Needlework Guild, a group of women who collected clothing for the needy—such activities as appeared among the society items dutifully reported by young Sue Gentry in the Independence *Examiner*. And for Bess that was quite enough. Her family was her life. She had no wish for more, no desire whatever for public attention or acclaim.

Margaret would remember her own life being nearly perfect. "I was an only child and I had lots of aunts and uncles with no children. And everything went to Margaret. It was lovely." The only disciplinarian in the household was her mother, whose eyes could turn steely and who on occasion spanked her, as her father never did. Her mother, Margaret recalled, was far more likely than her father to be hard on people who deserved it. "I could twist *him* around my little finger."

At dinner, Grandmother Wallace sat at the head of the table, Father at the other end. Margaret sat with her mother on one side, with Uncle Fred opposite. Dinner was served at 6:30. There was a white linen tablecloth, linen napkins, and good silver. Father did the carving, and "beautifully," according to Vietta Garr. The atmosphere was calm and proper, always. Grandmother Wallace did her hair a little differently for dinner and put on a fresh dress. "My manners were expected to be perfect," Margaret remembered. If her father and uncle discussed politics, her mother occasionally joined in, but never her grandmother, who did not care for politicians, or politics. "Her presence was very much felt. Even though she didn't talk a great deal."

The food, ordered each morning by Madge Wallace by telephone, was straightforward and ample—baked Virginia ham, standing rib roast, warm bread and old-fashioned biscuits, baked sweet potatoes, fresh vegetables in season, cakes, pies, peach cobbler. Harry particularly liked corn bread and Missouri sorghum. His favorite dessert was angel food cake, according to Vietta Garr, who, in all, would spend thirty-six years with the Truman family. "Yes, I spoiled him," she would say, "but he was always such a nice man."

On Sundays, Harry, Bess, and Margaret would drive to Grandview for a big, midday fried chicken dinner at the farm, where, as Margaret remembered, the atmosphere was "entirely different." It was not just that her father looked forward to these visits, but her mother as well. "She liked Mamma Truman immensely." Mamma was "full of spice," with opinions on nearly everything, including politics. The difference between this spry little "country grandmother" and the one in Independence was extreme. With Mamma Truman one felt in touch with pioneer times, with a native vigor and mettle that seemed ageless. Mamma still went rabbit hunting with Margaret's boy cousins, Vivian's sons. Once when she offered food to a tramp at the back porch and the tramp complained the coffee wasn't hot enough, she took the cup, went inside, and promptly returned with a shotgun. He could be on his way, she said, or she would warm more than his coffee for him.

It pleased Margaret to see the enjoyment her father took in Mamma's company. "Now Harry, you be good," she would say as they were leaving. But Mamma could also observe that "Being too good is apt to be uninteresting," a line they all loved.

With the Ogden sisters and a half-dozen other neighborhood girls, Margaret put on plays in the backyard at 219 North Delaware. For one called *The Capture of the Clever One,* with Margaret in the title role, the *Examiner* sent a photographer to make a portrait of the cast. Performances were after dark. A Ping-Pong table tipped on its side served as a backdrop, lights were strung, kitchen chairs set out for the audience. Harry attended dutifully. "I want her to do everything and have everything and still learn that most people have to work to live, and I don't want her to be a high hat," he had written to Bess.

He was habitually dutiful and responsible about all kinds of family matters, the sort of father who checked to see that the tires had good tread and 35 pounds of pressure, who had the oil changed every 1,000 miles without fail. "The car was washed every few days," Margaret would remember. "And the upholstery was vacuumed and cleaned and people did not throw gum wrappers around—they were put in the ashtray—and he did not like people to smoke because he had never smoked and because the smoke would get into the upholstery. . . . He was very particular about his cars." And about himself—his suits, ties, his shoes. He never went out the door without his hat, as few gentlemen of the day ever would, and his hat was always worn straight on his head. "Straight, absolutely straight," she remembered.

He was interested in the weather, like most farmers. "He read all the weather maps in the papers and he always had a barometer where he could see it."

He was a string saver. He could get two weeks' use out of a straight razor by stropping the blade on the palm of his hand before each shave. Interestingly, for all his years on the farm, for all he knew about tools and odd jobs, he did no repairs around the house, never cut the lawn or put up screens. Undoubtedly, his mother-in-law had some say in this. Such work was for the yard man.

"It never seemed like the Truman house," Sue Ogden remembered. "It was so clearly Mrs. Wallace's house. And she was clearly in charge of everything about it."

Another of Margaret's childhood friends, Mary Shaw, would remember hearing her parents say, "How does Harry put up with that?"

"It was *very* hard on my father," Margaret would concede long afterward, while showing a visitor through the house. "You know, my father was a very quiet, nontemperamental man at home. He got along. I mean, he made it his business to get along . . . because he loved my mother and this was where she wanted to live."

Up early every morning, well before dawn, and always before anyone else, he had the house to himself, to read the papers, including the comic strips which he loved, and especially Andy Gump. (Told that as county judge he could have any license plate number he wished, he had picked Number 369, because it was Andy Gump's number, a point he delighted in explaining to anyone who asked.)

In the evenings he would turn to his books and become wholly immersed. "You could talk to him if he were reading and you wouldn't get an answer." Indeed, Margaret could not recall her father sitting down quietly at home without a book in his hand.

He became a great joiner. In addition to the Masons, the American Legion, the Veterans of Foreign Wars, he belonged to the Elks, the Eagles, the International Acquaintance League. Monday nights he went uptown to the Square to play poker in a back room over the Farmer & Merchants Bank. It was a regular game among the same old friends, several of them Army pals like Edgar Hinde and Roger Sermon, a grocer who had become the town's mayor. They named themselves the Independence Harmonicon Society, or Harpie Club, because one of their number had once distinguished himself playing the harmonica, or French harp, extremely poorly but with exuberance in a contest at the local movie house. The game had a 10-cent limit. A little beer or bourbon was consumed, Prohibition notwithstanding, and the conversation usually turned to politics. Such was the social life of Judge Harry Truman in the early 1930s, the worst of the Depression, years when Adolf Hitler was rising to power and Japan invaded Manchuria.

As much as he enjoyed going out to the farm to see his mother and sister, he had no desire ever again to live in the country. He loved the town. "He liked his walk up to the courthouse square," said Margaret. "He liked people . . . he genuinely liked people and he liked to talk to them. . . ."

In many ways it was still the town he had grown up in. Farmers crowded the Square on Saturday nights, but the rest of the week, nights were quiet, broken only by the sound of passing trains and the striking of the courthouse clock. Margaret Phelps and Tillie Brown still taught history and English at the high school. The town directory listed most of the old names of the original settlers—Boggs, Dailey, Adair, McClelland, Chiles, Hickman, Holmes, Ford, Davenport, McPherson, Mann, Peacock, Shank, not to say Truman, Wallace, and Noland. Harry knew nearly all the family histories—it was good politics to know, of course, but he also loved the town.

His devotion to Bess appears to have been total, no less than ever. On his travels, at summer Army camp, he wrote to her nearly every day. How had he ever gotten along without her before they were married was a mystery he pondered in a letter from Fort Riley, Kansas, the summer of 1930. "Just think of all those *wasted* years. . . ."

"Have you practiced your music?" he wrote to Margaret from Camp Ripley, Minnesota, another summer. He had splurged and for Christmas bought her a baby grand piano, a Steinway, a surprise she did not appreciate. She had dreamed of an electric train. "I'm hoping you can play all those exercises without hesitation. If you can I'll teach you to read bass notes when I get back."

As early as 1931 there was talk of Harry Truman for governor, a prospect that delighted him. "You may yet be the first lady of Missouri," he told Bess. Whatever inner turmoil he suffered, however many mornings of dark despair he knew, the truth was he loved politics. He was as proud of the roads he had built and of the new Kansas City Courthouse as of anything he had ever accomplished, or hoped to. Work was progressing on the new Independence Courthouse, his courthouse, as he saw it, and everyone approved. "From the time of the establishment of Jackson County until now," wrote Colonel Southern in the *Examiner,* "men with the same indomitable courage of the county's namesake, Andrew Jackson, have dwelt in this 'garden spot of Missouri'—with eyes always fixed on the future greatness of this great domain and with the thought uppermost to build, build, build a county that the rest of the state would be proud of."

But the greater satisfaction for Harry was in what he had been able to do for ordinary people, without fanfare or much to show for it in the record books—things he could only have done as a politician. Years afterward, over lunch in New York with the journalist Eric Sevareid, he would describe how as a county judge in Missouri he had discovered that through a loophole in the law, hundreds of old men and women were being committed to mental institutions by relatives who could not, or would not, cope with their care or financial support, and how by investigating the situation he had restored these people to their rights and freedom. This, he said, had given him more satisfaction than anything.

"He loved politics," remembered Ted Marks, "and he strived for something and never let loose until he got there. I think no matter what job he held he put all he had into it. He enjoyed it and did the best he knew how. . . ."

He had not found his real work until late in life, not until he was nearly forty. But then, observed Ethel Noland, hadn't he been a late bloomer all along? "He didn't marry until he was thirty-five. . . . He didn't do anything early." Politics came naturally. "There," she said, "he struck his gait."

1

2

Harriet Louisa Gregg
Young and Solomon
Young.

Mary Jane Holmes Truman
and Anderson Shipp
Truman.

3

4

5

Martha Ellen Young
Truman and John
Anderson Truman
at the time of their
marriage, December 1881.

6

Harry S. Truman at about age ten.

8

The center of Independence, Jackson Square, at the turn of the century. The courthouse is on the right.

In a graduation portrait of the Class of 1901, seventeen-year-old Harry Truman stands fourth from the left at the back. Bess Wallace is on the far right, second row, and Charlie Ross sits on the far left in the front row. The Latin inscription over the door says: "Youth the Hope of the World."

7

Truman at about the time he was employed as a clerk at the National Bank of Commerce, Kansas City. "His appearance is good and his habits and character are of the best," wrote a supervisor.

Cousins Nellie and Ethel Noland, to whom he was the adored "Horatio."

11   The junior partner of J. A. Truman & Son, Farmers, stands with his mother and grandmother Young by the front porch of the house at Grandview.

The work day began with his father's call from the foot of the stairs at 5:30 A.M. Here, Truman rides the cultivator across a field of young corn.

13

Truman at the wheel of the second-hand, right-hand drive, 1911 Stafford touring car that transformed his life. With him are Bess Wallace (in front), sister Mary Jane Truman, and cousin Nellie Noland.

A summer outing on the Little Blue River with Harry at the oars, Bess with the fishing pole. "Harry was always fun," remembered Ethel Noland.

15

16

The portrait of Bess that Harry
carried to war in 1918. "Dear Harry,"
she wrote on the back, "May this
photograph bring you safely home
again from France."

His AEF identity card shows a newly commissioned
Captain Harry S. Truman with no glasses and a
regulation haircut.

17

With Harry "over there," Mary
Jane was left to run the farm.
"It was quite a blow to my
mother and sister," he later
conceded.

Truman (third from right) poses with some of his fellow artillery officers "somewhere in France."

18

19

Wounded soldiers from the Argonne are tended beneath an undamaged painting of the Ascension in a ruined church in Neuilly, September 1918.

20

The war over, Captain Truman (on the right) relaxes in the sunshine at Monte Carlo.

21   Harry and Bess Truman pose for their wedding portrait with bridesmaids Louise Wells (left) and Helen Wallace, Bess's brother Frank (center rear), who gave her away, and best man Ted Marks, who made the groom's suit on special order. The day, Saturday, June 28, 1919, was extremely hot and humid—standard for summer in Missouri.

22

The Gates-Wallace house, 219 North Delaware Street, Independence, as it looked at the time the Trumans moved in "temporarily" with Bess's mother, following their honeymoon.

Truman & Jacobson, "the shirt store," as Truman called it, opened for business on 12th Street, Kansas City, in November 1919. Above, on the left, haberdasher Harry S. Truman strikes a characteristic pose at the sales counter.

25

Thomas J. Pendergast, the "Big Boss" of Kansas City, beams for photographers at his daughter's wedding.

Michael Pendergast, whom Truman "loved as I did my own daddy."

James Pendergast, Michael's son and Truman's devoted friend.

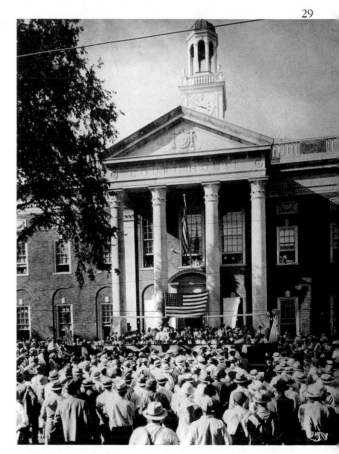

Judge Truman speaks at the dedication of the new Independence Courthouse on September 17, 1933, one of the proudest days of his life.

All but lost in floral tributes, Truman is sworn in for a second term as Presiding Judge of the Jackson County Court, January 1931.

Ten-year-old Margaret with her parents, the summer of
Truman's first campaign for the Senate, 1934.

Crisscrossing the state, the candidate spoke at one
county seat after another, his platform usually the
courthouse steps. Town loafers and boys on
summer vacation often represented a good part
of his "crowd." He was not a captivating or
impressive speaker, but people also had no
difficulty understanding what he meant and
seemed to feel better for having listened to him.
The punishing heat and time on the road
bothered him not at all.

31

Throughout the campaign Truman stressed his farm background. At right, for a publicity photograph, he sits on the porch swing at Grandview with the two other most important women in his life, his mother and sister Mary Jane.

32

33

At first "under a cloud" in the Senate because of his Pendergast connection, Truman nonetheless kept a portrait of "T.J." prominently displayed in his office.

John L. Lewis, head of the United Mine Workers (seated near left), makes a dramatic appearance before the Truman Committee, as Chairman Truman (far right) listens impassively.

35

34

A rare photograph of Truman and Tom Pendergast together was taken at the 1936 Democratic National Convention in Philadelphia. With them are Kansas City attorney James Aylward (center), FDR's political adviser, James A. Farley (the tall figure at rear), and David E. Fitzgerald, Sr., Democratic National Committeeman from Connecticut (right foreground).

36

Truman, who loved the Senate "club," became one of its most popular members. Here, in his office, he is surrounded by fellow Truman Committee members (from left to right) Homer Ferguson, Harold H. Burton, Tom Connally, and Owen Brewster.

In the midst of the 1944
Democratic National Convention
at Chicago, Truman signals his
feeling about the drive to make
him FDR's running mate.

38

Bess and Margaret at the moment Truman is
named the nominee for Vice President. Margaret
would be remembered cheering as if at a football
game. Bess, however, rarely smiled for
photographers.

37

Truman and Roosevelt smile for photographers at lunch in the Rose Garden at the White
House, August 18, 1944. Shocked by the President's appearance, Truman later told an aide,
"His hands were shaking . . . physically he's just going to pieces." This was one of the few
occasions when Truman and Roosevelt were seen together.

39

6

The Senator from Pendergast

Friends don't count in fair weather. It is when troubles come that friends count.

—HARRY TRUMAN

I

Francis M. Wilson, known to rural voters as the Red-Headed Peckerwood of the Platte, was a freckled, old-fashioned Missouri stump speaker who excelled at charming country crowds with his poetic tributes to the natural splendors of their beloved state. A convivial man, he had also attained, by age sixty-four, something of the air of a statesman, and in 1932, as the Pendergast choice for governor—and with Franklin Roosevelt heading the national ticket—he could look forward to certain election.

Though Wilson maintained a voting address in rural Platte County, his home was a fourth-floor walk-up apartment on East Linwood Boulevard, Kansas City, and it was there before sunup one morning in October 1932, just three weeks before the election, that he complained to his wife Ida of not feeling well. As only she and a few close friends knew, he had been suffering with bleeding ulcers. She immediately telephoned his brother, R. P. Wilson, a physician, who, with his wife and son, arrived as it was getting light.

At six o'clock Francis M. Wilson died. When someone mentioned calling the mortician, Ida Wilson said no. Once the mortician knew, the news would be out. She said to phone Tom Pendergast.

Dr. Wilson made the call, telling Pendergast only that he should come

193

at once. At seven o'clock T.J. arrived, breathing heavily from the climb up the stairs. The Wilson boy answered the door. "Mr. Pendergast didn't ask why or what or when," he later recounted. "He said, 'Have you called the mortician?'" Told they had not, T.J. asked what their wishes were about a replacement for Wilson in the election. The family said they thought it should be Guy B. Park, a Platte County circuit judge and neighbor, to which T.J. responded, "Who the hell is Guy Park?" After some discussion, Pendergast, who kept standing the whole time, told them he had to leave and that they should speak to no one until he called back.

They waited for nearly four hours, the body of Francis Wilson on the bed in the adjoining room. At eleven o'clock Pendergast called and said only three words, "Call the mortician."

Thus it was that white-haired, sober-looking Guy B. Park went to the governor's mansion, and Harry Truman did not.

Harry Truman had wanted more than anything to be the nominee for governor, and well before T.J. ever picked Francis Wilson. Encouraged by friends and complimentary comments in several papers suggesting he would make a good chief executive for the state, he had been hugely disappointed when Pendergast refused him the nod. Then came the stunning news of Wilson's death the afternoon of October 12, the same afternoon, it happened, that Harry and thirty-five thousand others were celebrating the completion of the road program at reputedly the biggest country barbecue ever put on in Jackson County. "It was my big day," he remembered bitterly.

Apparently he lost no time in getting to Tom Pendergast, only to be told once again he was not the choice, that Guy Park had been decided on. That night Harry drove to the little resort town of Excelsior Springs north of the river and checked into a hotel to remain in seclusion for several days.

His anguish over his future was deep-seated and painful. Having served two consecutive terms in the court, he was ineligible to run again for county judge, and unlike so many others in public life, he had no law practice or insurance business to fall back on, nor any private income. He questioned seriously whether he had made the right choice in life. In a letter of advice to a nephew, he wrote, "It will be much better for you to go to work for a bank or some mercantile institution and get real experience than to get a political job where you learn nothing and lose out when the administration changes." With the end of his term in 1934, Harry Truman would be fifty years old, and without the blessing of Tom Pendergast there was really not a lot more he could do in politics, whatever his aspirations. As he himself said, everything would be all right only as "long as the Big Boss believes in me. . . . "

The previous June he had traveled to Chicago with T.J. as part of the Missouri delegation to the Democratic National Convention that nominated Franklin Roosevelt. Pendergast had announced himself for former United States Senator James Reed of Missouri, who had begun his career as mayor of Kansas City in the era of Alderman Jim. The brilliant, egotistical Reed had been one of the "nine willful men" in the Senate who killed the League of Nations, and Harry consequently had no use for him. Pendergast's enthusiasm was mostly a pose to please Reed. In reality he was playing a somewhat complicated game of a kind new to Harry. Pendergast, Harry was later to say, "understood political situations and how to handle them better than any man I have ever known."

T.J. had already made a special trip to confer with Roosevelt at Albany before the convention. James A. Farley, Roosevelt's highly influential political adviser, had also been warmly received by the Kansas City organization at a lunch at the Muehlebach. If anything, T.J. was more enthusiastic about Roosevelt this time than in 1924. Still, he put on a show for Reed under the lights at Chicago Stadium, and Harry, swallowing his distaste for Reed, went through the motions, the dutiful soldier, until the Big Boss began letting votes go to Roosevelt, a little at a time, exactly as Jim Farley wanted, to keep the Roosevelt tally steadily building with each ballot. At the end, Pendergast, Harry, the whole Jackson County delegation had come home extremely pleased with the outcome.

By the following spring of 1933 Harry felt he was more in favor than ever before. "I had a fine talk with T.J. yesterday," he reported to Bess in high spirits, "and I am still *on top*. He told me to do as I pleased with the county payroll . . . he'd put the organization in line behind me. He also told me I could be Congressman or collector. Think of that a while."

The power of Tom Pendergast had become as great as or possibly greater than that of any political boss in the country. Major changes had taken place, promising larger roles for nearly everyone of ability in the organization.

In 1930, the year Harry was reelected presiding judge, T.J. had at last resolved the old, nettling problem of the Rabbits by simply convincing Joe Shannon that he belonged in Congress. The silver-haired, silver-tongued Shannon was put nicely out of the way in Washington, where he served six terms in the House, distinguishing himself as an apostle of the old-time faith of Thomas Jefferson. Only those who had been through the

Goat-Rabbit struggles of past decades could appreciate what a singular victory this was for the Big Boss, and all so smoothly done.

The year after, in 1931, Kansas City achieved "home rule," which meant control of its own police, who until then had been under state authority. Thus for all practical purposes, the organization now ran the police department.

In 1932, the Missouri legislature failed to establish new congressional districts as required by Congress, with the result that every candidate for the House had to be elected at large, instead of by districts. The possibilities in this for increased Pendergast power were almost too great to imagine, since the big Jackson County vote—the Pendergast vote—now bore directly on all congressional elections everywhere in the state. T.J. could not only name his own governor, but thirteen men for Congress as well. And that fall he had but one disappointment when Bennett Champ Clark of eastern Missouri made a vigorous campaign for the Senate and won, in open opposition to the Kansas City organization. (This was the same Bennett Clark, the son of Missouri's famous Champ Clark, who at the railroad station in France had fooled Harry Truman into believing an enemy air attack was imminent.) So by the start of 1933, with Park in office as governor, Pendergast was riding higher than ever. The Capitol in Jefferson City was spoken of now as "Uncle Tom's Cabin." With Franklin Roosevelt and his New Deal taking over in Washington, the prospects for the future looked boundless. In the small office at 1908 Main Street, a portrait of FDR now held the place of honor over T.J.'s rolltop desk.

Even in the depths of the Depression's worst years, Kansas City was enjoying a building boom. A new thirty-four-story Power & Light Building, the tallest skyscraper in Missouri, stood over the city like a shining statement of faith. Swinging his car out of the driveway each morning, heading to town on Van Horne Road, Judge Truman would see it rising proudly against the horizon, the very picture of progress.

A new Nelson Art Gallery was under construction at a cost of $3 million. As part of Kansas City's Ten-Year Plan, work began on a magnificent municipal auditorium that would fill an entire block, include an arena seating twelve thousand and an elegant music hall. A new police building was also part of the plan, along with a new waterworks system and a new public market. A few blocks from Judge Truman's skyscraper courthouse, a still larger City Hall was going up.

Compared to other cities, the Kansas City outlook was confident and expansive. There were jobs, and local government—the organization— was providing most of them. Under the direction of City Manager Henry McElroy, thousands were put to work with picks and shovels, while heavy machinery was left standing by unused, so that more men could be employed. (McElroy would later claim it was the Kansas City make-work program that inspired the New Deal's Works Progress Administration, the WPA.) One seemingly endless project involved paving mile after mile of Brush Creek with a thick bed of Pendergast's Ready-Mixed concrete.

If Judge Truman felt besieged by job applicants in these early Depression years, his was a small burden compared to what T.J. faced. The lines outside the yellow-brick building on Main Street began gathering before dawn most weekdays and by mid-morning stretched two or three blocks. He saw as many people as possible, on a first-come-first-served basis, no matter who they were, keeping the interviews to a few minutes at most, beginning about nine and ending promptly at noon when he stopped for lunch. Rarely was anyone sent away feeling empty-handed. Invariably courteous, Pendergast would listen attentively, ask a few questions, then scrawl a note on a slip of paper requesting somebody somewhere in one or another city or county organization, or in one of his own enterprises, to consider the needs of the bearer "and oblige," these final two words seeming to carry the full weight of his command. Actually, it depended on which color pencil he used. If the note was written in red, his "and oblige" meant the applicant should be given a job or granted a favor without delay. If, however, the Big Boss wrote in blue, then this was only someone to keep in mind should anything turn up. If the note was written with an ordinary lead pencil, the bearer was nobody to bother with.

When a reporter questioned Pendergast whether jobholders were ever asked to donate to the organization at election time, he said, "Why shouldn't they be? That's how they got their jobs."

Harry loved to tell the story of the day when there was a particularly large crowd waiting to see Pendergast, and his gatekeeper, "Cap" Matheus, went out to say that if there was anyone in line who had anything to *give* Tom, he should come directly in. But no one moved.

The old Pendergast policy that politics was chiefly a business of making friends placed no limits because of ethnic background, religion, or race. To be a Democrat was to be a Democrat. Tolerance was good politics. And while less was done to alleviate suffering in the desperate Negro wards, the attitude of the Pendergast organization was seen by black people as progress. As one of them remembered, "The machine did small favors mainly, but small favors were better than no favors at all."

Business people had few quibbles about the organization or the man who ruled it. Taxes were low. With a phone call or two, a talk with T.J. or young Jim, red tape wondrously dissolved, projects went forward. People in business found they could get quick, reliable answers to important questions, that problems with the city could be resolved with amazing dispatch. The comment most often heard about Tom Pendergast was that "he got things done."

Even the editors of the *Star* at this point were impressed by the executive ability of City Manager McElroy, a judgment they lived to regret. Kansas City probably had "the most efficient city government in its history," said the *Star* in 1930. Presiding Judge Truman was frequently cited as an exemplary public official.

But others, too, commanded respect and deservedly. Harry Truman was not, as sometimes implied later, the sole exception-to-the-rule in a wholly nefarious crowd. Jim Pendergast was able and honest and had, as remembered his priest, Monsignor Arthur Tighe, a remarkable "kind of gentleness about him for being a politician." Attorney James P. Aylward, T.J.'s friend and adviser, and chairman of the Democratic County Committee, was astute, hardworking, and well regarded within Kansas City professional circles.

Even Pendergast himself had lately acquired some of the trappings of respectability, a degree of polish unimaginable in earlier times. He dressed now in conservative, well-tailored suits. He and his wife had been to Paris. T.J. would expound on his love of Paris, without apology. He had developed a great fondness for French cooking, his friends knew. His new home on Ward Parkway, in the Country Club district, Kansas City's loveliest residential section, was an exact copy of a house he had seen in France, a red-brick mansion in the Regency style, perfect in every detail.

Life had never been better. And by the close of the year, with Prohibition ended in December 1933, the Pendergasts would be back in the legal liquor business again. Best of their line was "Old 1889 Brand," named for the year Tom first arrived in Kansas City. It was seven-and-a-half-year-old Kentucky bourbon, one hundred proof.

That gambling, prostitution, bootlegging, the sale of narcotics, and racketeering were a roaring business in Kansas City was all too obvious. Nor did anyone for a moment doubt that the ruling spirit behind it all remained Tom Pendergast. It was the Pendergast heyday. Never, not even in the gaudy era following the Civil War, had the city known such "wide-open" times. Forty dance halls and more than a hundred nightclubs were in operation, offering floor shows, dancers, comedians, and some of the best blues and jazz to be heard anywhere in America—the Bennie Moten Orchestra at the Reno, and later at the Reno, Count Basie and his Kansas City Seven doing "The One O'Clock Jump," trumpeter Hot Lips Page at the Subway, blues singer Julia Lee at the Yellow Front Saloon. Musicians from all over the country, most of them black and all hard hit by the

Depression, came to Kansas City, knowing there was work. "Every joint had music," one of them remembered, "every joint."

This, too, was heartland America, no less than the old-fashioned, country-town peace and quiet of nearby Independence.

"Dance All Night Long!" said an advertisement in the *Star* for the Musicians Ball at the Labor Temple, in the spring of 1932, at which Bennie Moten, Andy Kirk and his Clouds of Joy, Walter Page and his Blue Devils, the Nighthawks—in all, eight orchestras—played until sunup.

There were no closing hours. At the Subway, in a basement at 18th and Vine, thirty to forty musicians would "crowd in" to play. "Everybody played that wanted to play . . . and every night you could find music there. . . . It never really did open until after 1:00 [in the morning]." "A cracker town, but a happy town," Count Basie remembered.

The red-light district ran for blocks, on 13th and 14th Streets. One high-priced place called the Chesterfield Club offered a businessman's lunch served by waitresses clad only in high heels and cellophane aprons.

A lifetime resident of Kansas City named John Doohan, trying years later to describe the rollicking city it had been, would suddenly stop in mid-sentence, realizing how much he missed it. "See . . . there just wasn't any law," said Doohan, whose job in the research library at the *Star* required keeping watch on the unfolding history of the city.

> The clubs stayed open all night. Liquor flowed. There was a band in every place . . . and gambling, even around the *Star* [at Grand and 17th]. . . . On the northeast corner there was a bookmaker and gambling. On the southeast corner there was a bookmaker and gambling. Two doors north of the *Star,* there were two bookie joints. And then as you went on Main, there were gambling places at 31st . . . at 31st and Prospect, 34th and Main. . . .
>
> Gambling places . . . Prostitution—wide open. Knocking on windows. Two bits, quarter and fifty-cent places.

Whenever questioned about this, Tom Pendergast customarily replied, "Well, the rich men have their clubs, where they can gamble and have a good time. Would you deny the poor man an equal right?"

"Ours is a fine, clean, and well-ordered town," Pendergast would insist repeatedly, and John Doohan, too, would remember there being little fear of violent crime.

> I will say the town was safe. You never got mugged. You could walk around downtown any time of the day or night. You could walk through the colored district, and there weren't any problems. I mean things were . . . you know, there wasn't much crime. But there were the rackets.

Others, including respected, proper citizens, conceded privately that "wide open" was good business, particularly in hard times.

The head of the rackets, one of T.J.'s acknowledged "chief lieutenants," was a small, dapper Italian-American with a master-of-ceremonies personality named Johnny Lazia, who had earlier served a prison sentence for armed robbery. Lazia was the King of Little Italy, where, in 1926, he had seized power from T.J.'s old Ninth Ward leader, Mike Ross. T.J. had accepted Lazia as part of the organization largely because he had no choice and apparently with the understanding that Lazia would keep Al Capone and other out-of-town gangsters clear of the city. "Our Johnny," it seems, relied on his charm as well as his power, and he and Boss Tom soon were "fast friends." Also, importantly, T.J. had by this time become a heavy gambler on horse races and so was in continuous need of such "fast friends." At the office at 1908 Main, he had installed his own direct wire to tracks in the East, even set up betting cages at the rear of the clubroom. Across the Missouri River in Platte County he had established his own race track, the Riverside Park Jockey Club, where he also kept his own stable of horses.

In return for his support in the Ninth Ward, Lazia was to have control over liquor and gambling in the city, as well as a say in hiring policies at the police department. Allegedly, Lazia even had his own office at the police department. A federal agent sent to investigate Lazia's activities reported to Washington that when he called Kansas City police headquarters, Lazia answered the phone.

Lazia, too, knew how to be a friend in need. When former Senator James Reed's companion (later wife) Nell Donnelly was kidnapped in 1931, it was to Lazia that Reed went immediately for help, and Lazia who brought her safely home. Two years later, in 1933, when City Manager McElroy's stylish twenty-five-year-old daughter Mary was kidnapped, it was again "Our Johnny" who came to the rescue, this time producing the ransom money, $30,000 in cash, which he collected with astonishing speed from friends among the gamblers.

Through all this, only one brave voice was raised in protest, Samuel S. Mayerberg, the rabbi of Temple B'nai Jehudah, who in the spring of 1932 decided to speak out before a government study club, a meeting of perhaps forty people, most of whom were women. It was then that a reform movement began, though few, and clearly no one in the organization, seemed particularly concerned, nor was there a rush of good citizens to join his ranks. "One of my hardest jobs was not fighting the underworld," Mayerberg later said, "but in using my energy and time to convince thoroughly nice people, honorable men . . . that as respectable citizens, they ought to be in it [the fight] also."

When federal investigators started proceedings against Lazia for income tax evasion in 1933, T.J. wrote at once to Jim Farley, the new Postmaster General in Washington and part of FDR's inner circle, to stress how extremely important Lazia was to him. "Now Jim," he wrote, "Lazia is one of my chief lieutenants and I am more sincerely interested in his welfare than anything you might be able to do for me now or in the future. . . . "

But then, only weeks later, came the stunning news of Kansas City's "Union Station Massacre," one of the most sensational atrocities of the whole gangster era. On Saturday, June 17, 1933, three notorious bankrobbers and killers, Verne Miller, Adam Richetti, and "Pretty Boy" Floyd, armed with submachine guns, attempted to rescue another "public enemy," Frank ("Jelly") Nash, as Nash, in handcuffs, was being escorted by law officers from a train to a waiting car at Union Station, to make the short drive to the federal prison at Leavenworth. The three killers, who were waiting in the parking lot outside the station, made their move as Nash was being put in the car. One officer turned and fired with a pistol. The three then opened up with machine guns, killing five men—two Kansas City policemen, an agent of the FBI, a police chief from Oklahoma, and Nash—after which the killers vanished. And though none of the three had any known ties to Kansas City, a local racketeer named Michael James ("Jimmy Needles") LaCapra would later testify that it was Johnny Lazia who arranged to get them safely out of town. True or not, Lazia became the most talked-about man in Kansas City, drawing more popular attention even than Tom Pendergast.

In what was to be a long, often trying, and continuously eventful public life, some days for Harry Truman would stand out always as moments of great personal satisfaction. One was Tuesday, September 5, 1933, in the middle of what otherwise was a particularly difficult and uncertain time for him.

On Tuesday, September 5, the completed new $200,000 county courthouse at Independence—the fifth so-called "remodeling" of the building since 1836—was dedicated with ceremonies and festivities that began early in the morning and stretched on into the night. There were horseshoe-pitching contests, an old fiddlers' contest, a Negro dancing contest, music from seven marching bands and seven drum corps, a bathing beauty contest, a horse show, a street dance, a parade of floats by local merchants, and a historic pageant. The formal dedication itself took place in the afternoon, beginning at two by the old four-faced courthouse clock (it, too, newly refurbished and set now in a colonial cupola), and included speeches by Governor Park and Judge Harry S. Truman.

The day was warm and sunny, the large crowd in good spirits, everybody enjoying the occasion. The homely Victorian scruffiness of the old courthouse had been transformed into something larger, more spacious, and in a style vaguely like that of Philadelphia's Independence Hall, though the architect, Harry's brother-in-law Fred Wallace, was quoted in the day's special edition of the *Examiner* saying that his inspiration for the north and south porticos had been the Greek "Temple of the Winds."

The new building had little of the character of what had stood there before, but was neat and trim, it seemed, with its pink brick and columned porticos, its cupola and refurbished clock and marble lobby—a clear improvement to nearly everyone and to those especially who would work there, numbers of whom were looking down from the open windows upstairs as Judge Truman, in a white suit, delivered his brief, unexceptional remarks from the speaker's platform. The *Examiner* called the building "dignified, spacious, symmetrical" and praised the leadership of the man who, more than any other, had made it possible.

"During the six and one half years of his administration as presiding judge, Harry S. Truman, with the hearty cooperation of his associates on the county bench, has done a number of remarkably big things that will occupy a large place in the history of the county," said the paper, which then went on to list "a few": a $10 million road and bridge system built by two bond issues, a modern hospital at the Jackson County Home for the Aged and Infirm, a Girls' Home for Negroes on the County Farm, a new Kansas City Courthouse estimated to cost $4 million, and now the $200,000 Independence Courthouse. It was a record unmatched in the history of the county.

> During these years of strenuous service to Jackson County [the *Examiner* also wrote of Judge Truman] he has found time to serve as president of the National Old Trails Association, an office he still holds. He has become widely known throughout Missouri, and many of his friends have expressed the opinion that he will fill the office of governor someday. . . .

But to Judge Truman himself, his future remained a large mystery and a worry.

Later in the fall of 1933, outraged that the Roosevelt administration had appointed a Republican as director of the federal reemployment service in Missouri, Tom Pendergast complained to Washington, with the immediate result that the Republican was fired and the job given to Judge Truman. Having no wish to relinquish his place on the county court any sooner than necessary, Harry agreed to serve in this new federal post without pay. He waived the $300-a-month salary and began driving to and from the federal office in Jefferson City, halfway across the state, twice a week. The task was to channel unemployed laborers into jobs with contractors on federal public works, and, with his experience in county projects, he was ideally suited. The long drives also provided time to think about the future.

For Pendergast it was another giant step. In a few months *The Missouri Democrat* (a paper controlled by the organization) could report that 100,000 men and nearly 10,000 women were employed in the state under the new federal (Democratic) program.

Harry found himself reporting to Harry Hopkins, Roosevelt's public works official, and traveling to Washington on government business, something he had never done before.

At long last Harry made up his mind. He would run for Congress, he decided, against the wishes of his wife, who had liked the sound of the collector's job, with its high pay and security, and who greatly preferred staying in Independence. In Congress, Harry told her, he would have the chance for some "power in the nation."

But when he went to see T.J., he was told the choice was no longer his. Pendergast had picked another man, a circuit court judge named Jasper Bell (who would win handily in the primary, and again in November, and go on to serve six terms in Congress). Crestfallen, Harry found himself out in the cold again, "maneuvered out," as he said.

Weeks went by. Nothing more was mentioned, no further offer made. His spirits fell to a new low.

Then, in early May 1934, without warning, everything changed. Stopping at Warsaw, Missouri, on a speaking tour, he received a call from Jim Pendergast asking him to meet as soon as possible at the Bothwell Hotel in Sedalia. It was a matter of importance.

The drive to Sedalia took about half an hour. Pendergast had Jim Aylward with him and the three of them drew up chairs in a corner of the hotel lobby. Harry had no idea what was coming.

There had been a meeting, he was told. T.J. wanted him to run for the United States Senate. Harry was incredulous, almost speechless.

"The Boss is 95 percent for you," Aylward assured him.

"What's wrong with the other five percent?" Truman asked.

"Oh you know what I mean," Aylward said. "The Boss is for you."

He needed time to think, Truman said. They told him he had to do it for the good of the party, and this apparently settled the issue. He agreed to run but said he was broke. In another day or so, Aylward and Jim Pendergast each gave him $500 to get started.

As Harry learned soon enough, he was anything but T.J.'s first choice for the Senate. T.J. had asked at least three others to run, only to be turned down by all three. Jim Reed had been asked first, largely as a courtesy. (*The New York Times* had predicted Reed would be the choice.) When Reed said no, T.J. turned to Joe Shannon, who professed feeling too out of sympathy with the New Deal and said that at his age he preferred to remain in the House. The third and most serious choice was Aylward, who, everyone agreed, would have made a strong candidate and a first-rate senator if elected. His name had been mentioned repeatedly in the papers as a prime possibility. But Aylward had no longing for the life in Washington, he told T.J., no wish to give up time with his family or leave his law practice.

Other names came up. When Jim Pendergast suggested Harry Truman, whose name to this moment had never been on anyone's list, Aylward enthusiastically agreed. T.J. was skeptical. "Do you mean to tell me that you actually believe that Truman can be elected to the United States Senate," Aylward would remember Pendergast exclaiming. But Aylward and Jim persisted until T.J. agreed.

Joe Shannon, when consulted, said he thought T.J.'s initial reaction had been the right one. Truman was "too light," Shannon thought. "A very pleasant sort of fellow," Shannon would later explain to a reporter. "And he's clean. . . . On the other hand . . . I don't think he's heavy enough for the Senate. I can't imagine him there. . . ." But, added Shannon, "Tom hasn't got a field of world-beaters to pick from."

The Truman candidacy was announced on May 14, 1934. Before dawn that morning, alone in a room at the Pickwick Hotel, he had written:

> Tomorrow, today, rather, it is 4 A.M., I have to make the most momentous announcement of my life. I have come to the place where all men strive to be at my age and I thought two weeks ago that retirement on a virtual pension in some minor county office was all that was in store for me.

II

The state of Missouri comprises nearly 70,000 square miles, an area larger than all New England. The population in 1934 was 3.7 million, with more than 1 million people, roughly a third, concentrated in the two largest cities, St. Louis and Kansas City, some 260 miles apart at opposite ends of the state.

The landscape varied enormously, from the low alluvial cottonlands of the southeastern "Boot Heel," along the Mississippi, to the rugged Ozark Hills in the south-central section, to the prairie farmlands along the Kansas border. A dozen railroads crisscrossed the state and a half-dozen airlines flew in and out of St. Louis and Kansas City, while charter plane service was available for such smaller cities as St. Joseph, Springfield, and Joplin. But it was by automobile that Missouri Democrats waged their primary battles for Congress that summer of 1934, with candidates and campaign workers, hundreds of soldiers in the ranks, fanning out over the state, traveling many thousands of miles. And though the two major highways between Kansas City and St. Louis—Route 40 through Columbia, and Route 50 by way of Jefferson City—were the fastest, main-traveled roads, there was hardly a road anywhere, hardtop or dirt, that went untraveled, as each faction tried to win the courthouse towns in a state where there were a total of 114 county seats. And it was a task made no easier by the fact that the summer of 1934 in Missouri was the hottest on record.

The heat came up from the highways in shimmering waves, like a mirage on the desert. "It was 104 yesterday and 102 today," Kathleen Pendergast, the wife of Jim Pendergast, read in a letter from her husband, who had been on the road, "busy running hither and thither," as he said, ever since Harry Truman made his announcement. Jim Pendergast and Jim Aylward had driven first to Jefferson City, to be sure Guy B. Park was "in line," and to call on those state employees—a very great number indeed—who, like Governor Park, owed their jobs to the Kansas City organization. At the same time, some fifty others from Kansas City were traveling the state, dispatched to whichever county or small town they had originally come from, to drum up support for Judge Truman. Jim's assignment for the moment was to call on local newspapers. Distressed by the weather, he longed for a storm to clear the air. But in all the temperature would register 100 degrees or above for twenty-one days in July. Only Harry Truman appeared untroubled by the heat, a peculiarity that would be noticed often in times ahead.

It was Aylward, now chairman of the state committee, who ran the campaign, and the opening Truman rally at Columbia was a model operation, as "Kansas City took over Columbia." An estimated four thousand people filled the lawn in front of the Boone County Courthouse, close by the University of Missouri campus. Besides the busloads of people from Kansas City, a big Jefferson City turnout had been orchestrated—state employees from every department reportedly—and a "newfangled loud speaking truck" stood by to carry Judge Truman's speech, a sure sign, said the papers, of politics brought up to date. With the noise and color of the gathering crowds and an American Legion band pumping away, the mood seemed more like that of a homecoming game.

Harry had two opponents in the race, Jacob L. ("Tuck") Milligan from Richmond, and John J. ("Jack") Cochran from St. Louis, both of whom were Missouri congressmen experienced in the ways of Washington and far better known than Harry. Cochran, a big, friendly, humorous, and honest man, was favored to win. He was "a congressman's congressman," someone known to understand the "wheels-within-wheels" intricacy of government, and who, importantly, also had the support of the St. Louis counterpart of the Pendergast machine, the so-called "Igoe-Dickmann organization." Tuck Milligan, in his favor, was backed by Senator Bennett Clark—Milligan was seen as Clark's way of again challenging Tom Pendergast and gaining a second seat for himself in the Senate—and like his father before him, Clark was a colorful, two-fisted stump speaker.

Opening their campaigns weeks earlier, Milligan and Cochran had both focused on Harry Truman's one clear advantage in the race, the Pendergast power behind him, as his greatest liability, portraying him as a mere machine stooge. Their attacks, furthermore, came just as the excesses of the organization had again become lurid news, as violence in Kansas City's municipal elections left dozens of people injured and four dead. So Harry was an easy mark.

Now, at Columbia, in a speech carried statewide by radio, he lashed back. "It will be remembered that Mr. Milligan and Mr. Cochran journeyed to Kansas City two years ago and sought and received the endorsement of the Kansas City organization for their races for the nomination as congressman at large for Missouri." As for Bennett Clark, he only wanted more power, to make himself boss.

In days following, in Saline County and at Boonville, Harry tried to change the tone and subject. The Depression was the issue, he insisted, declaring his all-out faith in the New Deal. ("A New Deal for Missouri" said a placard in the window of the "newfangled loud speaking truck.") He talked of the capitalist domination of government in bygone Republican times, praised the determination of FDR to end the "rule of the rich" and give the average American a chance. Ninety percent of the wealth of the country was in the hands of 4 percent of the population, he said at Springfield. Roosevelt was "the man of the hour" to chase the money-changers from the temple, "so that the common people of the country could have a chance at the good things of life." The party of Jefferson,

Jackson, and Franklin D. Roosevelt was the party "for the everyday man just like you and me." He called for shorter working hours, higher pay, old-age pensions, payment of the soldiers' bonus. He also called his opponents in the primary his friends and said any remarks he might make about them would be of a purely political nature.

But the Pendergast issue would not go away. And since Milligan and Cochran were both stressing their own all-out support for Roosevelt, Pendergast was in practicality the only issue.

Then, on Tuesday, July 10, with Harry's campaign not yet a week old, the quiet of night in Kansas City exploded with machine-gun fire. It happened at 3:00 A.M. The victim this time was Johnny Lazia, cut down as he was about to open a car door for his wife in front of the Park Central Hotel. Two unknown assailants had been waiting in the dark. Lazia was hit eight times. "Why to me, to Johnny Lazia, who has been a friend to everybody?" he moaned to a doctor at the hospital. According to the account spread across the front page of the early morning edition of the Kansas City *Journal-Post,* he then delivered what were very nearly his last words: "If anything happens, notify Mr. Pendergast . . . my best friend, and tell him I love him."

Tom Pendergast and City Manager McElroy were prominent among the mourners at Holy Rosary Catholic Church for Lazia's funeral, the biggest ever seen in Kansas City, despite a temperature of 106 degrees. "There were at least ten thousand people down around the church who couldn't get in," Jim Pendergast recorded. "Of course a lot of them were simply curiosity seekers, but Johnny did have a world of friends."

The next night, across the state near St. Louis, at Washington, Missouri, Senator Bennett Clark, in support of Tuck Milligan, pulled off his tie, loosened his collar, and tore into Harry Truman as no one ever had until then. It was Missouri politics "with the bark off," the style Missouri loved.

It seems my old friend Judge Harry S. Truman finds it easier to abuse me than to set forth his own qualifications [the senator began slowly]. His opening speech at Columbia, which was attended almost exclusively by a mob from Kansas City—in fact I am informed the natives looked over the crowd to see if Dillinger was there—by a lot of state employees ordered out by their superiors as a condition to holding their jobs and herded over in buses like trucks carrying cattle to market, was largely an attack on me.

Harry fears that someone from the eastern part of Missouri may undertake to set up as boss. Harry Truman fears a boss in Missouri— God save the mark! Harry places the intelligence of the Democrats of Missouri so low and estimates their credulity so high that he actually

207

went into great length in promising people that if elected to the Senate he would not set up as a boss or undertake to dictate to anybody. Why, bless Harry's good kind heart—no one has ever accused him of being a boss or wanting to be a boss and nobody will ever suspect him of trying to dictate to anybody in his own right as long as a certain eminent citizen of Jackson County remains alive and in possession of his health and faculties. . . . In view of the judge's record of subserviency in Jackson County it would seem that his assurances against any assumption of boss-ship are a trifle gratuitous to say the least.

When all three candidates, plus Bennett Clark and Governor Guy B. Park, appeared at a huge picnic in Clay County, north of Kansas City, an annual affair sponsored by St. Munchins Catholic Church, Harry was clearly outclassed. Bennett Clark held the crowd spellbound, though it was Milligan who got the biggest applause. Ten thousand people sat resolutely through four hours of political oratory, as the sun beat down. "Deeply interested in the array of political lights that paraded across the rough board rostrum," wrote a reporter, "the perspiring crowd held its ground throughout."

The president of the Missouri Farmers' Association, William Hirth, joined the Cochran campaign and began referring to Truman as "Tom Pendergast's bellhop." "For this bellhop of Pendergast's to aspire to make a jump from the obscure bench of a county judge to the United States Senate is without precedent. When one contemplates the giants of the past who have represented Missouri this spectacle is not only grotesque, it is sheer buffoonery."

Striking back, Harry charged Milligan with padding the government payroll with relatives, but saved his harshest invective for Bennett Clark. The senator, said Harry, ran for office on his father's reputation, but his record proved there was nothing in heredity.

Many who thought they knew Judge Truman were astonished by the different man he became now, under attack. "Judge Truman is unobtrusive in his work," wrote a correspondent for the St. Louis *Globe-Democrat*. "His decisions are made in low tones; there is no braggadocio about him. He sees his job and does it quietly. But in a fight, this quiet man can and does hurl devastating fire. . . ."

Truman, said Bennett Clark, was conducting a campaign of "mendacity and imbecility" unmatched in Missouri history. "What Harry is really trying to do is to secure a good county job for himself on his retirement from the county court of Jackson County next January. . . . Harry himself told me of his hopes." Perhaps the heat was affecting Harry Truman, Clark surmised, because ordinarily he was neither vicious nor inventive enough to tell such lies. Further, Clark charged that seven or eight thousand state employees were out campaigning for Truman, all at the taxpayers' expense—but then such, alas, was the Pendergast way.

T.J., demonstrating that he still knew a few things about bringing politicians down to size, invited a reporter into his office and in the course of an affable, soft-spoken conversation remarked, "Why, Senator Clark is a friend of mine. He was in here just the other day."

Jack Cochran, to his credit, tried to keep the debate on a serious level. Mud slinging, Cochran said, was a luxury for prosperous times and had no place when conditions were so desperate and so many were suffering. In a speech in front of the Capitol at Jefferson City, Harry Truman, too, talked of his sadness over so much that he had seen traveling the countryside.

Farm prices, in steady decline since the Coolidge years, had gone from bad to worse. Eggs that normally sold for 25 cents a dozen were bringing 5 cents. Since 1930, more than eighteen thousand Missouri farms had been foreclosed. Abandoned houses, their windows boarded, fences falling, dotted the landscape. Sharecroppers were living in two-room, dirt-floor shacks, walls insulated with old newspapers. The look of the land, and in the faces of farm families in this summer of 1934, was as bleak as in anyone's memory. Certainly, Harry Truman had never seen anything comparable. It was both the worst of the Depression and the year dust storms on the western plains began making headlines. With no rain and the fierce heat continuing, crops were burning up all over Missouri. An editorial in the St. Louis *Post-Dispatch* assumed a biblical cadence in its description of the tragedy: "Under merciless summer suns the fields ached, and the corn withered, and the cattle perished, and the rivers became as scars of dust, as the drought droned its hymn of hate."

Conditions, said Truman in one speech, were "such as to make any human with a heart anxious to alleviate them."

He presented himself as a common-sense country boy. He was the good Baptist farmer from Grandview, repeatedly poking fun at his rivals as "city farmers." And he looked the part, deeply tanned from days in the sun, lean, fit, "hard as nails" by one account. He was fifty now and there was considerably more gray in his hair, yet he seemed much younger. He smiled constantly—a big politician's grin, his even, white teeth looking whiter than usual because of the tan, his eyes flashing behind the steel-rimmed glasses. Joe Shannon, among others, thought he smiled entirely too much.

One blistering day, on a road near Mexico, Missouri, seeing a farmer in a field having trouble with his binder, Harry stopped the car, climbed the fence, introduced himself, took off his coat, "and proceeded to set up the binder under a hot sun for his new found friend," as reported in the local paper in a story that did him no harm with the local farmers.

Truman and Cochran were both battling for the farm vote, knowing it could decide the election. Neither of them had a chance without the support of their respective big-city machines, but if the votes for Cochran in St. Louis and those for Truman in Kansas City proved equal, then it would be the farmers who named the winner. Jim Pendergast worried that the farmers were more concerned about the prospects for rain than about politics.

In six weeks candidate Truman covered the greater part of Missouri by automobile, by main highways and winding back roads, until he had appeared before, shaken hands, and "visited" with courthouse crowds in more than half of the 114 county seats. It was hot, exhausting, throat-parching day-and-night work and he greatly enjoyed nearly every moment. He had always liked being on the road. "Fact is, I like roads," he would say. "I like to move. . . ." He felt as good as if he were on vacation, he told reporters, and he looked it.

Again, as on the earlier cross-country courthouse survey, he was accompanied by Fred Canfil, whose hulking, blustery presence left some people wondering. If a man could be judged by the company he kept, why on earth would Judge Truman choose such a companion? But Canfil was as hardworking, as willing to put in ten to fifteen hours a day as ever. Besides, Harry found him amusing, good company, if eccentric and at times exasperating. Arriving at a hotel, Canfil would immediately check Harry's quarters to see that all was satisfactory—bathroom, sink, toilet, bathtub—and oblivious to the fact that he was scattering his cigarette ashes everywhere he went. Canfil and Truman were to be together for years, as things turned out, Truman refusing to abandon Canfil or to make apologies for him.

Some days that summer, they covered several hundred miles, stopping for food and gas and speeches at a dozen or more places. Some towns were good-sized, like Hannibal on the Mississippi, Mark Twain's town, which had grown to twenty thousand people, or Poplar Bluff, seat of Butler County, on the bright, clear, misnamed Black River, in the southeastern corner of the state. Poplar Bluff had a population of ten thousand. More often the candidate spoke in places like Laddadonia, Elmo, Liberty, or Benton, towns of six hundred people or less. At Benton, seat of Scott County, population four hundred and known for its chicken-calling contest on Neighbor Day each October, bobcats were still a sufficient menace in the 1930s to require an organized "drive" on them. At Liberty, just north of the Missouri River from Independence in Clay County, the little, two-story bank building on the northeast corner of the courthouse square looked no different from the day in 1866 when it was held up by Jesse James.

The crowds that turned out to hear Judge Truman were seldom large, no more usually than a cluster of a few hundred people standing quietly, attentively in the shade of a courthouse lawn, while in his rapid-fire fashion he spoke from the courthouse steps. A good part of his usual audience was composed of courthouse loafers, old-timers with nothing better to do, and, invariably, small boys free from school for the summer. The atmosphere was old-fashioned and neighborly, and though the response to him was rarely demonstrative, he seemed always to leave his crowds feeling better.

For a scrapbook of the campaign, Fred Canfil kept clipping the local papers along the way. One item dated August 3, from an unidentified paper, acknowledged that Judge Truman was no orator, but then this was an argument in his favor since there was already too much oratory in the United States Senate.

At a banquet in his honor at the Baltimore Hotel in Kansas City the week before the primary, Tuck Milligan brought seven hundred people to their feet cheering when, without mentioning Tom Pendergast by name, he said that anyone who perpetrated vote fraud in America ought to be treated as a common criminal. As for his opponent Harry Truman, who was still campaigning at the other end of the state, Milligan joked, "Why, if Harry ever goes to the Senate, he will grow calluses on his ears, listening on the long-distance telephone to the orders of his boss."

Milligan by now was clearly falling behind, while Cochran and Truman appeared to be neck and neck.

On the day of the primary, August 7, once the smoke blew away, as Harry said, he had won by 40,000 votes. The final tally was Truman, 276,850; Cochran, 236,105. Milligan, who ran a poor third, received 147,614.

Harry had done well with the farmers, but so had Cochran, carrying as many counties as Truman. The big margin of victory after all was in Jackson County, where a grand total of 137,000 votes had been rolled up for Truman, nearly half of all he received. Two years before, with Pendergast support in his race for Congress, Cochran had carried Jackson County by an overwhelming 95,000 votes. This time, with the organization against them, Cochran and Milligan together received all of 11,000 votes. In some Kansas City precincts Cochran failed to get a single vote.

Cochran felt his big mistake in the race had been to predict he would get 125,000 votes in St. Louis. This, he thought, had only made the Pendergast people work harder. As it was, Cochran's margin in St. Louis (and St. Louis County) was 112,000—25,000 votes less than what had been achieved by the machine at the other end of the state.

The Kansas City *Star* called it a Pendergast triumph pure and simple. The one consolation was that western Missouri would now have representation in the Senate. The St. Louis *Post-Dispatch* expressed the view that the winning of the Democratic nomination for United States Senator by Judge Harry S. Truman of Independence was "without significance."

No one seemed to think that Truman himself had had a thing to do with his victory, and he himself was quoted saying only how much he appreciated all that his friends had done for him.

As expected, the general election in the fall was a "pushover." Harry's Republican opponent was the incumbent who proudly carried the name of an infamous New York Republican of the Grant era, Roscoe Conkling. He was Roscoe Conkling Patterson. Harry's expenses in the primary had come to $12,286. In the general election they were $785.

Afterward, he and Jim Aylward made a flying visit to Washington to call on Bennett Clark, who had been the biggest loser in the primary fight and who now, looking to his own reelection a few years hence, preferred to forget all he had ever said against his "good friend" Harry Truman and the Kansas City organization.

In a talk before the Kansas City Elks Club, Harry said he hoped to keep his feet on the ground in Washington.

By December, the final touches were being added to the handsome new, twenty-one-story courthouse in Kansas City. On the day of its dedication, after Christmas, as her father beamed with pleasure, ten-year-old Margaret Truman helped pull the string to unveil Charles Keck's equestrian bronze of Andrew Jackson. Margaret had grown tall for her age, "skinny and all one color—faded blonde," a friend would remember, and clearly she enjoyed being her father's daughter.

As a reward for faithful service, Fred Canfil was made Building Director of Jackson County, a kind of glorified custodian or janitor for the new courthouse, and would, according to later testimony, prove "very energetic" and "very noisy and loudmouthed," and run things better than any other previous custodian.

They were exciting days for the Trumans. The week after, on January 3,

1935, Bess and Margaret, with Jim Pendergast, watched from the visitors' gallery in the United States Senate as Harry, "barely recognizable" in morning coat and striped pants, walked with Senator Clark down the blue-carpeted aisle to the dais, to take the oath of office from Vice President John Nance Garner.

On the day Harry bid goodbye to Tom Pendergast in Kansas City, Pendergast had told him, "Work hard, keep your mouth shut, and answer your mail."

III

Harry Truman had an unusually retentive mind. He remembered people—names, personal interests, family connections. He remembered things he had read or learned in school long before, often bringing them into conversation in a way that amazed others. He remembered every kindness he had ever been shown, the help given in hard times, and particularly would he remember those who treated him well when he first arrived in Washington, at age fifty, knowing almost no one and entirely without experience as a legislator. He would fondly recall Harry Hopkins, for example, because Hopkins had shown him kindness in this most difficult of times in his life. Another was William Helm, Washington correspondent for the Kansas City *Journal-Post,* to whom the new senator had gone for help at the start, confessing he was "green as grass" and in need of someone to show him around. At first, Helm took this as a joke. Here, he thought, was the eighth natural wonder of the world, a politician who didn't take himself too seriously, a friendly, likable, warmhearted fellow with a lot of common sense hidden under an overpowering inferiority complex.

Two other new Democratic senators, Carl Hatch of New Mexico and Lewis Schwellenbach of Washington, went out of their way to be friendly. Hatch was self-effacing and bookish, Schwellenbach "a real guy" and "a wheel horse." Among the older, veteran senators, Harry could count a half dozen from both sides of the aisle who gave encouragement, and like Hatch and Schwellenbach, they were all from the West, or were at least western in outlook.

Extremely important to Harry, as events proved, was Burton K. Wheeler, a lanky, independent-minded Montana Democrat, something of a rogue, who smoked big cigars and ran the powerful Interstate Commerce Committee.

Carl Hayden of Arizona, another Democrat, had come to Congress in

1911, as a territorial representative. "He took the trouble to explain some of the technicalities and customs of the Senate which appear pretty confusing to a newcomer," Harry would write. Republicans Arthur Vandenberg of Michigan and old William E. Borah, "the Lion of Idaho," never treated him as anything but an equal. And most memorable was seventy-two-year-old J. Hamilton ("Ham") Lewis of Illinois, the majority whip, who wore pince-nez, wing collars, spats, and a wavy pink toupee to match his pink Vandyke whiskers and sweeping mustache, and who one day came and sat down in an empty seat beside Senator Truman.

"Harry, don't start out with an inferiority complex," Lewis said kindly. "For the first six months you'll wonder how the hell you got here, and after that you'll wonder how the hell the rest of us got here."

He was liked also by the red-faced, hard-drinking Vice President, "Cactus Jack" Garner of Texas, who still dressed in a swallow-tailed coat and striped pants, and who, echoing T.J.'s parting words, told Truman to study hard and keep quiet until he knew what he was talking about. It was advice Garner always gave beginners, but that not all heeded. He, too, was a man of little formal education and obscure background. Now and then as time passed, he would ask Truman to take the Vice President's chair and preside over the Senate. On a day when Will Rogers came to Capitol Hill for lunch, Garner invited Harry to come along, a favor and an occasion Harry would never forget.

Such gestures were the exception, however. "I was under a cloud," he would say later. The Kansas City reputation had followed him to Washington. Bennett Clark was spoken of as the Senator from Missouri. Harry Truman was the Senator from Pendergast.

Bronson Cutting of New Mexico had a way of looking through Truman as though he didn't exist. Pat McCarran of Nevada later recalled, "I never considered him a Senator." George W. Norris of Nebraska, the great voice of reform in the Senate, thought he was "poison," and refused to speak to him.

When a congressional aide named Victor Messall, a native Missourian and an experienced hand on the Hill, was offered a job on Senator Truman's staff, he refused, fearing what the association might do to his career. "Here was a guy ... sent up [to Washington] by gangsters," he remembered. "I'd lose my reputation if I worked for him."

Messall only changed his mind after volunteering to help the senator hunt for an apartment, which they found on Connecticut Avenue—four rooms in the Tilden Gardens apartments for $150 a month. Later, they stopped at a piano store, where Truman sat down and played several before choosing one to rent for five dollars a month. From there they went to a bank. While Messall waited, the senator took out a loan for furniture.

This, Messall decided, was an altogether different kind of man from what he imagined and one he now wanted very much to work for. A slim, snappy dresser, his hair slicked back Fred Astaire style, Messall became number one of a staff of five in Truman's office. The reporter William Helm would describe him watching over the senator thereafter with "doglike devotion."

Making his first call at the White House in February, a nervous Senator Truman found Secretary of the Interior Harold Ickes, Secretary of Agriculture Henry Wallace, and one or two others high up in the administration sitting about the waiting room, busily talking and paying no notice of him. Though scheduled for fifteen minutes with the President, his time was cut to seven, during which he remained tongue-tied before Roosevelt. "It was quite an event for a country boy to go calling on the President of the United States," he remembered. His telephone calls to the White House in the months to follow often went unanswered.

"He came to the Senate, I believe, with a definite inferiority complex," wrote his boyhood friend Charlie Ross, who had become a Washington correspondent for the St. Louis *Post-Dispatch*. "He was a better man than he knew."

His diligence was noteworthy. Most mornings, he turned up at his office so early—about seven—and so in advance of everyone else in the building that it was decided he should have his own passkey, reportedly the first ever issued to a senator. Indeed, he would rise and be on his way so early in the morning that by mid-afternoon he would look in need of another shave. He carried himself straighter than a tall man would, walked considerably faster than customary in Washington. On good days he walked the several miles to the Capitol, moving along at a steady military clip of 120 paces a minute and stopping usually at Childs restaurant for breakfast. When he didn't walk, he took the trolley that ran down Connecticut Avenue, then swung east on Pennsylvania, past the White House, and on up to the Capitol.

"By the time his colleagues get down to work," wrote William Helm, "Senator Truman has been through the morning mail, dictated several hundred letters, fixed up as many deserving Democrats with jobs as possible and is rarin' to go."

That his ties to Tom Pendergast continued, he left no doubt. To one Kansas City job applicant who asked his support, he wrote, "If you will send us the endorsements from the Kansas City Democratic Organization, I shall be glad to do what I can for you." This, in his view, was how the game had always been played, not by Tom Pendergast only, but in American politics overall, from the beginning, and he was never to view it differently. To the victors went the spoils.

He saw to the appointment of hundreds of people to hundreds of different jobs in Missouri, including old friends and family. His brother Vivian would go to work for the Federal Housing Agency in Kansas City. Ted Marks was set up in a job with the Labor Department, in the Veterans Employment Service in Kansas City. Edgar Hinde became postmaster in Independence, a job he held for twenty-five years.

In the reception area of his office, over the marble mantelpiece where no one could possibly miss it, Senator Truman put a framed portrait of T. J. Pendergast.

His office was Number 248, on the second floor of the immense Senate Office Building (later named the Russell Building) northeast of the Capitol, his windows looking onto an interior courtyard. In the Senate Chamber he was assigned seat 94, one of seven newly installed behind the back row on the Democratic side to accommodate the disproportionate Democratic majority. To his right sat Sherman Minton of Indiana. The seat on the left remained empty until June when the newly elected Senator from West Virginia, Rush Holt, would turn thirty and thus be old enough, according to the Constitution, to take his place.

Of the ninety-six senators in this the 74th Congress, there were, including Senator Holt, sixty-nine Democrats and twenty-seven Republicans. Bennett Clark sat almost directly ahead, two rows down. Beyond Clark, about midway in the second row, was Tom Connally of Texas, who still wore the black bow tie and old-fashioned stand-up collar of the classic southern statesman. Alben Barkley of Kentucky and Hugo Black of Alabama, two senators of great importance to the administration, were also in the second row, and Ellison DuRant ("Cotton Ed") Smith of South Carolina, who was known for his orations on King Cotton and Southern Womanhood and his near-perfect aim with tobacco juice. In the majority leader's front-row seat on the aisle sat Joseph T. Robinson of Arkansas, while over near the other end of the first row, to Harry's left, in seat 17, was the storm center of the chamber, the place of Huey Long of Louisiana, whose rampant outbursts against the administration lately included the charge that Franklin Roosevelt was personally trying to destroy him.

The year before, Long had proclaimed his "National Share Our Wealth Program," promising to make "Every man a king, every girl a queen," and through Harry Truman's first months in the Senate, Long dominated, upstaging everyone. In early February he opened an assault on Jim Farley, charging that Farley's operations were steeped in corruption. Then, on February 20, calling Farley a "political monster," Long inserted in the *Congressional Record* an article from the *Post-Dispatch* describing how T. J. Pendergast had arranged with Farley to call off Internal Revenue investigations of Johnny Lazia. Long afterward told Harry it was only a little politics to please the home folks.

On the day of another Long tirade, when Harry was presiding in the Vice President's chair, most of the Senate got up and walked out. Later, when he and Long found themselves crossing the street together, heading for the Senate Office Building, Long asked how Harry had liked the speech. He had stayed, Harry said, only because he was in the chair and had no choice. Thereafter Long refused to speak to him. In September in Louisiana, Long would be shot and killed by an assassin.

But if repelled by someone like Huey Long, Harry cared little more for other celebrated "speechifiers" in the Senate. Admittedly fearful of making a speech himself, he seemed to resent particularly those who could and who made their reputations that way. They were the "egotistical boys" whose specialty was talk.

Watching Senator Truman from the press gallery, William Helm wrote, "He sits in the back row of the top-heavy Democratic side of the Senate at every session, listening, absorbing, learning. . . . His is the conventional way. He ruffles no oldster's feathers, treads on no toes."

Four months passed before he dared introduce his first bill. It concerned a subject he knew about from experience—"A Bill to provide insurance by the Farm Credit Administration of mortgages on farm property"—and was sent by Vice President Garner to the Committee on Banking and Currency, where it promptly died.

As customary for freshman senators, he was assigned to two major and several lesser committees. In former days, the Committee on Appropriations would have been a position of dignity, little work, and little significance, but in the New Deal Washington of 1935 it was the largest committee of all, its power unprecedented. The appropriation that January of $4.8 billion for work relief represented approximately half what the government spent. Interstate Commerce, the committee of which Burton K. Wheeler was chairman, seemed a natural place for Harry, with his background in roads and highways, his lifelong fascination with railroads. The smaller assignments included the Public Buildings and Grounds Committee, and the Printing Committee, headed by Carl Hayden and responsible primarily for the *Congressional Record*. (Mamma Truman had asked Harry to put her on the list for the *Record* and became a steadfast reader.) The one assignment he did not care for was the District of Columbia Committee, which eventually he quit. He thought the District ought to have self-government.

He worked exceedingly hard at his assignments. Indeed, his first years in the Senate were devoted almost exclusively to committee work. Seldom did he miss a meeting of the two major committees, where, it was also noted, "He speaks rarely, listens much." He was getting acquainted with the way things were done, which most veteran senators and staff people knew to be an art in itself. He was acutely aware of his limited formal education, and in a determined effort to compensate for it, he never let up. Assigned by Senator Wheeler to a new Interstate Commerce subcommittee investigating railroad finances, he searched the Library of Congress for books on railroad management, railroad history, until more than fifty volumes were piled in his office. "I'm going to be better informed on the transportation problem than anyone here," he vowed privately. What surprised and disappointed him was to find how few others from Congress ever used the Library.

He had come into national public life at the start of "the Second Hundred Days," the high tide of the New Deal. The crusade now was not just recovery from the Depression, but for reform, and he voted with the Democratic majority time after time, helping to pass some of the most far-reaching legislation in the history of Congress. He never once spoke for a measure, never took part in debate. He just voted—for the Wagner Labor Relations Act, guaranteeing the right of workers to join unions and to bargain collectively; for establishment of the Works Progress Administration; for the Social Security Act; and for rural electrification, which may have changed the way people lived more than any other single measure of the Roosevelt years. In his own state in 1935, nine out of ten farms had no electricity.

As a member of the Interstate Commerce Committee, he worked intensively on what became the Public Utility Holding Company Act, designed as a blow against public power cartels, and in the process had his first brush with big-time lobbying and high-powered witnesses. The lobby set up headquarters in a suite at the Mayflower Hotel.

He resolved to deny no one a hearing. "I'll take all the dinners he has to put out," he would later write of a lobbyist for a midwestern railroad, "and then do what I think is right." A true son of Missouri, he wanted all the facts. "I can see no harm in talking to anyone—no matter what his background. In fact I think everyone has a right to be heard if you expect to get all the facts."

At the hearings, witnesses for the public utilities included such prominent Wall Street figures as Wendell Willkie, president of the Commonwealth & Southern, and John W. Davis, the former Democratic presidential candidate. The "propaganda barrage," as Truman attested, was such as no county judge in Missouri had ever experienced. Constituents with utility stocks sent thirty thousand letters and telegrams. (He burned them all, Harry claimed years later, though Mildred Dryden, his secretary, would remember no such conflagration.) The lobby also sent people to Kansas City to see Tom Pendergast, who apparently took their side. But that too failed, according to Harry. In June, the bill passed the Senate by a wide margin as expected, with Senator Truman paired in favor. Detained "on important business," he had arranged to vote for the bill if the outcome looked close. (The important business was driving Bess and Margaret back to Independence for the summer. After five months, they had had enough of Washington.)

"I was a New Dealer from the start," he would say firmly and proudly later, and the record showed that few in the Senate could match his record of support for Franklin Roosevelt. Senator Robert Wagner of New York, author of so much New Deal legislation, was to praise Senator Truman as extremely useful. Yet in manner, background, language, age, choice of companions, he bore no resemblance to the ardent young New Dealers portrayed by one historian as "trained in the law, economics, public administration, or new technical fields, brilliant and dedicated ... nurtured on progressive ideals, schooled in the improved universities of the 1920's." Like so many things about Washington, liberals were a new experience for him, and generally speaking, he didn't care for them, unless they were of the Burton Wheeler variety, western in style and a bit rough about the edges. The rest seemed lacking in common sense, for all their education. He was heart and soul an Andrew Jackson–William Jennings Bryan–T. J. Pendergast kind of Democrat. He loved politics in large part exactly because it meant time spent with men like Cactus Jack Garner (who would be remembered for observing that the vice presidency was not worth a pitcher of warm piss). Privately he enjoyed poking fun at "the boys with the 'Hah-vud' accents," though never, as far as is known, at the Harvard man in the White House.

He voted with the President repeatedly because he genuinely wanted to do what was best for the common people at a time when so many were in desperate need of help. He considered himself one of them. He knew what they were suffering. But he knew also, of course, the value of voting with the President—the leader, "the Boss"—both as an article of faith and as a way ahead. Alben Barkley of Kentucky, assistant to the majority leader, would describe later how he had liked Harry Truman almost at once, instinctively. "As the old political saying goes, he 'voted right.' "

To many liberals in the Senate he was "go-along, get-along Harry," a decent, sincere man whose company they often enjoyed—"I liked Harry Truman," Claude Pepper of Florida remembered—but he was not someone to take seriously.

The President had told Congress it could not go home without passing his entire program. So Congress labored through the sweltering summer of 1935, the worst summer of the Dust Bowl, the summer when, for the benefit of the newsreel cameras, on a day the temperature hit 110 degrees, one Texas congressman fried an egg on the Capitol steps. Harry called it "a hot wave," in a letter to Bess and Margaret, but he never complained about the heat or the work, only about their being so far from him.

He gave up the apartment, moved to a hotel to save money, and wrote to them constantly, from his room or the office, or at his desk in the Senate and particularly if someone like Huey Long were "spouting." Long had begun calling the President a "faker" and predicting revolution if things didn't soon change. Once he held the floor for fifteen and one-half hours, sometimes reading from the Bible or offering recipes for Roquefort salad dressing.

Harry's spelling was not much improved from years past, for all he had advanced in station. He had trouble with words like "occasion," which he wrote "occation." He couldn't spell "Hawaii" and wrote of Senator Byrnes as "Senator Burns." He failed even with the spelling of his own home address, addressing envelopes repeatedly to Mrs. Harry S. Truman at 219 North "Deleware" Street.

In the month of July alone, he wrote thirty-four letters to her. To pass the evenings, he read Volume One of Douglas Southall Freeman's biography of Robert E. Lee. Or he would work his way through *The New York Times*. Always an ardent reader of newspapers, like most politicians, he was now taking the Washington *Star,* the Washington *Post,* and the Baltimore *Sun,* in addition to several Missouri papers, but he saved *The New York Times* for the quiet of evening. It was the summer Will Rogers was killed in a plane crash in Alaska, news that left Harry feeling devastated. Rogers had been a second Mark Twain, he told Bess. "No one has done more to give us common sense."

One evening, with a dozen others from the Senate, he crossed the Potomac to attend a party given by the chairman of the new Securities and Exchange Commission, Joseph P. Kennedy, at Kennedy's rented estate, Marwood, a thirty-three-room Renaissance château in the cool of the woods above the river. In a letter to Bess, Harry described it as "a grand big house a half mile from the road in virgin forest with a Brussels carpet lawn of five acres all around it, a swimming pool in the yard, and all the other trimmings." He had never been in such a house. He was told it had cost $600,000 to build. He felt complimented to be included in such a party, but of his host he had nothing to relate.

He was trying to find an apartment they could afford for the year ahead:

> Found a rather nice place at 1921 Kalorama Road. It was a northwest corner, fifth-floor apartment—two bedrooms, two baths, living room, small dining room, large hall, $125 per month. *No* garage. Then I looked at a house at 2218 Cathedral, a block north of Connecticut. . . . They were painting and papering it from cellar to attic. It had a two-car garage. . . . They wanted $90 per month. I then went down to the High-lands at California and Connecticut. They had a nice two-bedroom apartment on the southeast corner, fourth floor, at $125—better I think than 1921 Kalorama Road. Then I looked at the Westmoreland right behind the Highlands on California. They wanted $100 for a two-bed-room apartment on the sixth floor, and $79.50 for one on the fourth floor that had four rooms. It is an old place but the location and rooms were very nice. . . . I am going back to look at 2400 Sixteenth Street and the Jefferson tomorrow and a couple of houses. I bet I find something that'll suit before I quit.

Not only was he the Senator from Pendergast, he was one of the poor-est of senators, a point he felt acutely. He never ceased worrying about money and whether he could make ends meet in Washington on a salary of $10,000. In his letters to Bess he reported the amount of his bus fare (20 cents), the charge for six months of the Washington *Post* ($7.50), an old grocery bill ($9.53). Thinking he might go over to the Maryland seashore for the Fourth of July weekend, he was "extravagant" and bought a bathing suit, but then went to a public health dentist to have two teeth filled. He had always wanted to be able to buy house furnish-ings of his own choosing. He dreamed extravagant dreams, he told her— of paintings by Holbein and Frans Hals, of Bokhara carpets, Hepplewhite dining table and chairs, and mahogany beds ("big enough for two"). But she must have faith in him:

> I am hoping to make a reputation as a Senator . . . if I live long enough that'll make the money success look like cheese. But you'll have to put

up with a lot if I do it because I won't sell influence and I'm perfectly willing to be cussed if I'm right.

On three occasions in midsummer he traveled to New York to see Tom Pendergast, who was living like a potentate in a twenty-ninth-floor suite at the Waldorf-Astoria at a daily rate that would have covered Harry's rent for a month. To his surprise and delight, T.J.'s welcome was the warmest ever. "Pendergast was as pleased to see me as if I'd been young Jim," Harry reported to Bess after the first meeting. "We talked for three hours about everything under the sun." On the second visit, two weeks later, T.J. was "as pleased to see me as a ten-year-old kid to see his lost pal."

Hints of a huge insurance scandal were in the wind, involving a Pendergast man in the state government, R. Emmett O'Malley, Missouri's Superintendent of Insurance. Marquis Childs of the *Post-Dispatch* had been to the Waldorf to interview T.J. earlier in the spring, before T.J. sailed for France on the new *Normandie,* and in the course of the questioning, T.J. had said, "Yes, I told O'Malley to approve the insurance deal," adding angrily, "And what're you going to do about it?" which had been a mistake. (When Childs went to the ship later, to see T.J. off, he found him in a better mood. "Pendergast and the very blond Mrs. Pendergast were ensconced in the living room of their suite which was almost literally filled with flowers, orchids and lilies of the valley, expensive flowers. This was Pendergast, the Maharajah of Missouri, in all his glory.") But apparently Harry's conversations at the Waldorf included none of the truth of what was going on behind the scenes with O'Malley, even if to Harry it appeared as though he and T.J. had covered "everything under the sun."

One topic they did take up was a replacement for Governor Park, who by Missouri law could serve only a single term. Harry thought perhaps it should be a wealthy Pike County apple grower named Lloyd C. Stark. Harry and Stark had met through the American Legion—Stark, too, had served as an artillery officer in France—and had compared notes as time went on, Stark confiding his own political ambitions. Harry had been a guest at Stark's estate in Pike County, in northeastern Missouri, home of the Stark nursery, largest in the United States and famous for the Stark "Delicious" apple. At Stark's urging, Harry had provided him with a list of key people throughout the state and put in a word for him at 1908 Main Street. "Confidentially, I had a fine visit with our mutual friend in Kansas City last Friday," Stark had written Harry that spring of 1935, delighted by how things were shaping up.

But T.J. didn't like Stark and had already crossed him off as a possible governor at the time of Francis Wilson's death. (At Wilson's funeral, a news photographer happened to catch the massive Big Boss and the trim, elegantly tailored apple grower, each with cigarette in hand, deep in conversation among the parked cars.) Neither T.J. nor Jim Aylward thought Stark could be trusted and told Harry so.

"He won't do," said T.J. "I don't like the son-of-a-bitch. He's no good."

Long afterward, Harry would remark to a friend, "The old man had better judgment than I did."

However, as was said, the apple grower was also an accomplished apple polisher, and when Harry took both Stark and Bennett Clark with him on a third trip to the Waldorf that summer, T.J. at last consented. Stark was to have the organization's full support—which meant Stark could count on being the next governor—and, of course, with the implicit understanding that the organization could in turn count on Stark.

On the train back to Washington, Stark, "the most grateful man alive," promised to do anything to help Harry any time. He had only to say the word.

Relations with Bennett Clark, meanwhile, were also improving. Few in the Senate had been quite so contemptuous of Truman as Clark during Harry's first several months, and Clark still did little to make Harry's job any easier. Clark also seemed to go out of his way to annoy or embarrass the administration, and yet invariably it was Clark that Roosevelt worked with on federal appointments in Missouri, not Senator Truman, who voted consistently with the administration. It was Roosevelt's way of trying to win Clark over, and Clark's way of getting more than his share of patronage, all of which left Harry far out in the cold, trying to swallow his pride and resentment. Further, Clark had little time for what Harry called "the ordinary customers" from back home who had favors to ask or troubles to settle.

But Clark, as Harry recognized, was a man with an extraordinary mind, who knew the Constitution and parliamentary law as well as anyone in the Senate. He was hugely entertaining, a good host, a good cook—country ham with red-eye gravy and turnip greens his specialty—and like Cactus Jack Garner he enjoyed a sociable "libation" over lunch, or in mid-afternoon, or day's end, or most any time. Harry adored the banter and storytelling that went with this side of senatorial life. It was closer to the comradeship of Army life than anything else he had known. He enjoyed Clark's humor as they "took a little something to settle the nerves." At a lunch for the health faddist Bernarr Macfadden, they regarded each other with long faces across the table. "Kind of hard on Bennett and me to attend a dry lunch in this town," Harry noted.

In his office, for special guests like Clark, Harry kept a supply of T.J.'s best bourbon. ("And while I heard criticism aplenty of Pendergast himself," recorded William Helm, "I have yet to hear a noble senator raise his voice against the quality of Pendergast liquor.") Other "supplies for the thirsty" were kept by the Secretary of the Senate, Colonel Edwin Halsey (and later by his successor, Les Biffle), in an office only a short stroll across the hall from the chamber. Unlike Clark, Harry kept to a rule of one stroll, one drink only.

Though younger than Harry by six years, Clark was heavyset and jowly, and with his thinning hair looked both older and more senatorial. Clark's biography in the *Congressional Directory,* written by Clark himself, took up nearly three-quarters of a page of fine print. Senator Truman's, also self-penned, consisted of three lines.

A year later, in the summer of 1936, as the Democrats convened in Philadelphia to renominate Franklin Roosevelt for a second term, Harry was with T.J. again, and more conspicuously now than at any time in years past. Just back from still another European vacation—he had returned this time on the maiden voyage of the *Queen Mary*—T.J. came down to Philadelphia by train from New York, planning to commute back and forth every day from his suite at the Waldorf. He arrived Tuesday, June 23, the morning the convention opened. Jim Farley, chairman of the national committee, Jim Aylward, and Senator Truman clustered about him to pose for pictures on the convention floor, T.J. beaming as the flash cameras exploded.

All the big bosses of the Democratic Party were gathered in Philadelphia—Franklin Roosevelt's favorite, the urbane, affable, extremely powerful Edward J. Flynn of the Bronx; tall, natty Frank Hague of Jersey City, who would be remembered by history for his comment, "I am the law"; Mayor Edward J. Kelly of Chicago; E. H. ("Boss Ed") Crump of Memphis, former farm boy and noted bird lover; and T. J. Pendergast, a white carnation in his lapel, who the day before had celebrated his sixty-fourth birthday. At one time or other, Roosevelt had courted and worked with them all, depending on their help, and he would again. He called them all his friends. And all appreciated perfectly what wonders the Roosevelt magic had worked for them in four years. As Marquis Childs observed, "The vast expenditures of the New Deal had put into their hands power they had hitherto scarcely dreamed of." Though no one could know it at the time, the day was to mark T.J.'s last big public appearance. So, as a gathering of the era's big-city Democratic bosses, all figuratively on stage together, it was a final, historic moment.

Harry, who had driven up from Washington, had no real part to play.

He had been named to no committees of importance. He was only a delegate-at-large. He was there really to be with Pendergast, and indeed the group photograph taken on the convention floor is the only known picture of him at the Boss's side.

Returning by train to New York that night, Pendergast was suddenly taken ill. The doctors diagnosed coronary thrombosis. Harry, who had stayed on in Philadelphia but did not bother to remain for Roosevelt's speech the final night, apparently was not told for some time how serious the situation had become. In August, still confined to his hotel room, T.J. suffered another relapse and was rushed to Roosevelt Hospital for surgery. He had intestinal cancer and the operation required the closing of his rectum. For T.J. it meant the use of a tube in his side for the rest of his life.

Had T.J. only died that summer, Harry Truman would later reflect, his reputation would have been secure as the greatest political boss of the time. But it was not to be.

Not until September was Pendergast able to return to Kansas City, traveling by train in a special car and with great secrecy. By then the primaries were over, the organization having performed at peak efficiency: Lloyd C. Stark was the Democratic nominee for governor and as certain of election in November as was Franklin D. Roosevelt.

IV

During the second half of his first term in the Senate, Truman felt the cloud he was under begin to recede. His standing among his colleagues improved. He was assigned more spacious offices down the hall, suite No. 240, again looking onto the interior courtyard. By his own staff, by others on his committees, he was perceived as dogged, productive, respectful of the opinion of others, good-natured, and extremely likable. "We all found Truman a very nice man . . . [and] his heart was in the right place," recalled the historian Telford Taylor, who was then a young attorney on the Interstate Commerce Commission. The senator's patience, even with the dreariest assignments, seemed infinite. And though no one would have singled him out as exceptional in any particular way or predicted a brilliant future—"But he showed no signs of leadership," Taylor also remembered—his reputation was clearly on the rise.

The Republican Borah, one of the Senate's certified great men, made a point one day of throwing his arm about Senator Truman's shoulder in an open show of friendship. Truman was even attempting an occasional speech in the chamber by this time, reading always from prepared texts heavy with facts and figures. Once, in the middle of a debate, Arthur Vandenberg called on him to substantiate a point and after Truman obliged, Vandenberg told the Senate, "When the Senator from Missouri makes a statement like that we can take it for the truth." It was a gesture Harry would not forget.

"He was always going out of his way to do favors for others and you couldn't help but like his smiling, friendly manner," said Vic Messall, "...and he was that way with everyone. I never heard him say a cross word to his staff, and that's a real test...." Mildred Dryden, Truman's secretary, said, "Never in all the years that I worked for him did I ever see him lose his temper. He was always soft-spoken and very considerate to his staff...." She remembered no "salty language" either, never ever if women were present.

Alben Barkley, though he had liked Harry Truman "instinctively" from the start, said that his real appreciation of the man only came clear to him at the dramatic climax of the battle over Roosevelt's Court-packing plan, the contentious, frustrating issue that dominated in 1937.

In his acceptance speech at the Philadelphia convention—the speech Harry had missed hearing but called a masterpiece after reading it in the papers—Roosevelt said, "To some generations much is given. Of other generations much is expected. This generation of Americans has a rendezvous with destiny." In his second inaugural address in January 1937, the President became more specific. "I see one third of a nation ill-housed, ill-clad, ill-nourished," he said, and the Congress, like the country, had waited in anticipation to see what new legislation he would demand.

In the first week of February came the surprise. It was the Supreme Court he was out to "reform"—really to reshape to his liking—because the Court had found some earlier New Deal programs unconstitutional. His scheme was to enlarge the Court from nine members to fifteen if justices refused to retire at the age of seventy, and after the landslide in November, which gave him the largest majority in Congress ever enjoyed by a President, Roosevelt felt confident of having his way. He neither consulted with the leadership in Congress nor gave any advance word of what he was up to. The President was wrong in his approach; the whole attempt to influence the decisions of the Court by increasing its size was a blunder, damaging to Roosevelt and to the Senate.

Opposition in the Senate was fierce, and especially among Democrats, including not just conservatives like Carter Glass and Bennett Clark, but such formerly reliable Roosevelt men as Connally and Wheeler, who now led the fight against the Court-packing bill. Barkley, Truman, virtually every Democratic senator who had been a steadfast Roosevelt supporter now found himself caught between vehement pressure from the White House on the one hand and, on the other, outrage at home over the whole idea. By June, even Garner, Roosevelt's own Vice President, had become so infuriated over the affair that he packed his bags and went back to Texas. "The people are with me," Roosevelt had snapped when Garner took issue with him. A disappointed Carter Glass thought probably the Senate was with him, too, so great was the Roosevelt magic. "Of course I shall oppose it," said Glass. "I shall oppose it with all the strength that remains to me, but I don't imagine for a minute that it'll do any good. Why, if the President asked Congress to commit suicide tomorrow they'd do it."

Truman, like Barkley, decided to stand with the President, on the grounds that the size of the Court had been changed before in times past. But he took no part in the debate. He was preoccupied with the railroad investigations, where Wheeler, because of his part in the Court battle, had lost interest and left him most of the work, making Truman vice-chairman of the subcommittee. In June, in the midst of the Court fight, Harry ventured his longest, most daring speech thus far in the Senate, a preliminary report of the railroad investigations. As summer came on, he would have preferred greatly to stay free of the whole Court issue and like so many wished only that it had never happened. He found himself deluged with angry mail. Having announced his position on the bill, he was accused of being a Roosevelt stooge. His headaches returned.

At the White House the President's advisers were saying that if this fight were won, everything else he wanted would "fall into the basket."

But all strategies were suddenly shattered on July 14, when Majority Leader Joseph Robinson, who had been carrying the fight for Roosevelt, fell dead in his apartment across from the Capitol, the victim of a heart attack. Only days before Senator Royal Copeland, who was a physician, had slipped into a seat beside Robinson to warn him that he should slow down.

Bess, who was suffering acutely from Washington's oppressive heat, voiced worries about her own husband's stamina in a letter to Ethel Noland. "H. is worn out and is not well and will simply have to have a good rest or he will be really ill."

The fight on the Court was deferred until a new majority leader could be named. In the running were Barkley and the arch-conservative "Pat" Harrison of Mississippi, chairman of the Finance Committee. It was a critical juncture that could determine the future of the New Deal in the

Senate, and Roosevelt, determined to see Barkley win, wrote an open "Dear Alben" letter in which he referred to Barkley as the "acting" majority leader. To many in the Senate this seemed arrogant interference with what was solely Senate business, and so another bitter fight resulted.

From a private poll, Jim Farley calculated that Harrison stood to win by a single vote. Pressure from the White House grew intense—and not especially subtle. Senator William H. Dieterich of Illinois, who had pledged himself to Harrison, received a call from Boss Kelly of Chicago promising Dieterich a say in the appointment of two federal judges, should he vote as Roosevelt wished, which was quite enough to convince Dieterich to switch sides. On July 19, a day before the vote, Harry heard from Tom Pendergast, who had been called by the White House and asked to "tell" Harry Truman how to vote. Only in this instance no offer of patronage was forthcoming.

Harry told T.J. that he had already promised Pat Harrison his support and could not go back on his word. "Jim Aylward phoned me, too," Harry told William Helm an hour later. "I didn't mind turning Jim down, not so much, anyhow, but to say No to Tom was one of the hardest things I ever had to do." According to Harry, this was the one and only time T.J. had ever called him about a vote. Normally, T.J. made his views known by telegram.

But possibly T.J. did not like pressure from the White House any more than Harry, for as Harry also related, Pendergast had said it "didn't make a helluva lot of difference to him. . . ."

Why Harry had ever lined up with Harrison remains a mystery—he liked Barkley, nor had he any reason to oppose him—unless he saw it as a way to show the President he could not be taken for granted any longer.

He refused to be budged and was so furious with the people at the White House, the President included, that he could hardly contain himself. By going to Pendergast, rather than coming directly to him, they had left little doubt as to what they really thought of him. In their eyes, he was still truly the Senator from Pendergast. It was the worst insult he had suffered since coming to Washington and he decided to let Roosevelt know how he felt. Told that the President was not available, he talked to Steve Early, the press secretary. He was tired of being "pushed around" and treated like an office boy, Truman said. He expected the consideration and courtesy that his office entitled him to.

Senator Barkley, all the while, was under the impression that Harry Truman had given *him* his pledge of support. Barkley would later describe how Harry had come to him saying, "The pressure on me is so great [to vote for Harrison] that I am going to ask you to relieve me of my promise." It was this foursquare approach of Truman's that so impressed him, Barkley said. "I always admired him for the courage and character he displayed in coming to me as he did. Too often in politics the stiletto is slipped between your shoulder blades, while its wielder continues to smile sweetly. . . ."

On July 21 the Democratic members of the Senate met in the white marble Caucus Room of the Senate Office Building to vote for a majority leader by secret ballot. The winner was Alben Barkley by one vote. (Barkley would later speculate on how he might have felt about Harry Truman had he lost by one vote.) Harry immediately pledged Barkley his support and they were to be friends and allies thereafter.

The steam was gone from the Court bill. On July 22, by a margin of 50 votes, the Senate sent it back to the Judiciary Committee, where it died. The President had suffered his first and worst defeat since taking office, which to Harry's mind he richly deserved. The whole affair, Harry thought, had been a mistake and very badly managed by Roosevelt.

As time passed, in the comparatively few months of each year when Bess and Margaret were with him in Washington, the Trumans moved from one small, temporary apartment to another—to Sedgwick Gardens on Connecticut Avenue in the spring of 1936, to the Carroll Arms on 1st Street in early 1937, the Warwick Apartments on Idaho Avenue in 1938. In 1939 they were back again at Tilden Gardens, where they began. Margaret, who had grown taller and even more spindly, was attending Gunston Hall, a private school for girls, which was another financial worry for Harry. Independence, however, remained "home" for Margaret, as for Bess, who felt the constant pressure of her mother's need for her. Madge Wallace, who still believed Bess could have done better in the way of a husband, gave no sign of interest in Harry or his career.

The long separations grew no easier. "I just can't stand it without you," he wrote to Bess as the new session got under way in 1937. She was not only Juno, Venus, and Minerva to him, he wrote, but Proserpina, too, and urged her to look that up. Proserpina, as Margaret would remember ever after, was a goddess who spent half of each year in Hades with her husband Pluto, separated from her grieving mother.

His letters dutifully reported his modest social life. He went to the movies, played some penny-ante poker, listened to the symphony or opera on the radio. One weekend he drove to Gettysburg to hike over the battlefield with John Snyder, a St. Louis banker he had gotten to know at summer Army camp over the years. Another day he "played hooky" from the Appropriations Committee and went to the War College to hear

229

Douglas Southall Freeman lecture on Robert E. Lee, which he thought "one of the greatest talks I ever heard."

His health was uneven and he worried about it perhaps more than necessary. In the wake of the Court-packing fight, he felt so wretched he went to the Army-Navy Hospital at Hot Springs, Arkansas, for a checkup and complete rest. A month or so later, working harder than ever, nerves ragged, he was beset again by savage headaches. "This so-called committee work is nothing but drudgery and publicity," he wrote, "all so depressing sometimes." Vic Messall thought possibly he was drinking too much. William Helm wrote later that he had never known anyone who could hold his liquor so well as Senator Truman. On one occasion Helm had seen him take five drinks and show no effect. "Not once did I ever see him under the slightest influence of liquor."

The records from his stay at the Army-Navy Hospital at Hot Springs say only that he had developed severe headaches and "a sense of continually being tired," a "general malaise."

The President and his people continued to exhibit only supreme indifference toward him, which became especially grating whenever the governor of Missouri, Harry's friend Lloyd C. Stark, came to town. It had been Harry who arranged for Stark to meet Roosevelt for the first time, in October 1936, when Stark was running for governor. By mail and telegram Harry had urged the President to invite Stark and his wife to join him on board his train, as he campaigned across Missouri. "They are charming people," Harry had assured the President in a telegram from Independence. Now Stark went frequently to the White House and spoke warmly of Roosevelt as "the Chief." Stark was invited to join poker parties on the President's yacht on cruises down the Potomac, something Senator Truman could only dream of. Senator Truman often had difficulty getting the President's secretary even to return his calls.

Once, on a quick visit to Capitol Hill, Stark poked his head in at Harry's office door to say that some of the folks in Missouri were trying to get him to run for the Senate when Harry came up for reelection, but that Harry need not worry. When Stark had gone, Harry told Vic Messall, "That son-of-a-bitch is fixing to run against me."

Alone one night in October listening to the radio, he began to weep. "A couple of kids were singing 'They'll Never Believe Me' from the *Girl from Utah,*" he wrote to Bess, "and I sat here and thought of another couple of kids listening to Julia Sanderson and Donald Brian singing that beautiful melody and lovely sentiment, and I wished so badly for the other kid that I had to write her to sort of dry my eyes."

No one ever seemed to understand how sentimental he was, below the surface. He was lonely, homesick, feeling unappreciated, feeling sorry for himself, thinking often of times gone by. "Today is my father's birthday," he wrote on December 5. "He'd be eighty-six, if he'd lived. I always wished he'd lived to see me elected to this place. There'd have been no holding him."

The brighter side was an unlikely new friendship. A staff member of the railroad subcommittee, Max Lowenthal, had invited him to meet Justice Louis D. Brandeis, at one of the winter teas that Brandeis and his wife gave Sunday afternoons in an old-fashioned apartment on California Street. These Brandeis teas, as Marquis Childs would write, had become a "slightly awesome institution" in the capital, with Mrs. Brandeis presiding as umpire over a kind of musical chairs game designed to give the justice ten or fifteen minutes of individual conversation with as many guests as possible within an hour and a half. Truman was not accustomed to meeting such people, he had told Lowenthal candidly when the invitation was first issued. But to his surprise, Brandeis had spent more time with him than any of the other guests, wanting to hear about Harry's railway investigations and appearing extremely pleased to learn that Harry had read some of his books.

They sat in stiff, uncomfortable chairs in a large living room where little had changed since the time of Woodrow Wilson, the walls decorated with photographs of classical ruins. Brandeis, the first Jew to serve on the Supreme Court and the country's most distinguished Jeffersonian liberal, was by then in his eighties and to Harry, "a great old man." The day was cold, with snow forecast, but Harry felt warmed by the whole experience, a little out of place, yet more welcome than he had ever expected. "It was a rather exclusive and brainy party. I didn't exactly belong but they made me think I did."

He went several times again, and as he later wrote, he found that he and Brandeis were "certainly in agreement on the dangers of bigness." The influence of Brandeis was apparent soon enough.

On Monday, December 20, 1937, Senator Truman delivered the second of his assaults on corporate greed and corruption. In the earlier speech in June he had recalled how Jesse James, in order to rob the Rock Island Railroad, had had to get up early in the morning and risk his life to make off with $3,000. Yet, by means of holding companies, modern-day financiers had stolen $70 million from the same railroad. "Senators can see," he said then, "what 'pikers' Mr. James and his crowd were alongside of some real artists." Now, in a prepared address written and rewritten several times with the help of Max Lowenthal, he attacked the power of

231

Wall Street and the larger evil of money worship, sounding at times not unlike his boyhood hero, William Jennings Bryan. He had announced the speech in advance, so as to be heard by something more than an empty chamber. "It probably will catalogue me as a radical," he warned Bess, "but it will be what I think."

His lifelong hatred of high hats and privilege, all the traditional Missouri suspicion of concentrated power and of the East, came spouting forth with a degree of feeling his fellow senators had not seen or heard until now. He attacked the "court and lawyer situation" in the gigantic receiverships and reorganizations that destroyed railroads, and named the powerful law firms involved—Cravath, de Gersdorff, Swaine & Wood of New York; Davis, Polk, Wardwell, Gardner & Reed, also of New York; Winston, Strawn & Shaw of Chicago. He cited the immense fees taken by the attorneys for the receivers, told how some attorneys took their families on free vacations to California in the private cars of a bankrupt line, how a receivership judge on the federal bench had a private car on the bankrupt Milwaukee & St. Paul at his beck and call.

"Do you see how it pays to know all about these things from the inside?" he asked.

How these gentlemen, the highest of the high-hats in the legal profession, resort to tricks that would make an ambulance chaser in a coroner's court blush with shame? The same gentlemen, if the past is any guide to the future, will come out of the pending receiverships with more and fatter fees, and wind up by becoming attorneys for the new and reorganized railroad companies at fat yearly retainers; and they will probably earn them, because it will be their business to get by the Interstate Commerce Commission, to interpret, and to see that the courts interpret, laws passed by the Congress as they want them construed.

These able and intelligent lawyers, counsellors, attorneys, whatever you want to call them, have interviews and hold conferences with the members of the Interstate Commerce Commission, take them to dinner and discuss pending matters with them. The commission, you know, is the representative of the public and it has its lawyers also, but the ordinary government mine-run bureaucratic lawyer is no more a match for the amiable gentlemen who represent the great railroads, insurance companies, and Wall Street bankers than the ordinary lamb is a match for the butcher.

The underlying problem throughout, he said, was avarice, "wild greed."

We worship money instead of honor. A billionaire, in our estimation, is much greater in these days in the eyes of the people than the public servant who works for public interest. It makes no difference if the billionaire rode to wealth on the sweat of little children and the blood of underpaid labor. No one ever considered Carnegie libraries steeped in the blood of the Homestead steelworkers, but they are. We do not remember that the Rockefeller Foundation is founded on the dead miners of the Colorado Fuel & Iron Company and a dozen other similar performances. We worship Mammon; and until we go back to ancient fundamentals and return to the Giver of the Tables of Law and His teachings, these conditions are going to remain with us.

It is a pity that Wall Street, with its ability to control all the wealth of the nation and to hire the best law brains in the country, has not produced some statesmen, some men who could see the dangers of bigness and of the concentration of the control of wealth. Instead of working to meet the situation, they are still employing the best law brains to serve greed and self interest. People can stand only so much, and one of these days there will be a settlement. . . .

He saw the country's unemployment and unrest as the fault of too much concentration of power and population, too much bigness in everything. The country would be better off if 60 percent of all the assets of all insurance companies were not concentrated in four companies. A thousand insurance companies, with $4 million each in assets, would be a thousand times better for the country than the Metropolitan Life, with its $4 billion in assets. Just as a thousand towns of 7,000 people were of more value than one city of 7 million.

Wild greed along the lines I have been describing brought on the Depression. When investment bankers, so-called, continually load great transportation companies with debt in order to sell securities to savings banks and insurance companies so they can make a commission, the well finally runs dry. . . . There is no magic solution to the condition of the railroads, but one thing is certain—no formula, however scientific, will work without men of proper character responsible for physical and financial operations of the roads and for the administration of the laws provided by Congress.

The speech was front-page news in *The New York Times* and drew the immediate attention of labor leaders and reform-minded citizens across the country. Nor did anyone in the Senate doubt that he had done his homework. Not even the dullest of hearings seemed to wear him down

233

and some were as dull as any ever recorded at the Capitol. Many times he was the only senator present.

In the eyes of those working with him, he had also shown uncommon courage. Much of the focus had been on the financial finagling behind the bankrupt Missouri Pacific Railroad. Max Lowenthal, a former labor attorney, had written a critical analysis of railroad reorganization, *The Investor Pays*. As an expert on the subject, he warned the senator that the inquiries might produce some "pretty hot stuff," and that this could be embarrassing for him in Missouri. Truman instructed Lowenthal and the staff to proceed as they would with any other investigation. Pressures on him to call off the hearings, or at least to go easy, did become intense. But there was no letting up. Lowenthal did not think there were a half-dozen others in the Senate who could have withstood the pressure Truman took.

The hearings continued, the senator cross-examining witnesses in a courteous but persistent fashion. Lowenthal would remember that it seemed "an innate part of his personality to be fair and to know what is fair, and to exercise restraint when he possesses great power, particularly the power to investigate . . . the power to police. . . . He gave witnesses all the time they wanted."

Ironically, the senator whose own background had seemed so suspect was gaining a reputation as a skilled investigator.

Though it did not seem of particular importance at the time, Truman was also taking positions on civil rights that appeared to belie his Missouri background. He consistently supported legislation that would abolish the poll tax and prevent lynchings. In 1938, in a Senate battle over an anti-lynching bill, he voted to limit debate on the bill in an unsuccessful effort to break a filibuster against it.

Still more outspoken were his feelings on "preparedness," national defense. "We must not close our eyes to the possibility of another war," he warned an American Legion meeting at Larchmont, New York, in 1938, "because conditions in Europe have developed to a point likely to cause an explosion any time." He called for the establishment of an air force "second to none." No one could be more mistaken than the isolationists, he said. America had erred gravely by refusing to sign the Versailles Treaty and refusing to join the League of Nations. "We did not accept our responsibility as a world power." America couldn't pull back and hide from the world. America was blessed with riches and America wanted peace, but "in the coming struggle between democracy and dictatorship, democracy must be prepared to defend its principles and its wealth."

. . .

The end for Tom Pendergast was drawing near. The once robust, florid Big Boss looked dreadful, gray, drawn, physically diminished, and for all his high style of living he was close to financial ruin as a consequence of his chronic, consuming need to gamble. In one month he lost nearly $75,000 betting on the horses. His new private secretary at 1908 Main Street, Bernard Gnefkow, regularly kept tabs on bets of $5,000 to $20,000 on a single race. Later estimates were that T.J. may have squandered $6 million on the horses. But as would be shown, he had kept these transactions cleverly hidden from friends and family, as well as the government, by using cash only and devising fictitious names to conceal where the money came from and where it went. In the last part of the 1930s he had become so in debt to gamblers and bookmakers around the country as to be virtually in their control. They spoke of him not as "the Big Boss" but "the Big Sucker." To anyone who knew the story of the Pendergasts and their dynasty this seemed an odd turn of fate, since it was luck at the track that had given them their start, with Alderman Jim and his winnings on the horse called Climax.

Later, in an effort to explain the downfall of Boss Tom, his admirers, including Senator Harry Truman, would insist that he was "not himself," that failing health and the gambling fever drove him to do things he never would have done in his prime. A Kansas City police officer named John Flavin, a veteran of years on the force, would remember that on the day T.J. gave him his job, he had said, "Don't ever take any money that doesn't belong to you and you'll never have any trouble in life."

A new federal district attorney for Kansas City had begun investigations, focusing first on vote fraud in the '36 elections. He was Maurice Milligan, the younger brother of Tuck Milligan, and he, too, was Bennett Clark's man (Clark had arranged his appointment). But after the '36 elections Milligan's chief ally in the assault on Pendergast was Governor Lloyd C. Stark, whose own rise to office owed so much to T.J. and the whole Kansas City organization. Stark had turned on Pendergast as no one ever had—or ever dared try—determined to destroy him once and for all. It was Stark's conviction that his loyalty belonged to the people, not to any machine or its boss.

The documentation amassed by Milligan and a swarm of FBI agents revealed that approximately 60,000 "ghost" votes had been cast in Kansas City in 1936. Many precincts had registration figures exceeding the known population. Hundreds of defendants were brought to court and, as the *Star* reporter William Reddig noted, what surprised most people from Kansas City, who had heard about election thieves for years, was to find how many of them looked just like ordinary citizens, as indeed most were. The trials, lasting nearly two years, led to 279 convictions, and Milligan, a handsome, pipe-smoking "country lawyer," became a local hero.

But what would prove the crucial investigation began only after Governor Stark, accompanied by Milligan, went to Washington. Bennett Clark had given Roosevelt the tip that Pendergast had failed to report huge sums of income on his tax returns. Roosevelt notified the Treasury Department and it was then that Treasury investigators started looking into the story of the insurance bribe first described by Marquis Childs in the St. Louis *Post-Dispatch* in 1935. Before they were finished, Stark and Milligan had five federal agencies at work on special assignment.

They found that an official of the Great American Insurance Companies, Charles Street, had met with Pendergast in a Chicago hotel in January 1935, or just as Senator Truman was trying to learn his way about Capitol Hill. The Chicago meeting had been arranged by R. Emmett O'Malley, Missouri's Superintendent of Insurance. Charles Street, speaking for some eight different insurance companies, told Pendergast he wanted the settlement by O'Malley's office of an old issue over fire insurance rates that had kept nearly $10 million impounded. And that of course he was willing to pay for it. When Street offered $200,000, T.J. declined. When Street offered $500,000, T.J. said yes. Later, in the interest of speeding things along, the $500,000 was increased to $750,000.

A first installment of $50,000 in cash was delivered to T.J. personally at his Main Street office on May 9, 1935. An agreement releasing the insurance money was then worked out in a room at the Muehlebach Hotel by Street, O'Malley, and attorneys for the insurance companies, after which further payments on the bribe continued. One delivery to T.J.'s house on Ward Parkway in the spring of 1936 was for a total of $330,000 in cash in a Gladstone bag.

Though none of this was disclosed for some while, Stark fired O'Malley and rumors were rampant. How much or little Senator Truman knew is not recorded. Probably it was very little, in view of how hard he took the news when it broke. But when District Attorney Milligan's term expired early in 1938 and both Stark and Roosevelt were calling on the Senate to confirm his reappointment, Harry Truman found himself facing the nearly certain prospect of being the lone senator with objections. By senatorial custom, he could have blocked the reappointment simply by saying that Milligan was personally obnoxious to him. This he did not do, however, because Franklin Roosevelt called him on the phone and asked him not to, as a personal favor.

He could also, of course, have had nothing to do with the matter, and remained silent.

Instead, on Tuesday, February 15, 1938, he marched through the swinging doors of the Senate Chamber and delivered a full-scale attack on Milligan, as well as on the federal judges in Kansas City, a scathing, bitter speech that helped his reputation not at all, nor served any purpose other than to release a great deal of pent-up fury and possibly bring Tom Pendergast a measure of satisfaction. Milligan, he said, was Roosevelt's "personal appointment" and made to appease the "rabidly partisan press." He called Milligan corrupt, and charged the judges with playing politics, since they had been appointed by Republican Presidents Harding and Coolidge. "I say, Mr. President, that a Jackson County, Missouri, Democrat has as much chance of a fair trial in the Federal District Court of Western Missouri as a Jew would have in a Hitler court or a Trotsky follower before Stalin."

It was the one time he had ever attacked the President, the one time he had ever touched on, let alone defended his political origins in the Senate, and it was his worst moment in the Senate. Again he read from a prepared text. Yet he seemed out of control, grossly overreacting even if some of his points deserved hearing—the refusal of the courts, for example, to let anyone from Jackson County sit on the juries.

"The manner in which the juries were drawn," remembered a federal district judge in Kansas City years later, "and the fact that only Democrats were indicted in the polling precincts in which the vote fraud occurred, when it was obvious that the Republican judges and clerk of elections in the same precincts were equally guilty, distorted Truman's view beyond comprehension. He felt he had to blast, and blast he did—to his discredit."

Possibly, with a more measured, thoughtful defense, he could have taken his audience beyond the stereotypical picture of boss rule. By his own bearing, the decency and common sense that were so much a part of him, he might have encouraged appreciation of the accomplishments of the Kansas City organization that he himself so admired. As it was, he achieved nothing. When the time came to confirm Milligan by vote, he was the lone senator in opposition.

To his credit, it would be said only that he had made a brave gesture of loyalty to an old friend. At least he had not "run for cover."

So harsh were the expressions of disapproval issued at the White House that Truman began feeling his career was over. He brooded for days. In a confidential letter to a friend, he said that "in view of my speech on the Senate floor on Tuesday and the reaction to it from the White House," he would not be running for reelection in 1940—though later he would ask for return of the letter.

. . .

He had made matters no better, meantime, by announcing his intention to have his burly factotum, Fred Canfil, custodian of the Jackson County Courthouse, appointed a U.S. Marshal in Kansas City, an idea that met with immediate outrage there. The Justice Department sent FBI agents to begin inquiries and across one interdepartmental memorandum J. Edgar Hoover scrawled: "I want to make certain a very complete and thorough investigation is made of this man." By early March 1939, sensing the tide of opinion on Canfil was strongly against him, Truman said he was for Canfil or nobody. "I am for Canfil, first, last, and all the time." But Canfil was found unsatisfactory and rejected, chiefly because of the volume of adverse rumors and opinion gathered by the FBI. Five months earlier, in November, the senator had been assured through channels high up in the Justice Department that Canfil was acceptable and would be approved. "They figure they'll need Harry next session," he had said of the administration in a letter to Bess. But that was in November.

In Kansas City, by appearances, the functioning of the organization continued as before, T.J. somehow managing a serene face to the world. He went to his office as usual, except that now, because of his health, he rode the elevator in the adjacent hotel and crossed through to 1908 at the second-floor level, to avoid the stairs. In a municipal election in the spring of 1938, despite a new election board appointed by Governor Stark, despite the sensation of the vote fraud trials, the organization's candidates won by large margins. Considering the forces aligned against him, it was T.J.'s most impressive triumph ever, showing, as was said, that "the party in power . . . had lost none of its hold on honest voters." An exuberant, immensely gratified T.J. issued a rare statement to the press:

> If it is true . . . that the Democratic President of the United States was against us, that the Attorney General of the United States was against us, that the Governor of Missouri was against us, that the independent Kansas City *Star* newspaper was against us—I think under those circumstances we made a wonderful showing.

To Senator Truman it seemed to prove, as it did to many observers, that prior vote frauds had been unnecessary; the party would have won anyway.

How often or to what degree T.J. and Harry were in contact at this stage is again unknown. Mildred Dryden, Harry's secretary, could recall no correspondence from Tom Pendergast.

Only one communication written in T.J.'s own large, clear hand has survived, a note in red pencil on a single sheet of Jackson Democratic Club stationery: "Please help Sam Finklestein. He will explain. He has been my friend for 40 years. T.J. Pendergast." As Sam Finklestein did explain when he carried the note to Senator Truman in December 1938, he was trying to get two of his relatives out of Germany, Siegfried and Paula Finklestein of Berlin. Harry moved quickly, but in a report to T.J. mailed just before Christmas, Vic Messall could say only that the matter had been taken up with the American consul general in Berlin and that as soon as more information was available T.J. would be advised "immediately." For the moment the quota was full. Whether the Finklesteins ever succeeded in escaping to America is not known.

On Tuesday, April 4, 1939, J. Edgar Hoover himself arrived in Kansas City. On Friday, April 7, T. J. Pendergast was indicted for tax evasion. In Washington, Senator Truman was reported to have looked "hurt and astounded" at the news. "I am sure he had little inkling of his old friend's troubles before the grand jury returned its indictment," wrote William Helm. "Even then he seemed to cling to the hope that Pendergast somehow would prove his innocence. . . . " Asked for a comment by reporters, Harry said, "I am very sorry to hear it. I know nothing about the details . . . Tom Pendergast has always been my friend and I don't desert a sinking ship."

To Bess he would write, "The terrible things done by the high ups in K.C. will be a lead weight to me from now on."

On May 22, at the federal court in Kansas City, T.J. pleaded guilty. The total in evaded taxes, including fines, came to $830,494.73.

R. Emmett O'Malley and the director of the Kansas City police department were also convicted of tax evasion, as was Matthew S. Murray, the city's Director of Public Works. Charles Street, the insurance executive involved in the bribe, was dead. Edward L. Schneider, secretary treasurer of seven Pendergast companies, killed himself, or so it appeared, after making a full statement of his transactions to the grand jury. How many millions of dollars had been stolen from the city was never precisely determined. City Manager Henry McElroy, who also died while facing indictment, was found to have misplaced some $20 million with his unique system of bookkeeping, a figure nearly twice the city's annual budget. The assertion later by several of his friends that Harry Truman could have walked off with a million dollars during his time as presiding judge, had he chosen, seems an understatement.

"He was broke when he went to the Senate," Edgar Hinde would say.

239

"He didn't have a dime and he had all the opportunity in the world. He could have walked out of that office [as county judge] with a million dollars on that road contract. You know that would have been the easiest thing in the world. He could have gone to one of those contractors and said, 'I want ten percent.' Why you know they would have given it to him in a flash. But he came out of there with nothing."

"Looks like everybody got rich in Jackson County but me," Harry wrote privately to Bess from Washington.

At 8:45 A.M., May 29, accompanied by his son, T.J., Jr., and Jim Pendergast, T.J. arrived at the east gate of the federal penitentiary at Leavenworth to begin serving a sentence of fifteen months, reduced from three years in view of his age and health. On the day of his sentencing, the judge had remarked to reporters that he could well understand the feelings expressed for Pendergast by his friends. "I believe if I did know him I, too, might have been one of his friends. I think he is a man of character that makes friends."

In all that was revealed by the investigations there was nothing to suggest any involvement with illegal activities on the part of Harry Truman. As District Attorney Milligan, never a particular admirer of the senator, would state: "At no time did the finger of suspicion ever point in the direction of Harry Truman."

In its issue of April 24, 1939, *Life* magazine devoted six pages to the meteoric rise of Governor Lloyd C. Stark, the article illustrated with numerous lurid photographs of the Pendergast debacle. Governor Stark, said the magazine, was the new Democratic version of young Thomas E. Dewey, the Republican racket-buster of New York, and claimed that the major result of Pendergast's fall was to "catapult honest, efficient Lloyd Stark, an apple grower, right into the presidential ring." Or at the least to a seat in the United States Senate. (Elsewhere there had been talk of Stark as the next Secretary of the Navy.)

In Missouri, praise for Stark was overflowing. He was called "Missouri's Moral Leader," a figure of national importance, a presidential possibility, and in any event, "a man with a future."

"He has earned the high estimate," wrote the St. Louis *Post-Dispatch* in an editorial that Stark clipped and sent to Roosevelt.

He chose the hard way, and, of course, the right way, of meeting all the obligations of his office. He could have chosen the easiest way. He might have gone through the routine perfunctorily, basked in the approval of the all-powerful Pendergast machine that had supported him for the nomination, acquiesced in the Boss's few but salient demands, kept the peace.... The Governor entered his office under the shadow of the Kansas City machine. He had to live down the suspicion of being a Pendergast man....

The contrast to the path chosen by Senator Truman went without saying.

Life, too, acknowledged that Stark had accepted Pendergast support in 1936, but stressed there was nothing new in American politics about a governor turning on the machine that helped elect him. Theodore Roosevelt had done it in 1899, Woodrow Wilson in 1910, Franklin D. Roosevelt in 1932. All three became President, and "square-shouldered, poker-faced, dignified" Lloyd C. Stark, too, would like to be President, "quite definitely."

In September, Stark announced he was running for Truman's seat in the Senate.

V

It was the toughest campaign of Harry Truman's career. "If Governor Stark runs against me," he had told the papers, "I'll beat the hell out of him." But this was mostly bluff; he knew what the odds were.

Franklin Roosevelt, who could have made all the difference, only toyed with him awhile, leading Truman to think he was on his side. Truman had gone to the White House about some pending legislation and the President insisted instead on talking Missouri politics. He spoke of Stark as "funny," meaning phony, as Harry explained to Bess. "I do not think your governor is a real liberal," Roosevelt said. "He has no sense of humor.... He has a large ego." Later Harry had run into Bennett Clark, who, though "cockeyed," also promised his support. It was all too much for one day, Harry decided.

But Roosevelt gave no endorsement or even encouragement, no help at all except to let the senator know in roundabout fashion that he would be glad to appoint him to a well-paid job on the Interstate Commerce Commission. "Tell them to go to hell," Harry responded. If he couldn't come back as a senator, he didn't want to come back at all.

Clearly he would be on his own this time. Tom Pendergast was in prison, the organization in shambles. At best Roosevelt could be counted on to remain neutral, but then not even that was certain. For all his loyal service to the New Deal, Senator Truman was not someone Roosevelt was willing to stand by or utter a word for. In Washington, as columnist Drew Pearson observed, "the wise boys" wrote Truman off.

In Missouri every major paper was against him but one, the Kansas City *Journal-Post*. The St. Louis *Post-Dispatch* summed up Truman's chances as "nil." He was without money, while Lloyd Stark, riding a wave of publicity, had all the marks of a winner, including plenty of money and the apparent endorsement of Franklin Roosevelt. If ever anyone had a reason to detest Franklin Roosevelt, it was Harry Truman as 1940 approached.

Privately, he was in despair over Roosevelt, Pendergast, and the "terrible" state of the world. In late August 1939, Hitler and the Russians had signed a nonaggression pact. On September 1, Hitler invaded Poland. Britain and France declared war on Germany. Margaret had never known her father to be in such low spirits. He went to the Washington premiere of the new Frank Capra movie *Mr. Smith Goes to Washington,* hoping it would cheer him up, but came away, as he wrote to Bess, greatly discouraged by its blanket portrayal of senators as crooks and fools. Doubtless he was distressed too by the fact that the chief figure of corruption in the story was a fat, heavy-handed machine boss who acted much like Tom Pendergast and ruled a city called Jackson.

Public opinion of the New Deal seemed to be at a low ebb. Roosevelt was getting nowhere with Congress. New Deal cures for hard times had been insufficient, the Depression persisted. Eight million people were still unemployed.

Harry worried over money owed on his mother's farm. To meet notes coming due, Vivian had exchanged a mortgage on the farm for $35,000 from the Jackson County School Fund, this according to a law that allowed the loan of school money not currently needed. Harry's secret hope was to sell the farm and clear all the debt on it—he wished now it had been sold when he came home from France—but he knew how much the place meant to his mother. Giving it up at her age might be more than she could take.

For the record, he had kept out of the loan arrangement and later said he had known nothing about it, which was undoubtedly less than the truth, since, along with Vivian, Fred Canfil, too, had signed the papers.

The continued ranting of Adolf Hitler on the radio left him increasingly gloomy. He met for lunch in Washington with Robert Danford, his old superior officer at Camp Doniphan, now a general, and talking of events in Europe and Germany's apparent military superiority, they both became "mighty blue." Harry feared a Nazi world. He dug out some of his old Army maps of France and tacked them to his office wall to follow the fighting. In open opposition to such strident isolationists in the Senate as Wheeler, Borah, and his fellow Missourian, Bennett Clark, he spoke out still more and strongly for "preparedness," called on the President to summon a special session of Congress to revise the Neutrality Act of 1936, which he himself had voted for but now realized was a mistake. In a speech in Missouri in October, he said the three dictators, Stalin, Hitler, and Mussolini, had reverted to the code of "cave-man savagery." American neutrality was obsolete in the face of such reality, he said. The arms embargo must be lifted. "I am of the opinion that we should not help the thugs among nations by refusing to sell arms to our friends." With Senator James Byrnes of South Carolina, he urged larger appropriations for defense, an immediate buildup of the Army, and a Navy "second to none." He was outraged by the arguments of the America First movement and the speeches being made by Charles Lindbergh. On November 11, Armistice Day, he wrote to Bess: "You know it makes some of us who went on that first Crusade . . . wonder sometimes just what fate really holds for civilization."

But as so often in his life, he went ahead uncomplaining, determined to defeat the "double-crossing" Stark and return to the Senate, where, he knew, history was going to be made as never before. His back was up. He would find out who his real friends were.

Meantime, with five other senators, he flew off to Mexico and Central America on a so-called "fact-finding" trip—"a pleasure trip," he was frank to admit. There was "too much poverty" in San Salvador, he thought, but Costa Rica from the air looked like a painting by one of the old masters: "Smoking volcanoes, blue lakes and the Pacific Ocean all in view at the same time from 134 miles in the air," he wrote to Bess. In Panama, he toured the length of the Canal by plane, inspected the giant 16-inch defense guns, watched a ship pass through the Miraflores Locks, and found himself "treated royally" by everyone. One artillery officer whom he had known from summer camp at Fort Riley "treated me as if I were the President of the U.S.A."

In Nicaragua on the return route, President Somoza impressed him as "a regular fellow." In Mexico City, he tried to do some last-minute Christmas shopping. But it was arriving at San Francisco and stopping at the Fairmont Hotel on Nob Hill that he enjoyed most. He loved San Francisco. "This, you know, is one of the world's great cities and it is San Francisco —not Iowa, Kansas, Nebraska, and Oklahoma retired farmers as the city in southern California is," he wrote, referring to Los Angeles, a city he disliked. When others in the party went out on the town, on a "slumming expedition" in search of female companionship, he bowed out. "I guess I'm not built right," he told Bess. "I don't enjoy 'em—never did, even in Paris, and I was twenty years younger then."

.   .   .

At a first campaign strategy meeting in St. Louis, at the Hotel Statler in January 1940, fewer than half of those invited appeared and some only to explain sheepishly why they would be unable to take an active part. The few with serious interest included his old friend Mayor Roger Sermon of Independence, Harry Vaughan, John Snyder, and James K. Vardaman, who, like Snyder, was a St. Louis banker. They would support Harry no matter what, they said, though Roger Sermon, who was known as "a plodder" and "all business," thought Harry should understand the outlook was extremely bleak. "Harry, I don't think you can win and that's not merely my personal opinion but after inquiring around." Having heard several more comparably discouraging forecasts, Harry said only that he would appreciate a little talk about electing Senator Truman.

Jim Pendergast, who was unable to attend, had asked Vic Messall earlier to tell the senator that "if he gets only two votes in the primary one will be mine and the other will be my wife's." Jim Aylward decided to sit the campaign out. Congressman Joe Shannon wanted time to make up his mind. But Jim Pendergast, as surviving head of what was left of the organization, would work as few men ever did for Harry and produce considerably more than two votes.

On February 3, 1940, Truman announced formally that he was filing his declaration of candidacy for reelection to the United States Senate, and said further that he was both opposed to President Roosevelt's seeking a third term and that his own choice for President was Bennett Clark.

Seldom had he appeared more the politician, in the least complimentary understanding of the term. That he, Harry Truman, could honestly propose conservative, isolationist, alcoholic Bennett Clark for the presidency at any time, let alone now, with the world as it was, seemed so blatantly hypocritical and expedient as to be laughable. Nor did his promise, "as a faithful Democrat," to support Roosevelt, should he become the nominee, take any of the edge off the announcement. Clearly, it was Clark's support in eastern Missouri that he was after, that and a little satisfaction perhaps in letting Roosevelt know how he felt and that he too could play the game.

His opposition to a third term, however, was entirely sincere. The idea went against his fundamental political faith. "There is no indispensable man in a democracy," he wrote privately. "When a republic comes to a point where a man is indispensable, then we have a Caesar. I do not believe that the fate of the nation should depend upon the life or health or welfare of any one man."

To no one's surprise, the Bennett Clark presidential boom came to nothing.

. . .

Vaughan and Snyder raised what little money there was to begin with and set up headquarters in a "borrowed" room in the Ambassador Building in St. Louis. "We borrowed clerks, we borrowed furniture, we borrowed everything we could," Snyder recalled. Almost no one seemed willing to give money. Mildred Dryden, who had left the Washington office to help with the campaign, remembered having trouble finding money enough to buy stamps. One mailing of eight hundred letters asking for donations of a dollar produced about $200, hardly worth the effort. According to Rufus Burrus, an Independence lawyer and another of Harry's Army reserve friends, funds were so low at one point that there was not money enough for a hotel room, so the candidate slept in his car. "A United States Senator . . . sleeping in his car!"

The first of Harry's Senate friends to lend a hand was Lewis Schwellenbach, who arrived in time for the official opening of the campaign at Sedalia, in the heart of the state, the night of Saturday, June 15, 1940, one day after German troops occupied Paris. A crowd of several thousand turned out, which was fewer than expected, but having Schwellenbach there counted heavily with the candidate. Mary Jane and Mamma Truman were in front-row seats on the lawn. Bess and Margaret were seated on the platform. "At sixteen," Margaret later wrote, "I was able to feel for the first time the essential excitement of American politics—the struggle to reach those people 'out there' with ideas and emotions that will put them on your side." Mamma Truman, who was nearly eighty-eight, shook hands among the crowd, a campaign aide at her side to help with names. Probably, as one of her generation, she never thought of the people as "out there."

"Is he our friend?" she would ask about those she met.

More fellow Democrats from the Senate arrived in Missouri to lend a hand, an unusual gesture in a primary campaign and a very real measure of their regard and affection for Harry Truman. Carl Hatch, Sherman Minton, and Lewis Schwellenbach, three old friends, came to give vocal support. However pointedly Roosevelt ignored him, Truman was running hard on his New Deal record. "While the President is unreliable," he confided to Bess, "the things he's stood for are, in my opinion, best for the country. . . ." Senator Jimmy Byrnes, hearing of Truman's financial troubles, talked the New York financier Bernard Baruch into contributing a desperately needed $4,000 to the campaign. And at the last, Alben Barkley, too, would appear for speeches in St. Louis and Kansas City. But Bennett Clark appeared determined to do nothing. What had Harry Truman ever done for him, Clark is said to have remarked in Washington.

In full-page newspaper ads, the president of the Brotherhood of Rail-road Trainmen, A. F. Whitney, called for help for "our good friend" Harry Truman, and in another few weeks the railroad unions provided the only big money behind the senator, some $17,000. Harry, as always in his political life, refused to handle any money, leaving that to the others. Eventually, however, to meet expenses he had to borrow $3,000 on his life insurance policy.

Four years of investigations into railroad finances had resulted in the Truman-Wheeler Bill, still to be passed, providing protection for the railroads as a mainstay of the nation's transportation system. He had supported the Farm Tenancy Act of 1937, and after passage of the Agricultural Adjustment Act of 1938, giving farmers price supports, he had said on the floor of the Senate that until the farmer got his fair share of the national income there could be no real agricultural progress. In 1939 he had voted for expanding the low-cost housing program, for increased funds for public works, increased federal contributions to old-age pensions. Particularly was he proud of his part in the Civil Aeronautics Act (1938), to bring uniform rules to the burgeoning new aviation industry.

On the issues of national defense and how the country should meet the crises in Europe, he was adamant. America "ought to sell all the planes and materials possible to the British Empire," he said in a radio address on June 30.

It was the record he ran on, and tirelessly. Through July he crisscrossed the state in his own car, a '38 Dodge, again with Fred Canfil along to share the driving, or Vic Messall or his old Kansas City friend Tom Evans. When Harry drove, he drove fast—too fast, the others thought.

Between times he was traveling back and forth to Washington, where, because of the war in Europe, Congress was still in session. Yet he seemed to thrive on it all, just as in the last campaign. Tom Evans, who was twelve years younger, had to give up and go home, no longer able to keep the pace.

Truman's speeches were without charm. He made no attempt at eloquence or the kind of slowly building, tall-tale exaggeration and pleasure in words for their own sake that Missouri audiences traditionally adored. His voice was both flat and high-pitched—and the larger the crowd, the higher the pitch. In normal conversation he spoke in rather low, pleasing tones, but something happened as soon as he stepped to a podium. Trying to emphasize a point, he would chop the air rapidly, up and down, with both hands, palms inward, while at the same time, and in the same rhythm, bobbing up and down on the balls of his feet, a style some of his detractors loved to imitate.

He had little skill for making politics a good show. It was a talent he greatly admired in others, but that he did not have now any more than before. The Senate had taught him little in that respect. Compared to someone like Bennett Clark, who after half an hour on the stump was only warming up, he was a flat failure. Yet in his own face-to-face way of campaigning he could be very effective. Once, in the course of the campaign, he told a friend how to do it: "Cut your speech to twenty-five minutes, shake hands with as many people as you can for a little while. Afterward, even if you have time left, leave. If you have no place to go, you can always pull off the road and take a nap."

Moving among country crowds, pumping hands, he would say, "I just wanted to come down and show you that I don't have horns and a tail just because I'm from Jackson County."

He also took a stand on civil rights, and while by later standards what he said would seem hardly daring or sufficient, for Missouri in 1940 it was radical. He stated his position at the very start, in Sedalia, to a nearly all-white audience:

> I believe in the brotherhood of man; not merely the brotherhood of white men, but the brotherhood of all men before the law. . . . If any class or race can be permanently set apart from, or pushed down below the rest in political and civil rights, so may any other class or race when it shall incur the displeasure of its more powerful associates, and we may say farewell to the principles on which we count our safety. . . .
>
> Negroes have been preyed upon by all types of exploiters, from the installment salesman of clothing, pianos, and furniture to the vendors of vice. The majority of our Negro people find but cold comfort in shanties and tenements. Surely, as freemen, they are entitled to something better than this.

Privately, like the country people whose votes he was courting, he still used the word "nigger" and enjoyed the kind of racial jokes commonly exchanged over drinks in Senate hideaways. He did not favor social equality for blacks and he said so. But he wanted fairness, equality before the law. He had been outraged by reports of black troops being discriminated against at Fort Leavenworth and used his office to put a stop to it.

At the National Colored Democratic Association Convention in Chicago that summer, he told a black audience that raising educational opportunities for Negro Americans could only benefit all Americans. "When we are honest enough to recognize each other's rights and are good enough to respect them, we will come to a more Christian settlement of our

247

difficulties." Legal equality was the Negro's right, Truman said, "because he is a human being and a natural born American."

In one respect it was like 1934 all over again. There were three in the running and again one was named Milligan, for District Attorney Maurice Milligan had decided that he, not Lloyd Stark, was the one who had brought down Tom Pendergast and so deserved to be the next Senator from Missouri. Later speculation that Milligan was, in fact, cleverly maneuvered into the race by some of the Truman people—in order to divide the Stark vote—would never be substantiated, but that was what happened (just as Tuck Milligan had divided the vote for Cochran in 1934), and for Truman his entry into the contest could not have been more welcome.

In the first weeks the odds were heavily in favor of Stark, with Milligan second, Truman a very distant third. (A cartoon by Daniel Fitzpatrick in the *Post-Dispatch* showed two heavy trucks marked "Stark" and "Milligan" in head-on collision high above a tiny toy truck marked "Truman." "No place for a Kiddie car," said the caption.) The Milligan candidacy rapidly faded, however. It soon became a race between Stark and Truman, and one of Truman's chief advantages proved to be Stark himself, as Harry Truman seems to have known intuitively from the beginning. Over dinner at the Willard Hotel one evening in Washington, well before the campaign began, he had told friends he was sure Stark would attack him personally and that if he, Harry, were not even to mention Stark, then Stark would begin making mistakes—"enough errors to give me a definite opportunity."

As predicted, Stark tore into Truman at first chance, calling him a Pendergast lackey, a rubber-stamp senator, and a fraud. "The decent, honest, God-fearing, law-abiding citizens of Missouri," said Stark in a speech at Joplin, "know him for what he is—a fraudulent United States Senator, elected by ghost votes, whose entire record in public office has been devoted to one purpose alone, and that is to the service of the corrupt master who put him into power. . . . "

In Truman's files still was the letter from Stark thanking him for the introduction to Tom Pendergast. Learning of this, several on the campaign staff urged Harry to release it, certain it could settle the outcome of the election in one blow. But Harry refused, saying he would let Stark destroy himself.

Little things about Stark began to draw attention. It was noted, for example, that his chauffeur was required to give him a military salute. Then, with only weeks to go, Stark went to the national convention in Chicago as an announced candidate for the vice-presidential nomination, as well as for the Senate, and Bennett Clark, who had at last concluded that Harry Truman deserved his help, rose to the occasion in grand style. To a reporter for the St. Louis *Post-Dispatch,* Clark observed:

> Lloyd's ambitions seem to be like the gentle dew that falls from heaven and covers everything high or low. He is the first man in the history of the United States who has ever tried to run for President and Vice-President, Secretary of the Navy, Secretary of War, Governor General of the Philippines, Ambassador to England and United States Senator all at one and the same time. . . . I understand, too, that he is receiving favorable mention as Akhund of Swat and Emir of Afghanistan.

Stark was one of seventeen in a vice-presidential race that included Secretary of State Cordell Hull, Speaker of the House William B. Bankhead, William O. Douglas, Jimmy Byrnes, Henry A. Wallace, and Congressman Sam Rayburn. At Chicago, Stark passed out bushels of apples and wound up with 200 votes on the first ballot. The final decision, however, was made in Washington by Roosevelt, who had by then accepted the draft of the convention for a third term. He chose Henry A. Wallace, the Secretary of Agriculture, a former Republican from Iowa, a former editor of *Wallace's Farmer,* which had been founded by his grandfather, and an ardent liberal.

Truman had come to Chicago with the Missouri delegation and held a seat on the resolutions committee, an important role. The convention opened on July 15. But in Kansas City the following day, an event took place that rocked him as very little ever had. The Republicans who controlled the county court had decided to foreclose the court-held mortgage on the homeplace at Grandview, and on Tuesday, July 16, 195 acres of the farm were sold at auction on the courthouse steps in Kansas City. The *Star* carried a front-page picture of the auction crowd and a caption explaining that the farm belonged to Martha E. Truman, mother of the Missouri senator. How much warning Harry had is unknown, but clearly he was helpless to find the money to save his mother from eviction. He was also certain it had been done for political reasons only, to humiliate him in the middle of the campaign, which seems to have been exactly the case.

Two days later at the convention, in the middle of the fight over the vice-presidential nomination, Harry felt suddenly so tired and weak he thought he was having a heart attack. Reaching out desperately, he clutched at a railing and hung on for ten or fifteen minutes, totally unable to move, until someone, seeing what was happening, helped him to a chair.

The homeplace on Blue Ridge was gone—though it would be re-covered later. His mother and sister moved into a small, rented house in Grandview, where, not long afterward, Mamma Truman slipped on the unfamiliar steps and broke her hip. As broken hips were then often fatal, Harry thought it meant the end for her. But it was not, nor did she complain about the new quarters.

In a letter home, he asked Bess to try to imagine the shame she would feel if her mother were evicted from 219 North Delaware.

Election day for the primary would be August 6; from Washington in late July, he wrote, "I'm thinking August 6 all the time." Theodore Roosevelt had once written that "black care rarely sits behind the rider whose pace is fast enough." It seemed to be his own cure, too.

> Will call you from Sedalia tomorrow night. Taking train to arrive there at 9:30 P.M. Will start out at Salisbury at 10:00 A.M. Thursday, Keytesville at 2:00 P.M., Brunswick 4:00, and Carrollton at 8:00 P.M., Hardin at 9:00 P.M. Next day Cuba and Cape Girardeau. Saturday, Sikeston, Malden, and Poplar Bluff. Rest Sunday and start at Lamar, Nevada, Rich Hill, and Butler Monday. Harrisonville, Belton, and K.C. Tuesday. Will stay at home Tuesday night . . . and go to St. Louis, thirty-first. Barkley is coming to K.C. and St. Louis on thirtieth and thirty-first. Will stay in St. Louis until Saturday and then come home.

The night of the big speech with Barkley in St. Louis was a fiasco. In a hall big enough to seat more than three thousand people, a grand total of three hundred showed up.

And yet it was in St. Louis in the final week that events turned suddenly and unexpectedly in Harry's favor. When the campaign was over and the results final, he would comment to Bess, "Anyway we found out who are our friends. . . ."

As valuable as any, surprisingly, ironically, was Bennett Clark. From a hotel room in St. Louis, Clark began calling people all over the state. "He finally ended up in a hospital and we continued to push him even there," remembered a Truman campaign worker, "and he kept his telephone busy."

Still more important was Clark's influence on a hale, broad-shouldered young Irish-American named Robert E. Hannegan about whom until now Truman knew nothing. A St. Louis police chief's son, Hannegan had been a star athlete at St. Louis University and for a while, after law school, played semi-professional baseball. Since 1933, he had been extremely active in Democratic politics, in the rough school of the Dickmann organization, eventually becoming city chairman. But up to now, Hannegan had been working for Stark. Whatever it was that Bennett Clark said or promised to make him switch must have been extremely convincing, for with just two days to go before the primary, Hannegan suddenly deserted Stark and went to work feverishly for Truman. In hindsight, Harry would see it as the biggest break of the campaign, and thereafter the tall, good-looking young man in the loud neckties could do no wrong in Harry's estimation, though had anyone ever walked out on him as Hannegan had on Stark, it would have been seen as rank betrayal.

On election night Truman was heard to remark, "Well . . . I guess this is one time I'm beaten," to which his friend Edgar Hinde replied that it was a long time until morning.

Margaret, however, would remember her father going to bed after calmly announcing he would win. They had been listening to the returns on the radio in the living room. By eleven o'clock Stark had an 11,000-vote lead. For her mother, Margaret would write, it was one of the worst nights of her life. They were both in tears. When the phone rang in the middle of the night, after everyone was in bed, it was Bess who answered. A campaign worker in St. Louis, David Berenstein, wished to congratulate the wife of the Senator from Missouri. Bess took it as a bad joke and slammed down the receiver. But Berenstein called back. Truman was carrying St. Louis.

It was an extremely close shave, as Truman said. He won by not quite 8,000 votes out of 665,000 cast. And 8,411 votes were also his margin over Stark in St. Louis, where, thanks to Bennett Clark, Hannegan had done his last-minute work. But the black vote, too, had gone to Truman, and he did better with the farmers this time than he had in 1934. Most importantly, he carried Jackson County by 20,000 votes, which was only a fifth of his margin in 1934, but still 20,000 votes in the place where supposedly anyone ever associated with the Pendergasts was done for. His own standing with the people, the work of Jim Pendergast and what remained of the organization, had counted more than all the sensation of the scandals, the charges of his opponents, and the relentless opposition of the *Star*. It was truly an extraordinary victory.

Maurice Milligan sent his congratulations and promised Truman his support in the fall election. Governor Stark said nothing publicly, but in private correspondence with Roosevelt blamed his defeat on "the machine vote, backed by Bennett Clark with every force at his command," plus "virtually all the Federal appointees, including Postmasters and WPA workers," who had made the difference for Truman. Besides, said Stark, "our rural vote, which is strong for me," had failed to materialize, "due primarily to the severe drought."

In order to run in the primary Milligan had been required to quit as district attorney. When Milligan applied for reappointment, Truman wrote Roosevelt a letter saying that in fairness Milligan should have his job back. However, when Stark's term as governor expired and word reached Truman that Stark was being considered by Roosevelt for a position on the Labor Mediation Board, Truman saw that he did not get it. Stark, who had seemed so destined for glory, was to withdraw from politics in disgust, never again to hold public office.

Three days after the primary election, when Harry Truman walked into the Senate Chamber, both floor leaders and all the Democrats present "made a grand rush" to greet him. Les Biffle, Secretary to the Majority, told him that no political contest in memory had ever generated such interest in the Senate as had his race in Missouri. Biffle had arranged a surprise lunch in his honor. "I thought Wheeler and Jim Byrnes were going to kiss me," Harry later wrote Bess, his joy in the day still overflowing. "Barkley and Pat Harrison were almost as effusive. Schwellenbach, Hatch, Lister Hill, and Tom Stewart, and Harry Schwartz almost beat me to death. Dennis Chavez hadn't taken a drink since the Chicago convention but he said he'd get off the wagon on such an auspicious occasion, and he did with a bang. Minton hugged me. . . . Well, as you can see it was a grand party."

Though in the general election in the fall Truman failed to do as well as Franklin Roosevelt in his race with Wendell Willkie, he nonetheless won resoundingly, defeating his Republican opponent, Manvel Davis, by 44,000 votes.

His one last worry, before returning to Washington, was over delay of the papers certifying his reelection—papers that, by law, required the signature of Governor Lloyd C. Stark. "Has my certification of election been officially received by you?" he anxiously cabled the Secretary of the Senate, Colonel Edwin A. Halsey, on December 13. By return telegram Halsey assured him that all was in order.

In a brand-new pearl gray, two-door 1941 Chrysler Royal, a car that was to be in steady service for the next fifteen years, he and Bess set off again for Washington.

7

Patriot

War has many faces; or, rather, in war men and nations wear many faces.

—ERIC SEVAREID

I

In "Locksley Hall," the poem by Tennyson that young Harry Truman had copied down in his last year in high school, and that he carried still, neatly folded in his wallet, were lines describing an aerial war of the future, lines written well before the invention of the airplane:

Heard the heavens fill with shouting, and there rain'd a ghastly dew
From the nations' airy navies grappling in the central blue . . .

In July of 1940 began the first great air battle in history, the Battle of Britain, as day after day Hitler's *Luftwaffe* crossed the Channel to bomb British ports, airfields, and London, and the Spitfires and Hurricanes of the Royal Air Force went up to "grapple" in defense. It was all Tennyson had foreseen and worse. In a raid on London, September 7, there were 375 German bombers, an unprecedented force. Then the night raids began, and devastation from incendiary bombs that Americans read about in dispatches by correspondents Robert Bunnelle and Helen Kirkpatrick, or heard described firsthand by the dramatic radio voice of Edward R. Murrow. "As I watched those white fires flame up and die down, watched the yellow blazes grow dull and disappear," said Murrow in his broadcast of October 10 at five in the morning, London time, "I thought, what a puny effort is this to burn a great city." Hitler boasted that his air *Blitz* would break the will of the English people. On Sunday, December 29,

London was subjected to the most savage bombing yet. More than a thousand fires raged across the city.

In Washington that same night, Franklin Roosevelt was wheeled into the oval-shaped Diplomatic Reception Room on the ground floor of the White House to deliver by radio the "fireside chat" to be known as his "Arsenal of Democracy" speech. The Nazis, he said, were determined to enslave the world and he warned that stroking a tiger would never make it a kitten. He saw American civilization in graver peril than at any time since Plymouth and Jamestown. It was not war he wanted, but all-out, massive production for war to supply those nations under Nazi attack. "We must become the great arsenal of democracy. For this is an emergency as serious as war itself. . . ."

On January 6, 1941, at a joint session of the new Congress, Senator Harry Truman listened as Roosevelt delivered a second ringing summons to action, in support of those nations fighting in defense of what he called the Four Freedoms—freedom of speech, freedom of religion, freedom from want, freedom from fear. To Truman, it was the President at his best. A few days later came Roosevelt's plan for Lend-Lease, to send Britain arms on credit, and in both houses of Congress the fight was on. Isolationists in the Senate—Wheeler, Vandenberg, Bennett Clark, Gerald P. Nye, Taft of Ohio—objected bitterly, calling the bill the road to war. Wheeler, Truman's old mentor, was the most scathing of all, saying it would "plow under every fourth American boy," which Roosevelt called "the rottenest thing" that had been said in public life in his generation. Wheeler, Clark, and the others could not have been more wrong or shortsighted, Truman felt. Bennett Clark had made himself a favorite of the America First movement, praised Lindbergh, and claimed, "We have everything to lose and nothing to gain in a war." Clark opposed aid to Britain, opposed further involvement of any kind by the United States. If Hitler conquered Europe, he said, "we're better off defending the United States than frittering away our supplies in Europe."

Clark was destroying himself politically, Truman was certain, and plainly Clark was having increasing difficulty staying sober. Repeatedly, Truman voted against amendments designed to restrict Roosevelt's execution of the bill.

Truman was by now a member of both the Military Affairs Committee and the Military Subcommittee of the Appropriations Committee. In September he had voted for the first peacetime draft. By December, more than $10 billion had been awarded in defense contracts in a country that was officially still at peace. Testifying on the Hill, the Army's Chief of Staff, General George C. Marshall, had called for a force of 2 million men, and another $1 billion to cover expenses, and said the money was only a start.

Questioned whether he was not asking for more than necessary to meet the emergency, he replied, "My relief of mind would be tremendous if we just had too much of something besides patriotism and spirit."

Senator Truman, who was by now a colonel in the reserves, and who knew how critical was the shortage of qualified officers, went to Marshall's office in the rabbit warren of the old Munitions Building and tried to enlist. Pulling his reading glasses down on his nose, Marshall told him he was too old and could better serve his country in the Senate.

Events were moving rapidly. An older, simpler way of life in Washington was passing. It was becoming a different city overnight. All through the Depression years, even with the changes imposed by the New Deal since 1933, it had remained a small town in most ways, southern at heart and unhurried. Now there were new people everywhere, swarms of new federal employees, more automobiles, more rush and confusion. The year before, it appeared the old "temporaries" on the Mall, acres of unsightly structures like the Munitions Building put up during the First World War (as it was now being called), might at last be torn down and taken away. Instead, the demand was to increase their number. A hodgepodge of new war agencies was sprouting with names and initials difficult to keep straight—the NDMB, National Defense Mediation Board, the OPM, Office of Production Management, and later the OEM, Office of Emergency Management. There was the SPAB, Supplies Priorities and Allocations Board, and the DPC, Defense Plants Corporation.

Every month was adding five thousand people to the city's population. Already, the shortage of housing was more acute than in 1918. The Trumans were extremely lucky to find a new apartment, five small rooms at 4701 Connecticut Avenue, on the street side of the building, second floor, for $120 a month. And this time they would hold on to it, Bess—the Madam or the Boss, as the senator referred to her—having decided she and Margaret would stay through the year.

There were lines at movie theaters, constant crowds at Union Station. Hotel bars and the best restaurants were a hubbub of manufacturers' agents in search of defense contracts and influence peddlers claiming to have an inside track. The talk was different, more urgent and full of new expressions like "stockpile," "tooling up," and "mobilize." The New Deal was passé now, the Depression a bygone era. The hero of the hour, so different from the kind who had flocked to Washington in the early Roosevelt years, was the "dollar-a-year man," a high-powered, high-priced corporation executive who had taken a government post but kept his old corporate salary, an innovation that some, like Senator Truman, looked on with great skepticism.

Yet as fast as the pace was picking up, it was hardly enough, given the urgency of the crisis. To those like General Marshall who knew the truth of the country's military strength and were trying desperately to do something about it, the overriding worry was how slowly change was taking place.

In the beginning Truman had little idea what he was getting into.

Concerned about complaints from constituents of gross extravagance and profiteering in the construction of Fort Leonard Wood, a new camp for draftees in south-central Missouri, concerned also that his home state was not getting its share of defense contracts, he decided on "a little investigation" of his own. Setting off from Washington in the old Dodge, he drove south as far as Florida, then on into the Midwest, eventually swinging north to Michigan, stopping at Army installations and defense plants all along the way. It was another of his automobile odysseys, like the courthouse survey of earlier years, and he later claimed to have rolled up 30,000 miles, or 5,000 miles more than the distance around the world, which was preposterous. Still, he probably covered 10,000 miles, and the experience was an eye-opener, as he said. Hard times were plainly in retreat in the biggest boom in the history of the country. But great haste in the buildup for war was making unconscionably great waste. It was the same everywhere, he found. Millions of dollars were being squandered. Had there been such mismanagement of federal help for the poor and unemployed a few years earlier, he thought, the outcry would have been overwhelming. As it was, no one seemed to care or to be saying anything. If national defense was the issue, the sky was the limit.

At Fort Leonard Wood he found costly equipment and material lying about in the snow and rain "getting ruined, things that could never be used, would never be used...." The contractor had had no previous construction experience. "And there were men, hundreds of men, just standing around collecting their pay, doing nothing." Truman walked about this and other sites taking notes on what he saw and whatever people were willing to tell him. Unless asked, he seldom said who he was.

Much camp construction, he discovered, was being done on a cost-plus basis—the contractor was paid for all costs plus a fixed percentage profit —which could be virtually an open ticket for piling up excessive profits. He was disturbed, too, by the obvious fact that the vast part of defense work was going to a small number of large corporations and these mainly in the East. He feared that many of the safeguards usually observed in government transactions were being thrown aside. He felt the President should be informed at once.

Returning to Washington, he called the White House for an appointment and from the moment he was ushered into the Oval Office, his reception could not have been more cordial, or more gratifying personally. Roosevelt was in grand form. He gave the senator a hearty welcome from his chair, flinging one arm in the air in characteristic gesture. He called him "Harry," repeatedly, as for half an hour they talked across the clutter of papers and knickknacks covering the big mahogany desk. Yet, when the session ended, Truman came away wondering if he had made any impression at all. As he wrote to a friend, Roosevelt was so courteous and cordial it was hard to know just what he thought or where one stood with him. "Anyway," he concluded, "I'm going to lay it before the Senate."

He spent weeks preparing a speech, consulting other senators, asking for suggestions from friends and staff. He told William Helm he was outraged over the greed of big business at such a time, and of some of the labor unions. "There's too much that is wrong here!" he insisted.

On Monday, February 10, 1941, Truman stepped into the well of the Senate to describe the problem as he saw it and to propose the establishment of a special committee to look into the awarding of defense contracts. It was his own idea, his own moment. His obscurity in national life, and in the course of the war, was about to end—and it was of his own doing.

Reaction in the Senate was immediately favorable. (Besides sounding an alarm on the scandalous state of military spending, he struck a responsive chord everywhere on the Hill by calling it grossly unfair for the War Department to ignore the suggestions of members of Congress concerning defense contracts. "It is a considerable sin," he said, "for a United States Senator from a State to make a recommendation for contractors, although he may be more familiar with the efficiency and ability of our contractors than is anybody in the War Department.") Referred first to the Committee on Military Affairs, Resolution 71 was reported out unanimously in a matter of days. But then back it went to the Committee to Audit and Control the Contingent Expenses of the Senate. There it might have languished indefinitely, for the committee's chairman was Jimmy Byrnes of South Carolina, who was close to the administration, and the administration had no wish to see its method of handling things scrutinized or stalled by any congressional committee. Roosevelt's continuing admonition to everyone involved with defense production was, "Speed, speed, speed."

To bring some semblance of order to operations Roosevelt had established a National Defense Advisory Commission, then an Office of Production Management, but there was really no clearcut administrative system, or any one person in charge. In effect, the sprawling defense effort was being handled by the White House, where the last thing anyone wanted was a pack of congressional investigators to contend with. There was alarm, too, at the War Department. A single nettlesome senator could mean unending problems and bad publicity, let alone an ambitious chairman of an investigating committee whose main, underlying intent, more than likely, would be to advance his political fortunes. Constant congressional probing could well delay or deter the whole program.

Only one voice cautioned against a "resentful attitude"—Chief of Staff Marshall, who said it "must be assumed that members of Congress are just as patriotic as we."

Truman understood the potential peril in what he was proposing. From his reading of Civil War history he knew what damage could be done to a President by congressional harassment in a time of emergency, and the lives it could cost by prolonging the war. Abraham Lincoln had been subjected to unrelenting scrutiny by the powerful Joint Committee on the Conduct of the War, which caused continuing trouble and delays. Its Radical Republican leadership had insisted even on a say in the choice of field commanders and battle strategy, and as often as not it was the Confederates who benefited. Robert E. Lee once remarked that the committee was worth two divisions to him, an observation Truman would often cite. He had gone to the Library of Congress for the Civil War records to verify for himself what mistakes the committee had made.

Like others, Truman had little use for investigations after-the-fact such as those conducted by Senator Gerald P. Nye and his committee, who in examining the causes of the First World War had raised a conspiratorial theory of the role played by the munitions makers. The Nye Committee, Truman felt, had been a major cause of isolationist sentiment in the Congress and contributed more than anything else to the nation's woeful unpreparedness. It did no good, Truman said, to go digging up dead horses once a war was over. "The thing to do is to dig this stuff up now and correct it."

But what saved his proposal was another one put forward in the House by a belligerent Georgia Democrat, Eugene Cox, who openly despised Roosevelt and wanted the establishment of a joint congressional committee to investigate "all activities" involving national defense. At a White House meeting, Jimmy Byrnes stressed to the President how much better off he would be "in friendly hands"—with a Truman committee—and Roosevelt agreed. Byrnes also wanted Truman to be given an absurdly modest funding of $10,000, a shoestring, to keep watch on expenditures that in 1941 alone would exceed $13 billion; though Truman objected vigorously, he managed only to get the appropriation raised to $15,000.

Resolution 71 was reported out on a Saturday afternoon in March, when a total of sixteen senators were on the floor, none of whom objected as Byrnes asked for immediate adoption. The vote was unanimous. A week later in a late-night session, after beating back isolationist amendments, the Senate passed the Lend-Lease Bill, which called for the spending of another $7 billion.

Its formal title was the Senate Special Committee to Investigate the National Defense Program, but from the start it was spoken of almost exclusively as the Truman Committee. There were seven members, five Democrats, two Republicans. Except for Tom Connally of Texas, all, like the chairman, were junior senators and, in the words of one observer, distinguished only by their "unspectacular competence." The Democrats included Connally, Carl Hatch of New Mexico, Monrad C. Wallgren of Washington, and James Mead of New York. The Republicans were Joseph H. Ball of Minnesota and Owen Brewster of Maine.

"Looks like I'll get something done," Harry wrote to Bess. The summer before, in the midst of the primary, he had told her, "The political situation is going to be something to write history about next year, and if I do win watch out." He felt himself a participant in history again, as he had not since France. This second term in the Senate would be nothing like the first, he knew. Washington and the world were no longer the same. He was no longer the same. His proposal, as even his critics acknowledged, was a masterstroke. He had set himself a task fraught with risk—since inevitably it would lead to conflict with some of the most powerful, willful people in the capital, including the President—but again as in France, as so often in his life, the great thing was to prove equal to the task.

From his railway investigations he had learned the importance of a committee staff. Now, on the advice of Attorney General Robert Jackson, he hired a young Justice Department lawyer named Hugh Fulton, who had just convicted a federal judge for fraud. Fulton was only thirty-five years old and memorable, a big, apple-cheeked figure, over six feet tall and rotund, who wore a black derby and spoke with a piping voice. He told the senator he wanted a salary of $9,000, or more than half the whole appropriation. Truman hired him, confident that if they produced results, money would be no problem.

Like Truman, Fulton was an early riser and a steady worker. He was bright, tenacious, and, as time proved, a superb choice. For several months he would be all the committee could afford in a paid staff, though the problem was temporarily circumvented with the old senatorial device of "borrowing help" from some of the "downtown" (executive) agencies.

The first investigator hired was young Matthew J. Connelly from Boston, who had worked for a Senate committee investigating campaign expenses. Others included George Meader, who would later become a member of Congress; Harold Robinson, a former FBI agent; Agnes Strauss Wolf, the one woman in the group; Morris Lasker, a recent graduate of the Yale Law School; William Boyle, a young man from Kansas City who had worked his way up in the Pendergast organization from precinct captain to acting director of the Kansas City police; and the ever faithful Fred Canfil, who operated out of Truman's office in the Federal Building in Kansas City.

The only major change on Truman's senatorial staff was the departure of Vic Messall under somewhat mysterious circumstances. Apparently, for all his devotion to the senator, Messall had been dipping into campaign funds for his own purposes—or Truman thought so—and he was told to find work elsewhere.

As a replacement for Messall, Truman brought his jovial friend Harry Vaughan to Washington and made him both his secretary, as the position of administrative assistant was still called, and a liaison for the committee with the military services, Vaughan being a lieutenant colonel in the reserves. (Later, Vaughan would leave to go on active duty with the Army Air Corps.)

There was to be no whitewash or witch-hunt, Truman told his committee staff, no grandstanding for headlines or any attempt ever to forestall the defense effort. But neither were they to be cowed by rank or political pressure. The primary task was to get the facts. "There is no substitute for facts," he would say. They must know what they were about. "Give the work all you've got," he urged, warning them never to tell those under investigation they were doing a good job. "If you do and it is later found they haven't done a good job, then they can say our committee agreed with what they did."

Their time was to be spent only where there were clear and present problems. They were not to go looking for trouble where none was known—and this applied to staff investigators and committee members alike. Once, in a closed, or executive, session, a senator not on the committee, Alexander Wiley of Wisconsin, who was sitting in, asked out of curiosity, "What are you fishing for this morning?" It seemed a fair question, he thought, in an executive session.

Truman was offended. "This committee does not go on fishing expeditions," he answered.

"I think the distinguished chairman resented my question," Wiley observed.

"I do not like it," said Truman. "I resent it. We are not on a fishing expedition."

All findings were to be reported as the work of the full committee, not of any one senator or of the chairman. The committee would have no say on military strategy, military personnel, or the size or disposal of the defense effort.

What Truman came to appreciate most in Hugh Fulton was his "honesty of purpose," and Fulton's contribution overall was to be of such obvious value that some observers would later speak of him as the driving force of the committee. But this was not the case. The driving force was Senator Truman.

The long process began on April 15, 1941, with the appearance before the committee of a dozen highest-ranking officials, military and civilian, including the elderly Secretary of War, Henry Stimson, and Chief of Staff Marshall. When the problem of seniority in the Army was discussed, Marshall insisted on the need for selective promotion. "You give a good leader very little and he will succeed," he said, looking at the chairman; "you give a mediocrity a great deal and he will fail." Years later, Truman would say that his respect for George Marshall had its beginning at this first session of the committee hearings.

On April 23, the committee went to nearby Camp Meade in Maryland, the first of nine camps on a cross-country inspection tour. One camp, at Indiantown Gap, Pennsylvania, was found to have cost more than ten times the original estimate. Another, Camp Wallace in Texas, which was supposed to have been built for $480,000, wound up costing $2,539,000. In several instances the Army had shown "fantastically poor judgment" in selecting camp sites (Fort Meade was a prime example), and an estimated $13 million had been wasted just by renting trucks and other construction equipment instead of buying it all outright at the start.

The Army had made a special study of camp construction following the last war, when rampant waste and inefficiency had also prevailed, but as the committee discovered, this special study had been lost, news that left the chairman "utterly astounded." If plans for the country's military campaigns were comparable to those for construction, Truman reported to the Senate, the situation was truly deplorable.

The central problem was the system of cost-plus contracts. "There was no attempt to ask contractors what they had been in the habit of making in peacetime or even what they were willing to take," Truman would write. "Huge fixed fees were offered by the government in much the same way that Santa Claus passes out gifts at a church Christmas party."

Some contractors were making in a few months three to four times what they normally cleared in a year, and at no risk. One architect-engineer was found to have increased his income through an Army contract by 1,000 percent.

Lieutenant General Brehon B. Somervell, the hot-tempered Chief of Services of Supply, who was known for his efficiency, complained loudly about the committee as a creature "formed in iniquity for political purposes." It was "axiomatic," he said, that time and money could not be saved at the same time.

"General Somervell was a very brilliant general," remembered Matt Connelly, the chief investigator, "but he was also a martinet, and he resented any intrusion or stepping on his toes. But that did not impress Senator Truman. He went ahead anyway."

Later Somervell would concede that in fact the Truman Committee's investigations of Army camp building alone had saved the government $250 million. Further, as the committee had strongly recommended, the responsibility for camp construction was taken away from the Quartermaster Corps and given to the Corps of Engineers, as it should have been in the first place.

The senators on the committee worked extremely hard, almost without exception, and the chairman hardest of all. A few nights before the first interviews with Stimson and Marshall in April, Truman had what was diagnosed as a gallbladder attack. He had been wrenched from his sleep by such excruciating pains that Bess thought he must be having a heart attack. But there was no easing up on his schedule, and by June he was again badly exhausted.

"My standing in the Senate and down the street [at the White House] gets better and better," he wrote on June 19, 1941, in a letter to Bess, who was back in Missouri once more. "Hope I make no mistakes." If he weren't working so hard, from daylight until dark, he didn't know what he would do without her, he said, adding plaintively, "Hope I won't be long here alone."

On June 22 came the stunning news that Hitler had turned and attacked Russia along an 1,800-mile front. Asked what he thought of this colossal turn of events, Truman spoke his mind in a way no one could fail to understand and that would not be soon forgotten. "If we see that Germany is winning we ought to help Russia," he said, "and if Russia is winning we ought to help Germany, and that way let them kill as many as possible, although I don't want to see Hitler victorious under any circumstances." It was hardly an appropriate observation at this juncture, but like many Americans, and many in Congress, Truman saw little difference between the totalitarianism of Fascist Germany and Communist Russia, and particularly since the Nazi-Soviet Pact of 1939 and Russia's invasion of tiny Finland. Nor was he willing to close his eyes to the realities of the Soviet regime just because suddenly it was Russia under Nazi assault. Stalin was only getting what he had coming to him was the feeling, and one shared by a very large segment of the American people.

Worried about the world, worried about himself, he went to the Bethesda Naval Hospital for a checkup, only to be told there was nothing the matter with him beyond fatigue. He was suffering from severe headaches and nausea, he told the examining physician, who recorded in the senator's medical record:

> Last year he ran for reelection and had a particularly fatiguing campaign . . . in which a great deal of vilification was hurled at him. . . . The attack on him affected him and caused him much mental anguish. His symptoms increased more than ever from this time on. In the last few months there has been an increased amount of activity in the Senate . . . he felt that he would be unable to continue his present pace.

But back to work he went, the pressures on him only growing, his pace easing not at all, as increasingly the investigations seemed to cast a shadow on the White House. He refused to equivocate and people began taking notice as they had not before. In August, while speaking in the Senate, he was pressed by Senator Vandenberg to admit that the President was culpable. "In other words," said Vandenberg, a leading Republican, "the Senator is now saying that the chief bottleneck which the defense program confronts is the lack of adequate organization and coordination in the administration of defense. . . . Who is responsible for that situation?"

"There is only one place where the responsibility can be put," Truman answered.

"Where is that—the White House?"

"Yes, sir."

"I thank the Senator."

With others on the committee, senators and staff investigators, he traveled the length of the country—mostly by plane. They would put down at a city or military base, go through their routine for a day or so, and then be off again, like a roadshow, everybody by now knowing just what to do. War plants were inspected, hearings held in local hotels. In some places they found nothing out of line. They were in Memphis and Dallas in late August, then on to San Diego, Los Angeles, San Francisco, Seattle, and Spokane. Bess was kept posted nearly every day, by letter or phone call, often by both, no matter how grueling his schedule. Some letters spoke candidly of what they were finding:

Biltmore Hotel, Los Angeles, Calif.
Thursday, August 21, 1941

Dear Bess:

Well I spent yesterday at San Diego. The navy sent a big transport plane for us. We left the airport at 9:00 A.M., arrived at San Diego at 10:00, and Admiral Blakely took us in charge for the usual show around. Looked at marine barracks under construction and had lunch with the recruits. A Missouri boy from St. Louis waited on me, one from New York took care of Mead, and one from Washington, Wallgren.

Looked over the new marine base camp and then got another walk around a plane plant, the Consolidated—said to be the biggest of 'em all. The managers are all such liars you can't tell anything about the facts. Each one says he's having no trouble and everything is rosy but that the other fellow is in one awful fix. By questioning five or six of them separately I've got an inkling of the picture, and it's rather discouraging in some particulars but good in others. We are turning out a very large number of planes and could turn out more if the navy and army boys could make up their minds just what they want.

Labor is a problem. The same brand of racketeer is getting his hand in as did in the camp construction program. Some of 'em should be in jail. Hold some hearings today and tomorrow, spend Saturday and Sunday in San Francisco, and open in Seattle Monday. . . .

Kiss Margie, love to you,
Harry

Flying in and out of Washington's new National Airport, he looked down on the tremendous gouge in the mud flats along the Virginia side of the Potomac, downstream from Arlington Cemetery. It was the site of a gigantic new five-sided headquarters for the military, the Pentagon, a larger office building than any in the world and a clear sign of the direction the country was taking.

From modest beginnings and in only a few months, the committee proved its value, producing both results and attention. By fall its appropriation was increased from $15,000 to $50,000, its membership enlarged by one more Democrat, Harley Kilgore of West Virginia, and two Republicans, Harold Burton of Ohio, who was to become one of the most dedicated members, and Homer Ferguson of Michigan, a former judge, who, like Brewster of Maine, was to be a particularly tenacious interrogator at hearings. The staff, too, was expanded. Eventually there would be fifteen investigators and as many clerks and stenographers.

Hearings were held in the committee's headquarters on the fourth floor of the Senate Office Building, Room 449, or, in special cases, in the great marble Caucus Room on the third floor. Frequently business was also transacted in what was called the Dog House, a small room behind Truman's office with a few worn leather chairs, refrigerator, whiskey, and walls covered with Civil War scenes and photographs and cartoons telling the chairman's political life story.

At Truman's insistence any member of the Senate was welcome to sit in and take part in the hearings. When presiding, he seemed invariably well prepared and in charge, yet he seldom dominated. Instead, he would go out of his way to let other senators hold the stage. No one could remember congressional hearings being handled with such straightforwardness and intelligence. As in his earlier railroad investigations, witnesses were shown every courtesy, given more than ample time to present their case. There was no browbeating of witnesses, no unseemly outbursts tolerated on the part of anybody. One reporter wrote of a "studious avoidance of dramatics, no hurling of insults or threats of personal violence that characterize so many other congressional hearings." Yet Truman could be tough, persistent, in a way that took many observers by surprise. It was a side of the man that they had not known. Columnist Drew Pearson wrote that one of the most remarkable developments of the committee was its chairman. "Slightly built, bespectacled, a lover of Chopin and a shunner of the limelight, Truman is one of the last men in Congress who would be considered a hard-boiled prober. In manner and appearance he is anything but a crusader."

Above all the chairman was eminently fair. Once, during testimony from one of the dominant figures in the American labor movement, the flamboyant, pugnacious head of the United Mine Workers, John L. Lewis, Senator Ball questioned whether the witness was to be taken at his word when he said workers were going hungry:

"Mr. Lewis, you are not seriously trying to tell the committee that any large number of workers in the United States don't get enough to eat? That is demagoguery, pure and simple, and you know it."

Lewis, sitting forward on the edge of his chair, a dark scowl across his massive face, responded angrily in a deep stentorian voice that filled the room:

"If you ask the question, I will answer it. But when you call me a demagogue before you give me a chance to reply, I hurl it back in your face, sir."

Truman broke in. "Now, Mr. Lewis, we don't stand for any sassy remarks to the members of this committee," he said, "and your rights will be protected here just the same as those of everybody else. I don't like that remark to a member of the committee."

"Senator, did you object when the Senator called me a demagogue?" replied Lewis, a man of fierce pride.

"Yes," Truman said, "it works both ways. I don't think the Senator should have called you a demagogue."

The documenting of waste and mismanagement in the construction of Army camps had been comparatively easy work, a way to give the committee credence in about the least time possible, which was why Truman had started with the camps. The larger work—more difficult, more time-consuming, more important, and much more risky politically—was the investigation of defense production, the gathering of facts, figures, specific detail, and no end of opinion on the building of ships and warplanes, on ordnance plants, automobile plants, labor unions, government contracts, the roles played by the giant corporations and small business, the stockpiling of vital materials. And what the committee turned up was extremely alarming: bad planning, sloppy administration, sloppy workmanship, cheating by labor and management, critical shortages everywhere.

There was too little aluminum, so vital for warplanes, too little copper, zinc, and rubber. Even after drastic cutbacks in production for civilian use, the annual output of aluminum was only about half the demand for building planes. One producer, Alcoa, the Aluminum Company of America, had a near monopoly on the manufacture of the lightweight metal and kept claiming it could supply both domestic and defense needs, yet could not come even close. Production of magnesium was even more woefully behind, and the reason, when revealed, would cause a sensation. An arrangement had been made through an interlocking cartel, between Alcoa and the giant German firm of I. G. Farben. To safeguard its American market for aluminum, Alcoa had agreed to hold back on producing magnesium, also to sell what magnesium it owned to the Germans at a cut price, with the result that Germany had far more magnesium than the United States.

Standard Oil of New Jersey, through its agreements with I. G. Farben, had intentionally delayed the development of synthetic-rubber plants. "Standard Oil," reported Truman,

> had agreed with the German I. G. Farben Company that in return for Farben giving Standard Oil a monopoly in the oil industry, Standard

Oil would give the Farben Company complete control of patents in the chemical field, including rubber. Thus when certain American rubber manufacturers made overtures to Standard Oil Company for licenses to produce synthetic rubber, they were either refused or offered licenses on very unfavorable terms. . . . Needless to say, I. G. Farben's position was dictated by the German government.

There was no "unpatriotic motive" involved here, concluded the committee in its report. It was only "big business playing the game according to the rules," with a heavy price "to be borne by the entire nation."

The American government, too—specifically the Office of Production Management—had been negligent in seeing the need for a greatly increased output of copper, lead, and zinc. For his part, Truman worried that shortages of steel were the most serious of all.

Automobile manufacturers had been allowed to do as they wished, which was to keep turning out cars as usual in 1941, on the grounds, they said, that only 10 percent of their equipment could be used for war production anyway. Automobile production for the first eight months of 1941 actually exceeded production during the same months in 1940, and consumed quantities of strategic materials—some 18 percent of the nation's available steel, 80 percent of available rubber. The aircraft program was dawdling because the Army and the Navy had left it largely to the manufacturers to decide what planes to build. "There is no planned or coordinated program for the production of aircraft," Truman would report. The committee uncovered "negligence and willful misconduct" in the Navy Bureau of Ships. (When Admiral S. M. Robinson, Chief of the Bureau of Ships, said he believed the efficiency of private and Navy shipyards to be about the same, but told the committee that comparisons were difficult because of different bookkeeping systems, the committee declared that in a matter of such importance the Navy should take steps to ascertain the actual facts.) With private shipbuilders the Navy was found to be "extremely liberal." A representative of the Todd Shipyards Corporation in testimony about one contract with the Navy said that if it weren't for taxes the company could not have handled its profits with a steam shovel.

By late October the German Army had advanced to within seventy miles of Moscow and Roosevelt offered Stalin a billion dollars worth of supplies.

The root of most troubles and delays, the committee concluded, was the Office of Production Management, the President's own ungainly creation, where there were two heads instead of one, William S. Knudsen, formerly of General Motors, and labor leader Sidney Hillman, founder of the Amalgamated Clothing Workers. Roosevelt wanted the power divided. He had no wish to create a so-called "production czar," which, the committee decided, was exactly what was needed most, a strong man with clear authority. This was the conclusion of the committee's first annual report being prepared in the final months of 1941. Truman in particular had been outraged to discover Hillman withholding a construction contract from a low bidder because of his fear of trouble from "irresponsible" elements in the American Federation of Labor. "First of all," Truman told the Senate on October 29, "the United States does not fear trouble from any source. . . . If Mr. Hillman cannot, or will not, protect the interests of the United States, I am in favor of replacing him with someone who can and will."

The record of the OPM, said the report, was not impressive. Its leadership was inept. "Its mistakes of commission have been legion; and its mistakes of omission have been even greater. It has all too often done nothing when it should have realized that problems cannot be avoided by refusing to admit that they exist."

The committee had also decided it would be best for the country and for the defense effort to dispense as soon as possible with all dollar-a-year men, of whom there were more than 250 in the Office of Production Management. Such corporate executives in high official roles were too inclined to make decisions for the benefit of their corporations. "They have their own business at heart," Truman remarked. The report called them lobbyists "in a very real sense," because their presence inevitably meant favoritism, "human nature being what it is." They should be paid government salaries in keeping with other government positions of comparable responsibility, concluded the committee, and required to disassociate themselves from any other employment or any payment from companies with defense contracts. Divided loyalties, like the divided command at the top of the Office of Production Management, were a bad idea.

On October 30, the American destroyer *Reuben James* was attacked and sunk by a German U-boat off the coast of Iceland, with a loss of 115 men. Talk of war had become commonplace in Washington, though no one seemed to be doing anything very specific about it. Writing in his diary on December 2, during a stop in the city, David Lilienthal, head of the Tennessee Valley Authority, said it looked as if a war with Japan, not Germany, was only days off. Yet people seemed unconcerned. He wondered if the democratic system was capable of coping with the world as it was. On December 4, Secretary of the Navy Frank Knox declared, "No matter what happens the U.S. Navy is not going to be caught napping."

Having no wish to embarrass the administration—and thereby harm the defense effort—Truman saw that the President received an advance copy of the committee's findings, and in an eleventh-hour decision, before the report was released, Roosevelt disbanded the OPM and announced the establishment of an all-new War Production Board under a single head, Donald M. Nelson of Sears, Roebuck. Others had been pressing Roosevelt to make the change, including Secretary of War Stimson, but for the Truman Committee it was a signal victory. "We have fought to get you this job," Truman would tell Nelson later. "We are going to fight to support you now in carrying it out."

But by then the Japanese had bombed Pearl Harbor and it was Nelson's task to mobilize for all-out war. By then even the likes of Burton K. Wheeler were saying that the only thing left to do was beat the hell out of them.

Truman had been in Missouri the first week in December, busy with political chores. The night of December 6, he checked into a hotel in Columbia, hoping to catch up on some greatly needed sleep. How he heard the news the next day and managed to get back to Washington in time for Roosevelt's momentous address to Congress on December 8, he recounted a week later in a letter to Ethel Noland, probably because he had always seen her as the one in the family with the greatest feeling for history.

Dec. 14, 1941

Dear Ethel:

Well at last I am sitting at my desk, the office is empty for the first time since I returned. One reason is the doors are locked and it's Sunday. I came down to clean off my desk and find out just how many important letters were covered up on it. Do you remember that picture with W. C. Fields as the efficiency filing expert. Well my desk is just like his was. Whenever the girls can't find a letter in the files they are morally certain it's lost on my desk and the pitiful part about it is sometimes it's true.

Well there's been a lot of happenings since I was calling on you on my daddy's birthday [December 5]. I have been afraid it would come but not just the way it did. We're always surprised of course even when the expected happens—if it's war anyway. I left Saturday for Columbia to get a good night's sleep over the weekend before Monday at Jeff City. In fact I was hoping for two. Went to bed at the Pennant Hotel outside of town about seven o'clock Saturday night and had breakfast Sunday at 8. Called the madam and went back to bed. The boy who drove me down left about noon and at three o'clock called me from

Cross Timbers (I bet you never heard of it) and told me that the Japs had bombed Honolulu. The boy was a Deputy U.S. Marshal and he was on his way to Springfield. Well I phoned the St. Louis office of T.W.A. and told 'em I had to be in Washington the next morning and about that time Bess called and said the Sec. of the Senate had called to say there'd be a joint session Monday and that I should be there. Well I had no car and no driver so I called the little airport at Columbia right across the road from the hotel and the manager said he had a plane and would take me to St. Louis. We left at 4:50 and I was on the ground and in the station of the St. Louis Airport at 5:35. It took us just 40 minutes to fly 130 miles. Then my trouble began. I tried to go to Chicago and then tried Memphis and finally I think T.W.A. dumped somebody off and I got on the 11 P.M. plane for Pittsburgh. Sat up all night and listened to the radio, got to Pittsburgh at 3:30 where I met Senator Chavez of N. Mex who came from Chicago, Sen. Davis of Pa. who lives there and Curley Brooks, the great Republican Isolationist from Chicago. He's a new Senator from Ill, Legionnaire, fat, curly haired, has a small synthetic blonde wife and is a most important Chicago Tribune Senator. He looked as if he'd swallowed a hot stove and that's the way all those anti-preparedness boys looked the next day. It wasn't because they'd been up all night getting there either.

I went home (we got here at 5:30 A.M.), found Bess up getting breakfast. My new secretary, Harry Vaughan, was at the airport with my car and I was at home by 6 o'clock. Went to bed and slept until ten and then came to the Senate. It was quite an occasion. Guess you heard it on the radio. Then on the 11th we had to accept another invitation from Germany and Italy. Goodness knows where it will end. I wish I was 30 and in command of a Battery. It would be a lot easier. . . .

II

"Harry Truman was one of the liveliest, most vital Senators in my time," wrote a veteran Senate employee, the liaison for the press, Richard Riedel, who had first come to work as a Senate page at the age of ten in 1918. Riedel had observed them all, from the days of Henry Cabot Lodge, Sr., and doubted that any had ever enjoyed public life as much as Truman, or took it so in stride. "An easygoing joviality emanated from him . . . [he had] an interest in everything and everyone. . . ." But often at the hearings of his committee, Truman seemed to present a different face to the world. "When he got down to business, the twinkle in his eyes would be replaced by a look of concentration. At such times, at close range the thick lenses of his glasses gave his eyes a fearsome, eerie stare so stern that it gave the weird illusion that one was confronting an entirely different person." At such times, said Riedel, he was grateful Senator Truman was his friend.

In the frenzied, confusing weeks after Pearl Harbor, the Under Secretary of War, Robert Patterson, had urged the President to do away with the committee, saying it would "impair our activity if we have to take time out to supply the Truman Committee all the information it desires." But Roosevelt had no such wish, and as the work of the committee continued, the energy and effectiveness of its chairman drew increasing attention. The first annual report was presented to the Senate on January 15, 1942. In time would come 50 additional reports, as a consequence of extensive, careful research, and more than 400 hearings at which 1,798 witnesses appeared. Amazingly, all reports of the committee were to be unanimous. Asked how this could happen, Republican Owen Brewster said it was not hard to get men to agree when the facts were known.

Early 1942 was a dark time. Singapore fell to the Japanese, then Bataan, with the surrender of General Wainwright and some 75,000 American and Filipino troops, the largest surrender of an American fighting force since Appomattox. Leningrad was still under siege, after more than six months, and along the eastern seaboard of the United States, off shores long thought safe from Europe's wars, German U-boats were sinking oil tankers almost at will—and "so close," wrote Eric Sevareid, "that a chorus girl in a Miami penthouse could see men die in flaming oil." Washington made ready for air raids. Bess Truman had blackout curtains on order for the Connecticut Avenue apartment. The senator took his World War I helmet to the office and at night would lie awake tossing and turning, "fighting the war." In April, driving through North Carolina on committee business, he tried to think only of spring returning, "the return of Ceres from Pluto's palace." The dogwood and apple orchards were in bloom along the winding road, and at the hotel at Chapel Hill all was quiet and restful. Still he couldn't sleep, fretting over the course of the war.

In a speech on the Senate floor that summer of 1942, he called for a second front in Europe to relieve the Russians—as a matter of clear military necessity. In a speech at home in Jackson County he said the war was only a tragic continuation of "the one we fought in 1917 and 1918." The victors in that war, he argued, "had the opportunity to compel a peace that would protect us from war for many generations. But they missed the opportunity." A "spirit of isolationism" had brought the worse calamity of the present conflict. It must never happen again.

Disclosures produced by his committee were shocking. Curtiss-Wright was discovered manufacturing faulty airplane engines for delivery to combat forces. One inspector for Curtiss-Wright, a man with two nephews in the Army Air Corps, broke down and wept as he told a committee investigator what was going on. "If I were the executive in charge of a plant of that sort, I would know what was going on," Truman told an Air Corps officer who testified, "and I think it is plain negligence, and maybe worse than that . . . that they didn't know. They should have known." The officer agreed. "No doubt about it," said Truman. The Air Corps had denied that there were problems. Curtiss-Wright launched an advertising campaign stressing the company's contribution to winning the war. But the faulty engines were a reality, and as Truman surmised, more than negligence was involved. As an aftermath of the committee's investigation one Air Corps general involved was sent to prison.

Questioning the cause of troubles with the B-26 bomber built by the Glenn Martin Company, the committee was informed by Martin himself that the wings were not wide enough. Truman asked why the wings weren't fixed. Martin said plans were too far along and that besides he already had the contract. Truman said that if that was how Martin felt, then the committee would see the contract was ended. Martin said he would correct the size of the wings.

They saw a lot of the seamy side of the war effort, Truman once remarked, speaking for the committee. Yet for Truman the disclosures appeared to confirm many of his worst suspicions about big business in America. He was truly a Jeffersonian in spirit; William Jennings Bryan remained a political hero. The things Truman had said in the Senate in earlier years about the evils of big banks, big insurance companies, big corporations had been said in earnest. He had never really known any industrialists or heads of giant corporations, most of whom were Republicans. He had never counted such people among his personal or political friends.

Nor, at this stage, does he appear ever to have accepted the view that a certain amount of corporate stupidity and corruption was inevitable in an undertaking so massive and involving so many interests as the war effort. In fact, the American industrial powerhouse, America's phenomenal productivity was what would turn the tide against Germany and Japan. It would prove the decisive factor in the war, and Truman was to give too little credit to the vast majority of patriotic business people and industrialists who were making this happen. At times, in what he wrote and said, he made it seem as though the committee and its investigators were the only ones doing their duty. He didn't believe that, of course. Also, from what he and his investigators were finding, it is easy to understand why he might have felt as he did.

A classic case and one of the most memorable days of testimony concerned the United States Steel Corporation and its subsidiary, Carnegie-Illinois Steel. At issue was the quality of steel plate being produced for ships.

As frequently happened, the committee's first hint of trouble came in letters from employees who felt it their patriotic duty to report what was going on. At first little was done. The volume of similar complaints and warnings from around the country had become too great to handle. Much of it was obviously crank mail and to follow every lead would have been impossible. But when a newly launched ship, a tanker called *Schenectady* built by Henry J. Kaiser, broke in two at Portland, Oregon, in January 1943, the question of steel plate became one of vital importance.

At the Irvin Works, the Carnegie-Illinois rolling mill at West Mifflin, Pennsylvania, investigators for the Truman Committee found that at least 5 percent of the plant's production, or about 3,000 tons of steel per month, failed to meet Navy specifications, yet was being labeled and delivered as up to standard. The results of quality tests—chemical analysis conducted in the mill to determine the quantity of carbon and other elements in the steel—were simply altered (as were other tests for tensile strength) "to conform to what the customer expected to receive," in the words of the chief specifications examiner, a man named Murray Stewart. If the chemical analysis of a "heat" of steel wasn't known, he said, then they would just make one up for the record book.

Stewart was among the first to appear on the day of the hearing, March 23, 1943, and he provided some of the most damaging of all testimony, as well as a touch of unintended humor, when Hugh Fulton encouraged him to explain how exactly the system worked:

FULTON: In other words . . . you would make up a chemical analysis which you thought would fit what the steel should have been.
STEWART: That is right.
FULTON: And how would you deal with that in that particular record book?
STEWART: In order to keep our records so that we would know when it was an incorrect heat number, we would enter it in this book in pencil.
FULTON: How were the other entries made?
STEWART: They were made in ink.
FULTON: And did you, in addition to making them in pencil, put any prefix letter in front of them?
STEWART: It was a common practice to put an "F."
FULTON: What did "F" mean?

STEWART: Fake.

FULTON: You told our investigator originally that it meant phone.

STEWART: That is right.

FULTON: But now under oath you desire to state it meant fake?

STEWART: That is correct. The investigator was a stranger to me and I was sort of pressed for something to say at the moment.

An assistant metallurgist, David B. Ireland, Jr., testified—apparently hoping to put operations at the Irvin mill in a better light—that he learned how to fake the tests at the Edgar Thomson Works, another giant Carnegie-Illinois mill near Pittsburgh. Indeed, he had become so proficient, said Ireland, that he could readily fool a Navy inspector, whenever one was on hand. To date only one tester had been caught cheating by a Navy inspector, Ireland continued, but there was an explanation for that: "He cheated more than he was supposed to cheat."

Was the man fired, asked Senator Homer Ferguson. No, said Ireland, he was demoted. Was he demoted because he went too far, Chairman Truman asked a higher-ranking employee, chief metallurgist W. F. McGarrity.

"Yes, sir," said McGarrity.

"Going a little too far, he was demoted," repeated Truman. "He wasn't fired, he was just demoted."

"And through satisfactory work elsewhere he was brought back to a better paying job," added McGarrity.

Three investigators from the committee had gone to the Irvin Works earlier in March, or roughly two months after the *Schenectady* incident. They had called first at the Carnegie-Illinois headquarters in Pittsburgh, where they were told by the president of the corporation, J. Lester Perry, that they could speak to no employee unless a company attorney were present. Nor would they be permitted inside the mill until he, Perry, put through a call to Senator Truman to see what this was all about, a move that infuriated Senator Truman and made him immediately suspicious that Perry was trying to hide something. When the investigators arrived at Irwin about noon they were kept waiting for half an hour, then invited to lunch at the company cafeteria. They did not want lunch, they said, they wanted to see the record book from the mill at once. But they were kept waiting another hour, and when the book was at last made available at two in the afternoon, they learned it had been taken apart the night before and distributed among several people who were "doing work" for the company attorney. Two hours had been required to put it back together again. How much had been removed or altered they had no way of knowing, wrote one of the investigators in his report to Chairman Truman.

"I don't think that was exactly strong cooperation, Mr. Perry," Truman said when Perry took his place at the witness table, after Stewart, Ireland, and McGarrity had all completed their testimony. "And I was also rather surprised . . . that you didn't take immediate action to clean the plant and find why this procedure was followed. I want you to explain to the committee fully why that was."

"Senator Truman, it is not my intention to explain this and to be controversial," Perry answered smoothly.

"You can be as controversial as you like," said Truman. "It is your privilege."

He had never had any desire except to cooperate, Perry insisted. Perhaps he had not appreciated the full importance of the investigators' visit, perhaps he should have done more. He had demonstrated goodwill, he thought. As he recalled, it was only late in the day when the seriousness of the situation became clear to him. "That afternoon, late, it appeared definitely that they wanted to make an investigation," he said.

"We don't send investigators to plants just for fun," Truman snapped.

"I understand that now," replied Perry.

Truman pressed him again on what action had been taken to straighten things out in the mill. Had anybody been fired? What corrections had been made? Trying first to evade the questions, Perry admitted that as yet nothing had been done. He needed time to get all the facts, "the fullest implications." Truman found that unacceptable. If he had been president of the company, he said, he would have gotten to the bottom of the situation at once. "You had all this information as soon as our investigators had it."

It was Perry's position, as expressed in a prepared statement and in the course of testimony, that while management deplored such devious practices as had been disclosed by the committee's investigators—practices that higher management had no part in—even the substandard plates supplied by the mill were "entirely suitable for their intended use." If the Navy was not getting what it ordered exactly, what it was getting was good enough for the purpose. "The only explanation which can be given for the failure to carry out prescribed testing procedures is that a few individuals . . . grew lax under the pressure of heavy production. . . ." He found the word "cheat" as used in other testimony unacceptable. He preferred "misrepresentation."

Most important, concerning the *Schenectady*, he said that failure of steel plate in the ship had not been the cause of its breakup and even if that were the problem, the plate at the point where the break began was not a product of the Irvin Works.

Of the senators present, it was Ferguson and Brewster, the two Republicans, who bore down hardest on Perry, while Fulton or Truman would move in with a question or comment from time to time. Ferguson picked up quickly on the question of where the *Schenectady* plate had been made. It was not made at Irvin, Perry affirmed again. Then where, asked Ferguson. Homestead, admitted Perry.

"Didn't you hear the witness testify here that he was taught how to cheat down at the Homestead Works?" Ferguson asked.

"Senator, this word 'cheat' . . ."

"Have you a better one?"

Senator Brewster then read aloud from the report of an investigation conducted by the Bureau of Ships, stating quite plainly that "a very poor quality of steel" had been "most directly responsible" for the failure of the *Schenectady*. The plate was "of definitely inferior quality," Brewster read on. It was so brittle it was more like cast iron than steel.

Had Perry read the report? He had read parts of it, he replied. Brewster, his anger becoming more apparent, wondered how Perry might feel if he had a son going overseas in a ship made of such steel.

Perry answered, "Why, Senator, I don't for a moment condone poor steel, defective steel in ships or anywhere else that has to do with the war effort. Don't worry about how I feel about the sons going over there."

Truman interposed to explain that Senator Brewster had a son overseas in the war.

"If a customer asks you for a strength of 60,000 pounds, the breaking point on a test," Ferguson said, "and you give him a product of 57,000 pounds, but you represent to him in figures that you have tested it and it did test 60,000 pounds, is that a misrepresentation of a material fact?"

PERRY: Yes, sir.

FERGUSON: You understand that was done up to five percent of the material furnished?

PERRY: That is the evidence here this morning.

FERGUSON: Do you say that that was not selling a product to the United States Government under false representations?

PERRY: If that was done, to that extent it would be.

FERGUSON: You heard the testimony. Is there any doubt in your mind that it was done?

PERRY: There is a doubt in my mind as to whether it was done in regard to material that was furnished to Government specification and testing where the Government made the inspection or supervised the inspection.

FERGUSON: Do you mean to say—do I understand you now to say that you don't believe the testimony of your own men here under oath?

PERRY: Did they actually testify to that point that where inspection was made by the Navy . . . ?

FULTON: And also to the Navy where they said it was possible to cheat with the Navy inspector standing right there.

PERRY: I have stated that where that was done it was a misrepresentation.

FERGUSON: Do I understand that you still insist that no inferior material was sold to the Government?

PERRY: I still insist that it was not inferior for the end use to which it was put. . . .

FERGUSON: In other words, you are the man who is stating what you think the Government should buy, is that right?

PERRY: No, sir.

FERGUSON: Then, why don't you live up to the Government specifications?

PERRY: We should.

FERGUSON: Why didn't you?

PERRY: We will.

TRUMAN: I'll say you will. . . .

The hearing lasted five hours. When the company's attorney, testifying after Perry, talked of his need to master the technicalities of the steel business before "justifying this situation," Truman broke in to ask what knowledge of technicalities had to do with removing cheaters from jobs of critical responsibility. "I don't know anything about the steel business," Truman said, "and don't expect to know about it, but I can tell you when the books have been tampered with and when there is a bunch of crookedness going on. That is plain enough for me to see."

But the question of who ultimately had been responsible for what went on—of how high up the blame should go—was never really answered. No one above the chief metallurgist, McGarrity, would admit to any knowledge of rigging tests or falsifying records. Nor did the hearing disclose a substantial motive for passing off the inferior steel. Those in the mill involved in the deception had nothing to gain by their actions and everything to lose if found out. The one plausible explanation offered was that it was all in an effort to set an impressive production record.

In any event management promised to set everything straight, and in the final hour the president of U.S. Steel, Benjamin F. Fairless, promised Truman that whoever was responsible would "walk the plank."

"You realize, Mr. Fairless," said Senator Brewster, "how incredible it seems that subordinates in the company would risk their entire future without hope of reward of any character. That, of course, is what impresses the committee and makes it so amazing."

Senator Ferguson was curious whether Mr. Fairless thought, from what he had heard during the day, that the operation of Carnegie-Illinois Steel was an example of good management. "I certainly do not," said Fairless. "I consider it was very, very poor management."

At the close of the hearing, asked by a reporter for his personal comment on what had been divulged during the day, Truman said he did not think that could be printed.

On the issue of the dollar-a-year men on the War Production Board, Truman stood fast, stressing with great feeling the essential injustice of the system, but giving in at last, much against his better judgment, because the production czar he had helped create, Donald Nelson, argued otherwise. Nelson wanted no change in the system, insisting it was the way to get maximum results from industry. He had to have people who understood how industry worked, he told the committee. Asked why such men should be allowed to retain their corporate ties and benefits, he said people with big salaries had big expenses—mortgages, insurance, and the like—and could not make the change to government pay without suffering hardship.

"I don't think there should be any special class," Truman responded. Only that morning he had received a letter from a man who had been earning $25,000 a year, a reserve officer who had been called up for duty. "He is going to get $140 a month, and he can't draw his $25,000 while he is gone," Truman said. "He is satisfied to do that because he wants to win the war, just as you do and just as I do, by every means possible, no matter what it costs him, because if he doesn't win it his $25,000 a year won't be worth a cent. I am laboring, and have been, under the delusion, maybe, that if the government had the power to take these young men away from their jobs and their outlook on life for the purpose of this emergency, the dollar-a-year men could face the same situation and face it adequately, and would be glad to do it."

He was not opposed to the dollar-a-year men because they were businessmen—he wanted more businessmen in government, especially in the war effort—but he knew how "human" it was for a steel executive on loan to the war administration to hesitate in ordering any action that might injure the standing of his company or industry once the war was over. He had learned that certain high-ranking dollar-a-year men had initially delayed the construction of new furnaces when they were needed because of concern over what increased ingot capacity might do to their postwar profits.

But reluctantly he backed off, saying that if Nelson felt the system was what it took to win the war, then the committee should not stand in the way. In a letter to Nelson a few days later, he was more specific. The committee did not like having procurement matters entrusted to those who were such obvious hostages to fortune, he wrote.

> However, the committee believes that the best interests of the procurement program require that it be administered by a single head who will be able to do things in his way and who will be judged by his accomplishments as a whole. . . . The committee will, therefore, support you even on matters in which it disagrees with you. . . .

By pushing harder on the issue, he felt, the committee could run the risk of overreaching its power, to the point of dictating policy, like the intrusive Civil War committee.

In backing Nelson he was also standing by a fundamental conviction that control of the war effort must be kept in civilian hands. In just the first six months of 1942 military contracts added to the economy totaled $400 billion. He saw ambitious generals and admirals on all sides gaining influence over industry and agriculture and he worried what this could mean for the future. In the fall of 1942, on a broadcast for "The March of Time," he called the issue of civilian control the foremost of the day and warned it could shape the whole political and economic structure of the country after the war. "The function of generals and admirals is to fight battles," he said, "and to tell us what they need to fight battles with."

General Brehon Somervell, wearing three stars now, was again called before the committee to explain an incredible project, called Canol, after "Canadian oil." The scheme was to build a four-inch oil pipeline across 1,200 miles from Canada to Alaska, and it had been launched "on the nod" from Somervell, secretly, with little thought to the realities of terrain, climate, available materials, available manpower, or the views of oil experts, the Corps of Engineers, and the War Production Board. An item was added to the War Department budget of $25 million with no description except that it was for the construction of military facilities in Canada and Alaska.

The shroud of secrecy had been primarily to avoid interference from other civilian sides of government, and in particular the notoriously irascible Harold Ickes, Secretary of the Interior and head of the Petroleum Administration. Employees of the contractor, Stephen Bechtel, began calling Canol "the greatest project since the Panama Canal." But then Ickes found out about it and went before the Truman Committee to say the whole project "grew entirely out of a one-page memorandum from General Somervell, who was anxious to conserve paper. . . ." Ickes called the pipeline useless and the committee came to much the same conclusion, having heard more from Somervell's chief adviser for the project, James H. Graham, a dollar-a-year man who, Ickes said, was "worth every penny of it." Graham, the committee found, had no idea how long the pipeline was to be. He had made no estimate of the cost, nor did he believe anybody else had. "I don't regard cost in time of war," he told the committee more than once.

"The committee damns it up and down while the War Department is as usual scrambling desperately to save face instead of having the guts to admit a mistake frankly and go on from there," wrote a new observer on the scene, a young reporter for the United Press named Allen Drury, on the day of Somervell's appearance. "All the desperate assertions of an embarrassed incompetence have been hurried forth to justify the thing, but the committee is unimpressed."

Somervell had paraded into the hearings flanked by four brigadier generals and several majors. At one point, as Drury happily recorded in his journal, Somervell asked for some water, handing his glass to a brigadier who handed it to a major who, finding no one of lesser rank available, filled the glass himself and returned it to the brigadier who returned it to the general.

The committee hammered away at Somervell for four and a half hours, with Hugh Fulton and Senator Harley Kilgore doing most of the questioning. The chairman listened quietly. But in winding up the day Truman read Somervell a letter he had received from the Navy Department—a letter, he explained, written in answer to his own question whether the Navy had ever been asked for its opinion on Canol, or requested to participate. According to the letter, a search of Navy files had turned up no communication indicating such an inquiry. No officers or officials of the Navy Department had ever been questioned orally about Canol.

Somervell said he never implied that he had asked the Navy. "It is not a Navy situation. Not any more than a bakery we might build. . . ."

Truman suggested that very possibly it could have to do with the Navy, since ships burn a good deal of oil.

"Yes, sir," replied Somervell, who now said the Chief of Naval Operations and others had "expressed themselves in favor of the project."

"The Secretary of the Navy, however, has the other opinion," said Truman. "The committee will stand adjourned."

• • •

Worn down at day's end, he would complain to Bess that the pressures on him had begun to tell again. She knew of his headaches and exhaustion and worried he might push himself to the point of collapse. Witnesses at the hearings got on his nerves far more than he let on, he told her. He talked of just going away somewhere and reading Shakespeare and Plutarch "over and over and over."

Yet nothing about his public manner revealed any of this. He was brisk and cheerful as always. He radiated good health and youthful energy. In contrast to so many among the congressional brotherhood, the gray, double-chinned, food-stained veterans of Capitol Hill, he appeared abnormally fit and his good clothes, his one indulgence, were spotless. Though not a fancy dresser—he remained too much the midwesterner for that—he looked always, as Margaret said, as if he had just stepped from a bandbox. His suits were perfectly cleaned and pressed, his shirts immaculate. (He had had a time his first few years in Washington finding a dry cleaner who could do his clothes to his satisfaction.) He had dozens of suits—some old favorites custom-made by Ted Marks, others from Eddie Jacobson's new store in Kansas City or from Garfinckel's in Washington, mostly double-breasted, grays and blues, and cut to accentuate how trim he was. (He could still get into his old Army uniform, he liked to tell people.) Lately, too, he had begun wearing bow ties—a departure viewed by his wife and daughter with considerable disfavor—and there was always a fresh, perfectly folded handkerchief in the breast pocket showing five points, always the World War I service pin in his lapel. He looked crisp. He moved with a bounce, even in the heat of summer, his two-tone summer shoes clicking down the marble halls more rapidly than any. Richard Riedel, the young press liaison who prided himself in being able to get about the Capitol in double-quick time, remembered Truman's good-natured approval of the pace he set. "One day in a typical kidding mood he [Truman] started in behind me and walked lock-step through the Lobby to the amusement of all who saw him."

His vitality seemed greater than ever, in keeping with his new confidence. He had "arrived" in the Senate, as everybody knew, and it agreed with him. He was having a splendid time being Senator Harry Truman of the Truman Committee.

Yet he acquired no airs, for all this. He was as unpresuming, as accessible as always, despite the extraordinary new power he had and the urgent, wartime atmosphere of Washington. Self-importance was on display in the city in many quarters to a greater degree than ever in memory, but Truman seemed somehow unaffected. A reporter for the St. Louis *Globe-Democrat* described later how he had been sent by his editor to see the senator, who was reportedly back in town briefly after one of his committee forays and staying at the Jefferson Hotel on 16th Street:

> I went up to the front desk and asked the room clerk for the number of Senator Truman's room. He gave it to me. I went to a house phone and called the Senator's room. The phone was answered not by a security guard, not by an aide, not even by a secretary. It was answered by Harry Truman. I identified myself, and he said sure, come on up. I knocked on his door, and the door was opened by Senator Truman. He was alone, in his shirt sleeves, with a book held closed on a finger. He put the book aside, offered me a chair, poured us each a bourbon highball, and sat back with a friendly smile. We talked, without interruption, for almost an hour. What we talked about, what I later wrote, I have no real recollection of. All I remember is that the book he was reading was Volume III of Douglas Southall Freeman's biography of Robert E. Lee. That the bourbon we drank was Old Crow. That he was completely relaxed and responsive. And that there was no one else around.

Nearly everything being said about him in the papers was complimentary, and the committee and its work now had the respect of the administration. "I am more surprised every day at the respect with which the special committee is regarded by people in high places," he wrote to Bess, very pleased. "If I can just keep from making any real errors, we are on the way to really help win the war and to make the job more efficient and quicker. That means fewer of our young men killed and a chance for a more honorable settlement. So you must pray for me to go the right way."

In the Senate, where he was always well liked, he had achieved a new stature, even among liberals who, until now, had regarded him as pleasant enough and conscientious, but bland. "The man from Missouri," remembered Claude Pepper, "had dared to say 'show me' to the powerful military-industrial complex and he had caught many people in the act."

He was notable too for so much that he was not. He was not florid or promiscuous. He made no pretense at being superior in any regard. He did not seem to need the limelight, flattery, or a following. He did not want to be the President.

To his pleasure, he was recognized now in restaurants and hotel lobbies, as he had never been before except in Missouri, and not always there. "Now you've got to help me more than ever so I won't be a damn fool or stuffed shirt," he told Bess.

. . .

Margaret, now in her late teens, had begun singing lessons and was doing splendidly, he thought. She was talking already of a singing career. Neither he nor Bess was a singer. Margaret never heard him even try to sing, which seemed odd for someone with such love for music. But he did nothing to discourage her, said only that she must first finish college.

He called her "Margie" or "Miss Skinny." Alert and energetic, with a sunny disposition, she was one of the great satisfactions of his life.

They so clearly enjoyed one another's company that it gave pleasure to others. "One time, one Christmas," remembered a niece of Ethel Noland's, who lived in the Noland house on North Delaware, "Margaret was with him and they came across for a little visit Christmas morning. And I don't think I ever laughed any harder. . . . They just gave it back and forth. . . . They were as fun as can be. *Repartee!* He was so crazy about Margaret, just enjoyed being with her and talking with her and we sat there just entranced. . . ."

With friends in Washington he could talk about her by the hour, as she knew.

> You have a good mind, a beautiful physique and a possible successful future outlook—but that now is up to you [he wrote when she turned eighteen]. You are the mistress of your future. All your mother and dad can do is to look on, advise when asked and hope and wish you a happy one. There'll be troubles and sorrow a plenty but there'll also be happy days and hard work.
>
> From a financial standpoint your father has not been a shining success but he has tried to leave you something that (as Mr. Shakespeare says) cannot be stolen—an honorable reputation and a good name. You must continue that heritage and see that it is not spoiled. You're all we have and we both count on you.

Later, to Bess he would write, "Tell my baby she has a *most* beautiful voice—to keep it *natural* without any gimcracks, pronounce her words clearly and in *English* so they can be understood—and she'll be a great singer." She too must never become a damn fool or a stuffed shirt.

They remained an extremely close-knit family, their social schedule modest, their way of life private and quiet. At home in the small, simply furnished apartment on Connecticut, Truman's corner of the living room included a chintz-covered armchair, a reading lamp, his phonograph, and his record collection. In a small, free-standing bookcase within arm's reach was a leatherbound set of Plutarch's *Lives*, a two-volume *Andrew Jackson* by Marquis James, all four volumes of Freeman's *Lee*, the Bible, *Stories of the Great Operas*, a biography of John Nance Garner, and *Don Quixote*.

Bess, now in her fifties, looked plumper and more matronly by the year, and was enjoying Washington as she never had. The stepped-up pace of wartime agreed with her. He had put her on the office payroll, a not uncommon practice, but one he had criticized others for, most notably Tuck Milligan during his first Senate race. Her salary was $2,400. Truman worried about damaging publicity if ever this were known, but the extra income made a difference. How much real work she did would remain a matter of opinion among the staff, none of whom were as well paid. At one point he advised her privately to "only just drop in and do some signing" of letters. "It helps all concerned." She was working also at the USO one day a week, and reportedly "reveled" in the excitement he was causing on the Hill.

In a letter from Independence during a visit in June of 1942, she told him how much better he was sounding on the radio. A speech explaining the rubber shortage had been broadcast nationwide. She thought it his best yet, and Ethel Noland agreed. His consonants had all been pronounced just right, Ethel said.

The day before their twenty-third wedding anniversary, he sent Bess twenty-three roses, then telephoned her that night and wrote a letter the next morning:

> Washington, D.C.
> June 28, 1942
>
> Dear Bess:
> Well this is *the day*. Lots of water has gone over the dam. There've been some terrible days and many more nice ones. When my store went flooey and cost my friends and Frank [Wallace] money, when Margie came, don't think I ever spent such a day, although the pains were yours. And to name one more, when we thought Stark had won and when I lost actually for eastern judge. But the wins have far outweighed 'em. June 28, 1919, was the happiest day of my life, for I had looked forward to it for a lifetime nearly or so it seemed. When a man gets the right kind of wife, his career is made—and I got just that.
> The greatest thing we have is a real young lady who hasn't an equal anywhere. That's all the excuse we need for living and not much else matters.
> It was grand to say hello last night. I was so tired I could hardly sit up. Went to bed right away after playing Margie's song record and the Minuet (in G) and Chopin waltzes. It's pretty lonesome around here without you. . . .
> Kiss Margie, lots and lots of love and happy returns,
> Harry

In November 1942, after the American landing in North Africa, he was praised in the St. Louis *Post-Dispatch* in a way that would have been inconceivable a few years before. Harry Truman, wrote Marquis Childs, had become "one of the most useful and at the same time one of the most forthright and fearless of the ninety-six" in the Senate. In a book published that same fall, a brilliant portrait of Washington going to war called *I Write from Washington,* Childs also contrasted the appalling revelations of the Truman Committee to the kind of false picture presented by the Office of Facts and Figures, a new propaganda agency.

Truman and his committee were now known nationwide, observed the Washington *Star.* So great was their reputation, said *BusinessWeek,* that "often a threat to 'take everything to the Truman Committee' is sufficient to force a cure of abuses." The whole country was greatly indebted to Senator Truman and his colleagues, wrote *The Nation.*

Arthur Krock of *The New York Times* so admired the senator's "objectivity at the total expense of partisanship" in his running of the committee that he invited a select few of his fellow journalists to lunch with Senator Truman at the renowned Metropolitan Club and wrote later of the "excellent impression" he made.

By 1943 the committee had produced twenty-one reports covering a wide range of subjects—gasoline rationing, lumber, farm machinery, the loss of American shipping to U-boats. The week of March 8, 1943, "Investigator Truman" was on the cover of *Time.* In many ways, said *Time,* the Truman Committee was among the outstanding successes of the entire war effort. It was the "watchdog, spotlight, conscience and spark plug to the economic war-behind-the-lines," and a heartening sign that even in wartime a democracy could keep an eye on itself. Hardly less remarkable, said the magazine, was the transformation of Harry Truman, from Pendergast errand boy to able, energetic committee chairman just when he was needed:

> For a Congressional committee to be considered the first line of defense—especially in a nation which does not tend to admire its representatives, in Congress assembled—is encouraging to believers in democracy. So is the sudden emergence of Harry Truman, whose presence in the Senate is a queer accident of democracy. . . .

Truman himself, wrote *Time,* was "scrupulously honest. . . . His only vices are small-stakes poker, an occasional drink of bourbon." ("WHAT DO

285

THEY MEAN AN OCCASIONAL DRINK OF BOURBON?" Lewis Schwellenbach cabled from Spokane.)

In a poll of Washington correspondents conducted by *Look* magazine, Senator Truman would be named one of the ten men in Washington whose services had been the most important to the war effort. Further, he was the only one on the list from either branch of Congress.

On April 14, 1943, putting aside his committee work, Truman flew to Chicago to champion a cause that had little to do with the war effort and that seemed a bit surprising for a midwestern senator, a Baptist, a Mason, and proud member of the American Legion to involve himself with. He spoke at a huge rally called to urge help for the doomed Jews of Europe. Chicago Stadium was packed, the crowd estimated at twenty-five thousand. The chairman was a prominent Roman Catholic, Federal Judge William J. Campbell. The keynote speaker was Rabbi Stephen Wise of New York, head of the American Jewish Congress.

The war in which he and his comrades fought twenty-three years earlier, said Senator Truman in his speech, had been waged "not only that nations might be free but also that the people who make up those nations might be free." Now that freedom had been trampled to dust under the "iron heel of the barbarian." The Jews of Europe, through the edict of "a mad Hitler," were being "herded like animals" into concentration camps. It was time something was done about it.

In private, Truman was a man who still, out of old habits of the mouth, could use a word like "kike," or, in a letter to his wife, dismiss Miami as nothing but "hotels, filling stations, Hebrews, and cabins." But he spoke now from the heart, and with passing reference to Roosevelt's "Four Freedoms," made an implied criticism of the President for doing too little to help the Jews. Truman was not among those who refused to believe the Germans capable of such atrocities as were being reported from Europe.

> Merely talking about the Four Freedoms is not enough. This is the time for action. No one can any longer doubt the horrible intentions of the Nazi beasts. We know that they plan the systematic slaughter throughout all of Europe, not only of the Jews but of vast numbers of other innocent peoples.

Now was the time for fighting, he continued, but no less important was planning for the day when the war would end. "Today—not tomorrow—we must do all that is humanly possible to provide a haven and a place of safety for all those who can be grasped from the hands of the Nazi butchers." Free lands must be opened to them, he said.

> Their present oppressors must know that they will be held directly accountable for their bloody deeds. To do all this, we must draw deeply on our traditions of aid to the oppressed, and on our great national generosity. This is not a Jewish problem, it is an American problem— and we must and we will face it squarely and honorably.

It was a remarkable speech, one of the strongest he ever made. How very important it was that he felt as he did, neither he nor any of his audience could possibly yet know.

With other senators on the committee—Hatch, Ball, Harold Burton— Truman was giving more and more thought to problems of the postwar world. And though he played no direct part in the drafting of a Senate resolution for the establishment of a postwar international organization, a United Nations—a resolution sponsored by Senators Ball, Burton, Hatch, and Lister Hill, and hence known as B^2H^2—Truman was the acknowledged guiding spirit. The United States could "not possibly avoid the assumption of world leadership after this war," he was quoted in *The New York Times*. And with Republican Congressman Walter Judd of Minnesota, who had also fought in World War I, Truman set out on a Midwest speaking tour in the summer of 1943 to spread the internationalist word under the sponsorship of the United Nations Association. He kept hammering at the same themes over and over across Iowa, Nebraska, Kansas, and Missouri. "History has bestowed on us a solemn responsibility. . . . We failed before to give a genuine peace—we dare not fail this time. . . . We must not repeat the blunders of the past."

Not all the Truman Committee's efforts were successful. The Canol Project went on and wound up costing $134 million, all money that need never have been spent, and more serious even than the financial waste was the misuse of vitally needed manpower and materials. (At one point 4,000 troops and 12,000 civilians were involved.) Corporations and government agencies found to be bungling things or committing outright fraud, like Carnegie-Illinois Steel, were frequently let off the hook to keep production rolling. "We want aluminum, not excuses," Truman said after the committee's tangle with Alcoa.

Yet overall the committee's performance was outstanding. It would be called the most successful congressional investigative effort in American history. Later estimates were that the Truman Committee saved the country as much as $15 billion. This was almost certainly an exaggeration—no exact figure is possible—but the sum was enormous and unprecedented, and whatever the amount, it was only part of the service rendered. The most important "power" of the committee was its deterrent effect. Fear of investigation or public exposure by the committee was enough in itself to cause countless people in industry, government, and the military to do their jobs right, thereby, in the long run, saving thousands of lives.

It was not just that the production of defective airplane engines or low-grade steel had been exposed; the committee also made positive contributions to the production of improved military equipment. The most notable—and one that saved many lives—was the famous, hinge-prowed Higgins landing craft used for amphibious assault, which was built and ordered by the Navy's Bureau of Ships only after heavy prodding from the committee. With the new Higgins craft troops could be landed on a variety of shallow beaches, rather than just established harbors. It increased mobility for the offense, made obsolete much of the old coastal defenses. Yet until the committee looked at the subject with a fresh eye, Navy bureaucrats had been trying to force the adoption of a plainly inferior design.

The committee was also a continuing source of information about the war effort for the whole country. In its report on the loss to U-boats, for example, the committee said 12 million tons of American shipping were destroyed in 1942, an alarming figure. This was 1 million tons more than all the nation's shipyards were then producing. The Navy immediately denied the validity of the report. But when Secretary of the Navy Knox appeared before the committee in executive session, he admitted the committee was telling the truth.

Unquestionably, the relentless "watchdog" role, the attention to detail during the hearings, the quality as well as the quantity of the reports issued, all greatly increased public confidence in how the war was being run. Further, anyone called before the committee could count on a fair hearing. The chairman would have it no other way.

From what he had observed of Chairman Truman during the day of General Somervell's testimony, Allen Drury of United Press recorded: "He seems to be a generally good man, probably deserving of his reputation." But after watching several more sessions, including one in which Truman went out of his way to keep some of the other senators from browbeating a witness, Drury could hardly say enough for the head of the committee:

1

April 12, 1945: Harry S. Truman takes the oath of office from Chief Justice Harlan F. Stone in the Cabinet Room at the White House.

2

TRUMAN ENTERS OFFICE WITH FIRM HAND

THE INDEPENDENCE EXAMINER

The Nation's New Chief Executive, Who Vowed in Oath Last Night to "C_____ _ West and East" to a Successful Conclusion, Summons His Military Chiefs of Staff for Quick Conference.

L. 40   INDEPENDENCE, MO., FRIDAY, APRIL 13, 1945   NO. 284

MISSOURI LANGUAGE

Solomon Wise

To Roosevelt

he dooryard lilacs bloom,
vely nature wakes anew.
growing hearts a nation
rns

great chief, to you.

r now is home from sea,
nter home from hill,
the careful plans you

struggle to fulfill.

forgotten men, their tears
lingle with the great,
increasing purposes
tch and pray and wait.
—C. S. C.

Truman of Independence,
is President of the
ates. He will be a good
Of course we who know
ell and who love him so
humble but we are not
We have no fear and
s about the matter. We
e Harry Truman is hon-
atriotic and our ideal of
eal American should be
now that under his hand
of States will certainly
great destiny. We lift
in prayer and in faith.

Truman comes into the
office in the world with
eparation and training.
, ten good years, in the
the United States have
to know what it is all
experience has brought
to the mighty forces
sere on land. His train-
him to know where to
here is not a man in the
to Washington for that

CITY CHOKES ITS SORROW TO WISH ITS HARRY WELL

Independence Accepts the Death of Mr. Roosevelt and Elevation of Own Citizen With Mingled Emotions.

IS IN SAFE HANDS

Concensus of Opinion Is That Nation's Vice-President Is Equal to Momentous Task.

Independence at first too stunned to think, accepted President Franklin D. Roosevelt's death with mingled emotions. As the city gradually recovered from the immediate shock, its citizens realized that one of their own residents, Harry S. Truman, vice-president of the United States, would come to the nation's helm to take up where Mr. Roosevelt left off in this most crucial period in world history.

Political differences cleared away and one and all they remembered only the things they admired about the great humanitarian who had served his nation so long and so devoutly. Then there came a feeling of admiration and pride that Independence should provide the man who would carry on in his vital role in world affairs.

They silently wished "Harry" well, but there was a general feeling among many that they would like to have seen Mr. Roosevelt live through the coming San Francisco conference because of his experience and background. But tears were choked back and the city expressed pride in the recognition for President Truman began working, subconsciously in their minds.

PRESIDENT HARRY S. TRUMAN

'MAN OF HOUR' HAS A SOUND HEREDITY

LIGHT SHOWERS EXPECTED

The weather forecast for Independence and vicinity: Cloudy and slightly cooler this afternoon and tonight; occasional light showers ending early tonight; lowest tem-

MEMORIAL SERVICE HELD AT SCHOOLS

Assembly Programs Today Give Fitting Tributes Honoring the Late President, Franklin D.

MAYOR'S PROCLAMATION

Whereas the nation has suffered a great loss in the passing of Franklin D. Roosevelt, our President and leader, and,

Whereas all peace-loving people of the whole world mourn with the people of the United States in the death of this great humanitarian, and

Whereas, our late President dedicated his life in the service of his country and the work and in spite of pain and physical handicap carried on with the full knowledge he was hastening his own death;

Now therefore, I, Roger T. Sermon, mayor of Independence, Mo., request that the citizens of Independence pause in their usual activities and that the business houses close during the funeral hour of our late President in respect to his memory.

It is also requested that all traffic, including both public and private vehicles, stop for three minutes, beginning at 3 o'clock.

Roger T. Sermon, Mayor

Saturday to Be Day of Mourning President Says

Washington, April 13. (UP)—President Truman today proclaimed Saturday as a day of mourning and prayer throughout the United States in respect to the late Franklin D. Roosevelt.

The presidential proclamation was issued by Secretary of State, Edward R. Stettinius. At the same time by order of the President, Stettinius ordered that:

Flags remain at half-staff on all public buildings of the United States for one month, until the close of Monday, May 14; and

All executive departments and agencies of the government be closed tomorrow afternoon, the day of the funeral.

"I earnestly recommend the people to assemble in their respective places of divine worship," Mr. Truman's proclamation said, "to bow down in submission to the will of God and to pay out of full heart their homage of love and reverence to the member of the

ROOSEVELT ON WAY HOME

Funeral Cortege of Late President Who Died Thursday at Warm Springs, Ga., Will Reach Washington Tomorrow Afternoon for Services at 4 p. m., in the Big East Room of the White House.

Washington, April 13. (UP)—President Harry S. Truman today took over the White House responsibility and called into quick conference America's military chiefs to confirm his pledge to carry the war, in the West and in the East, to a victorious conclusion.

Shocked as all others by news of Mr. Roosevelt's death, the new President spoke his promise to the world a few minutes after taking the oath of office last night.

"The world may be sure," he said, "that we will prosecute the war on both fronts, East and West, with all the vigor we possess to a successful conclusion."

In simpler and considerably more forceful language he has expressed the same thought many times before.

"We've got to whip those so-and-sos," he would tell you, "and whip 'em good."

Conferences with Army and Navy leaders are understood to be high on the new President's list today. White House Secretary Jonathan Daniels said Mr. Truman would be on the job early.

The new President took the oath of office at 7:08 last night on word from Warm Springs, Ga., that Mr. Roosevelt was dead.

He asked Mr. Roosevelt's cabinet to "stay on" even before Chief Justice Harlan Fiske Stone administered the oath, which the new President took in the White House cabinet room, his family looking on.

Last night the Truman's slept in their five-room Connecticut Avenue apartment in Northwest Washington. There they will remain a little while before moving to the White House. But everything last night was beginning to change.

The secret service guard which had been somewhat of a formality —and a bit of an innovation, too—

should go on as scheduled April 25.

Mr. Roosevelt, at 63, had served 12 years, one month and eight days in the office whose cruel exactions killed him, but also stimulated his desire to stay on. No other man had served more than eight years.

Mr. Truman will be 61 on May 8.

Twice elected to the senate after a career in Missouri politics, Mr. Truman had been vice-president only since noon of last January 20. Then in the sequence of heartbeat yesterday, the unassuming man from Missouri became the head of the greatest acting concern on earth. The taking of an oath merely formalized fact. The White House has its common man.

Mr. Roosevelt is coming home, but not to the White House. He will be a brief pause there tomorrow after the Southern Railway funeral special arrives from Warm Springs. In the East Room where so often he had been easy host, there will be a funeral service at 4 p. m., Saturday. The late President will travel the last time to his beloved Hyde Park.

Expressions of grief, as well as confidence in Harry Truman, fill the front page of the Independence *Examiner*.

3

James F. Byrnes (left) and Henry A. Wallace, ardent candidates for the vice-presidential nomination only the summer before, wait with Truman for Roosevelt's funeral train at Washington's Union Station. Below: The new President of the United States at his desk.

4

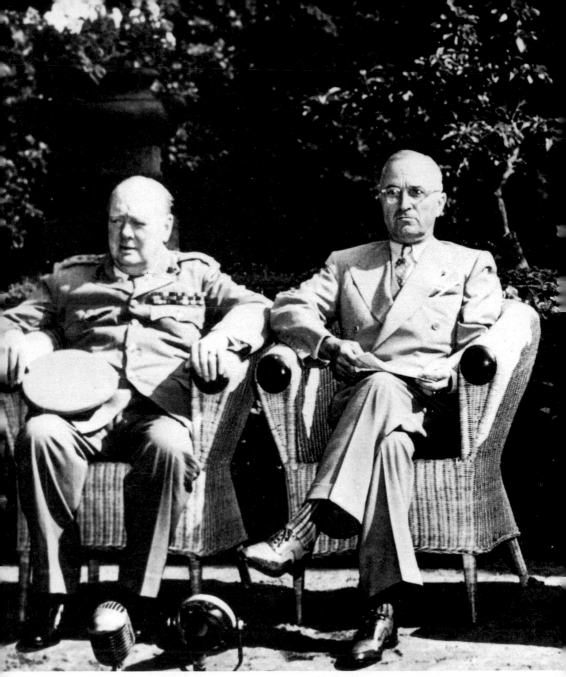

July 1945: Prime Minister Winston Churchill, President Truman, and Generalissimo Joseph Stalin, "The Big Three," meet at Potsdam, Germany.

6

Conference table, Cecilienhof Palace.

Truman in Berlin with Generals Eisenhower and Patton. Eisenhower was high on the new President's list of favorite generals; not so Patton.

7

5

8   Above: Truman's headquarters during the Potsdam Conference was No. 2 Kaiserstrasse,
the "nightmare" house where the decision on the atomic bomb was made.
Below: Truman's desk in the second-floor study.

9

Sec War

Reply to your 41011 suggestions approved Release when ready but not sooner than August 2.

HST

Above: Truman's order, handwritten in pencil to Secretary of War Stimson, to use the atomic bomb on Japan. Below: At his desk in the Oval Office, 7:00 P.M., August 14, 1945, Truman announces the surrender of Japan.

10

11

May 25, 1946: As he calls on Congress for the power to draft striking rail workers into the Army and thus break a nationwide shutdown, Truman is handed a note saying the strike has ended. Left: He and the First Lady had hosted a reception for wounded veterans the day before, just as worries over the rail strike were at their worst. The postwar burdens of his office bore heavily on Truman (opposite). But he had discovered a retreat away from Washington, the naval base at Key West, Florida, and aide Clark Clifford (shown below with Truman at Key West) had emerged as a bright new star on the White House staff.

14

17

Two who helped turn the tide in 1947: Left: Republican Senator Arthur H. Vandenberg shaking hands on March 12, as Truman is about to ask Congress for aid to Greece and Turkey—the speech that introduced the Truman Doctrine; and (opposite) Secretary of State George C. Marshall, the "great one," as Truman called him, who in a commencement speech at Harvard on June 5 proposed what came to be known as the Marshall Plan.

18

Eddie Jacobson, a behind-the-scenes key figure in the decision to recognize Israel, talks with his old friend and former business partner.

19

Chaim Weitzmann, the new president of Israel, presents Truman with the Torah scrolls during a first official call at the White House.

America's best-known walker steps out in a 35th Division Reunion parade in Kansas City.

Opposite: In the first address ever made by a President to the NAACP, Truman speaks from the steps of the Lincoln Memorial to a crowd of ten thousand, June 29, 1947.

Past 2:00 A.M., July 15, 1948, his hands chopping the air, Truman tells cheering convention delegates at Philadelphia, "Senator Barkley and I will win this election . . . and don't you forget that!" His odyssey began in September. Below: From the rear platform of the *Ferdinand Magellan* at Richmond, Indiana, Truman makes one of hundreds of "whistle-stop" speeches.

After Stalin clamped a blockade on Berlin on June 24 (the day Dewey was nominated), Truman launched the Berlin Airlift. Tensions over Berlin continued for months.

23

24

Republican candidate Thomas E. Dewey and his wife. According to the press, only a miracle or a series of unimaginable Republican blunders could save Truman from defeat.

In one of the most memorable photographs in the history of American politics, the "sure loser" holds aloft a premature Chicago *Tribune* headline. Heading east after the election, Truman's train had stopped at St. Louis where he was handed a copy of the paper. Below: Part of the throng that welcomed Truman back to Washington. Some 750,000 people filled the streets in the largest outpouring for a President that the capital had ever seen.

27

There are a number of times, when it is quite easy to find oneself thanking whatever powers there be that the country has Harry Truman in the Senate. He is an excellent man, a fine Senator and sound American. The debt the public owes him is great indeed. And Boss Pendergast put him in. Politics is funny business. . . .

III

For quite some time staff investigators had been picking up puzzling hints of a secret enterprise larger even than the Canol Project, odd bits and pieces of information indicating huge, unexplained expenditures for something identified only as the Manhattan Project. On June 17, 1943, Truman telephoned Secretary of War Stimson. Their conversation was brief:

STIMSON: Now that's a matter which I know all about personally, and I am the only one of the group of two or three men in the whole world who know about it.
TRUMAN: I see.
STIMSON: It's part of a very important secret development.
TRUMAN: Well, all right then—
STIMSON: And I—
TRUMAN: I herewith see the situation, Mr. Secretary, and you won't have to say another word to me. Whenever you say that to me that's all I want to hear.
STIMSON: All right . . .
TRUMAN: You assure that this is for a specific purpose and you think it's all right. That's all I need to know.
STIMSON: Not only for a specific purpose, but a unique purpose.
TRUMAN: All right, then.
STIMSON: Thank you very much.

Apparently, however, more information kept coming to Truman in one way or other, and by July he had been told enough to know the essential nature of the "very important secret development." Incredibly, he even put it in a letter to Lewis Schwellenbach, who had since left the Senate to become a federal district judge in Spokane. Schwellenbach had been concerned over sudden, enormous land condemnations for the DuPont Company along the Columbia River near a desolate railroad town called Hanford. Nearly half a million acres were involved and he had written to Truman to inquire about it. On July 15, 1943, Truman wrote to say he shouldn't worry.

"I know something about that tremendous real estate deal," he said, "and I have been informed that it is for the construction of a plant to make a terrific explosion for a secret weapon that will be a wonder." He added, "I hope it works."

This was a terrible breach of security on Truman's part, an astonishing lapse of simple good judgment—to have passed on such information in so offhand a fashion in an ordinary letter sent through the mail. It was exactly the sort of "insider" talk, one member of the senatorial "club" to another, that gave generals and admirals nightmares and little desire ever to tell politicians anything more than necessary. Truman had not bothered even to write in private, but dictated the letter to Mildred Dryden, which means that as of then she too was aware of the making of "a terrific explosion."

But apparently no one ever found out about the letter. Neither Schwellenbach nor Dryden said a word more on the subject, as far as is known.

Curiosity and concern over the DuPont operations at Hanford did not end there. Senator Elbert Thomas of Oklahoma wanted the situation investigated. He, too, apparently had been hearing stories. A staff man on the Truman Committee informed the chairman confidentially that complaints of waste and inefficiency at Hanford had become "chronic," and added, "In my humble opinion, I believe that this is another 'Canol,' wherein the guise of secrecy is being resorted to by the War Department to cover what may be another shocking example when the lid is finally taken off."

Truman felt pressured to know more, his agreement with Stimson notwithstanding.

On November 30, 1943, he informed Senator Thomas, "I have sent an investigator to look into it, and I hope we can find out what is wrong."

A few weeks afterward, Fred Canfil walked into a Western Union office in Walla Walla, Washington, and sent the following telegram, collect to Senator Truman. It must have made interesting reading to whoever put it on the wire:

COLONEL MATHIAS, COMMANDING OFFICER DUPONT PLANT, TOLD ME THAT YOU AND THE SECRETARY OF WAR HAD AN UNDERSTANDING THAT NONE OF YOUR COMMITTEE WOULD COME INTO THE PLANT. THROUGH ANOTHER AGENCY I FOUND THAT WITHIN THE LAST 10 DAYS A CONFIDENTIAL LETTER WAS RECEIVED FROM THE WAR DEPARTMENT . . . TO ARMY OFFICERS AND TO HIGH CIVILIAN ENGINEERS. . . . TO THE EFFECT THAT THESE PEOPLE WERE TO SEE THAT NO SENATOR OR ANYONE CONNECTED WITH THE SENATE WAS TO BE GIVEN ANY INFORMATION ABOUT THE PROJECT.

Canfil, who may not have known as much as Truman about the purpose of the plant, was only doing his duty. Truman thought him overly efficient. "Whenever he finds out that I want something," he once said of Canfil, "he never stops until it is done. . . ."

But after the wire from Walla Walla, committee interest in the Manhattan Project cooled. The understanding with Stimson was honored again. Nor is there anything in the record to suggest that Truman ever heard of separating plutonium from U-238 (the work going on at Hanford) or had any idea how "the terrific explosion" was to be made.

Only a few months later, Stimson, General Marshall, and Vannevar Bush, head of the Office of Scientific Research and Development, drove to the Capitol for a private meeting in Speaker Sam Rayburn's office. Present besides Rayburn were the House majority and minority leaders, John McCormack and Joe Martin. It was then, in February 1944, that Stimson and Marshall revealed "the greatest secret of the war" for the first and only time on the Hill. As Joe Martin wrote years later:

> The United States was engaged in a crash program to develop the atomic bomb before the Germans perfected one. Marshall described the design of the bomb in some technical detail. Stimson said that if the Germans got this weapon first, they might win the war overnight. They told us that they would need an additional $1,600,000,000 to manufacture the bomb. Because of an overriding necessity for secrecy, they made the unique request that the money be provided without a trace of evidence to show how it was spent.

The three legislators agreed to do what was necessary. Senator Truman was told nothing.

Yet according to Stimson's diary, the chairman of the investigating committee was soon after him once more. Truman was now asking that a member of the committee staff, General Frank Lowe, be taken into Stimson's confidence about the Hanford Works. Stimson by now was extremely annoyed with Senator Truman. Stimson thought he had an agreement. He told Truman no, a response Truman did not take lightly. "He threatened me with dire consequences. I told him I had to do just what I did," said Stimson in his diary, adding, "Truman is a nuisance and a pretty untrustworthy man. He talks smoothly but he acts meanly." Under no circumstances was Senator Truman to be told anything more.

8

Numbered Days

I hardly know Truman.

—FRANKLIN ROOSEVELT, JULY 1944

I

It was in early summer of 1943, one year in advance of the Democratic National Convention, that Senator Truman recorded on paper for the first time that in some circles he was being talked of as a candidate for Vice President, assuming the President were to run for a fourth term. He had been invited to Sunday lunch at the Washington home of Senator Joe Guffey, a staunch New Dealer who took him out into the garden to ask *"very confidentially"* what he thought of Vice President Henry Wallace. Truman had smiled and said Wallace was the best Secretary of Agriculture the country ever had. Guffey, laughing, said that was what he thought, too. "Then he wanted to know if I would help out the ticket if it became necessary by accepting the nomination for Vice President," Truman recorded. "I told him in words of one syllable that I would not. . . ."

And though the idea was talked about with increasing frequency thereafter, Truman, when asked his opinion, always gave the same answer. He wanted to stay in the Senate.

Moreover, he believed in being realistic. Franklin Roosevelt had shown no sign of dissatisfaction with the Vice President, nor any inclination to abandon him. And even if Roosevelt were to change his mind, there were a number of others—Jimmy Byrnes and Alben Barkley, to name the two most obvious possibilities—who were better known, more experienced, and who would leap to the opportunity. Jimmy Byrnes, a small, tidy, vivid man whom Truman greatly admired, was a southerner, a lapsed Catholic, and sixty-four years old, all of which could count against him. But he had done virtually everything there was to do in government, his experience ranging across all three branches, beginning with seven terms in the House before going to the Senate. Named to the Supreme Court in 1941, Byrnes had resigned after only one term to become Roosevelt's War Mobilization Director, with an office in the East Wing of the White House. Popularly referred to as "Assistant President," he was the consummate "insider" whose political judgment, whose ability to funnel money where needed in the party (such as to Senator Truman in 1940) were thought second to none. Roosevelt relied heavily on him and liked him. By contrast to such a man as Byrnes, Truman was small potatoes, as he well knew, and no closer to Roosevelt now than he had ever been.

In fact, lately, a distinct chill had been felt at the White House concerning Truman, ever since publication in *American Magazine* of a ghostwritten article about the findings of the committee that Truman had allowed to be published under his name without bothering to read it very carefully. Too late had he discovered how critical it was of the administration's handling of the war effort. ("Leadership is what we Americans are crying for," the article said. "We are fighting mad, and ready to tackle any job and to make any sacrifice. . . . All we ask is that we be intelligently and resolutely led.") He was certain that the President didn't like him, Truman told friends in the Senate.

Still the vice-presidential speculation continued, and with Truman's name spoken often, for the reason that certain influential figures in the Democratic Party had joined in a pact to keep Henry Wallace off the ticket.

They were only a handful, only a half dozen or so to begin with, but they were among the most powerful men in the party, and they had taken it upon themselves to talk down Wallace at every opportunity and begin organizing wider opposition to him. They included the chairman of the Democratic National Committee, Frank Walker, who had replaced Jim Farley as Postmaster General; Ed Pauley, a wealthy California oilman who was treasurer of the national committee; George E. Allen, a jovial man-about-Washington, lobbyist, and secretary of the national committee; and Robert E. Hannegan, Truman's last-minute savior in the 1940 campaign, who had since advanced to Commissioner of Internal Revenue and was now not only a great favorite of the President's but in line to replace Walker as national chairman. General Edwin "Pa" Watson, appointments secretary at the White House, had also agreed to clear the way whenever possible for anti-Wallace Democrats to see the President. Watson, it was hoped, could serve as counterbalance to Mrs. Roosevelt, a known champion of the Vice President.

But the key man in the "conspiracy" was Edward Joseph Flynn of the Bronx, who, since the downfall of Tom Pendergast, was considered the most powerful political boss in the country and who in looks and manner bore little resemblance to the usual picture of a successful Irish politician. At fifty-two, Flynn was tall and handsome, with thinning gray hair and gray eyes, beautifully dressed, well educated, an ardent gardener, a student of history. Most importantly, he was a devoted friend of Franklin Roosevelt and his influence on Roosevelt on political matters exceeded that of anyone inside or out of the administration. It was Ed Flynn who ran the President's successful bid for a third term in 1940, and it was Ed Flynn now, more than any of the others, who saw defeat in November unless something was done about the Vice President. For Henry Wallace was not their idea of a politician.

Henry Wallace was one of the most serious-minded, fascinating figures in national public life, a plant geneticist by profession who had done important work in the development of hybrid corn and whose Pioneer Hi-Bred Corn Company was a multimillion-dollar enterprise. He was an author, lecturer, social thinker, a firm advocate for civil rights and thorough New Dealer with a large, devoted following. With the exception of Franklin Roosevelt, he was the most popular Democrat in the country. Those who loved him saw him as one of the rare men of ideas in politics and the prophet of a truly democratic America. But he was also an easy man to make fun of and to these tough party professionals, Wallace seemed to have his head in the clouds. They had never wanted him for Vice President. He had been forced upon them in 1940, when Roosevelt threatened not to run again unless he could have Wallace as his running mate. Wallace was too intellectual, a mystic who spoke Russian and played with a boomerang and reputedly consulted with the spirit of a dead Sioux Indian chief. As Vice President he seemed pathetically out of place and painfully lacking in political talent, or even a serious interest in politics. When not presiding over the Senate he would often shut himself in his office and study Spanish. He was too remote, too controversial, too liberal —much too liberal, which was the main charge against him.

Of the group only Ed Flynn appears to have personally admired Wallace and his ideas, but as the political writer Richard Rovere observed of Flynn, he considered candidates only as good as their chances of winning.

None of this would have mattered greatly had the President said Wallace was again his choice. But Roosevelt preferred to let things slide. His mind was on the war. He was also just as happy to keep everyone guessing as long as possible.

· · ·

The first meeting with Roosevelt to discuss the "advisability" of ditching Wallace took place at the White House in January 1944, six months in advance of the national convention, and Truman's name figured prominently in a discussion of alternative choices that included Byrnes, Barkley, Sam Rayburn, Ambassador John G. Winant, Senator Sherman Minton, and Justice William O. Douglas, who had replaced the late Louis D. Brandeis on the Supreme Court. It was Hannegan who had the most to say about Truman, but Hannegan appeared equally enthusiastic about Byrnes, and as a whole the group was more against Wallace than for any one possible replacement.

Roosevelt declined to give a clear sign of what he wanted. As the historian James MacGregor Burns, then a member of the White House staff, later wrote, Roosevelt never pursued a more Byzantine course than in his handling of this question.

Truman, who was party to none of the discussions, thought Sam Rayburn would be the best nominee and said so publicly.

By spring Jimmy Byrnes looked like the clear favorite at the White House, though Wallace was leading in the polls. Harry Hopkins, the only one closer to Roosevelt than Byrnes, made a point of telling Byrnes that Roosevelt very much hoped he would be on the ticket. (Flying home from the Teheran Conference, looking out at the stars, Hopkins had asked the President who he thought would be the best man to take over his duties if something happened to the plane and it went down. "Jimmy Byrnes," Roosevelt said without hesitation.) When Byrnes appeared reluctant to try for the job, others began putting pressure on him.

For by then there was concern over more than just losing votes in November. The President's declining health could no longer be ignored, though in wartime nothing on the matter could be said publicly. After a bout of so-called "walking pneumonia" in April, Roosevelt, with much wartime secrecy, went to Bernard Baruch's estate in South Carolina for what was supposed to have been a two-week rest but that stretched to a month. Seeing the President after his return to the White House, Ed Flynn was so alarmed by his appearance that he urged Mrs. Roosevelt to use her influence to keep him from running again. "I felt," Flynn later said, "that he would never survive his term." Ed Pauley would say that his own determination to unseat Wallace came strictly from the conviction that Wallace was "not a fit man to be President . . . and by my belief, on the basis of continuing observation, that President Roosevelt would not live much longer." George Allen, remembering these critical months just before the 1944 convention, wrote that every one of their group "realized that the man nominated to run with Roosevelt would in all probability be the next President. . . ."

The worry aroused by the President's appearance was more than justified. His condition was worse than all but very few were aware of. Secretly, he was under the constant supervision of a cardiologist, who after a thorough examination in March reported that given proper care he might live a year.

In May, Roosevelt sent Henry Wallace on a mission to China, which many took as a sign that Wallace was finished. Then in early June, just after news of the Allied landings at Normandy, and with only a month to go before the convention, Hannegan dropped in on Byrnes at the White House, where, for several hours, he tried to convince Byrnes to become a candidate for Vice President. The President himself, Hannegan said, had told him Byrnes was the man he had really wanted as his running mate in 1940 and that he would rather have Byrnes on the ticket this time than anybody. Later, Pa Watson telephoned Byrnes to confirm everything Hannegan had said.

On June 27, Hannegan took things a step further. He told Roosevelt that Wallace had to come off the ticket. All he had to do, Hannegan said to the President, was to agree to Jimmy Byrnes and they could "sail through" the convention and the election.

"That suits me fine," Roosevelt responded. "He was my candidate for Vice-President four years ago [at the 1940 convention], but religion got messed up in it."

"That won't matter a damn bit," Hannegan answered. "I am a Catholic and I can talk on that subject. . . ."

While Truman had been a great backer of Hannegan, ever since the 1940 Senate race, it was Byrnes, with his influence with Roosevelt, who had had the most say in making Hannegan Commissioner of Internal Revenue and now the new chairman of the Democratic Party.

Roosevelt asked Byrnes to go with him to Shangri-la, the presidential retreat in the Catoctin Mountains of Maryland, to talk campaign strategy for a few days, after which, wrote Byrnes, "I did conclude that he was sincere in wanting me for his running mate. . . ."

Yet at the time, at the end of a long day, Byrnes also remarked to one of his aides, "Now, partner, let's not get too excited on this vice-president business. I know that man [FDR] more than anybody else."

Asked by two or three of his staff who were gathered about his desk what he thought of Harry Truman, Roosevelt said he didn't know much about him. But Henry J. Kaiser, the famous shipbuilder, he said, was somebody else "we have got up our sleeve."

Having completed a cross-country survey at Roosevelt's request, Ed Flynn told him that opposition to Wallace was greater even than anyone supposed. Both Flynn and Roosevelt knew the election in the fall would be close, that Roosevelt was by no means a certain winner. Wallace on the ticket, Flynn warned, could mean the loss of New York, Pennsylvania, New Jersey, and California, which was undoubtedly an exaggeration. The problem was to find someone who would hurt Roosevelt's chances least. So together, according to Flynn's subsequent account, the two of them ran down the list, weighing the negative sides of all the other candidates.

Byrnes was the strongest choice, Flynn agreed, but Byrnes, who had been raised a Catholic, had left the Church when he married, to become an Episcopalian, and in Flynn's view the Catholics "wouldn't stand for that." Organized labor had no enthusiasm for Byrnes since he had opposed sit-down strikes in wartime. But far more serious to Flynn was Byrnes's southern background and recorded positions on racial issues. This was the crucial flaw. In 1938, Byrnes had been in the forefront of those southern senators fighting against a proposed federal anti-lynching law, and in a speech on the Senate floor he had turned much of his fire on Walter White, head of the National Association for the Advancement of Colored People. "The Negro has not only come into the Democratic Party," Byrnes had said, "but the Negro has come into control of the Democratic Party." Then, pointing to the gallery where White was sitting, Byrnes exclaimed, "If Walter White . . . should consent to have this bill laid aside, its advocates would desert it as quickly as football players unscramble when the whistle of the referee is heard."

When asked who he thought should run with Roosevelt, Byrnes usually mentioned Truman, Rayburn, and Henry J. Kaiser.

Sam Rayburn was a good man, Flynn and Roosevelt agreed, but Rayburn was from Texas, another southerner, and so "couldn't be considered." When they went through the list of the entire Senate, only one fitted the picture, Harry Truman. As Flynn wrote:

> His record as head of the Senate Committee . . . was excellent, his labor votes in the Senate were good; on the other hand he seemed to represent to some degree the conservatives in the party, he came from a border state, and he had never made any "racial" remarks. He just dropped into the slot.

Flynn left the White House convinced he had an agreement, that Roosevelt saw Truman as the one who would do the ticket the least harm. This was not exactly a rousing endorsement for the Senator from Missouri, but it was what Flynn had wanted to hear, which is probably the main reason Roosevelt, given his manner of operation, sent him on his way with that impression.

. . .

About this same time, Roosevelt asked a favor of Mrs. Anna Rosenberg, a member of the War Mobilization Advisory Board, whose office, like that of Byrnes, was in the East Wing. Mrs. Rosenberg had become a favorite of the President's. A highly attractive woman, she dressed smartly, wore expensive perfume, and lent an air of femininity to the White House that he greatly welcomed. In contrast to Mrs. Roosevelt, she also appreciated good food and would on occasion smuggle in jars of caviar to the President, sometimes also baskets of paprika chicken cooked by her Hungarian mother, which she and Roosevelt would happily devour together in his office in secret, "like naughty children," she would remember. Roosevelt told her now that Byrnes was the best man, but asked her to go tell Byrnes he was not to be the vice-presidential choice, because of the Negro vote. Mrs. Rosenberg, who admired Byrnes greatly and wanted him on the ticket, said she couldn't do that. If the President wanted Byrnes to know he had no chance, then the President would have to tell him himself, she said. But Roosevelt never did, never could, as she knew.

Truman was trying to clear up his work and get away for a few days in Missouri before the convention opened in Chicago on July 19. With so little time remaining, gossip over the vice-presidential question had become intense. To any and all who asked if he was interested in the nomination, Truman said no—"no, no, no." The whole matter was getting on his nerves. He had not seen the President. It had been more than a year since he had seen the President. Nor would he make any effort to do so now.

"I don't want to be Vice President," he told William Helm as they were rushing along a hall in the Senate Office Building, and, as Helm wrote later, anyone who saw the look on his face would have known he meant it.

The number of other Democrats in the Senate reputedly in the running had grown to such a list, reporters were joking, that it was easier to tally those who were not candidates. On July 6, to judge by corridor gossip, Wallace had the nomination sewed up. On July 7, the word from "informed sources" was that the President wanted Wallace but he also wanted three or four "acceptable" names held in reserve, should the convention refuse to "swallow Henry." In that case Barkley was first choice. On July 9, it was noted that Senator Truman, by continuing to do battle with the War Production Board and the armed services, was killing whatever chance he might have had.

"The Vice President simply presides over the Senate and sits around hoping for a funeral," Truman explained to a friend. "It is a very high office which consists entirely of honor and I don't have any ambition to hold an office like that."

Max Lowenthal and Les Biffle were after him to run for Vice President. "The Madam doesn't want me to do it," he told Lowenthal. To Margaret he wrote, "It is funny how some people would give a fortune to be as close as I am to it and I don't want it." Then, making it unmistakable that his thoughts, too, were on the obvious mortality of Franklin Roosevelt, not to say his own advancing years, he added, "1600 Pennsylvania is a nice address but I'd rather not move in through the back door—or any other door at sixty."

The letter was written on July 9, just as he started the long drive home alone to Missouri.

On Monday, July 10, after an all-night flight from Seattle, an exhausted Vice President of the United States arrived in Washington at the end of a 51-day, 27,000-mile mission to China, and at 4:30 that afternoon he met with the President to report on what he had seen. Roosevelt was cordial as always. For a long while they talked about China and Wallace's venture to Outer Mongolia, where no American had set foot in seventeen years. (Wallace had brought Roosevelt some Mongolian stamps for his collection.) As Wallace recorded in his diary, it was Roosevelt who at last "opened up on politics saying that when I went out I should say that no politics were discussed."

Roosevelt assured Wallace that he was his choice as running mate and that he intended the fourth term to be "really progressive." He talked of the professional politicians who thought Wallace might mean a loss of 2 or 3 million votes (figures Ed Flynn had supplied). "Mr. President," Wallace interjected, "if you can find anyone who will add more strength to the ticket than I, by all means take him." Roosevelt warned Wallace of the ordeal he might face at Chicago trying to get the vice-presidential nomination and expressed concern about the pain this could mean for Wallace's family. "Think of the catcalls and jeers and the definiteness of rejection," Roosevelt remarked. Wallace said he was not worried about his family.

The next day, Tuesday, July 11, the President announced formally that he was running for another term. (Young Allen Drury wrote that he would never forget the look on the faces of Democratic senators when the news reached the Hill. "It was as though the sun had burst from the clouds and glory surrounded the world. Relief, and I mean relief, was written on every face. The meal ticket was still the meal ticket and all was well with the party.") At lunch that day, July 11, Hopkins again asked

Roosevelt who he thought would make the best President, Byrnes or William O. Douglas. "Jimmy Byrnes," Roosevelt said, "because he knows more about government than anybody around." Hopkins asked who the President thought would win the nomination if the convention were left free to decide. "Byrnes," Roosevelt said again.

Then that night, following dinner, in the President's blue Oval Study on the second floor of the White House, the full anti-Wallace coalition—Flynn, Hannegan, Walker, Allen, Pauley, plus one more exceptionally influential "practical" politician, Mayor Ed Kelly of Chicago—gathered with the President for what they were to regard as the decisive meeting.

Because of the muggy heat, everyone was in shirtsleeves. Drinks were passed, and again the full list of vice-presidential possibilities was taken up one by one. Again Byrnes and Rayburn were rejected. Now, for the first time, Barkley, too, was ruled out, and by Roosevelt, because Barkley was too old. Like Byrnes, Barkley was sixty-six, which made him Roosevelt's senior by only four years, but the Republicans at their convention in Chicago had just nominated for President Governor Thomas E. Dewey of New York, who was all of forty-two, the age Roosevelt's Republican cousin Theodore had been when he took office, and so age could very likely be an issue in the campaign.

Roosevelt thought a young man was needed on the Democratic ticket, and to the surprise of the others, he proposed William O. Douglas, an idea none of them had ever seriously entertained. Douglas, he said, was youthful (he was forty-six), dynamic, a good liberal, and he had a kind of Boy Scout quality that would appeal to voters. Besides, Roosevelt thought, Douglas played an interesting game of poker.

But the idea fell flat. No one wanted Douglas any more than Wallace.

Again the talk turned to Harry Truman, Roosevelt contributing little to the conversation except to observe that he had set Truman up in his committee (which was not so) and thought he was doing a commendable job. Truman was able and loyal to the administration, Roosevelt agreed, and "wise to the way of politics." Reportedly, the question of Truman's association with the Pendergast machine was "thoroughly discussed" and dismissed as irrelevant.

One point only troubled the President—Truman's age. He was not sure, Roosevelt said, but he thought Truman was nearly sixty. Hannegan, who knew Truman was already sixty, tried to change the subject, but Roosevelt sent for a *Congressional Directory* and the conversation continued. When the *Directory* arrived, Ed Pauley quietly took it and said no more.

As to which candidate might be best suited and prepared for the burdens and responsibilities of the presidency, there appears to have been little or no discussion. Apparently, only Roosevelt touched on the subject, saying again that, all in all, Jimmy Byrnes was the best-qualified man.

It would also be remembered how tired and listless the President was all through the stifling, hot evening. Frank Walker commented later that he had never known Roosevelt to stand so willingly on the sidelines "and let others carry the ball."

Exhausted he was, and preoccupied by the war. Since the Allied landings at Normandy on June 6, the Germans had launched their first V-1 "buzz bombs," Hitler's terrifying *Vergeltungswaffe,* the vengeance weapon, against London. In the Pacific, the American assault on the island of Saipan had been met with Japanese resistance as fierce as any since the fighting began. Just the week before, on the night of July 6, three thousand Japanese had hurled themselves against the 27th Division in one mass *banzai* charge, all to be killed. No one, and least of all Roosevelt, expected the final stages of the war to become anything but more and more costly.

At last, turning to Hannegan, Roosevelt said, "Bob, I think you and everyone else here want Truman."

Roosevelt had not said yet whether he himself wanted Truman, but at this point, Ed Pauley, still holding the *Congressional Directory,* rose and suggested they break up, then hurried everybody out of the room before Roosevelt had a chance to say anything more. Downstairs, as they were about to leave, Hannegan decided to go back up and get something in writing. By several accounts he returned with a note that Roosevelt had scrawled on an envelope: "Bob, I think Truman is the right man, FDR." But an offhand, personal note was hardly conclusive, and as George Allen observed in understatement, "Roosevelt was still free to change his mind. . . ."

A day or so later, writing in his diary, Harold Ickes, the Secretary of Interior, recorded that in a conversation with the President about the vice-presidential issue, little had been said about Senator Truman. "I gathered that he felt, as I do," wrote Ickes, "that Truman might do but that he might raise a political-boss issue that would be especially welcomed by Dewey whose rise to political prominence has been due to fighting political bosses."

It was a pattern. No matter how many talked to Roosevelt on the subject, each and all came away feeling he thought just as they did. For the moment anyway.

At first chance the morning of Wednesday, July 12, Hannegan went to see Henry Wallace at his apartment at the Wardman Park—a mission under taken, according to Hannegan's later account, at the request of the President. He told Wallace he would be a detriment to the ticket and must therefore withdraw. Wallace said they might as well understand one another. He was not withdrawing as long as the President preferred him.

On Thursday, the 13th, Wallace met for lunch with Roosevelt, who reported the meeting of the night of the 11th in some detail, explaining the preference of the professional politicians for Truman as "the only one who had no enemies and might add a little independent strength to the ticket." Wallace showed him a new Gallup Poll reporting 65 percent of Democratic voters in favor of Wallace, while Byrnes had but 3 percent, Truman 2 percent. The only other potential candidate with even a modest showing was Alben Barkley, with 17 percent.

It was his intention, Roosevelt said, to send a letter to the chairman of the convention, Senator Samuel Jackson, saying that if he were a delegate he would vote for Wallace. Would he offer any alternative name, Wallace asked. No, Roosevelt assured him, he would not.

The Vice President stood to leave. At fifty-five, he was slim and fit, a man who was regularly out of bed at 5:30 in the morning to play tennis. Yet he had an untidy look, which with his underlying shyness and the shock of reddish-gray hair that hung over the right side of his forehead, made him seem almost rustic, and so entirely different from the seated President.

"Well, I am looking ahead with pleasure to the results of next week no matter what the outcome," Wallace said.

Roosevelt, his head up, beaming, drew Wallace close and with a vigorous handclasp said, "While I cannot put it just that way in public, I hope it will be the same old team."

In another exchange earlier that same morning, Roosevelt had told Jimmy Byrnes he was certain Wallace could not win at Chicago, but that he would endorse no candidate other than Wallace. Byrnes pointed out that he had not allowed himself to become seriously interested until Bob Hannegan had told him, in effect, that he was the President's first choice. On the question of his standing with black voters, Byrnes said only that he didn't think that would matter, when all was said and done. He showed the President a photograph he had just received from Aiken, South Carolina, in which Mrs. Roosevelt was seen addressing a group of blacks. "Look at the expressions on their faces," Byrnes said. "That is idolatry. You can't tell me that because you have a Southerner on the ticket that those people are going to turn against Mrs. Roosevelt and the President who have done more for them than anybody. . . ." Roosevelt said he thought Byrnes was right.

"Mr. President, all I have heard around this White House for the last week is Negro. I wonder if anybody ever thinks about the white people. Did you ever stop to think who would do the most for the Negro. This is a serious problem, but it will have to be solved by the white people of the South. . . ."

He wanted an open convention, Roosevelt said, which Byrnes, understandably, took to mean that he himself had every chance for the nomination. "You are the best qualified man in the whole outfit and you must not get out of the race," Roosevelt told him. "If you stay in you are sure to win."

Meeting with Hannegan and Frank Walker for lunch the next day, Byrnes repeated what Roosevelt had said. Hannegan was incredulous. "I don't understand it," he said. Neither did Byrnes, who, determined to settle the matter, returned to his White House office and put through a call to Roosevelt, who by this time was at his home in Hyde Park, New York. Byrnes, who had once been a court stenographer, took down their conversation in shorthand.

Roosevelt said again he was not favoring anybody. "I told them so. No, I am not favoring anybody."

> BYRNES: Bob Hannegan and Frank Walker stated today that if at the convention they were asked about your views, they would be obliged to say to their friends that from your statements they concluded you did not prefer Wallace but did prefer Truman first and Douglas second, and that either would be preferable to me because they would cost the ticket fewer votes than I would.
>
> ROOSEVELT: Jimmy, that is all wrong. That is not what I told them. It is what they told me. When we all went over the list I did not say I preferred anybody or that anybody would cost me votes, but they all agreed that Truman would cost fewer votes than anybody and probably Douglas second. This was the agreement they reached and I had nothing to do with it. . . .

Byrnes pressed him. If Hannegan and his friends were to release any kind of statement saying the President preferred Truman and Douglas, that could make things very difficult for his own cause.

"We have to be damn careful about language," Roosevelt answered. "They asked if I would object to Truman and Douglas and I said no. That is different from using the word 'prefer.' That is not expressing a preference because you know I told you I would have no preference."

Roosevelt asked Byrnes whether he would try for the nomination. Byrnes said he was considering it, but he needed to know the President's views. Roosevelt replied, "After all, Jimmy, you are close to me personally and Henry is close to me. I hardly know Truman. Douglas is a poker partner. He is good in a poker game and tells good stories."

Finishing the call, Byrnes went directly down the corridor to Hopkins's office and repeated what the President had said. If anyone knew Roosevelt's mind supposedly it was Hopkins, who now told Byrnes the President was sure that if Byrnes entered the race he would win, he would be nominated.

According to Byrnes, it was then that he phoned Harry Truman in Missouri, though Truman would remember the call coming early in the morning, as he was about to leave for Chicago. Whether this was Friday morning or Saturday morning is not clear, nor important. But presumably Byrnes would not have called Truman until after he had talked with the President, so most likely it was Saturday morning.

Truman was staying at the President Hotel in Kansas City. Bess, Margaret, and Madge Wallace were visiting Fred Wallace at his new home in Denver.

Byrnes asked if Truman was serious when he told the newspapers he did not want the vice-presidential nomination. Yes, Truman replied, absolutely. He was not a candidate. Byrnes said he had been given the "go sign" from Roosevelt and would like nothing better than to have Truman make the nominating speech for him at Chicago. Truman accepted at once, saying he would be delighted and would do all he could to line up the Missouri delegation. Clearly he, too, was convinced by this time that Byrnes was both the President's choice and the best one, and his source for such confidence must have been Bob Hannegan. Otherwise, he would never have responded so affirmatively and without hesitation.

Again by Truman's recollection, he had no sooner put down the phone than it rang a second time. Alben Barkley now wanted him to make his nominating speech at Chicago. He was sorry, Truman replied, but he had just said yes to Jimmy Byrnes.

II

The turmoil at the Chicago convention was entirely over the vice presidency and at no time did the outcome appear inevitable. Ambitions were too large, the opportunities for deceit and maneuver and the play of emotion too plentiful, the dictates of Franklin Roosevelt too capricious and uncertain for there to have been even a momentary sense of events moving as if on a track. Things could have gone differently at any of several points, and with the most far-reaching consequences. As Alben

Barkley would write, the denouement in Chicago of all the plotting that had gone on in Washington was a fascinating political drama. It was politics for the highest stakes, politics at its slipperiest, and the only real drama of either national convention that summer.

A few weeks before, when the Republicans filled the same hotels and picked their nominees in the same steaming hall, there had been no contest and no surprises. Thomas E. Dewey was smoothly nominated on the first ballot and his only near rival, Senator John W. Bricker, was the choice for running mate. Now the assembling Democrats were to be denied the chance even to see their standardbearer, their hero, whose overwhelming endorsement for yet another term was a foregone conclusion. Roosevelt had declined to appear before the convention because of his duties as Commander in Chief, he said, just as he had agreed to run again because he saw it as his duty as a "good soldier" in time of war. His acceptance speech was to be delivered by radio hookup from some undisclosed location on the West Coast.

But as so many of the Democrats who converged on Chicago understood, the task of choosing a Vice President had unique importance this time. The common, realistic, and not unspoken view was that they were there to pick not one, but two presidents, and if the identity of the first was clear, that of the second was not.

Had there been a poll of the delegates as they checked in at the hotels, the choice of the majority would have been Henry Wallace. I. F. Stone, writing in *The Nation,* said that on the basis of his inside sources he could report for certain it would be Wallace. Yet the eminent radio commentator H. V. Kaltenborn virtually announced the nomination of Alben Barkley, while Arthur Krock of *The New York Times* said the prime contenders, after Wallace, were Byrnes, Barkley, and Douglas, in that order, and made no mention of Harry Truman. Speaking for the Democratic National Committee, George Allen thought it would be Truman but he couldn't be sure. Hannegan and Mayor Kelly, meantime, two of the most powerful figures on the committee, had concluded it would be Byrnes.

But, of course, nobody really knew, since so much depended on Franklin Roosevelt, and as George Allen also aptly observed, "Roosevelt could, of course, have named anybody."

Privately, and as he would tell no one until much later, Truman thought it would be Wallace.

Looking back on what happened, Alben Barkley would conclude that he had been sadly naive about the whole business. He had been in politics nearly forty years, this was his eleventh national convention, but he had never seen anything like what went on.

·   ·   ·

Truman drove to Chicago from Kansas City on Saturday, July 15, four days before the convention was officially to open, and the same day the President's westbound train made an unscheduled stop at Chicago.

As later disclosed, Roosevelt was en route to San Diego, where a cruiser would take him to Hawaii for meetings with General Douglas MacArthur. But at three that afternoon his train was shunted onto a siding so that Bob Hannegan could come aboard for a private talk in the President's new armor-plated private railroad car, the *Ferdinand Magellan,* another innovation resulting from the war. They were together approximately half an hour. "The train stood in the Chicago yards during this conference and none of us showed ourselves outside," wrote the President's secretary, Grace Tully. Though nearly everything said between Roosevelt and Hannegan was kept secret, one request by Roosevelt would become the best-known line of the convention. Whatever was decided, said the President, Hannegan must first "Clear it with Sidney," meaning that Sidney Hillman was to have the final say—Hillman, who now ran the CIO's well-heeled Political Action Committee, or PAC, which was something new in American politics.

Hannegan also came off the train with a letter on White House stationery, which, in lieu of a briefcase, he carried inside a copy of the *National Geographic Magazine.* The letter was postdated July 19:

> Dear Bob:
>   You have written me about Harry Truman and Bill Douglas. I should, of course, be very glad to run with either of them and believe that either one of them would bring real strength to the ticket.
>   Always sincerely,
>   Franklin Roosevelt

Whether it had been written earlier in Washington or was produced to order that day is not certain. Grace Tully, however, said Hannegan had come out of the President's sitting room with a letter in his hand naming two acceptable running mates, William O. Douglas first, Harry Truman second, and that Hannegan told her the President wanted it retyped with the order of the names reversed. To her, the reason for the switch seemed obvious. "By naming Truman first it plainly implied ... that he was the preferred choice of the President." Hannegan would later deny making any such switch, and since the first copy of the letter was thrown away by another secretary who did the actual typing, there was no way to confirm or disprove the story. Ed Pauley, who claimed to have been with Hannegan when he went to see Roosevelt, said later that Hannegan was back at his hotel before he discovered to his horror that Douglas was even mentioned. Also a note dated July 19 in Roosevelt's hand, as well as a typewritten duplicate on White House stationery, have survived with Truman's name listed first. But Grace Tully was not known for fabricating stories, nor was there any reason why she should have done so in this instance.

In any event, the handsome, gregarious Hannegan—Mr. Busyman Bob, as he would be remembered—was playing an extremely deceitful game at this his first national convention, possibly at Roosevelt's direction, and possibly not. For his next move was to call Jimmy Byrnes in Washington, a second call to Byrnes that day. The first, made by Mayor Ed Kelly in the morning, had been to tell Byrnes that he, Kelly, and Hannegan were no longer worried about losing the Negro vote if Byrnes were on the ticket, and that this was the message Hannegan would take to Roosevelt when the presidential train came in. Now, in the second call, Hannegan told Byrnes that the vice presidency was all set. Byrnes was the one. "The President has given us the green light to support you and he wants you in Chicago."

Byrnes left Washington for Chicago at once and, seeing Tom Connally on the train, confided triumphantly that the nomination was his. Roosevelt himself had passed the word. "Harry Truman will nominate me," Byrnes said.

Arriving in Chicago the morning of Sunday the 16th, Byrnes found a bright red fire chief's car and driver waiting at the station for him, courtesy of Mayor Kelly. He was taken directly to the mayor's apartment on Lake Shore Drive for a breakfast meeting with Kelly and Hannegan, who assured him he was the chosen man. "Well, you know Jimmy has been my choice from the very first. Go ahead and nominate him," they quoted Roosevelt as having instructed. A little afterward, Alben Barkley, too, was told by Kelly that "it was in the bag for Jimmy."

Hannegan and company spent most of the day with Byrnes mapping out strategy. Hannegan even ordered "Roosevelt and Byrnes" placards printed. By late afternoon, the word had spread among the delegates and reporters milling about in the hotel lobbies.

The Roosevelt letter to Hannegan was kept secret. Hannegan was showing it to no one, because of its mention of Douglas, he later said. And no one apparently had said anything about it as yet to Senator Truman, who by now had his nominating speech for Byrnes all prepared.

Sitting beside an open window in his hotel room that evening, the flat, gray-blue panorama of Lake Michigan in the distance, Truman talked at length to a St. Louis reporter, with the understanding that most of what he said was off the record. Although Bess and Margaret, due to arrive from Denver on Tuesday, would be staying at the Morrison Hotel, the senator had taken a suite in the Stevens, across the street from the venerable Blackstone, so that his "politicking" would not disturb their sleep. Jimmy Byrnes, his candidate, was also in the Stevens, six flights up on the twenty-third floor, in the hotel's plush Royal Skyway, the same rooms occupied a few weeks earlier by Thomas E. Dewey.

He was determined to stay out of the running, Truman said. He knew his Pendergast background would be dragged out again and he wished none of that. He had worked too hard to build a good name in the Senate. The reporter remarked that as Vice President he might "succeed to the throne." Truman shook his head. "Hell, I don't want to be president." He then described the failures and scorn experienced by every Vice President who had succeeded to the highest office, beginning with John Tyler and overlooking the most obvious example to the contrary, Theodore Roosevelt.

To another reporter that same evening Truman repeated much the same thing. Those who had succeeded dead presidents were ridiculed in office, had their hearts broken, and lost any vestige of respect they had before. "I don't want that to happen to me."

Nobody, it would seem, was avoiding the central issue of Roosevelt's health and what the vice-presidential nomination really meant. Truman's Kansas City friend Tom Evans later said Truman knew perfectly well that Roosevelt's days were numbered and this was precisely why he had no desire to be on the ticket. "I'm satisfied with where I am," Evans remembered him saying. "Just a heartbeat, this little," said Truman, making a tiny space between forefinger and thumb, "separates the Vice President and the President."

Since arriving in Chicago, he had hardly been able to sleep at night. He hated the thought of intrusions on his family's privacy, and what so much notoriety might do to Margaret at such an important stage in her life. He was worried about skeletons in the closet, he told Evans—about Bess being on the office payroll in Washington and what the papers would make of that. Writing years later, Margaret would say that most of all he feared what a disclosure and retelling of David Wallace's suicide would do to Bess and her mother.

Evans, an old Pendergast loyalist who had grown rich with a chain of drugstores that also sold quantities of Pendergast beer and whiskey, had come to Chicago at Truman's request for the supposed purpose of helping him fend off the nomination, as had Eddie McKim and John Snyder.

Scowling, heavy-handed Fred Canfil, too, was on hand in his role as general factotum and looking, noted one reporter, "as if he could throw a bull in two falls out of three." (Canfil would later complain of missing much of the drama on the convention floor because "somebody else wanted some booze and I had to help him.") Yet they all seem to have spent most of their time talking Truman up as the ideal choice—McKim liked to say it was a question of destiny—and trying to persuade Truman to change his mind.

Roy Roberts, the fat, hard-drinking, opinionated editor of the Kansas City *Star,* who was a Republican and a man Truman loathed, also came and went, perspiring heavily and acting like a kingmaker, which aggravated Truman greatly.

None of them lost sight of the point that it was really the presidency at stake. As McKim remembered, they "got Truman in a room and . . . explained the situation to him." After much talk, McKim told him, "I think, Senator, that you're going to do it." What gave him that idea, Truman snapped. "Because," said McKim, "there's a little, old ninety-year-old mother down in Grandview, Missouri, that would like to see her son President of the United States." Truman, in tears, stomped out of the room.

Bess, Margaret, Mildred Dryden, his little band of Missouri friends, as well as his brother Vivian, who was in Chicago to see his first national convention, were all sure he did not want the nomination and would all later stress how extremely stubborn he grew as pressures on him increased. Only Vic Messall, who was still out of favor but on hand as a spectator, thought differently. Truman was always politically ambitious, Messall said. "I'm sure he wanted to be Vice President. But he had to pretend he didn't."

Reflecting on Truman's frame of mind years later, John Snyder would say that it wasn't so much that Truman didn't want to be President but that he didn't want to succeed Franklin Roosevelt, which was different.

For Truman, in memory, the convention would always be "that miserable time" in Chicago, the most exasperating experience of his life. Marquis Childs, a practiced Truman observer, described him as plainly "scared to death."

The sensation of Monday, July 17, was the release by convention chairman Samuel Jackson of Roosevelt's letter about Wallace. A hundred reporters or more fought for the mimeographed copies. It had been written at Hyde Park on Friday, the same day as Roosevelt's reassuring telephone conversation with Jimmy Byrnes:

I have been associated with Henry Wallace during his past four years as Vice President [read the key paragraph of the instantly famous document], for eight years earlier while he was Secretary of Agriculture, and well before that. I like him and I respect him and he is my personal friend. For these reasons I personally would vote for his nomination if I were a delegate to the convention.

To many it seemed a kiss of death for Wallace—"the coolest and cruelest brushoff in all the long Roosevelt career," in the words of one account. Unquestionably, it threw the choice of a running mate wide open. He did not "wish to appear to be in any way dictating to the convention," Roosevelt had also written. If anybody benefited, said several papers, it was Jimmy Byrnes. The St. Louis *Post-Dispatch* called the letter a spur to the "already soaring campaign stock of energetic little Jimmy Byrnes." But the Wallace forces, including Sidney Hillman and Phil Murray of the CIO, took the announcement as a sign of hope, since theirs was the only candidate who now had something in writing from the President. "It was generally regarded as a Roosevelt endorsement," remembered Senator Claude Pepper of Florida, a Wallace floor leader, who, from his conversations with Roosevelt in Washington, was certain Roosevelt wanted Wallace.

It was only now, in response, that Hannegan began saying he, too, had a letter from the President, which named Truman. But no one was allowed to see it.

Hannegan's corner suite on the seventh floor of the Blackstone, Rooms 708–709, had become the convention nerve center, since Hannegan alone claimed direct telephone contact with the President. In the red-carpeted hall outside, reporters and photographers set up a round-the-clock vigil to see who came and went. At first Hannegan tried to discourage them, insisting that nothing was happening there. Mayor Kelly, who was in and out "continually," kept mentioning the Roosevelt letter. "Do you want to see it?" he asked a skeptical representative of the United Auto Workers. Indeed yes, said the man. "I haven't got it with me," Kelly replied, "but I'll show it to you tomorrow."

At a dinner that night arranged by Kelly in a private apartment on Chicago's North Side, a location kept secret from the press, Byrnes was man of the hour. It was only when everybody was about to leave that Hannegan mentioned one further detail, the need, as required by the President, to "Clear it with Sidney," a point Hannegan seemed to regard as only a formality.

· · ·

On Tuesday morning Senator Truman and Sidney Hillman had orange juice, eggs, and bacon sent up by room service to Hillman's suite at the Ambassador East, "the fancy hotel," as Truman called it. Born in Lithuania, educated to be a rabbi, Hillman had been an eight-dollar-a-week apprentice pants cutter in the garment district of New York when Truman was still riding a plow on the farm. He had led his first strike at twenty-three and founded the Amalgamated Clothing Workers of America by the time he was thirty. He had also joined the Socialist Party and still spoke with a slight accent, which would have been more than enough in places like Grandview, Missouri, to have made him seem a dangerous radical. To party chiefs like Hannegan and Kelly, he was an amateur and therefore not wholly trustworthy, whatever the power of his PAC or his allegiance to the President. Hillman wasn't even a registered Democrat. In addition, as co-director of the former Office of Production Management in Washington, he had come under heavy fire from the Truman Committee, which had been mainly responsible for his removal. And so Truman had no reason to expect much from him in the way of cooperation or favors.

Truman asked for Hillman's support for Byrnes. Hillman declined and refused to be budged. He was working hard for Henry Wallace, Hillman said. If it could not be Wallace, then he wanted either William O. Douglas or Harry Truman.

Truman said he was going to nominate Byrnes. Hillman said that would be a mistake.

Truman reported directly to Byrnes all that Hillman had said, but Byrnes seemed not to care, and with reason. By reliable reports he had already lined up more than 400 of the 589 votes needed to nominate.

When Ed Flynn arrived in Chicago later that morning, Tuesday the 18th, Hannegan rushed him into a corner to say it was all over. "It's Byrnes!" Flynn said it was no such thing and demanded a meeting of the select committee, the same group as the night before, which convened again in the same secret North Side apartment, except that this time Sidney Hillman was included and Jimmy Byrnes was not.

There was only one man to nominate, Flynn insisted, and that was Harry Truman, because Harry Truman was what they had agreed to with the President.

Flynn was extremely angry. "I browbeat the committee, I talked, I argued, I swore," he later wrote. Hillman declared Byrnes unacceptable to organized labor. Flynn said Byrnes would cost no less than 200,000 Negro votes in New York alone. Byrnes was a "political liability." Roosevelt could lose the election. Everyone agreed—Hannegan, the party's chairman, Pauley, Walker, Allen, Hillman for labor, Kelly the big-city boss. Reporters were to call them "the Harmony Boys."

Flynn put through a call to Roosevelt in San Diego and one by one each man got on the line. In the end Roosevelt agreed it should be Truman.

Though accounts differ somewhat, this appears to be what happened next: Within a short time that evening Byrnes and Truman were individually told what the President had said. Truman heard it from Hannegan, who came to his room at the Stevens, and also showed him a longhand note from the President saying, as Truman remembered, "Bob, it's Truman, F.D.R.," a different wording from what Roosevelt had supposedly scrawled for Hannegan the night of the 11th at the White House. Also, by Truman's recollection, the note he was now shown was written on scratch paper, not an envelope. Truman doubted Roosevelt had written it. "I still could not be sure this was Roosevelt's intent," he would recall.

An hour or so later Truman went alone to the Royal Skyway to square things with Byrnes. He asked to be released from his promise of support. Byrnes said he understood perfectly, given the circumstances. Whether he would stay in the race, Byrnes said, was a question he would have to sleep on. When Byrnes tried to get through to Roosevelt by phone, he was told the President was unavailable.

Word of the sudden turn in events spread fast. Ed Flynn had been in town less than a day and everything had changed. In a long account by Turner Catledge in *The New York Times* the next morning, Wednesday, July 19, opening day for the convention, was a revealing paragraph:

> Reports that Senator Truman was to be the choice of the anti-Wallace forces were heard in the New York state delegation. . . . Edward J. Flynn, New York national committeeman, in a conference with leaders, informed them that the decision of the Wallace opponents was to back Senator Truman, and that the New York delegation might be voting for him at least after the first ballot. The group agreed to accede to this decision.

Byrnes dropped out of the race and the talk everywhere was that the bosses killed his candidacy. In a release to the press, Byrnes said he was withdrawing "in deference to the wishes of the President." He then left for home in a fury, feeling he had been betrayed by Roosevelt. In a parting conversation with Alben Barkley, who was scheduled to nominate the President, Byrnes remarked sourly, "If I were you I wouldn't say anything too complimentary about him."

Barkley was as upset as Byrnes, furious over Roosevelt and his games at their expense. He was sick and tired of trying to determine which shell the pea was under, Barkley told a reporter, and threatened to tear up his nominating speech and be done with the whole affair.

For Truman, events were out of hand. These were three or four of the most critical days of his life and they were beyond his control, his destiny being decided for him by others once again. Speculation now centered on him. But as his stock rose, so did objections to him, because of the Pendergast connection. Jim Pendergast was prominent in the Missouri delegation, which was the first to name Truman its choice for Vice President, quite against his wishes. Running into his old high school classmate Charlie Ross, now a contributing editor for the St. Louis *Post-Dispatch,* Truman said, "Feel sorry for me. I'm in a terrible fix."

How much faith he had in Hannegan at this point, he never said, but to many it looked as though the young party head was out of line in taking such an overtly partisan role. He appeared to be constantly improvising, seldom sure of his ground. To prove he really did have something in writing from Roosevelt about Truman, he at last released the much-talked-of letter. But this only produced more grumbling and controversy. Why hadn't he said it mentioned Truman *and* Douglas? His claim of an endorsement for Truman was only half true and wasn't a half-truth as good as a lie? And how much credence should be given to a letter released on July 18 that was supposedly written on July 19?

Among those most surprised by the letter when he later saw accounts of it in the papers was William O. Douglas, who at the time of the convention was in Oregon hiking in the mountains. No one had told him he was being considered.

Meantime, Henry Wallace had arrived in Chicago, and at a packed press conference at the Sherman Hotel, sitting on a table with his long legs swinging, Wallace said he was there to fight to the finish. His supporters were claiming 400 votes on the first ballot. In a secret caucus of the political action committee at the Sherman, CIO president Phil Murray shook his fist and said in his deep Scottish burr, "Wallace . . . Wallace . . . Wallace. That's it. Just keep pounding."

A sluggish, entirely routine first session of the convention opened just before noon inside Chicago Stadium, the same giant arena where Roosevelt had been nominated in 1932 and again in 1940. From steel girders overhead hung a huge Roosevelt portrait used in 1940, only retouched a little to make him look a bit less pale. There was a prayer. There were speeches. The real business continued at the hotels.

III

Only narrow Balbo Street separated the Stevens from the Blackstone, and it was to the Blackstone, to Hannegan's seventh-floor suite, that Truman was "summoned" that afternoon, Wednesday, July 19. Hannegan, collar open, his shirt damp with perspiration, had assembled the inner core—Pauley, Walker, Kelly, Flynn—plus, for the first time, Boss Frank Hague of Jersey City, who had never cared particularly for Senator Truman and who until now had been telling delegates that he didn't want Truman because his nomination would only stir up the whole boss issue.

It was clearly a gathering arranged for effect, for Truman's benefit. (Barkley would later refer to Hannegan as "the stage manager" at Chicago.) The time had come for a decision from the senator. They were placing a call to San Diego.

Truman sat on one twin bed. Hannegan, phone in hand, sat on the other. "Whenever Roosevelt used the telephone," Truman remembered, "he always talked in such a strong voice that it was necessary for the listener to hold the receiver away from his ear to avoid being deafened, so I found it possible to hear both ends of the conversation."

"Bob," Roosevelt's voice boomed, "have you got that fellow lined up yet?"

"No," said Hannegan. "He is the contrariest goddamn mule from Missouri I ever dealt with."

"Well, you tell the Senator that if he wants to break up the Democratic party in the middle of the war, that's his responsibility." With that Roosevelt banged down the phone.

Truman said later that he was completely stunned. "I was floored, I was sunk." Reportedly his first words were "Oh, shit!" He himself recalled saying, "Well, if that's the situation, I'll have to say yes. But why the hell didn't he tell me in the first place?"

That evening Henry Wallace made a surprise appearance on the floor of the convention, and the roar of approval from the galleries astonished everyone, including, noticeably, Henry Wallace.

"Ye gods!" wrote Margaret Truman in her diary. "The Missouri delegation has decided to nominate Dad for V-P. Vice President Wallace is very strong so I doubt if we win, although the South doesn't want Wallace at all."

To judge by her use of the word "we," Bess, too, had resigned herself to the decision.

. . .

On Thursday, July 20, an immense crowd filling the hall, the convention became a thundering, old-fashioned political circus. Alben Barkley, bathed in spotlights on the podium, his broad face streaming with perspiration, his anger at Roosevelt forgotten for the moment, delivered a fulsome tribute to the great leader that set off a demonstration lasting forty minutes. In seconding the nomination, Henry Wallace gave one of the strongest speeches of his career, an impassioned, straight-from-the-shoulder declaration of liberal principles that brought the huge, roaring audience to its feet time after time. The only chance for the Democratic Party, he said, was to keep on its liberal course.

> In a political, educational and economic sense, there must be no inferior races. The poll tax must go. Educational opportunities must come. The future must bring equal wages for equal work regardless of sex or race. . . .

By evening, as time for the President's address approached, the crowd had grown far beyond what the arena was built to hold. It was packed to the roof with perhaps forty thousand people. Reportedly fifteen thousand counterfeit tickets had been printed and distributed with the blessing of Mayor Kelly, who for all his apparent Truman fervor was secretly hoping for a Truman-Wallace deadlock, so the prize would go to his own candidate, Illinois's favorite son, Senator Scott Lucas. But the ticket ploy resulted in thousands of additional Wallace supporters, many supplied by the CIO, who jammed the galleries and worked their way onto the convention floor, while thousands more milled about in the corridors. The Wallace people were determined to see the nomination decided there in the hall and not by the "big boys" in a smoke-filled room. The idea was to stampede the convention.

Nominations for the vice presidency were scheduled for the next day, but as the evening wore on, with more speeches and fanfare for Roosevelt, the surge for Wallace kept growing. The heat inside the hall was nearly unbearable.

At the Blackstone, Hannegan told Truman he might have to be nominated that night, depending whether they had the votes. They would have to be ready to move fast. Bennett Clark was supposed to nominate Truman, but no one knew where he was. Clark, whose wife had died the year before, had been drinking more than usual. Truman went to look for him. Hannegan started for the convention hall.

When the speeches and roll call ended, and the President was swiftly

315

renominated, the delegates settled down to hear his speech. The familiar voice came booming from a cluster of amplifiers, as the huge crowd sat watching the empty podium. Absolute silence hung over the darkened hall, even during the President's pauses. With no one on stage, the effect was eerie. Roosevelt was speaking from his railroad car in San Diego.

"What is the job before us in 1944?" the great, disembodied voice asked. "First, to win the war—to win the war fast, to win it overpoweringly. Second, to form worldwide international organizations, and to arrange to use the armed forces of the sovereign nations of the world to make another war impossible. . . ."

No sooner was the speech over than a Wallace demonstration erupted. From every corner of the stadium came a chant of "We want Wallace!" The organist, catching the spirit, began pumping away at the Wallace theme song, "Iowa, Iowa, That's Where the Tall Corn Grows," over and over. Ed Pauley, livid with rage, threatened to chop the wires to the amplifiers unless the tune was changed.

Bob Hannegan was seen hurriedly conferring with Mayor Kelly in the Illinois delegation. Then they were both up on the podium, heads together with Chairman Jackson. To several of the Wallace floor leaders it looked suddenly as if the time to nominate their man was then, that night, and the quicker the better.

"I sat there and watched the demonstration and I saw it growing in volume," remembered Claude Pepper, who, as head of the Florida delegation, was positioned on the aisle. "I stood up on my seat, and I could see the whole convention hall then. And I said [to myself], 'You know, that's a *real* demonstration. . . .' So after it got into full speed and steam, I said, 'If we could bring this nomination up right now, we could nominate Henry Wallace.' "

At the rear of the hall now, Hannegan had started throwing open the outer doors to let more people in, while, at the same time, Ed Kelly kept shouting about fire rules.

Desperate to get the chairman's eye, Pepper tried hopping up and down on his chair, waving the Florida banner, but to no avail. His floor microphone had been turned off.

He jumped down and started up the aisle, fighting his way through the crowd. Reporters, hundreds of delegates, and spectators saw him and knew at once what he was trying to do. If he could get to the podium, he would make the nominating speech himself with no more delay.

And then when I got to the little gate [remembered Pepper], the little fence around the podium where the Chairman presided . . . well, fortunately, there was a railroad labor man that was minding the gate. He was a friend of mine, so he opened the gate and let me in . . . I got up to about the second step from the top going just as hard as I could to get up that stairway, and I saw the Chairman look over there. He had seen me coming up the aisle. And so, immediately—by this time I got about nearly to the first step—the Chairman said, "Motion made. The convention adjourned. All in favor of the motion, let me know by saying 'Aye, aye.' " And, "That's it." And, "The convention's adjourned." And I by that time was just about to the top step. And they started roaring, "No, no, no, no."

Jackson later told Pepper he had hated to do what he did, but that he had promised the newspaper and radio people to hold the vice-presidential decision until the next day when they would be better prepared. Jackson admitted he had seen Pepper trying to get his attention, that he had an eye on him the whole time he was heading for the podium, and knew perfectly well why he was coming. What he did not tell Pepper was that he and Bob Hannegan had already made an agreement to shut things down that night before the Wallace people could start the nominations. The public explanation was that the decision was a matter of necessity, because of fire laws.

Harry Truman had witnessed none of this. He had spent the night in search of Bennett Clark, finding him finally in a room where he was not supposed to be, at the Sherman, and too drunk to say much more than hello. By then it was past midnight. "So I called Bob [Hannegan]," Truman remembered, "and said, 'I found your boy. He's cockeyed. I don't know whether I can get him ready or not, and I hope to Christ I can't.' "

Of all those in Missouri who had kept track of Harry Truman's activities and accomplishments in the Senate over the past nine years, none had been so attentive, appraising his every move, as his mother Martha Ellen Truman, who remained a close reader of the *Congressional Record* and a more partisan Democrat than almost anyone he knew. Once, introducing her to a political friend, Truman told her the man had grown up in Mississippi and had never seen a Republican until he was twelve. "He didn't miss much," she replied.

For days now, in her small parlor at Grandview, she had been sitting close to the radio, following the convention. Interviewed by reporters, she said she did not want her son to become Vice President. He should stay in the Senate, she said emphatically.

"I listened to all the Republican Convention, too. They keep predicting that Roosevelt will die in office if he's elected. The Republicans hope he will. They keep saying that I'll die, too, and I'm almost 92. I hope Roosevelt fools 'em."

The final session inside the stadium, Friday, July 21, lasted nine hours and would be described as the strangest, most bitter conclusion to a national convention in a very long time.

Senator Bennett Clark, after a great deal of black coffee, a shower, and some food, had, with Hannegan's help, pulled himself together sufficiently to appear on the podium. But his speech for Truman was short and had none of his usual flair. He moved the audience not at all. (In another few weeks, as Truman had anticipated, Bennett Clark went down to defeat in the Democratic primary in Missouri, thereby ending a career in the Senate that many, including Truman, had once thought could lead to the White House.)

Nor were the seconding speakers much of an improvement. A labor leader from Pennsylvania said that while he did not know the senator personally, he thought Truman would make the strongest possible running mate for the reason that he was a Democrat and an American.

By contrast, a vigorous speech for Henry Wallace, delivered by an Iowa judge named Richard Mitchell, touched off another noisy demonstration, and Claude Pepper, given a turn at the podium at last, made a moving plea to the Democratic Party not to repudiate the man who more than any other symbolized the democracy of Franklin Roosevelt. Wallace's delegate strength for the first ballot appeared to be gaining.

But Hannegan, Flynn, Kelly, and the others had been working through the night, talking to delegates and applying "a good deal of pressure" to help them see the sense in selecting Harry Truman. No one knows how many deals were cut, how many ambassadorships or postmaster jobs were promised, but reportedly, by the time morning came, Postmaster General Frank Walker had telephoned every chairman of every delegation.

The strategy of the Truman forces was to organize as many favorite-son nominations as possible and thereby keep Wallace from winning on the first ballot. The result was a total of sixteen nominations for Vice President, and as the speeches continued through the long afternoon, delegates in groups of twos and threes were seen going to and from a private air-conditioned room beneath the platform, Room H, at the end of a narrow, dark hall, where, for hours, Senator Truman stood shaking hands. Only later did he emerge to join Bess and Margaret in a box just behind the podium. Henry Wallace was waiting out the session in his hotel room, in keeping with custom, but Truman sat in full view munching on a hot dog and enjoying the spectacle.

The nominating session had drawn some interesting visitors, including film stars Gloria Swanson, who occupied a box close by, and Spencer Tracy, who was besieged by autograph hunters. Among the delegates were seventeen of Truman's fellow Democrats from the Senate. Ed Flynn and Frank Hague could be seen conferring on the platform, a tableau that caused some veteran observers among the press to recall earlier times when the "big boys" were more discreet about their conniving. But the crowds in the galleries were nothing like the night before. Mayor Kelly's police had been checking tickets, with the result that thousands of Wallace supporters had been kept out.

The first ballot began at 4:30 P.M. and Wallace stayed in the lead the whole way, rolling up 429 votes to Truman's 319, with the remainder divided among Alben Barkley and the favorite sons. By the time the tally became official, it was past six. The convention had been in session for nearly seven hours without pause and the crowd expected to recess for dinner, before the night session. But then Chairman Jackson stepped to the microphones to announce that a second ballot would be taken at once. The convention was still in its afternoon session, which meant no tickets for the night meeting would be honored—and therefore no more Wallace crowds admitted. It was a daring stroke by Hannegan.

On the second ballot the excitement began to build almost at once. Wallace was ahead until suddenly, just as had been forecast for the second ballot, Ed Flynn delivered to Truman 74 votes from the New York delegation, which had been divided the first time around. Now Truman moved out in front.

For a moment, the count narrowed again, Wallace pulling to within 5 votes of Truman. Then the break came. Alabama's favorite son, Senator John Bankhead, withdrew his name and cast 22 Alabama votes for Truman, which gave Truman nearly 500. Delegates rose from their chairs. South Carolina switched 18 votes from Bankhead to Truman and the stampede was on. Indiana, Wyoming, and Maine went over to Truman, while from the galleries came an insistent roar of "We want Wallace!" Photographers were clustering about the Truman box. The senator was smiling broadly. Even Bess, who had looked intermittently grumpy and skeptical through the first ballot, was seen beaming now and turning, as requested, to pose with her husband. Margaret was jumping up and down, cheering as if at a college football game. Over in the Illinois delegation Mayor Kelly shouted to Senator Lucas, "Christ Almighty, let's get in this thing." The whole crowd was on its feet.

Truman only needed one big state. Ohio announced for Truman, which would have been enough but a delegate challenged the count and Ohio passed. Then Senator David I. Walsh of Massachusetts declared that

Massachusetts changed its vote to 34 for Truman, and that did it. Senator Harry S. Truman of Missouri, "unofficially but conclusively," was the party's nominee for Vice President.

Illinois, a little late, piled on another 55 votes for Truman and more states followed. Bennett Clark started a Truman procession down the aisles, as a phalanx of police escorted the nominee to the platform. The official tally was running late, but at 8:14, Chairman Jackson formally announced the Truman victory. The final count was Truman 1,031, Wallace 105. William O. Douglas had 4 votes.

The acceptance speech, one of the shortest in American political history, lasted less than a minute. The nomination was an honor for Missouri, Truman said, and an honor that he accepted "with all humility." More than the speech, it was the shy, almost embarrassed way he stepped up to the bank of microphones, and the way he stood waiting for the crowd to settle down, that many people would remember. He looked out at the huge hall in tumult, his glasses glinting in the spotlight. Then he stepped back slightly.

"Now, give me a chance," he said.

He was called "the Missouri Compromise" and "the Common Denominator" of the convention. To many it had all been a sad spectacle. "I don't object to Truman," wrote Harold Ickes to Bernard Baruch, "but I react strongly against the method of his nomination and the seeming dominating position that the corrupt city bosses now have in the Democratic National organization." The senator's Pendergast roots figured in editorials across the country. The Pittsburgh *Post-Gazette* called him one of the weakest candidates ever nominated. *Time* magazine, which only the summer before had lauded his work on the Truman Committee, portrayed him now as a drab mediocrity, "the mousy little man from Missouri."

"Poor Harry Truman. And poor people of the United States," wrote Richard Strout in *The New Republic:*

> Truman and the people are the ones who will suffer from that convention deal between Roosevelt and the bosses. Truman is a nice man, an honest man, a good Senator, a man of great humility and a man of courage. He will make a passable Vice President. But Truman as President of the United States in times like these?

Yet, on balance, the reaction was favorable, if not enthusiastic. For all his machine background, said the Kansas City *Star,* Harry Truman had "unusual capacity for development." *The New York Times* praised his personal qualities and said he had the advantage of having been through the political mill.

> He has known the dust and heat of a political campaign, and has learned the art, not to be despised, of seeking that middle course which will appeal to a majority of the voters. He fought with distinction in the First World War; he has been a farmer; he has known firsthand the difficulties of a small businessman. He has had the kind of experience, in short, likely to make a realist sympathetic to the problems of the varied groups rather than to produce the doctrinaire or the zealot.

Astonishingly, the St. Louis *Post-Dispatch* called him an excellent choice. Even Richard Strout in his otherwise gloomy *New Republic* essay took heart from the idea that Truman, while not brilliant, had character.

Reflecting on the nomination in the privacy of his diary, reporter Allen Drury wrote:

> On the credit side, the Senator is a fine man: no one would do a better job of it in the White House if he had to. On the other side the Pendergast background made him entirely too vulnerable to Republican attack, and no one who knows him likes to see him subjected to that kind of smearing. . . . I think Senator Truman is one of the finest men I know.

Again at Chicago, as so consistently through the Truman career, it had been the system of politics, the boss system, that counted in deciding his fate. There had been no popular boom for him for Vice President. Nor had personal ambition figured. As Richard Rovere wrote, no one ever contrived less at his own elevation than Harry Truman at Chicago. And as time would tell, everything considered, the system, bosses and all, had produced an excellent choice.

In Independence a few days later, three thousand people streamed across the back lawn at 219 North Delaware to shake hands with the senator, who, in a white seersucker suit, stood beneath a blooming rose arbor beside his wife and daughter. Bess was performing the expected public role, though far from happily. At Chicago after the nomination, as they fought their way out through the crowds to a waiting limousine, with police pushing and shoving, she had turned and glared at her husband, demanding, "Are we going to have to go through this for the rest of our lives?" On the drive home through the smothering July heat of southern Illinois, the atmosphere inside their own car was, as Margaret recalled, "close to arctic." "Dad tried to be cheerful and philosophical simultaneously. Mother said little."

No sooner had they arrived in Independence than Margaret's Aunt Natalie Wallace, Uncle Frank's wife, took it upon herself to tell Margaret that her Grandfather Wallace had shot himself. Margaret ought to know, she said, since the story was bound to come out any time now. Shattered, disbelieving, Margaret rushed to the kitchen to ask Vietta Garr if this were true. Vietta nodded. Unable to face her mother, Margaret waited until evening to tell her father what she had heard, and for the first and only time in her life he turned his fury on her.

"He seized my arm in a grip that he must have learned when he was wrestling calves and hogs around the farmyard," she remembered. " 'Don't you *ever* mention that to your mother,' he said." Then Truman "rocketed" out the door to find Aunt Natalie.

> I wish I could tell you that years later I asked Mother if her anxiety about her father's death was the hidden reason for her opposition to Dad's nomination [Margaret would write years later]. But to the end of her life, I never felt free to violate the absolute prohibition Dad issued on that summer night in 1944.

Out-of-town reporters, looking over the old gray Victorian house for the first time, saw that it needed paint.

The defeated Henry Wallace immediately declared his all-out support for the ticket, exhibiting no bitterness, and in turn he was praised for his courage and forthrightness. Contrary to predictions, he had had real delegate strength after all and had nearly carried the convention despite all the forces aligned against him. Roosevelt would have had no trouble whatever getting him nominated, had he so decided. But then no one seemed nearer to understanding Roosevelt after the convention than before.

Eleanor Roosevelt wrote sympathetically to Wallace, "I had hoped by some miracle you could win out, but it looks to me as though the bosses had functioned pretty smoothly. I am told that Senator Truman is a good man, and I hope so for the sake of the country."

What was not perceived as yet, because so little was known of what went on behind the scenes at Chicago (as well as in Washington before the convention), was the critical part played by Ed Flynn—the fact that it was Flynn, more than anyone, who had convinced Roosevelt that Wallace was a liability and urged Harry Truman on him as the safest alternative;

that it was Flynn, the day he arrived in Chicago, who refused to accept Jimmy Byrnes as a fait accompli, as Kelly and Hannegan had; that it was Flynn, with perfect timing on the second ballot, who delivered the important New York vote.

Southern opposition to Wallace because of his views on racial equality was clear, as was the refusal of northern liberals to accept the southerner Byrnes for his opposing views on the same subject. What was not so clear still was the degree to which Flynn worried over the black vote in New York, the point he had stressed at the secret White House meetings in the spring. It was vital that Truman had no opposition from organized labor, as Byrnes did. It was important that Truman was seen by the conservative side of the party—the southerners' side—as the kind of politician they could work with, who would "go along" in the old phrase, as Wallace never could. It was also very important that Truman had no enemies, that nearly everybody liked Harry Truman, and especially in the Senate, where there would be much work to do when the war was over and the Senate once again, as after the first war, would take part in establishing the peace. But given Ed Flynn's concern about the black vote, it was, after all, Truman's record on civil rights—his stand in the Senate against the poll tax, his Sedalia speech in 1940, his talk to black delegates at the 1940 convention—that made him the right man, a somewhat ironic turn for the son of unreconstructed Missouri lineage who would soon be accused of having once been a member of the Ku Klux Klan.

Roosevelt declared himself well pleased with the outcome and wired Truman his congratulations. Harry Hopkins, somewhat in contradiction to what he had told Jimmy Byrnes, said later that the President had had an eye on Truman all along. "People seemed to think that Truman was just suddenly pulled out of a hat—but that wasn't true," said Hopkins. Bernard Baruch said that while everyone professed a willingness to do what the Boss—Roosevelt—wanted, the Boss did what Ed Flynn wanted.

Roosevelt's son Jimmy, a Marine officer who had been with him in San Diego at the time of the nomination, later wrote of his father's "irritability over what was happening in Chicago" and of his "apparent indifference as to whom the convention selected" as a running mate. "Although Father did not commit himself, I came away with the distinct impression that he really preferred Justice William O. Douglas as the vice-presidential nominee. But he professed not 'to give a damn' whether the delegates came up with Justice Douglas, Jimmy Byrnes, or Harry Truman."

On the very day of his renomination at Chicago, Roosevelt had had a seizure, as only his son Jimmy knew. He had suddenly turned deathly pale, with a look of agony in his face. "Jimmy, I don't know if I can make it—I have horrible pains," Roosevelt said, barely able to get the words out. Jimmy helped him lie down on the floor of the railroad car and watched over him for about ten minutes, terrified, until his father asked to be helped to his feet again. Soon afterward the Commander in Chief was driven to a hilltop above the Pacific where—chin up, smiling, intent —he watched ten thousand Marines storm ashore from Higgins boats in a dress rehearsal for an amphibious landing.

IV

On Tuesday, August 18, 1944, in the shade of a magnolia tree said to have been planted by Andrew Jackson, Franklin Roosevelt and Harry Truman had lunch on the South Lawn of the White House. Because of the heat, Roosevelt suggested they take off their jackets. So it was in their shirtsleeves, seated at a small round table set with crystal and silver from the Coolidge years, that the two men posed together for photographers for the first time.

In background, interests, personality, in everything from the sounds of their voices to the kind of company they enjoyed to the patterns of their careers, they could not have been much more dissimilar. Roosevelt was now in his twelfth year in office. He had been President for so long and through such trying, stirring times that it seemed to many Americans, including the junior Senator from Missouri, that he was virtually the presidency itself. His wealth, education, the social position he had known since boyhood were everything Harry Truman never had. Life and customs at the Roosevelt family estate on the upper Hudson River were as far removed from Jackson County, Missouri, as some foreign land. Roosevelt fancied himself a farmer. To Truman, Roosevelt was the kind of farmer who had never pulled a weed, never known debt, or crop failure, or a father's call to roll out of bed at 5:30 on a bitter cold morning.

Truman, with his Monday night poker games, his Masonic ring and snappy bow ties, the Main Street pals, the dry Missouri voice, was entirely, undeniably middle American. He had only to open his mouth and his origins were plain. It wasn't just that he came from a particular part of the country, geographically, but from a specific part of the American experience, an authentic pioneer background, and a specific place in the American imagination. His Missouri, as he loved to emphasize, was the Missouri of Mark Twain and Jesse James. In manner and appearance, he might have stepped from a novel by Sinclair Lewis, an author Truman is not known to have read. To anyone taking him at face value, this might have been George F. Babbitt having lunch with the President under the Jackson magnolia.

Roosevelt, on the other hand, was from the world of Edith Wharton stories and drawings by Charles Dana Gibson. He was the authentic American patrician come to power, no matter that he loved politics or a night of poker with "the boys" quite as much as the Senator from Missouri, or that he, too, was a Mason and chose a bow tie as many mornings as not, including this one. Roosevelt had been given things all of his life—houses, furniture, servants, travels abroad. Truman had been given almost nothing. He had never had a house to call his own. He had been taught from childhood, and by rough experience, that what he became would depend almost entirely on what he did. Roosevelt had always known the possibilities open to him—indeed, how much was expected of him—because of who he was.

Both were men of exceptional determination, with great reserves of personal courage and cheerfulness. They were alike too in their enjoyment of people. (The human race, Truman once told a reporter, was an "excellent outfit.") Each had an active sense of humor and was inclined to be dubious of those who did not. But Roosevelt, who loved stories, loved also to laugh at his own, while Truman was more of a listener and laughed best when somebody else told "a good one." Roosevelt enjoyed flattery, Truman was made uneasy by it. Roosevelt loved the subtleties of human relations. He was a master of the circuitous solution to problems, of the pleasing if ambiguous answer to difficult questions. He was sensitive to nuances in a way Harry Truman never was and never would be. Truman, with his rural Missouri background, and partly, too, because of the limits of his education, was inclined to see things in far simpler terms, as right or wrong, wise or foolish. He dealt little in abstractions. His answers to questions, even complicated questions, were nearly always direct and assured, plainly said, and followed often by a conclusive "And that's all there is to it," an old Missouri expression, when in truth there may have been a great deal more "to it."

Each of them had been tested by his own painful struggle, Roosevelt with crippling polio, Truman with debt, failure, obscurity, and the heavy stigma of the Pendergasts. Roosevelt liked to quote the admonition of his old headmaster at Groton, Dr. Endicott Peabody: "Things in life will not always run smoothly. Sometimes we will be rising toward the heights—then all will seem to reverse itself and start downward. The great fact to remember is that the trend of civilization is forever upward...." Assuredly Truman would have subscribed to the same vision. They were two optimists at heart, each in his way faithful to the old creed of human progress. But there had been nothing in Roosevelt's experience like the night young Harry held the lantern as his mother underwent surgery, nothing like the Argonne, or Truman's desperate fight for political survival in 1940.

Roosevelt, as would be said, was a kind of master conjurer. He had imagination, he was theatrical. If, as his cousins saw him, Harry Truman was Horatio, then Franklin Roosevelt was Prospero.

Truman was often called a simple man, which he was not. "I wonder why we are made so that what we really think and feel we cover up," he had once confided to Bess, and some who knew him well would, in retrospect, feel he had withheld too much of himself from public view, and that this was among his greatest limitations. But in contrast to Franklin Roosevelt—and it was Truman's destiny from this point forward to be forever contrasted to Roosevelt—he was truly uncomplicated, open, and genuine. In private correspondence Truman could be extremely revealing, whereas Roosevelt never dropped the mask, never poured his heart out on paper as did Truman in hundreds of letters and notes to himself, even after it was clear that he was to be a figure in history.

To many Americans, Truman would always be the "little man from Missouri." Roosevelt was larger than life, even in a wheelchair. He had that force of personality that Truman so admired in a leader and to a degree rarely equaled in the ranks of the presidency. This, too, was something Truman knew he did not have himself, as he knew he had no exceptional intellectual prowess, as had, say, Henry Wallace. "I am not a deep thinker as you are," he had told Wallace only a day earlier when asking Wallace for his help in the campaign ahead. Yet Truman, as Republican Congressman Joe Martin would write, was "smarter by far than most people realized."

In some ways Truman would have felt more in common, more at ease, with the earlier Roosevelt, Theodore, had he been host for the lunch. They were much more alike in temperament. They could have talked books, Army life, or the boyhood handicap of having to meet the world wearing thick spectacles. Or possibly the old fear of being thought a sissy. Like Theodore Roosevelt, and unlike Franklin, Truman had never known what it was to be glamorous.

The contrast in appearance between the President and his new running mate was striking. Truman looked robust, younger than his age. The President, though only two years older, seemed a haggard old man. He had returned only the day before from his long mission to the Pacific, and from the sag of his shoulders, the ashen circles under his eyes, it was clear the trip had taken its toll. Truman, who had not seen the President in more than a year, was stunned by how he looked. Even the famous voice seemed to have no energy or resonance.

The lunch was sardines on toast. The conversation dealt mainly with the campaign ahead and was not very private or revealing, since the President's daughter, Anna Roosevelt Boettiger, joined them. Truman would later repeat only one remark of Roosevelt's. The President told him not to travel by airplane, because it was important that one of them stay alive.

To his dismay, Truman noticed that Roosevelt's hand shook so badly he was unable to pour cream in his coffee.

"The President looked fine and ate a bigger lunch than I did," Truman told reporters afterward, already becoming party to the fiction of a steady hand at the helm. To Bess and Margaret, who were still in Independence, he described how Roosevelt had given him two roses, one for each of them. "You should have seen your Pa walking down Connecticut Avenue . . . with his hat blown up by the wind (so he looked like a college boy— gray hair and all) and two rosebuds in hand," he wrote, as if he hadn't a worry in the world. But arriving at his Senate office, he appeared notice- ably upset. He was greatly concerned about the President, he told Harry Vaughan, and described how Roosevelt's hand had trembled so pouring his cream in his coffee that he put more in the saucer than in the cup. "His hands were shaking and he talks with considerable difficulty. . . . It doesn't seem to be any mental lapse of any kind," Truman said, "but physically he's just going to pieces."

In September, Truman took Eddie McKim to a White House reception, where McKim was so shocked by the President's appearance he won- dered if Roosevelt would live long enough to be inaugurated, if Henry Wallace might become President after all. On the way out, as they were walking through the gate, McKim told Truman to turn and look back, because that was where he would be living before long. "I'm afraid you're right, Eddie," Truman said. "And it scares the hell out of me."

To his cousin Laura Delano, Roosevelt would later remark that he liked Harry Truman. "Harry is a fine man, intelligent, able, and has integrity. He doesn't know much about foreign affairs, but he's learning fast . . ."

How Truman honestly felt about Roosevelt can be deduced only from odd remarks to friends or in his private notes and correspondence, and the picture that emerges, though incomplete, is not complimentary. He called him Santa Claus. He called him a prima donna and a fakir. Writing about Bernard Baruch, whom he disliked, Truman would say, "There never was a greater egotist unless it was Franklin D." Another time, describing Roosevelt to Bess, he wrote, "He's so damn afraid that he won't have all the power and glory that he won't let his friends help as it should be done."

There was little subtle about Truman. He was never remote, rarely ever evasive. He had been raised on straight answers by people who nearly always meant what they said. Roosevelt wasn't that way. "You know how it is when you see the President," Truman once told Allen Drury. "He does all the talking, and he talks about what he wants to talk about, and he never talks about anything you want to talk about, so there isn't much you can do."

To Republican Owen Brewster, Truman said he had but one objection to the President and that was "he lies."

Such feelings, however, would never be publicly expressed, not by Senator Harry Truman of his President, his Commander in Chief and leader of the Democratic Party. That would be unthinkably disloyal, not to say politically unwise and unprofessional. On occasion Truman could also rise to Roosevelt's defense and in a manner not unlike that of his father. At a meeting in Boston in a room at the Ritz-Carlton Hotel that fall, halfway through the campaign, Joe Kennedy began vilifying Roosevelt. "Harry, what the hell are you doing campaigning for that crippled son-of-a-bitch that killed my son Joe?" Kennedy said, referring to his oldest son, who had died in the war. Kennedy went on, saying Roosevelt had caused the war. Truman, by his later account, stood all he could, then told Kennedy to keep quiet or he would throw him out the window. Bob Hannegan had to step in and take Truman aside to remind him of how important Kennedy's money was to the Democratic Party.

His first official speech of the campaign was delivered on a steamy, full-moon night in front of the old red-brick courthouse in Lamar, just up the street from the house where he was born. He spoke for half an hour, never once referring to himself. Experience was what the country needed in such critical times. Franklin Roosevelt was what the country needed. "You can't afford to take a chance. You should endorse tried and experienced leadership," Truman said, as if his own comparative inexperience were in no way part of the equation.

And this was the theme that he carried cross-country, traveling by rail in an old combination sleeper and dining car called the *Henry Stanley*. Hugh Fulton, Matt Connelly, Eddie McKim, and Fred Canfil were along to assist.

The youthful, handsome Connelly, whose own experience thus far had been only as an investigator for the Truman Committee, would remember how the senator recruited him as a political right-hand man:

> Truman came back from Chicago after the convention and the office was a madhouse . . . photographers, press, so at 5 I locked the door and said, "I think you've had enough for today."
>
> He said, "Yes, it was quite a day. Let's go back to the 'doghouse,' I want to talk to you." There he said, "How about a drink? You like that damn Scotch, don't you?"
>
> I said, "I'll mix them."
>
> He said, "No, I'm up to something. I'll mix them." So he made a drink and sat down. He said, "You know, I've got to make a campaign trip."
>
> I said, "I assumed you would."
>
> He said, "I want you to go along with me."
>
> "You want me to go along with you! What do I know about politics?"
>
> He said, "Never mind that. You've got a pretty good teacher."

The route was from New Orleans through Texas and New Mexico, then up the Pacific coast to Portland and Seattle, then east all the way to Boston, with a dozen stops en route. From Boston Truman went to New York, then Washington, where finally he turned homeward again, by way of Wheeling, Pittsburgh, and St. Louis.

At Uvalde, Texas, the morning the train stopped, old John Nance Garner was waiting on the station platform dressed in khaki work pants and a battered ten-gallon hat, his hands stained from picking pecans. "I'm glad to see you, Harry. Bless your old soul," said the former Vice President, who after falling out with Roosevelt had left Washington vowing never again to cross the Potomac River as long as he lived, a vow he kept. Somewhere in the world it must be twelve o'clock and time for a drink, Garner speculated. Truman told him to come right aboard.

In Seattle he addressed a crowd of ten thousand. At little Avery, Idaho, beside the Shoshone National Forest, only three women, schoolteachers, were waiting when the train stopped, but he spoke for fifteen minutes just the same. It wasn't their fault they were the only ones there, Truman would explain. "He's just like the rest of us," said Montana Congressman Mike Mansfield, introducing Truman at a lunch in Butte. On a drive through Pittsburgh he had a twenty-six-man motorcycle escort and huge crowds stretching for miles.

He was not an exciting speaker. It was not a colorful campaign. He just kept pounding away at the need for Roosevelt's leadership to win the war and establish the peace. There could be no return to the isolationism of the Republicans once the war was over, no Congress in the control of Republicans like Nye and Taft. To one reporter on the train, it was "the farmer-neighborliness," the "genuineness" of the candidate that made him appealing and believable, far more than anything he said.

Once, on the train, he was wrenched from his sleep by a vivid nightmare. He had dreamt Roosevelt was dead and he, Harry Truman, was President.

The Republicans tried hard to make him an issue. "Clear it with Sidney" became a Republican war cry. But all efforts by Republicans and reporters to turn up something unsavory from his Pendergast years came to nothing.

Bess's Senate salary was reported and deplored, just as he had feared. He was portrayed repeatedly as small-time, backwater Harry, the failed haberdasher. ("He couldn't even make good selling shirts.") A rumor spread that he was part Jewish, again, as in years past, on the basis that he had a grandfather named Solomon. He was not Jewish, Truman responded, but if he were he would never be ashamed of it.

The charge that he had been a member of the Klan, which he categorically denied, appeared first in the Hearst papers. The story broke shortly before he reached Boston, where, with the Irish-Catholic vote at stake, it might have done irreparable harm. To Truman and his entourage there was no question that the story had been purposefully planted to hit Boston just in time for his arrival and that the day was only saved by the celebrated former Governor of Massachusetts James Michael Curley, then a member of Congress, who spoke from the same platform with Truman.

"Jim Curley got up to make his little speech," remembered Matt Connelly, for whom it was one of the memorable moments of the campaign, "and [he] said, 'We have a very unusual candidate for Vice President. He goes to California, the word comes back to us he's a Jew; he arrives in the Midwest, the word comes back to us that he's a member of the Klan.' And he turned, 'Mr. Vice President, I invite you to join my lodge, The Ancient Order of Hibernians. We'd be glad to have you as one of our members, and I assure you, we will get out the vote.'

"I said to Mr. Truman, 'That takes care of the Klan.' "

But it was the old Pendergast association that dogged him most, and especially when coupled with the question of Roosevelt's health. Attacks by the Chicago *Tribune* were sharpest of all:

> If they confess that there is the slightest chance that Mr. Roosevelt may die or become incapacitated in the next four years, they are faced with the grinning skeleton of Truman the bankrupt, Truman the pliant

tool of Boss Pendergast in looting Kansas City's county government, Truman the yes-man and apologist in the Senate for political gangsters.

To the immense relief of the Trumans, nothing was said of the death of Bess's father, and Truman's anger erupted only over remarks by Republican Congresswoman Clare Boothe Luce, the glamorous wife of publisher Henry Luce, who, poking fun at the idea of Bess working on his Senate staff, began calling her "Payroll Bess." If, as Truman had said, his mother didn't bring him up to be a statesman, then she would not be disappointed, Mrs. Luce also declared.

In the normal rough-and-tumble of a campaign, Truman could take nearly anything said about him, but at any mention of his family, even an implied slight, he got "hotter than a depot stove." He would have nothing but contempt for Clare Boothe Luce from that point on, commenting privately that she spelled her name L-O-O-S-E.

Between Truman and the White House there was little or no communication. The real battle, after all, was the one Roosevelt was waging against Dewey, and to the delight of those close to the President, the battle revived him wonderfully. Though he made few public appearances, one before the International Brotherhood of Teamsters in Washington was considered the best campaign speech of his entire career. He seemed his old self, spontaneously adding a little extra to the prepared text, delivering it with great, feigned gravity and savoring the moment as only a seasoned performer could:

> These Republican leaders have not been content with attacks—on me, or my wife, or on my sons. No, not content with that, they now include my little dog, Fala. Well, of course, I don't resent attacks, and my family doesn't resent attacks, but [pause] Fala does resent them. . . .

As Robert Sherwood, his speechwriter, later observed, the Fala story put the needed excitement into the campaign. "The champ" was back. Ed Flynn, after all his anguish and exertions over the choice of a Vice President, would later tell friends that Roosevelt was in such fine form in the campaign that he could have won had he put Fala on the ticket.

The night the President spoke in Chicago, more than a hundred thousand people packed Soldier Field. He "improved visibly in strength and resilience," recalled Sherwood. In New York, in the face of a cold driving rain, he rode for hours in an open car, bare-headed, so millions of people could see him with their own eyes and know he was all right. It was an ordeal that could have put a younger, stronger man in the hospital, but at the end Roosevelt seemed exhilarated, glad for the chance to show what he could take.

Dewey had raised the specter of Communist infiltration in Washington. "Now . . . with the aid of Sidney Hillman . . . the Communists are seizing control of the New Deal . . . to control the Government of the United States," Dewey warned. Roosevelt had grown to detest Dewey as he never had a political opponent, and like the driving rain, this too seemed to brace him up.

The Trumans waited out the returns in Kansas City, in a suite at the Muehlebach, a throng of old political and Battery D friends on hand to help celebrate, and before the long night ended a large number of them were extremely drunk. "I was shocked," remembered Margaret.

One old political friend from southwest Missouri, Harry Easley, stayed on with Truman after everyone had left. Stretched out on a bed, Truman talked of how lonely he had felt through the campaign. He had seen the look of death in Roosevelt's face, Truman said. "And he knew . . . that he would be President before the term was out," Easley remembered. "He said he was going to have to depend on his friends . . . people like me, he said . . . he knew that he was going to be the President of the United States, and I think it just scared the very devil out of him . . . even the thought of it."

It was nearly four in the morning before Dewey conceded, and the victory was narrow, the closest presidential election since 1916. The Roosevelt-Truman ticket won by 3 million votes, carrying thirty-six of the forty-eight states. Yet a shift of just 300,000 votes in the right states would have elected Dewey and Bricker. Dewey asked all Americans to join him in the hope that "in the difficult years ahead Divine Providence will guide and protect the President of the United States."

Roosevelt, before turning in at Hyde Park, said, "I still think he is a son-of-a-bitch."

In deference to the tragedy of war and the President's limited strength, the inauguration at noon, January 20, 1945, was a somber affair lasting less than fifteen minutes. It was the first wartime inauguration since Lincoln and the first ever held at the White House, the ceremony conducted on the South Portico before a crowd that included numbers of disabled soldiers. A thin crust of snow covered the lawn. The day was grim. There were no parades. The red jackets of the Marine Band were the one note of cheer in the whole chill, muted scene.

Truman, wrapped in a heavy dark blue overcoat, his shoulders braced as if at attention, took the oath of office from Henry Wallace, a serious look on his face. Then the President was helped to his feet by his Marine son Jimmy and a Secret Service agent. Roosevelt wore only a thin summer-weight suit and moved slowly, stiff-legged from his braces, until he could reach out and grip the edge of the lectern. Mrs. Woodrow Wilson, standing close by, was suddenly reminded of how her husband had looked when he went into his decline.

V

Truman was Vice President for eighty-two days and as busy as he had ever been, doing what was customarily expected of a Vice President— presiding over the Senate, attending parties and receptions, shaking endless numbers of hands. Roosevelt was out of the country until the end of February. He had slipped away from Washington in strictest secrecy just two days after the inauguration, traveling by rail to Norfolk, where the cruiser *Quincy* carried him to the Mediterranean Sea, to the island of Malta. From Malta he went by plane to the old Black Sea health resort of Yalta, for his second Big Three conference with Churchill and Stalin. Jimmy Byrnes had gone, too, as a special adviser, and so had Ed Flynn, as a kind of official stowaway. Vice President Truman had been told only that if it was "absolutely urgent," he could make contact with the President through the White House. Since taking office, Truman had seen nothing of Roosevelt nor had he been told anything at all about the conference. Truman had not even met the new Secretary of State, Edward Stettinius.

To his surprise, however, he was enjoying himself. The round of social engagements not only didn't bother him, he delighted in it. "The amiable Missourian with the touch of country in his voice and manner," reported *Time,* "had conquered a schedule that had Mrs. Truman and Capitol society writers breathless."

Perle Mesta, heir to Oklahoma oil money and the widow of a wealthy Pittsburgh toolmaker, gave a party in the Vice President's honor that was described as "one of the most glittering in Washington's long history of glittery parties." Mrs. Mesta had come to Washington initially as a Republican, but "jumped the fence" to become a Democrat only the summer before, because the Republicans had refused to renominate Wendell Willkie. Now she had "taken up" Harry Truman.

[The party] had all the charm of an English court tea, the sparkle of a Viennese ball, and the razzle-dazzle of a Hollywood premiere. The best names in officialdom and society attended. Shirt fronts gleamed with star-ruby studs. Evening gowns fairly dripped with diamonds and pearls. Champagne, at $20 a bottle, flowed in cascades....

"He circulated around in as comfortable, unpretentious, and agreeable manner as could be," wrote the author John Gunther, after seeing Truman at a dinner party given by the foreign affairs editor of the Washington *Post*. Truman had been the first to arrive, Gunther noted.

> He was lively and animated . . . a guest among other guests.
> I had the impression of what you might call bright grayness. Both the clothes and hair were neat and gray. The gray-framed spectacles magnified the gray-hazel eyes, but there was no grayness in the mind. . . . His conversational manner is alert and poised. He talks very swiftly, yet with concision. You have to listen hard to get it all.

Later, during an interview on the Hill, when Gunther asked him what he liked most, Truman answered, "People."

Old friends on the Hill found him wholly unaffected by his new role, "homespun as ever." He kept his same quarters in the Senate Office Building, Room 240, using the Vice President's office in the Capitol mainly as a place to greet visitors, under the dazzle of a seven-tiered crystal chandelier.

For senators of both parties it became, as Charlie Ross wrote, "the most natural thing in the world" to drop in on Truman for a chat, or perhaps a nip of bourbon. "Many of them observed on these occasions that they had never been in the Vice President's office when Henry Wallace was there. Wallace to them was otherworldly. He didn't speak their language; Truman does."

He, Bess, and Margaret were still living in the same five-room apartment at 4701 Connecticut Avenue at the same $120-a-month rent. The only difference was that his mother-in-law, Mrs. Wallace, had also moved in.

"Harry looks better than he has for ages—is really putting on weight," Bess wrote to Ethel Noland. "Marg has gone to a picture show and Harry to a poker party," she told Ethel in another letter. "Mother is practically asleep in her chair—so it's very peaceful."

The one new personal convenience with the job was an official car, a black Mercury limousine, and a driver, Tom Harty, who picked the Vice President up each morning and returned him home again at day's end. En route to the Capitol, they would drop Margaret off at George Washington University, where she was in her junior year. Also, in the front seat rode a young man whom Truman at first assumed was a friend of Harty's who needed a lift. He was George Drescher, the first Secret Service man to be assigned to a Vice President. The idea had been suggested by Harry Vaughan, who had returned from active duty with the Air Corps to become Truman's military aide, another first for a Vice President. Appalled to find that no security arrangements had been made for Truman, Vaughan went to Secretary of the Treasury Henry Morgenthau and told him it seemed a bit incongruous to have seventy or a hundred people guarding the President and no one at all guarding the Vice President.

"I used to get down here to the office at 7 o'clock," Truman wrote his mother and sister from his office.

> But now I have to take Margaret to school every morning and I don't get here until 8:30. Reathel Odum [who had replaced Mildred Dryden as his stenographer] is always here at that time and we wade through a stack of mail a foot high. By that time I have to see people—one at a time just as fast as they can go through the office without seeming to hurry them. Then I go over to the Capitol gold-plated office and see Senators and curiosity seekers for an hour and then the Senate meets and it's my job to get 'em prayed for—and goodness knows they need it, and then get the business going by staying in the chair for an hour and then see more Senators and curiosity people who want to see what a V.P. looks like and if he walks and talks and has teeth.

What inner fear or concern Truman still felt over the President's health, he seems to have kept to himself. Nor did he appear to be making any effort to prepare himself for Roosevelt's death. It was as if all the dire speculation of the summer before, the nightmare he had had on the campaign train, were forgotten, locked away, now that the unthinkable was so much nearer at hand. The closest he came to open speculation on the future and its problems was an off-the-record conversation with a correspondent for *Time,* Frank McNaughton, who later wrote to his editor in New York:

> Truman says simply that he hopes to be of value to the administration through his contacts in the Senate, and he conceives the VP's job to be a sort of liaison between the executive and legislative branches. Truman is fervent in his declared hope that he can do this right up to the hilt.
>
> "There is a difficult situation after every war, and disagreements and misunderstandings spring up between the executive and legislative," Truman, an expert on history, says. "Madison encountered it, Andrew Jackson experienced it in an aggravated degree, and Woodrow Wilson

had to struggle with it. There is always a tremendous reaction after every such emergency. I don't think the human kind has changed so much, in that regard, but I have hopes that this will be a period in history when all will rise to the seriousness of the occasion and cooperate for the good of this country and the people."

We can't attribute it to Truman, but he is tremendously afraid that there will be a postwar struggle between executive and legislative, and between the Allied powers, that will wreck the peace once and for all. He believes it is going to take the greatest sagacity and diplomacy to prevent postwar national and international struggles for power and prestige, and he conceives it to be his job to effect, to the best of his ability, a smooth cooperation and liaison between the Senate and the President. . . .

His more immediate task was to help get Henry Wallace approved by the Senate as the new Secretary of Commerce. However, it was his part in two other events, both occurring in Roosevelt's absence, that drew the greatest attention.

In Kansas City, on January 26, less than a week after the inauguration, Tom Pendergast died at the age of seventy-two. Since his return from prison nearly five years before, Pendergast had been living in the big red brick house on Ward Parkway, where, in steadily declining health, he was seen by few outside his immediate family. His name rarely appeared in the papers any longer. His political influence was entirely gone. By court ruling, he was even restricted from setting foot ever again at 1908 Main Street. Truman is not known to have called on him from the time Pendergast left prison, but then to have done so would have been extremely difficult.

But on hearing of T.J.'s death, Truman decided at once that he would attend the funeral. He took off for Kansas City in an Army bomber and was among the several thousand mourners who filed past the bier at Visitation Catholic Church. He was photographed coming and going and paying his respects to the family, all of which struck large numbers of people everywhere as outrageous behavior for a Vice President—to be seen honoring the memory of a convicted criminal. Yet many, possibly a larger number, saw something admirable and courageous in a man risen so high who still knew who he was and refused to forget a friend.

Two weeks later he was back in the news, with more pictures, and again, to some, as a figure of ridicule. He had agreed to take part in a stage show for servicemen held at the Washington Press Club's canteen. He was playing an upright piano, to an audience of about eight hundred men in uniform, when actress Lauren Bacall, also part of the entertainment, was boosted on top of the piano to strike a leggy pose as the delighted crowd cheered and flashbulbs popped. "I was just a kid," she would remember. "My press agent made me do it." "Anything can happen in this country," a soldier was quoted at the time. The photographs of the Vice President serenading the glamorous Hollywood star were an instant sensation. What disturbed many people was that Truman appeared to be having such a good time, which he was. Bess was furious. She told him he should play the piano in public no more.

On March 1, in the House Chamber, at a solemn joint session of Congress, with Majority Leader John McCormack beside him, Vice President Truman sat on the dais behind the President as in slow, often rambling fashion Franklin Roosevelt reported on some of what had happened at Yalta. He read the speech sitting down, explaining it was easier not to carry 10 pounds of steel on his legs, which was the first time he had made public mention of his physical disability.

He appeared more pale and drawn than ever. His left hand trembled noticeably as he turned the pages. "It has been a long journey. I hope you will also agree it has been so far, a fruitful one." At times, losing his place, he ad-libbed. "Of course there were a few other little matters, but I won't go into them here." At times, his voice seemed to give out and his hand shook again as he reached for a glass of water. "Twenty-five years ago, American fighting men looked to the statesmen of the world to finish the work of peace for which they fought and suffered. We failed—we failed them then. We cannot fail them again, and expect the world to survive again."

Here and there in the chamber, listening to him speak, were more than a few who knew enough to have sensed what meaning could lie in these last words—John McCormack, Minority Leader Martin, Secretary Stimson, General Marshall, Henry Wallace, Jimmy Byrnes, Sam Rosenman, who had written much of the speech, Steve Early, the President's press secretary, and Eleanor Roosevelt, who was watching from the gallery, perhaps a dozen in total who knew the great secret about which the Vice President had been told nothing.

"I saw the President immediately after his speech had been concluded," Truman wrote. "Plainly, he was a very weary man." Roosevelt, as he told Truman, was leaving as soon as possible for Warm Springs, Georgia, and a rest.

In the stack of mail on his desk to be answered the morning of Thursday, April 12, was a letter from Jim Pendergast, who needed his old friend

Harry's help. "For about a year," Jim wrote, "the Pendergast Wholesale Liquor Company has been trying to get bottles and cartons in order to carry on their business. They have made three applications and these applications have all been approved by the local office of the War Production Board but when they get to Washington they have all been rejected." The company, Jim explained, had over eleven thousand barrels of straight bourbon whiskey stored in Kentucky but no bottles or cartons. The situation was serious.

"We will see what we can do right away," Truman dictated to Miss Odum.

He had dressed for the day with customary care, in a double-breasted gray suit with a white handkerchief in the breast pocket neatly folded so that three corners were showing, a white shirt, and a dark blue polka-dot bow tie. He looked scrubbed and well barbered, the picture of health and self-possession. In the Senate Chamber later in the day, reporters in the press gallery would comment on his obvious enjoyment of people as he moved among different groups of senators on the floor. "It's wonderful, this Senate," he had said in a press conference only the day before. "It's the greatest place on earth. . . . The grandest bunch of fellows you could ever find anywhere."

The rest of the mail took longer than usual, so that he was late getting over to the Senate Chamber, where the day's work had already begun, Alben Barkley substituting for him on the dais. The time of Truman's arrival was approximately 11:30 A.M.

Senator Willis of Indiana was just relinquishing the floor. Truman and Barkley shook hands and Truman, taking his seat, handed a few official communications to the reading clerk, who announced them to the Senate. One concerned plans being made by the town of Patton, Pennsylvania, for a welcome-home celebration in honor of General George S. Patton. Another was a request from the legislature of Alaska to increase the reindeer herds in Alaska's national parks by declaring open season on wolves and coyotes.

Many of those in the chamber were people Truman had known since he first came to the Senate ten years earlier. And for all that the world had changed, all the tumult and tragedy of the war, the old room itself looked much the same, except for a mass of ugly steel girders overhead, supports put up in 1940 to hold an old ceiling that had been on the verge of collapse. They had been installed as a temporary expedient only, but then, because of the war, the restoration work had to be postponed, and so there they remained, "barn rafters," beneath which the business of the Senate continued.

Senator Hawkes of New Jersey asked for printing in the *Congressional Record* of a petition from the Order of the Sons of Italy to invite Italy to the forthcoming San Francisco Conference to organize the United Nations. Senator Reed of Kansas asked that nineteen letters and telegrams be printed in the *Record,* all describing the critical shortage of boxcars for grain shipments. The boxcar situation, said the senator, was the worst he had ever seen; wheat was spoiling on the ground.

The main business before the Senate was the ratification of a water treaty with Mexico, affecting use of the Colorado and Rio Grande. As chairman of the Foreign Relations Committee, Senator Connally spoke first, followed by Ernest McFarland of Arizona. Both urged ratification. Truman had a page deliver a note to Republican Senator Saltonstall of Massachusetts, asking Saltonstall to come up and take his place. "I have a Missouri soldier boy in my office," explained Truman, who promised to be back in no more than an hour. Noticing an apple on the dais, Saltonstall asked what would happen if he ate it.

"You will take the consequences," Truman said.

Truman had always been a man of his word, Saltonstall would remember, telling the story years later. "He was back in an hour."

At another point, the Vice President was seen in a friendly huddle with Republicans Wiley of Wisconsin and Wherry of Nebraska. Allen Drury, watching from the press gallery, remarked to Tony Vaccaro of the United Press that Roosevelt was fortunate to have so good a man as Truman to deal with the Senate. Vaccaro, frowning, said Roosevelt would make no use of him. Vaccaro, who had lately been spending time with the Vice President, said, "Truman doesn't know what's going on. Roosevelt won't tell him anything."

As the record would show, Truman had met with the President exactly twice, except for Cabinet meetings, since becoming Vice President—once on March 8 and again on March 19, ten days before Roosevelt left for Warm Springs—and neither time was anything of consequence discussed.

About midway through the afternoon Senator Alexander Wiley, Republican of Wisconsin, commenced his remarks on the Mexican water issue, speaking not always to the point and in numbing detail when he did:

It may be noted that the report of the Bureau of Reclamation of the problems of the Imperial Valley and vicinity considered that 800,000 acres ultimately would be irrigated in Mexico, and that some storage would be required for this purpose. Under the present duty of water in the Mexico area, the 800,000 acres of land would require a diversion from the river of 4,800,000 acre-feet of water. The aggregate acreage under the two items to which the footnote in the above table applies is . . .

Truman decided to make other use of his time by writing a letter to his mother and sister, even though he had little news to report:

Dear Mamma and Mary—I am trying to write you a letter today from the desk of the President of the Senate while a windy Senator from Wisconsin is making a speech on a subject with which he is in no way familiar. . . .

Hope you are having a nice spell of weather. We've had a week of beautiful weather but it is raining and misting today. I don't think it's going to last long. Hope not, for I must fly to Providence, R.I., Sunday morning.

Turn on your radio tomorrow night at 9:30 your time and you'll hear Harry make a Jefferson Day address to the nation. I think I'll be on all the networks so it ought not to be hard to get me. It will be followed by the President, whom I'll introduce.

Hope you are both well and stay that way.

Love to you both.

Write when you can.

Harry

At the conclusion of Wiley's speech, Barkley moved for a recess. It was four minutes to five by the clock over the main lobby entrance.

Truman came down from the dais, went out through the swinging doors on his left, crossed the Senators' Private Lobby, and stepped into the Vice President's office to tell Harry Vaughan that he would be with Sam Rayburn should anybody want him.

Then, eluding his Secret Service guard, the Vice President walked the length of the Capitol, cutting through the Senate Reception Room, out past the eight-foot white marble statue of Benjamin Franklin, down the long, tiled corridor, around "Mark Twain's Cuspidor" (the columned well of the Senate Rotunda, so named by Twain because of the tobacco leaves on its columns), on through the main rotunda under the dome, through Statuary Hall (the old House Chamber), and briefly along another corridor to a stairway; down the stairs to the ground floor, left down one hall, right down another to Room 9, Sam Rayburn's private hideaway, known unofficially as "the Board of Education."

Rayburn, who referred to it simply as "downstairs," met there for a "libation" every afternoon, once the formal business of "upstairs" was concluded. It was an important part of his day, and to be invited to join him, even once or twice in a term, was considered the sign that one had arrived. Truman was among the regulars.

Moving along at his usual brisk pace, he would have covered the distance from the Vice President's office in less than three minutes. So it must have been just after five o'clock when he came in.

Though pictured often as small and plain, the room was about 20 feet in length, its ornate ceiling busy with painted birds and animals. The furnishings, too, were large, comfortable and utilitarian—big, worn black leather chairs, a long couch, a sink, and a large refrigerator that was camouflaged with veneer to more or less match the big desk, where Rayburn kept the whiskey.

Two others were already with the Speaker when Truman arrived, Lewis Deschler, the House Parliamentarian, and James M. Barnes, a staff man at the White House assigned to congressional liaison. The gray afternoon outside was fading, the room growing dim. No one had bothered yet to turn on the lights.

Apparently it was Deschler who reminded Rayburn that Truman had had a call from the White House.

"Steve Early wants you to call him right away," Rayburn said. Truman mixed himself a drink, then dialed the number, National 1414.

"This is the V.P.," he said.

Steve Early's voice sounded tense and strange. Truman was to come to the White House as "quickly and as quietly" as he could, and to enter by the main entrance on Pennsylvania Avenue.

As Lewis Deschler later recounted, Truman lost all his color. "Jesus Christ and General Jackson," he said, putting down the phone.

He was wanted at the White House right away, he told the others. They must say nothing.

He went out the door alone. Then he began to run, taking a different route. He kept to the ground floor this time, racing down a hall between a double line of bronze and marble Civil War generals and forgotten state governors, his shoes pounding on the marble floor. He ran through the echoing old Crypt, past the Senate barbershop, then up a flight of stairs with brass banisters to his office—to get his hat.

He told Harry Vaughan he was on his way to the White House and to keep that to himself. In minutes he was in the big Mercury with Tom Harty driving, but still no Secret Service guard, moving with all possible speed through the evening traffic. By now it was approximately 5:15 P.M.

What thoughts were rushing through his mind, he never fully revealed. "I thought I was going down there to meet the President," he later said.

"I didn't allow myself to think anything else." To his mother he would write it occurred to him that perhaps Roosevelt had returned from Warm Springs because the retired Episcopal bishop of Arizona, an old friend of the President's, had been buried that day. "I thought that maybe he wanted me to do some special piece of liaison work with the Congress and had sent for me to see him after the funeral."

But if this was so, why had he run back to his office? "I ran all the way," he told her. What did he imagine he was running toward? Or leaving behind?

At the White House, the long black car turned off Pennsylvania, through the northwest gate, and swept up the drive, stopping under the North Portico. The time was 5:25.

Two ushers were waiting at the door. They took his hat and escorted him to a small, oak-paneled elevator, more like an ornate cage, that had been installed in the Theodore Roosevelt era and that ascended now very slowly to the second floor.

In the private quarters, across the center hall, in her sitting room, Mrs. Roosevelt was waiting. With her were Steve Early and her daughter and son-in-law, Anna and John Boettiger. Mrs. Roosevelt stepped forward and gently put her arm on Truman's shoulder.

"Harry, the President is dead."

Truman was unable to speak.

"Is there anything I can do for you?" he said at last.

"Is there anything *we* can do for *you*," she said. "For you are the one in trouble now."

PART THREE

TO THE BEST OF
MY ABILITY

9

The Moon, the Stars,
and All the Planets

So ended an era and so began another.

—ALLEN DRURY

I

The news broke at 5:47 P.M., Eastern War Time, April 12, 1945.

International News Service was first on the wire, followed seconds later by the Associated Press, United Press, the four radio networks, and the Armed Forces Radio Service. In New York CBS interrupted a children's serial about Daniel Boone called "Wilderness Road." NBC broke into "Front-Page Farrell," ABC interrupted "Captain Midnight," and Mutual, "Tom Mix."

In minutes the bulletin had reached every part of the country and much of the world. The time in London was near midnight. In Berlin, where it was already another day, Friday the 13th, an ecstatic Joseph Goebbels, Nazi propaganda minister, telephoned Hitler personally to proclaim it a turning point written in the stars. In Moscow, the American ambassador, Averell Harriman, was hosting an embassy party when a duty officer called to report what he had heard on a late broadcast on the Armed Forces Radio Service. At the Armed Forces Radio Station in Panama, Sergeant James Weathers, assigned to answer incoming calls, began picking up the phone and answering, "Yes, it's true," "Yes, it's true," over and over again.

Franklin Roosevelt had died of a cerebral hemorrhage at the "Little White House" in Warm Springs, Georgia, at 4:45 in the afternoon (3:45, Warm Springs time). Two hours earlier, sitting at a card table signing papers, he had complained of a terrific headache, then suddenly collapsed, not to regain consciousness. As many accounts stated, his death at age sixty-three came in an hour of high triumph. "The armies and fleets under his direction as Commander-in-Chief were at the gates of Berlin and the shores of Japan's home islands . . . and the cause he represented and led was nearing the conclusive phase of success."

From the White House, Mrs. Roosevelt sent cables to her four sons in the service, saying their father had done his job to the end, as he would want them to do, a point Steve Early included in the initial White House announcement. To Early and Harry Truman she had also expressed a wish to fly to Warm Springs, but questioned whether it would be proper now for her to use a government plane. Truman, unhesitatingly, said she should. This and the arrival of Secretary of State Stettinius were among the few things he would remember from the scene in her study. Stettinius had appeared in the doorway with tears streaming down his face.

They agreed the Cabinet should be assembled at once and the Chief Justice summoned to administer the oath of office. Truman started downstairs for the West Wing. From the President's office he telephoned Les Biffle. He wanted the congressional leadership to come at once, and a car sent for Mrs. Truman and Margaret. He then called the apartment and told Bess what had happened. She had not had the radio on. It was the first she had heard.

The West Wing throbbed with activity and tension. Reporters, photographers, White House staff people, the Secret Service, and a few of Truman's own staff converged from several directions, crowding corridors and offices. Voices were hushed and tense. Telephones kept ringing. In the twilight outside, across Pennsylvania Avenue, in Lafayette Square, thousands of people gathered in silence.

By seven o'clock nearly everyone who was supposed to be there had assembled in the Cabinet Room: Stettinius and Chief Justice Harlan Stone, Sam Rayburn, John McCormack, Joe Martin, Henry Stimson, Henry Wallace, Harold Ickes, Attorney General Francis Biddle, Secretary of Agriculture Claude Wickard, Secretary of the Navy James Forrestal, Julius Krug, War Production Board Administrator, Fred M. Vinson, Director of the Office of War Mobilization, Admiral William Leahy, who was Roosevelt's personal chief of staff, Bob Hannegan, and Secretary of Labor Frances Perkins, the only woman present until the arrival of Bess and Margaret. Missing were Postmaster General Frank Walker, who was ill, and Alben Barkley, who had decided to stay with Mrs. Roosevelt. Uniformed White House guards were at the doors.

Truman sat by himself in a brown leather chair, looking dreadful, "absolutely dazed." When Bess came in, he crossed the room and took her hand. Little was said by anyone. Then, for what seemed an extremely long time, they all stood waiting while several of the staff went in search of a Bible. "It was a very somber group," Stimson would record.

Bess, who had been crying almost from the moment she heard the news, dabbed repeatedly at her eyes with a handkerchief. Margaret would remember feeling as if she were going under anesthesia. None of it seemed quite real.

The only Bible to be found was an inexpensive Gideon edition with garish red edging to the pages. It had been in the desk drawer of the fastidious head usher, Howell Crim, a short, stooped, bald-headed man who now made sure it was properly dusted before placing it on the table. Truman would later tell his mother he could have brought Grandpa Truman's Bible from his office bookcase had he only known.

He and Justice Stone took their places by the marble mantelpiece at the end of the room, beneath a portrait of Woodrow Wilson. Bess, Margaret, and the others filed in around them. A few reporters, photographers, and newsreel cameramen were told to come in. One of the staff recalled much milling about and confusion. The time on the clock on the mantel was 7:09, 2 hours and 24 minutes since Roosevelt's death.

Truman glanced at the clock. "It said nine past seven when I started to swear the oath—I remember," he later said. "I looked at it. And I remember the faces all around me. . . ."

He picked up the Bible and held it in his left hand. He raised his right hand.

"I, Harry Shipp Truman," Justice Stone began.

"I, Harry S. Truman," Truman corrected him.

". . . do solemnly swear that I will faithfully execute the office of the President of the United States, and will to the best of my ability, preserve, protect and defend the Constitution of the United States."

"So help you God," added the Chief Justice.

"So help me God."

His "sharp features taut," as a reporter noted, Truman looked straight ahead through his thick, round glasses. The sudden, fervent way he kissed the Bible at the end of the ceremony impressed everyone present. It had all taken not more than a minute.

Afterward he asked the Cabinet to remain.

They were assembled about the table when Steve Early came in to say the press wanted to know if the San Francisco Conference on the United Nations would open as planned in twelve days, on April 25. As several in the room knew, Roosevelt had often sat alone at the same table looking at the Wilson portrait, pondering the tragedy of Wilson's failure to create the League of Nations. The answer was emphatically yes, Truman said, making his first decision as President.

In his brief remarks to the Cabinet he said he intended to carry on with Roosevelt's program and hoped they would all stay on the job. He welcomed their advice. He did not doubt that they would differ with him if they felt it necessary, but final decisions would be his and he expected their support once decisions were made.

Stimson, the senior member, said it was time to close ranks. When the meeting ended, Stimson remained behind. There was a matter of utmost urgency to be discussed, he told Truman. It concerned a new explosive of unbelievable power. But he gave no further details, which left Truman no better informed than before.

In his diary later that night, Stimson wrote that the new President had conducted himself admirably, considering the shock he had been through and how little he knew.

Truman, before leaving for home, remembered that Eddie McKim was in town and that they had a date to play poker that night at McKim's room at the Statler. "I guess the party's off," Truman said, once the White House operator had McKim on the line.

By 9:30 he was back at 4701 Connecticut Avenue. Bess, Margaret, and Mrs. Wallace, he found, had gone to the apartment of neighbors next door, a general named Davis and his wife, where they were lingering over the remains of a turkey and cake. Margaret remembered her father saying little except that he had had nothing to eat since noon. Mrs. Davis fixed him a turkey sandwich and a glass of milk. Shortly, he excused himself, went to the apartment, and called his mother to tell her he was all right and not to worry. He then went to bed and, he later said, immediately to sleep.

Automobile traffic and streetcars passed beneath his open window as though nothing were different. People walking by took no more interest in the building than on other nights. Other residents, coming or going, some with dogs on leashes, were surprised to find reporters in the lobby and Secret Service men standing about.

The reporters had taken over two couches beside a stone fireplace. In a corner was the telephone switchboard for the building and a bank of mailboxes. Box 209 carried a printed card, "Mr. and Mrs. Harry S. Truman," with "Margaret Truman" handwritten in ink below. The switchboard operator said she regretted very much that the Trumans would be leaving. "Such lovely people," she said.

A widely repeated story in Washington that the switchboard at 4701 Connecticut Avenue was the busiest in town that night—because news of Roosevelt's death and Truman's swearing in meant there would soon be an apartment available in the building—is apparently apocryphal.

To the country, the Congress, the Washington bureaucracy, to hundreds of veteran New Dealers besides those who had gathered in the Cabinet Room, to much of the military high command, to millions of American men and women overseas, the news of Franklin Roosevelt's death, followed by the realization that Harry Truman was President, struck like massive earth tremors in quick succession, the thought of Truman in the White House coming with the force of a shock wave. To many it was not just that the greatest of men had fallen, but that the least of men—or at any rate the least likely of men—had assumed his place.

"Good God, Truman will be President," it was being said everywhere. "If Harry Truman can be President, so could my next-door neighbor." People were fearful about the future of the country, fearful the war would drag on longer now. "What a great, great tragedy. God help us all," wrote David Lilienthal, head of TVA. The thought of Truman made him feel physically ill. "The country and the world don't deserve to be left this way. . . ."

The fact that Roosevelt had died like Lincoln in the last stages of a great war, and like Lincoln in April, almost to the day, were cited as measures both of Roosevelt's greatness and the magnitude of the tragedy. But implicit also was the thought that Lincoln, too, had been succeeded by a lackluster, so-called "common man," the ill-fated Andrew Johnson.

Stettinius, who as Secretary of State was next in line now to succeed to the presidency, wondered privately if the parallel was not closer to what followed Woodrow Wilson, after the last war, if the country was in for another Harding administration, with cheap courthouse politicians taking over.

Senators, according to the conventional wisdom, didn't make strong presidents. Harding had been the only other President drawn from the Senate thus far in the century and the feeling was he had been taken from the bottom of the barrel. Theodore Roosevelt, Wilson, Franklin Roosevelt, even Coolidge had all been governors. And governors, from experience, knew something about running things.

In a house at Marburg, Germany, three American generals, Eisenhower, Bradley, and Patton, sat up much of the night talking about Roosevelt and speculating on the sort of man Truman might be. All three were greatly depressed. "From a distance Truman did not appear at all qualified to fill

Roosevelt's large shoes," Bradley wrote. Patton was bitter and more emphatic. "It seems very unfortunate that in order to secure political preference, people are made Vice President who are never intended, neither by Party nor by the Lord to be Presidents."

It had been an unusually difficult day for the three commanders, even before the news about Roosevelt. They had seen their first Nazi death camp, Ohrdruf-Nord, near Gotha. As they bid good night to one another, an aide recalled Eisenhower looking deeply shaken.

For thousands of men in the ranks, as for many at home, the question was not so much was Truman qualified, as who was he.

In the chill of dawn in Germany, a private named Lester Atwell remembered, his battalion had been lined up for breakfast beside a country road:

> "Men"—an officer came quickly along the line . . . "I have an announcement to make: President Roosevelt died last night."
>
> "*What?*" You heard it from all sides. "What? President Roosevelt? Roosevelt's *dead?*" We were astounded.
>
> The officer's voice continued. "We don't know any particulars, except that he's dead. I think it was very sudden. Probably a stroke. Truman, the Vice-President, will take over."
>
> "Who? Who'd he say?"
>
> "Truman, ya dumb bastard. Who the hell you think?"

There were some, however, who, facing the prospect of a Truman presidency, felt confident the country was in good hands. They knew the man, they said. They understood his origins. They had seen how he handled responsibility and knew the inner resources he could draw on. As before and later in his life, confidence in Harry Truman was greatest among those who knew him best.

"Truman is honest and patriotic and has a head full of good horse sense. Besides, he has guts," wrote John Nance Garner to Sam Rayburn, who was himself assuring reporters that Truman would make a good, sound President "by God," because, "He's got the stuff in him." To arch-Republican Arthur Vandenberg, writing the night of April 12, Truman was "a *grand person* with every good intention and high honesty of purpose." Could Truman "swing the job?" Vandenberg speculated in his diary. "I think he can."

Asked years later what his feelings were when he realized Truman was President, John J. McCloy, the Assistant Secretary of War, said, "Oh, I felt good. Because I *knew* him. I knew the kind of man he was."

Assistant Secretary of State Dean Acheson wrote to his son in the Navy that as a consequence of a long, recent meeting with Truman he had a definite impression:

> He was straightforward, decisive, simple, entirely honest. He, of course, has the limitations upon his judgment and wisdom that the limitations of his experience produce, but I think that he will learn fast and will inspire confidence. It seems to me a blessing that he is the President and not Henry Wallace.

Even I. F. Stone of *The Nation,* long an outspoken Wallace supporter, would write: "I hate to confess it, but I think Mr. Roosevelt was astute and farsighted in picking Mr. Truman rather than Mr. Wallace as his successor. At this particular moment in our history, Mr. Truman can do a better job."

At home in Independence, editor William Southern wrote in the *Examiner* that the country was "in the hands of an honorable man, not just a politician."

Among such old faithfuls as Eddie McKim, Ted Marks, John Snyder, Jim Pendergast, and Eddie Jacobson, there was never a doubt. "GET IN THERE AND PITCH. YOU CAN HANDLE IT," Jim Pendergast cabled immediately from Kansas City. "I wish people knew him as I do," Eddie Jacobson told a reporter.

At Grandview a day or so later, questioned by reporters, the mother of the new President offered as fair and memorable a comment as any: "I can't really be glad he's President because I am sorry President Roosevelt is dead. If he had been voted in, I would be out waving a flag, but it doesn't seem right to be very happy or wave any flags now. Harry will get along all right."

Truman was immensely pleased and proud of her. Her statement was "a jewel," he wrote in his diary. "If it had been prepared by [the] best public relations [advisers] it could not have been better."

Only gradually would he reveal his own feelings, making plain that if anyone was stunned by the turn of fate, or worried over the future, or distressed by the inadequacies of the man stepping into the place of Franklin Roosevelt, it was Harry Truman.

At the White House the difference was felt at once. Arriving at 9:00 the next morning at the West Wing, where a cluster of reporters were waiting, Truman stepped from the big White House Cadillac followed by Tony Vaccaro of the Associated Press. Vaccaro had gone early to the Connecticut Avenue apartment. He had been standing alone on the curb outside the building hoping to catch a glimpse of the new President as he started off for his first day. Truman told him to hop in if he wanted a ride.

"There have been few men in all history the equal of the man into whose shoes I am stepping," Truman had said as they headed downtown. "I pray God I can measure up to the task."

It was Friday, April 13, 1945, twenty-seven years to the day since he landed at Brest as a First Lieutenant in the American Expeditionary Force.

In the President's office everything was as Roosevelt left it, the arrangement of furniture, his ship models, his naval prints on the apple green walls. Only the desk had been touched, cleared of its pictures and knick-knacks by Jonathan Daniels of the Roosevelt staff, who stood by waiting now as Truman came in. He felt the presence of Roosevelt acutely, Truman later wrote, and so did Daniels, whose personal ties to Roosevelt went back to World War I, when his father, Josephus Daniels, the Secretary of the Navy, had been Roosevelt's boss. "It seemed still Roosevelt's desk and Roosevelt's room," Daniels remembered. "It seemed to me, indeed, almost Roosevelt's sun which came in the wide south windows and touched Truman's thick glasses." He watched as Truman sat in the President's high-backed leather chair, rolled back and forth, turned, leaned back, as if testing it, and he thought how pathetically undersized Truman looked.

The first visitor was Eddie McKim. "Eddie, I'm sorry as hell about last night," Truman greeted him, getting up from the desk. McKim, who was extremely nervous and straining at formality, felt he must remain standing as Truman sat down again. He didn't know what to do in front of a President, McKim blurted. Truman told him to come over and have a chair. When McKim remarked that he would be heading home that afternoon, Truman asked him to stay on, saying, "I need you."

He saw Secretary Stettinius twice, for forty-five minutes that morning and again at the end of the day. (At the conclusion of the morning meeting Truman asked Stettinius for a written report summarizing diplomatic problems in Europe and said he wanted it by the close of business.) Stimson, Marshall, Leahy, Forrestal, and Admiral Ernest J. King came in about an hour before noon to sketch in general terms the status of the war. And beginning about three o'clock he talked about "everything from Teheran to Yalta . . . everything under the sun," with Jimmy Byrnes, who had flown in from Spartanburg, South Carolina, the night before, as soon as he heard the news.

The White House was in a state of chaos meanwhile. Several of the Roosevelt staff had been up all night making arrangements for the funeral. Reporters jammed the press room and lobby. The President was granting no interviews, they were told, yet apparently the President was taking almost any out-of-town call from friends. Once Byrnes departed, the door was opened to Roy Roberts of the Kansas City *Star,* who squeezed his immense bulk into one of the maple armchairs beside the President's desk to carry on a half hour conversation that resulted in a widely syndicated article in which Roberts made much of the fact that Truman was the typical, average American. "What a test of democracy if it works!" he wrote.

But the big surprise of the day came at noon, when suddenly, defying tradition, Truman left the White House and drove to the Hill, saying he wanted to be with his friends. A lunch had been arranged in Les Biffle's office for a select seventeen from both parties and both houses, but mostly from the Senate. Truman arrived at the Capitol with full presidential entourage—cars, police, Secret Service— and walked surrounded by armed men down halls where only the day before he had walked free and alone. The lunch was private, reporters excluded. Pale and tense-looking, Truman took a drink and insisted on informality. The meal was salmon, cornbread, peas, and potatoes, and soon most of the group were calling him "Harry" again. He wanted to tell them in person, he said, that he needed their help in a "terrible job." He felt overwhelmed and he didn't mind saying so. What did they think of an address to a joint session on Monday, after the funeral? There was some discussion and indecision. He told them he would be coming and to prepare for it.

When, the lunch over, he came out into the hall still looking tense, a crowd of reporters stood waiting. "Isn't this nice," Truman said, his eyes suddenly filling with tears. "This is really nice." In his years in the Senate he had made no enemies among the working press. Reporters liked him, he was relaxed, easy with them, liked them individually, considered several real friends.

"Boys, if you ever pray, pray for me now. I don't know whether you fellows ever had a load of hay fall on you, but when they told me yesterday what had happened, I felt like the moon, the stars, and all the planets had fallen on me."

"For just a moment he had taken us into his confidence," wrote Allen Drury, "and shown us frankly the frightening thing that had happened to him—shown us, who represented something, a free and easy camaraderie and naturalness to which he knew he could never, for the rest of his life, quite return." Also, for a new, untried President to have come to the Hill in such fashion seemed an auspicious first move. "Characteristically he came to them. He did not, this first time, ask them to come to him," wrote Drury.

To Republican Arthur Vandenberg, Truman's surprise appearance on the Hill marked an end to years of "executive contempt for Congress" under Roosevelt. But among Roosevelt's people, the reaction was altogether different, as Jonathan Daniels recorded. They took it as a sign of regression, from a strong, independent presidency to a lonely, perhaps subservient one. Daniels himself felt crushed and resentful, anything but admiring of Truman.

Signing his first official document late the afternoon of his first day, a proclamation announcing Roosevelt's death, he felt strange writing his name, Harry S. Truman, President of the United States. Had he come into the office in normal fashion, there would have been two months grace after election day, time in which to get used to the idea and prepare himself. As it was, he had no time. He was President now and would be all the rest of the day, and all night, and all tomorrow and the next day and the next. He had been through the morning papers before breakfast. The war news ran on for pages. Ninth Army tanks had pushed beyond the Elbe River, nearly to the suburbs of Berlin. At some points, American and Russian forces were only seventy-five miles apart. The terrible Battle of Berlin was nearing its climax. In the Pacific, American infantry had landed on Bohol, last of the central Philippines still in enemy control. In one huge daylight raid more than four hundred B-29 Superfortresses had bombed Tokyo for two hours.

As the morning papers reported, the war thus far had cost 196,999 American lives, which, as Truman knew, was more than three times American losses in his own earlier war. The new total for American casualties in all categories—killed, wounded, missing, and prisoners—was 899,390, an increase in just one week of 6,481, or an average of more than 900 casualties a day. In the Pacific the cost of victory was rising steadily.

And he, not Roosevelt, was responsible now. He was the Commander in Chief—of armed forces exceeding 16 million men and women, of the largest naval armada in history, of 10 battleships, 27 aircraft carriers, 45 cruisers, of more planes, tanks, guns, money, and technology than ever marshaled by any one nation in all history, and in the critical last act of the most terrible war of all time. In their report that morning, the Chiefs of Staff had said fighting in Europe could last six months longer; in the Pacific, possibly another year and a half.

And what would follow? What might peace bring? Relations with Russia were deteriorating rapidly. The State Department report provided by Stettinius was hardly encouraging: "Since the Yalta Conference, the Soviet Government has taken a firm and uncompromising position on nearly every major question. . . ." In Poland, now occupied by Soviet forces, the situation was "highly unsatisfactory," with Soviet authorities failing repeatedly to keep agreements made at Yalta. The Russians were trying to "complicate the problem" by supporting their own Warsaw Provisional Polish Government to speak for Poland. There was no exchange of liberated prisoners. Direct appeals to Stalin had had little effect.

Until that afternoon the Soviets had been refusing to send their foreign minister, V. M. Molotov, to the San Francisco Conference. Now, suddenly, Stalin had changed his mind, as a gesture in memory of Franklin Roosevelt, a gesture that had been urged on him by the American ambassador in Moscow, Harriman. He would send Molotov, Stalin said, if the new President would request it—which Truman did at once, achieving thereby what appeared to be a first diplomatic breakthrough. But as Harriman himself wrote, the gesture resolved none of the basic difficulties. Churchill and the British government were more apprehensive than ever about Russia.

Truman had had no experience in relations with Britain or Russia, no firsthand knowledge of Churchill or Stalin. He didn't know the right people. He didn't know Harriman. He didn't know his own Secretary of State, more than to say hello. He had no background in foreign policy, no expert or experienced advisers of his own to call upon for help. Most obviously, he was not Franklin Roosevelt. How many times would that be said, thought, written?

Roosevelt had done nothing to keep him informed or provide background on decisions and plans at the highest levels. Roosevelt, Truman would tell Margaret privately, "never did talk to me confidentially about the war, or about foreign affairs or what he had in mind for peace after the war." He was unprepared, bewildered. And frightened.

"It is needless to say that President Truman comes into this gigantic assignment under a handicap," said the solemn editorial in that morning's Washington *Post*.

> He must pick up the work of a world-renowned statesman who had had more than 12 years of experience in the White House . . . [and] we should be less than candid at this grave moment . . . if we did not recognize the great disparity between Mr. Truman's experience and the responsibilities that have been thrust upon him.

He was the seventh man to have succeeded to the office after the death of a President, the first having been John Tyler of Virginia, to whom Truman mistakenly believed he was related through his great-grandmother, Nancy Tyler Holmes. John Tyler had replaced William Henry Harrison in 1841, the year Solomon and Harriet Louisa Young migrated to Missouri, and Tyler had set an important precedent, by deciding to be President in name and in fact and not the Vice President acting as President, which many at the time thought proper, the Constitution being somewhat ambiguous on the subject. Truman was born during the White House years of Chester A. Arthur, who succeeded to the presidency after the assassination of Garfield, and in Truman's lifetime two more vice presidents, Theodore Roosevelt and Calvin Coolidge, had become President following the deaths of McKinley and Harding. But with the exception of Andrew Johnson, no Vice President had ever succeeded so towering a figure as Franklin Roosevelt, and though Lincoln loomed larger than any President in history, Lincoln had not been a world leader, nor the Civil War a titanic, global conflict.

Truman felt great division within himself. Like John Tyler, he must *be* President, act presidential, but could he ever *feel* he was? "I'm still Harry Truman," he had said several times to different people since 7:09 the evening before.

A Pentagon information officer who had been sent to the White House that morning with a statement to the overseas troops for the President to sign, was asked to wait in the Fish Room and would remember always the moment when a "small, gray man" walked in, put out his hand, and said, "I'm President Truman," with the accent on the "I," as though there might be some other President Truman.

On the one hand he was determined to establish that he was in fact in charge. On the other, he felt the constant, nearly overbearing presence of Roosevelt. He would have a portrait of Roosevelt—Roosevelt in his Navy cape turned as if facing a storm—hung to the right of the desk and, pointing to it, would tell visitors, "I'm trying to do what he would like." Grace Tully, Roosevelt's secretary, complained to friends, "I still can't call that man [Truman] President." But then Truman himself still thought of Roosevelt as President. "He's the only one I ever think of as President," he would write to Mrs. Roosevelt months later.

His own favorite President of the century, Woodrow Wilson, had had a brilliant academic career. Herbert Hoover had been a world-famous engineer. Franklin Roosevelt, heir to a great name, had been the popular governor of New York, the nation's richest, most populous state. And who was he, Harry Truman? What qualifications had he beside such men, or so many others in public life who wanted the job?

Alben Barkley told Truman he must stop deprecating his ability to carry on. "Have confidence in yourself," Barkley said. "If you do not, the people will lose confidence in you."

Sam Rayburn came to deliver stern advice of another kind. "I have come down here to talk to you about you," Rayburn began.

You have got many great hazards, and one of them is in this White House. I have been watching this thing a long time. I have seen people in the White House try to build a fence around the White House and keep the very people away from the President that he should see. That is one of your hazards. The special interests and the sycophants will stand in the rain a week to see you and will treat you like a king. They'll come sliding in and tell you you're the greatest man alive—but you know and I know you ain't.

On Saturday morning, April 14, his second day in office, having decided to make John Snyder a federal loan official, Truman called Jesse Jones, head of the Reconstruction Finance Corporation, to tell him that "the President" had made the appointment. Jones, understandably, asked if the President had made the decision before he died. "No," snapped Truman. "He just made it now."

Secretary of the Treasury Henry Morgenthau arrived, intending to ask Truman a number of questions, as a way of assessing him. Truman said he did not wish to take up Morgenthau's time. He asked for a comprehensive report on the nation's financial standing and, as with Stettinius, he said he wanted it quickly, demonstrating that he, Harry Truman, was not on trial, Morgenthau was.

To Morgenthau, who had not known him, Truman seemed courteous as well as decisive. "But after all, he is a politician," added Morgenthau in his diary, "and what is going on in his head only time will tell."

When the train bearing Roosevelt's body came into Union Station from Warm Springs later the morning of Saturday the 14th, Truman was waiting on the platform beside the Roosevelt family and flanked by the two men who had the most reason to see themselves in his place, Henry Wallace and Jimmy Byrnes. Truman had asked them to accompany him to the station, knowing the photographers would record the moment. It was a generous, respectful gesture on his part, but seen also as a mark of confidence. Like the lunch at the Capitol, it seemed exactly the right thing for him to have done.

The day was extremely warm and muggy, the sun burning through a haze. To the steady beat of muffled drums, the three men in their dark suits rode together in the long, slow funeral procession to the White House. Tremendous crowds stretched the length of Constitution Avenue, waiting to see the caisson and casket roll past pulled by six white horses.

Never would he forget, Truman wrote, the sight of so many people in grief.

At midday the weather changed dramatically, with heavy clouds rushing in and the wind whipping the flags that stood at half-mast everywhere in the city. Then rain came in torrents. At the four o'clock service in the East Room, where several hundred had gathered—the Cabinet, Supreme Court, foreign diplomats, the Chiefs of Staff in uniform, Thomas E. Dewey, Mrs. Woodrow Wilson—not one person thought to stand when Truman entered, nor did he appear to notice. With Bess and Margaret beside him, he sat motionless through the service, staring straight ahead at the flag-draped casket.

His schedule had been crowded all day. With the capital and nation in mourning, with the Roosevelt family still in residence, he had wanted no more attention than necessary drawn to activities in the West Wing—no further official pronouncements, nothing until Roosevelt was decently buried. Still, in the time between the return from the station and the East Room service, there had been a steady procession in and out of his office —Harry Hopkins, Ed Flynn, Admiral Leahy, Jimmy Byrnes. The longest session was with Hopkins, who had left a sickbed in Minnesota to attend the funeral and looked like death itself. Truman asked him how he felt. "Terrible," Hopkins answered. "I knew what he meant," Truman wrote. For nearly two hours they reviewed the history of the Roosevelt years, talked about Stalin and Churchill, as the rain beat against the tall windows. Lunch was brought in and Hopkins pulled his chair up to the desk.

There were no eulogies in the East Room service, at Mrs. Roosevelt's request. Two hymns were sung, "Eternal Father, Strong to Save," and "Faith of Our Fathers." After the final prayer, Bishop Angus Dun, again as Mrs. Roosevelt wished, read the famous line from the 1933 inaugural address, "Let me assert my firm belief that the only thing we have to fear is fear itself. . . ."

On Sunday morning, April 15, after a night trip by presidential train, many of the same group were gathered at the graveside in the rose garden of Roosevelt's Hyde Park estate. The weather, mercifully, had turned fair and cool. It was a perfect spring day, the Hudson Valley glorious with spring green, the river sparkling. Truman stood with Bess and Margaret, hat in hand, his head bowed as Taps were sounded.

II

The first test was his address to Congress the afternoon of Monday, April 16, and he passed with flying colors. Indeed, for days, for weeks, he seemed to do nearly everything right. Congress, the press, the public liked what they saw and heard—even a little mix-up at the start of the speech, when Truman began before he was supposed to.

He came down the aisle to a standing ovation, went directly to the rostrum, opened a large black looseleaf notebook, and started in, addressing not just the packed chamber but an enormous radio audience. Speaker Rayburn leaned forward. "Just a minute, Harry, let me introduce you," he interrupted, his voice coming over clearly on the battery of microphones. In a phone call only that morning, Rayburn had told him, "Mr. President, you are not 'Harry' to me any more." But in his own excitement Rayburn had forgotten and the moment—amusing, poignant —would be recalled for years.

The speech lasted just fifteen minutes. Speaking slowly and carefully, Truman was interrupted by applause again and again, seventeen times before he finished.

"With great humility," he said, "I call upon all Americans to help me keep our nation united in defense of those ideals which have been so eloquently proclaimed by Franklin Roosevelt.

"I want in turn to assure my fellow Americans and all those who love peace and liberty throughout the world that I will support and defend those ideals with all my strength and all my heart. That is my duty and I shall not shirk it."

People everywhere felt relief, even hope, as they listened. He seemed a good man, so straightforward, so determined to do his job. The voice and accent would take some getting used to—he pronounced "United States" as "*U*-nited States," said "nation" almost as though it rhymed with "session," at times "I" came close to "Ah"—but he sounded as though he meant every word.

He would prosecute the war without letup, Truman said, work for a lasting peace, work to improve the lot of the common people.

All of us are praying for a speedy victory. Every day peace is delayed costs a terrible toll. The armies of liberation are bringing to an end Hitler's ghastly threat to dominate the world. Tokyo rocks under the weight of our bombs. . . . I want the entire world to know that this direction must and will remain—*unchanged and unhampered!*

"Our demand has been, and it *remains*—Unconditional Surrender," he declared, his voice rising suddenly in pitch on the last two words, which brought a storm of applause.

He spoke of the necessity for a "strong and lasting" United Nations organization. Isolationism was a thing of the past. There could be no more safety behind geographical barriers, not ever again.

"The responsibility of a great state is to serve and not to dominate the world."

The conservative columnist David Lawrence, watching from the press gallery, wrote that between the man on the rostrum and the audience before him there was a "bond of friendship" such as few presidents had ever experienced.

Much of the speech had been written on the train returning from Hyde Park. Jimmy Byrnes and Sam Rosenman, author of innumerable Roosevelt speeches, had played a large part. But the conclusion, delivered to a hushed chamber, was entirely Truman's own. His face lifted, his hands raised, in a voice of solemn petition, he said:

At this moment I have in my heart a prayer. As I have assumed my duties, I humbly pray Almighty God, in the words of King Solomon: "Give therefore Thy servant an understanding heart to judge Thy people, that I may discern between good and bad: for who is able to judge this Thy so great a people?" I ask only to be a good and faithful servant of my Lord and my people.

The old struggle to determine good from evil—it had been with him for so very long. "[I am] just a common everyday man whose instincts are to be ornery, who's anxious to be right," he had once told Bess Wallace in a love letter from the farm.

The applause, sudden and spontaneous, was such as few had ever heard in the chamber. Senators, members of Congress, old friends wanted him to succeed in a way they had not felt before. And because he wasn't Roosevelt, he would need all the help he could get. Because he wasn't Roosevelt, it was easier to feel a common bond. The morning after he became President, Republicans in the Senate had filed into their big conference room No. 335 and after passing a resolution of regret over Roosevelt's death, talked of Harry Truman's strengths and shortcomings, and decided it was no time to rock the boat. "He's one of us," reporters were told afterward. "He's a grand fellow, he knows us, thinks like us." Even those inclined to fight him felt obliged to help him get his feet on the ground. "We know how we'd feel thrust into such a job, and we know Harry Truman would be one of the first to help us."

Messages of approval poured into the White House. "I was tired of Eastern accents," wrote a woman from Indiana. Midwestern native good sense meant good things for the future, said a letter from Illinois. ("His diction comes out of the wide open spaces and will find an echo out of these same wide-open spaces," the Washington *Post* had said.) "Your modesty, your humility, your earnestness, have captivated the hearts of your American people," a woman in Georgia assured him. "Friend Harry," another letter began. There was heartfelt sympathy for his "tremendous burden," his "terrible responsibility." He was urged to trust in God, keep his health, get enough sleep, eat right. Labor unions, groups of company employees, veterans organizations, local chapters of the Communist Party, fraternal orders, and church groups pledged their cooperation. One correspondent from Port Jervis, New York, said that while he had "never known a man named Harry who really amounted to a damn," he would lend his support anyway.

From the Time and Life Building in New York, publisher Henry Luce informed Truman that at a meeting of his business friends he had found unanimous confidence in "your ability to discharge successfully the great duties of your office in your own way." In Topeka, a doctor who was delivering a baby during the broadcast of the speech stopped to shake hands with the newborn citizen—to congratulate him for making his entrance at so auspicious a moment in history. "May I say," wrote the doctor to Truman, "that in our locality I have never seen such unity of purpose as is manifest toward you and toward the administration you are beginning." And he was a Republican, the doctor said.

Every new President had his "honeymoon" with Congress and the country, of course, but this, the feeling that Truman was "one of us," was something more. The day of the speech the Trumans moved from their apartment to Blair House, across Pennsylvania Avenue from the White House, to stay temporarily until Mrs. Roosevelt moved out. For several days, his Secret Service convoy keeping step, Truman walked briskly across the street to work at about eight o'clock every morning. Once a taxi slowed, the driver put his head out the window and called, "Good luck, Harry," as if speaking for the whole country.

"Well, I have had the most momentous, and the most trying time anyone could possibly have," his mother and sister in Grandview read in a letter written from Blair House the night of April 16.

> This afternoon we moved to this house, diagonally across the street (Penn. Ave.) from the White House, until the Roosevelts have had time to move out of the White House. We tried staying at the apartment, but it wouldn't work. I can't move without at least ten Secret Service men and twenty policemen. People who lived in our apartment couldn't get in and out without a pass. So—we moved out with suitcases. Our furniture is still there and will be for some time. . . . But I've paid the rent for this month and will pay for another month if they don't get the old White House redecorated by that time.
>
> My greatest trial was today when I addressed the Congress. It seemed

to go over all right, from the ovation I received. Things have gone so well I'm almost as scared as I was when Mrs. R. told me what had happened. Maybe it will come out all right.

That same day the Russians had begun their final drive on Berlin, Marshal Georgi Zhukov concentrating twenty thousand guns to clear a path.

The first press conference, the next morning, April 17, was the largest that had ever been held in the White House, with more than three hundred reporters packed shoulder to shoulder in the President's office, those in front pressed against his desk. "The new President made an excellent impression. He stood behind his desk and greeted the correspondents smilingly. He answered their questions directly and avoided none of the queries put to him," recorded another of the Roosevelt staff, a press aide named Eben Ayers.

Truman began with a reading of the same wartime ground rules as established by Roosevelt. All off-the-record comments were to be kept in confidence. Background material must remain that only and not be attributed to the President, who was to be quoted directly only when he gave his express permission. With so much to do, Truman said, he expected to be able to hold only one press conference a week.

Would he go personally to the San Francisco Conference? No. Had he taken any steps to meet with Churchill and Stalin? Not as yet. What about David Lilienthal, whose term as head of TVA was about to expire? He was not ready to discuss appointments. How did he stand on race relations? His record in the Senate spoke for itself.

"Do you expect to see Mr. Molotov before he goes to San Francisco?"

"Yes. He is going to stop and pay his respects to the President of the United States. He should."

Admiral Leahy, who had witnessed so many Roosevelt press conferences, was delighted with the President's "direct" performance. Truman had already asked Leahy to stay on as Chief of Staff, with the understanding that he, Leahy, would always speak his mind. The old sailor, now past seventy, was also known for his "direct" performance.

The applause at the end of the session was unprecedented. To reporters long accustomed to Roosevelt, who had made every press conference a kind of circuitous game and charm show, the change was startling and to most, extremely welcome. Privately, Truman felt he had lived five lifetimes in five days.

Three days later, when he called them in again to say his old boyhood friend Charlie Ross was to be the new press secretary, replacing Steve Early, who had retired after twelve years in the White House, the announcement received unqualified approval. Ross had first come to the capital as a young reporter for the St. Louis *Post-Dispatch* in 1918, and in 1931 won a Pulitzer Prize for a study on the effects of the Depression. He was widely liked and respected. Steve Early had been hard-boiled. Many reporters were afraid of him. Ross was more professorial and patient, gentle-mannered, soft-spoken. "There is no more beloved or more highly regarded newspaperman in this city than Charlie Ross," said the Washington *Post.*

Hiring Ross had been Bess's idea. Truman had invited him to Blair House, where they talked for two consecutive evenings before Ross agreed. He was nearly sixty and understood perfectly how demanding the job would be. It also meant a severe cut in salary, from $35,000 a year at the *Post-Dispatch* to $10,000. "But Charlie," Truman told him, "you aren't the kind of man who can say 'no' to the President of the United States." Later they had put through a call to Independence to their old teacher, Tillie Brown, to tell her the news.

The reporters wanted to be sure they had her name right.

"Miss Tillie Brown," Truman said. "Matilda Brown. We always called her Tillie..."

Was that in grade school?

"High school. She taught Charlie and me English."

(In her own interview with reporters, Tillie Brown would remember Charlie as a "naturally smart boy," while Harry was "a bright boy who had to dig.")

On a first tour of the West Wing offices, Truman was annoyed to find that the half-dozen press photographers who covered the White House were allowed none of the comforts of the press room, but confined to a cramped, windowless space of their own. This was how it had always been, he was told. It was not the way it would be any longer, he said. Photographers were to have the same privileges as reporters, beginning immediately. "He made first-class citizens of us," remembered photographer George Tames of *The New York Times,* whose first presidential assignment, the year before, had been to photograph Roosevelt and Truman at lunch under the Jackson magnolia.

Reporters found they now had to be on duty at 8:00 in the morning, rather than 10:00 or 10:30 when Roosevelt's day had begun. They complained jokingly to Truman of having to get up in the middle of the night to be on time for work. "Stick with me and I'll make men of you yet," he assured them with a grin.

Among staff holdovers attitudes were changing appreciably, almost by the day, the more they saw of him. He was friendly, considerate, interested in them individually. His physical energy seemed phenomenal and the most startling difference of all from what had been. Lieutenant George M. Elsey, a young Naval Intelligence officer assigned to the top-secret Map Room, remembered being astonished by the simple realization that here was a President who *walked,* and quickly. "He was alert, sharp . . . he looked good, very vigorous, very strong," Elsey recalled. The Secret Service, long accustomed to a President who could move only when they moved him, found themselves suddenly on the go, with a man who could pick up and leave for lunch on the Hill, or anything else he wished, at any moment. With his braces and wheelchair, Roosevelt had been virtually their prisoner.

"See, with President Roosevelt, he was a man you had under control," remembered Floyd M. Boring of the White House Secret Service detail. "He couldn't move without you. . . . Now, here's a guy, you had to move when he moved. And he *moved fast*! He was a whiz, just like that! He'd go—*and went*! And you had to go with him. So, we had to revise our thinking, and the whole strategy of the place changed because of his ability to be in movement and motion."

One day at noon Truman decided to make an impromptu visit to the Hamilton National Bank a few blocks from the White House at 14th and G. He simply put on his hat and went out the door, with the result that he created a half-hour traffic jam. The lesson learned was that the bank would have to come to the President, not the President to the bank.

Jonathan Daniels, who at first had considered Truman "tragically inadequate," began to see him in new light. Here, Daniels decided, was no ordinary man. "The cliché of the ordinary American in the White House was a snob phrase," Daniels would write, "invented by those who, after Roosevelt's death, hoped to minimize the Presidency." Further, Truman was not poorly prepared for the presidency, as commonly said. Because he knew so much of American life, because he had experienced himself so many of the "vicissitudes of all the people," he was really exceptionally well prepared. (In time to come the historian Samuel Eliot Morison would take the same view, calling Truman as well prepared for the presidency as any of his immediate predecessors.) It was Truman's "too evident modesty" that was so misleading, Daniels decided. Asked by the President to stay on a while longer, he gladly agreed.

Sam Rosenman, a dedicated Roosevelt adviser, press aide Eben Ayers, David Niles, who had handled minority issues and patronage for Roosevelt, and Bill Hassett, Roosevelt's correspondence secretary, had all, like

Daniels, talked of quitting at first chance. Now, when asked to stay by Truman, they too accepted.

Bill Hassett, who had been with Roosevelt at the time of his death at Warm Springs, wrote in his diary on Monday, April 16:

> To the White House this morning at the usual time, but with a strange feeling—impossible to realize that F.D.R.'s day was done and another had taken over. . . . The President sent for me. He was very gracious; invited me to remain on the job; frank and forthright in manner. Said that unexpectedly he had been called upon to shoulder the greatest responsibilities, in the discharge of which he would need all the help and cooperation he could get and added, "I need you too." His attitude toward his duties and obligations magnificent.

None of the staff, however, thought much of the people Truman was installing. "Missourians are most in evidence," wrote Ayers privately, "and there is a feeling of an attempt by the 'gang' to move in." After a visit to the White House, the journalist Joseph Alsop wrote to his cousin, Eleanor Roosevelt, in dismay. In Franklin's time, it had been a great seat of world power. Now the place was like "the lounge of the Lion's Club of Independence, Missouri, where one is conscious chiefly of the odor of ten-cent cigars and the easy laughter evoked by the new smoking room story."

Eddie McKim, clearly out of his depth, made much of his own importance and on occasion drank too much. Jonathan Daniels thought McKim was "weird." Harry Vaughan, loud and jolly, seemed to serve no purpose beyond comic relief. A strange figure named Johnny Maragon, a former Kansas City bootblack who was in and out of Vaughan's office, claiming to be the new head of White House transportation, looked to Eben Ayers exactly like a Prohibition gangster. Hugh Fulton, meantime, bragged of his closeness to the President and the lead part he would be playing in policy matters as the President's speechwriter, once things settled down.

"We were all a strange lot to them and vice versa," remembered Sam Rosenman. "I had never heard of any of them before they moved in."

Only two of Truman's own people appear to have made a favorable impression—Matt Connelly, who would be the President's appointments secretary, and Rose Conway from Kansas City, a shy, industrious "little bird of a woman" in her late forties who had joined Vice President Truman's staff only weeks before and who would serve as the President's secretary.

But McKim would soon be gone. With great regret Truman told him it would be best if he went home to Omaha. ("Well, he was a sergeant in my battery once, I busted him and I can bust him again," Matt Connelly would remember Truman saying.) Nor was Hugh Fulton to have a place. As Truman had rid himself of the devoted Vic Messall after his first term in the Senate, so he now sent Fulton packing. Messall's downfall appears to have been some form of financial scheming that Truman found unacceptable. Fulton, it appears, was guilty primarily of sounding his own horn. To everyone's surprise, the long-serving, unquestionably astute Fulton was offered no official post, nothing whatever, and apparently because he had boasted too often and too conspicuously of his own importance. Truman, for all his reluctance ever to fire anyone, could not tolerate what he called "Potomac Fever," which he described as a prevalent, ludicrous Washington disease characterized by a swelling of the head to abnormal proportions.

Harry Vaughan, who struck many as the most miscast figure of the lot, remained, as the President's military aide. When Truman made him brigadier general, it seemed to many a bigger joke than the stories Vaughan told. Vaughan would become to the official family a figure not unlike Truman's Uncle Harry, a big, voluble, easygoing pal, which gave Vaughan singular importance. Truman seemed to need him around and would tolerate no criticism of him. "I'm still with ya, Chief," Vaughan would boom with a grin. Vaughan's stories, contrary to what was said, were not filthy, but more of the barnyard kind. Truman liked earthy humor but never told stories that had to do with sex, nor did he care to hear them. Also contrary to the popular impression, Vaughan never took a drink. Nobody disliked him, though some worried he could mean trouble down the line. "The fact is," wrote Ayers, "Vaughan, while likeable, seems to lack balance and tact and a sense of proportion."

In later years, it would be said by some who knew Truman well that for him Harry Vaughan was the fool in the Shakespearean sense, the fool who spoke wisdom, who could cut through the obfuscation and insincerity of so much that a President had to listen to day in, day out, who was incapable of posturing or pretense, and whose occasional uncouth moments, the very lack of "balance and tact and a sense of proportion" that upset people like Eben Ayers, provided not only laughter for Truman but a way of bringing everyone else back down to earth a little.

Truman liked a variety of people around him. He wanted contrasts in style and outlook. It was essential, he thought. The country, after all, was composed of all kinds and he understood how many Harry Vaughans there were. Importantly, Truman also knew from experience how extremely loyal Vaughan was, and for now he needed all the loyalty possible.

When Vaughan brought him some phone taps made by the FBI—a common practice under Roosevelt—and asked if he was interested, Truman glanced at a few pages that concerned the activities of the wife of a White House aide and said he had no time for such foolishness. "Tell them I don't authorize any such thing," he said.

Truman had little use for the FBI and its director, J. Edgar Hoover, in contrast to Franklin Roosevelt, who had liked the way Hoover got results and greatly enjoyed the spicy secrets Hoover passed on to him about the private lives of important people. It had been Roosevelt, in 1936, who had quietly ordered Hoover to begin gathering political information, a policy Truman strongly disliked. Truman considered Hoover and the FBI a direct threat to civil liberties, and he made no effort now, as Roosevelt had, to ingratiate himself with Hoover—as Hoover saw at once and found infuriating.

Hoover had chosen an FBI agent with a hometown, Truman connection, Morton Chiles, Jr., one of the big Chiles family of Independence, to call at the White House as Hoover's emissary—to explain to the President that if there was anything the FBI could do for him, he had only to say the word. But having courteously thanked the young man, Truman told him to inform Mr. Hoover that any time the President of the United States wished the services of the FBI, he would make his request through the Attorney General. From that point on, according to a later account by one of Hoover's assistants, "Hoover's hatred of Truman knew no bounds."

"We want no Gestapo or Secret Police," Truman would write in his diary after only a month as President. "FBI is tending in that direction. They are dabbling in sex-life scandals and plain blackmail.... *This must stop....*"

Very likely, Truman's dislike of Hoover had something to do also with the part Hoover and his agents had played in bringing down Tom Pendergast, though he is not known ever to have said so.

Vaughan, nonetheless, appears to have thought well of Hoover, or at least to have liked dealing with Hoover behind the scenes. In time Vaughan would request an FBI phone tap on Thomas Corcoran, the celebrated "Tommy the Cork," a former Roosevelt aide and Washington attorney, who was said to know everyone of importance in town and was thought to be working against Truman by leaking denigrating material to influential liberals and the press. Truman disliked and distrusted Corcoran, as Vaughan knew. The justification for the tap was White House security, but it was political surveillance pure and simple, and as much as Truman disapproved of such practices—and his contempt for Hoover notwithstanding—he gave his consent. The tap, as it turned out, produced nothing of consequence. Still, Hoover would continue to regard Vaughan as his friend at the White House.

In his first week as President, Truman signed a bill authorizing payment of $135.67 that for sixty-seven years the government had owed to one Charles Dougherty, Sr., for overtime work performed at the Brooklyn Navy Yard in the year 1879. He signed the Mexican Water Treaty that had been before the Senate his last day presiding there. He received his first foreign dignitary, the very elegant British Foreign Secretary Anthony Eden, who later telegraphed Churchill that the new President seemed "honest and friendly," and a delegation of Republican senators who had seldom ever set foot in the Executive Office in the Roosevelt years. Robert A. Taft, who led the group, had not been to the White House since 1932. George Aiken of Vermont, glad to see so much all-around good feeling for Truman, was sure it wouldn't last. "He'll make enemies sooner or later," Aiken told Allen Drury later. "If he doesn't make enemies he just won't be a very good President, that's all."

He saw Sam Rayburn, Bob Hannegan; Huseyin Ragip Baydur, the Turkish ambassador; Sergio Osmeña, president of the Philippines; T. V. Soong, foreign minister of China; Georges Bidault, the French ambassador; his own brother Vivian and Fred Canfil, who took turns sitting in his chair. He was photographed with three survivors of the Iwo Jima flag raising—Pfc. René Gagnon, Pharmacist Mate John H. Bradley, and Pfc. Ira Hayes—and with five-year-old Margaret Ann Forde, the child of a disabled serviceman, as she pinned a poppy on his lapel to launch a fund drive for the Veterans of Foreign Wars.

Between times, he decided to make Jimmy Byrnes his Secretary of State, and though the announcement would not be made until weeks later, word spread quickly. On Capitol Hill the feeling was he could have made no better choice. Byrnes knew the ropes in Washington as few men did; he understood the Senate and the workings of the White House from experience; he knew Churchill; he had met Stalin. Roosevelt had thought him the man best equipped to be President, and as Secretary of State, he, not Stettinius, would be next in line for the presidency, a consideration that weighed heavily in Truman's decision.

Sam Rosenman warned Truman that he was making a mistake. Rosenman had become highly cynical about Byrnes, considered him a man primarily interested in himself. "I don't think you know Jimmy Byrnes, Mr. President," Rosenman said. "You think you do. In the *bonhomie* of the Senate, he's one kind of fellow. But I think you will regret this and if I were you I wouldn't do it."

. . .

"It was a wonderful relief to preceding conferences with our former Chief to see the promptness and snappiness with which Truman took up each matter and decided it," Secretary of War Henry Stimson wrote after a Cabinet meeting. "There were no long drawn out 'soliloquies' from the President, and the whole conference was thoroughly businesslike so that we actually covered two or three more matters than we had expected to discuss."

Accompanied by Admiral Leahy, Truman went frequently to the Map Room, which had been established by Roosevelt on the ground floor of the main house as a means for him to follow the course of the war, an idea Roosevelt had borrowed from Churchill, who had a similar arrangement at 10 Downing Street. The low-ceilinged room was under tight security. There were blackout curtains at its single window and large maps covering the walls, these filled with colored pins indicating the latest disposition of ships and armies. To Truman, who had been trying to follow the war on his old World War I maps tacked to the wall of his Senate office, the place was a wonder. "Changes in the battle situation were immediately marked . . . as messages came in from commanders in the field," he wrote. "Messages came constantly throughout the day and night so that our military picture was always accurate up to the moment." Leahy was struck by how much world geography and military history Truman knew, and how quickly he absorbed new information. An assistant to the naval aide, Lieutenant William Rigdon, who had been on duty at the White House since 1942, said later of Truman that he never knew anyone to work so hard "to get on the inside of all that had taken place."

He saw the Director of the Bureau of the Budget, Harold D. Smith, who said he would always be bringing him problems, and on Friday, April 20, he saw Rabbi Stephen Wise, chairman of the American Zionist Emergency Council, to discuss the question of resettlement for Jewish refugees in Palestine. Buchenwald, largest of the Nazi death camps, had been liberated. "I pray you believe what I have said about Buchenwald," Edward R. Murrow had broadcast from the scene. However, a warning from the State Department that the problem of Palestine was "highly complex" had already crossed Truman's desk. Rabbi Wise, whose appointment was at 11:45, was given fifteen minutes only. At noon Ambassador Harriman arrived.

W. Averell Harriman was the son of E. H. Harriman, the "Little Giant" of Wall Street who ran the Union Pacific Railroad and was said to have feared neither God nor J. P. Morgan. The son looked nothing like his father. He was tall, slim, handsome as the man in the Arrow Collar, as was said, though somewhat cheerless in manner. His low, cultured voice could also lapse into a monotone that some who didn't know him mistakenly took as a sign of low vitality.

As heir to one of the great American fortunes, Harriman had grown up in luxury surpassing anything known by his friend Franklin Roosevelt. The Harriman estate on the Hudson comprised 20 square miles, included forty miles of bridlepaths and a stone château of one hundred rooms. Young Averell had been to Groton, then Yale, and after his father's death was virtually handed the Union Pacific, eventually becoming its chairman of the board. He was an art collector—Cézanne, Picasso—and at one point, the country's fourth-ranking polo player. But he was also a tenacious worker, who had built his own shipping empire and, at age forty, helped found the immensely successful and respected Wall Street banking firm of Brown Brothers, Harriman. Until joining the New Deal, he might have been the model for the kind of man that Harry Truman, with his Jacksonian Populist faith, believed to be the root cause of most of the country's troubles, and that Truman had earlier, in the heat of his railroad investigations, castigated unmercifully on the floor of the Senate. Harriman had what his number two man in Moscow, George Kennan, called "a keen appreciation of great personal power."

As ambassador to Russia since October 1943, he was known to work eighteen to twenty hours a day. His long, detailed reports were famous at the State Department. In all he had spent more time with Stalin than had any American, or any other diplomat. At the moment he appeared extremely tired and worried. There was a slight tick, a sort of wink, in his right eye.

Truman had never met Harriman until now, nor had he ever really worked with anyone of such background. Harriman was another new experience, and the first of several men of comparable education and eastern polish—Charles Bohlen, John J. McCloy, James Forrestal, Dean Acheson, Robert A. Lovett—who were to play vital roles in Truman's administration. Even the redoubtable Henry Stimson was as yet to Truman a remote presence.

Accompanying Harriman now were Stettinius, Under Secretary of State Joseph C. Grew, and Charles ("Chip") Bohlen, the department's Russian expert. Stettinius made the introductions, but in the half hour following, he, Grew, and Bohlen said very little.

Truman asked for a rundown of the most urgent problems concerning the Soviet Union.

The Russians had two contradictory policies, Harriman began. They wanted to cooperate with the United States and Great Britain, and they wanted to extend control over their neighboring states in Eastern Europe. Unfortunately, some within Stalin's circle mistook American generosity and readiness to cooperate as a sign of "softness" and this had led Stalin to think he could do largely as he pleased. Nonetheless, it was Harriman's view that the Soviets would risk no break with the United States. Their need of financial help after the war would be too great, and for this reason the United States could and should stand firm on vital issues.

Truman said he was not afraid of the Russians and intended to be firm. And fair, of course. "And anyway the Russians need us more than we need them."

Harriman had wondered how much Truman knew of recent correspondence between Churchill, Roosevelt, and Stalin, as well as his own dispatches, and was pleased to find it was quite a lot. Truman had been reading steadily from the Map Room files, night after night, so much that he feared he might be seriously straining his eyes.

Concerns about the Soviet Union had prevailed all through the war, but had taken a more serious cast by the winter of 1944–45, even before Yalta. "I can testify," wrote one State Department official, "that there was no time when the danger from the Soviet Union was not a topic of anxious conversation among officers of the State Department; and by the winter of 1944–45, as the day of victory approached, it became the predominant theme in Washington."

In March, Churchill warned that the Yalta agreements on Poland were breaking down, that Poland was losing its frontier, its freedom. Harriman reported that American prisoners of war who had been liberated by the Russians were being kept in Russian camps in "unbelievable" conditions. (At lunch one day with Anna Rosenberg, Roosevelt had banged his hand down on the arm of his wheelchair, saying, "Averell is right. We can't do business with Stalin.") In April an American-British effort to negotiate a surrender of the German armies in Italy brought a stinging cable from Stalin, who accused Roosevelt and Churchill of trying to bring off their own separate peace with the Nazis. Roosevelt, infuriated, had kept his response moderate:

> It would be one of the great tragedies of history if at the very moment of the victory, now within our grasp, such distrust, such lack of faith, should prejudice the entire undertaking after the colossal losses of life, material and treasure.

Churchill cabled Roosevelt urging a "blunt stand" against the Russians, and Roosevelt responded, "We must not permit anybody to entertain a false impression that we are afraid."

A secret OSS report for the President dated April 2, ten days prior to Roosevelt's death—a report since made available to Truman—warned that once the war was over, the United States could be faced with a situation more perilous even than the rise of Japan and Nazi Germany:

> Russia will emerge from the present conflict as by far the strongest nation in Europe and Asia—strong enough, if the United States should stand aside, to dominate Europe and at the same time to establish her hegemony over Asia. Russia's natural resources and manpower are so great that within relatively few years she can be much more powerful than either Germany or Japan has ever been. In the easily foreseeable future Russia may well outrank even the United States in military potential.

Russia might revert to the predatory tradition of the czars and "pursue a policy of expansion aimed at bringing all Europe and perhaps Asia under her control," the report warned. "If she should succeed in such a policy she would become a menace more formidable to the United States than any yet known...."

Harriman had become so exercised over the state of Soviet-American relations that he had wanted to fly home to Washington even before word came of Roosevelt's death. On April 6, in a lengthy cable to the State Department, he had said the time had come when "we must... make it plain to the Soviet Government that they cannot expect our cooperation on terms laid down by them."

"We now have ample proof that the Soviet government views all matters from the standpoint of their own selfish interest," he declared in another strongly worded report.

> The Soviet Union and the minority governments that the Soviets are forcing on the people of Eastern Europe have an entirely different objective. We must clearly recognize that the Soviet program is the establishment of totalitarianism, ending personal liberty and democracy as we know and respect it.

Roosevelt had undergone a profound change in outlook. Stalin was not a man of his word, he confided to Anne O'Hare McCormick of *The New York Times* before leaving for Warm Springs.

Still, he had refused to give up trying to work with the Russians. In a last message to Stalin sent the day of his death, Roosevelt said that in the future there must be no more mistrust between them, no more such "minor misunderstandings" as over the German surrender issue. (Before passing the message along to Stalin, Harriman had urged the deletion of the word "minor," but Roosevelt refused.) To Churchill that same day he wrote: "I would minimize the general Soviet problem as much as possible, because these problems, in one form or another, seem to arise every day, and most of them straighten out. . . . " He added only: "We must be firm, however, and our course thus far is correct."

Harriman told Truman that Russian control in Poland or Romania meant not just influence over foreign policy, but use of secret police and an end to freedom of speech. What they were faced with, Harriman said, using a phrase Truman would not forget, was a "barbarian invasion" of Europe.

American policy must be reconsidered. Any illusion that the Soviet Union was likely to act in accordance with the accepted principles in international affairs should be abandoned. He was not pessimistic, Harriman insisted. He believed workable relations with Russia were possible, with concessions on both sides.

Truman said he understood that 100 percent cooperation from Stalin was unattainable. He would be happy with 85 percent.

Molotov was due in Washington in two days. Truman said that if the Polish issue were not settled as agreed at Yalta, then the Senate would very likely reject American participation in the United Nations, and that he would tell this to Molotov "in words of one syllable."

Harriman told the President how relieved he was "that we see eye to eye."

On a first inspection tour of the private quarters at the White House, their future home, Bess and Margaret were crestfallen. "The White House upstairs is a mess . . . I was so depressed," wrote Margaret. The Roosevelts had lived comfortably among possessions shabby and fine, old, new, ordinary, and sentimental, with little concern for color harmony or ever any attempt at show. They had lived as they had at home, like an old-fashioned country gentleman's family of "comfortable circumstances." Mrs. Roosevelt had left untouched the $50,000 allocated by Congress for upkeep and repair on the house. Her focus was on other concerns.

Carpets were threadbare. Walls looked as if they hadn't been cleaned in years and were covered with lighter patches where pictures had hung. The scant remaining furniture was in sad disrepair. Some of the draperies had actually rotted. It looked like a ghost house, remembered the assistant head usher, J. B. West, who led the tour. Mrs. Roosevelt had told Bess she could expect to see rats.

•   •   •

The group that filed into the Oval Office for what was to be a landmark meeting at two o'clock the afternoon of Monday, April 23, was the same as Franklin Roosevelt would have assembled for the same purpose. There was no one from Truman's old Senate staff, no new foreign policy adviser or Russian expert of Truman's own choice, no Missouri "gang," no one at all from Missouri but Truman. They were all Roosevelt's people: Stettinius, Stimson, Forrestal, Marshall, King, Leahy, Harriman, Bohlen, Assistant Secretary of State James Dunn, and General John R. Deane, who was head of the Moscow military mission.

Molotov was expected shortly. He had arrived in Washington the day before, and he and Truman had already met briefly and quite amicably after dinner at Blair House, where Molotov, too, was staying. Truman had spoken of his admiration for the part Russia played in the war and told the Soviet minister he "stood squarely behind all commitments and agreements taken by our late President" and would do everything he could to follow that path. It had been Truman's first encounter with a Russian and it had gone smoothly. But now Stettinius reported the Russians were insisting on their puppet government in Poland regardless of American opinion. Truman remarked that so far agreements with the Russians seemed always a one-way street. If the Russians did not want to cooperate, they could "go to hell."

Asking for opinions, he turned first to the elderly Henry Stimson, who thought it extremely unfortunate the Polish issue had ever come to such a head. It seemed unnecessary, too hurried, too dangerous. Stimson was greatly alarmed, "for fear we are rushing into a situation where we would find ourselves breaking our relations with Russia. . . . " The United States must be very careful, try to resolve things without a "headlong collision."

Forrestal strongly disagreed. The situation in Poland was not an isolated example. The Russians were moving in on Bulgaria, Romania. Better to have a showdown now than later, he said. The real issue, added Harriman, was whether the United States would be party to a program of Soviet domination in Poland.

Admiral Leahy, from his experience at Yalta, was sure the Russians would never allow free elections in Poland, and warned that a break with the Soviet Union over Poland could be a "serious matter."

Truman broke in to say he had no intention of issuing an ultimatum to Molotov. He wanted only to be firm and clear.

Stimson interjected that in their concern about Eastern Europe, the Russians "perhaps were being more realistic than we in regard to their own security."

From his experience in Moscow, said General Deane, any sign of fear on the part of the United States would lead nowhere with the Russians.

Agreeing with Stimson, General Marshall urged caution. His great concern, Marshall said, was that Russia might delay participation in the war against Japan "until we have done all the dirty work."

Stimson found himself feeling pity for Truman, as he wrote later in his diary:

> I am very sorry for the President because he is new on his job and he has been brought into a situation which ought not to have been allowed to come this way. I think the meeting at Yalta was primarily responsible for it because it dealt a good deal in altruism and idealism instead of stark realities on which Russia is strong. . . .

As the meeting ended, it was clear the tone of American dealings with Russia would now take a different turn. Truman remarked that he would follow the advice of the majority.

"Indeed, he did," remembered Bohlen.

A survivor of revolutions, Siberia, purges, and war, Vyacheslav Molotov was one of the few original Bolsheviks still in power in the Soviet Union, his importance second only to that of Stalin. Molotov was tough and extremely deliberate in manner, with never a sign of emotion, not a hint of human frailty except for a stutter. In his customary dark blue European suit, with his pince-nez and small mustache, he looked like a rather smug English schoolmaster.

Molotov arrived at the President's office promptly at 5:30, accompanied by his interpreter, V. N. Pavlov, and the Russian ambassador, Andrei Gromyko. With Bohlen serving as his interpreter, Truman came directly to the point. He wanted progress on the Polish question, he said. The United States would recognize no government in Poland that failed to provide free elections. He intended to go ahead with the United Nations, irrespective of differences over "other matters," and he hoped that Moscow would bear in mind how greatly American foreign policy depended on public support, and that American economic assistance programs after the war would require the vote of Congress.

Molotov said the only acceptable basis for Allied cooperation was for the three governments to treat one another as equals. The Poles had been working against the Red Army, he insisted. Truman cut him short. He was not interested in propaganda, Truman said. He wished Molotov to inform Stalin of his concern over the failure of the Soviet government to live up to its agreements.

According to Bohlen's later account, Molotov turned "ashy" and tried to divert the conversation. Truman said he wanted friendship with Russia, but Poland was the sore point. The United States was prepared to carry out all agreements reached at Yalta. He asked only that the Soviet government do the same.

In Truman's recollection of the scene, Molotov responded, "I have never been talked to like that in my life."

"Carry out your agreements," Truman told him, "and you won't get talked to like that."

By Bohlen's account, however, this last exchange never happened. Truman just cut the conversation off, saying curtly, "That will be all, Mr. Molotov. I would appreciate it if you would transmit my views to Marshal Stalin." Thus dismissed, Molotov turned and left the room.

But whichever way the meeting ended, there had been no mistaking Truman's tone. Even Harriman admitted to being "a little taken aback . . . when the President attacked Molotov so vigorously." In retrospect, Harriman would regret that Truman "went at it" quite so hard. "I think it was a mistake. . . ."

Bohlen, for his part, thought Truman had said only about what Roosevelt would have in the same situation, except that of course Roosevelt would have been "smoother." The difference was in style.

When word of what happened reached Capitol Hill, Arthur Vandenberg called it the best news he had heard in a long time.

Stimson was gravely worried. There was more the President needed to know. "I think it is very important that I should have a talk with you as soon as possible on a highly secret matter," he wrote in a hurried letter to Truman.

> I mentioned it to you shortly after you took office but have not urged it since on account of the pressure you have been under. It, however, has a bearing on our present foreign relations and has such an important effect upon all my thinking in this field that I think you ought to know about it without much further delay.

At noon, Wednesday, April 25, Truman's twelfth day in office, the day after Molotov's visit and the same day as the opening of the United Nations Conference in San Francisco, Stimson again went to the White House, but this time alone. General Leslie R. Groves, head of the Manhattan Project, or S-1 as Stimson preferred to call it, was brought in a little later through a side door and by way of the ground floor, to avoid being seen, and asked to wait in a room adjoining the President's office. General Marshall stayed away entirely, so great was their concern over rousing curiosity among the press.

The war and a lifetime of service to his country had taken a toll on Stimson. On doctor's advice he was now going home for an afternoon nap whenever possible. The first President he had known was Theodore Roosevelt, who made him an assistant U.S. attorney for the Southern District of New York in 1905, at the time Truman was clerking in the Union National Bank. When Truman was learning about life on the farm, Stimson had become Secretary of War under William Howard Taft. Coolidge appointed him governor-general of the Philippines. Hoover made him Secretary of State. By the time Franklin Roosevelt made him Secretary of War again in 1940, Stimson was an elder statesman of seventy-two.

A graduate of Yale and the Harvard Law School, a lifelong Republican, Stimson was widely and correctly seen as a figure of thorough rectitude, if a bit old-fashioned and austere. He spoke with a faintly scratchy old man's voice, wore a heavy gold watch chain across his vest, and parted his hair in the middle, the bangs combed forward over the forehead, a style that had disappeared with wing collars. He was also one of the few men ever to admonish Franklin Roosevelt to his face. "Mr. President, I don't like you to dissemble to me," Stimson had once lectured, shaking a crooked, arthritic finger.

Reflecting on Stimson a few years later, Truman would describe him as "a real man—honest, straightforward and a statesman sure enough." Like Truman he had no patience with hypocrisy or circumlocution. Like Truman he was extremely proud of his service in the field artillery in France in 1918 and preferred still to be called "Colonel Stimson."

He had first learned of S-1 in November of 1941, when named by Roosevelt to a committee to advise the President on all questions relating to nuclear fission. Since then, he had overseen every stage of development.

He and Truman were alone in Truman's office. Stimson took from his briefcase a typewritten memorandum of several pages and waited while Truman read it. The words were Stimson's own and the first sentence especially was intended to shock. Stimson had finished writing it only that morning.

> Within four months we shall in all probability have completed the most terrible weapon ever known in human history, one bomb of which could destroy a whole city.

Although the United States and Great Britain had shared in the development of this "most terrible weapon," at present only the United States had the capability of producing it. Such a monopoly could not last, however, and "probably the only nation which could enter production within the next few years is Russia."

Stimson was anything but sanguine. Considering the state of "moral advancement" in the world, "modern civilization might be completely destroyed."

When Truman finished reading, General Groves was shown in to present another report of some twenty-five pages on the status of the Manhattan Project, which Truman was again asked to read.

> The President took one copy [Stimson wrote] and we took the other and we went over it and answered his questions and told him all about the process and about the problems that are coming up and in fact I think it very much interested him. . . . He remembered the time when I refused to let him go into this project when he was the chairman of the Truman Committee . . . and he said that he understood now perfectly why it was inadvisable for me to have taken any other course than I had. . . .

Stimson, said Truman later, seemed as concerned with the role of the atomic bomb in shaping history as in its capacity to shorten the war. Stimson asked for authorization to establish a special select committee to study the implications of "this new force" and to advise Truman—to help him in his decision. Truman told him to go ahead.

What questions Truman had asked, neither Stimson nor Groves later said, but in a memorandum for his files, Groves noted: "The President did not show any concern over the amount of the funds being spent but made it very definite that he was in entire agreement with the necessity for the project." Also, according to Groves, Truman had bogged down several times while reading the longer report, saying he didn't like to tackle so much all at once. Groves and Stimson replied there was no way they could be more concise. "This is a big project," Groves told the President.

In fact, S-1 was the largest scientific-industrial undertaking in history, and the most important and best-kept secret of the war. Overall responsibility had been given to the Army Corps of Engineers, with Groves, who had overseen the building of the Pentagon, in charge. It had been launched out of fear that the Nazis were at work on the same thing, which they were, though with nothing like the seriousness or success that were imagined. In less than three years the United States had spent $2 billion, which was not the least of the hidden truths, and, one way or other,

200,000 people had been involved, only a few having more than a vague idea of what it was about. That the diligent chairman of the Truman Committee had known so little was a clear measure of how extremely effective security had been. But then neither did General MacArthur or Admiral Chester A. Nimitz or a host of others in high command know what was going on.

While the United States and Great Britain shared in the secret and technical-scientific details, it was in all practicality an American project—initiated, supervised, financed, and commanded from Washington. Ultimately it was Franklin Roosevelt's project, his decision, his venture. Without his personal interest and backing it would never have been given such priority. For Truman it was thus another part of the Roosevelt legacy to contend with and again Roosevelt was of little help to him. Roosevelt had left behind no policy in writing other than a brief agreement signed with Churchill at Hyde Park the previous autumn saying only that once the new weapon was ready, "It might perhaps, after mature consideration, be used against the Japanese, who should be warned that this bombardment will be repeated until they surrender."

Whether the bomb would work, no one could say for certain. According to Groves, a first test would not be ready until early July.

The Washington *Star* needed to know what the President ate for breakfast (orange juice, cereal—usually oatmeal—toast, and milk, no coffee). Madame Tussaud's Wax Museum in London wrote for the President's exact measurements, requesting that the information be transmitted as soon as possible, and his office obliged: Height—5'9", chest measurement—42½, waist measurement—35½, size of shoes—9B, size of collar—15½, size of gloves—8, size of hat—7⅜.

He addressed the United Nations conference by radio hookup. A poor speech, it was full of windy, mostly meaningless pronouncements of exactly the kind Truman disliked and would never normally use. "None of us doubt," he said, "that with Divine guidance, friendly cooperation, and hard work, we shall find an adequate answer to the problem history has put before us." As I. F. Stone observed in *The Nation*, what Truman would normally have said was, "It's a tough job. I'm not sure we can do it. But we're going to try our best."

On the afternoon of April 25, he went to the Pentagon to talk to Churchill by the transatlantic "secret phone." There had been a secret German offer to negotiate, a peace feeler from Heinrich Himmler, received through Count Folke Bernadotte, head of the Swedish Red Cross. Himmler wanted to capitulate, but only to the Western Allies, not to the Russians. Obviously the Nazis would have to surrender to all the Allies simultaneously, Churchill said. "That is right. That is exactly the way I feel. . . . I agree to that fully," Truman responded. He would cable his news to Stalin at once.

Taking time out for his own first look at the White House living quarters, Truman moved through room after room "at a brisk trot," according to the assistant head usher J. B. West, for whom this was a first chance for a close-up look at the President. West was struck by how large Truman's glasses made his eyes appear. "I had the feeling he was looking at me, all around me, straight through me."

On April 27, fifty miles south of Berlin, American and Russian troops met at the Elbe. A day later came word that Mussolini had been killed by partisans, his body strung up by the feet like a slaughtered pig. On Tuesday, May 1, Hamburg Radio broke the sensational news that Hitler, too, was dead, by his own hand in the command bunker in Berlin. On May 2, the day Berlin fell to the Red Army, the President had to call a press conference to say there was no truth to the rumor of a final German surrender, though Churchill kept hinting at peace within the week.

The Postmaster General and the Secretary of Labor wished to retire. The Attorney General did not, but Truman wished he would. The Director of the Bureau of the Budget needed more of the President's time. The Secretary of War returned to go over a list of names for the special committee on S-1.

It would be hard to imagine a President with more on his mind.

From Grandview, Missouri, all the while, came a series of memorable letters from Mary Jane Truman—to keep Harry abreast of the trials *she* was enduring.

April 24, 1945

Dear Harry,

We have received so much mail I cannot remember all the details. . . . We try to read all about what you are doing and have kept up pretty well so far. I've lost seven pounds the last week, but no wonder, breakfast is the only meal we have had on time since you went into office. . . . someone called for pictures yesterday of Mamma, said he was an artist from Washington. I told him I was sorry but Mamma had had all the pictures she could pose for at present. . . .

Mary Jane's recurring theme through much of what she wrote was the considerable disservice he had done to them by becoming President. Of immediate concern was whether he could get home for Mother's Day or whether she and Mamma would have to come to Washington, as he had suggested.

May 1, 1945

Dear Harry,

I do hope that you can come, but if not I feel sure we can persuade Mamma to make the trip. And please tell me if you have any suggestion to make about what you would like me to bring in the way of clothes, for I want to look my best and also get Mamma fixed up all right too and it's a pretty large order on such short notice. . . .

May 7, 1945

Dear Harry,

I arrived home yesterday and found Mamma well and very much inclined to go Friday if possible. I had planned to go in [to Kansas City] today to get whatever is necessary, but it's pouring down rain and I have lost my voice, so Dr. Graham said I should stay in. Why do such things have to happen when I have so much to do? I am *hoping* and *hoping* that I can get everything ready to go Friday. However, you call me Wednesday instead of me putting the call through. If you can, call early as you can, for if I cannot go shopping tomorrow and Wednesday I don't see how I can get it all done. . . .

Understandingly, he wrote, "You both have done fine under this terrible blow."

The five-year-long war in Europe, the most costly, murderous conflict in history, ended on May 7, when the German High Command surrendered to the Allied armies. The terms were signed at 2:40 A.M., in a brick schoolhouse at Reims, Eisenhower's headquarters. The surrender was unconditional.

Churchill had wanted to make the announcement at once, but Stalin, with the situation on the Russian front still uncertain, insisted they wait. Truman agreed that the announcement would be made by all three Allies at the same time the following morning, May 8, V-E Day.

He broke the news to reporters in his office at 8:30. At 9:00, from the Diplomatic Reception Room where Roosevelt had so often broadcast to the country, he spoke to the largest radio audience yet recorded.

This is a solemn but glorious hour. I only wish that Franklin D. Roosevelt had lived to witness this day. . . . We must work to finish the war. Our victory is but half-won. . . .

381

In a separate statement he called on Japan to surrender, warning that "the striking power and intensity of our blows will steadily increase," and that the longer the war lasted the greater would be the suffering of the Japanese people, and "all in vain." Unconditional surrender, further, did "not mean the extermination or enslavement of the Japanese people."

New York, London, Paris, Moscow, cities around the world, had erupted in wild celebration, but not Washington, where it was raining and thousands of government workers, having listened to the broadcast, remained at their desks. "I call upon every American to stick to his post until the last battle is won," Truman had said.

May 8 was his sixty-first birthday. He had been President for three weeks and four days. The day before, Mrs. Roosevelt had moved out of the White House and the Trumans moved in, "with very little commotion," as he later wrote, "except that Margaret's piano had to be hoisted through a window of the second-floor living room." To move Mrs. Roosevelt out had required twenty Army trucks. To move the Trumans from Blair House across the street had required only one.

III

The "Russian situation" concerned Truman more than he let on. Patience must be the watchword if there was to be peace in the world, he wrote to Mrs. Roosevelt, knowing that she, like some others, was apprehensive about his approach to the Russians. To Joseph E. Davies, former ambassador to Moscow, he described how he had given Molotov a "straight one-two to the jaw," but then asked, "Did I do right?" The Russians, Truman told Henry Wallace, were "like people from across the tracks whose manners were very bad." Wallace had begun to worry that Truman was reacting too quickly, without sufficient information and thought.

Truman had made a sudden, arbitrary move to cut back on Lend-Lease not only to Russia but to France and Great Britain, as soon as the war in Europe ended. Ships already under way had been recalled. Apparently he signed the order without reading it, going on the word of State Department officials that Roosevelt had approved. It was a serious blunder, and he had quickly to countermand his own order.

Some nights he was so exhausted he went to bed at eight. One morning, after staying up much of the night to read the Yalta agreements again, he said that every time he went over them he found new meanings. "His sincerity and his desire to do what is right is continually evident," observed Eben Ayers.

In a top-secret telegram sent on May 6, even before the German surrender, Churchill had urged that the British and American armies "hold firmly" to their present positions in Germany and Eastern Europe and not pull back to the occupational line agreed to earlier with the Russians. It was essential, Churchill said, to "show them how much we have to offer or withhold." On May 9, Truman responded, saying, "it is my present intention to adhere to our interpretation of the Yalta agreements." In Germany this would mean withdrawing from the Elbe back as much as 150 miles, to as far west as Eisenbach.

On May 11 came two more cables from the prime minister, setting forth his anxieties over the Russians and the future of Europe. "Mr. President, in these next two months the gravest matters in the world will be decided," he said in the first cable. "I fear terrible things have happened during the Russian advance through Germany to the Elbe," he said in the second. Russian domination in Poland, eastern Germany, the Baltic provinces, Czechoslovakia, Yugoslavia, Hungary, Romania, Bulgaria, a large part of Austria, would constitute "an event in the history of Europe to which there has been no parallel." It was essential that the Allied armies not withdraw from their present positions "until we are satisfied about Poland and also about the temporary character of the Russian occupation of Germany," as well as "the conditions to be established" in the rest of Eastern Europe. All such matters, Churchill warned, could only be settled before American forces withdraw from Europe "and the Western world folds up its war machines."

In a telegram of May 12, Churchill's tone grew still more alarming:

> I am profoundly concerned about the European situation. . . . I learn that half the American air force in Europe has already begun to move to the Pacific Theater. The newspapers are full of the great movements of the American armies out of Europe. Our armies also are under previous arrangements likely to undergo a marked reduction. The Canadian Army will certainly leave. The French are weak and difficult to deal with. Anyone can see that in a very short space of time our armed power on the continent will have vanished except for moderate forces to hold down Germany.
>
> Meanwhile what is to happen about Russia?

"An iron curtain is drawn down upon their front," Churchill continued, using a new expression for the first time. "We do not know what is going on behind."

Both men agreed to the importance of meeting somewhere soon with Stalin, though Truman felt that for domestic political reasons he should not leave Washington until after June 30, the end of the fiscal year. In the meantime, he would send Harry Hopkins to see Stalin.

Writing to an old friend in Independence on May 13, a month to the day since he took office, Truman said, "It is a very, very hard position to fall into as I did. If there ever was a man who was forced to be President, I'm that man. . . . But I must face the music, and try to the best of my ability. You just keep on praying and hoping for the best."

Calling on Truman on May 14, to discuss the joint meeting with Stalin, Anthony Eden was struck by his "air of quiet confidence in himself."

"I am here to make decisions," Truman said, "and whether they prove right or wrong I am going to make them."

"To have a reasonably lasting peace the three great powers must be able to trust each other and they must themselves honestly want it," he wrote privately. "They must also have the confidence of the *smaller* nations. Russia hasn't the confidence of the small nations, nor has Britain. We have." Then, in frustration, he added, "I want peace and I'm willing to fight for it."

To Hopkins, he advised using either diplomatic language with Stalin or a baseball bat, whichever would work.

The Hopkins mission had been urged by Bohlen and Harriman, who had flown back to Washington from San Francisco greatly distressed that the United Nations conference was in trouble. Molotov was heading home. Hopkins, it was thought, might succeed in patching things up, since he would be seen by Stalin as both someone who had been close to Roosevelt and who had worked hard all along for a policy of cooperation with Russia. Hopkins could also handle arrangements for the Big Three conference. Though still gravely ill, Hopkins had at once agreed to go.

Meantime, accompanied by Mary Jane, ninety-two-year-old Martha Ellen Truman had arrived for her first visit ever to Washington, after her first flight in an airplane, for a first look at her oldest son since he had become President.

Truman had sent the presidential plane for them, the same four-motored, silver C-54, nicknamed *The Sacred Cow,* that had carried Roosevelt to Casablanca, Teheran, and Yalta, and to Truman's delight Mamma was a hit with the Washington press from the moment she stepped from the plane. "Oh, fiddlesticks!" she exclaimed, seeing how many had turned out to meet her. Had she known there would be such fuss, she said, she never would have come. Small and bent, but "chipper as a lark," she wore a large orchid on the lapel of a dark blue suit and a blue spring straw hat trimmed with a gardenia.

In the car on the way to the White House, Margaret asked Mamma teasingly if she would like to sleep in the Lincoln bed. Mamma, her Confederate blood rising, said if that was the choice she would prefer the floor. Truman thought she would be most comfortable in the Rose Guest Room, where so many queens had stayed, but his mother found the bed too high, the room too fancy. Offering it to Mary Jane, she chose a smaller room next door.

She had arrived in time for Mother's Day. She stayed a little more than a week, and charmed everyone at the White House. "Oh, you couldn't help but like her," Secret Service agent Floyd Boring would remember. "She was point blank, you know." The second Sunday, a brilliant, blue-sky day with the Capitol dome and Washington Monument gleaming in sunshine, Truman took her for a cruise on the Potomac in the presidential yacht.

Working with J. B. West and a Kansas City decorator, Bess was transforming the private quarters of the White House. Rooms were scrubbed, painted, furniture repaired or discarded. New furniture was purchased (mostly reproduction antiques). New curtains and draperies were installed, walls hung with paintings (landscapes primarily) borrowed from the National Gallery. Bess's mother moved in, taking a guest room over the North Portico. Reathel Odum, from Truman's Senate office, who was to serve both as Bess's personal secretary and as a companion for Mrs. Wallace, was given a room beside Mrs. Wallace.

Truman, Bess, and Margaret had separate rooms. Truman slept in an antique, canopied four-poster in the President's Bedroom, the room Roosevelt had used, just off the large, central oval room on the south side, which, again like Roosevelt, Truman would use as his private study. It was in this oval room that John Adams had held the first White House reception on New Year's Day 1801, and that Roosevelt had met with Bob Hannegan, Ed Flynn, and the others on the steaming July night less than a year earlier to decide who was to be number two on the Democratic ticket.

Bess had two rooms—sitting room and bedroom—adjoining the President's Bedroom, while Margaret was across the hall from her mother, in a corner room overlooking Pennsylvania Avenue. "My bedroom is pink with antique white furniture. Deep pink draperies and white window curtains," Margaret wrote happily in her diary. "It also has a fireplace and mirror. High (25 ft.) ceilings." She was the first young resident in the White House since the Wilson years and concerned mainly at this point with final exams at George Washington University.

For exercise, Truman had begun using the swimming pool Roosevelt had had built on the ground floor. Truman tried to do six or eight laps in his choppy, self-styled sidestroke, head up to keep his glasses dry, and hoped to get to where he could swim a quarter of a mile.

In the evening before dinner, he and Bess would relax with a cocktail in the so-called "sitting hall," but as J. B. West remembered, it took a while for the staff to learn their tastes.

On an evening when Bess first ordered old-fashioneds, the head butler, Alonzo Fields, a proudly accomplished bartender, had fixed the drinks his usual way, with chilled glasses, an ounce of bourbon each, orange slices, a teaspoon of sugar, and dash of bitters. But the night following she had asked that the drinks not be made quite so sweet and so Fields had tried another recipe.

This time she waited until morning to complain to J. B. West. They were the worst old-fashioneds she had ever tasted. She and the President did not care for fruit punch. West spoke to Fields, who, the third night, his pride hurt, poured her a double bourbon on ice and stood by waiting for the reaction as the First Lady took a sip.

"Now that's the way we like our old-fashioneds," she said, smiling.

Fields, a tall, handsome black man, would later say of Mrs. Truman that she would "stand no fakers, shirkers or flatterers," and that the only way to gain her approval was to do your job as best you could. "This done, you would not want a more understanding person to work for."

J. B. West, who had grown up in Iowa, found her down-to-earth and personable, "correct but not formal." He liked her. "Like most Midwestern women I'd known, her values went deeper than cosmetics."

The President impressed him as someone who knew who he was and liked who he was. And as a family all three were extremely fond of each other. "They were essentially very private people who didn't show affection in public," West wrote. "But they did everything together—read, listened to the radio, played the piano, and mostly talked to each other." In twelve years Franklin and Eleanor Roosevelt had never been in residence in the White House alone. Rarely had they ever taken a meal together.

The full staff for the main house—butlers, cooks, maids, doormen, plumbers, carpenters, electricians, gardeners—numbered thirty-two, of whom the highest ranking were the head usher, Howell Crim; the First Lady's social secretary, Edith Helm; and the housekeeper, elderly, gray-haired Henrietta Nesbitt, a favorite of Mrs. Roosevelt's, who had charge of the food and who was the only one who appeared to be a problem, since the food was uniformly dreadful. Ira Smith, who was Chief of Mails, had first come to work as a messenger at the White House in 1897. Samuel Jackson, the President's personal messenger, had begun his duties during the Taft administration, as had John Mays, the head doorman.

Truman got along splendidly with them all. In time he knew everyone's name and all about their families and years of service in the house. If there were guests, he would introduce each of the servants, something none of them had ever known a President to do before.

"He knew when a stenographer's baby caught a cold; when a White House servant lost a relative," Merriman Smith, White House correspondent for United Press, would remember. "He thought it was hilarious when LeRoy, the White House leaf-raker whom he knew and liked, fobbed himself off as an important official and was shown a box at Hialeah (Florida) race track."

One story would be told for a long time. On the night of the German surrender, May 8, Truman's birthday, the head cook, Elizabeth Moore, had baked him a cake. Dinner over, Truman had gone to the kitchen to thank her, and as Alonzo Fields would note, this was the first time a President had been in the White House kitchen since Coolidge, who had been in and out so often it was said he was only being nosy—to see no handouts were being given away.

"I always felt that he [President Truman] understood me as a man, not as a servant to be tolerated," Fields would write, "and that I understood that he expected me to be a man. . . . President Roosevelt was genial and warm but he left one feeling, as most aristocrats do, that they really do not understand one."

Harry Hopkins had told Truman he had made a mistake ever asking the Roosevelt Cabinet to stay. A President ought to have his own people around him, Hopkins lectured. Now the changes began.

Bob Hannegan, to no one's surprise, was named Postmaster General, the traditional reward for a party chairman, to replace the ailing Frank Walker, who had talked of retirement since before Roosevelt's death. Lewis Schwellenbach, Truman's old Senate friend and confidant, was to be the new Secretary of Labor, succeeding Frances Perkins, who had been the first to tell Truman she wished to step down. For Secretary of Agriculture, after the resignation of Claude Wickard, he picked Congressman Clinton Anderson of New Mexico. To replace Roosevelt's aristocratic Attorney General, Francis Biddle of Philadelphia, he named a relatively unknown Texan, Tom Clark, an assistant attorney general who had run the Criminal Division.

Announcement of the changes caused little stir. At his press conference Truman was asked only if Clark spelled his name with an "e" on the end.

Nor did Truman regret the departures. Walker he thought a decent enough man but lacking in ideas. Perkins, though "a grand lady," knew nothing of politics, and besides he didn't like the idea of a woman in the Cabinet. As for Biddle, Truman had never much cared for him.

The only sour note was Biddle's removal, which Truman mishandled. He had no heart for firing people. "Not built right, I guess, to man a chopping block," he had once observed to Bess. To avoid a confrontation with Biddle, he had one of the staff contact him by phone. Biddle, greatly insulted, said that if the President wished his resignation, the President could ask for it himself. A Cabinet officer should expect no less. So Truman sent for him and admitted he had gone about things the wrong way. He told Biddle he had not wanted to face him. He then asked for his resignation.

"The President seemed relieved," Biddle wrote in his version of the scene. "I got up, walked over to him and touched his shoulder. 'You see,' I said, 'it's not so hard.' "

The eventual announcement that Jimmy Byrnes would succeed Stettinius as Secretary of State brought the number of replacements to five, half the Cabinet. Just three of the old New Dealers remained—Wallace, Ickes, and Morgenthau—and the expectation was they wouldn't last much longer. Stimson intended to serve only until the war ended, which left Forrestal as the only one who seemed likely to stay.

In surface ways the new group was a projection of Truman himself. Everybody but Byrnes was from west of the Mississippi. There was no one who was notably brilliant or colorful or a vociferous liberal. All were good, solid Democrats, all perfectly safe choices. But most important, three of the five—Byrnes, Schwellenbach, and Anderson—had served in Congress. Truman was determined both to have a strong Cabinet to which he could delegate a large part of his responsibilities, and to get along with Congress better than Roosevelt had. Even Tom Clark was chosen chiefly on Speaker Sam Rayburn's recommendation.

To the regret of Admiral Leahy and other career Navy men, Truman also brought in a reserve officer, another Missourian, Navy Captain James K. Vardaman, Jr., to be his naval aide, an appointment approximately on a par to that of Harry Vaughan. Like Vaughan, Vardaman had stood by Truman when it mattered, in the 1940 Senate race. Like Vaughan, he knew how to amuse "the Boss." After one poker-party cruise on the Potomac in the presidential yacht with Vaughan, Vardaman, George Allen, and John Snyder, Truman wrote in his diary that his sides were sore from laughing.

. . .

One further appointment, however, was seen as a first sign of genuine political courage on Truman's part. Clearly it was not a case of politics as usual, or politics in the Roosevelt style.

With David Lilienthal's term as head of the Tennessee Valley Authority about to expire, Truman was under great pressure from conservative Democrats to dump him. Senator Kenneth McKellar of Tennessee, "Old Mack," the craggy, slouched president of the Senate and chairman of the Appropriations Committee, was in a "pow'ful tempuh," threatening to lead the biggest confirmation fight in memory if Truman dared reappoint the liberal Lilienthal, who insisted on merit rather than patronage appointments at TVA. To avoid trouble with McKellar, Roosevelt had already spoken of naming Lilienthal to another job.

Lilienthal, a steadfast, idealistic New Dealer who had been made nearly ill by the thought of Truman taking Roosevelt's place, was called to the White House. It was Truman's impression that Lilienthal had been doing a first-rate job and Truman told him so. Then, smiling, he asked if Lilienthal was ready to carry on at TVA. If so, he was reappointed. There would be troubles with McKellar, of course, Truman said, but he had tangled with McKellar before.

> And that was about all there was [recorded Lilienthal, incredulous and thrilled]. . . . No talk about what a "rap" he, as President, was assuming in naming me . . . no talk, such as . . . President Roosevelt had given me, about what McKellar could do to disrupt the peace if his wishes concerning me were not respected—none of that—just there it was.
>
> It was an admirable performance. Simple. No mock heroics. Nothing complex. Straightforward!

As it turned out, McKellar's opposition had little effect. The nomination was confirmed by the Senate on May 23.

Earlier, talking with his staff before seeing Lilienthal, Truman had said with a pleased look, "Old Mack is going to have a hemorrhage."

Another morning in late May, at their regular nine o'clock meeting, Truman told his staff he had done something about which there might be objection. He had invited Herbert Hoover to come see him. He had written Hoover in longhand the night before. The letter was already in the mail, so there was no use trying to stop it.

The former President had been *persona non grata* at the White House since Roosevelt first took office in 1933. Truman thought it was time that ended. He wanted to talk with Hoover, he said, about famine relief in

Europe. Also, as he did not say, Hoover was the one other mortal who had ever sat in his place, or who knew the feeling of being constantly compared to Roosevelt.

"Saw Herbert Hoover," Truman wrote in his diary, ". . . and had a pleasant and constructive conversation on food and the general troubles of U.S. Presidents—two in particular."

Things were going so well overall, Truman also recorded, that he hardly knew what to think. "I can't understand it—except to attribute it to God. He guides me, I think."

IV

Besides Henry Stimson, who served as chairman, the newly organized, entirely civilian and highly secret Interim Committee on S-1 included eight members, three of whom were eminent scientists involved with the project: James Bryant Conant, the president of Harvard, who was chairman of the National Defense Research Committee; Karl T. Compton, president of M.I.T.; and Vannevar Bush, president of the Carnegie Institute in Washington and director of the Office of Scientific Research and Development. Ralph A. Bard was Under Secretary of the Navy and a former Chicago financier. William L. Clayton was Assistant Secretary of State for Economic Affairs and a specialist in international trade. George L. Harrison was the president of the New York Life Insurance Company and Stimson's special assistant on matters related to S-1.

The eighth man was Jimmy Byrnes, who had been appointed by the President as his personal representative.

The first meeting was held on Wednesday, May 9, 1945, in Stimson's office at the Pentagon. "Gentlemen, it is our responsibility to recommend action that may turn the course of civilization," the venerable Secretary of War began. Meetings followed on May 14 and May 18. On Thursday, May 31, the committee convened for a crucial two-day session, joined now by an advisory panel of four physicists actively involved with development of the bomb: Enrico Fermi and Arthur H. Compton of the University of Chicago; Ernest O. Lawrence of the Radiation Laboratory at the University of California at Berkeley; and, most important, J. Robert Oppenheimer, head of the Los Alamos Laboratory, where the bomb was being assembled.

A wide range of subjects was covered at this final session, including relations with Soviets. General Marshall raised the possibility of inviting the Russians to send some of their scientists to witness the first test.

Byrnes objected, expressing a view agreed to by all present, that the best program would be to "push ahead as fast as possible in production and research to make certain that we stay ahead and at the same time make every effort to better our political relations with Russia."

After much discussion, the committee and scientific panel reached three unanimous conclusions:

1. The bomb should be used against Japan as soon as possible.
2. It should be used against war plants surrounded by workers' homes or other buildings susceptible to damage, in order "to make a profound psychological impression on as many inhabitants as possible." (Oppenheimer had assured them the "visual effect of an atomic bombing would be tremendous.")
3. It should be used without warning.

Byrnes went directly from the meeting to the White House to report to Truman, and Truman, according to Byrnes's later recollection, said that "with reluctance he had to agree, that he could think of no alternative. . . ."

Stimson, in the meantime, had received a long letter that impressed him greatly and that he passed on immediately to Marshall, calling it a "remarkable document" from an honest man. It was addressed to the President and had come through regular security channels. "I shall take the President's copy to him personally," Stimson wrote in reply, "or through Byrnes. . . ."

Dated May 24, it was from an unknown engineer named O. C. Brewster of 23 East 11th Street, New York, who had worked on uranium isotope separation for S-1, but who, since the defeat of Germany, had become tormented over what the release of the energy "locked up in the atom" might mean for the future. "The idea of the destruction of civilization is not melodramatic hysteria or crackpot raving. It is a very real and, I submit, almost inevitable result." In the early stages of the project, like many others, Brewster had hoped it would be conclusively proved impossible. "Obviously, however, so long as there was any chance that Germany might succeed at this task there was only one course to follow and that was to do everything in our power to get this thing first and destroy Germany before she had a chance to destroy us. . . . So long as the threat of Germany existed we had to proceed with all speed. . . . With the threat of Germany removed we must stop this project." He urged a demonstration of one atomic bomb on a target in Japan, but then no further production of nuclear material.

I do not of course want to propose anything to jeopardize the war with Japan but, horrible as it may seem, I know it would be better to take greater casualties now in conquering Japan than to bring upon the world the tragedy of unrestrained competitive production of this material. . . . In the name of the future of our country and of the peace of the world, I beg you, sir, not to pass this off because I happen to be unknown, without influence or name in the public eye. . . .

The letter reached the White House, but whether Truman saw it is not known. It was, however, returned shortly with no sign of presidential reaction.

The one hint of Truman's state of mind to be found in his own hand is a diary entry on Sunday, June 3: "Have been going through some very hectic days," is his only comment. Later, he would say that of course he realized an atomic explosion would inflict damage and casualties "beyond imagination."

Actually, no one was very clear on what power the weapon might have. Forecasts provided by the scientific panel for the explosive force varied from the equivalent of 2,000 tons of TNT to 20,000 tons.

Estimates by the scientists on how long it might take the Soviets to develop such a weapon ranged from three to five years, although General Groves personally reckoned as much as twenty years.

Stimson was thinking more of the larger historic consequences. At the final meeting of the committee he had said how vitally important it was to regard the bomb not "as a new weapon merely but as a revolutionary change in the relations of man to the universe," and like O. C. Brewster, he warned that the project might mean "the doom of civilization." It might be a Frankenstein monster, or it might mean "the perfection of civilization." (Ernest O. Lawrence of the scientific panel had forecast the day when it might be possible to "secure our energy from terrestrial sources rather than from the sun.") But no one knew.

On Wednesday, June 6, Stimson came to discuss the report with the President in more detail.

Stimson told Truman he was deeply troubled by reports of the devastation brought on Japan by the B-29 fire raids. He had insisted always on precision bombing, Stimson said, but was now informed by the Air Force that that was no longer possible, since in Japan, unlike Germany, industries were not concentrated but scattered among and closely connected with the houses of employees.

As Stimson appreciated, attitudes about the bombing of civilian targets had changed drastically in Washington, as in the nation, the longer the war went on. When the Japanese bombed Shanghai in 1937, it had been viewed as an atrocity of the most appalling kind. When the war in Europe erupted in 1939, Roosevelt had begged both sides to refrain from the "inhuman barbarism" of bombing civilians. His "arsenal of democracy" speech in December 1940 had had particular power and urgency because German bombers were pounding London. ("What a puny effort is this to burn a great city," Edward R. Murrow had said.) But the tide of war had turned, and the "ghastly dew" raining from the skies in the Tennyson poem that Truman still carried in his wallet had become more ghastly by far. That winter, in February 1945, during three raids on Dresden, Germany—two British raids, one American—incendiary bombs set off a firestorm that could be seen for 200 miles. In all an estimated 135,000 people had died.

A recent issue of *Life* carried aerial photographs taken after three hundred B-29 bombers swept such destruction on Tokyo, said *Life,* as was hitherto visited on the city only by catastrophic earthquakes. The magazine said nothing of how many men, women, and children were killed, but in one such horrendous fire raid on Tokyo the night of March 9–10, more than 100,000 perished. Bomber crews in the last waves of the attack could smell burning flesh. With Japan vowing anew to fight to the end, the raids continued. On May 14, five hundred B-29s hit Nagoya, Japan's third largest industrial city, in what *The New York Times* called the greatest concentration of fire bombs in the history of aerial warfare. On May 23, five square miles of Tokyo were obliterated. Thirty-six hours later, 16 square miles were destroyed. As weeks passed, other coastal cities were hit—Yokohama, Osaka, Kobe.

Stimson told Truman he didn't want to see the United States "outdoing Hitler in atrocities." But he was also concerned that targets in Japan might become so bombed out by conventional raids that S-1 would have no "fair background" to show its strength, an observation that seems to have struck Truman as so odd, coming on top of Stimson's previous worry, that he actually laughed, then added that he understood.

Neither Stimson nor General Marshall was concerned over whether the bomb should be used on Japan, only with how to use it to stop the slaughter as quickly as possible. Stimson's directive to General Groves in 1942 had been to produce the bomb at "the earliest possible date so as to bring the war to a conclusion."

As Stimson stressed, the committee's role was advisory only. The responsibility for a recommendation to the President was his alone, and he was painfully aware of all that was riding on his judgment.

The ultimate responsibility for the recommendation to the President rested on me [he would later write], and I have no desire to veil it. The conclusions of the Committee were similar to my own, although I reached mine independently. I felt that to extract a genuine surrender from the Emperor and his military advisers, there must be administered a tremendous shock which could carry convincing proof of our power to destroy the Empire. Such an effective shock would save many times the number of lives, both American and Japanese, that it would cost.

The possibility of dropping the atomic bomb on some target other than a city, as a harmless technical demonstration for the Japanese, had been considered by the committee and by the scientific panel and it had been rejected. General Marshall had thought initially that the weapon might first be used against such a "straight military objective" as a large naval installation, and then, if necessary, against manufacturing centers, from which the people would be warned in advance to leave. "We must offset by such warning methods," Marshall had said, "the opprobrium which might follow from an ill-considered employment of such force." But by now apparently Marshall had changed his mind, and besides, he was not formally a member of the committee. The scientists were able to propose no demonstration sufficiently spectacular to give the needed "tremendous shock." Probably only one bomb would be ready. There were worries it might not work, and that any advance announcement of a supposedly all-powerful secret weapon that failed would be worse than no attempt and only bolster Japanese resolve to fight on. Writing for the scientific panel, Oppenheimer said:

> The opinions of our scientific colleagues on the initial use of these weapons are not unanimous: they range from the proposal of a purely technical demonstration to that of the military application best designed to induce surrender. Those who advocate a purely technical demonstration would wish to outlaw the use of atomic weapons, and have feared that if we use the weapons now our position in future negotiation will be prejudiced. Others emphasize the opportunity of saving American lives by immediate military use, and believe that such use will improve the international prospects, in that they are more concerned with the prevention of war than with the elimination of this specific weapon. We find ourselves closer to these latter views; we can propose no technical demonstration likely to bring an end to the war; we see no acceptable alternates to direct military use.

Byrnes had introduced the further thought that if the Japanese were told in advance where the bomb was to be dropped, they might bring

American prisoners of war to the area. Oppenheimer, who supposedly knew the most about the bomb, stressed that the number of people killed by it would be considerably less than in a conventional incendiary raid. Oppenheimer's estimate was that twenty thousand would die.

Stimson told Truman what the committee had stressed, and what all his senior military advisers were saying, that it was the "shock value" of the weapon that would stop the war. Nothing short of that would work.

Okinawa was on Stimson's mind—Okinawa was on all their minds. An attack on the American armada by hundreds of Japanese suicide planes, the *kamikaze,* had had devastating effect—thirty ships sunk, more than three hundred damaged, including carriers and battleships. Once American troops were ashore on the island, the enemy fought from caves and pillboxes with fanatic ferocity, even after ten days of heavy sea and air bombardment. The battle on Okinawa still raged. In the end more than 12,000 Americans would be killed, 36,000 wounded. Japanese losses were ten times worse—110,000 Japanese killed—and, as later studies show, civilian deaths on the island may have been as high as 150,000, or a third of the population.

"We regarded the matter of dropping the bomb as exceedingly important," General Marshall later explained.

> We had just been through a bitter experience at Okinawa. This had been preceded by a number of similar experiences in other Pacific islands. [The first day of the invasion of Iwo Jima had been more costly than D-Day at Normandy.] . . . The Japanese had demonstrated in each case they would not surrender and they fight to the death. . . . It was to be expected that resistance in Japan, with their home ties, could be even more severe. We had had one hundred thousand people killed in Tokyo in one night of bombs, and it had seemingly no effect whatsoever. It destroyed the Japanese cities, yes, but their morale was affected, so far as we could tell, not at all. So it seemed quite necessary, if we could, to shock them into action. . . . We had to end the war; we had to save American lives.

Among some scientists connected with the project, but not party to the committee's discussions, there was sharp disagreement with such reasoning.

In early April, Leo Szilard of the University of Chicago, the brilliant Hungarian-born physicist who, with Einstein, had helped persuade Roosevelt to initiate the project in the first place, wrote a long memorandum addressed to Roosevelt saying that use of an atomic bomb against Japan would start an atomic arms race with Russia and questioning whether avoiding that might be more important than the short-term goal of knocking Japan out of the war. Because of Roosevelt's death, the memorandum was not sent. Instead, Szilard set about arranging an appointment with Truman through a friend and colleague at the University of Chicago's Metallurgical Laboratory, a mathematician named Albert Cahn, who came from Kansas City and had once, to pay his way through graduate school, worked for Tom Pendergast. A date was made for Szilard to see Matt Connelly, the new appointments secretary, and Szilard went to the White House. Connelly, having read Szilard's memorandum, agreed it was a serious matter. ("At first I was a little suspicious," he also said, "because the appointment came through Kansas City.") He told Szilard it was the President's wish that he see Jimmy Byrnes, and Szilard, who was unaware of Byrnes's role on the Interim Committee or that Byrnes was soon to become Secretary of State, took an overnight train to Spartanburg, accompanied by a University of Chicago dean, Walter Bartky, and another noted physicist, Harold Urey.

The three men saw Byrnes on May 27, just days before the crucial, last meeting of the Interim Committee. Reading the memorandum, Byrnes was at once annoyed by its tone. The true situation, it said, could be evaluated "only by men who have firsthand knowledge of the facts involved, that is, by the small group of scientists who are actively engaged in this work." Byrnes was put off also by Szilard himself, a notably eccentric man of expansive ego. "His general demeanor and his desire to participate in policy making made an unfavorable impression on me," Byrnes later wrote.

According to Szilard, Byrnes said he understood from General Groves that Russia had no uranium and that through possession of the bomb America could "render the Russians more manageable." Szilard felt certain it would have precisely the opposite effect.

According to Byrnes, what Szilard, Bartky, and Urey told him about the power of the bomb did nothing to decrease his fears of "the terrible weapon they had assisted in creating."

Szilard left Spartanburg determined to draw up a petition to the President opposing on "purely moral grounds" any use of atomic bombs on Japan. Stopping again in Washington en route to Chicago, he saw Oppenheimer.

Like Stimson, like so many, Oppenheimer by this time was worn out, his nerves on edge. There were problems at Los Alamos. Detonators were not firing as they should, the work was falling behind schedule. Oppenheimer looked a wreck. He had been stricken with chicken pox and lost 30 pounds. Though over six feet tall, he weighed all of 115 pounds.

"Oppenheimer didn't share my views," Szilard recalled. "He surprised me by saying, 'The atomic bomb is shit . . . a weapon which has no military significance. It will make a big bang—a very big bang—but it is not a weapon that is useful in war.'"

To what extent Byrnes discussed Szilard with Truman, if at all, is not recorded. But in his discussions about the atomic bomb, Admiral Leahy had been assuring Truman that "the damn thing" would never work. To Leahy it was "all the biggest bunk in the world."

On Saturday, June 2, after less than a month in residence, Bess, her mother, and Margaret had packed and left Washington by train to spend a long summer in Independence. Madge Wallace was not happy with life in the White House, nor was Bess. "We are on our way *home*, underlined, four exclamation points," wrote Margaret, who, to her father, seemed in a very unsatisfactory humor. "I hope—sincerely hope," he wrote privately, "that this situation (my being President) is not going to affect her adversely."

At home, the old house at 219 North Delaware was being patched up and repainted after years of neglect. It would be gray no more, but white now, with "Kentucky green" trim at the windows, as befitting the "summer White House."

After only a few nights alone, Truman began feeling desolate and more than a little sorry for himself. The first Sunday, giving no advance notice, he walked across Lafayette Square to St. John's Church and slipped into a back pew unnoticed by most of the congregation. It was where Lincoln had sometimes worshiped, he knew. "Don't think over six people recognized me," he wrote in his diary.

One evening Admiral Leahy stayed over for dinner and afterward he and Truman played hosts at a reception for White House employees and their families. But most nights were taken up with work in the upstairs Oval Study, where the long windows stood open to the mild spring air.

From sounds in the night, Truman became convinced the house was haunted and tried to imagine which former residents might be involved:

> June 12, 1945
>
> Dear Bess:
>
> Just two months ago today, I was a reasonably happy and contented Vice President. Maybe you can remember that far back too. But things have changed so much it hardly seems real.
>
> I sit here in this old house and work on foreign affairs, read reports, and work on speeches—all the while listening to the ghosts walk up

and down the hallway and even right in here in the study. The floors pop and the drapes move back and forth—I can just imagine old Andy and Teddy having an argument over Franklin. Or James Buchanan and Franklin Pierce deciding which was the more useless to the country. And when Millard Fillmore and Chester Arthur join in for place and show the din is almost unbearable. . . .

General Eisenhower made a triumphal return to the city, spoke to a joint session of Congress, and Truman gave a stag dinner for him at the White House, which everyone thought a big success. "He's a nice fellow and a good man," Truman reported to Bess. "He's done a whale of a job." There was talk everywhere of running Eisenhower for President, which, Truman told her, was perfectly fine by him. "I'd turn it over to him now if I could."

Alone in the old house he would poke about in the closets, adjust the clocks. He hated being by himself, hated having breakfast alone, or even going through the motions of dressing for the day. "I'm always so lonesome when the family leaves. I have no one to raise a fuss over my neckties and my haircuts, my shoes and my clothes generally," he lamented in his diary. "I usually put on a terrible tie not even Bob Hannegan or Ed McKim would wear just to get a loud protest from Bess and Margie. When they are gone I have to put on the right ones and it's no fun."

Yet the truth seemed to be that things were going exceedingly, inexplicably well for him. His popularity was beyond imagining. A Gallup Poll reported that 87 percent of the people approved his conduct of the presidency, which was a higher rating even than Roosevelt had ever received. Nor was the woeful man of the evening letters the one who turned up in the office each day. "And as usual, he is in good humor," Eben Ayers noted one Monday morning. Truman was pleased with his popularity on the Hill, pleased with his press conferences, his staff. He loved having Charlie Ross on duty. Most heartening was the "good progress" made by Hopkins, who returned from Moscow on June 12 and, with Joseph Davies, came for breakfast the next morning. Davies was back from a mission to London to see Churchill.

In long cables from Moscow Hopkins had given full account of his every conversation with Stalin. Though greatly offended by the manner in which Lend-Lease had been shut off, Stalin seemed willing to let the matter pass. He had agreed even to the American position on voting procedure in the United Nations Security Council, which in effect meant the San Francisco Conference was saved.

Churchill, in further cables, had been urging again that there be no withdrawal of American forces to the designated occupation zones in Europe. "Nothing really important has been settled yet," he warned Truman, "and you and I will have to bear great responsibility for the future." But Hopkins told Truman any delay in the withdrawal of American troops from the Soviet zone was "certain to be misunderstood by the Russians." Reportedly General Eisenhower also thought it unwise to keep American forces in the Russian zone. Truman, determined still to do nothing in violation of Roosevelt's agreements at Yalta, and believing this the best possible way to demonstrate America's good faith to the Russians and to induce them to carry out their own obligations in return, informed Churchill on June 11 that, as agreed, American troops would pull back, which Churchill saw as a terrible mistake. A few years later, Truman would write:

> We were about 150 miles east of the border of the occupation zone line agreed to at Yalta. I felt that agreements made in the war to keep Russia fighting should be kept and I kept them to the letter. Perhaps they should not have been adhered to so quickly....

Regarding Poland, Stalin had told Hopkins he was willing to talk. All of which meant the issue stood again where it was when Roosevelt came home from Yalta, except that now the place and time for such talk was settled. Truman had wanted to meet in Alaska. But as twice before—for both the Teheran and Yalta conferences—Stalin was granted his way. It would be Potsdam, a Berlin suburb in the zone held by the Red Army. The date chosen was July 15.

Truman was so pleased by what Hopkins had achieved, he even thought Hopkins, whose deathlike appearance stunned others at the White House, looked improved in health. The trip had done Hopkins good, Truman felt sure. The Russians, he wrote in his diary, had "always been our friends and I can't see why they shouldn't always be."

By leaving his sickbed to go to Moscow, Hopkins had performed heroic service for his country. Truman was enormously grateful to him and thanked him. Hopkins, who had worked so long and closely with Roosevelt, later told Charlie Ross that it was the first time he had ever been thanked by a President.

The President was trying to understand what to do in the Pacific, trying to fathom MacArthur, whom he had never met, but didn't like from what he had read and heard—"Mr. Prima Donna, Brass Hat, Five Star MacArthur," Truman referred to him in the privacy of his diary. "Don't see how a country can produce such men as Robert E. Lee, John J. Pershing, Eisenhower, and Bradley and at the same time produce Custers, Pattons, and MacArthurs."

His mind was on plans for the invasion and a proposed Navy blockade designed to starve Japan into submission. In a memorandum stamped URGENT, Admiral Leahy noted the President wanted to know the number of men and ships needed:

> He wants an estimate of the time required and an estimate of the losses in killed and wounded that will result from an invasion of Japan proper. ... It is his intention to make his decision on the campaign with the purpose of economizing to the maximum extent possible in the loss of American lives. Economy in the use of time and in money cost is comparatively unimportant.

"I have to decide Japanese strategy—shall we invade Japan proper or shall we bomb and blockade?" Truman pondered in his diary. "That is my hardest decision to date." S-1 was not mentioned.

Nor was it mentioned at the extremely important White House meeting to review the invasion plans the afternoon of Monday, June 18, 1945, and this, as the hour passed, struck one of Stimson's staff, Assistant Secretary of War John J. McCloy, as extremely odd. Things were proceeding, McCloy saw, as if the bomb did not exist.

The plan, as presented by General Marshall, was for a two-phase invasion, beginning in November with the southernmost of the Japanese islands, Kyushu, only 350 miles from Okinawa. The operation, said Marshall, would be as difficult as Normandy, but he thought it the only course to pursue. Casualties were hard to predict. He estimated that in the initial phase, the first 30 days only, losses would be similar to those on Luzon, which was about 31,000.

Admiral King said Okinawa would be a more realistic measure, and put the number at 41,000. Admiral Nimitz would forecast 49,000 casualties in the first 30 days, 7,000 more than at Normandy in an equal span of time. MacArthur's staff estimated 50,000, though MacArthur, who was all for the invasion, considered that too high.

Another estimate at the Pentagon included the invasion of both southern and northern Kyushu, as well as Japan proper, and the cost of this plan came to nearly a quarter of a million men. A memorandum of June 14, 1945, signed by General Thomas Handy of Marshall's staff, quoted the opinion of an unnamed "economist" (apparently Herbert Hoover) that 500,000 American lives or more could be saved by making peace and avoiding the invasion altogether. Such a figure was thought too high by some, including Handy. But Stimson, certain the Japanese would fight as never before, feared American casualties could reach a million. General Andrew Goodpaster, one of Marshall's strategic planners, would recall, "We anticipated that we would have losses of 500,000 killed or wounded, and the Japanese ten times that many."

The code name for the overall plan was "Downfall." The assault on Kyushu, called "Olympic," was to begin November 1. Operation Coronet, the larger invasion of Japan proper, the main island of Honshu, would follow in March 1946. Prior to the invasion of Honshu, air bombardment would be increased to an absolute maximum, to the point where, said one memorandum, "more bombs will be dropped on Japan than were delivered against Germany during the entire European War."

Truman approved the plan.

McCloy, who had expressed his own views to Stimson at length the night before, kept silent throughout the discussion. But as the meeting ended, he remembered, "We were beginning to get our papers together and the President saw me. 'McCloy,' he said, 'nobody leaves this room until he's been heard from.' I turned to Stimson and he said, 'Go ahead.'"

McCloy replied that the threat of the bomb might provide a "political solution." The whole invasion could be avoided. An immediate hush fell on the room, as if the mere mention of the ultra secret was out of order.

"I said I would tell them [the Japanese] we have the bomb and I would tell them what kind of a weapon it is. And then I would tell them the surrender terms." He thought the Japanese should also be told they could keep their Emperor. What if they refused, he was asked. "Our moral position will be stronger if we give them warning."

Truman indicated he would think about it.

He flew to San Francisco on *The Sacred Cow* to speak in the Opera House on June 26 at the official signing of the United Nations Charter. They were there, he told the delegates, to keep the world at peace. "And free from the fear of war," he declared emphatically, both hands chopping the air, palms inward, in rhythm with the words "free," "fear," and "war." San Francisco was his first public appearance since becoming President, and the reception the city gave him took his breath away. A million people turned out to cheer him as he rode in an open car.

A day later he flew into Kansas City for the first time as President, and to the biggest welcome home ever seen in Jackson County. "Dad loved every minute of it," remembered Margaret. He was photographed having his hair cut in Frank Spina's barbershop downtown. He dropped in at

Eddie Jacobson's Westport Men's Wear, drank bourbon and swapped stories with Ted Marks, Jim Pendergast, and seven or eight others from Battery D after dinner at the home of Independence Mayor Roger Sermon. When he spoke at the huge auditorium of the Reorganized Latter-Day Saints, every seat was filled. "I shall attempt to meet your expectations," he said humbly. "But do not expect too much of me."

The next day, after receiving an honorary degree from the University of Kansas City, he described how, on the flight from San Francisco, after a stop at Salt Lake City, he had looked down on the great plains and thought of his grandfather, Solomon Young. From Kansas City to Salt Lake and home again had taken Solomon Young three months each way. Now his grandson had done it in three and a half hours.

"I am anxious to bring home to you that the world is no longer county-size, no longer state-size, no longer nation-size," he said. "It is a world in which we must all get along."

On July 2, he went before the Senate to urge ratification of the United Nations Charter: "It comes from the reality of experience in a world where one generation has failed twice to keep the peace."

With the time for his departure for Berlin fast approaching, he spent longer hours in his office, which looked more as he himself wanted it to look. Everything belonging to Franklin Roosevelt had been removed. A Rembrandt Peale portrait of George Washington, on loan from the National Gallery, hung now to one side of the mantel facing him. On the other side was a portrait of Simon Bolívar given to him in 1941 by the Venezuelan ambassador. (The gift, on behalf of the Venezuelan government, was to the largest community in the United States bearing the name of the great liberator—Bolivar, Missouri.) Above the mantel was a Remington entitled *Fired On,* borrowed from the Smithsonian. It showed Indian fighters on horseback under attack in ghostly green moonlight, one horse rearing violently in the foreground, as Truman's own horse had reared the night in the Vosges Mountains when Battery D was fired on.

Roosevelt's naval scenes had been replaced with a series of prints of early airplanes. The Roosevelt portrait remained on the wall to Truman's right. On a table that once held a ship model was a bronze replica of the equestrian Andrew Jackson by Charles Keck that stood in front of the Kansas City Courthouse. Behind his desk, on a table in front of the windows, were portraits of Bess, Margaret, and Mamma Truman, and a hodgepodge of books.

Franklin Roosevelt's desk had been removed—given by Truman to Mrs. Roosevelt—and replaced with a seven-foot walnut desk that had belonged to Theodore Roosevelt. Its surface, by FDR's standards, was bare and tidy. Besides a large green blotter and telephone, there were several pairs of eyeglasses in separate cases, two small metal ashtrays for visitors, a model cannon, a clock, two pen sets (one fancy, one plain), pencils, date stamp, calendar, two magnifying glasses, paste jar, glass inkwell, and a battered old ice-water vacuum pitcher, the one item from among FDR's personal effects that Truman had asked to keep.

In a small silver frame was the 1917 photograph of Bess that he had carried with him to France. Another small frame held a motto of Mark Twain's, in Twain's own hand: "Always do right! This will gratify some people and astonish the rest."

There was no buzzer on or beneath the desk. Truman didn't like to "buzz" people. He would get up and go to the door instead. Further, he ordered the removal of a hidden recording device that Roosevelt had used now and then.

To an artist named S. J. Woolf, sent by *The New York Times* to do a sketch of the President at work, Truman seemed surprisingly relaxed, in view of all that must be on his mind. The responsibilities resting on a President, said Truman, were so heavy that if he were to keep thinking of them and considering what might happen as a result of the decisions he had to make, he would "soon go under."

Truman was sure the Russians wanted to be friends. He saw "no reason why we should not welcome their friendship and give ours to them." He looked forward to meeting both Stalin and Churchill, he said. But to Bess he wrote of feeling "blue as indigo" about going.

Henry Stimson, who had attended neither of the previous Big Three conferences, had not been invited to make the trip. This was out of consideration for his health, Truman told him. Acutely aware of how much could hang on last-minute developments concerning S-1, Stimson chose to invite himself. He would go by plane, arriving in Berlin in advance of the President.

Treasury Secretary Henry Morgenthau was also extremely eager to be included, and extremely upset when he found he was not. Morgenthau had a plan to strip Germany of all heavy industry and reduce it to an agricultural land, an idea Truman had never taken seriously and that Stimson ardently opposed, on the grounds that an economically strong and productive Germany was the only hope for the future stability of Europe. "Punish her war criminals in full measure," Stimson advised Truman. "Deprive her permanently of her weapons. . . . Guard her governmental action until the Nazi-educated generation has passed from the stage. . . . But do not deprive her of the means of building up ultimately a contented Germany interested in non-militaristic methods of civilization."

It had also been pointed out to Truman that if some unfortunate mishap were to occur on the trip to Berlin, and he and Secretary of State Byrnes were both to die, then, as the law of succession stood, Henry Morgenthau would become President, a thought that distressed Truman exceedingly; but whether this was because Morgenthau was a Jew—the reason Morgenthau suspected—is not indicated in anything Truman said or wrote.

Morgenthau came to see him in the Oval Office on July 5 to say, according to Truman's account of the meeting, that it was essential that he, Morgenthau, play a part at Potsdam, and that if he could not, he would resign. If such was the case, said Truman, then his resignation was accepted at once. The announcement was made the same day.

To replace Morgenthau at Treasury, Truman named Fred M. Vinson, who had served fourteen years in Congress, where he was considered an expert on fiscal matters, and five years as a judge on the Circuit Court of Appeals, before being named by Roosevelt to head the Office of Economic Stabilization and later the Office of War Mobilization and Reconversion. Vinson was a versatile, diligent public figure, if unimpressive in appearance. With his receding chin, the dark circles under his eyes, he had a weary, hound-dog look. He was also an affable old-style Kentucky politician—down-to-earth, humorous, shrewd—and in Truman's estimate one of the best men in government.

In his own diary account of the breakup Morgenthau made no mention of the Potsdam issue, only that Truman seemed "very weak and indecisive" about whether he wanted Morgenthau to stay on the job until the war ended. According to Morgenthau, he told Truman, "Either you want me to stay until V-J Day or you don't. . . . After all, Mr. President, I don't think it is conceited to say that I am at least as good or better as some of the five new people you appointed in the Cabinet, and on some of them I think you definitely made a mistake."

A number of years later, in a conversation with Jonathan Daniels, Truman would say, "Morgenthau didn't know shit from apple butter."

"I am getting ready to go see Stalin and Churchill," he wrote to his mother and sister. "I have to take my tuxedo, tails, Negro preacher coat, high hat, low hat and hard hat. . . . I have a briefcase filled up with information on past conferences and suggestions on what I'm to do and say. Wish I didn't have to go. . . ."

"How I hate this trip!" he wrote again in his diary on Sunday, July 7, on board the cruiser *Augusta,* under way to Europe once more for the first time since 1918.

10

Summer of Decision

Today's prime fact is war.

—HENRY L. STIMSON

I

Truman was accustomed to looking after himself on his travels. He had always bought his own train tickets, carried his own bags, paid his own hotel bills. Traveling by automobile, he liked to be the one to decide which route to take and where to stop for the night. In the glove compartment of the gray Chrysler were the logs he kept, thin little paperbound notebooks of the kind given away at Standard Oil gas stations. He made careful note of mileage and expenses, recorded that 10 gallons of gas at Roanoke had cost $2.25, or that lunch in Nashville was 45 cents, or that on the drive from Connecticut Avenue to 219 North Delaware Street he put 1,940 miles on the car. Even on campaign swings, with Fred Canfil along, he had preferred to do his own driving and make his own arrangements, which was why traveling now as President was such a change for him.

He could do almost nothing on his own any longer. Everything had to be planned for him. Hundreds of people had to be involved, as he had learned on the trip to San Francisco. For him to go anywhere was "like moving a circus," he said. So to transport him overseas was a production of phenomenal proportions. For the conference at Potsdam, the State Department, War Department, Army, Navy, and Air Corps, the White House staff and Secret Service were all involved. As were the British and the Russians. Just his own immediate party, a fraction of the total, numbered fifty-three, and the 10,000-ton cruiser *Augusta* that carried him across the Atlantic went accompanied by the light cruiser *Philadelphia*.

405

("It seems to take two warships to get your pa across the pond," he wrote to Margaret.) At the approach to the English Channel, a British cruiser and six British destroyers were waiting to escort him past the cliffs of Dover. At Antwerp, where the *Augusta* docked on Sunday, July 15, after eight days at sea, General Eisenhower headed the welcoming delegation. Driving south to an airfield at Brussels, Truman rode in a forty-seven-car caravan along a highway patrolled by the 35th Division, his old outfit, in full battle regalia. At the airfield, the presidential plane, *The Sacred Cow,* plus two other C-54 transports were waiting to take him and his party on the final leg, a three-and-a-half-hour flight to Berlin. Beyond Frankfurt he had an escort of twenty P-47 Thunderbolts.

The Germany passing below his window was an appalling spectacle. "You who have not seen it do not know what hell looks like from the top," General Patton would say in a speech. Truman could see shattered bridges, railroads, the wreckage of factories, entire cities in ruins, a scarred, burned land where, he knew, people were living like animals among the debris, scavenging for food. The threat of disease and mass starvation hung everywhere. Hundreds of thousands of displaced, home-less, and dispossessed people wandered the country. Not Abraham Lin-coln or Woodrow Wilson or Franklin Roosevelt, not any war President in American history, had ever beheld such a panorama of devastation.

His plane put down at Gatow airfield in the blazing heat of mid-after-noon and the reception this time included Secretary Stimson, Ambas-sador Harriman, Admiral King, two Russian generals, the Russian ambassador, Gromyko, and an honor guard from the 2nd Armored Divi-sion who had been waiting in the sun since early morning. From Gatow to his final destination, a drive of ten miles through the Soviet-controlled sector, the route was lined with Russian frontier guardsmen, elite Asiatic-looking troops in green caps who stood with fixed bayonets every twenty feet, mile after mile.

The number of Americans attending the conference would be four times greater than at Yalta. Truman's entourage included Byrnes, Leahy, Bohlen, Charlie Ross, Lieutenant Elsey and Captain Frank Graham from the Map Room; a physician, Captain Alphonse McMahon; a presidential valet, Arthur Prettyman, who had served Roosevelt; a Navy photographer; eleven Navy cooks and stewards; General Vaughan, Captain Vardaman, and, once again, Fred Canfil, the U.S. Marshal of Kansas City, who was temporarily attached to the Secret Service detail as a special bodyguard for the President. (Truman would take particular delight in introducing his burly former courthouse custodian to the Russians as Marshal Canfil, a title they took to signify military rank and so showed him utmost deference.) "He was the most vigilant bodyguard a President ever had," Truman would say later. "While the conferences were going on, he would stand by a window with his arms folded and scowl out the window . · everybody who passed . . . as if he would eat them alive if they bothered the President of the United States."

Food supplies, cases of liquor and wine, were flown in. A planeload of bottled water from France arrived daily. Because a planeload of pillows went astray, everybody below the rank of major general would be sleeping without one. So that Truman could maintain private communications with Washington, the Army had spent weeks installing wireless relays and teleprinter circuits across the 100 miles of Soviet-occupied territory separating the conference site from the American sector.

Truman, Churchill, and Stalin were to be quartered in three of twenty-five large houses that had been commandeered and hurriedly refurbished in a wooded Berlin suburb called Babelsberg, beside Lake Griebnitz, three miles from Potsdam. The lakeshore community had survived comparatively undamaged and was now under the intensely watchful eye of thousands of Russian troops and security agents, in addition to swarms of British and American military guards. The green-capped Russian soldiers were everywhere, along streets and highways, at every crossroad, and along the lakefront. They would appear out of the trees, look about, then be gone again. In all, the Russian complement—military, diplomatic, and security—exceeded twenty thousand people.

Truman was staying at Number 2 Kaiserstrasse, a three-story yellow-stucco villa on the lakeshore to be known as the "Little White House." He was told it had belonged to the head of the Nazi movie industry, who had been sent to Siberia. In fact, it had been the home of a noted publisher, Gustav Müller-Grote, and his large family, whose tragic story Truman would only learn years later in an extraordinary letter from one of the sons. Built before the turn of the century, the house had been for years a gathering place for German and foreign scientists, writers, and artists.

At the end of the war my parents were still living there, as indeed they lived there their whole lives. Some of my sisters moved there with their children, as the suburb seemed to offer more security from bombings. . . . In the beginning of May the Russians arrived. Ten weeks before you entered this house, its tenants were living in constant fright and fear. By day and by night plundering Russian soldiers went in and out, raping my sisters before their own parents and children, beating up my old parents. All the furniture, wardrobes, trunks, etc. were smashed with bayonets and rifle butts, their contents spilled and destroyed in an indescribable manner. The wealth of a cultivated house was destroyed within hours.

Told only that the house was to serve a "prominent purpose," the family was ordered to pack and be gone in an hour, after which the Russians stripped it of everything, including a library of rare books and manuscripts that were hauled away with a forklift truck to fill a bomb crater. The furnishings Truman found on arrival—dark, heavy Teutonic sideboards and tables, a huge carved desk, overstuffed chairs, a grand piano—had been confiscated elsewhere and rushed in at the last minute.

An American correspondent who managed to get a look inside some weeks later called it a "nightmare of a house." It was, wrote Tania Long of *The New York Times*, "oppressive and awesome in its gloom," filled with depressing still-lifes and hideous lamps. Truman, too, would use the word "nightmare" to describe the interior, though with his interest in architecture he was bothered more by the exterior. Remembering how he had once been quartered in such places as lovely little Montigny-sur-Aube, he called the house a ruined château—ruined, he said, by a German need to cover up anything French. "They erected a couple of tombstone chimneys on each side of the porch facing the lake so they could cover up the beautiful chateau roof and tower," he wrote in his diary. "Make the place look like hell but purely German. . . ."

There were no screens in the windows, and the mosquitoes, according to several in the party, were as plentiful as at Yalta. Bathroom facilities, in the words of the official log, were "wholly inadequate."

Still, Truman thought the place adequate under the circumstances, and was not told that the former owners were living in misery only a short distance away. His second-floor suite included a bedroom, living room, large office, and a porch with a view of the lake, which was narrow and winding and looked more like a river, with the woods beyond seeming very near at hand. On the lawn that sloped down to the water's edge stood three or four American MPs in their white gloves and leggings. It was said the Russians had thrown some German soldiers into the lake who were too severely wounded to walk.

Admiral Leahy was down the hall from the President; Secretary Byrnes and Chip Bohlen on the first floor. Charlie Ross, Vaughan, Vardaman, Canfil, and the Secret Service detail were on the third floor. The Map Room was set up in an L-shaped space off the stair landing, between the first and second floors. The telephone switchboard was in the basement.

Truman arrived appearing rested and well prepared. The weather on the Atlantic had been so fair, the crossing so smooth, he had suffered not at all from seasickness. With the war in Europe over, there had been no need any longer for a zigzag course or darkened ship at night—all very different from his crossing in 1918—and this time he had the admiral's cabin. There were movies on board and a number of "satisfactory" poker games with Ross, Vaughan, and some of the wire-service reporters who had been allowed to make the trip. Truman took early morning walks on deck and with binoculars watched gunnery practice. To the family in Grandview, he wrote of meeting a seaman on board named Lawrence Truman. "He comes from Owensborough, Ky., and is the great grandson of our grandfather's brother. He's a nice boy and has green eyes just like Margaret's."

But the week at sea had been primarily a working session with Byrnes, Leahy, and Bohlen, all of whom had been closely associated with Roosevelt and at his side at Yalta. The President had squeezed facts and opinions out of them all day, Leahy later said. Bohlen, too, was struck by how Truman "stuck to business," rarely taking up time with small talk. Averell Harriman would later find the President "astonishingly well prepared."

The central issues to be resolved at Potsdam were no different from those at Yalta: the political future of Eastern Europe (and Poland in particular); the occupation and dismantling of Germany; and a commitment from Russia to help defeat Japan, which Truman viewed as his main purpose in going. General Marshall and Admiral King had both stressed the need for Soviet action against Japan, to shorten the war and reduce American casualties. General MacArthur had twice insisted that Russian help was needed.

Truman also had a pet proposal of his own for ensuring free navigation on all inland waterways and the great canals, an idea he was sure would go far to guarantee future peace in the world.

But a further extremely important reason—in many ways the most important reason—for the meeting and for all the trouble and effort of coming so far was his need to get to know the other two of the Big Three ("Mr. Russia" and "Mr. Great Britain," Truman called them), to see them face to face and size them up, and they him. As American as anything about this thoroughly American new President was his fundamental faith that most problems came down to misunderstandings between people, and that even the most complicated problems really weren't as complicated as they were made out to be, once everybody got to know one another. He knew also the faith Roosevelt had in personal diplomacy as a consequence of his two meetings with Stalin, at Teheran and Yalta.

Truman had always wanted to succeed at whatever he undertook. There was no one who wanted to win "half so badly as I do," he had confided to Bess years before, and he had not changed. He knew the value of preparation, of homework—especially if he felt out of his depth, if he were thrown in among and were to be judged by others who appeared to know so much more. "I've studied more and worked harder in the last three weeks than I ever did in my life," he had written in 1918 from the elite artillery school at Montigny-sur-Aube, where everyone else in the class was a college graduate. "I'm going to be better informed on the transportation problem than anyone here," he had vowed after coming to the Senate.

But from boyhood he also prided himself in his gift for conversation. Given the chance to talk to people, he felt he could get pretty much anything he wanted. "Haven't you ever been overawed by a secretary," he had remarked only recently to a visitor in his office, "and finally, when you have reached the man you wanted to see, discovered he was very human?" He was sure that if he could meet Stalin and deal with him, then he could get to know Stalin and understand him; in this, like so many others before him, he was greatly mistaken.

On visits to Washington to see Roosevelt during the war, Winston Churchill had made a point of meeting those senators who were known to have influence. The junior Senator from Missouri, however, had not been on the prime minister's list. So, while Truman and Churchill had maintained steady correspondence in recent months, and talked by phone, the morning of Monday, July 16, 1945, when the familiar stout figure arrived at Number 2 Kaiserstrasse, marked their first meeting. Churchill had wanted his call on the President to be the first order of business. Truman had named the hour—11:00 A.M.—and Churchill arrived on the dot.

Churchill, too, had landed at Gatow the previous afternoon and was staying in a comparably large, if more attractive, lakeside house nearby. With him now were Foreign Secretary Anthony Eden, whom Truman had met, Sir Alexander Cadogan, the Permanent Under Secretary of Foreign Affairs, and the prime minister's daughter and driver, Mary Churchill, who was dressed in the uniform of a junior commander in the Auxiliary Territorial Service and who told Harry Vaughan her father had not been up this early in ten years.

Nor had Churchill prepared himself for the Big Three conference in anything like the way Truman had. He had bothered with no briefings, he came with no agenda. He required neither, he felt. He had spent a holiday near Biarritz painting, as his way of preparing for Potsdam.

Churchill was in the seventy-first year of a life in which he had seen and done more than all but a few. He had been a cavalry officer, foreign correspondent, a prisoner of war in South Africa, head of the British

Board of Trade, and First Lord of the Admiralty as early as 1911. He was the author of nineteen books, a painter, husband, father, ardent holiday bricklayer. Once, needing cash, he made $50,000 on a lecture tour in just five months. Born in a palace, he was the son of a lord, the grandson of a duke. His mother, as everyone knew, was an American, the brilliant, beautiful Jenny Jerome of New York. In politics he had begun as a Conservative, changed to a Liberal, switched back to a Conservative again. He had overcome political defeat and disgrace, survived his own recurring dark moods, and being struck down and nearly killed by an automobile in New York. As prime minister through the war, as the pungent, indomitable voice of British resolve, he had become the British lion incarnate, and the great words were *his* words, not the artifice of a ghost. "The nation had the lion's heart," he would say. "I had the luck to give the roar."

The scowl, the familiar upraised V-sign and jutting cigar, his command of the English language had made him a surpassing symbol and clearly one of the great figures of the age. If asked who in the world they most admired, now that Roosevelt was gone, most Americans would have said Churchill, and probably, after some thought, Truman would have, too. Yet the prospect of sharing the spotlight with such a man was extremely unsettling. Behind all of Truman's privately expressed apprehension over coming to Berlin was a great deal of plain stage fright—anxiety accentuated by memories of Churchill and Roosevelt together, posing for pictures, commanding attention and affection as few men ever had, and always with perfect confidence and obvious regard for one another. Roosevelt and Churchill had met nine times and exchanged, by Churchill's count, 1,700 messages. On visits at the White House, the prime minister had made himself so at home that Mrs. Roosevelt decided it was time an official guest residence be established, which led to the acquisition of Blair House. (If one favorite Washington story can be believed, she had found the prime minister padding down the hall in his nightshirt sometime before dawn one morning, a cigar and brandy in hand, saying he had still more to discuss with Franklin and must wake him at once.) He and Roosevelt saw the history of their times as Homeric drama and they the lead players, two professionals perfectly cast and at the top of their form.

"It is fun to be in the same decade with you," Roosevelt had told him, and in a recent letter to Truman, Eleanor Roosevelt had written how important it was that he get along with Winston. He should talk to him about books, she advised, or let him quote from his marvelous memory of everything from nonsense rhymes to Greek tragedy.

But Churchill had aged. He looked old, he sounded tired and disheartened. The empire he had led with such verve was nearly bankrupt, a great power no longer. On July 5, there had been a general election, the result of which would not be known for another ten days, when the soldier vote was in. The election could have been put off, but Churchill had gone ahead with it on the advice that his popularity was at a peak. While others were confident his victory would be substantial, he, privately, was not so sure.

It would become part of the mythology of the Truman presidency in time to come that Churchill, at their first meeting, thought little of Truman, an idea amplified by Churchill himself in a famous toast years later on board the presidential yacht. "I must confess, sir, I held you in very low regard," he would begin. "I loathed your taking the place of Franklin Roosevelt. . . ." But in fact Truman made a strong impression from the start. They talked for two hours, and, according to Truman, no business of the conference was considered; but walking back to his own quarters afterward, Churchill told his daughter how much he liked the new President. "He says he is sure he can work with him," Mary Churchill wrote to her mother. "I nearly wept with joy and thankfulness, it seemed like divine providence. Perhaps it is FDR's legacy. I can see Papa is relieved and confident."

Asked later by his friend and physician, Lord Moran, if Truman had ability, Churchill replied that he thought so. "At any rate, he is a man of immense determination," Churchill said. "He takes no notice of delicate ground, he just plants his foot down firmly upon it." To make his point, Churchill jumped a little off the wooden floor and brought both bare feet down with a smack.

Truman's impressions, recorded at the day's end in his diary, were not so favorable, however. As the White House butler, Alonzo Fields, had noted, commenting on Bess, flattery did not go far with the Trumans.

> We had a most pleasant conversation [Truman wrote of Churchill]. He is a most charming and a very clever person—meaning clever in the English not the Kentucky sense. He gave me a lot of hooey about how great my country is and how he loved Roosevelt and how he intended to love me etc. etc. Well. . . . I am sure we can get along if he doesn't try to give me too much soft soap.

Stalin, meanwhile, was nowhere to be seen. Where he was, or why, were not known, but the opening of the conference had to be postponed a day.

• • •

In the time since Truman had left Washington, the Japanese ambassador in Moscow, Naotake Sato, on orders from Tokyo, had begun discussions with the Soviets on the possibility of bringing an end to the war. On July 12, the Japanese Minister of Foreign Affairs, Shigenori Togo, sent a "Very Secret, Urgent" radio message to Ambassador Sato stating that the Emperor was "greatly concerned over the daily increasing calamities and sacrifices faced by the citizens of the various belligerent countries" and that it was "His Majesty's heart's desire to see the swift termination of the war." His Majesty wished to send Prince Konoye as a special envoy to Moscow to talk.

Sato responded that it was pointless talking about peace with the Soviets. Such proposed negotiations were entirely unrealistic, he stressed. Molotov was not interested. "In the final analysis," Sato bluntly told Togo, "if our country truly desires to terminate the war, we have no alternative but to accept unconditional surrender or something very close to it."

The messages were intercepted by American monitors (the Japanese code having been broken years before) and promptly reached Truman. And so, importantly, did Tokyo's repeated warnings to Sato that Japan would not consent to unconditional surrender.

Also available to the President was a Combined Intelligence Committee report warning that the Japanese might try to cause dissension among the Allies by just such peace overtures. And even had there been no such warning, there was for Truman, as for others trying to appraise the situation, the bitter memory of Japanese peace talks in Washington in December 1941 at the very time of the attack at Pearl Harbor.

On the afternoon of the 16th, his schedule open, Truman decided to see Berlin. A motorcade assembled in the drive outside Number 2 Kaiserstrasse and in ten minutes, with Byrnes and Leahy beside him in the back seat of an open Lincoln, he was speeding down the empty four-lane Autobahn. The day was stifling hot and the wind came as a great relief.

Halfway to the city they met the entire American 2nd Armored Division deployed for his inspection along one side of the highway, a double row of Sherman tanks and halftracks reaching as far as the eye could see. The motorcade drew up, Truman got out. It was the largest armored division in the world, he was told, and a spectacle of military power such as he might only have imagined until now. He climbed into a halftrack, and to review the formation rode standing, slowly, for twenty minutes, down a line of soldiers and equipment for a mile and a half—"good soldiers and millions of dollars of equipment, which has amply paid its way to Berlin," he thought.

Heading on, the motorcade passed miles of ruin and desolation, bomb craters, blackened burned-out buildings, and seemingly endless processions of homeless Germans plodding along beside the highway carrying or dragging bundles of pathetic belongings. They were mostly old people and children who appeared to be headed nowhere in particular, with nothing but blank expressions on their faces, no anger, no grief, no fear, which Truman found extremely disturbing. At the end of the last war, when the President of the United States, Woodrow Wilson, came to Paris, exuberant crowds had acclaimed him as a hero and savior. Now most of those trudging past never bothered even to look up.

In the center of Berlin, or what had been Berlin, the world's fourth largest city and capital of the Reich that was to have lasted a thousand years, the small presidential caravan moved down the famous old streets —Bismarckstrasse, Berlinerstrasse, and Unter den Linden, where the once celebrated Linden trees were no more. The Russians had cleared the main thoroughfares with bulldozers. Rubble on all sides was heaped two and three stories high, between the windowless, roofless hulks of bomb-gutted buildings. Everything was black with soot, and in the oppressive heat the smell of death and open sewers was nearly overpowering.

American and British bombers had laid waste to the city around the clock. Probably fifty thousand people had been killed, five times as many as in the London *Blitz*. Then, in April, came the Russian artillery and the Russian Army.

On Wilhelmstrasse, Truman's car pulled up beside the Reich Chancellery and the shell-blasted stone balcony where Hitler had harangued his Nazi followers. Truman did not get out. "It is a terrible thing," he began, knowing he was expected to say something, "but they brought it on themselves. That's what happens when a man overreaches himself." It was all he could find to say.

He saw the Brandenburg Gate and the wreckage of the Tiergarten, the city's once beautiful central park. In 1939, to honor his fiftieth birthday, Hitler had paraded columns of troops and tanks here, before a crowd of 2 million cheering Berliners.

Slowly the motorcade moved on, winding past the ruins of the Sports Palace, where huge crowds had shouted "Hail, the Führer," and "Leader, command, we follow," as Propaganda Minister Goebbels asked if they were true believers in the "final total victory" of the German people; then past the giant, gutted Reichstag, seat of parliament, where a fire set by the Nazis in 1933 and blamed on the Communists had given Hitler the excuse he needed to seize dictatorial power.

Despite all they had read, all they had been told in advance, the photographs and newsreels they had seen, the visiting Americans were unprepared for the reality of conquered Berlin. "I never saw such destruction," recorded Truman, who had seen his share in 1918. It was "absolute ruin." To Admiral Leahy, whose military career had begun with the famous voyage of the old *Oregon* around the Horn to Cuba in 1898, it was a calamity against the civilized laws of war. At a notably subdued dinner that night they talked quietly among themselves of the horrible destructiveness of modern war, now "brought home," as Leahy said, "to those of us who fought the war from Washington." Truman was as low as he had felt in a long time.

> I thought of Carthage, Baalbek, Jerusalem, Rome, Atlantis, Peking... [of] Scipio, Rameses II . . . Sherman, Jenghiz Khan [he wrote that night in his diary]. . . . I hope for some sort of peace—but I fear that machines are ahead of morals by some centuries and when morals catch up there'll be no reason for any of it.

He kept thinking of the devastated people he had seen wandering in the debris. But they had brought it on themselves, they did it, he would write to Bess.

Churchill, on a tour of Berlin of his own that afternoon, had spent half an hour exploring the Chancellery, the site of Hitler's bunker. ("This is what would have happened to us if *they* had won the war," Churchill was heard to say. "We would have been the bunker.") Truman had not wished to walk among the ruins, he said, because he would never want those unfortunate people to think he was gloating over them.

Because the reporters who had come to Berlin to cover the conference were excluded from all transactions of importance, denied access to the participants or even to the compound at Babelsberg, and provided with only occasional press releases by Charlie Ross, they had often to concoct stories from very little. Anne O'Hare McCormick speculated in a column for *The New York Times* that the mysterious Joseph Stalin, too, must have been there somewhere in Berlin that same afternoon, but had kept his presence unknown. It was hard to imagine the Soviet Generalissimo not wanting to survey the conquered city, she wrote, and she described all three men stalking about in the dust and wreckage.

> There are moments when the drama of our times seems to focus on a single scene. The meeting at Potsdam is one of those moments. We can hardly take in the sense of what happened until it is spelled

out in a picture like this. The picture of three men walking in a grave-yard. They are the men who hold in their hands most of the power in the world. . . .

Yet the devastation of Berlin was small scale compared to what had become possible that same afternoon of Monday, July 16. What Truman did not yet know, what none of them knew, was that at a remote part of the Alamogordo Air Base in the desert of New Mexico, at 5:29 in the morning (1:29 in the afternoon in Berlin) there had been a blinding flash, "a light not of this world," from the first nuclear explosion in history. Stimson received word at his Babelsberg quarters that evening at 7:30, a top-secret telegram from George Harrison in Washington, which Stimson took directly to Truman.

"Operated on this morning," it said. "Diagnosis not yet complete but results seem satisfactory and already exceed expectations." Details would follow.

II

"Promptly a few minutes before twelve, I looked up from the desk and there stood Stalin in the doorway," wrote the President in his diary.

It was midday, Tuesday, July 17, and from the high window behind Truman's shoulder, sunlight streamed into the room. A gilt-framed Victorian still-life of fruit and a dead duck hung over a small marble mantel-piece. His desk—a monstrous, deeply carved affair with huge clawed feet —had been positioned at an angle, facing the door, in the corner of a large Oriental rug. With the Generalissimo were Molotov and the inter-preter, Pavlov.

Stalin had arrived the night before and was staying in a thickly wooded area closer to Potsdam, but this, like the time of his arrival and the fact that he had traveled by train more than 1,000 miles from the Kremlin, were all kept secret. It was said he had been detained by official business. The truth was he came late primarily to accentuate his own importance.

Had Truman been outside waiting for Stalin's arrival, he would have seen a dozen heavily armed Russian guards materialize out of nowhere and surround the house, then, in minutes, the appearance of a long, closed Packard with bulletproof glass so thick that the figures inside were only a blur. As Stalin got out of the car, Harry Vaughan came bounding down the front steps to greet him like a fellow Rotarian, as George Elsey remembered. The Russian guards outside the yellow house were not quite sure what to do.

"I got to my feet and advanced to meet him," continues Truman's diary account. "He put out his hand and smiled. I did the same, we shook, I greeted Molotov and the interpreter. . . ."

Joseph Vissarionovich Djugashvili—Stalin, "the Man of Steel"—was the single most powerful figure in the world. He was the absolute dictator over 180 million people of 170 nationalities in a country representing one sixth of the earth's surface, the Generalissimo of gigantic, victorious armies, and Harry Truman, like nearly everyone meeting him for the first time, was amazed to find how small he was. "A little bit of a squirt," Truman described him, Stalin standing about 5 feet 5.

He was dressed simply in a lightweight khaki uniform with red epaulets and red seams down the trousers, and he wore no decorations except a single red-ribboned gold star, the Order of the Hero of the Soviet, over the left breast pocket, which gave him a kind of understated authority. His small, squinty eyes were a strange yellow-gray and there were streaks of gray in his mustache and coarse hair. He was badly pockmarked, his color poor—he had what in high Soviet circles was known as "Kremlin complexion," an unhealthy, indoor pallor made worse by a recent illness —and his very irregular teeth were darkly tobacco-stained. Truman had been told of his crippled left arm, the result of a childhood accident, but this was not especially noticeable. A chain smoker, Stalin held his cigarette in his right hand and gestured with his right hand only. He had unusually large, powerful-looking hands—hands as hard as his mind, Harry Hopkins once said.

Bohlen, who was standing by to translate for Truman, thought Stalin had aged greatly in just the few weeks since he and Hopkins had met with him in Moscow. Stalin moved slowly, stiffly, spoke little and in a very low tone. To Truman he seemed an old man, yet there was less than five years difference in their age. Born in abject poverty in Georgia in 1879, Stalin was the son of a semi-literate, drunken shoemaker and a doting mother who took in laundry. Initially, before turning revolutionary, he had studied for the priesthood.

Truman, in his freshly pressed double-breasted gray suit and two-toned summer shoes, looked a picture of vitality by contrast.

They sat in overstuffed chairs, flanked by Byrnes, Molotov, Bohlen, and Pavlov. Truman told Stalin he had been looking forward to their meeting for a long time. Stalin agreed solemnly that such personal contact was of great importance. In an effort to ease the tension, Byrnes asked Stalin about his habit of sleeping late. Stalin said only that the war had changed many of his habits. Truman tried an informal reference to Stalin as Uncle Joe, the nickname Roosevelt had used, but this too fell flat with the humorless Russian.

Truman said he hoped to deal with Stalin as a friend. He was no diplomat, Truman went on. He would not beat around the bush. He usually said yes or no to questions after hearing all the argument. Only then did Stalin appear pleased.

They talked briefly of the defeat of Germany, Stalin saying he was sure Hitler was alive and in hiding somewhere in Spain or Argentina. Then, abruptly, and entirely on his own initiative, Stalin said that as they had agreed at Yalta, the Soviets would be ready to declare war on Japan and attack Manchuria by mid-August. He had already assured the Chinese that Russia recognized Manchuria as part of China and that there would be no Soviet interference with internal political matters there.

Truman said he was extremely pleased. But Stalin, as if to be sure Truman understood, repeated that by the middle of August the Red Army would be in the war with Japan, "as agreed at Yalta," to which Truman expressed his every confidence that the Soviets would keep their word.

At this point Harry Vaughan slipped into the room to ask Truman in a whisper if he was going to invite "these guys" to lunch.

What was on the menu, Truman whispered. Liver and bacon, Vaughan said. "If liver and bacon is good enough for us, it's good enough for them," Truman replied.

When he asked Stalin to stay, Stalin protested, saying it would be impossible. "You could if you wanted to," Truman said. And Stalin stayed—for creamed spinach soup, liver and bacon, baked ham, Julienne potatoes, string beans, pumpernickel bread, jam, sliced fruit, mints, candy, cigars, which Stalin declined, and a California wine that he went out of his way to praise.

Truman thought the whole occasion went well, exactly because it was so spur of the moment and informal. He liked Stalin, he decided, "and I felt hopeful that we could reach an agreement satisfactory to the world and to ourselves."

But Stalin nearly always made a good impression on foreigners. Churchill, who once called Russia "a riddle wrapped in a mystery inside an enigma," and who warned both Roosevelt and Truman repeatedly of the Russian menace to Europe, confessed still to liking Stalin the man. Roosevelt had been convinced almost to the end that he could get along with "Uncle Joe." "The truth is," wrote Jimmy Byrnes, recalling Stalin's performance at Yalta, "he is a very likeable person." Joseph E. Davies, who had been ambassador to Russia briefly and would be at Truman's side daily at the Potsdam conference table, had said in a superficial and immensely popular book, *Mission to Moscow,* published in 1941, that Stalin was uncommonly wise and gentle. "A child would like to sit on his lap and a dog would sidle up to him," wrote Davies. Even Eisenhower, after a visit to Moscow later that summer, would describe Stalin in much the same fashion, as "benign and fatherly."

Truman, as he wrote, found Stalin to be polite, good-natured, business-like, "honest—but smart as hell." There had been not a hint of contention between them. The conference hadn't even begun, yet already Truman had achieved his main objective, as he recorded triumphantly in his diary. "He'll be in the Jap War on August 15. Fini Japs when that comes about. . . . I can deal with Stalin."

That Stalin was also secretive to the point of imbalance, suspicious, deceitful, unspeakably cruel, that he ruled absolutely and by terror and secret police, that he was directly responsible for destroying millions of his own people and the enslavement of many millions more, was not so clearly understood by the outside world at this point as it would be later. Still, the evil of the man was no secret in 1945. In a February issue, published just before Yalta, *Time* magazine had noted that Stalin and his regime had deliberately caused the deaths by starvation of at least 3 million peasants and liquidated another 1 million Communists who opposed his policies. Facts are stubborn things, said the article, borrowing a line from Lenin, and these were the facts. Actually the facts were more horrible. Probably 5 million peasants had died; probably 10 million had been sent to forced labor camps. "I was remembering my friends," the composer Shostakovich once remarked, "and all I saw was corpses, mountains of corpses."

Stalin himself had told Churchill in 1942 that "ten millions" of peasants had been "dealt with." At one point in 1940, during the Hitler-Stalin Pact, he had had many thousands of Polish officers murdered, in what became known as the Katyn Forest Massacre. In truth, "Uncle Joe" was one of the great mass murderers of all time, as much as Ivan the Terrible (his favorite czar), as much nearly as Adolf Hitler.

Yet, wrote Bohlen, "There was little in Stalin's demeanor in the presence of foreigners that gave any clue of the real nature and character of the man." Stalin had perfected a talent for disguise:

At Teheran, at Yalta, at Potsdam and during the ten days I saw him during the spring of 1945 with Hopkins, Stalin was exemplary in his behavior. He was patient, a good listener, always quiet in his manner and in his expression. There were no signs of the harsh and brutal nature behind this mask. . . .

The mask was the artifice of an accomplished actor and it rarely slipped. Once was at Teheran. Churchill had been arguing that a premature opening of a second front in France would result in an unjustified loss of tens of thousands of Allied soldiers. Stalin responded, "When one man dies it is a tragedy. When thousands die it's statistics."

Twenty years in politics had taught him a thing or two about people, Truman thought. He had only to look a man in the eye to know. "I was impressed by him," he would write of Stalin, remembering this first meeting. ". . . What I most especially noticed were his eyes, his face, and his expression."

With the lunch over and the opening session of the conference not scheduled to begin until five o'clock, Truman went upstairs in the "nightmare" house and took a nap.

III

The first of the plenary sessions of the Potsdam Conference, last of the wartime meetings of the Big Three, code-named "Terminal," was held in the Cecilienhof Palace at Potsdam, the former summer residence of Crown Prince Wilhelm of Prussia, which had served more recently as a military hospital, first for the Germans, then the Russians. A sprawling two-story, ivy-covered stone building in the neo-Tudor style, it looked very like a vast English country house, with gardens extending to the lake and an inner court where the Russians had planted a giant star of red geraniums.

The oak-paneled reception hall, a cavernous, dim space lit by heavy wrought-iron chandeliers, served as the conference room. The color scheme was dark red, black, and gold, and the effect rather foreboding, except for one immense window two stories tall looking onto the gardens and lake.

At the center of the room was a circular conference table 12 feet in diameter, covered in a burgundy cloth, and around it, evenly spaced, were fifteen chairs, five each for the three countries. The three chairs reserved for Churchill, Stalin, and Truman were immediately identifiable by their larger size and an incongruous pair of gilded cupids perched on the back of each. Additional chairs and several small desks were arranged in a larger circle behind, these for other members of the delegation, advisers and specialists, who would come and go as different topics arose.

To enter the room, the three leaders had their own separate doors, each of these heavily guarded by Russian soldiers. When everybody was assembled, the guards withdrew, the doors were closed.

Though wearing the same gray suit as earlier, Truman had put on a fresh white shirt and a bow tie. Churchill, like Stalin, was in a summer-weight khaki uniform and as they took their places, he lit up an eight-inch cigar. Stalin was carrying a briefcase, which he tossed onto the table, as if to say he was ready for business.

Truman sat with Byrnes and Leahy on his right, Bohlen and Davies on the left. In Churchill's group now was Clement Attlee, Churchill's Labor Party opponent in the general election, whom the prime minister had decided to include in the national interest, in the event that Attlee turned out to be his successor.

"Never in history has such an aggregation of victorious military force been represented at one conference," wrote *The New York Times;* "never has there been a meeting which faced graver or more complex issues; and never have three mortal men borne so heavy a responsibility for the welfare of their peoples and mankind."

No correspondents for the *Times* were present, however, nor any of the nearly two hundred other reporters who had made their way to Berlin to cover the story and were, as Churchill said, "in a state of furious indignation." For the "lid was on" at Potsdam, "everything conducted behind a ring of bayonets," as Stalin had insisted. Even the number of authorized people permitted in the room at any one time was strictly limited. Once when Byrnes's secretary brought him some papers and had to wait a few minutes, two women from the Russian staff entered immediately and took chairs until she left.

The conference was officially called to order at 5:10 P.M. Stalin spoke first, saying that President Truman, as the only head of state present, should preside. Churchill seconded the proposal. Truman expressed his appreciation. Then, as in his first speech to Congress, he plunged directly into his prepared remarks, moving rapidly down an item-by-item order of business that he thought the conference should follow. He proposed the establishment of a Council of Foreign Ministers to make the necessary preparations for a peace conference. Immediately Stalin was dubious, questioning any participation by China in a European peace settlement. Truman submitted a draft on how the administration of Germany should be handled. Churchill said he had had no opportunity to examine it. Truman read a prepared statement on implementation of the Yalta Declaration, which pledged the three powers to assist the people of all liberated European countries to establish democratic governments through free election. He was wasting no time getting to the sorest of subjects. "Since the Yalta Conference," he read, "the obligations assumed under this declaration have not been carried out." Of particular concern were Romania, Bulgaria, and Greece. Again Churchill said he needed time to consider the document.

Truman moved quickly on, calling for a change in policy toward Italy. As soon as possible, Italy must be included in the United Nations. Churchill now protested and to make his point invoked the memory of Roosevelt. They were trying to deal with too many important matters too hastily, said Churchill. He reminded Truman that Italy had attacked Britain at the time France was going down, and that Roosevelt himself had called this a stab in the back. The British had fought the Italians for two years in Africa before American forces ever arrived.

Truman paused, as if brought up short by the mere mention of Roosevelt.

Speaking more slowly now, he said he appreciated the honor of having been made chairman of the meeting. He had come to the conference with certain trepidation, he said. He had to replace a man who was irreplaceable. He knew full well the goodwill and friendship Roosevelt had achieved with the prime minister and the Generalissimo, both for himself and for the United States, and he, Harry Truman, hoped he might merit the same friendship and goodwill as time went on. It was simply and well expressed and what he should have said at the start, and the atmosphere changed at once, as Churchill responded in fulsome, Churchillian fashion. Though no official verbatim record was being kept, Llewellyn Thompson, from the American Embassy in London, and Ben Cohen of Byrnes's staff were both taking notes:

> Churchill [recorded Thompson] said he should like to express on behalf of the British delegation his gratitude to the President for undertaking the Presidency of this momentous Conference and to thank him for presenting so clearly the views of the mighty republic which he heads. The warm and ineffaceable sentiments which they had for President Roosevelt they would renew with the man who had come forward at this historic moment and he wished to express to him his most cordial respect. He trusted that the bonds not only between their countries but also between them personally would increase. The more they came to grips with the world's momentous problems the closer their association would become.

On behalf of the Russian delegation, said Stalin, he wished to say they "fully shared" the sentiments expressed by the prime minister.

It was a pattern that would prevail, Churchill rumbling on, Stalin being as direct and to-the-point as Truman.

Taking his turn now, his voice very low, Stalin spoke in short segments, leaving ample pauses between, as one practiced in working with an interpreter. He wished to discuss acquisition of the German Navy (which was then in British hands), German reparations, the question of trusteeships for the Soviet Union (by which he meant colonies), the future of Franco Spain, and the future of Poland.

Churchill agreed that the Polish question was foremost, but said the agenda for the next session should be left to the foreign ministers to decide (Eden, Byrnes, and Molotov). Stalin and Truman concurred.

"So tomorrow we will have prepared the points most agreeable," said Churchill.

"All the same, we will not escape the disagreeable," countered Stalin.

"We will feel our way up to them," said Churchill, who was ready to stop for the day.

Stalin turned again to the question of including China in preparations for the peace conference. Churchill thought it a needless complication to bring in China. Perhaps the matter could be referred to the foreign ministers, suggested Stalin, playing Churchill's game now. If the foreign secretaries decided to leave China out, said Truman, he had no objections.

"As all the questions are to be discussed by the foreign ministers, we shall have nothing to do," observed Stalin, producing the first laughter at the table.

Churchill thought the foreign ministers ought to provide three or four points for discussion per day, "enough to keep us busy."

Truman was on edge. This wasn't at all what he had come for. "I don't want to discuss," he said, "I want to decide."

"You want something in the bag each day," Churchill responded, as if he were just now beginning to understand the new American President.

Yes, and next time he wished to begin at an earlier hour, Truman said.

"I will obey your orders," responded Churchill, and at once Stalin stepped in, his eyes on Churchill.

"If you are in such an obedient mood today, Mr. Prime Minister, I should like to know whether you will share with us the German fleet?"

The fleet should either be shared or destroyed, exclaimed Churchill. Weapons of war were horrible things.

"Let's divide it," said Stalin. "If Mr. Churchill wishes, he can sink his share."

The Foreign Secretary thought the prime minister's performance had been pathetic. The "P.M." was "woolly and verbose," and too much under Stalin's spell, noted Anthony Eden, and he let others know, which annoyed Truman, who took it as an act of disloyalty to Churchill. Alexander Cadogan, in a letter to his wife, said the P.M. simply talked too much, while Truman was admirably businesslike.

It had made presiding over the Senate seem tame, Truman wrote to Bess, clearly pleased with himself and with the comments of his staff.

> The boys say I gave them an earful. I hope so. Admiral Leahy said he'd never seen an abler job and Byrnes and my fellows seemed to be walking on air. I was so scared I didn't know whether things were going according to Hoyle or not. Anyway a start has been made and I've gotten what I came for—Stalin goes to war August 15 with no strings on it. . . . I'll say that we'll end the war a year sooner now, and think of the kids who won't be killed! That is the important thing. . . .
> Wish you and Margie were here. But it is a forlorn place and would only make you sad.

The letter was written early on July 18 before the day began. To his mother and sister he wrote, "Churchill talks all the time and Stalin just grunts but you know what he means."

Mamma and Mary Jane had already written six times since he left Washington and he would keep them posted through the entire conference. This morning he had news he knew they would like. Sergeant Harry Truman, Vivian's oldest son, had joined him for breakfast.

> He was on the *Queen Elizabeth* at Glasgow, ready to sail [for New York]. I told them to give him the choice of coming to the conference or going home. He elected to come and see me. I gave him a pass to Berlin signed by Stalin and by me. Will send him home by plane and he'll get there almost as soon as if he'd gone on the *Elizabeth*. He sure is a fine looking soldier, stands up, dresses the part and I'm proud of him.

About mid-morning, Henry Stimson came in looking extremely excited. A second cable from George Harrison had arrived during the night:

> Doctor had just returned most enthusiastic and confident that the little boy is as husky as his big brother. The light in his eyes discernible from here to Highhold and I could have heard his screams from here to my farm.

The decoding officer at the Army message center had been amazed, assuming that the elderly Secretary of War had become a new father. Stimson explained the cable to Truman. The flash at Alamogordo had been visible for 250 miles (the distance from Washington to Highhold, Stimson's estate on Long Island), the sound carrying 50 miles (the distance to Harrison's farm in Virginia). Truman appeared extremely pleased and at lunch with Churchill, at Churchill's house, Number 23 Ringstrasse, he showed him the two telegrams. Stalin ought to be told, Truman offered. Churchill agreed that Stalin should know "the Great New Fact," but none of "the particulars." Better to tell him sooner than later, Churchill suggested. But how? In writing or by word of mouth? At a special meeting or informally?

Truman thought it best just to tell him after one of the meetings. He would wait for the right moment, Truman said.

They were dining alone. Churchill lamented the melancholy state of Great Britain, with its staggering debt and declining influence in the world. Truman said the United States owed Britain much for having "held the fort" at the beginning of the war. "If you had gone down like France," Truman told Churchill, "we might be fighting the Germans on the American coast at the present time."

They talked of the war in the Pacific and Churchill pondered whether new wording might be devised so that the Japanese could surrender and yet salvage some sense of their military honor. Truman countered by saying he did not think the Japanese had any military honor, not after Pearl Harbor. Churchill said that "at any rate they had something for which they were ready to face certain death in very large numbers, and this might not be so important to us as it was to them." At this Truman turned "quite sympathetic," as Churchill recounted, and began talking of "the terrible responsibilities upon him in regard to unlimited effusion of American blood."

"He invited personal friendship and comradeship," Churchill wrote. "He seems a man of exceptional character. . . ."

From the Churchill lunch Truman went to pay a return call on Stalin, accompanied now by Byrnes and Bohlen, and to his surprise found a second lunch waiting, an elaborate meal in his honor, which in Russian fashion called for numerous toasts.

Stalin told Truman of the secret Japanese peace feeler and passed the Sato message across the table. It might be best, said Stalin, to "lull the Japanese to sleep," to say their request for a visit by Prince Konoye was too vague to answer. Truman said nothing to indicate he already knew of the Japanese overtures. He would leave the answer up to Stalin, he said.

Bohlen would remember Stalin's disclosure of the Japanese proposal making a very great impression on Truman, as a sign the Russians might be ready after all to deal openly with them. To his delight Truman also discovered that Stalin, the supreme Soviet strong-man, was substitut-

ing white wine for what was supposedly vodka in his glass. The Generalissimo must visit the United States, Truman said. If Stalin would come,
Truman promised, he would send the battleship *Missouri* for him.

> He said he wanted to cooperate with U.S. in peace as we had coopera-
> ted in war but it would be harder [Truman recorded later]. Said he was
> grossly misunderstood in U.S. and I was misunderstood in Russia. I
> told him that we each could remedy that situation in our home coun-
> tries and that I intended to try with all I had to do my part at home. He
> gave me a most cordial smile and said he would do as much in Russia.

As the conference resumed that afternoon Churchill again grew extremely long-winded, and though an outward show of friendship continued around the table, an edge of tension could also be felt. In an
exchange with Truman, in a single sentence, Stalin hit on the hard reality
underlying nearly every issue before them, the crux of so much of the
frustration and divisiveness to come:

"We cannot get away from the results of the war," said Stalin.

The formal business was to be Germany and Truman had suggested
they begin at once. Churchill insisted on defining what was meant by
Germany. If it meant Germany as geographically constituted before the
war, then he agreed to discussion—his obvious point being that the
Germany of the moment was one with eastern boundaries being determined by the position of the Red Army.

> STALIN: Germany is what has become of her after the war. No other
> Germany exists. . . .
> TRUMAN: Why not say the Germany of 1937?
> STALIN: Minus what she has lost. Let us for the time being regard Ger-
> many as a geographical section.
> TRUMAN: But what geographical section?
> STALIN: We cannot get away from the results of the war.
> TRUMAN: But we must have a starting point.

Stalin agreed. Churchill agreed. "So it is agreed that the Germany of
1937 should be the starting point," said Truman, as if they had made a
major step forward.

They turned to Poland, a subject that moved Churchill to talk longer
even than usual, and so went the remainder of the session.

Truman was exasperated. He could "deal" with Stalin, as he said, but
Churchill was another matter. "I'm not going to stay around this terrible
place all summer just to listen to speeches," he wrote that night. To Bess,

426

earlier in the day, he had said Stalin's agreement to join in defeating Japan was what he came for. Now, his patience low at day's end, he wrote in his diary, "Believe Japs will fold up before Russia comes in. I am sure they will when Manhattan [the Manhattan Project, S-1] appears over their homeland."

At session three the day after, there was sharp talk across the table, much of it from Truman. When the subject of the German Navy was raised again, he said he agreed to dividing the ships three ways, but only after the surrender of Japan. Merchant ships especially were needed. "We will need every bomb and every ton of food." On the future of Franco Spain, a sore subject with Stalin, Truman said he had no love for Franco, nor had he any wish to take part in another civil war in Spain. "There have been enough wars in Europe." When the Yalta Declaration came up, Stalin insisted such matters be put off until another time.

Truman was impatient for progress of almost any kind. He was homesick, "sick of the whole business," he confided to Bess.

The day was saved only by the party he gave that night, a banquet for Churchill and Stalin at Number 2 Kaiserstrasse with music provided by a twenty-seven-year-old American concert pianist, Sergeant Eugene List, who was accompanied on the violin by Private First Class Stuart Canin. Stalin was charmed. To the Americans present it would remain the most memorable evening of the conference.

The two musicians, both in uniform, had been flown in from Paris at Truman's request. The grand piano had been moved onto the back porch overlooking the lake, where, after dinner, in the lingering light of the summer evening, the whole party gathered. At one point Truman himself played Paderewski's Minuet in G, the piece Paderewski had demonstrated for him in Kansas City forty-five years earlier. But the highlight was Sergeant List's performance of the Chopin Waltz in A Minor, Opus 42, which Truman had asked for specifically. List had not known the piece nor had there been time to learn it. Later, in a letter to his wife, he described what happened when he asked if someone in the audience would be good enough to turn the pages of the music for him.

> A young captain in the party started toward the piano mumbling something about not knowing how to read music but that he would take a stab at it if I would tell him when to turn. Whereupon . . . the President waved him aside with a sweeping gesture and volunteered to do the job himself! Just imagine! Well, you could have knocked me over with a toothpick!
>
> Thank goodness I was able to get through the waltz in creditable, if

not sensational, manner, despite the general excitement and the completely unexpected appearance of President Truman in the role of page-turner. Imagine having the President of the United States turn pages for you! . . . But that's the kind of man the President is.

Truman was delighted to see Stalin so obviously enjoying himself. "The old man loves music," he told Bess. "Our boy was good."

By Friday the 20th, the week nearly over, there was still no further word on the test explosion in New Mexico. But when Truman invited Generals Eisenhower and Omar Bradley to lunch, the talk, according to Bradley's later account, focused on strategy in the Pacific and use of the atomic bomb.

Bradley, a fellow Missourian, had never met Truman until now and liked what he saw. "He was direct, unpretentious, clear-thinking and forceful." To Bradley it seemed that Truman had already made up his mind to use the new weapon. Though neither Bradley nor Eisenhower was asked for an opinion, Eisenhower said he opposed use of the bomb. He thought Japan was already defeated. To Stimson earlier he had expressed the hope that the United States would not be the first to deploy a weapon so horrible. In time, however, Eisenhower would concede that his reaction was personal and based on no analysis of the subject.

Eisenhower also advised Truman not to beg the Russians to come into the war with Japan, though he acknowledged that "no power on earth could keep the Red Army out of that war unless victory came before they could get in."

If Truman, as implied in his diary, truly believed that "Manhattan" would bring such victory instantly, this would have been the time for him to have said so. But he did not, which suggests either that he was still less than sure about the bomb, or that, contrary to Bradley's impression, he had still to make up his mind.

"But all of us wanted Russia in the war," he would tell his daughter some years later. "Had we known what the bomb would do we'd never have wanted the Bear in the picture."

Lunch over, accompanied by the two generals, Truman went again to Berlin, to the American sector this time, to speak at the raising of the flag that had flown over the Capitol in Washington the day Pearl Harbor was attacked. The ceremony took place in a small cobbled square in glaring sunshine. Stimson and General Patton were present, the tall, theatrical Patton resplendent in buckled riding boots, jodhpurs, and a lacquered four-star helmet. Patton seemed to glow from head to foot. There were stars on his shoulders, stars on his sleeves, more stars than Truman had ever seen on one human being. He counted twenty-eight.

Truman spoke without notes and with obvious emotion, choosing his words carefully, as he stood shoulders braced, thumbs hooked in the side pockets of his double-breasted suit, his eyes shadowed by his very un-military western-style Stetson. It was his own kind of speech—exactly what his address to the United Nations was not—and the first public pronouncement by any of the Big Three since arriving in Germany:

> We are here today to raise the flag of victory over the capital of our greatest adversary . . . we must remember that . . . we are raising it in the name of the people of the United States, who are looking forward to a better world, a peaceful world, a world in which all the people will have an opportunity to enjoy the good things of life, and not just a few at the top.
>
> Let us not forget that we are fighting for peace, and for the welfare of mankind. We are not fighting for conquest. There is not one piece of territory or one thing of a monetary nature that we want out of this war.
>
> We want peace and prosperity for the world as a whole. [Here the thumbs came out of the coat pockets, his freed hands chopped the air in unison, the familiar gesture, as he stressed each word, *"peace and prosperity for the world as a whole."*] We want to see the time come when we can do the things in peace that we have been able to do in war.
>
> If we can put this tremendous machine of ours, which has made victory possible, to work for peace, we can look forward to the greatest age in the history of mankind. That is what we propose to do.

It was not what Abraham Lincoln might have said, or what Robert Sherwood might have written for Franklin Roosevelt, but it was deeply moving, even for hard-shelled reporters and old soldiers. "What might easily have been made a routine patriotic display," wrote Raymond Daniell of *The New York Times*, "and hardly a day passes without one in Berlin, was turned into a historic occasion by the President's simple, homely declaration of the faith that had sent millions of American boys into battle far from home for a belief few of them could express." As no one had anticipated, Truman made it a moment "of lasting inspiration to all of us who were there," recorded General Lucius D. Clay. "While the soldier is schooled against emotion," Clay wrote years later, "I have never forgotten that short ceremony as our flag rose to the staff."

On the ride back, Truman was in a generous mood. Turning to Eisenhower he said out of the blue, "General, there is nothing you may want that I won't try to help you get. That definitely and specifically includes the presidency in 1948."

Bradley remembered trying to keep a straight face. Eisenhower looked flabbergasted. "Mr. President," he replied, "I don't know who will be your opponent for the presidency, but it will not be I."

That night, recording his thoughts on the day's session at the conference table, Truman said only that "Uncle Joe looked tired and drawn today and the P.M. seemed lost." The main topic had been Italy. Little was accomplished.

Before noon on Saturday, July 21, Henry Stimson received by special courier the eagerly awaited report from General Groves, the first description of the first nuclear explosion and, as Stimson said, an "immensely powerful document." By early afternoon he and General Marshall had reviewed it together, and at 3:30 Stimson brought it to the President. Byrnes was summoned, the doors were closed. Stimson began to read aloud in his scratchy old man's voice.

The test had been "successful beyond the most optimistic expectations of anyone." The test bomb had not been dropped from a plane but exploded on top of a 100-foot steel tower. The "energy generated" was estimated to be the equivalent of 15,000 to 20,000 tons of TNT.

For the first time in history there was a nuclear explosion. And what an explosion. . . . For a brief period there was a lighting effect within a radius of 20 miles equal to several suns in midday; a huge ball of fire was formed which lasted for several seconds. This ball mushroomed and rose to a height of over ten thousand feet before it dimmed. The light from the explosion was seen clearly at Albuquerque, Santa Fe, Silver City, El Paso and other points generally to about 180 miles away. The sound was heard to the same distance in a few instances but generally to about 100 miles. Only few windows were broken although one was some 125 miles away. A massive cloud was formed which surged and billowed upward with tremendous power, reaching the substratosphere at an elevation of 41,000 feet, 36,000 feet above the ground, in about five minutes, breaking without interruption through a temperature inversion at 17,000 feet which most of the scientists thought would stop it. Two supplementary explosions occurred in the cloud shortly after the main explosion. The cloud contained several thousand tons of dust picked up from the ground and a considerable amount of iron in the gaseous form. Our present thought is that this iron ignited when it mixed with the oxygen in the air to cause these supplementary explosions. Huge concentrations of highly radioactive materials resulted from the fission and were contained in this cloud.

The report described how the steel from the tower had evaporated, and the greenish cast of the pulverized dirt in a crater more than 1,000 feet in diameter.

> One-half mile from the explosion there was a massive steel test cylinder weighing 220 tons. The base of the cylinder was solidly encased in concrete. Surrounding the cylinder was a strong steel tower 70 feet high, anchored to concrete foundations. This tower is comparable to a steel building bay that would be found in a typical 15 to 20 story skyscraper or in warehouse construction. Forty tons of steel were used to fabricate the tower which was ... the height of a six story building. The cross bracing was much stronger than that normally used in ordinary steel construction. The absence of the solid walls of a building gave the blast a much less effective surface to push against. The blast tore the tower from its foundations, twisted it, ripped it apart and left it flat on the ground. The effects on the tower indicate that, at that distance, unshielded permanent steel and masonry buildings would have been destroyed. . . . None of us had expected it to be damaged.

Groves also included the impressions of his deputy, General Thomas F. Farrell, who was with Oppenheimer at the control shelter.

"Everyone in that room knew the awful potentialities of the thing that they thought was about to happen," reported Farrell, who wrote of the explosion's "searing light" and a "roar which warned of doomsday," and described how, when it was over,

> Dr. Kistiakowsky . . . threw his arms around Dr. Oppenheimer and embraced him with shouts of glee. Others were equally enthusiastic. All the pent-up emotions were released in those few minutes and all seemed to sense immediately that the explosion had far exceeded the most optimistic expectations and wildest hopes of the scientists. All seemed to feel that they had been present at the birth of a new age. . . .

In his conclusion, Groves wrote, "We are all fully conscious that our real goal is still before us. The battle test is what counts. . . ."

To read it all took Stimson nearly an hour. Whether Truman or Byrnes interrupted with questions or comments is unknown. But when Stimson stopped reading, Truman and Byrnes both looked immensely pleased

The President, in particular, was "tremendously pepped up," wrote Stimson. "He said it gave him an entirely new confidence and he thanked me for having come to the Conference and being present to help him this way."

Indeed, all three men felt an overwhelming sense of relief—that so much time and effort, that so vast an investment of money and resources had not been futile. It was not just that $2 billion had been spent, but that it was $2 billion that could have been used for the war effort in other ways. The thing worked—it could end the war—and, there was the pride too that a task of such complexity and magnitude, so completely unprecedented, had been an American success.

Clearly, Truman was fortified by the news. It is hard to imagine that he would not have been. That he and Byrnes felt their hand might be thus strengthened at the bargaining table with the Russians in time to come is also obvious—and perfectly understandable—but by no means was this the primary consideration, as some would later contend.

Truman went directly from the meeting to the Cecilienhof Palace where, as the next session got under way, the change in him was pronounced. He was more sure of himself, more assertive. "It was apparent something had happened," wrote Robert Murphy, a political adviser to General Eisenhower. Churchill later told Stimson he could not imagine what had come over the President. (When Stimson went to see the prime minister the next day, to read him Groves's report, Churchill's response was more emphatic than Truman's by far: "Stimson, what was gunpowder?" exclaimed Churchill. "What was electricity? Meaningless. This atomic bomb is the Second Coming in Wrath.")

In an exchange across the table, Stalin said the three governments should issue a statement announcing a renewal of diplomatic relations with the former German satellite nations of Romania, Bulgaria, and Finland. When Truman disagreed, Stalin said the questions would have to be postponed.

"We will not recognize these governments until they are set up on a satisfactory basis," said Truman.

Again they addressed the thorny question of Poland. In vague language at Yalta it had been agreed that Poland was to get new territory on the west, from Germany, to compensate for what Russia had taken from Poland on the east. At issue was Poland's western border and the fact that the Polish government of the moment (and the Red Army) had already taken over what had been a sizable part of Germany. Truman thought such matters should be settled at the peace conference. It had been agreed, he said, that the Germany of 1937 was to be the starting point.

"We decided on our zones. We moved our troops to the zones assigned to us. Now another occupying government has been assigned a zone without consultation with us. . . . I am very friendly to Poland and sympathetic with what Russia proposes regarding the western frontier, but I do not want to do it that way."

In other words, the Russians could not arbitrarily dictate how things were to be, and there would be no progress on reparations or other matters concerning Germany until this was understood.

"I am concerned that a piece of Germany, a valuable piece, has been cut off. This must be deemed a part of Germany in considering reparations and in the feeding of Germany. The Poles have no right to seize this territory now and take it out of the peace settlement. Are we going to maintain occupied zones until the peace or are we going to give Germany away piecemeal?"

He was not contentious, only unequivocal. Churchill was delighted. Eden thought it the President's best day thus far, as did Leahy, though Leahy was certain the Russians had no intention of changing their course in Eastern Europe, regardless of what was said. Poland was a "Soviet *fait accompli,*" thought Leahy, and there was little the United States or Britain could do about it, short of going to war with the Russians, which was unthinkable.

There was no trace of tension at the lavish party given by Stalin that night, in honor of his Western Allies. Truman had the best time of his entire stay at Potsdam. Stalin's affair was a "wow," he reported to his mother and sister.

> Started with caviar and vodka and wound up with watermelon and champagne, with smoked fish, fresh fish, venison, chicken, duck and all sorts of vegetables in between. There was a toast every five minutes until at least 25 had been drunk. I ate very little and drank less, but it was a colorful and enjoyable occasion.
>
> When I had Stalin and Churchill here for dinner I think I told you that a young sergeant named List, from Philadelphia played the piano and a boy from the Metropolitan Orchestra played the violin. They are the best we have, and they are very good. Stalin sent to Moscow and brought his two best pianists and two feminine violinists. They were excellent. Played Chopin, Liszt, Tchaikowsky and all the rest. I congratulated him and them on their ability. They had dirty faces though and the gals were rather fat. Anyway it was a nice dinner.

To Bess he reported that the evening had meant more progress in his relations with Stalin and said again that he already had what he wanted, the promise of Russian support against Japan. Possibly Stalin may also have told him that a million Russian troops were now massed along the Manchurian border.

"He talked to me confidently at the dinner, and I believe things will be all right in most instances. Some things we won't and can't agree on, but I already have what I came for."

Churchill, who cared little for music, told Truman he was bored to tears and going home. Truman said he would stay until the party was over. So Churchill stalked off to a corner, where, with Leahy for another half hour—until the music ended—he "glowered, growled, and grumbled," as a delighted Truman would tell the story.

Two nights later, when it was his turn as host, Churchill had his revenge. He summoned a Royal Air Force band and instructed them to play as loud as possible all through dinner and afterward.

Possibly the hardest judge of character in the whole American delegation was Admiral Ernest J. King, Chief of Naval Operations, whose strong mind and long experience had made him invaluable to Roosevelt. A poised, impressive-looking man, King had played a part in every major conference of the war, beginning with the shipboard meeting of Roosevelt and Churchill that produced the Atlantic Charter in the summer of 1941. On the night of Stalin's dinner at Potsdam, King had leaned over to whisper to Lord Moran.

"Watch the President," he said. "This is all new to him, but he can take it. He is a more typical American than Roosevelt, and he will do a good job, not only for the United States but for the whole world."

Bohlen, who had been at Roosevelt's side as interpreter at Teheran and Yalta, later described his amazement at Truman's natural self-possession, his ease with people, the way he "moved through the conference with the poise of a leader of much greater experience."

The President's physical well-being impressed nearly everyone. "Churchill and Stalin were given to late hours, while I was an early riser," Truman would later comment. "This made my days extra long. . . ." Yet he seemed above fatigue. He was out of bed and dressed by 5:30 or 6:00 regularly every morning and needed no alarm clock or anyone to wake him. Subordinates found him invariably cheerful and positive. He was never known to make a rude or inconsiderate remark, or to berate anyone, or to appear the least out of sorts, no matter how much stress he was under. From first to last, he remained entirely himself. "There was no pretense whatever about him," recalled the naval aide, Lieutenant Rigdon, who was charged with keeping the daily log. The great thing about the President, said Floyd Boring, one of the Secret Service men, was that he never got "swagly." "He never came on as being superior. . . . He could talk to *anyone!* He could talk to the lowly peasant. He could talk to the King of England. . . . And that was, I think, his secret. . . . He never got swellheaded—never got, you know, swagly."

In Berlin the black market—trade in cigarettes, watches, whiskey—and prostitution were rampant. One evening at the end of an arduous session at the palace, a young Army public relations officer, seeing that Truman was about to leave alone in his car, stuck his head in the window and asked if he might hitch a ride. Truman told him to get in and Floyd Boring, who was driving, could not help overhearing the conversation as they headed off. The officer said that if there was anything the President wanted, anything at all he needed, he had only to say the word. "Anything, you know, like women."

"Listen, son, I married my sweetheart," Truman said. "She doesn't run around on me, and I don't run around on her. I want that understood. Don't ever mention that kind of stuff to me again."

"By the time we were home," Boring remembered, "he got out of the car and never even said goodbye to that guy."

Another member of the delegation, a State Department official named Emilio Collado, would recall a scene at Number 2 Kaiserstrasse on the afternoon of Saturday the 21st. Arriving with a document for the President to sign, Collado was shown into a large empty room overlooking the lake, where he saw seated at a grand piano "an alert small man in shirt sleeves with a drink on the corner of the piano." Gathered beside him, singing, were Byrnes and Leahy, both with their jackets off.

> I thought it was nice [Collado said years later]. . . . The President played the piano quite well, in a rather old-time, ragtime manner, and they were having a fine time. They weren't drunk or anything like that. They each had a drink. I have often thought of that picture: the five-star admiral, the Secretary of State and the President, together on a Saturday afternoon, having a little music. The fact of the matter is that Harry Truman was a very human man. They were having a little quiet relaxation. They had had their lunch. . . . They had a little free time and there they were. . . . I can't say that the singing was very high quality, but the piano playing was quite good.

IV

With the start of his second week at Potsdam, Truman knew that decisions on the bomb could wait no longer.

At 10:00 Sunday morning, July 22, he attended Protestant services led by a chaplain from the 2nd Armored Division. Then later in the morning he went to a Catholic mass conducted by his old friend Father Curtis Tiernan, the chaplain of Battery D, who was serving as Chief of Army Chaplains in Europe and had been flown to Berlin at Truman's request.

"I'm going to mass at 11:30 presided over by him," Truman wrote to Bess at mid-morning. "I've already been to a Protestant service so I guess I should stand in good with the Almighty for the coming week—and my how I'll need it."

Stimson had appeared at Number 2 Kaiserstrasse shortly after breakfast, with messages from Washington saying all was about ready for the "final operation" and that a decision on the target cities was needed. Stimson wanted Kyoto removed from the list, and having heard the reasons, Truman agreed. Kyoto would be spared. "Although it was a target of considerable military importance," Stimson would write, "it had been the capital of Japan and was a shrine of Japanese art and culture. . . ." First on the list of approved targets was Hiroshima, southern headquarters and depot for Japan's homeland army.

Early on Monday, Stimson came again to Truman's second-floor office. A warning message to Japan, an ultimatum, was nearly ready, the document to be known as the Potsdam Declaration. Stimson thought it unwise at this point to insist on unconditional surrender, a term the Japanese would take to mean they could not keep their Emperor. He urged a revision to read that the Allies would "prosecute the war against Japan until she ceases to resist." But Byrnes had vehemently opposed any such change. Unconditional surrender was an objective too long established, too often proclaimed; it had been too great a rallying cry from the time of Pearl Harbor to abandon now, Byrnes insisted. Truman had reaffirmed it as policy in his first speech to Congress on April 16. It was what the Nazis had been made to accept, and its renunciation with the Japanese at this late date, after so much bloodshed, the acceptance of anything less with victory so near, would seem like appeasement. Politically it would be disastrous, Byrnes was also sure. To most Americans, Hirohito was the villainous symbol of Japan's fanatical military clique. A Gallup Poll in June had shown that a mere fraction of Americans, only 7 percent, thought he should be retained after the war, even as a puppet, while a full third of the people thought he should be executed as a war criminal. Like others who had been advising Truman, Byrnes considered any negotiations with Japan over terms a waste of time and felt that if Hirohito were to remain in place, then the war had been pointless. Though Truman listened carefully, Stimson failed to convince him otherwise.

Tuesday, July 24, was almost certainly the fateful day.

At 9:20 A.M. Stimson again climbed the stairs to Truman's office, where he found the President seated behind the heavy carved desk, "alone with his work." Stimson had brought another message:

> Washington, July 23, 1945
>
> Top Secret
> Operational Priority
> War 36792 Secretary of War Eyes Only top secret from Harrison.
> Operation may be possible any time from August 1 depending on state of preparation of patient and condition of atmosphere. From point of view of patient only, some chance August 1 to 3, good chance August 4 to 5 and barring unexpected relapse almost certain before August 10.

Truman "said that was just what he wanted," Stimson wrote in his diary, "that he was highly delighted. . . ."

Later, Truman wrote of a consensus at Potsdam, among Byrnes, Stimson, Leahy, Marshall, and General Arnold, that the bomb should be used. He recalled that Marshall again stressed the number of lives that would be saved. "I asked General Marshall what it would cost in lives to land on the Tokyo plain and other places in Japan. It was his opinion that such an invasion would cost at a minimum a quarter of a million American casualties. . . ." He himself reached his own conclusion only "after long and careful thought," he wrote, adding, "I did not like the weapon."

Very possibly there was no one, clearcut moment when he made up his mind, or announced that he had. Most likely, he never seriously considered not using the bomb. Indeed, to have said no at this point and called everything off would have been so drastic a break with the whole history of the project, not to say the terrific momentum of events that summer, as to have been almost inconceivable.

Some critics and historians in years to come would argue that Japan was already finished by this time, just as Eisenhower had said and as several intelligence reports indicated. Japan's defeat, however, was not the issue. It was Japan's surrender that was so desperately wanted, since every day Japan did not surrender meant the killing continued. In theory, Japan had been defeated well before Truman became President. (Studies by the Japanese themselves had determined a year and a half before, by January 1944, that Japan had lost the war.) Yet in the three months since Truman took office, American battle casualties in the Pacific were nearly half the total from three years of war in the Pacific. The nearer victory came, the heavier the price in blood. And whatever the projected toll in American lives in an invasion, it was too high if it could be avoided.

"We had only too abundant evidence in those days that surrender was excluded from the Japanese ethos," remembered a captain in Military Intelligence, Charlton Ogburn, Jr. "Thousands of our Marines and soldiers had died rooting Japanese from their foxholes and bunkers when they were perfectly aware that their situation was hopeless." During the whole war, not a single Japanese unit had surrendered.

While intelligence reports indicated that Japan was beaten, they also forecast that the Japanese would hold out for months longer, meanwhile issuing intermittent peace feelers, both to bring the war to what they would regard as an acceptable conclusion, and "to weaken the determination of the United States to fight to the bitter end. . . . "

> The basic policy of the present [Japanese] government [said a combined Intelligence Committee report of July 8, 1945] is to fight as long and as desperately as possible in the hope of avoiding complete defeat and of acquiring a better bargaining position in a negotiated peace. Japanese leaders are now playing for time in the hope that Allied war weariness, Allied disunity, or some "miracle" will present an opportunity to arrange a compromise peace.

Nor, it must be stressed, was there ever anything hypothetical about preparations for the invasion—on both sides—a point sometimes overlooked in later years.

Truman had earlier authorized the Chiefs of Staff to move more than 1 million troops for a final attack on Japan. Thirty divisions were on the way to the Pacific from the European theater, from one end of the world to the other, something never done before. Supplies in tremendous quantity were piling up on Saipan. Japan had some 2.5 million regular troops on the home islands, but every male between the ages of fifteen and sixty, every female from seventeen to forty-five, was being conscripted and armed with everything from ancient brass cannon to bamboo spears, taught to strap explosives to their bodies and throw themselves under advancing tanks. One woman would remember being given a carpenter's awl and instructed that killing just one American would do. "You must aim at the abdomen," she was told. "Understand? The abdomen." The general in charge of defense plans told other senior officers, "By pouring 20 divisions into the battle within two weeks of the enemy's landing, we will annihilate him entirely and insure a Japanese victory." Thousands of planes were ready to serve as *kamikazes*.

To no one with the American and Allied forces in the Pacific did it look as though the Japanese were about to quit. On July 15, *The New York*

Times reported that twenty-five war-front correspondents from the United States and Australia had compared notes and their guess was the war would not end for nearly a year, not until June 1946. At the Pentagon, a long-remembered poster in the halls showed the face of a combat-hardened infantryman looking with grim determination at a map of the Japanese home islands, while across the top in bold letters was slashed the single word "Next!" There was no talk at the Pentagon of an early end to the war. The great concern was the likelihood of huge Japanese forces in China and Southeast Asia fighting on even if the government in Tokyo were to give up.

Truman foresaw unprecedented carnage in any attempted invasion. "It occurred to me," he would remark a few months later, "that a quarter of a million of the flower of our young manhood were worth a couple of Japanese cities, and I still think they were and are." But whether 250,000 or 20,000 casualties would result was not the issue at the moment, not if the shock effect of a single devastating blow, or two, could stop the war —and particularly when devastating blows, in the form of B-29 raids, had become the standard, almost daily routine.

"Today's prime fact is war," Henry Stimson had said at the start of one Interim Committee meeting. The Japanese were the despised enemy, perpetrators of the treacherous attack on Pearl Harbor (and then in the midst of peace talks), perpetrators of the bombing of Manila and the Bataan death march. They were the murderers of American prisoners of war, the fanatics who ordered the seemingly insane *kamikaze* attacks. The details of the Bataan death march had become known only in February and enraged the country. Other atrocities included the Palawan Massacre, during which Japanese soldiers on the Philippine island of Palawan lured 140 American prisoners of war into air-raid trenches, then doused them with gasoline and burned them alive. A few days after the German surrender in May, the papers had carried a photograph of a blindfolded prisoner of war, an American flyer down on his knees, his hands tied behind his back, about to be beheaded by a Japanese officer swinging a sword.

At Potsdam, as Bohlen was to write, "the spirit of mercy was not throbbing in the breast of any Allied official," either for the Germans or the Japanese.

And how could a President, or the others charged with responsibility for the decision, answer to the American people if when the war was over, after the bloodbath of an invasion of Japan, it became known that a weapon sufficient to end the war had been available by midsummer and was not used?

Had the bomb been ready in March and deployed by Roosevelt, had it shocked Japan into surrender then, it would have already saved nearly fifty thousand American lives lost in the Pacific in the time since, not to say a vastly larger number of Japanese lives.

Nor had anyone ever doubted that Roosevelt would use it. "At no time, from 1941 to 1945, did I ever hear it suggested by the President, or by any other responsible member of the government, that atomic energy should not be used in the war," wrote Stimson. "All of us of course understood the terrible responsibility involved . . . President Roosevelt particularly spoke to me many times of his own awareness of the catastrophic potentialities of our work. But we were at war. . . ."

Leahy later said, "I know FDR would have used it in a minute to prove that he hadn't wasted two billion dollars."

"I'll say that we'll end the war a year sooner now," Truman had told Bess in a letter the week before, speaking of Stalin's agreement to come in against Japan, "and think of the kids who won't be killed! That's the important thing." To him it was always the important thing. An invasion of Japan would be work for ground troops, dirty, God-awful business for infantry and artillery, as he knew from experience. For unlike Roosevelt or Woodrow Wilson, or any Commander in Chief since the advent of modern war, Truman had been in combat with ground troops. At the Argonne, seeing a German battery pull into position on the left flank, beyond his assigned sector, he had ordered his battery to open fire, because his action would save lives, even though he could face a court-martial. "It is just the same as artillery on our side," he would say later of the bomb, which would strike many people as appallingly insensitive and simplistic, but he was speaking from the experience of war.

Once, when presiding judge of Jackson County, he had, by his own private confession, allowed a crooked contractor to steal $10,000 in order to forestall the stealing of ten times the amount. He had permitted evil in order to prevent a larger evil and saw no other choice. Had he done right, had he done wrong, he had asked, writing alone late at night in the Pickwick Hotel. "You judge it, I can't."

Conceivably, as many would later argue, the Japanese might have surrendered before November and the scheduled invasion. Conceivably, they could have been strangled by naval blockade, forced to surrender by continued fire bombing, with its dreadful toll, as some strategists were saying at the time. Possibly the single sticking point was, after all, the Allied demand for unconditional surrender. But no one close to Truman was telling him not to use the new weapon. General Marshall fully expected the Japanese to fight on even if the bomb were dropped and proved as effective as the scientists predicted. Marshall saw the bomb more as a way to make the invasion less costly. That it might make the invasion unnecessary was too much to expect. "We knew the Japanese were determined and fanatical...and we would have to exterminate them man by man," he would later tell David Lilienthal. "So we thought the bomb would be a wonderful weapon as a protection and preparation for landings." Marshall had been so appalled by American casualties at Iwo Jima that he had favored using poison gas at Okinawa.

A petition drawn up by Leo Szilard, urging on grounds of morality that Japan be warned in advance, had been signed by seventy scientists but was not delivered to Washington until after Truman had left for Potsdam. Truman never saw it. But neither did he see the counter opinions voiced by those scientists urging that the bomb be used, and on grounds of morality. "Are not the men of the fighting forces...who are risking their lives for the nation, entitled to the weapons which have been designed," said one petition. "In short, are we to go on shedding American blood when we have available means to a steady victory? No! If we can save even a handful of American lives, then let us use this weapon—now!"

> It is hard to imagine anything more conclusive than the devastation of all the eastern coastal cities of Japan by fire bombs [wrote another scientist]; a more fiendish hell than the inferno of blazing Tokyo is beyond the pale of conception. Then why do we attempt to draw the line of morality here, when it is a question of degree, not a question of kind?

In a poll of 150 scientists at the Metallurgical Laboratory at Chicago, 87 percent voted for military use of the weapon, if other means failed to bring surrender. Arthur Compton was asked for his opinion:

> What a question to answer [he later wrote]! Having been in the very midst of these discussions, it seemed to me that a firm negative stand on my part might still prevent an atomic attack on Japan. Thoughts of my pacifist Mennonite ancestors flashed through my mind. I knew all too well the destruction and human agony the bombs would cause. I knew the danger they held in the hands of some future tyrant. These facts I had been living with for four years. But I wanted the war to end. I wanted life to become normal again.... I hoped that by use of the bombs many fine young men I knew might be released at once from the demands of war and thus be given a chance to live and not to die.

· · ·

441

Churchill was to write of the decision that was no decision, and in retrospect this seems to have been the case. "The historic fact remains, and must be judged in the after-time," Churchill wrote, "that the decision whether or not to use the atomic bomb to compel the surrender of Japan was never an issue. There was unanimous, automatic, unquestioned agreement around our table; nor did I ever hear the slightest suggestion that we should do otherwise."

"Truman made no decision because there was no decision to be made," recalled George Elsey, remembering the atmosphere of the moment. "He could no more have stopped it than a train moving down a track. . . . It's all well and good to come along later and say the bomb was a horrible thing. The whole goddamn war was a horrible thing."

For his part, Truman stated later:

> The final decision of where and when to use the atomic bomb was up to me. Let there be no mistake about it. I regarded the bomb as a military weapon and never had any doubt that it should be used. The top military advisers to the President recommended its use, and when I talked to Churchill he unhesitatingly told me that he favored the use of the atomic bomb if it might aid to end the war.

Though nothing was recorded on paper, the critical moment appears to have occurred at Number 2 Kaiserstrasse later in the morning of Tuesday, July 24, when, at 11:30, the combined American and British Chiefs of Staff convened with Truman and Churchill in the dining room. This was the one time when Truman, Churchill, and their military advisers were all around a table, in Churchill's phrase. From this point it was settled: barring some unforeseen development, the bomb would be used within a few weeks. Truman later told Arthur Compton that the day of the decision was the same day he informed Stalin, and that occurred late the afternoon of the 24th.

It happened at the end of a particularly contentious session at the Cecilienhof Palace. The meeting was just breaking up when Truman rose from his chair and alone walked slowly around the table to where Stalin stood with his interpreter.

"I casually mentioned to Stalin that we had a new weapon of unusual destructive force," Truman remembered. "All he said was that he was glad to hear it and hoped we would make 'good use of it against the Japanese.' "

Truman did not specify what kind of weapon it was—he did not use the words "atomic bomb"—or say anything about sharing scientific secrets. Stalin seemed neither surprised nor the least curious. He did not ask the nature of the weapon, or how it was made, or why he hadn't been told before this. He did not suggest that Soviet scientists be informed or permitted to examine it. He did not, in fact, appear at all interested.

To Bohlen, who was watching closely from across the room, Stalin's response seemed so altogether offhand that Bohlen wondered whether the President had made himself clear. "If he had had the slightest idea of the revolution in world affairs which was in progress his reactions would have been obvious," wrote Churchill, who had kept his eye on Stalin's face. Byrnes, too, was certain Stalin had "not grasped the importance of the discovery," and would soon be asking for more details. But this Stalin never did. He never mentioned the subject again for the remainder of the conference.

The fact was Stalin already knew more than any of the Americans or British imagined. Soviet nuclear research had begun in 1942, and as would be learned later, a German-born physicist at Los Alamos, a naturalized British citizen named Klaus Fuchs, had been supplying the Russians with atomic secrets for some time, information that in Moscow was judged "extremely excellent and very valuable." Stalin had understood perfectly what Truman said. Later, in the privacy of their Babelsberg quarters, according to Marshal Georgi Zhukov, Stalin instructed Molotov to "tell Kurchatov [of the Soviet atomic project] to hurry up the work." (Also, according to the Russian historian Dmitri Volkogonov, Stalin went even further that evening when he cabled Lavrenti Beria, who had overall supervision of the project, to put on the pressure.)

In years to come Truman often said that having made his decision about the bomb, he went to bed and slept soundly. He would be pictured retiring for the night at the White House, his mind clear that he had done the right thing. But in the strange "nightmare" house at Babelsberg, in the unremitting heat of the German summer, he was sleeping rather poorly and in considerably more turmoil than his later claims ever suggested.

"No one who played a part in the development of the bomb or in our decision to use it felt happy about it," recalled Jimmy Byrnes, who was quartered downstairs.

"We have discovered the most terrible bomb in the history of the world," Truman wrote in his diary on Wednesday, July 25, the day the general military order was issued to the Air Force to proceed with the plan, and "terrible" was the word he would keep coming back to. He wondered if the bomb might be "the fire of destruction" prophesied in the Bible. As if to convince himself, he wrote of how it would be used on military targets only, which he knew to be only partly true.

> This weapon is to be used against Japan between now and August 10th. I have told the Sec of War, Mr. Stimson, to use it so that military objectives and soldiers and sailors are the target and not women and children. Even if the Japs are savages, ruthless, merciless and fanatic, we as the leader of the world for the common welfare cannot drop this terrible bomb on the old capital [Kyoto] or the new [Tokyo, where the Imperial Palace had been spared thus far].
>
> He and I are in accord. The target will be a purely military one and we will issue a warning statement asking the Japs to surrender and save lives. I'm sure they will not do that, but we will have given them a chance. It is certainly a good thing for the world that Hitler's crowd or Stalin's did not discover this atomic bomb. It seems to be the most terrible thing ever discovered, but it can be made useful.

Whether this final thought—that it could be made useful—was his irrepressible, native optimism and faith in progress coming to the fore, or yet another way of trying to convince himself, or both of these, or merely means useful to end the war, is open to question.

V

It would be the thesis of some historians that the atomic bomb figured importantly at Potsdam as Truman's way of putting pressure on the Russians. But except for his private show of bolstered confidence after hearing Groves's report, Truman neither said nor did anything of consequence to support this theory and the whole idea would be vigorously denied by those who were present and witness to events. Once, sometime before the test at Alamogordo, Truman reportedly remarked to some of his aides that if the bomb worked, he would "certainly have the hammer on those boys," but whether by this he meant the Russians or the Japanese was unclear, and there was no intimation ever of a "hammer," no flaunting of power, in his dealings with Stalin. "The idea of using the bomb as a form of pressure on the Russians never entered the discussions at Potsdam," wrote Harriman. "That wasn't the President's mood at all. The mood was to treat Stalin as an ally—a difficult ally, admittedly—in the hope that he would behave like one."

At the conference session preceding Truman's disclosure to Stalin of the bomb secret, the Generalissimo had been as "difficult" as at any time thus far. Truman was firm in his positions, yet never belligerent or re-proachful. He had no intention to make reflection upon Stalin or his government, he stressed. The sharp exchanges were between Churchill and Stalin—Churchill having at last recovered much of his old spirit.

The topic on the agenda was the admission to the United Nations of Italy and the Balkan states formerly allied with Germany, the so-called "satellite countries." It was the American and British position that Italy should be admitted but that Romania, Bulgaria, and Hungary (all now firmly in Russian control) should not, until democratic governments were established. Stalin observed that since no democratic elections had been held in Italy either, he failed to understand this benevolent attitude toward Italy. The difference, said Truman, was that everyone had free access to Italy, while for the Western Allies there was no free access to the Balkan countries. (It was a point that Byrnes, too, had been making in meetings of the foreign ministers.)

"We are asking for the reorganization of the satellite governments along democratic lines as agreed upon at Yalta," Truman said.

Stalin's calm rejoinder was very simple: "If a government is not fascist, a government is democratic," he said.

Churchill pointed out that Italy was an open society with a free press, where diplomatic missions could go freely about their business. At Bucharest, by contrast, the British mission was penned up as if under arrest. An iron fence had descended, said Churchill darkly.

"All fairy tales!" exclaimed Stalin.

"Statesmen may call one another's statements fairy tales if they wish," answered Churchill.

As Bohlen was to write, no moment at the conference so revealed the gulf between the Soviet Union and the Western Allies.

Taking Churchill's side, Truman said that difficulties encountered by the American missions in Romania and Bulgaria had also been cause for concern. (That night Churchill would go on at length to Lord Moran about his admiration for Truman's plain, direct way with Stalin. "The President is not going to be content to feed out of anyone's hand; he intends to get to the bottom of things," Churchill would say, rubbing his eyes as if to remind himself he was not dreaming. "If only this had happened at Yalta." But then after a pause, he added sadly, "It is too late now.")

Truman tried to salvage the afternoon with progress in another direction. The previous day he had formally introduced his plan to internationalize the world's inland waterways, rivers, and canals, including the Danube, the Rhine, the Dardanelles, the Kiel Canal, the Suez and Panama canals. All nations, including Russia, were to have access to all the seas of the world. "I do not want to fight another war in twenty years because of a quarrel on the Danube," he had said. "We want a prosperous, self-supporting Europe. A bankrupt Europe is of no advantage to any country, or to the peace of the world." Stalin had said he wanted time to consider. So now Truman brought it up again, hoping for the best. Clearly it was important to him.

Stalin cut him off, declaring, "The question is not ripe for discussion."

On Wednesday, July 25, the conference was put on hold. Churchill was about to leave for London to face the final results of the general election. Anthony Eden and others of the British delegation were also to depart, as well as Churchill's opponent in the election, the quiet, mousy Clement Attlee, who dressed in a three-piece suit, despite the summer heat, and who seemed as convinced as everyone else that Churchill was certain to win and would return in a matter of days.

Churchill, privately, was full of foreboding. He had had a dream in which he saw himself lying dead beneath a white sheet in an empty room. He knew who it was, he told Moran, because he recognized the protruding feet.

"What a pity," Stalin said at the close of that morning's session, when Churchill announced he had no more to say.

Outside afterward, by the front door of the palace, Churchill, Stalin, and Truman posed for a final portrait. Truman, looking very much the American politician, stood in the middle with crossed arms, shaking hands with both men at once, smiling first at one, then the other, as a battery of photographers and newsreel cameramen recorded the moment. Even Stalin broke into a grin.

The next day from London came the stunning news that the Labor Party had won, Churchill was defeated, Clement Attlee was the new prime minister. Hardly anyone could believe it, but the Russians seemed most upset of all. How could this possibly be, Molotov kept demanding. How could they not have known the outcome in advance? Stalin postponed the conference for another few days and was seen by no one.

First Roosevelt, now Churchill, Truman noted privately. The old order was passing. Uneasily he wondered what might happen if Stalin were suddenly to "cash in" and a power struggle convulsed the Soviet Union. "It isn't customary for dictators to train leaders to follow them in power. I've seen no one at this Conference in the Russian lineup who can do the job." His feelings about Churchill were mixed, as much as he liked him. It was too bad about Churchill, he wrote to his mother and sister, but then he added that "it may turn out to be all right for the world," suggesting that this way, without Churchill around, he might make better progress with Stalin.

That same day, July 26, at the island of Tinian in the Pacific, the cruiser *Indianapolis* delivered the U-235 portion of an atomic bomb, nicknamed "Little Boy." That evening, Byrnes and Truman decided to release the Potsdam Declaration.

Phrased as a joint statement by Truman, Attlee, and Generalissimo Chiang Kai-shek, it assured the Japanese people humane treatment. They would not be "enslaved as a race or destroyed as a nation." Once freedom of speech and religion were established, once Japan's warmaking power had been eliminated and a responsible, "peacefully inclined" government freely elected, occupation forces would be withdrawn.

The words "unconditional surrender" appeared only once, in the final paragraph, and then specified only the unconditional surrender of the armed forces, not the Japanese nation. The alternative was "prompt and utter destruction."

The fate of Emperor Hirohito was left ambiguous. He was not mentioned. Nor was there any explanation of what form the "prompt and utter destruction" might take.

The declaration was picked up by Japanese radio monitors at six in the morning, July 27, Tokyo time, and Prime Minister Kautaro Suzuki and the Cabinet went into an all-day meeting. Meanwhile, over Tokyo and ten other Japanese cities, American planes were dropping millions of leaflets with a printed translation of the declaration.

Suzuki's decision was to ignore the matter. The declaration, he said at a press conference, was nothing but a rehash of old proposals and as such, beneath contempt. He would "kill [it] with silence," he said.

Clement Attlee and his new foreign minister, Ernest Bevin, arrived at Babelsberg the night of Saturday the 28th and Truman was impressed with neither—a couple of "sourpusses," he decided. Bevin looked as though he weighed 250 pounds.

> Mr. Attlee is not so keen as old fat Winston and Mr. Bevin looks rather rotund to be a Foreign Minister [Truman wrote to Margaret]. Seems Bevin is sort of the John L. Lewis type. Eden was a perfect striped pants boy. I wasn't fond of Eden—he is a much overrated man; and he didn't play fair with his boss. I did like old Churchill. He was as windy as Langer [Senator William Langer of North Dakota], but he knew his English language and after he'd talked half an hour there'd be at least one gem of a sentence and two thoughts maybe which could have been

expressed in four minutes. But if we ever got him on record, which was seldom, he stayed put. Anyway he is a likeable person and these other two are sourpusses. Attlee is an Oxford graduate and talks with that deep throated swallowing enunciation same as Eden does. But I understand him reasonably well. Bevin is a tough guy. He doesn't know of course that your dad has been dealing with that sort all his life, from building trades to coal mines. So he won't be new.

"We shall see what we shall see," he wrote to Bess.

Secretary of the Navy Forrestal, who had only just arrived, found Truman in an optimistic mood concerning the Russians, in contrast to others in the delegation. Harriman was "very gloomy." Byrnes was "most anxious to get the Japanese affair over with before the Russians got in."

All messages to the President from the War Department came in to Babelsberg a half block down the street from Number 2 Kaiserstrasse at the Army message center, where they were immediately decoded. From there they were taken to Number 2 Kaiserstrasse, to the officers on duty in the Map Room, who would give them to the President.

Late on Monday, July 30, another urgent top-secret cable to Truman was received and decoded, but held for delivery until morning in order not to disturb the President's rest. It was from Harrison in Washington:

> The time schedule on Groves' project is progressing so rapidly that it is now essential that statement for release by you be available not later than Wednesday, 1 August. . . .

The time had come for Truman to give the final go-ahead for the bomb. This was the moment, the decision only he could make.

The message was delivered at 7:48 A.M., Berlin time, Tuesday, July 31. Writing large and clear with a lead pencil on the back of the pink message, Truman gave his answer, which he handed to Lieutenant Elsey for transmission:

> Suggestion approved. Release when ready but not sooner than August 2.

Elsey, a lanky, earnest, good-looking young officer, a Princeton graduate who had a master's degree in history from Harvard, would not remember feeling that he was witness to one of history's momentous turning points. "*Everything* seemed momentous in those days at Potsdam," Elsey would recall. What impressed him was that Truman "didn't want anything happening until he got away from Stalin, away from Potsdam." All efforts now were to wind things up by August 2. Stimson was already back at the Pentagon. Marshall was to leave later that day.

The Potsdam Conference should have been a time of celebration. It should have been the most harmonious, most hopeful of the Big Three conferences, a watershed in history, marking the start of a new era of good feeling among the Allied powers now that the common foe, the detested Nazi, was destroyed. Such at least was the promise of Potsdam. But it wasn't that way, nor in practicality had there ever been much chance it would be. At lunch the first day they met, Stalin had told Truman he wanted to cooperate with the United States in peace as in war, but in peace, he said, that would be more difficult. It was what they all knew, and the underlying tensions felt at the beginning remained to the end.

Truman had kept insisting on results, not talk, something in the bag at the end of every day, as Churchill observed—it was why he was there, Truman would say—and as impatient as he grew, he seems to have felt right to the end that he could succeed. "We have accomplished a very great deal in spite of all the talk. . . . So you see we have not wasted time," he wrote to Bess just before Churchill departed. He wanted the future of Germany settled satisfactorily. Germany was the key, the overriding question. He wanted free elections in Poland, Eastern Europe, and the Balkans. He wanted Russia to join in the assault on Japan as soon as possible. But only on this last item could he feel he had succeeded. For the rest he faced ambiguity, delays, and frustration, Stalin having no wish to accept any agreement that threatened the control he already had, wherever the Red Army stood. Try as he might, Truman could make little or no progress with Stalin.

Could Roosevelt have done better? It was a question Truman must have asked himself many times. Chip Bohlen thought Roosevelt would have been less successful, since, with his personal interest in earlier agreements with Stalin, Roosevelt would have acted more angrily than Truman when faced with Stalin's intransigence. To Bohlen, Harriman, and others experienced in dealing with the Russians, Truman had acquitted himself well. "He was never defeated or made to look foolish or uninformed in debate," Bohlen would write. And since neither Stalin nor Molotov ever tried any tricks or subtleties, but only held stubbornly to their own line, the President's inexperience in diplomacy did not greatly matter after all. There was never any room for maneuver.

"Pray for me and keep your fingers crossed too," he wrote to Bess as the final week began.

> We are at an impasse on Poland and its western boundary and on reparations [he wrote in his diary]. Russia and Poland have agreed on the Oder and West Neisse to the Czechoslovakian border . . . without so much as a by your leave. I don't like it.

But the Red Army had pushed to the Oder River and the western Neisse River and so those rivers were agreed to as Poland's western frontier. Further, Poland was given the southern portion of East Prussia, including the port of Danzig, while the Soviet Union was granted the northern portion. As for free elections in Poland, it was agreed only that they should be held "as soon as possible," which in reality meant the Polish issue remained unresolved.

The future of Germany's former allies in the war—Italy, Bulgaria, Finland, Hungary, and Romania—was postponed, left to the Council of Foreign Ministers to resolve at some unspecified time in the future.

Germany, already portioned off into four zones of military occupation—American, British, Russian, and French—was in effect divided down the middle, between East and West. A complete demilitarization of the German state was agreed to. There was never an argument on that. Nazi war criminals were to be brought to justice. And there was no argument here either, not even over the place where the war crimes tribunal would sit—Nuremberg was the decision. And by a complicated formula for reparations the Soviet Union got the lion's share—mainly in capital equipment—in view of the fact that the Soviet Union had suffered the greatest loss of life and property.

In some instances Stalin did not get what he wanted—Soviet trusteeship over Italy's former colonies in Africa, a naval base on the Bosporus, four-power control over Germany's industrial Ruhr Valley. But it was the Western leaders who made the big concessions, because they had little choice—Russian occupation of Eastern Europe was indeed a fait accompli, as Leahy said—and because they hoped to achieve harmony with Stalin. It was never possible to get all you wanted in such situations, Truman would explain to the American people, trying to put a good face on the situation. "It is a question of give and take—of being willing to meet your neighbor halfway."

To such experienced Soviet specialists as Harriman and George Kennan, it was foolishness in the extreme to imagine the Russians ever keeping faith with such words as "democratic" and "justice." Or to see the arrangement agreed to for Germany as anything other than unreal and unworkable. Kennan, who was not present at Potsdam, would later despair over Truman's naivete. Harriman, who was present throughout, found himself so shut out of serious discussions by Byrnes that he decided it was time for him to resign.

Truman's waterways proposal got nowhere. On the next to final day of the conference, August 1, he made one last try, asking only that it at least be mentioned in the final communiqué. Attlee said this was agreeable with him, but again Stalin refused. Truman pointed out that the proposal had been discussed and that he was pressing only this one issue. "Marshal Stalin, I have accepted a number of compromises during this conference to confirm with your views," he said, "and I make a personal request now that you yield on this point . . ."

Stalin broke in even before his interpreter had finished with the President's statement.

"*Nyet!*" said Stalin. Then, with emphasis, and in English for the first time, he repeated, "No, I say no!"

It was an embarrassing, difficult moment. Truman turned red. "I cannot understand that man!" he was heard to say. He turned to Byrnes. "Jimmy, do you realize we have been here seventeen whole days? Why, in seventeen days you can decide anything!"

In a letter to his mother, Truman called the Russians the most pigheaded people he had ever encountered. He knew them now to be relentless bargainers—"forever pressing for every advantage for themselves," as he later said—and in his diary he left no doubt that he understood the reality of the Stalin regime. It was "police government pure and simple," he wrote. "A few top hands just take clubs, pistols and concentration camps and rule the people on the lower levels." Later he would tell John Snyder of an unsettling exchange with Stalin about the Katyn Forest Massacre of 1940. When Truman asked what had happened to the Polish officers, Stalin answered coldly, "They went away."

Still—*still*—Truman liked him. "I like Stalin. He is straightforward," he wrote to Bess near the windup of the conference. Stalin could be depended upon to keep his word, he would later tell his White House staff. "The President," wrote Eben Ayers, "seemed to have been favorably impressed with him and to like him." Stalin was a fine man who wanted to do the right thing, Truman would tell Henry Wallace. Furthermore, Truman was pretty sure Stalin liked him. To Jonathan Daniels, Truman would say he had been reminded of Tom Pendergast. "Stalin is as near like Tom Pendergast as any man I know."

Not for a long time, not for a dozen years, would Truman concede that he had been naive at Potsdam—"an innocent idealist," in his words—and refer to Stalin as the "unconscionable Russian Dictator." Yet even then he added, "And I liked the little son-of-a-bitch."

As Truman would later tell the American people, no secret agreements or commitments were made at Potsdam, other than "military arrangements." However, one secret agreement concerning "military operations in Southeast Asia" was to have far-reaching consequences. He, Churchill, and their combined Chiefs of Staff decided that Vietnam, or Indochina, would, "for operational purposes," be divided, with China in charge north of the 16th parallel and British forces in the southern half, leaving little chance for the unification or independence of Vietnam and ample opportunity for the return of the French. Truman so informed the American ambassador in China, Patrick J. Hurley, by secret cable the last day of the conference, August 1. At the time, given the other decisions he faced, both military and political, it did not seem overly important.

The thirteenth and concluding session at the Cecilienhof Palace that evening was devoted almost exclusively to the wording of the final communiqué and did not break up until past midnight. The struggle had come down to fine points. Molotov suggested an amendment in a paragraph that described Poland's western frontier as running from the Baltic through the town of Swinemünde. He wished to substitute the words "west of" for "through," Molotov said.
"How far west?" asked Byrnes.
"Immediately west," suggested Bevin.
"Immediately west will satisfy us," Stalin affirmed.
"That is all right," said Truman.
"Agreed," said Attlee.

Truman, in announcing that the business of the conference was ended, said in all sincerity that he hoped the next meeting would be in Washington.
"God willing," exclaimed Stalin, invoking the deity for the first and only time. Then, in a conspicuously unusual tribute, Stalin commended Byrnes "who had worked harder perhaps than any of us . . . and worked very well."
There was much hand shaking around the table and wishes for good health and safe journey. As it turned out, Truman and Stalin were never to meet again. Potsdam was their first and only big power conference.
In his private assessment, Stalin later told Nikita Khrushchev Truman was worthless.

VI

Packing had been going on at Number 2 Kaiserstrasse for several days, everyone, and especially the President, extremely ready to leave.

At 6:45 Thursday morning, August 2, his motorcade was drawn up in the driveway. By 7:15 they were on their way to Gatow airfield, where, at Truman's request, there were to be no ceremonies. At 8:05 *The Sacred Cow* was airborne, heading for Plymouth, England, to meet the U.S.S. *Augusta.* "That will save two days on the ocean because it takes so long to get out of the English Channel when we leave from Antwerp," he explained in a letter to his mother and Mary Jane. He would be having lunch with the English King, he wrote.

The lunch with King George VI took place on board the British battle cruiser H.M.S. *Renown,* which, with the *Augusta* and *Philadelphia,* was anchored in Plymouth Roads. To his surprise, Truman found the King "very pleasant," "a good man," and extremely interested in hearing all about Potsdam.

> We had a nice and appetizing lunch [Truman recorded]—soup, fish, lamb chops, peas, potatoes and ice cream with chocolate sauce. The King, myself, Lord Halifax [the British ambassador to Washington], a British Admiral, Adm. Leahy, [Alan] Lascelles [the King's private secretary], the Secretary of State in that order around the table. Talked of most everything, and nothing. . . . There was much formality etc. in getting on and off the British ship.

That afternoon, returning the call, the King came aboard the *Augusta,* inspected the guard, "took a snort of Haig & Haig" (as Truman happily recorded), and asked Truman for three of his autographs, one each for his daughters and the Queen.

Fifteen minutes after the King's departure, at 3:49, the *Augusta* was under way.

The following day, August 3, his first full day at sea, Truman called the few members of the press who were on board into his cabin. Seated at a small table covered with green felt, a looseleaf notebook open in front of him, he began telling them about the atomic bomb and its history. He spoke slowly, in measured tones. His emotions seemed divided. "He was happy and thankful that we had a weapon in our hands which would speed the end of the war," remembered Merriman Smith of the United Press. "But he was apprehensive over the development of such a monstrous weapon of destruction." How long the United States could remain the "exclusive producer," Truman wasn't sure. The material in the notebook was his statement for the country, which had been prepared in advance, before he left for Potsdam.

The frustration of the reporters was extreme. "Here was the greatest news story since the invention of gunpowder," wrote Smith. "And what could we do about it? Nothing. Just sit and wait."

On August 4, according to the official log, the President was up and strolling the decks at five in the morning, looking "completely rested from the strain of the long and tiring conference discussions." After an early breakfast, he spent the day studying conference reports and working on an address to the country. On Sunday, August 5, he attended church services, then returned to his work. Merriman Smith remembered the day as extremely tense and Truman looking worried. Smith and the other reporters tried to talk of other things. "The secret was so big and terrifying that we could not discuss it with each other." The ship, meantime, was boiling along at a full speed of 26.5 knots.

On the morning of Monday, August 6, the fourth day at sea, the President and several of his party spent time on deck enjoying the sun and listening to a concert by the ship's band. The ship had entered the Gulf Stream, south of Newfoundland. The sun was out, the weather considerably warmer. The crew had changed now to white uniforms that looked sparkling in the sunshine.

At noon the ship's position was latitude 39-55 N, longitude 61-32 W. The sea was calm.

Shortly before noon, Truman and Byrnes had decided to have lunch with some of the crew below deck in the after mess. Truman was seated with six enlisted men and just beginning his meal when Captain Graham, one of the Map Room officers, hurried in and handed him a map of Japan and a decoded message from the Secretary of War.

Hiroshima had been bombed four hours earlier. "Results clear-cut successful in all respects. Visible effects greater than in any test," Truman read. On the map Captain Graham had circled the city with a red pencil.

Suddenly excited, Truman grabbed Graham by the hand and said, "This is the greatest thing in history," then told him to show the message to Byrnes, who was at another table. It was just after noon. Minutes later a second message was brought in:

Big bomb dropped on Hiroshima August 5 at 7:15 P.M. Washington time. First reports indicate complete success which was even more conspicuous than earlier test.

Truman jumped to his feet now and called to Byrnes, "It's time for us to get home!" Like the scientists at Alamogordo at the moment of the first test, Truman was exuberant. Tapping on a glass with a fork, he called for the crew's attention. "Please keep your seats and listen for a moment. I have an announcement to make. We have just dropped a new bomb on Japan which has more power than twenty thousand tons of TNT. It has been an overwhelming success!"

With the crew cheering, he rushed out to spread the news. "He was not actually laughing," wrote Merriman Smith, "but there was a broad smile on his face. In the small dispatch which he waved at the men of the ship, he saw the quick end of the war written between the lines." At the officers' ward, telling the men to stay seated, he repeated what he had said in the mess, then added, "We won the gamble." He said he had never been happier about any announcement he had ever made.

All this happened very fast, and as George Elsey was to recall, the President's response seemed in no way inappropriate. "We were all excited. Everyone was cheering." Within minutes, the ship's radio was carrying news bulletins from Washington about the bomb. Then came the broadcast of the President's message, the text of which had been released at the White House only moments before, at 11:00 A.M. Washington time.

> Sixteen hours ago an American airplane dropped one bomb on Hiroshima.... It is an atomic bomb. It is a harnessing of the basic power of the universe.... We are now prepared to obliterate more rapidly and completely every productive enterprise the Japanese have above ground in any city. We shall destroy their docks, their factories, and their communications. Let there be no mistake; we shall completely destroy Japan's power to make war.... If they do not now accept our terms they may expect a rain of ruin from the air, the like of which has never been seen on this earth....

Not in this or any of the broadcasts was there mention of how much damage had been done at Hiroshima, since no details were yet known in Washington.

Excitement, feelings of relief swept the country—and especially among families with sons or husbands in the service. Surely the war would be over any day.

To the millions of men serving in the Pacific, and those in Europe preparing to be shipped to the Pacific, the news came as a joyous reprieve. One of them was the writer Paul Fussell, then a twenty-one-year-old lieutenant with an infantry platoon in France who was scheduled to take part in the invasion of Honshu, despite wounds in the leg and back so severe that he had been judged 40 percent disabled. "But even if my legs buckled whenever I jumped out of the back of the truck, my condition was held to be satisfactory for whatever lay ahead." After Hiroshima, he remembered, after the realization "that we would not be obliged to run up the beaches near Tokyo assault-firing while being mortared and shelled, for all the fake manliness of our facades we cried with relief and joy. We were going to live. We were going to grow up to adulthood after all."

Yet, even so, news of the bomb brought feelings of ambiguity and terror of a kind never before experienced by Americans. Children in households that had been untouched by the war would remember parents looking strangely apprehensive and wondering aloud what unimaginable new kind of horror had been unleashed. Could the poor world ever possibly be the same again?

"Yesterday," wrote Hanson Baldwin in *The New York Times* on August 7, "we clinched victory in the Pacific, but we sowed the whirlwind."

Editorial speculation was extremely grave. "It is not impossible," wrote the Chicago *Tribune,* "that whole cities and all the people in them may be obliterated in a fraction of a second by a single bomb." "We are dealing with an invention that could overwhelm civilization," said the Kansas City *Star,* and in St. Louis the *Post-Dispatch* warned that possibly science had "signed the mammalian world's death warrant and deeded an earth in ruins to the ants." The Washington *Post,* in an editorial titled "The Haunted Wood," said that with Truman's revelations concerning the new bomb it was as if all the worst imaginary horrors of science fiction had come true.

The weather in Washington had turned abnormally cool for August, making ideal nights for sleeping, but, observed James Reston of *The New York Times,* thoughtful people were not sleeping so well.

"Some of our scientists say that the area [in Hiroshima] will be uninhabitable for many years because the bomb explosion had made the ground radioactive and destructive of animal life," wrote Admiral Leahy, who had flown home ahead of the President. "The lethal possibilities of such atomic action in the future is frightening, and while we are the first to have it in our possession, there is a certainty that it will in the future be developed by potential enemies and that it will probably be used against us."

Robert Oppenheimer had predicted a death toll of perhaps 20,000. Early reports from Guam on August 8 indicated that 60 percent of Hiroshima had been leveled and that the number of killed and injured might reach as high as 200,000. In time, it would be estimated that 80,000 people were killed instantly and that another 50,000 to 60,000 died in the next several months. Of the total, perhaps 10,000 were Japanese soldiers.

Many thousands more suffered from hideous thermal burns, from shock, and from radioactive poisoning. Later also, there would be eyewitness accounts of people burned to a cinder while standing up, of birds igniting in midair, of women "whose skin hung from them like a kimono" plunging shrieking into rivers. "I do not know how many times I called begging that they cut off my burned arms and legs," a fifth-grade girl would remember.

Anne O'Hare McCormick, who had described Truman, Churchill, and Stalin poking about the graveyard of Berlin, wrote now of the bomb as the "ultimatum to end all ultimatums" because it was only a small sample of what might lie in store in laboratories where scientists and soldiers joined forces.

No one as yet was blaming the scientists or the soldiers or the President of the United States.

On the afternoon of August 7, just before 5:00 P.M., the *Augusta* tied up at Norfolk. Truman left immediately by special train for Washington and by the morning of the 8th the country knew he was back at his desk. There was still no word from Japan, no appeal for mercy or sign of surrender. At the Pentagon, Stimson and Marshall worried privately that the bomb had failed to achieve the desired shock effect.

On August 9, the papers carried still more stupendous news. A million Russian troops had crossed into Manchuria—Russia was in the war against Japan—and a second atomic bomb had been dropped on the major Japanese seaport of Nagasaki.

No high-level meeting had been held concerning this second bomb. Truman had made no additional decision. There was no order issued beyond the military directive for the first bomb, which had been sent on July 25 by Marshall's deputy, General Thomas T. Handy, to the responsible commander in the Pacific, General Carl A. Spaatz of the Twentieth Air Force. Paragraph 2 of that directive had stipulated: "Additional bombs will be delivered on the above targets as soon as made ready by the project staff. . . ." A second bomb—a plutonium bomb nicknamed "Fat Man"— being ready, it was "delivered" from Tinian, and two days ahead of schedule, in view of weather conditions.

Later estimates were that seventy thousand died at Nagasaki, where the damage would have been worse had the bombardier not been off target by two miles.

"For the second time in four days Japan felt the stunning effect of the terrible weapon," reported the Los Angeles *Times,* which like most papers implied that the end was very near. On Capitol Hill the typical reaction was, "It won't be long now."

Senator Richard B. Russell, Jr., of Georgia, one of the most respected, influential figures in Washington, sent a telegram to Truman saying there must be no letup in the assault on the Japanese.

> Let us carry the war to them until they beg us to accept unconditional surrender. The foul attack on Pearl Harbor brought us into the war, and I am unable to see any valid reason why we should be so much more considerate and lenient in dealing with Japan than with Germany. . . . If we do not have available a sufficient number of atomic bombs with which to finish the job immediately, let us carry on with TNT and fire bombs until we can produce them. . . . This was total war as long as our enemies held all the cards. Why should we change the rule now, after the blood, treasure and enterprise of the American people have given us the upper hand? . . .

Truman sent Russell a heartfelt answer written that same day, August 9:

> I know that Japan is a terribly cruel and uncivilized nation in warfare but I can't bring myself to believe that, because they are beasts, we should ourselves act in that same manner.
>
> For myself I certainly regret the necessity of wiping out whole populations because of the "pigheadedness" of the leaders of a nation, and, for your information, I am not going to do it unless it is absolutely necessary. It is my opinion that after the Russians enter into the war the Japanese will very shortly fold up.
>
> My object is to save as many American lives as possible but I also have a human feeling for the women and children of Japan.

That night, in his radio address on Potsdam, he made a point of urging all Japanese civilians to leave the industrial cities immediately and save themselves.

"I realize the tragic significance of the atomic bomb," he told the American people.

> Its production and its use were not lightly undertaken by this government. But we knew that our enemies were on the search for it. . . .
>
> We won the race of discovery against the Germans.
>
> Having found the bomb we have used it. We have used it against those who attacked us without warning at Pearl Harbor, against those who have starved and beaten and executed American prisoners of war,

against those who have abandoned all pretense of obeying international laws of warfare. We have used it in order to shorten the agony of war, in order to save the lives of thousands and thousands of young Americans.

We shall continue to use it until we completely destroy Japan's power to make war. Only a Japanese surrender will stop us.

Reflecting on the future and "this new force," he said with feeling: "It is an awful responsibility which has come to us."

On the morning Nagasaki was bombed, a crucial meeting of Japan's Supreme Council for the Direction of the War had been taking place in Prime Minister Suzuki's bomb shelter outside the Imperial Palace in Tokyo. The meeting was deadlocked, with three powerful military commanders (two generals and one admiral) arguing fervently against surrender. It was time now to "lure" the Americans ashore. General Anami, the war minister, called for one last great battle on Japanese soil—as demanded by the national honor, as demanded by the honor of the living and the dead. "Would it not be wondrous for this whole nation to be destroyed like a beautiful flower?" he asked. But when news of Nagasaki was brought in, the meeting was adjourned to convene again with the Emperor that night in the Imperial Library. In the end, less than twenty-four hours after Nagasaki, it was Hirohito who decided. They must, he said, "bear the unbearable" and surrender.

The Japanese government would accept the Potsdam Declaration with the understanding that the Emperor would remain sovereign.

Truman had been up early as usual the morning of Friday, August 10, and was about to leave his private quarters when, at 6:30, a War Department messenger arrived with the radio dispatch. Byrnes, Stimson, Leahy, and Forrestal were summoned for a meeting at 9:00. "Could we continue the Emperor and yet expect to eliminate the warlike spirit in Japan?" Truman later wrote. "Could we even consider a message with so large a 'but' as the kind of unconditional surrender we had fought for?"

Stimson, as he had before, said the Emperor should be allowed to stay. He thought it the only prudent course. Leahy agreed. Byrnes was strongly opposed. He wanted nothing less than unconditional surrender, the policy Roosevelt and Churchill had agreed to at the Casablanca Conference in 1943, and he was certain the American people felt the same. The Big Three had called for unconditional surrender at Potsdam, he reminded them. He could not understand "why now we should go further than we were willing to go at Potsdam when we had no atomic bomb and Russia was not in the war." Truman asked to see the Potsdam statement.

Forrestal thought that perhaps with different wording the terms could be made acceptable and this appealed to Truman.

He decided against Byrnes. He decided, as he recorded in his diary, that if the Japanese wanted to keep their emperor, then "we'd tell 'em how to keep him." The official reply, as worded by Byrnes, stated that the Emperor would remain but "subject to the Supreme Commander of the Allied Powers." If it was not unconditional surrender, it was something very close to it, exactly as Naotake Sato, the Japanese ambassador in Moscow, had warned Tokyo it would be a month before.

At a Cabinet meeting that afternoon, Truman reported these developments in strictest confidence. The Allied governments were being notified. Meantime, he had ordered no further use of atomic bombs without his express permission. (One more bomb was available at the time.) The thought of wiping out another city was too horrible, he said. He hated the idea of killing "all those kids."

To Henry Wallace afterward, Truman complained of dreadful headaches for days. "Physical or figurative?" Wallace asked. "Both," Truman replied.

Attlee cabled his approval that evening, but the Australians were adamantly opposed. "The Emperor should have no immunity from responsibility for Japan's acts of aggression.... Unless the system goes, the Japanese will remain unchanged and recrudescence of aggression in the Pacific will only be postponed to a later generation," said the Australians, who had been excluded from Potsdam and who had fought long and suffered greatly in the war with Japan.

At the same time shattering news was released in Washington, reminding the country that the war continued. On the night of July 29, the U.S.S. *Indianapolis,* the ship that had delivered the core of the Hiroshima bomb to Tinian, was torpedoed by a Japanese submarine. The ship sank in minutes, taking hundreds of its crew with it and leaving hundreds more drifting in the sea. They were there for days, many eaten by sharks. By the time rescue ships arrived, eight hundred lives had been lost.

Chiang Kai-shek cabled his agreement the next morning, Saturday, August 11, and so, reluctantly, did the Australians. The Soviets appeared to be stalling in the hope of having some say in the control of Japan and to drive farther into Manchuria, but eventually Stalin, too, agreed. A formal reply was transmitted to Tokyo. Then the wait began.

Bess Truman had arrived at the White House from Independence; after an absence of more than two months, a semblance of normal domestic life had resumed. On Sunday, Truman was at his desk writing a letter. It was his sister's birthday. He would have written sooner, he told her, but he had been too busy. "Nearly every crisis seems to be the worst one, but after it's over, it isn't so bad. . . ."

To reporters his composure was extraordinary. He took it all, "the drama and tenseness, the waiting and watching of war's end," in "cool stride markedly lacking in showmanship and striking for its matter-of-factness." Secretary Byrnes, who kept coming and going from the somber old State Department Building next door, seemed "a little frantic" by contrast. Rumors were everywhere. Peace was imminent. Crowds had gathered outside, expecting an announcement any moment.

But Sunday passed without word from the Japanese. And so did Monday the 13th. Truman confided to his staff that he had ordered General Marshall to resume the B-29 raids. Late in the day Charlie Ross told reporters the staff would remain on duty until midnight.

The wait continued the next morning. "It began like the days that had preceded it . . . reporters and correspondents jamming the press room and lobby, some of them worn and tired after hours of waiting and from the tenseness of the waiting and uncertainty," wrote Eben Ayers. The crowds outside grew noticeably larger by the hour. Across Pennsylvania Avenue thousands of people filled Lafayette Square, the majority of them servicemen and women in summer uniforms.

The answer reached the President at five minutes past four that afternoon, Tuesday, August 14. Japan had surrendered. At 6:10 the Swiss chargé d'affaires in Washington arrived at the State Department to present Secretary Byrnes with the Japanese text, which Byrnes carried at once to the White House.

(The document would have arrived ten minutes sooner but for the fact that a sixteen-year-old messenger, Thomas E. Jones, who picked it up at the RCA offices on Connecticut Avenue to deliver it to the Swiss legation, had been stopped by the police for making a U-turn on Connecticut.)

Just before 7:00 P.M., reporters jammed into Truman's office for the announcement. Truman stood behind his desk. Seated beside him, or standing in back, were Byrnes, Leahy, Bess, most of the Cabinet, and Sue Gentry of the Independence *Examiner,* who happened to be in town and had accepted an invitation to tea with Bess that afternoon. Truman had told her to stick around because she "might get a story." ("He'd just been for a swim," she remembered. "And I thought, 'Isn't it wonderful that he could be relaxed and go take a swim!' ")

It was still bright daylight outside, because of the summer clock. In

Lafayette Square at least ten thousand people were congregated, held in check only by a thin line of police barriers and Military Police along Pennsylvania Avenue.

Truman looked crisp and formal in a double-breasted navy blue suit, blue shirt, silver-and-blue striped tie with matching handkerchief. There was some shuffling among the reporters. Truman, smiling, said hello to one or two. A Secret Service man announced, "All in." Klieg lights were turned on for the newsreel cameras. Truman glanced at the clock. At exactly seven, his shoulders squared, he began reading slowly and clearly from a sheet of paper held in his right hand: "I have received this afternoon a message from the Japanese government. . . . I deem this reply a full acceptance of the Potsdam Declaration which specifies the unconditional surrender of Japan." General MacArthur had been appointed the Supreme Allied Commander to receive the surrender.

The reporters charged for the door. Truman and Bess returned to the living quarters, but the celebration outside kept growing.

In Grandview, Missouri, in the living room of her small clapboard house, Martha Ellen Truman excused herself to take a long-distance phone call in another room.

"Hello . . . hello," a guest heard her begin. "Yes, I'm all right. Yes, I've been listening to the radio. . . . Yes, I'm all right. . . . Now you come and see me if you can. . . . Yes, all right. . . . Goodbye."

"That was Harry," she said returning through the door. "Harry's a wonderful man. . . . I knew he'd call. He always calls me after something that happens is over. . . ."

In Lafayette Square someone had started a conga line. Within minutes throngs of people had broken past the barriers and MPs and surged across the street to crowd the length of the White House fence. Streetcars and automobiles stranded in the mob were quickly covered with sailors in white who clambered on top for a better view. Everyone was cheering. Bells were ringing, automobile horns blaring. The crowd set up a chant of "We want Truman! We want Truman!"

With the First Lady beside him, the President went out on the lawn to wave and smile. He gave the V-sign as cheer after cheer went up. "I felt deeply moved by the excitement," he remembered, "perhaps as much as were the crowds. . . ." He and Bess returned to the house, but the call for him continued, so he came out again onto the porch to make a few impromptu remarks over a microphone.

"This is a great day," he began, "the day we've been waiting for. This is

462

the day for free governments in the world. This is the day that fascism and police government ceases in the world." The great task ahead was to restore peace and bring free government to the world. "We will need the help of all of you. And I know we will get it." Another roar of approval reverberated through the trees, as it would have whatever he said.

He crossed the lawn again, coming closer this time to the high iron fence, beaming, waving until his arm ached, the crowds growing ever more exuberant, in what was to be the biggest night of celebration Washington had ever seen. Half a million people filled the streets. The crush around the White House grew to fifty thousand or more. As reported in the papers the next day, one jubilant soldier flung his arms around a civilian, shouting, "We're all civilians now!"

In just three months in office Harry Truman had been faced with a greater surge of history, with larger, more difficult, more far-reaching decisions than any President before him. Neither Lincoln after first taking office, nor Franklin Roosevelt in his tumultuous first hundred days, had had to contend with issues of such magnitude and coming all at once. In boyhood Truman had pored over the pages of *Great Men and Famous Women* and *Plutarch's Lives* and concluded that men made history, and he had never changed his mind. He remained old-fashioned in this as in other ways. But if ever a man had been caught in a whirlwind not of his making, it was he. "We cannot get away from the results of the war," Stalin had said at Potsdam, and it was just such results that had beset Truman since the night he raised his right hand and took the oath of office beneath the Wilson portrait. The launching of the United Nations, the menacing presence of the Red Army in Eastern Europe, Britain's bankruptcy, the revealed horrors of the Holocaust, the wasteland of Berlin, the advent of the nuclear age in New Mexico, Hiroshima, and Nagasaki—all were the results of the war, as indeed was his own role now, if one accepted the premise, as most did, that it was the strain of the war that killed Franklin Roosevelt.

What was most striking about the long course of human events, Truman had concluded from his reading of history, were its elements of continuity, including, above all, human nature, which had changed little if at all through time. "The only new thing in the world is the history you don't know," he would one day tell an interviewer. But clearly unparalleled power and responsibility had been thrust upon him at one of history's greatest turning points, and the atomic bomb, the looming shadow of the mushroom cloud, were absolutely "new things" in the world. The old rules didn't apply any longer. Europe was a ruin, Britain finished as a world power, Asia devastated and in a state of horrendous confusion. And who was to say about Stalin?

Only once did Truman suggest that history might be something other than he cared to say, that history had its own kind of direction and force —the "greater-than-man force" that Willa Cather wrote of, when describing the start of the earlier world conflict and its effect on the lives of so many small-town men such as he from the heartland of America. In a letter to his mother on August 17, Truman spoke of the past few days as a "dizzy whirl" in which he stood at the center trying to do something.

"Everyone had been going at a terrific gait," he wrote, "but I believe we are up with the parade now."

PART FOUR

MR. PRESIDENT

11

The Buck Stops Here

Look at little Truman now
Muddy, battered, bruised—and how!

—Chicago *Tribune*

I

"Everybody wants something at the expense of everybody else and nobody thinks much of the other fellow," Truman wrote to his mother and sister at the beginning of autumn, 1945.

There were more prima donnas per square foot in public life in Washington than in all the opera companies ever to exist, he told them another day, writing at his desk in October when the trees outside the White House had begun to turn.

On a bunting-draped platform at an American Legion fair at Caruthersville, Missouri, he said that after every war came an inevitable letdown. Difficulties would follow. "You can't have anything worthwhile without difficulties." Mistakes would be made. No one who accomplished things could expect to avoid mistakes. Only those who did nothing made no mistakes.

All Americans must cooperate, he said, dedicating a dam at Gilbertsville, Kentucky. It was time for everyone to "cut out the foolishness" and "get in harness."

A war President no longer, he was finding the tasks of peace more difficult and vexing than he ever imagined. "We want to see the time come when we can do the things in peace that we have been able to do in war," he had said with such conviction in July, at the small military ceremony in the cobbled square in Berlin. "If we can put this tremendous machine of ours . . . to work for peace, we can look forward to the greatest age in the history of mankind." But how? How possibly now, when no one wanted to cooperate any longer?

His troubles had begun with his first postwar message to Congress, only days after the Japanese surrender ceremonies on board the battleship *Missouri* in Tokyo Bay. Sent to the Hill on September 6, the message was 16,000 words in length (the longest since the Theodore Roosevelt era) and presented a 21-point domestic program that included increased unemployment compensation, an immediate increase in the minimum wage, a permanent Fair Employment Practices Committee, tax reform, crop insurance for farmers, a full year's extension of the War Powers and Stabilization Act, meaning the government would keep control over business, and federal aid to housing to make possible a million new homes a year.

> We must go on. We must widen our horizon further. We must consider the redevelopment of large areas of the blighted and slum sections of our cities so that in the truly American way they may be remade to accommodate families not only of low-income groups as heretofore, but every income group. . . .

It was an all-out, comprehensive statement of progressive philosophy and a sweeping liberal program of action that Truman had begun work on, dictating his thoughts to Sam Rosenman, on board the *Augusta* returning from Potsdam, and that he had since put in a full ten days of concentrated effort on, adding new sections, editing and revising. He had no wish to wait for his State of the Union address to present his domestic program. Nor did he intend to go to Congress with it on a piecemeal basis. He wanted one big message, and as time would tell, its significance was enormous, setting his domestic program on a liberal path at the very start. It was one thing to have voted for this kind of program in the Senate, when he was following the head of his party, Rosenman told him. It was quite another to be the head of the party and recommend and fight for it.

For those Republicans and conservative Democrats who had been happily claiming that the New Deal was as good as dead, that the "Roosevelt nonsense" was over at last, because they "knew" Harry Truman, it was a rude awakening. Not even FDR had ever asked for so much "at one sitting," complained House Minority Leader Joe Martin, and many of Truman's own party in Congress were equally distressed, equally disinclined to go along with him. The same conservative coalition of Republicans and southern Democrats that had stymied Roosevelt since 1937 stood ready now to block his successor. The House Ways and Means Committee, with fourteen Democrats and ten Republicans, voted to reject the unemployment compensation proposal, and shelved any further consideration of aid to the jobless. As the newspapers were saying, Truman's anticipated six-month "waltz with Congress" was over before it began.

Labor leaders demanded an end to wage controls, but a hold on prices. Business leaders demanded the opposite. Nobody wanted more inflation of the kind the war had brought. Yet while most everyday commodities were in short supply, nearly everyone seemed to have money to spend— billions of dollars put aside in war bonds and savings accounts.

Meanwhile, the Pentagon rushed to cancel billions of dollars in war contracts—$15 billion in less than a month. Boeing aircraft laid off 21,000 workers, Ford laid off 50,000, at the very moment when hundreds of thousands of soldiers were pouring home expecting to find jobs. Fully 12 million men and women were in uniform and hoping to return to "normal" life as soon as possible.

Prophecies of economic doom had become commonplace. His own downfall as a post-World War I haberdasher vivid in memory, Truman reminded Congress of what the country had experienced then. "We found ourselves in one of the worst inflations in our history, culminating in the crash of 1920 and 1921. We must be sure this time not to repeat that bitter mistake." Worse by far and closer to mind was the Great Depression, which had never really ended by 1939, when the war began in Europe. If the end of the war truly meant a return to what had been "normal" before the war, then the prospect was grim indeed.

As everyone knew, the nation had thrived on the war. Production of goods and services in 1945 was more than twice what it had been in 1939. If the cost of living was up by some 30 percent, the income of the average worker had also doubled and unemployment was less than 2 percent, an unbelievable figure. Farm income was five times what it had been when Truman was running the farm at Grandview. Never had Americans known such prosperity. Yet the certainty that hard times would return was also widespread and deeply ingrained. For a whole generation of Americans, fear of another Depression would never go away. It was coming "as sure as God made little green apples," fathers warned their families at the dinner table, and next time it would be "bad enough to curl your hair." Nor were the supposed experts any less pessimistic. In his report to the President at a Cabinet meeting on October 19, Secretary of Commerce Henry Wallace estimated that the drop in the gross national product in the coming months would be $40 billion, the drop in wages $20 billion, which by spring could mean 7 or 8 million unemployed—1939 all over again.

Even had there been time to plan and prepare, even if it had been possible to ignore the clamor to "bring the boys home" and demobilize in a slower, more orderly fashion, the problems of "reconversion" would have been staggering. As it was, sudden peace had caught the country almost as ill-prepared as had sudden war. A populace that had been willing to accept shortages and inconveniences, ceilings on wages and inadequate housing since 1941—because there was "a war on"—seemed desperate to make up for lost time, demanding everything at once.

By October, the country was facing the biggest housing shortage in history. In Chicago alone, reportedly, there were 100,000 homeless veterans. (The city of Chicago would shortly offer old streetcars for sale, for conversion into homes.) Among the letters pouring into the White House was one from a man in Los Angeles who told of meeting a homeless veteran, a medical sergeant, his pregnant wife and small child, and described how he had taken them in for the night because they had no place to go. "Do *something*," the writer urged the President.

Labor unions, free of their wartime pledges not to strike, called for "catch-up" pay hikes. Strikes broke out in nearly every industry. In New York, 15,000 elevator operators went out. Elsewhere 27,000 oil workers and 60,000 lumber workers walked off their jobs. In Washington, meantime, New Dealers were leaving the government in droves.

For Truman all this was extremely difficult to understand. He knew relatively little of economics and the economics of reconstruction were complicated. He failed to comprehend how a people who had shown such dedication and will through the war could overnight become so rampantly selfish and disinterested in the common good. "The Congress are balking, labor has gone crazy and management isn't far from insane in selfishness," he reported to his mother, who in her small frame house in Grandview remained an indispensable sounding board. He believed as ever in the ancient republican ideals of citizenship. Cincinnatus, the legendary Roman warrior who, after saving his country, laid down his arms and returned to the farm, remained a personal hero. As he liked to point out to visitors, he had replaced the model cannon on his desk with a shiny model plow.

His response was to work harder than ever, as if by keeping a fuller, busier schedule, moving faster, seeing more people, traveling more, he could at least set an example. On one not untypical morning he saw more than a dozen visitors in two hours, including Congressman Albert Gore of Tennessee, who brought him a bottle of Jack Daniel's; Senator Wheeler; his old Truman Committee aide, Max Lowenthal; the governor of the Virgin Islands; another congressman, Pat Cannon of Florida, who wanted to talk about hurricane damage; the young Democratic mayor of Minneapolis, Hubert Humphrey, and his wife; and a group of women sponsoring an Equal Rights amendment. ("A lot of hooey about equal rights," Truman noted on his appointment sheet as the last of these went out the door.) He "zipped" through work in what one account called "the decisive style that is now recognized as typically Truman." He made changes with "hurried" strokes of the pen, seldom anything earthshaking, "but everything brisk." At one press conference he took all of five minutes to announce that he was reorganizing the Labor Department, transferring authority over the Office of Economic Stabilization to the Office of War Mobilization and Reconversion under John Snyder, appointing Stuart Symington of St. Louis to a new Surplus Property Administration, accepting the resignation of Secretary of War Stimson, appointing Under Secretary Robert Patterson as Stimson's replacement, and naming Senator Harold H. Burton of Ohio to the Supreme Court. "Anything *else,* Mr. President?" asked a reporter, and the room erupted with laughter.

He greatly enjoyed such moments. He loved rewarding a loyal old friend like Snyder with the prestige and power of an important job. It was among the prime satisfactions of the successful politician's life, not to say what was expected of him as a good Jacksonian Democrat. He had always taken care of his own with jobs large and small, as best he could. He had hated firing Eddie McKim and eventually arranged a vague job for him with the Rural Finance Commission. When Jake Vardaman, the naval aide, began flaunting his supposed authority beyond bounds, irritating too many people at the White House, including Bess Truman, and Vardaman, too, had to be eased out, Truman put him on the Federal Reserve Board, a position for which Vardaman was plainly ill-suited. Even former Senator Bennett Clark of Missouri, who had so often made life difficult for him over the years, was not forgotten. On September 12, Truman made Clark a Judge of the U.S. Court of Appeals for the District of Columbia, and shortly afterward, when Clark was remarried in the little northern Virginia town of Berryville, Truman stood beside him as best man, something he had never done before.

Two official ceremonial duties that fall moved him deeply, which made both occasions especially memorable.

Before a small, sunny gathering in the Rose Garden on September 21, the day of Henry Stimson's retirement, Truman presented the elderly Secretary of War with the Distinguished Service Medal and did so with great simple dignity. As his staff had come to appreciate, it was at such occasions that Truman excelled. He was at his best with small groups, close-up and entirely himself, yet keenly aware of the meaning of the occasion. It was Stimson's seventy-eighth birthday and his last day in

Washington. "If anyone in the government was entitled to one [a medal] it is that good man," Truman wrote to Bess, who was back in Independence.

In November, in the courtyard at the Pentagon, at another no less moving farewell, this for General Marshall, Truman again presented the Distinguished Service Medal, which was the general's only American military decoration of the war. (Marshall had refused repeatedly to accept any such honors, saying it would be improper for him while men were dying overseas.) To Truman, Marshall, more than any other man, had been responsible for winning the war, and he spoke now of Marshall as a tower of strength to two presidents. "He takes his place at the head of the great commanders of history," Truman said, clearly meaning that exactly. Later, Truman said there wasn't a decoration big enough for General Marshall.

But such occasions were rare. More often he was feeling close to despair over how much needed to be done and how little real say he had, how little time there was ever to focus on any one problem. The strain began to tell. "The pressure here," he told his mother, "is becoming so great I hardly get my meals in, let alone do what I want to do."

His speaking trips around the country, intended as a way to bring his message to the people, too often resulted in adverse publicity that was seen as his own doing. At the American Legion fair at Caruthersville, Missouri, talking of the "difficulties" to be faced, he spoke seriously and thoughtfully of the atomic bomb. He had asked Congress for the establishment of a new Atomic Energy Commission under civilian, not military, control, saying, "the release of atomic energy constitutes a new force too revolutionary to consider in the framework of old ideas." Sounding like the naive Mr. Smith in *Mr. Smith Goes to Washington,* he told the crowd that the way to get along in the world was to apply the Golden Rule.

> We can't stand another global war. We can't ever have another war, unless it is total war, and that means the end of our civilization as we know it. We are not going to do that. We are going to accept that Golden Rule, and we are going forward to meet our destiny which I think Almighty God intended us to have.

But at Caruthersville, in the cotton country of Missouri's southeastern "Boot Heel," he also paused on a morning walk to spit in the Mississippi River—an old local rite, he explained to astonished reporters. He played the piano in the little hotel dining room, held open court in a drugstore, went to the races, signed autographs on napkins and blank checks, posed with Legionnaires on a mock locomotive, rang the bell, "did everything," said the Washington *Post,* "except have himself shot from the mouth of a cannon."

At a conference of several hundred Democratic congressmen and senators at a clubhouse on Jefferson Island in Chesapeake Bay, he encouraged everyone to call him Harry and joined a game of stud poker on the porch. An unnamed senator later reported that Harry Truman played "a damn good game," while another eyewitness (also unnamed), describing what a good time everyone had, said, "There was all we could eat and more than we could drink—only two people passed out."

The word "cronies" appeared with increasing frequency to depict the President's friends and associates. Harry Vaughan, his sudden eminence obviously having gone to his head, began holding his own press conferences and making speeches. Vaughan boasted of how at Potsdam he had sold a $55 watch to a Russian for $500, and in a talk before a group of Presbyterian women in Virginia, in an attempt to explain the difference between Presidents Roosevelt and Truman, he said that after a diet of caviar the country was ready for ham and eggs.

Several of the presidential staff grew concerned over the mounting confusion at the White House. Budget Director Harold Smith judged Truman to be a man of "fine keen intelligence," but regrettably disorganized. At a staff meeting in mid-October, Truman himself admitted to being "in the doldrums" over how things were going. He would cut back on his appointments, he said, cancel some trips—news that "delighted" everyone, wrote Eben Ayers, the assistant press secretary, who worried especially over stories about Harry Vaughan and poker games and drinking, certain that sooner or later they would bring trouble. An unobtrusive, soft-spoken man who was known among the White House press as "Mumbles," Ayers was secretly keeping a diary that would one day provide an invaluable "inside" record of the Truman years.

Outwardly, Truman appeared unchanged. Reporters described him as "chipper," "affable," "jaunty," looking "rested, fresh, and bouncy," looking always, wrote columnist Westbrook Pegler, "like his old maw just dressed him up and slicked his hair for the strawberry social." And he was still exceptionally popular, his approval rating at about 80 percent.

If Congress balked at his requests, he just asked for more. There was nothing unusual about a President being rebuffed by Congress. What was novel was a President who, when repeatedly rebuffed, refused to change his tactics.

He asked for national compulsory health insurance to be funded by payroll deductions. Under the system, all citizens would receive medical and hospital service irrespective of their ability to pay. And with the cry for demobilization at a peak, he went before a joint session to call for universal military training, an idea that stood no chance, but that he believed in fervently. "We must face the fact that peace must be built upon power, as well as upon good will and good deeds." Never again could the country count on the luxury of time to arm itself. He wanted mandatory training for one year for all young men between eighteen and twenty, not as members of the armed services, but as citizens who would comprise a trained reserve, ready in case of emergency.

One morning, standing at his desk, he presented to the press a new presidential flag, telling Harry Vaughan to hold it high enough so that everyone could see. "This new flag faces the eagle toward the staff," Truman explained, "which is looking to the front all the time when you are on the march, and also has him looking at the olive branch for peace, instead of the arrows for war. . . ." Both the flag and presidential seal had been redesigned for the first time since the Wilson years, and Truman meant the shift in the eagle's gaze to be seen as symbolic of a nation both on the march and dedicated to peace.

On October 26, he went to New York, to the Brooklyn Navy Yard to commission a huge new aircraft carrier, the U.S.S. *Franklin D. Roosevelt.* Later, from the deck of the battleship *Missouri,* he reviewed a line of fifty warships in the Hudson River, while overhead flew twelve hundred Navy planes. The eagle had never held such arrows. It was a spectacle of national power such as no Commander in Chief had ever beheld. And it was all rapidly dissolving. Had he tried then, in these last days of 1945, to halt the pell-mell demobilization under way and keep American fighting forces intact, he might have been impeached, so overwhelming was the country's desire for a return of its young men and women now that the war was won, the enemy crushed. It wasn't demobilization at all, he later remarked. "It was disintegration."

Riding in a caravan to Central Park to deliver a Navy Day speech (the first presidential address to be broadcast on television), he was cheered by tremendous crowds —3 to 5 million people at least, Mayor Fiorello LaGuardia told Truman and Admiral Leahy as they waved from the open car. To Leahy it was a triumphal procession such as no Roman emperor could have dreamed of.

Yet the press was already judging Truman only fair at his job. He was faulted for dealing with large issues in a "small-scale way," for too often "muddling through," while banking on "an apparently irrepressible and often-expressed belief that everything will always work itself out."

The labor situation grew steadily worse. Picket lines became an established sign of the times. And Truman wavered. In seeming support of labor, he called for reasonable pay raises through collective bargaining. Then, under pressure from both Democrats and Republicans to get tough with the unions, he asked Congress to forbid strikes in large national industries for thirty days, until the situation could be appraised by a fact-finding board—an idea that pleased neither labor nor management nor Congress. In the meantime, 175,000 employees of General Motors, workers in plants in 19 states, walked out in a strike that would last more than three months.

His was a thankless job, Truman told the writer John Gunther, who had not seen him since he was Vice President and was struck by the change. "Tiny lines had grown around his mouth," Gunther wrote. "He looked tired, perplexed, and annoyed."

On another day Robert Oppenheimer came to see him privately, and in a state of obvious agitation said he had blood on his hands because of his work on the bomb. For Truman, it was a dreadful moment. Oppenheimer's self-pitying, "cry-baby" attitude was abhorrent. "The blood is on my hands," he told Oppenheimer. "Let me worry about that." Afterward he said he hoped he would not have to see the man ever again.

In November the American ambassador to China, Patrick J. Hurley, who had returned to Washington for consultation, announced unexpectedly that he was resigning because of the way the State Department was siding with the Chinese Communists. Hurley broke the news in a speech at the Press Club, barely an hour after telling Truman that all was under control in China and that he would be returning there shortly. "To me, this was an utterly inexplicable about-face, and what had caused it I cannot imagine even yet," Truman would write years later. At the time he was more explicit. Tearing a yellow news copy from the White House ticker, he stormed into a Cabinet meeting saying, "See what a son-of-a-bitch did to me."

Clinton Anderson, the Secretary of Agriculture, suggested that the President immediately name General Marshall as the new special ambassador to China and thus take the headlines away from Hurley. It was an inspired suggestion. From the Red Room, Truman telephoned Marshall at his home in Leesburg, Virginia.

"General, I want you to go to China for me," he said.

"Yes, Mr. President," Marshall replied and hung up.

Truman had hated to make the call. Marshall by then had had all of six days of retirement. Marshall said later that he had ended the call abruptly because his wife walked into the room and he wished to explain to her himself, rather than have her overhear a telephone conversation.

At a Gridiron Club dinner in December, only half in jest, Truman declared that General William Tecumseh Sherman had been wrong. "I'm telling you I find peace is hell. . . ."

His health insurance plan was getting nowhere. Another message, and of equal importance to Truman, called for unification of the armed forces, under a single Secretary of Defense, an idea the Navy vehemently opposed and that Bob Hannegan thought politically unwise, arguing that it was foolish ever to wage an unnecessary fight that he might lose. But Truman insisted. He wanted to break up the power of the West Point and Annapolis cliques, to make the armed services more democratic—a noble aspiration, many around him agreed, but impossible, they felt. It was his duty to send the message, he said, because it represented his conviction.

To Sam Rosenman, who had grown immensely fond of Truman, the chief difference between Truman and Roosevelt was that Truman "paid much less attention to what his actions were doing towards his chances for reelection. . . . Truman did a great many things that Roosevelt, because he knew the effect it would have, never would have done."

To many it appeared that the President's easy familiarity with members of Congress—their talk of good old Harry and so forth—was proving a handicap. If his program was steadfastly in the Roosevelt tradition, they could be quite as obdurate as they had been with Roosevelt just before the war, only now without the fear that, like Roosevelt, Truman might take his case to the country with powerful effect. Truman couldn't "awe them," and as was said, in American politics "a fearsome respect" usually achieved better results than camaraderie.

Meantime, privately, Truman felt that Jimmy Byrnes, who was in Moscow at a Foreign Ministers' Conference, was failing to keep him sufficiently informed. To Henry Wallace he expressed concern that the peacetime use of atomic energy might so reduce the length of the working day that people would "get into mischief." Once, at a Cabinet meeting in December, Wallace politely but pointedly lectured him for not knowing how many atomic bombs were in stock and for saying further that he really didn't want to know. "Mr. President, you *should* know," Wallace insisted. "The President retreated in some confusion and said he guessed he should know and then covered up by saying, 'I do know in a general way,' " Wallace noted in his diary.

From Byrnes and Wallace both, Truman got the distinct impression that each thought his own judgment considerably superior to that of the President.

To many of the holdovers from the Roosevelt years, as to prominent liberals elsewhere, it appeared the administration was going to pieces. In the stridently liberal New York newspaper *PM,* columnist Max Lerner offered a scathing assessment of the President, calling him one of history's "wild accidents." There had been leaders in the past who had greatness thrust upon them by circumstance, but never one who wore the mantle of great office so uneasily, wrote Lerner, who had been to Missouri and felt he now understood Truman's strengths and defects. The President's "first quality" was personal honesty. He was also loyal to his friends and a hard worker. The overriding problem, said Lerner, was his "middle-class mentality":

> In a crisis the middle-class mind falls back on personal virtues and personal relations. In a crisis the middle-class mind shows itself more fearful of labor and strikes and labor's political power than of anything else. In a crisis the middle-class mind tries to assume a lofty detachment from the deep issues of the day, and tries to blink the real social cleavage and struggles.
>
> These struggles are not reconcilable by a personal appeal for cooperation. In the end you have to choose your side and fight on it.... In the end, President Truman's basic weakness lies in his failure to understand imaginatively the nature and greatness of the office he holds.

Though Bess, Margaret, and Madge Wallace departed for Independence a week before Christmas, Truman remained at the White House until Christmas morning when he decided to fly home despite dreadful weather. The first snow of winter had fallen on Washington two weeks earlier. On the 19th another five inches fell in a storm that hit much of the country. Christmas morning he awoke to a driving wind, sleet and rain. National Airport was sheathed in ice, he was told. All commercial flights were canceled. But after conferring with his pilot, Lieutenant Colonel Hank Myers, Truman decided to go, and when *The Sacred Cow* at last appeared out of the clouds over Kansas City, it was more than an hour overdue. Newspapers and radio commentators called the trip foolhardy —"one of the most hazardous 'sentimental journeys' ever undertaken" by a chief of state, said *The New York Times.* Had anyone known the sort of welcome he received on reaching the big gray house on North Delaware Street, the journey would have seemed even more unnecessary, his position still more pathetic. For Bess had been anything but sentimental or approving. At his desk in Washington three days later, Truman would write one of the most forlorn letters of his life:

477

December 28, 1945

Dear Bess:

Well I'm here in the White House, the great white sepulcher of ambitions and reputations. I feel like last year's bird's nest which is on its second year. Not very often I admit I am not in shape. I think maybe that exasperates you, too, as a lot of other things I do and pretend to do exasperate you. But it isn't intended for that purpose. . . .

You can never appreciate what it means to come home as I did the other evening after doing at least one hundred things I didn't want to do and have the only person in the world whose approval and good opinion I value look at me like I'm something the cat dragged in and tell me I've come in at last because I couldn't find any reason to stay away. I wonder why we are made so that what we really think and feel we cover up?

This head of mine should have been bigger and better proportioned. There ought to have been more brain and a larger bump of ego or something to give me an idea that there can be a No. 1 man in the world. I didn't want to be. But, in spite of the opinions to the contrary, *Life* and *Time* say I am. [He was on the cover of *Time* that week as "Man of the Year."]

If that is the case, you, Margie, and everyone else who may have any influence on my actions must give me help and assistance; because no one ever needed help and assistance as I do now. If I can get the use of the best brains in the country and a little help from those I have on a pedestal at home, the job will be done. . . .

Kiss my baby and I love you in season and out,

Harry

But thinking better of it, he never mailed the letter. It was tucked in a desk drawer together with its unused envelope.

The grim weather held as he struggled to keep control of events, his chief aggravation now the behavior of his Secretary of State.

Before returning from Independence, Truman had been notified by Charlie Ross that Byrnes, in winding up the Moscow conference, had released a communiqué in advance of any summary report to the President. To make matters worse, Byrnes, en route home, notified Ross to arrange air time on all the radio networks, so that he could report to the nation before seeing the President. Clearly, Byrnes had forgotten his manners.

Senator Vandenberg, disturbed that Byrnes had been too conciliatory with the Russians, rushed to the White House demanding to know what was going on.

This was on Friday, December 28, the day of Truman's plaintive letter to Bess. Afterward, he left for a cruise down the Potomac on the presidential yacht, *Williamsburg,* again disregarding the miserable weather. When Byrnes landed in Washington the following day, Saturday the 29th, a telegram from Truman was waiting for him: "Suggest you come down today or tomorrow to report your mission. . . . We can then discuss among other things the advisability of a broadcast by you. . . ."

The relationship between the two men had never been easy or entirely candid. Byrnes did indeed consider himself better equipped and more deserving than Truman to be President and he was not always successful in concealing that. Though Truman considered Byrnes extremely bright, his experience in government unequaled, he had never felt he could entirely trust him. En route to Potsdam, Truman had referred to him in a diary entry as his "able and conniving" Secretary of State. "My but he has a keen mind," Truman wrote. "And he is honest. But all country politicians are alike. They are sure all other politicians are circuitous in their dealings."

After a hurried flight by special plane, Byrnes went aboard the *Williamsburg* at Quantico, Virginia, and met with Truman privately in Truman's stateroom. A cold rain was falling on the river. Everything outside was gray and forbidding.

By Truman's account, written much later, he closed the door and gave Byrnes a sharp dressing down:

> I told him I did not like the way in which I had been left in the dark about the Moscow conference. I told him that, as President, I intended to know what progress we were making and what we were doing in foreign negotiations. I said that it was shocking that a communiqué should be issued in Washington announcing a foreign-policy development of major importance that I had never heard of. I said I would not tolerate a repetition of such conduct.

Byrnes, however, would insist the conversation was entirely pleasant, and according to others on board, it was not so much Truman as Admiral Leahy who gave Byrnes a hard time. (Leahy, as was known, considered Byrnes "a horse's ass.") Dean Acheson, who was not present, but who developed an understanding of both Truman and Byrnes, later speculated that both their impressions were genuine; that Truman, in recalling such encounters, was inclined to exaggerate his "bark," when in reality he was nearly always extremely considerate of the feelings of others; and that Byrnes, as a veteran of South Carolina politics, would never have taken as personal criticism Truman's demand to be kept informed.

In any event, the meeting marked a change in the relationship. There was no open break, but Truman's confidence in his Secretary of State was not to be the same again. Six days later, still steaming mad, he wrote a longhand letter to "My dear Jim," saying that while he wanted to give members of his Cabinet ample authority, he had no intention of relinquishing the authority of the President or "to forego the President's prerogative to make the final decision." He was intensely concerned about Russia, tired of "babying" the Soviets. "Unless Russia is faced with an iron fist and strong language another war is in the making. Only one language do they understand, 'How many divisions have you?'"

According to an account that Truman wrote years later, he then called Byrnes to his office and read the letter aloud. But again Byrnes declared that no such scene occurred—if it had, Byrnes said, he would have resigned at once. But for the record Truman noted on the letter in his own hand at the time: "Read to the Sec. of State and discussed—not typed or mailed." Later, in a conversation with Eben Ayers, Truman said he had most definitely read the letter to Byrnes, "right here in this office with him sitting right where you are. I told him I was not going to give him the letter but wanted to read it to him." Byrnes's face, said Truman, had turned "fiery red."

It was a letter like others to come in Truman's presidency. He called them his "longhand spasms," and there appears indeed to have been something sudden and involuntary about them. They seemed to serve some deep psychological need, as a vent for his anger, and were seldom intended for anyone to see. They cleared the air for him. He felt better almost immediately and, unsent, they did no one any harm. Yet in tone and content they bore little or no resemblance to the way he was ordinarily with people. "I have never heard him say, or heard of him saying a harsh, bitter, or sarcastic word to anyone, whatever the offense or failure," Dean Acheson would write.

II

With the new year under way, there was little time for brooding, seldom time enough for anything. A steel strike loomed, threatening the whole economy. Hurried meetings were held. Official cars came and went in the White House drive. "1946 is our year of decision," Truman had told the country in a radio broadcast. "This year we lay the foundation for our economic structure which will have to serve for generations."

The steel workers' union, headed by Phil Murray, called for a wage increase of 19½ cents an hour. The steel companies, represented by Benjamin Fairless of U.S. Steel, offered 15 cents. At the conclusion of a long, arduous session at the White House on January 12, Truman was able to announce that Murray had agreed to postpone the strike for one week. After another session on the 17th, and still no agreement, Truman proposed that the steel companies grant an increase of 18½ cents. Both sides wanted time to consider and were told that they had until noon the following day.

Murray accepted the President's proposal, but Fairless refused. On January 19, 1946, at more than 1,000 mills across the country, 800,000 steel workers walked off the job in the biggest strike in history.

The whole country was in the grip of strikes. Some 200,000 meatpackers had struck by now. There was a glass workers' strike, a telephone strike, a coffinmakers' strike, a huge strike at General Electric. In Pittsburgh a strike of 3,500 electric company employees caused plant closings that affected 100,000 other workers. Streetcars stopped running, office buildings closed. "This is a disaster," said Pittsburgh's Mayor David Lawrence in a radio plea to the strikers to go back to their jobs—and Mayor Lawrence, a Democrat, was long considered a solid friend of labor.

Pressed for a statement about the steel strike at his next press conference, Truman replied, "I personally think there is too much power on each side, and I think it is necessary that the government assert the fact that *it* is the power of the people."

But how would the government assert itself?

"We are doing everything we possibly can," he answered, giving no one much hope.

A week later, he could say only, "We have been working on it all the time."

No one who had never had the responsibility could possibly understand what it was like to be President, Truman would write later, not even his closest aides or members of his family. There was no end to the "chain of responsibility that binds him, and he is never allowed to forget that he is President." Problems and decisions of every conceivable variety wound up on his desk, as did criticism and blame. In the fall, Fred Canfil had given him a small sign for the desk. "The Buck Stops Here," it said. Canfil had seen one like it in the head office of a federal reformatory in El Reno, Oklahoma, and asked the warden if a copy might be made for his friend the President, and though Truman kept it on his desk only a short time, the message would stay with him permanently.

What sustained him, Truman said, was the belief that there was more good than evil in human beings. Now even that was being put severely to the test. Congress and labor had let him down. Mrs. Roosevelt was telling friends he had the wrong sort of people around him, a theme struck also by columnist Walter Lippmann. The "blunt truth," wrote Lippmann, was that the men nearest the President did "not have the brains, and have practically none of the wisdom from experience and education to help him be President. . . ." A cartoon in the arch-conservative Chicago *Tribune* pictured the President as Little Lord Fauntleroy being baited and knocked about by a gang of tough street urchins labeled "Labor," "Management," "Party Radical," "Party Conservative," and "Foreign Diplomacy." The caption was in verse:

Little Truman Fauntleroy
Famous as "that model boy"
Always trying to do good
In the name of brotherhood
Was the leader of his class
Temporarily—alas.

Look at little Truman now.
Muddy, battered, bruised—and how!
Victim of his misplaced trust,
He has learned what good boys must.

In the alley after school,
There just ain't no golden rule.

The *Saturday Evening Post,* which claimed to represent the views and values of middle America, said the Truman administration, after ten months in office, could be labeled "at best, undistinguished." Some Washington journalists, who admired the President's fundamental decency and determination, felt sorry for him. "It was a cruel time to put inexperience in power," wrote Richard Rovere.

In the new hit movie *The Best Years of Our Lives,* which had been written by Roosevelt's former speechwriter, Robert Sherwood, and was to win nine Academy Awards, actor Fredric March, playing one of the three heroes of the story, three returning veterans of the war, declared bitterly, "Last year it was kill Japs, this year it's make money," while at another point his teenage son voiced his fear of the future—of atomic bombs, guided missiles, "and everything."

People were "befuddled" and needed "time out to get a nerve rest," Truman wrote to his mother. He wouldn't mind going on strike himself, he said. As it was, he was planning a trip to Florida.

He had installed a new White House physician, a thirty-five-year-old Army doctor, Colonel Wallace H. Graham, who was the son of the Independence doctor who looked after Mamma Truman. Concerned that the President was working too hard, Graham urged a vacation. On Graham's orders, Truman had begun taking a brisk walk of two or three miles every morning before breakfast—walks, Truman told Charlie Ross, that were helping him sleep better.

To replace Henry Stimson as Secretary of War, he had named Robert Patterson, and for Chief of Staff, to replace George Marshall, General Eisenhower, both regarded as excellent appointments. But his choice for a new Under Secretary of the Navy had suddenly blown into storm. Truman had picked Ed Pauley, the California oil man and Democratic money raiser who helped engineer his nomination for the vice presidency and who, more recently, had been working on reparation problems in Europe and Japan. Truman liked Pauley, thought him tough, straightforward, and capable of getting things done. He intended that Pauley replace Forrestal eventually, then become the first Secretary of Defense once that office was created. ("I wanted the hardest, meanest son of a bitch I could get," Truman later said.) He also knew Roosevelt had been planning to make Pauley the Under Secretary of the Navy, and further, that Forrestal approved. But Pauley's business and political background made him an unwise choice, as others at the White House saw at once. "An oil man should not be head of the department which has such a vital interest in the conservation of the nation's oil reserve," noted Eben Ayers privately, "and a politician should not be at the head of the navy."

The trouble broke when Secretary of the Interior Harold Ickes was called to testify before the Senate Committee on Naval Affairs. On the train returning from Roosevelt's funeral, Ickes revealed, Pauley had had the nerve to question him on tidelands oil policy—Pauley's very unsubtle implication being that huge campaign contributions would be made available if California's jurisdiction over the tidelands went uncontested. Truman, when he heard what Ickes had said, was beside himself, for in a meeting with Ickes just prior to Ickes's testimony, Truman had told him that while of course he must speak the truth to the committee, Truman hoped he might also be "gentle" with Pauley.

Truman felt betrayed. Ickes felt he had had no choice but to tell what he knew. Asked by reporters if he would withdraw Pauley's nomination, Truman said he would not. Asked if his relations with Ickes had changed, he said Ickes could be mistaken the same as anyone.

Ickes resigned on February 13, declaring at his own press conference that he had been "unable to commit perjury for the sake of the party" and that he could not possibly serve in the Cabinet any longer and maintain his self-respect. He was against "government by crony," Ickes further stated, an expression that would not be forgotten.

Outraged that Ickes had implied that he, the President, had asked him to commit perjury, Truman not only accepted the resignation but told Ickes he had three days to clear out.

Though Pauley denied under oath that he had ever made any such proposition to Ickes, the appointment was doomed, and once the committee agreed to affirm Pauley's personal integrity, the nomination was withdrawn at his request.

The whole affair had been extremely unpleasant, recalling for many people memories of the Harding administration, with its Teapot Dome oil scandals. Ickes, celebrated as "Honest Harold" and the "Old Curmudgeon," was incurably hard to deal with, as everyone knew, but he had been an exceptional Secretary of Interior and served longer in the job than anyone. Except for Henry Wallace, Ickes was the last of the New Dealers in the Truman Cabinet and his departure, in combination with the bitterness of his parting remarks, was taken by liberals especially as still another extremely discouraging sign. "One has the feeling," wrote the New York *Post,* "that a poorer and poorer cast is dealing desperately with a bigger and bigger story."

Remembering Ickes years later, Truman would describe him as a chronic "resigner."

He reminded me of old Salmon P. Chase, who was Secretary of the Treasury in Lincoln's Cabinet, and he thought he ought to be President, that he'd be a better President than Lincoln, and he was always resigning. He must have resigned a dozen times. . . .

Lincoln said someplace that old Chase wasn't happy unless he was unhappy, and that was just about the case with Ickes. I knew he'd turned in his resignation a few times while Roosevelt was President. . . .

The whole thing . . . was a great pity because he'd been a good man in his day.

The Florida trip was canceled. Truman kept thinking each week that perhaps the next would not be so hectic, he told his staff, but then the next week was always worse. There was always a crisis just around the corner and he had to do something about it. Many in Washington wondered if this was to be the pattern—taking problems as they came, rather than working to achieve large, clear objectives.

His popularity was tumbling. From the record high of 87 percent approval in the months after Roosevelt's death, it had fallen by February to 63 percent, according to the Gallup Poll.

Some things of importance had been accomplished: A new Central Intelligence Group was organized, a civilian agency separate from the military and the State Department, to gather and analyze intelligence data for the President; Herbert Hoover was appointed to make a survey of the world food crisis; and an Employment Act had been passed by Congress, a landmark for the Truman administration. Though failing to call for full employment, as Truman wished, it did empower the federal government "to use all practical means" to foster "maximum employment," and set up a President's Economic Council, something new, to appraise the economic outlook and consider the effect of government programs on the economy.

In addition, Truman had become the first President to recommend statehood for Alaska and Hawaii.

His new Secretary of the Interior, to fill Ickes's place, was Julius Krug, who was young and widely respected. Privately, and somewhat bitterly, Truman mused that perhaps he should add some new Kitchen Cabinet secretaries as well: a Secretary of Inflation to convince everyone that however high or low prices went, it didn't matter; a Secretary of Reaction, to abolish airplanes and restore ox carts and sailing ships; a Secretary of Columnists, to read all the columns and report to the President on how the country should be run; and a Secretary of Semantics, to supply big words as well as to tell him when to keep quiet.

The trouble with the President, it was being said, was not that he spoke his mind too often or too candidly, but that he wanted too much to please, to get along with everybody, agree with everybody. It was an approach that might serve in the Senate but not in the Executive Office. In an article titled "Everyman in the White House," Kenneth G. Crawford wrote in *The American Mercury* that while Truman was proof of the great American myth that anyone could become President, he was a flat disappointment, "essentially indecisive ... essentially vacillating," too ready to see two sides to every argument.

"He does *so* like to agree with whoever is with him at the moment," wrote Henry Wallace, who, as Secretary of Commerce, had been seeing more of Truman than usual during the labor strife. Wallace's principal worry was American policy concerning the Soviet Union. Expressing his views privately with Truman—arguing that every effort must be made to get along with the Soviets—Wallace found that Truman invariably agreed

485

with him. Yet Wallace knew the contrary views the President was receiving from people like Harriman and Leahy, and felt sure that in private Truman agreed with them, too.

Leahy, for his part, saw Byrnes and others at the State Department as too ready to accommodate the Russians. He worried that "appeasement" would lead to war, as at Munich. In his diary in late February, Leahy recorded that the President "appears to consider it necessary to adopt a strong diplomatic opposition to the Soviet program of expansion. . . ."

In fact, Truman was not of one mind regarding the Soviets, any more than official Washington was, or the country. He did truly wish to get along with the Russians quite as much as did Wallace and, like Leahy, he was steadfastly against appeasement. Nor did he see why he should consider such attitudes contradictory. He had no clear policy or long-range objectives. He was facing events only as they came, trying to be patient, trying to be prudent and maintain balance. But at bottom he had no intention of being either belligerent or weak.

Then, in a rare public address in Moscow on February 9, Stalin declared that communism and capitalism were incompatible and that another war was inevitable. He called for increased production in a new five-year plan to "guarantee our country against any eventuality." Production of materials for national defense were to be tripled; consumer goods, Stalin said, "must wait on rearmament." Confrontation with the capitalist West, he predicted, would come in the 1950s, when America would be in the depths of another depression.

Washington was stunned. Even the liberal Supreme Court Justice William O. Douglas called it the "Declaration of World War III." Since Stalin had decided to make military power his objective, wrote Walter Lippmann, the United States was left with no choice but to do the same.

The Red Army was still in Manchuria. The Russian garrison in Iran's northernmost province, Azerbaijan, was still in place, in disregard of an agreement that it would be withdrawn within six months of the German surrender. On February 16, just a week after the Stalin speech, came the sensational news from Ottawa that a spy ring had been uncovered and charged with trying to steal information on the atomic bomb for the Russians, and the ring included a member of the Canadian Parliament.

But nothing so highlighted Truman's ambivalence about relations with the Soviets as events surrounding the speech given by Winston Churchill at Fulton, Missouri, in the first week of March 1946, a speech Truman had encouraged and that he knew about in advance and approved of, despite what he later said.

Located twenty miles north of Jefferson City in rolling farm land, the little town of Fulton was the site of tiny Westminster College, a Presbyterian men's school where Harry Vaughan had once played center on the football team. The idea to invite Churchill to speak there had been the inspiration of Dr. Franc L. McCluer, president of the college. McCluer had traveled to Washington to see Vaughan, who took him in to meet "the Boss." Truman was immediately enthusiastic and penned a postscript to Churchill at the bottom of the invitation: "This is a wonderful school in my home state. Hope you can do it. I'll introduce you. Best regards."

In reply, Churchill told Truman, "Under your auspices anything I say will command some attention. . . ."

In February, while vacationing in Florida, Churchill made a flying visit to Washington to talk with Truman about the speech. "The subject . . . will be the necessity for full military collaboration between Great Britain and the U.S. in order to preserve peace in the world," Admiral Leahy recorded. On March 3, returning again to Washington from Florida, Churchill conferred still further with Leahy, this time at the British Embassy, where, propped up in bed, puffing on a huge cigar, Churchill kept scattering ashes over the manuscript pages strewn about him. Leahy found "no fault" in the speech.

The following day, Monday, March 4, riding in Roosevelt's armored railroad car, the *Ferdinand Magellan,* Truman and Churchill left by special train for Missouri, accompanied by Leahy, Vaughan, Charlie Ross, Colonel Graham, and a half-dozen others from the White House staff, plus forty-three reporters and photographers. Truman's obvious high spirits impressed everyone. He was delighted to be traveling in such good company and bringing Churchill, the most famous speaker in the world, to a college in his home state that no one ever heard of. His mood was infectious. Churchill recited Whittier's "Barbara Fritchie" and drank five Scotches before dinner.

"Mr. President," Churchill said later at the card table, "I think that when we are playing poker I will call you Harry."

"All right, Winston," Truman replied.

As the evening passed, feigning ignorance of the game, Churchill would remark, to the great amusement of the others, "Harry, what does a sequence count?" Or, "Harry, I think I'll risk a shilling on a couple of knaves."

> He took a boy's delight in the game [wrote Charlie Ross]. He couldn't seem to get the hang of the joker as a wild card for aces, straights and flushes, and so at his suggestion we made the joker completely wild.

We played straight poker. The President and the rest of us would have liked to introduce some wild games, but the Prime Minister thought this would be too confusing. Colonel Graham was the principal winner.

About 2:30 in the morning, in the middle of a hand, Churchill put down his cards and said wistfully that if he were born again he would wish to live in the United States, though he deplored a few of its customs. Which customs did he have in mind, the others asked. "You stop drinking with your meals," he said.

The next morning, Tuesday, March 5, as the train raced along the banks of the Missouri River, Churchill made a few final changes in his speech, which was then mimeographed for distribution on board. It was, he said, the most important speech of his career. Truman, having read his copy, told Churchill it would "do nothing but good" and surely "make a stir."

Pointing to the President's seal on the wall of the car, Truman explained that he had had the eagle's head turned to face the olive branch. Churchill said he thought the eagle's head should be on a swivel.

The setting and reception at Fulton were all Truman could have wished for. The day was sunny, the temperature in the high sixties, the little town spruced up and looking exactly as he liked to think of Missouri. This was the America he knew best and that he wanted Churchill to see. Thousands of people, many in from the surrounding country, were waiting to cheer them as their motorcade rolled down the red-brick main thoroughfare. At a corner near the college, on the curbstone, sat a delegation of elderly gentlemen with old-fashioned high-topped shoes and canes, who waved colored balloons, and standing behind them were several sailors in uniform.

The Westminster campus, like the town, was decked with both British and American flags. Following lunch at the home of President McCluer, an academic procession started for the gymnasium, Churchill conspicuous in the scarlet robes and plush black cap of Oxford.

In his introduction, Truman said he had never met either Churchill or Stalin until Potsdam, and that he became fond of both. Then, calling Churchill one of the outstanding men of the ages, he said, "I know he will have something constructive to say to the world. . . ."

It was a great honor, perhaps almost unique, Churchill began, for a private visitor to be introduced to an academic audience by the President of the United States.

Amid his heavy burdens, duties, and responsibilities—unsought but not recoiled from—the President traveled a thousand miles to dignify and magnify our meeting here today and to give me an opportunity of addressing this kindred nation, as well as my own countrymen across the ocean, and perhaps some other countries too.

The President has told you that it is his wish, as I am sure it is yours, that I should have full liberty to give my true and faithful counsel in these anxious and baffling times. I shall certainly avail myself of this freedom. . . .

He had, he said, high regard for the Russian people and for his wartime comrade, Marshal Stalin. "We welcome Russia to her rightful place among the leading nations of the world. We welcome her flag upon the seas. Above all, we welcome constant, frequent and growing contacts between the Russian people and our own people on both sides of the Atlantic." Still, it was his duty, Churchill said, to present "certain facts." And thus he launched into that part of the speech that was to cause a sensation, giving his own kind of glowering, dramatic emphasis to the indisputable fact that an "iron curtain" had descended in Eastern Europe.

From Stettin in the Baltic to Trieste in the Adriatic, an iron curtain had descended across the Continent. Behind that line lie all the capitals of the ancient states of Central and Eastern Europe. Warsaw, Berlin, Prague, Vienna, Budapest, Belgrade, Bucharest and Sofia, all these famous cities and the populations around them lie in what I must call the Soviet sphere, and all are subject in one form or another, not only to Soviet influence but to a very high and, in many cases, increasing measure of control from Moscow. . . .

The Soviets did not want war, but rather the fruits of war, "and the indefinite expansion of their power and doctrine." What was needed in response was a union of the Western Democracies, specifically an English-speaking union of Britain and the United States. For he knew the Russians and there was nothing they so admired as strength, nothing for which they had less respect than weakness, and military weakness most of all.

From the expression on Truman's face, his applause at several points, it was obvious he approved, as did the audience.

The immediate reaction in the country, however, was strongly in opposition. Editorials accused Churchill of poisoning the already difficult relations between the United States and Russia. America had no need for alliances with any other nation, said *The Wall Street Journal*. Truman, declared *The Nation,* had been "remarkably inept" in ever associating himself with the occasion. To Walter Lippmann the speech was an "almost catastrophic blunder." In Moscow, Stalin said it was a "call to war" with the Soviet Union.

Truman was stunned by the criticism. Returning to Washington, he quickly backed off from responsibility, telling reporters he never knew what Churchill was going to say. It was a free country, he added. Churchill had had every right to speak as he pleased. To Henry Wallace, Truman was equally disingenuous, insisting he had never seen the speech in advance, and that Churchill had "put me on the spot." When reporters pressed him for his opinion of the speech, now that he had had time to think about it, Truman lamely pleaded "no comment."

To placate Stalin, he wrote a letter offering to send the *Missouri* to bring him to the United States and promising to accompany him to the University of Missouri so that he too might speak his mind, as Churchill had. But Stalin declined the invitation.

It was a bad time for Truman. To the press and an increasing proportion of the country, he seemed bewildered and equivocating, incapable of a clear or positive policy toward the Russians. Nor did the situation appear any more focused to those in the administration who were supposedly in the know. At the same time he was disavowing Churchill's speech, he was also telling Averell Harriman that the refusal of the Soviets to withdraw from Iran could mean war. Harriman, who had quit the Moscow Embassy and was now, at Truman's urging, to become ambassador to Great Britain, approved wholeheartedly of what Churchill had said, as did Leahy, Forrestal, and Dean Acheson, all of whom, like Harriman, would have welcomed a strong endorsement by the President, and blamed Byrnes, whom they saw as too much the compromising politician in his dealings with the Soviets.

In an 8,000-word message from the Moscow Embassy that was to become known soon as "the long telegram," George Kennan, the scholarly chargé d'affaires, had tried to dash any hopes the administration might have of reasonable dealings with the Stalin regime. The Kremlin, wrote Kennan, had a neurotic view of the world, at the heart of which was an age-old Russian sense of insecurity. For this reason, the Soviet regime was "committed fanatically" to the idea that in the long run there could be no "peaceful coexistence" with the United States, and further that "it is desirable and necessary that the internal harmony of our society be disrupted, our traditional way of life destroyed, the international authority of our state broken...." Stripped of the "fig leaf" of Marxism, Kennan said, the Soviets would stand before history "as only the last of a long session of cruel and wasteful Russian rulers who have relentlessly forced their country on to ever new heights of military power in order to guarantee external security for their internally weak regimes."

But Soviet power, he stressed, was highly sensitive "to the logic of force," and for this reason usually backed off when faced with strength.

The message had been received at the State Department in February, two weeks before the Churchill speech. Harriman sent a copy to Forrestal, who thought Kennan's thesis so important he had it mimeographed and circulated through the entire administration, to virtually anyone who had anything to do with foreign and military affairs. Truman, too, read it. But though its long-range influence would be considerable, it was not the immediately galvanizing document sometimes portrayed—not at the White House. On Truman in particular, it does not appear to have had any profound or immediate effect, and most likely for the reason that he had heard much the same case made by Harriman, with his talk of a "barbarian invasion of Europe" at their first meeting the year before. In any event, for attribution, he was taking no stand one way or the other.

At a Cabinet meeting on March 22, Truman expressed surprise over the fact that the Navy was inviting some sixty members of Congress to witness the series of atomic bomb tests scheduled to be held soon on the tiny Pacific atoll of Bikini. He didn't care how many went after July 1, Truman said, but until then Congress had business to attend. Byrnes questioned the wisdom of such tests, calling them "extremely ill-advised at this time" and warning of detrimental effect on relations with the Soviets. Vice Admiral William Blandy, who was in charge of the operation, reported that 37,000 men were already assigned to take part. When Truman said a decision was needed "here and now," Byrnes declared he would prefer no tests, but that later would be better. Wallace concurred. Truman said that if the tests were canceled, $100 million would be wasted. He decided the tests would be put off until summer.

The next night Charlie Ross went to the President's private quarters at the White House to see Truman about a statement announcing the postponement. "He was in his study, working . . . Mrs. Truman was away and he was waiting for Margaret to come in," wrote Ross. "We had a drink together. He seemed lonesome." To Ross, in confidence, Truman said he was less worried about Russia than were most other people.

When reporters questioned whether he shared Harriman's view of the Russian threat, Truman replied, "I have nothing to say about it." The easy camaraderie of his earlier press conferences had given way to an atmosphere of greater caution and tension. His sister Mary Jane, who had delighted in sitting in on several of his sessions with reporters during her stay at the White House the previous year, would describe how the questions then had come "thick and fast." To her it was a wonder that Harry could answer so quickly. "It just didn't seem to me that they gave him any time at all," she said, "and all of them got a big bang out of it." Everybody had seemed to be enjoying every moment. "Once in a while he got a kind of a smarty question," she remembered. "But...[he] had just as smarty an answer." Now the smarty answers were to be avoided. Increasingly at press conferences, on the advice of Ross and others on the staff, Truman's response was "No comment," or, "Your guess is as good as mine," or, "I'll cross that bridge when I come to it."

On April 1, April Fool's Day, John L. Lewis of the United Mine Workers called a nationwide coal strike. For hundreds of thousands of miners Lewis was a leader such as had only been dreamed of in years past. As he once told them, "I have pleaded your case not in the quavering tones of a mendicant asking alms, but in the thundering voice of the captain of a mighty host, demanding the rights to which free men are entitled." Understandably, their loyalty to him was unswerving. If he said it was time to strike, they struck. And in the weeks following, on the anniversary of Truman's first year in office, a flurry of newspaper and magazine articles appeared, appraising his performance as President to date. Truman, who still began the day with four or five morning papers and regularly saw a half-dozen different magazines, probably read them all.

The *Saturday Evening Post* said charitably that perhaps every President had to learn the hard way. (Truman might have added that that was about the only way he had ever learned anything in his life.) To reporters Bert Andrews and Jack Steele, writing in the New York *Herald-Tribune,* the central question was whether the President would grow in office. "New Dealers are still unhappy, conservatives are critical, middle-of-the-roaders uncertain. They still find it impossible to decide which way Truman is going."

Noel F. Busch, in an article in *Life,* noted a curious quality to be observed often again as time passed. Showing visitors about the presidential yacht, Truman would point out the lounge, the galley, and guest rooms, then say, "And this is the President's suite," as though the President were not aboard and he himself were merely an aide or guide.

Such remarks [wrote Busch] may serve as evidence of tact or humility or both. Taken in conjunction with many other traits of speech and behavior on Truman's part, they also show a curious reluctance or even inability to think of himself as President without a conscious effort of will.

To the editors of *Life*'s more overtly Republican sister publication, *Time,* it was by now quite clear that Truman was a mediocre man, the job too big for him.

A current Washington wisecrack was, "I'm just mild about Harry." Truman, went another joke, was the weakest President since Pierce. "What did Pierce ever do?" the listener was supposed to ask. "That's the point!" the teller would exclaim.

To Mrs. Robert A. Taft, wife of the conservative Republican senator from Ohio, was attributed the line, "To err is Truman."

Some observers, however, were not so quick to dismiss him. "Here is to be seen no flaming leadership," wrote Arthur Krock, chief Washington correspondent for *The New York Times,* "little of what could be called scholarship and no more that is profound. But it is very good and human and courageous. Common sense shines out. . . ."

III

Even without the coal strike it had become the longest, most costly siege of labor trouble in the nation's history. At one point more than a million workers were out on strike, and though the most crippling shutdown thus far, in the steel industry, was by now settled, the solution had been to grant not just higher wages but an increase in steel prices, all of which was certain to spur further inflation. Nor had its settlement of the steel strike done anything to improve the standing of the administration. Truman's offer of an 18½ cent increase to the steel workers' hourly wage had been made without even waiting for his own fact-finding board to report. So now an 18½ cent raise was what everyone wanted.

The General Motors strike dragged on. From the day John L. Lewis pulled his men out of the mines, every major industry was affected. Without coal, the steel plants were again banking their furnaces. Ford and Chrysler were forced to close. Freight loadings were off 75 percent. In Chicago the use of electricity was ordered cut by half.

The issue this time with Lewis was a proposed miners' welfare fund to be financed by a 5 cent royalty on every ton of coal produced. But Truman detested the hulking Lewis, remembering his bluster and arrogance before the Truman Committee and the strikes he had called during the war. Privately, Truman thought Roosevelt would have been justified if he had had Lewis shot as a traitor. When Truman announced his concern over the legality of the proposed welfare fund, Lewis answered, "What does Truman know about the legality of anything?"

Yet more worrisome still was the mounting threat of a nationwide railroad strike, a calamity no one seemed able to face or forestall and which, when it came, revealed more about Harry Truman than all but a few episodes in his entire presidency.

His public statements were models of restraint. On the surface he was all restraint, unrattled, entirely his familiar, chipper self, the double-breasted suits smoothly pressed, shoes shined, a spring to his step, a look of alert vitality behind the thick glasses. He had time still for streams of visitors—"the customers," he called them—time always to praise or thank those on the staff who had put in longer hours than usual. He rarely missed his half-hour nap after lunch, rarely avoided the variety of ceremonial chores expected of him, and whatever the occasion, he appeared always to be enjoying himself, as though there was nothing else on his mind. In early May, *Time* portrayed him meeting successive waves of crisis like a swimmer bobbing "lightheartedly" in the surf. "In the week of his 62nd birthday, apparently nothing could shake him."

Only now and then were there momentary flashes of temper of a kind not seen before. Asked by one of the regular White House reporters at a press conference why they had been given no advance notice of a Cabinet meeting, Truman snapped, "I can hold a Cabinet meeting whenever I choose. I don't have to tell you. . . ." In the notes he kept on his daily appointment sheets, he now had something caustic or derogatory to say about nearly everyone, including old Senate friends like Burton K. Wheeler, whom he now lumped with the "spineless liberals." His own ·recent choice as the American representative on the United Nations Atomic Energy Commission, Bernard Baruch, was described as wanting "to run the world, the moon and maybe Jupiter."

Inwardly Truman was an extremely frustrated, resentful, and angry man, worn thin by criticism, fed up with crises not of his making and with people who, as he saw it, cared nothing for their country, only their own selfish interests. "Big money has too much power and so have the big unions—both are riding to a fall because I like neither," he had written to his mother earlier, and his mood since had only worsened.

A railroad strike coming on top of the coal strike would mean almost unimaginable catastrophe, paralysis everywhere. Negotiations between railway management and twenty different railway unions had dragged on for months, with Labor Secretary Schwellenbach serving not very effectively as Truman's mediator, while assisted by a new man on the White House staff, a big, gregarious, gum-chewing, former economics professor and labor specialist from Alabama named John R. Steelman. The unions had demanded higher wages. Truman, invoking the Railway Labor Act that provided for a sixty-day mediation period, had ordered a delay in the strike. In April the negotiations fell apart and the strike was set for May

18. More talk followed, Steelman now replacing Schwellenbach as Truman's principal representative and apparently making progress. Of the twenty unions involved, all but two were ready to reach an accommodation.

The problem was that the two holdouts were the two major unions. What so exasperated Truman was that they were also headed by two of his old allies, A. F. Whitney, president of the Brotherhood of Railroad Trainmen, and Alvanley Johnston, president of the Brotherhood of Locomotive Engineers, the same pair who in his "hour of greatest need" in the 1940 senate race backed him when no one would, providing the lion's share of the money for his campaign. Moreover, at Chicago in 1944 they had been in the thick of the drive to make him Roosevelt's running mate.

Whitney and Johnston were two white-haired, veteran battlers, both now in their seventies. Whitney, whom Truman knew best and liked, had by far the greatest power, since he represented more than 200,000 trainmen in 1,145 "lodges" nationwide. Johnston, who looked like a cartoonist's version of a labor boss, with a girth so broad he had difficulty buttoning his suit jacket, spoke for 80,000 locomotive engineers. Between them they could shut down every railroad—all passenger service, all freight movement—from coast to coast and there appeared to be nothing anyone could do about it.

As the coal strike continued, John L. Lewis—large, theatrical, perpetually scowling under a broad-brimmed black fedora—was seen coming and going from the West Wing of the White House, his entrances and exits made always, for the benefit of the newsreel cameras, at a slow, ambling walk, a man very conscious of the fact that he was the center of attention. On May 13, Lewis agreed to a twelve-day truce. But only days later the coal negotiations collapsed and Truman, reading from a prepared statement, told reporters the country was truly in "desperate straits."

When, at a Cabinet meeting, Truman asked for constructive suggestions on how to handle the strike situation, nobody could offer any.

On May 17, with only a day remaining before the scheduled railroad walkout, Truman summoned Whitney and Johnston to his office. Whitney said they had to go through with the strike. "Our men are demanding it."

"Well then," Truman replied, hunching forward in his chair, "I'm going to give you the gun." As they watched, he signed an executive order for the government to seize and operate the railroads, effective the next day.

Not quite twenty-four hours later, on Saturday the 18th, the two labor leaders agreed to postpone the strike for another five days.

· · ·

On Sunday with apprehensions growing on all sides, Truman took off on a flying visit to Kansas City for the announced purpose of receiving an honorary degree from little William Jewell College at nearby Liberty, Missouri. He also wanted to see his mother. With the help of friends, he and Vivian had finally managed to buy back from the county all of the old homeplace on Blue Ridge, the farm she so loved, even though, because of her deteriorating health, she would be unable to move back there. (She and Mary Jane would continue on in the small yellow frame bungalow in Grandview, where they had been living since 1940.)

In conversation with friends in Missouri, Truman kept referring to Washington derisively as "that place," and to the graduating class at William Jewell he said leadership wasn't worth much without some followers. What the country needed was people who were willing to work, he said, speaking without notes.

> We have a society which is organized, and if one cog in the organization gives out the whole structure begins to shake loose. Now let me urge upon you: Get in line, get on the team, do a little work; help make the United States what it must be from now on: the leader of the world in peace, as it was the leader of the world in war. I urge you to be good workers in the ranks.

A White House reporter who made the trip, Felix Belair, Jr., of *The New York Times,* asked Truman's physician, Colonel Graham, if perhaps the President was working too hard. Graham agreed, adding with emphasis that there was also nothing anyone could do about it. "That's the way he is," said Graham. "I try using a little applied psychology, but you know the President has a pretty good psychology of his own. He does the best he can by his job and he knows there's no use worrying about it after that."

But two old Truman friends from Independence, Mayor Roger Sermon and Henry Bundschu, a dry goods merchant and neighbor of the Trumans, warned Belair to watch out for the President's temper. He might be "an easygoing fellow," but he was also no one to trifle with. "When the 'feuding blood' of his Kentucky ancestors was allowed to get the upper hand, Harry Truman was a man to be avoided," Belair wrote after talking with Sermon and Bundschu, who said they would prefer three or four ordinary men for enemies to one like Harry.

To Belair, the President was becoming an increasingly fascinating subject, not at all the simple man he had supposed but a "complex personality," something others had known for a long time and would talk of again. In Independence forty years later one of Truman's nephews, J. C.

Truman, Vivian's second son, would be asked by a visitor how he would describe his uncle Harry, beyond what everyone knew. After a long pause, he answered, "Complicated!"

On Tuesday, day three of the five-day postponement of the railway strike, Ed Flynn of the Bronx flew in to Washington to see if he could help sway Whitney and Johnston, but without success. Nothing seemed to work. No compromise appeared likely. On Wednesday, Truman ordered seizure of the coal mines and proposed an 18½ cent raise for the rail workers— again more than his own emergency fact-finding board had recommended—and still Whitney and Johnston "viewed the proposal unfavorably." By Thursday, May 23, the day the strike was scheduled to begin at 5:00 P.M., Washington time, the situation at the White House had become extremely tense.

The two union leaders were summoned one more time, along with officials representing management, and assigned to different rooms to resume bargaining, John Steelman moving back and forth between them. When Whitney and Johnston again refused Truman's offer, Steelman told them they simply couldn't say no to a President, insisting that that was just not done. Their response was that nobody paid attention to this President anyway.

"This was the fifth day of the postponement of the railroad strike and . . . [it] turned into one of the wildest days at the White House since the end of the war," wrote Eben Ayers in his diary:

> Newsmen thronged the lobby, tense and excited. The President was in his office as usual and met from time to time with Steelman, John Snyder and Schwellenbach. . . . This situation went on all day long. Early in the afternoon the President ordered John Pye, the colored messenger, who runs the executive lunchroom, to prepare some sandwiches . . . and they were sent in to the railroad people. I did not go out for lunch nor did my secretaries.
>
> During the course of the day Secretary of State Byrnes came over, secretly, so newspapermen did not know of his visit, and he argued with Whitney and Johnston for some time, trying to point out to them the effect upon our international relations of a general rail strike at this time.

At about four in the afternoon, with only an hour to go before the strike would begin, Truman went out to the South Lawn to host a reception for nearly nine hundred convalescent veterans from Walter Reed and other nearby military hospitals, among whom were amputees and others so severely disabled that they moved forward in the receiving line on crutches and in wheelchairs, attended by nurses in starched white uniforms. Such garden parties for hospitalized veterans had been an annual May tradition at the White House since 1919, but were discontinued during the war. Truman, some weeks earlier, had asked that the tradition be revived.

The spring afternoon was ideal, with bright sunshine, blue sky, and flowers in bloom. Several of the Cabinet were present with their wives, as were Admiral Nimitz and General Bradley. The Marine Band played. Strawberry ice cream and lemon punch were served, and for more than an hour Truman stood warmly greeting his guests, who were all in uniform and wearing their campaign ribbons.

Always moved by the sight of wounded veterans, Truman was struck especially now by the contrast between these respectful young men who had made such sacrifices for their country, and who were so plainly pleased to meet him, and the two contentious old union bosses inside. He kept smiling, chatting, patting the men on the back, asking where they were from, making every effort to see that they had a good time.

Only once was he seen glancing over his shoulder in the direction of the Cabinet Room, where the long French windows, under the colonnade, stood open to the air. Rumors were passed of progress in the negotiations. A soldier in a wheelchair said, "Draft all the strikers—all of them." Another claimed he wouldn't be President for anything. Truman drank a glass of punch. When a Strauss waltz was played, he walked over beside the band to sit and eat a heaping dish of ice cream, tapping his foot in time to the music. By then it was well past five and the strike was on.

There had never been a total railroad stoppage until now. Almost at once the whole country was brought virtually to a standstill. Of 24,000 freight trains normally in operation, fewer than 300 ran; of 175,000 passenger trains, all of 100 moved. Rush-hour commuters were stranded in New York and Chicago. In the West, coast-to-coast "streamliners" stopped and disgorged passengers at tiny way stations in the middle of the desert.

There were poignant scenes [reported *Newsweek*]: The Chicago woman kept from her father's deathbed in Minnesota; the 13-year-old Arizona boy en route for an emergency brain operation in California; the woman taking the body of her husband back to Cleveland for burial. Other less painful dilemmas: the Philadelphia Symphony Orchestra's

San Francisco-bound special train was abandoned by crewmen; ball clubs found their mid-season travels stymied; the circus, scheduled to leave for Philadelphia, was forced to give Boston an extra dose of the biggest show on earth. Everywhere, the stranded who refused to sleep on emergency cots set up in hotel basements or armories took to bus, airplanes, taxis, and hitchhiking. Washington cabbies had a field day; their price for a ride to Boston was $150, to Atlanta $100.

Newsreel camera crews rushed to film hundreds of freight cars standing motionless in railyards as far as the eye could see, loaded coal cars standing idle, and baggage piled head high in big-city stations.

There were reports of fortunes in lettuce and fruit rotting in Kansas and California. Officials in Washington announced that in Europe hundreds of thousands of people would starve if grain shipments were held up as much as two weeks. Panic buying for food and gasoline broke out everywhere in the country. No one, no community was untouched.

Telegrams flooding the White House came from every quarter and minced no words:

ALL TRAIN SERVICE OUT OF NEW YORK CANCELLED. WHAT NOW? . . .

HATCHERIES [in Henry County, Missouri] NOW PRODUCING MILLIONS OF CHICKS WEEKLY WHICH ARE A TOTAL LOSS UNLESS SHIPPED IMMEDIATELY BY RAIL WHEN HATCHED. . . .

THIS AGRICULTURAL AREA [Corning, Calif.] WILL BE RUINED IF THE STRIKE CONTINUES. . . .

MR. PRESIDENT, ZERO HOUR IS HERE. WHO IS TO RULE OUR NATION? THE LEGALLY CONSTITUTED AUTHORITIES OR ISOLATED DOMESTIC GROUPS? . . .

PLEASE FORGET SELFISH POLITICS LONG ENOUGH TO REMEMBER THAT OTHER PEOPLE BESIDES LABOR LEADERS HAVE TO LIVE AND EAT. THEY ALSO VOTE. . . .

IS THE PRESENT INCUMBENT IMPOTENT IN THE RAILROAD STRIKE? IF SO HE SHOULD RESIGN. . . .

WHY DON'T YOU GO AHEAD AND ACT IN THIS NATIONAL CRISIS. YOU'RE OUR LEADER. . . .

PROMPT ACTION IS THE ONLY THING THAT CAN SAVE OUR COUNTRY. . . .

LESS TALK AND MORE ACTION. . . .

QUIT PLAYING POLITICS. . . .

TIME TO GET TOUGH. . . .

RESPECTFULLY URGE YOU TO RISE TO THE OCCASION. . . .

Truman had had all he could take. Alone at his desk upstairs at the White House, on a small, cheap ruled tablet of the kind schoolchildren use, he began to write. It was the draft of a speech, a speech he had no intention of giving, but that he needed desperately to get off his chest. It was another of his "longhand spasms," and the worst.

He filled seven pages. All the pent-up fury of the past weeks, the feelings evoked by the wounded men on the South Lawn, his sense of betrayal at the hands of old friends Whitney and Johnston—and the sense that they were flouting the highest office, not to say belittling him personally—all his stubborn pride, came spewing forth in one of the most intemperate documents ever written by an American President. It was as though somewhere deep within this normally fair-minded, self-controlled, naturally warmhearted man a raw, ugly, old native strain persisted, like the cry of a frontier lynch mob, and had to be released. Probably he wrote in a state of exhaustion late that night. Possibly whiskey played a part. But no one knows. The "speech" could also have been written in the cold light of the next morning, which, if so, makes it still more appalling.

Under his constitutional powers as President, he would call for volunteers to support the Constitution, he said at the start. Then, after a few pages of praise for the Constitution and for the decisive role America had played in winning the war, he continued with what was on his mind:

At home those of us who had the country's welfare at heart worked day and night. But some people worked neither day nor night and some tried to sabotage the war effort entirely. No one knows that better than I. John Lewis called two strikes in war time to satisfy his ego. Two strikes which were worse than bullets in the back to our soldiers. He held a gun at the head of the Government. The rail unions did exactly the same thing. They all were receiving from four to forty times what the man who was facing the enemy fire on the front was receiving. The effete union leaders receive from five to ten times the net salary of your president.

Now these same union leaders on V.J. day told your President that they would cooperate 100% with him to reconvert to peacetime production. They all lied to him.

First came the threatened automobile strike. Your President asked for legislation to cool off and consider the situation. A weak-kneed Congress didn't have the intestinal fortitude to pass the bill.

Mr. Murray and his Communist friends had a conniption fit and Congress had labor jitters. Nothing happened. Then came the electrical workers' strike, the steel strike, the coal strike and now the rail tie-up. Every single one of the strikers and their demagogue leaders have been living in luxury, working when they pleased. . . .

I am tired of the government's being flouted, vilified and misrepresented. Now I want you men who are my comrades in arms, you men

500

who fought the battles to save the nation just as I did twenty-five years ago, to come along with me and eliminate the Lewises, the Whitneys, the Johnstons, the Communist Bridges [head of the maritime union] and the Russian Senators and Representatives and really make this a government of, by and for the people. I think no more of the Wall Street crowd than I do of Lewis and Whitney.

Let us give the country back to the people. Let's put transportation and production back to work, hang a few traitors, make our own country safe for democracy, tell the Russians where to get off and make the United Nations work. Come on boys, let's do the job.

It was patriotism run amok, as well as absurdly inaccurate. Rail workers earned nothing like forty times the pay of a soldier. The salaries of the union leaders were less, not more, than Truman's own of $75,000 a year, and to describe Whitney or Johnston or John L. Lewis as "effete" was laughable. He was even off in his math, calculating the time elapsed since his war of 1918.

What was very accurately reflected, however, was the intensity of his rage and his determination now to set things straight.

The look on Truman's face as he strode into a special meeting of the Cabinet Friday morning, May 24, was one White House reporters would not forget. The gray-blue eyes blazed behind his glasses. His mouth was "a thin, hard line pulled down at the corners," his back straight as a rod of steel. "In the manner of Lincoln and the Emancipation Proclamation," remembered Cabell Phillips of *The New York Times,* "he had summoned them not to solicit their views but to tell them what he was going to do." It was a Harry Truman they had not seen before, but that some on his staff knew well and liked.

"He's one tough son of a bitch of a man," Harry Vaughan would say. That was the key to understanding Harry Truman.

With the Cabinet assembled around the table, he asked for suggestions on operation of the railroads. No one had any.

He would go before Congress the following day, he told them, but first address the country by radio that night. He had decided to draft the striking rail workers into the Army.

There was a moment of stunned silence. The Attorney General, Tom Clark, questioned whether the President was overstepping the bounds of the Constitution. Truman was not interested in philosophy. The strike must stop. "We'll draft them and think about the law later," he reportedly remarked.

His seven-page speech draft was handed over to Charlie Ross, who, having read it, told Truman as an old friend that it wouldn't do. Sam Rosenman was sent for and a new speech written, with Rosenman, Ross, John Snyder, and Truman himself all contributing. But the main work, and at Truman's request, was done by a rising new star at the White House, Navy Captain Clark Clifford, who had been posted temporarily the summer before as assistant to Jake Vardaman, and then, when Vardaman was removed, had stepped in as naval aide. Clifford was thirty-nine years old, over six feet tall, broad in the shoulders, slim-waisted, and handsome as a screen actor, with wavy blond hair and a silky baritone voice. In his Navy uniform he looked almost too glamorous to be true, or to be taken seriously; but he was calm, clearheaded, polished as a career diplomat, and, as Truman had quickly perceived, exceedingly capable. Indeed, Clifford's almost chance presence on the staff would prove to be one of the luckiest breaks of Truman's presidency.

"I'd never been in the White House," Clifford would remember. "Never occurred to me I ever would be in the White House. Oh, it was exciting! And [at first] as naval aide, there wasn't much to do. You're kind of a potted plant. . . . The first time I arrived there, the first day, Vardaman took me in, he said, 'President Truman, this is Lieutenant Junior Grade Clifford who is going to look after my office.' And Truman looked up and said, 'Big fellow, isn't he!' "

Clifford had been raised in the fashionable west end of St. Louis. His father was an official with the Missouri Pacific Railroad, his mother a lecturer and author of children's books. An uncle, for whom he was named, Clark McAdams, had been a brilliant editorial page editor for the *Post-Dispatch*. Educated at Washington University, where he also took a law degree, Clifford himself had been a highly successful trial attorney in St. Louis before the war, while still in his early thirties.

"I think he did feel an affinity with those who had come from that part of the country and been schooled in that part of the country, and spoke very much as he did," Clifford would say of the President years later. "It was an important factor. I'm not sure he would have admitted to its being, but it happened to be so." But in no respect did Clifford resemble the other Missourians around Truman. He was of a different generation, an entirely different style, as even the sharpest critics of the administration would acknowledge. "Alone of all the Truman entourage, Clifford has the brains, the personal *élan,* and the *savoir-faire* requisite of a big-leaguer," Washington correspondents Robert S. Allen and William V. Shannon would soon write in a highly critical book called *The Truman Merry-Go-Round*. Clifford, they judged, was "really of White House class."

Clifford, who had had little knowledge of Truman, or any particular interest in him, prior to coming to the White House, soon found himself greatly impressed—devoted to the man in a way he would never have expected. "The President is intelligent, forthright and reasonable," Clifford had written to his mother. "I have developed a deep and abiding affection for him and hope and trust that I may be able to be of some small assistance to him. . . ."

Late the afternoon of the 24th, with no time to spare, Clifford went to work on his first major assignment. Alone at the long, polished table in the Cabinet Room, he labored as he would often again, "grubbing it out" with a yellow legal pad and a soft pencil. For all his many abilities, Clifford was not a facile or inspired writer, nothing like Sam Rosenman. He was not even a good writer, as he conceded, but he worked intensely, writing, erasing, and rewriting one sentence after another, laboriously down the page. He began at five o'clock. By eight a rough draft was ready, and by then a dozen people were in the President's office, waiting to take part. The revisions went on to the very last minute. Rose Conway, the President's secretary, was still typing the final pages of his reading copy as he went on the air.

Truman's own efforts on the ruled tablet paper, meantime, were tucked away in Clifford's file, to remain undisclosed for another twenty years.

Truman spoke to the country at ten o'clock, eastern time. Margaret, who had been in New York to see a play with her friend Drucie Snyder, John Snyder's daughter, and who, because of the strike, had had to borrow a car and drive back to Washington, fighting heavy traffic the whole way, arrived at the White House as her father's broadcast was about to begin. She would remember him looking as tired as she felt.

"I come before the American people tonight at a time of great crisis," he said. "The crisis of Pearl Harbor was the result of action by a foreign enemy. The crisis tonight is caused by a group of men within our own country who place their private interests above the welfare of the nation."

His voice was firm, deadly serious. It was "time for plain speaking." This was no contest between labor and management, but between two willful men and their government.

> I am a friend of labor . . . [but] it is inconceivable that in our democracy any two men should be placed in a position where they can completely stifle our economy and ultimately destroy our country.

He called on the striking railroad workers to return to their jobs as a duty to their country, and warned that if a sufficient number did not return by 4:00 P.M. the next day, he would call out the Army and do whatever else was necessary to break the strike.

He did not say anything about drafting the strikers. That he was saving for his speech to Congress the next afternoon.

Sam Rosenman, who was up most of the night working on the Congress speech, was opposed to the whole idea of drafting the rail workers. Attorney General Clark had also by now put his concerns in writing: "The Draft Act does not permit the induction of occupational groups and it is doubtful whether constitutional powers of the President would include the right to draft individuals for national purposes." Jimmy Byrnes, too, was strongly opposed. But Truman would not be budged.

The conference on the speech to Congress took place Saturday morning in Truman's office. John Steelman, meanwhile, had hurried off to see Whitney and Johnston at their suite at the Statler Hotel, determined to make one last try. Truman's appearance before Congress was scheduled for four o'clock.

The speech was nearly ready at three when Steelman called from the hotel to say he was making progress. The strike might be settled within the hour.

Rosenman and Clifford went into the Cabinet Room and wrote three or four alternative pages. At 3:35 Steelman called again, to report the situation still unresolved. By now it was past time for Truman to leave for the Capitol. Clifford, the new pages in hand, had to run to catch the President's car.

It was another sparkling day and as warm as summer. In the crowded House Chamber, even with the air conditioning on, many of the members sat mopping their brows. In the gallery Bess and Margaret could be seen quietly waiting.

When at a few minutes past four Truman walked in, a grim look on his face, the whole room resounded with the biggest ovation he had yet received as President, while in Sam Rayburn's office close by, Clifford was frantically on the phone again with Steelman, who now said a settlement was "awful close." Steelman had an agreement on paper in longhand, but it had still to be typed and signed. "He said they had verbally agreed to the points which they had in writing," Clifford remembered, "but there was no knowing whether they would finally sign." He would stay by the phone, Clifford told Steelman.

"For the past two days the Nation has been in the grip of a railroad strike which threatens to paralyze all our industrial, agricultural, commercial and social life. . . . The disaster will spare no one," Truman said from the rostrum. Strikes against the government must stop. The Congress and the President of the United States must work together—"and we must work fast."

In the packed press gallery behind him, reporters were writing furiously. "Spotlights blaze, cameras whir, his Missouri voice covers America," wrote Richard Strout of *The New Republic.*

He was calling, Truman said, for "temporary emergency" legislation "to authorize the President to draft into the Armed Forces of the United States all workers who are on strike against their government." The audience roared its approval.

At that moment, Les Biffle, Secretary of the Senate, hurried into the chamber and handed Truman a slip of red paper, a note from Clifford. Truman glanced at it, then looked up.

"Word has just been received," he said, "that the railroad strike has been settled, on terms proposed by the President!"

The whole Congress rose to cheer and applaud, everyone on both sides of the aisle. The sudden interruption by Biffle, the red note in Truman's hand, the surprise of his announcement had all been like something in a movie. (Some in the audience suspected the entire scene had been concocted for effect, which it had not.) Yet Truman himself made no attempt at dramatics. His grim expression never changed and having come that far in the speech, he continued on, delivering the rest of it as he would have anyway.

The President, who of late had seemed so often bewildered and inadequate, had proved himself extremely tough and decisive when the chips were down, and the reaction of the Congress—and of the country by and large—was instantaneous approval. His "bold action" was praised in the press and by leaders in both parties. He had "grown in national stature," said the Atlanta *Constitution.* He had "met magnificently one of the greatest tests of courage ever to face an American President," declared the Philadelphia *Record.* Harry Truman, wrote Felix Belair in *The New York Times,* had shown

> he could be tough—plenty tough—when the occasion demanded. He was no less "the average guy" on the streetcar . . . or driving with the family on Sunday such as he had always been pictured. But just now he was also a man who could rise to the occasion.

The House of Representatives gave him all he wanted, passing the bill to draft the strikers by a margin of 306 to 13, after a debate of less than two hours that same evening.

The Senate, however, refused to be stampeded, largely at the insistence of Senator Taft, who was outraged by the bill, certain that it violated every principle of American jurisprudence. And there were concerns among liberals on the Democratic side as well. Claude Pepper said he would rather give up his seat in the Senate than support such a measure.

A. F. Whitney declared that Truman had signed his own political death warrant. "You can't make a President out of a ribbon clerk," Whitney exclaimed at a cheering labor rally in New York's Madison Square Park. Placards in the crowd said: "Down with Truman," "Break with Truman." He was denounced as the country's number one strikebreaker, called a Fascist, a traitor to the union movement. Later, vowing revenge, Whitney claimed he would spend the last dollar in the treasury of the Brotherhood of Railroad Trainmen to defeat Harry Truman, should he dare run for reelection in 1948.

Prominent liberals were thunderstruck. Sidney Hillman, who was on his deathbed, spoke out against Truman as he never had. "Draft men who strike in peacetime, into the armed services!" wrote Richard Strout in *The New Republic*. "Is this Russia or Germany?" To Truman, Mrs. Roosevelt wrote politely that "there must not be any slip, because of the difficulties of our peacetime situation, into a military way of thinking."

Ultimately, the proposal to draft the strikers was defeated in the Senate, 70 to 13, the initial cries of Taft and Pepper having grown to a chorus.

But the strike was over, the trains were running again. To the great majority of Americans, Truman had exhibited exactly the kind of backbone they expected of a President. To most it seemed he had been left no other choice. He had done only what he had to do, and shown at last that somebody was in charge.

"I was the servant of 150 million people of the United States," Truman himself would later say, "and I had to do the job even if I lost my political career." He had no regrets.

Days later the coal strike, too, ended. On May 29, John L. Lewis met with the coal operators at the White House to sign a new contract. Lewis, it appeared, would be a problem no more, having achieved all he wished for his miners: an 18½ cent-per-hour raise, $100 in vacation pay, a guaranteed five-day workweek, and the 5 cent royalty on every ton of coal mined to go into a welfare fund. While other labor leaders continued the uproar over Truman, the habitually orotund Lewis at last, amazingly, kept silent.

For Truman himself the crisis had provided a chance finally to stand his ground, even take the offensive, none of which did his spirits any harm. Also, importantly, the crisis marked the emergence of Clark Clifford. In another few weeks, Clifford took Sam Rosenman's former position as legal counsel to the President, and would remain at Truman's side almost constantly.

IV

The lift that came from settlement of the rail and coal strikes was shortlived for Truman, and whatever confidence he had gained with the American people by his actions, he seemed incapable of holding onto it. As June came and went, as the summer wore on, criticism in the press, dissatisfaction on the Hill continued. Little went right, and with Bess and Margaret back in Independence through the hot months, Truman found himself beset again by loneliness. In August, when Congress left town for its first real break since before the war, and he attempted a vacation of his own, it got off in the wrong direction at first and ended in a storm. Then, in September, he stepped into a silly tangle with Henry Wallace that made him look more of a bumbler than ever in his career. As George Elsey was to remark years later, "Nothing about the Wallace affair was well done. It was miserably handled from one end to the other."

On June 6, without warning, Truman announced two major appointments, expecting wide approval. To replace Chief Justice Harlan Stone, who had died in April, he had picked Fred Vinson, the Secretary of the Treasury. To fill Vinson's place, he chose John Snyder. He thought they were exceptionally able men, and trusted both implicitly. Yet to many they were singularly uninspiring choices and seemed to have been made in haste, an impression Truman had only himself to blame for. Asked the day of the announcement when had he made up his mind on Vinson, he snapped, "About an hour and a half ago."

As Secretary of the Treasury, Vinson had seemed very suitably cast—solid, knowledgeable, with a broad understanding of government machinery. Truman, who had not known Vinson well in the Senate, had since come to admire him greatly, considered him a "devoted and undemonstrative patriot" with, as Truman would write, "a sense of personal and political loyalty seldom found among the top men in Washington." But Vinson was known more for political sagacity than judicial brilliance, and the choice of the colorless Snyder as his replacement seemed only to underscore the charge of "government by crony." Portrayed in the press as a "dour little St. Louis banker," Snyder seemed hardly adequate for the second highest ranking position in the Cabinet. To liberals and former New Dealers especially, Snyder was a pathetic choice. Unadmiring reporters described him as a "repressed" man, with a "pinched, unhappy look," who "occasionally tries to loosen up with a hefty intake of bourbon or by telling a dirty story." Among fiscal conservatives, the best that could be said for Snyder was that he might prove cautious. In fact, he was quite cautious, quite conservative, a "plugger" who worked long hours often seven days a week. His appearance to the contrary, he was also a man of much personal warmth, and though lacking in imagination, he had, like Vinson, a great deal of common sense—a quality Truman had often found wanting in more brilliant or charming men. In Tennyson's "Locksley Hall," the poem still neatly folded in his wallet, was the line affirming that it was "the common sense of most"—the common sense of ordinary humanity—which would ultimately "hold a fretful realm in awe."

In Paris in July, at another drawn-out, acrimonious session of the Council of Foreign Ministers, Secretary of State Byrnes was making little progress with Molotov in the peace treaty negotiations. In April, his relations with the President still strained, Byrnes had told Truman privately that he wished to resign, pleading health problems, but Truman had asked him to stay on at least until the end of the year. Confidentially, through General Eisenhower, Truman informed George Marshall in China that he wanted him to become the next Secretary of State, once Byrnes departed.

Senator Vandenberg, who was part of the American delegation in Paris, came home to report "appalling disagreement" over Germany, and "intense suspicions" between Russia and the West.

There were worries over Russia, worries over Europe, worries over China. In France and Italy, the Communists were emerging as the strongest single political units. In China, the Red Armies of Mao Tse-tung were making steady gains against the Nationalist government forces of Generalissimo Chiang Kai-shek. To a group of editors and executives from the McGraw-Hill Publishing Company who met with him informally in his office, Truman conceded that the difficulties with China were "very, very bad."

He was even having troubles back home in Jackson County. Infuriated by a congressman from his own district, Democrat Roger C. Slaughter, who, as a member of the House Rules Committee, had been stalling progress on the Fair Employment Practices bill, Truman decided not to support him for reelection and made a show of bringing Jim Pendergast to the White House to talk about it. "If Mr. Slaughter is right, I'm wrong," Truman told reporters. He had Pendergast back another candidate in the primary, Enos Axtell, with the result that some in the old Kansas City organization began resorting to their former ways, causing a storm of outrage in the Kansas City *Star*. When Truman returned to Independence the first week in August to vote in the primary, he discovered that the *Star* had a reporter staked out with binoculars keeping watch on 219 North Delaware, to record his every move. Seeing the reporter early the next day, Truman made a point of telling him in detail exactly how he had spent the morning thus far, including certain acts performed in the bath-room.

Axtell's victory in the primary was hailed by Bob Hannegan as a vote of confidence for the President. Reporters in Kansas City, however, turned up evidence of vote fraud, and though three federal judges found only minor violations in the election, Truman's involvement looked none too good, reviving old stories of his own past connection to the Pendergast machine, not to say doubts about his sense of propriety.

Clark Clifford remembered it as a summer of "wallowing." Even the President's health declined. He suffered from an ear infection and a re-turn of stomach pains such as he had not had in years, the result, said Wallace Graham, of "a nervous condition."

"Obviously, he needs a rest from the strain he's under," noted Charlie Ross in his diary, "though he looks the picture of health."

"Had the most awful day I've ever had Tuesday," Truman wrote to his mother and sister on July 31, "saw somebody every fifteen minutes on a different subject, held a Cabinet luncheon and spent two solid hours discussing Palestine and got nowhere. Today's been almost as bad but not quite. Got in a swim for the first time since February."

He was distressed about his mother's failing health. "She's on the way out," he wrote to Bess. "It can't be helped. . . . She's a trial to Mary, and that can't be helped either." He wished Bess would be more patient with them.

Bess and Margaret remained in Independence, Bess looking after her own mother, Margaret working with a voice teacher from Kansas City. "Be good and be tough," she advised her father at the close of one chatty, affectionate letter.

"I still have a number of bills staring me in the face," Truman wrote to Bess on August 10.

Byrnes called me from Paris this morning asking me not to veto a State Department reorganization bill, which I'd told Clark Clifford I was sure is a striped-pants boys' bill to sidetrack the Secretary of State. Jimmy told me it wasn't but I'm still not sure.

I have another one under consideration, which restores civil and military rights to a captain in the quartermaster department. He was court-martialed in 1926 in Panama for some seven or eight charges under the ninety-third and ninety-sixth articles of war. Dick Duncan [a federal district judge in Missouri and former congressman] is interested because the fellow's from St. Joe and he put the bill through the House and I put it through the Senate on two occasions, and Roosevelt vetoed it both times.

509

When I read the record I'm not so sure Roosevelt wasn't right! Ain't it awful what a difference it makes where you sit! I gave the whole thing to Clifford and told him to give me a coldblooded report on it.

I have another one which is a pain in the neck. Hayden [Senator Carl Hayden], my good friend, and [Congressman Cecil Rhodes] King want it signed. [Clinton] Anderson wants it disapproved and it looks like Anderson is right. It sure is hell to be President.

Longing for a vacation, eager to get away from both Washington and Independence, he had thought first of going to Alaska—he had always wanted to see Alaska—but decided instead on a cruise on the *Williamsburg* to New England in August and invited his old friend and best man, Ted Marks, to join an all-male party that included Snyder, Ross, Clifford, Vaughan, George Allen, Matt Connelly, and Colonel Graham, enough for an eight-handed game of poker.

Truman loved the *Williamsburg*. "It's just wonderful," he often told its commander, Donald J. MacDonald. "In ten minutes I'm away from everything." He loved cruising on the river, in placid waters, the green Virginia shoreline slipping by, other boats passing.

When he wasn't napping or playing cards [MacDonald remembered years later], President Truman was often up on the bridge with us, or sitting on deck. Boats would come alongside and [people] wave to him, which he seemed to enjoy. The boaters were just thrilled to see him. It was a different time, and no one thought of taking a potshot at him. In fact, I think the Secret Service thoroughly enjoyed whenever he went on the *Williamsburg,* because he became my responsibility. They just went along for the ride. I think often of this. . . .

The first few days, Truman gave up shaving and dipped into Arthur Schlesinger, Jr.'s, *The Age of Jackson.* But the poker and the comradeship were, as so often, what he obviously liked best and needed most. "Getting together with his old friends with whom he was completely comfortable was *the* greatest relaxation he had," remembered Clifford.

See, he had no airs. He never put on airs of any kind. He was much more relaxed with them. He didn't have to be careful with them. And if he wanted to have a couple [of drinks], why he felt perfectly at ease . . . nobody ever did it to excess, but that was part of the relaxation. And some of the jokes would be of the type that would not have been told in the White House, and they'd be awfully funny. And perhaps Missouri rural jokes of one kind, and then he had a wonderfully expansive, expressive laugh.

They were important [such times on the *Williamsburg*]—more important than most people might know because he felt the strains very, very much. He liked to pretend a little that he didn't. He'd say, "Oh, I sleep fine at night."

Asked once by a reporter what his attitude was toward card games, Truman replied with a twinkle in his eye, "Card games? The only game I know anything about is that game—let me see—I don't know what the name is, but you put one card down on the table and four face up, and you bet."

His enjoyment of poker came mainly from the companionship it provided. He was considered a "fairly good" player, but by no means exceptional.

He was what was called a "loose" player, rarely staying out of a pot and often betting freely with an occasional bluff. He was "full of mischief" at the table. Dealing left-handed, he loved to taunt anyone needing a particular card. Sometimes, after taking a poll of what the others wanted to play, he would deal something else. He liked games with wild cards, and especially a version of ordinary stud poker that he called "Papa Vinson," after Fred Vinson, who was a particularly skillful player.

"He always plays a close hand, I'll say that," Ted Marks remembered. "You can tell when he's winning, because there's a kind of smile on his face...." As Truman himself conceded, poker was by far his favorite relaxation, "my favorite form of paper work." It took his mind off other things more than anything else. It made no difference to him if the stakes were nickels and dimes, and no apparent difference to his enjoyment of the game if he won or lost. Wallace Graham thought the President played poker as much for what it revealed about the other players at the table as for the pleasure of the game itself. The fact that Vinson, for example, was an expert player was not incidental to Truman's high regard for Vinson.

Clifford, who had played little until coming to the White House, but had bought a book on the game and studied "assiduously," would remember that on this and other trips on the yacht, poker, except for meals, took up the better part of most days, but that lunch often lasted two hours or more, because of all the talk, Truman obviously enjoying every moment and contributing more than his share. "I will bet that the subject of his selection as Roosevelt's running mate in Chicago must have come up forty times . . . [all the] different facets about it."

The President's drinking, widespread stories notwithstanding, was

moderate. Some mornings on deck, he might squint at the sky and comment that it must be noon somewhere in the world, and ask for a bourbon. On occasion he would show the effects of several drinks, expressing
himself, as Clifford later wrote, "in language less restrained and more
colorful than he would otherwise use," and especially if he had had a
particularly vexing week. But he could also nurse a single drink through
a whole evening of talk and poker.

"The *Williamsburg,* being a commissioned vessel, was not supposed to
serve liquor," recalled MacDonald, but as Commander in Chief it was, "of
course," Truman's prerogative to drink on board if he so wished. "I made
no issue of that. . . . Old Grandad was his favorite."

When, at Narragansett Bay in Rhode Island, they hit cold winds, rain,
and fog, Truman ordered a change in plans. They turned and headed
south to Bermuda, which, he knew, had been Woodrow Wilson's favorite
retreat, and where finally, in ideal weather, he enjoyed a few days of
peace and uninterrupted sunshine. "This is a paradise you dream about
but hardly ever see," he wrote to Margaret on August 23.

But in Hampton Roads on the return to Washington, they sailed straight
into a storm. The 244-foot *Williamsburg,* built in 1930 as a private yacht
and purchased by the Navy at the outset of the war, had never been a
particularly good seagoing vessel, even after several hundred tons of pig
iron were put down in the bilges to improve stability. Now the ship "did
all sorts of antics," as Truman would tell his mother. Violently ill, he took
to his bed. "The furniture was taking headers in every direction," he told
Bess, "and it was necessary to stay in bed to keep your legs on." His
stateroom was a shambles. "Papers, books, chairs, clothing, yours, Margaret's, and Mamma's pictures mixed up with *Time, Newsweek, Reader's
Digest, Collier's, Saturday Evening Post,* luggage, pillows. Looked as if it
never would be in shape again. . . ."

The summer heat of Washington held, and again he was alone in the great
white jail, as he had begun calling the White House. Some of the servants
had been telling him how the ghost of Abraham Lincoln had appeared
over the years. Truman became convinced the house was haunted:

> Night before last [he reported to Bess] I went to bed at nine o'clock
> after shutting my doors. At four o'clock I was awakened by three dis-
> tinct knocks on my bedroom door. I jumped up and put on my bath-
> robe, opened the door, and no one there. Went out and looked up and
> down the hall, looked into your room and Margie's. Still no one. Went
> back to bed after locking the doors and there were footsteps in your

room whose door I'd left open. Jumped up and looked and no one there! Damn place is haunted sure as shootin'. Secret service said not even a watchman was up here at that hour.

More and more he disliked living there. Better it be made a museum, he thought, and give the President a rent allowance. That way, he told Bess, they could move back to the apartment on Connecticut Avenue, an idea he knew she would welcome.

"You better lock your door and prop up some chairs and next time you hear knocks, don't answer," Margaret advised him. "It'll probably be A. Jackson in person."

The little oak-paneled elevator that had carried him to the second floor the afternoon of Franklin Roosevelt's death was being replaced with new equipment. (The old elevator, dating from Theodore Roosevelt's day, had moved too slowly for Truman and on one occasion broke down, leaving him stranded between floors. He had to ring a gong and wait for the workmen to hurry to the basement and jiggle the apparatus back into motion.) New chandeliers were being installed, his bathtub fitted with a glass shower stall. But he had little faith in the old house.

The stock market was falling. A maritime strike that had begun on the West Coast was rapidly spreading. Next thing, he thought, the White House roof would cave in.

"I'm in the middle no matter what happens," he wrote mournfully the second week of September, on the eve of the Wallace fiasco.

At a press conference in his office the afternoon of Thursday, September 12, the President was asked by a reporter to comment on a speech scheduled to be given by the Secretary of Commerce at a political rally in New York at Madison Square Garden that evening, copies of which had already been distributed to the press. Truman said he couldn't answer questions about a speech that had not yet been delivered, at which Charlie Ross and others of the staff standing by appeared to breathe a sigh of relief. "If the President had only stopped there!" Ross later wrote.

The reporter, William Mylander of the Cowles newspapers, pressed on, saying Secretary Wallace referred in the speech to the President himself, which was why he had asked. There was laughter and Truman good-naturedly said that being the case perhaps he should hear the question.

Mylander, who held a copy of the speech in his hand, said it contained a sentence asserting that the President had "read these words" and that they represented administration policy.

That was correct, said Truman.

Was he endorsing a particular paragraph or the whole speech?

He had approved the whole speech, Truman said breezily. Reporters looked at one another.

"Mr. President," asked Raymond Brandt of the St. Louis *Post-Dispatch,* "do you regard Wallace's speech a departure from Byrnes' policy . . ."

"I do not," Truman snapped back, before Brandt could finish his sentence.

". . . toward Russia?"

"They are exactly in line," said Truman, in a manner implying the question was frivolous, and that he wished reporters would ask something harder.

In truth, he hadn't read all the speech—or hadn't been paying attention when Wallace went over it with him—and had given it no thought since. The President, noted Charlie Ross in his diary, had now been "betrayed by his own amiability."

According to Wallace's diary account, he and Truman had run through the speech together "page by page," and Truman agreed with everything in it. "He didn't have a single change to suggest," Wallace wrote. Clark Clifford, too, would remember Wallace reading through the speech for the President. But Truman, in his own diary, said he had been able to give Wallace only ten or fifteen minutes, most of which had been taken up with other matters. He had tried to skim through it, Truman wrote, assuming that Wallace was cooperating in all phases of administration policy, including foreign policy. "One paragraph caught my eye. It said that we held no special friendship for Russia, Britain or any other country, that we wanted to see all the world at peace on an equal basis. I said that is, of course, what we want." It was on the basis of this single paragraph only, according to Truman, that he gave his approval, "trusting to Henry to play square with me." In private conversation with Charlie Ross, he also admitted that he had looked at only parts of the speech, relying on Wallace's assurance that the rest was all right.

And most of the speech was indeed "in line" with administration policy. Wallace urged support for the United Nations, called for increased international trade and international control of atomic weapons. But he also condemned British "imperialism" and appeared to be advocating American and Russian spheres of interest in the world, a concept strongly opposed by Byrnes. The United States, Wallace said, had "no more business in the *political* affairs of Eastern Europe than Russia has in the *political* affairs of Latin America. . . ." Any "Get Tough" policy was foolhardy. " 'Get Tough' never brought anything real and lasting—whether for schoolyard bullies or businessmen or world power," Wallace said. "The tougher we get, the tougher the Russians will get."

At Madison Square Garden, departing from his prepared text, Wallace told an audience of twenty thousand—an audience, in part, vociferously pro-Soviet—"I realize that the danger of war is much less from Communism than it is from imperialism. . . ."

As James Reston wrote in *The New York Times* the following day, Truman appeared to be the only person in Washington who saw no difference between what Wallace had said and his own policy, or that of his Secretary of State in Paris, who, reportedly, was outraged. An angry Arthur Vandenberg declared there could be only one Secretary of State at a time.

Saturday morning, the 14th, his immediate staff gathered about his desk, Truman openly berated himself for having made so grave a "blunder." At a press conference that afternoon, he read a carefully prepared statement, and this time no questions were permitted. There had been "a natural misunderstanding," Truman said. His answer to Mr. Mylander's question had not conveyed the thought intended. It had been his wish only to express approval of Secretary Wallace's right to deliver the speech, Truman insisted, not approval of the speech itself.

Having stumbled into trouble, he was clumsily and obviously fabricating in a desperate effort to get himself out and get Byrnes "off the hook" in Paris. "There has been no change in the established foreign policy of our country," he also said, which was true but did no good. "The criticism continued to mount," wrote Ross, who had helped prepare the statement.

> Dispatches from Paris . . . indicated that Byrnes and his delegation felt that something more needed to be done. And, indeed, they were right. The question still remained whether Wallace was to be allowed to go on attacking in public the foreign policy line laid down by Byrnes at Paris. The press secretary's seat became warmer and warmer. I could only reply to questions that the President and Byrnes were not in communication.

The "Wallace episode" boiled on for days. As Wallace continued to tell reporters that he stood by his speech, Truman kept to a light schedule, saying nothing further for attribution.

Then Ross, too, blundered badly. Hearing that columnist Drew Pearson had obtained a long private letter written by Wallace to Truman two months earlier—a letter apparently "leaked" to Pearson by someone in the State Department—Ross, without approval from Truman, agreed with Wallace that the letter should be released to the press, in order to deny Pearson the limelight. When Ross informed the President of what he had done, Truman told him to call Wallace at once and stop release of the letter. But by then it was too late, the letter was out.

Dated July 23, it consisted of twelve single-spaced typed pages more critical even of administration policy than Wallace's speech had been. Forcefully advocating a new approach to the Soviet Union, Wallace charged, among other things, that certain unnamed members of the U.S. military command advocated a "preventive war" before Russia had time to develop an atomic bomb.

"I'm still having Henry Wallace trouble and it grows worse as we go along," Truman confided plaintively to his mother on Wednesday, September 18. Wallace was expected momentarily at the White House. "I think he'll quit today and I won't shed any tears. Never was there such a mess and it is partly my making. But when I make a mistake it is a good one."

To Wallace, too, Truman said he had only himself to blame for most of what had happened. He had not known so many sleepless nights since the convention at Chicago.

They talked alone in the Oval Office, Wallace giving no sign that he intended to quit. His mail, Wallace said, was running five to one in favor of his New York speech. "The people are afraid that the 'get-tough-with-Russia' policy is leading us to war," Wallace told him. "You yourself, as Harry Truman, really believed in my speech." He advised Truman to be far to the left when Congress was not in session, then move to the right when Congress returned. That was the Roosevelt technique, Wallace said. Roosevelt had never let his right hand know what his left hand was up to. "Henry told me during our conversation that as President I couldn't play square," Truman would report to Bess, ". . . that anything was justified so long as we stayed in power." If Truman would only lean more in his direction, Wallace said, it could mean victory for the Democrats in Congress in November. Truman told him he thought the Congress would go Republican in any event.

He asked Wallace to stop making foreign policy speeches—"or to agree to the policy for which I am responsible." But Wallace would not agree.

Still Truman refused to fire him. Indeed, he hardly dared offend him. As the last surviving New Dealer in the Cabinet, Wallace was too important symbolically—as Wallace knew, and as Wallace knew Truman knew. For countless liberal Democrats Wallace remained the rightful heir to the Roosevelt succession, while Truman was only a usurper. For Truman to have an open break with Wallace, anything like the Ickes affair, could be politically disastrous. The only agreement reached at last, after two and a half hours of talk, was that Wallace would say no more on foreign policy at least until Byrnes came home.

In the lobby afterward, when reporters asked if everything had been straightened out, Wallace replied, "Everything's lovely."

"Henry is the most peculiar fellow I ever came in contact with," Truman informed his mother. In his diary, he was more explicit. Wallace was unsound intellectually and "100 percent" pacifist.

> He wants to disband our armed forces, give Russia our atomic bomb secrets and trust a bunch of adventurers in the Kremlin Politburo. I do not understand a "dreamer" like that. . . . The Reds, phonies and "parlor pinks" seem to be banded together and are becoming a national danger.
> I am afraid they are a sabotage front for Uncle Joe Stalin. They can see no wrong in Russia's four-and-a-half million armed force, in Russia's loot of Poland, Austria, Hungary, Rumania, Manchuria. They can see no wrong in Russia's living off the occupied countries to support the military occupation.

At the Pentagon, at Truman's request, Secretaries Patterson and Forrestal issued a joint statement denying they knew of any responsible Army or Navy officer who had ever advocated or even suggested a policy or plan of attacking Russia.

From Paris, Byrnes sent Truman a long, reasoned message asking to be relieved at once:

> When the administration is divided on its own foreign policy, it cannot hope to convince the world that the American people have a foreign policy. . . . I do not want to ask you to do anything that would force Mr. Wallace out of the Cabinet. However, I do not think any man who professes any loyalty to you would so seriously impair your prestige and the prestige of the government with the nations of the world.
> . . . You and I spent 15 months building a bipartisan policy. We did a fine job convincing the world that it was a permanent policy upon which the world could rely. Wallace destroyed it in a day.

At 9:30, the morning of Friday, September 20, Truman called Wallace on the phone and fired him, and, as Truman confided to Bess, Wallace was "so nice about it I almost backed out." Then he added, "I just don't understand the man and he doesn't either."

Further, Wallace offered to return an angry, longhand letter—"not abusive, but . . . on a low level," as Wallace described it—that Truman had sent him the night before. "You don't want this thing out," Wallace told

Truman and Truman gratefully agreed. He was very happy to take it back. Later, Wallace crossed the street from his office and posed for photographers sitting peacefully on a park bench reading the comic papers.

When at a crowded, hurriedly called press conference in his office, Truman made the announcement, there were audible gasps from reporters and one long, low whistle. Once the room was cleared, Truman sat down at his desk and turning to Ross, who was standing nearby, said, "Well, the die is cast."

He had shown, Ross told him, that he would rather be right than President. "I would rather be *anything* than President," Truman said.

"No man in his right mind would want to come here [to the White House] of his own accord," he had written earlier to Margaret. Now, wishing as always to shine untarnished in her eyes, he tried to excuse his handling of the Wallace affair by saying he had no gift for duplicity. To be a good President, he told her, one had to be a combination Machiavelli, Louis XI of France, Cesare Borgia, and Talleyrand, "a liar, double-crosser and unctuous religio (Richelieu), hero and whatnot," and he didn't have the stomach for it, "thanks be to God."

He was mulling history and his own life more and more. On September 26, anniversary of the start of the Argonne offensive of 1918, reflecting on the intervening years, he wrote in his diary as follows, referring to himself only as "a serviceman of my acquaintance." The rage that filled his earlier rail strike "speech" was absent now, replaced by a kind of melancholy and disappointment, and an underlying resolve to face whatever he must:

> Sept. 26, 1918, a few minutes before 4 A.M. a serviceman of my acquaintance was standing behind a battery of French 75's at a little town called Neuville to the right of the Argonne Forest. A barrage was to be fired by all the guns on the Allied front from Belgium to the Swiss border.
>
> At 4 A.M. that barrage started, at 5 A.M. the infantry in front of my acquaintance's battery went over. At 8 A.M. the artillery including the 75 battery referred to moved forward. That forward movement did not stop until Nov. 11, 1918.
>
> My acquaintance came home, was banqueted and treated as returned soldiers are usually treated by the home people immediately after the tension of war is relieved.
>
> The home people forgot the war. Two years later, turned out the Administration which had successfully conducted our part of the war and turned the clock back.

They began to talk of disarmament. They did disarm themselves, to the point of helplessness. They became fat and rich, special privilege ran the country—ran it to a fall. In 1932 a great leader came forward and rescued the country from chaos and restored the confidence of the people in their government and their institutions.

Then another European war came along. We tried as before to keep out of it. We refused to believe that we could get into it. The great leader warned the country of the possibility. He was vilified, smeared, misrepresented, but kept his courage. As was inevitable we were forced into the war. The country awoke—late, but it awoke and created the greatest war production program in history under the great leader.

The country furnished Russia, Britain, China, Australia and all the allies, guns, tanks, planes, food in unheard of quantities, built, manned and fought the greatest navy in history, created the most powerful and efficient air force ever heard of, and equipped an army of 8½ million men and fought them on two fronts 12,000 miles apart and from 3,000 to 7,000 miles from the home base, created the greatest merchant marine in history in order to maintain those two battlefronts.

The collapse of the enemies of liberty came almost simultaneously in May for the eastern front and in August for the western front.

Unfortunately the great leader who had taken the nation through the peacetime and wartime emergencies passed to his great reward just one month before the German surrender. What a pity for this to happen after twelve long years of the hardest kind of work, three and a half of them in the most terrible of all wars.

My acquaintance who commanded the 75 battery of Sept. 26, 1918, took over.

The same elation filled the home people as filled them after the first world war.

They were happy to have the fighting stop and to quit worrying about their sons and daughters in the armed forces.

Then the reaction set in. Selfishness, greed, jealousy, raised their ugly heads. No wartime incentive to keep them down. Labor began to grab all it could get by fair means or foul, farmers began black-marketing food, industry hoarded inventories and the same old pacifists began to talk disarmament.

But my acquaintance tried to meet every situation and has met them up to now. Can he continue to outface the demagogues, the chiselers, the jealousies?

Time only will tell. The human animal and his emotions change not much from age to age. He must change now or he faces absolute and complete destruction and maybe the insect age or an atmosphereless planet will succeed him.

V

Harold Ickes called him "stupid." If the world had to depend on Truman and his administration to keep it out of trouble, wrote *Time,* then the world had much to worry about. Not in eighty years, not since Andrew Johnson, Lincoln's successor, had a President been the target of such abuse. He was made fun of for his mid-American mannerisms, his Missouri pals, the by now famous devotion to his mother. "Every day is Mother's Day in the White House," it was said with a snicker. According to one of the latest Washington jokes in the autumn of 1946, Truman was late for a Cabinet meeting because he woke up stiff in the joints from trying to put his foot in his mouth. A joke from Texas began with reflections on how Roosevelt might have handled the country's problems, then ended with the line, "I wonder what Truman would do if he were alive." A Chicago *Sun* cartoon that was reprinted widely showed him popeyed and befuddled, one hand on his aching head, asking, "What next?" In Boston, the Henry M. Frost Advertising Agency came up with an inspired two-word campaign slogan for the Republicans: "Had enough?"

Truman's popularity had vanished. Poll results released the first week in October, a month before the congressional elections, showed only 40 percent of the country approved his performance.

On the eve of Yom Kippur, the Day of Atonement, in what struck many as a bald play for the Jewish vote in New York, he called for admitting 100,000 Jewish refugees to the British protectorate in Palestine. But the fact was he had already made the same statement months before, and Republican Thomas E. Dewey, who was running for reelection as governor of New York, now quickly outbid him for Jewish support by demanding that several hundred thousand Jews be permitted to migrate to Palestine.

In another few weeks Truman's standing in the polls plunged to a low of 32 percent, nearly 50 points below where it had been the year before.

The depression that everyone had so feared had not come. Employment, even with all the strikes, was high. Money was plentiful. Business was booming. But the cost of living had also leaped 6½ points just since the end of 1945 and there were still acute shortages of the things people most wanted—housing, automobiles, refrigerators, nylon stockings, sugar, coffee. And, increasingly, meat. Speaker of the House Sam Rayburn, fearing a Democratic debacle at the polls, complained to a friend, "This is going to be a damned 'beefsteak election'!" As November drew closer and the meat shortage grew worse, the Republicans capitalized on a made-to-order issue. Cattle raisers staged a strike, refusing to send cattle to market. "Nothing on meat, Mr. President?" Truman was asked by reporters on October 10. "Nothing on meat," he said.

Democratic Party Chairman Bob Hannegan warned Truman that if controls on meat prices were not dropped, he could expect a Republican sweep. Truman told his staff he was sure to be damned whatever he did. If he ended controls, he would be accused of caving into pressure. If he left things as they were, he would continue to be seen as cause of all the trouble.

Talk of his Pendergast connection was encouraged, as Republicans stepped up the heat. He became, again, the little machine hack from backwater Missouri. New York showman Billy Rose suggested W. C. Fields for President in 1948, saying, "If we're going to have a comedian in the White House, let's have a good one." The chairman of the Republican National Committee, Congressman Carroll Reece of Tennessee, declared nothing remained of the Democratic Party but three distasteful elements: southern racists, big-city bosses, and radicals bent on "Sovietizing" the country.

Discontent over meat shortages was one thing, fear of Communist influence and infiltration was quite another and in the long run far more important. A Red scare was clearly on the rise. Edward T. Folliard of the Washington *Post* found "hatred of communism rampant" everywhere he traveled. Harry Truman, the Republicans charged, was pursuing a policy of appeasing the Russians abroad and fostering communism at home. The Democratic Party, said Senator Taft, was "so divided between Communism and Americanism that its foreign policy can only be futile and contradictory and make the United States the laughing stock of the world." John Taber, a Republican congressman from Auburn, New York, who had a voice like a bullhorn, warned of Communist infiltration of the universities, even the Army, while in California, another Republican congressional candidate, young Richard M. Nixon, castigated high officials "who front for un-American elements, wittingly or otherwise."

Yet such attacks were hardly different in spirit from Truman's own private anxieties over "Reds" and "parlor pinks," and who could say, after the uncovering of the Ottawa spy ring, that there was no cause for alarm? That summer, under pressure from Attorney General Clark, Truman had secretly agreed to continuation of electronic surveillance in cases where the national defense was involved, a policy instituted by Roosevelt, although, as Clark neglected to tell Truman, Roosevelt's original authorization in 1940 had been limited to aliens only In a speech at San Francisco,

J. Edgar Hoover of the FBI warned that no less than a hundred thousand Communists were loose in the country.

"The shrill pitch of abuse heaped upon the President continued to echo," wrote *Time*. "So mild a man as Harry Truman might well wonder at the temper of his countrymen."

Democrats were filled with despair. Bob Hannegan advised Truman that it would be best if he made no campaign appearances or political speeches, a decision Truman accepted. He kept to the White House. For days, for a portrait by Frank O. Salisbury, the British artist who had done Roosevelt, Truman posed in Charlie Ross's office, where three windows provided ample north light. On the afternoon the Supreme Court was to make its traditional White House call, he was listening to the deciding game of the 1946 World Series—the St. Louis Cardinals vs. the Boston Red Sox—when a staff aide told him the justices would soon be arriving in formal attire. Truman hurried upstairs and changed into striped trousers and a swallowtail coat, only to find at the reception that he alone was formally dressed.

Few campaigning Democrats even so much as mentioned the President's name. In some congressional contests, Democratic candidates resorted to playing old recordings of Roosevelt speeches to boost their chances. Senator Harley Kilgore, a warm friend and admirer of Truman, who was running for reelection in West Virginia, found that in the back hollows and coal fields the mere mention of Truman's name brought a chorus of boos and catcalls. "Here was a man who was actually doing an excellent job," Kilgore would recall, "but the most you could do was to defend him in a humorous fashion by using the old Western saloon refrain: 'Don't shoot our piano player. He's doing the best he can.'"

The capacity to smile when in trouble is a prime requirement for a politician, as Truman, a career politician, had long understood, and now, as so often before in difficult times, he revealed no sign of anger or gloom. He never complained, never acted sorry for himself, or blamed others. He was as cheerful and optimistic, as interested in others, as pleased to see them and to be with them, as ever. As Alonzo Fields, who saw him daily and close-up as only a butler could, later wrote of Truman, he "never seemed to have a problem," at this or any other time when worries beset him. "I am sure no one in the household could tell when he was troubled."

On October 14, three weeks before the election, Truman went on the radio to announce that reluctantly he was lifting price controls on meat. On October 23, he flew to New York to address the General Assembly of the United Nations at Flushing Meadow. "The course of history," he said in a well-reasoned speech, "has made us one of the stronger nations of the world. It has therefore placed upon us special responsibilities to conserve our strength and to use it rightly in a world so interdependent as our world today." Even the Russians complimented him.

"We went to the Waldorf [afterward]," he wrote Margaret. "Your Ma put on her best bib and tucker and we went down to the ballroom for a reception. Shook hands with 835 people in one hour flat. . . ."

Still he kept silent on politics. Traveling home by train to Independence to vote, he was greeted at Jefferson City by a crowd of cheering schoolchildren who set up a chant: "Make a two-hour speech; make it a full holiday." But Truman, all smiles, only waved and shook his head, then clamped one hand over his mouth.

The Republicans swept the election, carrying both houses of Congress for the first time since before the Depression, an era so distant to most people that it seemed another world. The margin in the House was 246 Republicans to 188 Democrats, in the Senate, 51 to 45. The Republicans took a majority of the state governorships as well, including New York, where Thomas E. Dewey was reelected by the largest margin ever recorded. In one city after another—Chicago, Detroit, Jersey City, New York —Democratic machines went down to defeat. In Kansas City, Truman's own handpicked candidate for Congress, Enos Axtell, lost to his Republican opponent by 6,000 votes, which Margaret Truman remembered as "mortifying" for her father.

The Chicago *Tribune* hailed the Republican triumph as the greatest victory for the country since Appomattox. The New Deal had been finally put to flight, the grip of the Democrats in Washington broken at last. Harry Truman, the "accidental" President, was now also a "minority" President. A young Democratic congressman from Arkansas, J. William Fulbright, was so distressed by the Republican landslide and the likelihood of a two-year stalemate in Washington that he proposed Truman appoint Arthur Vandenberg Secretary of State, then resign, and thus make Vandenberg President—an idea that led Truman to refer to Fulbright thereafter as "Halfbright."

Truman and his family started back to Washington on election day without waiting for the polls to close. By arrangement, however, the election returns were to be put on board the train every hundred miles or so.

That night, Charlie Ross came through the train to invite several Washington reporters to join the President in his private car for a poker game. "The game was hot and heavy until about 2 A.M.," remembered Merriman

Smith of United Press. "The returns had been arriving in a steady stream since 9 P.M. Not once did Truman look at them, nor did he refer to the elections."

At one point Margaret interrupted to say the results from Independence had come in. Truman, glancing at the slip of paper, shook his head and smiled up at her.

"Why bother with this sort of thing?" he said. "Don't worry about me —I know how things will turn out and they'll be all right."

"Probably no President since Andrew Johnson had run out of prestige and leadership more thoroughly than had Harry Truman when he returned almost unnoticed to Washington on that bleak, misty November morning in 1946," wrote Cabell Phillips. At Union Station Truman stepped from his car silent but smiling, a book under his arm.

12

Turning Point

This is a serious course upon which we embark....

—Truman to Congress, 1947

I

Was Harry Truman an ordinary provincial American sadly miscast in the presidency? Or was he a man of above-average, even exceptional qualities and character, who had the makings of greatness?

"What a test of democracy if it works!" Roy Roberts of the Kansas City *Star* had written on Truman's first day in office. Now, less than two years later, Walter Lippmann, like a great many others, was convinced the test had not worked. To Lippmann, regarded as the most thoughtful, authoritative political commentator of the time, Truman was an embarrassment. His bravado and quick decisions, Lippmann thought, were a facade for an essentially insecure man filled with anxieties. How could the affairs of the country be conducted by a President who not only had lost the support of his party, but was no longer in command of his administration?

In the years on the farm, when courting Bess—his first campaign—Truman himself had professed to being only a common everyday fellow. He could promise her no more. But he had written also that every farmer "thinks he's as good as the President or perhaps a little better," meaning that by the old Jeffersonian faith in which he had been raised, what was ordinary grass-roots American was as good as the best.

Questioned once by a reporter whether he considered himself the sublimation of the average man, Truman rejected the fancy phrase and asked in turn, "Well, what is wrong with being the average man?"

Since 1945 numbers of others had judged him as anything but ordinary. At Potsdam, Churchill immediately perceived the new President to be "a man of immense determination," and in the fateful spring of 1947, from Chartwell, his home south of London, where he was busy with his memoirs, Churchill would write to tell "My dear Harry" how much he admired "what you have done for the peace and freedom of the world. . . . " For Churchill, the presidency of Harry Truman had become the one cause for hope in the world.

Dean Acheson, who could be extremely hard, even contemptuous in his judgment of men he did not consider his equals, had described Truman, after Roosevelt's death, as straightforward, decisive, honest, and if inexperienced, likely to learn fast. And in the time since, Acheson had found no reason to think differently. On the morning in November 1946 when Truman arrived at Washington's Union Station, his political stock at an all-time low, Acheson alone of all the administration was waiting on the platform to greet him, a gesture that Truman, understandably, never forgot. Acheson looked to Truman as a leader. "The captain with the mighty heart," Acheson would call him.

Arthur Krock of *The New York Times,* foremost of Washington correspondents, was another who had seen something "very good and human and courageous" in this unlikely President, and at a point when many political commentators were ready to write him off. Felix Belair, White House correspondent for the *Times,* had decided that while Truman might look as much like "the average guy on the streetcar" as ever, he was a man to rise to the occasion.

So testament from experienced observers that this was a President of considerable substance—and that it would be a mistake to count him out —was already plentiful, even before the great change that came in 1947.

David E. Lilienthal, whom Truman had earlier reappointed head of the Tennessee Valley Authority (TVA), was a trim, agreeable-looking man in his mid-forties, the son of Jewish immigrants, a graduate of DePauw University and the Harvard Law School, and regarded still as a model New Dealer. TVA was a huge success. It had built dams, created lakes, forests, new industries, new farming methods, brought electricity to some 700,000 users, and, during the war, fueled the giant uranium plants at Oak Ridge. And Lilienthal, as much as anyone, had made TVA.

Unlike so many New Dealers who had quit since Roosevelt's death— who had fled government, as Clark Clifford said, "so fast they were falling all over each other"—Lilienthal had chosen to stay, not once, but twice. In October he had resigned from TVA to become Truman's designated, though still unconfirmed, head of the new Atomic Energy Commission, which Truman insisted be under civilian control. It was a position potentially as important as almost any in postwar Washington and one for which Lilienthal felt himself inadequately qualified. But then who was qualified? And the President had been extremely persuasive and patient, while Lilienthal went through days of soul searching.

Hardworking, articulate, Lilienthal was an exceptionally able man, if by some people's standards overly liberal, and his presence in the administration—like that of Byrnes, Marshall, Harriman (who had returned from London to replace Henry Wallace at the Department of Commerce), Acheson, Bohlen, and Clark Clifford—belied the whole idea that Truman had surrounded himself only with Missouri fools and mediocrities.

Lilienthal did not entirely approve of Truman's performance thus far. As a liberal he had been so shattered by Truman's call to draft the striking rail workers that after hearing Truman's speech over the radio, Lilienthal walked out into his garden in Tennessee and stood in a drenching rain, hoping it might wash away his misery. Still Lilienthal had faith in Truman, faith in the man—because Truman had shown such faith in him, but also because he saw qualities of courage and candor rare in a politician. Indeed, he felt better about working for the Truman administration, Lilienthal said, than he had working for Roosevelt, because now he could get straight answers.

Since November, Lilienthal had been extremely concerned about the effect so humiliating a defeat in the elections might have on Truman's self-confidence and thus on his program. Lilienthal's own appointment, as a prime example, was bound to stir up a hornets' nest, once the confirmation process began on the Hill, since the aging, vituperative Senator McKellar of Tennessee, who had fought to deny Lilienthal's reappointment at TVA and despised him no less than ever, had just been reelected to another term.

Not for a month after the elections did Lilienthal actually see the President, and then only by chance. It was at about five o'clock on an afternoon in early December, when Lilienthal and Clifford were working quietly in the Cabinet Room. The day was nearly over, it was growing dark outside. Clifford nudged him to look up at the French doors that opened to the outside passage to the main house. The President was standing on the other side of the glass, looking in at them and smiling. Not knowing what else to do, Lilienthal rose and bowed awkwardly. Truman waved, still smiling, then moved quickly on, a Secret Service man a half step behind.

Nothing had been said, the whole incident occupied only seconds, but to Lilienthal it was a moment of encouragement worth recording in his diary, as he would also record the hearty welcome Truman gave him a few days later in the Oval Office, when, with the four others on his new commission, Lilienthal came to make a brief progress report. The Army would relinquish no more control over atomic energy than it could possibly avoid, Truman warned. "I know how they are, they are trained not to give up. I know because I am one of them." Again he was smiling.

As the meeting ended and the group wished the President luck, Truman, thanking them, replied that his luck had been improving lately, this in reference to a recent test of wills with John L. Lewis. But what impressed Lilienthal was "the kind of grim gaiety in his tone and manner. . . ."

The change in the President became more obvious by the day. There had been a "showdown" with John L. Lewis, just after the November elections. At Clark Clifford's urging, Truman had challenged the legality of still another threatened coal strike. Except this time it was to be a "fight to the finish," as Truman said. "Oh, God, it was the chance of a lifetime," Clifford would remember. " 'Be right, be strong. Nobody's bigger than the President of the United States.' All the signs were right. It looked like Lewis had violated the law. . . . Roosevelt had toadied to him time and again. But now he pushed the President the wrong way. And he just said one day, 'Okay, we're going to go!' "

The administration took the powerful labor boss to court, on the grounds that he was violating the Smith-Connally Act, which prohibited strikes against government-held facilities, the coal mines being still technically under government seizure. An injunction was served, and when Lewis let the strike begin on November 20, a federal district judge ordered him to stand trial for contempt. Lewis refused. On December 4, the judge hit the United Mine Workers with a stunning $3 million fine, and fined Lewis personally $10,000. Truman, meanwhile, had been to Florida and back, for a few days of vacation at the Key West naval base. On December 7, Lewis gave up and ordered his men back to the mines, pending an appeal to the Supreme Court. (In March 1947 the Supreme Court upheld the contempt ruling, though the fine against the union was later reduced.)

It was a resounding victory for the administration and another step up for Clifford. Established now in Sam Rosenman's old office, the second largest and best office in the West Wing, Clifford was only twenty paces from the President's desk and saw him six or seven times a day. Often they ate together in the basement lunchroom.

Truman was hugely pleased by the collapse of Lewis. For the first time in months, he was being praised by the press—"Harry S. Truman stood fast, where Franklin Roosevelt met [Lewis] halfway," said *Newsweek*—and this, too, of course, he greatly enjoyed. But the real change, in the view of his old friend Charlie Ross and others, had come with the elections. It was the sweeping Republican triumph, ironically, that had given Truman a new lease on life, freeing him at last from the shadow of Franklin Roosevelt as perhaps nothing else could have. He owed no one anything any longer. He was free to take charge, to be himself, and show what he could do if he had to. He was on his own again, much as he had been in the 1940 Senate race, when Tom Pendergast was out of the picture and Roosevelt had abandoned him; or as he had been on the farm when his father died, or in France in 1918, when, with his new captain's bars, he stood alone, trembling, and speechless before his new command.

The President was "now a free man and can write a fine record," Ross wrote to his sister. "The real Truman administration," Ross told White House reporters, "began the day after the elections."

And clearly Truman agreed. In a letter to Bess from Key West, he had vowed, "I'm doing as I damn please for the next two years and to hell with all of them."

Far from being downcast or tentative about his new role as a "minority" President, he had returned from Florida tanned, rested, eager to get going. He had accepted the verdict of the people in the spirit, he said, that "all good citizens accept the results of any fair election." The change in Congress did not alter the country's domestic or foreign problems, and in foreign affairs especially it must be "a national and not a party program." Of course, conflicts would arise between a Republican Congress and a Democratic President. That was to be expected. But he, Harry Truman, would be guided by a simple idea: "to do in all cases . . . without regard to political considerations, what seems to me to be for the welfare of all our people. . . . "

In the new 80th Congress, Joe Martin would replace Sam Rayburn as Speaker of the House. In the Senate, instead of Alben Barkley, Taft and Vandenberg would hold the reigns of power, and with the tacit understanding that Taft would attend to domestic issues, Vandenberg to foreign affairs, as Chairman of the Foreign Relations Committee.

Truman knew the three Republican leaders from years of experience. Vandenberg, whom he knew best and liked best, had been a friend since Truman's first days in the Senate, and Truman considered him both able and trustworthy. A former newspaper editor from Grand Rapids, "Van" had been an all-out isolationist until the war, but Pearl Harbor, he liked to say, had ended isolationism for any realist. (Once in London during an attack of German robot bombs, Vandenberg remarked to a friend, "How can there be immunity or isolation when men can devise weapons like that?") It was a conversion of far-reaching consequence. Not only was Vandenberg one of the Senate's inner circle, and among Republicans the undisputed authority on foreign affairs, but he was a formidable force as a speaker. Large and hearty, he had the mannerisms of a somewhat pompous stage senator—the cigar, the florid phrase, and more than a little vanity, carefully combing a few long strands of gray hair sideways over the top of his bald head. When making a point on the Senate floor, he favored the broad gesture, grandly flinging out one arm in a sweeping arc. His prestige reached beyond national boundaries, and like Truman during his years in the Senate, he had made no enemies.

Vandenberg was the son of a harnessmaker, Joe Martin the son of a blacksmith, backgrounds Truman could identify with, as he could not with the privileged world of Robert A. Taft, whose father had been President William Howard Taft. Martin, who came from North Attleboro, Massachusetts, a factory town south of Boston, had arrived in Congress first in 1925, when his friend Calvin Coolidge was President. And for forty-two years Martin's outlook had remained fundamentally that of Coolidge. No legislation of importance had been attached to his name, no memorable declaration of political philosophy, but he was a good cloakroom organizer and known as dependable and fair-minded, "straight as a string," as was said in the home district. A short, square man, he wore poorly fitting three-piece navy blue suits and boxy black policeman's shoes. Even when speaking to small groups at home he would stand on a chair in order to be seen. A lock of dark hair that fell over the right side of his forehead had become a trademark.

Like his Democratic counterpart, Sam Rayburn, Martin was a bachelor. He neither drank, nor smoked, nor showed much interest in anything beyond politics and the hometown newspaper he owned, the North Attleboro *Chronicle*. Whatever was good for the district, Joe Martin held, was "pretty much good" for the nation.

On New Year's Day, busy placing calls to his Cabinet to wish them a Happy New Year, Truman decided to phone Vandenberg and Martin as well, and was encouraged by the results. Vandenberg was "very pleasant," Martin even more so, assuring the President that cooperation was uppermost in his mind. "He told me that he would be most happy to talk to me any time on any subject," Truman recorded. "I am inclined to believe that he meant what he said."

Taft, whom Truman did not call New Year's Day, was a remote, self-absorbed man, "a cold fish" in the view of many. ("Bob is not austere," his wife once explained. "He's just departmentalized.") Younger than

Truman by five years, Taft had been born into affluent, cultivated surroundings in Cincinnati. He had stood first in his class at Yale and later at the Harvard Law School. Though he had served in the Senate since 1938, he looked more like a banker than a politician. He wore rimless spectacles and, like Harry Truman, his hat at dead center. His Cheshire Cat grin was famous.

Often tactless, habitually brusque with those less intelligent than he, Taft was a poor "mixer," a poor public speaker. He had trouble remembering names. His reputation for hard work and standing by principle, however, his fund of knowledge and ability to cut to the heart of an issue were considered second to none in the Senate. He was "Mr. Republican," incorruptible, extremely conservative, and, unlike Vandenberg, a confirmed isolationist. But he could also be highly independent—and exasperate the old guard of his party—by advocating such liberal programs as federal aid to education, health, and housing. Senator Wallace H. White of Maine, a quiet, colorless figure, was to be the Republican majority leader in name only; Taft would be the one running things.

Taft, Vandenberg, and Martin were all determined to restore Congress to the prestige and authority that had been lost during the Roosevelt era. Martin would insist in his first address as Speaker, "Our American concept of government rests upon the idea of a dominant Congress." All three men, furthermore, were considered presidential prospects for 1948, and Taft in particular. Determined to follow in his father's footsteps, Taft had already tried for the Republican nomination in 1940. Now, with Harry Truman in office, his opportunity looked greater than ever.

Nor, importantly, was Taft interested in cooperating with the administration. "The purpose of the opposition is to oppose," he was fond of saying. And unlike Vandenberg and Martin, he had little regard for Truman, who to Taft was truly an ordinary man, deficient in background and education, ill-equipped in nearly every way for so heavy a responsibility, in addition to being overly susceptible to the bad advice of liberals.

Among the new faces in Republican ranks in the 80th Congress were Representative Richard M. Nixon of California, Senator Henry Cabot Lodge, Jr., of Massachusetts, and Senator Joseph McCarthy of Wisconsin. Among the relative handful of new Democrats elected was Representative John F. Kennedy of Massachusetts, the twenty-nine-year-old son of Joe Kennedy.

For all the labor strife of the year before, the country was prospering as it never had, just as Truman declared in his State of the Union message on January 6, 1947. Food production was at a new high. The national income was higher than ever before in peacetime. "We have virtually full employment," he said with satisfaction.

He looked like a man befitting the message, healthy and purposeful. At seven that morning he had walked from the White House to Union Station to meet the train from Missouri bringing Bess and Margaret, who sat now listening in the gallery.

He called for far-ranging improvements in labor-management relations, a strengthening of the anti-trust laws, a national health insurance program, including support for mental health, child care, and hospital construction. He wanted a "fair level of return" for farmers, aid to veterans, an "aggressive" program of home construction. He promised new progress in civil rights.

In no way was the speech a retreat from the domestic programs he had set forth in his message of 1945. Yet the tone was different, more reasonable, more optimistic. He advocated a balanced budget, a streamlining of the military establishment, international control of atomic energy. He ended with what would later seem a prescient line, about sharing America's bounty with the war-stricken peoples over the world.

Also, notably missing this time was any mention of Franklin Roosevelt.

Written in large part by Clark Clifford, with help from George Elsey, who like Clifford was in naval uniform no longer but serving as Clifford's assistant, the speech went far to raise Truman's standing with Congress. Even greater was the effect of the surprise announcement he made at the White House the following evening: George C. Marshall was to be the new Secretary of State. Jimmy Byrnes had resigned. Marshall was already en route from China.

The appointment of Marshall was one of the best, most important decisions of Truman's presidency. One wonders, as Truman must have in later years, how differently history might have unfolded had Marshall declined to serve as Secretary of State at that particular moment in world affairs. The reaction everywhere was immediate, virtually unanimous approval. Henry Stimson might have been speaking for the whole nation when he wrote to Marshall: "Your appointment as Secretary of State has filled me with a great sense of security so far as our country is concerned. Mr. Truman made a wise as well as a very shrewd appointment."

On Capitol Hill, Arthur Vandenberg pushed the nomination through the Foreign Relations Committee without a hearing or opposition, and by calling for a suspension of the rules, ran it through the Senate for unanimous approval the same day. The one possible shadow on the appointment, in the view of some Republicans, was the chance that it might set Marshall up as a future candidate for President, an idea Marshall himself put to rest the same morning he arrived in Washington. He would never be a candidate for any political office, he said, and being Marshall he was taken at his word.

He was sworn in at the White House by Chief Justice Vinson later that morning, Tuesday, January 21, 1947. When a beaming Truman shook his hand and said how much he appreciated Marshall's willingness to accept "this burden," Marshall replied simply that he would do his best.

At sixty-six, George C. Marshall was the first career soldier to become Secretary of State. He had been born on the last day of 1880 in Union-town, Pennsylvania, south of Pittsburgh, where through boyhood, from his businessman father, he heard repeated accounts of his distinguished Virginia ancestry, including the distantly related John Marshall, the great Chief Justice. "I thought that the continuing harping on the name John Marshall was kind of poor business," he later said. "It was about time for somebody else to swim for the family." Graduated from the Virginia Military Institute in 1901, he was commissioned a second lieutenant in the infantry and advanced steadily thereafter, serving in the Philippines, Oklahoma Territory, and Fort Leavenworth, until World War I when, as Pershing's aide, he directed the American advance to the Argonne. Between the wars, he had served three years in China. In 1939, Roosevelt made him chief of staff.

He was slightly under six feet tall, with sandy-gray, close-cropped hair and light blue eyes. His long face, with its long upper lip, had a home-spun, fatherly quality and often, in repose, he looked quite sad. With age his shoulders had begun to stoop slightly. As Dean Acheson would write, there was little military glamour about him, nothing pretentious. Rather it was an intangible aura that affected people. Like George Washington, with whom he was often compared, Marshall was a figure of such flawless rectitude and self-command he both inspired awe and made description difficult. Churchill called him "the noblest Roman." Bill Hassett on Truman's staff spoke of the "reverence" Marshall inspired. Imperturbable under pressure—"the imperturbability of a good conscience," George Kennan called it—invariably courteous, he was without a trace of petty vanity or self-serving ambition.

As one of his staff at the State Department later wrote, Marshall did not possess the intellectual brilliance of someone like Acheson, or the gift of eloquence, but he could distinguish what was important from what was unimportant, and this made him invaluable.

Acheson liked to recall in later years that the moment Marshall entered a room, one could feel his presence. "It was a striking and commanding force. His figure conveyed intensity, which his voice, low, staccato, and incisive, reinforced. It compelled respect. It spread a sense of authority and calm." At the Pentagon some lower-ranking officers had been known to exit from Marshall's office backwards, and no one of any rank, not even the President, called him "George," only "General Marshall," a title, as Acheson said, that suited him as though he had been baptized with it. Once, reportedly, when Roosevelt had called him "George," he responded, "It's General Marshall, Mr. President."

Truman described Marshall as "astute," "profound," and more of a listener than a talker. "He never made any speeches at you," Truman would gratefully recall. "Sometimes he would sit for an hour with little or no expression on his face, but when he had heard enough, he would come up with a statement of his own that would invariably cut to the very bone of the matter under discussion." But it was Marshall's rock-bound sense of duty, his selflessness and honesty that Truman especially prized. "He was a man you could count on to be truthful in every way, and when you find somebody like that, you have to hang on to them."

As Truman the politician also appreciated, Marshall stood high with Republicans on the Hill in a way almost no one else did, and this irrespective of the fact that he had worked so closely through the war with the Democrat they all liked least, Franklin Roosevelt. It had been Marshall who got the first peacetime draft past Congress, Marshall who had confided the secret of the atomic bomb to the congressional leadership, trusting them to keep the secret.

For Marshall, his recent mission to China had been a heavy disappointment. Trying to mediate a peace between the two Chinas of the Nationalist Kuomintang government under Chiang Kai-shek and the Communists of Mao Tse-tung, he had achieved only a tentative cease-fire. "I hate failure," he told a friend. But failure was what he had had to announce on the eve of his departure from China. "On the one hand the leaders of the Government are strongly opposed to a communistic form of government," he reported. "On the other, the Communists frankly state that they are Marxists and intend to work toward establishing a communistic form of government in China. . . . " His efforts with the Kuomintang had been frustrating in the extreme. It was a government riddled with corruption, overburdened with too many generals. "Though I speak as a soldier, I must deplore the dominating influence of the military." But the Communists fostered only chaos and violent anti-American propaganda, and with more than a million men under arms, their power was gaining.

Marshall had failed in his mission to China, yet no one blamed him for the failure, such was the scale of the problem and his own reputation. No one looked on his new assignment as anything but a very large step forward for the troubled Truman administration.

Marshall assumed his new duties at once and at once the difference was felt. Jimmy Byrnes had been a hardworking Secretary of State, and more effective than generally acknowledged, or than Truman would por tray him in his later reflections. But Byrnes had been maddeningly independent, determined to do everything himself, and continuously, uncurably on the move. In 546 days as Secretary, Byrnes had been away 241, and had shown little interest in the department itself. Under Marshall all that changed. "He gave a sense of purpose and direction. His personality infected the whole Foreign Service," Bohlen remembered. "There was greater clarity in the operation . . . than I had ever seen before . . . [and] Marshall never forgot, as Byrnes did, that Truman was President."

With Truman's blessing, a new Policy Planning Staff was established under the brilliant George Kennan, who had been recalled from Moscow. Organization overall was made more orderly and efficient. When section heads fell into dispute in his presence, Marshall would tell them, "Gentlemen, don't fight the problem. Solve it!"

Acheson, who had wished to return to private life, was persuaded to stay on as Under Secretary for another six months. Acheson found working with the general such a joy, wrote David Lilienthal after a dinner at Acheson's Georgetown home, that he could "hardly talk about anything else." Marshall, like Truman, was decisive. When Acheson informed Marshall that the State Department had outgrown its quarters in the old Victorian structure beside the White House, and that a new building was available near the Potomac, in the section called Foggy Bottom, Marshall said, "Move."

To no one was Marshall's presence more reassuring, or inspiriting, than to Truman. "The more I see and talk to him the more certain I am he's the great one of the age," Truman wrote not long after Marshall's swearing in. "Marshall is a tower of strength and common sense," he noted privately another time. It was admiration such as Truman felt for no other public figure, no one he had ever known, not Roosevelt, not Churchill, not anyone. Nor was he at all hesitant or concerned over having such a strong-minded man as his Secretary of State—Marshall, Harriman, Patterson, Forrestal, Lilienthal, Eisenhower, they were all strong-minded. Conceivably, Truman could have worried that someone of such immense reputation as Marshall in so prominent a role would diminish his own standing with the country, that he might suffer by comparison, and Marshall be perceived as more the sort of man who ought to be President. But Truman was neither jealous nor intimidated. He was not so constructed. "I am surely lucky to have his friendship and support," he wrote, and that was that.

• • •

By early February 1947 White House reporters were commenting on the President's greater ease and relaxation. "He no longer moans to every visitor that he doesn't want the job and never did," wrote Joseph Alsop to a friend. After a social call on the President, the former heavyweight boxing champion, Gene Tunney, said he had never seen a more solid citizen. "His eye is clear and he is just as solid as a wall. His jaw is square and his stomach is just as flat as an athlete's."

Truman's popularity in the polls, due in large measure to Marshall's presence, was back up to 48 percent.

The whole atmosphere was different. Truman had opened the White House to sightseers again after a six-year wartime ban on all but official callers. He and Bess reinstated formal receptions and state dinners for the first time since 1941, and the contrast between the Trumans "at home" in their private quarters and their official social life was amazing.

The President, with his sense of history, wanted White House entertaining done just so, "done to the minute," by rules that had not changed in half a century, except in wartime. "They brought back all the pageantry," assistant head usher J. B. West remembered approvingly, "all the formality, all the pomp that we had all but forgotten how to execute."

> We [the White House staff] had to work out the details, so that all the President and his wife had to do was to be in the right place at the right time. For a reception, they'd march down the stairs to the Blue Room and receive the guests, and then march back upstairs. But behind the scenes, we spent weeks of preparation and scheduling for each detail of that "right place" and "right time."

Attendance at the first reception, to honor the Supreme Court on December 10, had been 1,333. Dress was white tie, the Marine Band played. "The papers say today that Bess and I have shaken hands with 7,000 people this season," Truman wrote to his mother on February 9. At a full-dress affair for Senator Vandenberg in the State Dining Room, the gold service was used. The night of the diplomatic reception again more than a thousand attended. (Before the war only about five hundred people in total had been accredited to the embassies and legations in Washington.) For one occasion Truman asked Eugene List, the concert pianist, to perform for "the customers," and again, as at Potsdam, List played the President's favorite Chopin Waltz in A Minor, but this time without the President's help as page-turner.

> I was somewhat nervous through the entertainment [Truman told his mother], because Mr. Crim the usher and Jim Rowley [of the Secret

Service] came and told me that the engineers had found that the chain holding the center chandelier was stretching. . . . I let the show go and ordered the thing down the next day. If it had fallen I'd been in a real fix. . . .

Truman was glad to see Lent arrive and put an end to such affairs, he told his mother. He was tired of "smirking at people I don't like." On February 19, in another letter to Grandview, he could report that "the season" was over, "thank goodness." But the truth was he had had a fine time, every time. J. B. West would remember that "despite all the denying in the world (which he did), we could see the President enjoyed it. He was an extrovert, a friendly man, and he liked company."

Hearings on the Lilienthal nomination were causing a sensation, meanwhile, with Senator Kenneth McKellar insisting TVA was a "hotbed of Communism" and that David E. Lilienthal was more than a little suspect. The senator thought it was General Groves who had discovered the secret of splitting the atom and failed to understand why Groves should not therefore be left in command of his discovery.

Looking down from the bench, the senator asked Lilienthal where his parents had been born. When Lilienthal was unable to answer with certainty, McKellar acted as though he had scored an important point. He pressed the issue again another day. This time Lilienthal said he had been able to determine only that it had been in Austro-Hungary, somewhere near Pressburg, in what had since become Czechoslovakia. Again McKellar smiled at the audience as if everything were going his way—Czechoslovakia being under Soviet influence. But when he turned and abruptly asked Lilienthal to explain his views on "the communistic doctrine," the answer Lilienthal gave held the room spellbound. With his hands folded on the table in front of him, Lilienthal spoke for several minutes, his eyes not on McKellar or the committee, but on a spot somewhere just above his hands, almost as though he were talking to himself. He had felt a kind of smoldering within, he later wrote, "far from anger or temper, but some emotional tempo quite different, but definitely emotional." As he talked he kept saying to himself, "Don't deny; affirm."

I believe in, [he said] and I conceive the Constitution of the United States to rest, as does religion, upon the fundamental proposition of the integrity of the individual; and that all Government and all private institutions must be designed to promote and protect and defend the integrity and the dignity of the individual. . . .

Any forms of government, therefore, and any other institutions, which make men means rather than ends in themselves, which exalt that state or any other institutions above the importance of men, which place arbitrary power over men as a fundamental tenet of government, are contrary to this conception; and therefore I am deeply opposed to them. . . . The fundamental tenet of communism is that the state is an end in itself, and that therefore the powers which the state exercises over the individual are without any ethical standards to limit them. That I deeply disbelieve.

It is very easy simply to say one is not a Communist. And, of course, if despite my record it is necessary for me to state this very affirmatively, then this is a great disappointment to me. It is very easy to talk about being against communism. It is equally important to believe those things which provide a satisfactory and effective alternative. Democracy is that satisfying alternative.

And its hope in the world is that it is an affirmative belief, rather than simply a belief against something else. . . .

I deeply believe in the capacity of democracy to surmount any trials that may lie ahead provided only we practice it in our daily lives.

And among the things that we must practice is this: that while we seek fervently to ferret out the subversive and anti-democratic forces in the country, we do not at the same time, by hysteria, by resort to innuendo and sneers and other unfortunate tactics, besmirch the very cause that we believe in, and cause a separation among our people, cause one group and one individual to hate one another, based upon mere attacks, mere unsubstantiated attacks upon their loyalty. . . .

Hearsay and gossip had no place in courts of justice. If the principles of protection of an individual and his good name against gossip and hearsay were not upheld by legislatures in their investigating activities, that too would be a failure of the democratic ideal. Then, pausing, he unfolded his hands and said, "This I deeply believe."

For a moment the room was silent. Then, almost in a rush, members of the committee and people from the audience began crowding around him to praise Lilienthal for what he had said.

From the White House Truman let Lilienthal know that he would not only stand behind the nomination but was in the fight with all he had "if it took 150 years."

In the days following, a strain of anti-Semitism in the opposition to the appointment became increasingly apparent. Then, without warning, and without waiting for the committee report to reach the floor, Senator Taft announced he would oppose the nomination on the grounds that Lilienthal was not only a "typical power-hungry bureaucrat," and "temperamentally unfitted" for the job of heading the Atomic Energy Commission, but "soft on the subject of Communism." Until this point it had been McKellar's show, and thus largely personal and predictable. (In earlier days the senator had seen Communists behind the anti-poll tax bill, too.) But now with Mr. Republican stepping in, it became a distinctly partisan issue, and, as was said, a major Capitol crisis. The phrase "soft on Communism" caught on immediately.

Lilienthal did not see how he could possibly win with the Republican majority lined up against him. The Taft speech had been "a kick in the teeth." How long the confirming process might take, and at what toll, no one could say.

"Courage: What is it?" Lilienthal asked in his diary. "Isn't it the capacity to hang on?"

II

He had been trying for days to find time to write to her, Truman told his sister in a letter in February.

He was more concerned than usual about staying in touch. Mamma had had a fall and fractured her hip. Truman had flown home to see her, but remained gravely worried—and concerned, too, about the burden of care on Mary Jane. "Now Mary, don't you work too hard." If she needed help, she was to get it.

"Things have been happening here in a hurry," he told her. Foreign affairs were uppermost. Marshall was to leave for Moscow in little more than a week, for his first Foreign Ministers' Conference. He himself would be flying to Mexico in three days, for the first visit to Mexico ever by a President of the United States. "I am spending every day with Marshall going over policy and hoping we can get a lasting peace. It looks not so good right now."

The date was February 27, 1947. Six days earlier, on the 21st, a month to the day since Marshall took up his duties as Secretary of State, an urgent formal message, a so-called "blue paper," from the British ambassador, Lord Inverchapel, had been delivered to the State Department. Marshall had been out of town, speaking at Princeton University's bicentennial convocation. So it was Under Secretary Acheson who telephoned Truman that afternoon. Great Britain, its financial condition worsening, could no longer provide economic and military support for Greece and Turkey. The cost was too great. The Attlee government would withdraw forty thousand troops from Greece and all economic aid would halt as of March 31. The United States, it was hoped, would assume the responsibility.

The news was both momentous and not wholly unexpected. Britain was in desperate straits. All Europe had been hit by one of the worst winters on record. In France, the cold destroyed millions of acres of winter wheat. Snow fell in Paris for the first time in years. In Berlin, where temperatures hovered around zero, people were dying of the cold. Ice clogged the Kiel Canal from the Baltic to the North Sea. Food and fuel were scarce everywhere. In Prague, electric current was being shut off for three hours a day. But Britain was hit hardest, the whole country virtually snowbound. Factories and schools closed. Huge snowdrifts blocked highways and railroads, closed coal mines, and isolated hundreds of small towns. When a bus on a main coastal road ran into a ten-foot drift and a snowplow was brought to the rescue, reported *The Times* of London, the snowplow, too, was buried. "Weather Threatens Coal Supply," read the headline in *The Times* on February 6. To save power, London offices were being lit with candles. And the storms continued. On February 21, the day of Lord Inverchapel's message, it snowed again over most of the country.

On January 20, meantime, the British government had issued an economic White Paper describing Britain's position as "extremely serious." That Britain would soon have to cut back on its armed forces and overseas commitments was self-evident. The situation, wrote Walter Lippmann, would "shake the world and make our position highly vulnerable and precariously isolated."

Specific warnings had been crossing Truman's desk for weeks. As early as February 3, the American ambassador in Athens, Lincoln MacVeigh, reported rumors that the British were pulling out of Greece, where, since 1945, their troops and money had helped maintain a royalist government in a raging civil war with Communist guerrillas. On February 12, another dispatch from MacVeigh urged immediate consideration of American aid to Greece. A few days later, Mark Ethridge, publisher of the Louisville *Courier-Journal* and a member of a United Nations investigating committee, cabled from Athens that Greece was a "ripe plum" ready to fall into Soviet hands.

Warnings about Turkey had come even sooner. Turkey had "little hope of independent survival unless it is assured of solid long-term American and British support," cabled General Walter Bedell Smith, who had replaced Averell Harriman as the American ambassador in Moscow.

Truman himself, furthermore, had already made his concern for the future of Greece clear to the Greek government, if not, as yet, to the American people. In the fall of 1946, through Ambassador MacVeigh, Truman had acknowledged that Greece was of vital interest to the United States and promised substantial aid to maintain its independence, providing the Greek government could show that democracy survived there— a question of considerable importance, since the Greek government, as Truman knew and later wrote, "seemed to encourage irresponsible rightist groups."

But while the crisis in Greece and Turkey came not without warning, the formal announcement of British withdrawal did come, as Truman said, "sooner than we expected," and its very formality made it seem especially dramatic and unsettling.

February 21 was a Friday. Truman asked Acheson for a report by Monday, and Acheson, Bohlen, and others worked through the weekend at the old State Department, where packing boxes cluttered the halls in preparation for the move to Foggy Bottom. On Monday, Marshall and Acheson met with the President and urged "immediate action" to provide help for Greece, and, to a lesser degree, for Turkey as well. To Marshall the British announcement of withdrawal from Greece was tantamount to British withdrawal from the whole Middle East. He, too, saw the situation as extremely serious. The sum needed for Greece alone just for the remainder of 1947 was a quarter of a billion dollars.

Truman agreed. Greece would have to be helped, quickly and with substantial amounts.

But aid to Greece was only one aspect of the problem. It had been a year now since Kennan's "Long Telegram" and Churchill's "iron curtain" speech at Fulton. Something more than a simple aid bill was called for. On this Truman, Marshall, Acheson, Clifford—virtually all who had a say in policy—were agreed. One ranking State Department official, Joseph M. Jones, urged that Secretary Marshall, not the President, go before Congress, to rouse the nation to the reality of the crisis, because, as Jones wrote in an internal memorandum, Marshall was "the only one in Government with the prestige to make a deep impression."

Things were indeed "happening in a hurry," as Truman told his sister. The morning of the 27th, he called the congressional leaders to his office for a crucial meeting. They listened first to Marshall, who, in measured tones, told them, "It is not alarmist to say that we are faced with the first crisis of a series which might extend Soviet domination to Europe, the Middle East and Asia." The choice was "acting with energy or losing by default."

Acheson, who thought Marshall had failed to speak with appropriate force, asked to be heard. There was no time left for a measured appraisal, Acheson said. Greece was the rotten apple that would infect the whole barrel. "The Soviet Union was playing one of the greatest gambles in history at minimal cost. It did not need to win all the possibilities." When Acheson finished (according to his own later account), Vandenberg told the President in a sonorous manner that if he would say the same thing in the same way to Congress, then he, Vandenberg, would lend his support and so would a majority on Capitol Hill—his clear implication being that aid to Greece and Turkey could be had only if Truman shocked Congress into action. But in his memoirs, for all his regard for Acheson, Truman would make no mention of Acheson's remarks or the Vandenberg response as described by Acheson. Truman said only that Marshall had made it "quite plain" that the choice was to act or lose by default— "and I expressed my emphatic agreement to this."

The meeting ended at noon. Nothing was disclosed of what had been said.

The crowds in Mexico City were such as Truman had never experienced. Hundreds of thousands of people poured into the streets to see and cheer an American President for the first time. The trip had been Truman's idea and the acclaim was thrilling. He returned the *"Vivas!"* of the throngs (one woman shouted, *"Viva* Missouri!"), and several times broke away from his Mexican and Secret Service escorts to shake hands with people. "I have never had such a welcome in my life," he told the Mexican legislature, to whom he pledged anew Roosevelt's Good Neighbor policy. To a crowd of American citizens later, he said he hoped they would remember that they, too, were ambassadors.

The next morning, he announced suddenly that he wished to make an unscheduled stop at Mexico City's historic Chapultepec Castle, where, with one simple, unheralded gesture, he did more to improve Mexican-American relations than had any President in a century. Within hours, as the word spread, he had become a hero.

The long motorcade pulled into the shade of an ancient grove of trees. Truman stepped out of his black Lincoln and walked to a stone monument bearing the names of *Los Niños Héroes,* "the child heroes," six teenage cadets who had died in the Mexican-American War in 1847, when American troops stormed the castle. According to legend, five of the cadets had stabbed themselves, and a sixth jumped to his death from a parapet rather than surrender. As Truman approached, a contingent of blue-uniformed Mexican cadets stood at attention. As he placed a floral wreath at the foot of the monument, several of the cadets wept silently.

After bowing his head for a few minutes, Truman returned to the line of cars, where the Mexican chauffeurs were already shaking hands with their American passengers.

The story created an immediate sensation in the city, filling the papers with eight-column, banner headlines. "Rendering Homage to the Heroes of '47, Truman Heals an Old National Wound Forever," read one. "Friendship Began Today," said another. A cab driver told an American reporter, "To think that the most powerful man in the world would come and apologize." He wanted to cry himself, the driver said. A prominent Mexican engineer was quoted: "One hundred years of misunderstanding and bitterness wiped out by one man in one minute. This is the best neighbor policy."

President Truman, declared Mexican President Miguel Alemán, was "the new champion of solidarity and understanding among the American republics."

Asked by American reporters why he had gone to the monument, Truman said simply, "Brave men don't belong to any one country. I respect bravery wherever I see it."

The three-day whirlwind visit ended on March 6, when the presidential party departed on *The Sacred Cow* before dawn. Moonlight reflected on the plane's wings as Truman looked out the window. Despite the hour and the chill morning air, a thousand people had come to see him off.

Less than a year before, in July 1946, as only a few were aware, Truman had asked Clark Clifford to prepare a comprehensive analysis of Soviet-American relations, the first of its kind.

The project began at once, and though Clifford remained in charge, and with his editing gave the finished effort much of its tone and emphasis, the real work—research and writing—was done by his assistant, George Elsey, who had suggested the project in the first place. He had felt, Elsey later explained, that Truman was judging Russia on "too narrow a basis," his concerns limited too often to whether or not Russia was keeping its agreements.

By the time Elsey was finished in September 1946, the report ran to nearly 100,000 words. It was immensely detailed and clearly influenced by Kennan's "Long Telegram," but most of it had been drawn from interviews with or written reports from a dozen or more key people within the executive branch, including the State and War departments, and in all it was a far more alarming state paper than the "Long Telegram," even though, as Elsey himself later said, most of the material had been previously called to Truman's attention by Byrnes, Forrestal, Harriman, Leahy, even Harry Hopkins as early as April 1945.

Titled "American Relations with the Soviet Union," it began by stating that such relations posed the gravest problem facing the United States and that Soviet leaders appeared to be "on a course of aggrandizement designed to lead to eventual world domination by the U.S.S.R."

The Soviet Union was "consistently opposed" to British-American efforts to achieve world peace agreements, because the longer peace settlements were postponed, the longer Red Army troops could "legally" remain in "enemy" countries. Moreover, the Soviets were maintaining excessively large military forces in the satellite countries. The Soviets already dominated Finland, Poland, Czechoslovakia, Hungary, Romania, Bulgaria. In Austria only the presence of British, French, and American occupation troops prevented a Soviet takeover.

Communist parties were growing in France and Italy. In a weak and divided China, the USSR was "in a position to exert greater influence there than any other country." The Soviets were supplying the Communist forces in China, while in Korea, the Soviets had shown that they would consent to the unification of the country only if assured of a "friendly" government.

Most ominous was Soviet military power:

> Generalissimo Stalin and his associates . . . are supporting armed forces stronger than those of any potential combination of foreign powers and they are developing as rapidly as possible a powerful and self-sufficient economy. They are seizing every opportunity to expand the area, directly or indirectly, under Soviet control in order to provide additional protection for the vital areas of the Soviet Union.

The menace was gathering. Russia was rapidly developing "atomic weapons, guided missiles, materials for biological warfare, a strategic air force, submarines of great cruising range. . . ." The Soviet Union, the grim report continued, was also actively directing espionage and subversive movements in the United States.

Since the "language of military power" was the only language the Russians understood, it was necessary that the United States maintain sufficient military strength to "confine" Soviet influence. Therefore, the United States, too, must be prepared to wage atomic and biological warfare. "The mere fact of preparedness may be the only powerful deterrent to Soviet aggressive action and in this sense the only sure guarantee of peace."

In reviewing the situation in the Middle East, the report noted that the Soviets hoped for the withdrawal of troops from Greece to establish another of their "friendly" governments there. The Soviet desire for Turkey was a puppet state to serve as a springboard for the domination of the eastern Mediterranean.

Finally, the report concluded that in addition to maintaining its military strength, the United States "should support and assist all democratic countries which are in any way menaced or endangered by the U.S.S.R."

George Kennan, when asked to look at a nearly completed draft, judged it "excellent." Truman, who was up much of one night reading the final report, called Clifford at his home early the next morning to ask how many copies there were. Ten, Clifford said. Truman wanted the other nine put immediately "under lock and key." The report was so "hot," he told Clifford, that if it ever came out its effect on his efforts to resolve the East-West conflict peacefully would be "exceedingly unfortunate."

How much effect it had on Truman is difficult to gauge. He never said. Clifford, when recounting the Truman years, would stress its great far-reaching influence, while Elsey would be far more modest. "The impact of having it all drawn together may have had some influence on the President," Elsey would speculate. "Again, I don't think one can—you never know and neither the President nor anyone else is ever able—to say *exactly* what all the influences are that help make up his mind."

All the same, it was Clifford and Elsey who, after Truman's return from Mexico, put the finishing touches to the historic speech Truman would make before Congress concerning the situation in Greece, and much that was in the speech came directly from the report.

At a Cabinet meeting on March 7, Truman's first day back from Mexico, Acheson said the complete disintegration of Greece was only weeks away. "If we go in we cannot be certain of success in the Middle East and Mediterranean. If we do not go in there will be a collapse in these areas." There was also, of course, the possibility of "military risk."

Truman felt he faced a decision as difficult as any ever to confront a President. The money for Greece was only the beginning. "It means the United States is going into European politics. . . ." The President's staff viewed the speech as potentially the most important of his career.

A first draft had been prepared at the State Department, but Truman thought it too wordy and technical, more like an investment prospectus, as he later wrote. He also wanted the addition of a strong statement of American policy. Acheson made cuts and revisions, modified several passages, including a key sentence that essentially repeated what had been in the Clifford-Elsey report about helping countries in jeopardy from the Soviet Union, only here the Soviet Union was not to be mentioned by name.

"It is the policy of the United States to support free peoples who are resisting attempted subjugation by armed minorities or by outside pressures," the line read in its original state. Acheson changed it to, "I believe it must be the policy of the United States. . . ."

To Clifford, it was time to take a stand against the Soviets, time for "the opening gun" in a campaign to awaken the American people. As he had urged the President to stand fast against John L. Lewis, so Clifford now urged a strong response to Stalin.

George Kennan, on the other hand, thought the speech went too far, and in Paris, Marshall looked it over with Chip Bohlen, who was accompanying him to Moscow, and both felt there was "too much rhetoric."

When Bernard Baruch, who had no official position in the administration, let it be known that he too wished to have a say in the matter, Truman refused. "If you take his advice," Truman said, "then you have him on your hands for hours and hours, and it is *his* policy. I'm just not going to do it. We have a decision to make and we'll make it."

(Hearing the story later from Clifford, David Lilienthal wrote in his diary that "the President's comment interested me because it was so human: one of the few things a President can enjoy is to decide whom he will consult.")

Truman had Clifford and Elsey finish up the final draft as suited him. He was no Woodrow Wilson, who could sit down at a typewriter the night before addressing Congress at an historic juncture and tap out his own speech. But he knew what he wanted. "I wanted no hedging. . . . It had to be clear and free of hesitation or double talk."

In answer to Marshall's concern about "rhetoric," Marshall was told that in the opinion of the executive branch, including the President, the Senate would not approve the new policy without emphasis on the Communist threat. Probably that was correct.

"There is, you know, such a thing as being too intellectual in your approach to a problem," Clark Clifford would say years later in an interview.

> The man who insists on seeing all sides of it often can't make up his mind where to take hold.
> Without any disparagement, that was never a problem for Mr. Truman. He wanted all the facts he could get before he made up his mind. But if he could get only 80 percent of the facts in the time available, he didn't let the missing 20 percent tie him up in indecision. He believed that even a wrong decision was better than no decision at all. And when he made up his mind that was it. . . .
> We'd been through the greatest war in which the world had ever

been involved. . . . This is 1947. The war ended in August of 1945. There was every reason for Harry Truman to say, "This is not for us." And he kept worrying about it, thinking about it. . . . I remember thinking there was really nothing to impede the Soviet forces, if they chose to, from just marching straight west to the English Channel. . . . And yet he decided that it had to be done. . . . Harry Truman looks at this, and he just steps up to it. . . .

The speech setting forth what became known as the Truman Doctrine was delivered in the House Chamber before a joint session of Congress on Wednesday, March 12, 1947, beginning a few minutes past one o'clock. It was a straightforward declarative statement lasting eighteen minutes. Greece was in desperate need, the situation was urgent. The existing Greek government was not perfect, and the government of the United States, no less than ever, condemned extremist measures of the right or left. Though Turkey, unlike Greece, had been spared the destruction and suffering of the war, Turkey also needed American support.

One of the primary objectives of American policy, Truman said, was "the creation of conditions in which we and other nations will be able to work out a way of life free of coercion." This had been a fundamental issue in the war with Germany and Japan, countries that had tried "to impose their will, and their way of life, upon other countries."

Dressed in a dark suit and dark tie, he read from an open notebook slowly and with great force. His audience listened in silence. Hardly anyone moved. In the front row, John Snyder had his head bowed. Beside him the perfectly tailored Acheson sat as stiff and straight as if at a memorial service, hands folded in his lap. Further along in the same row, Senator Taft fiddled with his glasses, rubbed his face, then yawned. On the dais behind Truman, Speaker Martin and Senator Vandenberg were following the speech line by line in printed copies.

At the present moment in world history nearly every nation must choose between alternative ways of life. The choice is too often not a free one.

One way of life is based upon the will of the majority, and is distinguished by free institutions, representative government, free elections, guarantees of individual liberty, freedom of speech and religion, and freedom from political oppression.

The second way of life is based upon the will of a minority forcibly imposed upon the majority. It relies upon terror and oppression, a controlled press and radio, fixed elections, and the suppression of personal freedoms.

I believe that it must be the policy of the United States to support free peoples who are resisting attempted subjugation by armed minorities or by outside pressures.

I believe that we must assist free peoples to work out their own destinies in their own way.

I believe that our help should be primarily through economic and financial aid which is essential to economic stability and orderly political processes. . . .

Should we fail to aid Greece and Turkey in this fateful hour, the effect will be far reaching to the West as well as to the East.

We must take immediate and resolute action. . . .

To many who were listening there in the chamber and over the radio, it seemed an odd, ironic time for a crisis. The United States was the richest, strongest country in the world and prospering as few could have ever imagined. Production was up. Incomes were up. There were few strikes. There was no more waiting for new automobiles, no meat shortages any longer. White shirts, nylon stockings, fishing tackle, and golf balls were back on store shelves. Because of the GI Bill, more than 4 million veterans were attending college, as most never could have in other times. Yet the speech seemed disturbingly like a call to arms. "Well, I told my wife to dust off my uniform," an ex-soldier enrolled at the University of Oklahoma remarked to a reporter.

The cost of winning the war had been $341 billion. Now $400 million was needed for Greece and Turkey. "This is a serious course upon which we embark," Truman said at the finish, and the look on his face was serious indeed. "I would not recommend it except that the alternative is much more serious. . . . If we falter in our leadership, we may endanger the peace of the world, and we shall surely endanger the welfare of this nation."

The entire room rose in applause, but as Acheson later wrote, it was more as a tribute to a brave man than a unanimous acceptance of his policy. Truman, holding the closed notebook with the speech in front of his chest with both hands, nodded to the applause left and right, several times, but he never smiled.

Editorial reaction was overwhelmingly supportive. *The New York Times* compared the speech to the Monroe Doctrine. To the editors of *Time* and *Life* it was a great clearing of the air at long last. "Like a bolt of lightning," said *Life,* "the speech cut through the confused international atmosphere." The President, said *Collier's,* had "hit the popularity jackpot." But support was often expressed with troubling reservations—"Are we to shoulder the mantle of nineteenth century British imperialism?" asked the San Francisco *Examiner*—and some of the liberal press was outraged. *PM* charged Truman with scrapping Roosevelt's whole policy on Russia.

Most important was the objection of Walter Lippmann, who, though favoring aid to Greece, disapproved of the President's tone. "A vague global policy which sounds like the tocsin of an ideological crusade, has no limits," Lippmann warned. "It cannot be controlled. Its effects cannot be predicted."

That the speech was of immense importance, signaling a turning point, no one seems to have doubted. "If words could shape the future of nations," wrote *Newsweek,* "these unquestionably would. They had clearly put America into power politics to stay."

On Capitol Hill Senator Vandenberg was quick to stress that he did not consider Greek-Turkish aid as a "universal pattern," but something only "to fit a given circumstance." Acheson, too, told the Senate Foreign Relations Committee that the bill was not intended to establish a pattern for the future. The United States, he stressed, would "of course" act "according to the circumstances of each specific case."

Objections in Congress came from liberals and conservatives alike. Senator Pepper was sure such a policy would destroy all hope of reconciliation with Russia. Senators Byrd and McKellar were opposed chiefly because of cost. "I guess the do-gooders won't feel right until they have us all broke," said Republican Representative Harold Knutson of Minnesota.

Truman, within minutes after delivering the speech, had been on his way to the airport and another flight to Florida. The President, explained Wallace Graham, had been "going pretty hard lately" and needed a rest. In plain truth, the President was exhausted. Writing to Margaret from Key West, he said no one had any idea how "worn to a frazzle" he was by "this terrible decision." But the police state of communism was no different from the police state of the Nazis, he told her. He had known that since Potsdam.

In the time between Truman's dramatic appearance before Congress and the final vote on aid to Greece and Turkey, the fight in the Senate over the Lilienthal nomination grew intense and abusive. The opposition was nearly all Republican. Senator John Bricker of Ohio, who had been Dewey's running mate in 1944, warned that it might be the last chance ever to get the Atomic Energy Commission out of the hands of leftists. Capehart of Indiana said that especially now, in view of the situation in Greece and

Turkey, control of atomic energy ought to be returned to the Army, an idea that appealed also to Senator Taft. Brewster of Maine, who had once served on the Truman Committee, claimed Lilienthal's indifference to communism made him no less a threat than if he were an outright party member.

"If Mr. L. is a communist so am I," Truman wrote privately. He would carry the fight to the end, Truman vowed. "It is a matter of principle and we cannot let the peanut politicians ruin a good man. . . ." Taft, Truman thought, was succeeding only in making himself look like a fool.

A few Republicans—Knowland of California, Saltonstall of Massachusetts, Aiken of Vermont—declared support for the nominee. But the decisive moment came when Vandenberg spoke to a tense session on the afternoon of April 3, giving what many thought was his finest speech ever.

David Lilienthal, Vandenberg said, was "no part of a communist by any stretch of the imagination." When Vandenberg called for Lilienthal's confirmation, the galleries roared with applause.

There was a test vote on an amendment. Lilienthal was with Truman at the White House when Charlie Ross put his head in at the door to report the result. They had won by a margin of 14 votes, more than anyone had thought possible. Truman and Lilienthal shook hands. Atomic energy was "the most important thing there is," Truman remarked, looking subdued and thoughtful. "You must make a blessing of it, or," he said, pointing to a large globe in the corner, "we'll blow that all to smithereens."

The final, formal vote in the Senate came on April 9, when a total of twenty Republicans defied Taft to support Lilienthal. Of the southern Democrats, only four besides McKellar voted against him. The nomination was confirmed by 50 to 31. It was Truman's first test of strength with the new Congress and a sweet victory.

Yet the issue of loyalty—the issue of who was or who was not, in Taft's phrase, soft on communism—was by no means ended. The Republican leadership, having made communism a theme with such success in the fall elections, would keep up the demand for investigations, and Truman, to head off such attacks from conservatives in both parties, had by this time accepted the view of a special commission—and of Attorney General Clark and the director of the FBI, J. Edgar Hoover—that a program of loyalty reviews was necessary. The whole concept troubled him. In notes he made of a conversation with the President in May 1947, Clark Clifford wrote: "[He is] very strongly anti-FBI. . . . Wants to be sure to hold FBI down, afraid of 'Gestapo.' "

Further, much too much was being made of "the Communist bugaboo," Truman thought, and said so in a letter to a former Pennsylvania governor named George Earle. The country was "perfectly safe so far as Communism is concerned—we have far too many sane people."

The political pressures bore heavily, however. Attorney General Clark, conceding that the number of disloyal employees in the government was probably small, argued that even one such person posed a serious threat. J. Edgar Hoover wanted authority to remove anyone from public service whose views were politically suspect. Such people, Hoover warned, might well influence foreign policy in a way that could "favor the foreign country of their ideological choice." Like many Republicans on Capitol Hill, Hoover saw the State Department as the core of the problem. In his first speech as the new Speaker of the House, Joe Martin had declared there was "no room in the government of the United States for any who prefer the Communistic system." Accusations that the New Deal had been riddled with Communists were made repeatedly and widely believed, however unfounded. "The long tenure of the Democratic Party had poisoned the air we Republicans breathed," remembered Martin much later. "Fear of Communist penetration of the government was an ugly new phenomenon. Suspicion of the State Department was rife. We were disturbed and bewildered by the new power of the Soviet Union."

Truman worried particularly about the House Committee on Un-American Activities and the extremes it might go to under its vile-tempered, and to Truman contemptible, Republican chairman, Representative J. Parnell Thomas of New Jersey. By acting first on the loyalty issue, Truman hoped to head Thomas off. Also, importantly, he wanted no accusations of administration softness on communism at home just as he was calling for a new hard approach to communism abroad.

On Friday, March 21, 1947, nine days after his address to Congress, Truman issued Executive Order No. 9835, establishing an elaborate Federal Employees Loyalty and Security Program. And he did so with misgivings.

Roosevelt, in 1942, had empowered the Civil Service to disqualify anyone from government employment where there was a "reasonable doubt of loyalty," and by executive order Roosevelt later assigned the Justice Department and FBI to check on the loyalty of government workers. But that had been during the war. Until now, no such step had ever been taken in peacetime.

His purpose, Truman later wrote, was twofold: to guard against disloyal employees in the government work force, and to protect innocent government workers from unfounded accusations. To show that he had no intention of playing politics with the program, he put a conservative Republican, a prominent Washington lawyer named Seth Richardson, in charge of its Review Board.

All federal employees were to be subject to loyalty investigations, whatever their jobs. FBI files and the files of the House Un-American Activities Committee would be called into use. Anyone found to be disloyal could no longer hold a government job. Dismissal could be based merely on "reasonable grounds for belief that the person is disloyal," yet the term "disloyal" was never defined. Moreover, those accused would be unable to confront those making charges against them, or even to know who they were or what exactly the charges were. In addition, the Attorney General was authorized to draw up a list of subversive organizations.

To David Lilienthal, who well knew the torment that self-proclaimed Communist-hunters could bring down on a loyal government employee, the whole program looked ominous. Anyone serving in the government could be at the mercy of almost any malevolent accuser. "In practical effect," Lilienthal wrote in his diary, "the usual rule that men are presumed innocent until proved guilty is in reverse." Yet Lilienthal, too, conceded that something of the sort probably had to be initiated, and so staunch an upholder of liberal principle as the New York *Post* called the program a logical answer to subversion. At his next press conference, Truman was asked little or nothing about it. Of more interest was his letter to the former Pennsylvania governor. Was he truly so unconcerned about "the Communist bugaboo"?

"I am not worried about the Communist Party taking over the government of the United States," Truman replied, "but I am against a person, whose loyalty is not to the government of the United States, holding a government job." At the time it seemed all the answer anyone could ask for.

In another few months the FBI would begin running "name checks" on every one of the 2 million people on the federal payrolls, a monstrous, costly task. Over four years, by 1951, 3 million employees would be investigated and cleared by the Civil Service Commission, and another 14,000 by the FBI. Several thousand would resign, but only 212 would be dismissed as being of questionable loyalty. None would be indicted and no evidence of espionage would be found.

Clark Clifford would say sadly years later that the whole program had been "a response to the temper of the times," and that he did not see how Truman could have done otherwise.

But in an interview with the journalist Carl Bernstein, Clifford was considerably more blunt:

It was a political problem. [Clifford told Bernstein] Truman was going to run in '48, and that was it. . . .

My own feeling was there was not a serious problem. I felt the whole thing was being manufactured. We never had a serious discussion about a real loyalty problem. . . . the President didn't attach fundamental importance to the so-called Communist scare. He thought it was a lot of baloney. But political pressures were such that he had to recognize it. . . .

There was no substantive problem. . . . We did not believe there was a real problem. A problem was being manufactured. . . .

(To Bernstein, this was a particularly chilling revelation, since his own parents had been among victims of the Loyalty Program.)

And politically the effect of Executive Order No. 9835 was indeed pronounced, for the moment at least, as *Time*'s Capitol Hill correspondent, Frank McNaughton, described in a confidential report to his editors:

The Republicans are now taking Truman seriously . . . [his] order to root out subversives from government employment hit a solid note with Congress, and further pulled the rug from under his political detractors. The charge of "Communists in government" and nothing being done about it, a favorite theme of the reactionaries, simply will not stick any longer. . . . The Republicans are beginning to realize Truman is no pushover.

That Truman's concern over J. Edgar Hoover continued to trouble him there is no question. "If I can prevent [it], there'll be no NKVD [Soviet Secret Police] or Gestapo in this country," he wrote privately to Bess. "Edgar Hoover's organization would make a good start toward a citizen spy system. Not for me. . . . "

Writing in his memoirs years later, well after the pernicious influence of the Loyalty Program had become all too clear, Truman could say only in lame defense that it had started out to be as fair as possible "under the climate of opinion that then existed." In private conversation with friends, however, he would concede it had been a bad mistake. "Yes, it was terrible," he said.

On April 22, 1947, the Senate overwhelmingly approved aid to Greece and Turkey by a vote of 67 to 23. On May 9, the House, like the Senate, passed the bill by a margin of nearly three to one, 287 to 107. On May 22, while visiting his mother in Grandview, Truman sat at the Mission oak table in her small parlor and signed the $400 million aid package. The Truman Doctrine had been sanctioned.

Though it seemed so at the time, and would often be so presented in later accounts, the Truman Doctrine was not an abrupt, dramatic turn in American policy, but a declaration of principle. It was a continuation of a policy that had been evolving since Potsdam, its essence to be found in Kennan's "Long Telegram" and in the more emphatic Clifford-Elsey Report. It could even be said that it began with Averell Harriman's first meeting with Truman before Potsdam.

But, be that as it may, the Truman Doctrine would guide the foreign policy of the United States for another generation and more, for better or worse, despite any of the assurances by Acheson and Vandenberg that this was not the intent.

III

It could not have been a more exciting or important time, Clark Clifford would say, recalling events of 1947 and '48. "I think it's one of the proudest moments in American history. What happened during that period was that Harry Truman and the United States saved the free world."

Others felt the same. A young economic adviser at the State Department, Paul Nitze, would reflect after a long, eventful career in public service that nothing had given him such satisfaction as the work accomplished then. Dean Acheson, speaking for all of them, would write that they had been "present at the creation."

Their exhilaration derived in part from the tremendous urgency of the moment. Events moved rapidly. "There was much to be done and little time to do it," Truman would remember. Plans had to be conceived and clarified with minimum delay, imagination applied, decisions reached, and always with the realities and imponderables of politics weighed in the balance. The pressure was unrelenting. "You don't sit down and take time to think through and debate ad nauseam all the points," George Elsey would say, in response to latter-day critics. "You don't have time. Later somebody can sit around for days and weeks and figure out how things might have been done differently. This is all very well and very interesting and quite irrelevant."

With the stress of deadlines and long hours, emotions often ran high. The struggle to draw up a preliminary report for what would become the Marshall Plan was for George Kennan "an intellectual agony" greater than any he had known. So intense did a debate with his associates become one harried night at the State Department that Kennan had to leave the room and go outside, where he walked, weeping, around the entire building.

What they were attempting was, besides, different from what had gone before. They were pioneering, the state of the world being, as Acheson said, "wholly novel within the experience of those who had to deal with it."

Of great importance also to everyone's morale in the spring of 1947 was the changed outlook of the President, a subject which by now had drawn much attention. Dozens of articles appeared describing the "new" Truman, and for the reason that the change was truly striking. He was in "top spirits," reported *The New York Times;* the whole "political picture has changed in Washington." The President was "very different" now, "calm and forceful," wrote Alden Hatch in *Liberty* magazine. "The recent change in Harry Truman has been variously ascribed to new advisers, a difference of political climate, or a change in his nature. The fact is that it is not change, but growth." His voice, his whole manner had a "new authority," said *Collier's.* He was no longer Roosevelt's "stand in." Noting that Truman's public approval rating was up sharply, to 60 percent, *Time* lauded his "new sense of the dignity of his office." The President, said *Time,* had acquired "a new confidence and a new formula: be natural."

On an afternoon in mid-April, speaking extemporaneously to several hundred members of the American Society of Newspaper Editors who crowded into his office, Truman was as impressive as he had ever been before such a group—relaxed, sure of himself, convincing in a way that seemed to take many of them by surprise. The Truman Doctrine, he said, was no "sudden" turn in policy, and he traced the history of relations with Russia from the time of his first meeting with Molotov there in the same room two years before. He was sure a solution to the problems with the Soviets would be found and that a long era of peace was in store. "I believe that as sincerely as I am standing here." It was essential "to stand for what we believe is right," hard as the Russians were to negotiate with. "They deal from day to day, and what's done yesterday has no bearing on what's done today or tomorrow. We have to make up our mind what our policy is."

He had just been talking with a pilot who had flown around the world in sixty-eight hours, he told them. "We must catch up morally and internationally with the machine age. We must catch up with it ... in such a way as to create peace in the world, or it will destroy us and everybody else. And that we don't dare contemplate."

To his staff it was an inspiring performance, a long way from the fumbling press conferences of the previous year.

The morale of the staff had never been higher. Truman spoke of them proudly and affectionately as his "team." They were devoted to him, and increasingly as time went on, the better they knew him, quite as much as those who had served with him in the Army. They liked him as a man, greatly respected him as a leader, admiring his courage, decisiveness, and fundamental honesty. The President they worked for, the Harry Truman they saw day to day, bore almost no resemblance to the stereotype Harry Truman, the cocky, profane, "feisty little guy." Rather it was a quiet-spoken, even-tempered and uncommonly kind-hearted person, whose respect for the office he held enlarged their appreciation not only of him but of their own responsibilities.

"He was, as I'm sure you know, an extremely thoughtful, courteous, considerate man," George Elsey would tell an interviewer years later. "He was a pleasure to work for . . . very kindly . . . never too busy to think about members of his staff. . . . He had a tremendous veneration and re-spect for the institution of the Presidency. He demanded at all times respect for the President of the United States. . . ."

William J. Hopkins, an executive clerk who would serve nearly forty years in the White House, said later of Truman that no President in his experience had "set a comparable tone." Truman, Hopkins emphasized, "liked people, he trusted people, and in turn he engendered a feeling of unqualified loyalty and devotion among his staff."

A measure of the Truman manner and outlook was the way he con-ducted his regular morning meeting with the staff, one of the most im-portant events of their day, for the information and sense of direction provided, but also for its overall atmosphere. The staff numbered thir-teen, two more than in Roosevelt's time, and Truman was his own chief of staff. The meetings were informal, yet orderly and businesslike. Tru-man would open the door of his office on the dot of nine o'clock and one by one they would file in and take their seats.

> He was seated at his desk . . . the staff assembled in a semi-circle around his desk, and much of the day's business was gone over [remembered Hopkins]. He usually started with Matt Connelly, who would bring up matters relating to presidential appointments, what was on the agenda for the day and upcoming appointments. He would also bring to the President's attention requests for speeches throughout the country, getting the President's reactions and (in some cases) commitments. The President would then turn to Charlie Ross and see what problems might arise during the day in his relations with the press. Many matters

were discussed in terms of how to answer press questions and deal with certain problems.

Dr. Steelman, of course, was there, and Clark Clifford . . . and they brought up matters in their areas of responsibility. It was an opportunity to ·listen to the President's philosophy and get his directions for the day.

President Truman was a prodigious reader, and each night he would carry home a portfolio, often six or eight inches thick. The next morning, he would have gone through all that material and taken such action as was needed. He had a desk folder labeled for each of his staff members, and at this staff meeting, he would pass out to them documents in their area of responsibility, or on which he wished their advice or recommendations, or on matters he wanted raised with the various departments and agencies. In this way each staff member knew basically what the others were doing, knew to whom the President had given which responsibility—whether it was to respond to a certain request, or to follow through on the preparation of an Executive Order or a speech, or things of that nature.

Truman was as tidy about his desk as he was about his clothes. The "flow of paper was probably the best I have experienced," remembered Hopkins, whose job, as executive clerk, was to bring to the President and keep track of the immense range of documents requiring his attention or signature—enrolled bills, executive orders, proclamations, executive clemency cases, treaties, departmental directives, nominations for federal office, commissions, messages to Congress—in addition to "gleanings" from the incoming mail, which were routinely delivered to Truman's desk twice a day, in the morning and again after lunch.

Hopkins, who was himself extremely punctual, also noted admiringly of Truman, "When he went to lunch, if he left word that he would return at 2:00 P.M., he was back without fail, not at 2:05, not at 1:15, but at 2:00 P.M." The longer he was in office, the more conscious Truman seemed of time. On his desk now he had a total of four clocks, as well as two others elsewhere in the room and his own wristwatch.

Ross, Clifford, Elsey, could each tell his own stories of Truman's exceptional diligence, the long hours he kept, working as hard or harder than any of them. "Lots of times I would be down there [at the White House] in the evening," Clifford would remember, "and he'd be sitting upstairs, in the Oval Room upstairs, with an old-fashioned green eye shade on, like bookkeepers wear, and he'd be sitting there reading all this material . . . and we would talk together, and he took it *very, very* seriously. And the strain of the job was enormous."

"He spent virtually every waking moment working at being president," said Charles Murphy, a new man on the staff in 1947, who was Clifford's assistant. To convey the kind of sustained effort the presidency demanded, Murphy would compare it to cramming for and taking an examination every day, year after year, with never a letup.

Murphy particularly admired Truman's gift for simplification. "Not only could he simplify complex matters, he could also keep simple matters simple."

The staff was continuously amazed by the President's knowledge of the country, acquired from years of travel by automobile and from the territory covered at the time of the Truman Committee investigations. Charlie Ross claimed that Truman could look out of his plane at almost any point and name the exact region he was flying over.

They liked his sense of humor. "An economist," he told them, "is a man who wears a watch chain with a Phi Beta Kappa key at one end and no watch at the other." And all of them, it seems, admired his sense of history, which they saw as one of his greatest strengths. "If a man is acquainted with what other people have experienced at this desk," Truman would say sitting in the Oval Office, "it will be easier for him to go through a similar experience. It is ignorance that causes most mistakes. The man who sits here ought to know his American history, at least." When Truman talked of presidents past—Jackson, Polk, Lincoln—it was as if he had known them personally. If ever there was a "clean break from all that had gone before," he would say, the result would be chaos.

Once, that spring, at lunch on the *Williamsburg,* during a brief cruise down the Potomac, Truman and Bill Hassett, the correspondence secretary, began talking about the Civil War. As the others at the table listened, the conversation ranged over several battles and the abilities and flaws of various Union and Confederate generals, Truman, as often before, impressing everyone with how much he had read and remembered.

He would like to have been a history teacher, Truman said.

"Rather teach it than make it?" Clifford asked.

"Yes, I think so," Truman replied. "It would be not nearly so much trouble."

Clifford had become particularly important to Truman, in much the way Harry Hopkins had been to Roosevelt, and it was vital, they both knew, that Clifford understand Truman and what he was trying to accomplish in the long run. He did not want an administration like Roosevelt's, Truman said. Too many of those around Roosevelt had been "crackpots," he thought. "I want to keep my feet on the ground, don't feel comfortable unless I know where I'm going. I don't want any experiments. The American people have been through a lot of experiments and they want a rest from experiments." He disliked the terms "progressive" and "liberal."

What he wanted was a "forward-looking program." That was it, a "forward-looking program."

Perhaps more than Truman knew, they all appreciated the respect he showed them. Charles Murphy, a shy man who spoke only when spoken to, would later remark, "In many ways President Truman really was as tough as a boot, but with his personal staff he was extremely gentle . . . and his staff returned his kindness with an extraordinary amount of hard work, voluntary overtime, and wholehearted, single-minded devotion."

By later presidential standards the staff was small and unlike the White House staffs of some later presidencies, those serving Truman made no policy decisions. As George Elsey would remember, no one on Truman's staff would have dreamed of making policy or making decisions on fundamental economic or political issues, "or any other kind of issue."

> It just has to be said over and over again [Elsey would comment in an interview years later]. There was no vast foreign policy machinery at the White House. There was no vast machinery on *any* subject at the White House. . . . [And no one trying to] make their reputations by undercutting . . . by slitting the throat of a Secretary of State . . . by proving to the President, by trying to prove to the President, that they're smarter and more brilliant and their ideas are better [than the Secretary of State]. . . . None of that existed. Had *anybody* at the White House tried to behave that way, he would have been out of there in thirty seconds flat.

The loyalty of those around Truman was total and would never falter. In years to come not one member of the Truman White House would ever speak or write scathingly of him or belittle him in any fashion. There would be no vindictive "inside" books or articles written about this President by those who worked closest to him. They all thought the world of Harry Truman then and for the rest of their lives, and would welcome the chance to say so.

For Charlie Ross, the senior member of the staff and the one who had known Truman the longest—longer than anyone in the administration—serving with him, for all the strain of the job and the drastic cut in income it had meant, was the privilege of a lifetime, as Ross would write privately to Truman later that year, on Christmas Day, 1947:

> Dear Mr. President:
> There is nothing in life, I think, more satisfying than friendship, and to have yours is a rare satisfaction indeed.
> Two and a half years ago you "put my feet to the fire," as you said. I

am happy that you did. They have been the most rewarding years of my life. Your faith in me, the generous manifestations of your friendship, the association with the fine people around you—your good "team"—all these have been an inspiration.

But the greatest inspiration, Mr. President, has been the character of you—you as President, you as a human being. Perhaps I can say best what is in my heart by telling you that my admiration for you, and my deep affection, have grown steadily since the day you honored me with your trust.

Truman had rarely received a letter that meant so much to him.

To Dean Acheson it was Truman's "priceless gift of vitality, the life force itself," that was his strongest, most inspiriting quality, and always in the darkest, most difficult of times. The President's supply of vitality and good spirits seemed inexhaustible, wrote Acheson, who, to make his point, would quote from Shakespeare's *Henry V* the lines delivered the night before Agincourt:

> ... *every wretch, pining and pale before,*
> *Beholding him, plucks comfort from his looks.* ...
> *His liberal eye doth give to every one* ...
> *A little touch of Harry in the night.*

It was this "little touch of Harry" that "kept all of us going," Acheson would remember.

In addition, there was the example of General Marshall, who lent everyone confidence and raised morale not just at the State Department but throughout the administration. "Gentlemen, enlisted men may be entitled to morale problems, but officers are not," Marshall would tell those who served with him. "I expect all officers in this department to take care of their own morale. No one is taking care of my morale." Morale improved steadily.

As Acheson would stress, he and others at the State Department felt they were being led by two men of rare quality, the President and the Secretary. On Capitol Hill, in his speech in support of the Truman Doctrine, Sam Rayburn had said the nation "again has leaders asking for certain action," and his emphasis on leaders in the plural did not go unnoticed.

Marshall's entire personality inspired confidence, Truman would write. It was Truman's long-held conviction that men make history.

Clearly in the spring of 1947, with the Marshall Plan following on the heels of the Truman Doctrine, things of immense importance happened principally because a relative handful of men made them happen, almost entirely on their own, against great odds, and in amazingly little time.

On Saturday, April 26, 1947, Secretary Marshall returned to Washington from Moscow gravely worried and upset. His sessions with Molotov had been an ordeal, dragging on day after day with little purpose, Molotov acting all the while as if time and the frustrations of the Western Allies were of no concern. Marshall wanted an agreement on the future of Germany. Hoping he might do better dealing directly with Stalin, he made a courtesy call at the Kremlin. But Stalin had asked what difference it made if there was no agreement. "We may agree the next time, or if not then, the time after," Stalin said, as he idly doodled wolves' heads with a red pencil.

Stalin's indifference made a profound impression on Marshall. The Soviets, it seemed, were quite content to see uncertainty and chaos prevail in Europe. It served their purposes to let matters drift. Particularly, they had no wish for a return of order and stability in Germany, let alone a revived prosperity there. Marshall had thought the Russians could be negotiated with, but at Moscow he decided he had been mistaken.

Before leaving Washington, he received an urgent memo from Under Secretary for Economic Affairs Will Clayton warning that conditions in Western Europe were more serious than generally understood. During stops in Paris and Berlin, while going to and from Moscow, Marshall was stunned by what he saw and heard. On the plane back to Washington, he talked of little else but what could be done to save Western Europe.

Time was of the essence, Marshall stressed to Truman. "The patient is sinking while the doctors deliberate," he told the nation in a radio broadcast, April 28.

The next day Marshall summoned George Kennan, instructed him to assemble a special staff "immediately," and to report "without delay" on what should be done to save Europe. As Kennan later recalled, Marshall had only one piece of advice: "Avoid trivia."

The idea of economic aid to Europe had been on Truman's mind for some while. Two years past, in one of their earliest conversations in the Oval Office, Henry Stimson had pointedly told him that an economically strong, productive Germany was essential to the future stability of Europe, a concept Truman readily accepted. In his own State of the Union message in January, Truman had struck the theme of sharing American bounty with war-stricken peoples, as a means of spreading "the faith" of freedom

561

and democracy, and on March 6, even before announcement of the Truman Doctrine, he had said in a speech at Baylor University, "We are the giant of the economic world. Whether we like it or not, the future pattern of economic relations depends upon us."

Early in May, Truman sent Dean Acheson to fill in for him with a foreign policy speech in a remote little town in Mississippi called Cleveland, at the Delta State Teachers' College. Kennan and his special staff had as yet to make their report, but Truman had already made up his mind, from what Marshall had said after returning from Moscow, that Europe had to be rescued and quickly. The speech Acheson made was the alarm bell that Truman wanted sounded. The stricken countries of Europe needed everything and could afford to buy nothing. Financial help was imperative, but, as Acheson stressed, the objective was not relief, it was the revival of industry, agriculture, and trade. The margin of survival was so close in Europe that the savage winter just past had been nearly disastrous. Massive funding was needed if Europe was to be saved. "It is necessary if we are to preserve our own freedoms . . . necessary for our national security. And it is our duty and privilege as human beings."

What was Europe now, Winston Churchill asked rhetorically in a speech in London on May 14. "It is a rubble-heap, a charnel house, a breeding ground of pestilence and hate."

The Kennan Report, "Certain Aspects of the European Recovery Problem from the United States Standpoint," was delivered to Marshall on May 25. American response to world problems must be more than defensive reaction to Communist pressure, it said. An American aid effort in Europe "should be directed not to combating Communism as such but to the restoration of the economic health and vigor of European society." Two days later, Under Secretary Clayton, having just completed an inspection tour of Europe, sent another urgent memo. The situation was worse than anyone supposed. Millions of people were slowly starving. A collapse in Europe would mean revolution and a tailspin for the American economy.

Long sessions followed at the State Department and around the President's desk. With Truman's approval, Marshall decided to make a speech at Harvard, where he had been invited to receive an honorary degree at commencement exercises on Thursday, June 5, an idea Acheson opposed for the reason that no one ever listened to commencement speeches. When the moment came, at the podium in the sunshine of Harvard Yard, before an audience of seven thousand, Marshall read his remarks in a soft voice, his head down, as though he did not care especially if they were listening.

The speech had been written by Bohlen in about two days, drawing heavily on the Kennan Report. Whether Truman saw a copy in advance is not recorded, but given Marshall's extreme care to keep the President always informed, it is almost certain they discussed the matter.

As Marshall wanted, there were no oratorical flourishes. Nor was there any strident anti-Communist language.

> Our policy is directed not against any country or doctrine, but against hunger, poverty, desperation and chaos. Its purpose should be the revival of a working economy in the world so as to permit the emergence of political and social conditions in which free institutions can exist.

Two ideas were new and distinguishing. He was calling on the Europeans to get together, and, with American help, work out their own programs. And, by inference, he was leaving the door open to the Soviets and their satellite countries to take part.

> It would be neither fitting nor efficacious for this Government to undertake to draw up unilaterally a program designed to place Europe on its feet economically. That is the business of the Europeans. The initiative, I think, must come from Europe. The role of this country should consist of friendly aid in the drafting of a European program and of later support for such a program so far as it is practical for us to do so. The program should be a joint one, agreed to by a number, if not all, European nations.

Then, speaking directly to the American people, Marshall said it was virtually impossible by merely reading articles or looking at photographs to grasp the real significance of conditions in Europe—"and yet the whole world's future hangs on proper judgment, hangs on the realization by the American people of what can best be done, or what must be done."

The speech caught nearly everyone by surprise, in Europe no less than in the United States. "We grabbed the lifeline with both hands," said British Foreign Minister Ernest Bevin, who was the first to see the momentous import of what Marshall had said.

At a staff meeting the next day at the State Department, Marshall asked Kennan and Bohlen whether the Soviet Union would accept an invitation to join the plan. They did not think so, said the two Russian experts, but advised him to "play it straight" with the Soviets and exclude no one. It was a calculated gamble—since Congress was not likely to support any aid program that included the Soviets—but a gamble Marshall was willing to take and that Truman backed.

As Kennan later wrote, authorship of the plan was variously claimed and imputed, and he, Bohlen, Acheson, and Clayton were only some of a dozen or more who had had a hand in its creation. Marshall would praise Kennan's work in particular. Clark Clifford would stress the part Acheson played. But Clifford himself had been involved at every stage. In fairness it might have been called the Acheson-Clifford-Marshall Plan.

Truman would always give Marshall full credit. When Clifford urged that it be called the Truman Plan, Truman dismissed the idea at once. It would be called the Marshall Plan, he said.

More than once in his presidency, Truman would be remembered saying it was remarkable how much could be accomplished if you didn't care who received the credit. But in this case he insisted that Marshall be the one most honored because Marshall deserved no less.

He also commented realistically, "Anything that is sent up to the Senate and House with my name on it will quiver a couple of times and die."

But Truman was the President and so the Marshall Plan would be his inevitably, be it a success or failure. His confidence in Marshall could have misfired and brought embarrassment and trouble to the administration. A Marshall Plan that failed would assuredly have become a Truman Plan.

One member of the Policy Planning Staff, Louis J. Halle, later said of Truman that he had in Marshall a soldier of the highest prestige, in Acheson a man of both commanding intellect and fierce personal integrity who at critical moments, like Truman, was willing to risk his own career rather than abstain from doing what he conceived to be right, and in Kennan a man of Shakespearean insight and vision. Among Truman's own strongest qualities was "his ability to appreciate these men and to support them as they supported him."

The Republicans were determined to cut taxes and expenditures, and already since the war, $3 billion had been spent in foreign relief. In a single grant in 1946 the United States had loaned Britain $3.25 billion and now, it seemed, to little purpose. By Will Clayton's calculations, the Europeans would need $6 or $7 billion in the coming two or three years. When Arthur Vandenberg read this in *The New York Times,* in an article by James Reston, he telephoned Reston to say that surely he was misinformed. Congress, Vandenberg said, would never approve such sums, not to save anybody.

As all who were involved with the project appreciated, an enormous effort was called for if the people and the Congress were to be convinced, and the appeal would have to be to both American altruism and American self-interest—the same motivating factors that had propelled the idea from the beginning. When Truman called Sam Rayburn to the White House to brief him on what the cost might be, Rayburn was as incredulous as Vandenberg and insisted it would bankrupt the country. Truman said there was no way of telling how many hundreds of thousands of people would starve to death in Europe and that this must not happen, not if it could be prevented. He was also sure, Truman said, that if Europe went "down the drain" in a depression, the United States would follow. "And you and I have both lived through one depression, and we don't want to have to live through another one, do we, Sam?"

With Britain's Bevin taking the lead, a hasty conference was organized in Paris, to which the Soviets sent a sizable delegation headed by Molotov. The provisional and largely Communist-dominated government of Czechoslovakia had already indicated that it wished to be included in the program. Communist leaders in Poland and Romania had shown interest. But five days into the conference, after being handed a telegram from Moscow, Molotov stood up from the table and abruptly announced that the Soviet Union was withdrawing. The Marshall Plan, he said, was "nothing but a vicious American scheme for using dollars to buy its way" into the affairs of Europe.

Stalin had found unacceptable two particular American conditions, a pooling of resources that would include Soviet funds to rebuild parts of Western and Central Europe, and an open accounting of how American money was being spent. Eventually seventeen nations would take part; but under Soviet pressure, Czechoslovakia, Poland, Romania, and the other satellite countries of Eastern Europe did not.

By refusing to take part in the Marshall Plan, Stalin had virtually guaranteed its success. Sooner or later congressional support was bound to follow now, whatever the volume of grumbling on the Hill.

Officially it was called the European Recovery Program, or ERP, and the total sum requested was colossal indeed, $17 billion. Bohlen, Kennan, and others from the State Department were assigned to "sell" it to Congress, while a draft of specific plans was being drawn up by Paul Nitze, the young economic adviser. Arthur Vandenberg again played a vital role in the Senate. Marshall himself would eventually make a cross-country speaking tour, to convince business and civic groups, and with great effect, though the daring, wholehearted plan he proposed was not about to happen overnight.

Nor was there a letup in the pressure of events overall. That June, "to curb the powers of big labor," the Republican-controlled Congress passed by large majorities the Taft-Hartley Act, which outlawed the closed shop, made unions liable for breach of contract, prohibited political contributions from unions, required them to make financial reports, required their leaders to take a non-Communist oath. On Friday, June 20, after two weeks of deliberation, Truman vetoed the bill, calling it an attack on the workingman, though all the Cabinet but Schwellenbach and Hannegan had urged him to sign it, including John Snyder, his closest friend in the Cabinet. Clark Clifford, however, saw it as another chance to take a stand. Clifford wanted Truman to move more to the left on most matters, "to strike for new high ground," as he later said. "Most of the Cabinet and the congressional leaders were urging Mr. Truman to go slow, to veer a little closer to the conservative line," Clifford remembered. "They held the image of Bob Taft before him like a bogeyman." Thousands of letters pouring into the White House also favored the veto, and Truman, who genuinely believed it was a bad bill, knew a veto would go far to bring labor back into Democratic politics. As his daughter Margaret would one day write, remembering the Taft-Hartley veto, "While he was responding to his presidential conscience, my father did not by any means stop being a politician. The two are by no means incompatible."

It was only a matter of days until Congress voted to override the veto, and in the House more Democrats voted against the President than with him.

On July 25, Congress passed Truman's sweeping National Security Act, legislation he had sent to the Hill in February and that would mean mammoth change for the whole structure of power in Washington. Its primary purpose was to unify the armed services under a single Department of Defense and a single Secretary of Defense, a goal Truman had been striving for since taking office. It also established the Air Force as a separate military service, set up a new National Security Council, and gave formal authorization to the Central Intelligence Agency.

IV

Though he felt she needed more training before making a professional debut as a concert singer, Truman had supported his adored daughter Margaret in her ambitions all along. So also had her aunt Mary Jane and Mamma Truman, who had been the most enthusiastic, telling her to "go at it, hammer and tongs." Bess, however, was not pleased, and Grandmother Wallace declared that the stage was no life for a lady.

"If she wants to be a warbler and has the talent and will do the hard work necessary to accomplish her purpose, I don't suppose I should kick," Truman had written to his mother and sister. "She's one nice girl," he told them in another letter, "and I'm so glad she hasn't turned out like Alice Roosevelt and a couple of the Wilson daughters." To Margaret he wrote that it took "work, work and more work" to get satisfactory results, "as your pop can testify."

She talked for a while of singing under the name of Margaret Wallace, so as not to appear to be capitalizing on his position. But Mamma Truman, extremely displeased, couldn't understand any name being substituted for Truman.

Since the start of the year Margaret had been living in a small apartment overlooking Central Park in New York, working with her Kansas City teacher, Mrs. Thomas J. Strickler, who also stayed with her in the apartment as chaperon. Truman felt her absence acutely. Like his mother's precarious condition since her fall in February, it gave him a feeling of emptiness not easy to face. While he was so intensely preoccupied with his responsibilities, time was moving on, life passing him by.

For someone who had spent so much of his life in such male-dominated vocations as the military and politics, he had few close male friends and no real confidants among the men he knew or worked with, any more now than in boyhood. It was the four women in his life, Bess, Mamma, Mary Jane, and Margaret, who mattered above all, whose company and approval he most valued and needed. Now two of them, Mamma and Margaret, appeared to be deserting him.

"Margaret went to New York yesterday and it leaves a blank place here," he had written to his mother and sister in January 1947. "But I guess the parting time has to come to everybody. . . ."

In early March, with her first performance in the offing, she received a quick note from him:

> Here's a little dough in case you need R.R. tickets to some mysterious town.
> Now don't get scared, you can do it! And if anyone says you can't I'll bust him in the snoot.

Margaret Truman, coloratura soprano, made her radio debut in Detroit on March 16, 1947, as a guest on the Ford Motor Company's "Sunday Evening Hour," with the Detroit Symphony conducted by Karl Krueger. As reported in the papers, possibly no vocal performer in history had ever appeared for the first time under such pressure, or before so big an audience and so many critics. The broadcast was nationwide on ABC and reportedly 15 million people were listening, making it the largest radio audience ever for such a performance. "She could not help realizing," observed *The New York Times,* "that not only the immense listening public, but . . . every vocalist, every singing teacher and vocal student who has access to a radio set, was critically appraising her voice and her interpretations." In addition, singing with an orchestra was a new experience for her.

Scheduled to have appeared on the program the week before, she had had to back out at the last minute because of a sudden attack of throat and chest pains, diagnosed by Wallace Graham as bronchial pneumonia.

Truman was in Key West the night of the broadcast, still resting after his March 12 speech to Congress. The half hour he spent sitting by the radio, waiting for Margaret's turn on the show to come, was, he said afterward, as long as any he could remember. "Perhaps," she later wrote, "sheer naivete saw me through." She was the first daughter of a President ever to attempt a professional career of her own.

> I was aware that my father was glued to a radio in the Navy Commandant's quarters in Key West; that my mother was listening in the White House, that Mamma Truman was listening from her bed in Grandview, and that Grandmother Wallace, who didn't have much use for the stage, was listening critically in Independence. I couldn't let anybody down.

She sang three selections, beginning with the Spanish folk song "Cielito Lindo," then an aria from Félicien David's *La Perle du Brésil,* and finishing with "The Last Rose of Summer," a request of her father's.

The orchestra indicated its approval with spontaneous applause, and though the Detroit *Times* said she sang no better than a fairly talented student, the reviews were generally good—kinder than she deserved, she later acknowledged. Noel Straus, music critic for *The New York Times,* described her voice as "interesting," and said she had shown remarkable poise and self-control, considering the pressures she was under. Her phrasing was careful, the legato smooth throughout. "Miss Truman's work from start to finish," the reviewer concluded in a judgment that greatly pleased her father, "had an allure that resulted from deep sincerity and an unaffected simplicity of approach."

At home in Kansas City, to the delight of her father, the *Star* praised her for her courage and called it a "highly agreeable" occasion. The White House switchboard was so engulfed by calls of approval that it had to close down temporarily.

To reporters gathered around at Key West, Truman said he thought she had done "wonderfully," and for weeks after his return to Washington, it was obvious that nothing pleased him quite so much as to have visitors mention they had heard Margaret on the radio and enjoyed her singing.

Another performance, a full concert this time, was scheduled for May in Pittsburgh. Truman wanted only success for Margaret, but by no means should she become a prima donna.

> Wish I could go along and smooth all the rough spots—but I can't and in a career you must learn to overcome the obstacles without blowing up. Always be nice to the people who can't talk back to you. I can't stand a man or woman who bawls out underlings to satisfy an ego.

The Pittsburgh concert had to be postponed at the last minute, however, when word came that Mamma Truman had suffered a stroke and was not expected to live.

Truman flew from Washington immediately. It was his fifth trip home since his mother first fell and broke her hip. Ross, Wallace Graham, the whole presidential entourage were with him and set up headquarters on the eleventh floor of the Muehlebach Hotel. Mamma seemed to improve, knowing he was there, and he stayed on at the Muehlebach for nearly two weeks, driving out from Kansas City to Grandview every day. The weather was poor, chill and raining, and she slept most of the time. As the papers said, "the eyes of the world" were focused on the small yellow clapboard house day after day. Truman worked at the Mission oak table in the parlor. (It was then that he signed the bill for aid to Greece and Turkey.) "Whenever she wakes up," he told reporters, "she wants to talk to me. I want to be there."

But then to everyone's amazement she made a comeback and Truman returned to Washington. He called her nearly every day thereafter, returned for another visit in mid-June, and wrote regularly to Mary Jane, who would read the letters aloud for Mamma. He kept her posted on politics, as he knew she liked. "I've come to the conclusion that Taft is no good and Hartley is worse," he wrote. He also warned her he was about to make a speech she wouldn't like. It was for the National Association for the Advancement of Colored People. He would be quoting Abraham Lincoln, he said.

Delivered from the steps of the Lincoln Memorial, on June 29, to a crowd of ten thousand people, it was the strongest statement on civil rights heard in Washington since the time of Lincoln, and the first speech ever by a President to the NAACP. Full civil rights and freedom must be obtained and guaranteed for all Americans, Truman said, with Walter White, head of the NAACP, standing beside him.

When I say all Americans, I mean all Americans.

Many of our people still suffer the indignity of insult, the narrowing fear of intimidation, and, I regret to say, the threat of physical and mob violence. Prejudice and intolerance in which these evils are rooted still exist. The conscience of our nation, and the legal machinery which enforces it, have not yet secured to each citizen full freedom of fear.

We cannot wait another decade or another generation to remedy these evils. We must work, as never before, to cure them now.

He called for state and federal action against lynching and the poll tax, an end to inequality in education, employment, the whole caste system based on race or color. That someone of his background from western Missouri could be standing at the shrine of the Great Emancipator saying such things was almost inconceivable. As he listened, Walter White thought of Lincoln's Gettysburg Address. "I did not believe that Truman's speech possessed the literary quality of Lincoln's speech," he later wrote, "but in some respects it had been a more courageous one in its specific condemnation of evils based upon race prejudice . . . and its call for immediate action against them."

Late in 1946, at the urging of White and others, Truman had established his own blue-ribbon commission on civil rights, with Charles E. Wilson, the head of General Electric, as chairman. It was an unprecedented step and Truman, White was sure, had put his political fortunes on the line. "Almost without exception," White wrote, "Mr. Truman's political advisors from both South and North were certain that his authorization of inquiry into the explosive issue of civil rights was nothing short of political suicide. . . . Mr. Truman stood firm." The report of the commission would not be ready until October.

Taking his seat again after the speech, Truman turned to White and said he meant "every word of it—and I'm going to prove that I do mean it."

To his mother, Truman said it was a speech he wished he did not have to make. "But I believe what I say," he told her, "and I'm hopeful we may implement it."

He described for her the flowers in bloom at the White House, "down in the yard." With so much wet weather, were Vivian's sons able to get in the hay crop, he wanted to know.

He was thinking more than usual about times gone by. The morning of July 26, writing to Bess in Independence, he found himself reminiscing about Uncle Harrison and about Tasker Taylor, their high school classmate who had drowned in the Missouri River after graduation. July 26 had always been known to Missouri farmers as Turnip Day, the day to sow turnips, he told Bess. Once, in 1901, a particularly dry year, Uncle Harrison had walked into the seed store and declared he needed six bushels of turnip seed. Asked why so large an amount, Uncle Harrison said he understood turnips were 90 percent water and that maybe if he planted the whole farm in them the drought would break.

But he must not dwell on the past. "You see age is creeping up on me. Mamma is ninety-four and a half because she never lived in the past."

An hour or so later, Mary Jane telephoned from Grandview to say Mamma had pneumonia and might not live through the day. Truman ordered his plane made ready, but there was a delay. He wanted to sign the National Security Act and name James Forrestal the new Secretary of Defense before Congress recessed. A few congressional signatures were still needed. At the airport, he held off departure, waiting beside the plane for nearly an hour until the bill was brought to him. Minutes later the plane was airborne.

Somewhere over Ohio, dozing on a cot in his stateroom, he dreamt Mamma came to him and said, "Goodbye, Harry. Be a good boy." He later wrote, "When Dr. Graham came into my room on *The Sacred Cow,* I knew what he would say."

She had died at 11:30 that morning. "Well, now she won't have to suffer any more," Truman said. For the rest of the flight he sat by the window looking down at the checkerboard landscape and saying nothing.

Martha Ellen Young Truman had been born in 1852, when Millard Fillmore was President, when Abraham Lincoln was still a circuit lawyer in Illinois, when her idolized Robert E. Lee was Superintendent at West Point, overseeing the education of young men from both North and South. She had seen wagon trains coming and going on the Santa Fe Trail. She had been through civil war, survived Order No. 11, survived grasshopper plagues, flood, drought, the failures and death of her husband, the Great Depression, eviction from her own home. She had lived to see the advent of the telephone, electric light, the automobile, the airplane, radio, movies, television, short skirts, world wars, and her adored eldest son sitting at his desk in the White House as President of the United States. As Margaret would write in memory of her "country grandmother" some years later, "Everything had changed around her, but Mamma Truman had never changed. . . . Her philosophy was simple. You knew right from wrong and you did right, and you always did your best. That's all there was to it."

The funeral at the house in Grandview was simple and private. She was buried on the hillside at the Forest Hill Cemetery, next to her husband.

A few days later in Washington Truman asked Charlie Ross to bring the White House press into the Oval Office.

"I couldn't hold a press conference this week," Truman began quietly when they were assembled, "but I wanted to say to you personally a thing or two that I couldn't very well say any other way, so I asked Charlie to ask you to come in.

"I wanted to express to you all, and to your editors and publishers, appreciation for the kindness to me during the last week.

"I was particularly anxious to tell the photographers how nice they were to me, and to the family, and I didn't know any other way to do it but just call you in and tell you.

"I had no news to give you, or anything else to say to you, except just that, and I felt like I owed it to you.

"You have been exceedingly nice to me all during the whole business, and I hope you believe it when I say to you that it is from the heart when I tell you that."

To Margaret he wrote, "Someday you'll be an orphan just as your dad is now." Later, when she was on tour, he would tell her:

> You should call your mamma and dad *every time* you arrive in a town. . . . Someday maybe (?) you'll understand what torture it is to be worried about the only person in the world that counts. You should know by now that your dad has only three such persons. Your ma, you and your aunt Mary.

On August 24, Margaret sang at the Hollywood Bowl before nineteen thousand people. To the Los Angeles *Times* her performance was only "satisfactory," but the audience brought her back for seven curtain calls. On October 17, she returned to Pittsburgh to make her first full-length concert appearance at the city's immense old Syria Mosque auditorium, before a full house that included her mother, who was hearing her sing in public for the first time. Truman stayed away because he wanted Margaret to have all the attention.

Again her stage presence and rapport with the audience were remarkable for someone so young and inexperienced. The audience loved her. She had nine curtain calls, sang three encores. Everyone seemed to be pulling for her, even the ushers and the press, wrote the music editor of the Pittsburgh *Post-Gazette,* Donald Steinfirst. "You felt it in the waves of kindly feelings directed to this girl, standing assuredly with complete poise over the footlights in the spotlight. You wanted to feel that this young girl, who gave up most of the pleasures of White House living, if any such there might be, for a career in music, would realize her life's ambitions."

She was wearing a full-length, off-the-shoulder gown of pink taffeta, her blond hair in soft curls, and she sang, as she had in Detroit and Los Angeles, as if she were enjoying every moment. But this time the critics were considerably less kind.

> The bold fact is [wrote Steinfirst] that Miss Truman, judging from last night's performance, and with the usual allowances for youth and debut, is not a great singer; and, in fact, is not at this stage of her career, even a good singer. She is a young woman of a great deal of personal charm, considerable stage presence, apparently a fair knowledge of the fundamentals of singing, but she is not an artist by commonly-accepted standards.

Others said she had launched her career too soon, before she was ready, just as her father had worried she might. The critic in the Pittsburgh *Press* thought her training "very faulty."

"I called up Daddy after the concert, and he seemed to be satisfied," she remembered. "I can't say I was."

The tour went on. She sang in Fort Worth, Amarillo, Oklahoma City, Shreveport, and Tulsa, and she did better. "Margaret seems to be making a hit wherever she goes," Truman reported to Mary Jane. Fort Worth was a sellout. So was Amarillo. All the same, he wished she would come home and stay.

Sometimes, relaxing with friends, Truman liked to say that he and his small family might have been a hit as a vaudeville team. Margaret would sing, he would play the piano, and Bess would manage the act. He would then grin at Bess, while she responded with a skeptical look. It had become a family joke.

To those who knew Bess well the manager's role was perfect casting, and greatly to her husband's advantage. Margaret spoke of her mother as "the spark plug" of the family. Truman himself said many times he seldom made a decision without consulting "the Boss."

She had no more interest than ever in the limelight of public life, no desire to play any part beyond that of wife and mother.

Old friends from Independence or members of the White House domestic staff who saw her on an almost daily basis would speak warmly of her kindness, her "rollicking sense of humor." She would laugh so hard her whole body would shake, laugh, remembered one of the servants, Lillian Parks, "as if she had invented laughter."

No First Lady in memory had been so attentive to the welfare of the servants, and particularly in the summer months, before the advent of air conditioning in the White House. "It's too hot to work," she would say. "If it wasn't hot," remembered Lillian Parks, "she'd say, 'You've been working too long. Stop now.' [She] was the kind of First Lady who hated fussiness, loved cleanliness and neatness and an all-things-put-away look, but who didn't want her servants to keep working all the time and would order, yes *order,* them to rest."

To nearly everyone she seemed "the perfect lady," the phrase used so often to describe her mother. "She's the only lady I know who writes a thank you note for a Christmas card, and she writes it in a beautiful hand," a Kansas City friend would tell a reporter. Marquis Childs of the St. Louis *Post-Dispatch* called her the perfect *Missouri* lady. Once, when Childs and his wife gave a party at their Washington home for a poet who was an old friend, they invited the Trumans. "Mrs. Truman came with great apologies for her husband . . . who just couldn't possibly get away," Childs remembered. "And the wife of the poet had too much libation, and had to be taken off somewhere, put to bed somewhere. But Mrs. Truman was very polite and never made any fuss of this at all. She was a *very proper* woman. I think her whole life was Harry Truman. . . ."

Reathel Odum, her secretary, remembered Bess as "the white gloves type." Serene, shy, and stubborn were other words used often to portray her.

California Congressman Richard Nixon and his wife, attending their first White House reception, were impressed by the way both the President and Mrs. Truman made them feel at home. "They both had the gift of being dignified without putting on airs," Nixon wrote. "Press accounts habitually described Mrs. Truman as plain. What impressed us most was that she was genuine."

The longer people knew her, the more they appreciated her quiet strength and quality. Among her greatest admirers were Robert A. Lovett and his wife. Lovett, who, at the end of June 1947 replaced Dean Acheson as Under Secretary of State, was a suave, urbane New York investment banker, a partner at Brown Brothers Harriman, and a Yale graduate like Harriman and Acheson. To Lovett there was no question about the importance of Bess Truman. She was "one of the finest women I ever saw in my life," Lovett remembered. And, "of course," she helped Truman "immeasurably": "My wife and I absolutely loved her. She was simply superb. . . ."

Clark Clifford would later describe her as "a pillar of strength to her husband" and credit her with "better insight than her husband into the quality and trustworthiness of people who had gathered around him. . . ."

But if Truman relied on her, as he himself also attested, she clearly was extremely dependent on him. Years later, when asked by a friend what she considered the most memorable aspect of her life, Bess answered at once: "Harry and I have been sweethearts and married more than 40 years—and no matter where I was, when I put out my hand Harry's was there to grasp it."

Five foot four and stout, Bess Truman stood as straight as a drum major, head up, shoulders squared. She dressed simply and conservatively. There was nothing ever in any way mannered or pretentious about her. (Throughout her years in Washington, as Jonathan Daniels reported, she laughed at nothing so heartily as the sudden pretensions of some officials' wives.) She was exactly as she had always been and saw no reason to change because she had become First Lady. Some guests at the White House found her so natural and unprepossessing they had to remind themselves to whom they were speaking. *Time* said somewhat condescendingly that with her neatly waved gray hair and unobtrusive clothes she would have blended perfectly with the crowd at an A&P.

Asked once by reporters for his view of her appearance, Truman said he thought she looked exactly as a woman her age ought to look.

Many people, meeting Bess Truman for the first time, were surprised by how much younger and more attractive she appeared than in photographs, where her expression was often somber, even disapproving. Something seemed to come over her in public, and particularly when photographers pressed in on her. In receiving lines she often looked bored, even pained, as if her feet hurt—a very different person from the one her friends knew. A Louisiana congressman's wife, Lindy Boggs, would remember how vivacious the First Lady could be while arranging things for a reception, what delightful company she was behind the scenes. "And then . . . the minute the doors would open and all those people would begin to come in, she would *freeze,* and she looked like old stone face. Instead of being the outgoing, warm and lovely woman that she had been previously, the huge crowds simply made her sort of pull up into herself."

Where Eleanor Roosevelt had seen her role as public and complementary to that of her husband, Bess insisted on remaining in the background. "Propriety was a much stronger influence in her life than in Mrs. Roosevelt's," remembered Alice Acheson, the wife of Dean Acheson. It was widely known that Bess played cards—her bridge club from Independence had made a trip to Washington in the spring of 1946, stayed several days at the White House, and was the subject of much attention in the papers—and that she and Margaret, unlike the President, were movie fans. Bess also loved reading mysteries and was "wild" about baseball, going to every Senators game she could fit into her schedule. But she had no interesting hobbies for reporters to write about, no winsome pets, no social causes to champion or opinions on issues she wished to voice publicly. Her distaste for publicity was plain and to many, endearing. She refused repeatedly to make speeches or give private interviews or to hold a press conference, no matter how often reporters protested. "Just keep on smiling and tell 'them' nothing," she advised Reathel Odum. "She didn't want to discuss her life," Margaret remembered.

Two early public appearances had turned into embarrassments. She had been asked to christen an Army plane, but no one had bothered to score the champagne bottle in advance, so it would break easily. She swung it against the plane with no result, then kept trying again and again, her face a study in crimson determination. The crowd roared with laughter, until finally a mechanic stepped in and broke the bottle for her. Truman, too, had been amused, as was the country when the newsreel played in the movie theaters, but not Bess, who reportedly told him later she was sorry she hadn't swung that bottle at him.

The other episode concerned her acceptance, in the fall of 1945, of an invitation to tea from the Daughters of the American Revolution at Constitution Hall, a decision protested vehemently by Adam Clayton Powell, the flamboyant black congressman and minister of the Abyssinian Baptist Church in Harlem, whose wife, the pianist Hazel Scott, had been denied permission to perform at Constitution Hall because of her race. Bess, however, refused to change her mind. The invitation, as she wrote to Powell, had come before "the unfortunate controversy," and her acceptance of such hospitality was "not related to the merits of the issue." She deplored, she said, any action that denied artistic opportunity because of race prejudice. She was not a segregationist, but she was not a crusader either. Powell responded by referring to her publicly as "The Last Lady of the Land," which caused Truman to explode over "that damn nigger preacher" at a staff meeting, and like Clare Boothe Luce, Powell would never be invited to the White House.

When at last in the fall of 1947 Bess agreed to respond to a questionnaire from reporters, her answers were characteristically definite and memorable:

What qualities did she think would be the greatest asset to the wife of a President?

Good health and a well-developed sense of humor.

1   Truman, President in his own right, and Vice President Alben Barkley on the reviewing
stand, Inauguration Day, January 20, 1949.

Secretary of State Dean Acheson, by far the strongest, most brilliant, and most controversial member of Truman's Cabinet through all of the second term. "Do you suppose any President ever had two such men with him as you and the General [Marshall]?" Truman would later write to Acheson.

3

Truman's World War I pal and presidential military aide, General Harry Vaughan, who was seen as the ultimate White House "crony."

4

Alger Hiss, symbol of Republican charges that the administration was "soft on communism."

Republican Senator Joseph McCarthy, whom Truman loathed and mistakenly believed time and the truth would soon destroy.

5

6

Opposite: At midday, June 27, 1950, having announced that American forces would
intervene in Korea, Truman, accompanied by Attorney General J. Howard McGrath (left)
and Secretary of Defense Louis Johnson, heads from the White House to his temporary
residence across Pennsylvania Avenue at Blair House (above). It was at Blair House, after
meeting there with his advisers the two previous nights, that Truman reached his fateful
decision on Korea—the most difficult and important decision of his presidency, he felt.

8   On October 15, 1950, a month after the stunning success of General Douglas MacArthur's
surprise assault at Inchon (above), Truman and MacArthur met at Wake Island in the
Pacific, driving off for a first private talk in a battered Chevrolet (below). By all signs the
9   Korean War, Truman's "police action," was nearly over.

10

On his return from Wake, Truman is met at the airport by his Washington high command (from left to right): Special Assistant Averell Harriman, Secretary of Defense Marshall, Secretary of State Acheson, Secretary of the Treasury John W. Snyder, Secretary of the Army Frank Pace, Jr., and General Omar Bradley, Chairman of the Joint Chiefs.

11

In late 1950, as the Korean War entered its darkest time, Truman had also to oversee the complete reconstruction of the White House within the gutted shell of the old exterior walls (opposite). And on November 1, two fanatical Puerto Rican nationalists attempted to assassinate him (right, one lies wounded at the Blair House front steps).

12

13

On December 6 (left), a Washington *Post* music critic roundly panned his daughter Margaret's singing, eliciting from her father the most stinging letter of his presidency.

14

Pages from Truman's diary,
April 6 and 7, 1951.

15

16 General MacArthur addresses Congress, April 19, 1951.

17 MacArthur's replacement as Far East Commander, General Matthew B. Ridgway (with hand grenades strapped to his chest).

Though often called one of Truman's most courageous decisions as President, the firing of MacArthur was to Truman simply something that had to be done to keep control of the military where it belonged, in the Oval Office. Left: The outlook from the seat of responsibility and (below) a cartoon from the time by Herblock.

18

THE TUMULT AND THE SHOUTING DIES;
THE CAPTAINS AND THE KINGS DEPART

19

Chicago, July 26, 1952: Truman introduces to the Democratic National Convention the new, somewhat reluctant standard-bearer, Governor Adlai E. Stevenson of Illinois.

Oxford, England, June 20, 1956: The former President is congratulated by Lord Halifax, Chancellor of Oxford University, after receiving the honorary degree of Doctor of Civil Laws.

20

Washington, November 1, 1961: To the delight of President John F. Kennedy, the First Lady, and guests, Truman plays a bit of Paderewski's *Minuet* in the East Room, after an absence from the White House of eight years. The principal performer of the evening, Truman's favorite concert pianist, Eugene List, stands at right.

"COME, CHILDREN, MR. TRUMAN IS TALKING TO REPORTERS!"

60-342

Florence, Italy, May 27, 1956: Truman chats with Renaissance art authority Bernard Berenson, who found him very unlike the "Give 'Em Hell Harry" of the cartoon at left.

Margaret and
Clifton Daniel on their
wedding day, April 21, 1956.

24

25

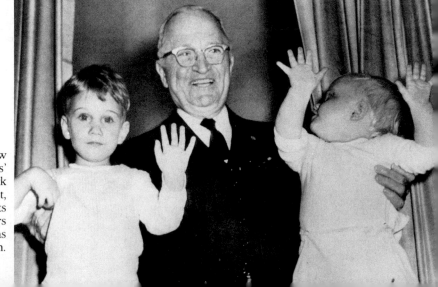

From the window
of the Daniels'
New York
apartment,
Truman greets
reporters
with grandsons
Clifton and William.

A resident of Independence for the last twenty years of his life, Truman said of his time as President, "I tried never to forget who I was and where I'd come from and where I was going back to."

Did she think there would ever be a woman President of the United States?

No.

Would she want to be President?

No.

Would she want Margaret ever to be First Lady?

No.

If she had a son, would she try to bring him up to be President?

No.

If it had been left to her own free choice, would she have gone into the White House in the first place?

Most definitely would not have.

What was her reaction to musical criticism of Margaret's singing?

No comment.

Did any of the demands of her role as First Lady ever give her stage fright?

No comment.

What would you like to do and have your husband do when he is no longer President?

Return to Independence.

"She seems to think Harry ought to run the country, not her," a Washington cab driver was quoted as saying. It was a sentiment widely shared, and according to Jonathan Daniels, Truman "conspired willingly" with her to protect her privacy.

Asked once if she was interested in any particular period of White House history, Bess said the Monroe years—an interesting observation that the press passed by. James Monroe's wife, another Elizabeth—Elizabeth Kortright Monroe—had followed the gregarious Dolley Madison, who had been as much the center of attention in her time as had Eleanor Roosevelt. A quiet aristocrat, Elizabeth Monroe married a hard-drinking politician and made a good marriage. In the White House, she had insisted on keeping her life a private matter.

As manager of household expenses, Bess was extremely frugal. She cut back on the size of the White House staff. Mrs. Nesbitt, the elderly housekeeper responsible for years of dreary food on the Roosevelt table, had been sent packing, with the result that both the cooking and the housekeeping improved. Most objectionable had been the cold, hard, dinner rolls, long a White House staple, but which to anyone raised as Bess had been on traditional hot southern biscuits—biscuits baked with Waggoner-Gates "Queen of the Pantry Flour"—were altogether inedible. "It was only on the command of President Truman," wrote the American correspondent for the BBC, Alistair Cooke, "that her recipe was passed on to the chef and the Trumans reverted to breaking the bread of their fathers."

"Mrs. Truman was no fussier than her predecessor. . . . It was just that she had been brought up to be house proud," recorded J. B. West. She kept close watch on the cost of food, kept her own books, went over all the household bills "with a fine tooth comb," and wrote every check herself.

According to West and Lillian Parks, both of whom later wrote books about their years of service in the White House, the staff felt closer to the Trumans than to any of the other presidents and their wives, which was saying a great deal, considering how long some of the staff had been employed. John Mays, a doorman who also cut Truman's hair every two weeks, had been on duty at the White House since the time of Woodrow Wilson. The way the Trumans lived, remembered West, the White House "might as well have been in Independence. As far as everyday living goes, they were no different." And for all the President's talk of not liking life in the White House, said West, "He liked living there better than living in his mother-in-law's house in Independence."

Truman's salary in his last years in the Senate, plus what Bess had earned, came to $14,500. As Vice President, his pay was $20,000; as President, it was $75,000. But nearly half of that would go to taxes, and while the government paid for the White House servants, Bess had to pay for their food, plus all meals for the family and guests. In Roosevelt's time, monthly food bills alone sometimes reached $7,000. Bess had been able to cut that back to about $2,000. In their twelve years in the White House the Roosevelts had never lived within the President's salary, but the Trumans had no family fortune to fall back on. Margaret would later describe her mother as a chronic penny pincher, of necessity. Still, she was able to save very little year to year. After expenses and taxes on his $75,000 salary, it was reported, the President had about $4,200 left.

In a smart Washington dress shop, browsing one day with Mrs. John Snyder, Bess told the sales clerk mildly but firmly there was no use for her to try on anything, since she couldn't afford the prices.

According to J. B. West, Bess guarded her privacy like a precious jewel, yet within that privacy played a role far exceeding what any but a few suspected. She did indeed advise Truman on decisions. "And he *listened* to her."

Margaret would later write that in her father's first months in office, Bess had felt shut out of his life, "more and more superfluous," and especially after the realization that he had not discussed with her his decision on the atomic bomb. The feeling of being left out, wrote Margaret, combined with Bess's original opposition to Truman's ever becoming President "to build a smoldering anger that was tantamount to an emotional separation," which may explain some of her long absences from Washington. Still, Margaret, too, would stress her mother's influence on her father, saying he constantly talked things over with Bess and would often do as she said. He was "very, very conscious" of her views and needed her approval. "Have you ever noticed Father when he's with Mother at any sort of public gathering?" Margaret remarked to a reporter at the time. "He's always trying to catch her glance to see if she approves of what he is saying or doing."

She remained, as she had been for more than thirty years, the most important person in his life.

Among family and old friends, he freely acknowledged the difference "Miss Lizzie" had made to the course of his life. "Suppose Miss Lizzie had gone off with Mr. Young, Julian Harvey or Harris," he wrote to Ethel Noland from the White House, recalling old suitors from days long past. "What would have been the result? For Harry I mean. He probably would have been either a prominent farmer in Jackson County or a Major General in the regular army. . . ."

To judge by the letters he wrote to Bess in the fall of 1947, while she was with her mother in Independence, he did indeed want her to know his mind and the details of the problems he faced in a "topsy-turvy world."

He was preoccupied with the immense projected cost of the Marshall Plan.

Marshall and Lovett were in yesterday and went over the European situation from soup to nuts with me. If it works out as planned it will cost us about 16 billion over a four-year period. . . . This amount of 16 *billion* is just the amount of the national debt when Franklin took over. He ran it up to 40 odd and then the war came along and it is 257 but we can't understand those figures anyway.

A few days later, on September 30, he went on, telling her more:

Yesterday was one of the most hectic of days. . . . I'm not sure what has been my worst day. But here is the situation fraught with terrible consequences. Suppose, for instance, that Italy should fold up and that Tito then would march into the Po Valley. All the Mediterranean coast of France then is open to Russian occupation and the iron curtain comes to Bordeaux, Calais, Antwerp, and The Hague. We withdraw from Greece and Turkey and *prepare for war*. It just must not happen. But here I am confronted with a violently opposition Congress whose committees with few exceptions are living in 1890; it is not representative of the country's thinking at all. But I've got a job and it must be done—win, lose, or draw.

Sent letters to Taber, Bridges, Vandenberg, and Eaton requesting them to call their committees together as soon as possible. Had my food committee together and will make a radio speech Sunday. To feed France and Italy this winter will cost 580 million, the Marshall Plan 16.5 billion. But you know in October and November of 1945 I cancelled 63 billion in appropriations—55 billion at one crack. Our war cost that year was set at 105 billion. The 16.5 is for a four-year period and is for *peace*. A Russian war would cost us 400 billion and untold lives, mostly civilian. So I must do what I can. I shouldn't write you this stuff but you should know what I've been facing. . . . I haven't resumed my walks yet but will in a day or two. Too much to read. General Bradley made a report to me today on his European trip and he remarked on my having had to make more momentous decisions than nearly any other President. He's right, and I hope most of 'em have been right. . . .

In a month's time that fall he wrote twenty-two letters to her. That he adored her as much as ever was also among his reasons for the letters. The following June, on their anniversary, he would write:

Dear Bess:
    Twenty-nine years! It seems like twenty-nine days.
    Detroit, Port Huron, a farm sale, the Blackstone Hotel, a shirt store. County Judge, defeat, Margie, Automobile Club membership drive, Presiding Judge, Senator, V.P., now!
    You still are on the pedestal where I placed you that day in Sunday school in 1890. What an old fool I am.

Except for Bess and Margaret, and his secretary, Rose Conway, few women ever had the opportunity to observe Truman close at hand or privately. There were no women on his staff in any but secretarial roles, none who sat in on staff meetings or who worked with him or accompanied him beyond the White House. But in that crucial year of 1947, a young Austrian-born artist named Greta Kempton came to the West Wing and with the help of two Secret Service agents set up her heavy wooden easel in the Cabinet Room. She was the first woman who had ever been invited to do a presidential portrait—Truman's official White House portrait as it would turn out—and she had never met the President. In all there would be five sittings.

"I was very impressed with him," she remembered. "He came in. I asked him to sit down. He had some papers, but I told him he couldn't study papers. 'Oh, no!' I said. 'This is the time *I'm* working. You are going to relax.'"

Unaware that the two who had helped her get set up were Secret Service men, she turned and said there would be nothing more, they needn't stay. Truman, amused, nodded to them and they left.

> He sat down . . . and I could only see a big important man and a big important portrait. I had to switch canvases. It had to be bigger. . . .
>
> The smaller the person, the more against posing they are, the more they feel they're doing you a favor. Not Mr. Truman. . . . He never seemed irritated or annoyed . . . never seemed impatient. He would settle down . . . and [the room] seemed to take on a feeling of grandeur and peacefulness. I felt very inspired. . . . He was always helpful. He wanted the finished portrait to be as good as I could possibly make it.
>
> The more he sat the more interested he became in the work, my work—the technique of painting, the canvas. He took a *serious* interest. . . .

She had told him at the start that under no circumstances was he to see the portrait until it was finished. But once, during a break, he decided to take "a little walk" around the enormous Cabinet table, his direction, as she remembered, "easing toward the canvas." Sensing what he was up to, she told him again there could be no peeking.

"You mean I can't have a look at my own portrait?" he said.

She told him no, and with good grace he went back to his chair.

When she had finished and asked if he would like to take a look, he stood in front of the easel for several minutes. "Well, I certainly do like that," he said, "but, of course, I wouldn't really know. I'll have to ask the Boss."

He telephoned Bess, who came at once, looked at the picture, and heartily approved. It was exactly as she saw him herself, she said.

Against a darkening sky, he sat foursquare, unsmiling, jaw firm, hands at rest on the arms of a wooden chair—a figure of strength and determination in a dark double-breasted suit, white shirt, dark striped tie, the familiar handkerchief in place, the service pin on his lapel, and in the distance, the Capitol Dome.

Now and then, during the sittings, Greta Kempton remembered, he had seemed a little hurried. "But in general I felt he had a great confidence in himself, as if, 'I know what I'm doing.' But also some humbleness. . . . I think he was very even."

In the summer of 1947, in the journal *Foreign Affairs,* George Kennan had published an article in which he introduced the idea of "containment," an expression already in use at the State Department by then. Kennan recommended "a policy of firm containment [of Russia] . . . with unalterable counterforce at every point where the Russians show signs of encroaching"—until the Soviet Union either "mellows" or collapses. The article was signed simply "X," but the identity of the author was known soon enough, and in another few months Walter Lippmann issued his own strong rebuttal to the concept in a book called *The Cold War,* an expression Bernard Baruch had used earlier in a speech, but that now, like the Iron Curtain, became part of the postwar vocabulary.

When and why the Cold War began—whether with announcement of the Truman Doctrine, or earlier, when Truman first confronted Molotov, or perhaps with the eventual sanction of the Marshall Plan by Congress— would be the subject of much consideration in years to come. But the clearest dividing point between what American policy toward the Soviets had been since the war and what it would now become was George Marshall's return from Moscow. The change came on April 26, 1947, when Marshall, of all men, reported to Truman what Truman had already privately concluded, that diplomacy wasn't going to work, that the Russians could not be dealt with, that they wanted only drift and chaos and the collapse of Europe to suit their own purposes.

Chip Bohlen, who had been witness to so much—Molotov's first call on Truman in the Oval Office, the meetings at Potsdam, Marshall's pivotal session with Stalin at the Kremlin—said the Cold War could really be traced to the seizure of power by the Bolsheviks in 1917. It had begun then, thirty years before.

Truman, looking back on his first years in office and the decisions he had made, would regret especially that he had been unable to stop wholesale demobilization after the war ended. It had been a grave mistake, he felt.

The Cold War was an expression he never much cared for and seldom used. He called it "the war of nerves."

In later years, he would be charged with acting too impulsively and harshly with the Russians, with making snap judgments as a new President, without the benefit of experience or understanding. But "patience, I think, must be our watchword if we are to have world peace," he had written to Eleanor Roosevelt less than a month after assuming office, and, in fact, it had taken two years to arrive at a policy toward the Soviets. He had moved slowly, perhaps too slowly, and always with the close counsel of the same people Franklin Roosevelt too had counted on, and particularly George Marshall.

In September, Truman received a handwritten note from Churchill, to say "how much I admire the policy into wh[ich] you have guided y[ou]r g[rea]t country; and to thank you from the bottom of my heart for all you are doing to save the world from Famine and War."

In a note of thanks, Truman said no man could carry the burden of the presidency and do it all right, but that he had good men around him now.

In mid-October, at an informal meeting in his office with newspaper editorial writers from around the country, he spent most of the time expounding on the vital need for the Marshall Plan. At the end, he was asked whether the United States would ever "get any credit . . . for sending this stuff to Europe?"

"I'm not doing this for credit," Truman answered. "I am doing it because it's right, I am doing it because it's necessary to be done, if we are going to survive ourselves."

The Marshall Plan was voted on by Congress in April 1948, almost a year after Marshall's speech at Harvard, and passed by overwhelming majorities in both houses. It was a singular triumph for the administration, "the central gem in the cluster of great and fruitful decisions made by President Truman," as Arthur Krock would write. Indeed, it was to be one of the great American achievements of the century, as nearly everyone eventually saw.

"In all the history of the world," Truman wrote privately a few days after final passage of the program, "we are the first great nation to feed and support the conquered. We are the first great nation to create independent republics from conquered territory, Cuba and the Philippines. Our neighbors are not afraid of us. Their borders have no forts, no soldiers, no tanks, no big guns lined up."

The United States wanted peace in the world and the United States would be prepared "for trouble if it comes."

13

The Heat in the Kitchen

If you can't stand the heat, you better get out of the kitchen.

—a favorite Truman saying

I

Exactly when Truman made up his mind to run for reelection is not known. Several times in 1947 he expressed reluctance to face another four years in the White House, "this goldfish bowl," and again he considered the idea of Eisenhower as the ideal candidate for the Democrats. He would "groom" the general to follow him, Truman said privately. But when once more he broached the subject to Eisenhower, early in 1947, Eisenhower again declined, saying he had no political ambitions—not that he was not a Democrat.

According to Secretary of the Army Kenneth C. Royall, Truman even offered to go on the ticket with Eisenhower as Vice President, if Eisenhower so desired. "Mr. Truman was a realist and from time to time doubted whether he could win in 1948," Royall later explained. Eisenhower was the most popular man in America. To judge by the polls he had only to nod his head and the presidency was his.

Except for the "reward of service," Truman told Secretary of Defense Forrestal, he had found little satisfaction in being President. Bess would "give everything" to be out of the White House, and he and Bess both regretted greatly the constrictions on Margaret's life. No man in his right mind, Truman wrote to his sister in November 1947, would ever wish to be President if he knew what it entailed.

> Aside from the impossible administrative burden, he has to take all sorts of abuse from liars and demagogues.... The people can never understand why the President does not use his supposedly great power

584

to make 'em behave. Well, all the President is, is a glorified public relations man who spends his time flattering, kissing and kicking people to get them to do what they are supposed to do anyway.

"President Truman did not want to run in 1948," John Steelman later said emphatically.

Yet to others equally close day to day, it was clear the job agreed with him and they were certain he would never willingly abandon it. The whole pattern of his life had been a succession of increasingly difficult tests of his capacity to prove equal to tasks seemingly too large for him. Nor had he failed to meet this latest and greatest of tests. The feelings of inadequacy that had so troubled him after Roosevelt's death were by now past. He liked being in charge. It showed in his face and in the way he carried himself.

He was a picture of health, his color good, his weight 175, blood pressure 120–128 over 80, which was considered excellent. He still took his daily walks and still at his old Army pace of 120 steps a minute, although lately, with the press of events, he often went in the evening instead of early morning.

He would complain at times of "the folderol" of the presidency, but unquestionably he enjoyed the power of the office and its trappings—the limousines, the yacht, the airplane, the special railroad car—as any vital, ambitious man would. The "abuse" he complained of to his sister was something he had long ago learned to live with. As Cabell Phillips of *The New York Times* would recall, Truman was "blessed with a tough hide and a secure conscience, so that he could roll with the punches . . . he responded with simple and exuberant delight to the flattery and deference that were showered upon him wherever he went in public life." And he did indeed value the "reward of service" in the presidency, as in every office he had held since entering public life. A career politician, he had attained the summit of his profession, and if it was fate that put him there, then that was all the more reason to win it now on his own merits. "The greatest ambition Harry Truman had," according to Clark Clifford, "was to get elected in his own right."

Having kept so silent and so uncharacteristically detached during the off-year elections in 1946, only to see his party and himself humiliated, Truman now relished the prospect of taking on the Republicans in an all-out, full-scale championship fight, as he said. He was nothing if not a partisan politician and this was the fight he simply could not walk away from. He had much he wished still to accomplish. And he knew how quickly his own and New Deal programs, the liberal gains of sixteen years, could be undone by a Republican President and a Republican Congress. He felt it his duty to "get into the fight and help stem the tide of reaction," as he later wrote. "They [the Republicans] did not understand the worker, the farmer, the everyday person. . . . Most of them honestly believed that prosperity actually began at the top and would trickle down in due time to benefit all the people."

He saw himself battling as Jefferson had against the Federalists, or Jackson staging a revolution "against the forces of reaction." In the long line of Republicans who had occupied the White House, he admired but two—Lincoln, for his concern for the common man; Theodore Roosevelt, for his progressive policies. To Truman, Woodrow Wilson and Franklin Roosevelt were the giants of the century, and he had no choice, he felt, but to fight for the Democratic heritage that had been passed on to him. "What I wanted to do personally for my own comfort and benefit was not important. What I could do to contribute to the welfare of the country was important. I had to enter the 1948 campaign for the presidency."

So by late autumn 1947 it was well known within the official family that he was in the race, and by the start of the new year nearly everyone in Washington had concluded he was running and that therefore just about anything he did or said was with that in mind, starting with his State of the Union address.

The speech, an uncompromising reaffirmation of his liberal program, delivered before Congress on Wednesday, January 7, 1948, evoked little applause and little praise afterward. The Republicans, as anticipated, did not like it at all, any more than did the southern Democrats. In less than an hour at the podium, Truman called again for a national health insurance program, a massive housing program, increased support for education, increased support for farmers, the conservation of natural resources, and a raise in the minimum wage from 40 to 75 cents an hour. To compensate for rising prices, he proposed a "poor man's" tax cut, whereby each taxpayer would be allowed to deduct $40 for himself and for each dependent from his final tax bill. ("Tom Pendergast had paid two dollars a vote," exclaimed the Republican chairman of the House Ways and Means Committee, Harold Knutson, "and now Truman proposes to pay forty dollars.") Further, Truman announced he would be sending Congress a special message on civil rights. "Our first goal," he said, "is to secure fully the essential human rights of our citizens." The distress among southern Democrats was considerable.

Three weeks later, on February 2, 1948, without conferring with his congressional leaders, he sent the civil rights message. Based on the findings of his own Civil Rights Commission, it was the strongest such program that had ever been proposed by a President. Indeed, until now there had never been a special message on civil rights.

Not all Americans were free of violence, it began.

> Not all groups are free to live and work where they please or to improve their conditions of life by their own efforts. Not all groups enjoy the full privileges of citizenship....
>
> The Federal Government has a clear duty to see that the Constitutional guarantees of individual liberties and of equal protection under the laws are not denied or abridged anywhere in the Union. That duty is shared by all three branches of the Government, but it can be filled only if the Congress enacts modern, comprehensive civil rights laws, adequate to the needs of the day, and demonstrating our continuing faith in the free way of life.

Truman called for a federal law against "the crime of lynching, against which I cannot speak too strongly." He wanted more effective statutory protection of the right to vote everywhere in the country, a law against the poll taxes that prevailed in seven states of the Old South, the establishment of a Fair Employment Practices Commission with authority to stop discrimination by employers and labor unions alike, an end to discrimination in interstate travel by rail, bus, and airplane. He announced also that he had asked the Secretary of Defense to look into discrimination in the military services and to see it was stopped as soon as possible.

In a final request, he asked Congress to act on the claims made by Americans of Japanese descent who, during the war, had been forced from their homes and kept in confinement "solely because of their racial origin"—claims that would not be met until years later.

It was a brave, revolutionary declaration, given the reality of entrenched discrimination and the prevailing attitudes of white Americans nearly everywhere in the country, but especially in the South, where the social status and legal "place" of black citizens had advanced not at all in more than half a century. That Truman believed in both the spirit and the specifics of the message there is no question. Asked at a press conference a few days later what he had drawn on for background, he replied, the Constitution and the Bill of Rights.

Whether the message was bad or good politics in the year 1948 was a matter of opinion. Clark Clifford was certain the President was doing the right thing, morally and politically. To Boss Ed Flynn of the Bronx, who was no less concerned about losing the black vote in New York than he had been in 1944, it was extremely welcome news. But the angry outcry on the Hill suggested that if Truman meant what he said, he was finished in the South and therefore in November as well. Southern congressmen lashed out in language often too raw to print. Harlem, it was said, had more influence with this administration than all the white South. Tom Connally of Texas, an old Truman ally in the Senate, called the message a lynching of the Constitution and vowed the South would not "take it lying down." Senator Olin Johnston of South Carolina boycotted the annual Jefferson-Jackson Day dinner at the Statler Hotel, where Truman was the guest of honor, because, as Johnston explained to reporters, he and his wife might be seated beside a "Nigra." (As it was, the three black Democrats attending the dinner were at a table in the rear.)

When several southern Democrats, meeting privately with the President, suggested all would turn out well if he "softened" his views, Truman, in a written reply, said his own forebears were Confederates and he came from a part of Missouri where "Jim Crowism" still prevailed.

> But my very stomach turned over when I learned that Negro soldiers, just back from overseas, were being dumped out of army trucks in Mississippi and beaten.
> Whatever my inclinations as a native of Missouri might have been, as President I know this is bad. I shall fight to end evils like this.

On racial matters, Truman had not entirely outgrown his background. Old biases, old habits of speech continued, surfacing occasionally off-stage, as some of his aides and Secret Service agents would later attest. Privately, he could still speak of "niggers," as if that were the way one naturally referred to blacks. His own sister told Jonathan Daniels that Harry was no different than ever on the subject. Daniels, who had gone to Missouri to gather material for a biography of the President, recorded in his notes that as Mary Jane drove him south from Independence to Grandview one morning, she turned and said, "Harry is no more for nigger equality than any of us"—a statement Daniels, as a southerner, found reassuring.

But Mary Jane, like others, failed to understand that Truman knew now, if they did not, that as President he could no longer sit idly by and do nothing in the face of glaring injustice. The findings of his Civil Rights Commission, in a landmark report entitled *To Secure These Rights,* had been a shocking revelation. When a friend from "out home" wrote to advise him to go easy on civil rights, appealing to Truman as a fellow southerner, Truman took time to answer privately and at length:

The main difficulty with the South is that they are living eighty years behind the times and the sooner they come out of it the better it will be for the country and themselves. I am not asking for social equality, because no such things exist, but I am asking for equality of opportunity for all human beings, and, as long as I stay here, I am going to continue that fight. When the mob gangs can take four people out and shoot them in the back, and everybody in the [surrounding] country is acquainted with who did the shooting and nothing is done about it, that country is in a pretty bad fix from the law enforcement standpoint.

When a mayor and a City Marshal can take a negro Sergeant off a bus in South Carolina, beat him up and put out one of his eyes, and nothing is done about it by the State Authorities, something is radically wrong with the system.

On the Louisiana and Arkansas Railway when coal burning locomotives were used, the Negro firemen were the thing because it was a back-breaking job and a dirty one. As soon as they turned to oil as a fuel it became customary for people to take shots at Negro firemen and a number were murdered because it was thought that this was now a white-collar job and should go to a white man. I can't approve of such goings on and I shall never approve of it, as long as I am here. . . . I am going to try to remedy it and if that ends up in my failure to be reelected, that failure will be in a good cause. . . .

The murder of four blacks by mob gunfire referred to in the letter had occurred in Monroe, Georgia, in July 1946. Two men and their wives were dragged from a car and gunned down so savagely their bodies were scarcely identifiable. One of the victims, Truman knew from the report of his Commission, had been a newly returned war veteran, and this, like the account of the men dumped from the truck in Mississippi, and of the young black sergeant, Isaac Woodward, who had been pulled from a bus in Batesburg, South Carolina, and brutally beaten and blinded by police, made an everlasting impression on Truman, moving him in a way no statistics ever would have.

"The wonderful, wonderful development in those years," Clark Clifford would reflect long afterward, "was Harry Truman's capacity to grow."

Of all the President's aides and Cabinet officers no one had done more than Clifford to push for a strong stand on civil rights, as part of a larger effort to, in Clifford's words, "strike for new high ground" whenever confronting the Republican Congress. And it was strategy based on close study, no less than moral conviction, for Clifford did nothing without careful preparation and planning. (On the golf course he was known as someone never to play behind, if it could be avoided, since he took so many practice swings before every shot.) A special, confidential report had been prepared on "The Politics of 1948," a document of thirty-two single-spaced typewritten pages prepared by a young Washington attorney and former Roosevelt aide named James A. Rowe, Jr., who had been talking with labor leaders, professional politicians, and newspaper people. It was a political forecast, with suggestions based, as Rowe stressed, solely on appraisal of "the politically advantageous thing to do." Because Rowe was a law partner of Thomas Corcoran, the influential "Tommy the Cork," whom Truman so disliked, Clifford decided not to tell Truman of Rowe's part in the report, but to submit it as his own. And with some editing and added refinements by Clifford and George Elsey it was perceived as, if not exactly a blueprint for the Democrats in 1948, then a guide to navigation.

That Rowe's authorship was so brushed aside then and later distressed Rowe very little. Such was the nature of the system. "This is, as you know, a typical and acceptable White House staff technique," he would write to a political scholar years later, "and one which I followed in the days when I was Administrative Assistant to President Roosevelt." Who got the credit was not the point. They were all there to serve the President. Roosevelt especially had preferred people working for him to be equipped with "a passion for anonymity."

In the Roosevelt and Truman years, George Elsey would remember, "staff was staff."

The Republican nominee, Rowe predicted, would be Dewey, and Dewey, a "resourceful," "highly dangerous" candidate, would be more difficult to defeat than in 1944. To win, the Democrats had to carry the West and the farm vote. Labor would have to be "cajoled, flattered and educated," not because labor might vote Republican, but because labor might "stay home" on election day. The liberals, on the other hand, had to be "fed" idealism. For while few in number, the liberals, like the manufacturers and financiers in the Republican ranks, were extremely influential: "The businessman has influence because he contributes money. The liberal exerts influence because he is articulate."

The black vote was crucial. "A theory of many professional politicians," Rowe reported, "is that the northern Negro vote today holds the balance of power in Presidential elections for the simple arithmetical reason that the Negroes not only vote in a block but are geographically concentrated in the pivotal, large and closely contested electoral states such as New York, Illinois, Pennsylvania, Ohio, and Michigan." Unless the administration made a determined campaign to help the Negro, Rowe insisted, the Negro vote was already lost.

No candidate since 1876, except Woodrow Wilson in 1916, had won the presidency without carrying New York, and crucial to New York, along with the black vote, was the Jewish vote, concentrated in New York City. But unless the Palestine issue was "boldly and favorably handled" by the administration, the Jewish vote was certain to go to the "alert" Dewey, or to Henry Wallace.

Housing and high prices would be the chief domestic issue. The foreign policy issue, of course, would be American relations with the Soviet Union, and, according to Rowe, there was "considerable political advantage" to the administration in its battle with the Kremlin. The Cold War made good election year politics.

> In times of crises the American citizen tends to back up his President. And on the issue of policy toward Russia, President Truman is comparatively invulnerable to attack because of his brilliant appointment of General Marshall, who has convinced the public that as Secretary of State he is nonpartisan and above politics.
>
> In a flank attack tied up with foreign policy, the Republicans are trying to identify the Administration with domestic Communists. The President adroitly stole their thunder by initiating his own Government employee loyalty investigation procedure and the more frank Republicans admit it. But their efforts will intensify as the election approaches. . . .

Leadership in the Democratic Party was moribund or worse. It had been so long in power that it was "fat, tired and even a bit senile." The old boss-run machines were a shambles.

The President appeared to be liked by the American people. "They know that he is a sincere and humble man and, in the cliché often heard, that he is a man 'trying to do his best.' " The problem was the people saw him still as fundamentally a politician, and the politician as such did not hold first place in the ranks of American heroes. The "public picture" of the President, unfortunately, was "not sufficiently varied." The people wanted more in a chief executive. To resolve the problem, Rowe suggested that Truman be seen less in the company of politicians and more often with such interesting people as famous scientists and best-selling authors. Further, the President should divest himself as rapidly as possible of any remnants of the "Missouri gang." Rowe (and subsequently Clifford in the final version of the report) proposed that Truman invite Albert Einstein to lunch at the White House, that Truman, as a matter of routine, be seen and photographed with not less than two interesting, admirable, nonpolitical figures per week

Most important of all, the President must be seen more by the people. He must get away from Washington, travel the country.

> Since he is President he *cannot be politically active* until after the July convention. . . . So a President who is also a candidate must resort to subterfuges—for he cannot sit silent. He must be in the limelight. He must . . . resort to the kind of trip which Roosevelt made famous in the 1940 campaign—the "inspection tour." No matter how much the opposition press pointed out the political overtones of those trips, the people paid little attention because what they saw was the Head of State performing his duties.

In several respects the report was decidedly mistaken. There was the assumption, for example, that Truman would agree to an idea like inviting Einstein to lunch. Truman had no patience with such public relations gimmickry. It would be synthetic and out of character and he wouldn't do it, he told Clifford. Nor was he about to cashier Harry Vaughan or Wallace Graham in order to enhance his standing in the public eye. But more striking was Rowe's mistaken confidence that the solid South would remain loyal to the Democratic Party. It was, he said, inconceivable that any policies initiated by the administration, no matter how liberal, could so alienate the South it would revolt in an election year. "As always the South can be considered safely Democratic. And in formulating national policy it can be safely ignored."

Since the Republicans controlled Congress, and since the southern Democrats who went along with the Republicans time and again were not about to change their attitudes, there was no reason to try to placate either faction.

"We were telling the President," Rowe later recalled, " 'You can't get anything done up there on the Hill, so, in effect, you want to send all the legislation you can up there and then give them hell for not doing anything about it. . . .' "

How much real influence the memorandum had on Truman is impossible to measure. Probably it was relatively little, certainly less than later claimed. According to Rowe—who was told by James Webb—Truman kept it in the bottom drawer of his desk and read it "every once in a while." But others would insist the memorandum made little if any impression on Truman, since he already knew most of the best that was in it. "To a politician of Harry Truman's experience and resourcefulness," remembered Robert Donovan of the New York *Herald-Tribune,* "the 'famous political memorandum' would have been a primer." And in any event Truman would be running the campaign his own way, according to his own ideas, his own political instincts.

As things developed, the boycotting of the Jefferson-Jackson Day dinner by Senator Johnston was only a mild preview of southern outrage. Fifty-two southern Democrats in Congress pledged themselves to fight any civil rights program in the Democratic platform and, by implication, any Democratic candidate for President who advocated such heinous liberal ideas. There were threats of a white southern march on Washington and Governor J. Strom Thurmond of South Carolina, speaking for a commit-tee of southern governors, pledged to defend white supremacy and warned the leadership of the Democratic Party that the South was no longer "in the bag." The Mississippi Democratic Committee said it would withdraw from the national convention unless "anti-Southern laws" were rejected.

Truman took all this very calmly. Then, on March 8, without fanfare, Senator J. Howard McGrath, Bob Hannegan's replacement as national chairman, announced formally that the President was in the fight for reelection, adding also that the President's position on civil rights remained unchanged.

Immediately Alabama's Senators Lister Hill and John Sparkman, two of the South's most liberal voices in Congress and old friends of Harry Truman, called on him to withdraw and said they would give him no support at the convention. Clearly, a southern rebellion of major proportions was under way.

Troubles of an entirely different nature were besetting Truman, meantime, some minor, even trivial, yet conspicuous and time-consuming just the same.

A huge stir of disapproval and ridicule—editorial indignation, jokes, cartoons—had erupted when he announced a plan to add a new balcony to the South Portico of the White House, extending from his upstairs Oval Study, so that he and his family could enjoy some outside "breathing space" with a degree of privacy. It would mean the first major change in the mansion since the time of Andrew Jackson, when the North Portico was added.

The balcony project was Truman's own idea and to his extreme annoy-ance, it met with instant disapproval from the Fine Arts Commission, as well as a large part of the press. He was called "Back Porch Harry" and accused of meddling with a structure that not only didn't belong to him, but that he was not likely to be occupying much longer. Republicans were delighted, as the "Truman Balcony" became an overnight sensation. Truman, his temper up, stood his ground, arguing that Jefferson himself had used just such upstairs galleries or balconies in his columned buildings at the University of Virginia. (The Washington *Star* expressed gratitude that the President had never seen the Taj Mahal or the old Moulmein Pagoda, or he might have had even more outrageous notions.) The balcony would make the White House "look right," Truman insisted. It would do away with the need for the unsightly awnings used in summer to shade the mansion's downstairs rooms on the south side. "The awnings you will remember were attached about halfway up the beautiful columns and looked always as if they'd caught all the grime and dirt in town," he wrote to his sister. "Had to be renewed every year [at a cost of $780] and cost $2,000 a year in upkeep. In eight years the portico will be paid for in awning cost and the White House from the south will look as it should." On his morning walks, when approaching the White House from the south side, he hated the sight of the dirty awnings and the way they "put the beautiful columns out of proportion." He would go ahead with his balcony. And that was that.

To compound his concerns over the old house, he was informed discreetly by Head Usher Howell Crim that the whole second floor was in imminent danger of falling down. After close examination, an engineer told Truman the ceiling in the State Dining Room was staying in place largely from "force of habit."

Charlie Ross was in a fury because Harry Vaughan insisted on making his own announcements to the press. The soft-spoken, thoughtful press secretary and the Falstaffian military aide had come to dislike one another more and more. Ross was "terrifically upset," warning there had to be a showdown; "it had to be either Vaughan or himself," recorded Eben Ayers.

Wallace Graham, the President's physician, was accused of gambling in grain futures at the very time the President had denounced commodity speculation as a contributing cause of inflation, and the implications were that Graham had benefited from inside information. Though at first Graham insisted he had "lost his socks" in the market, he eventually admitted to having made a profit of $6,000 on an investment of $5,700. Nonetheless he, like Harry Vaughan, remained on duty at the White House, and the more the press deplored their presence, the more Truman dug in his heels.

"You can guard yourself against the wiles of your enemies," Ross observed ruefully to Ayers, "but not the stupidity of your friends."

Henry Wallace, meantime, was crusading up and down the country and drawing huge crowds. His followers included ardent young liberals, working people, blacks, and, conspicuously, members of the American Communist Party. Attacking the Democrats and Republicans alike for their internal "rot," Wallace proposed turning America's atomic weapons over to the United Nations, and called for a massive reconstruction program for the Soviet Union to be financed by the United States. He repudiated the Marshall Plan as a marshal plan. He talked of nationalizing the country's coal mines and railroads. Truman's political strategists worried that the effect of the Wallace movement on Democratic loyalties could do more damage than defections in the South.

But above all, it was the urgent problem of what to do about Palestine that troubled Truman. Reflecting on her father's White House years long afterward, Margaret Truman would call this in some ways his most difficult dilemma of all.

II

The issue was complicated, baffling, and charged with emotion, "explosive," as Truman said, and in the heated climate of an election year, exceedingly sensitive. Its consequences in human terms—for the Jewish people, the Arab Palestinians, in its effect on Middle Eastern relations—could clearly be momentous and very far-reaching.

Truman felt pulled in several directions. Like the great majority of Americans, he wanted to do what was right for the hundreds of thousands of European Jews, survivors of the Holocaust, who had suffered such unimaginable horrors. His sympathy for them was heartfelt and deep-seated. As senator, at the mass meeting in Chicago in 1943, he had said everything "humanly possible" must be done to provide a haven for Jewish survivors of the Nazis. Often as senator, he had personally assured Zionist leaders he would fight for a Jewish homeland in Palestine. As President, he was further impressed by the report of an emissary sent the summer of 1945 to investigate displaced person camps in Europe and talk to Jewish survivors. Earl G. Harrison, dean of the University of Pennsylvania Law School and former U.S. Commissioner of Immigration, had supplied Truman with an exceedingly moving document describing misery that, as Truman said, "could not be allowed to continue." And it reinforced his own belief that Palestine was the answer. Palestine, reported Harrison, was "definitely and preeminently" the choice of the Jewish survivors in Europe. Only in Palestine would "they be welcomed and find peace and quiet and be given an opportunity to live and work.

No other single matter is, therefore, so important from the viewpoint of Jews in Germany and Austria and those elsewhere who have known the horrors of concentration camps as is the disposition of the Palestine question."

The two ardent champions of the Jewish cause on the White House staff were Clark Clifford and David K. Niles, Truman's special assistant for minority affairs. Niles, one of the holdovers from the Roosevelt years and himself a Jew, sensed in Truman a fundamental sympathy for the plight of the Jews that he had never felt with Roosevelt. Had Roosevelt lived, Niles later said, things might not have turned out as they did.

Niles was a short, dark, round-faced, nearsighted man with a receding hairline—as unremarkable in appearance as Clifford was striking—and an extremely shrewd, experienced political troubleshooter with long-standing contacts among Jewish leaders in every part of the country. To White House reporters, as to others on the White House staff, he seemed oddly secretive, even mysterious, spending long weekends in New York with theater people, or in Boston, his home town. It was a reputation Niles cultivated. His own "passion for anonymity" verged on being a mania. "I am a man of no importance," he would insist quietly. In his tiny, cluttered office on the second floor of the old State Department Building next door, he spent most of his time on the telephone. Between them, Niles and Clifford would keep key Zionists informed of what was going on in Washington and within the White House at almost every step.

Both men were keenly attuned to the politics of the Palestine issue, though Clifford vehemently objected to any charges, then or later, that the November election was the real heart of the matter, that it was all "just politics" to get the Jewish vote.

Support for a Jewish homeland was, of course, extremely good politics in 1948, possibly crucial in such big states as Pennsylvania or Illinois, and especially in New York where there were 2.5 million Jews. More important even than Jewish votes to the destitute Democratic Party could be Jewish campaign contributions. Nor was there any doubt that the Republicans stood ready to do all they could for the Jewish cause and for the same reasons. But beyond the so-called "Jewish vote" there was the country at large, where popular support for a Jewish homeland was overwhelming. As would sometimes be forgotten, it was not just American Jews who were stirred by the prospect of a new nation for the Jewish people, it was most of America.

Politics and humanitarian concerns and foreign policy were all closely, irrevocably intertwined. Yet for Truman unquestionably, humanitarian concerns mattered foremost. His sympathies were naturally with the underdog, but he was influenced too by a lifelong love of ancient history, his own remarkable grasp of the whole complicated chronicle of the Fertile Crescent. For Truman, Palestine was never just a place on the map.

And his own reading of ancient history and the Bible made him a supporter of the idea of a Jewish homeland in Palestine [Clifford remembered], even when others who were sympathetic to the plight of the Jews were talking of sending them to places like Brazil. He did not need to be convinced by Zionists. In fact, he had to work hard to avoid the appearance of yielding to Zionist pressure. . . . I remember him talking once about the problems of displaced persons. "Everyone else who's been dragged from his country has someplace to go back to," he said. "But the Jews have no place to go."

To Truman, as he himself wrote, it was "a basic human problem." When his Secretary of Defense, Forrestal, reminded him of the critical need for Saudi Arabian oil, in the event of war, Truman said he would handle the situation in the light of justice, not oil.

Any implication by Forrestal or officials from the State Department that he somehow failed to appreciate the complexities involved, Truman greatly resented. As President he could not possibly dismiss the strategic and economic importance to the United States and Europe of the rapidly developing Middle Eastern oil reserves. Like most Americans, he knew relatively little about the Arabs and their culture, but at the same time he had no wish to damage relations with the Arabs, whose hostility to the establishment of a Jewish state in their midst appeared implacable. American relations with the Arab states had been good until now and like Forrestal, the Chiefs of Staff, fearing an "oil-starved" war, put great stress on the importance of maintaining those relations. To the Arabs it seemed they were being made to pay for the crimes of Hitler.

Much blood had already been spilled in Palestine. Arab groups had attacked Jewish settlements. Jewish terrorists had attacked British troops. Zionist leaders had been jailed. In the summer of 1946, the Jewish terrorist group Irgun blew up the King David Hotel in Jerusalem, killing ninety-one people. And while Truman remained sympathetic to the claim of the Jews on Palestine and knew that more than 600,000 Jews were already there, he also knew the overwhelming numerical superiority of the Arabs. As he said many times, he had no wish to send American troops to guarantee the survival of the new Jewish state; and from the advice he was getting, that was exactly what would be required.

Also he found the mounting pressures on him by Jewish organizations extremely vexing. A good listener, he had been listening to their pleas and arguments since his earliest days in office, when Rabbi Stephen Wise first called on him, and he had become not just worn down by it all but increasingly suspicious, increasingly resentful of the politics of Palestine. In late 1947, the White House received more than 100,000 letters and telegrams concerning Palestine.

"Mr. President, it is up to you and the other leaders of the American people to set an example to the rest of the world. . . . Give your support to the Zionist Movement, just as the late President Roosevelt would have done," he read in a letter from Brooklyn. A telegram from the Philadelphia Womens Division of the American Jewish Congress said:

OUR GOVERNMENT IS HONOR BOUND BY ITS PLEASURES AND PROMISES AND MUST KEEP FAITH WITH HUMANITY. WE MUST GIVE OUR LEADERSHIP AND STRENGTH FOR THE ESTABLISHMENT OF A JEWISH STATE.

Truman became so exasperated by the flood of Jewish "propaganda," he told Senator Claude Pepper, that he took a great stack of such mail and "struck a match to it"—a claim that may have expressed his true desire but that appears to have no basis in fact. ("I don't remember that incident at all," his secretary Rose Conway later told writer Robert Donovan.)

"What I am trying to do is make the whole world safe for the Jews. Therefore I don't feel like going to war in Palestine," Truman wrote in response to one Zionist group, in a letter he never sent. To Mrs. Roosevelt, whom he had made a delegate to the United Nations, he wrote: "The action of some of our United States Zionists will eventually prejudice everyone against what they are trying to get done. I fear very much that the Jews are like all underdogs. When they get on top they are just as intolerant and as cruel as the people were to them when they were underneath. I regret this situation very much because my sympathy has always been on their side."

When a congressional delegation from New York came to see him about the issue, he sat at his desk irritably shuffling papers and said he wished more people would call on him about the country's problems, and not their own.

"I am not a New Yorker," he is supposed to have said at another meeting. "All these people are pleading a special interest. I am an American." He abhorred special interests of any kind, but several individuals had begun to get under his skin.

Particularly offensive to Truman was the attitude of Rabbi Abba Hillel Silver of Cleveland, who, with Stephen Wise, was co-chairman of the

American Zionist Emergency Council. A Republican and close ally of Senator Taft, Rabbi Silver had helped write a pro-Zionist plank in the 1944 Republican platform. At one point during a meeting in Truman's office, Silver had hammered on Truman's desk and shouted at him. "Terror and Silver are the causes of some, if not all, of our troubles," Truman later said, and at one Cabinet meeting he reportedly grew so furious over the subject of the Jews that he snapped, "Jesus Christ couldn't please them when he was on earth, so how could anyone expect that I would have any luck."

To his sister Mary Jane he wrote, "I'm so tired and bedeviled I can't be decent to people."

When several American diplomats, who had been called home from the Middle East to advise him, finished presenting the Arab point of view, Truman's comment was that he didn't have a great many Arabs among his constituents.

Forrestal's intense, repeated warnings of the importance of Arab oil, Forrestal's bitter opposition to any American action that would favor the Zionist cause, had also begun to play on Truman's nerves. And for his part, Forrestal found himself thinking less and less of a President who seemed so willing to cave in to cheap political expediency.

Truman had not, however, shut himself off from Zionist spokesmen, or, importantly, from contact with his old friend and former business partner, Eddie Jacobson. Like many American Jews, Jacobson was not a Zionist. But he looked to Zionist leaders to solve the problems of the Jewish refugees, and he had been trying to do his part, both for the refugees and for the cause of the Jewish homeland, by escorting small groups to the White House to explain the Zionist position. (Following one such visit in 1946, when he had accompanied Rabbi Arthur J. Lelyveld of New York, and Charles Kaplan, the vice president of a shirt company, to see the President, Jacobson quipped to reporters, "Kaplan sells shirts, I sell furnishings, and the Rabbi sells notions.")

Truman was as fond of Jacobson as ever. He knew him to be a devout Jew and a patriotic American and trusted him absolutely, and this was to give Jacobson a role of unusual importance as events unfolded. Until now, Jacobson had asked no favors of Truman or presumed ever to impose on his time. "And when the day came when Eddie Jacobson was persuaded to forego his natural reluctance to petition me and he came to talk to me about the plight of the Jews . . . I paid careful attention," Truman later wrote. Indeed, said Truman, it was "a fact of history" that Jacobson's contribution was of "decisive importance," a point quite unknown at the time.

. . .

The call to make Palestine a Jewish homeland had begun in the late nineteenth century, and prominent among American champions of the cause had been Truman's late friend Justice Louis Brandeis, who had helped win Woodrow Wilson's approval of the Zionist dream. In 1917, during the Great War, the British had seized Palestine from the Turks; that same year, in what became known as the Balfour Declaration, the British government formally endorsed the idea of a future Jewish home in Palestine, the ancient kingdom of Israel, a narrow streak on the map, at the eastern end of the Mediterranean, comprising all of 10,000 square miles, about the size of Sicily or Vermont.

The war over, Britain was granted a special mandate over Palestine by the League of Nations, with the understanding that independence would soon follow. But the British mandate had continued. Only after another world war, only in 1947, had the Attlee government announced that it would withdraw from Palestine, as from Greece, and turn the whole thorny issue over to the United Nations.

So, in effect, Palestine and the destiny of Europe's displaced Jews was another of those results of World War II—like the bomb and the presence of the Red Army in Eastern Europe—that had been left for Truman to face.

American policy, generally speaking, favored immediate independence for Palestine, which would then be divided, or "partitioned," into two separate states, one Jewish, one Arab, joined in an economic union. The United States also supported the idea of large-scale Jewish immigration to the new homeland.

Jews everywhere favored partition. The Arab states were vehemently opposed. The British thought the plan unworkable, and though Winston Churchill, at the peak of his power, had championed a Jewish homeland —"I am a Zionist," he had bellowed at a meeting in Cairo in 1944—the Attlee government opposed Jewish immigration to Palestine. To the British, Harry Truman seemed "carelessly pro-Zionist." When, in 1946, Truman had called for the admission of 100,000 Jews to Palestine, Foreign Secretary Ernest Bevin ascribed it to a crude desire for votes in New York and suggested Truman had no wish to see more Jews come to the United States, remarks that set Truman's teeth on edge.

The more attention given to the issue, the more divisive it became, dividing Jews from Arabs, British from Americans, and more and more in Washington threatening to divide the White House from the State Department, where it was strongly felt the Arabs would never accept partition except under force, and might very well turn to the Soviets for help—a move that could bring the Soviets into the Middle East on the pretext of keeping the peace.

Like the British, senior officers at the State Department favored a United Nations trusteeship over Palestine until the contention between Arabs and Jews could somehow be resolved. George Kennan considered the Palestine situation insoluble for the time being. More outspoken was the head of the Office of Near Eastern Affairs, Loy W. Henderson, a suave, knowledgeable career diplomat with a strong sense of duty who was convinced partition of Palestine had no chance of success. Henderson worried about the consequences to the Marshall Plan should Arab oil be cut off, Europe being dependent on the Arab states for 80 percent of its oil. The creation of a new Jewish state at this particular moment, he stressed to Marshall, could be disastrous to the long-range interests of the United States.

Relations between the State Department and such members of Truman's staff as Clifford and Niles grew extremely difficult. "Some White House men still believe that a number of positions taken by career men on this matter were based on anti-Semitism, not diplomacy," Jonathan Daniels was to write, naming no names. "And there are men in the State Department who believe that some of the presidential staff were clearly more concerned about Israel in terms of American politics than in terms of American security." If Clifford was reluctant to stress the domestic political stakes involved, Niles was not. Henderson would remember Niles turning to him at one point and saying sharply, "Look here, Loy, the most important thing for the United States is for the President to be reelected."

According to Dean Rusk, who was then Marshall's assistant secretary in charge of U.N. affairs, the real cause of difficulty was not any deviousness on the part of the State Department, but the "conflicting objectives" in the President's own mind. "This wasn't understood at the time. With Marshall and State working toward a long-range solution, the Zionists branded anyone not 1,000 percent behind the Zionist cause as having betrayed the president."

Clifford remained certain the State Department, "to a man," was doing everything possible to thwart the President's intentions, and he told Truman so. Truman thought Clifford unduly concerned. "I know how Marshall feels and he knows how I feel," Truman said, meaning if Marshall was with him, that was all he needed to know.

In Palestine, the whole time, violence and terrorism continued.

It was in late 1947, on Saturday, November 29, over the Thanksgiving weekend, that the United Nations, at the end of a dramatic two-and-a-half-hour session, voted for partition by a narrow margin, the United States taking a lead part behind the scenes to see the measure through. ("We went for it," Clifford told Jonathan Daniels. "It was because the White House was for it that it went through.") The Soviet Union, too, had joined the United States in support.

Eddie Jacobson recorded in telegraphic style his own chronicle of the unfolding drama:

> Nov. 6th—Wash.—Pres. still going all out for Palestine.
> Nov. 17th—Again to White House. . . .
> Wed., 26—Received call from White House—everything O.K.
> Nov. 27—Thanksgiving. Sent two page wire to Truman.
> Friday, received call from his secretary [Matt Connelly] not to worry.
> Nov. 29th—Mission accomplished.

Truman, Jacobson noted, had told him that "he [Truman] and he alone was responsible for swinging the votes of several delegations."

Zionists, Jews everywhere, were elated. In the lobby outside the General Assembly, at U.N. headquarters at Flushing Meadows, in what had been the New York City Building at the 1939 World's Fair, the Jewish delegation was swept up in the embrace of delegates and visitors from all but the Arab countries. In the hall itself, while members of the Arab delegations walked out, Zionists in the audience were rejoicing. "This is the day the Lord hath made!" a rabbi cried in the delegates' lounge. "There were Jews in tears, and non-Jews moved by the nobility of the occasion. Nobody who ever lived that moment will ever lose its memory from his heart," recalled Abba Eban, who was then a young liaison officer with the Jewish Agency, the official Zionist organization.

To the Zionist Organization of America, the vote was "a triumphant vindication" of the Zionist dream and "a victory for international equity." Rabbi Silver called it a turning point in history, and expressed particular appreciation for the part played by both the United States and the Soviet Union. Here, said the New York *Herald-Tribune,* was "one of the few great acts of courageous collective statesmanship which our shattered postwar world has been able to achieve." At a Zionist rally in New York to celebrate the occasion, twenty thousand people tried to jam into an auditorium on 34th Street, a crowd three times the seating capacity.

Britain announced that responsibility for Palestine would be turned over to the United Nations in less than six months, on May 14, 1948. The Arabs said partition meant war, and Truman was warned by the Chiefs of Staff that military intervention by the United States to protect a new Jewish state would require no less than 100,000 troops. (The British were about to withdraw 50,000 troops.) The Arabs, Forrestal told Clifford, would "push the Jews into the sea."

· · ·

The hard truth, as Forrestal reported to Truman, was that the deployable troops then available totaled less than 30,000, plus perhaps 23,000 Marines.

Nor was Palestine by any means the sole concern in early February 1948. In Czechoslovakia, a violent coup backed by the Red Army had imposed a pro-Communist government with bewildering speed. It was one of the traumatic events of the postwar era. A feeling of revulsion swept much of the world, as it had only ten years before when the Nazis seized Czechoslovakia. Italy and France appeared to be headed for the same fate.

Truman left for Key West for another greatly needed rest and change of scene which, after all, did little to improve his outlook. "Things look black," he told Margaret in a letter from Key West on March 3. Russia had kept none of its agreements. "So that now we are faced with exactly the same situation with which Britain and France were faced in 1938/39 with Hitler."

Two days later, on March 5, came a top-secret cable from General Lucius D. Clay in Berlin reporting a worrisome shift in Soviet attitudes in Berlin, "a new tenseness in every Soviet individual with whom we have official relations." Until recently, Clay had felt another war was not likely for at least ten years. His sense now was that war could come any time and "with dramatic suddenness."

If, as later suggested, the real purpose of Clay's message was to impress Congress on the need to reinstate the draft, this was not understood at the time and its effect on Washington was stunning and entirely real. General Bradley said later that it "lifted me right out of my chair." Secretary of the Army Royall checked with David Lilienthal to see how long it would take to move atomic bombs to the Mediterranean, closer to Russia. "The atmosphere of Washington today," wrote Joseph and Stuart Alsop in their column, "is no longer postwar. It is a prewar atmosphere."

"The Jewish pressure on the White House did not diminish in the days following the partition vote in the U.N.," Truman would write years later, bitter still over the memory. "Individuals and groups asked me, usually in rather quarrelsome and emotional ways, to stop the Arabs, to keep the British from supporting the Arabs, to furnish American soldiers, to do this, that, and the other. I think I can say that I kept the faith in the rightness of my policy in spite of some of the Jews."

Hundreds of thousands of postcards flooded the White House mail, nearly all from Jewish interest groups. Largely as a result of the efforts of the American Zionist Emergency Council, thirty-three state legislatures passed resolutions favoring a Jewish state in Palestine. Forty governors and more than half the Congress signed petitions to the President. David Niles grew so emotional at one meeting in Truman's office that he threatened to quit unless Truman moved more emphatically in support of the Jewish cause. Ed Flynn came down from New York to tell the President that he must either "give in" on Palestine or expect New York's opposition to his renomination in July.

Truman's patience wore thin. He refused to make further comment on Palestine, refused to see any more Zionist spokesmen, even ruling out a visit from Dr. Chaim Weizmann, the grand old man of world Zionist leaders, who, despite failing health, had sailed from London for the expressed purpose of seeing him. Weizmann, a renowned scientist, now seventy-four, had devoted a large part of his life to the dream of a Jewish homeland. Small, charming, and clever, he had been one of the architects of the Balfour Declaration. Also, he and Truman already knew and liked one another. At their first meeting, as Truman remembered, he had not known how to pronounce "Chaim." "So I called him 'Cham.' He liked it. He was a wonderful man, one of the wisest people I think I ever met . . . a leader, one of the kind you read about."

They had met secretly in the White House in November 1947, just before the U.N. vote on partition, and the effect on Truman was nearly as pronounced as it had been on the British Foreign Secretary, Lord Balfour, thirty years earlier. Spreading a map on Truman's desk, Weizmann had fascinated the former Missouri farmer with the agricultural possibilities in the Negev Desert, the future control of which was still at issue. Truman pledged his support for the inclusion of the Negev in the Jewish state. "You can bank on us," Truman had said, and as Weizmann would write with wry understatement, "I was extremely happy to find that the President read the map quickly and clearly."

But now Truman had closed the door to "the little doctor," and this to Weizmann and his American Zionist allies was an especially distressing sign. Through Clifford and Niles, they already knew in detail what opposition they faced at the State Department.

A secret paper from George Kennan's Policy Planning Staff recommended no further support for partition. A report from the new Central Intelligence Agency concluded that partition would not work and urged reconsideration. More important to Truman were the views of George Marshall who, at a meeting of the National Security Council on February 12, had said the United States was "playing with fire while having nothing with which to put it out."

Marshall saw America as gravely threatened by the Soviet Union, and as a soldier, he was acutely aware of the vital importance of Middle Eastern oil in the event of a war in Europe, which seemed more likely by the day. Marshall had besides a soldier's distaste for politics. Writing about the Palestine question in a letter to Eleanor Roosevelt, he had said candidly that "the political situation in this country doesn't help matters." At a press conference he was still more emphatic. As long as he was Secretary of State, there would be no "bending" to either political or military threats.

Clifford grew increasingly concerned. "On five occasions I told the President that our position on Israel was going sour," Clifford recorded. "On each time the President replied, 'No, Marshall knows how I feel.' "

At the State Department, thousands of letters were received demanding the dismissal of Loy Henderson for being "pro-Arab."

Henderson was summoned to Truman's office, to a meeting attended by Clifford and Niles, and asked to defend his position. Henderson felt Clifford and Niles were trying to humiliate him in front of the President. "I pointed out that the views which I had been expressing were those, not only of myself," Henderson remembered, "but of all our legations and consular offices in the Middle East and of all members of the Department of State who had responsibilities for that area." The cross-questioning by Clifford and Niles became more and more harsh, until finally Truman stood up and said, "Oh, hell, I'm leaving!"

> From his bearing and facial expression [Henderson remembered] I was not at all convinced that even at that late date the President had made the final decision to go all out for the establishment of the Jewish state. Although I was not in a position, of course, to know what his real feelings were, I had the impression that he realized that the Congress, the press, the Democratic Party, and aroused American public opinion in general, would turn against him if he should withdraw his support of the Zionist cause. On the other hand, it seemed to me he was worried about what the long-term effect would be on the United States if he should continue to support policies advocated by the Zionists. He was almost desperately hoping, I thought, that the Department of State would tell him that the setting up in Palestine of Arab and Jewish states as proposed by the U.N. Commission would be in the interest of the United States. This, however, the Department of State thus far had not been able to do.

On arriving at New York from London, Chaim Weizmann had taken ill from the "strain" of events. Every effort to make contact with Truman had failed. Then, late the night of February 20, as Weizmann lay in his room at the Waldorf-Astoria, the president of the national B'nai B'rith, Frank Goldman, put through a call to Eddie Jacobson in Kansas City, getting Jacobson out of bed to ask if he would be willing to help. No one, not even Ed Flynn, could budge the President, Goldman said.

In a hurried letter to Truman, Jacobson begged him to see Chaim Weizmann as soon as possible. But in response, in a letter from Key West dated February 27, Truman said there was nothing new that Weizmann could tell him. The situation, Truman added, was "not solvable as presently set up."

Jacobson refused to accept defeat. No sooner had Truman returned to Washington than Jacobson arrived from Kansas City. On Saturday, March 13, without an appointment, he walked into the West Wing of the White House, where, outside Truman's office, Matt Connelly warned him that under no circumstances was he to mention Palestine.

Entering Truman's office, shaking hands with his old friend, Jacobson was pleased to see how well he looked. Florida had done him good, Jacobson said. For a while they chatted about their families and Jacobson's business, a subject in which Truman, Jacobson said, "always had a brother's interest." They were alone, and with the West Wing largely unoccupied on Saturday, the hush of the room was greater than usual.

Jacobson brought up Palestine. Truman, suddenly tense and grim-faced, responded in hard, abrupt fashion, not at all like himself, Jacobson thought. "In all the years of our friendship he never talked to me in this manner, or in any way even approaching it," Jacobson would remember. Truman later told Clark Clifford he was not angry at Jacobson so much as at the people who were using Jacobson to get to him.

He had no wish to talk about Palestine or the Jews or the Arabs or the British, Truman said. He would leave that to the United Nations. He spoke bitterly of the abuse he had been subjected to, of how "disrespectful and mean" certain Jews had been to him. Jacobson thought suddenly and sadly that "my dear friend, the President of the United States, was at that moment as close to being an anti-Semite as a man could possibly be. . . ."

Jacobson tried arguing back—"I am now surprised at myself that I had the nerve," he later wrote—but Truman was unmoved. Jacobson felt crushed.

On a table to the right, against the wall, was one of the President's prized possessions, a small bronze of Andrew Jackson on horseback, the model of the statue by Charles Keck that Truman had commissioned for the Jackson County Courthouse in Kansas City. Jacobson had noticed it on other visits, but now, pointing to it, he found himself making an impassioned speech:

Harry, all your life you have had a hero. . . . I too have a hero, a man I never met, but who is, I think, the greatest Jew who ever lived. . . . I am talking about Chaim Weizmann. He is a very sick man, almost broken in health, but he traveled thousands of miles just to see you and plead the cause of my people. Now you refuse to see him just because you are insulted by some of our American Jewish leaders, even though you know that Weizmann had absolutely nothing to do with these insults and would be the last man to be party to them. It doesn't sound like you, Harry, because I thought you could take this stuff they have been handing out. . . .

As Abba Eban later wrote, the comparison between Weizmann and Andrew Jackson was unimaginably far-fetched. And it worked.

Truman began drumming his fingers on the desk. He wheeled around in his chair and with his back to Jacobson sat looking out the window into the garden. For what to Jacobson seemed "like centuries," neither of them said anything. Then, swinging about and looking Jacobson in the eye, Truman said what Jacobson later described as the most endearing words he had ever heard: "You win, you baldheaded son-of-a-bitch. I will see him."

From the White House Jacobson walked directly across Lafayette Square and up 16th Street to the bar at the Statler where, as never before in his life, he downed two double bourbons.

On March 16, the morning papers were filled with rumors of war. Truman's concern was extreme. The Marshall Plan was insufficient to check the Soviet menace. American military strength must also be reestablished and quickly. "It is the most serious situation we have faced since 1939," he wrote to Mrs. Roosevelt. "I shall face it with everything I have."

He must awaken the Congress and the country. "It was better to do that than be caught, as we were in the last war, without having warned the Congress and the people," he told his staff.

On March 17, a fine, bright St. Patrick's Day in Washington with the forsythia in bloom, he went before a joint session on the Hill to ask for immediate passage of the Marshall Plan, for universal military training still one more time, and for a "temporary reenactment" of the draft, to meet the rapid changes taking place in Europe that threatened national security. It was almost exactly a year since his speech from the same podium announcing the Truman Doctrine. And for the first time now, he identified the Soviet Union as the one nation blocking the way to peace. It was a forceful, historic statement:

Since the close of hostilities [World War II], the Soviet Union and its agents have destroyed independence and democratic character of a whole series of nations in Eastern and Central Europe.

It is this ruthless course of action, and the clear design to extend it to the remaining free nations in Europe, that have brought about the critical situation in Europe today. . . . I believe that we have reached the point at which the position of the United States should be made unmistakably clear. . . . There are times in world history when it is far wiser to act than to hesitate.

The will to peace, he said, must be backed by the strength for peace. "We must be prepared to pay the price for peace, or assuredly we shall pay the price of war."

But Congress was fundamentally unmoved.

To Arthur Krock of *The New York Times,* an acknowledged "hardliner," Truman deserved great praise for his courage, as well as his disregard for political considerations, since calling for the draft in an election year seemed the poorest possible political strategy. Yet to many in the audience, talk of the "growing menace" of the Russians seemed a blatant election year ploy, and, as such, a poor one. "Frankly, candidly," wrote Richard Strout in *The New Republic,* "we think Harry Truman is licked. We don't think any 'crisis atmosphere' will elect him."

A new Gallup Poll indicated that almost irrespective of what Truman might or might not do, he would lose in November to any of four possible Republican nominees: Dewey, Vandenberg, former Governor Harold E. Stassen of Minnesota, and General Douglas MacArthur.

"The simple fact is that Truman isn't the type of strong man to whom folks turn in time of national danger," concluded Strout. "The idea of Truman as a 'man on horseback' is just funny."

Shortly after dark on the evening of Thursday, March 18, to avoid being seen by reporters, Chaim Weizmann was ushered quietly into the White House by way of the East Wing. Truman, who had not informed the State Department of what he was up to, insisted the meeting be kept secret. Eddie Jacobson, by now a familiar face to the White House press, had agreed to stay away.

According to later accounts by both Truman and Weizmann, the meeting went well. They talked for three quarters of an hour. Truman said he wanted to see justice done without bloodshed and assured Weizmann that the United States would support partition. "And when he left my office," Truman would write, "I felt that he had received a full understanding of my policy and that I knew what it was he wanted." Recalling the event years later, Truman would also remember Eddie Jacobson being present—but then, in a sense, he was.

The situation, however, had become more complicated than Weizmann knew, or than Truman himself seems to have understood, as would be revealed quite dramatically in less than twenty-four hours.

And Truman was partly, if unintentionally, to blame for what happened. He had not only neglected to tell Secretary Marshall, or anyone at the State Department, of Weizmann's visit and what had transpired—possibly because Marshall was on the West Coast, or more likely because he refused to accept the possibility that he and Marshall might be working at cross-purposes—but he seems to have wholly misjudged the reaction of Jewish groups to the abrupt reversal of American policy that he himself had tacitly sanctioned several weeks before while in Key West and that his own ambassador to the U.N., former Senator Warren Austin, now presented, without warning, on Friday, March 19, the very day after Truman and Weizmann reached their "understanding."

To give all sides in the Palestine controversy time to cool down, Austin announced before the General Assembly, the United States recommended abandoning the partition plan and called for a temporary U.N. "trusteeship" over Palestine.

It was a complete, seemingly inexplicable turnabout by the administration, and for Jews everywhere shattering, almost unbelievable news. The American Jewish Congress, in an emergency meeting, charged the State Department with conduct both un-American and "thoroughly dishonorable." On Capitol Hill there were cries of "sellout." No more shameful decision in international politics had ever been made, charged Congressman Emanuel Celler, Democrat from New York, while a Democratic senator who chose to remain anonymous predicted that the antagonism of Jews in those states where their number was greatest could produce a revolt at the polls in November every bit as damaging to Truman as the anti-Catholic movement had been to Al Smith in 1928.

The New York Times accused the administration of unprecedented ineptness and of caving in to base material concerns:

A land of milk and honey now flows with oil, and the homeland of three great religions is having its fate decided by expediency without a sign of the spiritual and ethical considerations which should be determining at least in that part of the world. Ancient Palestine was once described as "not the land of philosophers but the home of prophets." It would take a prophet sitting on a rapidly spinning turntable to have

609

foreseen the course which our Government has pursued during the last few months.

The White House was deluged with letters, telegrams, and petitions to the President filled with alarm and outrage over such "whimsical and cynical action," such "vacillating" and "disastrous" policy. Nor were they all from Jews or Jewish organizations.

"This change can mean nothing but the complete annihilation of that wonderful home loving race of people who have demonstrated the wonders they can accomplish in that country which actually before God and man belongs to them," wrote a municipal court judge from Council Bluffs, Iowa, named John P. Tinley. "They must not be betrayed. For God's sake and the sake of humanity do something to correct this terrible blunder." "Oh, how could you stoop so low!" declared Professor Samuel A. Sloan of the Carnegie Institute of Technology in Pittsburgh. "Was your action of Friday a 'Gentleman's Agreement' with England and the Arab interests? This revolting move must and should be the death of the United Nations. . . . Won't you stop trying to be a statesman and act like a human being!"

For Eddie Jacobson in Kansas City, March 19 was "Black Friday." People enraged over the news kept calling him all day. How did he feel now that his friend Truman had turned out to be a traitor to the Jewish people? "There wasn't one . . . who expressed faith and confidence in the word of the President of the United States," remembered Jacobson, who felt so heartsick he had to take to his bed for the remainder of the weekend.

Not until Monday, when he was back at his store, did Jacobson hear from Chaim Weizmann, who called personally to tell him not to despair. Weizmann, who had more right than anyone to feel betrayed, was certain the President had meant what he said when they met. Jacobson must not forget, Weizmann stressed, that his friend Harry S. Truman was the single most powerful man in the world, and it was up to Jacobson to keep the White House door open.

Truman's first news of what had happened at the United Nations came in the morning papers, Saturday, the 20th, the day after Austin's speech. At 7:30 A.M. Truman was on the phone to Clifford at his home, telling him to get down to the White House immediately.

This morning I find that the State Dept. has reversed my Palestine policy [Truman wrote in a fury on his calendar]. The first I know about it is what I see in the papers! Isn't that hell? I'm now in the position of a liar and a double-crosser. I never felt so in my life.

There are people on the 3rd and 4th levels of the State Dept. who have always wanted to cut my throat. They are succeeding in doing it. . . .

Still unable to accept the idea that it might be Marshall who was opposing his position, or who misunderstood his position, he saw the State Department itself, "the striped pants boys," as the perpetrators of his troubles.

"Truman was in his office as disturbed as I have ever seen him," Clifford remembered. " 'I don't understand this,' he said. 'How could this have happened! I assured Chaim Weizmann . . . he must think I'm a shitass.' "

"The President's statement that the action [at the U.N.] had come without his knowledge seemed incredible," wrote Eben Ayers after an emergency staff meeting. "The political effect may be terrifically bad and it seemed impossible to believe that those responsible for the action could not have realized the reaction that would result."

Calling a press conference in Los Angeles that evening, Secretary Marshall said he regarded trusteeship over Palestine as "the wisest course." He himself had recommended it to the President, Marshall said, and the President had approved. The statement was brief, unadorned, accurate, and helped Truman not at all.

Marshall flew home the following day, Sunday the 21st, and on Monday the 22nd, at the White House he and Loy Henderson met with a calmer, more composed President, who now, in obvious deference to Marshall, said he had given approval to the idea of trusteeship as an intermediate step, and that it was only the "timing" of Austin's speech that had upset him.

But as he came out of the meeting, Truman was heard to mutter, "This gets us nowhere."

The fact was he had also specified earlier that nothing be done before the General Assembly that could be taken as a retreat from the partition plan. Further, he had insisted he be shown Austin's speech in advance. "Send final draft of Austin's remarks for my consideration," he had directed on February 22, which clearly the State Department had not done. As Charlie Ross observed in his diary, "No pronouncement of the momentous nature of Austin's should have been made without prior consultation with the P[resident] or someone on his staff." But as Ross also observed, it would be unthinkable now for Truman to disavow what Austin had said.

Though Truman made none of these points to Marshall, he felt them

acutely, as he felt still that it was those below Marshall who were determined to sabotage his policy, the "striped pants conspirators," as he now
referred to them in a letter to his sister.

At a press conference, speaking anything but plainly, he said trusteeship did not necessarily "prejudice the character of the final political
settlement." Was he then in favor still of partition at some future date?
"That is what I am trying to say here as plainly as I can."

He was straddling, obfuscating. He knew it, the reporters knew it, and
he felt miserable. "It was one of the worst messes of my father's career,"
Margaret would attest, "and he could do nothing but suffer."

Eleanor Roosevelt wrote to submit her resignation as a delegate to the
United Nations, while two of her sons, Franklin, Jr., and Elliott, joined a
disparate but growing number of worried Democrats who wanted to draft
General Eisenhower for the presidential nomination.

Truman refused to accept Mrs. Roosevelt's resignation and paid no
attention to her sons.

On April 9, writing to the President from New York, Chaim Weizmann,
after thanking Truman for "the personal kindness which you have so
often shown me" and for "the sympathetic interest which you have constantly devoted to the cause of our people," stressed the gravity of the
moment and Truman's own historic role in it:

> The choice for our people, Mr. President, is between statehood and
> extermination. History and providence have placed this issue in your
> hands and I am confident that you will yet decide it in the spirit of
> moral law.

On Saturday afternoon, April 11, to avoid the few reporters hanging
about the White House, Eddie Jacobson slipped in through the East Wing.
Again Truman reaffirmed—and "very strongly," according to Jacobson—
what he had told Weizmann. Moreover, he now assured Jacobson he
would recognize the new Jewish state. "And to this," wrote Jacobson later,
"he agreed with his whole heart." Harry Truman had made up his mind.

As the likelihood of war breaking out in Palestine grew more ominous
and the time before the British withdrawal grew shorter, tension at the
White House increased measurably and the strain on the President himself did not go unnoticed. "The President," wrote David Lilienthal after a
meeting on April 21, "looked worn—as I haven't seen him look since I
have known him."

There was never enough time. There was always more than one reasonable, prudent course of action to take. Nothing seemed simple.

At Griffith Stadium, throwing out the first ball at the start of the new baseball season—at a Senators-Yankees game—the ambidextrous President seemed hesitant even about which arm to use, then threw with his left.

News accounts described him as "whirling" about Washington. "Not once, but twice," Truman had "tootled off" to the National Gallery to see a collection of paintings by the old masters discovered by the American Third Army in a salt mine in Germany. He attended the Gridiron dinner, another rite of spring, and the funeral of a veteran White House clerk, Maurice C. Latta, who had been employed since 1898. From a flag-festooned platform on Constitution Avenue, he reviewed an Army Day parade and later at the White House welcomed the very nervous, young Prince Regent of Belgium with a state dinner. At the nearby Loew's Capitol Theater, accompanied by Bess and Margaret, he saw the premiere of Frank Capra's new movie, *State of the Union,* starring Spencer Tracy and Katharine Hepburn, which gave him a lift as nothing had in a long while. "It is a scream," he wrote to Mary Jane. "If you get a chance go see it. It gives the Republicans hell and, believe it or not, is favorable to your brother."

The latest Gallup Poll reported his approval rating at only 36 percent. Republicans were overjoyed, Democrats and the liberal press increasingly downcast. "Must it be Truman?" asked *The Nation.* "Truman Should Quit," said the front cover of *The New Republic.* "Harry Truman has none of the qualities demanded by the presidency." He was "colorless," "a little man" with a "known difficulty in understanding the printed word." In *The New York Times,* Arthur Krock wrote grimly:

> When he [Truman] vetoed what he called the "rich man's" tax bill, which Congress had substituted for his own "poor man's" bill, numerous Democrats in Congress jumped on the bandwagon to override the veto.
>
> The Democratic Party is imperiling the President's effectiveness as no major party in this country has done since the Republican radicals impeached Andrew Johnson. . . . A President whose defeat at the next poll is generally prophesied faces difficulties in performing his office that conceivably bring disaster. . . . At this writing, the President's influence is weaker than any President's has been in modern history.

Early in May, in advance of what was to be a crucial White House strategy conference on Palestine, Truman asked Clark Clifford to prepare the case for immediate recognition of the new Jewish state, which as yet had no name. He was to prepare himself, Truman told Clifford, as though presenting a case before the Supreme Court. "You will be addressing all of us present, of course," Truman said, "but the person I really want you to convince is Marshall."

Truman, as he told Clifford, was inclined to think that Marshall was opposed to such recognition. But this had nothing to do with Truman's regard for the general. Nor was there the least question about Marshall's own feelings. "I want you to know," wrote Marshall in a personal birthday greeting to the President on May 8, "that I am keenly aware of the remarkable loyalty you have given me. In return, I can only promise you to do my best and assure you of my complete loyalty and trust in you."

At a private birthday party for the President, Marshall had been still more emphatic, expressing his regard for the President in words no one present would forget. Indeed, it was one of the greatest tributes ever paid to Harry Truman. The party, at the nearby F Street Club, was given by Attorney General Tom Clark for some forty guests, including the President and Mrs. Truman, and marked one of the rare times that Marshall and his wife accepted an invitation to dine out in Washington. Clark and John Snyder each rose after dinner to offer toasts. Then, unexpectedly, Marshall stood up, pushed his chair out of the way, and leaning forward with his hands on the table began to speak, his expression very serious. Marshall, as everyone present was well aware, never complimented the people with whom he worked. It was not his way.

"The full stature of this man," he said, his eyes on Truman, "will only be proven by history, but I want to say here and now that there has never been a decision made under this man's administration, affecting policies beyond our shores, that has not been in the best interest of this country. It is not the courage of these decisions that will live, but the integrity of the man."

Truman, his face flushed, rose slowly to respond but was unable to speak. The silence in the room was stunning. He stood with his arms half outstretched trying to compose himself. Finally he could only gesture to Marshall and say, "He won the war," but he spoke with such simplicity and feeling that many guests were crying.

The meeting in the President's office on the afternoon of May 12 began at four o'clock, just two days and two hours before the British mandate in Palestine was to expire.

Present were Marshall, Robert Lovett, and two of their State Department aides, Robert McClintock and Fraser Wilkins; Clifford, Niles, and Matt

Connelly. Saying little, they took seats around Truman's desk, Marshall and Lovett on the President's left, with McClintock and Fraser just behind, Clifford sitting directly in front of the President, with Niles and Connelly to his left. Truman made a few preliminary remarks, in which he said nothing about recognition of Palestine, then turned to Marshall, who asked Lovett to present the case for trusteeship. Lovett spoke at some length, during which Marshall intervened briefly to report that during a recent conversation with Moshe Shertok of the Jewish Agency, he, Marshall, had warned that militarily the Jews were embarked on a very risky venture in Palestine, and should the tide turn against them, there was nothing to guarantee help from the United States.

Truman then called on Clifford, who for the first time mentioned recognition, proposing that the United States make the move quickly before the Soviet Union did. The United States should not even wait until the new Jewish state was declared but announce American recognition the very next day, May 13.

"As I talked," remembered Clifford, "I noticed the thunder clouds gathering—Marshall's face getting redder and redder."

"This is just straight politics," Marshall said. "I don't even understand why Clifford is here. This is not a political meeting."

"General," Truman answered softly, "he is here because I asked him to be here."

Clifford continued with his statement, speaking for perhaps fifteen minutes. He was calm, orderly, and unhurried, his rich voice, as always, beautifully modulated, one clear, perfectly structured sentence flowing smoothly, flawlessly after another. ("I had really prepared!" he would say, remembering the moment a lifetime later.) But Clifford was also twenty-six years younger than Marshall—and new to the experience of great power and large world decisions. Marshall's prestige was a palpable presence in the room and made especially memorable, especially intimidating, by his anger. He sat glaring at Clifford the entire time. Possibly it was Clifford's manner that upset Marshall, who was deeply worried about the world.

Recognition of the new Jewish state, Clifford said, would be wholly consistent with what had been the President's policy from the beginning. It would be an act of humanity, "everything this country should represent." The murder of 6 million Jews by the Nazis had been the worst atrocity of all time. Every thoughtful human being must feel some responsibility for the survivors, who, unlike others in Europe, had no place to go. He explained the Balfour Declaration. He cited lines from Deuteronomy verifying the Jewish claim to a Palestine homeland.

Behold, I have set the land before you: go in and possess the land which the Lord swear unto your fathers, Abraham, Isaac, and Jacob, to give unto them and to their seed after them.

There was no real alternative to the partition of Palestine, he said, or to recognition by the United States, since no postponement of the kind imagined by the State Department would ever be tolerated by the Jews. A separate Jewish state was inevitable. It would come to pass in a matter of days. "No matter what the State Department or anybody thinks, we are faced with the actual fact that there is to be a Jewish state." To think otherwise was unrealistic.

Lovett spoke again. To recognize a Jewish state prematurely, before its boundaries were even known or government established, would be buying a pig-in-a-poke. He produced a file of intelligence reports indicating that numbers of Jewish immigrants to Palestine were Communists or Soviet agents. The entire matter should remain a U.N. problem, Lovett argued. The United Nations was struggling to determine the future government in Palestine, and this at the specific urging of the United States. Any premature, ill-advised recognition of the new state would be disastrous to American prestige in the United Nations and appear only as "a very transparent" bid for Jewish votes in November.

On this note, Marshall broke in, speaking gravely and with all the weight of his reputation, his anger just barely in control.

Clifford's suggestions were wrong, Marshall said. Domestic political considerations must not determine foreign policy. At stake was "the great office of the President." Indeed, said Marshall, looking directly at Truman, if the President were to follow Clifford's advice, and if in the elections in November, he, Marshall, were to vote, he would vote against the President.

It was an extraordinary rebuke for Truman—"the sharpest rebuke *ever* for him," Clifford felt certain—coming as it did from Marshall, "the great one of the age," whose presence in his administration gave Truman such pride and feeling of confidence.

"That brought the meeting to a grinding halt. There was really a state of shock. The President, I think, was struck dumb by it," Clifford would say, trying years later to evoke the feeling in the room. "There was this awful, *total* silence."

Yet Truman showed no sign of emotion. His expression, serious from the start, changed not at all. He only raised his hand and said he was fully aware of the difficulties and dangers involved, as well as the political risks, which he himself would run. He was inclined to agree with General Marshall, but thought it best they all sleep on the matter.

Marshall and his retinue departed, Marshall refusing even to look at Clifford, who, seething within, began gathering up his papers. It was Marshall's "righteous goddamn Baptist tone" that was so infuriating, he would later tell Jonathan Daniels—Marshall "didn't know his ass from a hole in the ground." The President, Clifford could only conclude, had agreed with Marshall in order not to embarrass the general in front of the others.

"That was rough as a cob," Truman said to Clifford, once everyone was gone. Truman told him not to feel badly. As a trial lawyer, Clifford said, he had lost cases before.

"Let's not agree that it's lost yet," Truman said.

Would the United States recognize the new Palestine state, reporters asked the next day.

He would cross that bridge when he came to it, Truman replied.

But by then the bridge was already underfoot. Lovett had telephoned Clifford the evening before, less than an hour after the meeting broke up, to say he and Clifford must talk as soon as possible. Clifford had gone to Lovett's home in Kalorama, where, over drinks, they agreed something had to be done, or there could be a serious breach between the President and the Secretary. Conceivably, Marshall might resign, which, as Clifford knew, would be the heaviest possible blow to Truman's standing with the country and undoubtedly destroy whatever small chance he had of being reelected. "Marshall was the greatest asset he had," Clifford would recall. "He couldn't afford to lose him." It was painfully ironic: Marshall, who insisted there be no political considerations, Marshall who was so "above politics," had himself become the largest of political considerations.

Lovett asked Clifford to think about it, but when Lovett called Clifford the next morning, Clifford told him there was nothing he could do. Lovett would have to persuade Marshall he was wrong.

Truman's reaction, when Clifford reported all this, was that Marshall, in Truman's words, needed a little more time.

That was on Thursday, the 13th.

On Friday, May 14, the day the new Jewish state was to be declared at midnight in Jerusalem—6:00 P.M. Washington time—Clifford and Lovett met for lunch in the quiet of the F Street Club and worked out the wording of a statement to be released by the President. Lovett now urged only that there be no "indecent haste" in recognizing the new Jewish state, so that the American delegation at the United Nations could have ample warning. Clifford, however, could not promise that.

Sometime that afternoon, Marshall called the President to say that while he could not support the position the President wished to take, he would not oppose it publicly.

"That," said Truman to Clifford, "is all we need."

Clifford put through a hurried call to Elihu Epstein, an official at the Jewish Agency in Washington, to tell him that recognition would occur that day, and to get the necessary papers ready and over to the White House at once. When Epstein asked what was needed, Clifford had to say he didn't exactly know. "This is very unusual," Clifford said, "a new country asking for recognition—it doesn't happen every day."

Clifford called the State Department, then reported back to Epstein. When the papers finally arrived, the name of the new country had been left blank—to be filled in later—because it was still unknown.

The new Jewish state—the first Jewish state in nearly two thousand years —was declared on schedule at midnight in Jerusalem, 6:00 P.M. in Washington. Eleven minutes later at the White House, Charlie Ross announced *de facto* recognition by the United States of Israel, as it was to be called.

The American delegation at the United Nations was flabbergasted. Some American delegates actually broke into laughter, thinking the announcement must be somebody's idea of a joke. Ambassador Austin, the only one of the delegation who had been notified in advance and only at the last moment, was so upset he went home without telling any of the others.

At the State Department, meantime, Marshall had dispatched his head of U.N. affairs, Dean Rusk, by plane to New York to keep the whole delegation from resigning.

There was dancing in the streets in Brooklyn and the Bronx, a huge "salute-to-Israel" rally at the Polo Grounds. In synagogues across the country thanksgiving services were held. At 2210 Massachusetts Avenue in Washington, headquarters of the Jewish Agency, a new flag was unfurled—pale blue and white, with a star of David in the center.

In Kansas City, Eddie Jacobson packed his bags and left immediately by plane for New York to see Chaim Weizmann, who was to be the new President of Israel. Three days later, on May 17, Jacobson presented himself at the White House as Israel's "temporary, unofficial ambassador."

It would be pointed out as time went on that the United States had granted only *de facto* recognition of the new Jewish state, whereas the

Soviet Union followed with a more formal *de jure* recognition; that Truman in succeeding months, as Israel was under attack by Arab armies, refused to lift an American embargo on arms shipments to Israel; and that in the United Nations, through that summer and fall, the United States strongly supported a policy of mediation and compromise that the Israelis opposed. But such observations failed to diminish the larger symbolic force and importance of what Truman had done: it was the President of the United States of America who had granted the world's first recognition of the new Jewish nation. And while experienced observers, including most of his own experts on foreign affairs, considered much of his performance a sorry spectacle of mismanagement—"a comic opera performance," *Time* magazine said—there was immense approval in the country. An editorial in the Washington *Star* expressed well what most Americans felt:

> There is a great deal to be said against the past gyrations and topsy-turvy handling of American policy regarding Palestine. But that aspect of the situation is completely overshadowed at the moment . . . by the swift and dramatic decision of the United States to take the lead among all nations in recognizing the new Jewish State of Israel. It is a wise decision and a heartening one. . . .

As the popular radio commentator and world traveler Lowell Thomas said in his broadcast that evening, Americans in every part of the country would be turning to the Bible for some historical background for "this day of history."

Truman had no regrets. He had achieved what he intended and had, besides, established a point about who, after all, was in charge of American policy:

> The difficulty with many career officials in government [he would later write] is that they regard themselves as the men who really make policy and run the government. They look upon the elected officials as just temporary occupants. Every President in our history has been faced with this problem: how to prevent career men from circumventing presidential policy. . . . Some Presidents have handled this situation by setting up what amounted to a little State Department of their own. President Roosevelt did this and carried on direct communications with Churchill and Stalin. I did not feel that I wanted to follow this method, because the State Department is set up for the policy of handling foreign policy operations, and the State Department ought to take care of them. But I wanted to make it plain that the President of the United

States, and not a second or third echelon in the State Department, is responsible for making policy. . . .

He felt great satisfaction in what he had been able to do for the Jewish people, and was deeply moved by their expressions of gratitude, then and for years to come. When the Chief Rabbi of Israel, Isaac Halevi Herzog, called at the White House, he told Truman, "God put you in your mother's womb so you would be the instrument to bring the rebirth of Israel after two thousand years."

"I thought he was overdoing things," remembered David Niles, "but when I looked over at the President, tears were running down his cheeks."

Loy Henderson was removed from his job. Truman had him reassigned far from Washington and the concerns of American policy in the Middle East. He was made ambassador to India. Interestingly, Henderson would also remain a staunch admirer of Truman, considering him one of the great American presidents. "In my opinion," Henderson later said, "the morale and effectiveness of the [State] Department were never higher than during the period that Truman was President. . . . The morale of the department is usually higher when the President is a man who is not afraid to make difficult decisions and who is prepared to accept the responsibilities that flow from such decisions."

General Marshall continued in his duties as before. When some of Marshall's friends urged him to resign, Marshall allegedly replied that one did not resign because a President who had the constitutional right to make a decision made one. However, Marshall would not speak to Clark Clifford ever again.

Asked long afterward what he had thought to say to Marshall, to get him to agree at the last moment to American recognition of Israel, Robert Lovett said: "I told him that it was the President's choice."

III

The year of the birth of Israel, the year of the Republican tax cut and the Truman Balcony, would be remembered also as the year green (chlorophyll) chewing gum became a fad, the year of a new word game called "Scrabble," of tail fins on Cadillacs, and an unimaginably daring new bathing suit called the bikini, after the island where the atomic bomb tests were carried out the summer before.

The economy was booming. Profits were up. Farmers were prospering. American prosperity overall was greater than at any time in the nation's history. The net working capital of American corporations hit a new high of nearly $64 billion. For the steel, oil, and automobile industries, it was a banner year. Unemployment was below 4 percent. Nearly everyone who wanted a job had one, and though inflation continued, people were earning more actual buying power than ever before, and all this following the record year past, 1947, which, reported *Fortune* magazine, had been "the greatest productive record in the peacetime history of this or any other nation."

In London, the same summer of the 1948 national political conventions, American athletes—Bob Mathias, Harrison Dillard, Melvin Patton—swept the field in the first Olympic Games since 1936 in Berlin, winning thirty-eight medals.

It was a time of extraordinary technical and scientific achievement. A 200-inch telescope, the world's largest, was unveiled at Mount Palomar, California. Test pilot Chuck Yeager, flying a revolutionary rocket-plane, the Bell X-1, broke the sound barrier. The transistor was developed, a new antibiotic, Aureomycin, and cortisone to treat rheumatoid arthritis. A new kind of fuel, liquid hydrogen, promised, its inventor claimed, to "send men to the moon."

For evening entertainment the country was tuning in to such radio favorites as "Duffy's Tavern" and the Jack Benny Show. Radio dominated, for news and entertainment. But approximately one family out of every eight now owned a "television machine," as Truman called it, and 1948 would be remembered as the premier year for the "Camel Newsreel Theater," with John Cameron Swayze, the first nightly television news program. Also, for the first time ever, there would be television broadcasts of the political conventions, these to be held in the same city, Philadelphia, in order to make such coverage easier.

It was the year, too, of *Christina's World,* a haunting portrait by Andrew Wyeth of a crippled woman and a forsaken house on a bleak New England hill—a world bearing no relation to that of green gum and supersonic flight—that would become one of the most popular paintings ever done by an American.

The music being sung and danced to in 1948 included such hit songs as "Enjoy Yourself, It's Later Than You Think," "It's a Most Unusual Day," and a new rendition by Pee Wee Hunt of the old Kansas City favorite, "Twelfth Street Rag." Cole Porter's *Kiss Me Kate* was on Broadway, and several of the new motion pictures were some of the finest ever made— *The Treasure of Sierra Madre, The Red Shoes,* Laurence Olivier's *Hamlet.*

Among the best-selling books were Norman Mailer's *The Naked and the Dead,* Robert E. Sherwood's *Roosevelt and Hopkins,* Eisenhower's account of the war, *Crusade in Europe,* and *Sexual Behavior in the Human Male* by Alfred Kinsey, an Indiana University professor whose statistical revelations concerning male promiscuity in postwar American life caused a sensation.

In January, Mahatma Gandhi had been murdered while walking through a garden in New Delhi. In March, Czechoslovakian Foreign Minister Jan Masaryk, whose father founded Czechoslovakia as a free democracy, either jumped or was pushed to his death from a third-floor window in Prague, news that stirred grief and anger as almost nothing else had done since the end of the war. ("But let the world not misunderstand what he said, with that leap," wrote Dorothy Thompson. "He said: He who collaborates with Communism chooses slavery, treason, dishonor— or suicide.") In June would come a crisis in Berlin.

In July, one of Truman's favorite Americans, General John J. Pershing, died at age 87, and his body lay in state under the Capitol dome. Truman rode to the Capitol without police escort to pay his respects, as he said, "in my role as a Field Artillery Captain in World War I."

As time would tell, the politics of 1948 would also introduce a number of new words and expressions into common American usage—"whistle-stop," "Dixiecrat," and "red herring."

According to "scientific" polls given much attention in the press, 94 percent of the American people believed in God. According also to the polls, Harry Truman stood no chance of remaining President. "Obviously the Republican star is approaching its zenith," reported *Life,* the country's most popular magazine. Indeed, for all the change and tumult of the times, among the few accepted certainties was that it would be a Republican year, a dull campaign, and a debacle for Truman and the Democrats worse even than 1946.

Two experiences greatly influenced Truman's outlook through what remained of that spring, and on into summer and fall, giving him both courage and seemingly irrepressible confidence no matter how bleak the forecasts—and they grew steadily bleaker—or how many people deserted him—and there were to be many.

The first had happened eight years before. Nothing, no struggle, no road traveled, could ever again be so difficult or look so hopeless, he felt, as had his chances in the Senate primary of 1940, the summer he ran against Lloyd C. Stark. It was a segment of Truman's past that many political commentators and forecasters might well have studied closely in 1948.

Courage, the saying goes, is "having done it before," and in 1948 Truman knew he had done it before—against the odds, without money, without newspaper support, without the blessing of Franklin Roosevelt or any serious speculation by those supposedly in the know that he might actually wind up the winner. The persistent talk of his coming defeat in November, the tone of smug certainty in so much that was written and said, all had a very familiar ring to him.

Of greatest importance also was the more immediate experience of a much publicized "nonpolitical" tour made by rail cross-country in June, exactly as recommended in the Rowe Report. For while the two-week expedition was not without its blunders and embarrassments and seemed at times to have been a mistake, Truman found it exhilarating in a way nothing else could have been, and he returned to Washington looking and feeling as vigorous and sure of himself as at any time in his political life.

But courage and confidence, however important, would have been hardly enough without such other imponderable attributes as genuine sympathy for human feelings, humor, common sense, physical vitality— truly exceptional physical vitality for a man in his middle sixties—pride, determination, and a fundamental, unshakable Jacksonian faith in democracy, which to his mind mattered above all. Harry Truman trusted the American people. It would be said often, it sounded corny, and it was true. He loved the politician's work of "getting out among the people," loved seeing the country, loved the crowds. When local politicians came aboard the train to shake his hand, at one stop after another on this and later trips, and Truman took time for each of them, he was never just going through the motions, he genuinely liked such people, enjoyed seeing them.

As President he felt more than ever a need to see and make contact with what he called the everyday American. And he always felt better for it. On a recent evening in Washington, on one of his walks, he had decided to take a look at the mechanism that raised and lowered the middle span of the Memorial Bridge over the Potomac. Descending some iron steps, he came upon the bridge tender, eating his evening supper out of a tin bucket. Showing no surprise that the President of the United States had climbed down the catwalk and suddenly appeared before him, the man said, "You know, Mr. President, I was just thinking about you." It was a greeting Truman adored and never forgot.

In the primary summer of 1940 in Missouri, he had worked his way through small-town crowds pumping hands and saying, "I just wanted to come down and show you that I don't have horns and a tail just because I am from Jackson County." Now, across the West, the refrain, somewhat modified, was heard again: "I am coming out here so you can have a look at me and hear what I have to say, and then make up your mind as to whether you believe some of the things that have been said about your President."

His sixteen-car "Presidential Special" departed from Union Station the night of June 3, Truman traveling again in his special armor-plated car, the *Ferdinand Magellan,* and accompanied by about twenty of the White House staff, including Secret Service agents, and fifty-nine reporters and photographers, which made it a record press party.

The excuse for this "nonpolitical" tour was an invitation to receive an honorary degree and deliver a commencement address at the University of California at Berkeley, but no one took the nonpolitical claim seriously, least of all Truman, who began with his first brief stop at noon the next day, June 4, at Crestline, Ohio. "On this nonpartisan, bipartisan trip that we are taking here," he said to the obvious enjoyment of the crowd, "I understand there are a whole lot of Democrats present. . . ."

The principal reason for declaring it an official presidential trip was that the Democratic Committee had no money. The cost was thus charged to the President's annual travel fund, to the outrage of leading Republicans and much of the press.

What surprised everyone on board, and pleased Truman exceedingly, was the size of the crowds that turned out—1,000 people at little Crestline, 100,000 at Chicago, where he rode to the Palmer House in an open car.

At Omaha, an embarrassing foul-up caused by his old friend Eddie McKim produced much adverse publicity. Fewer than two thousand people attended a major speech, sitting down front in the huge Ak-Sar-Ben (Nebraska spelled backward) Auditorium, leaving eight thousand freshly polished, empty seats stretching behind. McKim, in charge of arrangements, had neglected to publicize the fact that the speech was open to the public and not just to Truman's old war outfit, the 35th Division, which was holding its reunion in Omaha. It was a stupid blunder. Photographs of the nearly vacant hall appeared all over the country, as a show not only of Truman's pathetically low popularity but of obvious political ineptitude. Yet Truman did not seem to mind. He went on stage as if speaking to a packed house. Nor did he blame or criticize McKim. "I don't give a damn whether there's nobody there but you and me," McKim would always remember him saying. "I am making a speech on the radio to the farmers. They won't be there—they'll be home listening to that radio. They're the ones I'm going to talk to."

Far more important to Truman, a better measure than the rows of empty chairs that night, was the welcome he had received in the streets of Omaha earlier the same day, when marching with the 35th Division. Wearing a light tan double-breasted gabardine suit and his favorite two-tone summer shoes, he stepped along at the head of his own Battery D, doffing a western-style hat right and left. He looked as happy as a man could be and the enormous crowd responded wholeheartedly—in Omaha, a Republican town. As Edward T. Folliard reported in the Washington *Post,* "They lined the streets in this Republican stronghold, 160,000 of them, and gave President Truman a welcome reminiscent of his 'honeymoon' days in the White House three years ago." Frank Spina, Truman's old barber, marched beside him, carrying the original Battery D guidon. Behind came Eddie Jacobson, Monsignor Tiernan, Eddie McKim, and Jim Pendergast.

> The onlookers were thrilled and charmed. Mr. Truman, sensing their friendliness, never looked more pleased [said the Omaha *Morning World Herald*].
> President Truman was at his best Saturday morning. . . . He marched jauntily, shoulders back. He smiled and waved his hat. Those watching the parade, astonished to see the President walking on the streets of Omaha, laughed and cheered.

In April, in a conversation in his office with Arthur Krock, in answer to Krock's question whether he detected any change in his own makeup since becoming President, Truman had said he could think of nothing, except a growing sense of being "walled-in." Now away from Washington, back among his own kind of people, people who would naturally laugh and cheer to see him walking their streets, he felt both free from the walls and much more himself. "The President, you know, is virtually in jail," he had told the crowd by the tracks at his first stop at Crestline. "He goes from his study to his office and from his office to his study, and he has to have guards there all the time . . . but when you go out and see people and find out what people are thinking about, you can do a better job. . . ." Now, again and again, he let his audiences know how much being with them was doing for him, how much it meant to him to see them, how buoyed up he felt by their numbers. "It almost overwhelms me to see all the people in western Nebraska in this town today," he said at little Sidney at the western end of the state, and he was "certainly happy to see this enthusiastic crowd!" at Laramie, Wyoming. "My goodness!" he exclaimed looking over the turnout at Dillon, Montana.

At Butte, a cheering throng lined the sidewalks several deep beside a four-mile parade route. When his train pulled into Missoula late at night and a crowd waited, hoping to catch a glimpse of him, he appeared in his pajamas and bathrobe. "I am sorry I had gone to bed," he said. "But I thought you would like to see what I look like, even if I didn't have on any clothes."

He was folksy—he just wanted to say "Howdy"—and often corny—he was on his way "down to Berkeley to get me a degree"—and the crowds grew steadily bigger.

> They told me at a little town in Idaho at 5:15 A.M. the whole town was out [he wrote to Mary Jane]. I wasn't up. At Pocatello, Id. at 7:15 there were 2000 people and at Ketchum, the P.O. for this place, everybody in the county was there.

There was another widely reported gaffe at Carey, a little town in southern Idaho. Dedicating the new Willa Coates Airport, Truman began to praise the brave boy who had died for his country, only to be informed by a tearful Mrs. Coates that "our Willa" was a girl and that she had died in a civilian plane crash.

Charlie Ross and Clark Clifford had been urging Truman to speak extemporaneously as much as possible, certain that with practice he could become as effective in front of a crowd as they had seen him be so often with small groups in his office. If only the public could know the Harry Truman he knew, Ross often said. In April Truman had spoken off-the-cuff to the American Society of Newspaper Editors, in May to a rally of Young Democrats in Washington, and both times with notable success. The press had commented favorably on "the new Truman." But at times now things he said made his staff cringe. "I have been in politics a long time, and it makes no difference what they say about you, if it isn't so," he declared unexpectedly at Pocatello. "If they can prove it on you, you are in a bad fix indeed. They have never been able to prove it on me."

Reporters on board began singing a many-versed song that included the refrain:

> *They can't prove nothing;*
> *They ain't got a thing on me.*
> *I'm going down to Berkeley*
> *For to get me a degree.*

Editorials in the East deplored the carnival air of the trip. The President, said the Washington *Evening Star,* was making "a spectacle of himself."

At Eugene, Oregon, recalling his meeting with Stalin at Potsdam, Truman suddenly confided to the crowd gathered about the rear platform of his car: "I like old Joe! He is a decent fellow." The remark sent reporters scrambling and caused an immediate sensation. From the State Department, Robert Lovett put through an urgent call to Clifford, who tactfully advised the President not to repeat the remark ever again. And Truman never did. "Well, I guess I goofed," he said, as he rolled on in good spirits.

Crossing into Washington, he made stops at Spokane, Ephrata, Wenatchee, Skykomish, Everett, Bremerton, Seattle, Tacoma, and Olympia. At Spokane, he judged, there were "about two acres of people." At Seattle more than 100,000 people turned out, the largest crowds seen in Seattle in thirty years. Not even Franklin Roosevelt had been given such a reception.

By now a decided pattern had begun to emerge in the speeches, a free-swinging style with Congress the main target.

"You know, this Congress is interested in the welfare of the better classes. They are not interested in the welfare of the common everyday man," he said at Bremerton.

"Pour it on, Harry!" someone shouted.

"I'm going to, I'm going to," Truman responded happily.

"Educate yourselves," he told his audience at Olympia. "You don't want to do like you did in 1946. Two-thirds of you stayed at home in 1946, and look what a Congress we got! That is your fault, that is your fault."

A remark to a reporter that the 80th Congress was the worst in history produced immediate howls of outrage from Republicans in Washington. Harry Truman, said House Majority Leader Charles Halleck, was the worst President in history, while Representative Cliff Clevenger of Ohio called him a "nasty little gamin" and a "Missouri jackass." Speaking in Philadelphia, Senator Taft deplored the spectacle of an American President "blackguarding Congress at whistle stops across the country," and Democratic Party Chairman Howard McGrath and his publicity director, Jack Redding, immediately saw an opportunity too good to miss. Telegrams went out to the mayors of thirty-five western towns and cities on Truman's route to ask if they agreed with Senator Taft's description of their community as a whistle-stop. "Must have the wrong city," responded the mayor of Eugene, Oregon. "Grand Isle was never a whistle-stop," came a reply from Nebraska.

In his commencement address at Berkeley, which was carried on a nationwide radio broadcast, Truman turned to foreign affairs and delivered one of the finest, most thoughtful speeches of his presidency. The

627

setting was the University of California's huge, sun-drenched football stadium, with fully 55,000 people present, twice the usual attendance at such
ceremonies.

The world, said Truman, was in a twilight time between a war so dearly
won and "a peace that still eludes our grasp." The chief cause of unrest
was the Soviet Union. The great divide was not between the United States
and the Soviet Union, but between the Soviet Union and all the free
nations of the world. The refusal of the Soviet Union to work with its
wartime Allies for world recovery and world peace was "the most bitter
disappointment of our time."

Different economic systems could live side by side and in peace, he
said, but only providing one side was not bent on destroying the other
by force.

> Our policy will continue to be a policy of recovery, reconstruction,
> prosperity—and peace with freedom and justice. In its furtherance, we
> gladly join with all those of like purpose.
>
> The only expansion we are interested in is the expansion of human
> freedom and the wider enjoyment of the good things of the earth in all
> countries.
>
> The only prize we covet is the respect and good will of our fellow
> members of the family of nations.
>
> The only realm in which we aspire to eminence exists in the minds
> of men, where authority is exercised through the qualities of sincerity,
> compassion and right conduct. . . .
>
> I believe the men and women of every part of the globe intensely
> desire peace and freedom. I believe good people everywhere will not
> permit their rulers, no matter how powerful they may have made them-
> selves, to lead them to destruction. America has faith in people. It
> knows that rulers rise and fall, but that the people live on.

Two days later, on June 14, at Los Angeles, an estimated 1 million
people packed both sides of his parade route from the railroad station to
the Ambassador Hotel. "They clung to the roofs of buildings, jammed
windows and fire escapes and crowded five deep along the sidewalk,"
reported the Los Angeles *Times*. It was the first visit to the city by a
President in thirteen years.

Los Angeles, said Truman with a grin that night at the Press Club, was
quite a whistle-stop. Stepping up the attack on Congress, he called for
action on price controls, housing, farm support, health insurance, and a
broader base for Social Security. Only that morning he had vetoed a
Republican bill that would have taken 750,000 people off Social Security.

Schools were overcrowded, he said, teachers underpaid. A bill for aid to education had passed the Senate and would take only ten minutes for the House to pass, but the House was "roosting on it," he said. "No action! No action!"

The one issue passed over, in this and other speeches along the way, was civil rights. Truman's advisers were divided over which would help him more, saying nothing about it for now, or speaking out. Truman had decided to say nothing for the time being.

When a smiling Jimmy Roosevelt turned up at the Ambassador Hotel for a private conference, and stood towering over Truman as they shook hands, Truman jabbed his forefinger into Roosevelt's chest, and according to the only witness to the scene, Secret Service Agent Henry Nicholson, said to him, "Your father asked me to take this job. I didn't want it . . . and if your father knew what you are doing to me, he would turn over in his grave. But get this straight: whether you like it or not, I am going to be the next President of the United States. That will be all. Good day."

Turning east, the train crossed Arizona, New Mexico, and Kansas, with stops the whole way, then on into Missouri, Indiana, Pennsylvania, and Maryland. The crowds continued large and friendly. "Are the special privilege boys going to run the country, or are the people going to run it?" he asked. This was the theme. The election, he was sure, would ride on it.

He covered 9,505 miles through 18 states, delivered 73 speeches, and was seen by perhaps 3 million people. The train reached Union Station on a steamy Washington afternoon, Friday, June 18. Truman, his sunburned nose peeling, his lips cracked, was, as reported, "full of bounce."

From the first day of the 1948 Republican National Convention, when former Congresswoman Clare Boothe Luce told the cheering, amused crowd that Harry Truman was a "gone goose," to the final celebration on the convention floor, there was never anything but a feeling of victory in the air.

The convention opened in Philadelphia on Monday, June 21. Of the five most publicized contenders for first place on the Republican ticket—Dewey, Taft, Vandenberg, Stassen, and Martin—Dewey, the favorite of the party's eastern liberal wing, showed almost overriding strength from the start and won on the third ballot, after Stassen refused to release his delegates to Taft. For his running mate, Dewey chose Governor Earl Warren of California, making it a "dreamboat of a ticket"—two popular, youthful, progressive governors of the two largest, wealthiest states in the Union. If Dewey seemed overly cool and self-assured in manner, Warren had more than compensating warmth. Nor had anyone forgotten how close Dewey had come the last time to defeating the Champion, Franklin Roosevelt. *Time* and *Newsweek* agreed that only a miracle or a series of unimaginable political blunders could save Harry Truman from overwhelming defeat.

Truman thought the Republicans had made a mistake. They would have been better off with Taft, he said privately; Taft was an honorable man who deserved the nomination and would have made a tougher opponent than Dewey.

In his acceptance speech, Dewey talked of national unity. "Our people yearn to higher ground, to find common purpose in the finer things which unite us . . ."

Truman had little time to dwell on the Republicans and their convention. On the day Dewey was chosen, Thursday, June 24, 1948, the Russians clamped a blockade on all rail, highway, and water traffic in and out of Berlin. The situation was extremely dangerous. Clearly Stalin was attempting to force the Western Allies to withdraw from the city. Except by air, the Allied sectors were entirely cut off. Nothing could come in or out. Two and a half million people faced starvation. As it was, stocks of food would last no more than a month. Coal supplies would be gone in six weeks.

Truman faced the issue with notable caution and firmness. It was suggested that the Allies force their way into Berlin by land, with an armored convoy. It was suggested that the United States retaliate by closing its ports and the Panama Canal to Russian ships. Truman rejected such ideas. When, at a meeting in his office with Forrestal, Lovett, and Secretary of the Army Royall, the question was asked whether American forces would remain in Berlin, Truman said there was no need for discussion on that: "We stay in Berlin, period."

Royall asked skeptically if the consequences had been thought through.

"We will have to deal with the situation as it develops," Truman said. "We are in Berlin by the terms of the agreement, and the Russians have no right to get us out by either direct or indirect pressure."

Lovett cabled the American ambassador in London that night: "We stay in Berlin."

General Clay, the American commander in Berlin, had already begun shipping supplies by air, on a very limited scale, a step considered little more than a palliative. On Monday, June 28, Truman ordered a full-scale airlift.

The same day he sent two squadrons of B-29s to Germany, the giant planes known to the world as the kind that dropped the atomic bombs on Japan. But in fact, these had not been modified to carry atomic bombs, a detail the Russians were not to know.

That the Berlin Airlift was about to become one of the most brilliant American achievements of the postwar era and one of Truman's proudest decisions, strongly affecting the morale of Western, non-Communist Europe, and the whole course of the Cold War, as well as Truman's own drive for reelection, was by no means apparent to anyone at this point. No one had any idea how things would turn out in Berlin, and Truman was no exception. General Bradley, who had replaced Eisenhower as Chief of Staff, thought the President was being far too vague, when, as Bradley later wrote, "we were nose to nose with massive Soviet military power." It hardly seemed realistic to expect a major city to be supplied entirely by air for any but a very limited time.

In making his decision, for all the political heat and turmoil of the moment, Truman had consulted none of the White House staff or any of his political advisers. Indeed, throughout the blockade, as George Elsey would recall, the White House staff "had no direct role whatever in any decisions or in the execution of any of the carrying out of the airlift." There was no talk of how the President's handling of the crisis would make him look, or what political advantage was to be gained. And neither did Truman try to bolster the spirits of those around him by claiming the airlift would work. He simply emphasized his intention to stay in Berlin and left no doubt that he meant exactly what he said.

Summer had arrived in Washington and that same evening, Monday, June 28, the President and the First Lady took their dinner on the South Porch of the White House, Truman seated so he could enjoy the view. A scrap of paper on which he recorded the scene would later be found among his papers:

> A ball game or two goes on in the park south of the lawn. Evidently a lot of competition, from the cheers and calls of the coaches. A robin hops around looking for worms, finds one and pulls with all his might to unearth him. A mockingbird imitates robin, jays, redbirds, crows, hawks—but has no individual note of his own. A lot of people like that. Planes take off and land at National Airport south of the Jefferson Memorial. It is a lovely evening. . . .

In imagination he pictured the old Chesapeake & Ohio Canal crossing the grounds of the Washington Monument, as it had long ago, barges anchored somewhere west of the Monument.

"I can see old J. Q. Adams going swimming in it and getting his clothes stolen by an angry woman who wanted a job," he wrote. "Then I wake up, go upstairs and go to work. . . ."

As Churchill had observed at Potsdam, Truman was a man of immense determination. "Stubborn as a mule," others often commented. And in nothing that Truman or anyone else wrote or said as 1948 unfolded is there any indication that once having made up his mind to run for reelection he was ever tempted to withdraw, or like the mockingbird, to sing a song not his own.

"I am not a quitter," he would say, and that was all there was to it.

Yet game as he may have been, as restored in spirit as he may have felt after his swing west, there was by all signs no cause for hope among Democrats. On the eve of the Democratic National Convention, his prospects could not have appeared much more grim. It was not just that he faced a strong, heavily financed, supremely confident Republican opponent, or the threat of the Wallace movement cutting away at his support among liberals. The whole Democratic Party, the famous, disparate Democratic "coalition" of labor, intellectuals, city bosses, and southern segregationists fabricated by Franklin Roosevelt, was coming to pieces. Harold Ickes, as if to settle old scores with Truman, wrote to tell him:

> You have the choice of retiring voluntarily and with dignity, or of being driven out of office by a disillusioned and indignant citizenry. Have you ever seen the ice on the pond suddenly break in every conceivable direction under the rays of a warming sun? This is what has happened to the Democratic Party under you, except that your party has not responded to bright sunshine. It has broken up spontaneously.

The biggest break came now from Ickes's own liberal side of the party, the doctrinaire New Dealers. The call for Eisenhower started by Roosevelt's sons had swelled to a chorus, with Claude Pepper, Chester Bowles, former head of the Office of Price Administration, who was now running for governor of Connecticut, Mayor Hubert Humphrey of Minneapolis, who was running for the Senate, all favoring an Eisenhower draft at the convention. The Americans for Democratic Action, the ADA, recently formed as a non-Communist liberal response to the Wallace movement and sometimes known as the "New Deal in Exile," voiced its preference for Eisenhower over Truman, and if not Eisenhower, then Justice William O. Douglas. Such professional Democrats as Jake Arvey of Chicago, Mayor William O'Dwyer of New York, and Boss Frank Hague of New Jersey also decided it was time for Eisenhower. Walter Reuther of the United Auto Workers and Phil Murray of the CIO joined the Eisenhower movement. And so did Alabama Senators Hill and Sparkman and South Carolina Governor Strom Thurmond, making it appear almost as though the old Roosevelt coalition were regrouping around the glamorous general, who by this time had become president of Columbia University.

And all this was made more remarkable by the fact that no one knew anything of Eisenhower's politics. No one could say even whether he was a Democrat, let alone what his position on issues might be—on civil rights, Social Security, taxes. Or how to keep peace with Stalin.

To Truman and those loyal to him, the revolt of the old New Dealers was especially grating. It seemed besides an act of personal betrayal, wholly unprincipled and intellectually dishonest. Truman had borne the banner of the New Deal as faithfully as any successor to Franklin Roosevelt possibly could have, was their feeling. No more progressive program had ever been put before Congress than the Truman program. That was a matter of record.

Though Eisenhower had stated publicly several times that he was not a candidate and did not want the nomination, this did little to dissuade his new admirers. Over the Fourth of July weekend, a week in advance of the Democratic Convention, the Eisenhower faction, led by Jimmy Roosevelt, wired each of the 1,592 delegates to choose the "ablest, strongest man available" as their candidate, adding that "no man in these critical days can refuse the call to duty and leadership implicit in the nomination and virtual election to the Presidency of the United States."

Truman, concluded the veteran *New York Times* political reporter James C. Hagerty, could look forward to "a hard and possibly losing fight for the nomination. . . ."

In six months he had faced some of the roughest abuse and difficulties of any President in history. He had been castigated by southern Democrats over civil rights, repudiated by a Republican Congress, ridiculed for his White House balcony and his Missouri cronies. He had faced the pressures of the Palestine issue, the increasing threat of war over Berlin, watched his popularity disintegrate in the polls, seen himself portrayed in the press as inept and pathetic. His party was broke. And now the New Dealers were abandoning him, and noisily. No President in memory, not even Herbert Hoover in his darkest days, had been treated with such open contempt by his own party.

"If you can't stand the heat, you better get out of the kitchen," Truman liked to say, an old line in Missouri that he had first heard in the 1930s, from another Jackson County politician named E. T. ("Buck") Purcell.

To a few former New Dealers the whole spectacle was appalling. "I am simply aghast at the unfair way in which President Truman is being 'judged,' if the current lynch-law atmosphere can be called 'judging'!" recorded David Lilienthal in his diary. "And the attitude of liberals and progressives, now whooping it up for Eisenhower or Douglas, is the hardest to understand or to be other than damn mad about."

> Truman's *record* [continued Lilienthal on July 5] is that of a man who, facing problems that would have strained and perhaps even floored Roosevelt at his best, has met these problems head on in almost every case. The way he took on the aggression of Russia . . . his civil rights program, upon which he hasn't welched or trimmed—My God! What *do* these people want?
>
> If it is said that he wobbled on veterans' housing or Palestine or this or that, did F.D.R. never wobble? Don't be funny; F.D.R. wobbled through the Neutrality Act and Arms Embargo (isolation of the very worst and blindest kind); he wobbled on economic matters all the time . . . Did F.D.R. ever stand up for public development of power, or human rights, or labor, essentially any more firmly than Truman? And who knows what Eisenhower would do on any of these issues! Bah!
>
> It is grossly unfair. They say the people want someone else; that the people aren't for him. Well, who in the hell but the Southern extremists and the perfectionist "liberals" together have created the impression (eagerly encouraged, of course, by the reactionaries and the Republicans) that the people don't have confidence in him?
>
> That makes me mad and rather ill, these hounders of a real man.

When Matt Connelly reported the defection of Frank Hague to Truman, he merely said, "All right, let him go. I never did like him anyhow." Writing in his diary later the same day, Truman would describe Hague, Jimmy Roosevelt, Jake Arvey, and the ADA as "double-crossers all," adding, "But they'll get nowhere—a double dealer never does." The Democratic leaders opposing his nomination were all acting very foolishly. He was certain Eisenhower was not a candidate, perhaps not even a Democrat. "I don't think he would be a candidate on the Democratic ticket anyway," he wrote to a friend. The influence of a sitting President—as leader of his party—was too great to be thwarted. Not even Theodore Roosevelt with all his popularity had been able to deny the Republican nomination to the incumbent Taft in 1912, he reminded his staff.

Did he think he would have enough pledged delegates to win on the first ballot at Philadelphia, Truman was asked at his press conference on July 1.

"Sure," he said.

· · ·

But he may not have been so sanguine as professed—not according to a story later recounted by Arthur Krock, whose source apparently was Kenneth Royall.

At a "bull session" over drinks among some half-dozen administration figures on the South Portico of the White House one evening shortly before the convention, Truman asked what they all thought would happen were Eisenhower's name put in nomination. Claude Pepper, already in Philadelphia, had proposed that the convention draft Eisenhower as a "national" rather than a party candidate. Everyone but Royall assured the President he would make short shrift of any such attempt. Truman, noticing Royall's silence, asked for his view. Ike would be nominated by acclamation, Royall said, causing a furor among the others. Truman said nothing, but afterward, at the White House door, an usher told Royall the President wished to see him upstairs. He found Truman in the Oval Study with John Snyder.

"I wanted to tell you," Truman said, "that I agree with you."

Then, according to the story, Truman asked how the presentation of Ike's name could be prevented, and Royall, assuring Truman that the general, too, had the same objective, agreed to see what he could do. "In a telephone conference with Ike," wrote Arthur Krock, "Royall worked out the statement that Eisenhower sent to Pepper and others that put an end to the effort to present his name."

On Friday, July 9, Eisenhower again said no, his refusal this time "final and complete," and "no matter under what terms." On reading the Eisenhower telegram, Boss Hague reportedly crunched out his cigar, saying, "Truman, Harry Truman. Oh my God!"

Claude Pepper, refusing to give up, declared it "no time for politics as usual" and announced he would run himself. His candidacy lasted a day.

Clark Clifford slipped in and out of Philadelphia to pass the word that the President had telephoned William O. Douglas, who was on vacation in Oregon's Wallowa Mountains. Douglas was Truman's choice for Vice President. He would give the ticket geographical balance. He was youthful, strong on civil rights, a solid New Dealer. Douglas only wanted time to consider.

Clifford was in the thick of things as usual, but more out of devotion to Truman than any high expectations. "None of us," he later admitted, "really felt at the time that the nomination meant very much. Our aim was just to get the President nominated. Because it would have been an unconscionable reflection on him, if after four years, the party had turned him down and gone to somebody else."

•   •   •

Though the Eisenhower boom had passed, it had been a measure of how intensely fearful Democrats had become of a debacle in November. It was not just that Harry Truman would fail to be reelected, but that he would pull everyone down with him. After sixteen years with the all-time winner, FDR, as their standardbearer, they now faced the prospect of a certain loser. And if there was anyone left banking on a revival of party spirit, once everybody was gathered in Philadelphia, the illusion was quickly disabused. The newly arrived delegates who wandered through the city's empty Sabbath streets on July 10, the day before the opening gavel, looked, it was reported, like nothing so much as mourners at a funeral.

"We got the wrong rigs for this convention," a cab driver was quoted. "They shoulda given us hearses."

Attendance was below expectations. Hotels that had been booked solid, their lobbies a continuous hubbub during the Republican Convention just weeks before, were receiving cancelations. Bunting and flags left over from the Republican affair looked pathetically shopworn.

"You could cut the gloom with a corn knife," remembered Alben Barkley. "The very air smelled of defeat."

The crowd expected for the opening day at Convention Hall failed to materialize. The galleries were largely empty. Delegates down on the floor milled about during the speeches, or shifted restlessly in their seats, fanning themselves furiously in the almost unbearable heat, for though the auditorium had been refurbished at great expense for this and the Republican Convention, there was no air conditioning and the big television lights, in combination with Philadelphia's oppressive summer weather, had made the place a steambath. The temperature at the rostrum was 93 degrees.

It was the presence and paraphernalia of television, the lights, cables, wires, microphones, amplifiers, cameras, the swarms of technicians, and the theatrics involved, that gave the event what novelty and interest it had. For many who attended, television would be the best-remembered part of the 1948 Democratic Convention.

Everything possible had been done to make the "political show" come off, and like their Republican counterparts, one Democrat after another now submitted to pancake makeup and eye shadow before going to the rostrum or in preparation for a "candid" off-the-floor interview. Several women addressed the convention wearing brown lipstick, because they were told it would look better on the black-and-white home screens. Reporters in the press gallery wore dark glasses in order to work in the fierce glare of the lights.

At the White House, arrangements had been made for Truman to watch as much or as little of the proceedings as he wished. A new console type DuMont television set with a 12-inch screen had been brought into his office and positioned against the wall to his left. So, in somewhat fuzzy black-and-white images, he would follow the proceedings right from his chair, like no President ever before. When television cameras were set up in the press room for the first time on the afternoon of the 12th, for an NBC broadcast of a half-hour discussion with several White House correspondents, Truman and his staff gathered about the new set to watch.

William O. Douglas had by now decided to refuse second place on the ticket, for the reason, he told Truman, that he wished to remain on the Supreme Court. Truman was deeply hurt. "I stuck my neck all the way out for Douglas and he cut the limb out from under me," he remarked to his staff. Reportedly Douglas had told others he did not want to be number two man to a number two man.

From the podium at Philadelphia that night, in a rousing keynote address, Alben Barkley brought the convention to life for the first time. The band played "My Old Kentucky Home." Delegates cheered and stomped. It was a speech made for the occasion, as the old warhorse politician, an orator of the old school and a sentimental, favorite Democrat who had been born in a log cabin, evoked the past glories of the New Deal and heaped unmerciful scorn on the opposition. And it was a speech, not incidentally, made for television. Truman, watching at the White House, was nearly as pleased as the crowd at Convention Hall.

Dewey, in his acceptance speech, had vowed to clean the cobwebs from Washington. Barkley, with perspiration pouring from his brow and nose, declared he was not an expert on cobwebs. "But if memory does not betray me, when the Democratic Party took over the government sixteen years ago, even the spiders were so weak from starvation that they could not weave a cobweb in any department of the government in Washington."

For the first time it seemed a real convention. Barkley was a hero and a favorite for second place on the ticket. There was even talk of Barkley for President.

Yet Barkley had never said a word about victory in November and mentioned Truman only once in a speech lasting more than an hour. Truman, as much as he had enjoyed the performance, commented that Barkley had all the markings of a man trying for the presidency.

Howard McGrath called from Philadelphia to find out if the President had seen the speech and to say it had put Barkley "out in front" for the nomination for Vice President. If Barkley was what the convention wanted, Truman said, then Barkley was his choice, too.

He tried to reach Barkley by phone that night, but Barkley had gone to bed.

Until now Truman had felt he needed someone like Douglas, a strong liberal, to run with him, and preferably someone younger than he. Barkley was neither. At seventy-one, he was seven years older than Truman, and coming from Kentucky, he would bring no geographical balance to the ticket. The contrast with the Republican ticket could be damaging.

But by phone the next morning Truman asked Barkley why he had never told him he wanted to be Vice President.

"I didn't know you wanted the nomination," Truman said.

"Mr. President, you do not know it yet," Barkley answered.

"Well, if I had known you wanted it, I certainly would have been agreeable," Truman said, which though hardly a ringing confirmation was sufficient for both to consider the decision settled, and almost immediately afterward in Philadelphia, McGrath told reporters that if the convention saw fit to nominate Senator Barkley for Vice President, the President would be "most happy." (Barkley, who had been available as a vice-presidential choice at every convention since 1928, told friends that if the nomination were to be his, he wanted it quickly. "I don't want it passed around so long it is like cold biscuit.")

As it was, Truman showed more distress over the Douglas refusal than enthusiasm over Barkley. To his staff, he seemed oddly, almost irresponsibly disinterested in the whole matter. He, if anyone, should have appreciated the potential importance of the decision. Yet there was no sign of thoughtful deliberation on his part. "Talking about the vice-presidency," wrote Eben Ayers, "the President said he never did care much who was nominated with him."

Excitement over Barkley was quickly eclipsed as a floor fight broke out over civil rights.

"A Negro alternate from St. Louis makes a minority report suggesting the unseating of the Mississippi delegation," Truman recorded, as he watched the drama unfold on the tiny black-and-white screen. "Vaughan is his name. He's overruled. Then Congressman Dawson of Chicago, another Negro, makes an excellent talk on civil rights. These two colored men are the only speakers to date who seem to be for me wholeheartedly."

The following day, Wednesday, July 14, the day scheduled for Truman's nomination and acceptance speech, the uproar over civil rights turned angry, as a vehement ADA faction headed by Mayor Hubert Humphrey demanded a stronger civil rights plank in the party platform. The existing plank was substantially what it had been in the 1944 platform—mild and ambiguous enough to mollify the southern delegations—and the wording had been agreed to at the White House, Truman and his advisers having decided now was no time to alienate the southerners. Humphrey was warned he would split the party and ruin his own career if he persisted.

But Humphrey and his forces held out for a plank that would emphatically endorse Truman's own civil rights program, item by item—anti-poll tax and anti-lynching legislation, fair employment laws, an end to segregation in the armed services. In bitter, heated sessions of the platform committee on the top floor of the Bellevue-Stratford, Humphrey charged that the administration plank was a "sellout" to states' rights over human rights. When the committee approved the moderate plank, the Humphrey forces took the fight to the convention floor. "We were inherently stronger than Truman's followers had believed," remembered one of them, Paul Douglas, a candidate for the Senate in Illinois.

As the majority report of the platform committee was being read before the convention and Humphrey sat near the rostrum waiting his turn to speak, Boss Ed Flynn beckoned Humphrey to show him the minority report, and having looked it over, Flynn said, "Young man, that's just what this party needs."

Unlike Jake Arvey and Frank Hague, Flynn had thought the whole Eisenhower idea silly, and that those who imagined otherwise were hacks and amateurs, blind to his own favorite political maxim: "Never confuse wishes with facts." There was no question that Harry Truman would be nominated, Flynn had been saying, and he wanted to see Harry Truman win.

Humphrey stepped to the podium, his face shining, the audience suddenly hushed. He spoke less than ten minutes and he made history. It was time for the Democratic Party to move forward. "There are those who say to you—we are rushing this issue of civil rights. I say we are a hundred and seventy-two years late. . . . The time has arrived for the Democratic Party to get out of the shadow of states' rights and walk forthrightly into the bright sunshine of human rights."

As the convention roared its approval, the California and Illinois delegations marched into the aisles. Others followed, joined by a forty-piece band led by James C. Petrillo, head of the American Federation of Musicians, while here and there glum, silent southern delegations kept their seats. At the podium Sam Rayburn of Texas, permanent chairman of the convention, looked down disapprovingly, fearing a southern "walkout" would destroy whatever slim chance Truman might have in November and devastate the party, possibly forever. Rayburn tried to stall a vote, but when it came the Humphrey forces won a resounding victory.

Told the Alabama delegation intended to lead a walkout that night, on the final roll call, Rayburn ordered a voice vote instead and the convention again thundered its approval.

At the White House, angered by the turn events were taking, Truman spoke of Humphrey and his followers as "crackpots" who hoped the South would bolt. But the fact was the convention that seemed so pathetically bogged down in its own gloom had now, suddenly, dramatically, pushed through the first unequivocal civil rights plank in the party's history; and whether Truman and his people appreciated it or not, Hubert Humphrey had done more to reelect Truman than would anyone at the convention other than Truman himself.

There were television cameras at Union Station for the President's departure that evening and there would be more cameras at the Philadelphia station when he arrived. "No privacy sure enough now," he wrote, though he remained calm and composed. He had a surprise for the convention and he knew what the effect would be. On their home screens, those still relatively few Americans who owned television sets in 1948 saw him sitting quietly at the window of his private railroad car waiting to leave the station.

The First Lady, Margaret, Charlie Ross, Clifford, Elsey, Ayers, Connelly, and Sam Rosenman were on board with him, and had dinner en route, while Truman kept to himself in his room going over his notes. It was by radio, approximately halfway to Philadelphia, that he heard the Alabama delegation and part of the Mississippi delegation stage their walkout. "Hard to hear," he noted. "My daughter and my staff try to keep me from listening. Think maybe I'll be upset. I won't be."

At Philadelphia, where a fine rain was falling, he stepped from the train at 9:15, looking relaxed and spotless in a white linen suit. From the station he was driven directly to the convention hall, now packed to capacity, the crowd noisy and full of anticipation—and suffering intensely from the heat, suit jackets long since discarded, ties and collars undone, shirts stained dark with perspiration.

The seconding speeches had begun and as they dragged on, Truman was kept out of sight, first in McGrath's so-called "office," a stifling room with no windows, then in the somewhat cooler air on an outdoor ramp near the stage entrance, overlooking an alley and the railroad tracks. He was joined by Alben Barkley and together they sat chatting side by side hour after hour, Truman in a straight-backed wooden chair, Barkley in a more accommodating red leather armchair that someone had borrowed from the speaker's platform.

To many who had attended other national conventions over the years, this one was as bungled, as badly managed as any in memory—*Newsweek* called it the worst-managed, most dispirited convention in American political annals—and the idea that a President of the United States had to wait his turn as Truman did, under such conditions, seemed the final straw. The scene would be portrayed in some accounts as one of the extreme low points of Truman's career. However, neither Truman nor Barkley saw it that way. Barkley would remember having "a very agreeable visit," during which they talked about "many things: politics, trivia, how to bring up daughters. . . ." To Truman, too, it was "an interesting and instructive evening," as he recorded in his diary. Tom Evans, remembering the "hot, horrible night," would describe Truman sitting calmly in his white suit, "and I give you my word of honor, there wasn't a wrinkle in it—he was cool . . . collected . . . it didn't seem to bother him at all."

To be a professional in politics required patience, often great patience, and the strength not to take things too personally, and Truman and Barkley were two veteran professional politicians.

"They did what you do under such circumstances," recalled George Elsey. "They waited."

Nearly four hours went by, as the seconding speeches were followed by the balloting for President. At 12:42 Truman was finally nominated, receiving 948 votes, while 263 votes went to Senator Richard Russell of Georgia, the last-minute candidate of the South. Then, by acclamation, Barkley was nominated for Vice President.

So it was nearly two o'clock in the morning when Truman and Barkley at last made their entrance, striding onto the platform as the band played "Hail to the Chief."

Considering the time, the fatigue of the crowd, it was a scene made for failure. Any radio or television audience that Truman might have hoped for was long since asleep. To make matters a little worse, the sister of a former Pennsylvania senator suddenly released a flock of white pigeons —"doves of peace" supposedly—from a floral Liberty Bell, where they had been held all night, cooped up in the heat. The distraught birds careened desperately into the air every which way, smashing into the balcony, the lights, bombarding spectators, and swooping so low over the rostrum that Chairman Rayburn had to fend off several at once, to the delight of the crowd as well as Truman and Barkley who were laughing uproariously. (Years later Truman would describe how one pigeon had actually landed on Rayburn's bald head, a claim that Rayburn, who saw nothing funny in the situation, stoutly denied, telling an interviewer, "Harry Truman's a goddamn liar. No pigeon ever lit on my head.")

Barkley spoke first, and briefly. Then came Truman's turn.

He advanced to the microphones, his natty white suit gleaming now in the full glare of the lights. And despite the hour, the heat, the discomfort and weariness of his audience, he did what no one would have thought possible. Wasting no time with pleasantries or grand phrases, his head up as he spoke without a script, his voice strong, hands chopping the air, he brought the convention immediately to its feet cheering.

"Senator Barkley and I will win this election and make these Republicans like it—don't you forget that." Not until this moment had anyone used the word "win" as though he meant it.

The Democratic Party would win in November because the Democratic Party was the people's party. The Republicans were the party of the privileged few, as always.

For the first time since 1945 he was speaking not as a leader by accident, by inheritance, but by the choice of his party. He was neither humble nor elegant nor lofty. The contrast with Dewey's stilted acceptance speech from the same platform could not have been greater. In manner as well as content he was drawing the line so there could be no mistaking one candidate for the other. Mere victory was not the purpose, Dewey had proclaimed, as if he had already been elected. "Our task," Dewey had said, "is to fill our victory with such meaning that mankind everywhere, yearning for freedom, will take heart and move forward. . . ." Truman declared: "Now it is time for us to get together and beat the common enemy." He was cracker-barrel plain, using words like "rotten" (for the Republican tax bill) and "poppycock" (for the Republican platform promise to increase Social Security benefits). *Life* magazine called it his "Li'l Abner Ozark style." It was exactly in the spirit of the vehement backcountry politics he loved, and where he knew he belonged, the tradition of Andrew Jackson and William Jennings Bryan, alive and full of fight.

He listed the gains for farmers, for labor and the poor achieved under sixteen years of Democratic leadership, and he tore into the Republican-dominated 80th Congress for holding up progress on housing, aid to education, medical care, and yes, civil rights.

Everybody knows that I recommended to the Congress the civil rights program. I did that because I believed it to be my duty under the Constitution. Some of the members of my own party disagree with me violently on this matter. But they stand up and do it openly. People can tell where they stand. But the Republicans all professed to be for these measures. But the Congress failed to act. . . .

Indeed, he said, there was a long list of promises in the new Republican platform, things of great importance that the Republicans claimed they wanted but that the Republicans who controlled Congress had prevented his administration from doing.

It was then he unveiled his surprise, his bombshell, and speaking so rapidly the words seemed to run together, as though all joined by hyphens.

I am, therefore, calling this Congress back into session July 26.

On the 26th of July, which out in Missouri we call "Turnip Day," I am going to call Congress back and ask them to pass laws to halt rising prices, to meet the housing crisis—which they are saying they are for in their platform. . . . I shall ask them to act upon . . . aid to education, which they say they are for . . . civil rights legislation, which they say they are for. . . .

The cheering and stomping in the hall was so great he had to shout to be heard.

Now, my friends, if there is any reality behind the Republican platform, we ought to get some action from a short session of the 80th Congress. They can do this job in 15 days, if they want to do it. They will still have time to go out and run for office.

He was calling the Republicans' bluff—"Let 'em make good!"—and the delegates were ecstatic. He had "set the convention on fire," said *The New York Times*. "He walked out there," remembered Clark Clifford, "and reached down within himself, found the strength and the inspiration to make that fiery speech which was necessary to put him over."

Critics on the left and the right found themselves grudgingly moved by such nerve and audacity in the face of the odds and by his effect on the crowd. "They sensed," wrote Max Lerner, "that this was the most militant Presidential acceptance speech in either party since Bryan. They liked the fact that he came out of his corner fighting. . . . It was a great speech for a great occasion, and as I listened I found myself applauding."

643

Even *The New Republic* bestowed the ultimate compliment: the speech was as "cannily suited" to the time and setting as any Franklin Roosevelt might have made. "For that night at least, Harry Truman was a real leader."

"You can't stay cold about a man who sticks out his chin and fights," *Time* reported one delegate exclaiming.

Truman was likened to the brave sea captain who rallies the crew to save the sinking ship. In fact, he was exactly like the Missouri artillery captain in the Vosges Mountains in 1918 who when his battery panicked under enemy attack stood by his guns and with a fierce harangue got his men back in order again.

The Republicans charged him with crude politics. The call for a special session of Congress was "the act of a desperate man," "the last hysterical gasp from an expiring administration."

"Of course, it was politics," wrote Jonathan Daniels, "and effective politics, tough and native."

What it did above all, as Truman intended, was to put the focus on Congress and thus on the split between those Republicans who, like Dewey and Earl Warren, favored much that had been set in motion since the 1930s by the New Deal, and those Republicans who remained obstructionists. It made the 80th Congress the issue, put the Republicans on the defense, and left Dewey with the dubious choice of either standing up for the 80th Congress, and thereby assume a share of responsibility for its failings, or remain aloof, which would seem less than courageous for a standardbearer.

As a political strategist Truman had been "devilishly astute," Speaker of the House Joe Martin later conceded. No President had called an emergency session of Congress in an election year since 1856. "On the 25th of July," went an old Missouri saying, "sow your turnips wet or dry." The Congress that met on the 26th (the 25th was a Sunday) would be known as the Turnip Congress.

"Arrived in Washington at the White House at 5:30 A.M., my usual time getting up," Truman jotted on his calendar for July 15, after the return from Philadelphia.

But go to bed at 6:00 and listen to the news. Sleep until 9:15, order breakfast and go to the office at 10:00. I called a special session of the Congress. My, how my opposition screams. I'm going to attempt to make them meet their platform promises before the election. That is according to the "kept" press and the opposition leadership "cheap politics." I wonder what "expensive politics" will be like!

In a red-brick auditorium in Birmingham, Alabama, two days later, a hurriedly assembled conference of states' rights Democrats, "Dixiecrats" as they now called themselves, waved Confederate flags and cheered Alabama's former Governor Frank M. Dixon as he denounced Truman's civil rights program as an effort "to reduce us to the status of a mongrel, inferior race," then unanimously chose Governor Strom Thurmond of South Carolina to be their candidate for President, and for Vice President, Governor Fielding L. Wright of Mississippi. The Dixiecrat platform called for "the segregation of the races and the racial integrity of each race." Their hope was to deny both Truman and Dewey a majority and thus throw the election into the House of Representatives.

Asked why he was breaking with the Democratic Party now, when Roosevelt had made similar promises as Truman on civil rights, Strom Thurmond responded, "But Truman really means it."

On July 27, once again at the Philadelphia Convention Hall, Henry Wallace's Progressive Citizens of America, with more than three thousand delegates—far more than at either the Republican or Democratic conventions—rallied to acclaim Wallace their candidate for the presidency, and Senator Glen H. Taylor, the "Singing Cowboy" of Idaho, as their improbable choice for a running mate. (Taylor, a Democrat, had campaigned for the Senate in 1944 singing, "Oh, Give Me a Home by the Capitol Dome.")

Black delegates were present in impressive numbers. Nearly a third of the delegates were women. Youth predominated. The average Progressive on hand in Philadelphia was described as twenty years younger and 30 pounds lighter than his or her Democratic or Republican counterpart. Comparably little alcohol was consumed and there were no "smoke-filled rooms" this time. But there was also a noticeable absence of political experience on hand, and though neither Wallace nor Taylor, nor any but a small minority of delegates, were Communists, the conspicuous presence of such celebrated pro-Communists as Paul Robeson and New York Congressman Vito Marcantonio, plus the obvious dominating presence of Communists throughout the whole new helter-skelter Progressive organization, was to many observers and much of the country deeply disturbing.

As he had from the start of his "crusade," Wallace refused to repudiate his Communist support. He would not repudiate any support that came to him, he said, "on the basis of interest in peace." Senator Taylor stressed the distinction between "pink" Communists and "red" Communists, telling reporters that the pink variety wished to change the American system through evolution rather than revolution, and that they would support the Progressive cause. In contrast, the red variety would be backing Dewey on the theory that revolution would inevitably follow another Hoover-style administration.

The Progressive platform that emerged from the convention was virtually no different from the Communist Party platform in its denunciation of the Marshall Plan, the Truman Doctrine, the new draft law, and called for the destruction of American nuclear weapons, which were still the only nuclear weapons known to exist. When a Vermont farmer named James Hayford introduced an amendment saying it was not the Progressive Party's intention to endorse the foreign policy of any other country, the idea was denounced as "the reflection of pressure from outside" and voted down—which Wallace knew to be a mistake but did nothing to stop.

Wallace delivered his acceptance speech at Philadelphia's Shibe Park before an exuberant crowd of more than thirty thousand people who had paid for their seats, a Progressive innovation to meet expenses. He blamed American policy for most of the world's troubles and tensions, never once criticizing the Soviet Union. Concerning Berlin, he said, there was nothing to lose by giving it up in the search for peace. "We stand against the kings of privilege who own the old parties . . . [who] attempt to control our thoughts and dominate the life of man everywhere in the world."

IV

In the stifling, relentless heat of summer in Washington, the Turnip Congress got reluctantly under way. Tension over Berlin increased almost by the hour. And to Truman's extreme annoyance, James Forrestal launched a campaign behind closed doors to turn custody of the atomic bomb over to the military chiefs.

From testimony being given before the House Un-American Activities Committee by a woman named Elizabeth Bentley and a *Time* magazine editor named Whittaker Chambers, both former Communists, it also appeared a major spy scandal was unfolding.

Visitors to the President's office found him looking tired and preoccupied. Bess and Margaret having made their annual summer departure for Missouri, he was feeling particularly alone again. "It is hot and humid and lonely," he wrote the night after putting them on the train. "Why in hell does anybody want to be a head of state? Damned if I know."

He had had no change of heart about Berlin. American forces would remain. That was his decision, he said again, meeting with Marshall and Forrestal on July 19, and he would stand by it until all diplomatic means had been tried to reach some kind of accommodation to avoid war. "We'll stay in Berlin—come what may. . . . I don't pass the buck, nor do I alibi out of any decision I make," he noted privately. He was convinced, as was Marshall, that the future of Western Europe was at stake in Berlin, not to say the well-being of the 2.5 million people in the city's Allied sectors. Stalin was obviously determined to force the Allies out of Berlin. "If we wished to remain there, we would have to make a show of strength," Truman later wrote. "But there was always the risk that Russian reaction might lead to war. We had to face the possibility that Russia might deliberately choose to make Berlin the pretext for war. . . ." The Allies had all of 6,500 troops in Berlin—3,000 American, 2,000 British, 1,500 French— while the Russians had 18,000 backed by an estimated 300,000 in the east zone of Germany.

With the airlift now in its fourth week, heavily laden American and British transports were roaring into Berlin hundreds of times a day, and in all weather. They came in low, one after another, lumbering just over the tops of the ruined buildings, as crowds gathered in clusters to watch. German children with toy planes played "airlift" in the rubble as the real drama went on overhead.

It had been General Clay's initial estimate that possibly 700 tons of food could be delivered to the beleaguered city by air in what would be a "very big operation." Already some days the tonnage was twice that and now, too, almost unimaginably, coal was arriving out of the sky by the planeload. Pilots and crew were making heroic efforts. At times planes were landing as often as every four minutes—British Yorks and Dakotas, American C-47s and the newer, much larger, four-engine C-54s, which had been dispatched to Germany from Panama, Hawaii, and Alaska. Most planes averaged three flights a day from Frankfurt to Berlin's Gatow or Templehof fields, a distance of 275 miles. Ground crews worked round the clock. "We were proud of our Air Force during the war. We're prouder of it today," said *The New York Times*. Already, three American crewmen had been killed when their C-47 crashed.

Still, the effort was not enough. On July 15, a record day, 1,450 tons were flown into Berlin. Yet to sustain the city 2,000 tons of food alone were needed every day, plus 12,000 tons of fuel and supplies. In winter, the demands for fuel would be far greater. The mayor of Berlin had said it would be impossible to provide the necessary food and coal supplies by air. "But every expert knows," reported a London paper, "that aircraft, despite their immense psychological effect, cannot be relied upon to provision Berlin in the winter months." Allied officials in Berlin worried about the increased activity of Russian Yak fighter planes in the air corridors.

Secretary of the Army Royall ordered General Clay to fly home to Washington to report to the President, which Truman thought a mistake. ("My muttonhead Secretary [of the] Army ordered Clay home from Germany and stirred up a terrific how-dy-do for no good reason," he wrote to Bess.) At a National Security Council meeting on July 22, Clay said the people of Berlin would stand firm, even if it meant further hardships. Probably the Russians would try to stop any attempt by an armed convoy to break through at this stage, but they were not likely to interfere with air traffic, unless, of course, they were determined to provoke a war. Did the Russians want war, Truman asked. Clay did not think so. No one could be sure. Truman rejected the convoy idea.

When Truman inquired what problems might result from increasing the airlift, General Hoyt Vandenberg, Air Force Chief of Staff, voiced concern that American air strength elsewhere in the world would dangerously be reduced. But that was a risk Truman would take. The airlift would be vastly increased, he decided, expressing again his "absolute determination" to stay in Berlin. More of the big C-54 transports would be sent. Clay ordered another Berlin airfield built and in response to his call, 30,000 Berliners went to work to clear the rubble and grade the runways.

"There is considerable political advantage to the Administration in its battle with the Kremlin," James Rowe had written in his effort to outline a political strategy for 1948. "In time of crisis the American citizen tends to back up his President." So by such reasoning, the Berlin crisis, if kept in bounds, was made to order for Truman. Yet in nothing he said or wrote is there a sign of his playing the situation for "political advantage." Rather, the grave responsibilities he bore as President at this juncture seem to have weighed more heavily on him than at any time since assuming office. He felt the campaign and its distractions, the drain it put on his time and strength, could not be coming at a worse time, as he told Churchill in a letter on July 10:

> I am going through a terrible political "trial by fire." Too bad it must happen at this time.
> Your country and mine are founded on the fact that the people have the right to express themselves on their leaders, no matter what the crisis. . . .

We are in the midst of grave and trying times. You can look with satisfaction upon your great contribution to the overthrow of Nazism and Fascism in the world. "Communism"—so-called—is our next great problem. I hope we can solve it without the "blood and tears" the other two cost.

Only the day before the National Security Council meeting about Berlin, on July 21, at the meeting arranged by Forrestal to discuss the custody of the atomic bomb, Truman had looked dreadful and in a moment of annoyance revealed as vividly as he ever would how much more he dwelt on the horror of the atomic bomb than most people, even those close to him, imagined, or than he wished anyone to know.

"The President greeted us rather solemnly. He looked worn and grim; none of the joviality that he sometimes exhibits, and we got right down to business," wrote David Lilienthal in his diary that night, when the whole scene and everything said were still fresh in his mind.

> It was an important session, and a kind of seriousness hung over it that wasn't relieved a bit, needless to say, by the nature of the subject and the fact that even at that moment some terrible thing might happen in Berlin. . . . I rather think it was one of the most important meetings I have ever attended.

Present besides Truman, Forrestal, and Lilienthal were the four other members of the Atomic Energy Commission, plus Secretary of the Army Royall, Secretary of the Air Force Stuart Symington, and Donald F. Carpenter, an executive of the Remington Arms Company who was chairman of the Military Liaison Committee of the National Military Establishment.

It was Carpenter who opened the discussion by reading aloud a formal letter requesting an order from the President that would turn custody of the atomic bomb over to the Joint Chiefs, on the grounds that those who would be ultimately responsible for use of the weapon should have it in their possession, to increase "familiarity" with it and to "unify" command. Truman, who did not appreciate being read to in such fashion, cut him off, saying curtly, "I can read." He turned to Lilienthal, who said the real issue was one of broad policy and that the bomb must not be the responsibility of anyone other than the President, because of his constitutional roles as both Commander in Chief and Chief Magistrate. Civilian control was essential, Lilienthal said.

But then Symington spoke, delivering an incongruously lighthearted account of a visit to Los Alamos where "our fellas" told him they should have the bomb just to be sure it worked, though one scientist had said he did not think it should ever be used.

"I don't either," Truman interjected, his face expressionless. He went on. "I don't think we ought to use this thing unless we absolutely have to. It is a terrible thing to order the use of something that . . . [and here, as Lilienthal recorded, Truman paused and looked down at his desk "rather reflectively"]—that is so terribly destructive, destructive beyond anything we have ever had. You have got to understand that this isn't a military weapon. ["I shall never forget this particular expression," wrote Lilienthal.] It is used to wipe out women and children and unarmed people, and not for military uses. So we have got to treat this differently from rifles and cannon and ordinary things like that."

In times past Truman had spoken of the bomb as a military weapon like any other. In times past he had spoken of Hiroshima and Nagasaki as military targets. Not any more. It was an extraordinary declaration, refuting absolutely—as Lilienthal understood—any thought that Truman was insensitive to the horror of the bomb or took lightly his responsibilities as Commander in Chief.

Yet Symington seemed not to understand Truman's point or the mood of the moment. "Our fellas need to get used to handling it," Symington repeated, referring now to the military.

They had to understand, Truman said sternly and solemnly, that he had other considerations to weigh. "This is no time to be juggling an atom bomb around."

He rose from his desk. He had had more than enough. The discussion was ended. The others stood and departed.

"If what worried the President, in part, was whether he could trust these terrible forces in the hands of the military establishment," wrote Lilienthal that night, "the performance these men gave certainly could not have been reassuring. . . ."

Two days later, at the close of a Cabinet meeting dealing with domestic issues, Truman held Forrestal a moment longer than the others to tell him the bomb would continue in civilian custody.

Privately, Truman had been expressing concern about Forrestal, who, as Truman said, seemed lately unable to "take hold."

"I went down the river on the yacht Friday at noon and slept around the clock," Truman wrote to Mary Jane first thing Monday morning, July 26.

I sure enough needed it. And I'll need some more before November. It's all so futile. Dewey, Wallace, the cockeyed southerners and then if

I win—which I'm afraid I will—I'll probably have a Russian war on my hands. Two wars are enough for anybody and I've had two.

I go to Congress tomorrow and read them a message requesting price control, housing and a lot of other necessary things and I'll in all probability get nothing. But I've got to try.

On Capitol Hill, the special session of Congress opened and later that same day Truman sprung another surprise. Without warning, he announced executive orders to end discrimination in the armed forces and to guarantee fair employment in the civil service.

His reception when he appeared before Congress the next day was noticeably cool. (As a show of their resentment, some members did not even rise from their seats as he entered.) He called for action on an eight-point program, including civil rights—controls on consumer credit, an excess profits tax, strengthened rent control, price controls, action on housing, farm support, aid to education, an increased minimum wage, and change in the Displaced Persons Act that discriminated against Catholics and Jews—all that he had asked for before and had been denied.

From his office in Albany, Governor Dewey said nothing one way or the other, but through his campaign manager, Herbert Brownell, encouraged Republican leaders in Congress to give careful consideration to the President's program. Taft absolutely refused, saying, "No, we're not going to give that fellow anything." To Taft, as to most Republicans and much of the public, the whole affair was a cheap political ploy.

The two-week session accomplished little, as Truman had anticipated, except to make his point that a Republican Congress was the great roadblock to social progress for the country and to show the gulf between Republican promises and Republican performance.

"They sure are in a stew and mad as wet hens," he told Bess. "If I can make them madder, maybe they'll do the job the old gods used to put on the Greeks and Romans. ..."

On August 4 on Capitol Hill, testifying before the House Un-American Activities Committee, the *Time* editor Whittaker Chambers charged that Alger Hiss, president of the Carnegie Foundation and once one of the "bright young men" of the New Deal, a former official in both the Roosevelt and Truman administrations, serving fourteen years in the State Department, had been his accomplice in a Communist network. "For a number of years, I, myself, served in the underground in Washington, D.C.," said Chambers. "I knew it at its top level. ... A member of this group ... was Alger Hiss." The news rocked the city. Official Washington was described as "stunned with anger and disbelief." Speaking off the record, Sam Rayburn told a reporter, "There is political dynamite in this Communist investigation. Don't doubt that."

But when, at his press conference the following day, Truman was asked whether he thought the "spy scare" on Capitol Hill was only "a red herring" to divert public attention from inflation, he said he agreed. The hearings were "a 'red herring' to keep from doing what they ought to do. . . . They are slandering a lot of people that don't deserve it."

Could they quote him, reporters asked. Yes, Truman replied, adding further to his troubles.

A week later, with the special session of Congress ended, he was fed another line by another reporter, but this time to his benefit. Did he think it had been a "do-nothing" Congress? "Entirely," Truman said. He thought that was quite a good name for the 80th Congress.

Upstairs at the White House the decline and fall of the old building was no longer theoretical. The floor of Margaret's sitting room, across the hall from his study, had caved in beneath her piano. His own bathroom, the President was informed, was about to collapse. Nothing of this was disclosed, however, nor would it be until after the elections. "Can you imagine what the press would have done with this story?" Margaret would recall. "The whole mess would have been blamed on Harry Truman."

"Margaret's sitting room floor broke in two but didn't fall through the family dining room ceiling," he reported to his sister on August 10. "They propped it up and fixed it. Now my bathroom is about to fall into the Red Parlor. They won't let me sleep in my bedroom or use the bath."

He was sleeping in the Lincoln Bedroom, in "old Abe's bed," he added, and finding it quite comfortable.

14

Fighting Chance

It will be the greatest campaign any President ever made.
Win, lose, or draw people will know where I stand. . . .

—Truman to his sister, autumn 1948

I

The *Ferdinand Magellan* was the only private railroad car ever fitted out for the exclusive use of the President of the United States. Eighty-three feet in length and painted the standard dark green of the Pullman Company, it had been built originally in 1928 as one of several luxury cars named for famous explorers—*Marco Polo, David Livingstone, Robert Peary*—then taken over by the government for Franklin Roosevelt's use during wartime, in 1942, when it was completely overhauled to become a rolling fortress.

The windows were three-inch, bulletproof glass, the entire car sheathed in armor plate—sides, top, bottom, ends, and doors—with the result that it weighed a colossal 142½ tons, or as much as a locomotive. Special trucks and wheels had to be built to carry the weight.

For security reasons during the war, only the word "Pullman" appeared on the outside, and still, in 1948, the only distinguishing exterior features were the presidential seal fixed to the rear platform and three loudspeakers mounted on top of the platform roof.

Inside everything was designed for comfort. At the forward end were galley, pantry, servants' quarters, and an oak-paneled dining room, which doubled as a conference room for the President, this furnished with china cabinets, a mahogany dining table, and six matching chairs upholstered in gold-and-green striped damask. Beyond, down a side aisle, were four staterooms, marked A, B, C, and D, the two middle rooms, B and C,

653

forming the Presidential Suite with joining bath and shower. Stateroom B, for the First Lady, was a pale peach color. Stateroom C, the President's room, had blue-green walls and carpet and satin chrome fixtures.

Past the staterooms, at the rear, was the observation lounge with blue and brown chairs and a blue sofa, walls covered with an attractive light brown tufted material resembling leather, blue velvet curtains at the windows and at the door opening onto the rear platform. The carpeting was dark green.

The whole car was air-conditioned—to its immense weight under way were added some 6,000 pounds of ice for the cooling system—and each room had a telephone that could be hooked up to a trackside outlet whenever the train was standing at a station.

To Truman, who loved trains and loved seeing the country, it was the perfect way to travel, and one he had enjoyed frequently since becoming President. There had been the memorable night of poker with Churchill on the way to Missouri for the "iron curtain" speech, the long "nonpolitical" swing west in June. More recently, he had made a quick one-day tour of Michigan for a Labor Day speech at Detroit's Cadillac Square, to open his campaign for reelection. Yet for all the miles covered, the days and nights spent on board the *Magellan,* these prior expeditions had been only prologue to the odyssey that began the morning of Friday, September 17, 1948, when the *Magellan,* at the end of a seventeen-car special train, stood waiting on Track 15 beneath the cavernous shed of Washington's Union Station. In June, he had gone 9,000 miles. Now, on what was to become famous as the Whistle-stop Campaign, he would travel all told 21,928 miles, as far nearly as around the world—as far nearly as the voyage of Magellan.

The idea was his own. "I want to see the people," he had said. There would be three major tours: first cross-country to California again, for fifteen days; then a six-day tour of the Middle West; followed by a final, hard-hitting ten days in the big population centers of the Northeast and a return trip home to Missouri.

"There were no deep-hid schemes, no devious plans," remembered Charlie Ross, "nothing that could be called, in the language of political analysts, 'high strategy.' " The President would simply take his case to the country in a grueling, no-quarter contest. Mileage meant crowds.

According to Ross, it had been Truman's original intention to go into all forty-eight states, including those of the Deep South. "He rather relished the prospect of facing up to the Dixiecrats on their homegrounds." (How did he expect to be received in the South, Truman was asked. "Why with courtesy, of course," he replied.)

The idea of a Southern trip held appeal [wrote Ross], because it would show that the Boss had courage, but the plan was ultimately ruled out on the ground that every ounce of energy should be used in places where material political gain might be expected. The political courage of the President had already been amply demonstrated.

So for a total of thirty-three days, more than a month, the *Magellan* was to be center stage for a fast-rolling political roadshow, which, as was said, had but one act and that one act built around just one performer. "We play more towns than the World of Mirth or Brunk's Comedians . . . and we work longer hours," an accompanying reporter would write. For Truman, away from the White House, the big private car would be home, office, presidential command center, campaign headquarters, and the place where, day after day, he would somehow, bravely, almost inconceivably keep hope alive.

No President in history had ever gone so far in quest of support from the people, or with less cause for the effort, to judge by informed opinion. Nor would any presidential candidate ever again attempt such a campaign by railroad.

As a test of his skills and judgment as a professional politician, not to say his stamina and disposition at age sixty-four, it would be like no other experience in his long, often difficult career, as he himself understood perfectly. More than any other event in his public life, or in his presidency thus far, it would reveal the kind of man he was.

"It's going to be tough on everybody," he told the staff. "But that's the way it's got to be. I know I can take it. I'm only afraid that I'll kill some of my staff—and I like you all very much and I don't want to do that."

The rest of the train was made up of diners, lounges, sleepers, a press car, a dynamo car for power, and a communications car (a converted baggage car operated by the Signal Corps), where radio teletype would provide continuous contact with Washington and thus the rest of the world, a point of critical importance to Truman, who had become more and more uneasy over the situation in Berlin. "I have a terrible feeling . . . that we are very close to war," he had written privately the night of September 13.

Security would be a major undertaking. Every grade crossing would have to be checked in advance by the Secret Service. A pilot train—a single locomotive and one car—would run five miles ahead of the President's train to "absorb" any possible trouble. The railroad official in charge, who had been handling presidential trips since the time of Warren G. Harding, admitted he was a nervous wreck. "Every grade crossing has to be manned when the train passes and I just can't tell you how many switches have to be spiked until we've moved on," he told a reporter. Once rolling the train would travel under the code name "POTUS," for "President of the United States," which gave it the right of way everywhere in the country.

Truman liked to move fast. Roosevelt, because of his infirmities, had preferred a smooth, easy pace of no more than 35 miles an hour when traveling in the *Magellan*. Truman liked to go about 80.

A cheer went up from the moderate-sized crowd gathered at the Union Station platform, the sound echoing under the vaulted roof as his limousine, easing through a break in the crowd, pulled right to the gate. Truman stepped out looking "positively buoyant," Margaret close behind. Marshall and Barkley had come to see him off. The First Lady would catch up with the caravan at Des Moines.

Charlie Ross, Clark Clifford, Matt Connelly, George Elsey, Charlie Murphy, White House physician Wallace Graham, and Rose Conway, the President's secretary, were all present and waiting to go on board, in addition to several White House stenographers, Jonathan Daniels, who would help with speeches, and three new speechwriters, David M. Noyes, Albert Z. Carr, and John Franklin Carter. Bill Boyle of Kansas City, an old Truman friend and aid who had served on the Truman Committee, would, like Matt Connelly, be handling political chores.

Counting the whole staff, the Secret Service detail, forty-four reporters and five photographers, the complete entourage numbered some seventy people. The one notable absentee was Harry Vaughan, who would remain out of sight—and out of contact with the press—for the duration of the campaign, at Truman's request.

With everything ready, Truman and Barkley posed together on the rear platform for a few last pictures.

"Mow 'em down, Harry," Barkley exhorted.

"I'm going to fight hard. I'm going to give 'em hell," said Truman, setting the theme at the start.

The odds against him looked insurmountable. The handicaps of the Truman campaign, wrote columnist Marquis Childs, one of the writers on board, "loomed large as the Rocky Mountains." Henry Wallace and the Dixiecrats had split the Democratic Party three ways. Conceivably, New York and the South were already lost to Truman. The victory of the Republicans in the elections of 1946 had been resounding, and ever since the Civil War, the party winning the off-year election had always gone on to win the presidency in the next election. At Washington dinner parties, as Bess Truman had heard, the talk was of who would be in the Dewey Cabinet. Some prominent Democrats in Washington were already offering their homes for sale. Even the President's mother-in-law thought Dewey would win.

In the West, where Truman had made an all-out effort in June, predictions were that at best he might win 19 of the 71 electoral votes at stake. Only Arizona, with 4 votes, looked safe for Truman. And the West was essential.

A Gallup Poll of farm voters gave Dewey 48 percent, Truman 38. And the farm vote, too, was essential.

On September 9, a full week before Truman's train departed Washington, Elmo Roper, a widely respected sampler of public opinion, had announced his organization would discontinue polling since the outcome was already so obvious. "My whole inclination," Roper said, "is to predict the election of Thomas E. Dewey by a heavy margin and devote my time and efforts to other things." The latest Roper Poll showed Dewey leading by an "unbeatable" 44 to 31 percent. More important, said Roper, such elections were decided early.

> Political campaigns are largely ritualistic.... All the evidence we have accumulated since 1936 tends to indicate that the man in the lead at the beginning of the campaign is the man who is the winner at the end of it.... The winner, it appears, clinches his victory early in the race and before he has uttered a word of campaign oratory.

The idea that the campaign was "largely ritualistic," a formality only, became commonplace. *Life,* in its latest issue, carried a picture of Governor Dewey and his staff under the headline: "Albany Provides Preview of Dewey Administration."

Yet, inexplicably, Truman had drawn tremendous crowds in Michigan on Labor Day. A hundred thousand people had filled Cadillac Square. By train and motorcade he rolled through Grand Rapids, Lansing, Hamtramck, Pontiac, and Flint, where to Truman and his staff the crowds were even more impressive. "Cadillac Square . . . that was *organized,*" remembered Matt Connelly. "But we rode from there up to Pontiac . . . [and] from Detroit to Pontiac I'd see people along the highway. This was not organized and there were a lot of them out there!" According to police estimates the turnout at Truman's six stops in Michigan totaled more than half a million people.

Often, in later years, the big Truman crowds would be remembered as a phenomenon of the final weeks of the campaign. But this was a misconception. They were there from the start, in Michigan and in traditionally Republican Iowa—in Davenport, Iowa City, Grinnell, Des Moines—beginning September 18, his first full day heading west.

"Newsmen were nonplused," reported *Time.* "All across Republican Iowa large crowds turned out . . . a good deal of the cheering was enthusiastic."

The main event of the day was the National Plowing Contest at Dexter, forty miles west of Des Moines, where Truman spoke at noon, in blazing sunshine, standing front and center on a high, broad platform, a sea of faces before him, a giant plowing scoreboard behind. The crowd numbered ninety thousand.

The long horizons were rimmed with ripening corn. The atmosphere was of a vast county fair in good times, with throngs of healthy, well-fed, sun-baked and obviously prospering people enjoying the day, as dust swirled in a steady wind and more families arrived in new trucks and automobiles. Lined up in an adjoining field, their bright colors gleaming in the sun, were perhaps fifty private airplanes.

It was a Republican crowd. Iowa had a Republican governor. All eight Iowa representatives in Congress, and both senators, were Republicans. In the last presidential election Iowa's ten electoral votes had gone to Dewey. But more important to Truman, nearly all his audience were farmers and in the Depression, he knew, Iowa farmers had voted for Roosevelt.

Years before, in 1934, when he had been running for the Senate the first time, a St. Louis reporter had written, "In a fight this quiet man can and does hurl devastating fire." Now at Dexter he ripped into the Republican "gluttons of privilege . . . cold men . . . cunning men," in a way no one had heard a presidential candidate speak since the days of William Jennings Bryan. The difference between Republicans and Democrats was a difference in "attitude":

> You remember the big boom and the great crash of 1929. You remember that in 1932 the position of the farmer had become so desperate that there was actual violence in many farming communities. You remember that insurance companies and banks took over much of the land of small independent farmers—223,000 farmers lost their farms. . . .
>
> I wonder how many times you have to be hit on the head before you find out who's hitting you? . . .
>
> The Democratic Party represents the people. It is pledged to work for agriculture. . . . The Democratic Party puts human rights and human welfare first. . . . These Republican gluttons of privilege are cold men.

They are cunning men. . . . They want a return of the Wall Street economic dictatorship. . . .

It was language that, to many, seemed oddly archaic and out of place in the midst of such obvious prosperity. The Des Moines *Register* would point to the "incongruity of being a prophet of doom to an audience in time of harvest of bumper crops." Truman, it was said, was sadly miscast as the new Bryan, his speech "harsh and demagogic." But he was leading to something quite specific.

In June, when rewriting the charter for the Commodity Credit Corporation (CCC)—the agency for federal farm loans—Congress had included an obscure provision prohibiting the CCC from acquiring additional grain-storage bins. It was meant as an economy measure. But since farmers were required to use storage facilities approved or maintained by the CCC in order to qualify for price supports, they stood to lose heavily in the event of wheat and corn crops too large for the existing facilities to handle. If there were no approved bins to store the surplus of a bumper yield, then for the farmers a bumper yield could mean not prosperity but heavy losses.

The bill had gone through unopposed by the Democrats and Truman had signed it. But that was in June when no one was paying it much attention. Now the prospect of a bumper year was no longer hypothetical. The corn harvest would not begin until October, but all that day crossing Iowa, since early morning, those on board the train had seen little else but corn in abundance. The talk in Iowa was of yields of 135 bushels to the acre.

It was the Republican Congress that rewrote the charter for the Commodity Credit Corporation, Truman now charged at Dexter. The Republican Congress, said Truman, had "stuck a pitchfork in the farmer's back." Nor would the Republicans stop with limits on grain storage. The "whole structure of price supports" was in jeopardy.

"I'm not asking you to vote for me. Vote for yourselves," he said, a theme he would strike over and over. To reporters covering the event, the huge crowd seemed friendly yet unmoved. But then who was to say.

Afterward, in a tent behind the platform, a perspiring President in his shirtsleeves pulled up a wooden folding chair to a long table with a red-check cloth and ate country fried chicken and prize-winning cake and pie with thirty farmers and their wives. Asked if he would please speak again, only on a more personal level this time, Truman agreed and returned to the platform.

Was it true he had once been able to plow the straightest furrows in his part of Missouri, he was asked. Yes, said Truman, but only according to an exceedingly partial witness, his mother. But he did have a reputation, he said, for never leaving a "skip place" when he sowed wheat. "My father always used to raise so much fuss about a skip place."

He talked of the 12-inch, horse-drawn gang plow he rode at Grandview and how it had taken him sometimes four days to plow a field. He didn't want to go back to those days. "I don't want to turn back the clock. I don't want to go back to the horse and buggy age, although some of our Republican friends do," he said, and this brought a warm cheer.

"He was delightful and the people were delighted," wrote Richard Rovere of *The New Yorker,* who had thought the earlier speech "deplorable."

Truman had begun the day at 5:45. There had been six stops and six speeches before Dexter. After Dexter, he spoke at Des Moines, Melcher, and Chariton, Iowa. "At each stop," reported the Des Moines *Register,* "the listeners massed for his rear platform talk were larger than the town's population."

"You stayed at home in 1946 and you got the 80th Congress, and you got just exactly what you deserved," he said at Chariton. "You didn't exercise your God-given right to control this country. Now you're going to have another chance."

He was on a crusade for the welfare of the everyday man, he said next, across the state line, at Trenton, Missouri. At Polo, Missouri, just after 8:00 P.M., he told the delighted crowd he had not been sure whether he would be able to stop there, but that the railroad had finally consented. It was his thirteenth speech of the day and he was sounding a little hoarse.

After a brief visit home in Independence the next day, Sunday, September 19, he was on his way again. Crossing Kansas that night, the engineer had the train up to 105 miles per hour, which Truman, from his chair in the lounge, decided was too fast, considering the weight of the *Magellan* and what might happen to the forward cars should the engineer suddenly have to stop. Calmly, quietly, he asked Charlie Ross to send word to the engineer that there was no great hurry. Eighty miles an hour would do.

"Understand me, when I speak of what the Republicans have been doing. I'm not talking about the average Republican voter," Truman told the twenty-five thousand people spread across the lawn of the State Capitol at Denver.

> Nobody knows better than I that man for man, individually, most Republicans are fine people. But there's a big distinction between the individual Republican voter and the policies of the Republican Party.

Something happens to Republican leaders when they get control of the Government . . .

Republicans in Washington have a habit of becoming curiously deaf to the voice of the people. They have a hard time hearing what the ordinary people of the country are saying. But they have no trouble at all hearing what Wall Street is saying. They are able to catch the slightest whisper from big business and the special interests.

He had just one strategy—attack, attack, attack, carry the fight to the enemy's camp. He hammered the Republicans relentlessly, in speeches at Grand Junction, Colorado, Helper, Springville, and Provo, Utah. "Selfish men have always tried to skim the cream from our natural resources to satisfy their own greed. And . . . [their] instrument in this effort has always been the Republican Party," he charged at Salt Lake City, to a standing-room-only crowd in the cavernous Mormon Tabernacle. At Ogden, he warned of "bloodsuckers who have offices in Wall Street." The 80th Congress, he said at Reno, Nevada, was run by a "bunch of old mossbacks still living back in 1890."

The country must not go backward, he would keep saying over and over, because he felt with all his heart that Americans were a forward-looking people and that his own program, as he had told Clark Clifford earlier, was a forward-looking program. If the old guard Republicans were to get control under a Republican administration, they would dismantle the progress made by the New Deal and in foreign affairs, retreat back into isolationism, which would be disastrous for the country and the world. He was certain of this and determined to keep it from happening.

To the crowd beside the Southern Pacific tracks at Roseville, California, he declared the Republican "do-nothing Congress tried to choke you to death in this valley," by cutting off appropriations for publicly owned electric power lines. "You have got a terrible Congressman here in this district. He is one of the worst," he told the citizens of Fresno, referring to Republican Bertrand W. Gearhart, who had once denounced George Marshall on the floor of the House.

One correspondent, Robert Donovan of the New York *Herald Tribune,* would later characterize the Truman campaign as "sharp speeches fairly criticizing Republican policy and defending New Deal liberalism mixed with sophistry, bunkum piled higher than haystacks, and demagoguery tooting merrily down the track."

Truman was at his best speaking to small crowds and without notes and, often, when the subject was himself, his family, his own pioneer background and outlook on life. He was described by some of the eastern reporters as a "feed mill type of talker" and "excellent indeed" with a small-town crowd. These "little speeches," thought Charlie Ross, were more important than the major addresses. "They got him close to the people."

At both Grand Junction, Colorado, and the Mormon Tabernacle in Salt Lake City, he reminisced about Grandfather Solomon Young and his journeys over the plains, his friendship with Brigham Young. "Oh, I wish my grandfather could see me now," he said spontaneously at Salt Lake, and the audience first laughed, then broke into prolonged applause. "Those pioneers had faith and they had energy," he said, seeming himself to embody an excess of both qualities.

Though he refused to put on Indian war bonnets or to kiss babies, he was thankful always for the gifts ceremoniously presented at stop after stop—hats, spurs, baskets of fruit ("I'll be eating peaches from now until I get to Washington"). And nearly always he had something to say about the local scenery, local history, local achievements and interests.

They tell me [he said at Mojave] that in 1883—that was the year before I was born—that a gentleman by the name of Webb built ten grand, big wagons here in this town, bought himself a hundred head of mules, and began to haul borax out of the Mojave Desert—and that was the origin of Twenty-Mule Team Borax which we always kept in the house when I was a kid. I never thought I would be here as President at the place where it originated and talking to you people about your interests in the welfare of the country.

He expressed love of home, love of the land, the virtues and old verities of small-town America, his America. "Naturally, if we don't think our hometown is the greatest in the world, we are not very loyal citizens. We all should feel that way," he told the loyal citizens of American Fork, Utah.

"You don't get any double talk from me," he declared from a brightly decorated bandstand first thing in the morning sunshine at Sparks, Nevada. "I'm either for something or against it, and you know it. You know what I stand for." What he stood for, he said again and again, was a government of and for the people, not the "special interests."

He was friendly, cheerful. And full of fight.

"You are the government," he said time after time. "Practical politics is government. Government starts from the grass roots." "I think the government belongs to you and me as private citizens." "I'm calling this trip a crusade. It's a crusade of the people against the special interests, and if you back me up we're going to win. . . ."

"The basic issue of this campaign is as simple as can be: it's the special interests against the people." "I'm here on a serious mission, and because it is so serious, I propose to speak to you as plainly as I can." "In 1940, you know, two-thirds of you stayed home and didn't vote. You wanted a change. Well, you got it. You got the change. You got just exactly what you deserved." "Now use your judgment. Keep the people in control of the government. . . ." "I not only want you to vote for me but I want you to vote for yourselves, and if you vote for yourselves, you'll vote for the Democratic ticket. . . ."

The crowds would be gathered at station stops often from early morning, waiting for him to arrive. Men and boys perched on rooftops and nearby signal towers for a better view. There would be a high school band standing by, ready to play the national anthem or "Hail to the Chief," or to struggle through the Missouri Waltz, a song Truman particularly disliked but that it was his fate to hear repeated hundreds of times over. His train would ease into the station as the band blared, the crowd cheered. Then, accompanied by three or four local politicians—usually a candidate for Congress or state party chairman who had boarded the train at a prior stop—Truman would step from behind the blue velvet curtain onto the platform, and the crowd, large or small, would cheer even more. One of the local politicians would then introduce the President of the United States and the crowd would cheer again.

At the ten-minute stops, he would speak for five minutes, beginning with praise for the local candidate for Congress or some issue of local interest, then moving quickly from the general to the particular. He would lambaste the Republican Congress for the high cost of living or failing to vote the grain-storage bins, for the Taft-Hartley Act or the "rich man's tax bill," for slashing federal support for irrigation and hydroelectric power projects in the West. It was the Republicans in Congress who were holding back progress in the Central Valley of California. Republicans at heart had no real interest in the West—not in water, not in public power. The Republicans who controlled the Appropriations Committees in the House and Senate, those upon whom the future of federal projects in the Central Valley depended were not Californians, they were not westerners: "They are Eastern Republicans."

"Give 'em hell, Harry!" someone would shout from the crowd—news accounts of his promise to Barkley to "give 'em hell" having swept the country by now. The cry went up at one stop after another, often more than once—"Give 'em hell, Harry!"—which always brought more whoops, laughter, and yells of approval, but especially when he tore into the 80th Congress.

("I never gave anybody hell," he would later say. "I just told the truth and they thought it was hell.")

At the close, he would ask if they would like to meet his family and the crowd never failed in its response. The routine became standard. He would first introduce Bess—"Miz Truman"—who would step out from behind the blue curtain, looking pleased and motherly. He would take her hand and she would stand at his right, saying nothing. If the crowd was small and especially friendly, he would refer to her as "the Boss." Then, proudly, he would present "Miss Margaret," whose appearance nearly always brought the biggest cheer of all, and to the obvious delight of her father. She would be carrying an armful of roses, a few of which she would throw to the crowd. Truman would lean over the brass rail to grasp one or two outstretched hands. Someone would signal the local band to start playing again, and with warning toots of the whistle, with reporters scrambling to get back on board, the crowd cheering and the three Trumans waving, the train would pull slowly out of the station.

No matter what the outcome of the campaign, wrote Richard Rovere, millions of Americans would remember for the rest of their lives this final tableau of the "Three Traveling Trumans."

> It will be a picture to cherish and it will stand Harry Truman in good stead for the rest of his life. Travelling with him you get the feeling that the American people who have seen him and heard him at his best would be willing to give him just about anything he wants except the Presidency.

It could be said also they had seen and heard for themselves a President who was friendly and undisguised, loyal to his party, fond of his family, a man who cared about the country and about them, who believed the business of government was their business, and who didn't whine when he was in trouble, but kept bravely, doggedly plugging away, doing his best, his duty as he saw it, and who was glad to be among them. He wasn't a hero, or an original thinker. His beliefs were their beliefs, their way of talking was his way of talking. He was on their side. He was one of them. If he stumbled over a phrase or a name, he would grin and try again, and they would smile with him.

"There is an agreeable warmheartedness and simplicity about Truman that is genuine," wrote Richard Strout for his column in *The New Republic*. A presidential train was probably the worst of all places to gauge public opinion, he added. "Nevertheless, reporters keep pinching themselves at the size of the crowds and their cordial response."

At Los Angeles, at Gilmore Stadium, with screen stars Lauren Bacall, Humphrey Bogart, and Ronald Reagan—all ardent liberal Democrats—seated prominently on stage beside him, Truman hit hard at Henry Wallace, warning liberal Democrats to "think again" if they thought a vote for the third party was a vote for peace. With Communists "guiding and using" it, the third party did not represent American ideals. A vote for Wallace only played into the hands of the Republican "forces of reaction." Now was the hour for the liberal forces of America to unite. "Think again. Don't waste your vote."

At San Diego, ten thousand turned out, despite threatening skies and the early hour of 9:00 A.M., and gave him the most enthusiastic welcome thus far. After the stop at Oceanside, California, where the train pulled within sight of the rolling surf of the Pacific, the route was east again.

By then, Friday, September 24, he had been on the road a week, and while some on board had already begun to show signs of strain, Truman, who bore much the heaviest burden, remained steady as a rock. Nor had he left the duties and concerns of the Oval Office. A White House pouch arrived daily—papers requiring his signature, letters to be signed, letters to be read, reports from department heads, reports to Congress, sealed manila envelopes marked "Confidential," as well as copies of the Kansas City *Star* and the Independence *Examiner*. A memorandum from Head Usher Howell Crim reported on the quantity of plaster descending in the East Room.

The Berlin crisis and the risks involved in the airlift weighed heavily on Truman. Though the quantity of supplies being flown into the city had increased since August, the disturbing truth was that the airlift was supplying less than half of what Berlin needed. "We are not quite holding our own," General Clay had cabled. In another few days, in Dallas, at Truman's request, General Walter Bedell Smith, the American ambassador to Moscow, would come quietly aboard the train to give his assessment to Truman of Stalin's mood and the chances of war.

Staff work on board had acquired a pattern of a kind, though little about it was systematic or efficient or ever very formal. Of the major speeches only the one at Dexter, Iowa, had been prepared well in advance. The rest—for Denver, Salt Lake City, Los Angeles—were produced under way, with the combined efforts of Ross, Clifford, Elsey, Murphy, and the new writers Noyes, Carr, and Carter. No speech was ever the work of one writer, and no speech failed to go through several drafts. Truman himself went over every line, worked "painstakingly" on every draft, and was the first to approve suggested deletions. "That's good," he would say. "Never use two words when one will do best." Convoluted structure and high-blown or evasive phrases greatly annoyed him. "That's not the way I would say it," he would remark as the group sat around the mahogany table in the dining room of the *Magellan,* working late into the night. "Let's just say what we mean."

"Nobody had any special pride of authorship, but we did get into heated arguments now and then," wrote Ross. "The President would grin and say, 'All right, you fellows fight it out and I'll decide.' " Ross wanted Truman to ease up on the abusive language and state his case in more dignified fashion. But Truman was determined to keep the heat on. He had also introduced a new line about the housing shortage that made the others wince. If they went to the polls and did their duty on November 2, Truman would tell the crowd with a smile, then he wouldn't have to go "hunting around in this housing shortage." He could stay right in the White House. It was a line he liked and that he was sure the people liked. So he kept it.

Background material, particularly material useful for the rear platform appearances, was provided by a "Research Division" of the Democratic National Committee—three or four "bright young men" who had been holed up in a small office off DuPont Circle in Washington and who, according to George Elsey, "worked like dogs and ground out an incredible amount of material. All kinds of historical, literary, political and economic data flowed through them, and news clippings, photostats of useful documents, anything that would give spark and vitality and originality and vigor to President Truman's campaign effort."

Elsey's task was to sort and edit it all, then keep the President supplied with pertinent items to choose from, and in proper order as they sped along. "I was the 'whistlestopper' on the job doing the outlines, getting the stuff together, and feeding these back to him," he remembered. "I felt I got twenty-five years exercise walking from my car to his car in the weeks of the campaign."

Bill Boyle would be credited with "planning every inch" of Truman's itinerary. Constantly in touch with state party leaders, he advised Truman on which towns mattered and why.

Traveling ahead of the train, as "advance men," were Oscar Chapman, the Under Secretary of Interior, and Donald Dawson, of the White House staff. They were responsible for all the details of local ceremonies, to make sure the local politicians knew where and when to come on board Truman's train, and that no such fiasco as the empty hall at Omaha in June ever happened again.

Between stops, in the comparative quiet and privacy of the *Magellan,* the candidate himself remained even-tempered and steadfastly confident.

The strain on him was unrelenting. Yet he showed no signs of wear-and-tear or faltering expectations. He knew he was behind and in private said so. But he was also sure he would catch up and move ahead by November, when it would count—a view shared by almost no one else on board, though few, other than the press, ever talked about it.

Once, late in an especially long day, a noticeably weary First Lady asked Clark Clifford if he thought the President really believed he could win and Clifford said yes. "He gives every appearance under *every* condition," Clifford answered.

"Oh," she said, "I don't know where it comes from."

Though several of his staff were gravely concerned about the split in the Democratic ranks—the campaigns under way by the Progressives and the Dixiecrats—Truman seems never to have taken the candidacies of Wallace and Thurmond as serious threats.

Henry Wallace was running hard. In August he had bravely campaigned through the South, decrying segregation and refusing to stay in hotels that enforced discrimination. In North Carolina angry crowds pelted him with eggs and rotten tomatoes. Traveling the rest of the country mainly by plane, he would eventually roll up more mileage even than Truman, his main theme remaining constant throughout: the Progressive Party was "the peace party" that could end the Cold War through direct negotiations with the Soviet Union. At Los Angeles, speaking at the same stadium where Truman had, Wallace drew a larger crowd than Truman had, and it was a paying crowd. But attendance overall at Wallace rallies and speeches was falling off, the excitement of his Progressive "crusade" plainly in decline, as he was perceived—and portrayed more and more in the press—as "playing Moscow's game." Of the Republicans and Democrats, he said they were "equally sinister" in their policies, both being in the grip of Wall Street and the Pentagon.

Strom Thurmond kept harping on states' rights and demanding that the "evil forces" in control of the Democratic Party be "cast out." He called Truman's Fair Employment Practices Committee "communistic." Racial integration of the armed services was "un-American." The South must hold the line. "There's not enough troops in the Army to break down segregation and admit the Negro into our homes, our eating places, our swimming pools and our theaters." He and the Dixiecrats would win 140 electoral votes in the South, Thurmond said, more than sufficient to force the election into the House. But almost no one took the claim seriously, and Truman least of all.

In his speeches, Truman never mentioned Wallace or Thurmond by name. But then never in the major addresses or in any of his largely extemporaneous remarks to small crowds in out-of-the-way places did he speak of Dewey by name. Dewey was always "my Republican opponent," or "the other fellow."

He never criticized or ridiculed Dewey in a personal way. Interestingly, Dewey was never even a subject of discussion on board the *Ferdinand Magellan*. There was no talk of Dewey's personality or failings, no gossiping about him, or ever any consideration of attacking him on personal grounds. It would not be recalled that the President ever even mentioned Dewey.

II

Governor Thomas E. Dewey had gone aboard his own campaign train at Albany on Sunday, September 19, two days after Truman left Washington, and Dewey, too, delivered his first major speech in Iowa, at Des Moines on Monday the 20th, two days after Truman spoke at the Dexter plowing contest. Starting later than Truman, Dewey would travel nowhere near so far, and at a much more leisurely pace. And he would deliver far fewer speeches—all this, like everything about the Dewey campaign, having been carefully thought out in advance. As the candidate and his advisers proudly informed the press, nothing was to be left to chance.

Press coverage of Dewey's advance across the country was also to be far greater than that Truman received. There were ninety-two reporters riding the "Dewey Victory Special"—ninety-eight by the time the train reached California—roughly twice the number traveling with the President, and they were catered to, their everyday needs handled with a skill and efficiency unknown on the Truman train. Copies of the candidate's speeches were nearly always available twenty-four hours in advance, as they seldom ever were on the Truman train. An internal public address system fed Dewey's remarks directly to the press car and dining cars, so reporters need not bother leaving their air-conditioned comforts. Coffee and sandwiches were provided to reporters at odd hours, their laundry attended to, their luggage moved from train to hotel for overnight stops. To those who had traveled with both candidates, the Truman operation, by comparison, was forty years behind the times.

"If you wanted anything laundered [on the Truman train], you did it yourself, in a Pullman basin," Richard Rovere informed his readers in *The New Yorker*.

When you detrained anywhere for an overnight stay, it was every man for himself. You carried your duffel and scrambled for your food. If a man was such a slave to duty that he felt obliged to hear what the President said in his back-platform addresses, he had to climb down off the train; run to the rear end, mingle with the crowd, and listen. Often this was a hazardous undertaking, for the President was given to speaking late at night to crowds precariously assembled on sections of roadbed built up fifteen or twenty feet above the surrounding land. The natives knew the contours of the ground, but the reporters did not, and more than one of them tumbled down a cindery embankment.

A condescending tone entered into a lot of what was written about Truman and his efforts. His whole campaign, as Jonathan Daniels said, was given a "sort of rube reputation" by the largely eastern press traveling with him. The Dewey campaign, by contrast, was described as "slick," "tidy as a pin," everything handled with "junior-executive briskness." The favored drink on board the "Dewey Victory Special" was the martini, not bourbon as on the Truman train. The favorite game was bridge, not poker. Dewey himself was cool, careful, "supremely self-confident," and from the start elevated in tone.

"Tonight we enter upon a campaign to unite America," he told the crowd at Des Moines, where, reportedly, he was leading Truman by a resounding 51 to 37 percent.

"We propose to install in Washington," Dewey said, "an administration which has faith in the American people, a warm understanding of their needs and the competence to meet them. We will rediscover the essential unity of our people and the spiritual strength which makes our country great. We will begin to move forward again shoulder to shoulder. . . ."

There were no harsh or divisive accusations, no pitting of farmers against Wall Street, no pitchforks in the back or angry, staccato assaults on any segment of government or society.

A Republican congressman from Minnesota, August H. Andresen, had written to warn Dewey of discontent among farmers, saying, "We cannot win without the farm vote." But Dewey refrained also from any mention of farm problems.

His voice was deep and resonant, as flowing as the smoothest radio preacher—everything Truman's voice was not. Dewey was dignified. He spoke ill of no one, offended no one. He had no surprises, he took no risks. And the pattern prevailed, his text seldom more rousing than a civics primer. "Government must help industry and industry must cooperate with government," he would say with a grand preacherlike sweep of the right arm.

"America's future is still ahead of us," he also said.

They were not speeches of the kind he had given in 1944, when he had hit hard and often, charging Franklin Roosevelt with failure to end the

Depression, failure to build American defenses before Pearl Harbor. At one point, he had called Roosevelt truly "the indispensable" man—"indispensable to the ill-assorted, power-hungry conglomeration of city bosses, Communists, and career bureaucrats which now compose the New Deal." But there would be no such harangue this time, because this time Dewey was not the challenger. This time he had the election sewed up.

It was an odd reversal of roles, with the incumbent President running as the challenger and his opponent performing as though he were already elected and the campaign a mere formality. Dewey had only to mark time, be careful, make no mistakes, say or do nothing silly or improper, and the presidency was his.

So the speeches were kept unceasingly positive. He was *for* unity, *for* peace, *for* "constructive change." He was not running against the New Deal. He was not even running against Harry Truman, whom he never mentioned, any more than Truman spoke of him, which was another odd turn. "Governor Dewey is deliberately avoiding any sharp controversy with the Democratic incumbent," reported *The New York Times* as the "Victory Special" rolled through California, passing, at one point, within only a few miles of the Truman train.

In some ways the two candidates were much alike. Both were efficient with their time, alert, and energetic. They always looked spanking clean and pressed. Both were men of medium stature, though Truman, the one so often referred to disparagingly as "the little man," was an inch taller than Dewey, who was 5 feet 8 inches. And unlike Truman, Dewey was extremely sensitive about his height.

They were each diligent, career public servants who genuinely believed that good government was possible and the best politics. They both loved music. Truman had dreamed of being a concert pianist, Dewey of being a concert singer and still loved to sing (especially "Oklahoma" in the bathtub). Each was devoted to his family. Dewey's wife, Frances, a particularly photogenic woman with a somewhat shy but winsome manner, was generally seen as an asset to his political career; and they had two teenage sons, Tom, Jr., and John.

Like Truman, Dewey was a product of small-town middle America. He had grown up in Owosso, Michigan, where his father, the editor of the local newspaper, was vitally interested in politics, just as John Truman had been.

Beyond there, however, the similarities ended. Where Truman was at heart a nineteenth-century man—raised, educated, formed in thought and outlook in the era before World War I—Dewey was of a different generation. Dewey had never lived with the burden of farm debt; he had never been to war, he had never been bankrupt. Born in 1902, eighteen years after Truman, he was the first candidate for President born in the twentieth century. His middle American origins, moreover, were hardly apparent any longer. Educated at the University of Michigan and the Columbia Law School in New York, he had made his entire career in the East, and with his homburg hats and cultivated voice, he had left Owosso far behind.

Where Truman had been, as Nellie Noland said, "a late bloomer all along," attaining prominence only past the age of fifty, Dewey had soared almost from the start, achieving national fame as the crusading district attorney of New York while still in his thirties. He was "the Gangbuster," a national hero. In 1938, at age thirty-six, he had made his first run for governor of New York. Trying again in 1942, he became New York's first Republican governor in twenty years. Running for a second term in 1946, he rolled up the biggest victory in the state's history, winning by nearly 700,000 votes.

As governor he cut taxes, doubled state aid to education, raised salaries for state employees, reduced the state's overall indebtedness by over $100 million, and put through the first state law in the country prohibiting racial discrimination in employment. If elected now, he would be, at forty-six, the youngest President since Theodore Roosevelt. Given his youth, ambition, his proven ability, it was not inconceivable that Thomas E. Dewey could serve as long as, or longer than Franklin Roosevelt. If he were to have four full terms, he would be in the White House until 1965, and even then would still be younger than was Truman in 1948.

But, as often noted, Dewey was also extremely cautious and cold in manner, at least in public, which for a politician was what mattered. On the campaign trail, he seemed not to care for the gifts he was offered or to mix with the crowd. He was incapable of unbending. Where Truman, at the end of a platform talk, would ask, "Would you like to meet my family?" Dewey would say stiffly, "I'm pleased to present Mrs. Dewey."

"Smile, governor," a photographer had called at a campaign stop in 1944. "I thought I was," said Dewey. A remark attributed to the wife of a New York Republican politician would be widely repeated. "You have to know Mr. Dewey well," she said, "in order to dislike him."

He was so self-controlled as to seem mechanical—Dewey came on stage, wrote Richard Rovere, "like a man who has been mounted on casters and given a tremendous shove from behind"—and there was a hard look in the dark eyes, a look that had served him well as a prosecutor. "Those eyes tell you this guy doesn't crap around," a staff man once said.

It was Dewey's small, dark "bottle-brush" mustache that the public knew him best for and that many people disliked, or wished he would get rid of, mustaches having been long out of fashion among public men. He had grown it on a bicycle tour of France years earlier and kept it because his wife approved. To the actress Ethel Barrymore, the mustache and Dewey's diminutive size made him look "like the bridegroom on the wedding cake," a remark greatly amplified by the acerbic, much-quoted daughter of Theodore Roosevelt, Alice Roosevelt Longworth, and that may have done Dewey real harm in the campaign.

To the reporters on board his train, he seemed aloof, even haughty. They were kept at a distance, and though they were certain he would win —and most believed he would make an efficient chief executive—almost none of them liked him, which was quite the reverse of how they felt about Truman. Dewey's "mechanical smile . . . and his bland refusal to deal with issues, have got under everybody's skin," wrote Richard Strout of the mood in the press car. Dewey, it was cracked, was the only man who could strut sitting down.

In sharp contrast to Truman, who had never wanted to be President, Dewey had started running for the job as early as 1939, in advance of the Republican Convention that nominated Wendell Willkie. Dewey believed it was his destiny to be President. "It is written in the stars," he said privately.

That it was written in the polls as well also carried enormous weight with him, for, unlike Truman, Dewey took such samplings with utmost seriousness. He was the first presidential candidate to have his own polling unit.

On several major issues Dewey, as a liberal Republican, held the same or very similar views as Truman. Dewey backed aid to Greece. He supported the Marshall Plan. He believed in a strong military defense, including Universal Military Training. He was for recognition of Israel. He supported the Berlin Airlift and wanted further progress made in civil rights. As he and his advisers saw things, the real struggle waited beyond November, not with the Democrats in Congress, but with Taft, whom Dewey intensely disliked. (On more than one occasion Dewey had been heard to say that the Ohio senator should have carnal relations with himself.)

The dominating strategy of the Dewey campaign, to say as little as possible, was Dewey's own—"When you're leading, don't talk," he would tell the Republican politicians who came aboard his train. The "Dewey high command," however, had more influence than did the people around Truman. They included campaign manager Herbert Brownell, Jr., whose headquarters were in Washington, but who talked to Dewey every night by phone; Paul Lockwood, Dewey's veteran executive assistant; and Elliott Bell, an old friend who wrote speeches and served as unofficial chief of staff on the train. These were able, experienced men. Brownell had been Dewey's campaign manager the last time, as well as chairman of the Republican Party. Lockwood had been with Dewey since his days as district attorney. Elliott Bell, a former financial writer for *The New York Times,* had managed Dewey's two triumphant campaigns for governor.

And they all agreed: the campaign was going fine. Nor had other Republican politicians objected thus far. "We always asked them what our strategy should be," remembered Bell, "and they all said that as matters stood Dewey was in and the thing to do was not stir up too much controversy and run the risk of losing votes." The consensus was that Dewey would have done better in 1944 had he not gone on the attack as he did. So why repeat the mistake?

"The tone of his campaign was set," wrote *Time* approvingly—*Time,* like its sister publication *Life,* having concluded that Dewey was as good as elected. The real concern among the Dewey staff, reported *Time,* was over what Truman might do between now and January to upset things, and particularly in the field of foreign policy. "The responsibilities of power already weighed on them so heavily that a newsman inquired blandly: 'How long is Dewey going to tolerate Truman's interference in the government?' "

Dewey, said *Life,* would keep his composure "no matter how much his rival taunted, teased and dared him to come out in the alley and scrap." Dewey himself remarked that he would never "get down in the gutter" with Truman. He would have preferred a more worthy opponent. In the seclusion of his private car, Dewey wondered aloud, "Isn't it harder in politics to defeat a fool, say, than an abler man?"

To help guarantee a Dewey victory, J. Edgar Hoover was secretly supplying him with all the information the FBI could provide. Dewey and Hoover were old friends and got along well. Hoover had put the resources of the bureau at Dewey's disposal months before, in the expectation that when Dewey became President he would name Hoover as his Attorney General. "The FBI helped Dewey during the campaign itself by giving him everything we had that could hurt Truman, though there wasn't much," remembered an assistant to Hoover, William C. Sullivan, who was one of those assigned to cull the files.

We resurrected the president's former association with Jim Pendergast ... and tried to create the impression that Truman was too ignorant to deal with the emerging Communist threat. We even prepared studies for Dewey which were released under his name, as if he and his staff had done the work. ... No one in the bureau gave Truman any chance of winning.

Only on the issue of Communists in government was Dewey willing to taunt Truman. "I suggest you elect an administration that simply won't appoint them in the first place," Dewey said at one stop after another, the line always drawing applause.

In Los Angeles, at the Hollywood Bowl, flanked on stage by Republican movie stars—Gary Cooper, Jeanette MacDonald, and Ginger Rogers, who came from Independence, Missouri—Dewey described communism on the march. "The tragic fact is that too often our own government ... seems so far to have lost faith in our system of free opportunity as to encourage this Communist advance, not hinder it. ... Communists and fellow travelers [have] risen to positions of trust in our government ... [and yet] the head of our own government called the exposure of Communists in our government 'a red herring.'"

Dewey did not try to inflame crowd passions. He opposed outlawing Communists. "We'll have no thought police," he said. Still the charge that the government was "coddling" Communists, a charge that had been injected into the campaign by the House Un-American Activities Committee, would be made again and again at nearly every stop.

Joseph Alsop described the typical Dewey speech as "over-rehearsed" and "a trifle chilling." Marquis Childs warned in his column that in the "very expertness" of his campaign, Dewey might be "laying up future trouble for himself." Privately among the Dewey people there was an increasing uneasiness over the size of the crowds, which, as *Time* conceded, were "good—but no more than good." At Salt Lake City, Dewey, like Truman, filled the Mormon Tabernacle to overflowing, but the turnout along the streets had been nothing like that for Truman. "We hit Salt Lake City about five P.M.," Elliott Bell would recall. "I was struck by the fact that there were very few people on the sidewalks—and a good many people walking hardly bothered to look at the motorcade."

"Then we went into Texas and everybody said Texas was going to be cold to the President," Truman would later tell a crowd in Neosho, Missouri, recounting his latest adventures.

And the first city we stopped in was El Paso, and everybody in El Paso was down at the station. The Chief of Police said he estimated the crowd at 25,000. Then we went over and had breakfast with John Garner, former Vice President, a good friend of mine, and he gave me a breakfast to write home about. We had chicken and white-wing dove, and we had ham and bacon and scrambled eggs and hot biscuits and I don't know what all. And the governor of Texas met me there as did Sam Rayburn, and we went across Texas, and I must have seen a million people in Texas.

Pounding his way across Texas, Truman had seemed to gather strength by the hour and give more of himself to the campaign with every stop. He was fighting for his political life and having a grand time at it.

"He is good on the back of a train because he is one of the folks," said Sam Rayburn. "He smiles with them and not at them, laughs with them and not at them."

With the rest of the Old South in revolt over his stand on civil rights, Truman had to hold on to Texas and its twenty-three electoral votes. Yet racial bias ran strong in Texas—segregation, poll taxes, outright race hatred. In Texas he was in Dixiecrat territory for the first time, which was why a "cold" reception had been assumed. There had even been rumors of threats on his life, of Dixiecrats claiming "they'd shoot Truman, that no-good son-of-a-bitch and his civil rights." It was the first time a Democratic nominee for the presidency had ever found it necessary to court Texas, and banking on friendships with such longstanding, powerful Democrats as Rayburn and Garner, Truman had decided to make it the most strenuous campaign ever waged there by a non-Texan.

A high point was the breakfast put on by "Cactus Jack" Garner at Uvalde, which, reporters discovered to their surprise, was a tree-shaded town with neat green lawns and no sign of anything remotely like cactus. Served on the glass-enclosed porch of Garner's big, buff-colored brick house, the breakfast was the best he had had in forty years, Truman later told the delighted crowd outside. Ten thousand people and a high school band had been at the Uvalde station to greet him at 6:50 that morning. Now several thousand cheered as he stood on the front porch with Garner, Rayburn, and Governor Beauford Jester, none of whom was known for his devotion to civil rights. (Jester, not long before, had called Truman's civil rights program a "stab in the back.")

John Garner and he had been friends "a long, long time," and they were going to be friends as long as they lived, Truman said. "I'm coming back for another visit sometime. I fished around for another invitation and got it."

Old friendships, old loyalties would hold, in other words, not only now for the sake of politics, but later, too, whatever changes were in the wind. The crowd understood what he meant and the crowd applauded.

So pleased was Bess Truman by the warmth of the reception that she broke precedent and stepped forward to the microphone to say thank you, proving thereby "beyond all doubt," reported Robert Donovan in the New York *Herald-Tribune,* "what an extraordinary occasion it was."

At San Antonio later the same day, Sunday, September 26, an estimated 200,000 people filled the streets, and at a dinner that night at the Gunter Hotel, speaking spontaneously and simply of his feeling for people and his wish for peace, Truman achieved what Jonathan Daniels called "an eloquence close to presidential poetry."

> Our government is made up of the people. You are the government, I am only your hired servant. I am the Chief Executive of the greatest nation in the world, the highest honor that can ever come to a man on earth. But I am the servant of the people of the United States. They are not my servants. I can't order you around, or send you to labor camps or have your heads cut off if you don't agree with me politically. We don't believe in that. . . .
>
> I believe that if we ourselves try to live as we should, and if we continue to work for peace in this world, and as the old Puritan said, "Keep your bullets bright and your powder dry," eventually we will get peace in this world, because that is the only way we can survive with the modern inventions under which we live.
>
> We have got to harness these inventions for the welfare of man, instead of his destruction.
>
> That is what I am interested in. That is what I am working for.
>
> That is much more important than whether I am President of the United States.

"Truman Gains Texas Votes by 'Human Touch' Method," read the headline in the San Antonio *Express.* When a reporter for the *Express* polled the correspondents on board the train, he found nearly all now thought Truman had at least "a fighting chance."

In not quite four days in Texas, he made twenty-four stops, spoke twenty-five times. He had perfect weather and enthusiastic crowds the whole way. Monday, September 27, the biggest day, began with a rear platform talk at San Marcos at 6:40 in the morning. As the day wore on he spoke at Austin, Georgetown, Temple, Waco, Hillsboro, Fort Worth, Grand Prairie, Dallas, Greenville, and the little rail stop of Bells, where he told the crowd, "I am going over to Bonham . . . and make the speech. . . . It's only 12 miles—why don't you just get in the car and come on over to Bonham, and I will give the Republicans the gun over there. I think you will like it!" The Bonham speech, last of the day, was carried by radio nationwide.

676

On board with him through the day were Rayburn, Governor Jester, and Congressman Lyndon Johnson, candidate for the Senate, who had just been certified by the Democratic State Convention as having defeated his rival in the primary, former Governor Coke Stevenson, by a total of 87 votes out of roughly 1 million cast.

At Waco a boy waved a Confederate flag and there were scattered boos from the crowd when Truman shook hands with a black woman. Otherwise, all was harmonious. But then neither did he mention civil rights.

At Rebel Stadium in Dallas, where authorities quietly did away with segregation for the day and blacks and whites were mingled in the cheering crowd as never before, Truman, for the first time, hit hard at the Republicans for the hypocrisy of their "high level" campaign—the Dewey speeches:

> So in making their speeches they put them on a very high level, so high they are above discussing the specific and serious problems which confront the people.... Republican candidates are apparently trying to sing the American voters to sleep with a lullaby about unity.... They want the kind of unity that benefits the National Association of Manufacturers ... the real estate trusts ... [the] selfish interests.... They don't want unity. They want surrender. And I am here to tell you people that I will not surrender....

Bonham, in the fertile Blackland Prairie, was Sam Rayburn's hometown, and at Bonham Truman went after Dewey again, saying Republican unity meant unity of the Tafts and the Martins of Congress—"unity in giving tax relief to the rich ... unity in letting prices go sky high ... unity in whittling away all the benefits of the New Deal." Was that really what they wanted, he asked the crowd.

> Some things are worth fighting for.... We must fight isolationists and reactionaries, the profiteers and the privileged class.... Our primary concern is for the little fellow. We think the big boys have always done very well, taking care of themselves.... It is the business of government to see that the little fellow gets a square deal.... Ask Sam Rayburn how many of the big money boys helped when he was sweating blood to get electricity for farmers and the people in small towns....

It was all language his audiences understood. He was truly, as Rayburn said, "one of the folks" and they let him know how much they approved.

At a reception later, at Rayburn's white frame house west of town, hundreds of people waited in a long line across the front lawn. "They came in droves and kept coming," remembered Margaret. When Truman's Secret Service detail, worried for his safety, refused to let him stand in the receiving line unless the names of all the guests were provided, Rayburn exploded, "I know every man, woman, and child here." They were all his friends, every one, Rayburn said; he would vouch for them personally.

So while Truman stood at the door shaking hands, and sipping now and then on a surreptitious bourbon-and-water, Rayburn called out each name. But then Rayburn exclaimed to the governor, "Shut the door, Beauford, they're comin' by twice."

For the Republicans money was never a problem. Talk of the big money behind Dewey was another sign supposedly of just how far out in front Dewey was, how certain his victory—on the theory that big money never followed a loser. But to find backing for Truman was nearly impossible. At small White House receptions for Democrats that spring and summer, Truman himself had had to ask for financial help, something he detested, just to get his campaign under way. At one such gathering in the Red Room in early September he had stood on a chair to say, in effect, that while he knew most people thought he was going to lose, he thought the President of the United States should have sufficient funds to take his case to the people, but that as things were he could not do that. There was no money to buy radio time. One of the most important parts of his speech in Detroit on Labor Day had to be cut, he said, because of insufficient funds to stay on the air. Now there was not money enough to get the train out of Union Station. His plea, reportedly, produced over $100,000.

When Truman asked Bernard Baruch to serve on the finance committee, Baruch refused, saying it was not his policy to play so partisan a role —an answer that infuriated Truman, who in sharp reply wrote, "A great many honors have passed your way . . . and it seems when the going is rough it is a one-way street." Baruch, his pride hurt, spoke of the President as "a rude, ignorant, uncouth man."

Others, too, turned him down, until finally he named for financial chairman Louis A. Johnson of Clarksburg, West Virginia, a former commander of the American Legion and Assistant Secretary of War who had headed the finance committee of the Democratic Party from 1936 to 1940. Johnson was a looming, bald-headed, headstrong corporation lawyer and millionaire who stood over six feet tall and weighed 250 pounds. A subject of controversy in the past, he would be again in time to come, to Truman's regret. But he took the job now when nobody else would, and he achieved amazing results, given the fact that no one other than Truman thought the ticket had the slightest chance.

Averell Harriman and Will Clayton were among the larger contributors. Harriman gave $5,000; Clayton, $9,000. Others included Stuart Symington; David Dubinsky of the International Ladies Garment Workers; Milton S. Kronheim, Sr., who controlled the wholesale liquor business in Washington; Jacob Blaustein, president of the American Jewish Committee; William Helis, a Louisiana oil man known as "the Golden Greek," who had been Governor Earl Long's biggest money backer; Cornelius Vanderbilt Whitney; and Pearl Mesta, the Washington hostess who came on board the Truman train at Gainesville, Texas, for the ride across Oklahoma, where her first husband had made a fortune in oil.

Floyd B. Odlum, the head of Atlas Corporation, a Wall Street investment company, put in $3,000, then rounded up another $20,000 from his associates. But the largest contribution seems to have come from Truman's old Kansas City friend Tom Evans, the drugstore king, who, after giving $3,000 himself, raised some $100,000 more in the Middle West.

As the train headed across Oklahoma, the weather remained ideal. Truman, in "fine fettle," spent much of the time out on the back platform waving at people as he sped along. If he was worried about campaign funds or anything else, no one would have known it. During a stop at Ardmore, having expressed his admiration for the Palamino horse of a cowboy who met the train, Truman examined the animal's mouth and declared it was six years old. "Correct!" exclaimed the delighted cowboy and the story appeared across the country: "Truman Gets Right Dope from Horse's Mouth."

The crowd at Ardmore was somewhere near forty thousand, more even, it was said, than for Gene Autry. At remote stations where no stops were scheduled people waited just to see the train go through. At Paul's Valley, Truman asked if it was true they grew taller corn than in Iowa and five thousand people happily roared yes. "Hello Harry," came shouts from the throng at Norman.

At Oklahoma City 100,000 turned out; 20,000 were at the State Fair Grounds for his speech. He had chosen Oklahoma as the time and place to answer Republican charges of communism in government and he was "strictly on the offensive." Such Republican tactics were only a "smoke screen" to hide their failure to deal with housing, price controls, education—*real* problems. His own Loyalty Program, he claimed, had proven the loyalty of 99.7 percent of all federal workers. It was not Republican talk that checked the Communist tide, but programs like the Truman Doctrine and the Marshall Plan, and that was "a plain and unanswerable fact." The government was not endangered by Communist infiltration. Publicity-seeking, electioneering Republicans with their irresponsible charges were doing more to damage national security than to strengthen it.

The speech was considered so important that for the first time the Democratic National Committee had dipped into its slim resources to pay for nationwide radio time.

But by then the money had run out. There was not enough even to move the train out of the station.

The crisis was resolved when Governor Roy J. Turner of Oklahoma, and a businessman from Shawnee, W. Elmer Harber, organized an emergency collection party on board the *Ferdinand Magellan* and raised enough contributions—"a substantial sum"—to keep the train rolling for another several weeks. But even so, remembered Charlie Ross, the campaign was never more than "one jump ahead of the sheriff."

The day following, Wednesday, September 29, was one of the biggest of the campaign. At Eufaula, Oklahoma, Truman gave his one hundredth speech. Before the day ended, he spoke sixteen times. There were crowds at Shawnee, Seminole, Wewoka, Muskogee, "tremendous" crowds at Tulsa. Crossing into Missouri, Truman told the throng at Neosho that he had already talked to 500,000 people that day—an understandable overstatement, given all he had seen. And so it went the rest of the journey through Missouri, Illinois, Indiana, Kentucky, and West Virginia. At Mount Vernon, Illinois, leaving his train to travel by motorcade, he stumped the down-state mining country for 140 miles, through five counties that had not gone Democratic in fifty years. "Mr. Truman [reported *The New York Times*] was the first Chief Executive to campaign in southern Illinois and the people turned out by the thousands, breaking through police lines, swarming around and through the procession of cars and yelling a noisy greeting."

With his headlong lambasting of Wall Street and "the special interests," the constant harkening to grim memories of the Depression, he sounded often as if he were running against Herbert Hoover. But at Carbondale, the sixth of nine stops in southern Illinois, he talked as he had not until now of the postwar era, of the "history" he himself felt responsible for and proud of, knowing how many in his audience remembered how differently things had gone after the first war.

A Democratic administration working with a Democratic Congress had seen to a swift reconversion in 1945, not only avoiding a postwar recession but achieving a peak of more jobs, a higher civilization, and better standards of living than ever before.

There is nothing like that in the history of the world after a great war. Bear that in mind. . . . Not very much has been said about that, but we had no riots and no bloodshed. We didn't have people crying for jobs. We didn't have farmers marching on Washington. We didn't have returning soldiers marching on Washington, because we took care of them in educational institutions and absorbing them back into the economy of the country without a debacle.

We enacted the Employment Act of 1946, pledging all our resources and efforts to the maintenance of prosperity.

We brought the United States to a position of unquestioned leadership in world affairs. Don't let anybody tell you anything different.

A warm reception in Kentucky had been anticipated, if for no other reason than Alben Barkley's presence on the ticket. But the crowds there surpassed all predictions. Truman was "never more human," reported the Louisville *Courier-Journal.* "He got down to earth and talked the language of the people. . . ." At Shelbyville, where a banner stretched in front of a wood-frame depot said: "Welcome Home President Truman and Family, Grandchildren of Shelby County," he talked of his grandfather, who had been married there. At Lexington, heart of the Bluegrass horse country, he reminded everyone that it didn't matter which horse was ahead or behind at any given moment in the race—it was the horse ahead at the finish that counted. To the several thousand gathered on the tracks at Morehead, Kentucky, pressing as close as possible to the rear platform of his car, he left no doubt what he expected of them:

Now, whatever you do, go to the polls early on election day, and don't waste any time. Just take that ticket and vote the Democratic ticket straight down the line, and you will be helping your country, and helping yourselves. You will not only be voting for me . . . but you will be voting for yourselves and your best interests. And I believe that is exactly what you are going to do.

At Montgomery, West Virginia, the final stop at 10:45 that night, Truman was so stunned by the size of the turnout at such an hour that before beginning his remarks he asked the photographers to turn their cameras around and take a picture of the people. That was the real news to show the country, he said.

· · ·

But what to make of the phenomenon of the Truman crowds?

Most correspondents attributed it to ordinary curiosity. Truman had made his campaign a vaudeville act, said *Time,* so naturally people would come out to see the show. The American people had a high regard for the office of President and so naturally wanted to see the man who occupied it, wrote Robert Donovan of the New York *Herald-Tribune,* who had been on the train from the beginning. Fletcher Knebel of the Cowles papers would remember in particular the stop at Shelbyville:

> The early morning haze was still hanging over the hills, and the sun wasn't up. But gathered around the railroad tracks, as far as you could see in any direction, was this incredible crowd of people—men holding kids up on their shoulders so they could see, little boys climbing trees and roofs, old grandpappies and men in overalls. Of course, we experts in the press car talked about the crowd, and we finally decided it didn't mean a damned thing. "Anybody will come out to see a man who is President of the United States, just to say they've seen one in the flesh. But that doesn't mean they'd vote for Harry Truman." He was going to lose. We believed it, because we wrote it every day.

Some correspondents, Jonathan Daniels noted, had convinced themselves that Truman's crowds were not Truman followers at all, but people wishing to see a very nice man on his way to oblivion.

To Walter Lippmann, who, as usual, was observing the world from his ivy-covered home in Washington, all such speculation was immaterial. Lippmann deplored the whole spectacle of a President chasing about the country devoting himself to parades and hand shaking, trying to "talk his way to victory." To Lippmann, who was secretly offering Dewey advice on foreign policy and who shared Dewey's contempt for Harry Truman, this was no time for a President to be away from his duties, and this President had been gone sixteen days. Unwittingly, wrote Lippmann, Truman had proven how little he mattered.

He had only begun to fight, Truman told the crowd waiting to welcome him at Union Station in Washington, Sunday morning, October 2. He would be heading off again in another few days. Others—his wife, daughter, his press secretary—looked exhausted, but not the President.

To his sister he wrote, "We made about a hundred and forty stops and I spoke 147 times, shook hands with at least 30,000 [people] and am in good condition to start out again. . . ." It would be the greatest campaign any President had ever made, he promised. "Win, lose, or draw people will know where I stand. . . ."

. . .

So much would be written and said about the Truman campaign of 1948, about the scrappy "Give-'em-hell-Harry" style that evolved, the headlong vigor and determination of the folksy, doomed candidate, that other factors bearing on the outcome were often overlooked. Truman was and remained his own show. Nor had any President ever worked harder at running for reelection. But other efforts behind the scenes were of considerable importance. Like all campaigns, his was a combination of many elements besides the candidate himself. Jack Redding, publicity director for the Democratic National Committee, would later write of the "classic unities of politics," saying they were as vital to a campaign as were the unities of time, place, and action to a successful drama. "When the unities fuse, the results achieved are far in excess of the sum of the parts." That Redding, Howard McGrath, and others worked as hard and effectively as they did was all the more remarkable given that they, too, knew perfectly what the odds were against them.

It was Redding, for example, who enlisted the services of the manager of a Polish-language newspaper in New York, Michel Cieplinski, who saw that all Truman press releases were translated into various foreign languages before being sent to foreign-language papers and radio stations around the country. Later, this would seem an obvious idea, but no one else had done it until then, and as Redding recalled, acceptance of the material was immediate. Truman stories were carried substantially as written—in Polish, German, Spanish, Italian, Russian, Swedish—and with 35 million people of foreign birth in America, or roughly 25 percent of the population, of whom 11 million were eligible to vote, this was no small break.

McGrath appreciated particularly the political importance of foreign-born Americans—it was with their support that he had been elected governor three times in Rhode Island—and he understood how greatly the Truman Doctrine and the Marshall Plan, as well as Truman's policy on immigration, mattered to such groups, that for no other reason than his stand on foreign policy, Truman had an excellent chance of winning their support.

It was arranged for the President to have his portrait painted by a beloved Polish artist, Tadé Styka, who, though an avowed Republican, became an immediate convert after hearing Truman speak to a group of Polish editors about the problems of the world as they affected Poland. ("Another hell of a day. I'm sitting for an old Polish painter, and I don't like to pose—but it's also part of the trial of being President," Truman had written in his diary on September 14. "He's painted a nice stuffed-shirt picture.") In October, after Styka presented the portrait at a formal ceremony at the White House, all seventy-two Polish papers in the country ran a picture of the painting, as well as Styka's personal praise for the President. To publicist Redding, it was a "political triumph."

Meantime, for the amusement of the press, a selection of the platitudes and banalities of the Dewey speeches was prepared and distributed:

"Our streams abound with fish."

"The miners in our country are vital to our welfare."

"Everybody that rides in a car or bus uses gasoline and oil."

"Ours is a magnificent land. Every part of it."

A sixteen-page, four-color comic-book biography was produced, *The Story of Harry Truman,* which, panel-by-panel, portrayed the Independence boyhood, the courtship of Bess Wallace, Truman's time on the farm, and how the neighbors judged him ("By crackies, in spite of Harry Truman's newfangled ideas about farmin', he's a durned good 'un!"). His part in the war took up two and a half pages, followed by his business failure ("You'd think the Republican Administration would do something to help small businessmen"), and the high points of his public service, including the presidency. To many the comic-book format seemed highly unfitting for a President. Several at the White House complained that it should never have been permitted without Truman's knowledge. But he had known and approved, and the book was a success. Three million copies quickly disappeared. In some places schools permitted distribution among students, who took the books home. *Time,* in a special feature, hailed it as "something new in 'campaign literature'," while regretting that it made no mention of "the late, great-bellied" Tom Pendergast.

Even more important and effective was a ten-minute Truman film, a "short" to be shown in movie theaters. (With approximately 20,000 theaters in the country, the weekly movie audience in 1948 was about 65 million.) Hearing that a Dewey film was being produced and paid for by the Republicans, Jack Redding, with no money available for films, threatened to have theaters picketed as unfair unless a "balancing" Truman story were made available. In response, the movie industry decided to produce a Truman film for nothing—Universal Newsreels lost the flip of a coin and did the work. With so little time left, and to keep costs to a minimum, *The Truman Story* was put together almost entirely from available newsreel footage, with the result that the finished production had a feeling of authenticity missing in the Dewey film, most of which had been staged. The candidate was seen as "neighbor Truman," shaking hands with people on the streets of Independence (including a black man in bib overalls). He was shown visiting Eddie Jacobson in his store, at Grand-view with his mother, but above all as the President, signing the Truman Doctrine, the Marshall Plan, addressing Congress, reviewing troops, conferring with Secretary Marshall beside the large globe in the Oval Office.

The two-reel film that had cost the Truman campaign nothing and was considered much more effective than its counterpart on Dewey would, in the final week before the election, play in theaters in every part of the country. "Thus, during the last six days of the campaign no one could go to the movies anywhere in the United States without seeing the story of the President," boasted Redding, who considered it the most important publicity break of the campaign.

Seventy-one-year-old Alben Barkley, meantime, was crisscrossing the country in a chartered DC-3 called *The Bluegrass*. In contrast to his much younger Republican counterpart and rival, Earl Warren, who was touring by train, Barkley had initiated what he called history's first "prop-stop" campaign. He flew 150,000 miles and delivered 250 speeches, mostly in small cities, farm towns, coal and railroad towns, labor halls, and small hotel dining rooms, his audiences sometimes numbering only in the hundreds. The press called him "the poor man's candidate," and Barkley enjoyed himself hugely, telling stories, speaking extemporaneously at almost any length, and giving no sign of wanting anything for himself, only to help the President and any number of local Democratic candidates. His own best help, he liked to say, came from the Republicans. Dewey's speeches reminded him, Barkley said, of an old Tennessee politician known as "Fiddlin' Bob" Taylor, who, in the era of the free silver issue, ran for governor by playing a violin and using his magnificent speaking voice to say as little as possible about anything specific, until finally he was pressed to state where he stood on the money question. "He paused dramatically," Barkley would say, savoring the story, "and he said, 'Here is where I stand. I am for a little more gold, a little more silver, a little more greenback—and a sprinkling of counterfeit.' "

When a reporter in New Haven, Connecticut, asked Barkley if he honestly thought the Democrats had a chance, Barkley replied, "Certainly. What do you think I'm running around for?"

One idea hatched behind the scenes by two of the new speechwriters proved a major embarrassment. David Noyes and Albert Carr, who were partial to the dramatic phrase or gesture—it was they who contributed the "pitchfork-in-the-back" line at Dexter—had concluded that the President needed to announce a bold move to dramatize his desire for world peace, and soon.

They proposed he send the Chief Justice, Fred Vinson, on a special mission to Moscow to see Stalin. That Vinson, as a member of the Supreme Court, had no connection with the diplomatic role of the executive branch, that Vinson knew nothing of the crisis in Berlin beyond what was in the papers, or had any experience in Soviet affairs, or in dealing with Stalin, were apparently not considered serious drawbacks.

Truman agreed to the scheme—a decision that suggested as nothing else would that for all his show of confidence he knew perfectly how desperate his situation was and was therefore willing to try almost anything. Undoubtedly, too, he hoped that so daring and unorthodox an approach might just give Stalin the chance to "open up," as he later wrote. He still thought Stalin could be reached, reasoned with, man-to-man. "If we could only get Stalin to unburden himself to someone on our side he felt he could trust fully, I thought perhaps we could get somewhere."

On his second day back at the White House, Sunday, October 3, without notifying George Marshall, who was at a United Nations General Assembly meeting in Paris trying to deal with the Berlin crisis, Truman called the Chief Justice to his office and asked him to make the trip.

Vinson was astonished. Members of the Court, he said, should confine themselves to their Court duties, and especially in an election year. But then, dutifully, Vinson consented to go.

The plan was for Truman to announce the mission on a special radio broadcast to the nation. Charlie Ross was instructed to arrange with the networks for a free, nonpolitical half-hour, for a statement of "major importance." The State Department was alerted, to make the necessary clearances with Stalin. Truman would remember requesting also that "every possible precaution" be taken against premature leaks.

The atmosphere at the White House was extremely uneasy. Nerves were on edge. Those of the staff who had been traveling with the President were still exhausted, while a number of those who had remained behind felt overworked and unappreciated. "There is much confusion and taut nerves [recorded the faithful diarist Eben Ayers], due to . . . the belief that the President is going to be defeated. There are a few optimists in the place. There are jealousies and undercurrents all through the staff."

The proposed "Vinson Mission" made tensions still worse. Clifford and Elsey argued vehemently against it, "almost violently," Elsey remembered.

But when Truman met with his advisers in the Cabinet Room on Tuesday, October 5, the majority view was that only a dramatic, "even desperate" measure could save the campaign.

Excusing himself from the meeting, Truman went to the Map Room to inform Marshall by teletype. But Marshall, appalled by the very idea of the Vinson scheme, vehemently objected, with the result that Truman immediately called the whole thing off.

When he returned to the Cabinet Room to report his decision, several at the table, including Jonathan Daniels, addressed him in no uncertain terms, arguing that the mission was his last, best chance. But Truman cut them off. "We won't do it," he said.

To Daniels, it was one of the most vivid moments of all he had witnessed in the White House. If ever there was a point when Truman seemed at his best, when he was more than large enough for the job, Daniels later wrote, it was then, and

> at a time when, by all reports, he seemed smaller than ever.
> He got up and went out of the glass-paned door to the terrace by the rose garden and walked alone—very much alone that day—back toward the White House itself. He was wrong, I thought, but he was strong, I knew. There were no dramatics about it. He never said he would rather be right than President. The next time I saw him he was laughing with the reporters, the politicians and the police as he got back on that long train which everyone seemed too sure was taking him nowhere.

He was gone just three days this time. A quick swing through eastern Pennsylvania, New Jersey, and upstate New York had been decided on, as an extra effort. The "Vinson Mission," presumably, was dead and buried, and no one the wiser. But there had been a leak. The radio networks, understandably, had insisted on knowing the nature of the "nonpolitical" announcement before relinquishing a free half hour in the middle of a presidential campaign. So Ross had told them "in confidence."

The story of the aborted peace mission broke wide open. Editorials accused Truman of attempted appeasement, of playing politics with foreign policy. "His attempted action was shocking because it showed that he had no conception whatever of the difference between the President of the United States and a U.S. politician," wrote *Time*. The campaign that had never had a chance was said to have been dealt a fatal blow. Dewey, publicly, decided to let the President's action speak for itself. Off the record, he told reporters huffily, "If Harry Truman would just keep his hands off things for another few weeks! Particularly, if he will keep his hands off foreign policy, about which he knows considerably less than nothing."

When Marshall flew in from Paris on Saturday, October 9, and stepped from his plane looking "ashen-faced," it was said he had come home to resign. In fact, though Marshall was in poor health, his relations with Truman were excellent. Indeed, Marshall assumed part of the blame for what had happened, apologizing to Truman for not having kept him better informed on the progress of negotiations in Paris.

Truman was not worried about the fuss in the papers. He found it hard to believe that the American people would fault a President too harshly for wanting to achieve peace in the world. He had been encouraged also by his three-day swing. At Albany, Dewey's own capital, ten thousand people had come down to the station in an early morning downpour to cheer and shout, "Give 'em hell, Harry!"

On Sunday, October 10, he was back on board the train, still behind in the polls, still exuding confidence, and with just three weeks to go.

III

Were one to pick a single representative day of all the many days in Harry Truman's drive for the presidency in 1948, a day that in spirit and content could serve as a classic passage in his whistle-stop odyssey, probably it would be Monday, October 11, when he barnstormed through central Ohio at the start of what was to prove a crucial swing into the Middle West.

Like the larger campaign, the day began in an atmosphere of gloom.

When Truman arrived in Cincinnati at 7:00 A.M., it was cold and raining. The streets from the railroad station to the Netherland Plaza Hotel, where he was to speak, were deserted. A reporter for the Des Moines *Register,* who had been traveling on board the Truman train for weeks, described him as looking that morning "like a man who had received bad news but felt the show must go on."

The morning was bleak and the whole plan for the day seemed pointless. At stake were Ohio's twenty-six electoral votes, but Ohio, the Buckeye State, was as formidable a Republican stronghold as any of the forty-eight states, with a Republican governor, nineteen Republican congressmen (as opposed to four Democrats), and two famous Republican senators, Taft and John Bricker, who had been Dewey's running mate in 1944. Moreover, Truman had decided to spend much of the day in rural Ohio, in places where, in 1944, the vote had run as much as 70 percent for Dewey.

It had been Bill Boyle who had urged Truman to campaign in Ohio and whose political sagacity Truman had decided to bank on. Boyle, who was still in charge of Truman's itinerary, was directing things now from an office at Democratic headquarters in Washington.

From Cincinnati, home of the Tafts, in the southwest corner of the state, Truman would head north on the B&O Railroad to Hamilton and Dayton, then on to a string of little towns, Sidney, Lima, Ottawa, and Deshler, where the train would turn east on the main line of the B&O, to stop at Fostoria, Willard, Rittman, and finally, that night, at industrial Akron, in the northeast corner. It was a trip of 350 miles. That Truman would even bother with towns like Ottawa or Willard struck many as a waste of time. But then to many observers the whole campaign was a waste of time. Dewey, who had carried Ohio against Roosevelt in 1944, was so sure of carrying it again, he would not actively campaign there. At one point while stopped in Ohio, Dewey did not trouble himself even to step out onto the rear platform, but sat in his compartment with the blind drawn. Told there was a crowd outside hoping to catch a glimpse of him, Dewey did not bother to raise the blind.

In eleven speeches at eleven stops, in the span of a fifteen-hour day, Truman hammered away steadily and happily at his same favorite themes —the high cost of living, the need for adequate housing, the intransigence and shortsightedness of the 80th Congress, the evils of the Taft-Hartley Act, and his desire for peace. He sang the praises of Franklin Roosevelt, and in the speech at Akron, the major speech of the day, he embraced as he never quite had in so many words the "entire philosophy" of the New Deal as his own, vowing "to build upon it an always better way of life."

There were no startling claims or announcements. He just kept pressing the attack, mindful always of where he was and to whom he was speaking. He praised the people of Hamilton for their wartime production record, a subject he knew about, he said, from his years on the Truman Committee. "I grew up on a farm and I always like to see good farming country," he said at rural Ottawa, then spent ten minutes describing the gains and prosperity achieved by farmers in the "Democratic years" since 1932.

At Lima, home of a locomotive factory, he shouted, "I've worn out three locomotives and we'll use three more before we get through, so that will make it good for business here...."

"Well, I say thank God for the whistle-stops of our country. They are the backbone of the nation," he told the citizenry of little Fostoria.

Bess and Margaret appeared on cue from behind the blue curtain and always to the delight of the crowd. "Would you like to meet the Boss?" Truman asked at Lima, adding that most married men had bosses at home. "He's the President," wrote the editor of the Lima *News,* and yet, "he's just an ordinary family man, proud of his wife and daughter. He has something in common with many who heard him."

(It was shortly after this that Bess told the candidate that if he called her "the Boss" one more time, she would get off the train.)

After the dreary start at Cincinnati the skies had literally cleared. The rain ended, the sun broke through. A crisp autumn wind was blowing, and with the maples beginning to turn gold and red, Ohio was a calendar picture for October in small-town, rural America.

From Hamilton on, the whole way, the crowds were big and responsive and Truman's vitality returned, as if he had been given a powerful injection. The sight of ten thousand people spilling out in all directions at Hamilton produced what the Des Moines reporter called "the most striking change in the Democratic candidate's demeanor I have witnessed in all our trips." Everyone was surprised by the size and mood of the crowds. Ohio's youthful, handsome former governor, Frank Lausche, who was running a "lone wolf" campaign for another try at the governorship, had come aboard at Cincinnati, not at all sure that being seen with Harry Truman was the best thing for his fortunes. But as he told Truman in dismay, he had never seen such throngs. At Dayton, where he and Truman rode in a motorcade, there were fifty thousand lining the route. Lausche, who had planned to get off the train at Dayton, decided he would stay on board.

No two of Truman's speeches were the same. Nearly all of what he said was spontaneous, his energy and enjoyment appearing to compound as the day went on, the more miles he covered, the more he talked of "the common people," "the American people," or "you good people of Deshler," or Dayton or Fostoria or Willard. As before, he played on fear of hard times, the memory of lean years, knowing from experience what so many who turned out to see him had been through, knowing, for example, how, among farmers, recollection of the 1920s in no way resembled the cliché, good-time picture of the Jazz Age. "If you don't want to go backward," he said at Ottawa, "if you don't want to slide downhill to bankruptcy and poverty the way you did in the Republican 12 years of rule back there in the 20's, you better get out early on election day and look after your own interests." He knew, he had been through it.

Take stock of your prosperity now, he was saying. Remember, it wasn't the Republicans who pulled the country back on its feet.

His opponent, he said, talked all the time of unity, because he didn't dare do anything else. "He's afraid that if he says anything, he will give the whole show away." Meantime, the real leaders of the Republican Party in the "do-nothing" 80th Congress had been "sent off into the bushes to hide until the campaign is over."

The people had a right to know where the candidates stood. That was why he had come to their town. They were entitled to know what the issues were, entitled to take a look at their President and hear what he had to say and decide for themselves. That was the idea of democracy: the people decide.

"They tell me that Seneca County is a Republican county," he said at Fostoria. "Well, that's all right with me. I want the Republicans of Seneca County to know what I think . . ."

His best trackside talk of the day was at Willard, in Huron County, Ohio, at 4:55 in the afternoon. It was a perfect example of Truman the barnstormer at top form.

A railroad town of plain, square frame houses and a population of four thousand, Willard had been called Chicago Junction until 1917, when it was renamed for Daniel Willard, president of the B&O Railroad. There was a surgical gloves factory in town, a Rotary Club, a good high school football team, and a World War II honor roll at the corner of Myrtle Avenue and Pearl Street listing 876 names. Will Rogers was known to have had lunch once in the restaurant in the red-brick, Italianate railroad station.

Truman's train stopped just east of the station, and Truman, looking west from the rear platform, the late afternoon sun full in his face, appeared still fresh and clean in a dark blue double-breasted suit and dark blue tie. Flags snapped in the wind. A crowd of several thousand pressed closer, cheering, waving to him, calling, "Hi, Harry!" As in so many other places, people who had brought small children held them on their shoulders, so they could say one day they had seen the President.

The excitement in Willard had begun building long before the train appeared down the tracks. When Franklin Roosevelt's train stopped at Willard during the campaign of 1944, and thousands of people had gathered, Roosevelt never appeared. They saw only his dog Fala.

Truman was introduced by Harlow A. Stapf, the proprietor of a popular bar and grill in Willard and president of Huron County's Young Democratic Club, who, to Truman's delight, was wearing a campaign necktie with Truman's portrait on it.

Truman began with a few customary words of appreciation for the warm welcome, which he followed with a note of local history, in this instance, Daniel Willard, who, as Truman said, was still fondly remembered for his generosity to suffering families of the town during the Depression. Several key themes were then sounded—housing, inflation, the 80th Congress—and Truman did a little advance drumbeating for the main speech to come, at Akron, which was to be carried by radio.

A personal observation on the value of opinion polls was also added at

Willard, for the first time. The complete talk, all spontaneous, lasted twelve minutes. Characteristically, it was without flourishes. There were no quotations for effect, no big words. He used no jargon, no stock jokes, nothing cute. But the intent of his thought was always clear. He spoke in good, solid, complete sentences—as indeed he did the whole way along, through the entire campaign. From what he said, his audience never had any trouble knowing what he meant.

I have had a most wonderful reception in Ohio today. It has been just like this all across the State of Ohio. We started in Cincinnati and came up the western border of the State, and now we are headed for Akron, and it seems as if everybody in the neighborhood and in every city has turned out, because they are interested in what is taking place in the country today and in the world.

It is good to be here in Willard this afternoon, even for a short stop. You people here in Willard have a great tradition, a tradition set by Dan Willard many years ago when he was President of the Baltimore and Ohio Railroad. I think it is significant that the name of Dan Willard is loved and respected all over the country, because he was the man who believed in the common people of the nation. He liked and respected the people who worked for him, and he recognized their right to join a union and bargain collectively.

Now, Dan Willard did not sneer at the "whistle-stops" of our country. He trusted people, and people trusted him. I think that is a good principle. It is a good way to run a railroad, and it is a good way to run a country. That is the way I have tried to run the country, but the Republican Congress would not cooperate, this 80th Congress.

Now, that is the way, with your help, we are going to run the country for the next 4 years.

The Republican candidate and the Republican Congress do not trust the people. They just work along at their old problem of trying to fool the people into voting for the interests of the few. They try to do it without telling you what they think. I have been out among the people now for nearly a month. I believe you have got a right to know what I think, and I have been telling you what I think.

Tonight, in Akron, I am going to talk over the radio about the Republican Taft-Hartley law. I am really going to tear the mask off the Republican Congress and the Republican candidate.

In Cincinnati this morning, at a splendid meeting, I talked about housing. I told the people there how your President had tried for 3 years to get a decent housing bill passed. At other places we stopped at in Ohio, I talked about prices. I told the people how your President had twice called Congress into special session in an effort to get something done about inflation that is picking your pockets.

Since I have been in the White House, there has not been a moment of doubt about where I stood on issues which are of concern to the people of America today. I have always spoken out and I have taken a stand on every issue as it has come up. I don't wait for any polls to tell me what to think. That is a statement some of the Republican candidates cannot make.

You know, since I started this campaign, I have talked to over 3 million people in various communities. They have come down to the train, just as you did this afternoon, because they were interested in this election. They know that the peace of the Nation and the peace of the world depend, to a large extent, on this election. They know that the continued prosperity of our Nation depends upon this election, and they want to know where the candidates stand on the issues. And that is what I have been telling you as simply and as plainly as I know how.

There is not a single, solitary man or woman in the United States today who can't find out in two minutes where I stand on the important matters like foreign policy, labor, agriculture, social security, housing, high prices, and all the other problems we as a nation have to face.

But there is not a single, solitary man or woman in the United States who has been able, within the last 2 months, to find out where the Republican candidate stands on these issues.

I think he is going to get a shock on the second of November. He is going to get the results of one big poll that counts—that is the voice of the American people speaking at the ballot box.

And he is going to find out that the people have had enough of such fellows as the one from this district who has been helping the 80th Congress to turn the clock back. And I think you are going to elect Dwight Blackmore to Congress in his place. And I think you are going to elect Frank Lausche Governor of Ohio.

If you do that, you will be voting in your own interests, and when you vote in your own interests on the second of November, you cannot do anything else but vote the straight Democratic ticket, and I won't be troubled with the housing problem. I will live in the White House 4 more years.

Now, that will be entirely to your interests. You will have a Congress who believes in the people, and you will have a President who has shown you right along that he believes in the welfare of the country as a whole, and not in the welfare of just a few at the top.

Akron, heart of the rubber industry, a big labor town, solidly Democratic, had been expected to give the Democratic standardbearer a good reception, however dismal his prospects. But the welcome at Akron was "tumultuous," everything that Cincinnati failed to provide, and more. People jammed the streets three and four deep, an estimated sixty thou-

693

sand, in what was reported in the national press as "the biggest political show in the city's history," everyone "cheering wildly" as Truman passed. The Akron Armory was packed. It was the perfect, grand finale for the day and Truman was radiant.

"I have lived a long time—64 years—and I have traveled a lot," he told the crowd, "but I have never seen such turnouts as I have seen all over this great country of ours. . . . The Republicans have the propaganda and the money, but we have the people, and the people have the votes. *That's* why we're going to win!"

Reporters traveling with Truman agreed it had been one of if not his best day of the campaign. By conservative estimates, the day's crowds totaled 100,000 people, even before Akron.

By eleven that night he was back on the train and heading west again. At 8:00 A.M. the next morning, at Richmond, Indiana, he was out on the rear platform ready to start another day.

It had been known for some while that *Newsweek* magazine was taking a poll of fifty highly regarded political writers, to ask which candidate they thought would win the election. And since several of the fifty had been on the train with Truman during the course of the campaign— Marquis Childs, Robert Albright of the Washington *Post,* Bert Andrews of the New York *Herald-Tribune*—there had been a good deal of speculation about the poll. It appeared in *Newsweek* in the issue dated October 11, and on the morning of Tuesday, October 12, three weeks before election day, at one of the first stops in Indiana, Clark Clifford slipped off the train to try to find a copy before anyone else. The woman at the station newsstand pointed to a bundle wrapped in brown paper, telling him to help himself. "And there it was!" remembered Clifford years afterward.

Of the writers polled, not one thought Truman would win. The vote was unanimous, 50 for Dewey, 0 for Truman. "The landslide for Dewey will sweep the country," the magazine announced. Further, the Republicans would keep control in the Senate and increase their majority in the House. The election was as good as over.

Returning to the train, Clifford hid the magazine under his coat. With the train about to leave, the only door still open was on the rear platform.

So I walked in. President Truman was sitting there, and so I cheerily said, "Good morning, Mr. President." He said, "Good morning, Clark." And I said, "Another busy day ahead." "Yes," he said. . . . So I walked off . . . and I got almost by him when he said, "What does it say?" And I

694

said, "What's that, Mr. President?" He said, "What does it say?" And I said, "Now what does what . . . ?" He said, "I saw you get off and go into the station. I think you probably went in there to see if they had a copy of *Newsweek* magazine." And he said, "I think it is possible that you may have it under your jacket there, the way you're holding your arm." Well, I said, "Yes, sir."

So I handed it to him. . . . And he turned the page and looked at it . . . [and] he said, "I know every one of these 50 fellows. There isn't one of them has enough sense to pound sand in a rat hole."

Truman put the magazine aside and made no further mention of it. "It just seemed to bounce right off of him," Clifford remembered.

There were three stops in Indiana, four crossing Illinois, where farmers on tractors waved small flags or held up hand-lettered "Vote for Truman" signs.

"I was with Truman in the central part of the state," wrote Paul Douglas, Democratic candidate for the Senate. "There was great applause, and there were constant shouts of 'Give 'em hell, Harry' . . . and he was at home with the crowd . . . he was simple, unaffected, and determined. We were proud of him."

At Springfield after dark old-time campaign flares burned, the streets were filled with people. No one could come to Springfield without thinking of Abraham Lincoln, Truman said in his speech.

I just wonder tonight, as I have wondered many times in the past, what Lincoln would say if he could see how far the Republican party has departed from the fundamental principles in which he so deeply believed. Lincoln came from the plain people and he always believed in them. . . .

He crossed into Wisconsin and Minnesota. At Duluth, where he rode in an open car with Hubert Humphrey, fully half the population, some sixty thousand people, lined Superior Street for two miles, crowding so close in places that the car brushed their clothes.

At St. Paul, an overflow crowd at Municipal Auditorium whistled, stamped, and shouted as he delivered one of the best fighting speeches of the campaign.

Now, I call on all liberals and progressives to stand up and be counted for democracy in this great battle. . . . This is one fight you must get in, and get in with every ounce of strength you have. After

November 2nd, it will be too late.... The decision is right here and now.

But we are bound to win and we are going to win, because we are right! I am here to tell you that in this fight, the people are with us.

The crowd at St. Paul numbered 21,000—15,000 inside the auditorium, another 6,000 outside. Dewey, in his appearance at St. Paul two days later, drew only 7,000.

Heading east again, Truman said there were going to be "a lot of surprised pollsters," come November 2.

Some of the Dewey people were beginning to worry. When Dewey asked his press secretary, Jim Hagerty, how he thought Truman was doing, Hagerty said, "I think he's doing pretty well." Dewey replied that he thought so, too.

When at Kansas City Dewey met privately with Roy Roberts of the *Star,* he was told the farmers of the Middle West were defecting from the Republican ticket in droves and that he had better do something about it quickly. *Time* was now describing Dewey's crowds as only "mildly curious," his speeches as "not electrifying."

"Our man is 'in,' " reporters were assured by the Dewey staff. "He doesn't have to win votes, all he has to do is avoid losing them." Dewey himself told Taft that he had found over the years that when he got into controversies he lost votes—an observation Taft thought disgraceful.

There was much that Dewey could have said in answer to Truman. The "do-nothing" 80th Congress was after all the Congress that had backed the Truman Doctrine and the Marshall Plan. Truman's assault on the Taft-Hartley Act failed to note that a majority of his own party in the House had voted approval and then to override his veto. The evil influence of Wall Street on the Republican Party, as described by Truman, might have been made to sound a bit hollow, had it been pointed out that such important figures within his own official family as Harriman, Lovett, and Forrestal had all come to Washington from Wall Street. Truman's dismissal of Henry Wallace had been a fiasco. His handling of the railroad strike might well have been made a major issue. "The only way to handle Truman," Taft wrote later, "was to hit every time he opened his mouth." But Taft was a cantankerous man and Dewey was determined to stick to his own strategy.

Meantime, a "slight misadventure" at a town called Beaucoup, in Illinois, had raised a stir. Just as Dewey was about to speak at Beaucoup, his train had suddenly lurched a few feet backward toward the crowd. There were screams, people fell back in panic. "That's the first lunatic I've had for an engineer," Dewey blurted angrily into the microphone. "He probably ought to be shot at sunrise. . . ."

The cold arrogance of the remark did Dewey great damage. The story appeared everywhere, and with it, the observation of the engineer—"the lunatic"—who said, "I think as much of Dewey as I did before and that's not very much."

With only two weeks to go, a new Gallup Poll showed Dewey's lead cut to six points. In the seclusion of the Governor's Mansion at Albany, Dewey ordered a showing of all the newsreels of the campaign and what he saw left him greatly disturbed. He was losing ground steadily, he was told. But when his campaign manager, Herbert Brownell, put through calls to some ninety Republican committeemen and women around the country, all but one urged him to keep to the present strategy.

Among professional gamblers, the betting odds against Truman on the average were 15 to 1. In some places, they were 30 to 1.

Besides the gamblers' odds, the opinion polls, the forecasts by columnists, political reporters, political experts, Truman by now had the majority of editorial opinion weighed heavily against him. His frequent claim that 90 percent of the papers opposed his election was a campaign stretch of the truth. It was 65 percent, which in fact meant overwhelming press support for Dewey, and especially since it included virtually all the biggest, most influential papers in the country. *The New York Times,* the Los Angeles *Times,* the Washington *Star,* the Kansas City *Star,* the St. Louis *Post-Dispatch,* and *The Wall Street Journal* all endorsed Dewey. The Detroit *Free Press* called Truman intellectually unqualified. The Chicago *Tribune,* though far from admiring the liberal Republican candidate, simply dismissed Truman as "an incompetent."

An editorial backing Truman, such as appeared in the Boston *Post,* under the heading "Captain Courageous," was a rare exception. Harry S. Truman, said the Boston paper, was

> as humbly honest, homespun and doggedly determined to do what is best for America as Abraham Lincoln.
>
> In standing by his party and its inherent principle of the greatest good for the greatest number, he has emulated other great Americans —Jefferson, Jackson, Cleveland, Wilson, Franklin Roosevelt and Alfred E. Smith. Like them, in the words of the old song, he—
>
> *Dared to be a Daniel,*
> *Dared to stand alone,*

TRUMAN

Dared to hold a purpose firm
Dared to make it known.
By that token he should win. America likes a fighter.

More representative were such conclusions as drawn in the Los Angeles *Times*: "Mr. Truman is the most complete fumbler and blunderer this nation has seen in high office in a long time."

Even papers that expressed an open fondness for the President as a man chose not to support him. "However much affection we may feel for Mr. Truman and whatever sympathy we may have for him in his struggles with his difficulties," said a front-page editorial in the Baltimore *Sun,* "to vote him into the presidency on November 2 would be a tragedy for the country and for the world."

For Charlie Ross, Clark Clifford, George Elsey, for everyone riding the Truman train, the campaign had become an unimaginable ordeal—interminable, exhausting in a way comparable to nothing in their experience.

"If you're winning, you'd be surprised how you can withstand fatigue," Clifford would say later. "If you're losing it becomes oppressive. . . . They were *long, long* days. I was young and strong, and in perfect health. From time to time I wasn't sure I was going to make it."

The candidate, who bore the main brunt, seemed indefatigable, his outlook entirely positive. Between speeches he could lie down and go immediately to sleep, however pressed others were, however rough the road bed. "Give me 20 minutes," he would say.

"Strain seemed to make him calmer and more firm," Jonathan Daniels recalled. At no point in the entire campaign did any of the staff, or the press, or his family ever see Truman show a sign of failing stamina, or failing confidence.

Once during a lull en route to St. Paul after the stop at Duluth, Truman had asked George Elsey to write down the names of the forty-eight states, after which he gave Elsey the number of electoral votes for each and told him how they would go. By his count he would win with 340 electoral votes. Dewey would have 108, Strom Thurmond 42, Henry Wallace none.

"He was not putting on a show for anybody," Elsey would recall. "Obviously he wasn't trying to influence or persuade or sell me. This is what the man himself *believed*."

"He either honestly believes he will win . . . or he is putting on the most magnificent and fighting front of optimism that any doubtful candidate ever did," wrote Bert Andrews of the New York *Herald-Tribune*.

The Truman staff was another matter, Andrews noted. They all appeared "a bit grim."

The work went on from seven in the morning until past midnight, day after day, until they lost all sense of time, until every day became merged with every other and everything became a blur. Margaret would remember the world beginning to seem like an endless railroad track. She would sit by the window and take idle snapshots of the passing country-side—telephone poles whizzing past, empty plains, country roads that seemed to lead nowhere.

As Ross wrote, the President was driving himself "unmercifully," and no one on the staff wished to do any less. Ross, "the old philosopher," suffered from arthritis and heart trouble, yet worked twelve, fourteen hours a day, knowing how much Truman counted on him. "For years afterward," Clifford said, "I'd sometimes wake up at night in a cold perspiration thinking I was back on that terrible train."

And day by day, steadily, the crowds grew larger. Clearly, something was happening. The mood of the crowds, their response to Truman was changing. People seemed always to be happier after hearing him speak.

"I remember thinking," said Clifford, " 'Well, I don't know whether we're going to make it or not, but, by God, I bet if we had another week we would surely make it.' There was something rolling. . . . We could sense it and the newspapermen could sense it."

Robert C. Albright, the veteran political correspondent for the Washington *Post,* speculated, "Could we be wrong?"

"We've got them on the run and I think we'll win," Truman wrote to his sister from the White House on October 20. After a day in Washington, he had flown to Miami, where 200,000 people filled the streets. From Miami he flew north to Raleigh, where there were "people all along the way from the airport which is fifteen miles out of town."

Things were looking decidedly more hopeful on several fronts. In Berlin, with improved landing facilities and more efficient air-traffic control after months of experience, the airlift was plainly succeeding at last, against all odds and forecasts. At his desk in the Oval Office on Friday, October 22, Truman authorized the dispatch to Berlin of still more of the giant C-54 transports, another twenty-six planes. "The airlift will be continued until the blockade is lifted," General Clay declared triumphantly in Berlin. Winter supplies for the city were guaranteed.

Back on his train again, Truman was telling a delighted crowd at Johnstown, Pennsylvania, that the GOP stood for "Grand Old Platitudes," and at a thunderous rally at Hunt Armory in Pittsburgh, he declared, "I am an old campaigner, and I enjoy it."

His opponent, Truman said, acted like a doctor whose magic cure for everything was a soothing syrup called unity. And here were the American people going for the usual once-every-four-years checkup.

"Say you don't look so good!" Truman said, acting the part of the doctor.

"Well, that seems strange to me too, Doc," he answered, as the voice of the people. "I never felt stronger, never had more money, and never had a brighter future. What is wrong with me?"

"I never discuss issues with a patient. But what you need is a major operation."

"Will it be serious, Doc?"

"Not so very serious. It will just mean taking out the complete works and putting in a Republican administration."

The audience roared with laughter. He had made the cool, letter-perfect Dewey a joke at last.

Chicago went all out. Politicians who had taken part in the great Roosevelt rallies of 1936 and 1940 said they had never seen anything like it. Possibly as many as fifty thousand people marched in the parade from the Blackstone to Chicago Stadium. Another half million lined the route. Marching bands blared, fireworks burst overhead. Yet, oddly, not everyone was cheering. Here and there, remembered Paul Douglas, were people with tears in their eyes. "The newspapers had convinced them that Truman was going to lose, and they believed that the gains they had made under the New Deal were going to be taken away. They seemed to feel something precious was about to be lost, and they wanted to come out and show their sympathy and support for the doughty little warrior who was doing battle for them against such great odds." Privately, Douglas felt that he, too, like Truman would go down to defeat in his bid for the Senate.

At the packed stadium, to a crowd of 24,000 Truman delivered his most savage speech of the campaign, a wild attack, uncalled for, in which he said a vote for Dewey was a vote for fascism. The authors of the speech were again David Noyes and Albert Carr, whose main purpose, Noyes later said, was to provoke Dewey into fighting back, a strategy Truman accepted. "An element of desperation comes into a campaign," Clifford would say in retrospect. "And fatigue leads to it."

Dewey was properly outraged, so much so he drafted a new speech for his own scheduled appearance at Chicago, but then was persuaded by his advisers to drop it, not to get into a slugging match with Truman. He mustn't get nasty, mustn't make mistakes with victory so close. Reportedly, Dewey's wife said that if she had to stay up all night to see him tear up what he had written, she would do it.

"They have scattered reckless abuse along the entire right of way coast to coast," Dewey would say only in Chicago, speaking of Democrats in general, "and now, I am sorry to say, reached a new low in mudslinging. ... This is the kind of campaign I refuse to wage...."

Truman offered no explanations or apologies. He was on his way east, and the "tide was rolling." Dewey's "Victory Special" would follow directly after him a day later.

At Boston a quarter of a million people banked Truman's parade route, cheered and yelled and enjoyed the obvious enjoyment written all over the candidate's face. To the packed house at Mechanics Hall, Truman said Republican talk of unity was all "a lot of hooey—and if that rhymes with anything, it is not my fault."

On Thursday, October 28, after nine stops and nine more speeches in Massachusetts, Rhode Island, and Connecticut, the Truman campaign reached New York, where the outpouring of humanity and enthusiasm exceeded everything thus far. Had Truman's whole career gone uncelebrated until now, the roaring, ticker-tape welcome that New York gave him would have made up for it. Over a million people turned out. Arriving at Grand Central Station in late afternoon, Truman set off on a nine-mile tour through the city, through the October twilight, led by a thundering motorcycle escort of a hundred machines. Truman was perched on the top of the back seat of an open car. Bess and Margaret followed six cars back.

> The confetti, ticker-tape and [shredded] telephone book demonstration along 42nd Street was extraordinary [wrote Meyer Berger in *The New York Times*]. It fell in great flurries and much of it landed on the open cars. It curled and twisted from high windows. It fell in other places like driven snow. Through it all, the President's figure, at times, was only dimly seen. He was smiling and he never stopped waving to curb crowds and to men and women clustered at high windows....

As he rolled through Seventh Avenue, in the garment district, loudspeakers, cranked to full volume, blared "Happy Days Are Here Again."

He made three rousing outdoor speeches—at Union Square, City Hall, and Sara Delano Roosevelt Park on the Lower East Side—spoke at a dinner at the Waldorf-Astoria, then again that night, his fifth speech of the day, at Madison Square Garden, where two of his old nemeses, Albert Whitney and Harold Ickes, joined him on stage while the band played "I'm Just Wild About Harry." A crowd of sixteen thousand roared its approval when Truman—evoking the memory of Al Smith, Robert Wagner, and Franklin Roosevelt—pledged his faith in the New Deal, pledged his support of Israel, and again, as at Pittsburgh, brought down the house with another doctor story. For weeks, he said, he had had the odd sensation that someone was following him. It had troubled him so he asked the White House physician about it, but the White House physician had said not to worry. "There is one place where that fellow is not going to follow you—and that's into the White House."

The race nearly over, Truman was determined to finish strong. Friday the 29th, under a clear blue sky, in what by now was being described as "Truman weather," he covered thirty-six sunlit miles through the city. He was seen and cheered, police said, by 1,245,000 people. There was not a discordant note through the whole day. Tugs on the East River tooted a greeting. In the Bronx, crowds screamed: "Hi, Harry" and "Hi, Margaret." "You can throw the Galluping polls right into the ash can," he told a delighted throng in Queens. If the campaign was only a ritual, as said so often, then it was a ritual people loved and they loved him for embracing it with such zest.

In Harlem he made his only civil rights speech of the campaign. It was no impassioned personal declaration, but focused on the work of his Civil Rights Commission and its "momentous" report. Nonetheless, his appearance marked the first time a major party candidate for President had stumped Harlem, and after reminding his almost entirely black audience that he had already issued two executive orders to establish equal opportunity in the armed services and federal employment, he vowed to keep working for equal rights and equal opportunity "with every ounce of strength and determination I have." The cheering in Harlem was the loudest of all.

When he rose to speak at the Brooklyn Academy of Music that evening, the audience gave him a twelve-minute ovation.

For months efforts had been made to persuade Eleanor Roosevelt to say something, anything, to help Truman—efforts that Truman himself refused to have any part in—but all to no avail. From Paris, where she was attending the United Nations session, she wrote to Frances Perkins that she had not endorsed Truman because he was "such a weak and vacillating person" and made such poor appointments. Now, at the last minute, she changed her mind, hoping to help the Democrats to carry New York.

"There has never been a campaign where a man has shown more personal courage and confidence in the people of the United States," she said in a broadcast from Paris.

· · ·

The scene of the final rally of the campaign, and the last platform appearance Harry Truman would ever make as a candidate for public office, was the immense Kiel Auditorium in St. Louis, where there was not an empty seat.

Discarding the speech efforts of his staff, he went on the attack, lashing out one last time at the Republican Congress, the Republican press, the Republican "old dealers," and the Republican candidate. The stomping, cheering crowd urged him on.

He felt afterward that he had done well. In any case, he had done the best he knew how.

The odyssey was over. Sunday, October 31, Halloween, was spent at home at 219 North Delaware Street. "Home!" remembered Margaret. "I couldn't believe it."

Truman worked on an election-eve radio address to be delivered from the living room the following night.

> From the bottom of my heart I thank the people of the United States for their cordiality to me and their interest in the affairs of this great nation and of the world. I trust the people, because when they know the facts, they do the right thing. . . .

Election day, up at five, he took his usual morning walk, read the papers, and had breakfast. Then, trailed by a swarm of reporters and photographers, he, Bess, and Margaret went to Memorial Hall three blocks away on Maple Avenue and voted.

A final Gallup Poll showed that while he had cut Dewey's lead, Dewey nonetheless remained a substantial five points ahead, 49.5 to 44.5. The betting odds still ranged widely, though generally speaking Dewey was favored 4 to 1.

The New York Times predicted a Dewey victory with 345 electoral votes. "Government will remain big, active, and expensive under President Thomas E. Dewey," said *The Wall Street Journal. Time* and *Newsweek* saw a Dewey sweep. The new issue of *Life* carried a full-page photograph of Dewey "the next President" crossing San Francisco Bay by ferry boat. Alistair Cooke, correspondent for the *Manchester Guardian,* titled his dispatch for November 1, "Harry S. Truman, A Study in Failure."

Changing Times, the Kiplinger magazine, announced on its front cover in bold, block type, "What Dewey Will Do." Walter Lippmann wrote about the work Dewey had cut out for him in foreign policy. Drew Pearson, who thought Dewey had run "one of the most astute and skillful campaigns in recent years," surveyed the "Dewey team," the "exciting, hardworking, close-knit clique" that would be moving into the White House. Marquis Childs questioned whether the Democratic Party could ever be put back together again, while in their final column before election day the Alsop brothers worried over "how the government could get through the next ten weeks with a lame-duck president: Events will not wait patiently until Thomas E. Dewey officially replaces Harry S. Truman."

For Truman there were but two irregular, entirely unprofessional samplings to take heart from. One was from Les Biffle, the Senate Secretary, who, on his own, posing as a "chicken peddler," had traveled about rural areas asking people how they felt about the election. Truman needn't worry, Biffle had reported—the common people were for him. The other was from the Staley Milling Company of Kansas City, which had taken a "pullet poll" among farmers who bought chicken feed in sacks labeled "Democratic" or "Republican." The Democratic feed had pulled well ahead, but then the company decided there must be something wrong and so abandoned its polling efforts.

Among the campaign staff, the state of physical and emotional exhaustion, the sense of relief that finally the ordeal was over, all but precluded any capacity for rational judgment of the outcome. Their devotion to the President was greater than ever, but that, of course, was another matter. Yet some now honestly thought he might just make it. In Washington, after a quiet day at the White House, Eben Ayers worked out his own remarkable assessment of the situation in the privacy of his diary:

> Were it not for all these predictions and the unanimity of the pollsters and experts, I would say the President has an excellent chance. All the signs that I see indicate it. The crowds which have turned out for him on his campaign trips have grown steadily.... I cannot believe they came out of curiosity alone. Other conditions are favorable to the President, the general prosperity of the country. It is contrary to political precedent for the voters to kick out an administration in times of prosperity.
>
> The Dewey personality and campaign has not been one to attract voters. He is not liked—there is universal agreement on that. I have repeatedly asked individuals, newspapermen and others, if they could name one person who ever said he liked Dewey and I have yet to find one who would say "yes." The Dewey campaign speeches have dealt only with national "unity," with the promise to do things better and more efficiently. He has not discussed issues clearly or met them head-on at any time. I have repeatedly asked my wife if it is possible that the American people will vote for a man whom nobody likes and who tells them nothing.

· · ·

Late in the afternoon of election day, Truman decided to disappear from the scene. It was an odd move and one never quite explained. The impression was he wanted to be alone, simply to get away from everyone and everything and be by himself. Only his immediate family and the Secret Service knew where he was going.

The Secret Service was about to have a changing of the guard at 219 North Delaware. At 4:30 a Secret Service field car, a black four-door Ford carrying the night shift, pulled into the driveway behind the house. The day shift was ready to leave, to drive back to Kansas City, to presidential headquarters at the Muehlebach Hotel.

A crowd had gathered in front of the house. Truman went out the kitchen door and climbed into the back seat of the Ford with Agents Henry Nicholson and Gerard McCann on either side of him. Agent Frank Barry took the wheel and Jim Rowley, head of the detail, got quickly into the front seat beside the driver. The car pulled away, drawing no attention.

They drove to Excelsior Springs, the little resort town across the Missouri in Clay County, and checked into the Elms Hotel, the same place Truman had escaped to sixteen years earlier, crushed by disappointment the night he learned he was not to be Tom Pendergast's choice for governor.

The sprawling three-story stone-and-timber hotel was the latest of several that had occupied the site since mineral springs were discovered there in the 1880s. Its chief attractions were seclusion, peace, and quiet. Franklin Roosevelt, John D. Rockefeller, and Al Capone were all known to have escaped from public view at the Elms. On this November night the place was nearly deserted.

The rooms picked by the Secret Service were on the third floor rear, at the end of a long hall. Truman, who had left home without baggage, borrowed bathrobe and slippers from the hotel manager and went for a steambath and a rubdown, after which, at 6:30, he had a ham and cheese sandwich and a glass of buttermilk sent up to his room. As he ate, he switched on the bedside radio.

The first final returns were from a town in New Hampshire called Hart's Location, where the vote, including two absentee ballots, was Truman 1, Dewey 11. By eight o'clock Missouri time, Dewey was ahead in such key eastern states as New York and Pennsylvania, but Truman was leading in the popular vote overall, nationally.

About nine, Truman called Jim Rowley into the room. He was going to get some sleep, Truman said, but Rowley was to wake him if anything "important" happened.

"We all, of course, stayed awake," remembered Agent McCann. "There was nothing to do but stay awake."

The head of the Secret Service, James J. Maloney, was in New York, having decided Governor Dewey was certain to be the next President. Maloney and five of his men had taken up positions outside an upper-floor suite at the Roosevelt Hotel, where Dewey was relaxing with family and friends, waiting to go down to the packed Roosevelt ballroom to announce his victory.

The crowd outside 219 North Delaware had grown larger, filling the sidewalks on both sides of the street and much of the front lawn. A stream of automobiles passed steadily by, their drivers slowing to see the excitement or to call to friends. Newspaper and radio correspondents had set up headquarters across the street, on the porches of the Luff and the Noland houses.

The night air was cool. Lights burned in every window of the Truman house, though the shades were all drawn except in the window of the upstairs hall, where a portrait of Franklin Roosevelt could be plainly seen.

Reporters were counting on the President to make an appearance. "We waited and waited and waited," remembered Sue Gentry of the *Examiner,* for whom, like others who lived in the neighborhood, it was turning into one of the most exciting nights ever in Independence. For by 11:00 P.M., though several commentators and the Republican chairman, Brownell, were still predicting a Dewey victory, Truman, incredibly, was still ahead in the popular vote. The crowd on the lawn began singing—"For He's a Jolly Good Fellow" and "Hot Time in the Old Town Tonight."

Then the porch light went on and Margaret came out. She stood on the porch smiling and making a hopeless gesture with both arms.

"Dad isn't here," she announced. "I don't know where he is," she said, which wasn't true.

The reporters were incredulous. "We *couldn't* believe it," remembered Sue Gentry. Some of the crowd began drifting away.

The lights in the windows remained on all night, as they would remain on in houses all over town and all over the country.

"What a night," Margaret wrote in her diary, conscious that she was at the center of history in the making. By midnight Truman was ahead in the popular count by 1 million votes.

I haven't been to bed at all. I've been running up and down the stairs all night answering the phone on the direct-line telephone [to the

Presidential Suite at the Muehlebach] to Bill Boyle who gave me the returns. We are ahead, but at about 1:30 A.M. we hit a slump—then gradually came up again. Dad has slipped away to Excelsior Springs and the reporters are going crazy trying to find him. They have offered me anything if I'll just tell them in which direction he went.

Sometime near midnight, Truman awoke and switched on the radio, picking up NBC and the clipped, authoritative voice of political commentator H. V. Kaltenborn, the voice that had reported Munich in 1938 and that to much of America was the very sound of the news. Though the President was ahead by 1,200,000 votes, Kaltenborn said, he was still "undoubtedly beaten." Truman switched him off, turned over, and went back to sleep.

Through their vigil over the next several hours, Agents Rowley, Nicholson, McCann, and Barry also stayed tuned to NBC. "And all of a sudden," remembered Rowley, "about four in the morning comes this thing that the tide has changed. And so I figured, '*This* is important!' And so I went in and told him. 'We've won!' And he turns on the radio."

Truman, Kaltenborn was saying, was ahead by 2 million votes, though Kaltenborn still did not see how Truman could possibly be elected, since in key states like Ohio and Illinois the "rural vote," the Dewey vote, had yet to be tallied.

"We've got 'em beat," Truman said. Rowley was told to get the car ready. "We're going to Kansas City."

IV

The black Ford pulled in front of the Muehlebach a few minutes before six o'clock, just as it was getting light. The street was empty.

At presidential headquarters, the penthouse on the seventeenth floor, Truman found only four who were up and about—Matt Connelly, Bill Boyle, and two Kansas City attorneys, Jerome Walsh and young Lyman Field, who had been barnstorming for Truman on his own all across Missouri, and who now, as the one nearest the door, had the honor of being the first to shake the President's hand and wish him congratulations.

Charlie Ross, sprawled across one bed, appeared to be dead drunk, but he was only exhausted. It had been a rough night for all of them, but for Ross especially. The press had been furious with him for not saying where

Truman was, and Ross, finally, had lost his temper, showing "his first case of nerves" since the campaign began. He didn't know where the President was, nor did Matt Connelly. None of them knew.

The rooms were a shambles. "There wasn't a drop of liquor around, by the way," wrote Jerome Walsh later, trying to describe the scene. "It was all black coffee and cigarettes and four telephones jangling. . . . At 6:00 we were out on our feet."

Truman, though unshaven, appeared rested and bright-eyed, "as refreshed as a man with two weeks' vacation behind him." Shedding his coat, he sat down on the couch and asked "how things were going."

Though Dewey had carried New York, New Jersey, Pennsylvania, and Michigan, Truman had won in Massachusetts, carried all the Old South but four states—South Carolina, Alabama, Mississippi, and Louisiana, which had gone to Thurmond—and was leading in Wisconsin, Iowa, and Colorado. He was ahead by slim margins in Illinois, Ohio, and, so far, crucially, in California. In the popular count he was ahead by nearly 2 million votes. Dewey had yet to concede.

But what most impressed those in the room was Truman's perfect calm at such a moment. To Lyman Field, the President seemed "wholly unconcerned." Here, by every sign, was a man on the verge of pulling off the biggest political upset in American history. He had confounded the experts, the professionals in both parties, not to say a nationwide chorus of columnists and poll takers. The President who had had to fight just to get the nomination from his own party was beating the opponent everybody had said was unbeatable. It was not only a supreme moment of triumph in a long political life, but one of the greatest personal victories of any American politician ever. Yet here he sat as if nothing out of the ordinary was happening. "He just seemed the same old Harry Truman," Field would say forty years later, the memory of that morning still a wonderment to him.

Jerome Walsh was so moved by Truman's total composure that he decided to record the scene while everything was still fresh in his mind, in a letter to a friend written just days later:

> He displayed neither tension nor elation. For instance someone remarked bitterly that if it hadn't been for Wallace, New York and New Jersey would have gone Democratic by good majorities. But the President dismissed this with a wave of his hand. As far as Henry was concerned, he said, Henry wasn't a bad guy; he was doing what he thought was right and he had every right in the world to pursue his course. Someone else pointed to a Kansas City *Star* headline which read, "Election in Doubt" or something like that. The President grinned. "Roy Roberts will change that in a few

hours," he said. I did not hear the name Dewey mentioned by the President.

I am trying to give you . . . a sense of the astonishment we all felt at the unbelievable coolness with which the President faced up to the whole situation, the manner in which he took the thing for granted, as if he had read the answer in a crystal ball two weeks before. At 6 A.M. there still was plenty of reason for Governor Dewey to refuse to concede. Conceivably Ohio might have switched in late returns. California or Illinois might have toppled and the President's lead been sharply reversed. . . . Actually, Mr. Truman, at 6 A.M., hardly seemed interested in the matter. To him the election was won, had always been won since the day he began carrying his fight to the people, and his mind was already turning to other aspects of his program. . . . The serenity of the President . . . suggested to all of us, I think, that his years of crisis in office have equipped him with a very large reserve of inner strength and discipline to draw upon.

Walsh, as he further wrote, could not help but think of Abraham Lincoln. "Is this sentimental outpouring?" he asked. "I don't think so."

Charlie Ross would remember being awakened by somebody shaking him at 6:30. "I looked up and there was the boss at my bedside—grinning. We all started talking at once."

Truman put through a call to Bess and Margaret, both of whom burst into tears at the sound of his voice.

He called in a barber, had a shave and a trim, then changed into a fresh white shirt, blue polka-dot tie and double-breasted blue suit.

By 8:30, Ohio went for Truman, putting him over the top with 270 electoral votes. A celebration broke out in the Presidential Suite. Vivian Truman, Ted Marks, Eddie Jacobson, Al Ridge, Tom Evans, and Fred Canfil arrived. The hall outside was jammed with exuberant well-wishers.

At 9:30 Truman was declared the winner in Illinois and California. By now, too, it was clear the Democrats had won control of both houses of Congress.

At 10:14 (11:14 at the Roosevelt Hotel in New York), Dewey conceded the election. A wild cheer went up on the seventeenth floor of the Muehlebach, and as the doors to the suite were thrown open, more friends, politicians, and reporters pushed their way in.

"Thank you, thank you," Truman kept saying, shaking hands, and behind the thick glasses there were tears in his eyes.

At Independence, minutes later, every bell, whistle, siren, and automobile horn seemed to go off at once. It had never occurred to anyone in town to plan a victory celebration, but now Mayor Roger Sermon quickly declared a holiday. Schools were let out and at day's end in a roaring spontaneous outpouring of pride and goodwill forty thousand people jammed the Square to see and honor the victorious native son.

Speaking from a small podium, visibly touched by what was the biggest crowd in the history of the town, with his courthouse behind him, Truman called it a celebration not for him but for the country.

V

The country was flabbergasted. It was called a "startling victory," "astonishing," "a major miracle." Truman, said *Newsweek* on its cover, was the Miracle Man.

He had won against the greatest odds in the annals of presidential politics. Not one polling organization had been correct in its forecast. Not a single radio commentator or newspaper columnist, or any of the hundreds of reporters who covered the campaign, had called it right. Every expert had been proven wrong, and as was said, "a great roar of laughter arose from the land." The people had made fools of those supposedly in the know. Of all amazing things, Harry Truman had turned out to be the only one who knew what he was talking about.

Actress Tallulah Bankhead sent Truman a telegram: "The people have put you in your place." Harry Truman, said the radio comedian Fred Allen, was the first President to lose in a Gallup and win in a walk.

A few papers had predicted a close election. A Washington correspondent for the Pittsburgh *Courier,* a leading black paper, had also described how, in theory, Truman might win. John L. Clark of the *Courier* had traveled with the Truman train part of the time and had taken seriously the size of the crowds. Victory for the President in twenty-three states outside the South, plus a break in the South, or an upset in California or New York, could spell victory for the President, Clark wrote, though he did not predict this would happen. Nor did the author Louis Bean, who, in a book published in July, *How to Predict Elections,* also offered the theoretical possibility of a Truman upset.

As it was, Truman carried 28 states with a total of 303 electoral votes, and defeated Dewey in the popular election by just over 2,100,000 votes. In the final tally, Truman polled 24,105,812, Dewey 21,970,065.

Dewey, who won in 16 states, had 189 electoral votes. Henry Wallace and Strom Thurmond each polled slightly more than 1,100,000 votes. Thurmond, with his victory in four southern states, had 39 electoral votes.

Wallace, who failed to carry a single state, thus received no votes in the Electoral College.

The outcome in the congressional races was 54 Senate seats for the Democrats, 42 for the Republicans. In the House the Democratic victory was overwhelming, 263 seats to 171.

Though Dewey had carried the three industrial giants of the Northeast, New York, New Jersey, and Pennsylvania, as well as his own home state of Michigan, Truman had defeated him soundly in thirteen of the country's biggest cities and captured the Republican stronghold of the rural Midwest, carrying Ohio, Illinois, Minnesota, Wisconsin, even Iowa, "the very citadel of Republicanism." Truman held on to seven states in the South, despite Strom Thurmond. He carried the four border states of West Virginia, Kentucky, Oklahoma, and his own Missouri, where he won by more than a quarter of a million votes. In the West, where at the start only Arizona had looked safe for the Democrats, he took every state but Oregon.

Truman also held Dewey to a smaller part of the total vote nationwide (45.1 percent) than Dewey had in 1944 running against Roosevelt.

As would be pointed out, Truman's margin of victory in such key states as Ohio, Illinois, and California had been narrow. He won Ohio by a bare 7,000 votes, Illinois by 33,000, California by 17,000. A switch in any two of these three states would have left him with less than a majority in the Electoral College and thrown the decision to the House of Representatives. Had Dewey won in all three states, then Dewey would have eked out victory in the electoral vote and thus won the presidency, while Truman finished in front in the popular tally. A cumulative shift of just 33,000 votes apportioned to the three states would have done it.

But it was also true that a similar shift in other states would have made Truman an even bigger winner. Truman very nearly won in New York, for example, and unquestionably would have had it not been for Henry Wallace, who rolled up half a million votes in the state (which was half Wallace's national total). "I think the mistake was not giving more time to New York. We should have carried New York," Clark Clifford would say. Dewey won there by only 61,000—in his own state—and New York meant 47 electoral votes. Had there been no Henry Wallace, or a Strom Thurmond, Truman might well have gained another 85 electoral votes, giving him an Electoral College landslide.

Efforts to explain why the impossible had happened began at once, as did, understandably, a great deal of soul searching among reporters, editors, and broadcasters who had fallen down on the job so very conspicuously.

To H. L. Mencken, who delighted in the outcome exactly because it "shook the bones of all ... [the] smarties," the answer was simply in the contrast of the two contestants as they presented themselves to the voters. "Neither candidate made a speech on the stump that will survive in the schoolbooks, but those of Truman at least had warmth in them," wrote Mencken in one of his last columns, at the close of a long career of appraising the American political scene. "While Dewey was intoning essays sounding like the worst bombast of university professors, Truman was down on the ground, clowning with the circumambient morons. He made votes every time he gave a show, but Dewey lost them."

To Dewey himself, it had all turned on the farm vote. "The farm vote switched in the last ten days," he claimed in a letter to Henry Luce, "and you can analyze figures from now to kingdom come and all they will show is that we lost the farm vote. . . ."

Joe Martin, who with the new Democratic majority in the House was to be Speaker no longer, said the fault was with the Republican Party, which had "digressed" too far from the people. Like many of the old guard, Martin and Taft both thought Dewey had run an abysmal campaign. "You've got to give the little man credit," said Arthur Vandenberg, in a somewhat patronizing tribute to Truman. Taft, furious, said, "I don't care how the thing is explained. It defies all common sense to send that roughneck ward politician back to the White House."

To the surprise of many, it would turn out that the Democrats had spent more on the campaign than the Republicans, the common impression to the contrary, $2,736,334 compared to $2,127,296—though many of the largest donations to the Democrats came pouring in after the fact, after November 2, some $700,000 in postdated checks.

A special study drawn up by the Republican Policy Committee would conclude, in essence, that the Republicans had only themselves to blame. They had "muffed" their best chance in sixteen years to win the presidency and keep control of Congress. The fault was mainly with the Dewey strategy and the Dewey performance, his "aloofness," speeches "high above the voters' heads," the mistake of "swallowing uncritically the Democratic propaganda." Dewey, said the report, had been "drugged" by the polls, and thus "sacrificed the initiative." Truman's hard-hitting assault on the 80th Congress, "however unprincipled and demagogic," had been "brilliant" since it had enabled him to "divert the battle" away from his own and his party's record. "He succeeded in arousing public indignation. . . . The Democratic sweep in Congress and its retention of the presidency is eloquent testimony to the brilliance of their strategy."

As amply substantiated by a number of studies, the farm vote, the labor vote, the black vote, and the vote of the West had all counted heavily in

Truman's success and in the Democratic sweep overall—just as the Rowe memorandum had forecast.

Nor was there any question about the value of the kind of campaign Truman chose to run. His big effort in Texas, for example, gave him the largest majority in Texas of any state. The extra swing by automobile that he made in the traditionally Republican counties of downstate Illinois turned the tide there and was decisive in carrying Illinois. The campaign through rural Ohio on October 11, the whistle-stop day that had seemed to others a wasted effort, apparently did make a difference. In counties that Dewey had carried in 1944, Truman was the winner.

Ethnic minorities voted strongly for Truman. Catholic voters, too, it was found, had gone Democratic in large majorities. In some predominantly Catholic wards in Boston and Pittsburgh the vote for Truman exceeded past tallies for Al Smith and FDR.

In the noise and excitement of the Presidential Suite after Dewey conceded, Truman reportedly said, "Labor did it." But while several of the biggest unions in the country did work hard to get out the vote and supplied major financial backing for his campaign, John L. Lewis and Alvanley Johnston were in Dewey's camp, and to lose in New York, New Jersey, Pennsylvania, and Michigan was hardly a sign that labor had carried the day.

More important, as Dewey said, was the farm vote and here, just as the Truman forces foresaw, the drop in the price of corn played a part. Once, in 1921, falling grain prices had bankrupt haberdasher Truman. Now they helped keep President Truman in the White House. Of the eight largest corn-producing states, he carried all but two.

Black support for Truman had been overwhelming. He polled more than two thirds of the black vote, a percentage higher than ever attained by Franklin Roosevelt. In such crucial states as Ohio and Illinois it could be said that the black voter had been quite as decisive as anyone in bringing about a Truman victory. Speaking of Truman's civil rights program and its impact on the election, J. Howard McGrath called it both honest statesmanship and politically advantageous. "It lost us three Southern states, but it won us Ohio, Illinois, would have carried New York for us if it had not been for Henry Wallace, and it was a great factor in carrying California."

The precarious state of the world also appeared to have benefited the Truman campaign, and particularly as it became clear that the Berlin Airlift was a resounding success. Several of Truman's sharpest critics, Walter Lippmann among them, now also grudgingly concluded that even the "inept" Vinson affair had proved a political net gain for Truman after all. "The bear got us," said Dewey's staff man, Elliott Bell, referring to the Russian menace.

Also, clearly, a host of strong Democratic candidates were a major factor. In Illinois, most notably, Truman's slim but crucial margin of 31,000 votes stood in sharp contrast to the resounding triumphs of Paul Douglas in his senate race and Adlai E. Stevenson, the Democratic candidate for governor. Douglas won by 400,000 votes, Stevenson by a still more astonishing 570,000 votes.

Hubert Humphrey had won his senate race in Minnesota. Estes Kefauver, who had campaigned in a coonskin cap, was the new Senator-elect from Tennessee, another state in the Truman column. Democratic candidates for governor had won in Connecticut and Massachusetts. Frank Lausche had been elected governor in Ohio by a margin of more than 200,000 votes.

Predictions of a Dewey landslide, it was widely believed, had lulled Republican voters into a state of false complacency. Had the polls not been so one-sided and unanimous, many argued, there would have been a bigger Republican effort, fewer Republican "stay-at-homes" on election day, and a Dewey victory. But a study of the campaign conducted by analyst Samuel Lubell for the *Saturday Evening Post* indicated quite the opposite. Republican victories in the industrial East, said Lubell, had been largely the fault of apathy among old Roosevelt voters who had concluded Truman didn't have a chance. "Far from costing Dewey the election, the [Democratic] stay-at-homes may have saved him almost as crushing a defeat as Landon suffered in 1936."

George Gallup, Elmo Roper, and other public opinion specialists were openly dumbfounded. He didn't know what happened, Gallup said. "I couldn't have been more wrong. Why I don't know," Roper admitted.

From later studies, it appears the polls were reasonably accurate up until mid-October, the point when Gallup completed his final survey of the campaign for the forecast that was released just before election day. The fault was probably not that the polls were imperfect, but that they were two weeks out of date. And it was in those final two weeks apparently that a massive shift took place.

Nearly everywhere in the country, it seems, a large number of people who agreed that Dewey was certain to win, and who no doubt would have bet on his winning, went to the polls and voted for Truman.

In Ohio, "up and down the state," reported William Lawrence of *The New York Times,* not a single Truman voter with whom he talked had expected Truman to win. "But a majority of the 'little people' from the mines, mills and farms, having made their decision quietly and thoughtfully, went out and voted for him anyway."

Two Ohio farmers, joking about the dissatisfaction of a neighbor who had voted for Dewey, were overheard saying, "What's the matter with that fellow anyway? Can't he stand four more years of prosperity?"

"I kept reading about that Dewey fellow," said another man, "and the more I read the more he reminded me of one of those slick ads trying to get money out of my pocket. Now Harry Truman, running around and yipping and falling all over his feet—I had the feeling he could understand the kind of fixes I get into."

He had talked all summer of voting for Dewey, a farmer in Guthrie County, Iowa, told a reporter. "But when voting time came, I just couldn't do it. I remembered . . . all the good things that have come to me under the Democrats."

She voted for Truman, said Freda Combs of Decatur, Illinois, because he was "the common man's man."

To his immense readership in every part of the country, Walter Lippmann explained the outcome as a posthumous triumph for Franklin Roosevelt. The election, Lippmann said, was simply another victory for the New Deal.

It was a view with which Truman modestly concurred. "It seemed to have been a terrific political upset when you read the papers here in this country," Truman would write in response to a letter of congratulations from Winston Churchill. "Really it was not—it was merely a continuation of the policies which had been in effect for the last sixteen years and the policies that the people wanted."

But to Edward Folliard of the Washington *Post,* as to most others who had witnessed the campaign firsthand, what it had all come down to was Harry Truman's own "gallant battle," his faith in himself and in the voters. As a barnstormer, the President was "surely the best of his time."

There was something in the American character that responded to a fighter, said the Washington *Post* on its editorial page. "The American people admire a man with courage even though they don't always agree with him," wrote Drew Pearson, who had been as blatantly mistaken in what he wrote prior to November 2 as almost anyone in journalism. "You just have to take off your hat to a beaten man who refuses to stay licked," conceded the ultra-conservative New York *Sun.*

Richard Strout, in *The New Republic,* would describe election night as an experience no political writer would ever forget:

There was personal humiliation for us as a prophet, but a glowing and wonderful sense that the American people couldn't be ticketed by polls, knew its own mind and had picked the rather unlikely but courageous figure of Truman to carry on its banner.

The feeling was widespread that so heavy a blow to the prestige of the polls could only be good for the country. As Eben Ayers wrote, "There has been a danger, it has seemed to me, that the polls would reach a point, if they continued to be right, where they could easily control the outcome of an election."

Some of the most intense and interesting of all postmortems went on at the New York headquarters of Time Incorporated, where telegrams from readers poured in saying, "Ha, Ha, Ha!" A "burden of doubt" had been cast over *Time* and *Life,* the editors were "deeply unhappy," said editor-in-chief Henry Luce in a confidential memorandum to his department heads. Luce blamed himself as much as anyone. "I personally paid less attention to this campaign than to any previous campaign in my lifetime," he admitted. Reporters and editors had been deluded not just by the polls but by politicians in both parties. Everybody should have known better, everybody should have taken his job more seriously, Luce said, and worked right to the end—"like Harry Truman did!"

To Luce the main cause for Dewey's defeat was Dewey. "His personality was against him."

The managing editor of *Time,* T. S. Matthews, took the position that there was nothing new about the press being wrong on elections. The press was often out of touch with the popular will.

> I think the press has been pretending to much more wisdom (or is it smartness?) than it had any right to claim, and has been getting away with murder for some time [Matthews wrote to Luce]. The plain fact now appears to be that (as far as politics is concerned, at least) the press hasn't known what time of day it is for years.

The great mistake now would be to see Truman as a political miracle-worker. "It was *not* a one-man miracle—that's too easy—but an unsuspected, overlooked, misreported national phenomenon."

But to the managing editor of *Life,* Joseph J. Thorndike, Jr., the problem centered on bias. "Of course, we did not intentionally mislead our readers," he wrote.

> But I do think that we ourselves were misled by our bias. Because of that bias we did not exert ourselves enough to report the side we didn't believe in. We were too ready to accept the evidence of pictures like the empty auditorium at Omaha and to ignore the later crowds. We were too eager to report the Truman "bobbles" and to pass over the things that were wrong about the Republican campaign: empty

Dewey speeches, the bad Republican candidates, the dangers of Republican commitments to big business. I myself had many misgivings about these things but thought that what the hell, the election was already decided, we could get after the Republicans later. . . .

Truman's victory, said Thorndike, was "primarily a personal triumph."

And this, as it turned out, was the conclusion of *Time* in its first issue after the election. "He did it all himself," said the magazine in tribute to Truman the politician. He was the "new champion" in American politics, "the absolute boss of a resurgent Democratic party."

"TRUMAN WORKS A POLITICAL MIRACLE," ran the headline on the lead story in *Life*. Truman was now "the durable hero in shining spectacles," "one of the fightin'est men" who ever went through a campaign.

To such staunch Truman loyalists as Sam Rayburn and George Marshall, to the weary White House staff workers who had been with him all the way, there was never any question as to why Truman won. He had done it by being himself, never forgetting who he was, and by going to the people in his own fashion.

Harry Truman deserved 90 percent of the credit, said Sam Rayburn. "You have put over the greatest one-man fight in American history," wrote Marshall to Truman on November 4. "You did exactly what you told me and what nobody else believed possible."

"I think that Harry Truman grew, too," wrote Charlie Ross, "grew spiritually." Truman had campaigned so hard, said Ross, because he genuinely believed the essential welfare of the country was at stake. He wanted peace in the world, prosperity at home, and he wanted to make the Democratic Party truly the party of the people. Also, wrote Ross, there was a "purely personal" motive. "He had been described as a little man, fumbling, inept, not measuring up to the President's job. He had a human desire to prove his detractors wrong."

Like others, Clark Clifford thought Dewey's people had done a poor job. "I think Dewey's whole campaign was a mistake. . . . They were greedy and dumb, and anxious to get back to power." But that was not the explanation for Truman's success. Nor did Clifford think it was due to extraordinary political acumen on Truman's part.

It wasn't in my opinion because he was a skilled politician that he won. He was a good politician . . . a sensible politician. . . . But that wasn't why he was elected President. . . . It was the remarkable courage in the man—his refusal to be discouraged, his willingness to go through the suffering of that campaign, the fatigue, the will to fight every step of the way, the will to win. . . .

It wasn't Harry Truman the politician who won, it was Harry Truman the man.

Early the morning of Thursday, November 4, as Truman stepped out onto the rear platform of the *Ferdinand Magellan* during a brief stop in St. Louis, photographers snapped the picture that would be remembered and enjoyed more than any other of the campaign. Truman was smiling, chatting with reporters, when someone handed him a copy of the Chicago *Tribune,* his least favorite newspaper, across the front of which ran the huge, soon-to-be famous headline: "DEWEY DEFEATS TRUMAN." Holding the paper aloft with both hands, grinning from ear to ear, the man who had been given no better than a fighting chance seemed to be saying not only, "Don't believe everything you read in the papers," but that in America it is still the people who decide.

Like some other photographs of other presidents—of Theodore Roosevelt in a white linen suit at the controls of a steam shovel in Panama, or Woodrow Wilson at Versailles, or Franklin Roosevelt, chin up, singing an old hymn beside Winston Churchill on board the *Prince of Wales* in the dark summer of 1941—this of Harry Truman in 1948 would convey the spirit of both the man and the moment as almost nothing else would.

On Friday, November 5, Truman returned to Washington in triumph. The welcome was the biggest, most enthusiastic outpouring for a President in the history of the capital. So great had been the excitement in the city the day before that the papers had forecast crowds of perhaps half a million people. But at least 750,000—two thirds of the city—lined his route from Union Station to the White House.

The day was warm, sunny, perfect. Truman, Bess, Margaret, Vice President-elect Barkley and his daughter, Mrs. Max Truitt, and Howard McGrath rode in a huge, seven-passenger open Lincoln, with two Secret Service men standing on the rear bumper. Truman and Barkley sat up on the back of the rear seat.

Passing the stone-fronted offices of the Washington *Post,* Truman looked up to see a big sign strung across the second floor: WELCOME HOME FROM CROW-EATERS.

The day after the election, the staff of the *Post* had sent a telegram asking him to attend a "Crow Banquet," to which all newspaper editorial writers, political reporters, pollsters, radio commentators, and columnists would be invited. The main course was to be old crow *en glâce.* Truman alone would be served turkey. Dress for the guest of honor would be white tie, for the others, sackcloth. In response Truman had written that he had "no desire to crow over anybody or to see anybody eat crow figuratively or otherwise. We should all get together now and make a country in which everybody can eat turkey whenever he pleases."

Confetti showered down. A band played "I'm Just Wild About Harry." Truman waved his hat and smiled.

At the White House, he stepped to a microphone on the North Portico to say thank you. The whole stretch of Pennsylvania Avenue, all of Lafayette Square, everywhere, as far as he could see, there were people, waving, cheering, calling out to him.

PART FIVE

WEIGHT OF THE WORLD

15

Iron Man

*Clearly he was conscious of the terrible responsibility his
victory had won him. His would be decisions affecting,
possibly, the very future of mankind. Ahead of Harry
Truman's America, nameless, half-imagined dangers lurked
in every shadow. None knew this better than he.*

—Washington *Evening Star,* Inauguration Day, 1949

I

Thursday, January 20, 1949, was chill and dazzling in Washington, with
a stiff wind out of the north and "100 percent" sunshine, as the National
Weather Bureau reported. The cloudless sky over the city was a vivid sea
blue. Colors everywhere stood out in the sparkling winter atmosphere.
Everything gleamed in sunlight—white marble, band instruments, scarlet
tunics, brass buttons, long lines of polished black official cars. From
Capitol Hill to the White House, along the whole length of Pennsylvania
Avenue, hundreds of flags whipped in the wind like the flags in patriotic
films.

It was a day made to glorify the occasion, "a perfect Inaugural Day," as
the President's daughter wrote in her diary. The temperature by noon
was in the high 30s, though with the wind, it felt colder.

There had been no full-scale inaugural festivities in Washington since
before the war, and this was to be the biggest, most costly inauguration
on record, the parade the greatest in the city's history. The year before,
when their return to presidential power had seemed such a certainty, the
Republicans who controlled the 80th Congress had voted an unprecedented $80,000 for the most lavish inaugural day ever. Now the jubilant
Democrats, with delighted approval from the President, had decided to
spend it all.

The size of the crowds was astonishing. More than a century before, in

1829, on a comparably bright winter day, Democrats had descended upon the city from "every point on the compass" to see Andrew Jackson take the oath in front of the East Portico of the Capitol. It was the first time the ceremony had been held there, and fifteen to twenty thousand people attended. At Jackson's famous White House reception afterward, the mob had grown so unruly that to relieve pressure and save the building, pails of whiskey had been carried out onto the lawn. Now, to see Harry S. Truman, the modern Jacksonian, another "man of the common people" and "hero of the great political drama of 1948," ride to the Capitol and take the same oath at the same place, more than a million people were gathered, more than ever before in history.

They had been pouring into the city for days, whole delegations in western hats, big-city politicians with their retinues, labor bosses, committeewomen, delegates from the American Legion, the NAACP, Boy Scout troops, Florida bathing beauties, and fifty extremely proud residents of Independence, Missouri, led by Mayor Roger Sermon, as well as ninety-eight veterans of Battery D of the 129th Field Artillery, with Monsignor Curtis Tiernan as their nominal leader. Entertainers and screen stars arrived—Gene Kelly, Jane Powell, Jane Froman, Lena Horne, Edgar Bergen, Abbott and Costello—and the big bands of Benny Goodman and Lionel Hampton, in addition to Phil Spitalny and his All-Girl Orchestra.

Most hotels were sold out, some at triple the normal rate, and for the first time in the city's history black guests were staying at several of the best hotels, since Truman, as no President before, had ordered that black Americans were to be as welcome as anyone at the main events of the inaugural.

The "invited guests" for the East Portico ceremony alone, those with seats beneath the inaugural stand, numbered 17,740, and another 44,000 paid $2 to $10 for seats in the wooden grandstands along the parade route.

It was also to be the first inauguration broadcast on television. As great as were the crowds on hand, another audience ten times greater would be watching—an estimated 10 million in fourteen cities connected by coaxial cable. This would make it the largest number of people ever to watch a single event until then. Indeed, more people would see Harry Truman sworn in as President on television on January 20, 1949, than had witnessed all previous presidents taking the oath since the first inauguration of George Washington. (As far away as St. Louis, the western limit of the cable, the pictures, like the day in Washington, were reported "bright and clear.") And 100 million more would be listening by radio.

Yet, as often said afterward, there was no one who took part, no one watching the parade, no one at the dinners and dances, who had a better time than the man at the center of the spectacle, for whom, by all signs, it was the happiest day of his life, "his day of days," as his daughter would say. "Weather permitting, I hope to be present," Truman had written in high spirits, in answer to his own invitation to the ceremonies.

It had been two months since the Key West vacation in November, and much had transpired. Because of conditions at the White House, the President and his family were now living across the way in Blair House, at 1651 Pennsylvania Avenue. The old Executive Mansion, as Truman had been informed the day of his return to Washington after the election, was in such a "dangerous" state it could collapse any moment. Ironically, the only safe place in the building was his new balcony. ("Doesn't that beat all!" he said.)

The facts of the situation were made public for the first time; the White House was closed to visitors. The President, the First Lady, and Margaret all departed for Key West—for Bess and Margaret it was a first visit to the "Little White House" in Florida—and with painters and decorators working night and day, Blair House was made ready, furniture moved in, in time for the family's return at Thanksgiving.

Privately Truman could not have been happier with the change and for the chance to make sure the White House was restored as it should be. With his love of building, love of history, he was genuinely interested in every detail of the project. "It is the President's desire that this restoration be made so thoroughly complete that the structural condition and all principal and fixed architectural finishes will be permanent for many generations to come," wrote Lorenzo Winslow, the architect in charge. At the time, it was thought the job would take a year.

The West Wing, built by Theodore Roosevelt in 1906, remained sound and would continue in service. So again Truman was "commuting" to the Oval Office on foot from across Pennsylvania Avenue, as he had in the first weeks after Franklin Roosevelt's death. Flanked by Secret Service agents, he would cross the street in the morning, twice again at lunchtime, and again at day's end. Traffic stopped, tourists gaped. Once, in early December, when a car with Virginia plates nearly ran him down, the driver, after a screeching stop, pressed his hands to his head, pondering what he had nearly wrought, but Truman walked on unconcerned. It was obvious from the President's stride, wrote *Life,* reporting the incident, that he was "a new and very happy man ... [who] knew where he was going. . . ."

Shortly after Thanksgiving, Truman had made one of the most fateful decisions of his presidency. George Marshall, who was soon to undergo surgery for the removal of a kidney, had said he wished to retire, and

Truman, after some deliberation, picked Dean Acheson to be the next Secretary of State, beginning with the new term. Truman had made the offer to Acheson privately at Blair House. At first speechless, Acheson had said he was not qualified to meet the demands of the office. This, responded Truman, was undoubtedly so, but then he could say the same for himself, or any man. The question was whether he would do the job?

Often in informal conversation, Truman would say there were probably a million men in the country who could make a better President than he, but that this was not the point. He, Harry Truman, *was* the President. "I have the job and I have to do it and the rest of you have to help me."

The Berlin Airlift, still proceeding with great effect, was never far from his mind. China was a worry, more and more, as the forces of Mao Tsetung won one smashing victory after another. From Tokyo, General MacArthur was warning that the "fall" of China imperiled America, while at home, the Red scare grew worse. On December 15, Alger Hiss had been indicted for perjury.

In Independence for Christmas, Truman took his daily walks, tipped his hat to neighbors, and, as reporters noted, carefully knocked the snow from his boots before going into the house. Between Christmas and the inauguration, his days grew increasingly crowded. Up regularly before dawn, he was busy every hour, except for a brief nap after lunch. Members of Congress and the Cabinet made a steady parade in and out of his office. He approved the withdrawal of the last American troops from Korea—a decision to which no great portent was attached by anyone at the time—and, on New Year's Day, issued a statement recognizing the new Republic of Korea. On Wednesday, January 5, 1949, he went to the Hill to deliver his State of the Union message to the new 81st Congress, calling again for the same progressive social measures he had championed the year before, except now he had a new name for his domestic program, "the Fair Deal," a name he had coined himself; and, unlike January 1948, when almost no one was listening, everyone now paid close attention.

At a news conference on January 7, visibly moved, he announced the retirement of Marshall and Acheson's appointment. Another day, he slipped out of the West Wing to fly to Pinehurst, North Carolina, to visit with the convalescing Marshall.

There was the new budget to present, calling for $41.9 billion, the largest ever in peacetime, half of which was to go for defense and foreign aid. There was his inaugural address to work on, meetings to prepare for, more press conferences, a Truman-Barkley Club dinner, and, the night before the inauguration, at the Mayflower Hotel ballroom, a full-dress Presidential Electors dinner, where he surprised and delighted his audience with an impromptu impersonation of H. V. Kaltenborn declaring on election night, in his hard, clipped style, that, "While the President is a million votes ahead in the popular vote . . . when the country vote comes in, Mr. Truman will .be defeated by an overwhelming majority." The audience exploded with laughter and applause. Truman seemed to glow with vitality and confidence.

He was a man with much to be pleased about, and at age sixty-four, after nearly four years in office and the most arduous political campaign ever waged by a President, he looked as he said he felt, "fit as a fiddle." His personal popularity, according to the latest polls, had bounced back up to 69 percent, as high as it had been in three years. Congress had raised his salary, from $75,000 to $100,000, and added an extra $50,000, tax-free, for expenses. Bess, all through the week before the inauguration, is said to have positively "bubbled" with good humor.

But there was also a strain of somber obligation in what he said to the crowd at the Mayflower. "I was not in any way elated over the election. In no sense did I feel anything unusual had happened to me. I felt only the responsibility, and that is what we are faced with now." Privately he worried about the dangers of being in the midst of such immense power and influence as to be found in Washington. "Every once in a while I notice it in myself," he confided to some of his staff, "and try to drag it out in the open."

His inaugural day had begun at 6:45, when, having had four and a half hours sleep following the gala of the night before, he stepped out onto the front stoop at Blair House. It was still dark. Pennsylvania Avenue was quiet. A pale moon hung over the great granite confection of the Old State Department Building across the street.

"Happy Inauguration Day, Mr. President," a reporter called from the sidewalk.

"Wonderful, wonderful," Truman said, glancing at the sky. "Looks like old man weather is going to be with us again."

He was wearing a dark overcoat, gray suit and gray fedora. He looked alert and rested. Secret Service men moved up and down the steps, or stood at the curb beside his waiting limousine. The move to Blair House was causing them increased concern, since the four-story building fronted directly on the busy avenue, nearly flush with the sidewalk, the front door only ten steps above street level. Scores of pedestrians passed by at all hours of the day. Every time the President came out the door he would be an easy mark. His bedroom, on the second floor, faced the street.

In minutes he was off in the car, again to the Mayflower for a reunion breakfast of Missouri ham and grits with "the boys" from Battery D, who, to the tune of "Tipperary," sang: "You're a great, great guy—Harry Truman, for you we'd march through hell." He didn't give a damn what they did after one o'clock that afternoon, he told them, but until then they were to stay sober.

"These boys are real," he told reporters. "They have no axes to grind. They don't want any jobs. They're just here. They don't call me Mr. President. They call me Captain Harry." He wanted them with him today, as a "kind of honor guard."

From the Mayflower the big car sped to the White House, flags snapping from the front fenders. Already crowds were converging on Lafayette Square. People waved as the car passed, or shielded their eyes against the morning sun, trying to catch a glimpse of him. From the West Wing, after perhaps fifteen minutes at his desk, he returned to Blair House to change. At ten on the dot, in inaugural attire, frock coat and striped trousers, and accompanied now by Bess and Margaret, he drove the two blocks to St. John's Episcopal Church on Lafayette Square, the historic "Church of the Presidents," for a prayer service. Only a small number attended—the Cabinet, a few friends, a few parishioners—since at Truman's request there had been no prior announcements of the service. Sitting in pew 63, traditionally reserved for the President since the time of James Madison, he joined in the opening hymn, "O God, Our Help in Ages Past," and read responsively from the 122nd Psalm: *"Pray for peace . . . Peace be within thy walls . . . Peace be within thee . . ."* During the prayers, as Bess and Margaret, both Episcopalians, knelt beside him, Truman sat with his head bowed. "With Thy favor . . . behold and bless Thy servant, Harry, the President of the United States, and all others in authority."

It was a day in which he would fill many roles, from Captain Harry to Servant Harry to President of the United States. For a time, technically, he was not even President but plain Citizen Harry again, for by law his term of office expired at noon and as the morning wore on, things began falling behind schedule.

He rode to the Hill with Alben Barkley, the two of them now in white silk scarfs and top hats, sitting up for all to see in the back of the huge open Lincoln. At the Capitol, the ceremonial greetings inside the Rotunda took longer than expected. By the time everyone was in place outside on the inaugural platform, by the time the invocation had been delivered, by Dr. Edward Pruden of Washington's First Baptist Church (Truman's church), the national anthem sung by tenor Phil Regan, and Alben Barkley, looking like an old Roman, sworn in as Vice President by Justice

Stanley Reed, and another prayer spoken by Rabbi Samuel Thurman of the United Hebrew Congregation of St. Louis, it was approaching 12:30.

Truman put aside his hat, scarf, and overcoat. He stood bareheaded in the wind, his right hand raised, a straight-backed, bespectacled figure with closely cropped gray hair, his expression deadly serious. Above him in the winter sun rose the immense white columns and dome of the Capitol. His wife and daughter and some fifteen members of his family sat nearby among the highest officials of the land, many of whom he had known since first coming to Washington. And it was Chief Justice Vinson, his mop of gray hair blowing in the wind, who administered the forty-three-word oath, which Truman repeated slowly and clearly, his left hand on two Bibles, a large facsimile of the Gutenberg Bible, a gift from the people of Independence, and, on top, the same small Gideon edition that had served under such different circumstances on April 12, 1945.

The oath completed, Truman, like Andrew Jackson at his inaugural, bent quickly and kissed the Bible.

It was 1:29, and for the first time as President in his own right, he turned to face the microphones and the expectant crowd.

> I accept with humility the honor which the American people have conferred on me. I accept it with a resolve to do all I can for the welfare of this nation and for the peace of the world. . . .

("How strange the matter-of-fact Missouri twang had sounded in the spring of 1945 to a world familiar with another man's phrase and another man's diction," wrote one reporter. "Today for listeners everywhere there was nothing strange about it. This simply was the President speaking.")

> Each period of our national history has had its special challenges. Those that confront us now are as momentous as any in the past. Today marks the beginning not only of a new administration, but of a period that will be eventful, perhaps decisive, for us and for the world.

He looked solemn and determined as he read from a looseleaf notebook. The voice was surprisingly strong. There was no hesitation, no stumbling over words. It was plain that he had worked on all of it, knew every line. Those close by on the platform could see his breath frosting the air.

The speech was devoted exclusively to foreign policy. Though a major

729

statement of American aspirations, its focus was the world—the "peace of the world," "world recovery," "people all over the world." He denounced communism as a false doctrine dependent on deceit and violence. The line between communism and democracy was clear:

> Communism is based on the belief that man is so weak and inadequate that he is unable to govern himself, and therefore requires the rule of strong masters.
> Democracy is based on the conviction that man has the moral and intellectual capacity, as well as the inalienable right, to govern himself with reason and fairness.
> Communism subjects the individual to arrest without lawful cause, punishment without trial, and forced labor as the chattel of the state. It decrees what information he shall receive, what art he shall produce, what leaders he shall follow, and what thoughts he shall think.
> Democracy maintains that government is established for the benefit of the individual, and is charged with the responsibility of protecting the rights of the individual and his freedom in the exercise of those abilities. . . .

The future of mankind was at stake, and without naming the Soviet Union, he stressed that "the actions resulting from the Communist philosophy are a threat to the efforts of free nations to bring about world recovery and lasting peace."

Democracy was the "vitalizing force" in the world. The American people stood "firm in the faith" that had inspired the nation from the beginning. Americans were united in the belief "that all men have a right to equal justice under law and equal opportunity to share in the common good."

He was affirmative in spirit, and characteristically he had specific proposals to make, four points, as he said. The United States would continue to support the United Nations; it would keep "full weight" behind the Marshall Plan; and the United States would join in a new "defense arrangement" among the freedom-loving nations of the North Atlantic, "to make it sufficiently clear . . . that any armed attack affecting our national security would be met with overwhelming force."

But it was the final proposal, his fourth point, that caught everyone by surprise. He called for a "bold new program" for making the benefits of American science and industrial progress available to "underdeveloped" countries. It was the first mention of what would become known as the Point Four Program.

The old imperialism—exploitation for foreign profit—had no place in the plan, Truman said. Half the people in the world were living in conditions close to misery, and for the first time in history the knowledge and skill were available to relieve such suffering. The emphasis would be on the distribution of knowledge rather than money.

> The material resources which we can afford to use for assistance of other peoples are limited. But our imponderable resources in technical knowledge are constantly growing and are inexhaustible. . . . Democracy alone can supply the vitalizing force to stir the peoples of the world into triumphant action, not only against their human oppressors, but also against their ancient enemies—hunger, misery, and despair.

The applause was immense and sustained. He was extending the promise of America beyond America. Poverty, he had said in his State of the Union address, was just as wasteful and just as unnecessary as preventable disease. Now he had extended that idea.

"Truman Proposes 'Fair Deal' Plan for the World," said the headline in the Washington *Post*. Moreover, he had been eloquent and moving, as he had seldom ever been. Many thought it the finest speech he had ever made. Franklin Roosevelt, Woodrow Wilson, Theodore Roosevelt, and Abraham Lincoln would all have approved and joined in the applause, said *The New York Times*.

Before the parade, in the interlude during which the President was to be received at lunch in the Capitol, a giant air armada like none ever seen over Washington roared across the sky, some seven hundred planes, including transports like those supplying Berlin and five gigantic new six-engined B-36 bombers that had flown, nonstop, 2,000 miles from Texas.

As the last of the planes passed, the grim President of the inaugural platform, the man with the weight of the world on him, became radiant Harry Truman once more, as he and Barkley, bundled again in overcoats and grinning broadly under their high silk hats, pulled away in the open Lincoln and started slowly back down Pennsylvania Avenue.

To either side now marched the Battery D honor guard, two lines of somewhat portly, gray-haired middle Americans swinging white ash walking canes, keeping pace with the big car rather smartly and all more or less in step as the delighted crowd cheered them on. (Only two would drop out in the mile-and-a-quarter route to the White House.)

The whole pageant struck countless viewers, including many who had witnessed numerous inaugurations, as profoundly stirring. It was a day of dedication for the democratic spirit, with all elements large and small momentarily in harmony.

The clear sunlight, the President's evident high spirits [said *The New York Times*], the patience and cheerfulness of the great crowds, such moving episodes as the presence of a guard of honor of Mr. Truman's comrades of the First World War . . . the slowly moving masses of men and vehicles coming down the Avenue from the seat of the national legislative power to the seat of its executive power, the booming of the Presidential salute, the planes overhead, the whole mood of the occasion—all these things seemed to speak of a confident and even exultant Americanism. . . . It was democracy looking homeward across a great continent, but also looking outward toward the world in which democracy will never again be impotent or ashamed or apologetic.

Behind the President, the procession stretched seven miles and would take, in all, three hours to pass. Truman, on reaching the White House, watched the show from a glass-enclosed reviewing stand and he missed none of it. West Point cadets, midshipmen from Annapolis, the Marine Band, the United States Army Band, all came swinging by, companies of WACS, WAVES, the Richmond Blues wearing white-plumed helmets, high school bands, police bands, drum majorettes, beauty queens, trick riders, state governors in open cars, a mounted posse of Kansas City "cowboys" —15,153 men, women, and children in costume, uniform, and civilian dress, more than 40 bands, 55 floats, trucks, jeeps, armored cars, more than 100 horses, 4 mules from Lamar, Missouri, and an old-time circus calliope tooting "I'm Just Wild About Harry." With Barkley beside him, Truman clapped his gloved hands, waved, chatted, laughed out loud, beat time to the Marine Hymn, swayed his head to the strains of "Dixie," bounced up and down on the balls of his feet to keep warm while sipping from a white paper cup of what was reportedly coffee but assuredly was not. "Like the honest Missouri extrovert that he is," wrote Roger Butterfield for *Life,* "he did not try to hide his moods—the crowds and the cameras saw them all."

Governor Adlai Stevenson passed by in advance of the Illinois float. General Eisenhower, in a spontaneous tribute that the crowd adored, stood in the back of his open car and saluted the President. Truman beamed and waved his top hat. When a Plymouth Rock float passed by, its cast of Pilgrims suddenly broke out cameras and began snapping pictures of him.

Every state, every size, shape, and color of American democracy, passed in review in the chilly afternoon sunshine. The last inaugural parade, eight years before, in 1941, when the country was arming for war, had been a grim procession of military might. The mood now was different. The crowd in the grandstand opposite the President, people in bright scarfs and winter coats, some wrapped in blankets, was a happy crowd;

just as it was now a larger, more plentiful America by far. Harry Truman was President of a nation of 147 million people, an increase in population of more than 15 million since the census of 1940. No President in history had ever taken office at a time of such prosperity and power. Industrial production outstripped any previous time in the nation's past, and all other nations of the world. The bumper harvest of the previous fall had been the biggest on record. "There never was a country more fabulous than America," the British historian Robert Payne would write in 1949, after an extensive tour of the country:

> She bestrides the world like a Colossus: no other power at any time in the world's history has possessed so varied or so great an influence on other nations. . . . It is already an axiom that the decisions of the American government affect the lives and livelihood of the remotest people. Half the wealth of the world, more than half the productivity, nearly two-thirds of the world's machines are concentrated in American hands. . . .

"The parade was the most fun I have ever had at a parade," wrote David Lilienthal. But the President, as the papers said, was "the fellow who was having the best time of anyone."

Only twice did he seem to register disapproval. When the Dixiecrat candidate, Governor Strom Thurmond of South Carolina, rode by waving happily, Truman gave him a cold stare. Then as Governor Herman Talmadge of Georgia, another champion of white supremacy, approached, Truman turned his back. But the only real snub was of Thurmond. Truman had turned as Talmadge passed because an electric heater beneath his feet had short-circuited, sending up smoke, and he was trying to put out the fire.

As the sun fell behind the Old State Department Building and the afternoon grew colder, a Texas delegation appeared, led by a car with a banner on its side: "Lieutenant Governor Shivers." The crowd and the President roared.

Truman stayed to the end, and at the inaugural ball that night at the armory, he was still going strong at nearly two in the morning. No dancer, he watched and waved from a balcony to a crowd of some five thousand people. He was dressed in white tie and tails, while Bess, "smiling and vivacious," wore a shimmering, full-length gown of silver lamé. With them were Mary Jane Truman, J. Vivian Truman and his daughter Martha Ann, Frank and Natalie Wallace, George and May Wallace, Nellie and Ethel Noland.

"Everybody looked wonderful," wrote Margaret, who wore pink tulle and spent most of the night on the dance floor. Happiest of all was her father, "whose face was shining like a new moon."

II

In contrast to his first years in office, and so much to follow, the first six months of the new term were a breather for Truman. Until midsummer 1949, things went well on the whole, the outlook remained hopeful. No calamitous domestic issues erupted. There were no sudden international crises to contend with. Greece and Turkey did not fall to Communist takeovers, nor would they. Nor would France or Italy. Best of all was a decided easing of tension over Berlin that began just days after the inauguration.

Realizing that the airlift was an established success, and that in fact the blockade had backfired on them, the Russians signaled "a change in attitude." Stalin was backing down. For the first time since Potsdam, the tide seemed to be turning. Secret negotiations followed—"It can almost be stated as a principle that when the Soviets are serious about something they do it in secret," Chip Bohlen observed—and on May 12, 1949, the blockade ended: The lights of Berlin came on again. The airlift was over, after a year and two months, 277,804 flights, and the delivery of 2,325,809 tons of food and supplies.

For Truman it was a momentous victory. Firmness and patience had prevailed without resorting to force. War had been averted.

On May 12 also, the Allied powers approved establishment of a new German Federated Republic, whereby the West Germans were to rule themselves with their own government at Bonn.

Things overall looked "fifty percent better" than a year ago, Truman confided to Lilienthal. Not even the advance of Communist forces in China seemed to discourage him. At Potsdam, Stalin had told him the people of North China would never be Communists and Truman thought that was "about right." The dragon was going to "turn over," he said, "and after that perhaps some advances can be made of it." With what Lilienthal described as a "big grin and a large dose of his particular brand of charm, which is not inconsiderable," Truman talked enthusiastically of what a program like TVA could mean for a country like China, "to put it on its feet."

By then, too, the North Atlantic Treaty had been signed in Washington on April 4, after much hard, skillful negotiation by Secretary of State Acheson. The United States, Canada, and ten Western European countries joined in a defense pact whereby an attack on any one would be taken as an attack on all: For the United States, it marked a radical departure with tradition—the first peacetime military alliance since the signing of the Constitution—but had such an agreement existed in 1914 and 1939, Truman was convinced, the world would have been spared two terrible wars. He ranked NATO with the Marshall Plan, as one of the proudest achievements of his presidency, and was certain that time would prove him right. And though Acheson and British Foreign Secretary Bevin had done most of the work, it was Truman who provided the commitment, unreservedly, just as he had with the Marshall Plan. His first major act after the election in November had been to instruct the State Department to open negotiations for the new alliance, and he rightly considered it his treaty. "We have really passed a milestone in history," he said in his toast at the state dinner at the Carlton Hotel, following the signing ceremony.

Objections in the Senate, among conservative Republicans, might be fierce, but he had no doubt the treaty would be approved. As it turned out, opposition in the Senate and the press was unexpectedly mild, approval broad. On July 21, the Senate voted ratification by a vote of 82 to 13.

The establishment of NATO, the success of the Berlin Airlift, the prospect of a prosperous, self-governing West Germany as part of the Western Alliance, all made for a greatly improved atmosphere for Truman. "He looks more relaxed . . . those drawn lines from his eyes across his cheekbones seemed to be considerably modified," Lilienthal noted.

In March he had taken off again for Key West, for another "working vacation," his sixth at Key West since becoming President. The place appealed to him as nowhere else. He loved the warm sea bathing and balmy tropical nights, as perhaps only an inland North American can. His quarters were in what had been the commandant's residence at the Key West naval base, a modest-sized white frame house in the West Indian style with jalousied porches, simply but comfortably furnished. Hibiscus and bougainvillaea bloomed in the garden. The cares, the pressures, the formality of the presidency, all began to subside almost from the moment he arrived.

He put on bright patterned sports shirts—"Harry Truman shirts," as they became known—and set off on his early morning walks through the picturesque old town of Key West, stopping sometimes for a cup of coffee at a local lunch counter. The White House pouch arrived daily; members of the Cabinet, congressional leaders, the Joint Chiefs, flew in and out for meetings, and some days he was on the phone far more than he liked; but he enjoyed a daily swim, or rather churning the turquoise water in his self-styled sidestroke, head up to keep his glasses dry, while one or two Navy boats stood guard, to keep other boats at a distance and to watch for barracudas. He loafed in the sun with members of the staff, joked, swapped stories, read, listened to classical music on the phonograph, took an afternoon nap, played poker on the porch nearly every evening, slept soundly, and started off each new day, before his walk, with a shot of bourbon.

His privacy on the base was complete. Nor was security ever a problem, which pleased the Secret Service. The staff all enjoyed themselves, as did the thirty-odd reporters who usually made the trip and who had little else to do but enjoy themselves. And with everyone so obviously pleased with his choice of vacation spot, so pleased to be included, pleased to be with him, Truman enjoyed himself that much more. "He was *great* down in Key West!" remembered Jim Rowley, by then head of the Secret Service detail.

Soon they were all sporting Harry Truman shirts. To Truman's great delight, even Sam Rayburn, during a visit in November, had put on one printed with flocks of cranes and swaying palm trees.

Back in Washington on May 8, at a party celebrating his sixty-fifth birthday in the ballroom of the palatial Larz Anderson House on Embassy Row, as toasts were raised, Truman looked better by far than he had since 1945, "like a man who had few qualms about the future," according to one account. "The President," said his physician, Wallace Graham, "is as close to being an iron man as anyone I know at his age."

The one distinct shadow on these "first sunny months" of 1949 was the tragic fate of Secretary of Defense James Forrestal, who as far back as the previous summer had begun looking weary and troubled and who, since the election, had been acting quite strangely. An intense, introverted, extremely dedicated man by nature, Forrestal had worked himself to a state of near collapse, yet wished only to hold on and work harder.

Truman had begun losing confidence in Forrestal even before the fall campaign. Struggling to bring about the reorganization of the military services—an unprecedented, killing task—Forrestal had become increasingly indecisive and absorbed in details. "He won't take hold," Truman complained. At one point, exasperated with Forrestal's handling of a problem, Truman had sent an uncharacteristically curt note saying, "This is your responsibility." Then, with the campaign under way, there had been suspicions about Forrestal's loyalty, whether his meetings with Thomas E. Dewey really concerned defense matters, as Forrestal said, or were arranged in the hope of staying on in the Dewey administration. Drew Pearson called it an open secret that Forrestal wanted to hold on to his job regardless of the outcome in November, and several of those closest to Truman grew convinced that politically the Secretary of Defense was no longer to be trusted.

Forrestal had also been one of the few members of the Cabinet since the departure of Henry Wallace to disagree with the President over policy —over Palestine and civilian control of the atomic bomb most notably— and now he was adamantly opposed to Truman's position on defense spending. To achieve a balanced budget, Truman insisted on a defense ceiling of $15 billion, a sum equal to more than a third of the entire federal budget, but that Forrestal thought dangerously low given the scale of the Soviet menace.

Criticism of Forrestal by the press had grown steadily since his unpopular stand on the Palestine issue, with Drew Pearson and Walter Winchell leading the attack in their columns and radio broadcasts. And for Forrestal, who had long courted the press, this was all extremely painful. He was called a tool of Wall Street and the oil companies, an imperialist, an anti-Semite. Pearson and Winchell tried to create doubt about his personal courage, with a trumped-up account of how years before, Forrestal had fled out the back door of his New York City home as jewel thieves accosted his wife. On an NBC Radio broadcast in January, a guest claimed that the I. G. Farben works in Frankfurt had not been bombed during the war because Forrestal owned I. G. Farben stock—a totally false charge that NBC later retracted.

The more amplified the attacks became, the more Truman, who hated to dismiss anyone under almost any circumstances, was inclined to keep Forrestal where he was. Truman would not have him leave "under fire." In February, Drew Pearson had attacked Harry Vaughan for accepting a decoration from the Argentine dictator Juan Perón, a decoration that several others, including Generals Eisenhower and Bradley, had received earlier, but about which nothing had been said. Pearson had called for Vaughan's immediate dismissal and Truman publicly responded by calling Pearson an "S.O.B.," which raised a new storm of adverse comment and gave Truman a great deal of satisfaction. "No commentator or columnist names any members of my Cabinet, or my staff," he said. "I name them myself. And when it is time for them to be moved on, I do the moving—nobody else." It was a sentiment that had been felt by other presidents before him and would be often again by more who followed in his place, but that none stated so openly in so many words.

Forrestal, as he told a friend, felt that Truman had always been very fair with him. Truman was "the best boss I have ever known." To another friend he wrote that the American people were fortunate to have in the highest office "a man who, while he reflects the liberal forces both in this country and throughout the world, is nevertheless conservative in the real sense of that word—a conserver of the things we hope to keep."

Forrestal was still greatly admired by several of those whose judgment Truman particularly valued. Eisenhower, whom Truman had recently asked to serve as an informal "presiding officer" of the Joint Chiefs, considered Forrestal one of the best men in public life and, as Eisenhower recorded privately, more perceptive than Truman concerning "the mess we are in due to neglect of our armed forces."

Except for my liking, admiration, and respect for his [Forrestal's] great qualities I'd not go near Washington, even if I had to resign my commission completely [Eisenhower wrote in his diary in January 1949]. To a certain extent these same feelings apply to H.S.T., but he does not see the problems so clearly as does Jim, and does not suffer so much due to the failure to solve the problems. I like them both.

But Forrestal, as Eisenhower also noted, was "looking badly. . . . He gives his mind no recess, and he works hours that would kill a horse."

(Eisenhower would himself soon find the bickering between the services all but intolerable. He was smoking four packs of cigarettes a day and worrying about his blood pressure. By mid-March he was suffering from severe stomach cramps, and Truman sent him off to recuperate for three weeks at the Little White House in Key West.)

A reporter seeing Forrestal on inauguration day was shocked by his "baffled" look. Afflicted with insomnia and loss of appetite, Forrestal appeared strangely drawn and aged, his shirt collars too large for him. Some days he would telephone the President several times on the same subject, which left Truman mystified. Privately, Forrestal told a few close friends his phone was being tapped. At meetings he would unconsciously scratch at a particular part of his scalp until it turned raw.

When, in early February, Forrestal told Truman he was resigning and would leave by June 1, Truman saw it would have to be sooner than that.

As Forrestal knew, Truman, for some time, had been considering Louis Johnson as his replacement—Johnson the headstrong financial wonder-worker of the Whistle-stop Campaign, who had once served as Roosevelt's Assistant Secretary of War—and Forrestal agreed with the choice, or so he said. Johnson, on meeting Forrestal to discuss the transition, concluded after an hour, as he later told Drew Pearson, that Forrestal was insane, or possibly taking drugs.

"Forrestal wanted to resign long before he did," Truman would write, "and I kept him from it, although I realized later that I should have let him quit when he wanted. He left because of failing health, and that's all there was to it."

On Tuesday, March 1, Truman summoned Forrestal to the White House to ask for his resignation. Truman also urged him to take a vacation, though he said nothing about seeking medical attention.

Forrestal maintained the necessary composure for public appearances in the following weeks, but only barely. He was present at the Pentagon on March 28 when Louis Johnson was formally installed as Secretary of Defense, and later in the day he stood mute at another ceremony at the White House, when Truman presented him with the Distinguished Service Medal. But the next day, Forrestal, "a very sick man," was flown to Florida, to Robert Lovett's home at Hobe Sound, where he told Lovett, "They're after me." In the days following he made at least one attempt at suicide.

Unaware of what was happening in Florida, but having now heard reports that Forrestal thought he was being followed by foreign agents, Truman asked the head of the Secret Service, U. E. Baughman, to look into the matter at once. The report, marked "Secret" and dated March 31, said Forrestal's suspicions were unfounded, that he had become of late "exceedingly nervous and emotional," and so distraught by the time of his last day as Secretary of Defense that he had not even known his own servants.

> As a result of his apparent lack of ability to make a positive decision and carry it out, he was assisted and escorted to the plane [to Florida] by two friends and former associates. When Mr. F. exhibited a last minute reluctance to make his departure, one of the friends reportedly said to the other: "We have to do something—we can't keep him around here."

Forrestal, the report concluded, was suffering from a "slight nervous breakdown," which apparently was as much as Truman had been told up to that point.

In Florida, a Navy psychiatrist and the renowned Dr. William C. Menninger had been sent for, and on April 2, Forrestal was flown back to Washington to be admitted to the Bethesda Naval Hospital for treatment of "nervous exhaustion."

Drew Pearson reported that Forrestal was "out of his mind" and claimed incorrectly that in Florida Forrestal had rushed out into the street screaming, "The Russians are coming."

Truman called on Forrestal at Bethesda the first week in May and thought Forrestal seemed "his old self."

Two weeks later, on Sunday, May 22, at two in the morning, Forrestal sat in his room on the sixteenth floor of the hospital copying lines from Sophocles' "Chorus from Ajax":

> *Worn by the waste of time—*
> *Comfortless, nameless, hopeless save*
> *In the dark prospect of the yawning grave . . .*

About three o'clock he walked across the hall to a small kitchen. After tying one end of the sash from his bathrobe to a radiator and the other end around his neck, he jumped from the unbarred window. His body was found on the roof of the third floor, the sash still around his neck.

The news rocked Washington. Suicide among high-ranking government figures was unknown. Other Cabinet members had resigned over the years, or been fired under a cloud, but none had ever taken his own life. Truman, in his words, was "inexpressibly shocked and grieved." The First Lady, haunted by memories of her father, was, as Margaret later revealed, "terribly shaken." At Easter, only the week before, Bess had sent Forrestal a bouquet of roses and in a note of appreciation he had said how much they had "helped brighten a bleak day."

> I am moved that you should trouble to send me a token but it's typical of your thoughtfulness. A Happy Easter to you and the President and Miss Truman. You all deserve it.

The President and Vice President, former President Hoover, the Cabinet, much of Congress, members of the Supreme Court, the Joint Chiefs, General Marshall, an estimated six thousand people were present for Forrestal's burial with full military honors at Arlington.

Truman, angry, troubled, doubtless remorseful that he hadn't acted sooner to relieve Forrestal from duty, accused Drew Pearson of "hounding" him to death. Pearson wrote that it was Truman's call for Forrestal's resignation that "undoubtedly worsened the illness." David Lawrence, in his column in the Washington *Star,* said it was not work that killed Forrestal, but the President's loss of confidence in him.

Questions about the tragedy persisted. Why had Forrestal, in his condition, with suicidal tendencies, been placed in a sixteenth-floor room? Had his priest been denied the chance to see him? As time went on, and fear of Communist conspiracy spread in Washington, it would be rumored that pages from Forrestal's diary had been secretly removed on orders from the White House—that Forrestal, the most ardent anti-Soviet voice in the administration, had in fact been driven to his death as part of a Communist plot and the evidence destroyed by "secret Communists" on Truman's staff.

But as ever in Washington, it was who was in power that mattered most and so the focus of attention swiftly shifted to the new Secretary of Defense, who, with his previous experience in the department, his reputation for getting things done, had seemed well equipped for the job. Louis Johnson was tough, hardheaded, and, importantly, committed to the President's policy of holding the line on spending. On the Hill, Democrats and Republicans liked what they saw. The Senate approved the appointment unanimously. But in little time Johnson's personal style and mode of operation made him a figure of extreme controversy. He hit the Pentagon like a cyclone.

Johnson's first move was to evict several high-ranking officers from the largest office in the building and make it his own. He resurrected General Pershing's old desk and installed Roosevelt's press secretary, Steve Early, as a deputy. Half of all Pentagon employees, some twenty-five thousand people, were shuffled about in a gigantic game of musical chairs. He did away with outdated service boards, cut back the use of official cars.

Johnson was doing what Truman had asked for. From his experience on the Truman Committee, Truman was convinced that huge sums were being wasted in defense spending. He had a basic distrust of generals and admirals when it came to spending money. In late April, with no advance warning to the President or the Secretary of the Navy, Johnson suddenly canceled construction of a new $186 million supercarrier, *United States,* a major component in the Navy's whole program—with the result that the Secretary of the Navy, John Sullivan, resigned in a rage. Truman, who liked Sullivan and did not blame him for resigning, nonetheless approved the cancelation. Still, Johnson's manner troubled him greatly.

In May, to the disbelief of the Joint Chiefs, Johnson ordered another $1.4 billion slashed from the military budget. To those who charged he was weakening the country's defense, Johnson boasted that the United States could "lick Russia with one hand tied behind our back."

Where Forrestal had been small, introverted, and apolitical almost to a fault, Johnson was a great boisterous bear of a man who shouted to make his point to an admiral or general, and exuded such overt political ambition, stirred such speculation as to his true motives, that he felt obliged after only a few months on the job to state publicly several times that he was *not* running for President. The press quoted an unnamed high official who said Johnson was making two enemies for every dollar he saved.

As was becoming rapidly apparent, Louis Johnson was possibly the worst appointment Truman ever made. In a little more than a year, many who worked with him, including Truman and Dean Acheson, would conclude that Johnson was mentally unbalanced. "Unwittingly," wrote General Bradley later, "Truman had replaced one mental case with another."

The President, the country read, was "in high good humor," "cheerful and chipper." And busy. He named Attorney General Tom Clark to the Supreme Court, made Howard McGrath the new Attorney General, put Bill Boyle, his old Kansas City protégé and whistle-stop mastermind, in McGrath's place at the head of the Democratic Party. He also picked Perle Mesta to be the new minister to Luxembourg, an appointment of no great importance but remembered fondly because it inspired a hit Broadway musical, *Call Me Madam,* with music by Irving Berlin, and Ethel Merman in the title role.

But even before spring vanished in the furnace heat of June and another long summer settled on the city, Truman's good cheer and optimism were being put to the test. The wave of anti-communism that had been gathering force since the charges against Alger Hiss erupted the previous summer now grew more serious, with Cardinal Spellman of New York, among others, saying America was in imminent danger of a Communist takeover. In December 1948, Hiss was indicted for perjury, but the real issue, everyone knew, remained the same: Was he or was he not a Communist spy? And how many more like him were there in government?

The country, Truman assured reporters, was not going to hell. They ought to read some history. America had been through such times before. "Hysteria finally died down, and things straightened out, and the country didn't go to hell, and it isn't now." When the Hiss trial ended in a hung jury in July, another trial was scheduled for the fall. As Truman failed to foresee, the issue was not going to go away.

Then at midsummer the outlook became dramatically worse. Indeed, by August 1949 Truman had entered a time of severe trial. Events beyond his control—in China and the Soviet Union—rocked the Western world as nothing had since the war, while on Capitol Hill, as if to provide a kind of perverse comic relief, Harry Vaughan was summoned before a Senate investigating committee.

The news from China had been grim all year, Truman's oddly sanguine remarks on the subject to David Lilienthal notwithstanding. The Chinese Nationalist regime of Chiang Kai-shek had been crumbling fast before the onrush of the Communists. The American military adviser to Chiang, General David Barr, reported that the military situation has deteriorated to the point where only the active participation of United States troops could effect a remedy. . . . No battle has been lost since my arrival due to lack of ammunition or equipment. . . . [The Nationalist] debacles, in my opinion, can all be attributed to the world's worst leadership . . . the widespread corruption and dishonesty through the [Nationalist] armed forces. . . .

In April a Communist army of a million men crossed the Yangtze River, south into the last provinces still loyal to Chiang. The outcome, the complete fall of China to the forces of Mao Tse-tung—an outcome implicit as early as 1946 in what George Marshall reported after his fruitless year in China—had by spring become a foregone conclusion.

Vehement alarm was sounded. Angry, vindictive charges were made against the administration by what had become known as the "China Lobby," whose numbers included religious and patriotic groups across the country, prominent Republicans in Congress, and *Time* and *Life* publisher Henry R. Luce, who was the son of missionaries to China. *Life* had carried an article by General MacArthur titled "The Fall of China Imperils the U.S." *Time* warned that the Red tide rising in Asia threatened to engulf half the peoples of the world.

Yet it was the administration's own attempt to account for its China policy, an effort intended to clarify what was about to happen in China before it happened, and thereby calm the country, that gave focus to this momentous turn of history as nothing else had, and with unexpected consequences.

At a morning press conference on August 4, Truman announced the release of a massive State Department report, *United States Relations with China: With Special Reference to the Period 1944–1949,* 409 pages in length, with another 645 pages of appended documents in smaller print. He had asked to have it compiled, Truman said, as a "frank and actual record . . . clear and illuminating . . . everything you want to know about the policy" from the 1840s forward.

As Dean Acheson stressed in a preface to the report, the United States had poured more than $2 billion into support for Chiang Kai-shek since V-J Day—money and arms to help destroy communism in China—but it had not been enough. The fault, said Acheson, was in the internal decay of the Nationalist regime, its rampant corruption, lack of leadership, its indifference to the aspirations of the Chinese people. "The unfortunate but inescapable fact is that the ominous result of the civil war in China was beyond the control of the . . . United States. . . . It was the product of internal Chinese forces, forces which this country tried to influence but could not."

Truman, his spelling no better than ever, had said in a handwritten note earlier that a "currupt" Nationalist government was the cause of China's woes. "We picked a bad horse," he told Arthur Vandenberg.

The "China White Paper" caused a sensation. Affection for China was widespread in the country. Generations of American children had carried nickels and dimes to Sunday School to support missionaries in China. Books by Pearl Buck about Chinese peasant life had won the hearts of millions of readers; Chiang Kai-shek, the Generalissimo, and his smiling, photogenic, Wellesley-educated wife had been America's loyal allies through the war. Now the State Department was declaring officially that China, the largest nation on earth, was lost to communism. Instead of serving as a palliative, as Truman and Acheson intended, the report inflamed the controversy. *The New York Times* judged it a "sorry record of well-meaning mistakes." More outraged critics called it a whitewash, a deliberate distortion, and worse, "a smooth alibi for the pro-Communists in the State Department who . . . aided in the Communist conquest of China." In the Senate, Republican William Knowland of California wondered aloud, and without a shred of evidence, whether Alger Hiss had helped shape China policy. The China Lobby raised the cry that Truman and Acheson had "lost" China, as though China had been America's to lose. A few Democrats, too, joined in the attack, including Representative John F. Kennedy of Massachusetts.

At the same time, Harry Vaughan was back in the news in what had all the signs of a full-blown White House scandal. A Senate subcommittee chaired by Democrat Clyde R. Hoey of North Carolina had begun investigating so-called "five percenters," those who, for 5 percent commissions, used their supposed influence to secure contracts or favored treatment from the government. Vaughan, it was revealed by several witnesses, had used his high position—"his general's stars, his White House telephone and his place in Harry Truman's affections"—to ease the way for such men-about-Washington as James V. Hunt, a former Army officer who claimed to be one of Vaughan's best friends, and "Mysterious" John Maragon, truly an old friend of Vaughan's, who in the first weeks of Truman's presidency in 1945 had been seen about the West Wing so often he was thought to be one of the staff.

When it was shown that Hunt had improper influence with the chief of the Army Chemical Corps and the Quartermaster General, Truman immediately ordered the retirement of the first and the suspension of the second officer.

Most of Vaughan's activities in behalf of such friends dated from just after the war. As a favor to Hunt he had helped obtain scarce lumber for construction of a California race track, a project being blocked by government restrictions on building materials needed for housing. For Maragon, he secured a permit for the purchasing of molasses, another scarce item. For a Chicago perfume manufacturer, another of Hunt's clients, he arranged a priority flight to Europe by Air Transport Command—at the time when Germany had just surrendered and virtually all transport facilities were preempted for military use—an arrangement whereby the Chicago manufacturer returned home with perfume essence valued at $53,000.

There was nothing illegal about the operations of the five percenters, nothing illegal about what Vaughan had done. But as had also been disclosed, the same Chicago perfume manufacturer, David A. Bennett, had made Vaughan a gift of a cold-storage food container, a "deep freezer," valued at approximately $400. Moreover, at Vaughan's suggestion, Bennett sent five more freezers: one to the First Lady, which broke down and had to be junked, one to Fred Vinson, who was then Secretary of the Treasury, one to J. K. Vardaman, who installed it in his Rappahannock County, Virginia, mountain retreat, another to Matt Connelly, and another to John Snyder, who returned it.

Summoned before the Hoey Committee, Vaughan insisted he had only been trying to be helpful. "I do these people a courtesy of putting them in contact with the persons with whom they can tell their story," he explained.

It was, of course, what every politician in Washington did almost daily. Nor was there a law against public officials accepting gifts from friends and constituents, as many news accounts were careful to point out. The President himself was constantly receiving and accepting gifts of all kinds —paintings, prize turkeys, country hams, Havana cigars, liquor, even a Ford automobile, during his first year in office. The freezers, said Vaughan, were "an expression of friendship and nothing more," and Chairman Hoey, after Vaughan's two days of testimony, acknowledged there was no evidence of corruption on Vaughan's part. Yet the damage was done. The freezers had been kept confidential and Vaughan's use of his privileged position, if not illegal, had been decidedly inappropriate and inept. His poor judgment, the almost ludicrous lack of propriety that had so long concerned others at the White House like Charlie Ross and Eben Ayers, had caught up with him.

Though his manner before the committee was calm and respectful, even impressive at times, by appearance Vaughan seemed anything but a figure of rectitude. Grossly overweight, his uniform, for all its brass and ribbons, looking about as military as pajamas, he was like a cartoonist's portrait of corruption. Thomas Nast would have gloried in the chance to draw him, as slouching back in his witness chair Vaughan lit up a big cigar.

The Republicans on the committee had prepared, as *Time* wrote, for a political barbecue with Vaughan as the pig on the spit. But the one who enjoyed it most, glowering at the witness, pointedly addressing the uniformed general as "Mr. Vaughan," was Senator Joseph McCarthy of Wisconsin.

Was it true, asked McCarthy, that he had taken campaign contributions from "Racket King" Frank Costello?

"Am I supposed to know Frankie Costello? . . . How did he get in here?" responded Vaughan, rightfully incredulous.

If the hearings had proven anything, it was only that Vaughan was an embarrassment who in the guise of a general played courthouse politics from the White House in a style reminiscent of the Harding days. "Five percenters" and "deep freezers" became odious new catchwords, to the extreme pleasure of the Republicans.

"Ross and I discussed the whole thing at some length," wrote Eben Ayers. "We agreed that Vaughan is entirely to blame for his troubles and the troubles he has brought on the President and others. But he seems to have no realization of what harm he has caused. . . ."

What Truman did was just what everyone who knew him well knew he would do. Had he been constituted differently, had he been able to see the commotion over Vaughan as justified, and not an attack on him personally—which was how he interpreted it—had he been able to see that Vaughan was a serious liability and been willing to sacrifice him for the sake of the public trust, not to say his own reputation, then things might have gone differently. But he did not, and this, as time would tell, was a mistake.

Beneath everything, Truman not only liked Vaughan, but liked how Vaughan conducted himself, and particularly with respect to the press. When, in the midst of the hearings, Vaughan had arrived back in Washington after a vacation and was confronted by reporters at Union Station, he had warned them to go easy on him. "After all I am the President's military aide, and you guys will all want favors at the White House someday." Asked about his connection with the five percenters, he said, "That's nobody's goddamn business and you can quote me," a response that so warmed Truman's heart when he read it that he pinned a mock decoration on Vaughan for "Operation Union Station."

"I think," Alben Barkley would later comment, "that Mr. Truman was far too kind and loyal to certain old friends who took advantage of him and whose actions sometimes were no credit to his administration."

When Vaughan offered to resign, Truman told him to say no such thing in his presence ever again. They had come into the White House together, Truman said, and they would go out together.

Only weeks later came the most stunning news of all, portending, as David Lilienthal wrote, "a whole box of trouble." An Air Force weather reconnaissance plane, flying at 18,000 feet from Japan to Alaska, had detected signs of intense radioactivity over the North Pacific, east of the Kamchatka Peninsula. Soon planes elsewhere over the Pacific were reporting radioactivity as much as twenty times above normal. The radioactive cloud was tracked by the Air Force from the Pacific nearly to the British Isles, where it was picked up by the RAF.

It took several days for scientists to analyze the data. Their conclusion was reached the afternoon of Monday, September 19. Lilienthal, who was on vacation at Martha's Vineyard, received the news that night in memorable fashion. As he and his wife were returning from a dinner party to their house near the northern shore of the island, they saw the figure of a man suddenly loom up out of the ground fog, caught in the glare of their headlights. It was General James McCormack, who looked bemused, thought Lilienthal, "as if I frequently found him on a windswept moor, in the dead of night, on an island. . . ."

Later, alone with Lilienthal in an upstairs room lit by a single kerosene lamp, McCormack gave Lilienthal his report.

> The coal-oil lamp between us [Lilienthal wrote], the shadows all around; outside, through . . . [the] windows, the Great Dipper and the North Star off toward the lights of New Bedford. . . . I took it with no outward evidence of anything more than a budget problem. . . .

Was he disturbed over something, his wife asked after they had gone to bed. "Oh some. One of those things," he said.

By 8:20 the next morning, he and McCormack were on their way to Washington in an Air Force C-47. Lilienthal was to see Truman at the White House that afternoon. By 11:30 he was at his office conferring with a hurriedly assembled advisory commission of nuclear scientists, chaired by J. Robert Oppenheimer, who looked frantic. There was no question, said Oppenheimer, the Russians had detonated an atomic bomb.

"Vermont affair, we are here," Lilienthal wrote, "Vermont" being the code name for the Russian bomb.

How was the President taking the news? Would he tell the country? And how soon?

Lilienthal saw Truman promptly at 3:45 and later, in his diary, in almost telegraphic style, he put down this extraordinary account of their half hour together:

> The President was reading a copy of the *Congressional Record,* as quiet and composed a scene as imaginable; bright sunlight in the garden outside. . . .
>
> He said: want to talk about this detection report—knew about it—knew it would probably come—German scientists in Russia did it, probably something like that. Be glad to call in the Joint Committee [on Atomic Energy] chairman, ranking minority member, tell them. . . . Not going to say anything myself now; later when this [Truman pointed to a newspaper with headlines about the devaluation of the British pound] quiets down, maybe in a week; realize may leak, lots people know—still take that chance, meet it when it comes.
>
> I said: may I have permission to state [my] views, despite fact you have reached conclusion? He took off his glasses, first time I saw him without them, large, fine eyes. Considerate, fine air of patience and interest. I tried to set out affirmative virtue of making it [the announcement] now and initiating matter rather than plugging leaks. . . . First, would show Pres. knows what is going on in Vermont [Russia]. . . . Second, Pres. knowing and saying so would show him not scared, hence others needn't be; third, would show Pres. will tell people when things come along they need to know that won't hurt being told.
>
> [The President agreed that] maintaining confidence of people in him, taking cue from his own calm, was good point, but not afraid of that. Can't be sure anyway [that the Russians actually had the bomb]. I stepped into that: is sure, substantial—and great surprise even to [the] most pessimistic. Really? —sharp look. . . .
>
> But [an announcement] by him [might] cause great fears, troubles. They [the Russians] changed . . . talking very reasonably again, things look better [since the end of the Berlin crisis]; this may have something to do with it. Not worried; took this into account; going to work things out. . . .

Three days later, the morning of Friday, September 23, with the White House press crammed into his office, Charlie Ross asked first that the door be closed, then passed out a mimeographed statement from the President. In an instant reporters were stampeding for the press telephones, smashing the head of a stuffed deer in their rush.

> I believe the American people, to the fullest extent consistent with national security, are entitled to be informed of all developments in the field of atomic energy. That is my reason for making public the following information.

> We have evidence that within recent weeks an atomic explosion occurred in the U.S.S.R. . . .

As the statement also said, the eventual development of "this new force by other nations was to be expected." Nonetheless, the news was three to five years ahead of most predictions and the realization came as an immense shock. The four-year American monopoly on the atomic bomb was over. And though there was no panic in the country, the fears and tensions of the Cold War were greatly amplified. It was a different world now.

A week later, on October 1 in Peking, the People's Republic of China, the most numerous Communist nation in the world, with more than 500 million people, one fifth of humanity, was officially inaugurated.

Very soon afterward, in October 1949, in a series of highly secret meetings at the offices of the Atomic Energy Commission, discussion began on the subject of a thermonuclear or hydrogen weapon—a superbomb, or "Super"—which would have more than ten times the destructive power of the bombs dropped on Hiroshima and Nagasaki. The Russian bomb, it was felt, had changed the situation "drastically." And if the Russians were capable of producing an atomic bomb, then the Russians too were in a position now to push forward with the more devastating weapon.

The initial proposal for the "Super" had come from Lewis Strauss of the Atomic Energy Commission, with strong support from the physicist Edward Teller.

James B. Conant, who had served on the President's Interim Committee on the first bomb, was flatly opposed. So was Oppenheimer. Enrico Fermi seemed at first to favor going ahead, then changed his mind. In the end, the scientific advisory committee expressed its opposition to the project on both technical and moral grounds. General Bradley was for it mainly for its "psychological" importance. Clearly, there would have to be a presidential decision.

Lilienthal had privately concluded that he, too, was against the Super. ("We keep saying, 'We have no other course!' Lilienthal wrote. "What we should be saying is, 'We are not bright enough to see any other course.' ") But the morning of Tuesday, November 1, he met with Dean Acheson to explain the "essence of the business," so Acheson might take it up with the President "soon," before he, Lilienthal, and others presented it in greater detail.

What a depressing world it was, Acheson remarked after listening to Lilienthal. He didn't know how Lilienthal had lived with "this grim thing."

. . .

In the evening of that same first day in November 1949, the President sat down to dinner at Blair House alone. Bess Truman, as she had been for most of the summer, was away in Independence, looking after her mother; Margaret was in New York, pursuing her singing career, and as always, their absence left him feeling downcast, if not occupied with work or people around him. Several times over the long, difficult summer, in letters home, he had grown more reflective than usual, recounting events that had brought him to where he was. "We can never tell what is in store for us," he had said to Bess. "Never in my wildest dreams did I ever think or wish for such a position," he told Nellie and Ethel Noland. He had "succeeded in getting myself into more trouble than Pandora ever let loose in the world."

If he felt Bess's absences more than usual, it was because their life together now, in Blair House, seemed such an improvement over what it had been across the avenue. The house itself, even with the quick cosmetics applied the year before, was not only nothing very grand, but a bit dowdy. It creaked and groaned, trembled noticeably whenever streetcars passed by outside. Its dark, old cellar was full of rats, as was well known by the Secret Service men, who hated ever having to go down there. And with Washington's Emergency Hospital located just around the corner on F Street, ambulance sirens screamed by in the street below the President's bedroom window often several times a night. Of all the presidents they had known, some of the Secret Service men would later say, only Harry Truman would have been willing to live in the place.

But with Margaret no longer at home, and without the burden of White House entertaining, the President and the First Lady had more time alone together, sitting in the small back garden reading, having lunch, or resting. Indeed, it was the first time in their married life that they had ever had a house to themselves. "Very discreet, very polite, they spent a lot of time behind closed doors in Blair House," remembered J. B. West. Maids joked about the "lovebirds" upstairs, and in recounting his memories of the Truman years, West would later provide the one known suggestion of the sexual attraction between these two very private, essentially Victorian people.

Sometime earlier that fall, when Bess had returned from a long stay with her mother in Independence, both she and the President had been so "jubilant," so obviously happy to be with each other again, that the whole domestic staff felt a lift of spirits. Everybody kept grinning, West remembered.

The next morning, when West reported to the First Lady's study at nine as usual, to go over the day's menu, she told him "in a rather small, uncomfortable voice" that there was a little problem with the President's antique bed. Two of the slats had broken during the night, she said, blushing.

He would attend to it immediately, said West, who had concluded, as he later wrote, that the Trumans were definitely not "antiques."

Now, the evening of November 1, with Bess back again in Independence, and after "another hell of a day," Truman penned one of the most delightful of all his diary sketches of himself—part melancholy, part amusing, entirely human and in character:

> Had dinner by myself tonight. Worked in the Lee House office until dinner time. A butler came in very formally and said, "Mr. President, dinner is served." I walked into the dining room in the Blair House. Barnett in tails and white tie pulls out my chair, pushes me up to the table. John in tails and white tie brings me a fruit cup. Barnett takes away the empty cup. John brings me a plate, Barnett brings me a tenderloin, John brings me asparagus, John brings me carrots and beets. I have to eat alone and in silence in a candle lit room. I ring— Barnett takes the plate and butter plates. John comes in with a napkin and a silver crumb tray—there are no crumbs but John has to brush them off the table anyway. Barnett brings me a plate with a finger bowl and doily on it—I remove finger bowl and doily and John puts a glass saucer and a little bowl on the plate. Barnett brings me some chocolate custard. John brings me a demitasse (at home a little cup of coffee— about two good gulps) and my dinner is over. I take a hand bath in the finger bowl and go back to work.
>
> What a life!

III

Of the nine members of his Cabinet, none was so conspicuous or had more influence on Truman than the elegant, polished Dean Acheson, Secretary of State. His place was unrivaled. Unlike Woodrow Wilson, whose portrait over the mantel in the Cabinet Room still kept watch over gatherings of the Cabinet each Friday morning at ten, Truman had no inside adviser like Colonel Edward House. Nor was there anyone serving as international troubleshooter the way Harry Hopkins had for Roosevelt. The relationship between Truman and Acheson was clear and unimpeded, as Truman wished. Acheson ran the vast operations of State, with its twenty-two thousand employees, but he was also the President's continuous contact with the world, his reporter and interpreter of world events, as well as his chief negotiator and spokesman on foreign policy. Apart from Cabinet meetings, where Acheson sat on Truman's immediate right, they saw each other regularly twice a week—Mondays and Thursdays at 12:30—and talked by phone almost daily.

Truman considered the importance of the office of Secretary of State second only to his own, and had filled the job three times now with men of proven ability and strong personality. Of Edward Stettinius, the Secretary he had inherited from Roosevelt and quickly replaced, Truman wrote, "a fine man, good looking, amiable, cooperative, but never an idea old or new." No figurehead Secretary, no mere dispenser of White House policy would answer. But in Acheson he had found his most exceptional Secretary, and one who, unlike either of his two predecessors, Byrnes and Marshall, had assumed the responsibilities of the office after years of experience in the department and after having already played a decisive part in the two landmark achievements of Truman's first term, the Truman Doctrine and the Marshall Plan.

There was no one in the administration, or in the Cabinet, or on the White House staff, whose views overall, whose sense of proportion, timing, sense of history, whose personal code and convictions concerning America's role in the world carried such weight with the President as Acheson, or whose trust and friendship were to mean as much in the long run.

"It was a great thing between Mr. Truman and me," Acheson would recall.

> Each one understood his role and the other's. We never got tangled up in it. I never thought I was the President, and he never thought he was the Secretary. . . . It is important that the relations between the President and his Secretary be quite frank, sometimes to the point of being blunt. And you just have to be deferential. He is the President of the United States, and you don't say rude things to him—you say blunt things to him. Sometimes he doesn't like it. That's natural, but he comes back, and you argue the thing out. But that's your duty. You don't tell him only what he wants to hear. That would be bad for him and for everyone else.

Truman often referred to Acheson as his "top brain man" in the Cabinet.

That Harry Truman of Missouri, product of the Pendergast machine, "bosom pal" of Harry Vaughan, could possibly have anything in common with Dean Gooderham Acheson, Groton '11, Yale '15, Harvard Law '19, or feel at ease in such a partnership, struck many as almost ludicrous.

Acheson was still another surprise in the presidency of this continuously surprising President.

He seemed to be everything Truman would find objectionable, the ultimate "striped pants boy," were one to judge by appearance—and in Acheson's case it was nearly impossible not to judge by appearance, since that, at first glance, was much the most impressive thing about him.

With his beautiful, chalk-stripe English flannel suits, his striking carriage, his bristling guardsman's mustache and luxuriant eyebrows, Acheson looked not quite real, more like an actor cast for the part of Secretary of State, a tall, slim, imperious, emphatically English-looking Secretary of State. Everything was in order—expensive English shoes rubbed to a fine gloss, the correct quantity of cuff showing spotlessly, hair brushed back from a noble brow. He was just over six feet tall, but the perfect tailoring and perfect posture, the lift of the head, made him seem taller still. He could not go unnoticed. Among the fond memories of Washington in these years would be the sight of the Secretary of State on his way to work in the morning, leather dispatch case in hand, walking the mile and a half from his home in Georgetown accompanied by Justice Felix Frankfurter, who, nearly a head shorter, seemed to take two steps for every one of the Secretary's. Two celebrated conversationalists, they talked the whole way, and reportedly never about government, while Frankfurter's car followed behind to drive him to the Court, once he and Acheson parted company at the steps of the State Department.

"If Harry Truman were a painter," said a Republican congressman, "and had never laid eyes on Acheson, and sat down to paint a picture of a foreign minister, he would come up with a life-size oil of Dean." For years Senator Lyndon Johnson entertained friends with his imitation of Acheson entering a committee room, nose in the air. Averell Harriman, who had known Acheson since they were undergraduates at Yale and who worried that Acheson's appearance might prove a handicap, urged him to at least get rid of the mustache, saying, "You owe it to Truman." But the mustache would stay, and if anything about Acheson's appearance or manner or background ever bothered Truman, he did not say so.

To Truman the State Department was "a peculiar organization, made up principally of extremely bright people who made tremendous college marks but who have had very little association with actual people down to the ground." They were "clannish and snooty," he thought, and he often felt like firing "the whole bunch." Yet no such feelings applied to the Secretary. Acheson was doing a "whale of a job." Truman hoped he would never leave the government.

Acheson, who was fifty-six years old in 1949, had been raised in the small-town America of other times, in Middletown, Connecticut, at the turn of the century, a setting not unlike Independence, Missouri. His mother was the heir to a Canadian whiskey fortune. His father, English by birth and a veteran of the Queen's Own Rifles, was an Episcopal minister, and later bishop of Connecticut, whose frequent admonition to his son was, "Brace up!" Like Truman, Acheson had had his first youthful brush with the "real world" working with a railroad crew. Like Truman, he relished history and biography. He, too, adored Mark Twain. If Acheson was a fashion plate, so, of course, was Truman in his way.

They had their morning walks in common. Both were men of exceptional physical vitality. Both were amateur architects. Truman spoke often of the influence Justice Brandeis had on him in his first years in Washington; Acheson had first come to the city, after law school in 1919, to clerk for Brandeis, from whom, he often said, he learned more than from anyone. Politically, like Truman, Acheson considered himself a little left of center.

His stiff appearance to the contrary, Acheson was also a warmhearted man with a wit of a kind that greatly appealed to Truman. Acheson enjoyed a convivial drink, a good story. (With his father a minister and his mother a distiller's daughter, he liked to say, he knew both good and evil at an early age.) And like Truman, he was devoted to his family. When his oldest daughter, Mary, was stricken with tuberculosis in 1944 and had to be sent to a sanatorium at Saranac, New York, for an extended cure, Acheson wrote to her every night, often revealing how much more of life he savored than was commonly understood.

> At lunch at the Capitol I was asked to sit at a table with Jessie Sumner of Illinois, the worst of the rabble rousing isolationists. . . . We got along famously. She is a grand old girl and reminded me of the madam in John Steinbeck's Cannery Row, sort of low, humorous and human. We became great friends and are going to lunch again. I often wonder whether I have any principles at all. It's a confusing world.

Writing once to Ethel Noland, Truman had said, "You know all of us have a very deep sentimental streak in us, but most of the time we are too timid or too contrary to show it." Acheson, when asked years later by Eric Sevareid how so much trust and affection could have developed between two such seemingly different men as he and the President, said the answer was complicated, but that much of it had to do with what he called Truman's "deeply loving and tender nature," adding, "This isn't the general impression of him at all." When Acheson's daughter had to undergo a serious operation while Acheson was out of the country, and it was not certain she would pull through, Truman personally called the hospital every day for a report, which he himself then transmitted to Acheson by overseas phone.

"Well, this is the kind of person that one can adore," Acheson later said. "You can have an affection for that man that nothing can touch."

Truman, Acheson knew, was far more sentimental than generally known, or than he wished people to know, far more touched by gestures that to many might seem routine. On board his plane later in the year, bound again for Key West, he would write Acheson a brief longhand note marked and underscored "Personal."

> It was good of you to see us off. You always do the right thing. I'm still a farm boy and when the Secretary of State of the greatest Republic comes to the airport to see me off on a vacation, I can't help but swell up a little.

"And then he was so fair," Acheson would say. "He didn't make different decisions with different people. He called everyone together. You were all heard and you all got the answer together. He was a square dealer all the way through."

Moreover, Truman welcomed other people's ideas. "He was not afraid of the competition of other ideas. . . . Free of the greatest vice in a leader, his ego never came between him and his job."

Felix Frankfurter, in listing the elements of Acheson's personal code, would put loyalty first, followed by truthfulness, and "not pretending to be better than you are." Truman had not forgotten that it was Acheson alone who was at Union Station to greet him, after the humiliation of the off-year elections in 1946. Acheson, Truman told David Lilienthal, was a fine man, "loyal, sensible, not like some men who are brilliant."

That Acheson had an exceptional capacity for hard work, that he also subscribed to the philosophy that civilization depended largely on a relatively small number of people who were willing to shoulder the hard work necessary, contributed greatly to Truman's regard for him. Acheson believed in clear, orderly thinking. He knew there were no easy answers, no quick remedies. With the world as it was, he said, Americans would have to get over the idea that the problems facing the country could be solved with a little ingenuity or without inconvenience.

He did not see the Cold War as an inevitable clash between good and evil. To say that good and evil could not exist in the world was absurd, he told an audience of military officers at the National War College in December 1949:

Today you hear much talk of absolutes ... people say that two systems as different as ours and that of the Russians cannot exist in the same world ... that one is good and one is evil, and good and evil cannot exist in the world. ... Good and evil have existed in this world since Adam and Eve went out of the Garden of Eden.

The proper search is for limited ends which soon enough educate us in the complexities of the tasks which face us. That is what all of us must learn to do in the United States; to limit objectives, to get ourselves away from the search for the absolute, to find out what is within our powers. ... We must respect our opponents. We must understand that for a long, long period of time they will continue to believe as they do, and that for a long, long period of time we will both inhabit this spinning ball in the great void of the universe.

As would become apparent to everyone soon enough, Acheson was not only the most important member of Truman's Cabinet, but the most important appointment Truman ever made. And unlike Byrnes and Marshall, he would serve as Secretary throughout a full term, despite vilification such as few in American public life had ever known. He would be seen as an immense political liability, called a fool and a traitor. Nor were his critics and adversaries to be found only among the ranks of the Republicans. One especially determined to challenge his authority at every chance, to see Acheson taken down several pegs, if not entirely, was Louis Johnson, who clearly disliked him and whose cutting remarks soon reached the White House. Greatly displeased, Truman warned Johnson to stop it. "Acheson is a gentleman," Truman told James Webb, the former Director of the Budget, who was now Acheson's under secretary. "He won't descend to a row. Johnson is a rough customer, gets his way by rowing. When he takes out after you, give it right back to him."

Others who knew Acheson thought that in a showdown Johnson wouldn't have a chance. Oliver Franks, the British ambassador and a close friend, described Acheson as "a romantic" and "a blade of steel."

He had a serious—a very serious—problem to decide before long, Truman told Lilienthal on November 7, Acheson having by then talked to him about the superbomb.

He hoped to have a full report from the Atomic Energy Commission (AEC) committee soon, Lilienthal replied.

Yes, said Truman. He wanted the facts, of course.

The report, with its unanimous conclusion by the advisory committee that the superbomb should not be developed, plus a concurring recommendation by the AEC, was delivered two days later, on November 9. The AEC had decided against the bomb by 3 to 2, with Lilienthal the deciding vote. The following day, Truman named Acheson, Johnson, and Lilienthal to act as a special committee of the National Security Council—the Z Committee, as it was called—to advise him whether to proceed with the Super and whether "publicity" should be given the matter. A week later all Washington knew a superbomb was under consideration.

A Washington *Post* reporter, Alfred Friendly, had picked up the first hint of the story from remarks made on a local television broadcast in New York by Democratic Senator Edwin Johnson of Colorado, a member of the Joint Congressional Committee on Atomic Energy, who made his disclosure while airing his fears about the ability of scientists to keep secrets. So suddenly the "H-bomb," a new word, was a public issue.

Physicists Edward Teller and Ernest Lawrence were lobbying hard for proceeding with it. Karl T. Compton, who served on the Interim Committee in 1945 and had only just retired as head of MIT, wrote to Truman saying that in the absence of an international agreement on the control of atomic energy, the United States had no choice but to go ahead with the Super.

At the State Department, stirred by moral outrage, George Kennan labored intensively on a close analysis of the problem and in a long memorandum to Acheson, a plea "as earnest and eloquent" as he knew how to make it, he not only declared against the project but urged that the United States set an example. The last hope for humanity was international control of all weapons of indiscriminate mass destruction. The United States should announce it was "prepared to go very far, to show considerable confidence in others, and to accept certain risk for ourselves," in order to achieve international agreement. To go forward with this still more fearsome next step would be to commit the country and the world to an indefinite escalation of destructiveness and cost.

So the voices against the Super were essentially three, Lilienthal, Kennan, and Oppenheimer, who apart from his own moral objections did not think such a bomb was technically feasible.

But Kennan, like Lilienthal, was about to retire, and the new head of the Policy Planning Staff at the State Department, Paul Nitze, agreed with the Joint Chiefs. To Nitze, Soviet possession of the atomic bomb meant not only that the United States must proceed with work on the H-bomb but build up its conventional forces as well.

Acheson, who, after Hiroshima, favored an atomic partnership with the Soviet Union, had by now come full circle. In effect, he told Kennan to take his Quaker ideas and go.

I told Kennan if that was his view he ought to resign from the Foreign Service and go out and preach his Quaker gospel but not push it within the Department. He had no right being in the Service if he was not willing to face the questions as an issue to be decided in the interests of the American people under a sense of responsibility.

"How can you persuade a paranoid adversary to 'disarm by example'?" Acheson asked rhetorically in conversation with another associate.

The top-secret debate went on for three months, from November 1949 to the end of January 1950, and much of it in Acheson's immense fifth-floor office at the State Department—a room that reminded him, he said, of the cabin-class dining salon on one of the old North German Lloyd ocean liners. But the three-man Z Committee of Acheson, Johnson, and Lilienthal met only twice, due primarily, as Acheson said, "to the acerbity of Louis Johnson's nature." Johnson and Lilienthal argued bitterly.

The first of these sessions was on December 22, the second and last on January 31.

Between times Truman kept to a full presidential schedule. He appointed Oscar Chapman as Secretary of Interior, after the resignation of Julius Krug. He received the new Shah of Iran on a first state visit; posed for photographs with five crippled children for the March of Dimes campaign; issued an executive order authorizing the Federal Housing Administration loans of $20 million for low-rent housing in twenty-seven states, the District of Columbia, and Puerto Rico; issued an executive order to the FHA to deny financial assistance to new housing projects with racial or religious restrictions; exchanged Christmas greetings with the Pope; and learned from the Secret Service that in 1949 alone there had been a total of 1,925 threats, written or oral, against him or his family. ("The day will come," said one, "when I will have your heart out and give it to the ants as food.")

Four days into the new year, in a recently redecorated House Chamber, he delivered his fifth State of the Union message. If American productive power continued to increase at the same rate as it had in the previous half century, he told the Congress, then national production fifty years hence would be four times as great, the average family income three times what it was in 1950, or $12,450 a year, which struck many as unimaginable. "Today, by the grace of God, we stand in a free and prosperous nation with greater possibilities for the future than any people have ever had before in the history of the world. . . ."

At a press conference on January 7, 1950, he presented his annual budget—a big green book the size and weight of a New York telephone directory—and answered questions about it. The total figure was $42.4

billion, which included an increase of $1 billion for domestic programs. But most, some $30 billion, was to pay for wars past and for the present national defense, listed to cost $13.5 billion. It was a budget that did not balance. The estimated deficit was $5 billion, which would mean a national debt by 1952 of $268.3 billion.

In a message to Congress he asked for a "moderate" tax increase to bring in an additional $1 billion.

For an hour at the Shoreham Hotel one night, he stood at the door of a private dining room shaking hands with virtually every Democrat in Congress. He addressed the A.F. of L. dinner and a civil rights conference; he held five more press conferences.

He also faced the fact that Clark Clifford and David Lilienthal, two of his best, were leaving in February, to return to private life. The loss of Clifford would be a real blow. But Clifford was worn out and deeply in debt, his living expenses over the past four years having run far ahead of his White House salary. He would stay on in Washington to practice law. Lilienthal, too, was exhausted and knew the time had come to move on. Truman, as he said, felt as though "the bottom had fallen out."

More serious, and worrisome, however, was the assault on Dean Acheson. In December, angry over the loss of China and the supposed infiltration of Communists everywhere, the Republicans in both houses of Congress called on Truman to fire Acheson. Then, in New York, on January 21, at the end of a long second trial, Alger Hiss was found guilty of perjury—he had lied about passing secret documents—and that night Republican Congressman Richard Nixon, who as the only lawyer on the House Un-American Activities Committee had played a leading part in the case against Hiss, went on the radio to accuse the administration of a "deliberate" effort to conceal the Hiss "conspiracy." On Wednesday, January 25, the day Hiss was sentenced to five years in prison, Acheson was asked at a press conference at the State Department if he had any comments.

The question was not unexpected. At his confirmation hearings the year before, Acheson had acknowledged that Hiss was a friend and remained a friend, adding that his own friendship was not easily given nor easily withdrawn. Hiss's brother, Donald, a partner in Acheson's law firm, had served as Acheson's assistant when Acheson was Assistant Secretary of State. Now to the throng of reporters he said, "I should like to make it clear to you that whatever the outcome of any appeal which Mr. Hiss or his lawyers may take in this case, I do not intend to turn my back on Alger Hiss."

It was no impulsive response. Acheson had thought long about what to say, and as many in the room sensed at once, it was a decisive moment in the history of the Truman administration. He continued, his voice full of emotion:

> I think anyone who has known Alger Hiss or has served with him at any time has upon his conscience the very serious task of deciding what his attitude is and what his conduct should be. That must be done by each person in the light of his own standards and his own principles. For me there is little doubt about those standards and principles. I think they were stated for us a very long time ago . . . on the Mount of Olives and if you are interested in seeing them you will find them in the 25th Chapter of the Gospel according to St. Matthew beginning with verse 34.

An aide stood at the door with a Bible ready for those reporters who wished to check the reference: "I was a prisoner and ye came unto me."

Perhaps the voice of the late bishop of Connecticut, Acheson's father, sounded in the citation, wrote the New York *Herald-Tribune,* one of the few papers to praise Acheson for what he had said.

> This newspaper has felt it necessary at times to criticize and oppose Mr. Acheson in his policies. . . . But of this statement made on Wednesday in a difficult hour, we are glad to declare in our judgment it was as courageous as it was Christian.

It was also a political disaster. The news reached Capitol Hill almost instantly. Senator Joseph McCarthy interrupted the flow of business in the Senate to report "the most fantastic statement" just made by the Secretary of State. Did this mean, McCarthy asked, that the Secretary would "not turn his back on any other Communists in the State Department?"

His press conference ended, Acheson went immediately to see Truman, who by then had seen the news ticker story. Acheson offered to resign. Truman, Acheson wrote to his daughter, was "wonderful about it . . . said that one who had gone to the funeral of a friendless old man just out of the penitentiary [Tom Pendergast] had no trouble knowing what I meant and proving it.

"So there we are," Acheson added, "and as the Persian King had carved on his ring, 'This, too, will pass.' "

But pass it did not. The damage done to himself and the President was worse than either knew. Richard Nixon called Acheson's statement "disgusting." Republican Senator Hugh Butler of Nebraska exploded in a tirade. "I look at that fellow, I watch his smart-aleck manner and his British clothes and that New Dealism in everything he says and does, and

I want to shout, 'Get out! Get out! You stand for everything that has been wrong in the United States for years!' "

The atmosphere in Washington, the atmosphere in which the decision on the hydrogen bomb was being weighed, had become charged with rancor and fear. At his press conference the next afternoon, Friday, January 27, Truman was asked first whether he too would refuse to turn his back on Alger Hiss—to which he replied, "No comment"—then, what his views were on the H-bomb, as though the two issues were directly connected. He would have nothing to say until he made a decision, Truman answered, thus acknowledging for the first time that the issue existed.

Comment and speculation on the bomb continued. Headlines called it the "Ultimate Bomb," the "Hell Bomb." *Life* ran an aerial photograph of Chicago showing how much of the city would be obliterated—50 square miles—by one such weapon. In the Washington *Post,* where for years he had been drawing the atomic bomb as a sinister presence looming over peace conferences or taking the measure of the world, cartoonist Herb Block now portrayed the atomic bomb holding the giant hand of an infinitely larger, more menacing creature labeled "Super-bomb," and asking a terrified Uncle Sam, "Want to meet my friend, too?"

Eleanor Roosevelt and Bernard Baruch announced their support for building the bomb. Harold Urey of the University of Chicago, a leader in atomic research who, in 1934, had won a Nobel Prize for his discovery of heavy hydrogen, declared in a speech in New York that the United States could not intentionally lose the armaments race without risking its liberties.

Rumors of bitter animosity within the administration, talk of who was for and who was against the H-bomb became a Washington obsession. On Capitol Hill, Democratic Senator Brien McMahon of Connecticut, chairman of the Joint Committee on Atomic Energy, was reportedly "almost in tears" over the prospect of the bomb not proceeding. War with the Russians was inevitable, the powerful senator assured Lilienthal. The thing to do was "blow them off the face of the earth, quick, before they do the same to us—we haven't much time." To Truman he wrote, "If we let Russia get the Super first, catastrophe becomes all but certain—whereas if we get it first, there exists a chance of saving ourselves."

The Joint Chiefs wanted a "crash program." General Bradley wrote that it was "folly to argue whether one weapon is more immoral than another. For, in a larger sense, it is war itself which is immoral, and the stigma of such immorality must rest upon the nation which initiates hostilities." Despite an understanding that deliberations on the bomb would be kept within the Z Committee, Louis Johnson quickly sent Bradley's memorandum to Truman.

> Like a patient sitting in a doctor's anteroom while the specialists discuss his case [wrote *Time*], the U.S. public . . . sat outside while the President, his military, scientific and diplomatic advisers debated whether to construct the . . . most powerful explosive weapon the world has yet dreamed of. . . . But since the principle of the hydrogen bomb was also known to the Russians, temporizing was risky and might be fatal. The simple fact, unpleasant though it might be, was that if the Russians are likely to build an H-bomb, the U.S. will have to build it, too.

When on Tuesday, January 31, 1950, Acheson, Johnson, and Lilienthal with several of their aides convened for the final session of the Z Committee in Room 216 of the Old State Department Building, it was Acheson who took charge. He had concluded that work should proceed on the hydrogen bomb and presented the draft of a statement to be made by the President.

Johnson agreed, but Lilienthal did not like rushing things through in an "atmosphere of excitement." A decision to go ahead with the bomb now would probably make a new approach to the atomic arms race impossible. He thought the country's almost sole reliance on this kind of weapon was extremely unwise and that going ahead with it would give the American people a "false and dangerous assurance . . . that when we get this new gadget 'the balance will be ours' as against the Russians." He questioned what the project would do to defense budgets and foreign policy.

Acheson, who greatly admired Lilienthal and who would later describe Lilienthal's objections as "eloquently and forcefully" expressed, said he could not overcome two "stubborn facts": that delaying work on the bomb would not delay Soviet work on their bomb; and that the American people would simply not tolerate a policy of delay.

"We must protect the President," Johnson said. And though he still had grave reservations, Lilienthal, too, agreed to sign the statement.

Accompanied by Admiral Sidney W. Souers, the executive secretary of the National Security Council, the three men walked to the White House. Their meeting had lasted two and a half hours. The meeting with the President took seven minutes.

Truman had already made up his mind, perhaps as much as ten days earlier, or at least that was the impression of his immediate staff, though he had said nothing specific. Acheson knew this. Apparently they all did. The President, wrote Lilienthal, was "clearly set on what he was going to do before we set foot inside the door."

As Truman looked over the statement, Acheson said Lilienthal had some additional views to express.

Truman, turning to Lilienthal, said he had always believed the United States should never use "these weapons," that peace was "our whole purpose." Lilienthal said that while he did not overrate the value of his own judgment, he felt he must express his grave reservations about the proposed course. Try as he might, he could not see it as the wisest move. However carefully worded, however issued, the statement would only magnify the essentially mistaken policy of relying on atomic weapons as the country's chief defense.

There was too much talk in Congress "and everywhere," Truman broke in. People were "so excited." He didn't see that he had any alternative.

"Can the Russians do it?" he asked the group. It was his only question. They all nodded.

"We don't have much time," interjected Admiral Souers.

"In that case," said Truman, "we have no choice. We'll go ahead."

As he signed the statement, Truman said he recalled another meeting of the National Security Council concerning Greece, when "everybody predicted the end of the world if we went ahead, but we did go ahead and the world didn't come to an end." It would be "the same case here," he said.

While the President went home to Blair House for lunch, Charlie Ross again handed out a mimeographed sheet.

It is part of my responsibility as Commander in Chief of the Armed Forces to see to it that our country is able to defend itself against any possible aggressor. Accordingly, I have directed the Atomic Energy Commission to continue its work on all forms of atomic weapons, including the so-called hydrogen or superbomb....

Lilienthal described the mood at the AEC afterward as that of a funeral party. For him it was a night of heartache. "I hope I was wrong, and that somehow I'll be proved wrong," he wrote. "We have to leave many things to God...." Albert Einstein, in a rare appearance on television, talked of the radioactive poisoning of the atmosphere and warned, "General annihilation beckons."

To what extent Truman had struggled with the decision, or dwelled on

763

it afterward, is not known. He left nothing in writing. Nor can Acheson's influence on him be readily gauged, though doubtless it was considerable. Acheson, as Truman said, was one of the most persuasive men he had ever known.

It would have been preferable surely—wiser, more prudent—to have given the entire question longer, closer examination, and under less stress, even assuming Truman would have decided no differently. The country could have been better prepared. There would have been time for a clear, explanatory presidential address to the nation, instead of a mimeographed announcement. So disquieting, so momentous, and so costly a step deserved better.

In any event, as anticipated, public and editorial approval of the decision was overwhelming—the President had made "the right and inevitable" decision. Then, in only a matter of days, the level of apprehension was raised still higher by news from London that Klaus Fuchs, a former atomic scientist at Los Alamos, had confessed to being a Russian spy, and by the sudden claim of Senator Joseph McCarthy that he had in his possession a list of more than two hundred known Communists employed at the State Department.

IV

With the onrush of so much sensational, seemingly inexplicable bad news—China lost, the Russian bomb, Alger Hiss, the treason of Klaus Fuchs—breaking with such clamor, all in less than six months, the country was in a state of terrible uncertainty.

"How much are we going to have to take?" asked Senator Homer Capehart of Indiana.

Life devoted much of one issue to show how vastly Russian military strength exceeded that of the United States—an army of 2,600,000 men, compared to an American force of 640,000, 30 Russian armored divisions to one American. The United States produced 1,200 new planes a year, the Russians 7,000. Only the American Navy stood first, but the Soviets already had a more powerful fleet than Germany had had at the start of the last war and three times the number of American submarines. While America spent 6 percent of its national income on military strength, the Russians were spending 25 percent. And so on. "War Can Come; Will We Be Ready?" asked the *Life* headline.

It was, of course, a question of paramount importance within the administration. For months behind the scenes Acheson had been arguing that Truman's $13 billion limit on defense spending was no longer realistic. Now with his decision to proceed with the hydrogen bomb Truman authorized a complete review of military policy. At both the State Department and the Pentagon, work began on a sweeping new report, and with the pressure on, relations between the Secretary of State and the Secretary of Defense grew steadily more contentious. At a meeting in March, Louis Johnson exploded with such temper—banging down his chair, shouting objections, hammering his fist on the table—that Acheson could only conclude that Johnson, like Forrestal, had cracked under the strain.

When Acheson reported to Truman what had happened, Truman was appalled. Probably it was then he knew that Johnson would have to go—when the time was right.

Fear gripped Washington and the country. "The air was so charged with fear," remembered Herb Block, "that it took only a small spark to ignite it." And the spark was McCarthy. When Block, in one of his cartoons in the *Post,* labeled an overflowing barrel of tar "McCarthyism," another new word entered the language along with the H-bomb.

Until that January, Joseph R. McCarthy, Wisconsin's forty-one-year-old junior senator, had been casting about for an issue that might lift him from obscurity. All but friendless in the Senate, recently voted the worst member of the Senate in a poll of Washington correspondents, McCarthy appeared to be a hopeless failure. Over dinner one evening at the Colony Restaurant, a Catholic priest, Father Edmund A. Walsh of Georgetown University, suggested he might sound the alarm over Communist infiltration of the government, and McCarthy, who had already made some loud, if unnotable, charges about Communist subversion, seems to have realized at once that he had found what he needed. A month later, in a Lincoln's Birthday speech in West Virginia, he waved a piece of paper, saying he had "here in my hand" the names of 205 "known Communists" in the State Department. The speech went largely unnoticed, but at Salt Lake City and Reno soon afterward he made essentially the same claim, except the number was cut to fifty-seven, and they were referred to now as "card-carrying" Communists. He made headlines across the country. Back at the Senate he carried on for five hours, claiming to have penetrated "Truman's iron curtain of secrecy" and come up with eighty-one names.

The charges were wild and unsupported. McCarthy had no names, he produced no new evidence. He was a political brawler, morose, reckless, hard-drinking, a demagogue such as had not been seen in the Senate since the days of Huey Long, only he had none of Long's charm or brilliance. The press called him desperate, a loudmouth and a character assassin. His Communist hunt was "a wretched burlesque of the serious and necessary business of loyalty check-ups." But he was no more bothered by such criticism than by his own inconsistencies, and whatever he said the press printed, his most sensational allegations often getting the biggest headlines. To more and more of the country it seemed that even if he might be wrong in some of his particulars, probably he was onto something, and high time.

Harry Truman, McCarthy charged, was the "prisoner of a bunch of twisted intellectuals" who only told him what they wanted him to know. Attacking Acheson, he said, "When this pompous diplomat in striped pants, with the phony British accent, proclaimed to the American people that Christ on the Mount endorsed Communism, high treason, and betrayal of a sacred trust, the blasphemy was so great that it awakened the dormant indignation of the American people." As McCarthy kept up the assault, Acheson received so much threatening mail that guards had to be posted at his house around the clock.

While numbers of his fellow Republicans silently deplored McCarthy's methods, others—Bridges, Brewster, Capehart, Mundt, Wherry—began lending support. "I will not turn my back on Joe McCarthy," said Brewster. Encouragement came too from Senator Taft, who had been the first to introduce the "soft on Communism" issue in the 1946 elections and who now admitted publicly that he was egging McCarthy on, to press the attack, to "keep talking and if one case didn't work out, to bring up another." All the anger and resentment felt by Republicans like Taft over Truman's surprise upset in 1948 had found an outlet.

Senate Democrats, meanwhile, called for a complete investigation of McCarthy's charges. A special subcommittee of the Foreign Relations Committee began hearings under the chairmanship of Millard Tydings of Maryland, one of the most respected, influential Democrats in the Senate. The assumption was that in the bright light of public exposure, McCarthy and his tactics could not long survive.

But the attention only magnified him. The hearings in the Senate's marble-columned Caucus Room gave him center stage and the full attention of the press day after day. "You are not fooling me," he said. "This committee [is] not seeking to get the names of bad security risks, but . . . to find out the names of my informants so they can be kicked out of the State Department tomorrow." By the end of March, in the six weeks since his initial outburst at Wheeling, McCarthy had not named a single Communist.

He announced he had the name of the "top Russian espionage agent" in the United States, indeed the "onetime" boss of Alger Hiss and his espionage ring. The man, said McCarthy, was Owen J. Lattimore, formerly of the State Department and currently director of the Johns Hopkins School of International Relations. As time would show, Lattimore was neither a Communist nor ever an influential figure at the State Department. He had worked for the department all of four months in 1946, as an adviser on a reparations mission in Japan. The accusation was a fraud. "If you crack this case," McCarthy told the committee, "it will be the biggest espionage case in the history of this country." He was willing, he said, to stand or fall on that.

In mid-February 1950, at about the time McCarthy's reckless charges were first making headlines, Truman agreed to an exclusive interview with Arthur Krock of *The New York Times,* during which he impressed Krock as a man of exceptional inner calm and strength.

> In an age of atomic energy, transmuted into a weapon which can destroy great cities and the best works of civilization, and in the shadow of a hydrogen detonant which could multiply many times that agent of destruction, a serene President of the United States sits in the White House with undiminished confidence in the triumph of humanity's better nature and the progress of his own efforts to achieve an abiding peace.

Harry S. Truman, said Krock, might seem to many a controversial figure. But to those who had the chance to talk with him intimately, his faith in the future had a "luminous" quality.

> He sits in the center of the troubled and frightened world. . . . But the penumbra of doubt and fear in which the American nation pursues its great and most perilous adventure . . . stops short of him. Visitors find him undaunted and sure that, whether in his time or thereafter, a way will be discovered to preserve the world from the destruction which to many seems unavoidable. . . .

David Lilienthal, who came to the Oval Office on February 14 for a final farewell meeting with the President, described it later as "one of the happiest sessions I've ever had with him."

"About these scientists," Truman said, "we need men with great intellects, need their ideas. But we need to balance them with other kinds of people, too."

Lilienthal, perhaps as much as anyone, knew the weight of the burdens Truman carried. Yet Truman looked "tip-top . . . his eye clear." Studying him, listening to him talk, Lilienthal was amazed. As he later wrote, "My admiration and wonder at his relaxed way of looking at things, and his obvious good health . . . reached a new high."

. . .

But his wife of thirty years knew differently, and to her alone, he portrayed himself differently. She grew increasingly concerned about his health, the stress the McCarthy attacks put on him. His headaches had returned. In mid-March Bess urged another retreat to Florida, to recover his strength. "You see everybody shoots at me, if not directly, then at some of the staff closest to me," he wrote to her from Key West.

In the Senate, Republican Styles Bridges had now joined McCarthy and stepped up the attack. Truman had liked Bridges, long considered him a friend. John Snyder had become a target lately. Rumors were Snyder was drinking too much.

Caustic comments in the press about Harry Vaughan, the almost constant abuse of Dean Acheson, and belittling comments on his own performance, all that he seemed impervious to, in fact bothered Truman greatly and he was feeling not just a little sorry for himself.

> The general trend of the pieces [he wrote to Bess] is that I'm a very small man in a very large place and when some one I trust joins the critical side—well it hurts. I'm much older and very tired and I need support as no man ever did.
>
> What has made me so jittery—they started on Snyder and have almost broken him, then Vaughan, whose mental condition is very bad. Now they are after my top brain man in the Cabinet. The whole foreign policy is at stake just as we are on the road to a possible solution. . . . I'm telling you so you may understand how badly I need *your* help and support now.

McCarthy, he felt, was a temporary aberration, "a ballyhoo artist who has to cover up his shortcomings by wild charges." Even so he had had enough. On March 30, midway through his Key West stay, Truman decided to speak out. By then, according to the polls, half the American people held a "favorable opinion" of the senator and thought he was helping the country. Truman's own standing, by stark contrast, had plunged to 37 percent, nearly as low as in the spring of 1948.

He called a rare press conference on the lawn beside the Little White House, where with sunny skies overhead and a breeze stirring the palms, talk of the junior senator from Wisconsin seemed strangely incongruous. Looking well tanned and fit in a light linen suit and open shirt, Truman sat in a white wicker chair, with reporters gathered about him in a circle.

Did he expect Senator McCarthy to turn up any disloyalty in the State Department?

"I think," he said with a hard look, "the greatest asset that the Kremlin has is Senator McCarthy."

And there were others, he said—Wherry and Bridges. The Republicans had been searching in vain for an issue for the fall elections. They had tried "statism," the "welfare state," "socialism." Some were even trying to dig up "that old malodorous dead horse called 'isolationism.' " He was furious. This "fiasco" going on in the Senate, he said, jabbing a finger in the air, was an attempt to sabotage bipartisan foreign policy. It was a dangerous situation, and it had to be stopped. Dean Acheson, he added emphatically, would go down in history as one of the great secretaries of state. There was no question about that.

Was Owen Lattimore a Russian spy?

"Why of course not. It's silly on the face of it."

It was a dramatic moment, a performance, reporters thought, that equaled Franklin Roosevelt at his angry best.

Taft accused Truman of having libeled McCarthy. "Do you think that's possible?" Truman responded, when a reporter raised the question at the next press conference, back in Washington.

To a gathering of the Federal Bar Association, he gave his assurance that no known instance of Communist subversion, or subversion of any kind, had gone uninvestigated by the FBI or as a result of his own Loyalty Program. "There is no area of American life in which the Communist Party is making headway, except maybe in the minds of some people. . . ." That his own Loyalty Program might have contributed to the overall atmosphere that gave rise to McCarthy is a thought he seems not to have entertained—not then at least.

"I think our friend McCarthy will eventually get all that is coming to him. He has no sense of decency or honor," Truman wrote to Owen Lattimore's sister.

> You can understand, I imagine, what the President has to stand—
> every day in the week he's under a constant barrage of people who
> have no respect for the truth and whose objective is to belittle and
> discredit him. While they are not successful in these attacks they are
> never pleasant so I know just how you feel about the attack on your
> brother. The best thing to do is to face it and the truth will come out.

Yet nothing Truman or anyone else said seemed to diminish McCarthy or the fear he spread in the government and the nation. When Truman, who had first refused to turn security files over to the Tydings Committee as a matter of principle, decided to let Tydings and the committee come to the White House to look at the files of the eighty-one people accused by McCarthy—in an effort to help Tydings discredit McCarthy and answer a Republican charge that he, Truman, was "covering up" evidence—it proved a bad decision. Now even the President appeared to be caving in to Joe McCarthy.

Tydings, in a state of near panic, was on the phone to the White House three and four times a day. Truman's staff grew extremely worried and on edge. Truman told them to stay calm. McCarthy would destroy himself, he said. The man was a liar. He would be found out and expelled from the Senate. That was how these things worked, and that was how it should be handled. Truman wondered only if there was anyone in the Senate with backbone enough to do the job.

When, in the first week of June, the senator with backbone turned out to be a Republican and the Senate's only woman, Margaret Chase Smith of Maine, who declared she did not want to see the Republican Party "ride to victory on the four horsemen of calumny—fear, ignorance, bigotry, and smear," Truman told his staff she had done "a fine thing," though he thought she should have been tougher still and more specific.

It was on a particularly glorious day that spring, on Sunday, April 9, 1950, with lilacs and azaleas blooming in profusion and the cherry blossoms coming full around the Tidal Basin, that Truman drafted a statement in his own hand that he planned to make public two years hence. April 11 marked the end of his fifth year in office, and he had decided not to run for another term.

In 1947, as a rebuke to the memory of Franklin Roosevelt and his four terms, the Republicans of the 80th Congress had passed the Twenty-second Amendment to the Constitution, an amendment Truman opposed, limiting presidents to two terms. With ratification by the states, it would become law in 1951. But since it had been worded not to include Truman, he was free to run again in 1952, as many if not most people assumed he would.

He had been thinking about the "lure in power," and the example set by his hero Cincinnatus, the Roman general who had turned away from power. He was neither discouraged nor angry over the course of events. He remained in many ways a man of iron, as Wallace Graham said, and more, "a happy man," in the words of one White House reporter, "and as far as the observer could tell boundlessly sure of himself." But quietly on his own, without discussion with anyone other than his wife, he had decided he would announce his retirement in the spring of 1952, when he would be sixty-eight:

I am not a candidate for nomination by the Democratic Convention.
My first election to public office took place in November 1922. I served two years in the armed forces in World War I, ten years in the

Senate, two months and 20 days as Vice President and President of the Senate. I have been in public service well over thirty years, having been President of the United States almost two complete terms.

Washington, Jefferson, Monroe, Madison, Andrew Jackson and Woodrow Wilson, as well as Calvin Coolidge stood by the precedent of two terms. Only Grant, Theodore Roosevelt, and F.D.R. made the attempt to break that precedent. F.D.R. succeeded.

In my opinion eight years as President is enough and sometimes too much for any man to serve in this capacity.

There is a lure in power. It can get into a man's blood just as gambling and lust for money have been known to do.

This is a Republic. The greatest in the history of the world. I want the country to continue as a Republic. Cincinnatus and Washington pointed the way. When Rome forgot Cincinnatus its downfall began. When we forget the examples of such men as Washington, Jefferson, and Andrew Jackson, all of whom could have had a continuation in the office, then we will start down the road to dictatorship and ruin. I know I could be elected again and continue to break the old precedent as it was broken by F.D.R. It should not be done. That precedent should continue—not by Constitutional amendment but by custom based on the honor of the man in office.

Therefore to reestablish that custom, although by a quibble I could say I have only had one term, I am not a candidate and will not accept the nomination for another term.

The tone, to be sure, was a bit self-congratulatory, and whether his confidence in reelection was altogether sincere or an added touch for the record—lest anyone see him retiring from the field in fear—is hard to say. The implied charge that Franklin Roosevelt had been something less than a man of honor by choosing to run more than twice was in keeping with his own position on the issue in 1940, but not in 1944, when he was the running mate. Still, it was a statement of conviction like none written by an American President. Nor is there any doubt of his devotion to the Cincinnatus ideal. As events would verify, this was no whim of the moment.

He said nothing on the matter. The two handwritten pages were quietly put away.

The explosive secret report on the country's military strength known as NSC-68 (Paper No. 68 of the National Security Council) was ready by the end of the first week in April. Produced primarily by Paul Nitze, under the direction of Dean Acheson and with the participation of the Defense Department, it was delivered to Truman on April 7 and discussed with him for the first time at a White House meeting of the National Security

Council on Tuesday, April 25. Like the Clifford-Elsey memorandum of an earlier day, it was intended to shock. Charlie Murphy, who had replaced Clark Clifford as special counsel to the President, would remember being so frightened by what he saw in an early draft that he spent a whole day reading it over and over.

An apocalyptic theme was struck at the start: "This Republic and its citizens, in the ascendancy of their strength, stand in their deepest peril. . . ." The American colossus, the report said in effect, was sadly wanting in real military might. Its policy of "containment," as advanced by George Kennan, was no better than a policy of bluff without the "superior aggregate military strength"—the conventional forces—to back it up. Nuclear weapons were insufficient and, in any event, the Soviets would probably achieve nuclear equality by 1954.

A massive military buildup was called for. This would put "heavy demands on our courage and intelligence." The financial burden would be extreme. Though no cost estimates were included, the figures discussed with Truman ranged from $40 to $50 billion a year, at least three times the current military budget.

"The whole success," Truman read in the concluding paragraph, "hangs ultimately on recognition by this government, the American people and all the peoples that the Cold War is in fact a real war in which the survival of the world is at stake."

So, while Albert Einstein was warning that annihilation beckoned, the Secretary of State and his associates, as well as the Defense Department, were saying anything short of a massive military buildup, including nuclear arms, was to put survival at risk.

In writing such papers, papers intended to shape national policy, Acheson would later explain, one could not approach the task as one would in writing a doctoral thesis. "Qualification must give way to simplicity of statement, nicety and nuance to bluntness, almost brutality, in carrying home a point." In the particular instance of NSC-68, he conceded, the purpose was to "bludgeon the mass mind of 'top government.' "

Truman, however, was not to be bludgeoned. His response was the same as it had been with the Clifford-Elsey Report. He put it away under lock and key. NSC-68 and *Life* magazine might both point up in dramatic fashion the perilous state of American military strength, but he refused to rush to a decision, even if he did not dispute their claims. His approach was essentially what it had been at the time of the Berlin crisis, essentially what it was in the face of McCarthy—he would make no drastic moves until he knew more.

Feeling the need for contact again with the American people, he set off by train in May for another "nonpolitical" cross-country tour, ostensibly to dedicate Grand Coulee Dam in Washington. Not once in two weeks of travel, never in more than fifty speeches in fifteen states, did he mention Joe McCarthy or sound a call to arms. Instead, he seemed to glow with patience and optimism. The Cold War would be "with us for a long, long time," he lectured. "There is no quick way, no easy way to end it." Yet even so, in the long run, there were no problems that could not be solved.

Whether he would have attempted anything like the buildup called for in NSC-68 had events not taken the calamitous turn they did in late June, will never be known. But it seems unlikely.

At his weekly press conference on June 1, he said he thought the world was closer to real peace than at any time in the last five years.

V

The silver plane of the President began its long, smooth descent over the farmland of Missouri at approximately 1:45, Central Standard Time, the afternoon of Saturday, June 24. Truman had planned a weekend at home with his family, nothing official on the schedule, "a grand visit—I hope," as he said in a note to a friend early that morning. "I'm going from Baltimore to see Bess, Margie and my brother and sister, oversee some fence building—not political—order a new roof for the farm house...."

He had begun his day at Blair House as customary, scanning the *Post,* the Baltimore *Sun, The New York Times,* all filled that morning with the spreading Communist scare. The University of California had fired 157 employees for refusing to sign an anti-Communist oath. At an annual convention in Boston, the NAACP had resolved to drive all known Communists from its membership. In Washington, a federal judge had denied pleas for acquittal to three screenwriters, part of the so-called "Hollywood Ten," who had refused to tell the House Un-American Activities Committee whether they were Communists. In a photograph on page 1 of the *Times,* a round-faced former Army sergeant named David Greenglass was being escorted in handcuffs from a New York court where he was charged with being part of the Klaus Fuchs spy ring at Los Alamos. On page 4 of the *Times,* the Secretary General of the United Nations, Trygve Lie of Norway, was reported responding angrily to a reporter's question as to whether he was, or ever had been, a Communist. "By God, there should be some respect for my integrity," he had exploded.

The one encouraging note for Truman was an announcement by Republican Senator Henry Cabot Lodge, Jr., a member of the Tydings Committee, that weeks of effort at the White House, going over the files of the eighty-one "cases" charged by Senator McCarthy, had produced no evidence of consequence.

The weather forecast, an item Truman never failed to check, called for a hot and humid day, with a high of 90 degrees and a chance of late thundershowers.

His plane, the *Independence,* took off from National Airport at mid-morning and before heading west, stopped briefly at Baltimore, where Truman dedicated the city's new Friendship Airport, with an eight-minute speech stressing peace and constructive confidence. ("We would not build so elaborate a facility for our air commerce if we did not have faith in a peaceful future. . . .") Through much of the flight afterward, huge thunderheads loomed in the distance. In a violent storm earlier in the day, a Northwest Airlines plane had gone down over Lake Michigan with fifty-eight people on board, all of whom were lost in the nation's worst air disaster. But Truman's trip was smooth and uneventful. Landing at Kansas City at two o'clock, he came down the steps from the plane looking fresh, relaxed, even "jaunty" in the Missouri heat.

At the house in Independence, a crowd of several hundred waited beside a new iron fence five feet high recently installed by the Secret Service. The time was now past when anyone could mingle on the Truman lawn.

As he stepped from the car, somebody shouted that he should have been at the Eagles' meeting the night before. "There are lots of places I'd like to go that I can't get to," Truman answered cheerfully with a wave, then started up the walk.

The baking summer afternoon passed quietly, the windows of the old house open wide to what little air was moving. Bess and Margaret had gone to a wedding. Automobiles passed on Van Horne, now renamed Truman Road—a gesture by the town that had pleased Truman not at all —but the sound was faint, mild compared to the steady hubbub outside Blair House. The lazy privacy of the interlude was just what Truman needed. He had not been home since Christmas.

Dinner was called by Vietta Garr at 6:30. Truman and Mrs. Wallace took their customary places at either end of the table. Margaret would recall a "very pleasant family dinner," after which they moved out onto a newly expanded, screened porch off the kitchen, where they sat talking, "small talk," until dark, when everyone moved back inside to the study.

By nine, Truman was ready for bed. It had been a long day. The time difference between Independence and Washington was two hours, since western Missouri was not on daylight saving time.

At about 9:20, the telephone rang in the hall. Dean Acheson was calling from his country house in Maryland.

"Mr. President," he said, "I have very serious news. The North Koreans have invaded South Korea."

There had been a report from John Muccio, the American ambassador in Seoul, Acheson explained. The North Koreans had crossed the 38th parallel, in what Muccio, an experienced officer, described as a heavy attack, not just a patrol foray of the kind there had been before.

Acting on his own initiative, Acheson had already notified the Secretary General of the United Nations to call a meeting of the U.N. Security Council.

He would leave for Washington at once, Truman said. ("My first reaction was that I must get back to the Capital," he later wrote.) Acheson, however, advised him to wait. There was no need to take the risk of a night flight, and it might alarm the country.

"Everything is being done that can be," Acheson said. "If you can sleep, take it easy." He would call tomorrow when he knew more.

According to Margaret, her father returned from the phone in a state of extreme agitation, having already concluded the worst. "My father," she wrote, "made it clear, from the moment he heard the news, that he feared this was the opening of World War III." It was to be a long night for the family.

Sunday morning, the feeling again was of full summer in Missouri, hot and humid.

Of the seventeen churches in Independence, the first to sound its bells, at eight o'clock, was St. Mary's, the old red-brick Catholic church on North Liberty, followed later by the new clarion at First Presbyterian, two blocks from the house, which played hymns until 10:45, by which time church bells all across town had begun their Sunday crescendo.

Bess and Margaret would leave for services at Trinity Episcopal shortly before eleven. But Truman by then had driven off to Grandview in a Secret Service car. They were all to act as normal and unconcerned as possible, "business as usual," he had instructed before leaving.

He stretched his stay at Grandview through most of the morning. Chatting amiably with his brother Vivian, he looked over a new milking machine, admired a new horse, and shook hands with Vivian's five grandchildren before moving on to see Mary Jane. To no one did he say anything about Korea, even though reports of the invasion were in the morning headlines and on the radio.

He reached 219 North Delaware shortly before noon to find Eben Ayers waiting with a copy of Ambassador Muccio's telegram: "IT WOULD APPEAR FROM THE NATURE OF THE ATTACK AND MANNER IN WHICH IT WAS LAUNCHED THAT IT CONSTITUTES AN ALL-OUT OFFENSIVE AGAINST THE REPUBLIC OF KOREA."

A swarm of reporters and photographers appeared at the front gate. On his way out, Ayers told them that naturally the President was concerned.

Bess and Margaret had only just returned from church when Acheson's second call came at about 12:30.

> Dad took it [Margaret recorded in her diary] and a few minutes later he went to pack and told me to call Kansas City and get Eben Ayers to call all the people who came out with him to say that he would arrive at the airport between 2:00 and 2:15.

The departure from Kansas City was so swift and sudden that some of Truman's own staff, as well as the White House correspondents who traveled by chartered plane, were left behind. As the *Independence* took off, Bess, Margaret, and Vivian Truman stood watching in silence, Bess looking much as she had the night of Franklin Roosevelt's death.

"Everything is extremely tense," wrote Margaret at home that night. "Northern or Communist Korea is marching in on Southern Korea and we are going to fight." Apparently from what she had seen and heard, she had no trouble knowing her father's mind.

The *Independence* touched down at National Airport at 7:15 that evening, Sunday, June 25. Dean Acheson, Louis Johnson, and Budget Director James Webb were waiting on the tarmac as Truman stepped from the plane looking grim and troubled. "That's all," he told photographers who were pressing for another shot. "We've got a job to do."

Webb would later recall Truman saying in the limousine as they sped to the city, "By God, I am going to let them have it," and Louis Johnson, in the jump seat in front of Truman, swinging about to shake his hand.

On the flight from Missouri, by radio, Truman had notified Acheson to summon an emergency meeting at Blair House, beginning with dinner at 7:30. His hours of privacy in the plane had provided opportunity for a lot of hard thinking, Truman later wrote. This was not the first time in his generation when the strong had attacked the weak. He had thought about Manchuria and Ethiopia.

> I remembered how each time that the democracies failed to act it encouraged the aggressors to keep going ahead. . . . If the Communists

were permitted to force their way into the Republic of Korea without opposition from the free world, no small nation would have the courage to resist threats and aggression by stronger Communist neighbors. If this was allowed to go unchallenged, it would mean a third world war, just as similar incidents had brought on the second world war.

The attack by North Korea had come as a total surprise. There had been incidents along the 38th parallel, Korea had been seen as a potential trouble point, but it was only one of numerous trouble points around the world and had never figured high on anyone's list. The last American troops had recently been withdrawn from South Korea. Describing the perimeter of American interests in the Pacific in an extemporaneous speech at the National Press Club in January, Acheson had not even included Korea. (The charge made later that the speech had thus inspired the Communist attack on South Korea would prove groundless.) Just that June, testifying on the Hill, Assistant Secretary of State for Far Eastern Affairs Dean Rusk had said he saw no likelihood of war in Korea. Indeed, among the manifold uncertainties at the moment was whether the invasion of South Korea was only a feint, a preliminary to a larger attack elsewhere, on Yugoslavia perhaps, or Formosa, or Iran.

As Truman had been notified en route to Washington, the U.N. Security Council had met that afternoon and adopted an American resolution calling for immediate cessation of "hostilities" and the withdrawal of North Korean forces to the 38th parallel. The vote was 9 to 0. There was no Soviet vote—no Soviet veto—because the Soviet representative, Jacob Malik, had walked out earlier in the year, when the Security Council refused to unseat Nationalist China, and he had not returned.

Besides the President, Acheson, Johnson, and Webb, the group gathered at Blair House included ten others: three from the State Department, Dean Rusk, Philip Jessup, and John Hickerson; the three service secretaries, Frank Pace, Jr., who had replaced Kenneth Royall as Secretary of the Army, Francis P. Matthews of the Navy, and Thomas K. Finletter of the Air Force; General Omar Bradley; and the three Chiefs of Staff, General Lawton Collins, Admiral Forrest Sherman, and Air Force General Hoyt Vandenberg. That made fourteen and they arrived, reported *The New York Times,* "as an atmosphere of tension, unparalleled since the war days, spread over the capital."

Drinks were served in the garden after Truman came downstairs from calling Bess to say he had arrived safely. He asked that there be no discussion of the crisis until dinner was over and the Blair House staff had withdrawn. Shortly after eight, dinner was announced by Alonzo Fields. They ate at the long mahogany table in the dining room, doors to the garden open to the warm evening air, and, for some reason, the hurriedly assembled meal—fried chicken, shoestring potatoes, asparagus, biscuits, vanilla ice cream with chocolate sauce—would be remembered as especially good and well served, "excellent," according to Acheson.

With the table cleared, it became the conference table and the meeting began, Acheson opening with a "darkening report," after which Truman asked for everyone's views.

The United States, said Rusk, had occupied South Korea for five years and had therefore a particular responsibility for South Korea, which, if absorbed by the Communists, would be "a dagger pointed at the heart of Japan." Bradley, who with Louis Johnson had just returned from Japan, and was feeling so ill he barely made it through the evening, said, "We must draw the line somewhere" and Korea was as good a place as any. (Acheson, some months later, was to say that if the best minds in the world had set out to find the worst possible location to fight "this damnable war," the unanimous choice would have been Korea.) Russia, in Bradley's view, was not ready for war, only "testing us."

There was no dissenting response. Nor did anyone present have the least doubt that what was happening in Korea was being directed from Moscow. But then this was also the prevailing view in the country and the press. It was the "Russian-sponsored" North Korean Army that had launched the invasion, according to bulletins in the papers. As Bradley would write, "Underlying these discussions was an intense moral outrage, even more than we felt over the Czechoslovakia coup in 1948."

That everyone at the table was in fundamental agreement became quickly clear, Truman's own obvious resolution having stiffened them all. "He pulled all the conferees together, by his show of leadership," one of them would say later, preferring to remain anonymous. Repeating Bradley's phrase, Truman agreed the line must be drawn "most emphatically." North Korea must be stopped. The Russians, he said, were trying to get Korea by default, gambling that the United States would be so fearful of starting another world war that it would put up no resistance.

"I thought we were still holding the stronger hand," he later wrote, "although how much stronger, it was hard to tell."

Admiral Sherman and General Vandenberg thought a combination of naval forces and air cover would be sufficient to do the job. And though Generals Bradley and Collins disagreed, they opposed any commitment of American ground forces in Korea, at least for the time being.

The possibility of active intervention by Soviet forces greatly concerned Truman. No one seemed to think the Russians were ready for a world war, but who was to say. Truman asked about Russian fleet strength in the Far East, Russian airpower, and requested an immediate intelligence report on "possible next moves" by the Soviets elsewhere in the world.

Recalling the evening, Truman would write that what impressed him most was "the complete, almost unspoken acceptance on the part of everyone that whatever had to be done to meet this aggression had to be done. There was no suggestion from anyone that either the United Nations or the United States should back away from it."

As Truman had determined, it was Acheson who led the meeting, Acheson who proposed the decisions Truman made. General MacArthur was to send arms and supplies to South Korea as swiftly as possible. American civilians in Korea were to be evacuated under the cover of American airpower. The Seventh Fleet would proceed from the Philippines to guard the Formosa Strait, to prevent any attack from Communist China on Formosa, or, as Acheson said, vice versa.

As the meeting was breaking up, Johnson made what in time would be remembered as a remarkable observation. Having just been with MacArthur in Japan, he thought it important that any instructions to the general be detailed, "so as not to give him too much discretion."

Truman, in an exchange with John Hickerson, the Assistant Secretary of State for U.N. Affairs, said the decisions he had just made had been for the United Nations. He had believed in the League of Nations with all his heart, Truman said, but the League had failed. The United Nations must not fail. "It was our idea, and in this first big test we just can't let them down."

As the group departed just before eleven, using the back door to avoid reporters, Truman said no one was to make any statement until he did.

It would be said of Harry Truman that without consulting Congress or the American people, he had rushed to judgment; that "as Hermann Goering, when he heard the word culture, reached for his gun, Harry Truman when he heard the word problem, reached for a decision." But the last thing Truman wanted was a war in Korea, or anywhere, and angry as he may have been over the attack, as determined as he obviously was to do what he felt had to be done, he had nonetheless, so far, made no irrevocable move.

On Monday, as the news from Korea grew worse, he issued a statement notable only for its generalities. The widespread impression was that the United States was going to take little or no action. According to the latest communications from MacArthur, the South Koreans appeared incapable of stopping the North Korean advance: "Our estimate is that a complete collapse is imminent."

That night, after supper alone, Truman summoned another emergency session, a second "war cabinet" meeting at Blair House, and decided to provide American air and naval support to the forces of South Korea and to press for immediate United Nations support.

No action should be taken north of the 38th parallel, he said, adding, "not yet."

In addition, he ordered an increase of American forces in the Philippines and a speedup of military aid to Indochina.

No ground troops had yet been committed to Korea. And no one at the meeting recommended that. General Bradley would remember Acheson "dominating" the meeting, as he had the night before. Bradley, as he wrote later, was gravely concerned over the possibility of a ground war in Asia. Whatever troops were sent, MacArthur would surely ask for more. Besides, "We had no war plan for Korea." Bradley suggested they "wait a few days." Acheson agreed.

"I don't want to go to war," Truman said with a force they would all remember.

"Everything I have done in the past five years," he remarked sadly as the meeting ended, "has been to try to avoid making a decision such as I had to make tonight."

Headlines the next day, Tuesday, June 27, reported North Korean tanks sweeping into the South Korean capital of Seoul. The government of South Korea had fled, its president, Syngman Rhee, bitterly describing American help as "Too little, too late." In a broadcast from Pyongyang, the capital of North Korea, Communist Premier Kim Il Sung vowed to "crush" South Korea as swiftly as possible.

At the White House events moved rapidly, as the leaders of Congress, the Secretary of State, Secretary of Defense, and Joint Chiefs rolled up to the West Wing in one official car after another. More than forty people were gathered. By 11:30 the doors of the Cabinet Room were closed. Half an hour later the meeting had ended. The congressional leaders had given the President their undivided support. No one had said a word against what he had decided. Further, he had been advised to proceed on the basis of presidential authority alone and not bother to call on Congress for a war resolution. A hundred reporters stood waiting anxiously in the lobby when minutes later Charlie Ross set off a "whirlwind," handing them the first word from Truman that he had ordered American air and naval forces to support South Korea in its hour of peril:

"The attack upon Korea makes it plain beyond all doubt that Communism has passed beyond the use of subversion to conquer independent nations and will now use armed invasion and war. . . ."

Cheers broke out in the House and Senate when the statement was read aloud. By a vote of 315 to 4, the House promptly voted a one-year extension of the draft law. In the Senate, Republican William Knowland called for "overwhelming support" for the President from all Americans regardless of party.

At the United Nations, debate began on a resolution to back the American decision—a resolution adopted that night at 10:45, the Soviet Union being still absent. For the first time in history, a world organization had voted to use armed force to stop armed force.

The response of the American people—by mail, telegrams, phone calls to the White House and Congress—the response of the press, of nearly everyone whose opinion carried weight in Washington and in the country, was immediate, resounding approval—a point that would be very soon forgotten. Editorials praised Truman for his "bold course," his "momentous and courageous act."

> Although the President was well and faithfully advised [wrote Joseph and Stewart Alsop], no one can fail to admire the blend of plain guts and homely common sense that has marked his own handling of his immense crisis. This, indeed, was one of the occasions when Truman seemed to sum up the good things in America.

James Reston said much the same thing in *The New York Times*. Truman, said the Washington *Post,* had given the free world the leadership it desperately needed.

> These are days calling for steady nerves, for a strict eye on the ball, and for a renewed resolve to keep our purposes pure in the grapple we have undertaken with men who would plunge the world into darkness. The occasion has found the man in Harry Truman.

The Wall Street Journal, Walter Lippmann, Thomas E. Dewey, George Kennan, General Eisenhower, all agreed it was time to draw the line. Eisenhower believed, "We'll have a dozen Koreas soon if we don't take a firm stand." Henry Morgenthau, Franklin Roosevelt, Jr., Phil Murray, Walter Reuther, and Sam Goldwyn sent telegrams in praise of Truman's decision. Cordell Hull called.

White House mail ran strongly in favor of the President's action. "You may be a whiskey guzzling poker playing old buzzard as some say," wrote a Republican from Illinois, "but by damn, for the first time since old Teddy left there in March of 1909, the United States has a grass roots *American* in the White House."

Even Taft and Henry Wallace gave their support, though Taft urged some congressional say in the matter. British Ambassador Oliver Franks reported to his government that virtually all shades of opinion backed the President. The entire mood in the capital had suddenly, dramatically changed. "I have lived and worked in and out of Washington for twenty years," wrote Joseph Harsch of the *Christian Science Monitor*. "Never before in that time have I felt such a sense of relief and unity pass through the city."

Appearing before a meeting of the Reserve Officers Association, an audience of a thousand people at the Mayflower Hotel, Wednesday morning, Truman received a standing ovation.

On Thursday, June 29, at his first press conference since the crisis began, he said with emphasis, "We are not at war." Could he be quoted? "Yes," Truman said. "We are not at war."

Would it be correct, asked a reporter, to call this a police action under the United Nations? "Yes," Truman replied. "That is exactly what it amounts to."

Later this would be called another of his press conference blunders—he had allowed a reporter to put words in his mouth. But it was no mistake. A "police action under the United Nations" was precisely how he wished it to be viewed. Nor, importantly, did anyone see reason then to fault him.

It was in the middle of the night in Washington, at 3:00 A.M. Washington time, Friday, June 30, that the Pentagon received still another report from General MacArthur, this based on his first personal inspection of the situation in Korea. "The only assurance for holding the present line and the ability to regain later lost ground," it said, "is through introduction of United States combat forces into the Korean battle area." Any further attempt to check the North Korean advance with air- and seapower alone would be a waste of time. So bleak were things at this stage, even an all-out U.S. effort—Army, Navy, and Air Force—might be "doomed to failure." Time was of the essence—"a clear-cut decision without delay is imperative."

When Frank Pace telephoned Blair House, it was still dark outside. Truman was already up and shaved. He took the call by his bedside at 4:47 A.M. Pace relayed the grim report. MacArthur wanted two divisions of ground troops.

Truman never hesitated. It was a moment for which he had been preparing himself for days and he made his decision at once.

Later he would say that committing American troops to combat in Korea was the most difficult decision of his presidency, more so than the decision to use the atomic bomb. He did not want to start another world war, he had been heard to say privately more than once during that most crucial week. "Must be careful not to cause a general Asiatic war," he now wrote in his diary, later that same day, Friday, June 30. What would Mao Tse-tung do? he wondered. Where would the next Russian move come?

"Now, your job as President," Acheson would observe years later, "is to decide. *Mr. Truman decided.*"

Later, too—many years later—Acheson would make public a note he received from the President that, as Acheson said, well illustrated the quality of the man who "bound his lieutenants to him with unbreakable devotion." It was written in longhand:

7/11/50

Memo to Dean Acheson
Regarding June 24 and 25—
Your initiative in immediately calling the Security Council of the U.N. on Saturday night and notifying me was the key to what followed afterwards. Had you not acted promptly in that direction we would have had to go into Korea alone.

The meeting Sunday night at Blair House was the result of our action Saturday night and the results afterward show that you are a great Secretary of State and a diplomat.

Your handling of the situation since has been superb.

I'm sending you this for your record.

Harry S. Truman

16

Commander in Chief

There was nothing *passive about Harry Truman. He was the commander in chief in law and in fact.*

—GEORGE ELSEY

I

In the five years since the nation was last at war, the President's office had changed very little, with one notable exception. The melodramatic, moonlit Remington, the painting called *Fired On* that had hung over the mantelpiece opposite Truman's desk in 1945, had been replaced by a commanding, full-figured portrait of George Washington, while below, in front of the fireplace, stood Truman's big office globe, his gift from General Eisenhower.

Thus from his desk now, Truman could look up at both the nation's first Commander in Chief, resplendent in full uniform, and the world at large, a subject that weighed on him more now than ever—the world and the threat of global war, the world and the imperative need not to repeat past mistakes, the world and Harry Truman.

He was not one to worry about decisions, once made, he told a reporter, but with the "Korean affair" he could not help worrying about the inevitable consequences. "Appeasement leads only to further aggression and ultimately to war," he would tell the nation in an historic radio and television broadcast the evening of July 19, still unwilling to call what was happening in Korea a war, but an "act of aggression" by the Communist leaders.

The Washington portrait, by Rembrandt Peale, was on loan from the National Gallery. The globe, which, with its heavy three-legged stand of polished mahogany, stood nearly chest high, had been Eisenhower's when he was Allied Commander in Europe. Truman had chosen the new arrangement himself. He was acutely conscious of everything in the room, liked it all just so. Once when Charlie Ross picked up Truman's engagement calendar from the desk to check something, then put it back down slightly askew, Truman, while chatting on, immediately lined it up again as before.

The globe especially gave the fireplace end of the room, the northern arc of the Oval Office, a weight and importance it had not had before. Photographers now, when posing the President, liked to have him stand there, particularly for portraits with his generals. He would be asked to put his right hand on the globe, as if explaining something, a natural pose, since in discussions with the Joint Chiefs—or members of the Cabinet or Congress or his own staff—Truman would frequently go to the globe to make a point. "Harry, don't you sometimes feel over-whelmed by your job?" he had been asked by Republican Senator Tobey of New Hampshire, and Truman had stepped to the globe and turning it slowly said, "All the world is focusing on this office. The nearest thing to my heart is to do something to keep the world at peace. We must find a way to peace, or else civilization will be destroyed and the world will turn back to the year 900."

Now, in the first weeks of the Korean crisis, he would put his finger on various spots in Europe or the Middle East—on the Elbe or the Iranian-Soviet border—then turning the globe, point to the pale gray of the Korean peninsula, between the Sea of Japan and the Yellow Sea, a place most Americans still had trouble finding on a map.

"This is the Greece of the Far East," Truman would say. "If we are tough enough now, there won't be any next time."

The whole of the Korean peninsula, north and south, was almost half again the size of Greece, roughly 84,000 square miles in total. The distance from top to bottom, from the Yalu River, which formed North Korea's border with Manchuria, to the southernmost tip of the peninsula, was about 600 miles, while the distance across varied from 125 to 200 miles.

The Republic of South Korea—everything below the arbitrary dividing line of the 38th parallel—was slightly larger than the state of Indiana. Its population of 20 million was double that of North Korea, and its economy chiefly agricultural, whereas most Korean industry was in the north.

The demarcation line of the 38th parallel had no basis in Korean history, geography, or anything else. It had been settled on hastily in the last week of World War II, as a temporary measure to facilitate the surrender of Japanese troops—those north of the line had surrendered to the Soviets, those south, to American forces. The decision had been made late one night at the Pentagon by then Colonel Dean Rusk and another young

Army officer named Charles Bonesteel, who picked the line of latitude 38 degrees north because it had the advantage of already being on most maps of Korea.

From Seoul, South Korea's fallen capital city, to Pusan, its largest port, at the southeastern end of the peninsula, was 275 miles by the main road and rail line—all extremely crucial miles just now, as news of the advancing North Korean "People's Army," the NKPA, grew steadily worse. July 1950 had become a wretched time in Korea and in Washington. News accounts portrayed Truman as "chipper" or "jaunty" no more, but as looking exhausted, seeming to "walk with the weary man's heavy tread." One Sunday, on a rare outing on the *Williamsburg* down the Potomac, he excused himself after lunch with his staff and slept the rest of the afternoon.

His press conferences were no longer held in his office but across the way in the old State Department Building, in the ornate, musty Indian Treaty Room, which offered more space for an expanding press corps. (He was also fed up with the way reporters spilled ink from their fountain pens on the rug in his office.) To repeated questions about his outlook, he maintained that "of course" he was hopeful. But as they knew from daily bulletins, and he knew better still from his morning briefings by Omar Bradley, the news from Korea was nearly all bad.

Bradley, one of the outstanding generals of World War II, was not given to exaggeration. Plain-mannered, likable, raised in Moberly, Missouri, he was Truman's kind of man, with more inner iron than generally understood and what his deputy chief of staff at the Pentagon, General Matthew Ridgway, described as "a fine, orderly mind." Until the Korean crisis, Bradley had reported to the President only on occasion, but he came now to the Oval Office every morning at 9:30 sharp, to unfold his map of Korea and commence his grim report in the dry, oddly high-pitched voice of a Missouri schoolteacher.

American ground forces and what was left of the Army of the Republic of Korea, the ROKs, were being rapidly chopped to pieces. The first American ground troops—all of 256 men, two and a half companies of the 24th Infantry Division—had gone into action south of Seoul, making a brave stand near Osan, on July 5, and they had been falling back ever since, fighting desperately to keep retreat from turning to rout. Airlifted from Japan, they had been rushed into action without adequate preparation. Many were young draftees with no combat experience; nearly all were soft from garrison duty in Japan; and, like their ROK allies, they were pathetically ill-equipped in the face of a highly disciplined enemy advancing in massive numbers and with heavy Russian T-34 tanks. As the newspapers were saying, it was all tragically reminiscent of the Nazi *Blitz-*

krieg in France in 1940. "The size of the attack, and the speed with which it was followed up," Truman would tell the nation, "make it perfectly plain that it had been plotted all along."

When at a meeting of the National Security Council on July 6, Vice President Barkley asked how many North Koreans were in the operation, Bradley said 90,000. American forces numbered about 10,000, the South Koreans 25,000.

In combat, American and ROK forces were often outnumbered three to one, or ten to one, in some places twenty to one. They had no tanks, no artillery, or any weapons capable of slowing the Russian tanks. (It had actually been American policy to keep the South Korean forces under-equipped before this, so as not to encourage aggressive action by South Korea against the North.) World War II bazookas bounced off the Russian tanks like stones. Matthew Ridgway would later say it was as if a few troops of Boy Scouts with hand weapons had tried to stop a German Panzer unit.

The retreat was fought in drenching rains and punishing heat, temperatures regularly over 100 degrees. July was the monsoon season in Korea. Weapons rusted, clothes rotted. With communications broken and mud roads clogged by tens of thousands of fleeing refugees, the chaos was overwhelming. American troops were wholly unfamiliar with the terrain. They knew nothing of the Korean people or the Korean language. They fought and fell back, fought and fell back, with little sleep or food, and in the terrible heat drank from drainage ditches by rice fields fertilized with human manure. As a consequence, violent dysentery ripped through their ranks. "Guys, sweat soaked, shitting in their pants, not even dropping them, moved like zombies," remembered an American infantryman. "I just sensed we were going to find another hill and be attacked, then find another hill and so forth, endlessly forever." Casualties were as high as 30 percent. "What a place to die," a young soldier was quoted in the papers. Some Americans cut and ran, victims of "bugout fever."

With his map propped on an easel before the President's desk, Bradley went over the situation one morning in mid-July, pointing out various units, noting the length of the American ROK line across the peninsula and the necessity of gradual withdrawal. The hope was to continue delaying actions—the most difficult kind of military maneuver—pulling back until a defensive, shortened line in the southeastern corner was reached and established.

American and ROK forces fell back from Osan to the Kum River, then to the temporary capital of Taejon, where a furious, house-to-house battle raged on July 19 (July 18 in Washington). With the city in flames, the commanding general of the 24th Division, William F. Dean, disappeared, reportedly last seen trying to stop an enemy tank with his Army .45 revolver.

Published accounts described suicidal enemy attacks, "waves" of North Koreans, a "Red tide." "For every ten we killed another ten came charging over the hill to replace them," an American soldier was quoted in the Washington *Post*. Before breakfast one morning at Blair House, Truman read on the front page of *The New York Times* of seven slaughtered American soldiers, prisoners of the North Koreans, who had been found by the roadside, their hands tied behind their backs and shot through the face.

"This is no orthodox war," wrote Marguerite Higgins of the New York *Herald-Tribune*, the only woman covering the war thus far.

"The stragglers are still coming in—small exhausted groups of them," reported a correspondent for the Baltimore *Sun*, a few days after the Battle of Taejon.

> Their wits and will to live carried them through enemy lines, over mountain trails, through sniper-infested country to this rain-soaked river bottom where camp is pitched.
>
> More than 200 of them had walked out. They had been forced to the hills after fighting in Taejon Thursday. By round-about trails that took them 50 miles through hostile country they reached safety before dawn today [July 22].
>
> Another group of 25 arrived later in the morning, led by a lieutenant colonel. They had started about 80 strong, but only this handful made it all the way. The others dropped from exhaustion along the route.

The retreat continued, through the steep passes of the Sobaek Mountains, to still another defensive line, on high ground behind the Naktong River. In seventeen days of savage fighting, American and ROK forces had fallen back seventy miles.

It was, in many respects, one of the darkest chapters in American military history. But MacArthur, now in overall command of the U.N. forces, was trading space for time—time to pour in men and supplies at the port of Pusan—and the wonder was the North Koreans had been kept from overrunning South Korea straightaway. Despite their suffering and humiliation, the brutal odds against them, the American and ROK units had done what they were supposed to, almost miraculously. They had held back the landslide, said Truman, who would rightly call it one of the most heroic rearguard actions on record.

On July 29, the tactical U.N. commander in the field, General Walton Walker, issued a "stand-or-die" order. There would be no more retreat, Walker said. Pusan must not fall. "There will be no Dunkirk, there will be no Bataan." Every man must fight to the death if necessary, until help arrived.

The speech, designed no doubt for home consumption, struck the troops as uncalled for. The prospect of another Dunkirk or Bataan had not occurred to them. "I never did like running," a private from Philadelphia told Marguerite Higgins.

One of Truman's important but little noted first moves in the fateful last week of June had been to recall Averell Harriman from Europe, where he had been a kind of roving ambassador, and make him a special assistant to help with war emergency problems; and one of Harriman's first moves in his new role was to press upon the President the need for congressional support for what he was doing in Korea. He urged Truman to call for a war resolution from Congress as soon as possible, while the country was still behind him. Dean Acheson, however, disagreed, insisting that such a resolution was unnecessary and unwise. The President, said Acheson, should rest on his constitutional authority as Commander in Chief. It was true that congressional approval would do no harm, but the process of obtaining it, Acheson thought, might do great harm. In the mounting anxiety over how things were going in Korea, the timing was wrong.

Truman sided with Acheson, telling Harriman further that to appeal to Congress now would make it more difficult for future presidents to deal with emergencies.

> Later when Robert Taft and others began criticizing the President [Harriman would recall] I was convinced the President had made a mistake. This decision, however, was characteristic of President Truman. He always kept in mind how his actions would affect future presidential authority.

In the first week of July MacArthur requested thirty thousand American ground troops, to bring the four divisions of his Eighth Army to full strength. Just days later, on July 9, the situation had become so "critical" that MacArthur called for a doubling of his forces. Four more divisions were urgently needed, he said in a cable that jolted Washington.

How much more could the United States commit to Korea, given the dangers in other parts of the world? General Bradley and the Joint Chiefs continued to view what was happening in Korea as a possible feint in a larger Kremlin strategy. Truman, at a meeting of the National Security Council, said he would "back out" of Korea only if a "military situation" had to be met elsewhere.

The hard reality was that the Army had only ten divisions. In Western

Europe there was but one, and as Winston Churchill noted in a speech in London, the full allied force of twelve divisions in Western Europe faced a Soviet threat of eighty divisions. The NATO allies were exceedingly concerned lest the United States become too involved in distant Korea.

Years of slashing defense expenditures, as a means to balance the budget, had taken a heavy toll. And while the policy of "cutting the fat" at the Pentagon had been pushed by Republicans and Democrats alike—with wide popular approval—and lately made a noisy crusade by Louis Johnson, it was the President who was ultimately responsible. It was Truman's policy—and along with the "fat," it was now painfully apparent, a great deal of bone and muscle had been cut. For all its vaunted nuclear supremacy, the nation was quite unprepared for war, just as such critics of the policy as James Forrestal had been saying.

Now, in these "weeks of slaughter and heartbreak," all that was to change dramatically and with immense, far-reaching consequences.

Truman himself had changed. Members of the White House staff spoke of the "aching pain" of the President's disappointment, since the Communist invasion of South Korea crushed his dream of peace. He was working eighteen hours a day and the strain showed. Margaret would write of her father's anguish as American troops were hurled back. Korea was "constantly" on his mind.

At the same time, Truman was undergoing extensive dental treatment. In three weeks beginning July 8, he had two bridges, four single crowns, and a filling replaced, in a series of twelve sessions at Walter Reed Hospital. And through all this, according to the records, he had anesthesia only once, for one of the crowns. Why he subjected himself to such an ordeal just then is puzzling, unless it was to safeguard his health overall, in anticipation of the stress of the war only growing worse.

Solemn, "war-conscious" crowds, as they were described, gathered outside Blair House every time word spread that he was meeting with his military advisers. Many Americans, perhaps most, had first thought of the Korean conflict as truly a "police action," a mere brushfire affair that would be quickly extinguished once American forces arrived. Now letters and telegrams poured into Washington, to the White House and Congress, decrying the way things were being handled. "It would seem General Vaughan is running the Korean situation," said one. "Are we being sabotaged by the State Department?" asked another. Those addressed to Truman were at one point running twenty to one against the war:

I wonder how well you have been sleeping these last nights? Mothers and fathers all over our beloved land are spending sleepless nights

worrying again over their boys being sent to fight wars on foreign soil
—wars that are no concern of ours. . . .

WE DEMAND THAT YOU STOP MURDERING AMERICAN BOYS AND KOREAN PEO-
PLE. . . .

In heaven's name, what are you doing? The blood hasn't dried from
World War 2. . . . We have nothing to do with Korea. These people are
capable of settling their own affairs. . . .

LET THEM HAVE THE ATOM BOMB NOW. . . .

I am the mother of a soldier in Korea. I am an American, I mean a
good American. I love this country and all it stands for. . . . I am writing
to you, because I want my son home, he is my only child, and very
young. Please, Mr. President, I implore you. . . .

YOU DID IT ONCE BEFORE STOP DROP ONE OVER THE KREMLIN AND GET IT
OVER WITH.

In the Senate, Taft called for Dean Acheson to resign. Owen Brewster
wanted to let MacArthur use the atomic bomb "at his discretion." Newspapers carried photographs contrasting the cheerful, confident President
of spring with the grave, lined President of summer. "The grin in which
his face was formerly permanently wreathed has disappeared," wrote the
Alsop brothers. "So, at last, has the euphoric presidential conviction that
'everything's going to be all right.' "

To the Alsops and others who had long deplored the decline of American military power, it was a case now of "we told you so." The influence
of Louis Johnson at the Pentagon had been "little less than catastrophic"
—"damn near treasonous," Joseph Alsop would later say privately. Truman had been naive at best. With the Korean crisis, however, Truman had
undergone a "complete change."

The great historic shift began at a meeting of the Cabinet on Friday,
July 14. Again, as at the fateful Blair House sessions, it was Acheson who
took the initiative, urging an immediate expansion of all military services
and huge increases in military spending. Truman agreed. And from this
point forward there was to be no turning back, not in his lifetime or in
that of any of those around the table.

On Wednesday, July 19, first in a special message to Congress, then in
an address to the nation, Truman said the attack on Korea demanded that
the United States send more men, equipment, and supplies. Beyond that,
the realities of the "world situation" required still greater American military strength. He called for an emergency appropriation of $10 billion—
the final sum submitted would be $11.6 billion, or nearly as much as the
entire $13 billion military budget originally planned for the fiscal year—

and announced he was both stepping up the draft and calling up certain National Guard units.

"Korea is a small country thousands of miles away, but what is happening there is important to every American," he told the nation, standing stone-faced in the heat of the television lights, a tangle of wires and cables at his feet. By their "act of raw aggression . . . I repeat, it was raw aggression," the North Koreans had violated the U.N. Charter, and though American forces were making the "principal effort" to save the Republic of South Korea, they were fighting under a U.N. command and a U.N. flag, and this was a "landmark in mankind's long search for a rule of law among nations."

As a call to arms it was not especially inspirational. Nor did he once use the word "war" to describe what was happening in Korea. But then neither was there any question about his sincerity, nor was he the least evasive about what would be asked of the country. The "job" was long and difficult. It meant increased taxes, rationing if necessary, "stern days ahead."

Possibly in time the strident warnings and enjoinders of NSC-68 would have effected such a turn in policy. But Korea made all that academic now. Truman's commitment to military power was theoretical no longer. In another televised address at summer's end, he would announce plans to double the armed forces to nearly 3 million men, saying such costs and obligations were to be part of the nation's burden for a long time to come.

Congress appropriated the money—$48.2 billion for military spending in fiscal 1950–51, then $60 billion for fiscal 1951–52.

Was he considering use of the atomic bomb in Korea, Truman was asked at a press conference the last week of July. No, he said. Did he plan to get out of Washington any time soon? No. He would stay on the job.

That Truman was extremely vexed with his Secretary of Defense, Louis Johnson, and less than fond or admiring of his Far Eastern Commander, Douglas MacArthur, was well known to his staff and a cause of gathering concern at the Pentagon. "He would have saved himself a lot of grief had he relieved both men at the onset of the war," was the subsequent view of General Bradley. Johnson had begun to show "an inordinate egotistical desire to run the whole government," Truman later recorded. "He offended every member of the cabinet . . . he never missed an opportunity to say mean things about my personal staff." His Secretary of Defense, Truman speculated, was suffering from a "pathological condition."

When Truman learned from Averell Harriman that Johnson had been praising Senator Taft—over the phone, and in Harriman's presence—for Taft's attacks on Acheson (and then promised Harriman to do all he could to make Harriman Secretary of State, once Acheson was out of the way), Johnson was, in effect, finished. From Eben Ayers' diary, it is known that the President confided Harriman's story to Charlie Ross on July 3. The next morning, July 4, Truman drove to Leesburg, Virginia, with Margaret for what was ostensibly a holiday visit with General Marshall, who, since recovering his health, had become head of the American Red Cross. "A most interesting morning," was all that Truman noted in his own diary.

Yet to fire Johnson then, with things going so badly in Korea, to shame the man who had been most conspicuous in carrying out Truman's own policies at the Pentagon, would not have been a move of the kind Truman admired. So weeks passed and Louis Johnson remained.

As for MacArthur, Truman's private view seems to have been no different from what it had been in 1945, at the peak of MacArthur's renown, when, in his journal, Truman had described the general as "Mr. Prima Donna, Brass Hat," a "play actor and bunco man." The President, noted Eben Ayers, expressed "little regard or respect" for MacArthur, called him a "supreme egotist" who thought himself "something of a god." But working with people that one did not necessarily like or admire was part of life—particularly the politician's life—and if removing Louis Johnson would have been difficult under the circumstances, firing the five-star Far Eastern Commander would have been very nearly unthinkable. John Foster Dulles told Truman confidentially that MacArthur should be dispensed with as soon as possible. Dulles, the most prominent Republican spokesman on foreign policy and a special adviser to the State Department, had returned from a series of meetings with MacArthur in Tokyo convinced that the seventy-year-old general was well past his prime and a potential liability. In a private conference in the Oval Office, Dulles advised Truman to bring MacArthur home and retire him before he caused trouble. But that, replied Truman, his blue-gray eyes large behind his glasses, was easier said than done. He reminded Dulles of the reaction there would be in the country, so great was MacArthur's "heroic standing."

In later years it would be stressed by some writers that Truman had little regard for generals, even viewed them with contempt, considering them limited in outlook and ability. He himself, in retirement, would say most generals were "dumb," "like horses with blinders on," and would fault their West Point education (the education he had so wanted as a youth but was denied). His bias, however, was not against generals overall, but such figures as MacArthur who seemed to feel they were above everyone else. Truman hated caste systems of any kind, disliked stuffed shirts of all varieties, and his experiences in France in 1918 had left him with an abiding dislike of the military caste system and its West Point stuffed shirts in particular.

However, his latter-day remarks notwithstanding, Truman's regard for such generals as Bradley and Ridgway (both West Pointers) could not have been much greater. He had long considered Bradley a model officer and very quickly that summer he had come to rely on Bradley as an adviser more than anyone in his administration except Acheson. Ridgway, too, greatly impressed Truman and would in time more than justify Truman's confidence in him. Then there were Eisenhower and Marshall—Eisenhower, the man Truman had been willing to step aside for, to make him President, and Marshall, "the great one," whom Truman revered above all men.

Nor, importantly, did Truman at this stage express any doubt concerning MacArthur's ability. If anything, he seems to have been banking on it.

By the first week in August, American and ROK forces, dug in behind the Naktong River, had set up the final defense line to be known as the Pusan Perimeter, a thinly held front forming an arc of 130 miles around the port of Pusan. On the map it looked like a bare toehold on the peninsula. On the ground the fighting went on as savagely as before. The monsoons had ended. Now the troops cursed the heat and dust so thick that supply trucks kept their headlights on at midday. But the retreat was over. Besides, the headlong advance of the North Koreans had cost them heavily—their casualties had been worse even than the Americans imagined. Their supply lines were now greatly overextended. U.N. forces controlled the sea and air, while at Pusan, the buildup of American tanks, artillery, and fresh troops was moving rapidly. At his briefing for the President on Saturday, August 12, in his customary, dry, cautious way, Bradley, for the first time, described the situation as "fluid but improving."

Averell Harriman, meanwhile, had returned from a hurried mission to Tokyo, bringing the details of a daring new MacArthur plan.

Harriman had been dispatched to tell the general of Truman's determination to see that he had everything he needed, but also to impress upon him Truman's urgent desire to avoid any move that might provoke a third world war. This was Truman's uppermost concern and there must be no misunderstanding. In particular, MacArthur was to "stay clear" of Chiang Kai-shek—a sore point since MacArthur had made a highly publicized flying visit to Formosa on July 31 to confer with Chiang, after which he had been photographed kissing Madame Chiang's hand. Chiang, Truman had instructed Harriman to tell MacArthur, must not become the catalyst for a war with the Chinese Communists.

Harriman, as Truman appreciated, had known MacArthur on a first-name basis since MacArthur was Superintendent at West Point in 1920.

Accompanied by Ridgway and General Lauris Norstad of the Air Force, Harriman had left for Tokyo on August 4, and on the morning of their return to Washington, August 9, Harriman went directly from the airport to Blair House, taking no time to shave or shower or have breakfast. As he would later explain, Harriman had scheduled his return so he could see the President at about 7:00 A.M., the best time to "catch him alone."

MacArthur had no reservations about the decision to fight in Korea, "absolutely none," Harriman reported. MacArthur was certain neither the Chinese Communists nor the Russians would intervene in Korea. Concerning Chiang Kai-shek, MacArthur had assured Harriman that of course, as a soldier, he would do as the President ordered, though something about MacArthur's tone as he said this had left Harriman wondering.

Of greater urgency and importance was what Harriman had to report of a plan to win the war with one bold stroke. For weeks there had been talk at the Pentagon of a MacArthur strategy to outflank the enemy, to hit from behind, by amphibious landing. The details were vague and the Joint Chiefs remained highly skeptical. But in Tokyo, Harriman, Ridgway, and Norstad had been given a grand unveiling, a brilliant, two-and-a-half-hour exposition delivered by MacArthur "with all his dramatic eloquence," as Ridgway wrote. The three men were completely won over, "enthralled," said Harriman, and ready to go home and argue for the plan. It could mean "our salvation," Harriman told Truman.

The idea was to make a surprise amphibious landing on the western shore of Korea at the port of Inchon, 200 miles northwest of Pusan. The problem was that Inchon had tremendous tides—tides of 30 feet or more —and no beaches on which to land, only sea walls. Thus an assault would have to strike directly into the city itself, and only a full tide would carry the landing craft clear to the sea wall. In two hours after high tide, the landing craft would be stuck in the mud.

To Bradley it was the riskiest military proposal he had ever heard. But as MacArthur stressed, the Japanese had landed successfully at Inchon in 1904 and the very "impracticabilities" would help ensure the all-important element of surprise. As Wolfe had astonished and defeated Montcalm at Quebec in 1759, by scaling the impossible cliffs by the Plains of Abraham, so, MacArthur said, he would astonish and defeat the North Koreans by landing at the impossible port of Inchon. But there was little time. The attack had to come before the onset of the Korean winter exacted more casualties than the battlefield. The tides at Inchon would be right on September 15.

"I made clear to the President the difficulties of the plan," Harriman later said, "including the very heavy tide which would make landing any reinforcements impossible until the next high tide."

Truman told him to see Johnson and Bradley "as fast as you can." Though Truman had made no commitment one way or the other, Harriman left the house convinced that Truman approved the plan.

At the Pusan Perimeter desperate fighting raged on, American casualties mounting—6,886 by August 25, by mid-September double that number. Soldiers who had fought in Europe were calling Korea a tougher war than any they had known. In a long, searing dispatch in *Time* and *Life,* correspondent John Osborne described it as "an ugly war," "sorrowful," "sickening," "an especially terrible war." No one who saw it firsthand would ever speak of it as a "police action." The savagery of the North Koreans was appalling, but that of some South Korean police was hardly less. Americans described seeing enemy troops within plain sight changing from the green uniforms of the North Korean Army to the common white trousers and blouses of the Korean peasants. The awful uncertainty of who was friend and who was foe had already forced American troops to their own appalling acts and attitudes.

> This means not the usual, inevitable savagery of combat in the field but savagery in detail—the blotting out of villages where the enemy *may* be hiding; the shooting and shelling of refugees who *may* include North Koreans in the anonymous white clothing of the Korean countryside, or who *may* be screening an enemy march upon our positions. . . .

The buildup of men and arms pouring into Pusan was phenomenal. Still, warned Osborne, "We may be pushed out of Korea."

By early August, General Bradley could tell the President that American strength at Pusan was up to 50,000, which with another 45,000 ROKs and small contingents of U.N. allies, made a total U.N. ground force of nearly 100,000. Still the prospect of diverting additional American forces for MacArthur's Inchon scheme pleased the Joint Chiefs not at all. Bradley continued to view it as "the wildest kind" of plan.

But on August 10, after a series of intense White House meetings, the Joint Chiefs and National Security Council approved the strategy in principle. As further sessions followed in Tokyo and in Washington, Bradley, Admiral Sherman, and General Collins expressed "the gravest misgivings," as Bradley reported to Truman at a briefing Saturday, August 26, the same day the Associated Press broke a statement from MacArthur to the Veterans of Foreign Wars, in which he strongly defended Chiang Kai-shek and the importance of Chiang's control of Formosa: "Nothing could be more fallacious than the threadbare argument by those who advocate appeasement and defeatism in the Pacific that if we defend Formosa we alienate continental Asia." It was exactly the sort of dabbling in policy that MacArthur had assured Harriman he would, as a good soldier, refrain from.

Truman was livid, "his lips white and compressed." Dispensing with the usual greetings at his morning meeting with Acheson, Harriman, Johnson, and the Joint Chiefs, he read the whole of MacArthur's statement aloud. Acheson, outraged, called it rank insubordination. To Bradley the message was "the height of arrogance." Harriman was the most upset of all. Truman would later say he considered but rejected the idea of relieving MacArthur of field command then and there and replacing him with Bradley. "It would have been difficult to avoid the appearance of demotion, and I had no desire to hurt General MacArthur personally."

Truman asked Louis Johnson to have MacArthur withdraw the statement. When Johnson demurred, Truman dictated the message himself and told Johnson to act on it at once.

But whatever his anger at MacArthur, to whatever degree the incident had increased his dislike—or distrust—of the general, Truman proceeded with discussion of the Inchon plan, and in spite of objections voiced by Bradley and the others, he decided to give MacArthur his backing. "The JCS inclined toward postponing Inchon until such time that we were certain Pusan could hold," remembered Bradley. "But Truman was now committed." On August 28, the Joint Chiefs sent MacArthur their tentative approval.

It was, they all knew, an enormous gamble. Several of MacArthur's own staff, as would later be known, thought the plan unwise. MacArthur himself called it a 5,000-to-1 shot. Bradley wrote that "a failure could be a national or even international catastrophe, not only militarily, but psychologically." Truman had been strongly influenced by Harriman and by a memorandum of support from Ridgway. But in the last analysis, he relied on his own instincts. "It was a daring strategic conception," he would write later. "I had the greatest confidence it would succeed."

In time to come, little would be said or written about Truman's part in the matter—that as Commander in Chief he, and he alone, was the one with the final say on Inchon. He could have said no, and certainly the weight of opinion among his military advisers would have been on his side. But he did not. He took the chance, made the decision for which he was neither to ask nor receive anything like the credit he deserved.

"Hell and high water every day," was Truman's description of the next several weeks. He had decided to show Louis Johnson the door.

On Wednesday, September 6, General Marshall came alone to the White House, and Truman, as he had twice before when he needed him, asked Marshall to return to service, this time as Secretary of Defense. Marshall warned Truman to consider carefully. "I'll do it," he said. "But I want you to think about the fact that my appointment may reflect upon you and your administration. They are still charging me with the downfall of Chiang's government in China. I want to help, not hurt you."

Greatly moved, Truman wrote to Bess, "Can you think of anyone else saying that?"

Three days later, Saturday, September 9, after one last Oval Office session on Inchon, the Joint Chiefs sent MacArthur a final go-ahead. The landing was to take place on September 15, in less than a week.

On Monday, the 11th, Truman summoned Louis Johnson and told him he must quit. Further, in announcing his resignation, Johnson was to recommend General Marshall as his successor.

Johnson looked as if he might faint. Truman felt dreadful. Johnson pleaded for time to think it over. He could have a day, Truman said, but there would be no change. Returning the next afternoon with an un-signed letter of resignation in hand, Johnson begged Truman not to fire him. When Truman insisted he sign the letter, Johnson broke down and wept. He had seldom ever been so miserably uncomfortable, Truman later said. He had known Johnson for thirty years.

The resignation of Johnson and the nomination of Marshall were an-nounced at once.

In the early hours of September 15—it was afternoon in Washington, September 14—the amphibious landing at Inchon began. As promised by MacArthur, the attack took the enemy by total surprise, and as also promised by MacArthur, the operation was an overwhelming success that completely turned the tables on the enemy.

The invasion force numbered 262 ships and 70,000 men of the Tenth Corps, with the 1st Marine Division leading the assault. Inchon fell in little more than a day. In eleven days Seoul was retaken. Meantime, as planned, General Walker's Eighth Army broke out of the Pusan Perimeter and started north. Seldom in military history had there been such a dramatic turn in fortune. By September 27 more than half the North Korean Army had been trapped in a huge pincer movement. By October 1, U.N. forces were at the 38th parallel and South Korea was in U.N. control. In two weeks, it had become an entirely different war.

In Washington the news was almost unbelievable, more by far than anyone had dared hope for. The country was exultant. It was a "military miracle." A jubilant President cabled MacArthur: "I salute you all, and say to all of you from all of us at home, 'Well and nobly done.'"

For nearly three months, since the war began, the question had been whether U.N. forces could possibly hang on and survive in Korea. Now suddenly the question was whether to carry the war across the 38th parallel and destroy the Communist army and the Communist regime of the north and thereby unify the country. MacArthur favored "hot pursuit" of the enemy. So did the Joint Chiefs, the press, politicians in both parties, and the great majority of the American people. And understandably. It was a heady time, the excitement of victory was in the air. Except for a few at the State Department—Chip Bohlen, Paul Nitze, George Kennan, who had returned to service temporarily—virtually no one was urging a halt at the 38th parallel. "Troops could not be expected . . . to march up to a surveyor's line and stop," said Dean Acheson. "As a boundary it had no political value."

Truman appears to have been as caught up in the spirit of the moment as anyone. To pursue and destroy the enemy's army was basic military doctrine. If he hesitated or agonized over the decision—one of the most fateful of his presidency—there is no record of it.

The decision was made on Wednesday, September 27. MacArthur's military objective now was "the destruction of the North Korean Armed Forces"—a very different objective from before. He was authorized to cross the 38th parallel, providing there was no sign of major intervention in North Korea by Soviet or Chinese forces. Also, he was not to carry the fight beyond the Chinese or Soviet borders of North Korea. Overall, he was free to do what had to be done to wind up the war as swiftly as possible. George Marshall, now Secretary of Defense, told him to "feel unhampered tactically and strategically," and when MacArthur cabled, "I regard all of Korea open for military operations," no one objected.

Carrying the war north involved two enormous risks—intervention by the Chinese and winter. But MacArthur was ready to move, and after Inchon, MacArthur was regarded with "almost superstitious awe."

By diplomatic channels came warnings from the foreign minister of the People's Republic of China, Chou En-lai, that if U.N. forces crossed the 38th parallel, China would send troops in support of North Korea. In Washington—at the State Department, the Pentagon, the White House—such warnings were judged to be largely bluff.

At the end of the first week of October, at Lake Success, New York, the United Nations recommended all "appropriate steps be taken to ensure conditions of stability throughout Korea," which meant U.N. approval for proceeding with the war. Just days later, on October 9, MacArthur sent the Eighth Army across the 38th parallel near Kaesong, and the day following, Truman made a surprise announcement. He was flying to an unspecified point in the Pacific to confer with General MacArthur on "the final phase" in Korea.

II

It was the kind of grand, high-level theater irresistible to the press and the American public. Truman and MacArthur were to rendezvous, as was said, like the sovereign rulers of separate realms journeying to a neutral field attended by their various retainers. The two men had never met. MacArthur had been out of the country since 1937. Truman had never been closer to the Far East than San Francisco.

The meeting place was a pinpoint in the Pacific, Wake Island, a minute coral way station beyond the international date line.

The presidential expedition was made up of three planes, the *Independence* with Truman, his staff, physician, and Secret Service detail; an Air Force Constellation carrying Harriman, Rusk, Philip Jessup, Army Secretary Pace, and General Bradley, plus all their aides, secretaries, and Admiral Arthur Radford, commander of the Pacific Fleet, who came on board at Honolulu; and a Pan American Stratocruiser with thirty-five correspondents and photographers. General MacArthur flew with several of his staff, a physician, and Ambassador John Muccio.

As a courtesy, Truman let MacArthur choose the place for the meeting, and for Truman, Wake Island meant a flight across seven time zones, a full round trip from Washington of 14,425 miles, while MacArthur had only to travel 4,000 miles from Tokyo and back. Events were moving rapidly in Korea, Truman would explain, "and I did not feel that he [MacArthur] should be away from his post too long."

To many the whole affair looked like a political grandstand play to capitalize on the sudden, unexpected success of the war and share in MacArthur's Inchon glory on the eve of the off-year elections in November. The President had been out of the headlines for some time, it was noted. Now he was back, and for those Democrats in Congress who were up for reelection, it was "the perfect answer to prayer and fasting." MacArthur himself, en route to Wake Island, appeared disgusted that he had been "summoned for political reasons." In fact, the idea for the meeting had originated with the White House staff as "good election year stuff," Charlie Murphy remembered, and at first Truman had rejected it for that very reason, for being "too political, too much showmanship." Apparently it was only after being reminded that Franklin Roosevelt had made just such a trip to meet with MacArthur at Hawaii in 1944 that Truman changed his mind.

Dean Acheson, who was conspicuously absent from the presidential entourage, had strongly disapproved and asked to be excused. "While General MacArthur had many of the attributes of a foreign sovereign . . . and was quite as difficult as any, it did not seem wise to recognize him as one," Acheson would write. "The whole idea was distasteful to me. I wanted no part in it and saw no good coming from it."

Truman, too, appears to have had second thoughts, even as he flew the Pacific. "I've a whale of a job before me," he wrote to Nellie Noland from the plane east of Hawaii. "Have to talk to God's right-hand man tomorrow. . . ."

That a dramatic meeting between the President and his Far East Commander could, at this juncture, have great political value was, of course, undeniable. But to many who took part in the meeting, the charge that it was only, or even primarily, a political ploy would be emphatically dismissed as absurd. "Sheer nonsense," said Bradley.

The importance of the occasion, like its drama, centered on the human equation, the vital factor of personality. For the first time the two upon whom so much depended, and who were so strikingly different in nature, would be able to appraise one another not at vast distance, or through official communiqué or the views of advisers only, but by looking each other over. As Admiral Radford commented at the time, "Two men can sometimes learn more of each other's minds in two hours, face to face, than in years of correct correspondence." Truman, after returning, would remark simply, "I don't care what they say. I wanted to see General MacArthur, so I went to see him."

Also what would be largely forgotten, or misrepresented by both sides in time to come, after things turned sour, was how the meetings at Wake Island actually went, what the President and the general actually concluded then, once having met.

Truman's plane put down at 6:30 A.M., Sunday, October 15, just as the sun rose from the sea with spectacular brilliance, backlighting ranks of towering clouds. The single airstrip stretched the length of the island.

MacArthur was there waiting. In a later account of Truman's arrival at Wake, as given to the author Merle Miller by Truman and Wallace Graham, MacArthur would be pictured deliberately trying to upstage Truman by circling the airstrip, waiting for Truman to land first, thus putting the President in the position of having to wait for the general. But it did not happen that way. MacArthur was not only on the ground, he had arrived the night before and was at the field half an hour early. Averell Harriman, whose plane had come in a few minutes before the *Independence* and who stood waiting with MacArthur, would remember MacArthur asking what the meeting was about. Harriman had said it was to discuss how a political victory could be attained in Korea, now that MacArthur had won such a brilliant military victory. "Good," said MacArthur. "The President wants my views."

With an eye on Truman's plane as it began its approach, MacArthur took Harriman by the arm and started walking toward the runway. Harriman spoke of the strong support the President had given the Inchon operation. MacArthur said that at Inchon, he, MacArthur, had taken "grave responsibility" upon himself. Perhaps, said Harriman, MacArthur should consider the responsibility the President had assumed in backing him, and to this, noted Harriman, MacArthur registered keen interest.

As Truman stepped from the plane and came down the ramp, Mac-Arthur stood waiting at the bottom, with "every appearance of warmth and friendliness." And while onlookers noted also that the general failed to salute the President, and though Truman seems to have been somewhat put out by MacArthur's attire—his open-neck shirt and "greasy ham and eggs cap" (MacArthur's famed, gold-braided World War II garrison cap)—the greeting between them was extremely cordial.

MacArthur held out his hand. "Mr. President," he said, seizing Truman's right arm while pumping his hand, which experienced MacArthur watchers knew to be the number one treatment.

"I've been waiting a long time meeting you, General," Truman said with a broad smile.

"I hope it won't be so long next time, Mr. President," MacArthur answered warmly.

Truman was dressed in a dark blue, double-breasted suit and gray Stetson. In Honolulu, he had outfitted his whole staff in Hawaiian shirts, but he looked now conspicuously formal, entirely presidential, and well rested, having slept during most of the last leg of the flight.

For the benefit of the photographers, he and MacArthur shook hands several times again, as a small crowd applauded. Then the two men climbed into the back seat of a well-worn black two-door Chevrolet, the best car available on the island, and drove a short distance to a Quonset hut by the ocean, where, alone, they talked for half an hour.

According to Secret Service Agent Henry Nicholson, who rode in the front seat beside Floyd Boring, the driver, Truman began talking almost immediately about his concern over possible Chinese intervention in Korea. Nicholson would distinctly recall Truman saying, "I have been worried about that."

At the Quonset hut, according to Truman's own account in his *Memoirs,*

MacArthur assured him victory was won in Korea and that the Chinese Communists would not attack. When MacArthur apologized for what he had said in his Veterans of Foreign Wars statement, Truman told him to think no more of it, he considered the matter closed—a gesture that so impressed MacArthur that he later made a point of telling Harriman.

What more was said in the Quonset hut is not known, since no notes were taken and no one else was present. But clearly the time served to put both men at ease. Each, to judge by his later comments, concluded that the other was not as he had supposed.

Like so many others meeting MacArthur for the first time, Truman was struck by the engaging manner, the remarkable physical bearing, the celebrated "presence." The general, Truman would write, "seemed genuinely pleased at this opportunity to talk with me, and I found him a most stimulating and interesting person. Our conversation was very friendly— I might say much more so than I had expected."

MacArthur, for his part, later told Harriman that newspaper accounts and magazine articles did not do the President justice. In his own *Reminiscences,* MacArthur would write: "I had been warned about Mr. Truman's quick and violent temper and prejudices, but he radiated nothing but courtesy and good humor during our meeting. He has an engaging personality, a quick and witty tongue, and I liked him from the start."

About 7:30 they reemerged in the brilliant morning sunshine and again drove off in the Chevrolet, now to a flat-roofed, one-story, pink cinderblock shack, a Civil Aeronautics administration building with a wind sock floating above, close to the beach where the Japanese had stormed ashore in 1941. Beyond the beach, blue Pacific rollers crashed over the dark hulks of two Japanese landing boats.

Others, some seventeen advisers and aides, were waiting in a large, plain room opening onto several smaller anterooms, these separated only by half-length, louvered swinging doors. Truman, setting a tone of informality, said it was no weather for coats, they should all get comfortable. He sat in his shirtsleeves at the head of a long pine table, MacArthur on his right, Harriman on the left, the rest finding places down the table or against the walls. MacArthur, taking out a briar pipe, asked if the President minded if he smoked. Everyone laughed. No, Truman said, he supposed he had had more smoke blown his way than any man alive.

The conference lasted less than two hours, during which Harriman, Bradley, Dean Rusk, and Philip Jessup each kept notes, and quite openly. A State Department stenographer, Vernice Anderson, who was sitting in an adjoining room just beyond one of the half doors, and could thus hear clearly most of what was said, also took notes in shorthand. She had been asked to wait outside until she was needed to type up a final communiqué at the close of the meeting, but she kept her shorthand record of the meeting "automatically," as she later explained, because it seemed the thing to do. No one had told her to and no one had told her not to. Because she remained out of sight, she would be portrayed later by MacArthur's admirers as a "planted" eavesdropper "lurking behind the door," her presence decried as "playing politics at about its lowest level." MacArthur was said to have been deeply offended when a transcript of the meeting, based on a composite of all the notes taken, including those by Anderson, was made public. Yet when MacArthur received copies of the transcript less than a week after the conference, he expressed no surprise or displeasure, and suggested no changes.

The meeting proceeded without formal agenda, and as MacArthur later wrote, no new policies or war strategies were proposed or discussed. But the discussion was broad-ranged, with MacArthur doing most of the talking, as Truman, referring only to a few handwritten notes, asked questions. As so often before, MacArthur's performance was masterful. He seemed in full command of every detail and absolutely confident. "He was the most persuasive fellow I ever heard," remembered Charlie Murphy; "indeed a military genius," said Frank Pace. The time moved swiftly.

MacArthur had only good news to report. The situation in Korea was under control. The war, "the formal resistance," would end by Thanksgiving. The North Korean capital, Pyongyang, would fall in a week. By Christmas he would have the Eighth Army back in Japan. By the first of the year, the United Nations would be holding elections, he expected, and American troops could be withdrawn entirely very soon afterwards. "Nothing is gained by military occupation. All occupations are failures," MacArthur declared, to which Truman nodded in agreement.

Truman's first concern was keeping it a "limited" war. What were the chances of Chinese or Soviet intervention, he asked. "Very little," MacArthur said.

> Had they interfered in the first or second months it would have been decisive. We are no longer fearful of their intervention. . . . The Chinese have 300,000 men in Manchuria. Of these probably not more than 100,000 to 125,000 are distributed along the Yalu River. They have no Air Force. Now that we have bases for our Air Force in Korea, if the Chinese tried to get down to Pyongyang there would be the greatest slaughter.

The Russians, MacArthur continued, were a different matter. The Russians had an air force in Siberia and could put a thousand planes in action.

A combination of Chinese ground troops and Russian airpower could pose a problem, he implied. But coordination of air support with operations on the ground was extremely difficult and he doubted they could manage it.

The support he had been given from Washington was surpassing, MacArthur stressed. "No commander in the history of war," he said, looking around the table, "has ever had more complete and adequate support from all agencies in Washington than I have."

How soon could he release a division for duty in Europe, Bradley wished to know. By January, MacArthur assured him.

Dean Rusk, concerned that the discussion was moving too fast, passed Truman a note suggesting he slow down the pace. Too brief a meeting, Rusk felt, would only fuel the cynicism of a press already dubious about the meeting. Truman scribbled a reply: "Hell, no! I want to get out of here before we get into trouble."

Much of the time was taken up with questions concerning the rehabilitation of Korea, now that victory was at hand. There were questions about costs, concern over what to do about war criminals, a question from Bradley on what was to be done with some sixty thousand North Korean prisoners. ("They are the happiest Koreans in all Korea," MacArthur said. "For the first time they are well fed and clean.") Then, briefly, the discussion moved to the French effort against the Communists under Ho Chi Minh in Indochina, a situation Truman and MacArthur both found puzzling. MacArthur could not understand why the French couldn't "clean it up" in a few months. He couldn't understand it either, Truman said. Later, talking with Dean Rusk, MacArthur said that all the French needed was an aggressive general.

When Truman said there was no need for discussion of Formosa, since he and MacArthur had already talked "fully" about it and were in "complete agreement," MacArthur said nothing—which suggests either that he and Truman covered more concerning Formosa than MacArthur's VFW remarks, or, more likely, that MacArthur had no inclination to disagree now, no desire to say anything that might detract from the rosy picture he was painting or disrupt the harmony of the moment.

As to the need for additional United Nations troops, MacArthur would leave that for Washington to decide, and it was then, at about 9:05, that Truman called a halt.

"No one who was not here would believe we have covered so much ground as we have been actually able to cover," he said. He suggested a break for lunch while a communiqué was prepared. But MacArthur declined, saying he was anxious to get back to Tokyo and would like to leave as soon as possible, which to some in the room seemed to border on rudeness. "Whether intended or not," wrote Bradley, "it was insulting to decline lunch with the President, and I think Truman was miffed, although he gave no sign."

"The communiqué should be submitted as soon as it is ready and General MacArthur can return immediately," Truman said. The conference had lasted one hour, thirty-six minutes.

In later studies, some historians would write that Truman had traveled extremely far for not much. But to Truman, at the time, it had all been worth the effort. He was exuberant. He had never had a more satisfactory conference, he told the reporters present. Tony Leviero of *The New York Times* described him beaming "like an insurance salesman who had at last signed up an important prospect."

As the communiqué was being drawn up, Truman and MacArthur, off to themselves, even talked politics. MacArthur asked the President whether he planned to run for reelection—the Emperor of Japan wished to know, MacArthur quickly added. Truman responded by asking Mac-Arthur what his own political ambitions were.

"None whatever," MacArthur said. "If you have a general running against you, his name will be Eisenhower, not MacArthur."

Truman laughed. He liked and admired Eisenhower, considered him a friend, but, said Truman, "Eisenhower doesn't know the first thing about politics."

The communiqué, which MacArthur read and initialed, stressed "the very complete unanimity of view" that had made possible such rapid progress at the conference table and called MacArthur "one of America's great soldier-statesmen." At the airstrip, in a little ceremony just before boarding his plane, Truman said still more as he honored MacArthur with a Distinguished Service Medal. He praised MacArthur for "his vision, his judgment, his indomitable will and unshakeable faith," his "gallantry and tenacity" and "audacity in attack matched by few operations in history."

Later, on the way home, in a speech at San Francisco carried worldwide by the Voice of America in twenty-six languages, Truman would refer repeatedly to MacArthur, the man who had written a "glorious new page" in military history. "It is fortunate for the world that we had the right man for this purpose—a man who is a very great soldier—General Douglas MacArthur."

There was no substitute for personal conversation with the commander in the field who knows the problems there from firsthand experience, Truman said in the speech. But he had felt also a "pressing need" to make clear that there was "complete unity in the aims and conduct of our foreign policy."

MacArthur, too, left Wake Island in high spirits. On the flight to Tokyo, according to Ambassador Muccio, MacArthur was at his "sparkling best," "effervescent." After listening to Truman's San Francisco speech, he immediately cabled the President his warm approval.

The whole spirit of Wake Island was one of relief and exhilaration. The awful bloodshed in Korea, the suffering, was all but over, the war was won. If MacArthur said there was "very little" chance of the Chinese coming in, who, after Inchon, was to doubt his judgment, and particularly if what he said confirmed what was thought in Washington? ("On this one MacArthur and the rest of us were all wrong," Dean Rusk would write in retrospect.) If Truman and MacArthur had disliked or distrusted one another before the meeting, they apparently did so no longer. If the conference had accomplished that alone, it had been a success.

As things looked late the morning of Sunday, October 15, 1950, on Wake Island, MacArthur would be winding up the war almost any day. "Come up to Pyongyang. It won't be long now," were his parting words to the Washington reporters who saw him off at the airstrip. The problems ahead in Korea, presumably, were to be problems only of peace and rehabilitation, problems of just the kind MacArthur, with his experience in postwar Japan, was equipped to handle.

For Truman, the Commander in Chief, his decision of June 30, to commit American arms and prestige to check aggression in Korea, the moves made to make it a United Nations effort, had never looked so sound. His "police action," for all the dark hours of summer, had succeeded. The Communist advance was thrown back. He had matched words with deeds. He had done what he felt he must for the good of America and the world, made the right choices after all, chosen the right general, backed him, gambled on his audacity. And it had all worked. Korea, it seemed, could be included now with the Truman Doctrine, the Marshall Plan, the Berlin Airlift, NATO, as among the proudest accomplishments of his presidency. With the Korean crisis settled, the war nearly over, the dreadful possibility of a larger world conflict was also passing, which, to Truman, exceeded all other considerations. If he was beaming like a successful insurance salesman, if MacArthur was "effervescent," they had good reason.

Truman believed and often said that how a person stood in history had a lot to do with the timing of his death. Had he or MacArthur died then or shortly after—had one of their planes gone down, or either succumbed to heart failure—their place in history and their record of achievement would have looked quite different from what would follow.

They said goodbye in the glaring sunshine of midday at Wake Island, as Truman boarded the *Independence*.

"Goodbye, sir," MacArthur said. "Happy landing. It has been a real honor talking to you."

It was their first and their last meeting. They never saw each other again.

III

By all signs Truman gave little thought to his own physical safety while President. When your time was up, it was up, was his feeling and it did not matter much what precautions were taken. He liked the Secret Service agents who watched over him, most of whom came from small towns or backgrounds much like his own and none of whom ever asked anything of him. "I like them more than all the top-notchers," he once told Margaret. Particularly he enjoyed chatting with the two or three who regularly accompanied him on his morning walks. He knew where they came from, whether they were married or had children, which church they attended. "He would treat us almost like sons," remembered one, Rex Scouten. "He talked nearly the whole time as we walked—about the Army [Truman liked the fact that Scouten, too, had been in the artillery], about his growing up in Missouri, and the Civil War. He'd go by a building and he'd tell you all about the building and why it was designed the way it was. . . ."

His interest in them, they knew, was more than passing. When Truman learned, for example, that Floyd Boring's wife had had a baby, he had another Secret Service man drive him to the hospital to visit with her and see the child.

But the unbroken presence of protectors, the feeling of being constantly under guard, grated on him. He never became accustomed to it. He would have much preferred less security than more. If after moving to Blair House he had any misgivings about the security problems it posed, he never said a word.

At midday on Wednesday, November 1, 1950, two weeks after the Wake Island conference, Truman returned to Blair House at the end of an extremely disquieting morning. According to a report from his new head of the CIA, General Walter Bedell Smith, it had been "clearly established" that the forces now opposing U.N. troops in North Korea included Chinese Communist soldiers, their numbers estimated as high as fifteen to twenty thousand.

The day in Washington was unseasonably hot—the hottest November day on record, 85 degrees in the shade along Pennsylvania Avenue.

Truman joined Bess and Madge Wallace for a quiet lunch, then went upstairs for a nap. At 2:50 he was scheduled to leave for Arlington Cemetery, to speak at the unveiling of a statue of British Field Marshal Sir John Dill, a member of the Combined Chiefs of Staff during World War II, who had died in Washington in 1944 as a result of his wartime service.

Because of the heat, Truman took off his clothes and stretched out on the four-poster bed in his underwear, the window open.

The rest of the house grew quiet. Bess and her mother had retired to another room. Downstairs, the front door stood open to the street, the screen door latched. On duty in the comparative cool of the front hall was Secret Service Agent Stuart Stout.

"The house was so quiet, the day so close, it was a struggle to stay awake," remembered the assistant head usher, J. B. West, who with head usher Howell Crim was in their small office just off the hall.

Outside, three White House police were posted, all sweltering in winter uniforms. Except for the heat, the afternoon was passing like any other. People strolled by beneath the President's window. Streetcars and automobiles moved along in the bright sun of the avenue. Autumn leaves floated down from the trees.

To ease the monotony somewhat, the guards worked on a rotation system, "the push," and at 2:15 the push began, placing Private Donald Birdzell at the bottom of the front steps, just under the canopy, where he stood facing the street. In two white-painted guard booths on the sidewalk to his left and right, about 30 yards apart, were two more uniformed White House guards. In the booth to the left, east toward Lafayette Square, Private Joseph Davidson sat talking with Agent Floyd Boring. ("I'd come out more or less to chat," Boring recalled. "[Davidson] had a pair of glasses on, and I'd never seen him with glasses on before. . . . I said, 'Why the glasses? To see these girls going by here?' ")

In the guard booth up the sidewalk, to the right, was Private Leslie Coffelt.

A fourth White House policeman, Joseph Downs, who had just been relieved by Coffelt, was starting for the basement door when two slim, neatly dressed men approached Blair House from opposite directions, coming along the sidewalk with the other pedestrians. The time was 2:19.

The two looked so subdued and unobtrusive in their dark suits and hats that a clerk in the hotel near Union Station where they stayed the night before had mistaken them for divinity students. The man approaching from the west, toward Leslie Coffelt's booth, was Griselio Torresola. He was twenty-five years old. The other, coming from the east, was Oscar

Collazo, who was thirty-six. They were both from New York, both Puerto Ricans, and fanatic Puerto Rican nationalists. To bring attention to their cause they had decided to kill the President.

Torresola was armed with a German Luger. Collazo, who had never fired a pistol before, carried a German Walther P-38. Between them they had sixty-nine rounds of ammunition.

Torresola paused at the window of Coffelt's booth and began saying something in a loud voice, apparently in an effort to divert attention from his partner, Collazo, who by then had walked directly past the other booth—past Davidson and Boring—and was heading straight for the Blair House stoop, where Donald Birdzell had his head turned, looking west toward Coffelt.

Birdzell would remember hearing a faint but unmistakable metallic click. Whirling about, he saw Collazo just eight or ten feet away, pointing the P-38 at him and trying to fire.

The gun went off, as Birdzell grabbed for his own pistol. Birdzell was hit in the right leg, but amazingly, instead of shooting back, and despite his leg, he had the presence of mind to run out into Pennsylvania Avenue, to draw the fire away from the President's quarters. As he moved, Collazo pivoted and kept firing, hitting him again. Birdzell crumpled by the streetcar tracks, but turned on one knee and shot back.

By now gunfire was exploding on all sides. Torresola had stepped to the open door of the west sentry booth and opened up on Coffelt point-blank. With bullets ripping his chest and stomach, Coffelt went down and began slowly to bleed to death. Torresola spun and fired at Joseph Downs, the White House policeman at the basement door, hitting him three times. Downs somehow struggled through the door yelling for help.

"It all happened so rapidly . . . I didn't really know what the hell was going on," Floyd Boring remembered. There were screams, shouting. People everywhere were running for cover. The noise of gunfire was terrifying—twenty-seven shots in two minutes.

Boring and Davidson opened fire on Collazo. A bullet clipped his ear, another his hat. With his second shot Boring hit him in the chest and Collazo went face down on the sidewalk, legs splayed out beside the front step, his hat still on.

Torresola, meantime, had wheeled and fired at Birdzell out by the streetcar tracks. Struck now in his good leg, Birdzell pitched forward, yet kept firing, his pistol braced on the pavement at arm's length. Then the dying Leslie Coffelt somehow got hold of his own pistol and brought Torresola down with a single shot through the head.

With that, suddenly, it was over and for a few seconds, strangely silent.

Then people came running from every direction—more police, photographers, Secret Service agents and reporters from the White House, a crowd of hundreds.

In the front hall, Agent Stout, who had rushed to the gun cabinet in the usher's office, stood ready now at the front door with a Thompson submachine gun.

J. B. West, stepping into the hall, saw the First Lady on the stairway. What was happening, she asked. There had been a shooting, West said. He remembered her gazing at him, "eyes wide," then hurrying back up the stairs.

Truman, in the roar of gunfire, had jumped from his bed and rushed to the window. Seeing him, someone on the sidewalk had shouted, "Get back! Get back!" until he moved away.

Ambulances nosed through the crowd outside. A rumor spread that the President had been murdered. Traffic backed up for blocks in every direction.

Birdzell lay motionless in the street, blood flowing onto the pavement from both legs. Coffelt was sprawled on his back beside his sentrybox. Downs, who had been dragged to a basement room, was asking for a priest.

Torresola was dead, doubled in a heap beneath a boxwood hedge. Collazo was still alive.

Truman quickly dressed and came downstairs. Looking out from the first floor, he could see a cluster of police bending over Collazo at the front stoop and Charlie Ross making his way through the police and up the steps. Would the President still be going to Arlington? "Why, of course," Truman said.

In another fifteen minutes, he was on his way out the back door, and with seven or eight Secret Service men following immediately behind in a big open car, some of them hanging onto the sides, his limousine wheeled out of the driveway and sped across the Potomac.

At Arlington, the several hundred people gathered for the ceremonies saw Truman step from the car looking grim but calm. No one knew what had happened, until ten minutes later when a motorcycle messenger arrived to pick up a photographer's film and immediately the word spread, a murmur running through the crowd. Standing beside the equestrian bronze of Sir John Dill, Truman kept to his prepared remarks as if nothing had happened. "It is important to the peace of the world to understand each other and have full faith in each other's sincerity. That is all we ask. That is all we want. . . ."

Only afterward, on hearing that Private Leslie Coffelt had died at the hospital, did Truman become extremely upset. As he would say later, when a plaque in Coffelt's memory was placed on a new iron fence in front of Blair House, Coffelt had been one of the best-liked officers on the White House force.

Officers Birdzell and Downs eventually recovered from their wounds and returned to their jobs.

Ironically, Truman had done more for Puerto Rico than any previous President. He favored the right of the Puerto Rican people to determine their political relationship with the United States and had said so several times. He had named the first native Puerto Rican as governor of the island, and extended Social Security to the people of Puerto Rico.

"But Truman was . . . just a symbol of the system," Oscar Collazo would insist in explanation. "You don't attack the man, you attack the system."

Convicted on four counts, including the murder of Coffelt, Collazo was sentenced to death in the electric chair. However, in 1952, and as a gesture to the people of Puerto Rico, Truman would commute the sentence to life imprisonment. In 1979, after twenty-nine years in Leavenworth Penitentiary, Collazo would be pardoned by President Jimmy Carter.

"A President has to expect these things," Truman told reporters as he set off on his morning walk the day after the shooting. The outing looked casual, as though nothing had changed. Truman, stepping out at his usual brisk pace through the quiet city, appeared no different than on other mornings. But he was being watched over now by at least a dozen more Secret Service men in addition to the four immediately beside him— some walking well ahead or across the street, others, more heavily armed, following in a slow-moving automobile.

Keeping his regular scheduled press conference that afternoon, Truman insisted in response to questions that he had never been in danger. The only thing one need worry about, he told Admiral Leahy, was bad luck and that was something he never had. But he kept thinking about what had happened. It had all been so "unnecessary," he said in a note to Acheson, "and the people who really got hurt were wonderful men." The gunmen had been fools, "stupid as they could be." "I know I could organize a better program than they put on," he wrote, a sign that he knew perfectly well how differently things might have gone. His plan to attend the ceremony at Arlington had been in the morning paper. The assassins had only to have waited another twenty minutes, until he came out of the house.

On November 5, in St. Louis, on his way to Independence to vote, he sat in a hotel room writing in his diary:

[Leaving the airport] we started for St. Louis in a closed car. It was cold and the wind was northwest. People all along the way wanted to see the President—not me! Some saw me and the usual "There he is!" "Hello, Harry" was the result. Most of the people in the U.S.A. are kindly happy people and they show it by smiling, waving and shouting. . . .

Because two crackpots or crazy men tried to shoot me a few days ago my good and efficient guards are nervous. So I'm trying to be as helpful as I can. Would like very much to take a walk this morning but the S[ecret] S[ervice] . . . and the "Boss" and Margie are worried about me—so I won't take my usual walk.

It's hell to be President. . . .

He was "really a prisoner now," he told Ethel Noland. The "grand guards" protecting him at Blair House had never had a fair chance. "The one who was killed was just cold bloodedly murdered before he could do anything."

In Washington henceforth there would be no more walking across the street from Blair House to the West Wing. Truman would be driven back and forth in a bulletproof car with a roof that, as he said, would "turn a grenade," a floor to "stop a land mine."

He had always imagined he might take care of any would-be assassin, as had Andrew Jackson, who, when shot at by a deranged assailant at the Capitol, went after the man with his cane.

IV

From November 1, the day of the assassination attempt, through December 1950 was a dreadful passage for Truman. Omar Bradley was to call these sixty days among the most trying of his own professional career, more so even than the Battle of the Bulge. For Truman it was the darkest, most difficult period of his presidency.

The off-year elections, though nothing like the humiliation of 1946, were a sharp setback for the Democrats and in some ways extremely discouraging. Local issues were decisive in many congressional contests, but so also were concerns over the war in Korea and what *Time* referred to as the suspicion that the State Department had "played footsie with Communists." "The Korean death trap," charged Joe McCarthy, "we can lay at the doors of the Kremlin and those who sabotaged rearming, including Acheson and the President, if you please." Senator Wherry said the blood of American boys was on Acheson's shoulders. In Illinois, Republican Everett Dirksen, running against Senator Scott Lucas, the Democratic majority leader, said, "All the piety of the administration will not put any life into the bodies of the young men coming back in wooden boxes."

McCarthy, who was not up for reelection, had vowed to get Lucas and Millard Tydings both, and both senators, two of the administration's strongest supporters, went down in defeat. Tydings especially was the victim of distortions and lies. In the campaign in Maryland, McCarthy and his aides circulated faked photographs showing Tydings chatting with Earl Browder, head of the Communist Party. In the California Senate race, Richard Nixon defeated Helen Gahagan Douglas by calling her, among other things, "pink down to her underwear."

One of the saddest things of all, Truman told a friend, was the way McCarthyism seemed to have an effect. In thirty years of marriage, Bess Truman had seldom seen him so downhearted, blaming himself for not keeping the pressure on McCarthy.

Fifty-two percent of the votes cast in the country had gone to the Republicans, 42 percent to the Democrats. The Democrats still controlled both houses of Congress, but the Democratic majority in the Senate had been cut from twelve to two, in the House from seventeen to twelve. And though Truman had taken no time for campaign speeches, except for one in his own state, in St. Louis on the way home to vote, the outcome was seen as a personal defeat. In the Senate, for all practical purposes, he no longer had control. Furthermore, Arthur Vandenberg, upon whom Truman had counted so long for nonpartisan support, was seriously ill and not likely to return.

"Some Republicans interpret the election as meaning that you should ask for the resignation of Mr. Acheson," a reporter said at his next press conference.

Mr. Acheson would remain, "Period," said Truman.

Was he blue over the elections? Not at all, he said. And in truth, the elections were a minor worry compared to what was happening in Korea.

That Chinese troops were in the war was by now an established fact, though how many there were remained in doubt. MacArthur estimated thirty thousand, and whatever the number, his inclination was to discount their importance. But in Washington concern mounted. To check the flow of Chinese troops coming across the Yalu, MacArthur requested authority to bomb the Korean ends of all bridges on the river, a decision Truman approved, after warning MacArthur against enlarging the war and specifically forbidding air strikes north of the Yalu, on Chinese territory.

Another cause of concern was MacArthur's decision, in the drive north, to divide his forces, sending the Tenth Corps up the east side of the peninsula, the Eighth Army up the west—an immensely risky maneuver that the Joint Chiefs questioned. But MacArthur was adamant, and it had been just such audacity after all that had worked the miracle at Inchon. "Then there were those," wrote Matthew Ridgway, "who felt that it was useless to try to check a man who might react to criticism by pursuing his own way with increased stubbornness and fervor."

With one powerful, "end-the-war" offensive, one "massive comprehensive envelopment," MacArthur insisted, the war would be quickly won. As always, he had absolute faith in his own infallibility, and while no such faith was to be found at the Pentagon or the White House, no one, including Truman, took steps to stop him.

Bitter cold winds from Siberia swept over North Korea, as MacArthur flew to Eighth Army headquarters on the Chongchon River to see the attack begin. "If this operation is successful," he said within earshot of correspondents, "I hope we can get the boys home for Christmas."

The attack began Friday, November 24, the day after Thanksgiving. Four days later, on Tuesday, November 28, in Washington, at 6:15 in the morning, General Bradley telephoned the President at Blair House to say he had "a terrible message" from MacArthur.

"We've got a terrific situation on our hands," Truman told his staff a few hours later at the White House, having waited patiently through the morning meeting, dealing with routine matters, as those around the room brought up whatever was on their minds.

The Chinese had launched a furious counterattack, with a force of 260,000 men, Truman said. MacArthur was going over on the defensive. "The Chinese have come in with both feet."

They were all the same, familiar faces around him—Charlie Ross, Matt Connelly, Harry Vaughan, Charlie Murphy, Bill Hassett, George Elsey, William Hopkins—with one addition, the author John Hersey, who was writing a "profile" of the President for *The New Yorker* and had been given permission to follow him through several working days, routine working days presumably. (It was unprecedented access for a writer, but Hersey had appealed to Truman on the grounds that what he wrote might be a contribution to history.)

Truman paused. The room was still. The shock of what he had said made everyone sit stiff and silent. Everything that had seemed to be going so well in Korea, all the heady prospects since Inchon, the soaring hopes of Wake Island were gone in an instant. As Hersey wrote, everyone present knew at once what the news meant for Truman, who would be answerable, "alone and inescapably," for whatever happened now in Korea. The decision to go beyond the 38th parallel had been his, just as the decision to risk the Inchon invasion had been his. Only this time the results had been different.

William Hopkins, the executive clerk, handed the President a stack of letters for his signature, most of them responses to correspondence about the assassination attempt. (In the weeks following the attempt, Truman received some seven thousand letters expressing gratitude that he was unharmed. He insisted that each of these be answered and he personally signed all seven thousand letters of acknowledgment.) As he wrote his name again and again, working down the pile, he talked of the "vilifiers" who wanted to tear the country apart. The news from Korea meant the enemy had misjudged American resolve. There had been an article in *Pravda* about deep divisions in Washington, he said. "We can blame the liars for the fix we are in this morning. . . . What has appeared in our press, along with the defeat of leaders in the Senate, has made the world believe that the American people are not behind our foreign policy. . . ."

He began outlining the immediate steps to be taken to inform the Cabinet and the Congress. Thus far he had shown no emotion. But now he paused again, and suddenly, as Hersey recorded, all his "driven-down" feelings seemed to pour into his face.

> His mouth drew tight, his cheeks flushed. For a moment, it almost seemed as if he would sob. Then in a voice that was incredibly calm and quiet, considering what could be read on his face—a voice of absolute personal courage—he said, "This is the worst situation we have had yet. We'll just have to meet it as we've met all the rest. . . ."

There were questions. Was the figure really 260,000 Chinese? Yes, Truman replied. Probably nothing should be announced yet, said Ross. Truman agreed. For the staff, watching him, the moment was extremely painful. Unquestionably, as he had said, it was the worst news he had received since becoming President.

But then he seemed to recover himself, sitting up squarely in his high-backed chair. "We have got to meet this thing," he said, his voice low and confident. "Let's go ahead now and do our jobs as best we can."

"We face an entirely new war," MacArthur declared. It had been all of three days since the launching of his "end-the-war" offensive, yet all hope of victory was gone. The Chinese were bent on the "complete destruction" of his army. "This command . . . is now faced with conditions beyond its control and its strength."

In following messages MacArthur called for reinforcements of the "greatest magnitude," including Chinese Nationalist troops from Formosa. His own troops were "mentally fatigued and physically battered." The directives under which he was operating were "completely outmoded by events." He wanted a naval blockade of China. He called for bombing the Chinese mainland. He must have the authority to broaden the conflict, MacArthur insisted, or the administration would be faced with a disaster.

That same day, November 28, at three o'clock in the afternoon, a crucial meeting of the National Security Council took place in the Cabinet Room —one of the most important meetings of the Truman years. For it was there and then in effect, with Truman presiding, that the decision was made not to let the crisis in Korea, however horrible, flare into a world war. It was a decision as fateful as the one to go into Korea in the first place, and stands among the triumphs of the Truman administration, considering how things might have gone otherwise.

General Bradley opened the discussion with a review of the bleak situation on the battlefield. Alben Barkley, who rarely spoke at such meetings, asked bitterly why MacArthur had promised to have "the boys home for Christmas"—how he could ever have said such a thing in good faith. Army Secretary Pace said that MacArthur was now denying he had made the statement. Truman warned that in any event they must do nothing to cause the commander in the field to lose face before the enemy.

When Marshall spoke, he sounded extremely grave. American involvement in Korea should continue as part of a United Nations effort, Marshall said. The United States must not get "sewed up" in Korea, but find a way to "get out with honor." There must be no war with China. That was clear. "To do this would be to fall into a carefully laid Russian trap. We should use all available political, economic and psychological action to limit the war."

Limit the war. Don't fall into a trap. The same points would be made over and over in time to come. "There was no doubt in my mind," Truman would write, "that we should not allow the action in Korea to extend to a general war. All-out military action against China had to be avoided, if for no other reason than because it was a gigantic booby trap."

"We can't defeat the Chinese in Korea," said Acheson. "They can put in more than we can." Concerned that MacArthur might overextend his operations, Acheson urged "very, very careful thought" concerning air strikes against Manchuria. If this became essential to save American troops, then it would have to be done, but if American attacks succeeded in Manchuria, the Russians would probably come to the aid of their Chinese ally.

The thing to do, the "imperative step," said Acheson, was to "find a line that we can hold, and hold it."

Behind everything they faced was the Soviet Union, "a somber consideration." The threat of a larger war, wrote Bradley, was closer than ever, and it was this, the dread prospect of a global conflict with Russia erupting at any hour, that was on all their minds.

The news was so terrible and came with such suddenness that it seemed almost impossible to believe. The last thing anyone had expected at this point was defeat in Korea. The evening papers of November 28 described "hordes of Chinese Reds" surging through a widening gap in the American Eighth Army's right flank, "as the failure of the Allied offensive turned into a dire threat for the entire United Nations line." The whole Eighth Army was falling back. "200,000 OF FOE ADVANCE UP TO 23 MILES IN KOREA" read the banner headline across *The New York Times* the following day. The two calamities most dreaded by military planners—the fierce Korean winter and massive intervention by the Chinese—had fallen on the allied forces at once.

What had begun was a tragic, epic retreat—some of the worst fighting of the war—in howling winds and snow and temperatures as much as 25 degrees below zero. The Chinese not only came in "hordes" but took advantage of MacArthur's divided forces, striking both on their flanks. The Eighth Army under General Walton Walker was reeling back from the Chongchon River, heading for Pyongyang. The choice was retreat or annihilation. In the northeast the ordeal of the Tenth Corps was still worse. The retreat of the 1st Marine Division—from the Chosin Reservoir forty miles to the port of Hungnam and evacuation—would be compared to Xenophon's retreat of the immortal ten thousand or Napoleon's withdrawal from Moscow.

"A lot of hard work was put in," Truman would remember of his own days in Washington.

For most of his time in office, Truman had enjoyed extremely good relations with the working press of Washington. He genuinely liked and respected most reporters—made himself available to them for questioning at regular weekly press conferences, or on his morning walks to any who felt up to it. "Remember, photographers are working people who sell pictures," he once advised Margaret. "Help them sell them. Reporters are people who sell stories—help them sell stories." And in turn reporters liked and respected him more perhaps than he realized. When he stepped before them in the Indian Treaty Room, at his press conference the day after the assassination attempt, the long applause they gave him was from the heart.

"No President of the last 50 years was so widely and warmly liked by reporters as Mr. Truman," Cabell Phillips would write.

> He "used" the press occasionally as most Presidents have done to test the wind. But he never tried to "con" them with flattery and devious favoritism. . . . Harry Truman worked less to ingratiate himself with people but succeeded better at it than any important public figure I have ever known. He did it, I think, because he was so utterly honest with and about himself, so free of what we call "side" or "put on."

Press Secretary Charlie Ross, too, deserved part of the credit for such feelings, for never had he thought it necessary to "sell" Truman to them.

It was the great press lords of the day, the powerful publishers and editors, and several of the syndicated columnists—the "paid columnists," the "guttersnipe columnists"—whom Truman despised: "What a test of democracy if it works!" Roy Roberts, editor of the Kansas City *Star,* had written in patronizing fashion on Truman's first day in office. Henry Luce considered Truman the *"reductio ad absurdum* of the common man." Michael Straight, editor of *The New Republic,* had written in 1948 that Truman had "a known difficulty in understanding the printed word." Westbrook Pegler, Walter Winchell, and Drew Pearson had all hit him hard, and in ways he would not forget.

Privately he spoke of the lot with vivid contempt. Roy Roberts was "a fat no-good can of lard," Pegler "a rat," Winchell and Pearson "newsliars." The Alsop brothers were "the Sop Sisters." He detested the newspapers of the Hearst and Scripps-Howard chains, and the lowest of all, still, was Colonel Robert ("Bertie") McCormick, owner of the Chicago *Tribune.* As Truman saw things, McCormick and his kind made their fortunes as character assassins, while those who did the dirty work for them, like some of the columnists, were no better than whores in that they offered their favors for money. "The prostitutes of the mind in my opinion . . . are much more dangerous to the future of mankind than the prostitutes of the body," he wrote in a letter he never mailed to Frank Kent, a columnist for the Washington *Star* whom he particularly disliked. That November, hearing from a friend that a Chicago *Tribune* writer named Holmes was in Kansas City asking questions about Truman and his family, Truman wrote in reply, "You might tell the gentleman named Holmes that if he comes out with a pack of lies about Mrs. Truman or any of my family his hide won't hold shucks when I get through with him."

But for those who covered him daily at the White House, who had traveled with him in 1948, who had been to Key West, he had no such feelings—Cabell Phillips and Tony Leviero of *The New York Times,* Edward Folliard of the Washington *Post,* Merriman Smith of United Press, Robert Donovan of the New York *Herald-Tribune,* Robert Nixon of the International News Service, Joe Short of the Baltimore *Sun.* And it was they, his friends, not the "newsliars" or the Bertie McCormicks, who again stood to ask their questions at a sensational press conference the morning of November 30, 1950, when Truman stumbled into still more trouble, blundering as he had never before with reporters, his remarks sending shock waves around the world.

The Indian Treaty Room was packed—more than two hundred stood as he came in—and at first all went well. He began by reading a prepared text, a strong, compelling statement of policy.

Neither the United States nor the United Nations had any aggressive intentions against China. What was happening in Korea, however, was part of a worldwide pattern of Russo-Communist aggression and consequently the world was threatened now with a serious crisis.

As he had once decided to take a stand at Berlin, Truman was now resolved to stay in Korea, and he said so. He was not bombastic, he was not eloquent, only clear and to the point.

> We may suffer reverses as we have suffered them before. But the forces of the United Nations have no intention of abandoning their mission in Korea. . . .
> We shall continue to work in the United Nations for concerted action to halt this aggression in Korea. We shall intensify our efforts to help other free nations strengthen their defenses in order to meet the threat of aggression elsewhere. We shall rapidly increase our military strength.

The statement had been worked over with extreme care by a dozen or more of the White House staff and State Department. It said nothing about the atomic bomb. The subject of the bomb had never even been discussed during preparation of the statement.

But then the questions began, reporters rising one by one, Folliard of the *Post* first asking Truman if he had any comments on the criticism of MacArthur in the European press.

"They are always for a man when he is winning, but when he is in a little trouble," Truman replied, "they all jump on him with what ought to be done, which they didn't tell him before." General MacArthur was doing "a good job."

Taking an exaggeratedly deep breath, Folliard then said the particular criticism was that MacArthur had exceeded his authority, went beyond the point he was supposed to go.

"He did nothing of the kind," Truman snapped.

Other reporters began pressing him. What if the United Nations were to authorize MacArthur to launch attacks across the Yalu into Manchuria?

Truman stood erect as always, his fingertips pressing on a tabletop as he spoke. Sometimes between questions he would sip from a glass of water or twist the heavy gold Masonic ring on his left hand.

"We will take whatever steps are necessary to meet the military situation, just as we always have."

Did that include the atomic bomb?

"That," said Truman unhesitatingly, "includes every weapon we have."

Did this mean there was "active consideration" of use of the bomb?

The room was still. The topic that had never been considered appropriate for a press conference had suddenly become the focal point. Truman should have cut off discussion of the bomb before this. But he seems not to have understood where the questions were leading him, while the reporters saw no reason to refrain from pressing him, if, as it appeared, he meant to rattle the bomb a little.

"There has always been active consideration of its use," Truman replied, adding, as he shook his head sadly, that he did not want to see it used. "It is a terrible weapon and it should not be used on innocent men, women, and children who have nothing whatever to do with this military aggression. That happens when it is used."

Merriman Smith, sensing that the President had said more than he meant to, offered him a chance to back off by asking for clarification. "Did we understand you clearly that the use of the bomb is under active consideration?"

Yet Truman insisted: "Always has been. It is one of our weapons."

Did this mean use against military objectives or civilian, another of the veteran White House press, Robert Nixon, started to ask, but Truman cut him off, saying, "It's a matter that the military people will have to decide. I'm not a military authority that passes on those things."

The correspondent for NBC, Frank Bourgholtzer, wished him to be more specific.

"Mr. President, you said this depends on United Nations action. Does that mean we wouldn't use the atomic bomb except on a United Nations authorization?"

"No, it doesn't mean that at all," Truman shot back. "The action against Communist China depends on the action of the United Nations. The military commander in the field will have charge of the use of the weapons, as he always has."

He had said far more than he ever intended and had been inaccurate besides, but the reporters had their story. The press conference ended at 10:30 A.M. By 10:47 a United Press bulletin was on the wire: *President Truman said today that the United States has under consideration use of the atomic bomb in connection with the war in Korea.* The Associated Press followed, adding that whether the bomb was used depended on American military command in the field, the clear implication being that the decision was being left to MacArthur. Huge headlines filled the early editions of the afternoon papers.

Truman's answers had been devastatingly foolish, the press conference a fiasco. The White House was besieged with calls. An exhausted Eben Ayers, writing privately that night, would describe it as one of the "wildest days" ever. The reaction in Europe was extreme alarm, and especially in Britain, where the news threw the House of Commons into a state of panic such as old-time members had never seen. Acheson hurried to the White House with the draft of a "clarifying" statement. Charlie Ross, under greater pressure than at any time since becoming press secretary, was called into the Oval Office to lend a hand in "damage control." The statement, ready by mid-afternoon, said that while "the use of any weapon is always implicit in the very possession of that weapon," only the President, by law, could authorize use of the atomic bomb, and "no such authorization had been given." Ross, as he presented the statement, looked and sounded completely spent, the circles under his eyes deeper and darker even than usual, his voice husky. The damage, he knew, had already been done.

By late afternoon came word from London that Prime Minister Clement Attlee was on his way to "confer" with the President. "PRESIDENT WARNS WE WOULD USE ATOM BOMB IN KOREA," said the front page of *The New York Times* the next morning. "NO NO NO," ran a headline in the *Times of India.*

The air of crisis rapidly compounded. The next morning, Friday, December 1, Truman met with the congressional leadership in the Cabinet Room to hear Walter Bedell Smith, head of the CIA, explain before a huge map of the Soviet Union and its satellites how events in Korea related to events in Europe. The Russians, Smith reported, had just completed maneuvers involving more than half a million men and consolidated their Siberian forces under a single command, an unusual step that "deserved watching."

There were joint State-Defense "crisis meetings" in the War Room at the Pentagon later in the day and again on Sunday, December 3, some six hours of talk.

As Acheson would write, all the President's advisers, civilian and military, knew something was badly wrong in Korea, other than just the onslaught of the Chinese. There were questions about MacArthur's morale, grave concern over MacArthur's strategy and whether on the actual battlefield a "new hand" was needed to replace General Walker. It was quite clear, furthermore, that MacArthur, the Far East Commander—contrary to the President's reassuring remarks at his press conference—had indeed deliberately disobeyed a specific order from the Joint Chiefs to use no non-Korean forces close to the Manchurian border.

But no changes in strategy were ordered. No "new hand" replaced Walker. No voices were raised against MacArthur. Regrettably, the President was ill-advised, Bradley later observed. He, Marshall, the Joint Chiefs, had all "failed the President." Here, in a crucial few days, said Acheson later, they missed their chance to halt the march to disaster in Korea. Acheson was to lament their performance for the rest of his life. Truman would never put any blame on any of them, but Acheson would say Truman had deserved far better. "I have the unhappy conviction," Acheson wrote nearly twenty years later, "that none of us, myself prominently included, served him as he was entitled to be served."

Matthew Ridgway would "well remember" his mounting impatience "that dreary Sunday, December 3," as hour after hour in the War Room discussion continued over the ominous situation in Korea.

> Much of the time the Secretaries of State and Defense participated in the talks, with no one apparently willing to issue a flat order to the Far East Commander to correct a state of affairs that was going from bad to disastrous. Yet the responsibility and authority clearly resided right there in the room. . . .

Unable to contain himself any longer, Ridgway spoke up, saying immediate action must be taken. They owed it to the men in the field and "to the God to whom we must answer for those men's lives," to stop talking and do something. For the first time, Acheson later wrote, "someone had expressed what everyone thought—that the Emperor had no clothes on." But of the twenty men who sat at the table, including Acheson, and twenty more along the walls behind, none spoke. The meeting ended without a decision.

Why didn't the Joint Chiefs just send orders and tell MacArthur what to do, Ridgway asked General Vandenberg afterward. Because MacArthur would not obey such orders, Vandenberg replied.

Ridgway exploded. "You can relieve any commander who won't obey orders, can't you?" he said. But Vandenberg, with an expression Ridgway remembered as both puzzled and amazed, only walked away.

The day following, in another closed session, this time at the State Department, Dean Rusk would propose that MacArthur be relieved of command. But again, no one chose to make further comment.

MacArthur, meanwhile, was being taken to task by the press, as he had never been. *Time,* which had long glorified him, charged him with being responsible for one of the worst military disasters in history. The "colossal military blunder" in Korea, declared an editorial in the New York *Herald-Tribune,* had shown that MacArthur would "no longer be accepted as the final authority on military matters." Unused to such criticism, his immense vanity wounded, MacArthur started issuing statements of his own to the press. He denied that his strategy had precipitated the Chinese invasion and said his inability to defeat the new enemy was due to restrictions imposed by Washington that were "without precedent."

Truman did not hold MacArthur accountable for the failure of the November offensive. But he deplored MacArthur's way of excusing the failure, and the damage his statements could do abroad, to the degree that they implied a change in American policy. "I should have relieved General MacArthur then and there," he would write much later.

As it was, he ordered that all military officers and diplomatic officials henceforth clear with the State Department all but routine statements before making them public, "and . . . refrain from direct communications on military or foreign policy with newspapers, magazines, and other publicity media." Dated December 6, the order was widely and correctly seen as directed to MacArthur. He was still expected to express his opinions freely—it was his duty to express his opinions—but only within the councils of the government.

Truman did not relieve the Far East Commander, he later explained, because he knew no general could be a winner every day and because he did not wish to have it appear that MacArthur was being fired for failing.

What he might have done had Acheson, Marshall, Bradley, and the Joint Chiefs spoken up and insisted that MacArthur be relieved is another question and impossible to answer.

For now the tragedy in Korea overshadowed everything. If MacArthur was in trouble, then everything possible must be done to help. "We must get him out of it if we can," Truman wrote in his diary late the night of December 2, following an intense session at Blair House with Acheson, Marshall, and Bradley that had left him feeling desperately low. "The conference was the most solemn one I've had since the Atomic Bomb conference in Berlin."

The talk had been of evacuating all American troops—of an American

Dunkirk in Korea after all. Marshall was not even sure such an operation would succeed, should the Chinese bring in their own airpower. "It looks very bad," Truman wrote.

Yet bad as it was, there was no mood of panic, and this, as those around him would later attest, was principally because of Truman's own unflinching response. "Mr. President, the Chinese simply must not be allowed to drive us out of Korea," Acheson said at one point, when things looked darkest, and Truman calmly agreed. When Clement Attlee arrived in Washington and argued, in effect, that the Far East should be abandoned in order to save Europe, Truman said no.

The bloody retreat in Korea continued. Pyongyang fell "to overwhelming masses of advancing Chinese," as the papers reported. General Walker's Eighth Army was heading for the 38th parallel. "World War III moves ever closer," said *Life*. "The Chinese Communist armies assaulting our forces . . . are as truly the armies of the Soviet Union as they would be if they wore the Soviet uniform." Everywhere in Washington the talk was of the "desperateness" of the situation. Senator McCarthy called on Acheson and Marshall both to resign and talked of impeaching Truman. But Truman remained calm and steady. "I've had conference after conference on the jittery situation facing this country," he wrote in his diary. "Attlee, Formosa, Communist China, Chiang Kai-shek, Japan, Germany, France, India, etc. I've worked for peace for five years and six months and it looks like World War III is here. I hope not—but we must meet whatever comes—and we will."

> [The President] thought that if we abandoned Korea the South Koreans would all be murdered and that we could not face that in view of the fact that they have fought bravely on our side and we have put in so much to help them [read the official minutes of his discussions with Attlee]. We may be subject to bombing from Manchuria by the Russians and Chinese Communists which might destroy everything we have. He was worried. He did not like to go into a situation such as this and then to admit that we were licked. He would rather fight to the finish. That was the way he had felt from the beginning. . . . He wanted to make it perfectly plain here that we do not desert our friends when the going is rough.

When Attlee urged that no decision be made on use of the atomic bomb without prior consultation with the British government, and possibly a formal agreement, Truman declined. He would not use the bomb without consulting the British government, Truman replied, but then neither would he state that in writing. If a man's word wasn't any good, he said, it wasn't made better by putting it on paper.

The goal of uniting Korea by force had been abandoned. The best hope now was to arrange an armistice back at the 38th parallel, and to this end the British agreed to help through the United Nations. On the policy that the war must not be widened, Truman and Attlee were in full agreement.

Attlee arrived in Washington on Monday, December 4. Little was said to the press about the substance of the first day's meeting, but at the end of the second day, Tuesday, December 5, in response to the pressures on him to release something, Charlie Ross met with some forty reporters at the White House. It was early evening, and Ross, like the President and the prime minister, was planning to attend a concert by Margaret Truman scheduled to begin in another few hours at Constitution Hall.

Limited as to how much he could say, Ross took time to describe in detail the luncheon held for the prime minister on board the *Williams-burg,* and with mock patience, spelled out such terms as "au jus" for the benefit of the reporters. "Charlie," wrote Eben Ayers, "seemed in good form. . . ."

The briefing over, Ross agreed to repeat the essence of what he had said for Frank Bourgholtzer and the NBC television crew. A microphone was set up on his desk. As he waited, Ross lit a cigarette and leaning back in his chair, smiled at his secretary, Myrtle Bergheim.

"Don't mumble," she kidded him.

"You know I always speak *very* distinctly," he joked, then fell over sideways.

Bourgholtzer thought he was clowning. Myrtle Bergheim grabbed for the phone and called Wallace Graham, whose office was on the floor below and who immediately dashed upstairs. But Charlie Ross was already dead of a coronary occlusion.

In the tribute he wrote shortly afterward in longhand, alone at his desk in the Oval Office, Truman said:

> The friend of my youth, who became a tower of strength when the responsibilities of high office so unexpectedly fell to me, is gone. To collect one's thoughts to pay tribute to Charles Ross . . . is not easy. I knew him as a boy and as a man. . . .
>
> Patriotism and integrity, honor and honesty, lofty ideals and nobility of intent were his guides and ordered his life from boyhood onward. He saw life steady and saw it whole . . .

But when Truman walked down the corridor to the press lounge where the reporters waited, he found he was unable to read what he had written. His voice broke on the first sentence.

"Ah, hell," he said. "I can't read this thing. You fellows know how I feel anyway . . ." He turned and with tears running down his face walked back to his office.

Ross had been sixty-five, a year younger than Truman. As Wallace Graham now revealed, Ross had had two or three prior mild heart attacks, but had refused to retire, preferring to remain on the job.

Concerned that the news of Ross's death would be too upsetting for Margaret before she went on stage, Truman gave orders that she was to be told nothing until after the concert, a decision she would later resent. Had she known, she could have said something in tribute to Ross, or possibly changed her repertoire.

The President and First Lady accompanied the prime minister to Constitution Hall, where all 3,500 seats were taken, the place aglow with a "brilliant audience." When Margaret came on stage, radiant in pink satin, and made her bow to the presidential box, Truman smiled and applauded. No President had ever been such a frequent concertgoer in Washington. He was a "regular" at Constitution Hall, at times, if the program included Mozart or Chopin, bringing the score with him. But tonight, even with his "baby" on stage, Truman looked extremely downcast.

She sang a light program that included selections from Schumann, Schubert, and a Mozart aria from *The Marriage of Figaro*. She drew waves of applause and was called back for four encores. A complimentary review in the Washington *Times-Herald* the next day would say she sang "better than ever before in her brief career." The Mozart aria was "fresh" and "unforced," her voice "charming."

"Afterward, Dad was effusive, even for him," she herself would write. "He hugged me and said he had never heard me sing better."

But others in the audience had found the performance wanting. She was "really pretty bad that night," recalled John Hersey. "She had a nice voice, but somebody, her coach, must have been pushing her too far." And the *Times-Herald* review was not the one her father saw first thing the next morning.

At Blair House at 5:30 A.M. Truman opened the Washington *Post* to a review in the second section, page 12, by music critic Paul Hume. "Margaret Truman, soprano, sang in Constitution Hall last night," it began.

Miss Truman is a unique American phenomenon with a pleasant voice of little size and fair quality. She is extremely attractive on stage.

... Yet Miss Truman cannot sing very well. She is flat a good deal of the time—more last night than at any time we have heard her in past years. There are few moments during her recital when one can relax and feel confident that she will make her goal, which is the end of the song.

Miss Truman has not improved in the years we have heard her ... she still cannot sing with anything approaching professional finish.

She communicates almost nothing of the music she presents. . . . And still the public goes and pays the same price it would for the world's finest singers. . . .

It is an extremely unpleasant duty to record such unhappy facts about so honestly appealing a person. But as long as Miss Truman sings as she has for three years, and does today, we seem to have no recourse unless it is to omit comment on her programs altogether.

It was a truly scathing review, though many of its harshest criticisms had been expressed before and Margaret, for some time now, had been advised by the Wagnerian opera star Helen Traubel not to rush her career, that her voice was as yet too small and inexperienced. Traubel, who liked Margaret and greatly admired her determination, said she needed five more years of study, at the least. When Traubel stressed this to the President, insisting that Margaret be able to stand on her own and not rely on his position, Truman, according to Traubel's later account, banged his fist on the desk in firm agreement. "That's exactly what I want."

It was the timing of the review in the *Post,* more than what Paul Hume had said, that caused Truman to explode. If it hadn't been the review, it might have been something else, given the stress he was under and his grief.

In the Blair House study, on a White House memo pad, he began what was to be his most notorious "longhand spasm" of all, a seething 150-word letter to Hume that he sealed in an envelope, addressed, fixed with a 3-cent stamp, and carried with him over to the White House.

To an elderly White House messenger named Samuel Mitchell, Truman asked if it was not an especially pleasant day. When Mitchell agreed, Truman suggested that he might like to take a stroll outside and on his way drop a letter in a mailbox on the street.

Had Charlie Ross still been on duty, the letter might have been stopped in time. Seeing the review, Ross would have known at once what Truman's response would be. "Charlie Ross would *never* have let the Paul Hume letter get out," George Elsey would say. "Charlie was . . . a calming fine influence on Truman, a tempering influence ... *much* more than a press secretary."

Though Hume and his editor at the *Post* decided to do nothing about the President's letter, copies were apparently made and in short order it appeared in full on page 1 of the tabloid Washington *News*.

Mr. Hume: I've just read your lousy review of Margaret's concert. I've come to the conclusion that you are an "eight ulcer man on four ulcer pay." [Truman here was quoting a phrase he had once heard used by Steve Early.]

It seems to me that you are a frustrated old man [Hume was thirty-four] who wishes he could have been successful. When you write such poppy-cock as was in the back section of the paper you work for it shows conclusively that you're off the beam and at least four of your ulcers are at work.

Some day I hope to meet you. When that happens you'll need a new nose, a lot of beefsteak for black eyes, and perhaps a supporter below!

[Westbrook] Pegler, a gutter snipe, is a gentleman alongside you. I hope you'll accept that statement as a worse insult than a reflection on your ancestry.

Margaret, who was by then in Nashville continuing her tour, refused to accept the news. She was positive, she said, that her father would not use such language. "In the first place, he wouldn't write a letter to Mr. Hume. My father wouldn't have time to write a letter." It was not hard to get hold of White House notepaper, she added, though she didn't know why anyone would do such a thing and sign her father's name.

Privately, Truman agreed he should never have written the letter, but now that he had, he would stand by it. To Margaret he said he had the right to be two people, the President and himself. It was Harry S. Truman the human being who wrote the letter, he told her.

But to the devoted White House staff, this inclination to see himself as both Truman the President and Truman the human being was not entirely a virtue or necessarily an admirable characteristic. Truman, remembered George Elsey, would forget that the rest of the country might not make such a differentiation. "When he would write a boiling hot letter to a music critic or would call Drew Pearson a son-of-a-bitch . . . behaving as Harry S. Truman, not as President of the United States . . . this caused embarrassment to him and I think reflected on the office, which, of course, was the last thing in the world he wanted to have happen."

Earlier embarrassing outbursts had included the angry letter to Bernard Baruch during the 1948 campaign that caused Baruch to call Truman a "rude, uncouth, ignorant man," and a letter in which Truman had said he wouldn't appoint John L. Lewis dog-catcher. In another, a letter to a congressman written the previous summer, he had called the Marine Corps "the Navy's Police Force" and accused the Marines of having "a propaganda machine that is almost equal to Stalin's," a charge for which he had publicly apologized. But nothing equaled the furor that erupted now over the Hume letter.

Hume himself, who greatly regretted that the letter had ever been made public, told reporters he was entirely sympathetic to the President. "I can only say that a man suffering the loss of a friend and carrying the burden of the present world crisis ought to be indulged in an occasional outburst of temper." But the gesture had little dampening effect.

The Chicago *Tribune* put the American people on notice that their President's "mental competence and emotional stability" were in question. A flood of letters-to-the-editor in papers across the country expressed shock over the President's "uncouthness," his lack of self-control. "It cuts to the quick to realize that we have a President who isn't even a gentleman," read one of hundreds of letters to the White House, and this from an "out-and-out" Democrat. "Truly we have chosen a 'common' man President. Yes—very common." There were suggestions also that Truman might begin to take himself and his daughter a bit less seriously. "My sympathy is with you about Margaret," wrote one man. "My four children cannot sing either."

While some who wrote took Truman's side, saying he had done only what any loyal, loving father worth his salt would have under the circumstances, such sentiments were in the minority. White House letters and telegrams ran nearly two to one against him and many, from mothers and fathers for whom the incident could only be seen in the context of the tragedy in Korea, voiced a deep-seated outrage that had to have touched Truman more than he ever let on.

> In times such as the present when the entire country is under abnormal duress and strain, your undue "concern" over your daughter's music career is completely ridiculous.

> Why don't you apologize to Mr. Hume, and then persuade your daughter to give up singing and take up some kind of war work where the public will appreciate her efforts.

> HOW CAN YOU PUT YOUR TRIVIAL PERSONAL AFFAIRS BEFORE THOSE OF ONE HUNDRED AND SIXTY MILLION PEOPLE. OUR BOYS DIED WHILE YOUR INFANTILE MIND WAS ON YOUR DAUGHTER'S REVIEW. INADVERTENTLY YOU SHOWED THE WHOLE WORLD WHAT YOU ARE. NOTHING BUT A LITTLE SELFISH PIPSQUEAK.

How many of these Truman actually saw is not known. But one letter from a Mr. and Mrs. William Banning of New Canaan, Connecticut, he both saw and held on to. It had been mailed with a Purple Heart enclosed.

Mr. Truman:

As you have been directly responsible for the loss of our son's life in Korea, you might just as well keep this emblem on display in your trophy room, as a memory of one of your historic deeds.

One major regret at this time is that your daughter was not there to receive the same treatment as our son received in Korea.

Truman put the letter in his desk drawer, keeping it at hand for several years.

V

It was Harry Truman's longstanding conviction that if you did your best in life, did your "damndest" always, then whatever happened you would at least know it was not for lack of trying. But he was a great believer also in the parts played by luck and personality, forces quite beyond effort or determination. And though few presidents had ever worked so hard, or taken their responsibilities so to heart in time of crisis as Truman had since the start of the war in Korea, it was luck, good and bad, and the large influence of personality, that determined the course of events time and again, and never more so than in late December 1950, in the midst of his darkest passage.

Two days before Christmas, on an icy highway north of Seoul, General Walton Walker, commander of the Eighth Army, was killed when his jeep ran head on into an ROK Army truck. Walker's replacement—as requested by MacArthur and approved immediately by Truman—was Matthew Ridgway, who left Washington at once, arriving in Tokyo on Christmas Day. At his meeting with MacArthur the next morning, Ridgway was told to use his own judgment at the front. "The Eighth Army is yours, Matt. Do what you think best." MacArthur, wrote Dean Acheson later, "never uttered wiser words."

That afternoon, Ridgway landed at Taegu, and in the weeks following came a transformation no one had thought possible. Rarely has one individual made so marked a difference in so little time. With what Omar Bradley called "brilliant, driving, uncompromising leadership," Ridgway restored the fighting spirit of the Eighth Army and turned the tide of war as have few commanders in history.

Since the Chinese onslaught of November 28, the Eighth Army had fallen back nearly 300 miles, to a point just below the 38th parallel, and for a while, Ridgway had no choice but to continue the retreat. Press reports described U.N. forces rolling back down the two main roads through Seoul as a continuous flow morning until night. "The retreating ROK soldiers were the most miserable troops I ever saw," wrote one correspondent. Millions of Korean refugees had also taken to the roads. "What are you going to do when the enemy doesn't care how many men he loses?" an American officer was quoted. Seoul was in flames again. President Rhee and his government had fled to Pusan. Abandoning Seoul, Ridgway withdrew as far as Oswan, near the very point where the first green American troops had gone into action in July. Now, instead of the murderous heat of summer, they fought in murderous cold.

The mood in Washington remained bleak. MacArthur continued to urge a widening of the war—again he proposed bombing and blockading China and utilizing the troops of Chiang Kai-shek—and as before his proposals were rejected. Dire consequences would follow, he implied, unless policy were changed.

> The troops are tired from a long and difficult campaign [MacArthur reported], embittered by the shameful propaganda which has falsely condemned their courage and fighting qualities . . . and their morale will become a serious threat in their battlefield efficiency unless the political basis upon which they are being asked to trade life for time is clearly delineated. . . .

Truman found such messages "deeply disturbing." When a general complained about the morale of his troops, observed George Marshall, the time had come for the general to look to his own morale.

The CIA was advising that it would be "infeasible under existing conditions . . . to hold for a protracted period a position in Korea." The best hope was an armistice. His primary consideration, MacArthur was told, was the safety of his troops and the defense of Japan.

> Under the extraordinary limitations and conditions imposed upon the command in Korea [MacArthur responded] . . . its military position is untenable, but it can hold, if overriding political considerations so dictate, for any length of time up to its complete destruction.

MacArthur called on the administration to recognize the "state of war" imposed by the Chinese, then to drop thirty to fifty atomic bombs on Manchuria and the mainland cities of China.

The Joint Chiefs, too, told Truman that mass destruction of Chinese cities with nuclear weapons was the only way to affect the situation in Korea. But that choice was never seriously considered. Truman simply refused to "go down that trail," in Dean Rusk's words.

Only once do I recall serious discussion about using nuclear weapons [Rusk later wrote]: when we thought about bombing a large dam on the Yalu River. General Hoyt Vandenberg, Air Force chief of staff, personally had gone to Korea, flown a plane over the dam, and dropped our biggest conventional bomb on it. It made only a little scar on the dam's surface. He returned to Washington and told us that we could knock the dam out only with nuclear weapons. Truman refused.

Truman also still refused to reprimand MacArthur. Rather he treated MacArthur with what Acheson considered "infinite patience"—too much infinite patience, Acheson thought, having by now concluded that the general was "incurably recalcitrant" and fundamentally disloyal to the purposes of his Commander in Chief. On January 13, 1951, Truman sent MacArthur a long, thoughtful telegram, generously praising him for his "splendid leadership" and stressing again the great importance of the whole costly effort in Korea as a means "to demonstrate that aggression will not be accepted by us or by the United Nations." But "great prudence" must be exercised, Truman stated.

> Steps which might in themselves be fully justified and which might lend some assistance to the campaign in Korea would not be beneficial if they thereby involved Japan or Western Europe in large-scale hostilities. . . .
> In the worst case, it would be important that, if we must withdraw from Korea, it be clear to the world that that course is forced upon us by military necessity and that we shall not accept the result politically or militarily until the aggression has been rectified.

Truman had by now declared a national emergency, announced emergency controls on prices and wages, and still greater defense spending—to the amount of $50 billion, more than four times the defense budget at the start of the year. He had put Charles E. Wilson, head of the General Electric Company, in charge of a new Office of Defense Mobilization, appointed General Eisenhower as Supreme Commander of NATO, and in a radio and television address to the nation on December 15, called on every citizen "to put aside his personal interests for the good of the country." So while doing all he could to avoid a wider war, he was clearly preparing for one.

As General Marshall later attested, "We were at our lowest point."

But then the morning of Wednesday, January 17, Marshall telephoned Truman to read an astonishing report just in from General Joe Collins, who had flown to Korea for talks with Ridgway. "Eighth Army in good shape and improving daily under Ridgway's leadership," Marshall read.

"Morale very satisfactory . . . Ridgway confident he can obtain two to three months' delay before having to initiate evacuation. . . . On the whole Eighth Army now in position and prepared to punish severely any mass attack."

Plainly MacArthur's bleak assessment of the situation, his forecasts of doom, had been wrong and the effect of this realization was electrifying. As the word spread through the upper levels of government that day, it would be remembered, one could almost hear the sighs of relief. The long retreat of the Eighth Army—the longest retreat in American military history—had ended. On January 25, 1951, less than a month after Ridgway's arrival, the Eighth Army began "rolling forward," as he said.

Ridgway had gone about his business with drive and common sense, seeing first to the basic needs of his troops—better food, warmer winter clothing, improved Mobile Army Surgical Hospitals (MASH units). He emphasized close communications, less dependence on roads and highways, more attention to holding the high ground, and better, more punishing use of airpower and artillery. With his own confidence, his natural vitality, his frequent and conspicuous presence at the front, dressed for battle with two hand grenades strapped to his chest, he set a strong example. The Army had been Ridgway's life, as it had been for his father before him. He was keenly intelligent, austere, superbly fit at age fifty-six, and already celebrated as the pioneer of the airborne assault in World War II. But Ridgway also understood MacArthur. He admired MacArthur's abilities and knew his limitations. More important, Ridgway both understood and approved of the administration's policy. Not only did he admire Harry Truman, he thought him a great and courageous man.

In Washington, every inclination now, as Bradley would write, was to look "beyond MacArthur" to Ridgway for reliable military judgments. Until now Washington had been almost entirely dependent upon MacArthur's headquarters for information, dependent on MacArthur's own opinions, his strategy. Now all that was over, his influence on planning was ended, a new phase of the war had begun. As far as military operations were concerned, wrote Bradley, MacArthur had become "mainly a prima donna figurehead who had to be tolerated."

With the Eighth Army on the offensive again, advancing relentlessly—to the Han River, to Inchon, then Seoul, retaking what was left of the capital city on March 15—morale in Washington revived. The advent of the new field commander was, as Acheson said, an event of immeasurable importance. "While General MacArthur was fighting the Pentagon, General Ridgway was fighting the enemy."

With a force of 365,000 men, Ridgway faced an enemy of more than 480,000, but Ridgway's use of concentrated artillery, "the really terrifying strength of our firepower," as he said, plus the spirit of "as fine a fighting field army as our country has yet produced," more than made up for the difference. By the end of March, having inflicted immense casualties on the Chinese, the Eighth Army was again at the 38th parallel.

Yet Ridgway's progress seemed only to distress MacArthur further. The American ambassador in Tokyo, William Sebald, found the Far Eastern Commander "tired and depressed." Unless he was allowed to strike boldly at the enemy, MacArthur said, his dream of a unified Korea was impossible. He complained of a "policy void." He now proposed not only massive attacks on Manchuria, but to "sever" Korea from Manchuria by laying down a field of radioactive wastes, "the by-products of atomic manufacture," all along the Yalu River. As so often before, his request was denied.

MacArthur's need to upstage Ridgway verged on the ridiculous. On the eve of a new Ridgway offensive in late February, MacArthur flew to the front and standing before a dozen correspondents, while Ridgway remained in the background, declared he had "just ordered a resumption of the offensive," when in fact he had had nothing to do with any part of the operation.

Talking to journalists on March 7, MacArthur lamented the "savage slaughter" of Americans inevitable in a war of attrition. When by the middle of March, the tide of battle "began to turn in our favor," as Truman wrote, and Truman's advisers both at the State Department and the Pentagon thought it time to make a direct appeal to China for peace talks, MacArthur refused to respond to inquiries on the subject. Instead he decried any "further military restrictions" on his command.

To MacArthur, as he later wrote, it appeared that Truman's nerves were at a breaking point—"not only his nerves, but what was far more menacing in the Chief Executive of a country at war—his nerve."

Truman ordered careful preparation of a cease-fire proposal. On March 21, the draft of a presidential statement was submitted for approval to the other seventeen U.N. nations with troops serving in Korea. On March 20 the Chiefs of Staff had informed MacArthur of what was happening—sending him what Truman called the "meat paragraphs" of the statement in a message that seems to have impressed MacArthur as nothing else had that there was indeed to be no all-out war with Red China. His response so jarred Washington as to leave a number of people wondering if perhaps he had lost his mind—first there had been Forrestal, then Louis Johnson, now MacArthur. Years afterward Bradley would speculate that possibly MacArthur's realization that his war on China was not to be "snapped his brilliant but brittle mind."

On the morning of Saturday, March 24, in Korea (Friday the 23rd in Washington), MacArthur, without warning, tried to seize the initiative in a manner calculated only to inflame the situation. He issued his own florid proclamation to the Chinese Communists, which in effect was an ultimatum. He began by taunting the Red Chinese for their lack of industrial power, their poor military showing in Korea against a U.N. force restricted by "inhibitions." More seriously, MacArthur threatened to expand the war.

> The enemy, therefore, must by now be painfully aware that a decision of the United States to depart from its tolerant effort to contain the war to the areas of Korea, through an expansion of our military operations to his coastal areas and interior bases, would doom Red China to the risk of imminent military collapse.

In conclusion, MacArthur said he personally "stood ready at any time" to meet with the Chinese commander to reach a settlement.

All Truman's careful preparations of a cease-fire proposal were now in vain. MacArthur had cut the ground out from under him. Later MacArthur would dismiss what he had said as a "routine communiqué." Yet his own devoted aide, General Courtney Whitney, would describe it as a bold effort to stop one of the most disgraceful plots in American history, meaning the administration's plan to appease China.

The news reached Washington after nightfall.

MacArthur, with his "pronunciamento," wrote Acheson, had perpetrated a major act of sabotage. To Acheson, it was "insubordination of the grossest sort"; to Bradley, an "unforgivable and irretrievable act."

At eleven o'clock that night in Washington, Friday, March 23, Acheson, Lovett, Rusk, and two other senior State Department officials, Alexis Johnson and Lucius Battle, met at Acheson's house in Georgetown and talked until past midnight. Lovett, ordinarily a man of imperturbable temperament, was angriest of all. MacArthur, he said, must be removed at once. Acheson agreed and quoted Euripides: "Whom the gods would destroy they first make mad."

At Blair House, Truman sat in an upstairs study reading and rereading the text of the MacArthur ultimatum. "I couldn't send a message to the Chinese after that," he would say in later years, trying to recall the disappointment and fury he felt. "I was ready to kick him into the North China Sea . . . I was never so put out in my life. . . . MacArthur thought he was the proconsul for the government of the United States and could do as he damned pleased."

In his *Memoirs,* Truman would write that he now knew what he must do about MacArthur.

> This was a most extraordinary statement for a military commander of the United Nations to issue on his own responsibility. It was an act totally disregarding all directives to abstain from any declarations on foreign policy. It was in open defiance of my orders as President and as Commander in Chief. This was a challenge to the President under the Constitution. It also flouted the policy of the United Nations. . . .
>
> By this act MacArthur left me no choice—I could no longer tolerate his insubordination. . . .

And yet . . . MacArthur was not fired. Truman said not a word suggesting he had reached such a decision. At a meeting with Acheson, Lovett, and Rusk in the Oval Office the next day, Saturday the 24th, Truman, by Acheson's account, appeared to be in a state of mind that combined "disbelief with controlled fury." Acheson and Lovett, for all their own anger, worried about adverse public reaction, given the mood of the country and MacArthur's immense prestige. People were fed up with the war. MacArthur was promising victory. If the President challenged that, he would appear to be, as Lovett said, "on the side of sin." Truman's decision was to send MacArthur only a restrained reprimand, a message he himself dictated to remind MacArthur of his order of December 6 forbidding public statements that had not been cleared with Washington.

Truman was moving with extreme caution. Some, later, would call this an act of political guile. Others would see it as another of those critical moments, like the Berlin crisis, when he drew on his better nature as President, refusing to act impulsively or irresponsibly, whatever his own feelings.

Meantime, on March 14, the Gallup Poll had reported the President's public approval at an all-time low of only 26 percent. And by the end of March, there were appalling new statistics on the war from the U.N. Secretariat: U.N. forces had now suffered a total of 228,941 casualties, the greatest part of them by far being South Korean (168,652) and American (57,120).

Truman was dwelling on the relationship between Abraham Lincoln and General George B. McClellan during the Civil War, in the autumn of 1862, when Lincoln had been forced to relieve McClellan of command of the Army of the Potomac. Truman had sent one of his staff to the Library of

Congress to review the details of the Lincoln-McClellan crisis and give him a report. Lincoln's troubles with McClellan, as Truman knew, had been the reverse of his own with MacArthur. Lincoln had wanted McClellan to attack and McClellan refused time and again. But then, when Lincoln issued orders, McClellan, like MacArthur, ignored them. Also like MacArthur, McClellan occasionally made political statements on matters outside the military field. Asked what he thought about this, Lincoln, according to a story Truman loved, said it reminded him of the man who, when his horse kicked up and stuck a foot through the stirrup, said to the horse, "If you are going to get on, I will get off."

> Lincoln was patient [Truman later wrote], for that was his nature, but at long last he was compelled to relieve the Union Army's principal commander. And though I gave this difficulty with MacArthur much wearisome thought, I realized that I would have no other choice myself than to relieve the nation's top field commander. . . .
>
> I wrestled with the problem for several days, but my mind was made up before April 5, when the next incident occurred.

On Thursday, April 5, at the Capitol, House Minority Leader Joe Martin took the floor to read the text of a letter from MacArthur that Martin said he felt duty-bound to withhold no longer.

In February, speaking in Brooklyn, Martin had called for the use of Chiang Kai-shek's troops in Korea and accused the administration of a defeatist policy. "What are we in Korea for—to win or to lose? . . . If we are not in Korea to win, then this administration should be indicted for the murder of American boys." Martin had sent a copy of the speech to MacArthur, asking for his "views." On March 20, MacArthur had responded and virtually all that he said was bound to provoke Truman, as Martin well knew. Since MacArthur's letter carried no stipulation of confidentiality, Martin had decided to make it public.

The congressman was right in calling for victory, MacArthur wrote, right in wanting to see Chinese forces from Formosa join the battle against communism. The real war against communism was in Asia, not in Europe: ". . . here [in Asia] we fight Europe's war with arms while the diplomats there still fight it with words . . . if we lose the war to Communism in Asia the fall of Europe is inevitable, win it and Europe most probably would avoid war and yet preserve freedom. . . . There is no substitute for victory."

The letter was on the wires at once. At the White House, a new assistant press secretary named Roger Tubby took the ticker bulletin and rushed to the Oval Office, to find Truman sitting quietly reading General Bradley's book, *A Soldier's Story*. Truman appeared unconcerned.

"Mr. President," said Tubby, "this man is not only insubordinate, but he's insolent, and I think he ought to be fired."

Truman looked again at the ticker sheet. "Well," he said, "I think they are maneuvering the general out of a job."

At the Pentagon, Bradley called a meeting of the Joint Chiefs. "I did not know that Truman had already made up his mind to relieve MacArthur," Bradley remembered, "but I thought it was a strong possibility." The Joint Chiefs, however, reached no conclusion about MacArthur.

On Friday, April 6, official Cadillacs filled the White House driveway. Marshall, Bradley, Acheson, and Harriman met with the President for an hour. Saying nothing of his own views, Truman asked what should be done. When Marshall urged caution, Acheson agreed. To Acheson it was not so much a problem of what should be done as how it should be done.

> The situation could be resolved [remembered Acheson] only by relieving the General of all his commands and removing him from the Far East. Grave trouble would result, but it could be surmounted if the President acted upon the carefully considered advice and unshakable support of all his civilian and military advisers. If he should get ahead of them or appear to take them for granted or be impetuous, the harm would be incalculable.

"If you relieve MacArthur," Acheson told Truman, "you will have the biggest fight of your administration."

Harriman, reminding the President that MacArthur had been a problem for too long, said he should be dismissed at once.

"I don't express any opinion or make known my decision," Truman wrote in his diary. "Direct the four to meet again Friday afternoon and go over all phases of the situation."

He was a model of self-control. MacArthur, in his own memoirs, would describe how, having read Truman's letter to the music critic, he saw himself "at the apex of a situation that would make me the next victim of such uncontrolled passion." But those close to Truman knew that "uncontrolled passion" was never a problem. Under the pressures of this tensest of times, with so much of his own stature and political welfare riding on his every move, he was at his steadiest. For the next several days an air of unnatural calm seemed to hang over the White House. "The wind died down," remembered Joe Martin. "The surface was placid . . . nothing happened."

Truman telephoned the Vice President. Given all that had happened, Barkley concluded reluctantly, a compromise was out of the question—

MacArthur would have to go. When Truman called Chief Justice Vinson and Speaker Sam Rayburn to the Oval Office, Vinson, like Marshall, advised caution. What Rayburn said is not known.

On Saturday, Truman met again with Marshall, Acheson, Bradley, and Harriman, and again nothing was resolved. Marshall and Bradley were still uncertain what to do. They were hesitating in part, according to Bradley's later account, because they knew the kind of abuse that would be hurled at them personally—an understandable concern for two such men at the end of long, distinguished careers. The previous fall, in acrimonious Senate debate over Marshall's confirmation as Secretary of Defense, Republican William E. Jenner of Indiana had called Marshall "a front man for traitors" and a "living lie." Firing MacArthur now, wrote Bradley, was certain to provoke more such savage assaults on Marshall by those Acheson called the "political primitives." Nor could he, Bradley, expect to escape similar treatment.

On Monday, April 9, the same foursome convened with the President once more, this time at Blair House. But now the situation had changed. The Joint Chiefs had met the afternoon before and concluded that from a military point of view, MacArthur should be relieved. Their opinion was unanimous.

"There was no question about the Chiefs being in thorough agreement on this," Bradley's aide, Colonel Chester Clifton, would later say:

They had become disenchanted with MacArthur . . . and on military rather than on political grounds.

A part of their dissatisfaction was with some of his strategic and tactical decisions, such as splitting his forces in Korea and jumping off on his November offensive with inadequate field intelligence about the enemy. . . .

What really counted was that MacArthur had lost confidence in himself and was beginning to lose the confidence of his field officers and troops. There is nothing in the book that more seriously undermines a commander's effectiveness than this. When it happens, he's through. . . .

And when he committed the final error of insubordination to the Commander-in-Chief—and there's absolutely no question about that —they had no trouble at all deciding what had to be done.

Now at Blair House, Acheson, Marshall, Bradley, and Harriman all agreed that MacArthur should be relieved, and only after each had spoken, Truman, for the first time, said he was of the same opinion. He had made his decision. He told Bradley to prepare the necessary papers.

· · ·

"Rarely had a matter been shrouded in such secrecy at the White House," reported the Washington *Post* the morning of Tuesday, April 10. "The answer to every question about MacArthur was met with a 'no comment' reply."

On Capitol Hill, an unidentified "congressional official" told the *Post* that the President had decided against removing the Far East Commander. Representative Martin said he favored bringing MacArthur home to report to Congress. In Tokyo, according to a United Press dispatch, a member of MacArthur's staff said meetings between the general and Secretary of the Army Pace were "going forward with an air of cordiality"—thus seeming to refute rumors that Pace had been sent to dismiss MacArthur. A photograph on page 1 of the *Post* showed a smiling MacArthur welcoming an even more smiling Pace on his arrival at the Tokyo airport.

A *Post* editorial, meantime, expressed concern that MacArthur's repeated efforts "to run away with the diplomatic ball" had "excited little more than a ripple among the American people," and blamed the administration for its "muting" of the issue. Civil supremacy was at stake. The President ought to take a firm hand. "Any reassertion of the President's authority as Commander in Chief and initiator of the country's foreign policy would win him, we feel sure, the support of the American people. That's what they are crying out for—leadership. . . ."

The morning cartoon by Herb Block showed "Captain Harry Truman" asleep on his World War I army cot, trembling in fear, too terrified to challenge the five-star general.

At the end of a routine morning staff meeting, the President quietly announced—"So you won't have to read about it in the papers"—that he had decided to fire General MacArthur. He was sure, Truman added, that MacArthur had wanted to be fired.

He was sure also that he himself faced a political storm, "a great furor," unlike any in his political career. From beyond the office windows, the noise of construction going on in the White House was so great that several of the staff had to strain to hear what he was saying.

At 3:15 that afternoon, Acheson, Marshall, Bradley, and Harriman reported to the Oval Office, bringing the drafted orders. Truman looked them over, borrowed a fountain pen from Bill Hassett, and signed his name.

They were to be sent by State Department channels to Ambassador Muccio in Korea, who was to turn them over to Secretary Pace, who by now was also in Korea, with Ridgway at Eighth Army headquarters. Pace was to return at once to Tokyo and personally hand the orders to Mac-

Arthur—this whole relay system having been devised to save the general from the embarrassment of direct transmission through regular Army communications. All aspects of the issue thus far had been kept secret with marked success, but it was essential there be no leaks in the last critical hours, as Truman made clear to his new press secretary, Joe Short, the White House correspondent for the Baltimore *Sun* whom Truman had picked to replace Charlie Ross. Announcement of the sensational MacArthur news was not to be made until the following morning.

The next several hours passed without incident, until early evening, after Truman had returned to Blair House. Harriman, Bradley, Rusk, and six or seven of Truman's staff were working in the Cabinet Room, preparing material for release, when Joe Short received word that a Pentagon reporter for the Chicago *Tribune*, Lloyd Norman, was making inquiries about a supposed "major resignation" to take place in Tokyo—the implication being that somehow MacArthur had already learned of Truman's decision and was about to resign before Truman could fire him.

Bradley telephoned Truman at about nine o'clock to report there had been a leak. Truman, saying he wanted time to think, told Bradley to find Marshall and Acheson. Marshall, it was learned, had gone to a movie with his wife, but Acheson came to the White House immediately, and like Rusk and George Elsey, he thought it would be a mistake to do anything rash because of one reporter's inquiry. As he had from the start, Acheson again stressed the importance of the manner in which the general was dismissed. It was only fair and proper that he be informed before the story broke.

Harriman, Charlie Murphy, Matt Connelly, Joe Short, and Roger Tubby argued that MacArthur must not be allowed to "get the jump" on the President. The story must come from the White House, not Tokyo. The announcement should be made that night.

Such a decision, thought Elsey, would look like panic on the part of the White House. It would be undignified, unbefitting the President. But as Elsey later recalled, "There *was* a degree of panic."

> There was concern that MacArthur might get wind of this and might make some grandstand gesture of his own. There were rumors flying around that he was going on a world-wide broadcast network. . . . And in effect, the White House was, I'm afraid, I'm sorry to say it, panicked by the fear that MacArthur might get the jump.

Meantime, something apparently had gone wrong with the transmission of the President's orders. Nothing had been heard from Muccio about their receipt.

Had George Marshall been present that night—or Charlie Ross—possibly things would have been handled differently.

Truman would remember Bradley "rushing over" to Blair House at a late hour. Actually, the time was just after ten and Bradley came accompanied by Harriman, Rusk, Joe Short, and Matt Connelly. By 10:30, Truman had decided.

Short telephoned Roger Tubby at the White House to have all the orders— those relieving MacArthur, as well as those naming Matthew Ridgway his successor—mimeographed as quickly as possible.

"He's not going to be allowed to quit on me," Truman is reported to have said. "He's going to be fired!" In his diary, Truman recorded dryly, "Discussed the situation and I ordered messages sent at once and directly to MacArthur."

From a small first-floor study in his Georgetown home, Dean Acheson began placing calls to Tom Connally, Les Biffle, and John Foster Dulles, to tell them what was about to happen. At the State Department, Rusk spent a long night telephoning the ambassadors of all the countries with troops in Korea. "Well, the little man finally did it, didn't he," responded the ambassador from New Zealand.

At the White House, switchboard operators began calling reporters at their homes to say there would be an extraordinary press conference at 1:00 A.M. And at 1:00 A.M. in the White House press room, Wednesday, April 11, Press Secretary Short handed out the mimeographed sheets.

Truman, in his second-floor bedroom at Blair House, was by then fast asleep.

General MacArthur learned of his recall while at lunch in Tokyo, when his wife handed him a brown Signal Corps envelope.

If Truman had only let him know how he felt, MacArthur would say privately a few hours later, he would have retired "without difficulty." Where the *Tribune* reporter got his tip was never learned. MacArthur would later testify that he had never given any thought to resigning.

According to what MacArthur had been told by an unnamed but "eminent" medical authority, Truman's "mental instability" was the result of malignant hypertension, "characterized by bewilderment and confusion of thought." Truman, MacArthur predicted, would be dead in six months.

TRUMAN FIRES MACARTHUR

The headline across the early edition of the Washington *Post,* April 11, 1951, was the headline everywhere in the country and throughout much of the world, with only minor variations. The reaction was stupendous, the outcry from the American people shattering. Truman had known he would have to face a storm, but however dark his premonitions, he could not possibly have measured what was coming. No one did, no one could have. One southern senator in the course of the day described the people in his part of the country as "almost hysterical." The senator himself was almost hysterical. So were scores of others on Capitol Hill and millions of Americans.

The day on Capitol Hill was described as "one of the bitterest . . . in modern times." Prominent Republicans, including Senator Taft, spoke angrily of impeaching the President. The full Republican leadership held an angry emergency meeting in Joe Martin's office at 9:30 in the morning, after which Martin talked to reporters of "impeachments," the accent on the plural. "We might want the impeachments of 1 or 50." A full-dress congressional investigation of the President's war policy was in order. General MacArthur, announced Martin, would be invited to air his views before a joint session of Congress.

Senator Nixon demanded MacArthur's immediate reinstatement. Senator Jenner declared the country was "in the hands of a secret coterie" directed by Russian spies. When, on the floor of the Senate, Jenner shouted, "Our only choice is to impeach President Truman and find out who is the secret invisible government which has so cleverly led our country down the road to destruction," the gallery broke into applause.

A freshman Democrat from Oklahoma, Senator Robert Kerr, rose to defend the President. If the Republicans believed the nation's security depended on following the policy of General MacArthur, Kerr said, then they should call for a declaration of war against Red China. Otherwise, Republican support of MacArthur was a mockery. Tom Connally reminded his colleagues that Americans had always insisted on civilian control over the military, and three Senate Republicans, Duff of Pennsylvania, Saltonstall and Lodge of Massachusetts, spoke in agreement.

But such voices were lost in a tempest of Republican outrage. The general's dismissal was "another Pearl Harbor," a "great day for the Russian Communists." MacArthur had been fired "because he told the truth." "God help the United States," said Senator James P. Kem, Republican of Missouri.

In New York two thousand longshoremen walked off their jobs in protest over the firing of MacArthur. A Baltimore women's group announced plans for a march on Washington in support of the general. Elsewhere enraged patriots flew flags at half-staff, or upside down. People signed petitions, fired off furious letters and telegrams to Washington. In Worcester, Massachusetts, and San Gabriel, California, Truman was burned in effigy. In Houston, a Protestant minister became so angry dictating a telegram to the White House that he died of a heart attack.

The legislatures of four states—Florida, Michigan, Illinois, and California—voted resolutions condemning the President's action, while the Los Angeles City Council adjourned for a day of "sorrowful contemplation of the political assassination of General MacArthur." In Chicago, in a front-page editorial, the *Tribune* called for immediate impeachment proceedings:

> President Truman must be impeached and convicted. His hasty and vindictive removal of Gen. MacArthur is the culmination of a series of acts which have shown that he is unfit, morally and mentally, for his high office. . . . The American nation has never been in a greater danger. It is led by a fool who is surrounded by knaves. . . .

"IMPEACH THE IMBECILE" . . . "IMPEACH THE LITTLE WARD POLITICIAN STUPIDITY FROM KANSAS CITY" . . . "SUGGEST YOU LOOK FOR ANOTHER HISS IN BLAIR HOUSE," read telegrams typical of those pouring into Washington. In the hallways of the Senate and House office buildings, Western Union messengers made their deliveries with bushel baskets. According to one tally, of the 44,358 telegrams received by Republicans in Congress during the first 48 hours following Truman's announcement, all but 334 condemned him or took the side of MacArthur, and the majority called for Truman's immediate removal from office.

Republicans were overjoyed. "This is the biggest windfall that has ever come to the Republican Party," exclaimed Senator Styles Bridges.

A number of prominent liberals—Eleanor Roosevelt, Walter Reuther, Justice William O. Douglas—publicly supported Truman. Douglas, who had told Truman as early as October that MacArthur should be fired, wrote, "In the days ahead you may need the strength of all your friends. This note is to let you know that I am and will be in your corner . . . I know you are right."

While by far the greatest clamor came from those in the country outraged over what Truman had done, there was no lack of conviction, even passion, among people who felt he was in the right, that a fundamental principle was at stake. And to many of these same people, how one felt about Harry Truman personally was immaterial.

"It makes not the slightest difference if Mr. Harry Truman is an ignorant person who never graduated from college, who once worked in a haberdashery shop, who was a protégé of one of our worst city bosses and came into the presidency through accident," the Reverend Dr. Duncan E.

Littlefair said in a sermon at the Fountain Street Baptist Church in Grand Rapids, Michigan.

> Neither does it make any difference if General MacArthur is a man of astounding personality, tremendous achievement, graduated first in his class in the great College of the Army and has had a distinguished career and has proven a wonderful administrator of the Japanese people or that we like him better than we do Harry S. Truman. Principle, *principle,* must always be above personality and it must be above expediency. The principle here we recognize . . . [is] that control of this country must come through the president and the departments that are organized under him and through Congress, and that any decision that comes from that person through those means is not to be dismissed because we don't like the personality who expressed it, nor is it to be overridden because we have a conquering hero. . . .

Another letter of support addressed to the President came from the Washington *Post* music critic, Paul Hume.

Throughout Europe, MacArthur's dismissal was greeted as welcome news. "MAC IS SACKED," declared the London *Evening Standard.* The French, reported Janet Flanner in *The New Yorker,* were "solidly for Truman." Not a single paper in Paris had failed to support his decision.

But most impressive was the weight of editorial opinion at home, despite vehement assaults in the McCormick, Hearst, and Scripps-Howard newspapers, or the renewed glorification of MacArthur in Henry Luce's *Time* and *Life.*

The Washington *Post, The New York Times,* the New York *Post,* the Baltimore *Sun,* the Atlanta *Journal,* the Miami *Daily News,* the Boston *Globe,* the Chicago *Sun-Times,* the Milwaukee *Journal,* the St. Louis *Post-Dispatch,* the Denver *Post,* the Seattle *Times,* the *Christian Science Monitor,* all these and more endorsed Truman's decision. Importantly the list also included such staunch Republican papers as the Des Moines *Register and Tribune* and the New York *Herald-Tribune,* which went out of its way to praise Truman as well for his strength of character:

> The most obvious fact about the dismissal of General MacArthur is that he virtually forced his own removal. In high policy as in war there is no room for a divided command. . . . General MacArthur is a soldier of the highest abilities . . . to lose his service and his talents is in a very true sense a tragedy for the nation, yet he is the architect of a situation which really left the President with no other course. With one of those strokes of boldness and decision which are characteristic of Mr. Tru-

man in emergencies, a very difficult and dangerous problem has been met in the only way it could have been met. . . .

In his "Today and Tomorrow" column, Walter Lippmann commended Truman and Marshall both for having "done their duty." And the working press, according to the *Saturday Review,* privately sided with Truman by a margin of six to one, though most reporters thought the dismissal had been poorly handled.

The clamor in the country, the outrage, the noisy hostility to Truman, the adulation of MacArthur continued, however, and would grow greater still when MacArthur made his triumphal return. Nothing had so stirred the political passions of the country since the Civil War.

At the heart of the tumult was anger and frustration over the war in Korea. Nobody liked it. Senator Wherry had begun calling it "Truman's War," and the name caught on. People were sick of Truman's War, frustrated and a bit baffled by talk of a "limited war." America didn't fight to achieve a stalemate, and the cost in blood had become appalling. If it was a United Nations effort, then the United States seemed to be bearing the heavy side of the burden. According to the latest figures, there were more than ten thousand Americans dead, another fifty thousand wounded or missing in action. The country wanted it over. MacArthur at least offered victory.

To a great part of the country MacArthur was a glorious figure, a real-life, proven American hero, the brilliant, handsome general who had led American forces to stunning triumph in the greatest of all wars wherein there had never been any objective but complete and total victory. "Douglas MacArthur was the personification of the big man . . . Harry Truman was almost a professional little man," wrote *Time* in a considerably less than unbiased attempt to appraise the national mood, but one that nonetheless applied to a large part of the populace. For someone of Truman's modest attainments, a man of his "stature," to have fired Douglas MacArthur seemed to many Americans an act smacking of insolence and vindictiveness, not to say dreadful judgment. Nor did the way it happened seem right. Reportedly, the firing had been carefully timed so as to make the morning papers "and catch the Republicans in bed." Rumors also attributed the announcement to another of Truman's dead-of-the-night temper tantrums, or heavy drinking. In a speech in Milwaukee, having called Truman a "son-of-a-bitch," Joe McCarthy charged that the decision had been influenced by "bourbon and Benedictine." Even to more fair-minded Republicans than McCarthy and others of the party's vociferous right wing—as to a great many Democrats—it seemed to have been a graceless, needlessly unkind way to terminate a great career. Who did "little Harry Truman" think he was?

Old admirers of Franklin Roosevelt speculated on how differently "the master politician" might have handled things—made MacArthur ambassador to the Court of St. James's, perhaps.

But in a larger way, for many, the firing of MacArthur was yet another of those traumatic turns of events of recent years—like the fall of China to Communist control, like the advent of the Russian bomb—that seemed to signal a world out of joint, a world increasingly hard to understand and threatening.

According to a Gallup Poll, 69 percent of the country backed General MacArthur. The fact that the country and nearly every leading Republican had strongly supported Truman's decision to go into Korea the previous June, the fact that in November MacArthur, the supreme military strategist, had presided over one of the worst debacles in American military history, or that only 30 percent of the country expressed a willingness to go to war with China, were all overlooked.

Truman was not to appear at a big public event until April 20—not until after MacArthur had made his return and appeared before Congress —and when he did, to throw out the first ball at the opening game at Griffith Stadium, he was booed to his face, something that had not happened since Herbert Hoover attended a ball game in 1931.

Except for a brief broadcast from the White House the night following his dismissal of MacArthur, April 11, Truman had maintained silence on the matter. General MacArthur was "one of our greatest military commanders," he told the nation, but the cause of world peace was far more important than any single individual.

> The change in commands in the Far East means no change whatever in the policy of the United States. We will carry on the fight in Korea with vigor and determination. . . . The new commander, Lieutenant General Matthew Ridgway, has already demonstrated that he has the great qualities of military leadership needed for this task.
>
> We are ready, at any time, to negotiate for a restoration of peace in the area. But we will not engage in appeasement. We are only interested in real peace. . . .
>
> We do not want to widen the conflict. . . .

He went about his schedule as though all were normal. On April 13, he had his picture taken as, smiling confidently, he began his seventh year in the Oval Office. One evening he and Bess went to the theater, another to see a British film of Offenbach's *Tales of Hoffman*.

MacArthur landed at San Francisco Tuesday, April 17, to a delirious reception. He had been away from the country for fourteen years. Until now, the American people had had no chance to see and cheer him, to welcome the hero home. Ten thousand were at the San Francisco airport. So great were the crowds on the way into the city, it took two hours for the motorcade to reach his hotel. "The only politics I have," MacArthur told a cheering throng, "is contained in a simple phrase known to all of you—God Bless America."

When Truman met with reporters the next day, April 18, at his first press conference since the start of the crisis, he dashed all their expectations by refusing to say anything on the subject. Scheduled to appear before the American Society of Newspaper Editors on Thursday, April 19, the day MacArthur was to go before Congress, Truman canceled his speech, because he felt it should be the general's day and did not wish anything to detract from it.

Only in a few personal letters did Truman touch on the matter, and then briefly, simply, and without apologies or complicated explanations. "I was sorry to have to reach a parting of the way with the big man in Asia," he wrote to Eisenhower, "but he asked for it and I had to give it to him."

There would be "hell to pay" for it for perhaps six or seven weeks, he told his staff and the Cabinet. But eventually people would come to their senses, including more and more Republican politicians who would grow doubtful of all-out support for the general. Given some time, MacArthur would be reduced to human proportions. Meanwhile, Truman could withstand the bombardment, for in the long run, he knew, he would be judged to have made the right decision. He had absolutely no doubt of that. "The American people will come to understand that what I did had to be done."

As a boost for failing spirits, someone circulated among the White House staff a mock "Schedule for Welcoming General MacArthur" to Washington:

12:30	Wades ashore from Snorkel submarine
12:31	Navy Band plays "Sparrow in the Treetop" and "I'll Be Glad When You're Dead You Rascal You"
12:40	Parade to the Capitol with General MacArthur riding an elephant
12:47	Be-heading of General Vaughan at the rotunda
1:00	General MacArthur addresses Members of Congress
1:30–1:49	Applause for General MacArthur
1:50	Burning of the Constitution

1:55	Lynching of Secretary Acheson
2:00	21-atomic bomb salute
2:30	300 nude D.A.R.s leap from Washington Monument
3:00	Basket lunch, Monument grounds

As it was, a cheering crowd of twelve thousand people waited until past midnight at National Airport to welcome MacArthur when his plane landed.

Secretary Marshall, General Bradley, and the Joint Chiefs were at the foot of the ramp to greet him, as Truman had agreed was only proper. But so also was Major General Vaughan, whose presence may have been Truman's idea of a small joke of his own.

At 12:31 P.M., Thursday, April 19, in a flood of television lights, Douglas MacArthur walked down the same aisle in the House of Representatives as had Harry Truman so often since 1945, and the wild ovation from the packed chamber, the intense, authentic drama of the moment, were such as few had ever beheld.

Neither the President's Cabinet, nor the Supreme Court, nor any of the Joint Chiefs were present.

Wearing a short "Eisenhower" jacket, without decoration, the silvery circles of five-star rank glittering on his shoulders, MacArthur paused to shake hands with Vice President Barkley, then stepped to the rostrum, his face "an unreadable mask." Only after complete silence had fallen did he begin.

"I address you with neither rancor nor bitterness in the fading twilight of life, with but one purpose in mind: to serve my country."

There was ringing applause and the low, vibrant voice continued, the speaker in full command of the moment.

The decision to intervene in support of the Republic of Korea had been sound from a military standpoint, MacArthur affirmed. But when he had called for reinforcements, he was told they were not available. He had "made clear," he said, that if not permitted to destroy the enemy bases north of the Yalu, if not permitted to utilize the 800,000 Chinese troops on Formosa, if not permitted to blockade the China coast, then "the position of the command from a military standpoint forbade victory. . . ." And war's "very object" was victory. How could it be otherwise? "In war, indeed," he said, repeating his favorite slogan, "there can be no substitute for victory. There were some who, for varying reasons, would appease Red China. They were blind to history's clear lesson, for history teaches, with unmistakable emphasis, that appeasement begets new and bloodier war."

He was provocative, and defiant. Resounding applause or cheers followed again and again—thirty times in thirty-four minutes. He said nothing of bombing China's industrial centers, as he had proposed. And though he said "every available means" should be applied to bring victory, he made no mention of his wish to use atomic bombs, or to lay down a belt of radioactivity along the Yalu. He had been severely criticized for his views, he said. Yet, he asserted, his views were "fully shared" by the Joint Chiefs—a claim that was altogether untrue and that brought a deafening ovation. Republicans and most spectators in the galleries leaped to their feet, cheering and stamping. It was nearly a minute before he could begin again.

To those who said American military strength was inadequate to face the enemy on more than one front, MacArthur said he could imagine no greater expression of defeatism. "You cannot appease or otherwise surrender to Communism in Asia without simultaneously undermining our efforts to halt its advance in Europe." To confine the war to Chinese aggression in Korea only was to follow a path of "prolonged indecision."

"Why, my soldiers asked of me, surrender military advantages to an enemy in the field?" He paused, then, softly, his voice almost a whisper, he said, "I could not answer."

A record 30 million people were watching on television and the performance was masterful. The use of the rich voice, the timing, surpassed that of most actors. The oratorical style was of a kind not heard in Congress in a very long time. It recalled, as one television critic wrote, "a yesteryear of the theater," and it held the greater part of the huge audience wholly enraptured. Work had stopped in offices and plants across the country, so people could watch. Saloons and bars were jammed. Schoolchildren saw the "historic hour" in classrooms or were herded into assemblies or dining halls to listen by radio. Whether they had any idea what the excitement was about, they knew it was "important."

"When I joined the Army, even before the turn of the century, it was the fulfillment of all my boyish hopes and dreams," MacArthur said, his voice dropping as he began the famous last lines, the stirring, sentimental, ambiguous peroration that the speech would be remembered for.

The hopes and dreams have long since vanished. But I still remember the refrain of one of the most popular barracks ballads of that day which proclaimed most proudly that, "Old soldiers never die. They just fade away." And like the old soldier of the ballad, I now close my military career and just fade away—an old soldier who tried to do his duty as God gave him the light to see that duty.

Goodbye.

A "hurricane of emotion" swept the room. Hands reached out to him. Many in the audience were weeping. "We heard God speak here today, God in the flesh, the voice of God!" exclaimed Republican Representative Dewey Short of Missouri, a former preacher. To Joe Martin, it was "the climaxing" of the most emotional moment he had known in thirty-five years in Congress. Theatrics were a part of the congressional way of life, Martin knew, but nothing had ever equaled this.

It was MacArthur's finest hour, and the crescendo of public adulation that followed, beginning with a triumphal parade through Washington that afternoon, and climaxing the next day in New York with a thunderous ticker-tape parade, was unprecedented in American history. Reportedly 7,500,000 people turned out in New York, more than had welcomed Eisenhower in 1945, more even than at the almost legendary welcome for Lindbergh in 1927. It was "awesome," wrote *Time*. "Everybody cheered . . . a man of chin-out affirmation, who seemed a welcome contrast to men of indecision and negation."

But, in fact, not everybody cheered. There were places along the parade route in New York where, as MacArthur's open car passed, people stood silently, just watching and looking, anything but pleased. In Washington, one senator had confided to a reporter that he had never feared more for his country than during MacArthur's speech. "I honestly felt that if the speech had gone on much longer there might have been a march on the White House." Even *Time* noted that while Republicans in Congress might consider MacArthur a godsend, few were ready to endorse his proposals.

Truman had not listened to MacArthur's speech, or watched on television. He had spent the time at his desk in the Oval Office, meeting with Dean Acheson as usual at that hour on Thursdays, after which he went back to Blair House for lunch and a nap. At some point, however, he did read what MacArthur had said. Speaking privately, he remarked that he thought it "a bunch of damn bullshit."

As Truman had anticipated, the tumult began to subside. For seven weeks in the late spring of 1951, the Senate Foreign Relations and Armed Services committees held joint hearings to investigate MacArthur's dismissal. Chaired by Democratic Senator Richard B. Russell, the inquiry opened on May 3 in the same marble Caucus Room, 318 of the Senate Office Building, where the Truman Committee had conducted its sessions. Though the hearings were closed, authorized transcripts of each day's sessions, edited for military security reasons, were released hourly to the press.

MacArthur, the first witness, testified for three days, arguing that his way in Korea was the way to victory and an end to the slaughter. He had seen as much blood and disaster as any man alive, he told the senators, but never such devastation as during his last time in Korea. "After I looked at that wreckage and those thousands of women and children and everything, I vomited. Now are you going to let that go on . . .?" The politicians in Washington had introduced a "new concept into military operations— the concept of appeasement," its purpose only "to go on indefinitely . . . indecisively, fighting with no mission. . . ."

But he also began to sound self-absorbed and oddly disinterested in global issues. He would admit to no mistakes, no errors of judgment. Failure to anticipate the size of the Chinese invasion, for example, had been the fault of the CIA. Any operation he commanded was crucial, other considerations were always of less importance. Certain that his strategy of war on China would not bring in the Soviets, he belittled the danger of a larger conflict. But what if he happened to be wrong, he was asked. What if another world war resulted? That, said MacArthur, was not his responsibility. "My responsibilities were in the Pacific, and the Joint Chiefs of Staff and various agencies of the Government are working night and day for an over-all solution to the global problem. Now I am not familiar with their studies. I haven't gone into it. . . ." To many, it seemed he had made the President's case.

The great turning point came with the testimony of Marshall, Bradley, and the Joint Chiefs, who refuted absolutely MacArthur's claim that they agreed with his strategy. Truman, from the start of the crisis, had known he needed the full support of his military advisers before declaring his decision on MacArthur. Now it was that full support, through nineteen days of testimony, that not only gave weight and validity to the decision, but discredited MacArthur in a way nothing else could have.

Speaking solemnly, Marshall began by saying it was "a very distressing necessity, a very distressing occasion that compels me to appear here this morning and in effect in almost direct opposition to a great many views and actions of General MacArthur. He is a brother Army officer, a man for whom I have tremendous respect. . . ."

The administration was not turning its back on an easy victory in Korea, Marshall said, because there could be no easy or decisive victory in Korea short of another world war. The present policy might indeed seem costly, but not compared to an atomic war. There had been complaints of stalemate, demands for quick, decisive solutions at the time of the Berlin crisis, too, he reminded the senators. The war in Korea was in its tenth month, but the Berlin crisis had lasted almost fifteen months before ending in a "notable victory."

Just what did Secretary Marshall consider the "Korean business," he was asked. "A police action? A large or small war? . . ."

"I would characterize it as a limited war which I hope will remain limited," Marshall replied evenly.

Bradley, his first day in the witness chair, testified with unexpected vigor and delivered a telling blow with what would be the most quoted line of the hearings. MacArthur's program to step up and widen the war with China, Bradley said, would "involve us in the wrong war, at the wrong place, at the wrong time, and with the wrong enemy."

Never, said the Joint Chiefs, had they subscribed to MacArthur's plan for victory, however greatly they admired him.

From a purely military standpoint, General Collins was asked, had General MacArthur's conduct of the war in Korea been compatible with General MacArthur's outstanding conduct of the war in the Pacific from 1941 to 1945? That, said Collins, was a question he would prefer not to answer, and no one insisted.

The dismissal of MacArthur, said all of them—Marshall, Bradley, the Joint Chiefs—was more than warranted, it was a necessity. Given the circumstances, given the seriousness of MacArthur's opposition to the policy of the President, his challenge to presidential authority, said Marshall, there had been "no other course but to relieve him."

The fidelity of the military high command to the principle of civilian control of the military was total and unequivocal.

Such unanimity of opinion on the part of the country's foremost and most respected military leaders seemed to leave Republican senators stunned. As James Reston wrote in *The New York Times,* "MacArthur, who had started as the prosecutor, had now become the defendant."

The hearings ground on and grew increasingly dull. The MacArthur hysteria was over, interest waned. When in June, MacArthur set off on a speaking tour through Texas, insisting he had no presidential ambitions, he began to sound more and more shrill and vindictive, less and less like a hero. He attacked Truman, appeasement, high taxes, and "insidious forces working from within." His crowds grew steadily smaller. Nationwide, the polls showed a sharp decline in his popular appeal. The old soldier was truly beginning to fade away.

The furor of the MacArthur crisis had taken a heavy toll. It had spread confusion and increasing doubt about the war in Korea, increasing skepticism about the leadership in Washington and particularly about the President himself. Politically, the damage to the administration and to the Democratic Party had been serious. Even among Truman's strongest supporters, he was criticized for both the way the dismissal had been handled and for failing to convince the country that he was right. Where was the eloquence, the power of "the bully pulpit" of the presidency when it was so desperately needed? "Having made this courageous decision, Truman failed to mobilize the country behind him," Bradley would write in retrospect. Truman's address to the nation the night of the MacArthur dismissal had been, in Bradley's estimate, "a complete flop."

A Gallup Poll in late May showed that while support for MacArthur had dropped to 30 percent, support for Marshall and Bradley was only 19 percent, and three out of four of those polled regarded the MacArthur hearings as "just politics."

Many then, and more in time to come, would say that Truman's biggest mistake had been not firing the general months before, a view with which Truman himself wholeheartedly concurred.

Truman would regard the decision as among the most important he made as President. He did not, however, agree with those who said it had shown what great courage he had. (Harriman, among others, would later speak of it as one of the most courageous steps ever taken by any President.) "Courage didn't have anything to do with it," Truman would say emphatically. "General MacArthur was insubordinate and I fired him. That's all there was to it."

But if the firing of MacArthur had taken a heavy toll politically, if Truman as President had been less than a master of persuasion, he had accomplished a very great deal and demonstrated extraordinary patience and strength of character in how he rode out the storm. His policy in Korea—his determined effort to keep the conflict in bounds—had not been scuttled, however great the aura of the hero-general, or his powers as a spellbinder. The principle of civilian control over the military, challenged as never before in the nation's history, had survived, and stronger than ever. The President had made his point and, with the backing of his generals, he had made it stick.

"Truman's conflict with MacArthur," wrote Dean Rusk, "was more than a clash of egos or contest of wills; Truman was concerned about the presidency. . . . I am convinced that 95 percent of Truman's decision to fire MacArthur hinged on the relationship of the president as the Commander in Chief to his general and on civilian control of the military."

MacArthur did truly believe that he was above the President. MacArthur himself later told the historian Samuel Eliot Morison that a theater commander should be allowed to act independently, with no orders from the President, the United Nations, or anyone; then, to be sure that there could be no mistaking his meaning, MacArthur repeated the statement.

President Harry S. Truman was President and Commander in Chief still, and he was Harry S. Truman still, anything but disconsolate or defeated.

Already, before the Senate hearings ended, he had reemerged and begun fighting back in his own way, sounding often as he had in the 1948 campaign. Speaking at an Armed Forces Day dinner on May 18 at the Statler, Truman reminded his full-dress audience that even as "we sit here tonight . . . partaking of food on white tablecloths and enjoying ourselves . . . there are men fighting and dying . . . to reach that peace for which we have been striving since World War II. . . . You must quit your bickering here at home . . . you must quit playing petty politics. . . ."

Of the war in Korea, he said, "We are fighting for time . . . for us. There is always an emphasis on the casualties in Korea. . . . But did it ever occur to you that [they] will be one small drop in the bucket from one of those horrible bombs of which we talk so much.

"Think—think—think," he said, his voice low, almost shaking, "what a responsibility your President faces. If you would think, and think clearly, you would get behind me and help win this peace. . . . It is up to you."

If "victory" in Korea meant risking a world war—a war of atomic bombs—Truman would settle for no victory in Korea. That was the line he had drawn. There was a substitute for victory: it was peace. And he would stand by his policy of limited war for that specific objective.

"And look at the alternatives these critics have to present," he said in a speech at Tullahoma, Tennessee.

> Here is what they say. Take a chance on spreading the conflict in Korea. Take a chance on tying up all our resources in a vast war in Asia. Take a chance on losing our allies in Europe. Take a chance the Soviet Union won't fight in the Far East. Take a chance we won't have a third world war. They want us to play Russian roulette with the foreign policy of the United States—with all the chambers of the pistol loaded.
>
> This is not a policy. . . . No president who has any sense of responsibility for the welfare of this great country is going to meet the grave issues of war and peace on such a foolish basis as that.

In the same speech, delivered June 25, almost a year to the day since his decision to go into Korea, he said, in effect, that he was ready to negotiate a settlement of the war at the 38th parallel.

Russia's deputy foreign minister, Jacob Malik, had just proposed a Korean armistice. At Tullahoma, Truman gave the Soviets his fast answer.

"We are ready to join in a peaceful settlement in Korea now, just as we have always been."

17

Final Days

I have tried to give it everything that was in me.

—TRUMAN

I

In the summer of his seventh year in office, the sixty-seven-year-old President looked the picture of health. His color was good; his clothes, impeccable as always, fit perfectly; his walk was firm and full of purpose. He saw people all day, yet seemed to have time for everyone. Visitors to the Oval Office found a man who stood immediately to greet them, shoulders back and smiling, and who, at his desk, gave them his full attention. Radiating vitality and confidence, he seemed completely at home in his job, as one could only be with experience. *Mens sana in corpore sano* was the old adage he had learned in high school Latin, "a sound mind in a sound body." Clark Clifford, who dropped by on occasion, would say he never knew anyone of the President's age who remained physically and psychologically so sound and solid.

He still walked two miles "most every morning," Truman had recorded in his diary.

> I eat no bread but one piece of toast at breakfast, no butter, no sugar, no sweets. Usually have fruit, one egg, a strip of bacon and half a glass of skimmed milk for breakfast; liver and bacon or sweet breads or ham or fish and spinach and another nonfattening vegetable for lunch with fruit for dessert. For dinner I have a fruit cup, steak, a couple of non-fattening vegetables and an ice, orange, pineapple or raspberry . . . So —I maintain my waist line and can wear suits bought in 1935!

The morning bourbon—an ounce of Old Grandad or Wild Turkey taken after the two-mile walk and a few setting-up exercises and the rubdown that usually followed the morning walk—had also become routine. Whether the bourbon was on doctor's orders, or a bit of old-fashioned home medicine of the kind many of his generation thought beneficial to the circulation past age sixty ("to get the engine going"), is not known. But it seemed to agree with him.

And how Harry Truman looked, how he carried himself, the timbre of his voice, his air of confidence were all subjects of increasing interest in the summer of 1951, once the MacArthur crisis had passed, as a means of divining whether he intended to carry on in the job beyond the next election. Did he or did he not plan to run again in 1952?

At a press conference, a visiting reporter from Macon, Georgia, said with a drawl, "Mr. President, this is my first conference. My impression of you is that you look a lot younger than I thought you would." With everyone in the room, Truman laughed.

"Could you tell me if you feel like you are in better physical condition now than you were when you first became President?"

He never felt better, Truman said, looking pleased. "I am still young enough to make a good race—foot race, I mean." And there was more laughter.

"That wouldn't be an announcement, would it?"

"No, no."

To those at the White House who saw him daily, at all hours and often under extremely trying circumstances, he was still the Truman of old, hardworking, cheerful, never short with them, never petty. He seemed to have some kind of added inner balance mechanism that held him steady through nearly anything, enabling him not only to uphold the fearful responsibilities of his office and keep a killing schedule, but to accept with composure the small, silly aggravations that also went with the job. It was a level of equanimity that at times left those around him hugely amused and even more fond of him.

At still another banquet at the Statler one evening, the head table waiters managed to confuse the orders they had about a special meal for Joe Short, who had ulcers. It was Truman who was served a bowl of milk toast, which he ate without complaint, thinking that perhaps Dr. Graham had requested it for him.

One day on the *Williamsburg,* Graham sat on the fantail dictating into a recording machine, his lap full of letters, mostly inquiries about the President's health, his weight, diet, manner of exercise. Truman walked over, picked up the letters from Graham's lap, and threw them overboard. "You constantly tell me to relax. Now you relax," Truman said laughing.

His resilient cheerfulness was both a wonder and, to some who worked with him, disconcerting at times. It was almost as though he did not fully understand how serious his troubles were, how truly grim and menacing his horizons appeared, even with the MacArthur crisis out of the way. Only in the eyes, behind the thick glasses, could the fatigue sometimes be seen. Only on rare off moments would he say something to suggest how much else he felt.

Once, while paying a visit to the office of the engineer in charge of the White House renovation, General Glen E. Edgerton, whose desk was in a shack on the South Lawn amid a cluster of temporary buildings put up when the work began, Truman had paused to read a framed verse on the wall. Written for Edgerton by a plumbing contractor named Reuben Anderson, it so appealed to Truman that he read it aloud:

> *Every man's a would be sportsman, in the dreams of his intent,*
> *A potential out-of-doors man when his thoughts are pleasure bent.*
> *But he mostly puts the idea off, for the things that must be done,*
> *And doesn't get his outing till his outing days are gone.*
> *So in hurry, scurry, worry, work, his living days are spent,*
> *And he does his final camping in a low green tent.*

"Hurry, scurry, worry, work!" Truman sighed. "That's the way it is."

Another day, in September, riding in his limousine on the way to make a speech to a gathering of churchmen, he again sighed and said that sometimes he wondered if it was all worth the effort.

Though peace talks had begun in Korea, at Kaesong on July 8, the war was grinding on with unabated savagery. Joe McCarthy continued to spew charges of treason and espionage, the worst of his venom aimed now at George Marshall. Congress was stalling on a raise in taxes to pay for the war, threatening to cut foreign aid, and there were new charges of further scandal within the administration. Earlier, in the lull after the MacArthur hysteria, Herb Block, in a Washington *Post* cartoon titled "The tumult and the shouting dies; the captains and the kings depart," had shown Truman working alone into the night, his desk piled with reports labeled "Korea," "Europe," "A-Bomb," "H-Bomb," "Troops," "Planes," "United Nations," "Economic Program," "Peace," and "War." In the time since his burdens had only increased.

By midsummer, American troops had been fighting and dying in Korea for as long nearly as Truman and his generation had fought and died in France in World War I, and the struggle in Korea had become increasingly like World War I. The seesaw swings of fortune, the sweeping end runs and pellmell retreats and advances, were past now, the fighting concentrated near or along the 38th parallel. Some of the bloodiest, most desperate battles of the war were fought for limited topographical features —a numbered hilltop or ridgeline—where often, as in France in 1918, the enemy was heavily dug in, fortified with barbed wire, mines, and elaborately camouflaged tunnels. Newspapers and news broadcasts were filled with accounts of the Battle of Hill 1179, Bloody Ridge, Heartbreak Ridge. American casualties ran sometimes as high as three thousand a week, never less than three hundred. By late August the peace talks had broken down. By summer's end total American casualties had passed 80,000, with 13,822 dead. Losses among the ROK and other U.N. forces were greater still. What the costs had been to the enemy in dead and wounded, or to the people of Korea, were as yet undetermined.

The war Truman had never wanted or expected, but knew to be of utmost importance to the future of the world—the most important decision of his presidency, he believed—had come to overshadow his whole second term. He knew what the reality was in Korea. "I know what a soldier goes through," he would say with feeling. He knew the anguish of families at home. But when would it end? Who could say? What could he do that he was not already doing? The worries and frustrations were incessant.

One August morning at Blair House, he read in the papers that the body of an American soldier killed in action, Sergeant John Rice, had been brought home for burial in Sioux City, Iowa, but that at the last moment, as the casket was to be lowered into the grave, officials of the Sioux City Memorial Park had stopped the ceremony because Sergeant Rice, a Winnebago Indian, was not "a member of the Caucasian race" and burial was therefore denied. Outraged, Truman picked up the phone. Within minutes, by telephone and telegram, it was arranged that Sergeant Rice would be buried in Arlington National Cemetery with full military honors and that an Air Force plane was on the way to bring his widow and three children to Washington. That, as President, was the least he could do.

The scourge of Joe McCarthy, that Truman had thought would end soon, was poisoning the entire political atmosphere all the while. McCarthy's attack on Marshall from the floor of the Senate in mid-June was his most vile yet, a wild harangue lasting nearly three hours. The "mysterious, powerful" Marshall and Dean Acheson were part of a Communist conspiracy, a conspiracy of infamy so immense, said McCarthy, that it surpassed any "such venture" in history. It was Marshall who had created the disastrous China policy, Marshall whose military strategy had made the war in Korea a pointless slaughter. Harry Truman, no longer master of his house, was being guided by a "larger conspiracy, the world-wide web of which has been spun in Moscow." In the final hour of the speech McCarthy was addressing a virtually empty chamber—all but three senators had walked out. The press deplored these "senseless and vicious charges," but McCarthy carried on, traveling the country. He still had no evidence. He exposed not a single Communist in government. Yet none of that seemed to matter, as he shouted and threatened and waved fistfuls of so-called "documentation."

One night in the dining room at Blair House, Truman had called a secret meeting attended by Attorney General McGrath, four Democratic senators—Anderson, Monroney, Hennings, and Sparkman—a veteran Kentucky congressman named Brent Spence, Solicitor General Philip B. Perlman, Democratic Party Chairman William Boyle, Clark Clifford, who again sat in, and the author John Hersey as a kind of witness to history. Truman wanted confidential advice. What could be done about McCarthy?

As Hersey would recall, Truman gave a "pithy and bitter" summary of McCarthy's methods—"his hectoring and innuendo, his horrors and dirty tricks . . . his bully's delight in the ruin of innocents." All this was tearing the country apart, Truman said. But what antidote could he as President use against such poison?

Senator Clinton Anderson mentioned a "devastating" dossier that had been assembled on McCarthy, complete with details on his bedmates over the years, enough to "blow Senator McCarthy's whole show sky high." Suggestions were made that the material be leaked to the press. But Truman smacked the table with the flat of his hand, and as Hersey remembered, "His third-person self spoke in outrage; the President wanted no more such talk."

Three pungent comments of Harry Truman's on the proposal that had just been made have stuck in my mind ever since [Hersey would write]. This was their gist:

You must not ask the President of the United States to get down in the gutter with a guttersnipe.

Nobody, not even the President of the United States, can approach too close to a skunk, in skunk territory, and expect to get anything out of it except a bad smell.

If you think somebody is telling a big lie about you, the only way to answer is with the whole truth.

Now repeatedly at press conferences when asked his views on the senator or the influence of McCarthyism, Truman, though plainly seething, would answer only, "No comment."

Marshall, too, refused to respond, saying privately that if at this point in his life he had to explain that he was not a traitor, then it was hardly worth the effort.

To what degree the attacks by McCarthy influenced Marshall's decision to retire is not clear. But on September 12, with great reluctance, Truman announced that the Secretary of Defense was stepping down for the final time, the extraordinary career was over. No man, said Truman, had ever given his country more distinguished and patriotic service.

There was a gathering sense of strong, central figures leaving the stage. Arthur Vandenberg had died of cancer in the spring. Admiral Forrest Sherman, Chief of Naval Operations and one of the keenest and best of Truman's military advisers, dropped dead of a heart attack in August. Now Marshall, Truman's "strong tower," was departing.

Nor were Truman's days in the West Wing quite the same without Charlie Ross. Press secretary Joe Short was highly professional, but a taut, intense man, very different from the gentle, wise Ross. The only one left on the staff who came close to filling Ross's place in Truman's affections was Bill Hassett, the correspondence secretary, who was of the same generation as Truman, and whose kind-hearted outlook, interest in history, and sense of humor greatly appealed to Truman. Hassett would bring him funny items clipped from magazines, joke with him about the endless obligatory letters that had to be cranked out to every conceivable kind of organization, the absurd proclamations that were called for. And from years of experience as a Vermont newspaperman and working for Roosevelt, Hassett had his own kind of wisdom to contribute. But Hassett was seventy-one years old and an alcoholic, as Truman knew.

With charges of scandal—mounting evidence of favoritism, outright corruption—filling the headlines again, the whole atmosphere in the West Wing grew increasingly strained. Joe Short, Roger Tubby, George Elsey, and Bill Hassett were seething with indignation over the damage done by the "chiselers" within. They saw the President being used by so-called loyal associates for their own pernicious ends, and his continuing tolerance of them could only mean shame and trouble ahead, not just for Truman but for the Democratic Party.

"My house is always clean," Truman had said at a press conference in March. Somehow, he seemed incapable of imagining any of his people doing anything illegal or dishonorable. The accusations and innuendo coming from the Hill, the reports in the papers were all exaggerated, Truman insisted.

"He tended to live a day at a time and do the best he could each day as it came along," George Elsey remembered. "Maybe it was the farmer in him. You go out and do the day's work."

. . .

In February 1951 a Senate subcommittee chaired by Arkansas Democrat J. William Fulbright had issued a preliminary report called *Study of Reconstruction Finance Corporation: Favoritism and Influence* that implied misconduct in the operations of the Reconstruction Finance Corporation (RFC), which dispensed low-interest government loans to business. Among those implicated were Democratic Party Chairman William Boyle, White House aide Donald Dawson, who was Truman's administrative assistant in charge of personnel, and a former RFC examiner and friend of Dawson's named E. Merl Young, whose wife, Loretta, also worked at the White House, as an assistant to Rose Conway, Truman's secretary.

The implication was of an influence ring, the power of which stemmed directly from the White House itself. Newspaper accounts indicated that Boyle and Dawson both had been unduly active in support of loan applicants. Dawson, reportedly, had exercised "considerable influence" over certain RFC directors, even "tried to dominate" the agency. But the one mentioned most frequently and who attracted the most attention was E. Merl Young. Though he was no relation to Truman, Young, for years, had allowed people to think he was, supposedly through Truman's grandparents, Solomon and Harriet Louisa Young, and the odd part was that Young looked enough like Truman to be taken for his son. As a high-paid, fast-talking Washington "expeditor," Young traded on his former association with the RFC, his friendship with Dawson; and as now disclosed he had lately given his wife, the White House stenographer, a $9,540 pastel mink coat paid for by the attorney for a firm that received an RFC loan. Overnight the mink coat, like Harry Vaughan's deep freezers, became a symbol of corruption in the Truman White House. The fact that Boyle, Dawson, and E. Merl Young were also all from Missouri—like Vaughan, like Wallace Graham, who had had his troubles earlier over speculation on grain futures—served not only to renew old charges of "government by crony," but to recall Truman's past connections to the Pendergast machine.

After careful study of the "peculiar Washington species known as the influence peddlers," wrote *Time,* the Senate investigating subcommittee had discovered some distinctive markings and characteristics:

> The finest specimens claim Missouri as their habitat, have at least a nodding acquaintance with Harry Truman, a much chummier relationship with his aides and advisers, and can buzz in and out of the White House at will. They also have a great fondness for crisp currency.

Truman denounced the report, called it "asinine," because while its insinuations were in effect serious charges, it also piously stressed that no charges were being made. "Well, now," he told reporters, recalling his own experience as head of a Senate investigating committee, "when I made a report to the Congress, I made specific charges if I thought they were necessary." But like his dismissal of the Hiss case as a "red herring," the word "asinine" struck sparks, infuriating Senator Fulbright, who announced he would begin public hearings. Nor did Truman improve matters by portraying Fulbright as "an overeducated S.O.B."

Truman had somebody from the White House staff make a fast check of RFC correspondence and was told, as he had anticipated, that the RFC files contained hundreds of "pressure letters" from members of Congress, including a number from Fulbright himself and Senator Paul Douglas of Illinois, another Democrat on the investigating committee. (Douglas, quickly checking his own files, found three such letters, which he immediately read into the record, conceding that probably he had "gone too far.") His temper up, Truman put through a call to the Capitol and had Senator Charles Tobey of New Hampshire, the leading Republican on the committee, summoned away from an executive session. Tobey, a veteran on the Hill, was a man Truman had long liked and admired, but now Truman angrily warned him to watch his step. Paul Douglas would later write that Tobey returned from the call looking pale and solemn. Truman had told him the "real crooks and influence peddlers" were members of the committee, as they might soon find out.

But when Democrats Fulbright and Douglas went to the White House to meet with Truman, to urge him to "clean house" and allow Dawson to testify before the committee, they found him disarmingly subdued.

"You have been loyal to friends who have not been loyal to you," said Douglas, who would remember the silence that followed as Truman turned in his chair and looked sadly out the window at the slanting rain.

"I guess you are right," he said softly.

In May, Truman put Stuart Symington in as head of the RFC and Symington moved expeditiously to straighten things out.

There was an increasing sense nationwide that the moral fabric was breaking down all about. For a year now, Democratic Senator Estes Kefauver of Tennessee had been staging televised hearings in one city after another, looking into activities of organized crime, and the testimony of such big-time underworld figures as Joe Adonis and Frank Costello had caused a sensation.

"You bastards. I hope a goddamn atom bomb falls on every goddamn one of you," said the girlfriend of gangster Bugsy Siegel, Virginia Hill

Hauser, who wore a $5,000 silver-blue mink stole the day of her appearance before the Kefauver Committee.

The New York advertising firm of Young & Rubicam took a full page in the newspapers to register concern:

> With staggering impact, the telecasts of the Kefauver investigation have brought a shocked awakening to millions of Americans.
>
> Across their television tubes have paraded the honest and dishonest, the frank and the furtive, the public servant and the public thief. Out of many pictures has come a broader picture of the sordid intermingling of crime and politics, of dishonor in public life.
>
> And suddenly millions of Americans are asking:
>
> What's happened to our ideals of right and wrong? . . .
>
> What's happened to our principles of honesty in government?
>
> What's happened to public and private standards of morality?

That summer of 1951 came the shocking news that ninety West Point cadets, including a large part of the Army football team, were expelled for cheating on examinations. Truman was sickened by the West Point scandal. It made him feel discouraged, he said, in a way nothing else had in a long time. When other colleges began making offers to the dismissed football players, he felt even worse.

As time passed and Dawson, Young, and Boyle testified on the Hill, along with scores of others, it often became difficult to distinguish truth from hearsay, or to tell how much that had gone on was illegal or only an impropriety, or old-fashioned, petty political wangling and stockjobbing. Corporations of questionable stability had been propped up or rescued by multi-million-dollar RFC loans, and too often, it appeared, because of political influence. A director of the RFC named Walter L. Dunham testified that Donald Dawson had told him to clear all top personnel matters of the RFC with the White House, and Dunham's telephone log showed 45 calls from or about Dawson, 151 calls from Bill Boyle or his office, mostly all to urge Dunham to see some "very dear friend" or other on an RFC matter. Yet Dunham also stressed that Dawson had never tried to influence him on an RFC loan.

Dawson, in his turn, insisted he had done no wrong. Acknowledging that he had stayed without charge at a Miami hotel on three different occasions, Dawson said he understood this was a common practice, that even some senators were on the hotel's free list, a point no one on the committee chose to press. A handsome man with a smooth, ingratiating manner, Dawson gave the appearance of someone who definitely knew his way around, yet claimed he never realized that the Miami hotel had a

$1.5 million RFC loan. "I did nothing improper, but I would not do it again," said Dawson. In conclusion, Senator Fulbright assured Dawson that the object of the hearings was not to embarrass him. "You were sort of a necessary background," Fulbright said. As Senator Douglas later conceded, Dawson made a "good showing," only "minor peccadilloes" were proved against him.

While the RFC hearings continued, a House committee began investigations of irregularities in the tax administration, looking into charges of bribes, shakedowns, and gross negligence.

To his staff, Truman said it was all politics and all aimed at him. He could not see that either Dawson or Boyle had done anything seriously out of line and refused even to reprimand them. He liked people, he told Bill Hassett privately, and was loath ever to think of anyone as evil or unredeemable.

"Mr. President," Joe Short warned, "I don't think this business is going to blow over."

Meanwhile, Merl Young, who, because of his wife, had a White House pass, would breeze in cheerfully after work to pick her up. Seeing Young one evening, Roger Tubby had a momentary urge to slam into him. "He was dressed in flashy sport clothes and talked almost gaily to Officer Ken Burke at the door," Tubby wrote later, still angry.

It was the appearance of wrongdoing, the presence of someone like Merl Young at the White House, that Truman seemed unwilling to respond to with appropriate action, and the appearance of wrongdoing, whether representative or not, only grew worse.

In July the St. Louis *Post-Dispatch* broke a story charging that Bill Boyle had received $8,000 for arranging a half-million-dollar RFC loan for a St. Louis printing firm, the American Lithofold Corporation, and that part of the fee had been paid after Boyle became chairman of the Democratic Party.

"Ah, me," wrote Roger Tubby, after returning to the White House from a vacation. "I wonder if this is all as bad as it appears—yes—then, is it as bad or worse than the stuff which goes on in every presidency?" Tubby was forty, a bright, idealistic Yale graduate and former Vermont newspaper reporter who had been a press aide at the State Department before coming to the White House and who in the time since had become devoted to Truman. Like his predecessor as assistant press secretary, Eben Ayers, Tubby was keeping a diary. He was also a great worrier, with premonitions of Truman ending up, as some critics were saying, like Warren G. Harding. "Poker, poker, I wonder why he played so much," Tubby had commented on Truman in his diary at Key West in April, "a feeling of vacuum otherwise, no struggle, excitement? . . . companionship, banter, escape from the pressing problems of state?" Now Tubby wrote:

T[ruman] has to take strong action to save himself. . . . There are rumors of new exposés in Internal Revenue—let the W[hite] H[ouse] take the lead in checking and cleaning up, instead of appearing to be forced to action as in RFC business. Check, then fire Boyle. Lay about with a good broom. It probably won't be done—probably too late anyhow . . . to do good politically . . . never too late otherwise.

In Vermont for two weeks—yes, guess that's right, Truman and Acheson made good decisions. BUT WHAT ABOUT THE MINK COAT? WHAT ABOUT THAT LETTER TO THE MUSIC CRITIC?

So he has an Achilles heel, maybe two of 'em. But he fights doggedly on for the right things. But why, why, why doesn't he make it easier for himself, for all of us, really, in the world?

Another day, Tubby would write of the President, "He does not like to dwell upon the weakness and foibles of his party, or even of the GOP—he is a builder, looking far into the future. . . ."

Once when he had served as budget director, prior to becoming Secretary of the Army, Frank Pace had asked the President why he continued to tolerate the influence of machine politicians on his administration, and Truman, with a chuckle, had replied, "Frank, you make a splendid director of the budget, but a lousy politician."

For Truman, the attack on Boyle was cutting close to the bone. He had known Boyle since Boyle was a child in Kansas City, growing up in a prosperous Irish Catholic family where politics was a life force. Boyle's mother, Clara, had been a Pendergast precinct worker, an energetic, God-fearing woman still honored and respected in Kansas City, and someone Truman greatly admired, calling her "one of the best Democrats Missouri ever produced." By age sixteen Boyle had organized a Young Democrats Club in the city's affluent Fourth Ward, and until now he had never been accused of misconduct or dishonesty. Truman liked him. He had put Boyle in one job after another over the years, and from the time Truman first brought him to Washington, as an assistant counsel for the Truman Committee, Boyle had remained a staunch, resourceful enthusiast, working hard for the Roosevelt-Truman ticket in 1944 and harder still for the Truman campaign in 1948, while between times prospering as a Washington lawyer. Boyle was commonly credited as one of the "masterminds" of Truman's upset victory in 1948. Once Truman installed him as chairman of the Democratic National Committee he became truly, as the papers said, a political power-house.

No one seeing Bill Boyle in the lobby of the Mayflower or the Statler would have had trouble guessing his occupation. A well-dressed, six-foot, fleshy "good fellow" with a round Irish face, he was the picture of a professional politician. He had a "nice way" about him, an "index card memory" for names, and though not known for efficiency or a particularly sharp mind, he knew politics from experience in a way that others, like most of Truman's staff, never would. He talked the language, he had "the feel."

Boyle's chief trouble was with alcohol, and this had infuriated Truman more than once in times past. On the night of the 1944 presidential election, Boyle had been one of those in the suite at the Muehlebach who got so drunk that Bess and Margaret left in disgust. "Your views on Mr. Boyle and the other middle-aged soaks are exactly correct," Truman had written to Margaret afterward, apologetically.

I like people who can control their appetites and their mental balance. When that isn't done I hope you will scratch them off your list. It is a shame about Boyle. I picked him up off the street in Kansas City, because I thought he'd been mistreated by the people out there for whom he'd worked. He had the chance of a lifetime to become a real leader in politics and to have made a great name for himself. John Barleycorn got the best of him and so far as I'm concerned I can't trust him again. . . .

But Truman had not scratched him from his own list, he did trust Boyle again, and remained genuinely fond of him. "Bill's all right! Don't let anybody tell you differently!" he had told those gathered for a huge black-tie dinner in Boyle's honor at the Kansas City Municipal Auditorium in September 1949. Truman and Barkley both had flown from Washington for the occasion. "All these are friends to tie to," Truman had continued, sparkling with warmth for Boyle, McGrath, and Bob Hannegan, his three party chairmen since becoming President. "They are there when you need them, and that's the kind of friends I like to have around me." It was the old professional creed—politics as a matter of friends—and his Kansas City audience gave a roar of approval.

But conspicuously present among the more than two thousand at the dinner had been several well-known North Side gamblers, including the ruling Kansas City racketeer of the day, Charles Binnagio, who only months later was shot to death in a gangland killing reminiscent of the city in its worst days. The press had taken careful note of such "friends" present to honor Boyle, just as the press highlighted the fact that Binnagio had been gunned down in a Democratic clubhouse located on Truman Road and that his bullet-riddled body fell beneath a poster-sized portrait of President Harry S. Truman.

To many on the White House staff Boyle now looked like a very large liability.

"So Boyle is not only stupid and inefficient, but also, it seems, a crook," wrote Roger Tubby, so angry he could hardly contain himself.

He should of course resign, or offer his resignation. But these chiselers who use, and who do terrible damage to, the President don't resign. He should be fired as soon as the President is satisfied there has been wrong doing. . . . The important thing is that the President be saved from his friends.

Bill Hassett urged Truman to rid himself of Boyle without delay. "Your friends will destroy you," Hassett pleaded.

"It's all right, Bill," Truman said, as if trying to calm a child. "It's all right."

Truman quietly ordered a confidential investigation by Charlie Murphy, his precise, scrupulously honest counselor whose importance was far greater than generally understood. Murphy's report was ready by midsummer, and at a subsequent press conference, Truman said he would stand by Boyle. No one connected with the Democratic National Committee ought ever to take fees for favors or services, Truman said, and it was his impression that Boyle had not. "I have the utmost confidence in Mr. Boyle. And I believe the statements that he made to me."

In his memorandum, Murphy reported that a thorough search of the RFC records had revealed "no effort of any kind whatever" by Boyle to influence the loan made to the American Lithofold Corporation.

Monthly reports filed by the Company with the St. Louis office of the RFC during 1949 and 1950, while the loan was outstanding, indicate that the Company paid Boyle $1500 in the Spring of 1949. . . . This appears to be entirely consistent with the statement which Boyle has made that he was retained by the Company for general legal services for two and one half months in the Spring of 1948, that he gave up the account voluntarily in April 1949, when he became a full-time, salaried employee of the Democratic National Committee. . . .

The RFC examiner for the Lithofold loan had never met Boyle, never communicated with him directly or indirectly on that particular subject or any other. Murphy had concluded there was nothing "fishy" about the RFC loan. "I believe that the facts I have developed substantiate the statement Mr. Boyle himself has already issued concerning this matter, and that they indicate pretty clearly that he had nothing to do with the granting of the loans in question and that there is no reason why he should be subjected to criticism, express or implied, on that account."

Murphy's report could only have pleased Truman greatly, while also reinforcing his own natural inclination to see attacks on any of his people as fundamentally political and directed at him. It might sound egotistical, Truman remarked, but he thought he was as good a judge of people as anyone who had ever sat in his chair. He had made some mistakes, and he had had to fire some people consequently. But, he added, "You can't punish a man for not seeming to be right if he isn't wrong."

In October, a new revelation relieved considerably the sting of the Boyle accusations. The chairman of the Republican National Committee, Guy George Gabrielson, testified that he had been paid $25,000 for "looking after" the loans of a Texas corporation, Carthage Hydrocel, Inc., and had intervened many times with the RFC on behalf of the firm. Gabrielson found it amusing that anyone might think his activities improper. "It is inconceivable to me," he told the committee, "to believe that a chairman of a party that is not in power could have any possible influence." But as reported, embarrassed Republicans in Congress did not think it would sound so inconceivable to the voters.

When, in time, the Senate committee issued its final report, Boyle would be cleared of any wrongdoing. In the oddly inverted wording of the report, he was guilty only of conduct that was "not such that it would dispel the appearance of wrong-doing." But by then, "for reasons of health," Boyle had also resigned as Democratic national chairman and scandals in the tax bureau loomed larger than any thus far.

For more than a year, Treasury Secretary John Snyder had been trying to get to the bottom of persistent rumors of corruption in various tax collectors' offices around the country. But Snyder had made little progress. Then in April 1951, the collector in St. Louis, James P. Finnegan, resigned only after being cleared by a grand jury. In July, Truman had to fire two more collectors, Denis W. Delaney in Boston and James G. Smyth in San Francisco. Eight of Smyth's associates were also suspended, and a few months later, the collector in Brooklyn, Joseph P. Marcelle, was fired.

All four men—Finnegan, Delaney, Smyth, and Marcelle—had been appointed by Bob Hannegan, when Hannegan was head of the Bureau of Internal Revenue under Roosevelt, and all had taken their jobs with the understanding that tax collection need only be a part-time responsibility, that they were free to do other things as well. Like Hannegan, all four men were also the products of big-city Democratic machines, and in fact corrupt practices—or at the least flagrant "irregularities"—had been rampant during their terms of office. Finnegan was indicted for bribe taking and misconduct, Delaney, the Boston collector, for taking bribes to "fix" tax delinquencies. In San Francisco, Smyth, too, was indicted—for fixing tax fraud claims—and in Brooklyn, Marcelle was found to have cheated on his own tax returns and amassed, through his law practice, nearly a quarter of a million dollars beyond his $10,750-a-year salary as tax collector.

Meantime, the Commissioner of Internal Revenue, George J. Schoeneman, had suddenly resigned "for reasons of health," and the resignations of the assistant commissioner, Daniel A. Bolich, and the bureau's chief counsel, Charles Oliphant, followed almost immediately.

In November, Truman had to fire the head of the tax division at the Justice Department, Assistant Attorney General T. Lamar Caudle. A House investigating committee would conclude that Caudle, though undoubtedly an honorable man, had been naive in his dealings with tax fixers.

By December, George Elsey would report in a White House memorandum that signs of corruption were spreading so fast the staff was unable to document them all.

In Truman's defense, it was stressed that the tax collectors under fire were holdovers from the Roosevelt administration. Also, Truman had moved swiftly and forcefully to clean house in the tax bureau, a point no one could contest. By December, 113 employees of the Internal Revenue Bureau, including six regional collectors, had been fired from their jobs. When Boyle was replaced by a new Democratic national chairman, Frank E. McKinney, Truman also determined that collectors of the Internal Revenue would no longer be patronage jobs but put under civil service.

Nonetheless, corruption in the tax bureau was truly appalling, the housecleaning long overdue, and if Bob Hannegan had made his key appointments under Roosevelt, Hannegan had also been known as a thorough Truman man, another Missouri crony. Hannegan had himself been a first-rate head of the tax bureau, but Hannegan was no longer available to speak in his own defense—he had died of heart failure in October 1949. And whatever the comparative guilt or stupidity of an unfortunate figure like T. Lamar Caudle, it would be remembered that his wife, too, was the recipient of a mink coat, a Christmas present from an attorney who had dealings with the tax division.

Would he be taking drastic action to clean up the government, Truman was asked at a press conference in December. "Let's say *continue* drastic action," he replied.

"Wrongdoers have no house with me," he said, an expression that left reporters looking puzzled and that Truman later told his staff he had used since boyhood. (*Time* would report that it was a colloquialism as old at least as *Romeo and Juliet,* where Juliet's father, angry with her for refusing to marry Paris, tells her: "Graze where you will, you shall not house with me.")

Did he ever feel as though he had been "sold down the river" by his friends?

"Well, who wouldn't feel that way," he snapped angrily. But beyond that he would say no more.

"Boss, you're going to have to run in '52," Harry Vaughan told him one day, as Truman sat at his desk. "Who else is there?"

"We'll get someone," Truman answered, a twinkle in his eye.

"You know there isn't anybody else. You'll have to run."

"We'll see," said Truman, and Vaughan came out of the office convinced the President would run again.

Vaughan, as he told the others, had no misconceptions about what was ahead for him personally, should Truman not run.

"Once I'm outa the White House," Vaughan said one noon hour in the staff lunchroom downstairs, "I know perfectly well that these jokers who bow and scrape and call me General would pass me by on the street and if they saw me say, 'Why there goes that fat god-damned son-of-a-bitch!' "

It was one of those moments when several of the staff were reminded why, after all, the President had kept Vaughan around for so long.

The only one not pointedly urging Truman to run again was Bill Hassett, who was due to retire soon himself and who told Truman that for his own sake and the sake of his family, he should do the same.

In Korea, though peace talks had resumed, now at Panmunjom, the war went on. The sticking point in the talks was the fate of 132,000 North Korean soldiers held prisoner by the U.N. Command. Originally, it had been agreed that the end of hostilities would bring an immediate exchange of all prisoners. But now the United States opposed that policy, since nearly half of the North Korean prisoners of war, some 62,000, had no wish to be repatriated. Truman insisted that they be given the choice of whether to go home. At the end of World War II Stalin had executed or sent to Siberia thousands of Soviet soldiers whose only crime was to have been captured by the enemy. "We will not buy an armistice by turning over human beings for slaughter or slavery," Truman declared, and he would not be budged.

American casualties in Korea were now far less than in the first year of the war. Still every week meant more death and suffering. Korea was consuming lives and resources, poisoning American politics, devastating Truman's presidency. No one wanted the war ended more than he. According to the polls, half the American people favored using the atomic bomb to get it over with. And though determined to keep to his policy of restraint, even he had his own fantasies about the ultimatum he might hand the Soviets. In another of his solitary ventings of anger and frustration, a lengthy private soliloquy in longhand, he wrote:

> Dealing with Communist Governments is like an honest man trying to deal with a numbers racket king or the head of a dope ring. . . . It seems to me that the proper approach now would be an ultimatum with a ten day expiration limit, informing Moscow that we intend to blockade the China coast from the Korean border to Indo-China, and that we intend to destroy every military base in Manchuria, including submarine bases, by means now in our control, and if there is further interference we shall eliminate any ports or cities necessary to accomplish our peaceful purposes.
>
> That this situation can be avoided by the withdrawal of all Chinese troops from Korea and the stoppage of all supplies of war and materials by Russia to Communist China. We mean business. We did not start this Korean affair but we intend to end it for the benefit of the Korean people, the authority of the United Nations and the peace of the world.
>
> We are tired of these phony calls for peace when there is no intention to make an honest approach to peace. . . .
>
> Stop supplying war materials to the thugs who are attacking the free world and settle down to an honorable policy of keeping agreements which have already been made.
>
> This means all out war. It means that Moscow, St. Petersburg, Mukden, Vladivostock, Pekin[g], Shanghai, Port Arthur, Dairen, Odessa, Stalingrad and every manufacturing plant in China and the Soviet Union will be eliminated.
>
> This is the final chance for the Soviet Government to decide whether it desires to survive or not.

But no one heard him ever say such things. He had no such intentions. The seven sheets of desk notepaper that he had filled were put away in a drawer and on he went with the hard work of his responsibilities. "I know of no easy way to be President," he would say.

At Washington dinner parties, and increasingly to reporters, prominent Republicans talked almost gleefully of the "damndest" campaign ever in 1952 on the issues of communism, corruption, and Korea. Taft was already running. Others, Republicans and Democrats, spoke more and more of Eisenhower as the ideal candidate. By December, Attorney General McGrath was being questioned by the House committee investigating the Internal Revenue scandals and Truman's standing in the polls had fallen to an all-time low. Only 23 percent of the country approved of how he was handling his job.

But by then the staff had been told. In mid-November, during a brief vacation at Key West, Truman had gathered them about the poker table on the porch at the Little White House to read aloud the statement he had written on April 12, 1950, and that he planned to release in the coming spring, in April 1952, well in advance of the Democratic National Convention. He was not running again; but for the next five months, he cautioned them, there must be utmost secrecy. He was only telling them now, he explained, so they could start making their own plans. Once having told them, he seemed greatly relieved.

"From that day forward," Roger Tubby was to write several months later, "I have not discerned any difference in any of our feelings for, or relations with the President—we are, and I think it proper to generalize for the staff, devoted to him as before."

Later still, it would be seen as a measure of that devotion that none of those who knew Truman's plans for 1952 ever said a word. The secret was kept for five months, as he had asked.

In the first week of the new year, on January 5, 1952, Winston Churchill, who in recent months, at seventy-seven, had returned to office as prime minister, arrived for a brief visit. Churchill had sailed on the *Queen Mary*. Truman sent the *Independence* to New York to bring him to Washington and Truman was there at National Airport to welcome him. Churchill, white-haired, wearing the familiar derby and smoking a long cigar, looked greatly aged, more stooped than ever, his walk slower. But to those watching as he and Truman greeted one another, he was "the old warrior," "the old lion" still, with an air of dramatic dignity about him. To Truman, Churchill was the greatest public figure of the age, as he often said. To Dean Acheson, this was an understatement. One would have to go back four centuries to find his equal, Acheson insisted. "What Churchill did was great; how he did it was equally so. . . . Everything felt the touch of his art—his appearance and gestures. . . ."

That evening, following dinner on board the *Williamsburg*, the table cleared, Churchill began talking of the state of the world, the menace and paradoxes of the Soviet empire. He acknowledged the importance of American nuclear power, and warmly praised Truman's leadership of the free world, including, as Churchill said, Truman's "great decision" to commit American forces in Korea. For Acheson, Averell Harriman, and others present, it was an occasion to be long remembered.

Looking at Truman, Churchill said slowly, "The last time you and I sat across the conference table was at Potsdam, Mr. President." Truman nodded.

"I must confess, sir," Churchill went on, "I held you in very low regard then. I loathed your taking the place of Franklin Roosevelt." He paused.

"I misjudged you badly. Since that time, you more than any other man, have saved Western civilization."

In a dark period for Harry Truman, a winter of tawdry scandal, of interminable war in Korea and greatly diminished public confidence in his leadership, the gallant old ally had again, and as only he could, served as a voice of affirmation.

II

During his initial years in the White House, Truman had often referred to it derisively as "the great white jail," "the great white sepulcher of ambitions," or "the taxpayers' house." He had found living there difficult, often very lonely. But he was also the President who, with the war over, reestablished state dinners and receptions in the grand, formal rooms of the mansion, insisting on respect for tradition in most every detail. He and the First Lady had returned "pageantry" to the White House, as J. B. West said, and plainly this had given him great pleasure.

As much perhaps as anyone who had ever lived there, Truman felt the aura of the old structure's past, the lingering presence of the strong personalities who had been its occupants down the years, even to the point, some nights, of hearing their ghosts stalking the center hall upstairs or knocking at his door. As Ethel Noland and others had observed, history for Truman was never just something in a book, but part of life, and of interest primarily because it had to do with people. Often when he spoke of Andrew Jackson or John Quincy Adams or Abraham Lincoln, it was as if he were talking about someone he knew. One cold Saturday morning near the end of 1950, he had led John Hersey on a tour of the White House renovation, at a time when the inside of the building looked like any big construction project, with steel beams, raw concrete floors, and metal ductwork contained within the shell of the old exterior walls. There were no partitions. Nothing remained of the original interior. It looked, thought Hersey, as if someone had decided to set up a modern office inside a deserted castle. Yet Truman stepped briskly along describing the historic features of one room after another, as though they were all still there, everything in place. The tour became a kind of fantasy, "a game of imagining," as Hersey wrote. Truman pointed out the Red Room, the Blue Room, the Green Room, then, at the far end, the East Room.

"You know, the White House was started in 1792," he said, "and the first ones to move in were John Adams and his wife, in 1800, and when they moved in, only six rooms in the whole building were ready to be lived in. This East Room was just a stone shell, so Abigail Adams used to string up her wash to dry in here. Imagine it! Later on, when the room was dolled up, Jackson bought twenty spittoons to go in here. They cost twelve-fifty apiece."

When Hersey asked if the intention was to restore the interior more or less as it had been before the building was dismantled, Truman answered emphatically, "Oh, yes indeed!"

History aside, Truman also understood the building's immense power as symbol. Since his first weeks in office, he had made steady use of such lesser symbols as the presidential yacht, the presidential plane, railroad car, and limousines. It was not just that he enjoyed them, but that he knew the degree to which they represented the dignity and importance of the office. Now, in an ironic bit of timing, as his tormentors in the press and opposition party made much over the "mess in Washington" by use of such other symbols as deep freezers and mink coats, Truman found some relief from his daily burdens, welcome diversion from war and scandals and politics, in the work of saving and returning to service the ultimate symbol of his high place in American life. The creator of acclaimed Missouri roads and courthouses—and of what had become the nation's best-known balcony—could be a builder again, restorer and guardian of one of democracy's shrines, the oldest building of the federal city. And little else that he was able to accomplish in these last years of his presidency would give him such satisfaction.

From its beginning stages he had cared intensely about the project. "It is the President's desire," the official White House architect, Lorenzo Winslow, had written in the spring of 1949, "that this restoration be made so thoroughly complete that the structural condition and all principal and fixed architectural finishes will be permanent for many generations to come."

The first dismantling had begun December 13, 1949, after six months of planning. Truman had hoped to have full responsibility for the project—it was, after all, the President's house—but was turned down by Congress. A Congressional Commission on the Renovation of the Executive Mansion was established, its six members appointed by the President, including two from the Senate, two from the House, the president of the American Society of Civil Engineers, and the president of the American Institute of Architects. The senior member of the commission, old Kenneth McKellar of Tennessee, the president pro tempore of the Senate, who was by then eighty, became chairman, while Glen E. Edgerton, a retired major general from the office of the Army Chief of Staff, was made executive director of the work. But it was the White House architect, Winslow, who worked most directly with Truman, and it was to be Truman, in the last analysis, who made nearly all the major decisions and a good many others as well.

The last major overhaul of the old mansion had been in Theodore Roosevelt's day, in 1902. Under the direction of Charles McKim of the renowned New York architectural firm of McKim, Mead, & White, the main floor especially had been transformed from something resembling a dowdy Victorian hotel to a kind of Beaux-Arts elegance, with the added touch of magnificent new electrical light fixtures and chandeliers. But the work was fundamentally cosmetic and accomplished in a huge rush. Structural needs had been bypassed, making the house in all less stable than it had been before. It had been truly a "botch job," as Truman said, and a principal cause of the conditions Truman faced forty-seven years later.

Although the exterior sandstone walls, the roof, and a fire-resistant third floor that had been added in the 1920s, during the Coolidge era, were in stable condition, the rest of the house was on the verge of collapse and a fearful fire hazard. Great loads had been put on the interior bearing walls. Beams had been notched or cut for plumbing or electrical wiring. The entire second floor, most of which had been rebuilt after British soldiers burned the house in 1814, was unsafe. "The character and extent of structural weakness were found to be truly appalling," said the Commissioner of Public Buildings in his report. (Winslow had claimed he could prove mathematically that it was impossible for the house to remain standing.) The plumbing was all largely makeshift and long outdated, the heating system and electrical wiring all inadequate and obsolete.

The main question to be decided in 1949 was whether to remove the existing interior of the house below the third floor, keeping the outside walls, and then rebuild everything within; or to take down the whole building, preserving and numbering the exterior stones in the process, so they could be reassembled when the new building went up. In the words of a later report, "The decision between these plans presented a matter of not inconsiderable complexity, especially since there were involved not only the construction factors, but the compelling sentimental aspects of the matter." To have proceeded by dismantling the outside walls would have made the project less difficult and less costly, saving as much as $300,000 or $400,000. But only one member of the commission, Democratic Congressman Louis C. Rabaut of Michigan, had argued for that approach. To the rest, tearing down the White House was unacceptable. It would have seemed an act of desecration. Truman never considered the idea.

Had he and the commission decided otherwise, the walls of the White House would have begun coming down in early 1950, as McCarthy was beginning his assault. The country would have had to have seen the complete demolition of the building, down to the ground, at about the time the news from Korea had turned so dreadful the following summer, with American troops fighting desperately to hang on at the Pusan Perimeter.

As it was, the exterior remained intact, while within, everything below the third floor was removed, piece by careful piece to begin with—after which came the full-scale demolition until the entire inside was hollowed out and the house had become a cavernous empty shell, the old outside walls held in place by steel framing. Trucks and bulldozers moved in to begin excavation for two entirely new basement levels. It was an extraordinary sight. "They took the insides all out," Truman wrote in his diary. "Dug two basements, put in steel and concrete like you've never seen in the Empire State Building, Pentagon or anywhere else." He loved making inspection tours, often using the workers' catwalks, high above ground.

The work was projected to cost $5,412,000 and be completed by December 1951. John McShain, Inc., of Philadelphia was, as low bidder, made general contractor. The firm had built the Pentagon, the Jefferson Memorial, and had a high reputation in Washington, but when Truman, walking over from Blair House one morning, saw a big McShain sign on the North Lawn of the White House, he told head usher Howell Crim to have "that thing" removed at once.

The project was far bigger and more complicated than commonly appreciated. Most of Washington and the country never realized all that was involved or the extent to which it was to become the house that Harry Truman built.

For 149 years the outside walls of the house had been standing on clay. Now, for proper underpinning, 4-foot-square pits were dug to a depth of about 25 feet, down to a firm stratum of gravel—some 126 pits in all, these filled with reinforced concrete, thereby forming the foundation for the structural steel frame of the house that went up within the original walls. The old brick of the interior bearing walls—the backing for the stone—was also found to be too soft and had to be removed, thus for the first time revealing the inside surfaces of the original stones, many of which, to Truman's delight, bore the mark of Masonic symbols. (He was also pleased to learn that on the Saturday in October 1792 when the Free Masons of Georgetown had laid the first stone, in the presence of President George Washington and the architect of the house, James Hoban, they had afterward paraded back to Georgetown, to "Mr. Sutter's Fountain

Inn," where toasts were raised to the fifteen United States, the President, and "masonic brethren throughout the universe.")

Original ornamental plaster cornices designed by James Hoban were found in the East Room hidden behind plaster put on in 1902. A well dug by Thomas Jefferson was discovered beneath the east wall. In his temporary office out on the South Lawn, General Edgerton kept an assortment of curiosities uncovered: a brick with a dog's footprint in it, a pike blade found buried under the North Portico, an ancient pair of workman's shoes.

All the principal rooms of the main floor—those used for state occasions—were to be rebuilt as "faithful reproductions" of the original rooms. The second and ground floors, too, would be restored with only minor changes.

The best of the original furnishings, beyond what was already at Blair House, had been put in storage at the National Gallery. Old mahogany doors and window sashes, mantelpieces, hardware, and floorboards deemed worth saving for reuse in the building, all paneling from the East Room and State Dining Room, were numbered, tagged, and carried away to federal warehouses across town. Twenty surplus mantels were given to museums, while some 95,000 old bricks were trucked off to Mount Vernon for the restoration of garden walls and to reconstruct George Washington's orangery.

The public, too, was offered the choice of a dozen different White House relic "kits," these ranging from a single foot-long piece of original, hand-split lath, for 25 cents, to a single brick ("as nearly whole as possible") for a $1, to enough old pine to make a walking stick or gavel, for $2. The charge was intended only to cover the cost of distribution. A small metal "authentication plate" was also provided with each item. For $100, one could get enough bricks to surface a fireplace.

Truman had warmly endorsed the idea of offering such souvenirs, and receipts wound up exceeding expenses by $10,000. Originally he had said he wanted to send gavels made of White House wood to all forty-eight state governors. When the stones showing the original stonemasons' marks were uncovered, he ordered a large number of them removed, some to be reset in the walls of the restored ground-floor kitchen, the rest to be sent to the grand lodges of the Masonic orders of every state, as a token of the bond between Freemasonry and the founding of the nation.

But as the pace of demolition stepped up, an immense quantity of material that might have been saved was not. Tons of old pine flooring, scrap lumber, ancient plumbing fixtures, pine doors, brick, and stone were hauled away to Forts Belvoir and Myer in nearby Virginia, some of it to be used in construction, but the large part as landfill. Chair rails, door frames, beautiful plaster moldings (once they had been measured and cast for reproduction) were scrapped, as part of the wreckage. For nearly a month, trucks loaded with White House "debris" went rolling back and forth across the Potomac to Virginia.

By the standards of latter-day preservation work, this was a needless and tragic loss. The justification would be cost and the President's own desire to see the job finished in reasonable time.

Before the renovation, there had been sixty-two rooms in the mansion, twenty-six halls and corridors, fourteen bathrooms. With the project complete, there were to be more than one hundred rooms, forty corridors and halls, and nineteen bathrooms. There would be 147 windows, 412 doors, 29 fireplaces, 12 chimneys, 3 elevators. There would also be a television broadcast room and a bomb shelter, two definite and costly signs of the times.

Most of the additional rooms and baths were on the third floor (thirty-one rooms and nine baths) and in the new basement levels, which, when finished, would resemble the off-stage service and utility complex of an up-to-date 1950s hotel. There were storage rooms, a laundry, a dental clinic, medical clinic, staff kitchen, barbershop, pantries, everything very institutional-looking. Few buildings anywhere in the country had such advanced mechanical and electrical equipment as went into the new White House that was emerging. The main electrical control board looked big enough for a theater. Plumbing, heating, air conditioning, kitchen appliances, elevators, incinerator, fire alarm systems, wall safes—all were the most advanced of the day, and cost well over $1,250,000. To accommodate the refrigeration compressors for the air conditioning, a tremendous additional excavation had to be made outside, next to the North Portico.

To make the lowest basement bombproof, an additional $868,000 was spent, and with no questions asked. The Secret Service and Truman's military advisers had convinced him of the necessity. The decision was made in the grim first months of the Korean War, when it seemed a third world war could come any time. "The President has authorized certain protective measures at basement level in and adjacent to the wings of the White House," the commission was informed on August 16, 1950. "Plans for this work are now being developed by the Architect of the White House. . . ."

The change meant many tons of additional steel and concrete in corridor walls and the floor above, work that was rushed ahead full speed.

The bomb shelter was completed in less than a year, long before the upstairs levels were even close to finished.

The entrance, at the end of a subterranean passage at the northeast end of the house, was a four-inch steel door with a narrow window at eye level, like the entrance to a speakeasy. In the event that the President and those with him reached the shelter after an atomic attack had already occurred, they were to shed their clothes once inside a small entrance hall, then, naked, proceed into another somewhat larger hall, where they would shower—to remove any radioactive material—and put on emergency clothing, which by the summer of 1951, like everything else in the shelter, was all ready and waiting.

Beyond was a large room with some seventy army cots neatly stacked against one wall, gas masks, chemical toilets, and acetylene torches (in case the occupants had to cut their way out of the steel door). In adjacent rooms were an emergency generator, a larder of Army rations, and a communications center, with radios, cryptographic machines, and telephone switchboard with direct lines to the Pentagon, state police headquarters, and a secret military relocation center near Leesburg, known as Mt. Weather. Accommodations for the President and his family consisted of an 8 by 10-foot room, four bunk beds, a toilet, and a supply of books.

Those inside, Truman was informed during a first visit to the shelter, would probably survive an atomic attack. The facility, however, would not sustain a direct hit. As the Secret Service and most of his staff already knew, Truman intended, in the event of an attack, to remain at the White House or in the shelter, both during and afterward, largely for "morale reasons."

(Once when a radar operator incorrectly reported the approach of twenty-five unscheduled, unidentified planes—which turned out to be one plane—and several of the White House staff went below to the shelter, Truman did not.)

In the early months of the White House project, the work had proceeded ahead of schedule; but with the onset of the Korean War, and increasing shortages of building materials, progress slowed, costs began to rise. About 250 men were on the job. The work went on six days a week. Truman came and went repeatedly, so often as time passed that the men scarcely bothered to glance up or take notice.

"He considered it *his* project. He was saving the White House," remembered Rex Scouten, one of the Secret Service agents who regularly accompanied the President on such rounds and who, years later, would become head usher, then curator of the White House. "He was also showing his desire to get it done with."

Truman wanted everything handled correctly, on the job and on paper. When he learned of a movement within the commission to dispense with making complete plans of the installations in the new building—as a way of cutting costs—he responded at once with a terse memorandum to the head of the General Services Administration:

> It is absolutely essential that the conduits, both wire and water, and all the complicated arrangements underneath the floors and the air conditioning service, be put on paper so that future mechanics of the White House can find things when it is necessary to make repairs. One of the difficulties with the old White House was that nobody knew where anything went and why it was there.
>
> Now there just isn't any sense in not having in the Archives, in the General Service Headquarters and in the White House complete plans of all installations. I want this done and if it requires an extra appropriation to get it done we will get that done too.

His own principal contribution to the design of the building concerned the grand stairway, which he insisted be relocated to the east side of the main entrance hall and made more open, more fitting for the ceremonial processions of the President and his guests of honor. Before, the stairway had been largely out of sight.

Often over the years, Truman had told friends and members of his staff that had he been forced as a young man to choose a profession other than politics, he would have been either a farmer, an historian, or an architect. Now, working with Winslow, he could pore over plans and drawings to his heart's content, as he had once with Edward Neild, when building the Kansas City Courthouse; and at first, he and Winslow got along extremely well. A tall, personable, highly gifted man, Winslow had been an important figure at the White House since the 1930s. He cared intensely about the building, knew and loved its history. Privately, he even communed with the spirits of a few departed presidents. ("Franklin Roosevelt appeared and presented a rose to me as did Andrew [Jackson]," Winslow had recorded in his diary after an evening over a Ouija board in the summer of 1950.) A married man, he was also romantically involved with several women, and while Truman seems to have been aware of this, he appears only to have grown annoyed by it when the project started to fall behind schedule. Losing his patience, Truman could often become quite abrupt with Winslow.

Most of the time, however, they worked smoothly together, each admiring the other's strengths and pleased to find how often they agreed. Winslow would write long memoranda reporting on progress, or listing current problems, and Truman would give his answers in the margins or between paragraphs in longhand. When, for example, Winslow reported that the commission intended to dismantle the temporary sheds on the South Lawn and set up various storage rooms and facilities for the workers in the new basement areas, Truman scrawled, "No! HST."

It is probable [Winslow continued] that ground floor areas will be . . . used for contractor's offices [and] without a doubt there will be considerable damage done to the various interior finishes that cannot be repaired satisfactorily at the last minute.
Don't use them. HST

The basement areas should be kept as clean as possible after being finished. For any of these areas to be put into use as storage and dressing rooms for laborers and mechanics is inconceivable in a residence of this kind.
Just do not do it. HST

I am inclined to believe that the sheds on the south lawn should remain until nearly all the work is finished throughout the interior of the building. If this is done all tools, paints and other materials may remain stored outside the building where they properly should be stored.
Right.

As each room is completely finished it should be locked and kept locked until the furnishings are moved in for occupancy. After that time no workmen or government personnel should be permitted free access throughout the building without specific permission from the Executive Director of the Commission.
Right as can be. HST

In August 1951 the plasterers went out on strike for two weeks, slowing progress still more. The laying of the fine parquet floors, a slow process at best, seemed to go on endlessly, since few craftsmen could be found who knew how the work should be done and those available were often advanced in years and worked very slowly.

The contract for furnishing and decorating the house went to B. Altman & Company of New York, which did the entire project at cost. When a number of socially prominent New Yorkers who had served on a White House advisory committee in years past began pressing for the chance to contribute their views, Truman wrote that

I want it distinctly understood that this matter will be closely watched by me and that no special privileged people [will be] allowed to decide what will be done. . . .

I am very much interested in the proper replacement of the furniture in the White House in the manner in which it should be placed, and since I am the only President in fifty years who has had any interest whatever in the rehabilitation of the White House, I am going to see that it is done properly and correctly.

This settled, the work went on, directed principally by B. Altman's young chief of design, Charles T. Haight, who was tireless, forceful, and got along well with both the President and the First Lady, even as Truman made his presence felt more and more.

He kept pressing for greater speed. He wanted everything ready by Christmas 1951. He hoped to have at least a year in the house, before his term of office expired. As the new year began, work on the floors was still behind schedule. Installation of marble and paneling was incomplete. Bath fixtures had yet to arrive, and though some twenty painters were at work, only the third floor, the guest and servant quarters, had been finished.

There was no letup in the racket and confusion. In February 1952, the main floor was a thicket of scaffolding, paint buckets, and stacks of lumber, as Truman led a half-dozen reporters on a preview tour. The builders were speeding things up, he said, obviously pleased. He had "taken a curry comb to them." He intended to move in by April. The reporters confessed difficulty in imagining how the finished interior would look.

On March 15, *The New York Times* reported that things were "moving at the double quick" at the White House.

Two large moving vans stood under the White House front portico. From them movers carried furniture through the White House double doors. Graders were smoothing off a new front lawn just ahead of landscapers who were rolling down turf that arrived in great truck-loads. . . .

Twelve days later, late in the afternoon on Thursday, March 27, Truman arrived back in Washington after a week's stay at Key West and, joined by Bess, was driven to the White House, entering by the north gate on Pennsylvania Avenue.

It was spring again and the mansion looked warm and cheerful in the dusk, with lights glowing from every window on the ground floor. As a further note of cheer, a large cherry tree in full blossom had been planted just that day in the front lawn.

Beneath the North Portico several of the White House staff, members of the commission, and others stood waiting, with a cluster of reporters, photographers, and newsreel cameramen. Along the sidewalk, by the iron fence, a crowd applauded and called welcome.

Head usher Howell Crim greeted the President at the door. John Mays, the veteran doorkeeper who had been at the White House since the time of William Howard Taft, took the President's coat.

Truman, "tanned and appearing in excellent health," "obviously highly pleased," as reporters jotted in their notebooks, stepped inside. After an absence of three years, four months, the President of the United States was again in residence at the White House.

Every light was burning, everything shimmered with light—crystal chandeliers and red carpets, window glass, marble columns, gilt-framed mirrors. Wood floors shone like polished glass. Walls and ceilings glistened with new paint. The effect was stunning. It all looked much the same as before, yet brighter, more spacious, and finished to perfection.

With Bess, Truman toured the whole of the first floor. To the white and lemon-gold splendor of the East Room had been added new mantelpieces of Tennessee marble, in honor of the chairman of the commission, Senator McKellar. Except for two magnificent grand pianos standing in opposite corners and two newly acquired Adam benches against the far wall—eighteenth-century benches designed by John Adam of Edinburgh —the room was bare of furniture, its parquet floor shining like glass beneath the same two crystal chandeliers that had hung there before but that had been reduced slightly in scale. The Green Room—once Jefferson's bedroom, later a dining room, later still a diplomatic reception room—looked no different from before, with the same silk on the walls, the same white Carrara marble mantels ordered by James Hoban in 1816. Above the entrance to the Blue Room, however, was a new presidential seal. Previously the seal had been embedded in the floor of the main hallway, but Truman had insisted it be moved—he didn't like the idea of people walking on it.

The oval-shaped Blue Room itself had been changed from dark to royal blue, with a large motif in gold on its silk damask walls, while the Red Room had new damask walls, new draperies and valances—all very red —setting off another Hoban mantel of lustrous white Carrara marble. Truman was particularly fond of a small French clock on the mantel in the Red Room and of four portraits on the walls: of William McKinley, Grover Cleveland, Theodore Roosevelt, and Woodrow Wilson. The painting of Roosevelt, by John Singer Sargent, was, Truman liked to say, "the most expensive picture" in the house.

Where the State Dining Room had been formerly rather subdued, even somber, with dark oak paneling, it was now painted a soft green, a "lovely color," Truman thought, and a large portrait of Abraham Lincoln by George P. A. Healy hung now over the mantel in a heavy gilt frame.

Because Bess had made a previous commitment to appear at a Salvation Army dinner at the Statler that evening, Truman dined alone, in the family dining room, off the State Dining Room, under a recently donated antique cut-glass chandelier and a spotless replacement of the ceiling where Margaret's piano had once poked a hole.

"Bess and I looked over the East Room, Green Room, Blue Room, Red Room, and State Dining Room," he recorded that night. "They are lovely. So is the hall and state stairway. . . . I spent the evening going over the house. With all the trouble and worry, it is worth it. . . ." The cost had been $5,832,000. It could have been done for less, he thought, and taken less time, if he had been fully in charge. But he was extremely pleased all the same. He had been told by the architect and engineers that it had been built to last another five hundred years. He hoped it would be a thousand years.

On Tuesday, April 22, when the White House was reopened for public tours, 5,444 people went through. On Saturday afternoon, May 3, with the pride of a new householder, Truman led his own television tour of the mansion. The broadcast was carried by all three networks and three network announcers—Walter Cronkite of CBS, Bryson Rash of ABC, and NBC's Frank Bourgholtzer—took turns accompanying him and asking questions. Thirty million people were watching, the largest audience ever for a house tour. There was no script and Truman was at his best, relaxed, gracious, amusing, and knowledgeable. "His poise, his naturally hearty laugh, and his intuitive dignity made for an unusual and absorbing video experience," wrote Jack Gould, television critic for *The New York Times*. In the East Room, to demonstrate the tone of the magnificent Steinway— "the most wonderful tones of any piano I have ever heard," Truman told Frank Bourgholtzer—he sat down and gave an impromptu performance of part of Mozart's Ninth Sonata, then crossed the room to the Baldwin, an American-made piano, as he said, and from a standing position, played a few more bars on it as well.

He spoke of Alice Roosevelt's wedding in the East Room and recalled that Franklin Roosevelt had lain in state there.

The President was an inexhaustible source of information [wrote Jack Gould]. He explained the decor and furnishings and offered a host of anecdotes on former occupants of the White House. Yet through his narratives there always ran an underlying note of deeply sincere and moving awe for the historic continuity of the Presidency.

Time called his performance "outstanding." The country loved the new White House and, for the moment, very much liked the man who occupied it.

III

For quite some time, Truman had been thinking about the question of a successor, someone to head the Democratic ticket in November 1952 and take his place in the White House after inauguration day in January 1953. The Republicans, he expected, would choose Taft, and the prospect of Taft as President was intolerable to Truman. There must be no isolationist takeover that would destroy everything he had worked for.

By late summer 1951, he appears to have concluded that the ideal Democratic candidate, "the most logical and qualified," was Chief Justice Fred Vinson. But Vinson declined, saying he had been out of politics too long. In November Truman tried again, inviting Vinson to Key West where they could talk freely in the privacy of the Little White House, but not until after Truman had had a meeting with Eisenhower over which there was to be a good deal of controversy.

Whether Eisenhower, still the nation's number one hero, would run for President, remained the great imponderable, though to judge by reports coming from his NATO headquarters in Paris, he was warming to the idea.

The first week of November, on a brief visit to Washington, the general had lunch with Truman at Blair House and reportedly Truman again offered his full support if Eisenhower would accept the Democratic nomination. The meeting took place on the 5th. On the 7th, Arthur Krock broke the story in *The New York Times.* Krock's source, he later disclosed, was Justice William O. Douglas, who told Krock he had heard it from Truman himself and in the presence of Chief Justice Vinson and one or two others from the Court, during a reception at Blair House later the same day as Truman's lunch with Eisenhower. "You can't join a party just to run for office," Eisenhower was described saying to Truman. "What reason have you to think I have ever been a Democrat? You know I have been a Republican all my life and that my family have always been Republicans."

At Key West a week later, Truman denied the story, as had Eisenhower in Paris, both publicly and privately. "He told me Arthur Krock's story that Truman had offered him the Democratic candidacy in 1952 wasn't really true," Krock's colleague on the *Times,* C. L. Sulzberger, recorded after an evening with Eisenhower in Paris.

> He told me this twice—before dinner and after dinner. When he first met Truman on this trip, they winked at each other and by mutual agreement said right away there was one subject they weren't going to talk about, and that was the closest they ever came to politics.

When Vinson arrived at Key West, Truman told him the nomination was his if he would accept. Vinson was tentative, saying he needed time to discuss the matter with his wife. Later, in Washington, Vinson told Truman he did not think the Supreme Court should be seen as a stepping stone to the White House. When Truman countered with the example of Chief Justice Charles Evans Hughes, who as the Republican candidate in 1916 nearly defeated Woodrow Wilson, Vinson declined for reasons of health, and apparently to Truman's great surprise. But Vinson, who had always looked sallow, was indeed in poor health. He would die two years later, in September 1953, at age sixty-one.

As the year ended, Truman seems to have been in something of a quandary, even about his own intentions, as implied in a longhand letter to Eisenhower dated December 18, 1951:

> Dear Ike:
>
> The columnists, the slick magazines and all the political people who like to speculate are saying many things about what is to happen in 1952.
>
> As I told you in 1948 and at our luncheon in 1951, do what you think best for the country. My own position is in the balance. If I do what I want to do I'll go back to Missouri and *maybe* run for the Senate. If you decide to finish the European job (and I don't know who else can) I must keep the isolationists out of the White House. I wish you would let me know what you intend to do. It will be between us and no one else.
>
> I have the utmost confidence in your judgment and your patriotism.

He, too, would like to live a semi-retired life with his family, Eisenhower wrote in reply to Truman. "But just as you have decided that circumstances may not permit you to do exactly as you please, so I've found that fervent desire may sometimes have to give way to conviction of duty." He would not seek the presidency, Eisenhower said. Further, "you know, far better than I, that the possibility that I will ever be drawn into political activity is so remote as to be negligible."

Eisenhower's letter was dated New Year's Day, 1952. Five days later, Senator Henry Cabot Lodge announced in Washington the formation of an Eisenhower-for-President campaign, and the following day in Paris, January 7, Eisenhower announced he was prepared to accept the Republican nomination.

Asked at his next press conference what he thought of the announcement, Truman had only praise for Eisenhower. He was "a grand man," Truman said. "I am just as fond of General Eisenhower as I can be. I think he is one of the great men produced by World War II. . . . I don't want to stand in his way at all, because I think very highly of him, and if he wants to get out and have all the mud and rotten eggs thrown at him, that's his business. . . ."

As the Eisenhower boom gathered force, Truman would remark to his staff, an edge of sadness in his voice, "I'm sorry to see these fellows get Ike into this business. They're showing him gates of gold and silver which will turn out copper and tin."

With Vinson no longer a possibility for the Democratic nomination, Truman decided the best choice would be Governor Adlai E. Stevenson of Illinois. Alben Barkley, at seventy-four, was too old. The presidency would kill Barkley in three months, Truman thought. ("It takes him five minutes to sign his name," Truman noted sadly in his diary.) Averell Harriman, whom Truman judged "the ablest of them all," had never run for office and would be severely handicapped by his Wall Street background. ("Can we elect a Wall Street banker and railroad tycoon President of the United States on a Democratic ticket?") Senator Estes Kefauver, a possibility, was a man Truman instinctively disliked and distrusted, a feeling shared by most of the party regulars. Privately, Truman referred to him as "Cowfever."

Adlai Stevenson, by contrast, was comparatively young at fifty-one. He was able, progressive, the governor of a major industrial state, a champion of honest government, and a new face. Stevenson had carried Illinois in 1948 by an overwhelming 570,000 votes, in his first campaign for any office, a point that greatly impressed Truman. "He proved in that contest," Truman would write, "that he possessed a knowledge and 'feel' for politics, that he understood that politics at its best was the business and art of government, and that he had learned that a knowledge of politics is necessary to carry out the function of our form of free government."

That Truman should turn to Stevenson was greatly to Truman's credit, for not only was Stevenson still a political unknown nationally, but a man altogether unlike Truman. A graduate of Princeton, well born, a prosperous lawyer, eloquent, witty, urbane—and divorced—Stevenson could hardly have been more different from Truman, or from most political figures of the day. Further, Truman hardly knew him. But Truman had read Stevenson's speeches; he liked what he heard, admired Stevenson's political philosophy, his Midwest background, his political heritage—the fact that Stevenson's grandfather, the first Adlai E. Stevenson, had been a Democratic congressman and Vice President under Grover Cleveland. ("He comes of a political family," Truman noted approvingly.) Also, several of the younger aides at the White House were keenly interested in Stevenson, seeing in him qualities of the kind needed to revitalize the Democratic Party.

Dispensing with any pretense of round-about overtures, Truman asked the governor to come see him, and for an hour or more, the evening of Tuesday, January 22, 1952, they met alone in the seclusion of Blair House —once Stevenson had talked his way past the guards outside who had never heard of him.

As Truman later recounted the conversation, he spoke to Stevenson at length about the office of the presidency, then asked him to take it, saying he need only agree and the nomination was his. He could count on Truman's unqualified endorsement. "I told him I would not run for President again," Truman recorded in notes made afterward, "and that it was my opinion he was best fitted for the place."

> He was overcome. . . . [I] offered to have him nominated by the Democratic Convention in July. I had to explain to him that any President can control his party's convention. Then I cited Jackson, Hayes, Teddy Roosevelt, Wilson, Franklin Roosevelt and myself at Philadelphia in 1948. I reminded him that Washington picked John Adams, that Jefferson did the same with Madison and Monroe before conventions were used . . . I told him I could get him nominated whether he wanted to be or not. Then I asked what he'd do in that case. He was very much worried and said that no patriot could say no to such a condition.

But that night Stevenson said no. "He apparently was flabbergasted," concluded Truman, who refused to give up.

Stevenson, according to a close friend, came away filled with admiration for Truman, who had been sitting by the fire reading the Bible when Stevenson arrived.

> Stevenson was impressed with this self-contained, internally secure man that Truman was [remembered Carl McGowan]. A simple man of

great strength. Stevenson, with his own churning around, was impressed with the calm, serenity, self-contained quality.

As Stevenson later confided to James Reston, Truman had said Stevenson was the man to defeat Eisenhower, who would most likely be the Republican candidate. Eisenhower's intentions were good, Truman had said, but he was inexperienced in politics and bound to become the captive of Taft and so destroy Truman's foreign and domestic programs. It was therefore essential that a Democratic administration be continued in the White House. The President wanted him to save the world from Dwight Eisenhower, Stevenson told Reston, highly agitated.

According to another Stevenson friend, George Ball, who had driven Stevenson to and from Blair House that night, Truman had also observed at one point, "Adlai, if a knucklehead like me can be President and not do too badly, think what a really educated smart guy like you could do in the job."

But Stevenson had said no to Truman. Not only did he wish to remain governor of Illinois, he was less than certain that a change in Washington, a Republican administration, would be a bad thing for the country. Privately he wondered if the Democrats had been in power too long. And, in any event, he did not feel that being Truman's handpicked candidate would be necessarily an advantage, given the woeful state of Truman's popularity. If Eisenhower were the Republican candidate, Stevenson told George Ball, nobody could beat him.

On March 4, Truman and Stevenson met again at Blair House, this time at Stevenson's request.

> [He] came to tell me that he had made a commitment to run for re-election in Illinois [Truman wrote] and that he did not think he could go back on that commitment honorably. I appreciate his view point.... He is an honorable man. Wish I could have talked with him before his announcement. He is a modest man too. He seems to think that I am something of a superman which isn't true of course ... he argued that only I can beat any Republican be he Taft, Eisenhower or Warren, or anyone else! My wife and daughter had said the same thing to me an hour before. What the hell am I to do? I'll know when the time comes because I am sure God Almighty will guide me.

For several weeks Truman toyed with the prospect of running again. Some of the staff felt sure he had changed his mind and was about to announce his candidacy.

On March 11, Estes Kefauver won a stunning victory in the New Hampshire primary, having stumped the state wearing his trademark coonskin cap and accusing the administration of doing too little to get rid of corruption. Truman had allowed his name to be entered, but did not campaign. He thought primaries were a lot of "eye-wash." Still, Kefauver had challenged a President and won handily.

At a small private dinner at Blair House for a few close advisers, including the new Democratic chairman, Frank McKinney, Truman polled the table. Should he become a candidate to succeed himself? The answer, put as tactfully as possible, was no.

Truman left for Key West and on March 22 called Clark Clifford and asked him to come down. The following day, they sat alone in the garden behind the Little White House. Clifford told the President he hoped he would not run again. Truman expressed concern over the effect his withdrawal might have on the war in Korea. Clifford answered that the course of the war had long been established.

The same day from Key West, March 23, a White House aide named David Lloyd, who had once worked with Stevenson when Stevenson was with the State Department, wrote to the governor without Truman's knowledge, urging him to reconsider, and in large part because of Truman:

> Anybody who works closely with that man loves him, so I am prejudiced, and think, like the others, that he ought to have what he wants. Because of all he has put into the job, because of the way he has given himself to it, because of the things he has done for us all, I feel that if he wants to quit, and wants you to take the job, he ought to have his way. This may sound a little rough on you. But there is more to it than my personal feelings about him. We have to support him because of the things he represents, which are the things we believe in. If we don't support him, then we signify to the world that we aren't really taking seriously the things we talk about and work for, and the world will cease to take us seriously. . . .

On their way to the Jefferson–Jackson Day dinner, the huge, annual $100-a-plate black-tie gathering of Democrats held the evening of March 29 in the National Armory, Alice Acheson asked her husband if he thought the President might disclose his political future in his after-dinner speech. "Not at all," said the Secretary of State in what, as she subsequently told him, was a notably superior manner. It would be too early for the President to announce an intention not to run again, Acheson explained, and too disappointing to many at the dinner were he to announce the contrary.

Truman appeared at the podium looking tanned and uplifted by the occasion. At the end of a lively, fighting speech, having duly assaulted the Republicans and championed his own record, he put aside his prepared text and gave his answer:

"I shall not be a candidate for re-election. I have served my country long, and I think efficiently and honestly. I shall not accept a renomination. I do not feel that it is my duty to spend another four years in the White House."

It was said without buildup, almost matter-of-factly, and for a few seconds the immense audience sat silent and confused. Then followed a strange mixture of automatic applause and shouted cries of "No," even from some of those who had hoped he would step down. "I found myself shouting 'No' with vigor," recalled Arthur Schlesinger, Jr., who had tried to stop Truman's nomination in 1948. "Then I wondered why the hell I was shouting 'No,' since this is what I had been hoping would happen for months. Still the shouts of 'No' seemed the least due to the President for a noble and courageous renunciation."

Truman left the hall quickly, smiling, waving, yet looking somewhat tense, though the First Lady had a very different expression. "When you made your announcement," Harry Vaughan later told the President, "Mrs. Truman looked the way you do when you draw four aces."

At the White House, as the President and First Lady arrived, many of the household staff who stood waiting at the door were crying.

Did he plan to run for the Senate, Truman was asked a few days later, at his next press conference. No, he said. (Mrs. Truman did not want him to, he had told his staff.) Did he favor Governor Stevenson for the nomination? No comment.

From Springfield, Stevenson had written:

I was stunned by your announcement Saturday night after that superb speech. I can only accept *your* judgment that the decision was right, although I had hoped long and prayerfully that it might be otherwise. As for myself, I shall make no effort to express the depth of my gratitude for your confidence. I hope you don't feel that I am insensitive to either that confidence or the honor you have done me.

Replying immediately, Truman said he appreciated Stevenson's letter "most highly." The need was for a man who would "carry on the Foreign Policy of the United States as it was established in 1938 by President Roosevelt and carried through by me, to the best of my ability. . . . We must also have a President who believes in the domestic policies which have made the Foreign Policy possible," for the one was not possible without the other. "I sincerely hope you will not take yourself completely out of the picture."

Characteristically, whatever his frustrations with Stevenson, Truman would keep trying.

IV

How the President got through the first weeks of April, wrote Roger Tubby, was a testimony to his amazing stamina. Tubby himself, as he wrote, felt more dead than alive.

On April 3, Truman fired Attorney General McGrath, who for months had appeared to be obstructing the investigations Truman ordered into corruption in the Bureau of Internal Revenue. Feeling he had been "sold down the river" by people whom he trusted, Truman had turned the "cleanup job" over to McGrath in January 1952, which raised charges of an attempted whitewash, since McGrath was a former chairman of the Democratic National Committee. McGrath had then named a respected New York lawyer, a Republican, Newbold Morris, to head the investigation. But Morris had soon quarreled with McGrath and annoyed Congress. When Morris issued a long, intricate questionnaire to be filled out by all federal employees, including the Cabinet, listing all assets and sources of income, McGrath exploded, calling the questionnaire an invasion of privacy and a violation of individual rights. McGrath refused to fill out the questionnaire, and after reading a copy, Truman, too, decided it should not be used.

Truman despaired over McGrath's "inability to get on top" of his job. He liked McGrath—"I don't think there was the slightest thing wrong with Howard personally at all," he would later say—but found his performance frustrating. When, on April 3, McGrath announced he had fired Newbold Morris, and apparently with the idea that this was what Truman wanted, Truman fired McGrath.

With this farcical denouement, as Cabell Phillips would write, the administration's housecleaning effort seemed to have blown to pieces. "It had been a miserable performance from start to finish, almost a burlesque of executive management, and the net result was to underline 'the mess in Washington' as a good deal more than a gloating Republican catchphrase." Truman felt wretched about it all. In his *Memoirs* he would say nothing of the episode, but shortly afterward he wrote to McGrath, "I want you to know that my fondness for you has not changed one bit. Political situations sometimes cause one much pain."

And by then, Truman was caught up in telephone and telegraph strikes, and the threat of another nationwide steel strike. He was showing the strain as those close to him had seldom seen. He looked stern in repose, his face deeply lined. After one morning staff meeting, when William Hopkins put the usual stack of papers in front of him to sign, Truman begged off until later, "when I'm not so shaky." He was tired, terribly tired, he admitted. At the White House the evening before, he had fallen asleep in his chair, something he almost never did.

He seemed overburdened by his duties and decisions in a way he had never been before. It was as if the decision not to run again, the prospect of not being President, had taken something from him.

In his diary, Roger Tubby wrote:

> McGrath, Korean truce talks perhaps heading up to a settlement, the steel, telegraph and telephone strikes, and his decision not to run again have been among the recent events draining on his emotional reserves ... we were urging him to take a weekend off, to cut down on his afternoon appointments. He brightened, said he thought [it] a good idea to go down river on the Williamsburg.... But Matt reminded him he could not get away, there was a wreath laying ceremony Sunday at the Jefferson Memorial. "God, what a three weeks," he said with feeling.

His appointment schedule for Tuesday, April 8, the crucial day, was typical and did not even include what was to be the most important event of the day.

```
9:45—      Hon. Mon. C. Wallgren
               (Called Mr. Connelly)
10:00—     (Staff)
10:30—
11:00—     Hon. Fred Lawton, Director of the Budget
               (Wants half hour)
11:15—
11:30—     Hon. Clark Thompson, Congressman from Texas
               (Leaving for Texas Apr. 9th and asked to see the President
                   before that time)
11:45—     Hon. Morgan Moulder, Congressman from Missouri
               (Leaving soon for Missouri and asked to come in)
12:00—     Hon. Ellsworth Bunker, newly appointed American
                   Ambassador to Italy
               (In city April 7 to 9 and asked through State to see the
                   President)
```

```
12:15—    Mr. Alfred Kirsch
              (Mr. Kirsch is President and Treasurer of the West
                 Disinfecting Co., Long Island City—called Mr.
                 Connelly)
12:30—    The Secretary of Defense
              (Usual weekly appointment)
1:00—     Lunch at Supreme Court
              (Justice Minton called the President)
THE PRESIDENT WILL LEAVE WHITE HOUSE AT 12:45 P.M.
3:00—     Hon. Joseph Keenan, A F of L
              (Called Mr. Connelly)
3:15—     Hon. Harley M. Kilgore, Senator from West Virginia
              (Called Mr. Connelly)
3:30—     Mr. James Patton, President of the Farmers Union
              (In city this week and requested appointment)
3:45—     Hon. J. Russell Young, Commissioner for District of
                 Columbia
              (to submit his resignation—called Mr. Connelly)
4:00—     Hon. Lister Hill, Senator from Alabama
              (Called Mr. Connelly)
7:50—     The President will leave White House to attend dinner at
              Shoreham given by National Conference on International
              Economic and Social Development—This is meeting in
              connection with Point Four. The President will speak at
              9:45 P.M.
```

As it turned out, he did not speak at the Shoreham as scheduled —the Secretary of State took his place—for it was that night, in a nationwide radio and television broadcast from the White House, that he announced he was seizing the steel mills.

It was one of the boldest, most controversial decisions of his presidency, and like so much else, the seriousness of the crisis was compounded by Korea, the war that had come to overshadow his whole second term and that was rarely ever out of his thoughts. "These are not normal times," he would stress in his broadcast. "I have to think of our soldiers in Korea . . . the weapons and ammunition they need. . . ." Also, it being an election year, with, as he saw it, his whole domestic and foreign program at issue, he had no wish to alienate labor.

From his reading of history, Truman was convinced his action fell within his powers as President and Commander in Chief. In a state of national emergency, Lincoln had suspended the right to *habeas corpus,* he would point out. Tom Clark, now on the Supreme Court, had once, as

Attorney General, advised him that a President, faced with a calamitous strike, had the "inherent" power to prevent a paralysis of the national economy.

Truman's legal advisers supported his views. And so, significantly, did Fred Vinson. According to later comments by John Snyder, the Chief Justice had confidentially advised the President that, on legal grounds, he could go ahead and seize the mills. Such counsel clearly violated the division between branches of government and was particularly improper in this instance, since a seizure of the steel industry was bound to be challenged in the courts and thus Vinson himself, very likely, would wind up having to weigh the case. But out of friendship and loyalty, Vinson offered advice that was taken quite to heart.

The path was clear, Truman told the ever cautious Snyder, who opposed seizing the mills. "The President has the power to keep the country from going to hell," Truman would assure his staff.

A steel crisis had been a long time coming. Driven by the demands of the war, the mills were producing record tonnage. Profits, too, were on the rise. Yet steel workers, unlike workers in the auto and electrical industries, had had no pay raise since 1950. In November 1951, the 650,000 United Steel Workers, who were part of the CIO and headed by Phil Murray, called for a boost in wages of 35 cents an hour. Management refused to negotiate. The union gave notice that it would strike when its contract expired on December 31. On December 22, Truman referred the dispute to his Wage Stabilization Board, and to maintain production, the union agreed to postpone the strike until April 8. When, after weeks of hearings, the Wage Stabilization Board recommended an hourly raise of 26 cents, and the union quickly agreed, the companies denounced the proposal as unreasonable, unless they could add a hefty increase of $12 a ton to the price of steel.

Negotiations continued, only to end in deadlock. With the April deadline approaching, the country, as said in the press, was caught "squarely on the griddle." To Truman, the pay increase proposed by the Wage Stabilization Board seemed both "fair and reasonable," and the most direct way to prevent a strike that would not only be a national emergency but would critically impair the flow of munitions to Korea and to the buildup of NATO forces in Europe, which he saw as crucial.

Secretary of Defense Lovett [Truman later wrote] said emphatically that any stoppage of steel production, for even a short time, would increase the risk we had taken in the "stretch-out" of the armament program.

He also pointed out that our entire combat technique in all three services depended on the fullest use of our industrial facilities. Stressing the situation in Korea, he said that "we are holding the line with ammunition, and not with the lives of our troops." Any curtailment of steel production, he warned, would endanger the lives of our fighting men.

Truman refused to invoke the Taft-Hartley Act—by which the government could enjoin a strike for eighty days pending an impartial study—because he saw no sense in delaying a settlement still further and felt the facts were already well known. Also, the steel workers had remained on the job voluntarily for nearly three months as it was. For them to continue thus another eighty days with no change in pay seemed to him unfair. Nor did the prospect of resorting to a law he disliked, and that labor despised, have any appeal.

But it was Truman's fundamental feeling about the giants of the steel industry, the old distrust of big corporations that he had voiced with such passion during his years in the Senate, that moved him now, more than sympathy for the position of the steel workers. He considered the industry's proposed price increase little better than profiteering, and saw the steel companies, with U.S. Steel in the lead, attempting to force a compromise that would ultimately play havoc with his anti-inflation policies and raise the cost of the war. "The attitude of the companies seemed wrong to me, since under the accelerated defense program the government was by far the biggest customer for steel and steel products. To hike prices at this time meant charging the government more for the tools of defense."

While conceding that a modest ($4.50) increase in steel prices might be tolerated, Truman stubbornly rejected industry demands out of hand and went over the head of his own director of defense mobilization, Charles E. Wilson, who saw validity in the industry position. As a result Wilson resigned, a turn of events that Truman regretted and that brought down still more criticism on him.

To Truman, seizure of the mills was a temporary last resort. On Tuesday, April 8, only hours before the mills were scheduled to be struck, he made his move, signing Executive Order No. 10340.

"The plain fact of the matter is that the steel companies are recklessly forcing a shutdown," he told the country when he went on the air at 10:30 that night.

They are trying to get special, preferred treatment. . . . And they are apparently willing to stop steel production to get it. As President of the United States it is my plain duty to keep this from happening. . . . At midnight the Government will take over the steel plants. . . .

The broadcast over, on his way to his room, Truman looked so exhausted Joe Short thought he might collapse.

In some ways it was as though, in the last act of his presidency, with less than a year to go, he had reverted to the man he had been in the spring of 1946, after less than a year in office, when, faced by the great railroad impasse, he had tried to draft the striking workers into the Army.

At some eighty-eight steel mills across the country, the morning of April 9, 1952, things appeared the same as usual. The morning shifts arrived, production continued, the mills worked by the same men and managed by the same officials. The one clearly visible sign of change were the American flags that flew over the mills. In Washington, the Secretary of Commerce, Charles Sawyer, had assumed legal command of the industry.

But Truman had brought on an additional crisis, a constitutional crisis, just as he would have in 1946 had the railroad unions not agreed at the last minute to settle the strike. The outcry now was instantaneous and as scathing nearly as what he had faced after the firing of MacArthur. He was called a Caesar, a Hitler, a bully and lawbreaker. In reporting his action to Congress, in a special message delivered to the Hill immediately that same day, April 9, he stressed that his action had been taken with utmost reluctance: "The idea of government operation of the steel mills is thoroughly distasteful to me and I want to see it ended as soon as possible." He acknowledged the power of Congress to supersede his policy and act on its own to pass a new law enabling the government to operate the mills as an emergency measure. Such legislation, he said, might be "very desirable." But Congress did not choose to grant him such power. Instead, there were calls for congressional investigations, calls for his impeachment.

The President's "evil deed" had no precedent in history, said the head of Inland Steel, Clarence Randall, in a radio and television broadcast. *Time, Newsweek, U.S. News and World Report,* all attacked Truman. The "Truman talent for trouble," said *Newsweek,* gave him and the nation no rest. *The New York Times* accused him of acting on "almost inconceivably bad advice." The Washington *Post* predicted his seizure of the mills would probably go down in history as one of the most high-handed acts ever committed by an American President. Truman, said the *Post,* had grossly usurped the power of Congress, and in a constitutional democracy there was no more serious offense against good government. "Nothing in the Constitution can be reasonably interpreted as giving to the Commander in Chief all the power that may be necessary for building up our defenses or even for carrying on a war."

If he could seize the steel mills under his inherent powers, could he therefore, Truman was asked at a press conference, also seize the news-papers and radio stations?

"Under similar circumstances, the President of the United States has to act for whatever is best for the country," he answered abruptly and im-prudently, stirring speculation that he was indeed planning to seize the press, an idea that had never occurred to him and that he couldn't imag-ine happening.

The steel industry sued to get its property back. Swiftly, a federal district judge, David A. Pine, determined that seizure of the steel industry was illegal and the Supreme Court announced it would hear the case.

"I believe," wrote Judge Pine in a 4,500-word opinion, "that the con-templated strike, if it came, with all its awful results, would be less inju-rious to the public than the injury which would flow from a timorous judicial recognition that there is some basis for this claim to unlimited and unrestrained Executive power...."

He had read the Pine opinion, Truman told his staff—"read it, read it and read it"—and still could not understand why he had been judged wrong. To Secretary of Commerce Sawyer, he confided that he would be "terribly shocked, disappointed and disturbed," should the Supreme Court, too, decide against him.

The President was depressed, recorded Roger Tubby after a morning staff meeting.

> [I] had never seen him so quiet and down. Occasionally there seemed to be ... [an] effort by him to laugh at our sallies, but the laughs were brief, his countenance mostly serious.... Of course the steel wrangle has troubled him, the touch-and-go situation in Korea, the Democratic Party uncertainties—and he's been terribly tired.

He would, of course, abide by the Court's ruling, Truman told report-ers. He had no ambition to be a dictator. He just wanted to keep the country running.

The case against the President was argued in the Supreme Court by the attorney for the U.S. Steel Corporation, white-haired John W. Davis, who had been the Democratic candidate for President in 1924 when he lost to Calvin Coolidge, and who in a distinguished career had argued more than a hundred cases before the Court. Defending the President was Solicitor General Perlman, whom Truman would later describe as an "outstanding" lawyer who presented the government's case ably and forcefully.

On Monday, June 2, the Court declared the President's action unconsti-tutional by a crushing majority of 6 to 3. Those in the majority were Hugo

L. Black, who delivered the official opinion, Felix Frankfurter, Robert H. Jackson, William O. Douglas, and, as infuriated Truman, Tom Clark.

"We cannot with faithfulness to our constitutional system hold that the Commander in Chief of the Armed Forces has the ultimate power as such to take possession of private property in order to keep labor disputes from stopping production," Justice Black read slowly and calmly. "This is a job for the Nation's lawmakers, not for its military authorities."

"Today," wrote Justice Douglas, in a concurring opinion, "a kindly President uses the seizure power to effect a wage increase and to keep the steel furnaces in production. Yet tomorrow another President might use the same power to prevent a wage increase, to curb trade unionists, to regiment labor as oppressively as industry thinks it has been regimented by this seizure."

The Chief Justice, who strongly upheld the President, arguing that he had acted entirely within his constitutional responsibilities, was joined in the minority by Justices Stanley F. Reed and Sherman Minton. Any man worthy of the office of the presidency, Vinson argued, should be "free to take at least interim action necessary to execute legislative programs essential to survival of the nation." Nor was there any question that "the possession [of the steel industry] was other than temporary in character and subject to Congressional approval, disapproval," or regulation of "the manner in which the mills were to be administered and returned to the owners."

For Truman it was a humiliating defeat, and at the hands of old friends and fellow spirits. It was a liberal Court. Hugo Black had been an ardent New Dealer. All nine justices had been appointed either by Truman or Roosevelt. That Tom Clark had gone against him would anger Truman for years. Putting that "damn fool from Texas" on the Supreme Court, he would one day tell the author Merle Miller, was the biggest mistake he made as President, though this, like others of his observations to Miller, was more harsh than he meant or than he indicated at the time.

As a gesture of friendship and goodwill, Hugo Black invited the President and the justices to a party at his beautiful home across the river in Old Town Alexandria. At the start of the evening, Truman, though polite, seemed "a bit testy," remembered William O. Douglas. "But after the bourbon and canapes were passed, he turned to Hugo and said, 'Hugo, I don't much care for your law, but, by golly, this bourbon is good.' "

The steel strike that began after the Court decision of June 2 dragged on for seven weeks, until midsummer 1952, making it the longest, most costly steel strike in the nation's history. Losses in production, losses in wages were unprecedented—21 million tons of steel and $400 million in wages, as 600,000 steel workers and 1,400,000 others in related industries were idle. The military output scheduled for 1952 was cut by a third. "No enemy nation could have so crippled our production as has this work stoppage," said Robert Lovett bitterly. "The weird and tragic thing is that we have done this to ourselves."

The settlement called for a 21 cent an hour raise for the workers and a steel price increase of $5.20 a ton, which was the same as the $4.50 offered by the government months earlier, plus 70 cents for increased freight rates.

In the long weeks of the strike, Truman had grown increasingly distressed over congressional inaction. Congress declined to do anything more than request—rather than direct—him to use the Taft-Hartley Act, thus sending the problem—and responsibility for the decision—right back to him. And whether steel production would resume, were he to invoke Taft-Hartley, was highly debatable.

"The Court and Congress got us into the fix we're now in," he told his staff. "Let Congress do something about getting us out."

Discouraged that so few Democrats on the Hill had come to his support, discouraged that practically no Democrats "up there" were fighting for his foreign aid bill, he grumbled that maybe it might be good for the Democrats to be out of power for a while.

For the first time since taking office, he felt ill. At the Army's Walter Reed Hospital, years earlier, a special Presidential Suite had been set up on the third floor, in the event that he needed medical attention, but it had never once been used. Truman had never been sick until the morning of July 16, when he awoke feeling "poorly" and Wallace Graham found he was running a low fever. Two days later, with what Graham called a mild virus, he was driven to Walter Reed. He stayed three days, during which he was gone over by some eight different specialists. He ate well, slept well, signed more than two hundred bills, and, as he later told his staff, spent a lot of time thinking about what he would say at the Democratic Convention. He delivered his speech to the bedpost, Truman said. "If the doctor had come in then he would have found my temperature up two degrees and might have thought me off my trolley." He wanted to talk not only about his record, "but about the future and what we can make of it."

What could be done about the steel strike, Joe Short asked him his first morning back at the Oval Office, July 21, when Truman still looked pale and subdued. He didn't know, Truman said.

"It's a lockout, that's what it is. U.S. Steel is against the little fellows, want to take them over, and of course they're against labor and against me."

Three days later, on July 24, he summoned Phil Murray and the head of U.S. Steel, Benjamin Fairless, to his office, demanded a settlement, and got it. "This should lead to a speedy resumption of steel production," he said in a brief formal announcement that the strike was over.

The following day, he left for Chicago and the convention that was already under way.

V

Truman's distress over the choice of a Democratic standardbearer had grown extreme. Firm in his belief that any red-blooded Democrat ought to be ready and willing to run against any Republican, he had become increasingly annoyed with Adlai Stevenson, whose reluctance to commit himself had begun to strike Truman as not only tiresome but perhaps something of an act.

As the press was saying, nearly all the old Democratic bosses were gone now. Jim Farley was long past his prime. Tom Pendergast and Bob Hannegan were dead. Ed Flynn was ill. Frank Hague no longer ruled in New Jersey, and Kefauver, with his primary campaigns, had eclipsed Ed Crump of Tennessee. "There was no one to supply party-wide leadership except the President," reported *Newsweek,* and he was "under tremendous pressure to name his preference for the nomination. . . ."

Truman continued to wait, holding out for Stevenson. It was only a week before the convention, his patience gone and resolved to do almost anything to stop Kefauver, that he at last suggested that Barkley would be a good choice—and then wished he hadn't because Averell Harriman, having declared himself a candidate, was proving a spirited champion of the whole New Deal–Fair Deal program in a way that made Truman glow.

When someone raised the point that Harriman had never run for public office, and so might not be up to a sustained campaign, Truman remarked, "You never know what's in you until you have to do it."

The Republicans opened their convention in Chicago on July 7. Taft had the largest number of committed delegates. Attacking what he called the "me-too" Republicanism of the party's eastern liberals—the Dewey people who were backing Eisenhower this time—Taft said it was time to give the American people a clear choice. The floor fight before the balloting turned bitter. "We followed you before and you took us down the road to defeat," declared Senator Everett Dirksen from the podium, shaking his finger at the New York delegation, where Dewey sat. "And don't do this to us again." But such were the tactical skills of the Eisenhower managers, combined with the glamour of the Eisenhower band-wagon, that the general swept to victory on the first ballot—as no doubt he would have done at the Democratic Convention, too, had he been willing.

Of the Democratic candidates, on the eve of the Democratic Convention, Kefauver was far in the lead, claiming 257 delegates, or nearly half what was needed for the nomination. Richard Russell, running as the candidate of the South, had 161, Harriman 112, Stevenson a mere 41, while Truman, it was believed, could swing at least 400 votes to whomever he chose. As *Time* reported, Truman's hold on Democratic leaders continued remarkably strong because they saw him as the smartest practical politician around. "If Harry Truman turns out to have an enormous influence on the convention, it will not be a case of delegates doing his bidding, but of their following his highly respected judgment."

A Barkley boom began and gathered surprising force, only to be abruptly terminated when the leaders of organized labor met with Barkley and told him the blunt truth. It was not that they objected to him on issues, as they had with Jimmy Byrnes in 1944, he was just too old.

Barkley called Truman to say he was withdrawing, and on the afternoon of July 24, the day of the steel strike settlement at the White House, Stevenson telephoned from Illinois to ask Truman if it would embarrass him were he, Stevenson, to allow his name to be placed in nomination. Truman, as he later said, chose some "rather vigorous" words. "I have been trying since January to get you to say that," he told the governor. "Why would it embarrass me?" Stevenson could count on his full support. As far as Truman was concerned, Stevenson was as good as nominated.

On the floor of the immense international amphitheater at the Chicago Stock Yards, a headlong Stevenson boom was already under way, as a result of the governor's own brilliant welcoming address to the convention. James Reston in *The New York Times* called Stevenson "a leaf on a rising stream." When, during the first ballot the next afternoon, Friday, the 25th, the Missouri delegation was polled, the President's own alternate, an old Pendergast stalwart named Tom Gavin, was seen voting for Stevenson just as the President and First Lady were leaving from Washington on the *Independence*. On television the two events were shown simultaneously on a split screen.

Heading west, Truman watched the convention on television "all the way" in flight, something no President had done before. He saw the results of the first ballot—Kefauver 340, Stevenson 273, Russell 268, Harriman 123—and the start of the second. By the end of the second ballot, at 6:00 P.M. Chicago time, with Stevenson gaining but still no decision, Truman was at the Blackstone working on his speech in Room 709, the same corner suite where he had taken the fateful call from Franklin Roosevelt eight years before. To others in the presidential entourage, he appeared in high gear.

With the convention in recess until nine o'clock, Truman went by motorcade and booming motorcycle escort to the Stockyards Inn and dinner in a private dining room with Jake Arvey, Sam Rayburn, and Democratic Chairman Frank McKinney. From there, he also sent word to the governors of Massachusetts and Arkansas, as well as to Averell Harriman, to release their delegates to Stevenson. Charlie Murphy was the messenger sent to see Harriman, who, as it happens, had already decided on his own to withdraw in favor of Stevenson.

The convention's dramatic turn to Stevenson came on the third ballot, with the release of the Harriman delegates. But it was past midnight before the vote was made unanimous, and not until 1:45 in the morning, as late nearly as four years before, when the nominee and the President entered the hall arm in arm, down the floodlit runway to the rostrum, Truman exuberant, a spring to his step, Stevenson, a short, rather dumpy figure, looking slightly uncertain.

They had picked a winner, Truman assured the crowd. "I am going to take my coat off and do everything I can to help him win."

Stevenson spoke briefly and eloquently. "The people are wise," he said, "wiser than the Republicans think. And the Democratic Party is the people's party, not the party of labor, not the farmer's party—it is the party of no one because it is the party of everyone." The ordeal of the twentieth century was far from over. "Sacrifice, patience, understanding and implacable purpose may be our lot for years to come. Let's talk sense to the American people. . . ."

Later, Stevenson, Truman, Rayburn, McKinney, and four or five others met backstage. Stevenson asked for advice on a running mate. The Republicans had chosen Senator Richard Nixon as their vice-presidential candidate. Stevenson mentioned Kefauver, but when Truman vigorously objected, Rayburn and McKinney backed him. Barkley and Russell were also mentioned and rejected. Finally, the choice was Senator John Sparkman of Alabama. "Stevenson made his decision with Harry Truman's help," one of those present explained afterward to a reporter.

In his room that morning at 6:40, Saturday, July 26, having slept perhaps an hour, if at all, Truman wrote a warm letter to the nominee on a sheet of Blackstone Hotel stationery; a letter such as he himself had never received from Franklin Roosevelt.

Dear Governor:

Last night was one of the most remarkable I've spent in all my sixty-eight years. When thousands of people—delegates and visitors—are willing to sit and listen to a set speech and introduction by me, and then listen to a most wonderful acceptance speech by you, at two o'clock in the morning, there is no doubt that we are on the right track, in the public interest.

You are a brave man. You are assuming the responsibility of the most important office in the history of the world.

You have the ancestral, political and educational background to do a most wonderful job. If it is worth anything, you have my wholehearted support and cooperation.

When the noise and shouting are over, I hope you may be able to come to Washington for a discussion of what is before you.

But though Stevenson sent a gracious reply and would eventually meet with Truman at the White House, he was no less determined than before not to be seen as Truman's candidate. "He was affronted by the indifferent morality and untidiness of the Truman Administration and was frantic to distance himself from Truman," his friend George Ball would remember. In quick succession, Stevenson replaced Truman's party chairman, McKinney, with a Chicago friend, Stephen A. Mitchell, an attorney with little political experience, and announced that Democratic headquarters henceforth would be in Springfield, Illinois, not Washington—decisions certain to offend Truman. Nor did he make any effort to solicit Truman's advice on plans for the campaign.

Stevenson's attitude toward him was a "mystery," Truman would write in his *Memoirs*. But in a letter he never sent, Truman told the nominee, "I have come to the conclusion that you are embarrassed by having the President of the United States in your corner. . . . Therefore I shall remain silent and stay in Washington until Nov. 4." He did not like being treated as a liability. Frank McKinney, he wrote, had been the best party chairman in his memory. "I can't stand snub after snub by you. . . ."

In August, to make matters worse, Stevenson carelessly signed a letter prepared by an assistant in answer to a question from the *Oregon Journal*. "Can Stevenson really clean up the mess in Washington?" the editor of the Portland paper had asked. "As to whether I can clean up the mess in Washington," read the Stevenson reply, "I would bespeak the careful scrutiny of what I inherited in Illinois and what has been accomplished in three years." The Republicans quickly made the most of the letter, as confirmation by Stevenson himself that there was truly a mess in Washington, and Truman, in another letter he never mailed, said Stevenson had now made the whole campaign "ridiculous."

I'm telling you to take your crackpots, your high socialites with their noses in the air, run your campaign and win if you can. Cowfever could not have treated me any more shabbily than have you.

At a later point, Stevenson sent Chairman Mitchell to tell Truman that it would greatly help the campaign if Dean Acheson were to announce his plan to retire as Secretary of State once the election was over—an idea Truman bluntly rejected.

But as his daughter Margaret would recall, Truman was more sad than angry. "Oh, Stevenson will get straightened out," he told his staff. "The campaign hasn't really started." And in time to come, he would write that Stevenson conducted himself magnificently in the campaign:

> His eloquence was real because his words gave definition and meaning to the major issues of our time. He was particularly effective in expressing this nation's foreign policy. He made no demagogic statements. . . . While some felt he may have talked over the heads of some people, he was uncompromising in being himself. His was a great campaign and did credit to the party and the nation. He did not appeal to the weakness but to the strength of the people. He did not trade principles for votes. What he said in the South he would say in the North, and what he said in the East he would say in the West. It will be to his credit that, although given provocation by the opposition, he stayed away from personalities and accusations. . . . I hold him in the highest regard for his intellectual courage.

On August 12, Stevenson came to the White House at Truman's invitation to have lunch with the Cabinet and be briefed at length on the state of the Union. In the course of three hours of discussion, Truman said more than once that he wanted to do everything possible to be of help. He did not wish to direct or dominate the campaign in any way. Stevenson was the boss, Truman stressed. "I think the President wants to win this campaign more than I do," Stevenson remarked. "As much as you do," interrupted Truman, who appeared to be greatly enjoying himself, until the meeting ended and he and Stevenson stepped outside to talk to the press.

Truman came out the door first, as customary, only now the photographers shouted to him, "Wait for the Governor, Mr. President." A new order had clearly begun. "That's your point of contact right there, Governor," Truman said, gesturing to the microphones.

Stevenson joked about the size of the lunch he had just enjoyed, saying if he had another he would be too fat to campaign. Truman, usually the first to laugh at such banter, barely smiled, as if his thoughts were elsewhere. "There was just a hint of tension in the atmosphere," wrote Andrew Tully of *The New York Times,* "and of sadness—as Harry Truman watched this man taking over. . . ." When Stevenson finished, Truman did not linger, but turned and walked back to his office, "slowly, head erect."

Several of the White House staff watched in pain. Secret Service Agent Floyd Boring turned to Roger Tubby and remarked, pointing to the President, "There's a man of granite. And him [pointing to Stevenson], he looks like a sponge."

With the campaign under way in September, Truman quickly forgot any injured pride he felt and joined the fray with all his old zest. Though not the candidate, he saw the election as a referendum on his presidency. Nor, constituted as he was, could he possibly have stayed out once the fight was on. "We didn't have to ask Mr. Truman to get into the campaign," remembered the new party chairman, Stephen Mitchell. "He was raring to go . . . and he put on a great show."

He took to the rails, crisscrossing the country again in the *Ferdinand Magellan.* Stevenson traveled by plane and they kept entirely different schedules, never appearing on the same platform. Stevenson was eloquent as no presidential candidate had been in more than a generation. Truman was the fighter, the believer. "When you vote the Democratic ticket . . . you are voting for your interests because the Democrats look after the interests of the everyday man and the common people," he said, sounding very like the candidate of 1948. He praised Stevenson. He evoked the memory of Franklin Roosevelt, heaped scorn on the Republican Party, stoutly championed his own Fair Deal programs. Toward the Republican candidate he was unexpectedly gentle at first. It was Taft he attacked.

He liked Ike, too, Truman would say, seeing Eisenhower buttons or signs in a crowd. But he liked him as a general in the Army. As it was, Ike didn't seem to know what he was doing. "I think Bob Taft and all the Republican reactionaries are whispering in his ear, and pulling his leg," he told the people of Whitefish, Montana. "If you like Ike as much as I do, you will vote with me to send him back to the Army, where he belongs."

The truth was he did still like Ike. Even when Eisenhower refused Truman's invitation to the same kind of briefing as he had given Stevenson, Truman had written to Eisenhower privately to express his friendship as much as his distaste for those now advising the general:

What I've always had in mind was and is a continuing foreign policy. You know that is a fact, because you had a part in outlining it.

Partisan politics should stop at the boundaries of the United States. I am extremely sorry that you have allowed a bunch of screwballs to come between us. . . .

May God guide you and give you light.

From a man who has always been your friend and who always wanted to be!

In conversation on board his train, Truman could swing from premonitions of Eisenhower as a dangerous President, "a modern Cromwell," to open expressions of sympathy. "You know, I still feel sorry for Ike. He never should have gotten into this." When it was revealed in mid-September that Eisenhower's running mate, Nixon, had been subsidized by a secret fund subscribed by California millionaires, and others traveling with Truman were cheered by the news, he commented only, "This will help us, but I'm sorry to see it happen, for it lowers public opinion of politics."

As so often before, the grueling business of a campaign seemed to restore and enliven him. He would be remembered rolling along at night in the dining room of the *Ferdinand Magellan,* eating fried chicken with his fingers, enjoying stories and "matching wits" with his staff, while every now and then in the darkness outside a lonely light flashed by. He would be remembered washing his socks in the bathroom sink in California and after a day of eight speeches from Ohio to upstate New York, sitting in a hotel in Buffalo playing the piano at 1:30 in the morning.

The pace and heat of the contest picked up rapidly.

The Republicans, campaigning under the slogan "Time for a Change," had no intention of repeating Dewey's bland glide to defeat. Much of what was said by both sides became very unpleasant. "I nearly choked to hear him," Truman remarked privately after Eisenhower, stepping up the attack, assaulted the foreign policy that, as Truman saw it, Eisenhower himself, as Chief of Staff and head of NATO, had helped shape and implement. Eisenhower, Truman now charged, had become "a stooge of Wall Street." He was "owned body and soul by the money boys." Eisenhower, because of his career in the Army, knew little of the realities of life, didn't "know the score and shouldn't be educated at public expense."

Eisenhower, for his part, deplored the "top-to-bottom mess" in Washington, "the crooks and cronies," while Nixon hammered at what became known as "K_1C_2"—"Korea, Communism and corruption." When Nixon accused Truman, Stevenson, and Dean Acheson of being "traitors to the high principles in which many of the nation's Democrats believe," Truman understood this to mean Nixon had called him a traitor, and he would not forget it.

There was no Charlie Ross to help this time, no Clark Clifford. Press Secretary Joe Short had recently been hospitalized for what was thought to have been a mild heart condition. When Truman received word that Joe Short was dead, he took it very badly, feeling acutely, personally responsible. "I feel as if I killed them," he said, remembering Ross as well.

Stevenson "has the most wonderful command of the language and he is delighting audiences wherever he goes," recorded Roger Tubby, who took over in Short's place.

> [Stevenson's] humor, his gift of satire and the devastating barb are irrepressible and so, thank God, the nation is being treated as it has not in some time, perhaps not since Lincoln.... Nevertheless some observers wonder whether S[tevenson] is "getting across" to the people, and compare his style unfavorably with the President's, which is simple, declarative sentences, blunt and hard-hitting. Ike meanwhile goes blundering along, often badly tangled in his thoughts and words, but sticking persistently to a couple of simple themes: get rid of corruption, throw the rascals out....

Most newspapers backed Eisenhower. The Republicans were also outspending the Democrats by more than two to one. But Truman's crowds at times were as large and friendly as in 1948. In West Virginia, Pennsylvania, New Jersey, across New England, his crowds were often bigger than those that turned out for Eisenhower.

The searing moment of the campaign for Truman came in early October, when Eisenhower went into Wisconsin, Joe McCarthy's home state, where McCarthy in a drive for his own reelection continued to vilify George Marshall. Many of Eisenhower's backers, many of his own aides, were confident he would eventually repudiate McCarthy and speak up for Marshall, and as he crossed Illinois, heading for Wisconsin, Eisenhower decided now would be the time, "right in McCarthy's backyard." A personal tribute to Marshall was prepared for a speech at Milwaukee. But then Eisenhower's political advisers adamantly objected. McCarthy himself flew to Peoria, Illinois, and crossed into Wisconsin on board the general's train. Reportedly, when McCarthy argued against any mention of Marshall, Eisenhower reacted with "red-hot anger." Still, in a speech at Green Bay, Eisenhower expressed his gratitude to the senator for meeting him in Illinois and told his audience it was only in methods, not objectives, that he and McCarthy differed. Then in the speech at Milwaukee, with McCarthy seated behind him on stage, Eisenhower declared that a national tolerance of communism had "poisoned two whole decades of our national life," thus creating "a government by men whose very brains were confused by the opiate of this deceit." The fall of China, he charged, the "surrender of whole nations" in Eastern Europe could be attributed to the Reds in Washington. There was no mention of Marshall; the tribute had been cut. But because Eisenhower's aides had been telling reporters all day about the Marshall tribute they would hear, its removal made more news than the rest of the speech. Even staunch Eisenhower supporters were appalled.

"Do I need to tell you that I am sick at heart?" Arthur Hays Sulzberger, publisher of *The New York Times,* wired Eisenhower's personal campaign manager, Sherman Adams.

To Truman, with his devotion to George Marshall, Eisenhower had committed an act of unpardonable betrayal. Truman tried to contain his fury. The spectacle of the Republican candidate campaigning against his own record, his own better nature and principles, was "very sad and pathetic," Truman said in Oakland, California.

> And I wish for the sake of history, and for the sake of future generations who will read about him in the schoolbooks, that he had not so tarnished his own bright reputation as a commander of men. And I mean that with all my heart.

Heading east, Truman remarked to his staff that probably he should "lay off Ike for a while . . . got to be very careful we don't overdo the attacks." But the outrage within seemed to gather force by the day, the more he thought about Marshall, the more he thought about Eisenhower and McCarthy, the more Eisenhower attacked his foreign policy and handling of the Korean War.

"The general whose words I read, whose speeches I hear, is not the general I once knew. Something, my friends, has happened to him," he told the crowd at Colorado Springs. "I thought he might make a good President," he said at Muncie, Indiana, "but that was a mistake. In this campaign he has betrayed almost everything I thought he stood for."

Finally, in a rear platform speech at Utica, New York, Truman lashed out full force. Eisenhower, he said, had betrayed his principles, deserted his friends.

> He knew—and he knows today—that General Marshall's patriotism is above question . . . [he] knows, or he ought to know, how completely dishonest Joe McCarthy is. He ought to despise McCarthy, just as I expected him to—and just as I do.
>
> Now, in his bid for votes, he has endorsed Joe McCarthy for re-election—and humbly thanked him for riding on his train.

I can't understand it. I had never thought the man who is now the Republican candidate would stoop so low. I have thought about this a great deal. I don't think I shall ever understand it. . . .

And he never did, never really got over Eisenhower's ingratitude to the man who had made him. For years to come Truman would harbor intense anger. "Why, General Marshall was responsible for his whole career," he would say. "When Roosevelt jumped him from lieutenant colonel to general, it was Marshall's recommendation. Three different times Marshall got him pushed upstairs, and in return . . . Eisenhower sold him out. It was just a shameful thing."

Eisenhower, stunned by Truman's attack, was enraged. "Just how low can you get?" He would never ride down Pennsylvania Avenue with Truman on inauguration day, he vowed.

The polls showed Eisenhower well in the lead. The polls also showed that the stalemate in Korea was what worried most voters. The election had become a referendum on Korea, and Eisenhower stepped up the attack on the administration's handling of the war. On October 24 at Detroit, in a blistering speech broadcast on national television he called Korea "the burial ground for twenty-thousand American dead," and promised to end the war. If elected, Eisenhower declared dramatically, "I shall go to Korea."

Truman issued a statement stressing that the general had been in agreement with administration policy concerning Korea from the start. To a crowd at Winona, Minnesota, Truman warned, "No professional general has ever made a good President. The art of war is too different from the art of civilian government."

If Eisenhower had a way of ending the war in Korea, he should tell him now, Truman said. "Let's save a lot of lives and not wait. . . . If he can do it after he is elected, we can do it now." Such "demagoguery used in connection with this tragic situation is almost beneath contempt," he would write to Stevenson. No man, Truman thought, had less right than Eisenhower to use Korea for political advantage.

At the Pentagon, Eisenhower's old friends among the Joint Chiefs were hardly less furious than the President. "Ike was well informed on all aspects of the Korean War and the delicacy of the armistice negotiations," recalled Omar Bradley. "He knew very well that he could achieve nothing by going to Korea."

In the final days of the campaign, Truman was still going strong. A local reporter in Iowa noted that the President "never looked more fit or pleased with the rigorous job of 'giving 'em hell.' "

But with his dramatic promise to go to Korea, Eisenhower had decided the election, as Truman seemed to know. "Roger, we may be up against more than we can control," he told his press secretary.

The Eisenhower victory was overwhelming—he carried all but nine of forty-eight states, including Stevenson's Illinois and Truman's Missouri, his percentage of the popular vote was bigger than any Democratic victory since Roosevelt in 1936—and the issue that cut deepest was Korea. But with his radiant smile, the unequaled place he held in the affections of the people, Eisenhower had also proven an exceptional candidate. His popularity had made him all but impregnable. And prevalent as the feeling may have been that a change was due in Washington after so long a Democratic reign, it was clearly an Eisenhower, not a Republican, triumph. In Congress the Republicans barely gained control. Their margin in the Senate was one seat.

As Truman would comment privately, probably no one could have beaten Eisenhower in 1952. That some observers, including the Kansas City *Star,* were saying that he, Truman, had done Stevenson more harm than good left him feeling deeply hurt.

He sent Eisenhower his congratulations and offered him use of the *Independence* to fly to Korea, but not without adding, "if you still desire to go to Korea," a final partisan jab that not surprisingly infuriated Eisenhower, who declined the offer.

Eisenhower flew to Korea by military plane and under greatest security at the end of November. For three days he toured the front lines, then flew home having concluded only that the situation was intolerable.

"I sincerely wish he didn't have to make the trip," Truman had written in his diary on November 15. "It is an awful risk. If he should fail to come back I wonder what would happen. May God protect him."

With no hesitation or the least sign of bitterness, Truman immediately invited Eisenhower to the White House to discuss the turnover of power. He was determined, as he wrote to the general, to guarantee "an orderly transfer of the business of the executive branch." The gesture was unprecedented, and to those around Truman a vivid example of his ability to separate his personal feelings from the larger responsibilities of his office. He would do all he could to help the new President. He only wished someone had done as much for him.

Eisenhower arrived at the White House just before two o'clock, the afternoon of Tuesday, November 18, for a meeting first with Truman in his office, then an extended briefing in the Cabinet Room by Truman, his Cabinet and staff. All went very formally and without incident, though Eisenhower remained unsmiling and wary—"taciturn to the point of surliness," thought Acheson. To Truman, Eisenhower was a man with a chip on his shoulder. He would remember Eisenhower's "frozen grimness throughout."

When Truman offered to give Eisenhower the big globe that Eisenhower had given him years before, and that for Truman had come to symbolize so much of the weight of his responsibilities, Eisenhower accepted it, though "not very graciously," in Truman's view. Nor from Eisenhower's reactions during the briefing in the Cabinet Room did Truman feel the general truly comprehended the extent or complexity of the task that faced him. "I think all this went into one ear and out the other," Truman recorded. Later, at his desk, talking with some of the staff, he would remark, "He'll sit right here and he'll say do this, do that! And nothing will happen. Poor Ike—it won't be a bit like the Army. He'll find it very frustrating."

VI

Upstairs at the White House a death watch had begun. In the bedroom across from Truman's study, ninety-year-old Madge Gates Wallace lay in a coma.

"The White House is quiet as a church," Truman wrote in his diary at five in the morning, November 24. "I can hear the planes at the airport warming up. As always there is a traffic roar—sounds like wind and rain through the magnolias.

"Bess's mother is dying across the hallway. . . ."

She had never been an easy person to get along with. Even as a resident of the White House she had let it be known in small ways to some of the servants and staff that she still thought Harry Truman not quite good enough for her Bess. But Truman, who had never been known to say anything critical about her, even by inference, was greatly saddened. "Since last September Mother Wallace has been dying . . . but we've kept doctors and nurses with her day and night and have kept her alive. We had hoped—and still hope—she'll survive until Christmas. Our last as President." When she died, on December 5, he wrote, "She was a grand lady. When I hear these mother-in-law jokes I don't laugh."

For a while the mood overall seemed one of a death watch over his own presidency. New poll results showed that only 32 percent of the people approved of the way he was handling his job; and 43 percent thought it had been a mistake for the United States to go to war in Korea. But polls meant no more to him now than ever before. "I wonder how far Moses would have gone if he'd taken a poll in Egypt?" he wrote privately, in an undated memo to himself. "What would Jesus Christ have preached if he'd taken a poll in Israel? . . . It isn't polls or public opinion of the moment that counts. It's right and wrong."

To Ethel Noland, he wrote that no one knew what responsibilities the job entailed, except from experience—"It bears down on a country boy." The people had never been better off, yet they wanted a change. He felt "repudiated." The people were fine about supporting the President in time of crisis, he told his staff, recalling the first weeks of the Korean War, "but when there is a long row of corn to shuck, they want an easy way out."

A new census report confirmed that gains in income, standards of living, education, and housing since Truman took office were unparalleled in American history. As Truman would report in his final State of the Union message to Congress, on January 7, 1953, 62 million Americans had jobs, which was a gain of 11 million jobs in seven years. Unemployment had all but disappeared. Farm income, corporate income, and dividends were at an all-time high. There had not been a failure of an insured bank in nearly nine years. His most important accomplishments, he knew, were in world affairs. Yet he could rightly point with pride to the fact that the postwar economic collapse that everyone expected never happened, that through government support (the GI Bill) 8 million veterans had been to college, that Social Security benefits had been doubled, the minimum wage increased. There had been progress in slum clearance, millions of homes built through government financing. Prices were higher, but incomes, for the most part, had risen even more. Real living standards were considerably higher than seven years earlier.

Truman had failed to do as much as he wanted for public housing, education, failed to establish the medical insurance program he knew the nation needed, but he had battled hard for these programs, set goals for the future. He had achieved less in civil rights than he had hoped, but he had created the epoch-making Commission on Civil Rights, ordered the desegregation of the armed services and the federal Civil Service, done more than any President since Lincoln to awaken American conscience to the issues of civil rights. Until the onset of the Korean War, he had also kept the budget in line, actually reduced the national debt.

With the establishment of a unified Defense Department, the National Security Council, and the CIA, he had changed the structure of power in Washington in ways surpassing even the sweeping measures of FDR. With the creation of the Atomic Energy Commission, he had kept the control of nuclear power in civilian hands.

Reminiscing with his staff, and occasionally with reporters, he talked of the accomplishments he was most proud of—aid to Greece and Turkey, the Marshall Plan, NATO, Point Four (which, if not a massive program, had also set a goal for the future), the Berlin Airlift. And Korea, "the supreme test," as he called it. The nation's military power had been restored, the nation's prestige was high.

In an extraordinary article in *Look* magazine the summer before, the historian Henry Steele Commager had written that by all normal measures the Truman administration had been one of almost uninterrupted, unparalleled success—a view that not only conflicted with popular opinion at the moment but with which the editors of the magazine specifically expressed their own disagreement.

"We cannot know what verdict history will pronounce upon it [the Truman record], but we can make a pretty good guess," wrote Commager.

It will perhaps record the curious paradox that a man charged with being "soft" on communism has done more than any other leader in the Western world, with the exception of Churchill, to contain communism; that a man charged with mediocrity has launched a whole series of far-sighted plans for world reconstruction; that a man accused of being an enemy to private enterprise has been head of the Government during the greatest period of greatest prosperity for private enterprise; that a man accused of betraying the New Deal has fought one Congress after another for progressive legislation.

Reviewing the record—for his message to Congress, for his farewell broadcast—improved Truman's spirits. He was in "high good humor," "vigorous, hearty," obviously happy as he worked to wind things up properly. He insisted on writing his farewell speech himself, and at the big table in the Cabinet Room one evening, the staff gathered, he read it aloud, stopping at the end of each page for their comments. Recounting the decision on Korea, he described how he had flown from Independence to Washington, the fateful Sunday in June 1950. "Flying back over the flatlands of the Middle West," he read, "I had a lot of time to think." Roger Tubby suggested he make it *"rich* flatlands"—"rich flatlands" would sound better, Tubby said. "The parts of southern Illinois, Indiana, and Ohio that I flew over are not rich, Roger," Truman replied. Plain "flatlands" it remained.

Pictures came down from his office walls. His desk was cleared of knickknacks, clocks, everything personal. Packing boxes lined the halls of the West Wing, as painters moved from room to room. Already he was making plans for his presidential library. Some four hundred steel file cabinets filled with his private and presidential papers had been shipped to Missouri. When his old friend Senator Kilgore came by for a last visit, Truman told him that if he had known there would be so much work in leaving, he would have run again.

Questioned whether he wanted to live in Washington, Truman said no. Asked about his future plans, he said he had none as yet.

He was "full of bounce" at his last press conference—his 324th—and applauded lustily at the end by some three hundred reporters. There were farewell letters to write. "You have been my good right hand," he wrote to Dean Acheson.

> Certainly no man is more responsible than you for pulling together the people of the free world, and strengthening their will and their determination to be strong and free.
>
> I would place you among the very greatest of the Secretaries of State this country has had. Neither Jefferson nor Seward showed more cool courage and steadfast judgment.

There was a last meeting with the Cabinet, a final session with his staff, a round of farewell dinners. The closer inauguration day drew, the happier Truman became. "Why, you'd have thought the President won the election the way he acts," the White House valet, Arthur Prettyman, told a reporter for the Washington *Post*.

Bennett Clark, Louis Johnson, Clark Clifford, and Senator-elect John F. Kennedy, among others, came to say goodbye. A select few reporters and writers were given the chance for a final, private interview. He felt much as he had when he was heading home from France after World War I, not knowing what the future held in store for him, Truman told Tony Leviero of *The New York Times*.

The critic and author John Mason Brown, who came and went several times, was surprised to find Truman looking "anything but old" and in "the most benevolent of valedictory moods," gentle, self-possessed.

> "In personality, conversation, and manner he bore no resemblance, even coincidental, to the quick-to-anger or the "pour-it-on Harry" of the whistle-stop tours. . . .
>
> Whenever I saw him, Truman was unfailingly equable and considerate of everyone on every level who worked with him or came to see him. The dreadful responsibilities he still bore, the appalling daily schedule which continued to be his, the abuse that had been heaped upon him, the annoyances of moving, the pangs of farewell, the drastically changed life that would soon face him, the uncertainties of his own future, and the verdict of history—none of these disturbed him.

The President's physical and mental "resilience," wrote Brown, was incredible. In fact, Truman, at sixty-eight, was leaving office in better health than when he came in in 1945 and better than any departing President since Theodore Roosevelt left the White House at age fifty in 1909.

Churchill arrived for a farewell call at the West Wing and to host a dinner for "Harry" at the British Embassy. Considerably more spry than on his last visit, Churchill was in "rollicking form" and Truman hugely enjoyed his company.

From Pennsylvania Avenue now, the White House was all but obscured behind the wooden grandstands set up for Eisenhower's inauguration.

Truman's farewell address was delivered from his desk in the Oval Office by radio and television the night of Thursday, January 15, 1953, at 10:30 Washington time. It was a speech without rhetorical flourishes or memorable epigrams and it was superb, Truman at his best. In what it forecast concerning the Cold War, it was more extraordinary than could possibly have been understood at the time. He was clear, simple, often personal, but conveying overall a profound sense of the momentous history of the times, the panoramic changes reshaping the world, and the part that he, inevitably, had had to play since that desolate day when he was summoned to the White House and told of Roosevelt's death. It was not a nostalgic farewell. He hated to think he was writing a valedictory, he had said privately beforehand. "I'm not through. I'm just starting."

"Next Tuesday," he began, "General Eisenhower will be inaugurated as President of the United States. A short time after the new President takes office, I will be on the train going back home to Independence, Missouri. I will once again be a plain, private citizen of this great Republic. That is as it should be. . . ."

Four years earlier, in his inaugural address, his emphasis had been on the world—democracy looking outward to the world. Now, reviewing his full time as President, he again struck the same theme. His very first decision as President, he reminded his audience, had been to go forward with the United Nations. He recalled the German surrender, his meeting with Churchill and Stalin at Potsdam, the first atomic explosion in the New Mexico desert, his decision to use the atomic bomb to end the war with Japan—all this, as he said, within a little more than four months. He did not say, as he could have, that no President in history had had to face so many important problems in so brief a time, or found it necessary to make so many momentous decisions so quickly or with such little preparation. What he said was that the greatest part of a President's responsibilities was making decisions. A President had to decide. "That's his job."

Yet it was not for the decisions of his first months in office that he would be remembered, Truman speculated.

> I suppose that history will remember my term in office as the years when the Cold War began to overshadow our lives.
> I have had hardly a day in office that has not been dominated by this all-embracing struggle.... And always in the background there has been the atomic bomb.
> But when history says that my term of office saw the beginning of the Cold War, it will also say that in those eight years we have set the course that can win it. . . .

The decision to go into Korea, he said, was the most important of his time in office. Korea was the turning point of the Cold War. Whereas free nations had failed to meet the test before—failed to stop Japanese aggression in Manchuria, the Nazi takeover in Austria and Czechoslovakia—"this time we met the test." Yet the horrific potential of modern war had not been allowed to get out of hand. That was what was so important to understand. The issue was world peace in the nuclear age.

In his State of the Union message of the week before, which he had sent to Congress rather than delivering personally before a joint session, Truman had reported that in recent thermonuclear tests at Eniwetok Island in the Pacific, "we have entered another stage in the world-shaking development of atomic energy," which was correctly understood to mean that the age of the H-bomb had arrived. The President who had ushered in the atomic bomb in 1945 was departing in 1953 at the start of a new era of destructive power "dwarfing," as he reported to Congress, "the mushroom clouds of Hiroshima and Nagasaki."

His intent in Korea, he now said, was to prevent World War III. "Starting an atomic war is totally unthinkable. . . ."

How then would the Cold War end, he asked. How and when?

He offered a simple forecast, a long-range prediction that, at heart, was a statement of faith. His whole life Truman had been moved primarily by faith. Now in this last chance to talk to the country, in his attempt to read the history of the future, he trusted again to an unwavering faith. To millions who listened then, it seemed a striking expression of the best instincts of America. Read many years later, in the light of what happened at the end of the Cold War, it would seem utterly extraordinary in its prescience. He appeared to know even then the essence of what in fact would transpire, and, more importantly, why.

> As the free world grows stronger, more united, more attractive to men on both sides of the Iron Curtain—and as the Soviet hopes for easy

expansion are blocked—then there will have to come a time of change in the Soviet world. Nobody can say for sure when that is going to be, or exactly how it will come about, whether by revolution, or trouble in the satellite states, or by a change inside the Kremlin.

Whether the Communist rulers shift their policies of their own free will—or whether the change comes about in some other way—I have not a doubt in the world that a change will occur.

I have a deep and abiding faith in the destiny of free men. With patience and courage, we shall some day move on into a new era....

He was "glad the whole world will have a chance to see how simply and how peacefully our American system transfers the vast power of the Presidency...." Looking back at his time in office, he said, he had no regrets, and he thanked the people for their support.

When Franklin Roosevelt died, I felt there must be a million men better qualified than I, to take up the Presidential task. But the work was mine to do, and I had to do it. And I have tried to give it everything that was in me....

Good night and God bless you all.

The speech, indeed Truman's whole handling of his departure, was praised on all sides. The speech was the finest of his presidency, it was said; he had finished strong. Walter Lippmann, who had been so consistently critical for years, wrote that

in the manner of his going Mr. Truman has been every inch the President, conscious of the great office and worthy of it.

His farewell messages are those of the man of whom it can fairly be said that he had many opponents and few enemies, that he had many more who wished him well and liked him than he had political supporters. He was often enough angry himself, and it was not hard to become angry with him. But neither he nor his critics and opponents were able to keep on being angry. For when he lost his temper, it was a good temper that he was losing. He has the good nature of a good man, and with his wife and daughter who are universally respected and liked, there is no bitter after-taste as the Truman family leave the White House.

Inauguration day was as sunny as it had been four years earlier, only warmer, with blue skies and again tremendous crowds. The ceremonies for Dwight David Eisenhower, the thirty-fourth President of the United States and the first Republican to hold the office in twenty years, went smoothly.

Up early, Truman spent an hour or so winding up odds and ends in his office and saying goodbye to the secretarial staff and Secret Service agents. Relaxed, exuding good cheer, he popped in and out of the other offices. "Looks mighty bare in here," he said. He was wearing the formal gray-striped trousers and Oxford gray coat that had been decided on as the inaugural attire. Many of the staff had brought their children to see him and say goodbye. At 10:30 there was a small reception for the Cabinet and their wives in the Red Room, as Truman waited for the President-elect to arrive.

The papers had been making much of a presidential hat crisis. Without consulting Truman, Eisenhower had announced he would be wearing a homburg, instead of the traditional top hat. So what would Truman wear, it was wondered? He had no wish to have his last quarrel over a hat, Truman told his staff. He would wear a homburg.

Further speculation had followed over whether the Eisenhowers would call on the President and First Lady before Inauguration Day, as was customary. Truman's hopes, it was said, "remained touchingly, almost boyishly high" that the tradition would be honored, and when the Eisenhowers declined an invitation to lunch, he felt insulted. Reportedly the general did not wish to enter the house until he was President. When, at 11:30, the Eisenhowers arrived at the North Portico, to start the drive to the Capitol, they refused to come in for a cup of coffee, but sat in the car waiting. Only when the Trumans appeared did they step out of the car to greet them.

"It was a shocking moment," recalled CBS correspondent Eric Sevareid, who was on the porch close by. "Truman was gracious and he had just been snubbed. He showed his superiority by what he did."

From the way the two men looked as they drove off in the big open Lincoln, J. B. West remembered, "I was glad I wasn't in that car."

"I ride with Ike in car No. 1 along with Joe Martin and Styles Bridges. Bess and Margie ride with Mrs. Ike," Truman recorded in his diary. "Conversation is general—on the crowd, the pleasant day, the orderly turnover, etc."

Later accounts of what was said would differ, but both Truman and Eisenhower would recall an exchange over the presence of Eisenhower's only son, Major John Eisenhower, at the inaugural ceremonies. Eisenhower asked Truman who had ordered John back from Korea, and according to Eisenhower, Truman said simply, "I did." But according to Truman what he said was, "The President thought it was right and proper for your son to witness the swearing-in of his father to the Presidency." In any event, three days later, Eisenhower would send Truman a gracious letter thanking him for "the very many courtesies you extended to me and mine during the final stages of your Administration . . . I especially want to thank you for your thoughtfulness in ordering my son home from Korea . . . and even more especially for not allowing either him or me to know that you had done so."

Truman had been President for seven years, nine months, for 2,841 days, and at noon it was over. He tried to pay attention to Eisenhower's inaugural address, he later wrote, but his mind was on other things.

Less than half an hour later, he was being driven in a closed limousine back from the Capitol toward Georgetown when at 7th and D streets the driver stopped for a red light. It was the first time that a car in which Truman was riding had had to stop for a traffic light since 1945.

A farewell luncheon for the Trumans, before their train, had been arranged at the Achesons' home. It was to be a small, private party for the Cabinet, White House aides, and a few close friends, but as the car swung into P Street a crowd of several hundred people, massed in front of the red-brick house, set up a cheer. Truman was astonished. "The street in front of Dean's house," he wrote, "was full of people who cheered as if I were coming in instead of going out."

Swallowing hard, he told them, "I appreciate this more than any enthusiastic meeting I attended as President, Vice President and Senator. I'm just plain Mr. Truman now, a private citizen."

Elsewhere in the city, as the Eisenhower inaugural parade filled Pennsylvania Avenue, others were telephoning friends to say that perhaps, even with the city tied up in traffic, they ought to try to get down to Union Station so that at least someone would be there to see the Trumans off.

Margaret would describe the lunch at the Achesons' as "an absolutely wonderful affair full of jokes and laughter and a few tears." By the time the party broke up, the crowd in P Street reached the length of the block. Traffic was backed up far beyond. When the Trumans went for their train, thousands were at the station to see him, wave to him, cheer and call, "So long, Harry!" "Good luck, Harry!" People pressed forward reaching for his hand.

The *Ferdinand Magellan,* provided as a courtesy by the new President, had been attached to a regular B&O train bound for Missouri. The police formed a flying wedge to get the Trumans through the crowd.

Old friends, Democratic senators, Supreme Court justices, members of the Cabinet, generals and ambassadors, piled aboard to shake Truman's hand one more time. "There's the best friend in the world," Acheson said above the noise, when a reporter tapped him on the arm. "There's nothing like that man."

He kept smiling, waving. Bess looked radiant.

"I can't adequately express my appreciation for what you are doing. I'll never forget it if I live to be a hundred," Truman said from the rear platform. Then, chopping his hands in the air with the familiar gesture, he said with a grin, "And that's just what I intend to do!"

At 6:30, with the crowd singing "Auld Lang Syne," the train began pulling slowly out of the station, until it was beyond the lighted platform. It had been a long road from Independence to the White House, and now Truman was going home.

"Crowd at Harper's Ferry . . . and it was reported to me at every stop all night long," he recorded. "Same way across Indiana and Illinois."

PART SIX

BACK HOME

18

Citizen Truman

Been going over a book on what former Presidents did in times past. Maybe I can get some ideas.

—TRUMAN TO DEAN ACHESON, APRIL 1953

I

For as far back nearly as he could remember, Truman had held to the ideal of the mythical Roman hero Cincinnatus, the patriot farmer who assumes command in his country's hour of peril, then returns to the plow. "Who knows, maybe I'll be like Cincinnatus and be elected constable someday," the farmer from Grandview had written long ago to Bessie Wallace. It was an ideal upon which the nation had been founded. Truman and Dwight Eisenhower, in their inaugural procession through the Rotunda of the Capitol, had passed by John Trumbull's immense painting of George Washington as Cincinnatus—Washington resigning his commission to the Congress as commander-in-chief of the Army, Washington, farmer and hero, turning away from power in 1783. Now, in 1953, having become considerably more than constable, having turned by his own choice from the most power ever vested in a single human being in all history until then, Truman would note in his diary that Cincinnatus knew not only when but how to lay down power.

It was the common belief in America, Truman wrote, that anyone could become President, and then, when the time was up, go back to being "just anybody again." Recalling his years in the White House, he would say, "I tried never to forget who I was and where I'd come from and where I would go back to." In actual practice, however, it was not so simple. A cartoon in the *Saturday Review* showed a small boy with glasses and a book under his arm, a boy very like Truman had been, walking beside a friend who said, "O.K., so you grow up to be President, and you

927

even get reelected, that's still only eight years. What do you do with the rest of your life?" With his pen, Truman scrawled boldly across the bottom, "God *only* knows!!!"

He had traveled home from Washington unprotected by Secret Service agents and there were to be none watching over him. He had come home without salary or pension. He had no income or support of any kind from the federal government other than his Army pension of $112.56 a month. He was provided with no government funds for secretarial help or office space, not a penny of expense money, and while he and Bess had managed to put aside part of his $100,000-a-year salary as President during his second term, primarily in government bonds, it was in all probability a modest amount. Estimates at the time ranged as high as a quarter of a million dollars, but there was no evidence to support such a figure, or any sum. In fact, it is known that Truman had been forced to take out a loan at the National Bank in Washington in his last weeks as President, to tide him over, though the amount was never disclosed.

With his brother and sister, he had inherited Martha Ellen Truman's farm land at Grandview, and while official disposition of the old house at 219 North Delaware had yet to be made, he and Bess would soon become joint owners. Certainly, as things were, there could be no extravagant living. In effect they were land-rich only. The estate of the supposedly well-to-do Madge Wallace, not including the house, totaled all of $33,543.60, which after being divided four ways among Bess and her brothers, left Bess with a cash inheritance of $8,385.90. Indeed, among the reasons why they had come back to Independence and the old house was that financially they had little other choice.

The town buzzed with speculation over where the Trumans might live now, whether they would stay on in "the old Wallace place," which to many seemed unlikely for someone who had been President of the United States. "Rumors have it that they will buy a fine home and live in Kansas City," wrote Sue Gentry in the *Examiner*. "Other rumors predict they will build a home on farm land Mr. Truman owns at Grandview, a part of his old home place." A local attorney and old friend of the family, Rufus Burrus, had picked out an elegant house in a new section of town that he thought perfect, much more suitable for a former President. But all such talk was beside the point, finances notwithstanding. The Trumans had no intention of living anywhere else, no interest in living somewhere warmer or less expensive or more glamorous.

Herbert Hoover, the country's one other surviving former President, was a man of wealth who lived in style at the Waldorf Towers in New York. Theodore Roosevelt, William Howard Taft, Woodrow Wilson, none of those who had faced the prospect of being a former President since the start of the century, had had worries about money; none but Calvin Coolidge who, downcast over the death of a son and in poor health, lived less than three years after leaving office. Theodore Roosevelt had gone storming off to Africa to hunt big game; Taft became a professor of law at Yale, then Chief Justice of the United States. Wilson, with his wealthy second wife, retired in style to a twenty-two-room house on S Street in Washington and lived a few more years in semi-seclusion. For his part, Truman had neither wealth to sustain him nor any particular prospects at the moment, no plans for future employment. His only intention, as he said, was to do nothing—accept no position, lend his name to no organization or transaction—that would exploit or "commercialize" the prestige and dignity of the office of the President.

He had had a number of offers already from undisclosed organizations for jobs paying $100,000 a year or more, and calling for little commitment of his time. A letter from a Miami real estate developer inviting him to become "chairman, officer, or stockholder, at a figure of not less than $100,000" would turn up later in his files, but what the other propositions were is not clear, though none apparently was from a corporation or organization of particular renown. In any event, he had turned them all down and would continue to do so. His name was not for sale. He would take no fees for commercial endorsements or for lobbying or writing letters or making phone calls. He would accept no "consulting fees," nor any gifts that might appear as a product endorsement on his part. Offered a new Toyota, by Toyota's American public relations firm, as a demonstration of improved good feelings between Japan and America, he flatly refused. Moreover, he wrote in response, there was no possibility of his ever driving a foreign car of any make. He believed in driving cars made in America.

He liked to say he was just a plain American citizen again. It confirmed his democratic philosophy. It pleased people and pleased him. But the difficulties in practice were more than he had anticipated. "I still don't feel like a completely private citizen and I don't suppose I ever will," he told a reporter. "It's still almost impossible to do as other people do, even though I've tried. You can't always be as you want to be after you've been under those bright lights."

Further, he missed the bright lights. He missed the pace of the presidency, felt strange without the constant pressures. He missed the people terribly. In thanking Dean Acheson for the farewell luncheon, he wrote that he had never been to such a party "where everybody seemed to be having the best time they ever had." Then he added, "I hope we will never lose contact."

•   •   •

The cheering throng that welcomed the Trumans home at the Independence depot the night of their return exceeded all expectations. Perhaps ten thousand people were waiting in the cold when the train came round the bend at 9:03, an hour late because of other crowds at earlier stops across Missouri. Truman was astonished, overjoyed. "Well, Harry, this makes it all worth it," Bess said to him.

They had arrived the night of Wednesday, January 21. The morning after, asked by NBC correspondent Ray Scherer what was the first thing he planned to do, Truman said he was going to "carry the grips up to the attic," a remark that would become famous. (Scherer, like Tony Vaccaro of the Associated Press, had accompanied Truman from Washington on the train, as had Roger Tubby.) But in another hour, Truman was on his way out the door, heading downtown to Kansas City in a state highway patrol car, riding up front with Sergeant Art Bell, a former Battery D "boy" who had been assigned by the governor as a temporary driver. Truman went to see his new offices, four corner rooms on the eleventh floor of the Federal Reserve Bank Building, at 10th and Grand. The faithful Rose Conway was already on duty sorting through several thousand letters, mostly expressions of praise and gratitude, all of which Truman felt obliged to answer.

There was no official welcome in Kansas City, but this seemed to bother him not at all. When, with Roger Tubby, he walked five blocks to the Muehlebach for lunch with his brother Vivian, and few passers-by took notice, Truman kept on smiling and talking as though all were perfectly fine.

The following day the weather turned foul, with a sudden drop in temperature—down to the 20s—accompanied by a biting north wind, sleet, and snow. Ignoring the weather, Truman set off for Grandview, to look over the site for the library he planned to build. Roger Tubby had arranged for some of the local press to join him and the group made a memorable picture, the old President, his collar up against the wind, tramping across the snow-covered fields, talking rapidly of his childhood and of his $1,500,000 project and what it would mean to the young students "who will take over the destiny of our country," while a half-dozen reporters, his former White House press secretary, and one-time comrade-in-arms Sergeant Bell in his state police uniform, all tried their best to keep up and stay warm.

The library was the "big interest now." Truman's papers, for the time being, were stored at the county courthouse in Kansas City. Since the time of George Washington, it had been commonly understood that a President's papers were his own personal property, and that he was free to do with them as he wished. The Franklin Roosevelt Library had been established at Hyde Park, New York, the first so-called "Presidential Library," on the grounds of the Roosevelt estate on the Hudson, but Roosevelt had not lived to take part in the project. Truman, before leaving office, had sent George Elsey out from Washington to look over the farm with his brother Vivian and architect Edward Neild. Vivian had led them to the spot where he thought the library ought to go: a low-lying, swampy corner close to the railroad tracks. When Elsey and Neild pointed to a more attractive site on a high rise with views in all directions, Vivian objected. That was good land, Vivian said, and he saw no reason to waste good land on "any old dang library."

Truman had already made some sketches. He wanted the building to look like his Grandfather Solomon Young's house, the big house of his own childhood memories. Truman had made a rough drawing of the house as best he could remember it.

"A cold wind whipping around us," Roger Tubby would record in his diary, "and he talks of the library. 'This America of ours . . . we look out over the prairies, envision cities or universities and lo, they arise!' "

The former President, reported the *Examiner,* seemed to enjoy the brisk weather.

A few days later, on a Sunday, he set off early, before it was fully light, on his first walk through town, free of Sergeant Bell or bodyguards of any kind for the first time in more than seven years. He covered some fifteen blocks, rounding Jackson Square en route, and nothing he had done thus far, he later wrote, had given such a striking sense of being on his own at last. "More than any other single thing, this marked the abrupt change in my life."

Speaking at a huge welcome-home banquet at the auditorium of the Reorganized Latter-Day Saints, Truman said simply and from the heart, "There never is and never can be anything like coming back home."

He bought Bess a new car, a four-door black Chrysler with white-wall tires, and started driving himself again. As sightseers and the curious kept coming around the house almost daily, he decided not to have the iron fence taken down. Often whole delegations—Girl Scouts, tourists—stood outside looking through the fence. "Is this where Truman lives?" a man called to him at seven one morning from a car at the curb.

He kept to the routine of the morning walks, kept up with the mail pouring into the office in Kansas City—72,000 pieces in the first two weeks alone. He refused to be idle. His name was painted in black block letters on the door marked 1107. He arrived regularly before nine each morning.

Nearly anyone who wished could come into the office to shake hands with him or visit. As he told a friend, "You don't need an appointment to see me now." Yet he was worse than alone, his friend Tom Evans would remember. "He was utterly *lost*. After all those years in the White House with somebody around to do everything for him, he didn't know how to order a meal in a restaurant. He didn't know when to tip. He didn't even know how to call a cab and pay for it." But as Evans also remembered, Truman never said a word of complaint.

At home the house seemed "quiet and too big," with only Bess and Vietta Garr, who went to her own home after dinner. Every night, he and Bess would call Margaret in New York.

By early February, less than a month since the return, it began to look as though their financial worries were over. He was about to sign a book contract for a "fantastic sum," Truman wrote to Acheson, and on February 12, the press reported that he had sold the exclusive worldwide rights to his memoirs to *Life* magazine for an undisclosed amount. In fact, the figure was $600,000—truly a fantastic sum in 1953—which, by a contract negotiated for him by Sam Rosenman, was to be paid in installments over five years.

At the end of March, he, Bess, and Margaret went off on a dream vacation trip to Hawaii, traveling first to San Francisco as the guests of Averell Harriman in his private railroad car. From San Francisco, they sailed on the *President Cleveland,* of the American Presidents Line, down the bay and out under the Golden Gate Bridge. Of the morning they arrived off Oahu, Truman wrote: "Diamond Head and then Honolulu with the Pali in the background, rainbows, clouds, sunshine and a beautiful city all in one scene."

It was one of the most enchanting experiences of their lives. Hawaii was "Paradise," and they stayed a month, as the guests of Ed Pauley at his estate on little Coconut Island, in Kaneohe Bay, on the windward side of Oahu. Long a champion of statehood for the islands, Truman was given an effusive Hawaiian welcome from the moment the ship landed. Government and military officials, the press, a dozen different reception committees rushed on board to escort him ashore. "[They] covered us with leis and smothered us with questions and flash bulbs." He accepted an honorary degree at the University of Hawaii, toured Oahu, and on a flying visit to the big island of Hawaii in a Navy C-47, soared over the saddle between the snow-capped volcanoes, Mauna Kea and Mauna Loa. When, on the return flight to Oahu, he spotted a school of whales off Maui, the Navy pilots told him it meant good luck. He swam, loafed, read, and thoroughly enjoyed "the wonderful people" of the islands . . . And then the month was over and he was home again at North Delaware Street, where the house was still quiet and too big.

. . .

He bought another car, this one for himself, a two-tone green Dodge coupe, to drive to his office. He loved cars no less than ever and was as fussy as ever about their appearance.

"This morning at 7 A.M., I took off for my morning walk," begins a diary entry from that spring.

> I'd just had the Dodge car washed a day or so ago and it looked as if it had never been used.
>
> The weather man said it would rain so I decided to put the washed car in the garage and use the black car which was already spotted and dusty. My sister-in-law, watching me make the change, which required some maneuvering due to the location of several cars in the driveway, wanted to know if I might be practicing for a job in a parking station!

He knew he must get started on his memoirs, but dreaded the prospect. Hawaii had made him "lazy as hell." He wished he had never agreed to do the book.

On his walk that same spring morning he stopped to watch a construction project, the widening of Truman Road.

> A shovel (automatic) and a drag line were working as well as some laboring men digging in the old fashioned way. The boss or the contractor was looking on and I asked him if he didn't need a good strawboss. He took a look at me and then watched the work a while and then took another look and broke out in a broad smile and said, "Oh yes! You *are* out of a job aren't you."

He felt a constant need to be on the move. So in the heat of June, he and Bess started for Washington in the new Chrysler. He wanted to give the car "a real tryout," he said. Bess was delighted. Friends and family tried to talk them out of going. He and Bess had not traveled on their own by automobile in nine years, not since their return from the Chicago convention in 1944. Yet off they went, making an early start, Truman at the wheel. Wasn't it good to be on their own again, she said. They got as far as Hannibal before stopping for lunch at a roadside restaurant, only to find how difficult being on their own was going to be. As Truman later wrote to his old Army friend, Vic Householder, "Everything went well until a couple of old-time County Judges came in and saw me. They said, 'Why there's Judge Truman'—and then every waitress and all the customers had to shake hands and have autographs."

At Decatur, Illinois, 150 miles later, Truman pulled into a Shell station where he had often stopped for gas in years past, traveling to and from

Washington. An elderly attendant who kept studying him while filling the tank, finally inquired if he wasn't Senator Truman.

> I admitted the charge [Truman continued in his letter to Householder] and asked him if he could direct me to a good motel in town. We'd never stayed at one and wanted to try it out and see if we liked it. Well he directed us but he told everybody in town about it. The Chief of Police got worried about us and sent two plain clothes men and four uniformed police to look after us. They took us to dinner and to breakfast the next morning and escorted us out of town with a sigh of relief.

Bess insisted he keep to the 50-mile-an-hour speed limit. But going "so slowly," as he said, meant others passing had a chance to look them over. "Hi, Harry!" people shouted as they went by. "There goes our incognito," he told her. At the hotel where they stopped in Wheeling, West Virginia, the lobby was jammed with reporters and photographers.

But there was no doubt that he loved the attention. When, at Frederick, Maryland, he saw several familiar faces from the Washington press corps waiting in a car to escort him into the city, he greeted them like long-lost brothers. "You're a sight for sore eyes," he exclaimed. Pulling up at the Mayflower Hotel, he stepped from the car in his shirtsleeves to be immediately surrounded by a crowd of more reporters and photographers and hotel employees, all trying to shake his hand. He was there only to have a good time, he said, his face beaming in the late afternoon sunshine—"carefree as a schoolboy in summer," according to the account in the *Post* the next morning. To all questions concerning Congress, the President, the Korean War, Truman said, "No comment, no comment, no comment."

A steady stream of old friends, members of his Cabinet, Democratic senators, members of Congress came to call. It was "like a dream," Truman later wrote. "The suite we stayed in at the Mayflower could have been the White House. . . . Everything seemed just as it used to be—the taxi drivers shouting hello along the line of my morning walks, the dinners at night with the men and women I had worked with for years, the conferences, the tension, the excitement, the feeling of things happening and going to happen. . . ."

And the "good time" continued over the next weekend, when he and Bess drove on to New York and checked in at the Waldorf-Astoria. With Margaret they dined at the Twenty-one Club and saw Leonard Bernstein's *Wonderful Town* at the Winter Garden. As they came into the theater, the whole audience rose and applauded.

Cab drivers in New York did not just call to him, they pulled to the curb and jumped out to shake his hand. He was still their man, he was assured. "If you'd go again tomorrow, Harry, you'd win."

Heading home for Missouri, "perking along" on the Pennsylvania Turnpike, Truman was signaled to pull over by the police. According to what State Trooper Manly Stampler told reporters, "Mr. Truman" had twice cut in front of vehicles trying to pass him. "He was very nice about it and promised to be more careful." But according to Truman, who had never had a traffic violation, the young man had only wanted to shake hands.

It was his last venture with Bess on their own by automobile. Thereafter, they would go by train, plane, or ship.

On March 5, in Moscow, after nearly three decades in power, Joseph Stalin had died of a cerebral hemorrhage at age seventy-three. Ten days later, Stalin's successor, Georgi M. Malenkov, declared in a speech that there was no issue between Moscow and Washington that could not be resolved by peaceful means. Two weeks after Malenkov's speech, the Communists in Korea suddenly agreed to an exchange of wounded prisoners and said that this should lead to a "peaceful settlement" of the entire prisoner issue. Then in the final week of July, as Truman, in the heat of high summer in Missouri, was beginning work on his memoirs, an armistice was signed at Panmunjom; the Korean War was over.

It was an armistice with voluntary repatriation, and the dividing line between North and South Korea was to remain the 38th parallel. So President Eisenhower had achieved essentially the very same settlement that had eluded Truman—a "no-win" agreement, as Truman's Republican critics would have called it. As Senator Paul Douglas observed, Truman "would have been flayed from one end of Washington to the other if he had accepted the present agreement."

Stalin's death had unquestionably had an effect; so also had Eisenhower's threats to use newly developed tactical nuclear weapons in Korea.

The war had caused terrible bloodshed and destruction—perhaps as many as 2 million civilian dead according to some estimates, 4 million casualties overall. The Americans killed in battle numbered 33,629 and another 20,617 Americans died of other causes.

To many Americans at home, it seemed the war had resolved nothing. But to Truman, as to a great many others, it was a major victory for the United States and the United Nations. Military aggression had been stopped. The Communist advance in Asia had been checked; South Korea and possibly Japan as well had been saved from what had seemed an inexorable "Red tide." The United Nations had been shown to be something more than a world debating society "As for the United States [wrote

The New York Times], the action in Korea represented something of a regaining of our national soul and conscience. We did a difficult and costly thing because we thought it was right."

Asked for his opinion about the armistice settlement, Eisenhower said simply, "The war is over, and I hope my son is coming home soon." Truman said nothing for attribution. Though undoubtedly and understandably resentful that his successor had achieved what he himself had failed to attain, and without resulting political rancor, he kept silent. Privately he thanked God it was ended. "Of course I'm happy about the truce in Korea," he wrote to a friend. "It doesn't make any difference about the credit for holding back Soviet aggression. The fact that the shooting has stopped is a very satisfactory one."

The following October, when Eisenhower came to Kansas City for a speech to the Future Farmers of America, and was staying at the Muehlebach, Truman tried to reach him at the hotel by phone, to say he would like to drop by to pay his respects, but was told by an aide that the President's schedule was too full, a meeting would be impossible. Truman was shattered. In explanation, Eisenhower's office later said that whoever answered the phone must have thought it was a crank call.

II

With the task of the memoirs that he had been putting off finally under way, and with his efforts to launch the library, Truman found himself more occupied than he had ever anticipated. "The book is doing fine but what a slave it's made of me," he would report to Dean Acheson in the fall.

Of all the presidents until then, only Herbert Hoover had written his own story in his lifetime. ("How much is lost to us because so few Presidents have told their own stories," Truman was to say in the preface to his own work.) John Quincy Adams and James K. Polk had written extensively about their time in office, but in their private diaries. Ulysses S. Grant, dying of cancer, had spent his final days laboring heroically on his memoirs as a means to provide financial security for his family, but Grant chose not to include his shadowed years in the White House. Even Theodore Roosevelt, with his sense of history and of his own importance to history, was oddly superficial when describing his presidency in his popular autobiography. Nor had Herbert Hoover, in telling his story, been obliged to recount anything approaching the world-shaking tumult, the watershed history, of the Truman years. The closest thing to what Truman would be attempting was Winston Churchill's magisterial history of World War II, which had also appeared first in *Life,* and against which, as Truman knew, whatever he produced was bound to be compared.

"I'm not a writer!" those working with him on the project were to hear him say many times. He was not after their sympathy, only stating what he saw as the heart of the problem. Before the task was finished a full dozen people would be involved.

The first called in to help were William Hillman and David Noyes, both of whom had served on the White House staff as speechwriters and whose loyalty to Truman verged on adoration. Hillman, a hulking veteran newspaper correspondent, had already published a eulogizing Truman portrait called *Mr. President,* a book of photographs with text compiled mainly from Truman quotes and selections from his private papers. Noyes was in advertising in California, a short, wiry, talkative man, who had worked on the 1948 campaign and was best known for initiating the controversial scheme to send Chief Justice Vinson to Moscow. His claim to have been one of Truman's key advisers was greatly exaggerated.

Promising to "protect" Truman from the publisher, Hillman and Noyes set up a working procedure for the memoirs. They offered advice and they came and went, flying in and out of Kansas City, as need be, every month or so, while a paid staff of three was established in Room 1002, on the floor below Truman at the Federal Reserve Bank Building. The plan was for Truman to "talk" the book. For months, he talked to a recording machine supplied by *Life*—a device he hated—responding to questions put to him by the hour by a University of Southern California professor of journalism named Robert E. G. Harris. Meantime, two young research assistants checked all that Truman said against what was in the files. By late fall, more than 100,000 words had been transcribed, all beautifully typed and arranged in looseleaf notebooks. But there was very little in the way of an actual manuscript, and what Truman saw of this, he didn't like. "Good God, what crap!" he scrawled across the top.

Professor Harris was dismissed, his place taken by another academic scholar, Morton Royce, a highly disorganized, excessively profane man, who continued on with the interviews, but ever so slowly, pressing Truman over and over for more complete and detailed answers, often returning to the same questions several times, and particularly about the atomic bomb. As a consequence, Truman grew extremely annoyed with Royce and the whole process.

The editor of *Life,* Ed Thompson, flew in from New York for a first look early in 1954. Truman had agreed to deliver 300,000 words by June 30, 1955. As it was, perhaps thirty-five pages of manuscript were ready. The raw material, Truman's own recollections, Thompson thought "lively" and "honest." But far greater progress was needed, and soon.

Morton Royce departed and two new writers were taken on, young Herbert Lee Williams, a doctoral candidate from the University of Missouri, and Francis H. Heller, an associate professor of political science at the University of Kansas.

Williams would remember being astonished by the volume of official and private papers at hand:

> The cream of the White House communications mix from 1945 to 1952 had been systematically ladled into 50 large metal file cabinets which now lined the walls of the eleventh-floor suite, Truman's offices [upstairs]. In these were all of the personal and official correspondence of the President: transcripts of 2,003 public speeches and 324 press conferences; a multitude of inter-office memoranda and directives; minutes of countless executive sessions; copies of more than 31,000 dictated letters, plus handwritten notes to Mamma or sister Mary. . . .
>
> The first bundle of files I was given, to take down to 1002 where I was to digest the contents and regurgitate them in memoirs form, covered the entire lend-lease story, from the time that Truman inherited it from FDR. . . .

Entering Truman's office one morning in search of a reference book, Williams was also astonished to find the former President fixing himself a drink. (As Williams strongly disapproved of drinking, he would, as time went on, decline invitations to join Truman for lunch, which customarily began with "a little H_2O flavored with bourbon," as Truman would say.)

As manuscript chapters began to emerge, they were reviewed page by page during lengthy sessions in Truman's office, a good-sized room comfortably furnished with leather chairs, a flag, portraits of Jackson and Jefferson, and books across one wall. The windows faced west over a panoramic view of the city and the distant hills of Kansas. As someone on the staff read aloud, Truman would sit listening intently. "His approval or criticism was solicited almost paragraph by paragraph. The whole idea was to jog the memory of the man who had been there, to add the auto to the biography," Williams would recall in an article somewhat vainly and inaccurately titled, "I Was Truman's Ghost." In fact, he was only a minor ghost among the several enlisted, and his participation was to be relatively brief.

As time went on, various members of Truman's White House staff, as well as Dean Acheson, John Snyder, General Bradley, and others of Truman's Cabinet would come to Kansas City to take part in these review sessions.

· · ·

The man who had been rising early and going off to work every morning most of his long life had by now settled again into the old pattern. At the house on North Delaware the lights started coming on well before dawn, usually at 5:30, at the sound of the courthouse clock. His morning paper, the Kansas City *Times,* arrived shortly afterward, tossed over the iron fence from a passing car, and he would unlatch the front door and come down the porch steps in his shirtsleeves to retrieve the paper from the front walk.

About seven he would emerge again from the front door, in suit jacket and hat now, a walking cane in hand. He would go out the front gate—in turn unlocking, closing, and checking to see it was secure—then start off on his walk, a half hour tour that took him through the same neighborhoods, over much the same ground in memory, that he was covering in the memoirs. Across the street still was the little Victorian Noland house, occupied still by his Noland cousins, Ethel and Nellie. Rounding the corner from North Delaware, left onto Maple and heading east, "uptown" to the Square, he would pass the red-brick First Presbyterian Church where he and Bess had met in Sunday School. (*She had golden curls and has, to this day, the most beautiful eyes,* he was saying in the memoirs.) At the Square, Clinton's drugstore was now Helzberg Jewelers, but looked not greatly different from when he had worked there so diligently as a boy (*. . . mopping the floors, sweeping the sidewalk, and having everything shipshape when Mr. Clinton came in*).

The courthouse, the "new" courthouse as his generation still called it, *his* courthouse, held sway over the Square no less than ever, its white cupola catching the morning sun ahead of the rest of the town. Tourists would ask which was his office, which were his windows. (*The judges of these Missouri county courts are not judges in the usual sense, since the court is an administrative, not a judicial body. . . .*)

The town had greatly changed in the two decades since he had first gone to Washington. The town was still changing, growing. New sections of new houses seemed to spring up overnight. Traffic was heavier. The population was now past 40,000, more than five times what it had been when he was a boy. More and more, Independence was becoming a suburb of Kansas City. Yet the old part of town, the Square, the neighborhoods of his boyhood looked much like they always had, and he felt great affection for all of it.

Others who were up and about early often made an effort to say hello, to introduce themselves and shake his hand as he came down the sidewalk at his steady clip. "I always try to be as pleasant as I can," he wrote in his diary. "They, of course, don't know that I walk early to get a chance to think over things and get ready for work of the day." If he didn't know them, he usually knew something about someone they were related to or descended from, and these recollections always pleased him.

"Well, I went to Maple Ave., turned left 'toward town' and spoke to several people, turned south on Pleasant Street," continues the diary account of one such morning.

> After I'd passed the light at Lexington I met a young man, Frank A. Reynolds, who introduced himself as John Strother's son-in-law. We talked a few minutes and I thought of the Strother family—one of the best old families in the County.
>
> John was Democratic Committeeman from Blue Township (Independence) from the time I was road overseer in Washington Township until I went to Washington as U.S. Senator from Missouri. He was a grand man—but wouldn't tell his age! He was my father's generation and he always wanted to be young with the young men. He was a good lawyer and an honest one too.
>
> Just as I started to leave Mr. Strother's son-in-law—and there were other great Strothers: Sam, who was a pillar of the Democratic Party in Kansas City; a second generation Judge, Duvall, and many others—as I say, just as I started to walk again a car stopped across the street and the man jumped out and came over to shake hands and said, "I'm sure you can't remember me—it's been so long since you've seen me." I did though. I told him whose son he is and who his grandfather was! Some feat for a man who has met millions of people.
>
> He belonged to the Pugh family. His grandfather, Noah E. Pugh, was one fine man. He came out to Missouri in 1894 or 1895 and settled on my mother's part of her father's estate, 160 acres south east of the farm about three miles. Mr. Pugh had several sons and daughters older and younger than I. Conley Pugh was a few years older than I and was married to a nice Grandview girl when they were very young. It was a happy marriage and the man who stopped me is Conley's oldest boy. He told me he had four children. It is remarkable indeed how time flies and makes you an old man whether you want to be or not.

His mother had never looked back, always forward, he liked to remind himself. It was part of her strength. With the work on his memoirs, and these daily tours through the old neighborhoods now after so many years, he was thinking more than ever of both parents.

He varied his route one day to another, but it hardly mattered. Whichever way he went was a walk through the past. The boyhood home at River and Waldo was still standing, as was the old house on South Crysler, near the depot. (*When we moved to Independence in December 1890, my father bought a big house on South Crysler Street with several acres of land. . . .*)

There was to be only one chapter about his early life, taking him from boyhood to his return from France in 1919. But it was a part of the story only he could tell, for which there were no file drawers to search, and the words would be his.

(In the fall of 1892 Grover Cleveland was re-elected over Benjamin Harrison, who had defeated him in 1888. My father was very much elated by Cleveland's victory. He rode a beautiful gray horse in the torchlight parade and decorated the weather vane on the tower at the north-east corner of the house with a flag and bunting. The weather vane was a beautiful gilded rooster.)

Once at the White House, a magazine writer had remarked to him that his father had been a failure. How could he be called a failure, he had answered, if his son became President of the United States.

During the half hour or so that he was gone from the house, at about 7:15, Vietta Garr would arrive by taxi at the side gate to begin fixing breakfast. The schedule rarely varied. He would return through the front gate at 7:30, not to reemerge until roughly 8:15, but from the back porch this time and carrying an aluminum briefcase, with the manuscript pages he had brought home the night before. He would head for the garage. Then the two-tone green Dodge would be seen backing cautiously out the driveway and off he would go, west down Truman Road, the Kansas City skyline dead ahead and on sunny mornings shining like an artist's picture of America on the rise.

His regular parking space was in an open lot a block from the office. He would pay a dollar in advance and walk to the bank building. Entering in the lobby, he would tip his hat to the elevator operator, Kay Walker, and greet her by name. By 8:45, he was at his desk.

"I have been working on the opening chapter of my purported memoirs," Truman wrote to Dean Acheson from the office on January 28, 1954, trying to get to the bottom of why he found the task so very difficult.

I have tried to place myself back into the position I was on April 12, 1945. I have read letters to my mother and sister, to my brother and cousins. I have read telegrams to and from Churchill and Roosevelt, to and from Stalin and Roosevelt. I've read memos I made of visits to the White House from April 12th back to July 1944. I've read Ike's, Leahy's, Churchill's, Grew's, Cordell Hull's books. Memos from Hopkins, Stimson, Assist. and Acting Secretary of State Dean Acheson; reports from Marshall, Eisenhower, King, Bradley. Communiqués of Teheran, Cairo, Casablanca, Quebec, Yalta, Byrnes' book on it, etc., etc. ad lib and still I am living today. . . .

So you see the past has always interested me for use *in the pres-*

ent and I am bored to death with what I did and didn't do nine years ago.

But Andrew Johnson, James Madison, even old Rutherford B. Hayes I'm extremely interested in as I am [in] King Henry IV of France, Margaret of Navarre, Charles V and Philip II of Spain and Charlie's Aunt Margaret.

Wish to goodness I'd decided to spend my so called retirement putting Louis XIII, Gustavus Adolphus, Richelieu and five tubs of gold together instead of writing about me and my mistakes. . . .

On St. Patrick's Day, he wrote again to tell Acheson he was thinking still about the relationship between history and government. "Our tribal instinct has not been eliminated by science and invention. We, as individuals, haven't caught up physically or ethically with the atomic age. Will we?"

Perhaps their grandchildren would do better, though, he added, in his case this remained a hypothetical statement. (Margaret as yet had shown no signs of getting married.)

He sensed a change in how the country regarded him and was heartened by it. "The tone of my mail has changed completely. It still comes in by the bushel but there's hardly a mean one in two hundred. . . ."

The increase in interest and appreciation at home in Independence was even more striking. Automobiles and sightseeing buses now cruised slowly by on North Delaware nearly all day. When Bess sent some of his clothes to her church rummage sale, word spread that one item, an overcoat, had been worn at Potsdam—a silly claim since the meeting at Potsdam had taken place in midsummer, but the coat brought a big price just the same. A sign at the depot now proclaimed: "Independence, the Home of Harry S. Truman, 33rd President of the United States"—a sign that annoyed Truman, who, with his concern for historical accuracy, insisted he was the thirty-second president since Cleveland served twice.

Some people in town, mainly among Republicans, thought no better of him than they had before. But they were a decided minority. By strong consensus the town thought it wonderful that the Trumans were home to stay. People liked the way they had both stepped modestly back into the life of the town, and especially the way "Mr. Truman" conducted himself, as a fellow citizen. They were as proud of him for his lack of side, his fundamental small-town genuineness after all, as they were of anything about him. "I used to say that Harry Truman lived around the corner from me," his old friend and ardent Republican, Henry Bundschu, told a magazine writer from the East, "now there isn't a day goes by that I don't tell myself that you live around the corner from Harry Truman and don't you forget it."

Largest and most generous of the town's gestures, and much the most appreciated by Truman, was the donation of a town park north of the Square as a site for his library. He could not have been more pleased. Independence would be a far more appropriate location than Grandview and more accessible. Slover Park, a quiet, picturesque 13-acre knoll, was just beyond U.S. Highway 24. To have turned over a comparable portion of the Grandview farm, furthermore, would have meant a major financial sacrifice not only for Truman, but Vivian and Mary Jane, for the land at Grandview was becoming more valuable all the time. Also, the Independence site was only a mile from 219 North Delaware, nothing at all for a good walker.

"All partisanship and selfishness were left behind months ago and this home city of this world-famous statesman is the most logical place to establish such a national shrine as the Harry S. Truman Library," wrote the Kansas City *Times*.

Besides the work on the memoirs, Truman threw himself into raising money for the library, attending dinners, making speeches around the country, and writing thousands of letters. A fund-raising auction for the library at the National Guard Armory in Independence went on for seven hours. The government in Washington was to contribute nothing to the cost of creating the library. He would raise all the money himself. It was another campaign for him, and in a year and a half he would build a fund of more than $1 million. "The pace he set absolutely terrified me," Margaret would remember.

Past the age of seventy, Truman often said, one was living on borrowed time. Yet in the spring of 1954, turning seventy, he gave no sign of exerting or enjoying himself any less than ever. He was putting in seventeen hours a day on the book, the mail, and seeing the "customers" who came by the office, he reported to Acheson on May 28. Nor was that all on his mind:

> I'm worried about our world situation. We are losing all our friends, the smart but inexperienced boys at the White House are upsetting NATO and throwing our military strength away. Yet they seem to want to intervene in Indo-China. . . .

In June, when the Irving Berlin hit musical *Call Me Madam*, about Perle Mesta, came to Kansas City's outdoor theater, Truman happily

943

agreed to make a surprise appearance in the last act, playing the part of himself. Waiting backstage, the night of June 18, he was suddenly ill with violent pains in his stomach. Bess rushed him home and the lights were on at the house all night. On June 20, in an emergency operation at Research Hospital, he had his gallbladder and appendix removed by Wallace Graham, who, since leaving the White House, had resettled in Kansas City to practice surgery. Infection set in. Graham grimly reported that, due to an "unusual hypersensitivity" to modern drugs, the former President was in serious condition. For several days there was extreme concern. It was "a hell of a time," Truman later said. "They gave me about five or ten gallons of antibiotics by sticking needles in veins. But they just couldn't kill me."

But the crisis passed and Truman, improving rapidly, was the model patient. Nothing seemed to bother him. Western Missouri was in the grip of a fierce heat wave. By midday thermometers outside the hospital windows ranged between 110 and 114 degrees and the hospital had no air conditioning. Nevertheless, he was content. When the director of the hospital insisted on putting an air conditioner in his room, he refused. He wanted no special treatment. It was only after Tom Evans pointed out that Bess, who had been sitting with him day after day, was suffering from heat if he wasn't, that Truman sent for the director and had the air conditioning installed immediately.

"When the papers tell us that you had a gangrenous gall bladder," wrote Acheson, "I was at once prepared to tell Doc Graham how you got it. It comes from reading the newspapers. No one can escape some malady from this cause. With me it has taken the form of an attack of gout. . . ."

For Truman's convalescence, Acheson sent a copy of *The Reason Why*, Cecil Woodham-Smith's account of the disastrous Charge of the Light Brigade. "When you get acquainted with Lords Raglan, Cardigan and Lucan you will be reminded of a certain General we know," Acheson said, meaning MacArthur.

To Bess, Acheson wrote, "It is touching the way so many people—elevator boys, our cook, taxi drivers, people on the street—keep asking me about the President. He is deeply loved—even by the press."

More than a hundred thousand cards and letters poured in to Truman, wishing him a speedy recovery, and enough flowers, as he said, "to supply every customer" in the hospital.

From his hospital room on July 6, he pledged to do "everything possible" to get his library started and finished as soon as possible. Once released from the hospital, he was immediately back at work.

· · ·

Ed Thompson flew in from New York in November to find that the "raw material" of the memoirs had grown beyond limits, yet the manuscript was still far from ready. Tactfully he proposed to the former President that one of *Life*'s best staff writers, Ernest Havemann, be sent in to do some reshaping and polishing. But Truman declined. "More important to me," he wrote to Thompson, "especially at this stage, than style or organization of the material are the facts . . . so that the record of the years of my Presidency may be correct. Until this part of the job is completed I would like you to hold up sending Mr. Havemann; or anyone else. . . ."

Havemann's turn came three or four weeks later, and for the first time, Truman had an experienced writer working with him. Francis Heller would recall how much he himself learned from Havemann—though Havemann did no actual writing—and how hard everyone worked, six, sometimes seven days a week, "going great guns," as Truman said. "The damned thing is turning out much better than I thought it would," he reported to Acheson. But apparently Havemann found the former President a difficult collaborator, and the staff even more troublesome to work with. After a month, he asked to be relieved.

Another writer, Hawthorne Daniel, was recruited, now at the request of Doubleday, the publisher that would be bringing out the book, once *Life* had launched its installments. Eventually, too, Doubleday's editor-in-chief Ken McCormick would take part in the cutting and refining, and both Dean Acheson and Sam Rosenman would be asked by Truman to go over the whole "accumulation." Acheson's comments were to be of particular value.

> The material is more interesting and gripping when you are talking about your own life and your own ideas than it is when you are giving lists of callers at the White House and the activities of the Truman Committee which do not reveal much about you as a man [Acheson advised in one extended critique].
>
> Page 114, line 3. You use the cliché, "striped pants boys in the State Department." I should like to see you change this to "people in the State Department," not merely because the phrase is tiresome, but because it gives quite a wrong impression of the tremendous support which you gave to the career service and for which they will be forever grateful.

In places, as he told Truman, Acheson found the manuscript brusque, didactic, and superficial, "quite contrary to what you are."

Acheson's lengthy, single-space typed comments, running to many pages, would be gone over closely by the staff, who, in turn, would give Truman their own lengthy comments on Acheson's comments.

Ken McCormick sensed that Bess Truman was also playing more of a role than met the eye, since Truman seemed to make better decisions about the manuscript, seemed to improve in his judgments, after having talked with her at home in the evenings. "She was his true North, I think," McCormick said years later, remembering how the work had gone.

The financial burden of all this for Truman was mounting, for as yet he had received no money. The first payment of his $600,000 from *Life* was not due until June 30, when he was supposed to deliver the finished manuscript.

By early 1955, the manuscript had grown to approximately 2 million words, whereas the contract had called for only 300,000. After some negotiations, *Life* agreed to accept 580,000 words, but still the project was behind schedule. Hillman and Noyes now spent more time in Kansas City, cutting and trimming.

Doubleday, faced with the size of the manuscript, decided to bring the memoirs out in two volumes, and so through the first six months of 1955, all concentration was on finishing up Volume One—dealing with only the first sixteen months of the presidency, plus the one chapter on his early life and two others covering the political career prior to Roosevelt's death.

Things were moving fast. And things were changing. Acheson and his wife Alice arrived—Acheson to help with the manuscript—and were overnight guests at 219 North Delaware, an event that had the whole town talking, both because there had never before been a former Secretary of State in residence in Independence and because there had never before been "house guests" at 219 North Delaware, as far as anyone could recall.

On May 8, Truman's seventy-first birthday, with some two thousand people gathering in Slover Park, he turned the first spade of earth at an old-fashioned home-style groundbreaking ceremony for his library, complete with band music. Then, as they had also never done before, he and Bess hosted a buffet dinner at home for some 150 people. It was a sight, wrote Margaret, that she never thought she would see. There was her mother standing at the door of her "sanctuary," welcoming each guest.

Flying to San Francisco on June 24, to attend a tenth anniversary of the founding of the United Nations, Truman looked out over Wyoming and the Rockies from the vantage point of 14,000 feet, and as he wrote in his room that night in the Fairmont Hotel, he couldn't help but think of Solomon Young.

We'd left home at 7 A.M. and at 11 A.M. were all past the high mountains. Grandpa would have left home at what is now Grandview at four A.M. and in all probability would have been ten or twelve miles west of the

946

Missouri line. What an age we live and have our being in! We had a mountain lake trout lunch and before we realized it were descending into the Great Salt Lake Valley. . . .

With the deadline pressure on in the offices at the Federal Reserve Bank Building, the work hours grew longer. In the final days of June, some of the staff were working round the clock.

Truman handed over a 500,000-word manuscript to Ed Thompson in Kansas City on July 4, 1955, and told him, "I never really appreciated before what is involved in trying to write a book."

His first check was for $110,000, and with it came five promissory notes for the rest of the $600,000, the last installment not to be paid until January 1960.

The opening installment of the *Memoirs*, titled "The Most Momentous First 18 Days," appeared in the September 25 issue of *Life*, with a cover photograph of the former President and First Lady standing in front of their Independence home. Doubleday's publication of Volume One, called *Year of Decisions*, followed five weeks later, with an author's autographing party in the grand ballroom of the Muehlebach, on Tuesday, November 2, 1955.

To the delight of the publisher, Truman had agreed to sign books for all who came. "I expect to use, probably, a couple of $1.75 fountain pens that I bought at the Twenty-five Cent Store, along with a half dozen others that I happen to have, and I don't want to be in any advertising stunt [for the pens] whatever," Truman had written to Samuel Vaughan, Doubleday's advertising manager. "I will go along with any party arrangements which you make for Doubleday, but don't get me into any advertising for pens, cakes or anything, because I won't do it."

Arriving in Kansas City a few days in advance to make arrangements, Vaughan was distressed to hear people asking why they would want to come to such an occasion for Truman, "when we see him all the time anyway." Greatly concerned, Vaughan worked to line up Battery D veterans, the Boy Scouts, anyone he could think of, to be sure there was a crowd. But he need not have bothered. More than three hundred people were already in line waiting before the party began.

"Hand Firm to the End" was the headline in the next morning's paper.

It was almost unbelievable. "I had no idea it would be anything like this," Truman said as he saw the crowds grow, the people still coming, hour after hour. His hand fairly flew as he signed books, until he was doing six to eight autographs a minute. If ever there was a demonstration of his extraordinary vitality, this was it. He kept going hour after hour, not only signing his name but greeting people. "There, that one's all slicked up," he would say with satisfaction, finishing his signature and handing over the book.

By the end of the first session, he had signed over a thousand copies. In all, incredibly, he turned out four thousand autographs in just five and a half hours. Reporters on hand, his publishers, watched in amazement. Earlier, when Ken McCormick of Doubleday had suggested to Truman that perhaps he might prefer to have the autographs done by a machine, Truman had replied, "I will autograph as many as I can. I am not an expert with a machine, and I would rather do it by hand."

Reviewers rightly treated the book as a major event. "The first volume of Harry Truman's *Memoirs* (Doubleday) provides a more detailed report on life at the summit of American politics than a President has given since the early days of the Republic," wrote Richard Rovere in *The New Yorker*. Truman was commended for his contribution to history, his understanding of presidential power, his clarity, attention to detail, "his appealing mixture of modesty and confidence," as the historian Allan Nevins wrote on the front page of *The New York Times Book Review*. There was too little autobiography, it was thought, too much that read like an official paper worked over by many hands. (In the preface, Truman freely acknowledged the help he had been given.) Richard Rovere, having covered Truman for years, missed the characteristic pungent manner of expression, Truman in his own words, and wished there were more of what was to be found in Truman's letters to his mother, eighteen of which were included in the book, providing, as Rovere said, not only relief from the state-paper style but "wonderful insights" into Truman's style as a human being.

As the reviewers implied, too many people had been involved in the task. Truman had been homogenized. He had been made at times even tedious. Acheson's warnings should have been taken more to heart. Truman himself—the vitality, the vividness of his letters, his own way of expressing himself—was missing through great portions of the book. But to a large degree, of course, Truman himself had been responsible for this, by agreeing to the process by which the work was produced. Also, from the start, he seems to have seen the task more as one of recording history than telling his own story. Francis Heller, for example, would never recall Truman speaking of the work in progress as "memoirs," only as "my history."

The inevitable comparisons with Churchill's history of the war were made, though not so unfavorably as might have been supposed. As a literary performance, said Allan Nevins, Truman's book did not rank among the best memoirs of the era. Nevertheless, Nevins emphasized, this was a "volume of distinction." His praise exceeded his criticism and the review, like others, became as much a judgment of the author as of the book. If not one of the landmark memoirs of the century, it was nonetheless an admirable work by one of the most important figures of the century.

> Altogether, it well expressed one of the most conscientious, dynamic and (within his horizons) clearsighted Presidents we have ever had [wrote Nevins]. . . . His penetrating shrewdness has been underrated. . . . We are equally impressed by his exceptionally high conception of the Presidency and his determination to live up to it. . . . In ordinary affairs he seemed commonplace, and in small matters he could make curious blunders. But he grew in his office as few Presidents have ever done; and he was sustained by an unusual knowledge of American history and a firm grasp of our best traditions. To the major crisis he brought statesmanlike insight, energy, and courage. There was greatness in the man. . . .

The large effect of the book and the series in *Life*—and Volume Two, which appeared the next spring—was to create renewed interest in Truman and a reconsideration of his presidency. And while his account of events also stirred controversy—protests and rebuttals by such major protagonists as Jimmy Byrnes and Henry Wallace—publication of the *Memoirs* marked the beginning of what was to be a steady revival of Truman's reputation, and the beginning of an exceptionally happy time for him. Indeed, it may be said that publication of the *Memoirs* marked the opening of one of the happiest passages in his long life.

III

Truman had always wanted a son. It was why he had called Margaret "Skinny" as she grew up, he recently explained in a letter to Acheson. "But I wouldn't trade her for a houseful of boys although I always wanted a couple and another girl."

In mid-March 1956, at a press conference at the Carlyle Hotel in New York, Margaret announced she was engaged to be married to Elbert Clifton Daniel, Jr., who was an assistant foreign news editor of *The New York Times* and at forty-two, ten years older than his fiancée. The news was a surprise. Though her parents had known for several weeks, Margaret had succeeded in keeping her romance private.

Margaret and Clifton, as he was called, had known each other for more than a year. He was of slightly less than medium height, slim, handsome, well dressed, and spoke with a trace of a British accent, acquired, it was said, from ten years as a foreign correspondent in England. He appeared very polished and sophisticated, but as the country soon learned, he, like Margaret, had grown up in a small town, Zebulon, North Carolina, where his father, Elbert Clifton Daniel, Sr., had a drugstore.

Alone at his office desk, Truman took up one of his $1.75 pens and wrote a two-page letter to Acheson. Their friendship, the great trust and mutual admiration, the enjoyment they found in exchanging news on life's turns and human folly, everything that had made the seemingly incongruous bond between them so important during the presidency, had come to mean still more to Truman now. The truth was that the number one citizen of Independence, Missouri, the President who had come home to be "plain Mr. Truman" again, sorely missed the company and stimulation of just such people as the worldly Acheson. The letters to and fro between them would steadily increase, Truman speaking his mind—writing from the heart—as he had only, until now, to the women who were dear to him. He even told Acheson, as once he had told Bess Wallace, that he wrote sometimes just to get a letter in return. "When I hear from you I always feel better," he would write. "Wish I could sit and talk with you for an hour or thirty minutes or even for five minutes. My morale would go up 100%."

Unexpectedly and most happily, at this late date, Truman found his life enlarged by this close, if distant friend, a brother in spirit, a confidant—indeed a male friend such as he had never had before—and this as much as anything was to account for his great increased enjoyment of these years.

Now he addressed himself to the latest turn in his personal life. "Margie has put one over on me and got herself engaged to a news man!" he began, the words advancing steadily across the page, the bold certainty of every stroke looking no different from the handwriting in letters written to Bess Wallace from Grandview nearly fifty years before.

> He strikes me as a very nice fellow and if Margaret wants him I'll be satisfied. He seems to be very highly thought of in newspaper circles and particularly by *The New York Times* people.
>
> The young lady told us about it just a week or two before the announcement and swore us to secrecy. In fact, she made me hang up while she told her mother. Did your daughter do you that way? I was forbidden to tell my brother and sister. Like a couple of amateurs they went to North Carolina to see his mother and father (nice people by the way) and then had dinner with Jonathan Daniels, of all people,

hoping to keep a secret! The next day they called Daddy and wanted to know what to do. Well Dad announced the engagement the next morning without a chance to tell his friends. Again did your daughter do that?

Well, we've had at least two thousand letters and telegrams and she's had twice as many—serves her right. As every old man who had a daughter feels, I'm worried and hope things will work out all right. Can't you give me some consolation?

Acheson replied at once:

Consolation is just what I can give. In the first place about Margaret's choice. She has always had good judgment and has shown it again here. Alice and I had dinner with them here on her birthday—just a year before we celebrated it in Independence with you. I was completely captivated by Clifton Daniel. He has charm and sense and lots of ability. On the way home I told Alice that there was romance in the wind and that I was all for it. She somewhat acidly remarked that I had so monopolized Mr. Daniel that she hadn't been able to get any idea of Margaret's view of him, and that I was getting to be an old matchmaker. This only made my triumph all the sweeter when the announcement came. I stick by my guns and am sure that the man Margaret has chosen is first class and just the one for her. Marriage is the greatest of all gambles. But character helps and my bets are all on the success of this venture.

Now as to the behavior of daughters and the position of the father of the bride. Daughters, I have found, take this business of marriage into their own hands and do as they please. So do sons—or perhaps someone else's daughter decides for them. I explained most lucidly to Mary and David that they should wait until the end of the war to get married. So they got married at once. All in all, the father of the bride is a pitiable creature. No one bothers with him at all. He is always in the way—a sort of backward child—humored but not participating in the big decisions. His only comforter is a bottle of good bourbon. Have you plenty on hand?

The wedding took place in Independence on Saturday, April 21, 1956, in little Trinity Episcopal Church on Liberty Street, where Bess Wallace and Harry Truman had been married in 1919. It was also followed by a small reception at the home of the bride that was not greatly different from the reception there in 1919—except the party this time was held indoors, out of view of the hundreds of reporters and photographers at the iron fence and the carloads of sightseers passing the house bumper to bumper. The temperature was in the 80s, the shaded lawn clipped and green, the spirea bushes by the porch in bloom. Margaret wore an ankle-length, full-skirted pale beige wedding dress, fashioned of two-hundred-year-old Venetian lace. At the church, when arriving by limousine with Margaret, and later during the ceremony, the father of the bride appeared "a pitiable creature" indeed, unhappy and unsmiling. Later at the reception he brightened noticeably—possibly by Acheson's remedy.

Less than a month after, he and Bess departed on what was described as a honeymoon of their own, the finest trip of their lives, across Europe in grand style.

They were gone seven weeks, touring Europe by train—France, Italy, Austria, West Germany, France again, Brussels, the Netherlands, England. It rained a good part of the time—"rain, rain, rain, day after day, with sometimes a peep of sun," he wrote in his diary—yet nothing seemed to lessen his spirits.

Bringing the suitcases down from the attic the morning they left home, Truman had slipped on the stairs and twisted his ankle, so that it swelled to the size of two, as he said. But he took a shiny black cane and carried on, covering whatever ground had to be covered the first few days only a little slower than usual. They departed from the Independence depot at 7:15, the morning of May 8, his seventy-second birthday. A crowd of friends and family came to see them off. A birthday cake was cut and passed out—"a grand party"—and there were to be crowds everywhere from then on.

The reason given for the trip was a longstanding invitation to Truman to accept an honorary degree at Oxford, and the ceremony at Oxford on June 20 would prove the highlight. "I was so afraid I'd let you down at Oxford, but apparently I didn't," he told Acheson, who, like George Marshall, had already been honored there.

Former President Ulysses S. Grant, as part of a famous trip around the world, had spent months touring Europe where he was received as royalty, and in 1910, at the end of his African safari, former President Theodore Roosevelt delivered a series of lectures across Europe and at Oxford, where he received an honorary degree. For Truman it was a third trip to Europe, but his first as a private citizen. (He was carrying his first passport.) He and Bess had long dreamed of a chance to travel abroad. For both it was the trip of a lifetime, and for Bess a first venture ever overseas. They would be two of the 500,000 American tourists in Europe that year.

Sailing from New York on the *United States,* accompanied by Stanley Woodward, who had been Truman's chief of protocol, and his wife Sara, they landed at Le Havre. From there they went directly by train to Paris.

By midday May 17, his first full day in Paris, Truman was sitting happily at a small outdoor table, sipping coffee at the venerable Café de la Paix, close to the Opéra, where only after a while did heads begin to turn and passers-by stop to stare. He had been there before, he explained, during World War I. At home the papers carried a wire-service photograph of the former President strolling the Place de l'Opéra swinging his cane like a boulevardier.

Reporters dogged his steps wherever he went. Several hundred had been waiting at the Gare Saint-Lazare when he arrived in the city and there were scarcely ever less than a dozen at his side afterward. "Mr. Truman is as popular in Europe as he is in Missouri," readers of the Independence *Examiner* learned in a United Press story from Paris. He was cheered and welcomed by people in the street. In Rome the welcome at the railroad station was tumultuous, with a crowd of hundreds shouting, "Viva Truman!" and even, in English, "Hi, Harry!" He and his party stayed at the Hassler Hotel at the head of the Spanish Steps.

For a conducted tour of Rome's ancient monuments, Truman had as a guide, of all people, Henry Luce, who was filling in for his wife, Clare Booth Luce, the American ambassador to Italy, who had taken ill. The sight of Harry Truman and Henry Luce side by side speculating on the vanished empire of the Romans as they sat in the Colosseum was one not to be forgotten.

Scores of American tourists cheered Truman and followed along. On Rome's Capitol Hill, in front of the giant equestrian statue of Marcus Aurelius, he started introducing himself and shaking hands.

"How are you? I'm Harry Truman."

"I'm Paul Schultheiss of Rochester, New York," responded the amazed tourist.

He and Bess had a rare Sunday audience with Pope Pius XII, that marked the first time an American President had been received at the Holy See since Woodrow Wilson's formal visit on Pope Benedict XV in 1919. Bess wore black and a lace veil over her head, Truman a black cutaway coat, striped trousers, and a top hat. A "most happy visit indeed," he said.

Then, in two weeks' travels through Italy, they saw Mt. Vesuvius, the ruins of Pompeii, the ancient Greek temples of Paestum, near Salerno. They explored the green hills of Umbria where St. Francis once lived with the birds and animals; they shopped for leather goods on the centuries-old Ponte Vecchio over the Arno in Florence, gazed at the Botticellis in the Uffizi Gallery. In Venice, he and Bess, like every other tourist, strolled St. Mark's Square and rode together in a gondola down the Grand Canal.

Between times Truman told reporters that the weather in Italy reminded him of Texas. He declared that victory for the Democrats in the presidential election in the fall was not probable but inevitable, and got himself in a good deal of hot water by saying that the bloody World War II battles of Salerno and Anzio had been unnecessary and the fault of "some squirrel-headed general."

He was having a glorious time, enjoying immensely the setting of so much of the history he had loved since boyhood—and enjoying immensely the attention he received. At Naples, the crowds had tossed flowers in his path. "This is fantastic!" he said, openly astonished.

If the picture of Truman with Henry Luce amid the ruins of ancient Rome had seemed the unlikeliest of holiday vignettes, Truman succeeded in topping it at Florence, when he, Bess, and the Woodwards were the luncheon guests of Bernard Berenson at Berenson's famous villa, I Tatti, overlooking the city. It was a luminous setting of incomparable paintings, sculpture, a library of 55,000 volumes, and the place where the legendary Berenson, "B.B.," widely regarded as the consummate connoisseur, "the world's last great aesthete," held court. A Lithuanian Jew by birth, a graduate of Harvard, and a leading authority on Italian Renaissance art, he had made I Tatti his home—shrine, institution—since before World War I, when Truman was still on the farm. A tiny, frail, but godlike figure with a white beard, now nearly ninety-one, Berenson was still immensely vital and talkative. His flow of guests, of celebrated literary and theatrical figures, was unending—J. B. Priestley, Robert Lowell, Alberto Moravia, Laurence Olivier, Mary McCarthy. They came to listen—since customarily "B.B." did most of the talking—and, of course, to be able to say they knew the great man.

"We just had to look him up. He was the best in his line," Truman would later tell Merle Miller.

In his diary at the time, Truman said he found Berenson as "clear headed and mentally alert as a man of 35 or 40."

He is considered the greatest authority on Renaissance Art and is noted for his epigrams, one of which struck me forcibly. We were discussing world affairs and he remarked that modern diplomacy had degenerated into "Open insults openly arrived at." We discussed the causes of the first World War, the Austrian Prime Minister at that time, the Serbian situation and the whys and wherefores of the Austrian ultimatum which started the war.

Truman was greatly stimulated by Berenson's company and delight in conversation, much as he had been years ago at the Sunday afternoon teas with Louis Brandeis. In a letter to Berenson later, recalling the pleasant visit, Truman wrote in a postscript: "I wish the Powers-that-be would listen, think, and mock at things as you have."

But more remarkable was Berenson's reaction to the former American President, which Berenson recorded in his own diary at the time:

[Harry] Truman and his wife lunched yesterday. Came at one and stayed till three. Both as natural, as unspoiled by high office as if he had got no further than alderman of Independence, Missouri. In my long life I have never met an individual with whom I felt so instantly at home. He talked as if he had always known me, openly, easily, with no reserve (so far as I could judge). Ready to touch on any subject, no matter how personal. I always felt what a solid and sensible basis there is in the British stock of the U.S.A. if it can produce a man like Truman. Now I feel more assured about America than in a long time. If the Truman miracle can still occur, we need not fear even the [Senator Joe] McCarthys. Truman captivated even Willy Mostyn-Owen, aged twenty-seven, ultra-critical, and like all Englishmen of today hard of hearing anything good about Americans, and disposed to be condescending to them—at best.

At Salzburg, in Truman's honor, the organist of Salzburg Cathedral played Mozart's Ninth Sonata on a 250-year-old organ, and at Mozart's birthplace, Truman himself played a Mozart sonata on Mozart's own clavichord. ("I found that it was somewhat different from the modern piano but it makes beautiful music. . . . This Mozart town has certainly been a joy to me. . . .")

From Salzburg, the expedition moved on to Bonn, capital of the West German Republic that Truman had helped create, and during a brief rain-soaked stay he met with Konrad Adenauer for the first time. Swinging back through France again, the tourists kept to a steady schedule, stopping at Versailles, which Truman did not much enjoy (he kept thinking of how the money to build it had been "squeezed" from the people), Chartres Cathedral, which he loved despite the pouring rain, then Chenonceau, the lovely sixteenth-century château in the Loire Valley, which he had wanted particularly to see because of its connection to Catherine de Médicis, one of his favorite historic figures. ("Of course, there are all sorts of traditions and stories about the happenings of the days of Catherine," he observed in his diary, "but she was a remarkable woman and a Medici, all of whom believed in government by deviation as set out in *The Prince* by Machiavelli. Catherine was the mother of ten children, three of whom became kings of France and two of whom became queens. Quite a record for a tough conspiratorial old woman.")

Truman was tireless, determined to see everything, and fascinated by nearly all he saw. Bess tried valiantly to keep the pace, seldom smiling, at least in view of the photographers. The itinerary would have exhausted people half their age.

Their route in France, interestingly, included no return visits to the Vosges Mountains, the Argonne, or Verdun, Truman apparently having no wish to see any of those places ever again.

There were big crowds to cheer him at the train stations in Brussels, The Hague, and Amsterdam, where at the Dutch State Museum he and Bess saw the largest exhibit of Rembrandts ever held, and had lunch with Queen Juliana at the Royal Soestdikk Palace.

Then, on June 17, they were on their way to England, the part of the trip Truman had looked forward to most of all. "We crossed the Channel on the night boat," he recorded, "and landed at the English side in beautiful sunshine. . . ."

It may be fairly said that in his long, eventful life, in an extraordinary career with many surprising turns and times of great fulfillment, there were few occasions that meant so much to Truman as the ceremony that took place at Oxford on Wednesday, June 20, 1956. Wearing the traditional crimson robe and crushed black velour hat of Oxford, the man who had never been to college, nor ever made a pretense of erudition, walked at the head of the procession, beside the Public Orator, at one of the world's oldest, most distinguished universities.

"Never, never in my life," he had whispered to a reporter, "did I ever think I'd be a Yank at Oxford."

The ceremony, called the *Encaenia* and conducted in Latin, was held in Oxford's 300-year-old Sheldonian Theatre, designed by Christopher Wren. The audience numbered more than a thousand people. As Truman stood in the center facing the crimson-robed professors of Oxford, he heard the Public Orator present "*Harricum Truman*," for an honorary degree of "*Doctoris in Iure Civili*" (Doctor of Civil Law). Then the towering, ornately robed Earl of Halifax, chancellor of the university and former British ambassador to Washington, admitted Harricum Truman into the ancient fellowship of Oxford, lauding him, in Latin, as

> Truest of allies, direct in your speech and in your writings and ever a pattern of simple courage . . . *(sociorum firmissime, qui missis ambagibus et loqueris et commentarios scribis veraeque constantiae specimen semper dedisti)*.

The applause that followed went on for a full three minutes. Truman, moved to tears, searched beneath his academic gown for a handkerchief.

An elderly professor told a reporter that he had attended many such convocations but had never heard such applause. "Mr. Truman is very popular in this country," he said. Recovering himself, Truman smiled broadly.

That night he was honored at a white-tie dinner for four hundred returning graduates of Christ Church College. "Every person born in the twentieth century is entitled to the benefits of the twentieth century," he said in his speech.

> ... we must declare in a new Magna Carta, in a new Declaration of Independence, that henceforth economic well being and security, that health and education and decent living standards, are among our inalienable rights.

Every man and woman was entitled to the full benefit of the best in medicine, he added, striking an old theme. Every child was entitled to a first-rate education. There should be no economic worries for the elderly in their declining years.

"Give 'em hell, Harricum!" the students of Oxford called from their windows as he departed.

A still more dazzling white-tie dinner followed the next night in London, at the Savoy—the annual stag dinner of the Pilgrims, the leading Anglo-American society dedicated to maintaining close ties between the two nations. And again Truman was a triumph, Lord Halifax paying him what to most present was the ultimate compliment. "I think we in this room feel that you are the sort of chap with whom all of us would be quite happy to go tiger hunting."

He had been getting along very well in England, Truman said, at the start of his remarks. So far, he had not needed an interpreter.

"A good many of the difficulties between our two countries," he continued, "spring not from our differences but from the fact that we are so much alike.... Another problem we have ... is that in election years we behave somewhat as primitive peoples do at the time of the full moon." But the essence of his warning was that "a great, serene and peaceful future can slip from us quite as irrevocably by neglect, division and inaction, as by spectacular disaster." He hoped that both nations would never become careless about "our strength and our unity."

> And—not least of all—let us escape from this modern idea of the mass psychologists that we should be guided not by what we honestly

believe is wise and right, but by some supposed reflecting of what other people think of us. I am ready to give up the complexity of propaganda, with its mass psychology, in favor of Mark Twain's simpler admonition:

"Always do right. It will please some people and astonish the rest."

He was "most happy" to see London, Truman wrote in his diary. "Never been here. It is a wonderful city."

Visiting the House of Commons on Home Affairs Day, he listened to the opposition ask questions "about everything from roads to bawdy houses and gangsters." At the House of Lords he sat through a long-winded speech as "boresome" as any in the United States Senate.

> England is prosperous, cordial and courteous [he recorded]. From Lords to taxi drivers and policemen they recognize and wave and bow to the former President. When they have a chance they show by word and deed that they still like us and appreciate our friendship. It is heart warming.

On June 24, at Chartwell, the Churchill family estate 40 miles south of London, Sir Winston and Lady Churchill, daughters Sarah and Mary and Mary's husband, Christopher Soames, and Lord Beaverbrook were in the driveway waiting as the Trumans arrived for lunch in a chauffeur-driven Armstrong Siddeley. "This is just like old times," Truman said, as he and Churchill greeted each other. Inside, a butler brought a tray of drinks, and before a bronze bust of Franklin Roosevelt the two men made what appeared to be a silent toast. Lunch finished, each swinging a walking stick, they strolled in the gardens.

"It was all over too soon," Truman wrote in his diary.

> The house faces a hill covered with rhododendrons, which were in full bloom. Behind the house is a beautiful garden and below that a valley containing a lake in the distance, a lovely view which Sir Winston called the Weald of Kent.
> He showed me a large number of his paintings in the house and told me he had some 400 more in his studio in the valley below the house. We didn't have time to visit the studio. It was a very pleasant visit and a happy one for me.

Churchill, Truman thought, seemed as alert mentally as ever. "But his physical condition shows his 82 years. He walks more slowly and he doesn't hear well."

He told me that he could do whatever had to be done as he always did but that he'd rather not do it. He walked around and up and down steps with no more effort than would be expected of a man his age. He remarked that it would be a great thing for the world if I should become President of the United States again. I told him there was no chance of that.

They said goodbye not knowing if they would ever see one another again, and they did not.

On June 26, as reported in the Independence *Examiner,* "Mr. and Mrs. Truman joined the Queen and the Duke of Edinburgh at Buckingham Palace" for lunch. On June 28, from Southampton, their grand tour over, the Trumans sailed for home.

During the visit at Chartwell, Lord Beaverbrook had told Truman that on his European trip he had made the greatest ambassador of goodwill America ever had. Now, the same refrain was heard repeatedly.

"Too bad he's not campaigning for anything in this country," an American reporter overheard an English spectator remark as Truman boarded the boat train in London. "He'd win any election." The London *Evening Standard* headlined the visit as the "Truman Triumph." The *Daily Telegraph* described him as the "living and kicking symbol of everything that everyone likes best about the United States."

In the tradition of homespun Benjamin Franklin, he had charmed Europe by being himself. "Never [said the United Press] has an 'ordinary' American been given such a red carpet treatment from the brass and such a warm welcome from the people as was accorded that jaunty traveler from Missouri."

On reaching home, Truman never let up the pace. He was scarcely unpacked before plunging into election-year politics, in a determined and unsuccessful effort to see Averell Harriman, rather than Adlai Stevenson, win the Democratic nomination. Arriving in Chicago for the convention in August, Truman backed Harriman, who had been elected governor of New York two years earlier, because, as Truman said, he thought the country needed a President who wanted the job. Stevenson "lacks the kind of fighting spirit we need to win," Truman charged at a jammed press conference at the Blackstone. (A few weeks earlier, while stopping at the Blackstone for a Truman Library dinner, Truman had talked privately with Stevenson, who asked what he was doing wrong. Truman had gone to the window and pointing to a man in the street below said, "The thing you have to do is learn how to reach that man.") For a time it appeared Truman might turn things on end.

Harry S. Truman had the Democratic party chewing its fingernails down to the cuticle today and he loved every second of it [wrote Russell Baker in *The New York Times*].

While the party's other demi-gods fretted and stewed and guessed, Mr. Truman was as exhilarated as a small boy given free run of the circus.

At the height of the suspense, he blithely took off from the politicians and went down to the south side of town to lead a parade. There for Chicago's vast Negro population, it was Bud Billiken Day. Bud Billiken is a mythical heroic godfather for the town's Negro children. In the parade Mr. Truman drove 2½ miles to the enthusiastic cheers of 100,000 spectators.

But in fact his efforts came to nothing. The nomination went easily to Stevenson, and to many it seemed Truman had succeeded only in making himself a contradictory, even pitiful figure who confused his popularity with real power. Truman, however, showed no signs of bitterness or regret, and immediately endorsed the nominee—Stevenson's chances in November were "perfectly wonderful"—and pledged the full support of the "old man from Missouri."

Besides, as he liked to say, he had had himself a time.

"When I arrived in Chicago," he wrote to Acheson, "things were dead, no life, no nothing. I decided to wake them up.... I am going to do all I can to help win this election. How I wish I were ten years younger!"

He campaigned actively for the ticket, traveling to Milwaukee, Texas, Boston, New York, San Francisco, Gary, Indiana, and Pittsburgh, where he and Eisenhower were staying at the same hotel but never met.

A month after Stevenson's defeat and Eisenhower's reelection, Truman was writing to Lyndon Johnson, the Democratic majority leader in the Senate, "I have never wanted to pose as a prophet, nor do I intend to be one now, but I do want to keep the Democratic Party a party of the people. We can never win unless it is."

Nineteen fifty-seven was a landmark year for Truman. On June 5, in New York, Margaret had a baby son, and both Trumans were on the train heading east the very next day. On June 7 *The New York Times* carried a photograph of the proud grandparents at the hospital looking through the window at the baby, Clifton Truman Daniel. When, in another few days, Margaret and the baby came home to the Daniels' New York apartment and her father asked if he might hold the baby, she insisted he first take off his jacket and be seated. "Dad sat there for a long time, rocking him back and forth."

Less than a month later, Truman was moving out of the Federal Reserve

Bank Building and into an all-new suite of offices at the new Truman Library. Formal dedication of the building took place on July 6. The two things he had said he wanted most after leaving the White House—to become a grandfather and to see his library established—had both come to pass.

Former President Hoover, Eleanor Roosevelt, Speaker Sam Rayburn, four United States senators, nine governors (including Averell Harriman), Dean Acheson, John Snyder, some dozen or more from Truman's White House staff, his family, neighbors, a crowd in all of five thousand people were present for the dedication, a fortunate few seated in the shade of the trees, the majority taking the full force of the Missouri summer sun. In the history of Independence there had been no occasion like it. ("I expect to be knee deep in 'Big Shots' July 6th and I want you and Alice to be here to help me out of what Huey Long would call a deep 'More Ass!'" Truman had written excitedly to Acheson. "Be sure and come.") The main speaker, addressing the crowd from the steps of the building, was the former governor of California and Republican candidate for Vice President, Earl Warren, now the Chief Justice of the United States, who acclaimed the library as a milestone in American history, and Harry S. Truman as a man of action, "tireless, fearless, and decisive," adding that he himself had personally learned to appreciate the former President's "dynamic, fighting qualities" in the fall of 1948.

> Mr. Truman, who has an abiding interest in our national history, has arranged for the preservation of his papers in this library in such manner that his administration will be one of the "clearest ages" of history. It is in compliance with his public-spirited generosity that I dedicate this building as a museum and a library to safeguard, exhibit, and facilitate the use of its valuable resources that the American people, and all the peoples of this earth, may gain by their wide and wise use understanding of ourselves and our times, and wisdom to choose the right paths in years that lie ahead.

The building was long and low, crescent-shaped and built of Indiana limestone in an architectural style that no one was quite able to categorize —"modern" seemed to apply, though the main entrance with its square columns also had a decidedly classic Egyptian look. It had been designed by a local architect, Alonzo H. Gentry, assisted by Edward Neild, who came up with a scheme quite unlike what Truman had been expecting but that he decided not to reject. Though only one story tall, the building, with its full basement, had a total of 70,000 square feet of floor space. Finished in two years, it had cost thus far $1,800,000. Two Truman Library dinners in New York and Philadelphia in 1954 had raised $45,000 each. More than thirty different labor unions had contributed generously— $25,000 from Sidney Hillman's Amalgamated Clothing Workers, $10,000 from the American Federation of Musicians, $10,000 from John L. Lewis, $250,000 from the United Steel Workers. Dean Acheson, Averell Harriman, Ed Pauley, and William Clayton made substantial private donations. But in all, the money had come from some 17,000 contributions large and small, from every part of the country, and Truman acknowledged every gift, regardless of the amount.

The 3.5 million documents already in the library were only the beginning of the collection that was to be amassed as time went on, when other figures from the Truman administration such as Acheson contributed their own papers.

For Truman personally from this point on, the library was to be the focus of his life. If the immense effort devoted to the memoirs had proven something of a disappointment, his library was to be an unqualified success.

He was also successful in convincing Congress—working through Democratic Representative John McCormack of Massachusetts—that all existing presidential papers should be indexed and put on microfilm. As he said, this was something that should have been done generations earlier. Yet until he raised the issue, no one had bothered to make the effort—a point for which he deserved far more credit than he received.

With the library established and in operation in Independence, a large part of the Truman land at Grandview was sold to a Kansas City developer, B. F. Weinberg & Associates. The old farmhouse, its barn and immediate acres were kept in the family, but some 224 acres of the prime land where Solomon Young had long ago staked his claim, and where Truman had labored so many seasons, were now to give way to the advance of suburbia and become a shopping center. For Truman it meant the end of a heritage that had come to mean more and more to him, partly out of sentiment but also from a realization of how much his own makeup and attitudes derived from his rural background. He took particular pleasure —obvious pride—in describing himself as a retired farmer. "Hey there, farmer!" Sam Rayburn would greet him over the telephone, knowing how it pleased him.

"I sure hate to see the old place go," he was quoted in the Kansas City *Star*.

But the sale, as he also said, meant financial security at last, for Truman, as for Vivian and Mary Jane. And while, with the transaction went a good deal of sadness, it affirmed the old faith that come what may, land was wealth to count on. It wasn't Truman's rise to political power or his world renown, his books or lectures or the legacy of his wife's family that saw him through in the end, but the old farm at Grandview.

The sale was announced in January 1958. What the final figure was, what his share came to, are not known. However, a tallying up of all his bank balances a year and a half later, dated August 14, 1959, has survived and shows him with a total of $208,548.07. And this did not include what he had in government and municipal bonds and a few stocks.

The final financial returns on his *Memoirs,* after expenses and taxes, were turning out to be very much less than anticipated. Even with his payments from *Life* extended over five years, he had still to pay 67 percent federal and state income taxes, and this he found particularly discouraging, since in 1949 General Eisenhower had been permitted by the Internal Revenue authorities to treat his sale of *Crusade in Europe* for $635,000 as a capital gain, on the grounds that he was not a professional author; Eisenhower had paid a tax of only 25 percent. At the time the Eisenhower question was at issue, the White House had intervened; now the Eisenhower White House declined to become involved. Truman's expenses for the *Memoirs,* for staff and office space, had amounted to $153,000, according to a letter he wrote to John McCormack. His net profit, over the five-year period, would end up, he figured, at about $37,000.

"Had it not been for the fact that I was able to sell some property that my brother, sister and I inherited from our mother I would practically be on relief, but with the sale of that property I am not financially embarrassed."

He was not asking for a pension, he told McCormack. He wanted justice. He thought the least a former President merited was a government allowance covering perhaps 70 percent of the necessary office expenses and overheads to meet his responsibilities.

> As you know, we passed a Bill which gave all five star Generals and Admirals three clerks, and all the emoluments that went with their office when they retired.
>
> It seems rather peculiar that a fellow who spent eighteen years in government service and succeeded in getting all these things done for the people he commanded should have to go broke in order to tell the people the truth about what really happened. It seems to me in all justice a part of this tremendous overhead should be met by the public.

With the help of Charlie Murphy, he took his case to Speaker Rayburn and Senate Majority Leader Lyndon Johnson, with the result that in 1958

Congress passed a law providing former presidents with a $25,000 annual pension, money for staff, office space, and free mailing privileges.

For quite some time, since even before Truman left the White House, Dean Acheson had been eager to arrange for him to come to Yale. Truman would be the recipient of what was known at Yale as a Chubb Fellowship, whereby he would be the honored guest of the university for several days, to lecture and to meet with students and faculty.

The prospect delighted Truman. He thought highly of Yale, out of regard for Acheson—and such other Yale graduates in his administration as Harriman, Lovett, and Roger Tubby—but also because Yale, as Truman said, was the kind of great university he wished he had been able to attend. What pleased him most was that Acheson wanted him to do it.

"I would be proud to appear anywhere with you from Yale to 1908 Main in Kansas City. (That's the address of the Pendergast Club)," Truman had written in 1952, obviously enjoying the picture of his elegant Secretary of State hobnobbing with the "Boys" at 1908 Main—as he knew Acheson would, too.

Acheson, who was a member of the Yale Corporation, had set things in motion, and in a letter to Professor Thomas G. Bergin, who would be Truman's host, Acheson provided what stands as one of the finest, most perceptive descriptions ever written of his friend the President:

> Mr. Truman is deeply interested in and very good with the young. His point of view is fresh, eager, confident. He has learned the hard way, but he has learned a lot. He believes in his fellow man and he believes that with will and courage (and some intelligence) the future is manageable.
>
> This is good for undergraduates. He is easy, informal, pungent. He should not be asked to do lectures for publication. The pressures on him are too great, and it is not his field. It is not what he says but what he is which is important to young men and this gets communicated. . . .
> I should want Mr. Truman to be received at Yale with honor, with simplicity—not as a show, not with controversy, not as a lecturer in a field which I do not believe is yet a discipline, "political theory or science"—but as one who could, if in some way we were wired for spirit, give our undergraduates more sense of what their lives are worth (how to spend them for value) than anyone I know.

As it was, Truman did not go to Yale until the spring of 1958. He stayed three days and was an immediate hit with students and faculty. Even the crusty Yale librarian, an arch-Republican who had openly stated his distaste for Truman, refusing at first to receive "that man" when Truman expressed interest in seeing the Franklin Papers, wound up wanting Truman to stay longer, so they might talk at greater length, and afterward told others he had had no idea how much the President knew or how far-ranging were his interests. On his early morning walks through campus, Truman was trailed by students and local reporters. There were dinners in his honor and repeated warm applause, and he loved it all. "I have never had a better time anywhere," he wrote Acheson. "Yale still rings in my ears. What a time we had," he said again, in another letter.

He was in steady demand now, with two to three hundred speaking invitations a month. At home he seemed to radiate good feeling. "He's so damn happy," said a friend, "that it makes me happy just being around him."

Tom Evans had asked him to join a regular group for noontime bourbon, lunch, and poker at the Kansas City Club, an exclusive gathering known as the 822 Club, for the suite it occupied. Though Truman had been an honorary member of the Kansas City Club since he was elected to the Senate, he had never felt particularly welcome by its members, most of whom were Republicans. The Kansas City Club had never been exactly his crowd. He had been looked down upon as both a Democrat and a politician, not the sort one would want to know personally. But in no time he had become the most popular member of the group, the pride of the 822 Club, an "elevating influence," as was said. "It was just terrific. He really bowled them over," Evans told *Life* writer John Osborne for an article titled "Happy Days for Harry." Osborne was struck by Truman's "phenomenal vigor," the pleasure of his company to others. "Why, goddamnit, Mr. President, I'm going to raise you," he heard exclaimed over the poker table at the 822 Club.

The "major achievement of his latter years," wrote Osborne, was "a rare one of its kind, and it has a place in the story of our times. . . . At the age of 74, in the bright winter of his life, Harry Truman is a genuinely happy man."

At a benefit performance of the Kansas City Philharmonic, Truman in white tie and tails conducted the orchestra in Sousa's *Stars and Stripes Forever*. Soon he and Bess were off again for another summer sojourn in Europe, a more private, quiet tour this time, through the South of France accompanied by Sam and Dorothy Rosenman.

That fall, in the 1958 congressional campaign, Truman was back on the trail again, delivering some twenty-five speeches in twenty different states. Lecturing at Columbia University the next year, he referred to himself as "an old stiff," but few people in the busiest part of their lives were as active as he.

Truman, reported Cabell Phillips, was getting a bigger kick out of life than ever before. In an article for *The New York Times Magazine* on the former President as he turned seventy-five, Phillips quoted a Kansas City friend saying, "Harry feels that he's square with the world, that he gave it his best, and got its best in return. Now he's enjoying the dividends. . . ."

"I found him looking pink and fit, with the same crisp smile and sparkling eyes and the same firm handshake which I remembered from earlier years," wrote Phillips. And increasing numbers of writers, reporters, and well-wishers made the pilgrimage to see him at the Truman Library, to try to divine what the magic was.

To Dean Acheson, Truman's salient quality was his vitality. Here was "a man overflowing with life force, with incurable curiosity . . . no brooding image in a history book . . . [but] vigorous, powerful . . . full of the zest of life."

Margaret had told her father that he talked too much. "She says I am just like my two year old grandson," Truman cheerfully related to a reporter from out of town. "She says that he runs all the time, never walks, and talks all the time and never says anything."

Showing visitors "the layout" of "my library," he would move briskly down the halls talking a steady stream, pausing frequently to greet groups of visitors and especially if they were students. The library proper—the actual collection of presidential papers—would not be open to researchers until May of 1959, but for now there was the museum to see, with displays of photographs, gifts to the President, everything from an ear of Iowa corn to a jewel-encrusted sword from Ibn Saud; there was a small auditorium and a replica of the Oval Office, which though slightly reduced in scale, was furnished as it had been during his years in the White House.

"I want this to be a place where young people can come and learn what the office of the President is, what a great office it is no matter who happens to be in it at the time." He did not "care a damn" about all the attention on himself. "They said it was necessary to put me all over the place just to show how one particular President worked." But clearly the focus on his life and achievements pleased him very much indeed.

He loved his office, a bright, spacious room with books and sliding glass panels that opened onto a private patio and garden. His desk was the same big mahogany desk he had used in the upstairs study at the White House. He was there nearly every day, Sunday included, except when he was traveling. As was often said, the most interesting item on display at the Truman Library was Truman himself.

He was always on the job early. Some mornings, at his desk before the staff arrived, he would answer the phone himself, telling callers what the library hours were, or, in reply to further questions, saying he knew because it was *his* library. "This is the old man himself."

About noon, if not going into town to the 822 Club, he would go home for lunch. Bess remarked privately that if she never saw another sardine or peanut butter sandwich, she would be very happy.

> You know this five day week doesn't work with me [he told Acheson]. I guess I'm old fashioned. I work every day and Sunday too even if Exodus 2–8.9.10 and 11 and Deuteronomy 5–13 and 14 say I shouldn't. I think probably those admonitions were the first labor laws we know about. . . . But someone had to fix things so the rest can work five days —coffee breaks and all.

Having the library gave purpose to his days. The most satisfactory part of the whole effort of creating the library, said David Lloyd, a former White House aide who had taken the leading part in the fund raising and organization of the project, was that it provided Truman with a base, "where he can sit happily among his beloved books, conducting his tremendous correspondence, saying what he thinks and doing as he pleases . . . able to carry on his old fashioned American occupation of being himself."

He was there in total six and a half days a week for nine years, longer than his two terms in the White House. And as at the White House, the staff adored him. "Mr. Truman was one of the most thoughtful persons we have known," remembered Dr. Philip C. Brooks, the first director.

> [He] had an optimistic outlook, and a conversation with him never failed to give one's spirits a lift. . . . Many times people have written about Mr. Truman as having a temper and "shooting from the hip" in his remarks. We never saw the temper, though we saw plenty of candor. . . . He was rarely wrong. . . .

David Lloyd and the Archivist of the United States, Wayne Grover, had convinced Truman that there ought to be a mural in the main lobby, to enliven the space and strike an appropriate historic theme for visitors as they entered the building. When Lloyd and Grover recommended the Missouri painter Thomas Hart Benton, whose great-uncle and namesake had been one of Missouri's first two U.S. senators, as the perfect artist to undertake the work, Truman bluntly said no. He thought Benton had made a mockery of Tom Pendergast in a mural at the Capitol in Jefferson City done in 1936. Further, he did not care for Benton's style. Shown a

Benton painting called *The Kentuckian,* Truman recalled that both of his grandfathers were from Kentucky and neither looked like "that long-necked monstrosity."

Nevertheless, a meeting was arranged by Lloyd and Grover who were sure that Truman and Benton would like each other if given the chance to discover how much they had in common. Benton, gruff, opinionated, outspoken to a fault, often profane and extremely vital, had been born, like Truman, in southwestern Missouri, in little Neosho in 1889, and had grown up with politics. His father had served several terms in Congress. Truman went with Lloyd and Grover to visit Benton at his studio in Kansas City in the spring of 1957. As predicted, the two men quickly became fast friends. A contract was signed in 1958, and with the mural under way, Truman took obvious pleasure in Benton's company, pride in Benton's friendship, and at one point, at Benton's urging, climbed up the scaffold to help him paint a corner of the sky.

The first day Truman offered Benton a drink in his office, pulling a bottle of bourbon from his desk and saying, "I hear you like this," Benton took it as a calculated provocation by Truman, a way to test him.

"This performance on the part of a president of the United States embarrassed me," Benton remembered. "There is no good reason why it should have, because it was a common act of human hospitality, but there was still about Harry Truman an aura of power. . . ."

Later, as the bourbon ritual became more established, and Benton would ask for a second drink, Truman would tell him no. "Tom, you're driving a car. You can't have another because you've got some work to do around here and I'm not going to take any risks with you."

"I was now, in effect, his man," Benton wrote, "and he was going to protect me. And he did."

The theme for the mural was arrived at only after considerable discussion. Truman had first thought it should be about Jefferson and the Louisiana Purchase, with the emphasis on Jefferson's foresight. Benton had said there was no way he could paint foresight. "Well, what the hell is it you can paint?" Truman said. Benton suggested that the mural be about Independence and its importance in the opening of the West, and so it was agreed.

"I thought at first that the President would also want to be included in the mural," Benton later told an interviewer, "but he very emphatically turned that down."

Benton's fee was $60,000. The work took him two years. Completed in 1961 and titled *Independence and the Opening of the West,* the mural included no specific events of written history nor any identifiable personages. The theme was expressed with symbolic figures, the great human stream that had passed through—with Plains Indians, trappers, hunters, French *voyageurs* giving way to a tide of settlers and their black slaves. It was robust, colorful, romantic, and as literal as a magazine illustration, with two additional lower panels showing the Missouri River landing and Independence Square in the 1840s, the time when Truman's grandparents arrived. Truman thought it was wonderful. Showing visitors about the library, he rarely failed to stop in front of the mural, to praise it and explain the history portrayed. His friend Tom Benton, he now liked to say, was the "best damn painter in America."

Attendance at the library was up to more than 150,000 people a year, a figure that delighted him. In May 1960, Margaret had a second child, another boy, William Wallace Daniel. Meantime, Truman was finishing up another book to be called *Mr. Citizen,* a collection of essays on life and the world at large written originally for *The American Weekly,* the Sunday supplement owned by Hearst, Truman's past nemesis. He had liked particularly being paid and publicized by Hearst. There was no praise sweeter, he said, than the praise of old enemies.

As Acheson observed, Truman was no brooding image in a history book. He expressly disliked the term "elder statesman" as applied to him. "When a good politician dies he becomes a statesman," he would say. "I want to continue as a politician for a long time." It had become a standard line. "I like being a nose buster and an ass kicker much better," he told Acheson privately.

To mark his seventy-fifth birthday on May 8, the Democratic National Committee staged a nationwide celebration, a star-spangled television broadcast that included appearances by Adlai Stevenson, Eleanor Roosevelt, Jack Benny, Leonard Bernstein, Isaac Stern, H. V. Kaltenborn, and such old personal friends as Monsignor Curtis Tiernan, in a series of spoken and musical tributes, much of the broadcast originating at a $100-a-plate dinner for Truman at the Waldorf-Astoria in New York. A few days earlier in Washington, he had said he had no favorite candidate for 1960 as yet, only that he wanted to see the party nominate a man who could win and he had every intention of taking part. "What do you think? How are you going to keep me home?"

In October 1959, George Marshall had died, and for Truman it was another and the heaviest of a succession of personal blows, as slowly but steadily close friends and favorite members of his former official family began to pass from the scene. Fred Vinson had died in 1953, Eddie Jacobson in 1955, Alben Barkley in 1956, Admiral Leahy in July 1959. Hearing that Marshall was dying, Truman had telephoned Marshall's wife in North Carolina to say he was on his way by plane. But she told him not to come because the general would not know him. "She and I spent most of my call weeping," Truman wrote to Acheson.

"Do you suppose any President of the United States ever had two such men with him as you and the General?" he would say in another letter.

At a brief Episcopal funeral service for Marshall in the chapel at Fort Myer, Virginia, Truman and Eisenhower sat side by side in the same pew at the front, their common grief partly easing the strain between them.

A new generation of politicians was bidding to take power. With Eisenhower retiring from office and Richard Nixon the probable choice for a Republican nominee, the chance of a Democratic victory looked promising. Of those Democrats in the running, Truman's favorites were Stuart Symington and Lyndon Johnson, neither of whom had much of a chance. Truman refused to consider Stevenson for a third try. Nor was he enthusiastic about John F. Kennedy, whom he considered too young and inexperienced. He did not want a Catholic—it was not that he was against Catholics, only that he was against losing. Remembering what had happened to Al Smith, he did not think a Catholic could be elected. He also thought Kennedy had been too approving of Joe McCarthy and he disliked Kennedy's father quite as much as ever. Joe Kennedy had spent over $4 million to buy the nomination for his son, Truman told Margaret. To others he quipped, "It's not the pope I'm afraid of, it's the pop."

John Kennedy had called on Truman at the Mayflower Hotel in January 1960, during one of Truman's visits to Washington. According to Kennedy's own notes on the meeting, he urged Truman not to announce his support for any candidate until he, Kennedy, had had a chance to come to Independence and "give him all the facts as I saw them." If, at the convention, the contest became a deadlock, then, Kennedy suggested, Truman could intervene in the name of party unity. But until then it was important, Kennedy said, to let the primary process run its course. Truman expressed warm regard for both Kennedy and Hubert Humphrey, the other leading contender, and ended the meeting by telling Kennedy he would do nothing to hurt him.

Bess Truman was advising her husband to stay out of the whole affair. "She refused to get excited about the Democratic party and told Dad he was crazy if he went to another convention at the age of seventy-six," remembered Margaret. "Let the next generation fight it out among themselves—that was her attitude." But like John Strother, the man he had recalled when meeting the son-in-law on his morning walk—"the grand old man" who wouldn't tell his age—Truman, too, wanted "to be young with the young men."

He sometimes felt forgotten. On Capitol Hill in Washington late one evening, a young Senate aide answered the phone. The operator said she had a long-distance, person-to-person call for Senator Symington. When the aide said the senator had gone for the day and asked if he might know who was calling, he heard a familiar, clipped voice come on the line. "Just tell him Harry S. Truman called. Used to be President of the United States."

In April, Acheson wrote to tell Truman that if Kennedy were to "stub his toe" in the West Virginia primary, then probably the nomination would go to Stevenson. "I hate to say this but I think the only possible alternative is Stu and I doubt very much, though I am for him, that he can make it. He just doesn't seem to catch hold. Maybe we should all give Jack a run for his money—or rather for Joe's."

In May, with Kennedy out in front after an upset victory over Hubert Humphrey in West Virginia, Truman announced his support for Missouri's own Symington, calling him "without doubt" the best qualified for the presidency. Asked what objections he had to Kennedy, Truman said, "None whatever. He's a fine young man and I know and like him. The only thing is, he lives in Massachusetts."

Acheson grew greatly concerned that Truman might now go on the attack against Kennedy and say things that could cause long-lasting harm, not only about Kennedy but about civil rights. For lately Truman had been expressing views that left many feeling chagrined and disappointed, and especially those who knew how committed he was to equality before the law. Truman strongly disapproved of the methods of the civil rights movement, the sit-ins and marches. The leaders of the movement, it seemed to him, were flouting the law, resorting to mob rule, which was not his idea of the right way to bring about progress. He also appeared to take seriously the view of J. Edgar Hoover that much of the movement was Communist-inspired.

On June 27, his greatest admirer and most devoted friend, Dean Acheson, wrote to set him straight in no uncertain terms and to ask him to agree to a few specific "don'ts" concerning the weeks ahead. It was a remarkable letter, attesting not only to Acheson's exceptional skill and value as an adviser, but to the confidence he had in the strength of their friendship:

Dear Boss:

As the Convention approaches we partisans are likely to become, shall we say, emphatic in our statements to the press. Could we make a treaty on what we shall *not* say?

On the positive side we can, and doubtless will, say that our candidate—yours and mine—has all the virtues of the Greats from Pericles through Churchill. St. Peter and Pee-pul forgive this innocent though improbable hyperbole. But there are some things that no one should, and few will, forgive.

These fall into several groups, but the common denominator is the harm that comes from allowing the intensity of the personal view to dim a proper concern for the common cause. The list of the "It's not dones," as I see it, goes like this:—

I.   About other Democratic Candidates:
      (a) Never say that any of them is not qualified to be President.
      (b) Never say that any of them can't win.
      (c) Never suggest that any of them is the tool of any group or interest, or is not a true blue liberal, or has (or has used) more money than another.

The reason: At this point public argument is too late—Deals may still be possible. I just don't know. But sounding off is sure to be wrong. If our candidate is going anywhere—which I doubt—it will not be because of public attacks on other candidates. And such attacks can do a lot of harm when they are quoted in the election campaign.

II.   About the Negro sit-in Strikes:
      (a) Do not say that they are communist inspired. The evidence is all the other way, despite alleged views of J. Edgar Hoover, whom you should trust as much as you would a rattlesnake with the silencer on its rattle.
      (b) Do not say that you disapprove of them. Whatever you think you are under no compulsion to broadcast it. Free speech is a restraint on government; not an incitement to the citizen.

The reason: Your views, as reported, are wholly out of keeping with your public record. The discussion does not convince anyone of anything. If you want to discuss the sociological, moral and legal interests involved, you should give much more time and thought to them.

III. About Foreign Policy:
      (a) For the next four months do not say that in foreign policy we must support the President.

The reason: This cliché has become a menace. It misrepresents by creating the false belief that in the recent disasters the President has had a policy or position to support.

This just isn't true. One might as well say "Support the President," if he falls off the end of a dock. That isn't a policy. But to urge support for him makes his predicament appear to be a policy to people who don't know what a dock is.

So, please, for just four months let his apologists come to his aid.

We have got to beat Nixon. We shall probably have to do it with Kennedy. Why make it any harder than it has to be. Now, if ever, our vocal cords ought to be played on the keyboard of our minds. This is

so hard for me that I have stopped using my cords at all. By August they
will be ready to play "My Rosary."

So I offer you a treaty on "don'ts." Will you agree?

In reply, Truman wrote, "You'll never know how very much I appreciated your call and your good letter. I tried my best to profit by both . . .
thanks to a real friend and a real standby."

When it appeared that Kennedy already had the nomination in hand,
Truman kept insisting it would be an open convention and, by inference,
one he would influence if not control. "A bandwagon only begins to roll
after the third or fourth ballot," he told reporters. He was greatly looking
forward to the convention. "I am going to Los Angeles and make the best
fight I can," he wrote to Agnes Meyer, wife of the owner of the Washington *Post.* "I am not a pessimist and always fight until the last dog dies. . . ."

In reality, Kennedy had all but settled the matter, as Truman's ever
devoted advisers Hillman and Noyes reported to him from Los Angeles.
The game was over. "Your coming here is considered routine and not
calculated to make any significant change. This is the judgment of even
those who are partial to you." But they urged him to say nothing about
the convention being "rigged—or you will be charged with November
defeat—a prospect that seems all but certain."

But Truman—angry, bitter—would speak his mind. On July 2, at a
dramatic televised press conference at the Truman Library, he lashed out
at Kennedy in a way certain to infuriate a great many Democrats, exactly
as Acheson had urged him never to do. He not only announced he would
not attend the convention as a delegate, because the Kennedy forces had
it "rigged," but, facing the television cameras, leveled his remarks directly
at Kennedy: "Senator, are you certain that you are quite ready for the
country, or that the country is ready for you in the role of President in
January 1961?" He had no doubt, Truman said, about the political heights
to which Kennedy was destined to rise.

> But I am deeply concerned and troubled about the situation we are
> up against in the world now and in the immediate future. That is why I
> hope that someone with the greatest possible maturity and experience
> would be available at this time. May I urge you to be patient?

Kennedy responded quickly and smoothly. If fourteen years in major
elective office was insufficient experience, he said, then that would have
ruled out all but a handful of presidents, including Wilson, Roosevelt, and
Truman.

No one applauded Truman for what he had done. Acheson wrote to
him after the convention:

I listened to your press conference and regretted that you felt impelled to say anything, though what you said was better than what you first told me that you intended to say. It seemed quite inevitable that Jack's nomination would occur and that all you and Lyndon said you would both have to eat—as indeed you have.

Poor Lyndon came off much worse, since he is now in the crate on the way to the county fair and destined to be a younger and more garrulous—if that is possible—Alben Barkley. It is possible that being a smart operator in the Senate is a special brand of smartness which doesn't carry over into the larger field. . . . Jack and his team were the only "pros" in Los Angeles, so far as I could see. . . .

Well, we're off to the races. . . . I hope it is still true that the Lord looks benignly after children, drunks and the U.S.A. . . .

Again as in 1956, Truman was ready to join forces and do his part. When Kennedy called him from Hyannis Port on August 2, he said at once that he was ready to help. "He could not have been kinder to me," Kennedy remarked privately.

Truman's own disappointment and anger had to be put aside. He was "blue as indigo" over what had happened at Los Angeles, he wrote in a letter to Acheson that he decided not to send. The choice of Kennedy or Nixon was a bleak prospect. "You and I are stuck with the necessity of taking the worst of two evils or none at all. So—I'm taking the *immature* Democrat as the best of the two. Nixon is impossible. So, there we are."

Accompanied by Stuart Symington, Kennedy came to the Truman Library, where Truman, who was old enough to be Kennedy's father, met him at the door. "Come right on in here, young man. I want to talk to you."

Two days later Truman wrote to Sam Rosenman, "Don't get discouraged. The boy is learning—I hope."

To the surprise of no one who knew him, Truman joined the campaign. The Kennedy-Nixon contest of 1960 was to be his "last hurrah," as assuredly he knew, and he pitched in for all he was worth.

"Now you are in for it," wrote Acheson. "Just don't exhaust yourself through sheer nonsense."

Traveling by plane, train, and automobile, Truman covered nine states, delivered 13 speeches. He rode in parades, held press conferences, shook hands, waved, smiled, kept everyone with him on the run, and as always thrived on it. The one thing he insisted on was his midday nap. "A nap after lunch is imperative and cannot be missed under any consideration," his aide, David Stowe, was instructed.

Only in overcrowded rooms, when people began pushing and shoving to meet him, did he show the strain.

Although he moves into and through situations with the same good humor and smiles [wrote Stowe in his notes], apparently this problem bothers him to some extent because it became a frequent topic of conversation. Conceivably, it is a warning to those who work with him to be on our toes to avoid in our planning any large gatherings in which he can be mauled and shoved around. After all he is 76.

"The campaign is ended and we have a Catholic for President," Truman wrote to Acheson on November 21.

It makes no difference, in my opinion, what church a man belongs to, if he believes in the oath he takes to support and defend the Constitution. . . .

If our new President works on the job, he'll have no trouble. You know, I wish I'd been young enough to go back to the White House and make Alibi Ike wear a top hat!

The day after Kennedy's inauguration in January 1961, Truman was welcomed back to the White House and the Oval Office for the first time in eight years, for which, as he wrote the President, he was extremely grateful. The following November, the Trumans and Margaret and Clifton Daniel were guests at the White House for a white-tie dinner in Truman's honor and for an overnight visit. The grouse served at dinner was so tough as to be nearly inedible, but with many of his old Cabinet assembled for the occasion, and with the hospitality shown by the President and First Lady, Truman was radiant. For the after-dinner entertainment, in the East Room, the Kennedys had arranged a piano concert of Truman's favorites—Mozart and Chopin—played by Eugene List, who had first performed for Truman at Potsdam. When, at one point, List invited the former President to take a turn at the big Steinway, Truman obliged, looking as pleased as a man could possibly be.

IV

With the passing of time, old political wounds began to fade. Truman made amends, restored friendship with one former adversary or critic after another—Henry Wallace, Joe Martin, Joe Alsop, Drew Pearson, even Paul Hume, the Washington *Post* music critic who came to Kansas City to review a concert of Maria Callas and decided to drive out to the Truman Library. As Hume later recounted, he and Truman had a "wonderful visit," Truman taking an hour to talk and show him about the library. "I've had a lot of fun out of you and General MacArthur over the years," Truman said as Hume was leaving. "I hope you don't mind."

At the concert that night, Hume found himself sitting across the aisle from the Trumans. When he went over to say hello, Truman turned to Bess and said, "See, I told you that Paul Hume was in my office today."

(Following the performance, Truman went backstage to meet Maria Callas and later, catching up with friends walking to their cars in the garage across the street, Truman, looking tremendously pleased, said, "You know, she remembered me!")

Only three remained for whom he had little or nothing good to say: Eisenhower, MacArthur, and Richard Nixon. The man he had hated most, Joe McCarthy, was dead, of acute alcoholism at age forty-eight in 1957.

In November 1961, at Sam Rayburn's funeral in Bonham, Texas, with twenty thousand people standing in the cold outside the packed church, Truman was seated with both Kennedy and Eisenhower, all three in the same front pew, Truman and Eisenhower looking—as the nation saw on television—like very elder statesmen indeed, next to the young President. For Truman, with his fond memories of Rayburn, it was a particularly painful ceremony; but like the Marshall funeral, it was another step in what was becoming a slow but steady reconciliation with Eisenhower.

For eight years, Truman had hoped Eisenhower would sometime call on him for advice or ask him to take on a project, as Truman had asked Herbert Hoover, but it had never happened. Nor did it now with Kennedy, and Truman felt terribly let down. "You are making a contribution," he told Acheson, who was being called on by Kennedy for advice. "I am not. Wish I could."

The morning walks continued, though he went accompanied now by a bodyguard, a big, solid-looking Independence police officer in plain clothes named Mike Westwood, who was being paid by the town and would stay at Truman's side in all seasons.

His chief pleasures remained constant—his books, his library, his correspondence with Acheson, his family. To Clifton Daniel, he was the ideal father-in-law, "just great," never interfering, always considerate. " 'Give-'em-hell Harry' didn't give anybody hell at home," Daniel would remember.

Needless to say, I was always respectful of him both as a father-in-law and a former President. In public I addressed him as "Mr. President" and in private, after our first son was born, as "Grandpa." Before I avoided calling him anything whenever I could. It would have made us both uncomfortable for me to say "Dad," and for his generation and mine "Harry" was unthinkable. I used "Sir" as much as possible.

. . .

In the summer of 1961, Truman had begun work on what was to be a
series of television films about the presidency, but dealing primarily with
his own years in the White House. It was still another effort, like the
Memoirs and the Truman Library, intended to educate the country, and
especially young Americans. "I'm mostly interested in children," he often
said. The films were to be produced and financed by David Susskind and
his company, Talent Associates. The writer and general "organizer" of the
project was Merle Miller, a novelist and former reporter for *Yank,* who
had been chosen not only to add a "creative spark," but because it was
felt that he and the former President had much in common. Miller, too,
had grown up in the Midwest, a book-loving boy with eyeglasses and
early dreams of glory. But more important and influential than the films
that eventually resulted was the portrait that Miller would compile from
recorded conversations with Truman in a book called *Plain Speaking*—a
book that would not be published for another dozen years.

Ironically, because of his background, Miller had not expected to like
Truman, imagining him to be far too much like people he had known
growing up in Marshalltown, Iowa. "I had thought he was not what we
want in a President," Miller remembered. "I think we want in a President
something somewhat regal. . . ."

But here, he remembered, was

an extraordinarily intelligent, informed human being.
    If I had a father who was smart, or if I had a father who read a book,
if I had a father who knew how to get along with people . . . this was
he. . . . How could you not like him! He was such a decent human being
with concern, a *genuine* concern, for your welfare. "Well, how are
you?" "How's your hotel?" "How's the food?" . . . He wanted to make
you comfortable, and he *did* make you comfortable. I never had an
uncomfortable moment with him except toward the end when it appeared that there was never going to be a show. . . .

With Truman, Miller felt, "You could reach out and there was somebody there. There was a person there! . . . *He was there for you.*"

The producer assigned to the series, Robert Alan Aurthur, found Truman brisk, opinionated, and during one morning session, Aurthur
thought, possibly more fortified with bourbon than ever the doctor ordered.

"Don't try to make a play actor out of me!" Truman insisted to them. A
day of shooting was arranged at the Army Command and General Staff
School at Fort Leavenworth, Kansas. Truman was to sit with a selected

group of officers and talk about Korea. Everyone had expected Truman to be at his best in such a setting, with nothing rehearsed. Instead, he was "terrible," as Robert Aurthur remembered. Truman was told how good he had been, but clearly he knew better. "You're trying to make a play-actor out of me . . . and it won't work."

Using a tape recorder, Miller and Aurthur spent hours—eventually days—interviewing Truman. The stories, the pithy observations came pouring forth. Listening to him, Merle Miller thought Truman had been ill-served by those who had worked with him on the *Memoirs*. "I think there were people, Noyes and Hillman being foremost among them, who wanted to make him something he wasn't, largely dull."

Truman still told stories wonderfully and with an infectious enjoyment. He was also inclined to exaggerate, even invent. Miller was reminded of Huck Finn's comment about Mark Twain, "He told the truth, mainly. There were things which he stretched, but mainly he told the truth."

Truman described the old Democratic picnics at Lone Jack and the oratorical mannerism of the old-time politicians, and particularly Colonel Crisp, who had said, "Goddamn an eyewitness, he always spoils a good story." He described seeing William Jennings Bryan sitting at lunch in Kansas City with a bowl full of radishes and a plate of butter. "He'd just sit there buttering the radishes and eating them. Ate the whole bowl."

When Miller asked if he ever "identified" with Huck Finn or Tom Sawyer when growing up, "No," Truman said. "I wasn't in that class, I was kind of a sissy when growing up." Wearing glasses, he said, "makes a kid lonely and he has to fight for everything he wants. Oh, well, you had to be either intellectually above [the others] or do more work than they did. . . . Then you have to be careful not to lord it over those that you've defeated in that line."

He talked of political bosses. ("The boss is not the boss unless he has the majority of the people with him.") He talked of Franklin Roosevelt. ("He had something like Bryan had. He could make people believe what he wanted to do was right.") He told the story of the Chicago convention of 1944, recounting how he had felt when he put down the telephone in Bob Hannegan's room after talking to Roosevelt and described how the others in the room looked, waiting to hear what he would do. ("I walked around there for about five minutes and you should have seen the faces of those birds! They were just worried to beat hell.") He described how, during the 1944 campaign, he had threatened to throw Joe Kennedy out the window of the Ritz-Carlton Hotel in Boston, when Kennedy kept maligning Roosevelt. "I haven't seen him since." But then he warned Miller not to use the story, "because his son's President of the United States and he's a grand boy."

An optimist was a person who thinks things can be done. No pessimist ever did anything for the world. Billy Graham said the end of the world was coming, but Truman didn't believe it. Courtesy mattered greatly to him. He had heard a story of a gas attendant who refused to fill Tom Dewey's tank, and Truman strongly disapproved. Later he would chide the press for calling the First Lady "Jackie."

The great men of the Roman Republic were not military men, he said. Hadrian was the greatest; his own favorite, however, was Marcus Aurelius, who thought always of the welfare of his people.

Listened to long afterward the tapes would be extremely difficult to follow, full of static, full of the sound of other voices in Truman's office, as people came and went. His own voice was strong, lower and more appealing than his platform voice. Often everyone would break into laughter. The mood was one of a good time, good fellowship, and clearly Truman delighted in it.

Unlike the day at Fort Leavenworth, some of the filming sessions went extremely well. His answers "came back rich with detail, and with all the sharp authority of the man who'd been there," remembered Robert Aurthur of one particularly good session in New York. "Two or three times it was Mr. Truman who asked for another try, saying he could do better." When, at one point, concern was voiced over whether the President was wearing the same necktie as he had during previous sessions in Independence, Truman asked if that really mattered. "Because if while I'm talking about Korea people are asking each other about my necktie it seems to me we're in a great deal of trouble."

To Miller and Aurthur, he seemed exceptionally alert and fit. His first impression, Miller remembered, was, "My God, he's not old at all!" But in fact Truman had begun to slow down, even slip a little. To those who had worked with him at the White House, those who had known him from years past in Independence and Kansas City, he was noticeably different from the man he had been. He moved with less authority. He had become slightly hard of hearing. Responding to questions, he was often inclined to give a quick abrasive answer for effect, an old man's wisecrack. He had been asked so many of the same questions so often in recent years that he had developed a set of pat answers that sounded no better than pat answers. Sometimes he talked as if quoting his own books or old speeches. Other times, and only in the company of men, he used more profanity than in days past. And while the famous smile, the cheerful, personable demeanor remained, his private disdain of certain people and trends of the moment was greater than ever before. He hated the fashion of long hair on young men, and greatly disliked being called "senior citizen." Asked if he thought there would ever be an expedition to the moon, he said probably, but he could not imagine why.

In private, every once in a while, he could revert still to old habits of the mouth as if he were not aware of what he was saying. "People in Independence haven't changed a darned bit," he remarked at one point. He had nothing against Mormons, he told Miller, they were exceedingly hardworking people. But a lot of old-timers in town "hate them just as bad as they ever did," Truman said, and "for the same reason some people hate to eat at the same table with a nigger." It was prejudice, he said.

He worried about the mounting national debt and "this poor broke government of ours." He intensely disapproved of what he saw happening to politics because of television. "I don't like counterfeits and the radio and television make counterfeits out of these politicians."

He hated to see the town being swallowed up by tract houses, billboards, gas stations, and traffic. And ironically, sadly, it was the automobile and the highway, two of the loves of his life, causing the change. Most mornings now, he had to stop and pick up litter—beer cans and candy wrappers—thrown into his front yard.

His lingering anger over General MacArthur seemed excessive. "There were times," Merle Miller remembered, "when you wanted to say to him, 'Look, you know, you had the last word. Leave it lay and bask in your triumph.'"

Of Eisenhower, he could hardly say anything without resorting to profanity.

But then Kennedy, too, seemed nearly as misguided to him as had Eisenhower. Truman was utterly appalled by the Bay of Pigs fiasco, as was Acheson.

There was an unfortunate preoccupation at the Kennedy White House with "image," Acheson wrote to Truman.

> This is a terrible weakness. It makes one look at oneself instead of at the problem. How will I look fielding this hot line drive to short stop? This is a good way to miss the ball altogether. I am amazed looking back to how far you were from this. I don't remember a case where you stopped to think of the effect on your fortunes—or the party's for that matter—of a decision in foreign policy.

"Keep writing," Truman replied, "it keeps my morale up—if I have any."

"You must remember our head of State is young, inexperienced and hopeful," he told Acheson in another letter. "Let's hope the hopeful works."

Hearing that the Democratic Party, at Kennedy's suggestion, was going to put on a $1,000-a-plate dinner, Truman was appalled. "If as and when that happens we'll just quit being democrats with a little d." Nobody had consulted him on the matter. "To hell with these millionaires at the head of things."

Of Attorney General Robert Kennedy, he said, "I just don't like that boy, and I never will." In May of 1960, Matt Connelly had begun serving a prison sentence for income tax evasion. Convinced of Connelly's innocence, and like others, convinced that Connelly was being made the victim of a Republican vendetta, Truman had done all he could, including helping to raise money to defray Connelly's legal expenses. In March 1961 he had written to Bobby Kennedy to urge a pardon for Connelly, who was by then out of prison on parole. But Kennedy had responded by saying only that he was studying the problem. In May, Truman wrote again, providing more detailed background information, and again Kennedy guaranteed his personal attention. But nothing happened, and by the start of 1962, a furious Truman wrote in longhand to the Attorney General:

> Matt Connelly has been abused and mistreated as I told you in my original letter. I want him pardoned and his full rights restored. I've never spoken to your brother about this and I don't intend to. But if you think that I enjoy mistreatment and injustice to one of my best employees, you are mistaken. So don't smile at me any more unless you want to do justice to Matt Connelly, which is the right thing—a full pardon.

In November 1962, Connelly was pardoned by President Kennedy, and it was to the President that Truman sent his letter of gratitude.

Bess, who had been suffering increasingly with arthritis in her knees and hands, had discovered a lump in her breast. Although reported to be benign, it had invaded the lymph nodes and Wallace Graham performed a mastectomy.

The ordeal had been extremely distressing for Truman, who was also later hospitalized, in January 1963, to be operated on for an intestinal hernia—a "little butchering" as he said. In fact, it was an extremely serious operation for someone his age, and he was a long time recovering.

The man who had always loved clocks—who on restless nights had wound the clocks at the White House and kept eight or nine in the Oval Office, who had always wanted to be on time wherever he went—now saw time as the enemy, the pursuer. "That old lady 'Anno Domini' has been chasing me and I have to slow up a little bit," he wrote to Acheson, "particularly since she has a partner in Mrs. Truman." All three of Bess's younger brothers, Frank, George, and Fred Wallace, were dead by now.

"At 79 you go to funeral after funeral of your friends, most of whom are younger than 79—and you sometimes wonder if the old man with the scythe isn't after you," Truman said in another letter in May 1963, following his birthday.

The murder of John F. Kennedy that fall left him feeling devastated. He had been having lunch at the Muehlebach when he heard the news that Kennedy had been shot, but it was not until later, in his car driving home, that he learned that Kennedy was dead.

"Having come so close to that fate himself," wrote Margaret, "Dad was terribly shaken by it. For the first time in his life he was unable to face reporters."

As I was preparing to fly to Washington [Truman later wrote in reply to a query from the author William Manchester] I received a call from President Johnson telling me that a plane was being sent for me and I was able to arrive the day before the funeral. I went directly to Blair House. Shortly after arriving there we rode over to the White House to call on Mrs. Kennedy. I found her as I expected, remarkably self possessed and poised, but to me the deep sadness in her eyes came through. She said to me her husband, the President, spoke of me often and with much feeling and understanding of what we tried to do, and I found myself choked up with emotion.

It is difficult for one who has lived through the Presidency and the trials and burdens that go with it, not to realize the enormity of the tragedy that had befallen the nation and the tragic blow that was visited on his family, and particularly the wife of the President.

Bess had been ill and unable to make the trip. Margaret and Clifton had come down from New York to stay with Truman at Blair House. Seeing her father, Margaret grew concerned. He looked dreadful. A doctor was sent for. Truman obediently went upstairs to his room and was served his dinner in bed. But he was back on his feet the next day to attend the funeral and graveside services, after which he returned to Blair House in the same car with the Eisenhowers. For about an hour in the front parlor at Blair House the two men sat talking. Then Eisenhower returned to his home in Gettysburg and Truman flew back to Missouri.

In the aftermath of the Kennedy tragedy, a bill was passed by Congress authorizing Secret Service protection for former presidents, and so a Secret Service detail arrived in Independence. But when one of the agents called at the Truman house to introduce himself, and told the

President that he would no longer have a need for his own bodyguard, Mike Westwood, Truman told him, "Well, I no longer have a need for you, so get out of here."

Neither of the Trumans had any wish for the Secret Service to return to their lives. Margaret described her mother reacting as if they had just told her she was going to have to spend four more years in the White House. Bess, too, refused to allow the agents on the property. But then President Johnson personally telephoned one evening and convinced Bess that the Secret Service should be reinstated and the Trumans agreed. They were to be watched over from then on, though Mike Westwood continued accompanying the President as before.

Celebrations of Truman's eightieth birthday in May 1964 went on for more than a week in Independence, Kansas City, and Washington. There was a huge lunch in his honor in Independence and another at the Muehlebach. In Washington on May 8, he celebrated with "characteristic verve and vinegar," drawing cheers and praise wherever he went. Invited to address the Senate, he sat in a front seat, a rose in his lapel, and listened to glowing tributes from twenty-seven senators, including two of his favorites from his own years in the Senate, Republicans George Aiken and Leverett Saltonstall. It was an historic occasion, the first time the Senate was making use of a new rule, adopted the year before, whereby former presidents could be granted "the privilege of the floor"—a point that Truman felt so deeply that when he rose he was scarcely able to speak.

> Thank you very much. I am so overcome that I cannot take advantage of this rule right now. It is one of the greatest things that has ever happened to me in my whole lifetime.
> It is unique. It is something that has never been done before. And between you, and me, and the gatepost, since I profit by it, I think it is a good rule.

"You can wish me many more happy birthdays, but I'll never have another one like this," he said as senators crowded about him to shake his hand.

Five months later, on October 13, 1964, Truman tripped on the sill going into the upstairs bathroom at 219 North Delaware. He fell, cracking his head against the washbasin, his glasses shattering and cutting him badly over the right eye. He then fell against the bathtub, fracturing two ribs. Though still conscious, he was unable to move.

The police were called and he was taken to the hospital in an ambulance. Two days later, Wallace Graham reported that his patient was "much improved," his condition "very satisfactory." But though Truman was soon home again and eventually returned to something like his old routine, he never fully recovered from the fall. He began losing weight, his face becoming drawn, the eyes behind the thick glasses appearing disproportionately large. "He doesn't look a thing like he used to," his sister Mary Jane said. "He always had a full face and always looked so well. He takes a miserable picture now, he is so thin. He's always taken such a nice picture."

Yet on he went, taking his morning walks with Mike Westwood, or on occasion with Thomas Melton, pastor of the First Presbyterian Church, who lived just across Truman Road—the pace a little slower each year, but Truman doing most of the talking, as Melton remembered. Passing an enormous gingko tree on Maple Street, one of the largest, most spectacular trees in town, Truman would customarily speak to it, too.

And what would the President say to the tree, Melton would be asked by a visitor years later. "He would say, 'You're doing a good job.'"

He and Bess became steady patrons of the Independence Public Library. In another new Chrysler, this a light green model, Mike Westwood would drive them, Truman riding in front, Bess in back. At the library she would go in and return with an armload of books.

The correspondence with Acheson also continued, Acheson writing at length to keep Truman posted on the Johnson presidency, as he knew Truman wanted. But Truman dictated his letters now and had less and less to say.

In the summer of 1965, Vivian Truman died at age seventy-nine. "His passing has meant a great loss to me," Truman told Acheson. Within days Ted Marks, too, was dead and Truman attended both funerals.

When, on July 30, 1965, President Johnson came to Independence, to sign the new Medicare bill in Truman's presence at the Truman Library, there was, in the words of one account, "sad amazement" expressed in the large Washington contingent over Truman's pitifully frail appearance. His voice, however, remained firm and he talked of several projects he planned for the library.

Sitting at Johnson's elbow, a cane in his lap, he watched the signing into law of legislation for health care for the aged such as he had proposed twenty years before.

"You have made me a very, very happy man," Truman told the President.

Nellie Noland died, and Jim Pendergast. Among the private sorrows of Truman's final years had been a falling out with his old friend Jim Pendergast. There had been a misunderstanding in 1958 over the endorse-ment of a local Democratic candidate, which left each of them convinced the other had betrayed their friendship. It was a sad, unfortunate impasse, and when Jim Pendergast, after a long battle with cancer, died in the spring of 1966, Truman, who attended the funeral, knew another chapter of his life was closed and not at all as he wished.

Attending funerals had become a part of his life. Thomas Melton, the Presbyterian pastor, would later recount an unforgettable graveside scene one grim winter day in Independence:

> Quite often we have committals for people who are not from this area when they die. It was in February if I recall correctly and it was very cold and bitter, a lot of snow that year. And we were going to have a committal at the city cemetery. So I went to the appointed place. . . . There was no one there but the undertaker . . . no pallbearers. And we thought we'd wait until the appointed time [as announced] in the news-papers, in case anybody would come. . . . In came this green Chrysler and I recognized the car immediately. I knew it was Mr. Truman's car. The Secret Service man got out and stood in his position and Mr. Truman walked over to the bier, and I was amazed. I went ahead with the committal. Snow was still in the air, cold. . . . After I had my bene-diction, I asked him, I said, "Mr. President, why are you here? It's cold and bitter. Did you know this gentleman?" And he said, "Pastor, I never forget a friend." And I was just speechless. This was the President of the United States.

Lyndon Johnson came to Independence several times again, hoping to enlist Truman's endorsement of the war in Vietnam. But Truman, who as President had first pledged American support for the French against Ho Chi Minh, made no statement about the war. Privately, he had become more and more disillusioned with Johnson's leadership.

In 1967, in his eighty-fourth year, Truman stopped coming to the li-brary on a regular basis. Nothing was said in explanation; he just was not there much any more.

When, in early 1969, the new President, Richard Nixon, expressed a desire to come see Truman, he and Bess agreed. The President and First Lady called at 219 North Delaware on March 22. They were with the Trumans for half an hour, then drove to the library, where Truman, who was not having one of his best days, stood expressionless while Nixon, at a concert grand piano outside Truman's office, played "The Missouri Waltz." To many who were present, and who knew how much Truman disliked the song, it was a difficult moment. But when Nixon finished, Truman turned to Bess and asked what it was he had played.

Margaret and Clifton Daniel had had two more children by now—
Harrison and Thomas—making a family of four sons. Twice with the
Daniels, in late March 1968 and again the same time the next year, the
Trumans returned to Key West, where, with the four boys, Grandpa
would be seen walking the streets of the old town wearing a blue blazer
and a baseball cap, enjoying the air and sunshine as in times past. These
would be remembered as among the happiest weeks for all of them. He
felt "damn good for an old man," Truman told reporters.

But he had been hospitalized for the flu that winter and was beginning
to feel like the last leaf on the tree. Adlai Stevenson, Churchill, Douglas
MacArthur were all dead. During the stay at Key West came the news of
the death of Eisenhower. Truman wrote a gracious tribute.

On June 28, 1969, the Trumans celebrated their fiftieth wedding anniversary at home. There was no party. Only a few friends dropped by. As
Bess explained to reporters, the President was not up to standing for a
long time shaking hands.

Once, in 1913, writing from the farmhouse at Grandview, he had told
her, "It seems a hollow week if I don't arrive at 219 Delaware at least one
day in it." Now, there were few days that he did not spend there. His
books became his life more and more. Cars passing on Truman Road,
neighbors out for a walk in the evening, could see him in the window,
sitting with a book under his reading lamp. What would her father's idea
of heaven have been, Margaret would be asked years later. "Oh," she
said, "to have a good comfortable chair, a good reading lamp, and lots of
books around that he wanted to read." Once in New York, when Ken
McCormick of Doubleday had called on him early in the morning at his
hotel, Truman had been sitting in a chair in the bedroom with several
new books stacked on a table beside him. Did the President like to read
himself to sleep at night, McCormick asked. "No, young man," said Truman, "I like to read myself awake."

Thomas Hart Benton came to the house to sketch the frail, old figure
in his chair with his books, and the drawing Benton made was one few
Americans would have recognized as Harry Truman. Benton thought
there was more character in the face now.

"I was greatly pleased by your kind and generous letter on my eighty-
seventh birthday," Truman wrote to Acheson on May 14, 1971. "Coming
from you, this carries a much deeper meaning for me." The signature
was still recognizable as his own, but just barely.

Ethel Noland died that summer. Then, on Tuesday, October 12, at his
farm in Sandy Spring, Maryland, Acheson was found slumped over a desk
in his study, dead of a heart attack at age seventy-eight. "Oh, no," Bess
Truman said when called by *The New York Times.* Mr. Truman, she said,

would have no immediate comment, but added, "I know he'll be very disturbed."

The summer of 1972 Truman was hospitalized—first after another fall, then for two weeks with gastrointestinal troubles.

Late the afternoon of Tuesday, December 5, he was taken again to the hospital, leaving the house on North Delaware by ambulance for the last time. His condition, as given to reporters at Research Hospital by Wallace Graham that night, was "fair." He was suffering from lung congestion.

On December 6, his condition listed as "critical," bulletins were issued throughout the day. The doctors were trying to unclog his lung with antibiotics and oxygen, but were hampered because the former President was also suffering from bronchitis and because hardening of the arteries was causing his heart to race periodically.

Margaret, who was in Washington for a reception celebrating her new book about her father, *Harry S. Truman,* flew to Kansas City immediately in a White House jet provided by President Nixon.

In another few days, Truman appeared to rally and was taken off the critical list. But as his battle went on, Wallace Graham could say only that his condition was "very serious."

Bess and Margaret were with him daily in his room on the sixth floor. Mary Jane Truman dropped by. She too was a patient in the hospital, having injured herself in a fall several weeks before. Truman was reported awake and smiling. Asked how he was feeling, he answered, "Better." There were Christmas decorations in his window, reporters were told. Mrs. Truman "remained in good spirits." "He smiled at us and gave yes and no answers to our questions," Margaret told the press on December 10. On the night of December 11, when asked how he felt, Truman reportedly said, "I feel all right." Asked if he hurt anywhere, he said, "No." On December 14, he was reported no longer able to talk.

The struggle went on for three weeks, during which Margaret returned to her family in New York. By now he was suffering from lung congestion, heart irregularity, kidney blockages, and a failing digestive system.

One of the special duty nurses who had been with him as his night nurse since he was first admitted on December 5, Mrs. Walter Killilae, described him later as "warm, sweet and most appreciative of anything you did for him." On Sunday morning, December 24, her night duty ended, she leaned over to tell him she was to have the night off, Christmas Eve, and asked him if he would be there when she got back. "He squeezed my hand," she later said, "which leads me to believe his mind was still responsive. . . ."

On Christmas Eve, he grew progressively weaker. On Christmas morn ing he was reported in a deep coma and near death. Margaret arrived by plane from New York. A 2:00 P.M. bulletin reported his condition "unimproved" and the hospital's chief of staff, Warren F. Wilhelm, called his chances of survival "very, very small." Asked why Mr. Truman was being kept alive this long, Dr. Wilhelm replied, "It's an ethical question. Who would decide? You can always hope that he will rally."

Bess, who had been staying overnight in the hospital and was with her husband through most of every day, had reached a point of almost total exhaustion. Greatly concerned, Margaret persuaded her mother to go home with her to Independence that Christmas night. "Dad was in a coma and there was nothing we could do to help him."

Truman died in Kansas City's Research Hospital and Medical Center on Tuesday, December 26, 1972, at 7:50 A.M. Central Standard Time.

An elaborate, five-day state funeral had been planned years before, with everything to be conducted by the Fifth Army from Fort Sam Houston, Texas. "O Plan Missouri," as it was called, ran to several hundred pages, with everything specified in elaborate detail. Originally, Truman's body was to be flown to Washington to lie in state in the Rotunda of the Capitol, then returned to Missouri for burial. As it was, in the three weeks when he lay dying in the hospital, the Army's aging "Black Jack," the horse that had become such a symbol of tragedy for the nation during the Kennedy state funeral, was taken up in a plane several times to prepare him for the flight to Missouri.

Truman had been shown the entire plan one day in his office at the library and approved nearly all of it, subject to changes his family might wish. He thought it sounded like a "fine show" and was sorry to have to miss it, he said. He objected only to lying in state in Washington. He wanted to be buried "out there," he had said, turning in his chair to look into the courtyard. "I want to be out there so I can get up and walk into my office if I want to."

But the funeral on December 27 was greatly reduced in scale, to be more what Bess wanted. "Keep it simple, keep it simple," she told Margaret and Clifton Daniel. Even so, the military presence was to be substantial, as several thousand troops arrived in Independence to take part in the ceremonies.

After a private service for the family at Carson's Funeral Home, the body was taken to lie in state in the lobby of the Truman Library, the hearse moving slowly through the streets of the town—along Lexington, River Boulevard, Maple, and North Delaware, all lined with soldiers. An honor guard was posted at the library steps. Six howitzers lined the front lawn.

President and Mrs. Nixon came to pay their respects and to place a wreath of red, white, and blue carnations on the casket. Lyndon Johnson was present with all of his family. Johnson, who looked gaunt and greatly aged, would himself die just three weeks later.

For the rest of the day and through the night and on into the morning, thousands of people—seventy-five thousand people, it would be estimated—passed by the closed casket in the lobby of the Truman Library in front of the Benton mural. The line stretched half a mile, to beyond the highway. "This whole town was a friend of Harry's," one man told a reporter.

That afternoon, Thursday, December 28, as he had wished, Truman was buried in the courtyard of the library. With space for the service in the library auditorium limited, only 250 people were invited. Among those present were Averell Harriman, Clark Clifford, Charlie Murphy, Rose Conway, Harry Vaughan, and Sam Rosenman.

Bess Truman, Margaret and Clifton and their four sons, sat behind a green curtain, screened from the others. It was an Episcopal service, as Bess wished, though a Masonic rite was included and a Baptist minister read a prayer. There was no eulogy, no hymns were sung.

Outside afterward, at the gravesite, it was cold and raw, and as the howitzers roared a twenty-one-gun salute and Taps was sounded, the day seemed to turn dramatically colder still. Later, there was snow in the air, and a few of the library staff would remember standing at a window looking out into the empty court and feeling great sympathy, as assuredly Truman would have too, for the men who were working in the cold and dark to fill in the grave.

V

"He was not a hero or a magician or a chess player, or an obsession. He was a certifiable member of the human race, direct, fallible, and unexpectedly wise when it counted," wrote Mary McGrory in the Washington *Star* the next day, in one of hundreds of published tributes.

He did not require to be loved. He did not expect to be followed blindly. Congressional opposition never struck him as subversive, nor did he regard his critics as traitors. He never whined.

He walked around Washington every morning—it was safe then. He met reporters frequently as a matter of course, and did not blame them for his failures. He did not use the office as a club or a shield, or a hiding place. He worked at it. . . . He said he lived by the Bible and history. So armed, he proved that the ordinary American is capable of grandeur. And that a President can be a human being. . . .

He was remembered in print and over the air waves, in the halls of Congress and in large parts of the world, as a figure of courage and principle. Even *Time* and *The Wall Street Journal,* publications that had often scorned him in years past, acclaimed him now as one of the great figures of the century.

The obituary in *The New York Times* ran seven pages. (When the writer, Alden Whitman of *The Times,* had been preparing it in advance years before and went to Independence to interview Truman himself, feeling extremely uneasy about the whole assignment, Truman greeted him with a smile, saying, "I know why you're here and I want to help you all I can.")

In a day of memorial tributes in the Senate chamber that he so loved, he was eulogized as the president who had faced the momentous decision of whether to use the atomic bomb, praised for the creation of the United Nations, for the Truman Doctrine, the Marshall Plan, the Berlin Airlift, the recognition of Israel, NATO; for committing American forces in Korea and for upholding the principle of civilian control over the military—"decisions many of us would pale before," said Senator William Proxmire of Wisconsin.

He was remembered as the first president to recommend Medicare, remembered for the courage of his stand on civil rights at the risk of his political fortunes. The whistle-stop campaign was recalled as one of the affirming moments in the history of the American political system.

His lack of glamour, the "cronies" and loud Florida shirts, the angry letters and the taint of the "Truman scandals," seemed to fade in memory. The scandals, squalid as they were, would with time appear almost tame in contrast to the corrupt excesses of later administrations.

The frequently quoted view of Sam Rayburn that Truman was right on all the big decisions, wrong on all the little ones, was hardly accurate. His Loyalty Program, a very large decision, had been woefully wrong—as was the appointment of Louis Johnson, as was the high-handed seizure of the steel industry—while the restoration of Herbert Hoover to public service and public esteem was not only a right and generous "small" decision, but one that said much about Truman's essential human quality.

That he would later be held accountable by some critics for the treacheries and overbearing influence of the CIA, as well as for the Vietnam War, was understandable but unjustified. He never intended the CIA to become what it did. His decisions concerning Vietnam by no means predetermined all that followed under later, very different presidents.

His insistence that the war in Korea be kept in bounds, kept from becoming a nuclear nightmare, would figure more and more clearly as time passed as one of his outstanding achievements. And rarely had a president surrounded himself with such able, admirable men as Stimson, Byrnes, Marshall, Forrestal, Leahy, Acheson, Lovett, Eisenhower, Bradley, Clifford, Lilienthal, Harriman, Bohlen, and Kennan—as time would also confirm. It was as distinguished a group as ever served the country, and importantly, he had supported them as they supported him.

Born in the Gilded age, the age of steam and gingerbread Gothic, Truman had lived to see a time of lost certainties and rocket trips to the moon. The arc of his life spanned more change in the world than in any prior period in history. A man of nineteenth-century background, he had had to face many of the most difficult decisions of the unimaginably different twentieth century. A son of rural, inland America, raised only a generation removed from the frontier and imbued with the old Jeffersonian ideal of a rural democracy, he had had to assume command of the most powerful industrial nation on earth at the very moment when that power, in combination with stunning advances in science and technology, had become an unparalleled force in the world. The responsibilities he bore were like those of no other president before him, and he more than met the test.

Ambitious by nature, he was never torn by ambition, never tried to appear as something he was not. He stood for common sense, common decency. He spoke the common tongue. As much as any president since Lincoln, he brought to the highest office the language and values of the common American people. He held to the old guidelines: work hard, do your best, speak the truth, assume no airs, trust in God, have no fear. Yet he was not and had never been a simple, ordinary man. The homely attributes, the Missouri wit, the warmth of his friendship, the genuineness of Harry Truman, however appealing, were outweighed by the larger qualities that made him a figure of world stature, both a great and good man, and a great American president.

"Watch the President," Admiral King had whispered to Lord Moran at Potsdam. "This is all new to him, but he can take it. He is a more typical American than Roosevelt, and he will do a good job. . . ."

With his ability to "take it," his inner iron, his bedrock faith in the democratic process, his trust in the American people, and his belief that history was the final, all-important judge of performance, he was truly exceptional. He never had a doubt about who he was, and that too was part of his strength, as well as the enjoyment of life he conveyed.

He was the kind of president the founding fathers had in mind for the country. He came directly from the people. He *was* America. In his time, in his experience, from small town to farm to World War in far-off France in 1918; from financial failure after the war to the world of big-city machine politics to the revolutionary years of the New Deal in Washington to the surge of American power during still another terrible World War, he had taken part in the great chronicle of American life as might have a character in a novel. There was something almost allegorical about it all: The Man of Independence and His Odyssey.

The "lesson" of Truman's life, said Senator Adlai E. Stevenson III of Illinois, was a lesson about ourselves: "an object lesson in the vitality of popular government; an example of the ability of this society to yield up, from the most unremarkable origins, the most remarkable men."

Dean Acheson had called him the Captain with the Mighty Heart; George Marshall, in 1948, had said it was "the integrity of the man" that would stand down the ages, more even than the courage of his decisions. Eric Sevareid, who observed at close range so much of the history of the era and its protagonists, would say nearly forty years later of Truman, "I am not sure he was right about the atomic bomb, or even Korea. But remembering him reminds people what a man in that office ought to be like. It's character, just character. He stands like a rock in memory now."

He had lived eighty-eight years and not quite eight months. Bess Truman lived on at 219 North Delaware for another ten years. She died there on October 18, 1982, and was buried beside him in the courtyard of the Truman Library.

ACKNOWLEDGMENTS

For a biographer, the great body of surviving letters, diaries, private memoranda, and autobiographical sketches written by Harry S. Truman is a treasure beyond compare. There is really nothing like the Truman manuscript collection at the Harry S. Truman Library in Independence. The letters he wrote between 1910 and 1959 to the idolized love of his life, Bess Wallace Truman, are thought to number 1,302—but no one really knows what the exact total may be—and there are thousands more in his own hand, to his mother, his sister, to his cousins Nellie and Ethel Noland, to old Army friends, Dean Acheson, fellow politicians, newspaper editors, friend, and foe, as well as long diary entries. Truman poured himself out on paper with vigor and candor all of his adult life. For a latter-day writer trying to understand him and tell his story in the context of his times, it is Truman himself, again and again, who makes it possible to go below the surface, to know what he felt, what he wanted, his worries, his anger, the exceptional and the commonplace details of his days. Few Americans of any era, irrespective of background or profession, have left such a vivid personal record, quite apart from the immense volume of his official papers, and it is almost certain that we will never again have a President who leaves so candid and revealing an account. Or one written in such a clear hand. In addition to all else that he did for his country, Harry Truman gave us a very large part of himself and his times in his own words, and in my efforts to write his life, during ten years of work on this book, there has been no one to whom I have felt more gratitude.

The staff archivists, librarians, and other specialists at the Harry S. Truman Library have been helpful in countless ways, instructive, patient, generous with their time, generous with ideas and advice, since the morning I first walked in the door one very cold winter day early in 1982. Though they are in no way responsible for any errors of fact or judgment in these pages, there is no part of the book in which they have not played a role, both in what they have helped to uncover in the library collection and in what they themselves know of Truman's life from years of interest and study. In my experience, there is no more agreeable place in which to do research than the Truman Library. Nor has there been anyone on the staff who has not shown an interest in my work or failed to be helpful. I am grateful to them all. But for their particular help and friendship over the years I wish to express my utmost thanks to: Benedict K. Zobrist, director, and George Curtis, assistant director; archivists Philip D. Lagerquist, Erwin J. Mueller, and Dennis Bilger; photographic librarian Pauline Testerman; the very good-natured, resourceful Elizabeth Safly, research librarian and creator and keeper of the so-called vertical file, a mine of marvelous information; Vicky Alexander, Clay Bauske, Robin Burgess, Carol Briley, Millie Carol, John Curry, Patricia Dorsey; J. R. Fuchs, Ray Geselbracht, Anita Heavener, Jann Hoag, Niel Johnson, Earl Pennington, Warren Ohrvall, Ruth Springston, and Mark Beveridge, who knows more about World War I than anyone I know.

I wish also to express my particular indebtedness to the following published works about Truman: his own two-volume *Memoirs* and Margaret Truman Daniel's *Harry S. Truman,* a lively, often moving memoir by an adoring daughter; *The Man of Independence* by Jonathan Daniels, which though incomplete as a biography and anything but impartial (it was written while Truman was still President and Daniels served on Truman's staff), nonetheless contains much on Truman's early life not to be found elsewhere; *Truman* by Roy Jenkins, a too-brief survey of the Truman presidency, but very valuable for its insights; John Hersey's *Aspects of the Presidency,* which includes his deft *New Yorker* profile of Truman, written after an unprecedented chance to follow the President through several crucial days during the second term; *The Truman Presidency, The History of a Triumphant Succession* by Cabell Phillips, who wrote from firsthand observation as a correspondent for *The New York Times;* and *Plain Speaking,* Merle Miller's popular compilation of reminiscences by the elderly former President and others close to him. Though not altogether reliable as to fact, it has the vitality of its subject and contains much of value.

The three leading Truman scholars of our day are Alonzo L. Hamby, Robert J. Donovan, and Robert H. Ferrell, and I have benefited greatly from their work—from Professor Hamby's many articles; from Robert Donovan's comprehensive two-volume study of the Truman presidency, *Conflict and Crisis* and *The Tumultuous Years,* fine books by a writer who covered the Truman White House as a reporter for the New York *Herald Tribune.*

and from Robert H. Ferrell for his advice, friendship, and a whole shelf of Truman books, including *The Autobiography of Harry S. Truman,* a skillful stitching together of Truman's own sketches about himself, and two collections of Truman letters and other writings, *Off the Record: The Private Papers of Harry S. Truman* and *Dear Bess: The Letters from Harry to Bess Truman, 1910–1959.* Everyone who writes about Truman is indebted to Professor Ferrell for these invaluable books.

My bibliography follows, with the principal sources of manuscript and published works, and includes the names of the more than 125 people who agreed to be interviewed for this book. I thank each and all many times over. A number of the interviews were done over several days, and at intervals of several years. Most of the longer interviews were taped, unless this was against the wishes of the interviewee. When a tape recorder was not used, I kept notes. And while all those who generously gave of their time contributed to my understanding of the subject—and including many who are not directly quoted in the book—I want to thank the following especially: Margaret Truman Daniel for three long interviews, including an all-day session in the Truman home at Independence done for the public television series *Smithsonian World;* Clifton Daniel, who talked for several hours over lunch in New York and during a thirty-block walk back uptown; Clark Clifford, who gave many hours of his time over a span of ten years and whose recollections and insights were of greatest possible value; George Elsey, who, like Clark Clifford, played a key role in the Truman administration and whose memory for details and sense of history has helped to give life and balance to my recounting of events in ways that would never have been possible otherwise; Rex Scouten, Curator of the White House, and Floyd Boring, both of whom were part of President Truman's Secret Service detail and who not only spent hours recalling people and events, but took a Saturday afternoon to walk me through what happened at Blair House, inside and out, the day the Puerto Rican nationalists tried to kill the President; James and Martha Ann Truman Swoyer of Oskaloosa, Kansas, who, in addition to talking with me at length about their Uncle Harry, let me see and make notes from his high school workbooks, wonderful, important documents that are quoted here for the first time; the late Merle Miller, who gave me one of the earliest, most interesting of the interviews, and granted me exclusive access to his recorded conversations with former President Truman which are on file at the Lyndon Baines Johnson Library but closed to researchers at Miller's request; the late Stephen Slaughter, who grew up next door to the Truman farm, who knew Harry Truman when he was a farmer, and whose superb book, *History of a Missouri Farm Family,* and personal recollections of life in Grandview helped immeasurably in recreating that vanished time and way of life; Joe Pruett of Kansas City, who helped track down former members of the Pendergast organization, who took me to 1908 Main, up the narrow stairs, to see where Tom Pendergast once ruled, and who, with his wife Catherine Pendergast Pruett, let me examine a wealth of Pendergast family letters, photographs, and memorabilia, and talked with great candor and understanding about the whole Pendergast era; and Sue Gentry, who began writing about life in Independence in the 1930s as a reporter for the *Examiner* and is still going strong, in her "Local Gentry" column in the paper. From the vantagepoint of her home on West Waldo, around the corner from the Truman house, she knows "the whole story."

For their very valuable comments and suggestions on various portions of the manuscript, I thank Paul Horgan, Charlton Ogburn, Anna Loomis McCandless, John T. Galvin, John Zentay, Paul Nagel, George Elsey, Mark Beveridge, Liz Safly, Erwin Mueller, Lyman Field, the late John Oliver, Charles Guggenheim, and Richard Baker, Historian of the United States Senate.

Richard Baker also arranged for me to retrace the steps of Vice President Harry Truman at the Capitol the fateful evening of April 12, 1945, and with Capitol police officers William E. Uber and John D. Roach, we ran, as Truman did, from one end of the Capitol to the other, from what was Sam Rayburn's hideaway back along the lower halls and corridors to the Vice President's office. When I first inquired if it would be possible for me to make the run, Dr. Baker said, "Only if I can come too."

Paul Nagel, Pat O'Brien, and Brent Schondelmeyer, three historians and authors who grew up in Independence and share a passion for Missouri history, gave me a wonderful day's tour of Jackson County for which I will always be grateful. Lyman Field recalled his

ACKNOWLEDGMENTS

memorable experience with President Truman the morning after the 1948 election and introduced me to dozens of people in Kansas City who took an interest in my project.

I wish to thank also for their continuing help and interest: the staff of the Boston Athenaeum, and especially director Rodney Armstrong and research librarian Jan Malcheski; David Wigdor and others of the Manuscript Division, the Library of Congress; Carol Dage of the Liberty Memorial Library in Kansas City; the staff of the National Archives, and particularly Military Historian Edward Reese, who saved me many hours and much frustration in documenting the casualty estimates anticipated in an invasion of Japan in 1945; the staff of the Jackson County Historical Society; Norman J. Reigle and others of the National Park Service who do such an excellent job at the Truman home—the Harry S. Truman National Historic Site; Aurora Davis of the Kansas City *Star* Library; Ralph Graves, former Editor-in-Chief of Time, Inc., who arranged access to the *Time-Life* files; Harry Middleton and his staff at the Lyndon Baines Johnson Library; Helen Bergen of the Martin Luther King, Jr., Library, Washington, D.C.; the Yale University Library; the West Tisbury Public Library; the Cornell University Library; the Smithsonian Institution.

To the following I am also indebted in many ways: Henry Adams; Clarence A. Barnes, Jr., Mary Margaret Bell of the Kentucky Historical Society; the late Walter H. Bieringer; Robert Blafield; Barrington Boardman; Walt Bodine; Daniel J. Boorstin; Charles Burke; Brian Burns; the late Martin Carr; Major General William A. Carter; Carl Charlson; Bernice J. Conley, County Clerk at the Kansas City Courthouse; Paul W. Cook, Jr.; L. P. Cookingham, Frances Cottingham and the Shelby County Historical Society; Annette Curtis; Albert A. Eisele; Christa Fischer; Pauline Fowler; Andrew J. Glass; Neil Goodwin and Margot Barnes Street; Katherine Graham; William and Joyce Graves; Shannon Gregory; David Grubin; Janet Helm; Thomas Hill; William F. P. Hugonin; Oliver Jenson, who let me borrow his complete bound set of *Life* for the Truman years; Emerson and Matilee Johnson; Alvin M. Josephy, Jr.; Chester and Joan Kerr; James Ketchum; Richard Ketchum; Arthur M. Klebanof; Jill Kneerim; the late Kathleen Moore Knight; Professor Robert Knowles; Laurelle O'Leary; Mark Mazer; John Mayhew; Harry McPherson; Cynthia Miller; Richard Miller; Wilson D. Miscamble; James Mongello; James Morrison; Royall O'Brien; Pat O'Neill; Margaret K. Olwine; Harlene Stapf Palkuti; Arva Parks; Eleanor R. Piacenza; Monty B. Poen; Barbara J. Potts, former mayor of Independence; Henry Hope Reed; Donald Ritchie; Judge Howard Sachs; Professor William Sand; Francis N. Satterlee; Michael Shapiro of the St. Louis Art Museum; Al Silverman; Robert C. Smith; Raymond W. Smock, Historian of Congress; Richard Snow; Marie-Cecile and Alfred E. Street; Audrey Stubbart; the late Barbara Tuchman; Geoffrey Ward; Laura and Robert Wilson; Philip F. Ziedman; William Zinsser.

I am deeply grateful to: the John Simon Guggenheim Memorial Foundation for a fellowship grant that helped make possible an additional year of research; J. Gordon Kingsley, president of William Jewell College in Liberty, for the opportunity to learn about Missouri by living there, as writer-in-residence at William Jewell; Haroldine Helm, who provides welcome comforts of home for researchers at the Truman Library, even researchers and their families; the tireless, resourceful Mike Hill, research specialist, who helped through thick and thin; Shirley Mayhew, Sarah Mayhew, Lynn S. Worthington, Ed Wise, and Eric Moe, who, with Mike Hill, assisted with the source notes.

For the design and production of the book I gratefully acknowledge the work of three splendid people, Eve Metz, Frank Metz, and Sophie Sorkin of Simon & Schuster. I thank Wendell Minor for his stunning original portrait of Truman for the dust jacket. And for the immensely helpful contributions she has made as copy editor, I thank Ann Adelman.

To Richard Snyder and Peter Schwed of Simon & Schuster, for their initial enthusiasm for a Truman biography, my wholehearted appreciation. I thank especially my editor, Michael Korda. With his professional advice and good cheer, my friend and literary agent Morton L. Janklow has been a mainstay throughout, for which I am extremely grateful.

For all their efforts typing the manuscript, I thank Patricia Kendall and Kathryn Harcourt. I thank again my daughter Melissa and her husband John McDonald, for a wealth of favors and interest; my son David, for his invaluable suggestions on the manuscript; my son Bill, for research assistance in Missouri and for traveling with me as driver, photographer, companion, and "interpreter" across France, following Captain Harry Truman through World War I; my son Geoffrey, for his help with research at the Library of Congress; and

ACKNOWLEDGMENTS

my daughter Dorie, who uncovered valuable material about the White House, who, when the end seemed near, warned me not to let up, and to whom the book is happily, proudly dedicated.

And with all my heart I thank my wife, Rosalee Barnes McCullough, who took part every step of the way and always to the benefit of the work and the author.

—David McCullough
Washington, D.C.; Liberty, Missouri;
Ithaca, New York; West Tisbury, Massachusetts

January 11, 1992

NOTES
BIBLIOGRAPHY
INDEX

Source Notes

PART ONE

1. BLUE RIVER COUNTRY

16 "Lord, grant": Gilbert, *Westering Man*, 21.
17 One side-wheel steamer: Blue Springs (Missouri) *Examiner*, April 26, 1989.
18 One traveler described: Waugh, "Desultory Wanderings . . . ," *Missouri Historical Society*, April 1950.
18 "The Missouri is constantly": Parkman, *Oregon Trail*, 14.
19 in a letter from Missouri dated July 24, 1846: Nancy Tyler Holmes to Mary Jane Holmes, Harry S. Truman Library (cited hereafter as HSTL).
20 "As for myself": Anderson Shipp Truman to Mary Truman, September 16, 1846, HSTL.
20 "grand prairie ocean": Gregg, *Commerce of the Prairies*, 59.
20 "Mules, horses": Parkman, *Journals*, Vol. 2, 419.
21 "To live in a region:" *History of Jackson County*, 73.
21 "rich and beautiful uplands": Gregg, 163.
22 "without other warrant": *History of Jackson County*, 255.
22 Mormons must leave or be "exterminated": Ibid., 268.
22 a lone assassin: Ibid., 257.
23 "Awful cold": Quoted in Slaughter, *Missouri Farm Family*, 45.
23 "a gun and an axe": John W. Meador, Oral History, HSTL.
24 "She was a strong woman": HST quoted in Miller, *Plain Speaking*, 62.
25 In 1850, his recorded wealth: U.S. Census, 1850.
25 at nearly $50,000: U.S. Census, 1860.
25 a man "who could do pretty much anything": HST quoted in Miller, 62.
25 "The wagons were coupled": Deseret *News*, August 15, 1860, 188.
26 In the spring of 1849: *History of Jackson County*, 96.
26 In 1851 cholera struck again: Ibid.
27 "Come on then, gentlemen": Quoted in Oates, *To Purge This Land with Blood*, 80.
27 "enough to kill every God-damned abolitionist": Ibid., 89.
27 John Brown . . . come to "regulate matters": Ibid., 130.
28 A Jackson County physician named Lee: *History of Jackson County*, 272.
28 "They asked me": Ibid., 300.
29 Quantrill struck Kansas: Monaghan, *Civil War on the Western Border*, 286; Josephy, *Civil War*, 373.
29 Jim Crow Chiles: Sheley, "James Peacock and 'Jim Crow' Chiles," *Frontier Times*, May 1963.
30 In the formal claim Harriet Louisa Young filed. U.S. House of Representatives, 59th Congress, 1st Sess., Sen. Doc. No. 901, June 19, 1906.
31 Recollection of Martha Ellen Young: Berger, "Mother Truman's Life Not All Frontier Toil," Kansas City *Times*, June 30, 1946 (reprinted from *The New York Times*).
32 "It is heartsickening to see": Brownlee, *Gray Ghosts of the Confederacy*, 126–27.
32 "I hope you have not turned": John Truman to Anderson Truman, October 8, 1861, HSTL.
33 the Red Legs had arrived: Daniels, *Independence*, 36.
33 Anderson loaded his five slaves: Ethel Noland, Oral History, HSTL.
33 "They never bought one": Ibid.
33 He was "universally hated": Mary Paxton Keeley, Oral History, HSTL.
33 To black people he was a living terror: Donald R. Hale, "James Chiles—A Missouri Badman," *The West*, October 1968.
34 "to see them jump": Ibid.
34 the confrontation on the west side: Ibid.
36 it was said of John A. Truman: *History of Jackson County*, 986.

36 a three-drawer burl walnut dresser: Martha Ann Truman Swoyer, author's interview.
36 The couple's own first home: Kornitzer, "The Story of Truman and His Father," *Parents Magazine,* March 1951.
37 Lamar *Democrat:* June 28, 1883.
37 a Baptist circuit rider: Steinberg, *The Man from Missouri,* 20.
37 "Baby is real sick now": Letter of Mary Martha Truman, April 7, 1885, HSTL.
38 he was chasing a frog: *Autobiography,* 3.
38 his mother, for fun: Ibid.

2. MODEL BOY

39 the happiest childhood: Harry S. Truman, *Memoirs* (cited hereafter as *Memoirs*), Vol. I, 113.
39 The farm was "a wonderful place": Ibid., 115.
40 "I became familiar with every sort of animal": Ibid.
40 "there were peach butter": Ibid., 114.
40 The child liked everybody: Ibid., 124.
41 "flat eyeballs": Daniels, *The Man of Independence,* 49.
41 Mamma taught that punishment followed: *Autobiography,* 33.
41 enough to "burn the hide off": HST quoted in Miller, *Plain Speaking,* 63.
42 John Truman acquired a house: *Memoirs,* Vol. I, 115.
42 "I do not remember a bad teacher": Ibid., 118.
42 "When I was growing up": Ibid., 124–25.
43 "He just smiled his way along": Jackson (Mississippi) *Daily News,* December 21, 1947.
43 diphtheria: *Memoirs,* Vol. I, 116–17.
43 "didn't scare easy": Daniels, 53.
44 "not once," he said: Quoted in Miller, 48.
44 "It was just something you did": Ibid., 52.
44 "Harry, do you remember": Daniels, 57.
45 "It's a very lonely thing": Quoted in Miller, 277–78.
45 Caroline Simpson taught: Steinberg, *The Man from Missouri,* 24.
45 "To tell the truth": Quoted in Miller, 32.
45 "They wanted to call him": Henry P. Chiles, Oral History, HSTL.
46 "intended for a girl" anyway: HST to EW, April 8, 1912, in Ferrell, ed., *Dear Bess* (cited hereafter as *Dear Bess*), 80.
46 He patented a staple puller: Original patents, HSTL.
46 automatic railroad switch: *Parents Magazine,* March 1951.
46 "A mighty good trader": Ibid.
47 "fight like a buzz saw": Quoted in Steinberg, 17.
47 "A fiery fellow": Stephen Slaughter, author's interview.
47 "No one could make remarks": *Memoirs,* Vol. I, 124.
47 "He had no use for a coward": *Parents Magazine,* March 1951,
48 "Our house became headquarters": *Memoirs,* Vol. I, 117–18.
49 "Harry was always fun": Ethel Noland, Oral History, HSTL.
49 "If I succeeded in carrying": "Pickwick Papers," May 14, 1934, HSTL.
50 "No! No! Harry was a Baptist": Mary Paxton Keeley, Oral History, HSTL.
51 men with their blazing torches: Paxton, *Memoirs,* 22.
52 cows to milk: *Autobiography,* 30.
52 "in regard to integrity": *An Illustrated Description of Independence, Missouri,* ca. 1902.
52 "There was conversation": Quoted in Miller, 32.
52 "No town in the west": *An Illustrated Description of Independence, Missouri.*
53 "Harry always wanted to know": Amanda Hardin Palmer, Oral History, HSTL.
54 "The community at large": Independence (Missouri) *Examiner,* August 23, 1901.
54 "Never, never give up": *Parents Magazine,* March 1951.
54 "In those days": Quoted in Miller, 62.

55 "Oh! Almighty and Everlasting God": HST Diary, in Ferrell, ed., *Off the Record* (cited hereafter as *Off the Record*), 188.
55 "There must have been a thousand": *Memoirs,* Vol. I, 121.
56 "In a little closet": Ibid., 122.
57 "the biggest thing that ever happened": Ibid.
58 "I don't know anybody": Noland, Oral History, HSTL.
58 "He had a real feeling for history": Quoted in Miller, 50.
58 "Reading history, to me": *Memoirs,* Vol. I, 119.
59 "the salt of the earth": Ibid., 118–19.
59 "It cultivates every faculty": *Course of Study and Rules and Regulations of the Independence Public Schools,* March 15, 1909, HSTL.
59 HST composition books: Collection of James F. and Mary Ann Truman Swoyer.
61 "Mothers held him up as a model": Leviero, "Harry Truman, Musician and Music Lover," *The New York Times Magazine,* June 18, 1950.
61 he genuinely adored the great classical works: Ibid.
62 "all right," John Truman said: *Parents Magazine,* March 1951.
63 picnics every August at Lone Jack: Miller, 66–67.
63 HST at 1900 Democratic National Convention: Daniels, 58.
64 Caesar's bridge: Miller, 33.
64 "over a good deal": Noland, Oral History, HSTL.
64 "'Progress' is the cry": *The Gleam,* Independence High School Annual, May 1901.

3. THE WAY OF THE FARMER

67 "I'm fine. And you?": Quoted in Miller, *Plain Speaking,* 12.
67 "plunged" into railroads: Ethel Noland, Oral History, HSTL.
67 "He got the notion he could get rich": Daniels, *The Man of Independence,* 59.
67 "mud horse": Ibid.
67 Tasker Taylor tragedy: Independence *Sentinel,* August 23, 1902.
68 "A very down-to-earth education": *Memoirs,* Vol. I, 123.
68 "He's all right": Jonathan Daniels interview notes, July 28, 1949, HSTL.
68 "Are you good at figures?": April 24, 1903, HSTL.
69 "He is an exceptionally bright young man": A. D. Flintom to C. H. Moore, April 14, 1904, HSTL.
69 "Trueman," as Flintom spelled it: A. D. Flintom to C. H. Moore, July 27, 1904, HSTL.
69 "never so happy as when": *Autobiography,* 20.
69 Wallace suicide: Jackson *Examiner,* June 19, 1903.
70 "an attractiveness about him": Ibid.
70 "Why should such a man": Ibid.
70 wedding of Madge Gates to David Wallace: Kansas City *Journal,* June 15, 1883.
70 "[Bessie] was walking up and down": Mary Paxton Keeley, Oral History, HSTL.
71 "Ties Collar Cuffs Pins": HST Expenses Diary, HSTL.
71 A note from "Horatio": HST to EN, February 2, 1904, HSTL.
71 A performance by Richard Mansfield: *Autobiography,* 22.
71 "They wanted to see him grin": Quoted in Miller, *Plain Speaking,* 84.
72 "I was twenty-one": *Autobiography,* 27.
72 dress uniform episode: Ibid., 28.
72 "when a bachelor": Dahlberg, *Because I Was Flesh,* 1.
72 Virgil Thomson, who was to become: Thomson, *Virgil Thomson,* 3.
73 "Harry and I had only a dollar a week": Daniels, 70.
73 Trumans move back to Grandview: Steinberg, *The Man from Missouri,* 32.
73 His friends were sure: Noland, Oral History, HSTL.
73 "and woe to the loafer": *Autobiography,* 36.
74 "Well, if you don't work": Robert Wyatt, Oral History, HSTL.
74 "The simple life was not always": Stephen Slaughter, author's interview.
74 "My father told me": Quoted in Daniels, 76.
74 Yet John Truman was happier: *Parents Magazine,* March 1951.

75 "Yes, and if you did a good job": Gaylon Babcock, Oral History, HSTL.
75 A few days later: Renshaw, "President Truman. His Missouri Neighbors Tell of His Farm Years," *The Prairie Farmer,* May 12, 1945.
75 Harry also kept the books: HST Account Books, HSTL.
76 "The coldest day in winter": HST to EW, May 19, 1913, *Dear Bess,* 125.
76 "finest land you'd find": Quoted in Miller, 89.
77 "always bustling around": *The Prairie Farmer,* May 12, 1945.
77 "The ground was terribly hard": Ibid.
77 "He was so down-to-earth": Pansy Perkins, Oral History, HSTL.
78 "He always looked neat": Slaughter, author's interview.
78 "Harry was a very good lodge man": Babcock, Oral History, HSTL.
78 "Frank Blair got Harry interested": Slaughter, author's interview.
79 "Papa buys me candy": HST to EW, April 27, 1911, *Dear Bess,* 30.
80 "To be a good farmer in Missouri": Vivian quoted in *Parents Magazine,* March 1951.
80 "You know as long as": HST to EW, October 16, 1911, *Dear Bess,* 52.
80 "Well, I saw her": Truman, *Bess W. Truman,* 32.
81 "Isn't she a caution?": HST to EW, March 19, 1911, *Dear Bess,* 25.
81 "I'm always rattled": HST to EW, postmark illegible, ibid., 134.
82 "Say, it sure is a grand thing": HST to EW, February 13, 1912, ibid., 73.
82 "It is necessary to sit": HST to EW, July 8, 1912, HSTL.
82 "This morning I was helping": HST to EW, January 26, 1911, *Dear Bess,* 21.
82 "I have been to the lot": HST to EW, April 1, 1912, ibid., 80.
83 "I'm horribly anxious for you": HST to EW, April 8, 1912, ibid., 81.
83 "You know when people can get excited": HST to EW, March 19, 1911, ibid., 25.
83 "you've no idea": HST to EW, May 17, 1911, ibid., 33.
83 "I am by religion": HST to EW, February 7, 1911, ibid., 22.
83 "Lent and such things": HST to EW, March 19, 1911, ibid., 24.
83 "I have been reading *David Copperfield*": HST to EW, May 3, 1911, ibid., 31.
84 "you know, were I an Italian": HST to EW, June 22, 1911, ibid., 39.
84 "You know that you turned me down": HST to EW, July 12, 1911, ibid, 40.
85 In August, he announced: HST to EW, August 27, 1911, ibid., 44; September 5, 1911, 45.
85 "I was reading Plato's *Republic*": HST to EW, November 6, 1912, ibid., 103.
85 "He had found he could get": HST to EW, May 23, 1916, ibid., 200.
86 "girl mouth": HST to EW, November 19, 1913, ibid., 145.
86 "so long as he's honest": HST to EW, June 22, 1911, ibid., 39.
86 "Did you ever sit": HST to EW, November 1, 1911, ibid., 57.
86 "We never rated a person": Slaughter, author's interview.
86 "Just imagine how often": HST to EW, November 1, 1911, *Dear Bess,* 57.
87 "hat-full of debts": HST to EW, December 21, 1911, ibid., 64.
87 two reasons for wanting to be rich: HST to EW, January 25, 1912, ibid., 69.
87 "I really thought once I'd be": HST to EW, May 23, 1911, ibid., 36.
87 "I am like Mark Twain": HST to EW, May 17, 1911, ibid., 34.
87 "You know a man has to be": HST to EW, July 12, 1911, ibid., 41.
87 "who knows, maybe I'll be": HST to EW, May 23, 1911, ibid., 36.
87 "Sucker! Sucker!": HST to EW, October 22, 1911, ibid., 53.
88 three hundred bales of hay: HST to EW, August 12, 1912, ibid., 93.
88 "I have been working like Sam Hill": HST to EW, September 30, 1913, ibid., 137.
88 father in a "terrible stew": HST to EW, postmarked November 11, 1913, HSTL.
89 "Politics is all he ever advises me": HST to EW, August 6, 1912, *Dear Bess,* 92.
89 "I don't think we would have traded him for anybody": Slaughter, author's interview.
89 "I never understood": Ibid.
89 "Politics sure is the ruination": HST to EW, postmark illegible, *Dear Bess,* 132.
90 "I told him that was a very mild remark": HST to EW, May 26, 1913, ibid., 126.
90 He was the one person: Noland, Oral History, HSTL.
90 another try in an Indian land lottery: HST to EW, September 30, 1913, *Dear Bess,* 138.
90 "all puffed up": HST to EW, November 4, 1913, ibid., 141–42.

91   "How does it feel to be engaged to a clodhopper": HST to EW, November 10, 1913, ibid., 143.

91   "I know your last letter word for word": HST to EW, November 19, 1913, ibid., 145.

91   "Oh please send me another like it": Ibid.

91   "Mrs. Wallace wasn't a bit in favor of Harry": Ardis Haukenberry, author's interview.

92   "We have moved around quite a bit": HST to EW, February 16, 1911, *Dear Bess*, 24.

92   "Yes, it is true that Mrs. Wallace did not think": May Wallace, author's interview.

92   mother's operation for a hernia: HST to EW, March 20, 1914, *Dear Bess*, 161.

92   "I hope she lives to be": HST to EW, January 26, 1914, ibid., 157.

92   Mamma gave him the money for an automobile: HST to EW, May 12, 1914, ibid., 168.

93   "Harry didn't like onions": May Wallace, author's interview.

93   "I started for Monegaw Springs": HST to EW, no postmark. *Dear Bess*, 183.

94   "Imagine working the roads": HST to EW, August 8, 1914, ibid., 172.

95   "If anyone asks him how he's feeling": HST to EW, September 28, 1914, ibid., 176.

95   "good letters" helped "put that backbone into me": HST to EW, September 17, 1914, ibid., 175.

95   his father, who refused to let the nurse: HST to EW, November 1914, ibid., 178.

95   "I remember the Sunday afternoon": Slaughter, *History of a Missouri Farm Family*, 71.

95   "I was with him": Daniels, 74.

96   "Harry and I often got up": *Parents Magazine*, March 1951.

96   "An Upright Citizen": Independence *Examiner*, November 3, 1914.

96   "I have quite a job on my hands": HST to EW, November 1914, *Dear Bess*, 178.

96   "quiet wheat-growing people": Cather, *One of Ours*, 143.

97   "gave it everything he had": Quoted in Miller, 90.

97   "I almost got done planting": HST to EW, April 28, 1915, *Dear Bess*, 182.

97   "It's right unhandy to chase": HST to EW, Grandview, 1915, ibid., 181.

97   he traveled to Texas; HST to EW, February 16, 1916, ibid., 185.

97   "There's no one wants to win": HST to EW, February 19, 1916, ibid., 187.

98   "This place down here": HST to EW, date illegible, ibid., 193.

98   "I don't suppose": HST to EW, June 3, 1916, ibid., 201.

99   "I can't possibly lose forever": HST to EW, April 24, 1916, ibid., 198.

99   "The mine has gone by the board": HST to EW, May 19, 1916, ibid., 199.

99   He could "continue business": HST to EW, May 23, 1916, ibid., 200.

99   "It's about 111 degrees in the shade": HST to EW, July 30, 1916, ibid., 206.

99   "Wish heavy for me to win": HST to EW, July 28, 1916, ibid.

99   "Keep wishing me luck": HST to EW, August 4, 1916, ibid., 207.

99   buying and selling oil leases: Steinberg, 39.

100   "signed also by Martha E. Truman": Ibid., 39.

100   "came up every time with something else": HST to EW, August 5, 1916, *Dear Bess*, 209.

100   "Truman was surrounded by people, people, people": Daniels, 81.

100   "If this venture blows": HST to EW, January 23, 1917, *Dear Bess*, 213.

100   "In the event this country": Daniels, 83.

100   Teeter Pool discovered: *Memoirs*, Vol. I, 127.

101   He said $11,000 at the time: Truman, *Bess W. Truman*, 56.

101   If his part in his father's debts: HST to EW, April 28, 1915, *Dear Bess*, 182.

101   he was never meant for a farmer: Noland, Oral History, HSTL.

101   "Riding one of these plows all day": HST, "Autobiographical Sketch," HSTL.

101   "It takes pride to run a farm": HST to MET and MJT, September 18, 1946, in Ferrell, ed., *Off the Record*, 96.

4. SOLDIER

102   "It is the great adventure": HST to EW, September 15, 1918, *Dear Bess*, 271.

102   "we got through": Quoted in Miller, *Plain Speaking*, 93.

102   Some people thought her the best looking: Gaylon Babcock, Oral History, HSTL.

103 "It was quite a blow": Steinberg, *The Man from Missouri,* 42.
103 She must not tie herself: HST to EW, July 14, 1917, *Dear Bess,* 225.
103 the reasons to go to war: HST to EW, January 18, 1918, HSTL.
103 there wasn't a German bullet: HST to EW, February 1, 1918, *Dear Bess,* 242.
104 "Galahad after the Grail": *Autobiography,* 41.
105 passes eye exam: U.S. Army Medical Records, August 9, 1917, HSTL.
105 On July 4, 1917, when Harry turned up: HST to EW, July 4, 1918, HSTL.
105 "It was sure enough cold": HST to EW, October 9, 1917, HSTL.
105 "A tent fifty yards away": HST to EW, October 18, 1917, *Dear Bess,* 231–32.
106 "all the Lillian Russells": HST to EW, September 30, 1917, ibid., 228.
106 artillery terms: Lee, *The Artillery Man,* 326.
106 "I have been squads east": HST to EW, February 3, 1918, *Dear Bess,* 242.
106 "I learned how to say Verdun": HST to EW, October 27, 1918, HSTL.
106 "He made us feel": HST to EW, January 27, 1918, *Dear Bess,* 241.
107 "one of our most effective officers": Thomson, *Virgil Thomson,* 35.
107 "I have a Jew in charge": HST to EW, October 28, 1917, *Dear Bess,* 233.
107 "Each day Harry would write a letter": Mayerberg, "Edward Jacobson: President Truman's Buddy," *Liberal Judaism,* August 1945.
107 "I guess I should be very proud": HST to EW, February 3, 1918, *Dear Bess,* 242.
107 "real good conversation": HST to EW, February 23, 1918, ibid., 245–46.
107 "Jacobson says he'd go": HST to EW, November 24, 1917, ibid., 238.
107 "I didn't know how crazy": HST to EW, January 10, 1918, ibid., 240.
108 Tiernan provides whiskey: HST to EW, October 23, 1917, ibid., 232.
108 "We elected Klemm": Truman interview with Jonathan Daniels, November 12, 1949.
108 "He taught me more about handling men": *Autobiography,* 44.
109 "You speak pretty good English": Ted Marks, Oral History, HSTL.
109 "No man can be that good": *Memoirs,* Vol. I, 128.
109 Berry would stalk up and down: Steinberg, 43.
109 "I suppose you will have to spend": HST to EW, March 16, 1918, HSTL.
110 "I'd give anything in the world": HST to EW, March 20, 1918, *Dear Bess,* 251.
110 "The phone's yours": *Memoirs,* Vol. I, 129.
110 "On leave in New York": HST to EW, March 24 and March 26, 1918, *Dear Bess,* 252–53.
110 a "Kike town": HST to EW, March 27, 1918, ibid., 254.
110 "Israelitist extraction": HST to EN, ca. 1918, HSTL.
110 "I imagine his vision": Harry Vaughan, Oral History, HSTL.
111 "There we were watching": *Autobiography,* 45.
111 He ached for home: HST to EW, April, 1918, *Dear Bess,* 256.
111 arrival at Brest: *Autobiography,* 45.
112 At the hotel in Brest: HST to EW, April 14, 1918, *Dear Bess,* 257.
112 The whole surrounding countryside: HST to EW, April 23, 1918, ibid., 260.
112 "The people generally treat us fine": HST to EW, April 12, 1918, ibid., 259.
112 "I'm for the French more and more": HST to EW, June 27, 1918, ibid., 264.
113 They also knew how to build: HST to EW, May 19, 1918, ibid., 262.
113 "They are the most sentimental people": HST to EW, June 2, 1918, HSTL.
113 *"Je ne comprends pas"*: HST to EW, April 17, 1918, *Dear Bess,* 259.
113 determined to drink France dry: HST to EW, April 14, 1918, ibid., 258.
113 "Wandering through dark streets": Quoted in Freidel, *Over There,* p. 80.
113 "Personally, I think Harry": Edgar Hinde, Oral History, HSTL.
113 "Wish I could step in": HST to EW, April 17, 1918, *Dear Bess,* 259.
113 the first-class coach: HST to EW, May 17, 1918, HSTL.
113 account of château: HST to EW, April 28, 1918, *Dear Bess,* 260.
114 "You'd never think that a war": HST to EN, May 1, 1918, HSTL.
114 "and then the clock on the Hôtel de Ville": HST to EW, April 28, 1918, HSTL.
115 "I've studied more and worked harder": HST to EW, May 26, 1918, HSTL.
115 "We had a maneuver yesterday": HST to EW, May 26, 1918, HSTL.
115 Sundays at church: HST to EW, April 28, 1918, *Dear Bess,* 261.

115 "and I'm for helping them": HST to EW, May 5, 1918, ibid.
115 discovered volumes of music: HST to EW, May 19, 1918, HSTL.
115 "He had maps": Arthur Wilson, Oral History, HSTL.
116 "I just barely slipped through": HST to EW, June 14, 1918, *Dear Bess,* 263.
116 "old rube" from Missouri: HST to EW, June 27, 1918, ibid., 263.
116 value of a university education: HST to EW, July 22, 1918, ibid., 267.
116 "No I haven't seen any girls": HST to EW, June 27, 1918, ibid., 264.
116 "I look like Siam's King": HST to EW, June 19, 1918, HSTL.
116 "That was one of the things": Cather, *One of Ours,* 319.
116 "Dear Harry, May this photograph": EW inscribed photograph, HSTL.
117 "They were a pretty wild bunch": Hinde, Oral History, HSTL.
117 "a sitting duck": Eugene Donnelly quoted in Miller, 97.
117 "a stirring among the fellows": Ibid., 96.
117 "a rather short fellow": Vere Leigh, Oral History, HSTL.
117 "You could see that he was": Edward McKim, Oral History, HSTL.
117 "I could just see my hide": *Autobiography,* 46.
117 "Never on the front": "Pickwick Papers," HSTL.
117 Ridge recollection: Miller, 96.
117 "He was so badly scared": "Pickwick Papers," HSTL.
117 "And then we gave Captain Truman": Leigh, Oral History, HSTL.
117 "He didn't hesitate at all": Ibid.
117 "I didn't come over here": Daniels, *The Man of Independence,* 95.
118 "Well, I would say": Wilson, Oral History, HSTL.
118 "You soldier for me": Ibid.
118 "soldier, soldier, all the time": Lee, 33–34.
118 "Talk about your infantryman": HST to EN, August 5, 1918, HSTL.
118 "You've no idea what an immense responsibility": HST to EW, August 13, 1918, HSTL.
120 train passing close enough to Paris: War Diary of Captain Keith W. Dancy, Battery A, Liberty Memorial, Kansas City, Missouri.
120 "It was just a quiet sector": Frederick J. Bowman, Oral History, HSTL.
121 "It was surely some steep hill": HST to EW, November 23, 1918, HSTL.
121 "we were firing away": Leigh, Oral History, HSTL.
122 "gasping like a catfish": Columbus (Kansas) *Daily Advocate,* August 16, 1950.
122 "I led the parade!": Walter Menefee, Oral History, HSTL.
122 "I got up and called them everything": Daniels, 96.
123 "The men think I am not much": HST to EW, September 8, 1918, HSTL.
123 "It was literally true": Lee, 67.
123 Bennett Clark incident: Steinberg, 47.
124 "Well, I was scared green": HST to EW, November 23, 1918, HSTL.
124 "September 10. Leave Coyviller": HST War Diary, HSTL.
124 "Who can ever forget": Lee, 75.
124 "So slow was our progress": Ibid., 72.
125 "American drive begins": HST War Diary, HSTL.
125 "The great adventure": HST to EW, September 15, 1918, *Dear Bess,* 271.
125 "We were doing our best to finish": HST to EW, September 15, 1918, HSTL.
126 "And there was an order out": Floyd Ricketts, Oral History, HSTL.
126 "like a crazy man": McKim, Oral History, HSTL.
126 Tiernan's coat: Ibid.
126 "The Colonel insults me shamefully": HST War Diary, HSTL.
127 "The weather was bad": Ricketts, Oral History, HSTL.
127 "the history of the world": Miller, 101.
127 "If all priests were like him: Ibid., 103.
127 "I stripped the battery for action": HST to EW, November 23, 1918, HSTL.
128 "Everything was now in readiness": Lee, 93.
128 "Just a word to you": Toland, *No Man's Land,* 403.
129 Captain Eddie Rickenbacker, who took off: Ibid., 432.
129 "That gun squad worked": Harry E. Murphy, Oral History, HSTL.

SOURCE NOTES

129 "My guns were so hot": HST to EW, November 23, 1918, HSTL.
129 "confusing in the extreme": Marshall, *Memoirs of My Services in the World War,* 160.
130 At a crossroads near Cheppy: Truman, "The Military Career of a Missourian," HSTL.
130 "Truman didn't panic": Leigh, Oral History, HSTL.
130 "Truman sent back the data": McKim, Oral History, HSTL.
130 "You know . . . when you're in the artillery": Leigh, Oral History, HSTL.
131 "The artillery fire has been something": Minder, *This Man's War,* 328.
131 "Well, men," Miles said: Lee, 167.
131 "The coolness, the steady courage": Ibid., 168.
132 "It isn't as bad as I thought": HST to EW, October 8, 1918, *Dear Bess,* 274.
132 "He was the Captain": Leigh, Oral History, HSTL.
132 "The most terrific experience": HST to EW, October 8, 1918, *Dear Bess,* 274.
132 "all the comforts of home": HST to EW, October 30, 1918, ibid., 276.
132 consistently clean and dapper: Vaughan, Oral History, HSTL.
133 "where every time a shell lights": HST to EW, November 1, 1918, *Dear Bess,* 277–78.
133 "When the moon rises": HST to EW, October 30, 1918, ibid., 276.
133 sends a poppy: HST to EN, November 1, 1918, HSTL.
134 "He handed me a piece": Meisburger quoted in Peoria *Journal-Star,* May 6, 1970.
134 "My battery fired the assigned barrages": Weintraub, *A Stillness Heard Round the World,* 169.
134 "When the firing ceased": Ibid.
134 "People went so wild": Ibid., 170.
134 "You've no idea": HST to EN, December 18, 1918, HSTL.
135 "We were just—": Leigh, Oral History, HSTL.
135 "what you'd expect at the Gaiety": HST to EN, December 18, 1918, HSTL.
135 Paris tour: HST to EW, November 29, 1918, *Dear Bess,* 283.
135 "as wild as any place": HST to EN, December 18, 1918, HSTL.
135 "a dandy place": HST to EW, November 29, 1918, *Dear Bess,* 283.
136 "beautifully sung": HST to EW, December 18, 1918, ibid., 284.
136 "To keep from going crazy": Steinberg, 50.
136 "Every day nearly someone": HST to EW, January 12, 1919, *Dear Bess,* 292.
136 "Would as leave lost a son": HST War Diary, HSTL.
137 "It's some trick to keep": HST to EN, January 20, 1919, HSTL.
137 the possibility of running for political office: HST to EW, November 1, 1918, *Dear Bess,* 277.
137 "I can't see what on earth": HST to EW, December 19, 1918, ibid., 287.
137 "thirsted for a West Point education": HST to EW, December 14, 1918, ibid., 286.
137 "back to God's country again": HST to EW, November 1, 1918, ibid., 277.
137 "Maybe have a little politics": HST to EW, December 14, 1918, ibid., 285.
137 "We'll be married anywhere": HST to EW, February 18, 1919, ibid., 296.
138 "You may invite the entire 35th Division": Truman, *Bess W. Truman,* 77.
138 "As far as we're concerned": HST to EN, January 20, 1919, HSTL.
138 he bought a wedding ring: Truman, 78.
138 violently seasick nearly the whole way: HST to EW, April 24, 1919, *Dear Bess,* 297–98.

PART TWO

5. TRY, TRY AGAIN

141 "I've had a few setbacks": Quoted in Miller, *Plain Speaking,* 70.
141 nineteenth-century man: Ibid., 43.
142 "I want you to be happy": HST to EWT, July 9, 1925, *Dear Bess,* 319.
142 "It was characteristic": Leuchtenburg, *Perils of Prosperity,* 83.
142 "I have always wondered": *Memoirs,* Vol. I, 127.
142 answering letters from the mothers and fathers: Miller, 97.

143 "Well, I remember when he came back": Ethel Noland, Oral History, HSTL.
143 last heated argument: HST to EWT, June 29, 1949, *Dear Bess,* 558.
143 Truman wedding: Truman, *Bess W. Truman,* 79–80.
144 "I hope you have the same success": Unidentified letter from member of Battery D, Waco, Texas, to HST, July 45, 1919, HSTL.
144 "Well, Mrs. Truman, you've lost Harry": Ted Marks, Oral History, HSTL.
144 Mary Jane had cooked noon dinner: Miller, 107.
144 "You've just never seen such a radiant": Noland, Oral History, HSTL.
145 "a very, very difficult person": Miller, 106.
147 "I didn't know": Quoted in Daniels, *The Man of Independence,* 100.
147 "Twelfth Street was in its heyday": Ibid., 105–06.
147 "We'd all drop in": Edward McKim, Oral History, HSTL.
147 "But Harry seemed glad": Miller, *Harry S. Truman,* 155.
147 "You can't quit them": Quoted in Miller, *Plain Speaking,* 92.
148 "I see no reason": Unidentified letter to HST, December 14, 1919, HSTL.
148 "Well, sir, don't forget me": Eugene Donnelly to HST, October 4, 1920, HSTL.
148 "We'd have done anything for him": Quoted in Miller, *Plain Speaking,* 97.
148 husband never worked as hard: Ibid., 112.
149 Battery D reunion: E. J. Becker to HST, March 22, 1921, HSTL.
149 "He would get out and go": Marks, Oral History, HSTL.
149 Dr. A. Gloom Chaser: HSTL.
150 war memorial ceremonies: Kansas City *Times,* October 17, 1921.
150 "That was when we took": Quoted in Daniels, 119.
150 "high jinks": McKim, Oral History, HSTL.
150 a sign of anti-Semitism: Miller, *Plain Speaking,* 106.
151 Eddie's frayed suit: Daniels, 109.
151 "It was a nice store": Edgar Hinde, Oral History, HSTL.
151 "There goes Harry": Gaylon Babcock, Oral History, HSTL.
151 "a nice boy": HST to EWT, September 20, 1921, *Dear Bess,* 312.
152 "I've got friends": Quoted in Reddig, *Tom's Town,* 28.
152 "There is no kinder hearted": Kansas City *Times,* March 26, 1892.
152 "No deserving man": Quoted in Dorsett, *The Pendergast Machine,* 21.
153 reputation of saloon keepers: Kansas City *Star* files, undated.
153 "I never needed a crooked": Quoted in Reddig, 32.
153 "His support of any man": Ibid., 72.
153 "Brother Tom will make": Ibid.
154 Thomas Joseph Pendergast: Ibid., 33.
155 "Yes. Why not?": O. K. Armstrong, "Crusade in Kansas City," *This Week,* March 13, 1938.
155 "He was a master!": Matt Devoe, author's interview.
155 "that fellow could probably talk": Conn Withers, author's interview.
155 "Oh, he was a wonderful man": Geraldine Ketchum, author's interview.
155 "No, I never had a sense of evil": Monsignor Arthur Tighe, author's interview.
155 Tom kept to himself: Mason, *Truman and the Pendergasts,* 33.
155 "You can't make a man good": St. Louis *Post-Dispatch,* September 12, 1937.
155 "We have the theory": Ibid.
155 "Let the river take its course": Mason, 25.
156 "Politics is a business": Kansas City *Star,* March 31, 1966.
156 "When a man's in need": St. Louis *Post-Dispatch,* September 12, 1937.
156 happy to be "repeaters": Ketchum, author's interview.
156 woman in the hospital laundry: Ibid.
156 "Oh, I knew it was illegal": Ibid.
157 "When we come over the hill": Reddig, 34.
157 "Stealing elections": Quoted in Mason, 46.
157 Fifty-Fifty Agreement: Dorsett, 62–63.
158 "enforcer of loyalty": Reddig, 97.
158 "tenacious fighting type": Unidentified obituary of Pendergast, September 2, 1929.

158   Mike passed over because of temper: Robert Pendergast, author's interview.
159   idea of running Harry: Joseph and Catherine Pruett, author's interview.
159   If Captain Truman was all Jim said: Ibid., and Robert Pendergast, author's interview.
159   "They are trying to run me": HST to Ernest Schmidt, February 4, 1922, HSTL.
159   "Now, I'm going to tell you": Quoted in Daniels, 114.
160   "Old Tom Pendergast wanted": Harry Vaughan, Oral History, HSTL.
160   "Went into business all enthusiastic": "Pickwick Papers," HSTL.
160   "I loved him as I did my own daddy": Ibid.
160   "feeling fairly blue": Daniels, 109.
160   "Well, I've got to eat": Ibid., 121.
161   "mess up" his life with politics: Ibid., 110–11.
161   "They always like to pick winners": Noland, Oral History, HSTL.
161   auditorium at Lee's Summit: Lee's Summit *Journal,* March 9, 1922.
161   "thoroughly rattled": Quoted in Truman, *Mr. Citizen,* 156.
161   "I was scared worse": HST Diary, September 23, 1952, in Ferrell, ed., *Off the Record,* 271.
162   "I knew Harry Truman": Stephen Slaughter, author's interview.
162   "the poorest effort of a speech": Hinde, Oral History, HSTL.
162   "If you're going to be in politics": Quoted in Miller, *Plain Speaking,* 128.
162   "We'd do whatever was necessary": Ibid.
163   sacks of cement: *Memoirs,* Vol. I, 137.
163   to arrive by airplane: McKim, Oral History, HSTL.
163   "I am now going to tell you": Independence *Examiner,* July 18, 1922.
163   "I want men for road overseers": Quoted in Daniels, 142.
164   "You have heard it said": Ibid., 118.
164   Edgar Hinde urged Harry: Hinde, Oral History, HSTL.
165   "They didn't just hate Catholics": Quoted in Reddig, 113.
165   "The smell of old 'alky' ": Independence *Examiner,* August 1, 1922.
166   Shannon henchmen: Ibid., August 2, 1922.
166   Gibson's 45-caliber: Ibid.
167   Fifty-Fifty was finished: Kansas City *Times,* September 2, 1929.
167   "We ran the county": *Memoirs,* Vol. I, 137.
167   "When a road project": Independence *Examiner,* July 9, 1919.
168   suffered a second miscarriage: Truman, 88.
168   "I wish you would send me": HST to Ralph Truman, February 23, 1923, HSTL.
168   "It is now 10:20": Quoted in Truman, 90.
168   She would wait for hours: Ibid.
168   "You be a good girl": HST to EWT, July 21, 1923, *Dear Bess,* 314.
169   Nurse Kinnaman's account of baby's birth: From reporter Champ Clark's files dated February 1951, Time-Warner archives.
169   "He has the most magnetic personality": Quoted in Schlesinger, *The Crisis of the Old Order,* 376–77.
170   "He kept his feelings to himself": Quoted in Miller, *Plain Speaking,* 127.
170   "The record of the county court": Kansas City *Star,* July 17, 1924.
170   "To even talk about throwing": Independence *Sentinel,* undated, General Family Files, HSTL.
170   Klan rally: Daniels, 126.
171   "You did what your gang told you": Henry P. Chiles, Oral History, HSTL.
171   Kansas City Automobile Club: *Autobiography,* 59.
171   "This is almost like campaigning": HST to EWT, November 9, 1926, *Dear Bess,* 323.
172   "If one thing did not work": Marks, Oral History, HSTL.
172   called the Citizens Security: Daniels, 134–35.
172   "kind of a cold bird": Mary Salisbury Bostian, author's interview.
172   "Anybody who's ever been a friend": Hinde, Oral History, HSTL.
172   "used me for his own ends": "Pickwick Papers," HSTL.
172   "a no-good bastard": Jonathan Daniels interview notes, September 25, 1949, HSTL.
173   run for county collector: *Memoirs,* Vol. I, 139.

SOURCE NOTES

173   Collector's job: Daniels, 138.
173   "No criticism or scandals": Independence *Examiner,* July 27, 1928.
174   "Every subject of debate": *New Republic,* April 30, 1945.
174   "We intend to operate": Independence *Examiner,* January 3, 1927.
175   spinning about in Judge Truman's swivel chair: Robert Pendergast, author's interview.
175   nervous breakdown: Ibid.
176   "You can't do it": Quoted in Daniels, 145.
176   "I told the voters": Ibid., 146.
177   "Here were hundreds of square miles": *Results of County Planning,* 7, 9.
178   Farm on Blue Ridge Boulevard: Ibid., 97.
178   "Oh! If I were only John D. Rockefeller": "Pickwick Papers," HSTL.
178   "a loudmouthed, profane, vulgar": FOIPA No. 297,745, FBI.
179   "What the hell do you do": Ibid.
179   The facts about Canfil: Ibid.
180   "Fred's a little rough": Quoted in Steinberg, *The Man from Missouri,* 257.
180   "Character excellent": FOIPA No. 297,745, FBI.
180   an equestrian bronze of Andrew Jackson: Steinberg, 95.
180   "I wanted a real man": Quoted in Miller, *Plain Speaking,* 139.
180   "that I either had to run away": HST to EWT, February 12, 1931, *Dear Bess,* 343.
180   "and every person I've ever had": "Pickwick Papers," HSTL.
181   exceptionally fit: U.S. Army Personnel Records, 1925, 1936, HSTL.
181   "I haven't had a headache": HST to EWT, July 13, 1927, *Dear Bess,* 329.
181   "We didn't have any equipment": Vaughan, Oral History, HSTL.
181   "I've been around Legion conventions": Hinde, Oral History, HSTL.
181   "Three things ruin a man": Quoted in New York *Post,* December 29, 1972.
181   "I never wanted power": Ibid.
182   Truman buying seat covers: Kansas City *Star,* November 14, 1990.
183   attempt to kidnap Margaret: From reporter Champ Clark's file dated February 1951, Time Warner archives.
183   "While it looks good": HST to EWT, August 27, 1933, *Dear Bess,* 358.
183   "Politics should make a thief": HST to EWT, May 7, 1933, ibid., 353.
184   "The Boss wanted me": "Pickwick Papers," HSTL.
184   Meeting with Pendergast: Daniels, 146–47.
184   Harry's later account: "Pickwick Papers," HSTL.
185   "Didn't I tell you boys": Daniels, 147.
185   "And that's God's truth": Miller, *Plain Speaking,* 137.
185   "He, in times past": "Pickwick Papers," HSTL.
185   "loved the ladies": Ibid.
185   "Since childhood at my mother's": Ibid.
186   "This sweet associate of mine": Ibid.
186   Pendergast lecturing: Ibid.
187   To little Sue Ogden: Sue Ogden Bailey, author's interview.
188   "And this was a disaster!": Margaret Truman Daniel, author's interview.
188   Sue Ogden's memories: Bailey, author's interview.
188   "I never heard a squabble": Vietta Garr quoted in Kansas City *Star,* April 18, 1945.
188   "I was an only child": Margaret Truman Daniel, author's interview.
188   "I could twist *him*": Ibid.
189   "My manners were expected": Truman, 109.
189   "Her presence": Margaret Truman Daniel, author's interview.
189   "Yes, I spoiled him": Kansas City *Star,* April 18, 1945.
189   "She liked Mamma Truman": Truman, 109.
189   Once when she offered food: J. C. Truman, author's interview.
189   *The Capture of the Clever One:* Margaret Truman Daniel, author's interview.
190   "I want her to do everything": HST to EWT, July 17, 1929, *Dear Bess,* 338.
190   "The car was washed": Margaret Truman Daniel, author's interview.
190   "Straight, absolutely straight": Ibid.

190   "He read all the weather maps": Ibid.
190   "How does Harry put up": Mary Shaw Branton, author's interview.
190   "It was *very* hard": Margaret Truman Daniel, author's interview.
190   picked Number 369: Sue Gentry in Independence *Examiner,* April 25, 1979.
191   Harpie Club: Daniels, 152.
191   "He liked his walk": Margaret Truman Daniel, author's interview.
191   the town directory: *Independence City Directory,* 1934.
191   "Just think of all those *wasted* years": HST to EWT, July 22, 1930, *Dear Bess,* 339.
191   "Have you practiced your music?": HST to EWT and MT, July 10, 1932, ibid., 347.
192   "You may yet be the first lady": Daniel, 117.
192   over lunch with . . . Eric Sevareid: Sevareid, "A Truly Great Man," *McCall's,* March 1973.
192   "He loved politics": Marks, Oral History, HSTL.
192   hadn't he been a late bloomer: Noland, Oral History, HSTL.
192   "There, he struck his gait": Ibid.

6. THE SENATOR FROM PENDERGAST

193   "Friends don't count": *Autobiography,* 74.
193   Francis M.Wilson: Kansas City *Star,* February 2, 1982.
194   "It was my big day": *Autobiography,* 71.
194   Excelsior Springs seclusion: Ibid.
194   "It will be much better": HST to Robert Ragland, January 17, 1923, HSTL.
195   "long as the Big Boss": HST to EWT, April 14, 1933, *Dear Bess,* 348.
195   "understood political situations": *Autobiography,* 83.
195   Big Boss began letting votes go: Dorsett, *The Pendergast Machine,* 106–07.
195   "I had a fine talk": HST to EWT, April 23, 1933, *Dear Bess,* 350.
196   "Uncle Tom's Cabin": Kansas City *Star,* July 4, 1976.
197   McElroy would later claim: Art Brisbane, "Kansas City Needs an Honest Boss Tom," Kansas City *Star,* May 3, 1982.
197   Pendergast would listen attentively: Kansas City *Times,* April 21, 1986.
197   "Why shouldn't they be?": St. Louis *Post-Dispatch,* September 12, 1937.
197   "The machine did small favors": Dorothy Davis Johnson, author's interview.
198   "the most efficient city government": Reddig, *Tom's Town,* 128.
198   "kind of gentleness": Monsignor Arthur Tighe, author's interview.
199   "See . . . there just wasn't any law": John Doohan, author's interview.
199   "The clubs stayed open all night": Ibid.
200   Kidnapping of McElroy's daughter: Reddig, 255–56.
201   "Now Jim": *Congressional Record,* February 20, 1934.
201   "Union Station massacre": Reddig, 257–59.
201   new county courthouse: Independence *Examiner,* September 7, 1933.
202   "During the six and one half years": Ibid.
202   "During these years of strenuous service": Ibid.
203   "maneuvered out": Quoted in *Memoirs,* Vol. I, 141.
203   Truman meeting with Jim Pendergast and Aylward: James Aylward, Oral History, HSTL; correspondence in the collection of Joe and Catherine Pruett.
204   Pendergast offer to Joe Shannon: Daniels, *The Man of Independence,* 167.
204   "A very pleasant sort of fellow": Quoted in Helm, *Harry Truman,* 32–33.
204   "Tomorrow, today, rather": "Pickwick Papers," HSTL.
205   "It was 104 yesterday": Letter from Jim Pendergast to Kathleen Pendergast, postmarked July 4, 1934, Pruett Collection.
205   opening Truman rally: Kansas City *Star,* July 7, 1934.
206   "a congressman's congressman": Quoted in Childs, *I Write from Washington,* 96–97.
206   "wheels-with-wheels": Ibid.
206   "It will be remembered that": *News-Press,* July 6, 1934, Fred Canfil Scrapbooks, HSTL.
207   Johnny Lazia killing: Kansas City *Journal-Post,* July 10, 1934.

207 "tell him I love him": Ibid.
207 "There were at least ten thousand": Jim Pendergast letter to Kathleen Pendergast, undated, Pruett Collection.
207 "It seems my old friend": Kansas City *Star,* July 11, 1934.
208 a huge picnic in Clay County: *News-Press,* July 16, 1934, Fred Canfil Scrapbooks, HSTL.
208 "For this bellhop of Pendergast's": Kansas City *Star,* July 29, 1934.
208 "Judge Truman is unobtrusive": St. Louis *Globe-Democrat* (undated), Fred Canfil Scrapbooks, HSTL.
208 "mendacity and imbecility": El Dorado Springs (Missouri) *Gazette,* July 23, 1934.
209 "Why, Senator Clark is": United Press, July 30, 1934, Fred Canfil Scrapbooks, HSTL.
209 Since 1930, more than eighteen thousand: *Missouri Historical Review,* Vol. 29, July 1935.
209 "such as to make any human": Kansas City *Star,* July 31, 1934.
210 "Fact is, I like roads": Hersey, *Aspects of the Presidency,* 37.
210 Canfil would check out room: HST to EWT, October 25, 1942, *Dear Bess,* 491.
211 scrapbook of the campaign: Fred Canfil Scrapbooks, HSTL.
211 "why, if Harry ever goes": Kansas City *Times,* August 1, 1934.
211 On the day of the primary: *Autobiography,* 67.
212 "without significance": St. Louis *Post-Dispatch,* August 8, 1934.
212 a "push-over": *Autobiography,* 68.
212 "skinny and all one color": Mary Shaw Branton, author's interview.
212 Fred Canfil descriptions: FOIPA No. 297,745, FBI.
213 "green as grass": Quoted in Helm, 7.
213 Hatch and Schwellenbach friendly: Ibid., 70.
214 "He took the trouble": *Memoirs,* Vol. I, 144.
214 "Harry, don't start out with": Ibid.
214 the Senator from Pendergast: Miller, *Plain Speaking,* 158.
214 "Here was a guy": Steinberg, *The Man from Missouri.* 125.
215 "doglike devotion": Quoted in Helm, 13.
215 "It was quite an event": Steinberg, 130.
215 "He came to the Senate": St. Louis *Post-Dispatch,* April 15, 1945.
215 "He was a better man": Ibid.
215 his own passkey: Kansas City *Journal-Post* (undated), Messall Scrapbooks, 1933–41, HSTL.
215 "By the time his colleagues": Ibid.
215 "If you will send us": HST to L. T. Slayton, February 5, 1935, HSTL.
217 "political monster": *Congressional Record,* February 30, 1935, 2352–59.
217 Thereafter Long refused to speak: *Memoirs,* Vol. I, 146.
217 "He sits in the back row": Kansas City *Journal-Post* (undated), Messall Scrapbooks, 1933–41, HSTL.
218 "He speaks rarely": Ibid.
218 "I'm going to be better informed": HST to EWT, December 11, 1935, *Dear Bess,* 382.
218 "I'll take all the dinners": HST to EW, December 6, 1937, ibid., 408.
219 He burned them all: *Memoirs,* Vol. I, 157.
219 "I was a New Dealer from the start": Ibid., 149.
220 "As the old political saying goes": Quoted in Barkley, *That Reminds Me,* 155.
220 "I liked Harry": Claude Pepper, author's interview.
220 "a hot wave": HST to EWT, August 15, 1935, *Dear Bess,* 377.
220 read Southall Freeman: HST to EWT, July 9, 1955, ibid., 369.
220 "No one has done more": HST to EWT, August 19, 1935, ibid., 378.
221 "a grand big house": HST to EWT, June 29, 1935, ibid., 366.
221 "Found a rather nice place": HST to EWT, July 17, 1935, ibid., 372.
221 bus fare and bathing suit: HST to EWT, July 3, 1935, ibid., 367.
221 "big enough for two": HST to EWT, December 5, 1937, ibid., 407.
221 "I am hoping to make": HST to EWT, June 28, 1935, ibid., 365.
222 "Pendergast was as pleased": HST to EWT, July 29, 1935, ibid., 374.

222 "as pleased to see me": HST to EWT, August 11, 1935, ibid., 376.
222 "Pendergast and the very blond": Childs, 111.
222 "Confidentially, I had a fine visit": Lloyd C. Stark to HST, March 22, 1935, HSTL.
222 Pendergast at Wilson's funeral: Kansas City *Star* archives.
223 "He won't do": Jonathan Daniels interview notes, November 12, 1949, HSTL; Daniels, *The Man of Independence,* 181.
223 "The old man had better judgment": Quoted in Daniels, 181.
223 "the most grateful man": *Autobiography,* 73.
223 "Kind of hard on Bennett": HST to EWT, June 22, 1935, *Dear Bess,* 365.
224 "And while I heard": Quoted in Helm, 10.
224 "The vast expenditures": Childs, 110.
225 Pendergast ill: Kansas City *Times,* January 27, 1945.
225 "We all found Truman": Quoted in Louchheim, ed., *The Making of the New Deal,* 243.
225 "But he showed no signs": Ibid.
226 "When the Senator from Missouri": Quoted in Steinberg, 127.
226 "He was always going out of his way": Ibid., 126.
226 "Never in all the years": Mildred Dryden, Oral History, HSTL.
226 liked Harry Truman "instinctively": Barkley, 155.
227 "H. is worn out": EWT to EN, undated, HSTL.
228 "tell" Harry how to vote: Helm, 51.
228 "Jim Aylward phoned me": Ibid.
228 By going to Pendergast: Daniels, 180.
228 tired of being "pushed around": Helm, 53.
228 "The pressure on me": HST quoted in Barkley, 155–56.
229 "I always admired him": Ibid.
229 "I just can't stand it": HST to EWT, January 5, 1935, *Dear Bess,* 391.
229 he "played hooky": HST to EWT, February 11, 1937, ibid., 397.
230 "This so-called committee work": HST to EWT, November 7, 1937, ibid., 403.
230 "Not once did I ever see him": Quoted in Helm, 11.
230 "a sense of continually being tired": U.S. Army Medical Records, September 13, 1937, HSTL.
230 "They are charming people": HST to Marvin McIntyre, October 11, 1936, FDRL.
230 "That son-of-a-bitch": Steinberg, 167.
230 "A couple of kids": HST to EWT, October 29, 1937, *Dear Bess,* 402.
231 "Today is my father's birthday": HST to EWT, December 5, 1937, ibid., 407.
231 Brandeis teas: Daniels, 185–86.
231 "slightly awesome institution": Childs, 43.
231 not accustomed to meeting such people: Daniels, 186.
231 Brandeis had spent more time: HST to EWT, December 13, 1937, *Dear Bess,* 409.
231 "It was a rather exclusive": HST to EWT, December 13, 1937, ibid., 100.
231 "certainly in agreement on the dangers": HST quoted in Miller, 151.
231 December 20, 1937, speech: *Congressional Record,* December 20, 1937, 2482–95.
232 "It probably will catalogue me": HST to EWT, December 12, 1937, *Dear Bess,* 409.
233 The speech was front-page news: *The New York Times,* December 21, 1937.
234 Max Lowenthal comments about pressure: Daniels, 185.
234 "an innate part of his personality": Gosnell, *Truman's Crises,* 129.
234 "We must not close our eyes": Messall Scrapbooks, HSTL.
235 Pendergast betting: Reddig, 278; Kansas City *Star,* December 27, 1974.
235 "Don't ever take any money": Quoted in Kansas City *Star,* March 1, 1984.
237 Truman speech on February 15, 1938: *Congressional Record,* February 15, 1938, 1962–64.
237 "The manner in which the juries": John Oliver, author's interview.
237 "in view of my speech": Kansas City *Star,* September 15, 1978.
238 "They figure they'll need": HST to EWT, November 17, 1938, *Dear Bess,* 412.
238 "If it is true": Reddig, 303–04.
239 "Please help Sam Finklestein": T. J. Pendergast to HST, undated, HSTL.

239   "I am sure he had": Helm, 47.
239   "I am very sorry": St. Louis *Post-Dispatch,* undated, Messall Scrapbooks, HSTL.
239   "The terrible things": HST to EWT, October 1, 1939, HSTL.
239   "He was broke": Edgar Hinde, Oral History, HSTL.
240   "Looks like everybody got rich": HST to EWT, October 27, 1939, *Dear Bess,* 426.
240   "I believe if I did know him": Kansas City *Star,* May 22, 1939.
240   "At no time": Quoted in Daniels, 196.
240   "He has earned the high estimate": St. Louis *Post-Dispatch,* April 12, 1939.
241   "If Governor Stark runs": Associated Press (undated), Messall Scrapbooks, HSTL.
241   "I do not think": HST to EWT, August 8, 1939, *Dear Bess,* 418.
241   "Tell them to go to hell": Truman, *Harry S. Truman,* 130.
241   "the wise boys": Quoted in Drew Pearson column (undated), Messall Scrapbooks, HSTL.
242   Washington premiere: HST to EWT, October 18, 1939, *Dear Bess,* 426.
242   mortgage on the farm: Daniels, 192.
242   "mighty blue": HST to EWT, September 22, 1939, *Dear Bess,* 419.
243   "I am of the opinion": Miscamble, "The Evolution of an Internationalist," *Australian Journal of Politics and History,* August 1977.
243   "You know it makes some of us": HST to EW, November 11, 1939, *Dear Bess,* 428.
243   "a pleasure trip": HST to EWT, November 16, 1939, ibid., 430.
243   "a regular fellow": HST to EWT, November 22, 1939, ibid., 431.
243   "This, you know": HST to EWT, December 1, 1939, ibid., 432.
243   "I guess I'm not built": HST to EWT, December 1, 1939, ibid.
244   "Harry, I don't think": Quoted in Daniels, 198.
244   "if he gets only two votes": Quoted in Helm, 126.
244   reelection announcement: St. Louis *Post-Dispatch,* February 5, 1940.
244   opposed to FDR third term: Ibid.
244   "There is no indispensable man": Hassett, "The President Was My Boss," *Saturday Evening Post,* November 28, 1953.
245   "We borrowed clerks": John Snyder, Oral History, HSTL.
245   "A United States Senator . . . sleeping": Quoted in Miller, 166.
245   "At sixteen": Quoted in Truman, *Harry S. Truman,* 139.
245   "While the President is unreliable": HST to EWT, September 24, 1939, *Dear Bess,* 420.
245   Bernard Baruch contribution: Byrnes, *All in One Lifetime,* 101.
246   America "ought to sell": Miscamble, "Evolution of an Internationalist."
246   Tom Evans, who was twelve years: Evans, Oral History, HSTL.
247   "Cut your speech": Quoted in Daniels, 202.
247   "I just wanted to come down": Ibid.
247   "I believe in": HST quoted in Helm, 137.
247   "When we are honest enough": Speech before National Colored Democratic Association Convention, July 14, 1940, HSTL.
248   St. Louis *Post-Dispatch* cartoon: March 29, 1940.
248   "enough errors to give me": Quoted in Daniels, 205.
248   "The decent, honest": St. Louis *Globe-Democrat* (undated), Messall Scrapbooks, HSTL.
248   Truman urged to release letter: Daniels, 205.
248   Stark's chauffeur: Truman, *Harry S. Truman,* 141.
249   "Lloyd's ambitions": Ibid., 132–33.
249   foreclosure on farm: Kansas City *Star,* July 17, 1940, Messall Scrapbooks, HSTL.
249   thought he was having a heart attack: HST to EWT, November 15, 1941, *Dear Bess,* 468.
250   the shame she would feel: HST to EWT, August 13, 1940, ibid., 442.
250   "I'm thinking August 6": HST to EWT, June 23, 1940, ibid., 440.
250   "Will call you from Sedalia": Ibid.
250   "Anyway we found out": HST to EWT, August 9, 1940, ibid., 441.
250   "He finally ended up": Daniels, 209.

250 Bob Hannegan: St. Louis *Post-Dispatch,* July 24, 1944.

251 "Well . . . I guess": Hinde, Oral History, HSTL.

251 it was Bess who answered: Truman, *Harry S. Truman,* 145.

251 "the machine vote": Lloyd C. Stark to FDR, August 9, 1940, FDRL.

252 "I thought Wheeler and Jim Byrnes": HST to EWT, August 10, 1940, *Dear Bess,* 441.

252 "Has my certification of election": Edwin A. Halsey, telegram to HST, December 13, 1940, HSTL.

7. PATRIOT

253 "War has many faces": Sevareid, *Not So Wild a Dream,* 164.

253 "Locksley Hall" poem in wallet: Hillman, ed., *Mr. President,* 206.

253 "As I watched those white fires": Quoted in Flower and Reeves, eds., *The Taste of Courage,* 135.

254 "We have everything to lose": Kansas City *Times,* May 2, 1941.

254 Clark was destroying himself: HST to EWT, October 3, 1941, *Dear Bess,* 466.

255 "My relief of mind": Pogue, *George C. Marshall: Ordeal and Hope,* 59.

255 Marshall told him he was too old: HST "Autobiographical Sketch," HSTL.

255 Washington a different city: Green, *Washington,* 466–73; Brinkley, *Washington Goes to War.*

256 "a little investigation": *Memoirs,* Vol. I, 165.

256 automobile odysseys: Ibid.

256 "getting ruined . . . And there were men": Quoted in Miller, *Plain Speaking,* 175.

257 "There's too much that is wrong": Helm, *Harry Truman,* 151.

257 "It is a considerable sin": Schlesinger and Bruns, *Congress Investigates. A Documented History, 1792–1974,* 3121.

258 it "must be assumed that": Pogue, 108.

258 Nye Committee: Baruch, *Public Years,* 269.

258 "The thing to do": *Time,* March 8, 1943.

258 Byrnes $10,000 committee funding: *Memoirs,* Vol. I, 166.

259 "Looks like I'll get something": HST to EWT, March 19, 1941, *Dear Bess,* 456.

259 "The political situation": HST to EWT, August 1, 1939, ibid., 416.

259 Hugh Fulton: *Memoirs,* Vol. I, 167.

260 departure of Messall: Tom Evans, Oral History, HSTL.

260 "What are you fishing for?" Executive Session, June 8, 1942, *Special Committee to Investigate the National Defense Program,* United States Senate, NA.

261 "You give a good leader": *Papers of George C. Marshall,* Vol. 2, 483.

261 "There was no attempt": *Memoirs,* Vol. I, 171.

262 saved the government $250 million: Riddle, *The Truman Committee,* 147.

262 gallbladder attack: U.S. Army Medical Records, 1941, HSTL; Truman, *Bess W. Truman,* 200–01.

262 "My standing in the Senate": HST to EWT, June 19, 1941, *Dear Bess,* 457.

262 "If we see that Germany": *The New York Times,* June 24, 1941.

263 "Last year he ran": U.S. Army Medical Records, 1941, HSTL.

263 pressed by Vandenberg: Schlesinger and Bruns, 3127.

264 "Well I spent yesterday": HST to EWT, August 21, 1941, *Dear Bess,* 461–62.

265 "studious avoidance of dramatics": Salter, ed., *Public Men In and Out of Office,* 12.

265 "Slightly built, bespectacled": *Tri-County News,* Long City, Missouri (undated), Messall Scrapbooks, HSTL.

265 "Mr. Lewis, you are not seriously": John L. Lewis testimony, March 26, 1943, *Special Committee to Investigate the National Defense Program,* United States Senate, NA, 55.

267 "Standard Oil" and I. G. Farben: HST Broadcast, "Rubber in America," Blue Network, June 15, 1942, printed copy, HSTL.

268 "First of all": Truman before Senate, October 29. *Congressional Record,* 77th Congress, 1st Sess., 1941, Vol. XXCVII, 8303.

268   The record of the OPM: January 15, 1942, *Special Committee to Investigate the National Defense Program,* United States Senate, 77th Congress, 2nd Sess., 6.

268   Lilienthal on war with Japan: Lilienthal, *Journals,* Vol. I, 408.

268   "No matter what happens": Boardman, *From Harding to Hiroshima,* 250.

269   "We have fought to get you": Schlesinger and Bruns, 3131.

269   "Well at last I am sitting": HST to EN, December 14, 1941, HSTL.

270   "Harry Truman was one of the": Riedel, *Halls of the Mighty,* 173–75.

271   it would "impair our activity": Gosnell, *Truman's Crises,* 161.

271   unanimous reports: McCune and Beal, "The Job That Made Truman President," *Harper's,* June 1945.

271   "so close that a chorus girl": Sevareid, 213.

271   "the return of Ceres": HST to EWT, April 26, 1942, *Dear Bess,* 473.

271   Still he couldn't sleep: HST to EWT, April 30, 1942, ibid., 474.

271   he called for a second front: Miscamble, "Evolution of an Internationalist," *Australian Journal of Politics and History,* August 1977.

272   "If I were the executive": Closed Hearing on Wright Aeronautical Corporation, May 24, 1943, *Special Committee to Investigate the National Defense Program,* United States Senate, NA, 13.

272   Glenn Martin Company: *Memoirs,* 184.

272   Carnegie-Illinois Steel hearing: March 23, 1943, *Special Committee to Investigate the National Defense Program,* United States Senate, NA, 820.

273   Stewart testimony: Ibid., 817.

274   "He cheated more than he was supposed": Ibid., 833.

274   McGarrity testimony: Ibid., 837.

274   Irwin Works investigation: Ibid., 843–74.

277   "I don't know anything about": Ibid., 886.

277   Benjamin Fairless testimony: Ibid., 896–97.

278   asked by a reporter for his personal comment: Washington *Post,* March 24, 1943.

279   Canol Project: Testimony of General Brehon Somervell, December 20, 1943, *Special Committee to Investigate the National Defense Program,* United States Senate, NA.

280   "The committee damns it up and down": Drury, *A Senate Journal,* 29.

280   "all the desperate assertions": Ibid.

281   reading Shakespeare and Plutarch: HST to EWT, June 18, 1942, *Dear Bess,* 477.

281   as if he had just stepped: Margaret Truman Daniel, author's interview.

281   "One day in a typical": Riedel, 174.

282   "I went up to the front desk": *The New Yorker,* November 23, 1987.

282   "I am more surprised every day": HST to EWT, August 21, 1942, *Dear Bess,* 487.

282   "The man from Missouri": Pepper, with Gorey, *Pepper,* 129.

283   never heard him even try: Margaret Truman Daniel, author's interview.

283   "One time, one Christmas": Ardis Haukenberry, author's interview.

283   "You have a good mind": HST to MT, March 13, 1942, Truman, *Letters from Father,* 40.

283   "Tell my baby": HST to EWT, July 22, 1942, *Dear Bess,* 480–81.

284   to "only just drop in": HST to EWT, April 30, 1942, ibid., 474.

284   "Well this is *the day*": HST to EWT, June 28, 1942, ibid., 480.

285   "one of the most useful": Helm, 228.

285   Truman and his committee known nationwide: Washington *Star* (undated), HSTL.

285   that "often a threat": *Business Week,* June 26, 1943.

285   The whole country was greatly indebted: *The Nation,* January 24, 1942.

285   "objectivity at the total expense": Krock, *Memoirs,* 220.

286   *Look* poll: May 16, 1944.

286   He spoke at a huge rally: Chicago *Daily News,* April 15, 1943.

286   "hotels, filling stations": HST to EWT, December 21, 1939, *Dear Bess,* 436.

286   merely talking about the Four Freedoms: Chicago *Daily News,* April 15, 1943.

287   Summer 1943 speaking tour: Miscamble, "The Evolution of an Internationalist."

287   "History has bestowed": Ibid.,

287   "We want aluminum": Schlesinger and Bruns, 3129.

288 saved . . . as much as $15 billion: *Memoirs*, Vol. I, 186.
288 "He seems to be a generally": Drury, 29.
289 "There are a number of times": Ibid., 106.
289 "Now that's a matter": Telephone conversation between HST and Stimson, June 17, 1943, HSTL.
290 "I know something about": HST to Lewis Schwellenbach, July 15, 1943, HSTL.
290 "In my humble opinion": Memorandum to Mildred Dryden, December 3, 1943, HST Senate Papers, HSTL.
290 "I have sent an investigator": HST to Senator Thomas, November 30, 1943, HST Senate Papers, HSTL.
290 "COLONEL MATHIAS": Fred Canfil to HST, December 7, 1943, HSTL.
291 "Whenever he finds out": HST to EWT, October 25, 1942, *Dear Bess*, 491.
291 "The United States was engaged": Martin, *My First Fifty Years in Politics*, 100–01.
291 "He threatened me with dire consequences": Stimson Diary, Yale University.

8. NUMBERED DAYS

292 being talked of as candidate: HST to EW, May 7, 1943, HSTL.
293 "Leadership is what we Americans": Truman, "We Can Lose the War," *American Magazine*, November 1942.
294 key man in the "conspiracy": Quoted in HST memorandum to Jonathan Daniels, HSTL.
294 Flynn admires Wallace: *The New Yorker*, September 8, 1945.
295 First meeting with FDR: Flynn, *You're the Boss*; Allen, *Presidents Who Have Known Me*.
295 "I felt that he would never": Flynn, 179.
296 Secretly, he was under: Bishop, *FDR's Last Year*, 94.
296 Hannegan on Wallace: Brown, *James F. Byrnes of South Carolina, A Remembrance* (manuscript), 255–56.
296 Byrnes influence on FDR: Ibid., 259.
296 "I did conclude": Quoted in Byrnes, *All in One Lifetime*, 221.
296 "Now, partner": Quoted in Brown, 258.
296 somebody else "we have got": Quoted in Daniels, *The Man from Missouri*, 243.
297 Loss of New York: Flynn, 180.
297 "The Negro has not only": Quoted in Brown, 264–66.
297 When they went through the list: Flynn, 181.
297 "His record as head": Ibid.
298 FDR asked a favor: Anna Rosenberg, author's interview.
298 smuggle in jars of caviar: Ibid.
298 "I don't want to be": Quoted in Helm, *Harry Truman*, 220.
298 the word from "informed sources": Drury, *A Senate Journal*, 215–16.
299 "The Madam doesn't want": Max Lowenthal, Oral History, HSTL.
299 "It is funny": HST to MT, July 9, 1944, Margaret Truman, *Letters from Father*, 55.
299 "opened up on politics": Wallace, *The Price of Vision*, 361.
299 "Mr. President, if you can find": Ibid., 362.
299 "Think of the catcalls": Ibid.
299 "It was as though": Drury, 216.
300 "Jimmy Byrnes": Quoted in Brown, 269.
300 the decisive meeting: Allen, 128–29.
301 "I gathered that he felt": Ickes Diary, July 16, 1944, LC.
302 "the only one who had": Wallace, 366.
302 a new Gallup Poll: Allen, 130.
302 "Well, I am looking": Wallace, 367.
302 "Look at the expressions": Quoted in Brown, 276.
303 "Mr. President, all I have heard": Ibid.
303 "You are the best qualified": Quoted in Byrnes, 222.
303 "I don't understand it": Ibid., 223.

303 "I told them so": Ibid., 224–25.
303 "We have to be": Ibid.
304 Byrnes went directly down: Ibid.
304 Truman accepted at once: Ibid., 226.
304 Truman to nominate Barkley: Barkley, *That Reminds Me,* 189.
305 As Alben Barkley would write: Ibid., 190.
305 Arthur Krock: *The New York Times,* July 16, 1944.
305 "Roosevelt could, of course": Allen, 130.
306 "The train stood": Tully, *F.D.R., My Boss,* 276.
306 "Dear Bob": Robert Hannegan to FDR, July 14, 1944, HSTL.
306 "By naming Truman": Tully, 276.
307 "The President has given": Quoted in Byrnes, 226.
307 "Well, you know Jimmy": Ibid., 226–27.
307 Hannegan showing note to no one: St. Louis *Post-Dispatch,* July 21, 1944.
308 He was determined to stay out: Salter, ed., *Public Men In and Out of Office.* 4–5.
308 "Hell, I don't want": Ibid.
308 "I don't want that": Quoted in Truman, *Harry S. Truman,* 183.
308 "I'm satisfied": Tom Evans, Oral History, HSTL.
308 Writing years later, Margaret: Truman, *Bess W. Truman,* 227.
309 they "got Truman": Edward McKim, Oral History, HSTL.
309 "I'm sure he wanted": Quoted in Steinberg, *The Man from Missouri,* 203.
309 it wasn't so much: John Snyder, author's interview.
309 "that miserable time": HST to Mrs. Emmy Southern, May 13, 1945, in Ferrell, ed., *Off the Record,* 23.
309 "scared to death": Childs, "He Didn't Want the Job," *Liberty,* September 23, 1944.
310 "I have been associated": Washington *Post,* July 18, 1944.
310 "the coolest and cruelest": Drury, 218.
310 "already soaring campaign stock": St. Louis *Post-Dispatch,* July 18, 1944.
310 "It was generally regarded": Claude Pepper, author's interview.
310 Hannegan's corner suite: *Life,* July 31, 1944.
310 "Do you want to see it?": Washington *Post,* July 28, 1944.
310 "Clear it with Sidney": Quoted in Byrnes, 227.
311 Sidney Hillman: *Time,* July 24, 1944.
311 Hillman's support: HST "Autobiographical Sketch," HSTL.
311 "It's Byrnes!": Quoted in Flynn, 182.
311 "I browbeat the committee": Ibid.
311 200,000 Negro votes: Byrnes, 228.
312 "Bob, it's Truman": Steinberg, 213.
312 An hour or so later: Byrnes, 229.
312 Turner Catledge account: *The New York Times,* July 19, 1944.
312 "If I were you": Quoted in Barkley, 190.
313 "Feel sorry for me": St. Louis *Post-Dispatch,* July 19, 1944.
313 secret caucus: *Time,* July 31, 1944.
314 "the stage manager": Barkley, 191.
314 "Whenever Roosevelt": *Memoirs,* Vol. I, 192.
314 "Oh, shit": George Elsey, Notes, Ayers Papers, HSTL.
314 "Well, if that's the situation": *Memoirs,* Vol. I, 193.
314 "Ye gods!": Truman, *Souvenir,* 66.
315 "In a political": Wallace, 368; *Time,* July 31, 1944.
316 "What is the job": Quoted in Burns, *Roosevelt: The Soldier of Freedom,* 507.
316 "I sat there": Claude Pepper, author's interview.
316 "And then when I got": Ibid.
317 "So I called Bob": Quoted in Miller, *Plain Speaking,* 194.
317 Martha Ellen Truman: Ibid., 149.
317 Interviewed by reporters: Washington *Star,* July 20, 1944.
318 Bennett Clark . . . pulled himself together: Miller, 194.
318 "a good deal of pressure": *The New York Times,* July 22, 1944.

318 Truman and hot dog: Truman, *Souvenir,* 67.
319 "Christ Almighty": *Time,* July 31, 1944.
320 he accepted "with all humility": *The New York Times,* July 22, 1944.
320 "Now, give me a chance": St. Louis *Post-Dispatch,* July 22, 1944.
320 "the Missouri Compromise": *Life,* July 31, 1944.
320 "the Common Denominator": Kansas City *Star,* July 22, 1944.
320 "I don't object to Truman": Baruch, *The Public Years,* 339.
320 one of the weakest candidates: Pittsburgh *Post-Gazette,* July 23, 1944.
320 "the mousy little man": *Time,* July 31, 1944.
320 "Poor Harry Truman": *New Republic,* July 31, 1944.
321 "unusual capacity": Kansas City *Star,* July 22, 1944.
321 "He has known the dust": *The New York Times,* July 22, 1944.
321 an excellent choice: St. Louis *Post-Dispatch,* July 22, 1944.
321 Even Richard Strout: *New Republic,* July 31, 1944.
321 "On the credit side": Drury, 220.
321 "Are we going to have to": Quoted in Truman, *Bess W. Truman,* 231.
322 "Dad tried to be cheerful": Ibid., 233.
322 Margaret learns of grandfather's suicide: Ibid., 234.
322 "He seized my arm": Ibid.
322 "I wish I could tell you": Ibid., 235.
322 looking over the old gray Victorian house: *Life,* August 21, 1944.
322 "I had hoped": Walton, *Henry Wallace, Harry Truman and the Cold War,* 20–21.
322 the critical part played by Ed Flynn: *The New Yorker,* September 8, 1945.
323 "People seemed to think": Daniels, 259.
323 his father's "irritability": Roosevelt and Shalett, *Affectionately, F.D.R.,* 351–52.
323 FDR seizure: Ibid.
324 FDR lunch with Truman: There has been speculation that at this lunch Roosevelt told Truman about the atomic bomb. The source is an interview with Truman's friend Tom Evans made many years later as part of the Truman Library's oral history program. There is no possibility that it is correct, since the President's daughter, Anna Roosevelt Boettiger, was also present at the lunch, as were a half dozen or so photographers, cameramen, and servants. Nor would Roosevelt have brought up the matter on such an occasion in any event.
326 "I wonder why we are made": HST to EWT, December 28, 1945, *Off the Record,* 75.
326 "I am not a deep thinker": Wallace, *The Price of Vision,* 373.
326 "smarter by far": Martin, *My First Fifty Years in Politics,* 176.
327 FDR told Truman not to travel: *Memoirs,* Vol. I, 5.
327 FDR's hand shook: Truman, *Harry S. Truman,* p. 203.
327 "You should have seen": Ibid., 201.
327 He was greatly concerned: Harry Vaughan, Oral History, HSTL.
327 Ed McKim and Truman: McKim, Oral History, HSTL.
327 "Harry is a fine man": Hatch, *Franklin D. Roosevelt,* 376.
327 "There never was a greater": HST to EWT, June 15, 1946, *Dear Bess,* 526.
328 "He's so damn afraid": HST to EWT, December 21, 1941, ibid., 470.
328 "You know how it is": Drury, 327.
328 "he lies": Ickes Diary, December 16, 1944, LC.
328 "Harry, what the hell": Quoted in Miller, 199; also Miller Tapes, LBJL.
328 "You can't afford": Audio Collection, HSTL.
329 Recruitment of Matt Connelly: Matt Connelly, Oral History, HSTL.
329 "I'm glad to see you, Harry": Steinberg, 225.
330 it was "the farmer-neighborliness": McNaughton and Hehmeyer, *This Man Truman,* 182.
330 Truman dream about FDR: Pearson, "The Man Who Didn't Want to Be President," Vertical file, HSTL, April 16, 1945.
330 A rumor spread: Truman, *Harry S. Truman,* 204.
330 Klan story: Hearst papers, October 26, 1944.
330 Curley speech: Connelly, Oral History, HSTL.

330   Chicago *Tribune* attacks: October 17, 1944.
331   "hotter than a depot stove": HST to EWT, July 25, 1945, *Dear Bess,* 521.
331   Teamsters appearance: Burns, *Roosevelt: The Soldier of Freedom,* 523.
331   "He improved visibly": Sherwood, *Roosevelt and Hopkins,* 825.
332   "I was shocked": Truman, *Bess W. Truman,* 240.
332   "And he knew": Harry Easley, Oral History, HSTL.
332   "I still think": Quoted in Hassett, *Off the Record with F.D.R.,* 294.
333   only if it was "absolutely urgent": Leuchtenburg, *In the Shadow of FDR,* 6.
333   "The amiable Missourian": *Time,* February 5, 1945.
334   "He circulated around": Gunther, *Procession,* 256–57.
334   Truman answered, "People": Ibid., 260.
334   "the most natural thing": St. Louis *Post-Dispatch,* April 15, 1945.
334   "Harry looks better than he has": Truman, *Bess W. Truman,* 247.
335   "I used to get down here": HST to MET and MJT, April 11, 1945, *Off the Record,* 13.
335   "Truman says simply": Frank McNaughton Papers, December 14, 1944, HSTL.
336   Pendergast's death: Washington *Post,* January 27, 1945.
336   Pendergast funeral: Miller, 210.
337   "I was just a kid": Lauren Bacall, author's interview.
337   "Anything can happen": Washington *Post,* February 11, 1945.
337   Bess was furious: Truman, *Bess W. Truman,* 245.
337   "I saw the President": *Memoirs,* Vol. I, 3.
337   April 12 Pendergast letter: T. J. Pendergast to HST, April 7, 1945, HSTL.
338   "We will see": Ibid.
338   "It's wonderful, this Senate": Drury, 410.
339   Senator Hawkes: *Congressional Record,* April 12, 1945, 3284.
339   Senator Reed: Ibid., 3285.
339   "I have a Missouri": *Remarks by Former President Harry S. Truman,* 88th Congress, 2nd Sess., Sen. Doc. No. 88, May 8, 1964.
339   remarked . . . that Roosevelt was fortunate: Drury, 410.
339   "Truman doesn't know": Ibid.
340   "Dear Mamma and Mary": HST to MET and MJT, April 12, 1945, HSTL.
340   Tells Harry Vaughan: HST to MET and MJT, April 16, 1945, HSTL.
341   "Steve Early wants you": *Memoirs,* Vol. I, 4.
341   as "quickly and as quietly": HST to MET and MJT, April 16, 1945, HSTL.
342   "I ran all the way": HST to MET and MJT, April 16, 1945, HSTL.
342   "Harry, the President is dead": *Memoirs,* Vol. I, 5.
342   "Is there anything *we*": Ibid.

PART THREE

9. THE MOON, THE STARS, AND ALL THE PLANETS

345   "So ended an era": Drury, *A Senate Journal,* 412.
345   "Yes, it's true": Quoted in *Yank,* 122.
346   "The armies and fleets": *The New York Times,* April 13, 1945.
346   Stettinius . . . with tears streaming: *Memoirs,* Vol. I, 6.
347   "It was a very somber": Stimson Diary, April 12, 1945, Yale University.
347   Margaret feeling as if under anesthesia: Truman, *Harry S. Truman,* 229.
347   Truman would later tell his mother: HST to MET and MJT, April 16, 1945, HSTL.
348   first decision as President: HST Diary, April 12, 1945, in Ferrell, ed., *Off the Record,* 15–16.
348   brief remarks to the Cabinet: *Memoirs,* Vol. I, 9–10.
348   a matter of utmost urgency: Ibid., 10.
348   had conducted himself admirably: Stimson Diary, April 12, 1945.
348   "I guess the party's off": Edward McKim, Oral History, HSTL.
348   immediately to sleep: Miller, *Plain Speaking,* 215.
349   "What a great, great tragedy": Lilienthal, *Journals,* April 14, 1945, Vol. I, 693.

349   "From a distance": Bradley and Blair, *A General's Life,* 429.
350   "It seems very unfortunate": Ibid.
350   Eisenhower shaken: Eisenhower, *Eisenhower at War, 1943–1945,* 763–64.
350   Lester Atwell: Quoted in Flower and Reeves, eds., *The Taste of Courage,* 996.
350   "He's got the stuff": Quoted in McNaughton Papers, April 13, 1945, HSTL.
350   "a *grand person*": Vandenberg, ed., *The Private Papers of Senator Vandenberg,* April 13, 1945, 167.
350   "Oh, I felt good": John J. McCloy, author's interview.
351   He was straightforward: Acheson, *Present at the Creation,* 104.
351   "I hate to confess it": Stone, *The War Years 1939–1945,* 274.
351   "GET IN THERE": Telegram from Jim Pendergast to HST, April 12, 1945, HSTL.
351   "I can't really be glad": Quoted in *Off the Record,* 17.
351   "a jewel": HST Diary, April 15, 1945, ibid., 19.
352   "There have been few men": *Memoirs,* Vol. I, 13.
352   Truman later wrote: Ibid., 29.
352   "It seemed still": Quoted in Daniels, *The Man of Independence,* 27.
351   "Eddie, I'm sorry": Quoted in Truman, *Harry S. Truman,* 234.
352   "everything from Teheran": HST Diary, April 13, 1945, *Off the Record,* 17.
353   "What a test": Kansas City *Star,* April 15, 1945.
353   Truman left the White House: Drury, 412.
353   "Isn't this nice": Quoted in ibid., 413.
353   "Boys, if you ever pray": *Memoirs,* Vol. I, 19.
353   "For just a moment": Drury, 413.
354   "executive contempt for Congress": Vandenberg, April 13, 1945, 167.
354   Stettinius report: Quoted in *Memoirs,* Vol. I, 15.
355   "never did talk": Truman, *Letters from Father,* March 3, 1948, 106.
355   "It is needless": Washington *Post,* April 13, 1945.
356   "I'm President Truman": Paul Horgan, Oral History, HSTL.
356   "I still can't call": Wallace, *The Price of Vision,* 448.
356   "He's the only one": HST to Eleanor Roosevelt, September 1, 1945, *Off the Record,* 63.
356   "Have confidence": Barkley, *That Reminds Me,* 197.
357   "I have come down here": Quoted in Hardeman and Bacon, *Rayburn: A Biography,* 311–12.
357   "No . . . He just made it": HST Diary, April 14, 1945, *Off the Record,* 18.
357   not on trial: Bishop, *FDR'S Last Year,* 646.
357   "But after all": Morgenthau, *Diaries,* Vol. III, 423.
358   "Terrible": *Memoirs,* Vol. I, 31.
359   "Mr. President": Ibid., 42.
359   "With great humility": *Public Papers of the Presidents of the United States. Harry S. Truman . . .* (cited hereafter as PP, HST), April 16, 1945, 2.
360   "bond of friendship": Washington *Star,* April 17, 1945.
360   "At this moment": PP, HST, April 16, 1945, 3.
360   "He's one of us": McNaughton Papers, April 14, 1945, HSTL.
361   "your ability to discharge": Henry Luce to HST, April 17, 1945, HSTL.
361   "May I say": Archibald John Brier to HST, April 17, 1945.
361   "Good luck, Harry": Quoted in Donovan, *Conflict and Crisis,* 19.
361   "Well, I have had": HST to MET and MJT, April 16, 1945, HSTL.
362   First press conference: PP, HST, April 17, 1945, 8–13.
362   "direct" performance: Leahy, *I Was There,* 349.
362   lived five lifetimes: *Memoirs,* Vol. I, 53.
362   Three days later: PP, HST, April 20, 1945, 16–19.
363   "naturally smart boy": *Newsweek,* August 15, 1949.
363   "He made first-class citizens": George Tames, author's interview.
363   "Stick with me": Quoted in Smith, ed., *Merriman Smith's Book of Presidents: A White House Memoir,* 56.

364 "He was alert": George Elsey, author's interview.
364 "See, with President Roosevelt": Floyd Boring, author's interview.
364 "tragically inadequate": Daniels, 27.
365 "To the White House this morning": Hassett, "The President Was My Boss," *Saturday Evening Post,* November 28, 1953.
365 "Missourians are most in evidence": Ayers Diary, April 17, 1945, HSTL.
365 "the lounge of the Lion's Club": Quoted in Steinberg, *The Man from Missouri,* 13.
365 McKim was "weird": Jonathan Daniels, Oral History, HSTL.
365 Prohibition gangster: Ayers Diary, April 17, 1945, HSTL.
365 "We were all a strange lot": Rosenman, "Harry S. Truman: Man from Independence," *American Heritage* (unpublished), 70.
365 "Well, he was a sergeant": Matt Connelly, Oral History, HSTL.
366 "The fact is": Ayers Diary, May 14, 1945, HSTL.
366 "balance and tact": Ibid.
367 "Tell them I don't authorize": Harry Vaughan, Oral History, HSTL.
367 "Hoover's hatred": Sullivan, *The Bureau,* 38.
367 "We want no Gestapo": HST Memorandum, May 12, 1945, *Off the Record,* 22.
368 "honest and friendly": Quoted in Churchill, *The Second World War.* Vol. VI: *Triumph and Tragedy,* 484.
368 "He'll make enemies": Drury, 418.
368 "I don't think you know": Samuel Rosenman, Oral History, HSTL.
369 "It was a wonderful relief": Stimson Diary, April 18, 1945.
369 "Changes in the battle situation": *Memoirs,* Vol. I, 51.
369 Leahy was struck: Leahy, 348.
369 "to get on the inside": Rigdon, with Derieux, *White House Sailor,* 183.
369 "I pray you believe": Quoted in Snyder, *The War,* 520.
370 "a keen appreciation": Kennan, *Memoirs, 1925–1950,* 233.
371 "And anyway the Russians": *Memoirs,* Vol. I, 70–71.
371 "I can testify": Quoted in Halle, *The Cold War as History,* 38.
371 "Averell is right": Quoted in Truman, *Harry S. Truman,* 255.
371 "It would be one": Harriman and Abel, *Special Envoy to Churchill and Stalin,* 437.
371 "We must not permit": Quoted in Truman, *Harry S. Truman,* 437.
372 "Russia will emerge": OSS File, April 2, 1945, HSTL.
372 April 6 cable: Gaddis, *The United States and the Origins of the Cold War,* 201.
372 not a man of his word: Morgan, *F.D.R., A Biography,* 762.
372 "minor misunderstandings": Harriman and Abel, 439–40.
373 "I would minimize": Ibid.
373 "barbarian invasion": *Memoirs,* Vol. I, 73.
373 happy with 85 percent: Gaddis, 203.
373 "The White House upstairs": Quoted in Truman, *Bess W. Truman,* 260.
373 like a ghost house: West, with Kotz, *Upstairs at the White House,* 58.
374 "go to hell": Quoted in *Forrestal Diaries,* 50.
374 "for fear we are rushing": Stimson Diary, April 23, 1945.
374 Forrestal strongly disagreed: *Forrestal Diaries,* 50.
374 no intention of issuing: *Memoirs,* Vol. I, 78.
375 "until we have done": Ibid., 79.
375 "I am very sorry": Stimson Diary, April 23, 1945.
376 "I have never been talked to": *Memoirs,* Vol. I, 82.
376 Bohlen's account: Bohlen, *Witness to History,* 213.
376 "a little taken aback": Harriman and Abel, 453.
376 the best news he had heard: Vandenberg, 176.
376 "I think it is very important": *Memoirs,* Vol. I, 85.
377 "Mr. President, I don't like": Quoted in Morison, *Turmoil and Tradition,* 609.
377 "a real man": HST to Jonathan Daniels, February 26, 1950, unsent, *Off the Record,* 174.
377 "Within four months": Stimson Diary, April 25, 1945.

378 "The President took": Ibid.
378 Truman told him to go ahead: Stimson and Bundy, *On Active Service in Peace and War,* 616.
378 "The President did not show": Quoted in Sherwin, *A World Destroyed,* 293.
378 "This is a big project": Quoted in Rhodes, *The Making of the Atomic Bomb,* 625.
379 "It might perhaps": Quoted in Sherwin, 284.
379 Truman measurements: Paul Shinkman to Eben Ayers, May 10, 1945, HSTL.
379 "It's a tough job": Stone, *The War Years. 1939–1945,* 281–82.
380 "He ought to surrender it": *Memoirs,* Vol. I, 91.
380 "at a brisk trot": West, with Kotz, 61.
380 "We have received so much mail": MJT to HST, April 24, 1945, HSTL.
381 "I do hope": MJT to HST, May 1, 1945, HSTL.
381 "I arrived home": MJT to HST, May 7, 1945, HSTL.
381 "You both have done": HST to MET and MJT, April 21, 1945, HSTL.
381 "This is a solemn": PP, HST, May 8, 1945, 44.
382 "straight one-two to the jaw": Sherwin, 172.
382 "like people from across": Wallace, 450–51.
382 "His sincerity": Ayers Diary, May 26, 1945, HSTL.
383 "show them how much": Churchill, 437.
383 "it is my present intention": *Memoirs,* Vol. I, 216.
383 "Mr. President, in these next two months": Churchill, 497.
383 May 12 Churchill telegram: Gilbert, *Winston Churchill. Never Despair,* 6.
384 "It is a very, very hard position": HST to Mrs. Emmy Southern, May 13, 1945, *Off the Record,* 23.
384 "air of quiet confidence": Eden, *Memoirs,* 621.
384 "To have a reasonably": HST Diary, May 22, 1945, *Off the Record,* 35.
384 Martha Ellen Truman's visit: *The New York Times,* May 12, 1945.
385 prefer to sleep on the floor: Truman, *Harry S. Truman,* 266.
385 "Oh, you couldn't help but": Floyd Boring, author's interview.
385 "My bedroom is pink": Truman, *Souvenir,* 98.
386 story of the old-fashioneds: West, with Kotz, 75.
386 "stand no fakers": Fields, *My 21 Years at the White House,* 122.
386 "correct but not formal": West, 58.
387 "He knew when a stenographer's": Smith, 60.
387 "this was the first time": Fields, 120.
388 "Not built right": HST to EW, March 19, 1941, *Dear Bess,* 455.
388 "The President seemed relieved": Quoted in Donovan, 28.
389 "And that was about all": Lilienthal, *Journals,* Vol. I, 698.
390 "Saw Herbert Hoover": HST Diary, June 1, 1945, *Off the Record,* 40.
390 "I can't understand it": HST Diary, May 27, 1945, ibid., 38.
391 "push ahead as fast": Quoted in Rhodes, 646.
391 "visual effect of an atomic bombing": Quoted in Sherwin, 208.
391 "with reluctance": Quoted in Wyden, *Day One,* 163.
391 "a remarkable document": Ibid., 154.
391 "The idea of": Yale University Atomic Bomb File, HSTL.
392 "Have been going through": HST Diary, June 1, 1945, *Off the Record,* 39.
392 "as a new weapon": Stimson Diary, May 31, 1945.
392 June 6 Stimson meeting: Stimson Diary, June 1 and 6, 1945.
393 "What a puny effort": C. L. Sulzberger, *World War II,* 114.
393 "outdoing Hitler": Stimson Diary, June 6, 1945.
393 "the earliest possible date": Quoted in Morison, 621.
393 "The ultimate responsibility": Stimson and Bundy, *On Active Service in Peace and War,* 617.
394 "straight military objective": Cray, *General of the Army,* 538.
394 "We must offset": Quoted in Pogue, *George C. Marshall: Statesman 1945–1959,* 17.
394 "The opinions of our scientific": Quoted in Bundy, *Danger and Survival,* 71.
395 "shock value": Stimson, *On Active Service,* 617.

395 "We regarded the matter": Quoted in Mosley, *Marshall*, 337–38.
396 "only by men": Quoted in Rhodes, 637.
396 "His general demeanor": Quoted in Wyden, 143.
396 "render the Russians": Ibid., 142.
397 "Oppenheimer didn't share": Ibid., 143.
397 "the damn thing": Quoted in Phillips, *The Truman Presidency*, 54.
397 "We are on our way": Quoted in Truman, *Souvenir*, 109.
397 "I hope—sincerely hope": HST Diary, June 1, 1945, *Off the Record*, 40.
397 "Don't think over six": Ibid.
397 "Just two months ago": HST to EWT, June 12, 1945, *Dear Bess*, 515–16.
398 "He's a nice fellow": HST to EWT, June 19, 1945, Ibid., 516.
398 "I'm always so lonesome": HST Diary, June 1, 1945, *Off the Record*, 40.
398 A Gallup Poll: Donovan, 21.
398 "And as usual": Ayers Diary, June 18, 1945, HSTL.
399 "Nothing really important": *Foreign Relations of the United States, Conference of Berlin (Potsdam), 1945,* Vol. I, 92.
399 "always been our friends": HST Diary, June 7, 1945, *Off the Record*, 44.
399 "Mr. Prima Donna": HST Diary, June 17, 1945, *Off the Record*, 47.
400 "He wants an estimate": Quoted in Sherwin, 336.
400 "I have to decide": HST Diary, June 17, 1945, *Off the Record*, 47.
400 June 18, 1945, meeting: Feis, *The Atomic Bomb and the End of World War II,* 10.
400 Handy memo, Sherwin, *World Destroyed,* 350–55.
401 Goodpaster, *New York Times,* August 11, 1993.
401 "We were beginning": John J. McCloy, author's interview.
401 June 26, 1945, speech: PP, HST, June 26, 1945.
402 "I shall attempt": HST, Speech Files, June 27, 1945, HSTL.
402 "I am anxious": Truman, *Harry S. Truman,* 279–280.
402 July 2, 1945, speech: PP, HST, July 2, 1945, 153–55.
403 no buzzer: Woolf, "President Truman Talks About His Job," *The New York Times Magazine,* July 15, 1945.
403 he would "soon go under": Ibid.
403 "Punish her war criminals": Stimson Diary, May 16, 1945.
404 Morgenthau meeting: Morgenthau, 466.
404 Morgenthau didn't know: Jonathan Daniels interview with HST, November 12, 1949, HSTL.
404 "I am getting ready": HST to MET and MJT, July 3, 1945, HSTL.
404 "How I hate": HST Diary, July 7, 1945, *Off the Record*, 49.

10. SUMMER OF DECISION

405 "Today's prime fact": Stimson quoted in Compton, *Atomic Quest,* 219.
405 "like a moving circus": HST to MET and MJT, January 27, 1947, HSTL.
406 "It seems to take two warships": HST to MT, July 14, 1945, HSTL.
406 "You who have not seen": Film Collection, HSTL.
406 Truman on Fred Canfil: Hersey, *Aspects of the Presidency,* 39.
407 "At the end of the war": O. Müller Grote to HST, February 10, 1956, HSTL.
408 a "nightmare of a house": *The New York Times,* August 3, 1945.
408 "They erected a couple of": HST Diary, July 16, 1945, in Ferrell, ed., *Off the Record,* 50.
408 "wholly inadequate": *Foreign Relations of the United States, Conference of Berlin (Potsdam), 1945,* Vol. II, 9.
409 "He comes from Owensborough": HST to MET and MJT, January 27, 1947, HSTL.
409 Bohlen, too, was struck: Bohlen, *Witness to History,* 226.
409 "astonishingly well prepared": Harriman and Abel, *Special Envoy to Churchill and Stalin,* 485.
409 "Mr. Russia" and "Mr. Great Britain": HST Diary, July 7, 1945, *Off the Record*, 49.
409 "half so badly": HST to EWT, February 19, 1916, *Dear Bess*, 187.

410 "I've studied more": HST to EWT, May 26, 1918, HSTL.
410 "Haven't you ever been": Woolf, "President Truman Talks About His Job," *The New York Times Magazine,* July 15, 1945.
411 Prime Minister padding down the hall: Wilroy and Prinz, *Inside the Blair House,* 7–8.
411 Eleanor Roosevelt had written: Lash, *Eleanor: The Years Alone,* 29.
412 "I must confess, sir": See note for page 874, Chap. 17.
412 "He says he is sure": Gilbert, *Winston S. Churchill. Never Despair,* 61.
412 "We had a most pleasant": HST Diary, July 16, 1945, *Off the Record,* 51.
413 "Very Secret, Urgent": *Foreign Relations of the United States, Conference of Berlin (Potsdam), 1945,* Vol. I, 876.
413 Sato responded: Ibid., 883.
413 "good soldiers and millions": HST Diary, July 16, 1945, *Off the Record,* 52.
414 "It is a terrible thing": *The New York Times,* July 17, 1945.
415 "I never saw such destruction": *Memoirs,* Vol. I, 341.
415 "absolute ruin": HST Diary, July 16, 1945, *Off the Record,* 52.
415 modern war . . . "brought home": Leahy, *I Was There,* 396.
415 "I thought of Carthage": HST Diary, July 16, 1945, *Off the Record,* 52.
415 He kept thinking: HST to EWT, July 20, 1945, *Dear Bess,* 520.
415 "This is what would have happened": Gilbert, 61.
415 Anne O'Hare McCormick column: *The New York Times,* July 18, 1945.
416 "Operated on this morning": *Foreign Relations of the United States, Conference of Berlin (Potsdam), 1945,* Vol. II, 1360.
416 "Promptly a few minutes": HST Diary, July 17, 1945, *Off the Record,* 53.
416 The truth was: Volkogonov, *Stalin: Triumph and Tragedy,* 499.
416 As Stalin got out of the car: George Elsey, author's interview.
417 "I got to my feet": HST Diary, July 17, 1945, *Off the Record,* 53.
417 "A little bit of a squirt": Film Collection, HSTL.
418 Stalin sure Hitler was alive and in hiding: Byrnes, *Speaking Frankly,* 68.
418 "as agreed at Yalta": *Foreign Relations of the United States, Conference of Berlin (Potsdam), 1945,* Vol. II, 1586.
418 "You could if you wanted to": *Memoirs,* Vol. I, 541.
418 "and I felt hopeful": Ibid., 342.
418 "The truth is he is a very likeable person": Byrnes, 45.
419 "honest—but smart as hell": HST Diary, July 17, 1945, *Off the Record,* 53.
419 "He'll be in the Jap War": Ibid.
419 *Time* magazine on Stalin: *Time,* February 5, 1945.
419 "There was little in Stalin's demeanor": Bohlen, 340.
420 "When one man dies": Antonov-Ovseyenko, *The Time of Stalin: Portrait of Tyranny,* 278.
420 "I was impressed": *Memoirs,* Vol. I, 340–42.
421 "Since the Yalta Conference": *Foreign Relations of the United States, Conference of Berlin (Potsdam), 1945,* Vol. II, 643.
422 "Churchill said he should like": Ibid, p. 54.
423 "So tomorrow we will have prepared": Ibid., 61.
423 "Let's divide it": Ibid, p. 59.
423 "woolly and verbose": Gilbert, 65.
423 HST took as act of disloyalty: HST to MT, July 29, 1945, HSTL.
424 "The boys say": HST to EWT, July 18, 1945, *Dear Bess,* 519.
424 "Churchill talks all the time": HST to MET and MJT, July 18, 1945, HSTL.
424 "Doctor had just returned": *Foreign Relations of the United States, Conference of Berlin (Potsdam), 1945,* Vol. II, 1360–61.
425 HST appeared extremely pleased: Churchill, 554.
425 "at any rate they had something": Ehrman, *Grand Strategy,* 302–03.
425 "lull the Japanese": *Foreign Relations of the United States, Conference of Berlin (Potsdam), 1945,* Vol. II, 1588.

425 Stalin's disclosure: Bohlen, 236.
426 The Generalissimo must visit: HST Diary, July 18, 1945, *Off the Record,* 54.
426 "We cannot get away": *Foreign Relations of the United States, Conference of Berlin (Potsdam), 1945,* Vol. II, 96.
426 "I'm not going to stay": HST Diary, July 18, 1945, *Off the Record,* 54.
426 To Bess, earlier in the day: HST to EWT, July 18, 1945, *Dear Bess,* 519.
427 "Believe Japs": HST Diary, July 18, 1945, *Off the Record,* 54.
427 "sick of the whole business": HST to EWT, July 20, 1945, *Dear Bess,* 520.
427 "A young Army captain": *The New York Times,* August 14, 1945.
428 "The old man loves music": HST to EWT, July 20, 1945, *Dear Bess,* 520.
428 "He was direct, unpretentious": Bradley and Blair, *A General's Life,* 444.
428 Eisenhower opposed use of the bomb: Eisenhower, *Crusade in Europe,* 443.
428 Eisenhower would concede: Eisenhower, *Eisenhower at War, 1943–1945,* 692.
428 truly believed that "Manhattan": HST Diary, July 18, 1945, *Off the Record,* 54.
428 "But all of us wanted": Truman, *Bess W. Truman,* 316.
429 "We are here today": PP, HST, July 20, 1945, 195.
429 "of lasting inspiration": Clay, *Decision in Germany,* 44–45.
430 "General, there is nothing": Bradley and Blair, 444–45.
430 "Uncle Joe looked": HST Diary, July 20, 1945, *Off the Record,* 55.
430 "immensely powerful document": Stimson Diary, July 21, 1945.
430 "successful beyond the most optimistic": Groves Memorandum, *Foreign Policy of the United States, Conference of Berlin (Potsdam), 1945,* Vol. II, 1362.
431 HST and Byrnes both looked pleased: Stimson Diary, July 21, 1945.
432 "It was apparent": Murphy, *Diplomat Among Warriors,* 273.
432 "We will not recognize": *Foreign Relations of the United States, Conference of Berlin (Potsdam), 1945,* Vol. II, 216.
433 the Russians had no intention: Leahy, 406.
433 "Started with caviar": HST to MET and MJT, July 23, 1945, HSTL.
434 "He talked to me confidently": HST to EWT, July 22, 1945, *Dear Bess,* 521.
434 "Watch the President": Moran, *Diaries,* 303.
434 "There was no pretense": Rigdon, with Derieux, *White House Sailor,* 183–84.
435 "swagly." "He never came on": Floyd Boring, author's interview.
435 "I thought it was nice": Emilio Collado, Oral History, HSTL.
436 "I'm going to mass": HST to EWT, July 22, 1945, HSTL.
436 "Although it was a target": Stimson and Bundy, *On Active Service in Peace and War,* 625.
436 "prosecute the war against Japan": *Memoirs,* Vol. I, 391.
437 "alone with his work": Stimson Diary, July 24, 1945.
437 July 23, 1945, cable: *Foreign Relations of the United States, Conference of Berlin (Potsdam), 1945,* Vol. II, 1374.
437 "said that was just what he wanted": Stimson Diary, July 24, 1945.
437 HST wrote of a consensus: *Memoirs,* Vol. I, 415.
437 "I asked General Marshall": HST to Professor F. Cate, undated letter, HSTL.
437 battle casualties during HST's three months in office: Army Battle Casualties and Nonbattle Deaths in World War II, Department of the Army.
438 "We had only too abundant": Charlton Ogburn, Jr., author's interview.
438 "The basic policy of the present": Combined Intelligence Committee Report, July 8, 1945, HSTL.
438 conscription of Japanese people: *The New York Times,* August 5, 1985.
439 "the spirit of mercy": Bohlen, 231.
440 "At no time, from 1941 to 1945": Stimson and Bundy, 613.
440 "I know FDR": Daniels, *The Man of Independence,* 281.
440 "I'll say that we'll end": HST to EWT, July 18, 1945, *Dear Bess,* 519.
440 "It is just the same as artillery": *The New York Times,* May 3, 1959.
441 "We knew the Japanese were determined": Lilienthal, *Journals,* Vol. II, 198.
441 A petition drawn up: Wyden, *Day One,* 180.

SOURCE NOTES

441   "Are not the men": Compton, 242.
441   "It is hard to imagine": Evan J. Young of Clinton Laboratories to M.D. Whittaker, undated, HSTL.
441   "What a question": Compton, 247.
442   "The historic fact": Churchill, 553.
442   "Truman made no decision": George Elsey, author's interview.
442   "The final decision": *Memoirs*, Vol. I, 419.
442   HST later told Arthur Compton: Compton, 245.
442   "I casually mentioned to Stalin": *Memoirs*, Vol. I, 416.
443   Stalin's response offhand: Bohlen, 237.
443   "If he had had the slightest idea": Churchill, 580.
443   "not grasped the importance": Byrnes, 263.
443   "No one who played": Ibid., 265.
443   "We have discovered": HST Diary, July 25, 1945, *Off the Record*, 55.
444   "The idea of using the bomb": Harriman and Abel, 490.
445   "We are asking for the reorganization": *Foreign Relations of the United States, Conference of Berlin (Potsdam), 1945,* Vol. II, 360.
445   "If a government": Ibid.
445   an iron fence had descended: Ibid., 362.
446   "I do not want to fight": *Foreign Relations of the United States, Conference of Berlin (Potsdam), 1945,* Vol. II, 313.
446   "The question is not ripe": Ibid., 373.
446   Churchill full of foreboding: Moran, 306.
446   "What a pity": *Memoirs*, Vol. I, 389.
446   old order passing: HST Diary, July 30, 1945, *Off the Record*, 58.
446   It was too bad about Churchill: HST to MET and MJT, July 28, 1945, HSTL.
447   "enslaved as a race": *Memoirs*, Vol. I, 392–93.
447   "kill it with silence": Sherwin, *A World Destroyed*, 236.
447   "Mr. Attlee is not so keen": HST to MET and MJT, July 29, 1945, HSTL.
448   "We shall see": HST to EWT, July 29, 1945, *Dear Bess*, 522.
448   HST in an optimistic mood: *Forrestal Diaries*, 79.
448   "The time schedule on Groves' ": *Foreign Relations of the United States, Conference of Berlin (Potsdam), 1945,* Vol. II, 1374.
448   "Suggestion approved": Declassified "Urgent—Top Secret Message," Stimson to HST, July 30, 1945: HST's handwritten message on back, HSTL.
448   *"Everything* seemed momentous": Elsey, author's interview.
449   "We have accomplished a very great deal": HST to EWT, July 25, 1945, *Dear Bess*, 521.
450   "Pray for me": HST to EWT, July 29, 1945, ibid., 522.
450   "We are at an impasse": HST Diary, July 30, 1945, *Off the Record*, 58.
450   "It is a question of give and take": PP, HST, August 9, 1945, 209.
450   foolishness in the extreme: Kennan, *Memoirs,* 259, 290.
451   "Marshal Stalin I have accepted": Murphy, 278.
451   Stalin broke in: Ibid., 279.
451   HST called Russians pigheaded: HST to MET and MJT, July 31, 1945, HSTL.
451   "police government": HST Diary, July 26, 1945, *Off the Record,* 57.
451   "They went away": Donovan, 73.
451   "I like Stalin": HST to EWT, July 29, 1945, *Dear Bess,* 522.
451   "The President seemed to have been": Ayers Diary, August 7, 1945, HSTL.
451   Stalin was a fine man: Wallace, *The Price of Vision,* 490.
451   "Stalin is as near": Daniels, *The Man of Independence,* 23.
452   "an innocent idealist": HST to Dean Acheson, March 15, 1957, unsent, *Off the Record,* 348–49.
452   "for operational purposes": *Foreign Relations of the United States, Conference of Berlin (Potsdam), 1945,* Vol. II, 1321.
452   Discussion of Poland's frontier: Ibid., 597–601.
452   Stalin on HST: Khrushchev, *Khrushchev Remembers,* 221.

453 "That will save two days": HST to MET and MJT, July 31, 1945, HSTL.
453 HST found the King "very pleasant": HST Diary, August 5, 1945, *Off the Record,* 59.
454 "Here was the greatest news story": Smith, *Thank You, Mr. President,* 256.
454 "completely rested": Official log of the *Augusta,* HSTL.
454 "Results clear-cut": *Memoirs,* Vol. I, 421.
454 "This is the greatest thing": Smith, 257.
454 "Big bomb dropped": *Memoirs,* Vol. I, 421.
455 "Please keep your seats": *The New York Times,* August 7, 1945.
455 "He was not actually laughing": Smith, 258.
455 "We were all excited": Elsey, author's interview.
455 "Sixteen hours ago": PP, HST, August 6, 1945, 196–200.
456 "But even if my legs": Kansas City *Star,* July 28, 1965.
456 "Some of our scientists": Leahy Diary, August 8, 1945, LC.
457 "ultimatum to end all ultimatums": *The New York Times,* August 8, 1945.
457 Stimson and Marshall worried: Mosley, *Marshall. Hero for Our Times,* 338.
457 "Additional bombs": *Memoirs,* Vol. I, 420.
457 "For the second time": L.A. *Times,* August 9, 1945.
458 Russell telegram to HST: Richard B. Russell to HST, undated, HSTL.
458 HST note to Russell: HST to Richard B. Russell, August 9, 1945, HSTL.
458 "I realize the tragic significance": PP, HST, August 9, 1945, 212.
459 "Would it not be wondrous?": Washington *Times,* August 6, 1985.
459 "Could we continue": *Memoirs,* Vol. I, 428.
459 Stimson said the emperor: Ibid.
460 "we'd tell 'em how to keep him": HST Diary, August 10, 1945, *Off the Record,* 61.
460 "subject to the Supreme Commander": *Memoirs,* Vol. I, 429.
460 "all those kids": Wallace, 474.
461 "Nearly every crisis seems to be": HST to MET and MJT, August 12, 1945, HSTL.
461 "it began like the days": Ayers Diary, August 14, 1945, HSTL.
461 "might get a story": Sue Gentry, author's interview.
462 "I have received this afternoon": PP, HST, August 14, 1945, 216.
462 "I felt deeply moved": *Memoirs,* Vol. I, 437.
462 "This is a great day": *The New York Times,* August 15, 1945.
463 "The only thing new": Miller, *Plain Speaking,* 69.
464 "Everyone had been going": HST to MET and MJT, August 17, 1945, *Off the Record,* 62.

PART FOUR

11. THE BUCK STOPS HERE

467 "Everybody wants something": HST to MET and MJT, September 22, 1945, HSTL.
467 more prima donnas per square foot: HST to MET and MJT, October 23, 1945, HSTL.
467 "You can't do anything worthwhile": PP, HST, October 7, 1945, 380.
467 "cut out the foolishness": Ibid., October 10, 1945, 394.
468 "We must go on": Ibid., September 6, 1945, 291.
469 Wallace's estimate of drop in GNP: Wallace, *The Price of Vision,* 495.
470 "The Congress are balking": HST to MET and MJT, October 23, 1945, HSTL.
471 "Anything *else,* Mr. President?": PP, HST, September 18, 1945, 326.
472 "If anyone in the government": HST to EWT, June 22, 1945, *Dear Bess,* 523.
472 "The pressure here": HST to MET and MJT, October 13, 1945, HSTL.
472 "We can't stand another global war": PP, HST, October 7, 1945, 381.
473 "did everything . . . mouth of a cannon": Quoted in Phillips, *The Truman Presidency,* 129.
473 "in the doldrums": Ayers Diary, October 19, 1945, HSTL.
474 call for universal military training: PP, HST, October 23, 1945, 404, 413.
474 HST shows new presidential flag: Ibid., October 25, 1945, 415–417.
474 "It was disintegration": *Memoirs,* Vol. I, 509.

SOURCE NOTES

475   "Tiny lines had grown": Gunther, *Procession,* 260.
475   Encounter with Oppenheimer: Lilienthal, *Journals,* Vol. II, 118.
475   "See what a son-of-a-bitch": Quoted in Wallace, 519.
475   Marshall ends call abruptly: Miller, *Plain Speaking,* 252.
476   "paid much less attention": Samuel Rosenman, Oral History, HSTL.
476   "Mr. President, you *should* know": Wallace, 530.
477   "wild accidents": Quoted in Lerner, *Actions and Passions,* 219.
477   "one of the most hazardous": *Time,* December 8, 1947.
478   "Well I'm here in the White House": HST to EWT, December 28, 1945, *Dear Bess,* 523–24.
479   "able and conniving": HST Diary, July 7, 1945, in Ferrell, ed., *Off the Record,* 49.
479   "I told him I did not like": *Memoirs,* Vol. I, 550.
479   "a horse's ass": Clifford quoted in Jonathan Daniels interview notes, HSTL.
479   Acheson impressions of HST: Acheson, *Present at the Creation,* 136.
480   HST longhand letter for Byrnes: HST to James F. Byrnes, January 5, 1946, unsent, *Off the Record,* 79–80.
480   "1946 is our year of decision": PP, HST, January 3, 1946, 1.
481   "This is a disaster": Quoted in Goulden, *The Best Years 1945–1950,* 113.
481   "I personally think there is": PP, HST, January 24, 1946, 92.
482   The "blunt truth": *Time,* January 14, 1946.
482   Chicago *Tribune* cartoon: Reprinted in *Time,* February 4, 1946.
482   "at best, undistinguished": MacKaye, "Things Are Different in the White House," *Saturday Evening Post,* April 20, 1946.
482   People were "befuddled": HST to MET and MJT, January·23, 1946, HSTL.
483   "An oil man": Ayers Diary, January 18, 1946, HSTL.
483   Ickes resignation: *The New York Times,* February 14, 1946.
484   a chronic "resigner": Quoted in Miller, 226.
484   "There would have been no rest": HST to MET and MJT, February 7, 1946, HSTL.
485   *American Mercury* article: Crawford, "Everyman in the White House," February 1946.
486   "appears to consider it necessary": Leahy Diary, February 21, 1946, LC.
486   Stalin statement on war: Donovan, 187.
486   Justice Douglas reaction: Ibid.
487   "I will call you Harry": Ross Diary, March 7, 1946, HSTL.
487   "Harry, what does a sequence count?": Quoted in Daniels, *The Man of Independence,* 279.
487   "He took a boy's delight": Ross Diary, March 7, 1946, HSTL.
488   Churchill wish to be born American: Gilbert, *Winston Churchill. Never Despair,* 146.
488   "You stop drinking": Ibid., 147.
488   "do nothing but good": Ibid.
488   HST and Churchill on eagle's head: Ross Diary, March 9, 1946, HSTL.
489   "Iron curtain" speech: Quoted in Gilbert, 198.
490   HST denies knowing what Churchill would say: Wallace, 558.
490   HST pleads "no comment": PP, HST, March 8, 1946, 145.
490   "the Long Telegram": Donovan, 187–88.
491   "here and now": Matt Connelly Papers, HSTL.
491   "He was in his study": Ross Diary, March 23, 1946, HSTL.
492   Mary Jane's reaction to HST press conference: Mary Jane Truman, Oral History, HSTL.
492   *Life* article: Busch, "A Year of Truman," April 8, 1946.
493   "Here is to be seen": *The New York Times Magazine,* April 7, 1946.
494   *Time* article: May 6, 1946.
494   "I can hold a Cabinet meeting": PP, HST, May 2, 1946, 227.
494   "Big money has too much": HST to MET and MJT, January 23, 1946, HSTL.
495   "I'm going to give you the gun": Quoted in Daniels, 325.
496   "We have a society": *The New York Times,* May 22, 1946.
496   "That's the way he is": Ibid., May 26, 1946.
496   a "complicated": J. C. Truman, author's interview.
497   "This was the fifth day": Ayers Diary, May 23, 1946, HSTL.

SOURCE NOTES

498   HST meeting with veterans: Washington *Star,* May 24, 1946.
498   "There were poignant scenes": *Newsweek,* June 3, 1946.
499   Telegrams flooding the White House: White House Correspondence File, HSTL.
500   "At home those of us": HST speech draft, undelivered, Clifford Papers, HSTL.
501   "In the manner of Lincoln": Phillips, 115.
502   "I'd never been in the White House": Clark Clifford, author's interview.
502   "Alone of all the Truman entourage": Quoted in Allen and Shannon, *The Truman Merry-Go-Round,* 61.
503   "The President is intelligent": Clifford, with Holbrooke, *Counsel to the President,* 274.
503   "I come before the American people": PP, HST, May 24, 1946, 274.
504   "He said they had verbally agreed": Clifford interview, Daniels notes, HSTL.
504   "For the past two days": PP, HST, May 25, 1946, 277.
505   "Spotlights ablaze": *New Republic,* June 3, 1946.
505   "he could be tough": *The New York Times,* May 26, 1946.
506   "Draft men who strike": *New Republic,* June 3, 1946.
506   "I was the servant": Film Collection, HSTL.
507   "Nothing about the Wallace affair": George Elsey, author's interview.
508   "If Mr. Slaughter is right": PP, HST, July 18, 1946, 350.
509   HST's health: Ross Diary, July 20, 1946, HSTL.
509   "Had the most awful day": HST to MET and MJT, July 31, 1946, HSTL.
509   "She's on the way out": HST to EWT, August 9, 1946, *Dear Bess,* 530.
509   "Be good and be tough": MT [Margaret Truman] to HST, June 14, 1946, Truman, *Letters from Father,* 142.
509   "I still have a number of bills": HST to EWT, August 10, 1946, *Dear Bess,* 530.
510   "It's just wonderful": MacDonald, "President Truman's Yacht," *Naval History,* Winter 1990.
510   "See, he had no airs": Clifford, author's interview.
511   "He always plays a close hand": Ted Marks, Oral History, HSTL.
512   "The *Williamsburg*": MacDonald, "President Truman's Yacht."
512   "This is a paradise": HST to MT, August 23, 1946, Truman, *Letters from Father,* 69.
512   "did all sorts of antics": Truman, *Harry S. Truman,* 366.
512   "The furniture was taking headers": HST to EWT, September 2, 1946, *Dear Bess,* 534.
512   "Night before last": HST to EWT, September 9, 1946, ibid., 535.
513   disliked living there: HST to EWT, September 3, 1946, ibid., 534.
513   "You better lock your door": Truman, *Letters from Father,* 144.
513   "I'm in the middle": HST to EWT, September 10, 1946, *Dear Bess,* 536.
513   HST press conference: PP, HST, September 12, 1946, 426–29.
513   "If the President": Ross Diary, September 21, 1946, HSTL.
514   Wallace account: Wallace, 612–13.
514   tried to skim through it: HST Diary, September 17, 1946, *Off the Record,* 94.
515   Reston column: *The New York Times,* September 13, 1946.
515   "The criticism continued to mount": Ross Diary, September 21, 1946, HSTL.
516   "I'm still having Henry Wallace trouble": HST to MET and MJT, September 18, 1946, HSTL.
516   "Henry told me": HST to EWT, September 20, 1946, *Dear Bess,* 539.
517   "Everything's lovely": Quoted in Acheson, 192.
517   "Henry is the most peculiar fellow": HST to MET and MJT, September 20, 1946, HSTL.
517   "He wants to disband": Quoted in Donovan, 227.
517   Byrnes telegram: Byrnes, *Speaking Frankly,* 241–42.
517   "so nice about it": HST to EWT, September 21, 1946, *Dear Bess,* 539.
518   "I would rather be *anything*": HST to MET and MJT, September 20, 1946, HSTL.
518   "No man in his right mind": HST to MT, September 9, 1946, Truman, *Letters from Father,* 71.
518   "a liar, double-crosser": HST to MT, September 17, 1946, ibid., 75.
518   "Sept. 26, 1918": HST Diary, September 26, 1946, *Off the Record,* 98.
520   Ickes called him "stupid"; *Time,* September 30, 1946.

520 32 percent poll results: Gallup, *The Gallup Poll: Public Opinion 1935–1971*, 604.

521 "Nothing on meat": PP, HST, October 10, 1946, 447.

521 Truman continues electronic surveillance: Gentry, *J. Edgar Hoover*, 344.

522 "The shrill pitch of abuse": *Time*, October 28, 1946.

522 he alone was formally dressed: Ibid.

522 "Here was a man": Kilgore quoted in Steinberg, *The Man from Missouri*, 288.

522 "never seemed to have a problem": Fields, *My 21 Years in the White House*, 187.

523 "We went to the Waldorf": HST to MT, October 26, 1946, Truman, *Letters from Father*, 81.

523 Jefferson City stop: *Time*, November 11, 1946.

524 "Probably no President": Phillips, 161.

12. TURNING POINT

525 "This is a serious course": PP, HST, March 12, 1947, 179.

525 Lippmann on HST: Steel, *Walter Lippmann and the American Century*, 455.

526 "My dear Harry": WC to HST, May 12, 1947, quoted in Gilbert, *Winston S. Churchill. Never Despair*, 326.

526 Acheson alone . . . was waiting: Acheson, *Present at the Creation*, 200.

526 "The captain with the mighty heart": Ibid., dedication page.

526 "so fast they were falling all over": Clark Clifford, author's interview.

527 Lilienthal in rain: Lilienthal, *Journals*, Vol. I, 54.

528 "the kind of grim gaiety": Ibid., 118.

528 "Oh, God, it was the chance": Clifford, author's interview.

529 "now a free man": Quoted in *Time*, April 7, 1947.

529 "I'm doing as I damn please": HST to EWT, November 18, 1946, *Dear Bess*, 540.

529 "How can there be immunity": Goldman, *The Crucial Decade—And After*, 29.

530 "He told me that he would": HST Diary, January 1, 1947, in Ferrell, ed., *Off the Record*, 107.

530 "Bob is not austere": *Time*, January 20, 1947.

532 HST walks to Union Station: Ayers Diary, January 6, 1947, HSTL.

532 "your appointment as Secretary of State": Mosley, *Marshall: Hero for Our Times*, 390.

533 "I thought that the continuing harping": Cray, *General of the Army*, 17.

533 Marshall did not possess the intellectual brilliance: Halle, *The Cold War as History*, 113.

533 "It was a striking and commanding force": Acheson, 140–41.

533 exit office backwards: Paul Horgan, author's interview.

534 "He never made any speeches": Miller, *Plain Speaking*, 251.

534 "Sometimes he would sit": *Memoirs*, Vol. II, 112.

534 "He was a man you could count on": Quoted in Miller, 250.

534 "On the one hand": Pogue, *George C. Marshall. Statesman*, 141–42.

535 "He gave a sense of purpose": Bohlen, *Witness to History*, 259.

535 "Gentlemen, don't fight": Quoted in Pogue, 148.

535 Acheson found working with the general: Lilienthal, *Journals*, Vol. II, 159.

535 "The more I see and talk": HST appointment sheet, February 18, 1947, *Off the Record*, 109.

535 "Marshall is a tower": HST Diary, May 7, 1948, ibid., 134.

535 "I am surely lucky": HST appointment sheet, February 18, 1947, ibid., 109.

536 "He no longer moans": Gaddis, *The United States and the Origins of the Cold War, 1941–1947*, 347.

536 "His eye is clear": Quoted in *Time*, January 27, 1947.

536 48 percent poll rating: *Time*, February 10, 1947.

536 "They brought back all the pageantry": West, with Kotz, *Upstairs at the White House*, 91.

536 "The papers say today": HST to MET and MJT, February 9, 1947, *Off the Record*, 108.

536 "I was somewhat nervous": HST to MET and MJT, February 13, 1947, HSTL.

537 "despite all the denying": West, 91.

537 Lilienthal nomination hearings: Lilienthal, *Journals,* Vol. II, 141–42.
537 "far from anger or temper": Ibid., 141.
537 "I believe in": Ibid., Appendix B, 646–48.
538 HST supports Lilienthal: Ibid., 144.
538 Taft opposes nomination: *Time,* February 24, 1947.
539 "Courage: What is it?": Lilienthal, *Journals,* Vol. II, 160.
539 "Now Mary, don't you work too hard": HST to MET and MJT, February 27, 1947, HSTL.
540 Lincoln McVeigh reported rumors: *Memoirs,* Vol. II, 99.
540 Greece a "ripe plum": Ibid.
540 "little hope of independent survival": Quoted in Donovan, *Conflict and Crisis,* 277.
541 "the only one in Government": Gaddis, 346, note.
541 "It is not alarmist": Quoted in Pogue, 164.
542 "The Soviet Union was playing": Acheson, 219.
542 Vandenberg told the President: Ibid.
542 "and I expressed my emphatic": *Memoirs,* Vol. II, 103.
542 Mexico City visit: *Newsweek,* March 17, 1947.
543 Clifford memo: appears in full in Krock, *Memoirs,* Appendix, 419–82.
545 "The impact of having it all": George Elsey, Oral History, HSTL.
545 "If we go in": Matt Connelly Papers, HSTL.
545 most important of his career: Ayers Diary, March 8, 1947, HSTL.
546 "I believe it must be": Clifford, *Counsel to the President,* 136.
546 "too much rhetoric": Bohlen, 261.
546 "If you take his advice": Lilienthal, *Journals,* Vol. II, 163.
546 "I want no hedging": *Memoirs,* Vol. II, 105.
547 Truman Doctrine speech: PP, HST, March 12, 1947, 176–80.
548 "Well, I told my wife": *Time,* March 24, 1947.
549 "A vague global policy": Quoted in Steel, 438–39.
549 a "universal pattern": Hartmann, *Truman and the 80th Congress,* 61.
549 would "of course" act: Acheson, 225.
549 "I guess the do-gooders": *Newsweek,* March 24, 1947.
550 "If Mr. L is a communist": HST, draft unreleased statement, March 1947, *Off the Record,* 113.
550 "no part of a communist": Vandenberg, ed., *The Private Papers of Senator Vandenberg,* 355.
550 "the most important thing": Lilienthal, *Journals,* Vol. II, 166.
550 "[He is] very strongly anti-FBI": Clark Clifford Papers, HSTL.
551 "The long tenure": Martin, *My First Fifty Years in Politics,* 163.
552 "I am not worried": PP, HST, April 3, 1947, 190.
553 "It was a political problem": Bernstein, *Loyalties,* 195–98.
553 "The Republicans are now taking": Frank McNaughton Papers, March 28, 1948, HSTL.
553 "If I can prevent": HST to EW, September 27, 1947, *Dear Bess,* 550.
553 "Yes, it was terrible": Joseph Rauh quoted in Bernstein, 196.
554 "I think it's one of the proudest": Clifford, author's interview.
554 "There was much to be done": *Memoirs,* Vol. II, 104.
554 "You don't sit down": Elsey, Oral History, HSTL.
555 Kennan leaves the room: Kennan, *Memoirs,* 328, note.
555 meeting with newspaper editors: PP, HST, April 7, 1947, 207–10.
556 "He was . . . an extremely thoughtful": Elsey, Oral History, HSTL.
557 "When he went to lunch": Quoted in Heller, *The Truman White House,* 46.
557 "Lots of times I would be": Clifford, author's interview.
557 "He spent virtually every waking": Quoted in Heller, 119.
558 HST would like to have been history teacher: Ayers Diary, April 26, 1947, HSTL.
558 Clifford insists HST not be FDR: Markel, "Truman As the Crucial Third Year Opens."
559 "In many ways President Truman": Quoted in Heller, 120.
559 "It just has to be said": Elsey, author's interview.
559 "There is nothing in life": Quoted in Farrar, *Reluctant Servant,* 195.

560 "priceless gift of vitality": Acheson, 730.
560 the nation "again has leaders": Hardeman and Bacon, *Rayburn: A Biography,* 328.
561 Marshall's return of April 26, 1947: *Memoirs,* Vol. II, 112; Bohlen, 262–63; Kennan, 325.
561 The Soviets, it seemed: Marshall quoted in Pogue, 196.
561 "The patient is sinking": Ibid., 200.
561 "Avoid trivia": Kennan, 326.
562 Clayton memo: Pogue, 206.
562 Marshall speech: Mosley, 404–05.
563 "We grabbed the lifeline": Quoted in Pogue, 217.
563 "play it straight": Bohlen, 264.
564 part played by Acheson: Clark Clifford address, American Ditchley Foundation, April 5, 1984.
564 "anything that is sent up": Clifford, author's interview.
564 Halle's comments on staff: Halle, 115–16.
565 "And you and I have both lived": Quoted in Miller, 264.
566 "While he was responding": Truman, *Harry S. Truman,* 383.
566 "If she wants to be a warbler": HST to MET and MJT, January 30, 1947, HSTL.
567 "She's one nice girl": HST to MET and MJT, February 19, 1947, HSTL.
567 Mrs. Thomas J. Strickler: Kansas City *Star,* April 18, 1946.
567 "Margaret went to New York": HST to MET and MJT, January 30, 1947, HSTL.
567 "Here's a little dough": HST to MT, February 28, 1947, Truman, *Letters from Father,* 89.
567 Margaret Truman's radio debut: Kansas City *Star,* March 7, 8, 9, and 17, 1947.
568 "Perhaps, sheer naivete": Truman, *Souvenir,* 162.
569 "Wish I could go along": HST to MT, May 14, 1947, Truman, *Letters from Father,* 92.
569 "Whenever she wakes up": *Time,* June 2, 1947.
570 "When I say all Americans": PP, HST, June 29, 1947, 311–13.
570 "I did not believe": White, *A Man Called White,* 348.
570 "Almost without exception": White, *How Far the Promised Land,* 74.
570 he meant "every word of it": White, *A Man Called White,* 348.
570 "But I believe what I say": HST to MJT, June 28, 1947, HSTL.
570 reminiscing to Bess: HST to EWT, July 26, 1947, *Dear Bess,* 549.
571 "Goodbye, Harry": HST Diary, November 24, 1952, *Off the Record,* 275.
571 "Well, now she won't have to suffer": Steinberg, *The Man from Missouri,* 295.
571 "Everything had changed": Truman, *Souvenir,* 174.
572 "I couldn't hold a press conference": PP, HST, August 5, 1948, 365.
572 "Someday you'll be an orphan": HST to MT, August 1, 1947, Truman, *Letters from Father,* 96.
572 "You should call your mamma": HST to MT, December 3, 1947, Truman, *Harry S. Truman,* 404–05.
573 "I called up Daddy": Truman, *Souvenir,* 191.
573 a hit as a vaudeville team: Daniels, "The Lady from Independence," *McCall's,* April 1949.
574 She would laugh so hard: Parks and Leighton, *My Thirty Years Backstage at the White House,* 28.
574 "She's the only lady I know": Randall Jessee quoted in the Dallas *Morning News,* February 9, 1976.
574 "Mrs. Truman came with great apologies": Marquis Childs, author's interview.
574 "the white gloves type": Reathel Odum, author's interview.
574 "They both had the gift": Nixon, *In the Arena,* 231.
574 "one of the finest women": Robert Lovett, Oral History, HSTL.
575 HST's reliance on Bess: Quoted in Means, "What Three Presidents Say About Their Wives," *Good Housekeeping,* August 1963.
575 Bess laughs at pretensions: Daniels, "The Lady from Independence."
575 "And then . . . the minute the doors": Lindy Boggs, author's interview.
575 "Propriety was a much stronger influence": Alice Acheson, author's interview.

576   "Just keep on smiling": Truman, *Bess W. Truman,* 265.
576   "She didn't want to discuss": Margaret Truman Daniel, author's interview.
576   Bess Truman questionnaire: *Time,* November 10, 1947.
577   "She seems to think Harry": Asbury, "Meet Harry's Boss, Bess," *Collier's,* February 2, 1949.
577   Bess interested in Monroe administration: Daniels, "The Lady from Independence."
578   "Mrs. Truman was no fussier": West, 83.
578   "might as well have been in Independence": J. B. West, author's interview.
578   "And he *listened* to her": Ibid.
578   Bess's emotional separation: Truman, *Bess W. Truman,* 272.
579   "Suppose Miss Lizzie": HST to EN, June 22, 1949, *Off the Record,* 157.
579   "Marshall and Lovett": HST to EWT, September 23, 1947, *Dear Bess,* 549–50.
579   "Yesterday was one of the most hectic": HST to EW, September 30, 1947, ibid., 550–51.
580   "Twenty-nine years!": HST to EWT, June 28, 1948, *Dear Bess,* 554.
580   Greta Kempton portrait: Greta Kempton, author's interview; Kempton letter to the author, June 20, 1984; Kempton, "Painting the Truman Family," *Missouri Historical Review,* April 1973; "An Interview with Greta Kempton," *Whistlestop,* Vol. 15, no. 2, 1987.
583   a handwritten note from Churchill: Gilbert, *Winston Churchill. Never Despair,* 351.
583   "In all the history of the world": HST speech draft, undelivered, April 1948, *Off the Record,* 133.

13. THE HEAT IN THE KITCHEN

584   Eisenhower again declined: Donovan, *Conflict and Crisis,* 338.
584   "Mr. Truman was a realist": Quoted in Phillips, *The Truman Presidency,* 197, note.
584   "give everything": Ayers Diary, January 19, 1948, HSTL.
584   "Aside from the impossible": HST to MET and MJT, November 14, 1947, HSTL.
585   "President Truman did not want to run": Quoted in Donovan, 338.
585   "blessed with a tough hide": Phillips, 140.
585   "The greatest ambition": Quoted in Ross, *The Loneliest Campaign,* 9.
586   "get into the fight": *Memoirs,* Vol. II, 171–72.
586   "What I wanted to do personally": Ibid., 174.
586   speech before Congress: PP, HST, January 7, 1948, 1.
586   message to Congress: Ibid., February 2, 1948, 121.
587   press conference on civil rights: Ibid., February 5, 1948.
588   black Democrats at rear table: *Time,* March 1, 1948.
588   "But my very stomach turned": Truman, *Harry S. Truman,* 429.
588   Privately could speak of "niggers": Rex Scouten, author's interview; Miller, *Plain Speaking,* 195.
588   "Harry is no more": Jonathan Daniels interview with Mary Jane Truman, October 2, 1949, HSTL.
589   "The main difficulty": HST to Ernest W. Roberts, August 18, 1948, in Ferrell, ed., *Off the Record,* 146.
589   murder of four blacks: *To Secure These Rights: Report of the President's Committee on Civil Rights,* 22.
589   "The wonderful, wonderful development": Clark Clifford, author's interview.
589   "strike for new high ground": Quoted in Ross, 19.
589   Clifford on golf course: David Acheson, author's interview.
590   Clifford decided not to tell HST: Clifford, author's interview.
590   "This is, as you know": James Rowe, Jr., to William Sand, July 8, 1971.
590   "In the Roosevelt and Truman years": George Elsey, author's interview.
590   "The Politics of 1948": Memorandum by James H. Rowe, Jr., Miscellaneous Historical Documents, HSTL.
592   "We were telling the President": James H. Rowe, Jr., author's interview.
592   HST kept memo in bottom drawer. Ibid.

SOURCE NOTES

592   "To a politician of Harry Truman's": Washington *Post,* undated, Vertical Files, HSTL.
593   Hill and Sparkman call for HST's resignation: Ayers Diary, March 23, 1948, HSTL.
593   instant disapproval: Washington *Star,* May 25, 1965.
593   "Back Porch Harry": *Time,* January 26, 1948.
594   Jefferson himself: PP, HST, April 15, 1948, 217–18.
594   Washington *Star:* Donovan, 351.
594   "The awnings you will remember": HST to MJT, January 30, 1948, HSTL.
594   "Had to be renewed": HST to George Rothwell Brown, January 20, 1948, HSTL.
594   danger of second floor falling: Ayers Diary, March 6, 1948, HSTL.
594   Ross "terrifically upset": Ibid., February 6, 1948, HSTL.
594   "You can guard yourself": Ibid., December 30, 1947, HSTL.
595   his most difficult dilemma: Truman, *Harry S. Truman,* 416.
595   "humanly possible": Chicago *Tribune,* April 15, 1948.
595   "could not be allowed to continue": *Memoirs,* Vol. II, 138.
595   "definitely and preeminently": Harrison quoted in Eban, *An Autobiography,* 59.
595   "would they be welcomed": Ibid.
596   Niles sensed HST's sympathy with Jews: Steinberg, *The Man from Missouri,* 304.
596   "I'm a man of no importance": Steinberg, "Mr. Truman's Mystery Man," *Saturday Evening Post,* December 24, 1949.
596   "just politics": Clifford, author's interview.
597   "And his own reading": Weisberger, interview with Clark Clifford, *American Heritage,* December 28, 1976.
597   justice not oil: HST quoted in Wallace, *The Price of Vision,* 607.
597   no wish to send American troops: PP, HST, August 6, 1945, 228.
598   "What I am trying to do": HST to Joseph H. Ball, November 24, 1945, unsent, HSTL.
598   "The action of some of our American Zionists": Truman, *Harry S. Truman,* 420.
598   he wished more people: Donovan, 319
598   "I am not a New Yorker": Quoted in Wallace, 605
599   "Terror and Silver": HST Memorandum to David Niles, May 13, 1947, HSTL.
599   "Jesus Christ couldn't please them": Quoted in Wallace, 607.
599   "I'm so tired": HST to MJT, February 11, 1948, HSTL.
599   not a great many Arab constituents: Donovan, 322.
599   Forrestal thought less of HST: *Forrestal Diaries,* 309, 363.
599   "Kaplan sells shirts": Quoted in Donovan, 317.
599   "And when the day came": Washington *Star and Daily News,* December 31, 1972.
600   "carelessly pro-Zionist": Jenkins, *Truman,* 116.
601   Kennan on Palestine: Pogue, *George C. Marshall: Statesman.* 356.
601   Henderson worried about consequences: *The New York Times,* March 26, 1986.
601   "Some White House men": Daniels, *The Man of Independence,* 317.
601   "Look here, Loy": Loy Henderson, Oral History, HSTL.
601   "conflicting objectives": Rusk, *As I Saw It,* 147–48.
601   "I know how Marshall feels": Quoted in Daniels, 318.
601   "We went for it": Clark Clifford interview with Jonathan Daniels, October 26, 1949.
602   Eddie Jacobson account: Washington *Post,* May 6, 1973.
602   "he [Truman] and he alone": Ibid.
602   Jewish delegation swept up: *The New York Times,* November 30, 1947.
602   "There were Jews in tears": Eban, 99.
602   "a triumphant vindication": *The New York Times,* November 30, 1947.
602   turning point in history: New York *Herald-Tribune,* November 30, 1947.
602   "one of the few great acts": Ibid., December 1, 1947.
602   "push the Jews": Weisberger interview with Clark Clifford, *American Heritage,* December 28, 1976.
603   Forrestal report to HST: *Forrestal Diaries,* March 4, 1948, 386.
603   "Things look black": HST to MT, March 3, 1948, Truman, *Letters from Father,* 108.
603   "a new tenseness": *Forrestal Diaries,* 387.
603   "lifted me right out": Smith, *Lucius D. Clay,* 466–67.

SOURCE NOTES

603 to move atomic bombs: Lilienthal, *Journals,* Vol. I, 302.
603 "The Jewish pressure": *Memoirs,* Vol. II, 160.
604 Niles grew so emotional: Letter from Joseph Alsop to Martin Sommers, June 1, 1948, LC.
604 either "give in": Ibid.
604 "So I called him 'Cham' ": Film Collection, HSTL.
604 They had met secretly: *Memoirs,* Vol. II, 161.
604 "You can bank on us": Daniels, *The Man of Independence,* 318.
604 "I was extremely happy": Weizmann, *Trial and Error,* 459.
604 Kennan's paper: Donovan, 370.
604 "playing with fire": *Forrestal Diaries,* 373.
605 "the political situation": Lash, *Eleanor: The Years Alone,* 127.
605 no "bending": Pogue, 361.
605 "On five occasions": Clark Clifford interview with Jonathan Daniels, October 26, 1949.
605 "pro-Arab": Loy Henderson, Oral History, HSTL.
605 "I pointed out that the views": Ibid.
605 "Oh, hell, I'm leaving": Ibid.
606 Frank Goldman call to Jacobson: Kansas City *Times,* May 13, 1965.
606 Connelly warned Jacobson: Adler, *Roots in a Moving Stream,* 210.
606 "always had a brother's interest": Kansas City *Times,* May 13, 1965.
606 HST suddenly tense: Ibid.
606 "In all the years of our friendship": "Two Presidents and a Haberdasher—1948," *American Jewish Archives,* April 1968.
606 "disrespectful and mean": Ibid.
607 "Harry, all your life": Ibid.
607 HST reaction to Jacobson: Ibid.
607 Jacobson has drink: Kansas City *Times,* May 13, 1965.
607 "It is the most serious situation": HST to Eleanor Roosevelt, March 16, 1948, *Off the Record,* 126.
607 "It was better to do that": Ayers Diary, March 16, 1948, HSTL.
607 Joint Session speech: PP, HST, March 17, 1948, 182–86.
608 "And when he left my office": *Memoirs,* Vol. II, 161.
609 HST and Weizmann reached "understanding": Ibid.
609 "A land of milk and honey": *The New York Times,* March 21, 1948.
610 "whimsical and cynical action": Letter from Tucson Jewish Community Council, undated, White House Correspondence File, HSTL.
610 "vacillating": Letter from Democratic Council, undated, Whittier, California, White House Correspondence File, HSTL.
610 "This change can mean": Judge P. Tinley to HST, March 25, 1948, HSTL.
610 "Oh, how could you stoop": Samuel A. Sloan to HST, March 19, 1948, HSTL.
610 "Black Friday": "Two Presidents and a Haberdasher—1948."
610 "There wasn't one": Ibid.
610 Weizmann certain what HST had meant: Adler, 211.
610 Jacobson must not forget: "Two Presidents and a Haberdasher—1948."
610 "This morning I find": HST Diary, March 20, 1948, *Off the Record,* 127.
611 "the striped pants boys": HST to MJT, March 21, 1948, HSTL.
611 "Truman was in his office": Clark Clifford interview with Jonathan Daniels, October 26, 1949; Daniels interview notes, HSTL.
611 "The President's statement": Ayers Diary, March 20, 1948, HSTL.
611 "the wisest course": *The News York Times,* March 21, 1948.
611 "This gets us nowhere": Quoted in Steinberg, *The Man from Missouri,* 307.
611 "Send final draft": *Foreign Relations of the United States.* Vol. V: *The Far East, South Asia and Africa,* 645.
612 "striped pants conspirators": HST to MJT, March 21, 1948, HSTL.
612 "prejudice the character": PP, HST, March 25, 1948, 190, 192.
612 Eleanor Roosevelt resignation: Lash, 130.

SOURCE NOTES

612 "The choice for our people": Weizmann, 474.
612 "very strongly": "Two Presidents and a Haberdasher—1948."
612 "the President looked worn": Lilienthal, *Journals,* Vol. II, 320.
613 "It is a scream": HST to MJT, April 8, 1948, HSTL.
613 Gallup Poll: Gallup, *The Gallup Poll: Public Opinion 1935–71,* 727.
613 "When he [Truman] vetoed": *The New York Times,* April 4, 1948.
614 "You will be addressing all of us": Weisberger interview with Clifford.
614 "I want you to know": George C. Marshall to HST, May 8, 1948, HSTL.
614 Marshall speech: As reported in Frank McNaughton Papers, December 18, 1948, HSTL.
614 May 12, 1948, meeting: Clay, *General of the Army,* 658, 661.
615 "As I talked": Address by Clark Clifford, American Ditchley Foundation, April, 5, 1984; Clark Clifford, author's interview.
615 "This is just straight politics": Ibid.
615 "General, he is here": Ibid.
615 "I had really prepared!": Clifford, author's interview.
615 "everything this country should represent": Ibid.
616 "Behold, I have set the land": Clifford, letter to the author.
616 "No matter what the State Department": Clark Clifford interview with Jonathan Daniels, October 26, 1949, HSTL.
616 "the sharpest rebuke *ever*": Clifford, author's interview.
616 "the great one of the age": HST appointment sheet, February 18, 1947, *Off the Record,* 109.
616 "That brought the meeting": Clifford, author's interview.
617 "righteous goddamn Baptist": Clark Clifford interview with Jonathan Daniels, October 26, 1949, HSTL.
617 "didn't know his ass": Ibid.
617 "That was rough as a cob": Clifford, author's interview.
617 "I will cross that bridge": PP, HST, May 13, 1948, 253.
617 "Marshall was the greatest asset": Clifford, author's interview.
617 Lovett would have to persuade: Ibid.
617 Marshall called HST: Ibid.
618 "That is all we need": Ibid.
618 "This is very unusual": Ibid.
618 name of new country left blank: Ibid.
618 reaction of American delegation: *The New York Times,* May 16, 1948.
618 "temporary, unofficial ambassador": Adler, 212.
619 "There is a great deal to be said": Washington *Star,* May 16, 1948.
619 "The difficulty with many career": *Memoirs,* Vol. II, 165.
620 "God put you in your mother's womb": Quoted in Steinberg, 308.
620 "In my opinion": Henderson, Oral History, HSTL.
620 Marshall never spoke to Clifford again: Pogue, 377.
620 "I told him that it was": Isaacson and Thomas, *The Wise Men,* 433.
624 Crestline, Ohio: PP, HST, June 4, 1948, 284.
624 Omaha stop: Ayers Diary, June 7, 1948, HSTL.
624 "I don't give a damn": Edward McKim, Oral History, HSTL.
625 "President Truman was at his best": Omaha *Morning World-Herald,* June 8, 1948.
625 "walled-in": Krock, *Memoirs,* 242.
625 "It almost overwhelms me": PP, HST, June 6, 1948, 288.
625 "My goodness!": Ibid., June 8, 1948, 303.
626 Butte, Montana, stop: Idaho *Daily Statesman,* June 9, 1948.
626 "I am sorry I had gone to bed": New York *Sun,* June 9, 1948.
626 "down to Berkeley": Donovan, 400.
626 "They told me at a little town": HST to MJT, June 8, 1948, HSTL.
626 Carey Airport gaffe: Montana *Standard,* June 9, 1948.
626 "I have been in politics": PP, HST, June 8, 1948, 301.
626 a many-versed song: Kansas City *Star,* March 23, 1969.

626 "a spectacle of himself": Steinberg, 312.
627 Eugene, Oregon, stop: PP, HST, June 11, 1948, 329.
627 "about two acres of people": Ibid., June 14, 1948, 348.
627 "You know, this Congress": Ibid., June 10, 1948, 314.
627 "blackguarding Congress": Redding, *Inside the Democratic Party,*178.
627 telegrams to mayors: Ibid.
627 Berkeley commencement address: PP, HST, June 12, 1948, 336–40.
628 "Our policy will continue": Ibid., 340.
628 "they clung to the roofs": *Los Angeles Times,* June 15, 1948.
629 HST jabbed his forefinger: Donovan, 401.
629 June 18 return to Washington: *Time,* June 28, 1948.
629 a "gone goose": Ibid.
630 Dewey acceptance speech: *Time,* July 5, 1948.
630 "We stay in Berlin": *Forrestal Diaries,* 454–55.
630 "We stay in Berlin": Pogue, 301.
631 "we were nose to nose": Bradley and Blair, *A General's Life,* 481.
631 "had no direct role whatever": George Elsey, Oral History, HSTL.
631 "A ball game or two": HST Diary, June 18, 1948, *Off the Record,* 140.
632 "I am not a quitter": Krock, 241.
632 "You have the choice": Ickes quoted in Donovan, 389.
633 decided it was time for Eisenhower: Hartmann, *Truman and the 80th Congress,* 186.
633 Eisenhower did not want nomination: Steinberg, 309–10.
633 Jimmy Roosevelt wired: Goulden, *The Best Years, 1945–1950,* 381.
633 "a hard and possibly losing fight": Ross, 113.
634 "I am simply aghast": Lilienthal, *Journals,* Vol. II, 378–79.
634 "All right, let him go": Ayers Diary, July 6, 1948, HSTL.
634 "double-crossers all": HST Diary, July 6, 1948, *Off the Record,* 141.
634 "I don't think he would be a candidate": HST to James W. Gerard, April 27, 1948, HSTL.
635 Krock story: Krock, *Memoirs,* 242.
635 Pepper proposing Eisenhower draft: *Newsweek,* July 19, 1948.
635 "I wanted to tell you": Krock, 243.
635 "In a telephone conference": Ibid.
635 "final and complete": *Newsweek,* July 19, 1948.
635 "Truman, Harry Truman": Goldman, *The Crucial Decade—and After,* 83.
635 "no time for politics as usual": Ross, 115.
635 "None of us": Phillips, 218.
636 'We got the wrong rigs": *The New York Times,* July 12, 1948.
636 "You could cut the gloom": Barkley, *That Reminds Me,* 200.
637 Douglas wished to stay on Court: HST Diary, July 12, 1948, *Off the Record,* 141.
637 "I stuck my neck": Ayers Diary, July 13, 1948, HSTL.
637 "But if memory does not betray": Redding, 188–89.
638 If Barkley was what convention wanted: *Newsweek,* July 26, 1948.
638 Barkley gone to bed: HST Diary, July 13, 1948, *Off the Record,* 142.
638 Barkley never told HST he wanted to be VP: Ross, 119.
638 "I don't want it passed": Truman, *Harry S. Truman,* 12.
638 "Talking about the vice-presidency": Ayers Diary, July 13, 1948, HSTL.
638 "A Negro alternate from St. Louis": HST Diary, July 13, 1948, *Off the Record,* 142.
639 "sellout" to states' rights: Ross, 121.
639 "We were inherently stronger": Douglas, *In the Fullness of Time,* 137.
639 "Young man, that's just what": Goulden, 385.
639 "There are those who say": Ross, 125.
640 southern "walkout" would destroy: Hardeman and Bacon, *Rayburn: A Biography,* 337.
640 as "crackpots": HST Diary, July 14, 1948, *Off the Record,* 143.
640 "No privacy sure enough": Ibid.
640 "Hard to hear": Ibid.

641 "a very agreeable visit": Barkley, 203.
641 "an interesting and instructive evening": HST Diary, July 14, 1948, *Off the Record,* 143.
641 "hot, horrible night": Tom Evans, Oral History, HSTL.
641 "They did what you do": Elsey, author's interview.
642 "Harry Truman's a goddamn liar": Hardeman and Bacon, 338.
642 "Senator Barkley and I": PP, HST, July 15, 1948, 406.
642 "Our task is to fill": Smith, 500.
642 "Now it is time for us": PP, HST, July 15, 1948, 406.
643 "Everybody knows that I recommended": Ibid., 408.
643 "He walked out there": Clifford, author's interview.
643 "They sensed": Lerner, *Actions and Passions,* 233.
644 "Of course, it was politics": Daniels, 356.
644 "devilishly astute": Martin, *My First Fifty Years in Politics,* 178.
644 "Arrived in Washington": HST Diary, July 15, 1948, *Off the Record,* 144.
645 "to reduce us to the status": Ross, 131.
645 "the segregation of the races": Ibid.
645 "but Truman really means it": Steinberg, 315.
645 "on the basis of interest": Ross, 158.
646 "We stand against the kings": *Time,* August 2, 1948.
646 Forrestal and atomic bomb: HST to EWT, July 23, 1948, *Dear Bess,* 555.
646 "It is hot and humid": HST Diary, July 19, 1948, *Off the Record,* 145.
647 "We'll stay in Berlin": Ibid.
647 "If we wished to remain": *Memoirs,* Vol. II, 124.
647 a "very big operation": Davidson, *The Berlin Blockade,* 105.
647 "We were proud of our Air Force": Quoted in Tusa, *The Berlin Airlift,* 167.
647 "But every expert knows": Quoted in Davidson, 125.
648 "My muttonhead Secretary": HST to EWT, July 23, 1948, *Dear Bess,* 555.
648 "There is considerable political": Memorandum by James H. Rowe, Jr., Miscellaneous Historical Documents, HSTL.
648 "I am going through a terrible": HST to WC, July 10, 1948, Truman, *Letters from Father,* 110.
649 "The President greeted us rather solemnly": Lilienthal, *Journals,* Vol. II, 388–89.
650 "This is no time": Ibid., 391.
650 "If what worried the President": Ibid.
650 Truman held Forrestal: *Forrestal Diaries,* 461.
650 seemed lately unable to "take hold": Lilienthal, *Journals,* Vol. II, 386.
650 "I went down the river": HST to MJT, July 26, 1948, HSTL.
651 "No, we're not going to give": Quoted in Donovan, 411.
651 "They sure are in a stew": HST to EWT, July 23, 1948, *Dear Bess,* 66.
651 "For a number of years": Phillips, 369.
652 "a 'red herring' ": PP, HST, August 5, 1948, 433.
652 "Entirely": Ibid., August 12, 1948, 438.
652 floor of Margaret's room: HST to MJT, August 10, 1948, HSTL.
652 "Can you imagine?": Truman, *Bess W. Truman,* 329.
652 "Margaret's sitting room": HST to MJT, August 10, 1948, HSTL.
652 "old Abe's bed": Ibid.

14. FIGHTING CHANCE

653 "It will be the greatest": HST to MJT, October 5, 1948, HSTL.
654 "There were no deep-hid schemes": Ross, "How Truman Did It," *Collier's,* December 24, 1948.
655 "It's going to be tough": Ibid.
655 "I have a terrible feeling": HST Diary, September 13, 1948, in Ferrell, ed., *Off the Record,* 149.
655 "Every grade crossing": *The New Yorker,* October 9, 1948.

SOURCE NOTES

656 "I'm going to give 'em hell": *Time,* September 27, 1948.
657 Gallup Poll: Gallup, *The Gallup Poll: Public Opinion 1935–1971,* 757.
657 "My whole inclination": *Time,* September 13, 1948.
657 "Cadillac Square": Matt Connelly, Oral History, HSTL.
658 "You remember the big boom": PP, HST, September 18, 1948, 504.
659 plow the straightest furrows: Ibid., 506.
660 "You stayed at home in 1946": Ibid., 501.
660 "Understand me, when I speak": Ibid., September 20, 1948, 518.
661 "Selfish men have always": Ibid., September 21, 1948, 531.
661 "sharp speeches": Donovan, *Conflict and Crisis,* 425.
662 These "little speeches": Ross, "How Truman Did It."
662 "Oh, I wish my grandfather": PP, HST, September 21, 1948, 531.
662 "They tell me [he said at Mojave]": Ibid., September 23, 1948, 554.
663 "I'm here on a serious mission": Ibid., September 22, 1948, 544.
663 "In 1946, you know": Ibid., September 20, 1948, 512, 514.
663 "Give 'em hell": Clark Clifford, author's interview.
663 "I never gave anybody hell": *The New York Times,* December 27, 1972.
664 "It will be a picture": *The New Yorker,* October 9, 1948.
665 Los Angeles speech: PP, HST, September 24, 1948, 559.
665 "We are not quite holding our own": Tusa, *The Berlin Airlift,* 235.
665 "That's good": Ross, "How Truman Did It."
666 a "Research Division": George Elsey, Oral History, HSTL.
667 "He gives every appearance": Clifford, author's interview.
667 the "evil forces": *Time,* October 11, 1948.
668 HST never mentioned Dewey: Clifford, author's interview.
668 "If you wanted anything": *The New Yorker,* October 16, 1948.
669 "sort of rube reputation": Daniels, *The Man of Independence,* 358.
669 Description of Dewey campaign: *The New Yorker,* October 16, 1948.
669 "Tonight we enter upon a campaign": Ross, *The Loneliest Campaign,* 193.
669 "We cannot win without": Quoted in Donovan, 420.
671 "Smile, governor": Smith, *Thomas E. Dewey and His Times,* 26.
671 "You have to know Mr. Dewey well": Ross, *The Loneliest Campaign,* 32.
671 "like a man who has been": *The New Yorker,* October 16, 1948.
672 "It is written in the stars": Smith, 17.
672 carnal relations: Ibid., 34.
672 "When you're leading": Ibid., 30.
673 "We always asked them": Ross, *The Loneliest Campaign,* 166.
673 "How long is Dewey": *Life,* October 25, 1948.
673 "get down in the gutter": Quoted in Smith, 515.
673 "Isn't it harder in politics?": *New Republic,* November 1, 1948.
674 "We resurrected the president's": Sullivan, *The Bureau,* 44.
674 "The tragic fact is": *Time,* October 4, 1948.
674 "We'll have no thought police": Quoted in Smith, 508.
674 "We hit Salt Lake City": Quoted in Ross, *The Loneliest Campaign,* 207.
674 "Then we went into Texas": PP, HST, September 29, 1948, 629.
675 "He is good on the back": Quoted in Hardeman and Bacon, *Rayburn: A Biography,* 340.
675 "they'd shoot Truman": Quoted in Steinberg, 325.
676 "an eloquence close to": Daniels, 362.
676 "Our government is made up": PP, HST, September 26, 1948, 210.
676 "I am going over to Bonham": Ibid., September 27, 1948, 591.
677 "So in making their speeches": Ibid., 589.
677 "Some things are worth fighting for": Ibid., 593, 595.
677 "They came in droves": Truman, *Souvenir,* 231.
678 "I know every man, woman, and child": Hardeman and Bacon, 341.
678 "Shut the door, Beauford": Quoted in Truman, *Harry S. Truman,* 37.
678 "A great many honors": Baruch, *The Public Years,* 399.

680 "one jump ahead of the sheriff": Ross, "How Truman Did It."
681 "There is nothing like that": PP, HST, September 30, 1948, 650.
681 "Now, whatever you do": Ibid., October 1, 1948, 664.
682 "The early morning haze": Quoted in Goulden, *The Best Years 1945–1950,* 399.
682 "We made about a hundred and forty": HST to MJT, October 5, 1948, HSTL.
683 "classic unities of politics": Redding, *Inside the Democratic Party,* 202.
683 "Another hell of a day": HST Diary, September 14, 1948, *Off the Record,* 149.
684 selections from Dewey speeches: Goulden, 400.
684 HST campaign movie: Redding, 254.
685 "He paused dramatically": Barkley, *That Reminds Me,* 204.
686 "If we could only get Stalin": *Memoirs,* Vol. II, 215.
686 "every possible precaution": Ibid., 216.
686 "There is much confusion": Ayers Diary, October 6–7, 1948, HSTL.
687 "He got up and went out": Daniels, 29.
687 "If Harry Truman would just": Goulden, 414.
689 Dewey with blind drawn: Smith, 536.
689 "I grew up on a farm": PP, HST, October 11, 1948, 737.
690 If HST called Bess the Boss: Truman, *Bess W. Truman,* 330.
690 "If you don't want to go": PP, HST, October 11, 1948, 736–37.
691 Willard, Ohio, stop: Willard *Times;* Joseph Dush, author's interview; materials supplied by Harlene Staptf Palkuti.
692 "I have had the most wonderful": PP, HST, October 11, 1948, 740.
694 "I have lived a long time": Ibid., 743, 747.
694 "And there it was!": Clifford, author's interview.
694 "So I walked in": Ibid.
695 "I was with Truman": Douglas, *In the Fullness of Time,* 138.
695 "I just wonder tonight": PP, HST, October 12, 1948, 760.
695 "Now, I call on all liberals": Ibid., October 13, 1948, 774.
696 "a lot of surprised pollsters": *Time,* October 25, 1948.
696 "I think he's doing pretty well": Ross, *The Loneliest Campaign,* 215.
696 "The only way to handle Truman": Patterson, *Mr. Republican. A Biography of Robert A. Taft,* 424–25.
697 "That's the first lunatic": *Time,* October 25, 1948.
697 Boston *Post* editorial: October 27, 1948.
698 "If you're winning": Clifford, author's interview.
698 "Strain seemed to make him": Daniels, 361.
698 "He was not putting on": Elsey, author's interview, and Oral History, HSTL.
699 "For years afterward": Clifford, Oral History, HSTL.
699 "We've got them on the run": HST to MJT, October 20, 1948, HSTL.
699 "The airlift will be continued": Tusa, 245.
700 "Say you don't look so good!": PP, HST, October 23, 1948, 839.
700 "The newspapers had convinced them": Douglas, 138.
700 attack on Dewey: Ross, *The Loneliest Campaign,* 235.
700 "An element of desperation": Clifford, author's interview.
701 "They have scattered reckless abuse": Smith, 536.
701 "The confetti, ticker-tape": *The New York Times,* October 29, 1948.
702 "There is one place": Quoted in Ross, *The Loneliest Campaign,* 237.
702 "Such a weak and vacillating": Lash, *Eleanor: The Years Alone,* 153.
702 "There never has been a campaign": *The New York Times,* November 1, 1948.
702 "I became President": PP, HST, October 30, 1948, 934.
704 "pullet poll": *Life,* November 15, 1948.
704 "Were it not for all": Ayers Diary, November 1, 1948, HSTL.
706 "We all, of course, stayed awake": Gerard McAnn, author's interview.
706 Maloney and his men: Smith, 40.
706 "We waited and waited": Sue Gentry, author's interview.
706 "We *couldn't* believe it": Ibid.
706 "What a night": Truman, *Souvenir,* 242.

707 "And all of a sudden": Jim Rowley, author's interview.
708 "his first case of nerves": Letter from Jerome K. Walsh to Morris J. Ernst, undated, HSTL.
708 "He just seemed the same old": Lyman Field, author's interview.
708 "He displayed neither tension": Letter from Jerome K. Walsh to Morris J. Ernst, undated, HSTL.
709 "Thank you, thank you": *Time,* November 8, 1948.
710 Bankhead telegram: Goulden, 421.
711 "I think the mistake was": Clifford, author's interview.
711 "shook the bones": Baltimore *Sun,* November 7, 1948.
712 "The farm vote switched": Thomas Dewey to Henry Luce, undated, L. C.
712 "You've got to give the little man": Vandenberg, *Private Papers,* 460.
712 Taft comment: Steinberg, 332.
712 Republican Policy Committee Report: December 17, 1948, HSTL.
713 "Labor Did It": Ross, *The Loneliest Campaign,* 255.
713 "The bear got us": Smith, 543.
714 "Far from costing Dewey": Quoted in Phillips, 250–51.
714 "I couldn't have been more wrong": *Life,* November 15, 1948.
715 "What's the matter with that fellow": *The New York Times,* November 28, 1948.
715 "I kept reading": Goldman, *The Crucial Decade,* 87.
715 "But when voting time came": Ibid.
715 "the common man's man": *Life,* November 15, 1948.
715 "It seemed to have been": Donovan, 438.
715 "There was personal humiliation": *New Republic,* November 15, 1948.
716 "There has been a danger": Ayers Diary, November 4, 1948, HSTL.
716 Luce memo: November 11, 1948, *Time-Warner* archives.
716 "His personality was against him": Henry Luce memorandum, November 5, 1948, Ibid.
716 "I think the press": T. S. Matthews memorandum to Henry Luce, November 4, 1948, Ibid.
716 "Of course, we did not intentionally": J. J. Thorndike, Jr., memorandum to Henry Luce, November 5, 1948, Ibid.
717 90 percent of the credit: Hardeman and Bacon, 342.
717 "You have put over": George C. Marshall to HST, November 4, 1948, HSTL.
717 "I think that Harry Truman grew": Ross, "How Truman Did It."
717 "I think Dewey's whole campaign": Clifford, author's interview.
719 "no desire to crow": HST to the Washington *Post,* November 6, 1948, HSTL.

PART FIVE

15. IRON MAN

723 "Clearly he was conscious": Washington *Evening Star,* January 20, 1949.
725 "his day of days": Truman, *Souvenir, 255.*
725 *"It is the President's desire":* Seale, *The President's House,* Vol. II, 1027.
726 "I have the job": Washington *Post,* January 20, 1949; *Time,* January 31, 1949.
726 State of the Union message: PP, HST, January 5, 1949, 1.
727 H. V. Kaltenborn impersonation: Ibid., January 19, 1949, 110.
727 "I was not in any way elated": Ibid.
727 "Wonderful, wonderful": Washington *Post,* January 21, 1949.
728 Battery D reunion: Washington *Evening Star,* January 20, 1949.
728 prayer service: Washington *Post,* January 21, 1949.
729 inaugural address: PP, HST, January 20, 1949, 112–16.
729 "How strange": Washington *Evening Star,* January 20, 1949.
732 "The clear sunlight": *The New York Times,* January 21, 1949.
732 "At the reviewing stand": J. B. West, author's interview.
733 "There never was a country": Payne, *Report on America,* p. 3.

733 "The parade was the most fun": Lilienthal, *Journals,* Vol. II, 448.
733 "the fellow who was having": Washington *Post,* January 22, 1949.
734 "It can almost be stated": Bohlen, *Witness to History,* 284.
734 "fifty percent better": Lilienthal, *Journals,* Vol. II, 527.
735 "He looks more relaxed": Ibid., 463–64.
736 "He was *great* down in Key West!": James Rowley, Jr., author's interview.
736 "The President is as close to being": *Time,* May 16, 1949.
736 "He won't take hold": Lilienthal, *Journals,* Vol. II, 386.
737 "No commentator": *Time,* March 7, 1949.
737 HST fair with Forrestal: *Forrestal Diaries,* 551.
737 "The best boss I have ever known": Truman, *Bess W. Truman,* 345.
738 "a man who, while he reflects": *Forrestal Diaries,* 529.
738 "the mess we are in": *Eisenhower Diaries,* 152–53.
738 his "baffled" look: Washington *Post,* January 21, 1949.
738 Forrestal was insane: Pearson, *Diaries, 1949–1959,* 42.
739 "a very sick man": Krock, *Memoirs,* 253–57.
739 Secret Service Report: March 31, 1949, HSTL.
739 "out of his mind": Lilienthal, *Journals,* Vol. II, 506.
740 Bess was "terribly shaken": Truman, *Bess W. Truman,* 346.
741 25,000 Pentagon employees: *Time,* June 6, 1949.
742 "Unwittingly": Bradley and Blair, *A General's Life,* 503.
742 "in high good humor": *Time,* April 25, 1949.
742 Cardinal Spellman: Goldman, *The Crucial Decade—and After,* 130–31.
742 "Hysteria finally died down": PP, HST, June 16, 1949, 294.
743 "The military situation": Acheson, *Present at the Creation,* 305.
743 morning press conference: PP, HST, August 4, 1949, 408.
743 "The unfortunate but inescapable": Acheson, 303.
744 "his general's stars": *Time,* August 22, 1949.
745 "I do these people a courtesy": Dunar, *The Truman Scandals and the Politics of Morality,* 70.
745 "an expression of friendship": *Time,* September 12, 1949.
746 Was it true, asked McCarthy: Ibid.
746 "Ross and I": Ayers Diary, August 12, 1949, HSTL.
746 "After all I am": Abel, *The Truman Scandals,* 42–43.
746 "I think that Mr. Truman": Barkley, *That Reminds Me,* 212.
747 When Vaughan offered to resign: Dunar, 64.
747 "a whole box of trouble": Lilienthal, *Journals,* Vol. II, 569.
747 "as if I frequently found him": Ibid.
748 "The President was reading a copy": Ibid., 570–71.
748 "I believe the American people": PP, HST, September 23, 1949, 485.
749 "We keep saying": Lilienthal, *Journals,* Vol. II, 577.
749 "this grim thing": Ibid., 584.
750 "We can never tell": HST to EWT, June 29, 1949, in Ferrell, ed., *Off the Record,* 158.
750 "Never in my wildest dreams": HST to EN, September 8, 1949, ibid., 163–64.
750 rats in the White House: Floyd Boring and Rex Scouten, author's interviews.
750 "Very discreet": West, with Kotz, *Upstairs at the White House,* 111.
751 "Had dinner by myself": HST Diary, November 1, 1949, *Off the Record,* 168–69.
752 "a fine man": HST to Jonathan Daniels, February 26, 1950, unsent, ibid., 174.
752 "It was a great thing": Dean Acheson, Oral History, HSTL.
753 Acheson descriptions: *Time,* February 28, 1949; *The New Yorker,* November 12 and 19, 1949; *The New York Times,* October 13, 1971; Clark Clifford and George Elsey, author's interviews.
753 "You owe it to Truman": Isaacson and Thomas, *The Wise Men,* 547.
753 "a peculiar organization": HST to David H. Morgan, January 28, 1952, *Off the Record,* 235.
754 "At lunch at the Capitol": Acheson, 107.
754 "You know all of us": HST to EN, September 24, 1950, *Off the Record,* 194.

SOURCE NOTES

754 "deeply loving and tender nature": Sevareid, *Conversations with Eric Sevareid,* 73.
755 "Well, this is the kind of person": Ibid.
755 "It was good of you to see us off": HST to Dean Acheson, November 28, 1949, HSTL.
755 "And then he was so fair": Sevareid, 74.
755 "He was not afraid of the competition": Acheson, 732–33.
755 "not pretending to be better": McLellan, *Dean Acheson,* 19.
756 "Today you hear much talk": Ibid., 173–74.
756 "Acheson is a gentleman": Lilienthal, *Journals,* Vol. II, 565.
757 "I told Kennan": McLellan, 176.
758 "How can you persuade": Isaacson and Thomas, 487.
758 "The day will come": *Time,* January 23, 1950.
758 "Today, by the grace of God": PP, HST, January 4, 1950, 3.
759 "I should like to make it clear": Acheson, 360.
760 "I think anyone who has known": Ibid.
760 "This newspaper has felt": New York *Herald-Tribune,* January 27, 1950.
760 "wonderful about it": Acheson, 360.
760 "I look at that fellow": Quoted in Goldman, 125.
761 "blow them off the face of the earth": Lilienthal, *Journals,* Vol. II, 585.
762 "Like a patient": *Time,* January 30, 1950.
762 an "atmosphere of excitement": Lilienthal, *Journals,* Vol. II, 628–29.
762 "eloquently and forcefully": Acheson, 349.
762 "We must protect the President": Lilienthal, *Journals,* Vol. II, 630.
763 he felt he must express: Ibid., 632.
763 "Can the Russians?": Quoted in Donovan, *Tumultuous Years,* 156.
763 "It is part of my responsibility": PP, HST, January 31, 1950, 138.
763 "I hope I was wrong": Lilienthal, *Journals,* Vol. II, 633–34.
763 "General annihiliation beckons": Quoted in Goldman, 137.
764 "How much are we going": Weinstein, *Perjury: The Hiss-Chambers Case,* 507.
765 "The air was so charged": Block, *The Herblock Book,* 144.
765 205 "known communists": Reeves, *Life and Times of Joe McCarthy,* 224, 237.
766 "When this pompous diplomat": Bernstein and Matusow, eds., *The Truman Administration,* 407.
766 "I will not turn my back": Washington *Post,* June 25, 1950.
766 "keep talking and if one case": Reeves, 263.
766 "top Russian espionage agent": *Time,* April 3, 1950.
767 "In an age of atomic energy": Krock, *In the Nation: 1932–1966,* 145–46.
767 "One of the happiest sessions": Lilienthal, *Journals,* Vol. II, 635.
768 "You see everybody": Truman, *Bess W. Truman,* 351.
768 "What has made me so jittery": Ibid.
768 "a ballyhoo artist": Donovan, 166.
768 plunged to 37 percent: *Time,* April 24, 1950.
768 Little White House press conference: PP, HST, March 30, 1950, 232–38.
769 Federal Bar Association speech: Ibid, April 24, 1950, 269.
769 "I think our friend": Quoted in Donovan, 170.
770 Maragaret Chase Smith: Acheson, 365.
770 the "lure in power": HST Diary, April 16, 1950, *Off the Record,* 177.
770 "I am not a candidate": Ibid.
771 NSC-68: Acheson, 374.
772 "bludgeon the mass mind": Ibid.
773 "with us for a long, long time": PP, HST, May 9, 1950, 335.
773 "a grand visit": HST to Stanley Woodward, June 24, 1950, *Off the Record,* 184.
774 "We would not build": PP, HST, June 24, 1950.
774 nation's worst air disaster: *The New York Times,* June 25, 1950.
774 "There are lots of places": St. Louis *Post-Dispatch,* June 25, 1950.
775 Dean Acheson call: *Memoirs,* Vol. II, 332.
775 "My first reaction": Ibid.
776 "It would appear": *Memoirs,* Vol. II, 334.

SOURCE NOTES

776   "Dad took it": Truman, *Souvenir,* 275.
776   departure so swift: *Memoirs,* Vol. II, 332.
776   Bess looking as she had the night FDR died: *The New York Times,* June 26, 1950.
776   "By God, I am going to": Quoted in Donovan, 197.
776   "I remembered how": *Memoirs,* Vol. II, 332–33.
777   Rusk had seen no likelihood of war: Rusk, *As I Saw It,* 161.
777   Blair House meeting: *Memoirs,* Vol. II, 333.
777   dinner meeting: Smith, "Why We Went to War in Korea," *Saturday Evening Post,* November 11, 1950.
778   a "darkening report": Acheson, 406.
778   "a dagger pointed at the heart": Rusk, 162.
778   "We must draw the line": Bradley and Blair, 534–35.
778   "Underlying these discussions": Ibid., 535.
778   "He pulled all the conferees together": *The New York Times,* June 28, 1950.
778   "I thought we were still holding": *Memoirs,* Vol. II, 335.
779   "the complete, almost unspoken": Ibid., 334.
779   "so as not to give him too much": Bradley and Blair, 536.
779   "It was our idea": Donovan, 199.
779   "as Hermann Goering": Jenkins, *Truman,* 164.
779   "Our estimate is that a complete collapse": *Memoirs,* Vol. II, 337.
780   adding "not yet": Department of State Memorandum for the Secretary, June 30, 1950, HSTL.
780   "We had no war plan": Bradley and Blair, 539.
780   "Everything I have done": Phillips, *The Truman Presidency,* 289.
780   "Too little, too late": Washington *Post,* June 27, 1950.
780   "The attack upon Korea": PP, HST, June 27, 1950, 492.
781   "Although the President": Alsop, "Why Has Washington Gone Crazy?", *Saturday Evening Post,* July 29, 1950.
781   "These are days": Washington *Post,* June 28, 1950.
781   "We'll have a dozen Koreas": *Eisenhower Diaries,* 175.
781   "You may be a whiskey guzzling poker playing": Harry Abel to HST, June 27, 1950, HSTL.
782   "I have lived and worked": *Time,* July 10, 1950.
782   "We are not at war": PP, HST, June 29, 1950, 504.
782   "The only assurance for holding": MacArthur, *Reminiscences,* 334.
783   "Must be careful not to cause": HST Diary, June 30, 1950, *Off the Record,* 185.
783   "Now, your job as President": Sevareid, 74.
783   "Memo to Dean Acheson": Acheson, 415.

16. COMMANDER IN CHIEF

784   "There was *nothing* passive": Elsey, "Memoir: Some White House Recollections, 1942–1953," *Diplomatic History,* Summer 1988.
785   "This is the Greece": Quoted in Phillips, *The Truman Presidency,* 297.
786   "walk with the weary man's": *Time,* July 10, 1950.
786   Bradley meeting with HST: *Time,* August 21, 1950.
787   "The size of the attack": PP, HST, July 19, 1950, 538.
787   as if a few troops of Boy Scouts: Ridgway, *The Korean War,* 17.
787   "Guys, sweat soaked": Knox, *The Korean War, Pusan to Chosin,* 71.
787   "What a place to die": New York *Herald-Tribune,* July 6, 1950.
789   Acheson, however, disagreed: Acheson, *Present at the Creation,* 414.
789   "Later when Robert Taft": Heller, *The Truman White House,* 13.
789   HST said he would "back out": *Memoirs,* Vol. II, 340.
790   her father's anguish: Truman, *Bess W. Truman,* 357.
791   telegrams and letters to White House: White House Correspondence File, HSTL.
791   "The influence of Louis Johnson": Joseph Alsop, author's interview.
791   July 14 meeting: Acheson, 421.

SOURCE NOTES

791   July 19 message to Congress: PP, HST, July 19, 1950, 527–37.
792   press conference: Ibid., July 27, 1950, 560–64.
792   "He would have saved himself": Bradley and Blair, *A General's Life*, 542.
792   "an inordinate egotistical desire": HST Diary, September 14, 1950, in Ferrell, ed., *Off the Record*, 192.
792   a "pathological condition": Bradley and Blair, 542.
793   HST confiding Harriman's story: Ayers Diary, July 3, 1950, HSTL.
793   "A most interesting morning": HST Diary, September 14, 1950, *Off the Record*, 192.
793   "Mr. Prima Donna": HST Diary, June 17, 1945, ibid., 47.
793   "little regard or respect": Ayers Diary, July 1, 1950, HSTL.
793   Dulles advised HST: Ibid.
793   HST's little regard for generals: HST memorandum, April 24, 1954, *Off the Record*, 303.
793   "likes horses with blinders on": Miller, *Plain Speaking*, 220.
794   "fluid but improving": Ayers Diary, August 12, 1950, HSTL.
794   HST's uppermost concern: *Memoirs*, Vol. II, 351.
795   "catch him alone": Quoted in Heller, 14.
795   MacArthur assured HST: *Memoirs*, Vol. II, 351.
795   "with all his dramatic eloquence": Bradley and Blair, 546.
795   the riskiest military proposal: Ibid., 544.
795   "I made it clear to the President": Quoted in Heller, 14.
796   "as fast as you can": Bradley and Blair, 546.
796   "This means not the usual": Osborne, *Life* and *Time*, August 21, 1950.
796   "the wildest kind": Bradley and Blair, 556.
796   "the gravest misgivings": Ibid., 547.
797   "Nothing could be more fallacious": Manchester, *American Caesar*, 568.
797   "his lips white": Bradley and Blair, 551.
797   rank insubordination: Ibid.
797   "the height of arrogance": Ibid.
797   HST rejects idea of relieving MacArthur: *Memoirs*, Vol. II, 355–56.
797   HST asks Johnson to have MacArthur's statement withdrawn: Bradley and Blair, 551.
797   "The JCS inclined toward postponing": Ibid., 547.
797   "a failure could be a national": Ibid., 545.
797   "It was a daring strategic conception": *Memoirs*, Vol. II, 358.
798   "Hell and high water": HST to EWT, September 7, 1950, *Off the Record*, 189.
798   "I'll do it": Ibid.
798   "Can you think of anyone?": Ibid.
798   Johnson told he must quit: HST Diary, September 14, 1950, ibid., 193.
799   a "military miracle": Ridgway, 44.
799   "I salute you all": Quoted in Phillips, 313.
799   "Troops could not be expected": Acheson, 445.
799   to "feel unhampered": Ridgway, 45.
799   "an almost superstitious awe": Ibid., 61.
799   warnings a bluff: Spanier, *The Truman-MacArthur Controversy and the Korean War*, 87.
800   "and I did not feel": *Memoirs*, Vol. II, 368.
800   "the perfect answer": Wiltz, "Truman and MacArthur: The Wake Island Meeting," *Military Affairs*, December 1978.
800   "good election year stuff": Donovan, *Tumultuous Years*, 284.
801   "While General MacArthur": Acheson, 456.
801   "I've a whale of a job": HST to Nellie Noland, October 13, 1950, *Off the Record*, 196.
801   "Two men can sometimes learn": *Time*, October 23, 1950.
801   "I don't care what they say": Ibid.
801   MacArthur had arrived the night before: Ibid.
802   Harriman exchange with MacArthur: Bradley and Blair, 573.
802   "grave responsibility": Ibid.
802   MacArthur greeting: New York *Herald-Tribune*, October 15, 1950.

SOURCE NOTES

802 "I have been worried": Quoted in Donovan, 285.
803 MacArthur assured him victory was won: *Memoirs,* Vol. II, 365.
803 "seemed genuinely pleased": Ibid.
803 "I had been warned": MacArthur, *Reminiscences,* 361.
803 Vernice Anderson incident: Jessup, "Research Note/The Record of Wake Island—A Correction," *The Journal of American History,* March 1981.
804 when MacArthur received transcript: Bradley and Blair, 575.
804 "He was the most persuasive fellow": Quoted in Manchester, 592.
804 "the formal resistance": *Substance of Statements Made at Wake Island Conference on October 15, 1950,* compiled by General Omar Bradley, declassified, 1, HSTL.
805 By January: Ibid.
805 Dean Rusk concerned: Rusk, *As I Saw It,* 169.
805 "Hell no!": Ibid.
805 "They are the happiest": *Foreign Relations of the United States, 1950.* Vol. VII: *Korea,* 953.
805 the French couldn't "clean it up": *Substance of Statements Made at Wake Island Conference,* 17.
805 MacArthur declined lunch: Ibid.
806 "Whether intended or not": Bradley and Blair, 576.
806 "The communiqué should be submitted": *Substance of Statements Made at Wake Island Conference,* 23.
806 MacArthur asked the President: MacArthur, *Reminiscences,* 362.
806 "Eisenhower doesn't know the first thing": Ibid., 363.
806 "the very complete unanimity of view": PP, HST, October 15, 1950, 672.
806 "his vision, his judgment": Donovan, 288.
806 a "glorious new page": PP, HST, October 17, 1950, 674.
807 "On this one": Rusk, 169.
807 "Come up to Pyongyang": *Newsweek,* October 23, 1950.
808 "Goodbye, sir": *Time,* October 23, 1950.
808 "I like them more": Truman, *Letters from Father,* 97.
808 "He would treat us": Rex Scouten, author's interview.
808 Floyd Boring's wife: Floyd Boring, author's interview.
809 "The house was so quiet": West, with Kotz, *Upstairs at the White House,* 116.
809 "I'd come out more or less": Boring, author's interview.
809 mistaken for divinity students: *Life:* November 13, 1950.
809 assassination attempt: Boring, author's interview; Scouten, author's interview; *Life,* November 13, 1950; *The New York Times,* November 2, 1950; *Time,* November 12, 1950; *Whistle Stop,* Fall 1979.
811 "Why, of course": *Time,* November 12, 1950.
811 "It is important": PP, HST, November 1, 1950, 693.
812 "But Truman was . . . just a symbol": Kansas City *Times,* September 11, 1979.
812 "A President has to expect": *The New York Times,* November 2, 1950.
812 HST insisted he was in no danger: PP, HST, November 2, 1950, 696.
812 so "unnecessary": HST to Dean Acheson, November 2, 1950, HSTL.
813 "[Leaving the airport]": HST Diary, November 5, 1950, *Off the Record,* 198.
813 "really a prisoner now": HST to EN, November 17, 1950, ibid.
813 "The Korean death trap": Donovan, 295.
813 "All the piety": Ibid., 297.
814 Bess had seldom seen HST so downhearted: Truman, *Bess W. Truman,* 363–64.
814 "Some Republicans interpret": PP, HST, November 16, 1950, 714.
815 "Then there were those": Ridgway, 61.
815 "If this operation is successful": Manchester, 606.
815 "a terrible message": Ibid., 608.
815 "We've got a terrific": Hersey, *Aspects of the Presidency,* 27.
815 "The Chinese have come in": Ibid.
815 "alone and inescapably": Ibid., 28.
816 seven thousand letters: Heller, 47.

816   "We can blame the liars": Ibid., 30.
816   "His mouth drew tight": Ibid., 28.
816   "We have got to meet this thing": Ibid., 30.
816   "We face an entirely new war": Quoted in Acheson, 469.
817   November 28, 1950, meeting: Ibid., 469, 471.
817   "There was no doubt": *Memoirs,* Vol. II, 378.
817   "We can't defeat the Chinese": Acheson, 471.
818   the "imperative step": Ibid.
818   "The threat of a larger war": Bradley and Blair, 599.
818   "hordes of Chinese Reds": Washington *Star,* November 28, 1950.
818   "A lot of hard work": *Memoirs,* Vol. II, 388.
818   "Remember, photographers are": Truman, *Letters from Father,* 99.
819   "He 'used' the press": Phillips, *The New York Times,* December 31, 1972.
819   "a fat no good can of lard": HST to MJT, July 25, 1947, *Off the Record,* 115.
819   "the Sop Sisters": HST to EWT, June 11, 1950, Ibid., 179 and 41, note.
819   "The prostitutes of the mind": Poen, *Strictly Personal and Confidential,* 24.
819   "You might tell the gentleman": HST to Joseph J. McGee, November 22, 1950, *Off the Record,* 199.
820   November 30, 1950, press conference: PP, HST, 724–728.
821   "No, it doesn't mean": Ibid., 727.
822   the "wildest days" ever: Ayers Diary, November 30, 1950, HSTL.
822   "the use of any weapon": PP, HST, November 30, 1950, 727.
823   HST ill-advised: Bradley and Blair, 604.
823   in a crucial few days: Acheson, 466.
823   "I have the unhappy conviction": Ibid.
823   "well remember": Ridgway, 61.
823   "someone expressed what everyone": Acheson, 475.
823   "You can relieve any commander": Ridgway, 62.
824   Rusk proposes relieving MacArthur: Acheson, 476.
824   "I should have relieved": *Memoirs,* Vol. II, 384.
824   "We must get him out": HST Diary, December 2, 1950, *Off the Record,* 202.
825   "It looks very bad": Ibid.
825   "Mr. President, the Chinese": Rusk, 170.
825   "I've had conference after conference": HST Diary, December 9, 1950, *Off the Record,* 204.
825   "[The President] thought that if": Quoted in Donovan, 317.
825   He would not use the bomb: Ibid., 318.
826   "Charlie seemed in good form": Ayers Diary, December 5, 1950, HSTL.
826   Death of Charlie Ross: Washington *Post,* December 6, 1950.
826   "The friend of my youth": PP, HST, December 5, 1950, 737.
827   "Ah, hell": Truman, *Harry S. Truman,* 545–46.
827   previous Ross heart attacks: Washington *Post,* December 6, 1950.
827   HST keeps Ross death from Margaret: Truman, *Harry S. Truman,* 546.
827   "Afterward, Dad was effusive": Truman, *Bess W. Truman,* 366.
827   "really pretty bad that night": John Hersey, author's interview.
827   Hume review: Washington *Post,* December 6, 1950.
828   "That's exactly what I want": Traubel, *St. Louis Woman,* 211.
828   "longhand spasm": HST to Dean Acheson, April 8, 1957, HSTL.
828   "Charlie Ross would *never* have": Elsey, author's interview.
829   "Mr. Hume: I've just read": HST to Paul Hume, December 7, 1950.
829   "In the first place": *Time,* December 18, 1950.
829   To Margaret he said: Truman, *Harry S. Truman,* 547.
829   "When he would write": Elsey, Oral History, HSTL.
830   "a propaganda machine": *Time,* September 18, 1950.
830   "I can only say": *Time,* December 18, 1950.
830   letters and telegrams to White House: General Correspondence File, HSTL.
831   letter from the Bannings: HSTL.

SOURCE NOTES

831 "The Eighth Army is yours": Ridgway, 83.
831 "never uttered wiser words": Acheson, 512.
831 "brilliant, driving": Bradley and Blair, 608.
832 "The troops are tired": Ibid., 619.
832 "Under the extraordinary": Quoted in Donovan, 346.
832 to recognize the "state of war": Manchester, *The Glory and the Dream,* 550.
832 atomic bombs: Schaller, *Douglas MacArthur,* 225.
832 "go down that trail": Rusk, 170.
833 "infinite patience": Acheson, 515.
833 "steps which might in themselves": *Memoirs,* Vol. II, 438, 436.
833 "We were at our lowest": Bradley and Blair, 620.
833 "Eighth Army in good shape": Ibid., 623.
834 "rolling forward": Ridgway, *The Korean War,* 106.
834 to look "beyond MacArthur": Bradley and Blair, 623.
834 Ridgway thought HST a great and courageous man: Ridgway, author's interview.
834 "mainly a prima donna": Bradley and Blair, 623.
834 "While General MacArthur was fighting": Acheson, 517.
835 "the really terrifying strength": Ridgway, 111.
835 "tired and depressed: Goulden, *Korea,* 453.
835 "just ordered a resumption": Ridgway, 109.
835 "not only his nerves": MacArthur, *Reminiscences,* 393.
836 "snapped his brilliant": Bradley and Blair, 626.
836 "The enemy, therefore": MacArthur, 388.
836 his "pronunciamento": Acheson, *The Korean War,* 101.
836 "unforgiveable and irretrievable act": Bradley and Blair, 627.
836 "Whom the gods would destroy": Acheson, *Korean War,* 100.
836 "I couldn't send a message": Truman, *Harry S. Truman,* 559.
837 "This was a most extraordinary": *Memoirs,* Vol. II, 441–42.
837 "disbelief with controlled fury": Acheson, *Korean War,* 102.
837 "Gallup Poll: *The Gallup Poll: Public Opinion 1935–1971,* 970.
838 "If you are going to get on": *Memoirs,* Vol. II, 443–45.
838 "What are we in Korea for": Martin, *My First Fifty Years in Politics,* 203.
839 "Mr. President, this man is not": Roger Tubby Diary, April 5, 1951.
839 "I did not know": Bradley and Blair, 629.
839 "The situation could be resolved": Acheson, *Korean War,* 104.
839 "If you relieve MacArthur": *Memoirs,* Vol. II, 447.
839 "I don't express any opinion": HST Diary, April 5, 1951, *Off the Record,* 211.
839 "at the apex of a situation": MacArthur, 394.
839 "The wind died down": Martin, 207.
840 because they knew the kind of abuse: Bradley and Blair, 633.
840 MacArthur firing would provoke: Ibid.
840 "There was no question": Phillips, 346–47.
840 He told Bradley to prepare: *Memoirs,* Vol. II, 448.
841 Speculation about MacArthur: Washington *Post,* April 10, 1951.
841 "So you won't have to read about it": Tubby Diary, April 12, 1951.
842 a supposed "major resignation": Bradley and Blair, 636.
842 "There *was* a degree of panic": Elsey, author's interview.
843 "He's not going to be allowed": Phillips, 343.
843 "Discussed the situation": HST Diary, April, 9, 1951, *Off the Record,* 211.
843 "Well, the little man": Rusk, 172.
843 would have retired "without difficulty": Schaller, 239.
843 HST's "mental instability": Donovan, 360; Goulden, 495.
844 "Our only choice": Washington *Post,* April 12, 1951.
844 Tom Connally reminded: Ibid.
845 Chicago *Tribune* editorial: April 12, 1951.
845 "This is the biggest windfall": Washington *Post,* April 18, 1951.
845 "In the days ahead": Letter from W. O. Douglas to HST, April 11, 1951, HSTL.

SOURCE NOTES

845 "It makes not the slightest": The President vs. the General," Sermon by Dr. Duncan E. Littlefield, April 15, 1951, Fountain Street Baptist Church, Grand Rapids, Michigan, HSTL.
846 "The most obvious fact": New York *Herald-Tribune*, April 13, 1951.
847 "bourbon and Benedictine": St. Louis *Post-Dispatch*, April 14, 1951.
848 Gallup Poll: Goldman, *The Crucial Decade*, 203.
848 HST booed at Griffith Stadium: Washington *Post*, April 21, 1951.
848 April 11, 1951, broadcast: PP, HST, April 11, 1951, 223–27.
849 "The only politics I have": *Time*, April 30, 1951.
849 "I was sorry to have to reach": HST to Eisenhower, April 13, 1951, HSTL.
849 mock "Schedule for Welcoming...": HSTL.
850 "I address you": New York *Herald-Tribune*, April 20, 1951.
851 "When I joined the Army": MacArthur, 405.
851 "The hopes and dreams": Quoted in Manchester, 661.
852 "We heard God speak": Ibid.
852 "I honestly felt that if the speech": Truman, *Harry S. Truman*, 563.
852 "a bunch of damn bullshit": Quoted in Miller, *Plain Speaking*, 337.
853 "After I looked at that wreckage": *Time*, May 14, 1951.
853 "a very distressing necessity": Ibid.
855 "Having made this courageous decision": Bradley and Blair, 637.
855 "Courage didn't have anything": Quoted in Phillips, 350.
855 "Truman's conflict with MacArthur": Rusk, 172.
855 MacArthur to Samuel Eliot Morison: Morison, *The Oxford History of the American People*, 1072.
856 May 18 dinner: PP, HST, May 18, 1951, 292–93.
856 Tullahoma, Tennessee, speech: Ibid., June 25, 1951, 357–63.

17. FINAL DAYS

857 "I have tried to give it": PP, HST, January 15, 1953, 1202.
857 "I walk two miles": HST Diary, January 3, 1952, in Ferrell, ed., *Off the Record*, 226.
858 "Mr. President, this is my first": PP, HST, July 12, 1951, 387.
858 HST served bowl of milk toast: Tubby Diary, May 21, 1951.
858 "You constantly tell me to relax": Ibid., April 13, 1952.
859 a framed verse: Hersey, *Aspects of the Presidency*, 108.
859 it was all worth the effort: Tubby Diary, October 15, 1951.
860 "I know what a soldier goes through": PP, HST, January 15, 1953, 1200.
860 Sergeant John Rice: *The New York Times*, August 29, 1951.
860 "mysterious, powerful" conspiracy: Reeves, *The Life and Times of Joe McCarthy*, 372.
861 a "pithy and bitter" summary: Hersey, 137–38.
861 "Three pungent comments": Ibid.
862 HST announces Marshall stepping down: PP, HST, September 12, 1951, 516.
862 Hassett would bring him funny items: Tubby Diary, June 24, 1951.
862 Hassett an alcoholic: Ibid., September 18, 1951.
862 the "chiselers" within: Ibid., early June, 1951.
862 "He tended to live": George Elsey, author's interview.
864 "an overeducated S.O.B.": Douglas, *In the Fullness of Time*, 222.
864 he had "gone too far": Ibid., 223.
864 "real crooks and influence peddlers": Ibid.
864 "You have been loyal to friends": Ibid., 224.
864 "You bastards": Quoted in Goldman, *The Crucial Decade—and After*, 196.
865 "With staggering impact": Ibid., 198–99.
865 HST and Army football scandal: Tubby Diary, August 3 and 8, 1951.
866 "I did nothing improper": Douglas, 224.
866 He liked people: Tubby Diary, August 3, 1951.
866 "He was dressed in flashy": Ibid., September 13, 1951.
866 "Ah, me. I wonder": Ibid., early June, 1951.

866 like Warren G. Harding: Ibid., September 13, 1951.
866 "Poker, poker": Ibid., April 2, 1951.
867 "Truman has to take strong action": Ibid., early June, 1951.
867 "He does not like to dwell": Ibid., October 15, 1951.
867 Boyle background: Kansas City *Star,* August 31, 1951.
868 "I like people who can": HST to MT, December 3, 1944, Truman, *Letters from Father,* 60.
868 Charles Binnagio: *The New York Times,* April 7, 1950; *Life,* April 17, 1950.
869 "So Boyle is not only stupid": Tubby Diary, early June, 1951.
869 "It's all right": Ibid.
869 "I have the utmost confidence": PP, HST, August 9, 1951, 454.
869 Murphy memorandum: Charles S. Murphy to HST, August 9, 1951, HSTL.
870 Gabrielson revelations: *Time,* October 15, 1951.
871 Elsey report: Dunar, *The Truman Scandals,* 128.
871 "Let's say *continue*": PP, HST, December 13, 1951, 641.
872 "Boss, you're going to have to run": Tubby Diary, October 15, 1951.
872 "Once I'm outa the White House": Ibid.
873 Gallup Poll: *The Gallup Poll: Public Opinion 1935–71,* 1032.
874 "From that day forward": Tubby Diary, January 16, 1952.
874 "Dealing with Communist Governments": HST, private longhand note, January 27, 1952, HSTL.
874 Churchill trip to Washington: Gilbert, *Winston Churchill, Never Despair,* 675.
874 "What Churchill did was great": Acheson, *Present at the Creation,* 595.
874 Churchill acknowledged American nuclear power: Tubby Diary, January 16, 1952.
874 HST's "great decision": Gilbert, 676.
874 "The last time you and I sat": This often repeated tribute appears to have been recorded by Joe Short, who was on board the *Williamsburg.* It is paraphrased in Roger Tubby's diary and would later appear in Margaret Truman Daniel's book about her father and in several obituaries at the time of Truman's death.
875 "the great white jail": HST to EWT, September 13, 1946, *Dear Bess,* 536.
875 Hersey tour of White House: Hersey, 88.
876 "It is the President's desire": Winslow Diary, January 14, 1949, OCWH (Office of the Curator, White House).
874 Congressional Commission established: Seale, *The President's House,* Vol. II, 1029.
877 "The character and extent": *The White House Report of the Commission of Public Buildings,* 91.
877 "The decision between these plans": Ibid., 48.
877 Rabaut argued for dismantling: *Renovation Commission Hearing Minutes,* July 19, 1949, HSTL.
878 "They took the insides all out": HST Diary, March 2, 1952, *Off the Record,* 243.
878 for proper underpinning: Seale, Vol. II, 1034.
879 "faithful reproductions": *The White House Report of the Commission of Public Buildings,* 93.
880 "The President has authorized": Seale, Vol. II, 1039.
881 description of bomb shelter: Tubby Diary, July 26, 1951.
881 for "morale reasons": Ibid.
881 False radar report: Ibid.
881 "He considered it *his* project": Rex Scouten, author's interview.
882 "It is absolutely essential": HST to Les Larson, June 12, 1951, HSTL.
882 HST forced into politics: Hersey, 88.
882 communing with White House spirits: Seale, Vol. II, 1047.
883 Winslow memo to HST: H. G. Grim to Lorenze S. Winslow, September 13, 1951, HSTL.
883 "I want it distinctly": HST to William Adams Delano, August 25, 1950, HSTL.
884 "moving at the double quick": *The New York Times,* March 15, 1952.
886 "Bess and I looked over": HST Diary, March 27, 1952, *Off the Record,* 246.
886 "The President was an inexhaustible": *The New York Times,* May 4, 1952.

887   "the most logical and qualified": *Memoirs,* Vol. II, 489.
887   Eisenhower lunch with HST: Krock, *Memoirs,* 267–68.
887   "You can't join a party": Ambrose, *Eisenhower, Soldier and President,* 259–60.
888   "He told me Arthur Krock's story": Sulzberger, *A Long Row of Candles,* 693.
888   "Dear Ike: The Columnists": HST to Dwight D. Eisenhower, December 18, 1951, *Off the Record,* 220.
889   "a grand man": PP, HST, January 10, 1952, 21, 22.
889   "I'm sorry to see these fellows": Tubby Diary, April 13, 1952.
889   "Can we elect?": HST Diary, July 6, 1952, *Off the Record,* 261.
889   "He proved in that contest": *Memoirs,* Vol. II, 491.
890   "He comes of a political family": Ibid.
890   Stevenson talked his way past the guards: Martin, *Adlai Stevenson of Illinois,* 523.
890   "I told him I would not run": *Memoirs,* Vol. II, 491.
890   "He was overcome": HST Diary, March 4, 1952, *Off the Record,* 245.
890   "He apparently was flabbergasted": *Memoirs,* Vol. II, 492.
890   "full of admiration": Quoted in Martin, 523.
890   "Stevenson was impressed": Ibid., 524.
891   "Adlai, if a knucklehead like me": McKeever, *Adlai Stevenson, His Life and Legacy,* 179.
891   "If Eisenhower were the Republican": Ibid., 178.
891   "[He] came to tell me": HST Diary, March 4, 1952, *Off the Record,* 245.
892   Clifford advice to HST: Clifford, with Holbrooke, *Counsel to the President,* 283.
892   "Anybody who works closely": Quoted in Martin, 544–45.
892   "Not at all": Acheson, 632.
893   "I shall not be a candidate": *Memoirs,* Vol. II, 492.
893   "I found myself shouting": Quoted in Martin, 547.
893   "When you made your announcement": Tubby Diary, April 3, 1952.
893   Did he plan to run: PP, HST, April 3, 1952, 233–34.
893   "I was stunned by": Quoted in Martin, 553.
893   HST response to Stevenson: Ibid.
894   his amazing stamina: Tubby Diary, April 13, 1952.
894   "inability to get on top": Dunar, 119.
894   with this farcical denouement: Phillips, *The Truman Presidency,* 413.
894   "I want you to know": Dunar, 119.
895   "when I'm not so shaky": Tubby Diary, April 13, 1952.
895   "McGrath, Korean truce talks": Ibid.
895   HST appointment schedule: HSTL.
896   "These are not normal times": PP, HST, April 8, 1952, 246.
897   "The President has the power": Tubby Diary, April 6, 1952.
897   "Secretary of Defense Lovett": *Memoirs,* Vol. II, 469.
898   "The attitude of the companies": Ibid., 468.
898   "The plain fact of the matter": PP, HST, April 8, 1952, 249.
899   HST looked so exhausted: Tubby Diary, April 13, 1952.
899   "very desirable": PP, HST, April 9, 1952, 251.
899   one of the most high-handed acts: Washington *Post,* April 10, 1952.
899   "Nothing in the Constitution": Ibid.
900   "Under similar circumstances": PP, HST, April 17, 1952, 273.
900   "I believe that the contemplated strike": *Time,* May 12, 1952.
900   "read it, read it": Tubby Diary, May 3, 1952.
900   "[I] had never seen him": Ibid.
900   an "outstanding" lawyer: *Memoirs,* Vol. II, 475.
901   "We cannot with faithfulness": Donovan, "Truman Seizes Steel," *Constitution,* Fall 1990.
901   "Today a kindly President": Ibid.
901   "damn fool from Texas": Miller, *Plain Speaking,* 242.
901   "a bit testy": Donovan, "Truman Seizes Steel."
902   "No enemy nation could": *Newsweek,* August 4, 1952.

902   "The Court and Congress got us": Tubby Diary, May 30–June 1, 1952.
902   "If the doctor had come in": Ibid., July 21, 1952.
902   "It's a lockout": Ibid.
903   "This should lead to": PP, HST, July 24, 1952, 501.
903   any red-blooded Democrat: *Time,* July 7, 1952.
903   "You never know what's in you": Tubby Diary, July 2, 1952.
903   "We followed you before": *Time,* July 21, 1952.
904   "If Harry Truman turns out": Ibid., July 7, 1952.
904   "I have been trying": *Memoirs,* Vol. II, 496.
905   "I am going to take my coat off": Ibid., 497.
905   "The people are wise": *Time,* August 4, 1952.
905   "Sacrifice, patience": Quoted in McKeever, 201.
905   "Stevenson made his decision": *Time,* August 4, 1952.
906   "Dear Governor: Last night": HST to Adlai Stevenson, July 26, 1952, *Off the Record*
      263.
906   "He was affronted by": Quoted in McKeever, 198.
906   "I have come to the conclusion": HST to Adlai Stevenson, early August 1951, *Off the*
      Record, 266.
906   "Can Stevenson really clean up": Martin, 644.
906   "rather ridiculous": HST to Adlai Stevenson late August 1952, unsent, *Off the Record,*
      268.
907   "Oh, Stevenson will get": Tubby Diary, August 21, 1952.
907   "His eloquence was real": *Memoirs,* Vol. II, 497.
907   HST would do everything possible: Tubby Diary, August 13, 1952.
908   "There's a man of granite": Ibid.
908   "When you vote the Democratic ticket": PP, HST, September 29, 1952, 621.
908   "What I've always had in mind": HST to Dwight Eisenhower, August 16, 1952, *Off the*
      Record, 263–64.
909   "a modern Cromwell": Tubby Diary, September 17, 1952.
909   "This will help us": Ibid., September 22, 1952.
909   "I nearly choked to hear him": Ibid., September 14, 1952.
910   "I feel as if I killed them": Ibid., September 22, 1952.
910   "red-hot anger": Reeves, 439.
911   "Do I need to tell you": Ibid., 440.
911   "very sad and pathetic": PP, HST, October 4, 1952, 711.
911   "lay off Ike for a while": Tubby Diary, early October, 1952.
911   "The general whose words": PP, HST, October 7, 1952, 738.
911   "betrayed his principles": Ibid., October 10, 1952, 784.
912   "Why, General Marshall was responsible": Quoted in Miller, 370.
912   "Just how low": Quoted in Donovan, 401.
912   "Ike was well informed": Bradley and Blair, *A General's Life,* 650.
913   no one could have beaten Eisenhower: HST memorandum, December 22, 1952, *Off*
      the Record, 282.
913   "if you still desire": Donovan, 402.
913   "I sincerely wish": HST Diary, November 15, 1952, *Off the Record,* 273.
913   "an orderly transfer": *Memoirs,* Vol. II, 505.
913   he wished someone had done: Tubby Diary, November 24, 1952.
914   "not very graciously": HST Diary, November 20, 1952, *Off the Record,* 274.
914   "He'll sit right here": Truman, *Harry S. Truman,* 603.
914   "The White House is quiet": HST Diary, November 24, 1952, *Off the Record,* 275.
914   "Since last September Mother Wallace": Ibid.
914   "She was a grand lady": HST Diary, December 6, 1952, ibid., 279.
914   32 percent: Gallup, 1102.
914   43 percent: Ibid.
914   "I wonder how far Moses": HST Memorandum, 1954(?), *Off the Record,* 310.
915   "It bears down on a country boy": HST to EN, January 2, 1952, *Off the Record,* 287.
915   felt "repudiated": Tubby Diary, February 1, 1953.

915   reminiscences with staff: Ibid., February 2, 1953.
916   *Look* magazine article: Commager, "A Few Kind Words for Harry Truman," *Look,* August 1951.
916   "Flying back over the flatlands": Tubby Diary, February 3, 1953.
917   "Certainly no man": PP, HST, January 16, 1953, 1203.
917   "In personality, conversation": Brown, *Through These Men,* 41.
918   farewell address: PP, HST, January 15, 1953, 1197–1202.
920   "in the manner of his going": New York *Herald-Tribune,* January 19, 1953.
920   Inauguration day: HST Diary, January 20, 1953, *Off the Record,* 287.
921   "I was glad I wasn't": West, with Kotz, *Upstairs at the White House,* 126.
921   "I ride with Ike": HST Diary, January 20, 1953, *Off the Record,* 257.
921   "the very many courtesies": Ambrose, 296.
921   "It was a shocking moment": Eric Sevareid, author's interview.
922   "The street in front of Dean's house": HST Diary, January 20, 1953, *Off the Record,* 288.
922   "an absolutely wonderful affair": Truman, *Harry S. Truman,* 610.
922   "There's the best friend": Washington *Post,* January 21, 1953.
923   "I'm just Mr. Truman": *The New York Times,* January 21, 1953.
923   "Crowd at Harper's Ferry": HST Diary, January 20, 1953, *Off the Record,* 288.

PART SIX

18. CITIZEN TRUMAN

927   "Been going over": HST to Dean Acheson, April 18, 1953, HSTL.
927   "Who knows": HST to EW, May 23, 1911, *Dear Bess,* 36.
927   "I tried never to forget": Miller, *Plain Speaking,* 10.
928   "Rumors have it": Independence *Examiner,* January 22, 1953.
928   Burrus had picked out house: Rufus Burrus, author's interview.
929   exploit or "commercialize": Associated Press, January 23, 1953.
929   a Miami real estate developer: Samuel Q. Goldman to HST, October 7, 1952, HSTL.
929   Toyota offer: HST to Paul Butler, March 3, 1959, HSTL.
929   "I still don't feel": Quoted in Ferrell, *Harry S. Truman and the Modern American Presidency,* 153.
929   "where everybody seemed": HST to Dean Acheson, February 7, 1953, HSTL.
930   "take the grips up": Ray Scherer, author's interview.
930   HST set off for Grandview: Tubby Diary, February 5, 1953; Independence *Examiner,* January 23, 1953.
931   That was good land: George Elsey, Oral History, HSTL; author's interview.
931   "A cold wind whipping": Tubby Diary, February 5, 1953.
931   "More than any other single": Harry S. Truman, *Mr. Citizen,* 25.
932   "He was utterly *lost*": Osborne, "Happy Days for Harry," *Life,* July 7, 1958.
932   "Diamond Head": HST Diary, April 1953, in Ferrell, ed., *Off the Record,* 290.
933   "This morning at 7 A.M.": HST Diary, May 20, 1953, Ibid., 292.
933   "A shovel (automatic)": Ibid.
933   "a real tryout": Truman, 64.
933   "Everything went well": HST to Vic H. Householder, November 29, 1953, *Off the Record,* 298.
934   "I admitted the charge": Ibid.
934   "There goes our incognito": Truman, 65.
934   "You're a sight for sore eyes": *The New York Times,* June 22, 1953.
934   "like a dream": Truman, 67.
935   "If you'd go again": *The New York Times,* June 29, 1953.
935   "He was very nice": St. Louis *Post-Dispatch,* July 6, 1953.
936   "The book is doing fine": HST to Acheson, November 5, 1953, HSTL.
935   Paul Douglas observation: Quoted in Manchester, *The Glory and the Dream,* 663.
935   "As for the United States": July 27, 1953.

936 "The war is over": Manchester, 663.
936 "Of course I'm happy": HST to Bela Kornitzer, August 7, 1953, HSTL.
937 "I'm not a writer!": Francis Heller, author's interview.
937 Hillman and Noyes: Miller, 20.
937 Promising to "protect" HST: Heller, author's interview.
937 recording machine: Heller, "The Writing of the Truman Memoirs," *Presidential Studies Quarterly,* Winter 1983.
937 Royce highly disorganized: Heller, author's interview.
937 HST annoyed: Heller, "The Writing of the Truman Memoirs."
937 "lively" and "honest": Elston, *The World of Time Inc.,* 299.
938 "The cream of the White House": Williams, "I Was Truman's Ghost," *Presidential Studies Quarterly,* Spring 1982.
938 "His approval or criticism": Ibid.
939 HST begins his day: Erskine, "Truman in Retirement," *Collier's,* February 4, 1955.
939 "She had golden curls": *Memoirs,* Vol. I, 116.
939 "I always try to be": HST Diary, July 8, 1953, *Off the Record,* 293.
940 "After I'd passed": Ibid.
940 "When we moved": *Memoirs,* Vol. I, 115.
941 "In the fall of 1892": Ibid., 116.
941 How could father be called failure: Steinberg, *The Man from Missouri,* 15.
941 "I have been working on": HST to Acheson, January 28, 1954, HSTL.
942 "Our tribal instinct": HST to Acheson, St. Patrick's Day, 1954, HSTL.
942 "I used to say": Osborne, "Happy Days for Harry."
943 auction at the Armory: Independence *Examiner,* November 19, 1954.
943 "I'm worried about our world": HST to Acheson, May 28, 1954, HSTL.
943 Truman stricken at *Call Me Madam*: Kansas City *Star,* June 19, 1954.
944 gall bladder operation: *The New York Times,* June 21, 1954.
944 "a hell of a time": HST to Acheson, October 14, 1954, HSTL.
944 "When the papers tell us": Acheson to HST, June 21, 1954, HSTL.
944 "When you get acquainted": Ibid.
944 "It is touching": Acheson to EWT, June 30, 1954, HSTL.
945 "going great guns": HST to Acheson, January 11, 1955, HSTL.
945 "The material is more interesting": Acheson to HST, June 21, 1955, HSTL.
945 "Page 114, line 3": Ibid.
946 "She was his true": Ken McCormick, author's interview.
946 "We'd left home": HST Diary, June 24, 1955, *Off the Record,* 317.
947 "I never really appreciated": Elston, 299.
947 "I expect to use, probably": HST to Samuel S. Vaughan, October 22, 1955, HSTL.
947 "when we see him": Samuel S. Vaughan, author's interview.
947 "I had no idea": Ibid.
948 "There, that one's all slicked up": Paul Horgan, author's interview.
948 "I will autograph": HST to Ken McCormick, July 1, 1955, *Off the Record,* 319.
948 only as "my history": Heller, author's interview.
949 "Altogether, it well": *The New York Times Book Review,* November 6, 1955.
949 called Margaret "skinny": HST to Acheson, January 11, 1955, HSTL.
950 "When I hear": HST to Acheson, January 25, 1955, HSTL.
950 "Margie has put one over": HST to Acheson, March 26, 1956, HSTL.
950 "He strikes me as a very nice": HST to Acheson, March 26, 1956, HSTL.
951 "Consolation is just what": Acheson to HST, March 27, 1956, HSTL.
952 "rain, rain, rain": HST Diary, June 21 (?), 1956, *Off the Record,* 336.
952 "I was so afraid": HST to Acheson, July 20, 1956, HSTL.
953 welcome in Rome: *Time,* May 28, 1956.
953 Henry Luce tour: *The New York Times,* May 20, 1956.
953 Paul Schultheiss: Independence *Examiner,* May 19, 1956.
954 "He is considered the greatest": HST Diary, May 27–29, 1956, *Off the Record,* 329.
955 "[Harry] Truman and his wife lunched": Berenson, *Sunset and Twilight,* 436.
955 "I found that it was somewhat": HST Diary, June 4, 1956, *Off the Record,* 332.

955   "squeezed" from the people: HST Diary, June 1956, ibid., 333.
956   "We crossed the Channel": HST Diary, June 21 (?), 1956, ibid., 336.
956   "Never, never in my life": Kansas City *Times,* June 20, 1956.
956   "Truest of allies": *The New York Times,* June 21, 1956.
957   "Mr. Truman is very popular": Kansas City *Times,* June 20, 1956.
957   "Every person born": Ibid., June 21, 1956.
957   "Give 'em, hell, Harricum!": Ibid.
957   "I think we in this room": *The New York Times,* June 22, 1956.
957   "A good many of the difficulties": *The Times* (London), June 22, 1956.
957   "And—not least of all": Ibid.
958   visit to London: HST Diary, June 21 (?), 1956, *Off the Record,* 336.
958   "England is prosperous": Ibid., 337.
958   "It was all over too soon": HST Diary, June 24, 1956, ibid., 338.
959   "He told me that he could do": Ibid.
959   "Too bad he's not campaigning": Kansas City *Times,* June 29, 1956.
959   "Never [said the United Press]": Independence *Examiner,* June 28, 1956.
959   "lacks the kind of fighting spirit": McKeever, *Adlai Stevenson,* 376.
960   "Harry S. Truman had the Democratic": *The New York Times,* August 12, 1956.
960   "When I arrived in Chicago": HST to Acheson, August 29, 1956, HSTL.
960   "I have never wanted to pose": HST to LBJ, December 11, 1956, LBJL.
960   "Dad sat there for a long time": Truman, *Harry S. Truman,* 621.
961   "I expect to be knee deep": HST to Acheson, June 7, 1957, HSTL.
961   "Mr. Truman, who has abiding": *The New York Times,* July 7, 1957.
962   labor union contributions: "Contributions of Labor Unions to Harry S. Truman Library, Inc.," HSTL.
962   "Hey there, farmer!" HST telephone conversation with Sam Rayburn, July 15, 1958, *Off the Record,* 364.
963   net profit: Kirkendall, ed., *The Harry S. Truman Encyclopedia,* 129.
963   "Had it not been": HST to John W. McCormack, January 10, 1957, *Off the Record,* 346.
963   "As you know, we passed": Ibid.
964   "I would be proud": HST to Acheson, October 15, 1952, HSTL.
964   "Mr. Truman is deeply": Acheson to Thomas Bergin, July 12, 1954, HSTL.
964   HST and Yale librarian: Chester Kerr, author's interview.
965   "I have never had a better time": HST to Acheson, April 16, 1958, HSTL.
965   "Yale still rings": HST to Acheson, May 15, 1958, HSTL.
965   "He's so damn happy": Osborne, "Happy Days for Harry."
966   getting a bigger kick: Phillips, "Truman at 75," *The New York Times Magazine,* May 3, 1959.
966   "a man overflowing with life": Ibid.
966   "She says I am just like": St. Louis *Post-Dispatch,* May 10, 1959.
967   "You know this five day week": HST to Acheson, April 10, 1968, HSTL.
967   "where he can sit": Unidentified article, February 3, 1960, Vertical Files, HSTL.
967   "Mr. Truman was one of the most thoughtful": Essay by Phillip C. Brooks, February 16, 1971, HSTL.
968   HST and Benton's drinking: Kansas City *Star,* March 14, 1989.
968   "Well, what the hell": Benton, *An Artist in America,* 351.
969   "When a good politician": Kansas City *Star,* April 27, 1959.
969   "I like being a nose buster": HST to Acheson, April 20, 1955, HSTL.
970   "She and I spent": HST to Acheson, February 19, 1959, HSTL.
970   "Do you suppose any President": HST to Acheson, November 24, 1959, HSTL.
970   "It's not the pope": Miller Tapes, LBJL.
970   Kennedy's notes: "Interview with Truman," Dictated to Mrs. Evelyn Lincoln, 12:00 Noon, January 10, 1959, HSTL.
971   "Just tell him it was Harry Truman": John Zentay, author's interview.
971   "stub his toe": Acheson to HST, April 14, 1960, HSTL.
971   "I hate to say this": Ibid.
971   "without doubt": Kansas City *Star,* May 13, 1960.

SOURCE NOTES

971   Acheson letter: Acheson to HST, June 27, 1960, HSTL.
973   "You'll never know": HST to Acheson, July 9, 1960, HSTL.
973   "I am going to Los Angeles": HST to Agnes E. Meyer, June 25, 1960, *Off the Record,* 386.
973   "Your coming here is considered": Memorandum from Hillman and Noyes to HST, undated, Post-Presidential Files, HSTL.
973   "rigged—or you will be charged": Ibid.
973   HST press conference: *The New York Times,* July 3, 1961.
974   "I listened to your press": Acheson to HST, July 17, 1960, HSTL.
974   "He could not have been": Notes from Conversation of United Press Newsman with JFK, undated, HSTL.
974   "blue as indigo": HST to Acheson, August 26, 1960, unsent, *Off the Record,* 390.
974   "Don't get discouraged": HST to Samuel Rosenman, August 22, 1960, HSTL.
974   "Now you are in for it": Acheson to HST, August 12, 1960, HSTL.
974   "A nap after lunch": "Memo on Mr. Truman's Trips," David Stowe Papers, HSTL.
975   "Although he moves into and through": "Notes on Truman Trips During 1960 Presidential Campaign," David Stowe Papers, HSTL.
975   "The campaign is ended": HST to Acheson, November 21, 1960, HSTL.
976   "I've had a lot of fun": HSTL research staff phone conversation with Paul Hume, December 21, 1979, HSTL.
976   "See, I told you": Ibid.
976   "You know, she remembered": Peggy Scott, author's interview.
976   "You are making a contribution": HST to Acheson, July 7, 1961, *Off the Record,* 395.
976   "Needless to say": Ibid.
977   "I had thought he was not": Merle Miller, author's interview.
977   "Don't try to make a play actor": Aurthur, "The Wit and Sass of Harry S. Truman," *Esquire,* August 1971.
978   "I think there were people": Miller, author's interview.
978   inclined to exaggerate: Miller, 13.
978   "Goddamn an eyewitness": Miller Tapes, LBJL.
978   "He had something like Bryan": Ibid.
978   "I haven't seen him": Ibid.
979   "He was a good man": Ibid.
979   "came back rich with detail": Aurthur, "Harry Truman Chuckles Dryly," *Esquire,* September 1971.
979   "Because if while I'm talking": Ibid.
979   "My God, he's not old": Miller, author's interview.
979   hated long hair: Byron Stewart, Jr., author's interview; Miller, 456.
980   "People in Independence": Miller Tapes, LBJL.
980   "There were times": Miller, author's interview.
980   HST appalled by Bay of Pigs: HST to Acheson, May 3, 1961, HSTL.
980   "This is a terrible weakness": Acheson to HST, July 14, 1961, HSTL.
980   "Keep writing": HST to Acheson, July 18, 1961, HSTL.
980   "You must remember": HST to Acheson, September 25, 1961, *Off the Record,* 397.
981   "If and when that happens": HST to Acheson, December 20, 1962, HSTL.
981   "I just don't like": Schlesinger, *Robert Kennedy and His Times,* 230.
981   "Matt Connelly has been": HST to RFK, January 24, 1962, HSTL.
981   HST sends letter of gratitude: HST to JFK, December 3, 1962, HSTL.
981   "That old lady": HST to Acheson, May 14, 1963, *Off the Record,* 407.
982   "Having come so close": Truman, *Bess W. Truman,* 418.
982   HST put to bed at Blair House: Wilroy and Prinz, *Inside Blair House,* 117.
982   Secret Service protection: Robert Lockwood, author's interview.
983   "Thank you very much": *Remarks by Former President Harry S. Truman, Being the Occasion of Mr. Truman's 80th Birthday,* May 8, 1964, 88th Congress, 2nd Sess., Sen. Doc. No. 88.
983   HST falls: HST to Acheson, January 12, 1965.

SOURCE NOTES

984   "He doesn't look a thing": Ferrell, *Harry S. Truman and the Modern American Presidency,* 159.

984   "He would say 'You're doing . . .' ": Thomas Melton, author's interview.

984   "sad amazement" at HST's appearance: Merriman Smith, UPI, July 31, 1965.

985   "Quite often we have": Melton, author's interview.

985   Nixon visit: Independence *Examiner,* March 21, 1969.

985   asked what he had played: Elizabeth Safly, author's interview.

986   HST with grandchildren in baseball cap: Photo Archives, HSTL.

986   "Oh, to have a good comfortable": Margaret Truman Daniel, author's interview.

986   "No, young man": Ken McCormick, author's interview.

987   December 5 illness: Research Hospital and Medical Center, press release, December 5, 1972, HSTL.

987   December 6 "critical": Ibid., December 6, 1972, 10:23 P.M. CST, HSTL.

987   "very serious": Ibid., December 14, 1972, 9:00 A.M., CST, HSTL.

987   he answered, "Better": Ibid., December 10, 1972, 2:00 P.M., HSTL.

987   "warm, sweet and most appreciative": Quoted in Belton (Missouri) *Star-Herald,* December 28, 1972.

987   "He squeezed my hand": Ibid.

988   "very, very small": *The New York Times,* December 26, 1972.

988   Bess almost exhausted: Truman, *Bess W. Truman,* 421.

988   "Keep it simple": Ibid., 422.

989   "This whole town": *Time,* January 8, 1973.

989   staff watching grave filled in: Safly, author's interview.

989   "He was not a hero": Washington *Star,* December 29, 1972.

990   Alden Whitman interview: Whitman, *Come to Judgment,* xvii.

992   "I'm not sure": Eric Sevareid, author's interview.

Bibliography

Author's Interviews

Alice Acheson, Washington, D.C. • David Acheson, Washington, D.C. • Pat Acheson, Washington, D.C. • Joseph Alsop, Washington, D.C. • James P. Aylward, Jr., Kansas City, Missouri • Lauren Bacall, Washington, D.C. • Sue Bailey, Lincoln, Nebraska • Lindy Boggs, Washington, D.C. • Richard Bolling, Crumpton, Maryland • Floyd Boring, Washington, D.C. • Mary Salisbury Bostian, Independence, Missouri • Bernard Brannon, Kansas City, Missouri • Mary Shaw Branton, Kansas City, Missouri • Ellsworth Bunker, Washington, D.C • Rufus Burrus, Independence, Missouri • Hilary Bush, Kansas City, Missouri • Jack Capps, West Point, New York • Liz Carpenter, Austin, Texas • Jimmy Carter, Atlanta, Georgia • Marquis Childs, Washington, D.C. • Clark Clifford, Washington, D.C. • Wilbur Cohen, Austin, Texas • John Sherman Cooper, Washington, D.C. • Bill Crotty, Kansas City, Missouri • Clifton Daniel, New York City • Margaret Truman Daniel, New York City • Matt Devoe, Kansas City, Missouri • John Doohan, Kansas City, Missouri • Peggy Dow, Copenhagen, Denmark • Joseph Dush, Willard, Ohio • Alfred Eisenstaedt, Menemsha, Massachusetts • George Elsey, Washington, D.C. • Lyman Field, Kansas City, Missouri • Stanley Fike, Washington, D.C. • Francis Fitzgerald, Kansas City, Missouri • Gerald Ford, New York City • Polly Fowler, Independence, Missouri • Clayton Fritchey, West Tisbury, Massachusetts • Virginia Geier, Kansas City, Missouri • Sue Gentry, Independence, Missouri • Rosalind Gibson, Independence, Missouri • D. W. Gilmore, Kansas City, Missouri • T. Sterling Goddard, Grandview, Missouri • Wallace Graham, Kansas City, Missouri • John Hahn, Washington, D.C. • Elliott Harris, Kansas City, Missouri • Steve Harrison, Independence, Missouri • Ardis Haukenberry, Independence, Missouri • Ken Hechler, Boston, Massachusetts • John Hersey, Vineyard Haven, Massachusetts • Anna Rosenberg Hoffman, Bedford, New York • Bernard Hoffman, Kansas City, Missouri • Robert Hopkins, Washington, D.C. • Paul Horgan, Middletown, Connecticut • Dorothy Davis Johnson, Kansas City, Missouri • Lady Bird Johnson, Austin, Texas • J. Walter J. Jones, Kansas City, Missouri • Greta Kempton, New York City • Chester Kerr, New Haven, Connecticut • Geraldine Ketchum, Kansas City, Missouri • Kathleen Moore Knight, Vineyard Haven, Massachusetts • Philip Lagerquist, Independence, Missouri • Johanna Laughlin, Kansas City, Missouri • Tom Leathers, Kansas City, Missouri • Sol Linowitz, Washington, D.C. • Robert B. Lockwood, Independence, Missouri • Eugene McCarthy, Woodville, Virginia • Gerrard McCann, Norfolk, Virginia • John J. McCloy, New York City • Ken McCormick, New York City • Harry McPherson, Washington, D.C. • David Melton, Independence, Missouri • Thomas Melton, Independence, Missouri • Merle Miller, Brewster, New York • Grace Minor, Independence, Missouri • Gerald Mitchell, Kansas City, Missouri • Paul Nagel, Independence, Missouri • Terence O'Brien, Kansas City, Missouri • Reathel Odum, Charleston, South Carolina • Charlton Ogburn, Beaufort, South Carolina • Gertrude Field Oliver, Kansas City, Missouri • John W. Oliver, Kansas City, Missouri • Jacqueline Kennedy Onassis, Chilmark, Massachusetts • Frank Pace, Jr., Boston, Massachusetts • Beverly Pendergast, Kansas City, Missouri • Robert Pendergast, Kansas City, Missouri • Claude D. Pepper, Washington, D.C. • Catherine Pruett, Kansas City, Missouri • Joseph Pruett, Kansas City, Missouri • Jennings Randolph, Washington, D.C. • Ronald Reagan, Washington, D.C. • James Reston, Washington, D.C. • Richard Rhodes, Kansas City, Missouri • Abe Ribicoff, New York City • Matthew Ridgway, Pittsburgh, Pennsylvania • Franklin D. Roosevelt, Jr., Chautauqua, New York • James H. Rowe, Jr., Washington, D.C. • James Rowley, Washington, D.C. • Liz Safly, Independence, Missouri • Harrison Salisbury, Vineyard Haven, Massachusetts • Dwight Salmon, Chilmark, Massachusetts • Frank Sayre, Vineyard Haven, Massachusetts • Ray Scherer, Washington, D.C. • Peggy Scott, Chilmark, Massachusetts • Rex Scouten, Washington, D.C. • Eric Sevareid, Washington, D.C. • Robert Sherrod, Washington, D.C. • Stephen Slaughter, Grandview, Missouri • John Snyder, Charleston, South Carolina • John Steele, Washington, D.C. • Byron Stewart, Jr., Independence, Missouri • Charlotte Stewart, Independence, Missouri • Nathan Stinnette, Crescent City, Florida • Chris J. Stolfa, Kansas City, Missouri •

BIBLIOGRAPHY

David Stowe, Washington, D.C. • Richard L. Strout, Boston, Massachusetts • James Swoyer, Oskaloosa, Kansas • Martha Ann Truman Swoyer, Oskaloosa, Kansas • James Symington, Washington, D.C. • George Tames, Washington, D.C. • Arthur Tighe, Kansas City, Missouri • J. C. Truman, Independence, Missouri • Roger Tubby, Washington, D.C. • Regna Vanatta, Grandview, Missouri • Sam Vaughan, New York City • May Wallace, Independence, Missouri • J. B. West, Falls Church, Virginia • David Wheeler, Kansas City, Missouri • Conn Withers, Liberty, Missouri • John Zentay, Washington, D.C. • Benedict K. Zobrist, Independence, Missouri

UNPUBLISHED SOURCES

MANUSCRIPT COLLECTIONS CONSULTED AT THE HARRY S. TRUMAN LIBRARY, INDEPENDENCE, MISSOURI

Papers of Harry S. Truman
Papers of: Dean Acheson • Eben A. Ayers • James P. Aylward • Jordan Bentley • Henry A. Bundschu • Fred Canfil • Oscar L. Chapman • Tom C. Clark • Will L. Clayton • Clark M. Clifford • Matthew J. Connelly • Clifton Daniel and Margaret Truman Daniel • Jonathan Daniels • Robert L. Dennison • Harry Easley • George M. Elsey • Tom L. Evans • Alonzo Fields • Hugh Fulton • Harold F. Gosnell • William D. Hassett • Lou E. Holland • Edward Jacobson • Joseph M. Jones • Mary Paxton Keeley • Edward B. Lockett • J. Howard McGrath • Frank McNaughton • Edward P. Meisburger • Victor R. Messall • Charles S. Murphy • Philleo Nash • David K. Niles • Mary Ethel Noland • Frank Pace, Jr. • William M. Rigdon • Samuel I. Rosenman • Charles G. Ross • John W. Snyder • L. Curtis Tiernan • Jerome K. Walsh

OTHER ARCHIVAL PAPERS

Congressional Quarterly Library • Democratic National Committee • Miscellaneous Historical Documents • President's Committee on Civil Rights • Special Committee to Investigate the National Defense Program • U.S. Army 35th Division Records • White House Daily Schedule Logs • White House General Correspondence • White House Reconstruction Commission • White House Social Office • White House Telephone Office

ORAL HISTORY TRANSCRIPTS

Dean Acheson • Eben A. Ayers • Gaylon Babcock • Thomas Hart Benton • Frederick J. Bowman • Welbern Bowman • Oscar L. Chapman • Henry P. Chiles • Tom C.Clark • Lucius D. Clay • Clark M. Clifford • Emilio G. Collado • Matthew J. Connelly • Clifton Daniel • Jonathan Daniels • Donald S. Dawson • Mildred Lee Dryden • Harry Easley • George M. Elsey • Tom L. Evans • Stanley R. Fike • Edward T. Folliard • Sue Gentry • Esther M. Grube • William D. Hassett • Loy W. Henderson • Edgar G. Hinde • Johannes U. Hoeber • William J. Hopkins • Mary Paxton Keeley • Leon H. Keyserling • Vere C. Leigh • Katie Louchheim • Robert A. Lovett • Max Lowenthal • Ted Marks • Edward D. McKim • George Meader • John Meador • Walter B. Menefee • Charles T. Morrissey • John H. Muccio • Charles S. Murphy • Harry E. Murphy • Robert G. Nixon • Mary Ethel Noland • Edwin G. Nourse • Frank Pace, Jr. • Amanda Hardin Palmer • Pansy Perkins • Floyd T. Ricketts • Samuel I. Rosenman • Pauline Sims • John W. Snyder • John J. Strode • Richard L. Strout • George Tames • Mary Jane Truman • Roger Tubby • Regna Vanatta • Harry H. Vaughan • Fred M. Vinson • Margaret Weddle • Arthur W. Wilson • John Woodhouse • Robert B. Wyatt

DISSERTATIONS

Heed, Thomas J. *Prelude to Whistlestop: Harry S. Truman the Apprentice Campaigner.* Ed. D. dissertation, Columbia University, 1975
Schmidtlein, Eugene F. *Truman the Senator.* Ph.D. dissertation, University of Missouri, 1962

AUDIO-VISUAL ARCHIVAL SOURCES

Audio Collection • Newsreel, Film and Motion Picture Collection • Photographic Collection

BIBLIOGRAPHY

OTHER LIBRARY AND ARCHIVAL SOURCES

Franklin D. Roosevelt Presidential Library • Independence *Examiner* files • Jackson County Historical Society • Joint Collections of the University of Missouri Western Historical Manuscript Collection and the State Historical Society of Missouri, Columbia, Missouri • Kansas City *Star* Archives • Liberty Memorial Research Archives

Library of Congress Manuscript Division—Papers of Joseph Alsop • William O. Douglas • Philip C. Jessup • Kathleen S. Louchheim • Robert A. Taft
Lyndon Baines Johnson Presidential Library
National Archives, Washington, D.C.—Genealogy Division • Military Reference Branch • Records of the Commission on the Renovation of the Executive Mansion • Time-Warner Incorporated—Time Magazine Archives • U.S. Department of Justice, Federal Bureau of Investigation • Yale University Library—Papers of Henry L. Stimson

OTHER UNPUBLISHED MATERIALS

American Heritage, eds. *Harry S. Truman. Man from Independence.* Narrative text by Louis Koenig • Brown, Walter, J. *James F. Byrnes of South Carolina. A Remembrance.* Manuscript. • Chiles, Mary Sue. "A Brief History of the Six Mile Territory," Joint Collection of the University of Missouri Western Historical Manuscript Collection and the State Historical Collection of Missouri Manuscripts, Columbia, Missouri • Sherrod, Robert. Transcript of interview with Harry S. Truman, April 9, 1964. • Tubby, Roger. Journal—1950–1951.

PUBLISHED SOURCES

OFFICIAL AND SEMI-OFFICIAL PUBLICATIONS

Ballou, M. E. *Official Report on the Resources and Opportunities of Jackson, County, Missouri.* 1926.
Biographical Directory of the American Congress 1774–1971. Washington, D.C.: Government Printing Office, 1971.
Budget Fiscal Year, 1934. Jackson County, Missouri.
Congressional Record, Washington, D.C.
Course of Study and Rules and Regulations of the Independence Public Schools. March 15, 1909.
Foreign Relations of the United States, Diplomatic Papers. The Conference of Berlin (The Potsdam Conference) 1945. Vols. I and II. Washington, D.C.: Government Printing Office, 1960.
Foreign Relations of the United States 1948. The Near East, South Asia, and Africa. Vol. V. Washington, D.C.: Government Printing Office, 1976.
Gallup Political Almanac for 1948. Compiled by the American Institute of Public Opinion, Princeton, New Jersey. Manchester, New Hampshire: Clarke Press, 1948.
Guide to Research Collections of Former United States Senators 1789–1982. Washington, D.C.: Historical Office, United States Senate, 1983.
Harry S. Truman National Historic Site, Independence, Missouri. Cultural Landscape Report. United States National Park Service, 1989.
Harry S. Truman National Historic Site, Independence, Missouri. Historic Structures Report. Restoration Associates, 1987.
Harry S. Truman National Historic Site, Independence, Missouri. Historic Structures Report: History and Significance. United States National Park Service, Midwest Regional Office, 1984.
Hearings Before the Committee on Rules of the House of Representatives on H. Res. 505. Losses of Thirty-fifth Division During the Argonne Battle. Washington, D.C.: Government Printing Office, 1919.
Hiroshima and Nagasaki. The Physical, Medical and Social Effects of the Atomic Bombings. The Committee for the Compilation of Materials on Damage Caused by the Atomic Bombs in Hiroshima and Nagasaki. New York: Basic Books, 1981.

BIBLIOGRAPHY

Historic Furnishings Report. Harry S. Truman Home, National Historic Site, Independence, Missouri. United States National Park Service, 1986.

History of United States Senate Roof and Chamber Improvements and Related Historical Data (Sen. Doc. 20, 82nd Cong., 1st Sess.). Washington, D.C.: Government Printing Office, 1951.

Interim Report of Special Committee to Investigate the National Defense Program—Supplementary Remarks. Congressional Record. Washington, D.C.: Government Printing Office, January 19, 1942.

Kansas City. A Place in Time. Landmarks Commission of Kansas City, Missouri, 1977.

Letter from the Assistant Clerk of the Court of Claims Transmitting a Copy of the Findings Filed by the Court in the Case of Harriet L. Young, Administratrix of Solomon Young, Deceased, Against the United States (Sen. Doc. No. 901, 59th Cong., 1st Sess.). Washington, D.C.: Government Printing Office, 1906.

Memorial Services in the Congress of the United States and Tributes in Eulogy of Harry S Truman. Late President of the United States. Washington, D.C.: Government Printing Office, 1973.

Meuse-Argonne American Cemetery and Memorial. The American Battle Monuments Commission. Washington, D.C.: Government Printing Office, 1986.

Missouri. A Guide to the "Show Me" State. Compiled by the Workers of the Writers' Program of the Work Projects Administration in the State of Missouri. New York: Duell, Sloan and Pearce, 1941.

Morton, Louis. *The Decision to Use the Atomic Bomb. Extracted from "Command Decisions."* Office of the Chief of Military History, Department of the Army, Washington, D.C., 1971.

National Register of Historic Places Inventory-Nomination Form. Harry S. Truman Farm Home. United States Department of the Interior, National Park Service, National Register of Historic Places, Washington, D.C., 1978.

Official Congressional Directory, 74th Congress, 1st Sess. Washington, D.C.: Government Printing Office, 1935.

Official Inaugural Program 1949. Commemorating the Inauguration of Harry S. Truman, President of the United States of America, and Alben W. Barkley, Vice President of the United States, January 20, 1949.

Official Report of the Proceedings of the Democratic National Convention Resulting in the Re-nomination of Franklin D. Roosevelt of New York for President and the Nomination of Harry S. Truman of Missouri for Vice-President, Chicago, July 19 and July 21, 1944.

Oregon Trail. Compiled and written by the Federal Writers' Project of the Works Project Administration. New York: Hastings House, 1972.

Polk's Independence (Jackson County, Missouri) City Directory, 1934. Kansas City, Missouri: Gate City Directory Co., 1933.

Provisional Drill and Service Regulations for Field Artillery (Horse and Light). 1916. Vol. 1, Parts I, II and III. War Department, Office of the Chief of Staff, Document No. 538. New York: Military Publishing Co., 1916.

Public Papers of the Presidents of the United States. Harry S. Truman. Containing the Public Messages, Speeches and Statements of the President. 1945–1953. 8 vols. Washington, D.C.: Government Printing Office, 1961–66.

Remarks by Former President Harry S. Truman. Being on the Occasion of Mr. Truman's Eightieth Birthday (Sen. Doc. No. 88, 88th Cong., 2nd Sess.). Washington, D.C.: Government Printing Office, 1964.

Results of County Planning. Jackson County, Missouri, May 1932.

Rural Electrification in Missouri. Official Manual. State of Missouri, 1951–52.

Soil Survey of Jackson County, Missouri. United States Department of Agriculture, Soil Conservation Service, Washington, D.C., 1984.

35th Division. Summary of Operations in the World War. American Battle Monuments Commission. Washington, D.C.: Government Printing Office, 1944.

To Secure These Rights. Report of the President's Committee on Civil Rights. New York: Simon and Schuster, 1947.

BIBLIOGRAPHY

Trumans of Independence. Historic Resources Study. Harry S Truman National Historic Site, Independence, Missouri. United States National Park Service, Midwest Regional Office, 1985.

War of the Rebellion. A Compilation of the Official Records of the Union and Confederate Armies. Washington, D.C.: Government Printing Office, 1891.

Washington, D.C. Compiled by the Workers of the Writers' Program of the Works Project Administration for the District of Columbia. New York: Hastings House, 1942.

The White House Report of the Commission on the Renovation of the Executive Mansion. Washington, D.C.: Government Printing Office, 1952.

Yearbook of Agriculture. United States Department of Agriculture. Washington, D.C.: Government Printing Office, 1936.

BOOKS

Abbott, Shirley. *Womenfolks. Growing Up Down South.* New Haven, Connecticut: Ticknor and Fields, 1983.

Abel, Jules. *The Truman Scandals.* Chicago: Regnery, 1956.

Abell, Tyler, Ed. *Drew Pearson. Diaries 1949–1959.* New York: Holt, Rinehart and Winston, 1974.

Acheson, Dean. *Among Friends: Personal Letters of Dean Acheson.* David S. McClellan and David C. Acheson, eds. New York: Dodd, Mead, 1980.

———. *Morning and Noon.* Boston: Houghton Mifflin, 1965.

———. *Present at the Creation. My Years in the State Department.* New York: Norton, 1969.

———. *Sketches from a Life.* New York: Pantheon, 1989.

———. *The Korean War.* New York: Norton, 1971.

Adler, Frank J. *Roots in a Moving Stream: The Centennial History of Congregation B'nai Jehudah of Kansas City, 1870–1970.* Kansas City, Missouri. Published by the Congregation: 1972.

Alexander, Robert. *Memories of the World War, 1917–1918.* New York: Macmillan, 1931.

Alinsky, Saul D. *John L. Lewis, an Unauthorized Biography.* New York: Putnam, 1949.

Allen, Frederick Lewis. *Since Yesterday.* New York: Bantam, 1961.

———. *The Big Change. America Transforms Itself 1900–1950.* New York: Harper, 1952.

Allen, George E. *Presidents Who Have Known Me.* New York: Simon and Schuster, 1950.

Allen, Robert S., and William V. Shannon. *The Truman Merry-Go-Round.* New York: Vanguard, 1950.

Alsop, Joseph. *F.D.R. 1882–1945. A Centenary Remembrance.* New York: Viking, 1982.

Ambrose, Stephen E. *Eisenhower. Soldier and President.* New York: Simon and Schuster, 1990.

———. *Eisenhower. Soldier. General of the Army. President-Elect. 1890–1952.* New York: Simon and Schuster, 1983.

———. *Rise to Globalism. American Foreign Policy Since 1938.* 5th rev. edn. New York: Penguin, 1988.

American Heritage, eds. *The American Heritage History of World War I.* New York: American Heritage, 1964.

———. *The History of the Atomic Bomb.* New York: American Heritage, 1968.

Anderson, Patrick. *The President's Men.* Garden City, New York: Doubleday, 1968.

Antonov-Ovseyenko, Anton. *The Time of Stalin. Portrait of Tyranny.* New York: Harper and Row, 1981.

Applewhite, E. J. *Washington Itself. An Informal Guide to the Capital of the United States.* New York: Knopf, 1981.

Arrington, Leonard J., and Davis Bitton. *The Mormon Experience. A History of the Latter-Day Saints.* New York: Vintage, 1979.

Asbell, Bernard. *When FDR Died.* New York: Holt, Rinehart and Winston, 1961.

Attlee, Clement R. *As It Happened.* New York: Viking, 1954.

Baker, Richard Allen. *Conservation Politics. The Senate Career of Clinton P. Anderson.* Albuquerque, New Mexico: University of New Mexico Press, 1985.

BIBLIOGRAPHY

Barber, James David. *The Presidential Character. Predicting Performance in the White House.* 2nd edn. Englewood Cliffs, New Jersey: Prentice-Hall, 1977.

Barkley, Alben W. *That Reminds Me—The Autobiography of the Veep.* Garden City, New York: Doubleday, 1954.

Barry, Louise. *The Beginning of the West. Annals of the Kansas Gateway to the American West 1840–1854.* Topeka, Kansas: Kansas State Historical Society, 1972.

Baruch, Bernard M. *Baruch: The Public Years.* New York: Holt, Rinehart and Winston, 1960.

Benton, Thomas Hart. *An Artist in America.* Columbia, Missouri: University of Missouri Press, 1983.

Berenson, Bernard. *Sunset and Twilight. From the Diaries of 1947–1958.* New York: Harcourt Brace and World, 1963.

Bergamini, David. *Japan's Imperial Conspiracy.* New York: Pocket Books, 1972.

Berman, William C. *The Politics of Civil Rights in the Truman Administration.* Columbus, Ohio: Ohio State University Press, 1970.

Bernstein, Barton J., and Allen J. Matusow, eds. *The Truman Administration. A Documentary History.* New York: Harper and Row, 1966.

———. *The Atomic Bomb: The Crucial Issues.* Boston: Little, Brown, 1976.

Bernstein, Carl. *Loyalties. A Son's Memoir.* New York: Simon and Schuster, 1989.

Biddle, Francis. *In Brief Authority.* Garden City, New York: Doubleday, 1962.

Bird, Leah M. *Grandview, Missouri.* Grandview, Missouri: Neal-Settle, 1959.

Bishop, Jim. *FDR's Last Year: April 1944–April 1945.* New York: William Morrow, 1974.

Blair, Clay. *The Forgotten War, America in Korea 1950–1953.* New York: Times Books, 1987.

Bland, Larry I., Sharon R. Ritenour, and Clarence E. Wunderlin, Jr. *The Papers of George Catlett Marshall.* Vol. 2. Baltimore: Johns Hopkins University Press, 1986.

Block, Herbert. *The Herblock Book.* Boston: Beacon, 1952.

Blum, John Morton. *The Morgenthau Diaries. Years of the War 1941–1945.* Vol. III. Boston: Houghton Mifflin, 1967.

———, ed. *The Price of Vision: The Diary of Henry A. Wallace, 1942–1946.* Boston: Houghton Mifflin, 1973.

Boardman, Barrington. *From Harding to Hiroshima. An Anecdotal History of the United States 1923–1945.* New York: Dembner Books, 1988.

Bohlen, Charles E. *Witness to History. 1929–1969.* New York: Norton, 1973.

Boyer, Paul. *By the Bomb's Early Light.* New York: Pantheon, 1985.

Bradley, Omar N., and Clay Blair. *A General's Life. An Autobiography.* New York: Simon and Schuster, 1983.

Breihan, Carl W. *The Killer Legions of Quantrill.* Superior, 1971.

Brinkley, Alan. *Voices of Protest. Huey Long, Father Coughlin and the Great Depression.* New York: Vintage, 1983.

Brinkley, David. *Washington Goes to War.* New York: Knopf, 1988.

Broun, Heywood. *The A.E.F. with General Pershing and the American Forces.* New York: Appleton, 1918.

Brown, A. Theodore, and Lyle W. Dorsett. *K.C. A History of Kansas City, Missouri.* Boulder, Colorado: Pruett, 1978.

Brown, John Mason. *Through These Men. Some Aspects of Our Passing History.* New York: Harper, 1956.

Bundschu, Henry A. *Harry S. Truman. The Missourian.* Reprint from the Kansas City *Star,* December 26, 1948 (pamphlet).

Bundy, McGeorge. *Danger and Survival. Choices About the Bomb in the First Years.* New York: Random House, 1988.

Burns, James MacGregor. *Roosevelt: The Soldier of Freedom.* New York: Harcourt Brace Jovanovich, 1970.

Byrnes, James F. *All in One Lifetime.* New York: Harper, 1958.

———. *Speaking Frankly.* New York: Harper, 1947.

Cather, Willa. *One of Ours.* New York: Vintage, 1971.

Catton, Bruce. *The War Lords of Washington.* New York: Harcourt, Brace, 1948.

BIBLIOGRAPHY

Caute, David. *The Great Fear. The Anti-Communist Purge Under Truman and Eisenhower.* New York: Simon and Schuster, 1978.

Chafe, William H. *The Unfinished Journey. America Since World War II.* New York: Oxford University Press, 1986.

————, and Harvard Sitkoff, eds. *A History of Our Time. Readings on Postwar America.* New York: Oxford University Press, 1983.

Childs, Marquis W. *I Write from Washington.* New York: Harper, 1942.

Churchill, Winston S. *The Second World War.* Vol. VI, *Triumph and Tragedy.* London: Cassell & Co., 1954.

Clay, Lucius D. *Decision in Germany.* Garden City, New York: Doubleday, 1950.

Clifford, Clark, with Richard Holbrooke. *Counsel to the President. A Memoir.* New York: Random House, 1991.

Cochran, Bert. *Harry Truman and the Crisis Presidency.* New York: Funk and Wagnall's, 1973.

Coit, Margaret L. *Mr. Baruch.* Boston: Houghton Mifflin, 1957.

Collins, J. Lawton. *War in Peacetime. The History and Lessons of Korea.* Boston: Houghton Mifflin, 1969.

Compton, Arthur Holly. *Atomic Quest. A Personal Narrative.* New York: Oxford University Press, 1956.

Congdon, Don. *The Thirties. A Time to Remember.* New York: Simon and Schuster, 1962.

Cooke, Alistair. *America Observed: From the 1940s to the 1980s.* New York: Knopf, 1988.

————. *One Man's America.* New York: Knopf, 1952.

Craig, William. *The Fall of Japan.* New York: Dial Press, 1967.

Crane, Katherine Elizabeth. *Blair House. Past and Present.* Washington, D.C.: U.S. Department of State, 1945.

Cray, Ed. *General of the Army. George C. Marshall. Soldier and Statesman.* New York: Norton, 1990.

Dahlberg, Edward. *Because I Was Flesh.* New York: New Directions, 1963.

Daniel, Clifton. *Lords, Ladies and Gentlemen.* New York: Arbor House, 1984.

Daniel, Margaret Truman (*see also under* Truman, Margaret). *Bess W. Truman.* New York: Macmillan, 1986.

————. *Harry S. Truman.* New York: William Morrow, 1972.

Daniels, Jonathan. *The Man of Independence.* Philadelphia: Lippincott, 1950.

Davis, Elsie Spry. *Descendants of Jacob Young of Shelby County Kentucky—Including President Harry S. Truman.* Coronado, California: Elsie Spry Davis, 1980.

Davis, James Martin. *Top Secret. The Story of the Invasion of Japan.* Omaha, Nebraska: Ranger Publications: 1986 (pamphlet).

Davison, W. Phillips. *The Berlin Blockade. A Study in Cold War Politics.* Princeton, New Jersey: Princeton University Press, 1958.

De Jonge, Alex. *Stalin, and the Shaping of the Soviet Union.* New York: William Morrow, 1986.

De Voto, Bernard. *The Year of Decision, 1846.* Boston: Little, Brown, 1943.

Diggins, John Patrick. *The Proud Decades. America in War and Peace, 1941–1960.* New York: Norton, 1988.

Dimont, Max I. *The Jews in America. The Roots, History, and Destiny of American Jews.* New York: Simon and Schuster, 1978.

Divine, Robert A. *Foreign Policy and U.S. Presidential Elections 1940–1948.* New York: New Viewpoints, 1974.

Djilas, Milovan. *Conversations with Stalin.* London: Rupert Hart-Davis, 1962.

Donner, Frank J. *The Age of Surveillance. The Aims and Methods of America's Political Intelligence System.* New York: Knopf, 1980.

Donovan, Robert J. *Conflict and Crisis. The Presidency of Harry S Truman, 1945–1948.* New York: Norton, 1977.

————. *Tumultuous Years. The Presidency of Harry S. Truman, 1949–1953.* New York: Norton, 1977.

Dorsett, Lyle W. *The Pendergast Machine.* Lincoln, Nebraska: University of Nebraska Press, 1968.

BIBLIOGRAPHY

Douglas, Paul H. *In the Fullness of Time. The Memoirs of Paul H. Douglas.* New York: Harcourt Brace Jovanovich, 1972.

Douglas, William O. *Go East, Young Man. The Early Years.* New York: Random House, 1974.

Dower, John W. *War Without Mercy. Race and Power in the Pacific War.* New York: Pantheon, 1986.

Druks, Dr. Herbert. *From Truman Through Johnson. A Documentary History.* New York: Robert Speller and Sons, 1971.

Drury, Allen. *A Senate Journal. 1943–1945.* New York: McGraw-Hill, 1963.

Dubovsky, Melvyn, and Warren Van Tine. *John L. Lewis: A Biography.* New York: Quadrangle/New York Times Book Co., 1977.

Dunar, Andrew J. *The Truman Scandals and the Politics of Morality.* Columbia, Missouri: University of Missouri Press, 1984.

Dush, Joseph F. *History of Willard, Ohio.* Willard, Ohio, 1974.

Eban, Abba. *An Autobiography.* New York: Random House, 1977.

Eccles, Marriner S. *Beckoning Frontiers: Public and Personal Recollections,* Sidney Hyman, ed. New York: Knopf, 1951.

Eden, Anthony, Earl of Avon. *Memoirs. The Reckoning.* Boston: Houghton Mifflin, 1965.

Ehrman, John. *Grand Strategy,* Vol. 6, edited by James Ramsey Montague Butler. London: Her Majesty's Printing Office, 1956.

Eisenhower, David. *Eisenhower at War, 1943–1945.* New York: Random House, 1986.

Eisenhower, Dwight D. *Crusade in Europe.* Garden City, New York: Doubleday, 1948.

———. *The White House Years. Mandate for a Change. 1953–1956.* Garden City, New York: Doubleday, 1963.

Elston, Robert T. *The World of Time Inc. The Intimate History of a Publishing Enterprise 1941–1960.* New York: Atheneum, 1973.

Farrar, Ronald T. *Reluctant Servant. The Story of Charles G. Ross.* Columbia, Missouri: University of Missouri Press, 1969.

Feis, Herbert. *Between War and Peace: The Potsdam Conference.* Princeton, New Jersey: Princeton University Press, 1960.

———. *From Trust to Terror. The Onset of the Cold War.* New York: Norton, 1970.

———. *The Atomic Bomb and the End of World War II.* Princeton, New Jersey: Princeton University Press, 1970.

Fellman, Michael. *Inside War. The Guerilla Conflict in Missouri During the American Civil War.* New York: Oxford University Press, 1989.

Fermi, Laura. *Atoms in the Family. My Life with Enrico Fermi.* Chicago: University of Chicago Press, 1954.

Ferrell, Robert H. *American Diplomacy: A History.* New York: Norton, 1980.

———, ed. *Dear Bess. The Letters from Harry to Bess Truman, 1910–1959.* New York: Norton, 1983.

———. *Harry S. Truman and the Modern American Presidency,* Oscar Handlin, ed. Boston: Little, Brown, 1983.

———, ed. *Off the Record. The Private Papers of Harry S. Truman.* New York: Penguin, 1980.

———, ed. *The Autobiography of Harry S. Truman.* Boulder, Colorado: Colorado Associated University Press, 1980.

———. *The Eisenhower Diaries.* New York: Norton, 1981.

———, ed. *Truman in the White House. The Diary of Eben A. Ayers.* Columbia, Missouri: University of Missouri Press, 1991.

Fields, Alonzo. *My 21 Years in the White House.* New York: Coward-McCann, 1961.

Flower, Desmond, and James Reeves, eds. *The Taste of Courage.* New York: Harper & Row, 1960.

Flynn, Edward J. *You're the Boss.* New York: Viking, 1947.

Foerster, Bernd. *Independence, Missouri.* Independence, Missouri: Independence Press, 1978.

Forrestal, James. *The Forrestal Diaries.* Walter Millis, ed. New York: Viking, 1951.

Fredericks, Pierce G. *The Great Adventure.* New York. Dutton, 1961.

BIBLIOGRAPHY

Freeland, Richard M. *The Truman Doctrine and the Origins of McCarthyism: Foreign Policy, Domestic Politics, and Internal Security, 1946–1948*. New York: Knopf, 1972.

Freidel, Frank. *Over There. The Story of America's First Great Overseas Crusade*. Boston: Little, Brown, 1964.

Friedman, L., and F. L. Israel, eds. *The Justices of the United States Supreme Court. 1789–1969*. New York: Chelsea House, 1969.

Fussell, Paul. *The Great War and Modern Memory*. New York: Oxford University Press, 1977.

Gaddis, John Lewis. *The United States and the Origins of the Cold War, 1941–1947*. New York: Columbia University Press, 1972.

Galbraith, John Kenneth. *The Great Crash 1929*. New York: Avon, 1979.

Gallu, Samuel. *"Give 'Em Hell Harry": Reminiscences*. New York: Viking, 1975.

Garwood, Darrell. *Crossroads of America. The Story of Kansas City*. New York: Norton, 1948.

Gentry, Curt. *J. Edgar Hoover. The Man and the Secrets*. New York: Norton, 1991.

Gies, Joseph. *Harry S Truman. A Pictorial Biography*. Garden City, New York: Doubleday, 1968.

Giglio, James N., and Greg G. Thielen. *Truman in Cartoon and Caricature*. Ames, Iowa: Iowa State University Press, 1984.

Gilbert, Bil. *Westering Man: The Life of Joseph Walker*. New York: Atheneum, 1983.

Gilbert, Martin. *Winston Churchill, Never Despair 1945–1965*. Boston: Houghton Mifflin, 1988.

Gimbel, John. *The Origins of the Marshall Plan*. Stanford, California: Stanford University Press, 1976.

Giovanneti, Leo, and Fred Freed. *The Decision to Drop the Bomb*. New York: Coward-McCann, 1965.

Gleam. The Independence (Missouri) High School Annual. 1901.

Goldman, Eric F. *Rendezvous with Destiny. A History of Modern American Reform*. New York: Vintage, 1956.

———. *The Crucial Decade—And After. America, 1945–1960*. New York: Random House, 1960.

Goldwater, Barry M., with Jack Casserly. *Goldwater*. New York: St. Martin's Press, 1988.

Goodchild, Peter. *J. Robert Oppenheimer. Shatterer of Worlds*. Boston: Houghton Mifflin, 1981.

Gosnell, Harold F. *Truman's Crises. A Political Biography of Harry S. Truman*. Westport, Connecticut: Greenwood Press, 1980.

Goulden, Joseph C. *Korea. The Untold Story of the War*. New York: Times Books, 1982.

———. *The Best Years 1945–1950*. New York: Atheneum, 1976.

Graham, Otis L., Jr., and Meghan Robinson Wander. *Franklin D. Roosevelt. His Life and Times. An Encyclopedic View*. Boston: G. K. Hall, 1985.

Gray, Richard S. *Gray Ghosts of the Confederacy: Guerilla Warfare in the West, 1861–1865*. Baton Rouge, Louisiana: Louisiana State University Press, 1984.

Green, Constance McLaughlin. *Washington, Capital City, 1879–1950*. Princeton, New Jersey: Princeton University Press, 1963.

Greenstein, Fred I., ed. *Leadership in the Modern Presidency*. Cambridge, Massachusetts: Harvard University Press, 1988.

Gregg, Josiah. *The Commerce of the Prairies*. New York: Citadel Press, 1968.

Groueff, Stephane. *Manhattan Project. The Untold Story of the Making of the Atomic Bomb*. Boston: Little, Brown, 1967.

Groves, Leslie R. *Now It Can Be Told: The Story of the Manhattan Project*. New York: Harper, 1962.

Gunther, John. *Procession*. New York: Harper and Row, 1965.

Halle, Louis, J., Jr. *Spring in Washington*. New York: Sloane and Associates, 1947.

———. *The Cold War as History*. New York: Harper and Row, 1968.

Hamby, Alonzo L. *Beyond the New Deal: Harry S. Truman and American Liberalism*. New York: Columbia University Press, 1973.

BIBLIOGRAPHY

Hardeman, D. B., and Donald Bacon. *Rayburn: A Biography*. Austin, Texas: Texas Monthly Press, 1987.

Harriman, W. Averell, and Elie Abel. *Special Envoy to Churchill and Stalin, 1941–1946.* New York: Random House, 1975.

Hart, Liddell. *A History of the World War*. Boston: Little, Brown, 1935.

Hartmann, Susan M. *Truman and the 80th Congress*. Columbia, Missouri: University of Missouri Press, 1971.

Hassett, William D. *Off the Record with F.D.R. 1942–1945.* New Brunswick, New Jersey: Rutgers University Press, 1958.

Hastings, Max. *The Korean War*. New York: Simon and Schuster, 1987.

Hatch, Alden. *Franklin D. Roosevelt: An Informal Biography*. New York: Henry Holt and Co., 1947.

Haynes, Richard F. *The Awesome Power, Harry S. Truman as Commander in Chief.* Baton Rouge, Louisiana: Louisiana State University Press, 1973.

Hechler, Ken. *Working with Truman. A Personal Memoir of the White House Years.* New York: Putnam's, 1982.

Heller, Francis H. *The Korean War. A 25 Year Perspective.* Lawrence, Kansas: Regents Press of Kansas, 1980.

————. *The Truman White House. The Administration of the Presidency 1945–1953.* Lawrence; Kansas: Regents Press of Kansas, 1980.

Heller, Mikhail, and Aleksandr M. Nekrich. *Utopia in Power. The History of the Soviet Union from 1917 to the Present.* New York: Summit Books, 1986.

Helm, William. *Harry Truman. A Political Biography.* New York: Duell, Sloan and Pearce, 1947.

Herken, Gregg. *The Winning Weapon: The Atomic Bomb in the Cold War 1945–1950.* New York: Knopf, 1980.

Hersey, John. *Aspects of the Presidency*. New Haven, Connecticut: Ticknor and Fields, 1980.

————. *Hiroshima*. New York: Knopf, 1946.

Hillman, William, ed. *Mr. President*. New York: Farrar, Straus and Young, 1952.

History of Jackson County, Missouri. Cape Girardeau, Missouri. Kansas City: Union Historical Company, 1881 (reprint, Ramfre Press, 1966).

Hodgson, Godfrey. *America in Our Time. From World War II to Nixon. What Happened and Why*. New York: Vintage, 1976.

————. *The Colonel. The Life and Wars of Henry Stimson 1867–1950.* New York: Knopf, 1990.

Hofstadter, Richard. *The Age of Reform*. New York: Vintage, 1955.

Horgan, Paul. *Josiah Gregg and His Vision of the Early West*. New York: Farrar, Straus & Giroux, 1972.

Horne, Alistair. *The Price of Glory. Verdun 1916*. New York: Viking, 1986.

Horne, Charles, ed. *Great Men and Famous Women*. 4 vols. New York: Selman, Hess. 1894.

Howard, Gerald, ed. *The Sixties. The Art, Attitudes, Politics, and Media of Our Most Explosive Decade*. New York: Washington Square Press, 1982.

Hulston, John K. *An Ozark Lawyer's Story*. Republic, Missouri: Western Printing, 1976.

Humphrey, Hubert H. *The Education of a Public Man: My Life and Politics,* Norman Sherman, ed. Garden City, New York: Doubleday, 1976.

Huthmacher, J. Joseph, ed. *The Truman Years: The Reconstruction of Postwar America.* Hinsdale, Illinois: Dryden, 1972.

Illustrated History of Independence, Missouri. Jackson County Historical Society (ca. 1902).

Independence, Missouri. Centennial 1827–1927. Official Souvenir (pamphlet).

Isaacson, Walter, and Evan Thomas. *The Wise Men. Six Friends and the World They Made.* New York: Simon and Schuster, 1986.

James, D. Clayton. *The Years of MacArthur 1941–1945*. Boston: Houghton Mifflin, 1975.

————. *The Years of MacArthur 1945–1964*. Boston: Houghton Mifflin, 1985.

Jenkins, Roy. *Truman*. London: Collins, 1986.

Johnson, Lady Bird. *A White House Diary*. New York: Holt, Rinehart and Winston, 1970.

Johnson, N. R. *The Harry S. Truman Birthplace Home. Lamar, Missouri.* 1973.

BIBLIOGRAPHY

Johnson, Paul. *Modern Times. The World from the Twenties to the Eighties.* New York: Harper and Row, 1983.

Jones, Joseph Marion. *The Fifteen Weeks, February 21–June 5, 1947.* New York: Viking, 1955.

Josephy, Alvin M., Jr. *On the Hill. A History of the American Congress. From 1789 to the Present.* New York: Simon and Schuster, 1979.

———. *The Civil War in the American West.* New York: Knopf, 1991.

Jungk, Robert. *Brighter Than a Thousand Suns. A Personal History of the Atomic Scientists.* New York: Harcourt, Brace, 1958.

Kansas City School of Law Catalogue. Kansas City, Missouri, 1923.

Kennan, George F. *American Diplomacy 1900–1950.* Chicago: University of Chicago Press, 1951.

———. *Memoirs 1925–1950.* Boston: Little, Brown, 1967.

———. *Sketches from a Life.* New York: Pantheon, 1989.

Kennedy, David M. *Over Here. The First World War and American Society.* New York: Oxford University Press, 1980.

Kennedy, John F. *Profiles in Courage.* New York: Harper & Row, 1964.

Kingsley, J. Gordon. *Frontiers. The Story of Missouri Baptists.* Jefferson City, Missouri: Missouri Baptist Historical Commission, 1983.

Kirkendall, Richard S. *The Harry S. Truman Encyclopedia.* Boston: G. K. Hall, 1989.

———. *The Truman Period as a Research Field.* Columbia, Missouri: University of Missouri Press, 1967.

Knox, Donald. *The Korean War. Pusan to Chosin. An Oral History.* San Diego, California: Harcourt Brace Jovanovich, 1985.

Koenig, Louis W. *The Chief Executive.* New York: Harcourt, Brace and World, 1964.

———. *The Truman Administration. Its Principles and Practice.* New York: New York University Press, 1956.

Kolko, Gabriel. *The Politics of War: The World and United States Foreign Policy, 1943–1945.* New York: Random House, 1968.

Kolko, Joyce and Gabriel. *The Limits of Power: The World and United States Foreign Policy, 1945–1954.* New York: Harper and Row, 1972.

Krock, Arthur. *In the Nation: 1932–1966.* New York: McGraw-Hill, 1966.

———. *Memoirs. Sixty Years on the Firing Line.* New York: Funk and Wagnall's, 1968.

Lacey, Michael, ed. *The Truman Presidency.* Woodrow Wilson Center Series. Cambridge, England: Cambridge University Press, 1989.

LaFeber, Walter. *America, Russia and the Cold War (1946–1971).* 2nd edn. New York: Wiley, 1972.

———. *The American Age. United States Foreign Policy at Home and Abroad Since 1750.* New York: Norton, 1989.

Lait, Jack, and Lee Mortimer. *Washington Confidential. The Low-Down on the Big Town.* New York: Crown, 1951.

Lamont, Lansing. *Day of Trinity.* New York: Atheneum, 1965.

Laqueur, Walter. *A History of Zionism.* New York: Holt, Rinehart and Winston, 1972.

Larrabee, Eric. *Commander in Chief. Franklin Delano Roosevelt, His Lieutenants and Their War.* New York: Harper and Row, 1987.

Lash, Joseph P. *Dealers and Dreamers. A New Look at the New Deal.* New York: Doubleday, 1988.

———. *Eleanor and Franklin.* New York: New American Library, 1971.

———. *Eleanor: The Years Alone.* New York: Norton, 1972.

Leahy, William D. *I Was There: The Personal Story of the Chief of Staff of Presidents Roosevelt and Truman Based on His Notes and Diaries Made at the Time.* New York: Whittlesey House, 1950.

Lee, Jay M. *The Artilleryman. The Experiences and Impressions of an American Artillery Regiment in the World War. 129th F.A., 1917–1919.* Kansas City, Missouri: Spencer, 1920.

Lerner, Max. *Actions and Passions. Notes on the Multiple Revolution of Our Time.* New York: Simon and Schuster, 1949.

BIBLIOGRAPHY

————. *America as a Civilization*. New York: Simon and Schuster, 1957.

Leuchtenburg, William E. *Franklin D. Roosevelt and the New Deal 1932–1940*. New York: Harper and Row, 1963.

————. *In the Shadow of FDR. From Harry Truman to Ronald Reagan*. Ithaca, New York: Cornell University Press, 1983.

————. *The Perils of Prosperity 1914–1932*. Chicago: University of Chicago Press, 1958.

Lewis, Sinclair. *Babbitt*. New York: Harcourt, Brace, 1922.

————. *Main Street*. New York: Harcourt, Brace, 1922.

Liebowich, Louis. *The Press and the Origins of the Cold War 1944–1947*. New York: Praeger, 1988.

Lilienthal, David E. *The Journals of David E. Lilienthal. 1945–1950*. 2 vols. New York: Harper and Row, 1964.

Link, Arthur S. *American Epoch: A History of the United States Since the 1890's*. New York: Knopf, 1959.

Louchheim, Katie, ed. *The Making of the New Deal. The Insiders Speak*. Cambridge, Massachusetts: Harvard University Press, 1983.

Luce, Robert B., ed. *The Faces of Five Decades. Selections from Fifty Years of The New Republic. 1914–1964*. New York: Simon and Schuster, 1964.

MacArthur, Douglas. *Reminiscences*. New York: McGraw-Hill, 1964.

Manchester, William. *American Caesar. Douglas MacArthur 1880–1964*. Boston: Little, Brown, 1978.

————. *The Glory and the Dream. A Narrative History of America, 1932–1972*. Boston: Little, Brown, 1974.

Marcus, Maeva. *Truman and the Steel Seizure Case. The Limits of Presidential Power*. New York: Columbia University Press, 1977.

Marcus, Robert D. *A Brief History of the United States Since 1945*. New York: St. Martin's Press, 1975.

Markowitz, Norman D. *The Rise and Fall of the People's Century: Henry A. Wallace and American Liberalism 1941–1948*. New York: Free Press, 1977.

Marshall, George. *Memoirs of My Services in the World War*. Boston: Houghton Mifflin, 1974.

Martin, Joe, as told to Robert J. Donovan. *My First Fifty Years in Politics*. New York: McGraw-Hill, 1960.

Martin, John Bartlow. *Adlai Stevenson of Illinois*. Garden City, New York: Doubleday, 1976.

Mason, Frank. *Truman and the Pendergasts*. Evanston, Illinois: Regency, 1963.

Matusow, Allen J. *Farm Policies and Politics in the Truman Administration*. Cambridge, Massachusetts: Harvard University Press, 1967.

McCarthy, Eugene. *Up 'Til Now. A Memoir*. San Diego, California: Harcourt Brace Jovanovich, 1987.

McCoy, Donald R., and Richard Ruetten. *Quest and Response: Minority Rights in the Truman Administration*. Lawrence, Kansas: University Press of Kansas, 1973.

McDermott, John Francis, ed. *Travels in Search of the Elephant: The Wanderings of Alfred S. Waugh, Artist, in Louisiana, Missouri, and Santa Fe, in 1845–1846*. St. Louis, Missouri: Missouri Historical Society, 1951.

McKeever, Porter. *Adlai Stevenson, His Life and Legacy*. New York: William Morrow, 1989.

McLellan, David S. *Dean Acheson. The State Department Years*. New York: Dodd, Mead, 1976.

McNaughton, Frank, and Walter Hehmeyer. *Harry Truman: President*. New York: Whittlesey House, 1948.

————. *This Man Truman*. New York: McGraw-Hill, 1945.

McNeal, Robert H. *Stalin, Man and Ruler*. New York: New York University Press, 1988.

McPherson, Harry. *A Political Education. A Washington Memoir*. Boston: Houghton Mifflin, 1988.

McReynolds, Edwin C. *Missouri. A History of the Crossroads State*. Norman, Oklahoma: University of Oklahoma Press, 1975.

Medved, Michael. *The Shadow Presidents. Top Aides in the White House from Lincoln to the Present*. New York: Times Books, 1979.

BIBLIOGRAPHY

Mee, Charles L., Jr. *The End of Order. Versailles 1919*. New York: Dutton, 1980.
———. *Meeting at Potsdam*. New York: Evans, 1975.
Meyer, Karl E. *Pundits, Poets, and Wits. An Omnibus of American Newspaper Columns*. New York: Oxford University Press, 1990.
Miller, Merle. *Plain Speaking. An Oral Biography of Harry S. Truman*. New York: Berkley, 1974.
Miller, Richard Lawrence. *Harry S. Truman, The Rise to Power*. New York: McGraw-Hill, 1986.
Miller, William "Fishbait," as told to Frances Spatz Leighton. *Fishbait. The Memoirs of the Congressional Doorkeeper*. Englewood Cliffs, New Jersey: Prentice-Hall, 1977.
Milligan, Maurice M. *Missouri Waltz: The Inside Story of the Pendergast Machine by the Man Who Smashed It*. New York: Scribner's, 1948.
Minder, Charles F. *This Man's War. The Day-to-Day Record of an American Private on the Western Front*. New York: Pevensey Press, 1931.
Moley, Raymond. *27 Masters of Politics*. New York: Funk and Wagnall's, 1949.
Monaghan, Jay. *Civil War on the Western Border, 1854–1865*. Lincoln, Nebraska: University of Nebraska Press, 1955.
Moran, Charles McMoran Wilson, Baron. *Churchill: The Struggle for Survival, 1940–1965, Taken from the Diaries of Lord Moran*. Boston: Houghton Mifflin, 1966.
Morgan, Ted. *F.D.R. A Biography*. New York: Simon and Schuster, 1985.
Morison, Elting E. *Turmoil and Tradition: A Study of the Life and Times of Henry L. Stimson*. Boston: Houghton Mifflin, 1960.
Morison, Samuel Eliot. *The Oxford History of the American People*. New York: Oxford University Press, 1965.
Mosley, Leonard. *Marshall. Hero for Our Times*. New York: Hearst, 1982.
Mosteller, Frederick, Herbert Hyman, Philip J. McCarthy, Eli S. Marks, and David B. Truman. *The Pre-Election Polls of 1948. Report to the Committee on Analysis of Pre-Election Polls and Forecasts*. New York: Social Science Research Council, 1949.
Murphy, Robert. *Diplomat Among Warriors. The Unique World of a Foreign Service Expert*. Garden City, New York: Doubleday, 1964.
Nagel, Paul C. *Missouri. A History*. New York: Norton, 1977.
Nathan, Pearson W., Jr. *Goin' to Kansas City*. Chicago: University of Illinois Press, 1987.
Nettl, Paul. *Mozart and Masonry*. New York: Philosophical Library, 1957.
Neustadt, Richard E. *Presidential Power: The Politics of Leadership from FDR to Carter*. New York: John Wiley, 1980.
Nichols, Major General K.D., U.S.A. (Ret.). *The Road to Trinity. A Personal Account of How America's Nuclear Policies Were Made*. New York: William Morrow, 1987.
Nicolson, Nigel, ed. *The Diaries and Letters of Harold Nicolson*. Vols. 2 and 3. New York: Atheneum, 1967.
Nixon, Richard. *In the Arena. A Memoir of Victory, Defeat and Renewal*. New York: Simon and Schuster, 1990.
Oates, Stephen. *To Purge This Land with Blood*. New York: Harper and Row, 1970.
O'Brien, William Patrick. *Independence Square. A Convenient Guide to the Past for Today's Pioneers*. Amerifax, 1985 (brochure).
Overland, Orm. *America Perceived: A View from Abroad in the 20th Century*. West Haven, Connecticut: Pendulum Press, 1974.
Paige, Glenn D. *The Korean Decision (June 24–30, 1950)*. New York: Free Press, 1968.
Palmer, R. R., and Joel Colton. *A History of the Modern World*. 4th edn. New York: Knopf, 1971.
Parkman, Francis. *The Journal of Francis Parkman*. 2 vols. New York: Harper, 1947.
———. *The Oregon Trail*. New York: New American Library, 1950.
Parks, Lillian Rogers, and Frances Spatz Leighton. *My Thirty Years Backstairs at the White House*. New York: Fleet, 1961.
Parmet, Herbert S. *Richard Nixon and His America*. Boston: Little, Brown, 1990.
———. *The Democrats: The Years after FDR*. New York: Macmillan, 1976.
Parrish, William E., Charles T. Jones, Jr., and Lawrence O. Christensen. *Missouri. The Heart of the Nation*. St. Louis, Missouri: Forum Press, 1980.

BIBLIOGRAPHY

Paterson, Thomas G., ed. *Cold War Critics. Alternatives to American Foreign Policy in the Truman Years.* Chicago: Quadrangle, 1971.

Patterson, James T. *Mr. Republican. A Biography of Robert A. Taft.* Boston, Houghton Mifflin, 1972.

Paxton, Mary Gentry. *Mary Gentry and John Gallatin Paxton. A Memoir.* Privately published, 1967.

Payne, Robert. *Report on America.* New York: John Day Co., 1949.

Pearson, Drew. *Diaries, 1949–1959.* New York: Holt, Rinehart, 1974.

———, and Jack Anderson. *The Case Against Congress. A Compelling Indictment of Corruption on Capitol Hill.* New York: Simon and Schuster, 1968.

Pepper, Claude Denson, with Hays Gorey. *Pepper. Eyewitness to a Century.* San Diego, California: Harcourt Brace Jovanovich, 1987.

Perrett, Geoffrey. *America in the Twenties. A History.* New York: Simon and Schuster, 1982.

Persico, Joseph E. *Edward R. Murrow. An American Original.* New York: McGraw-Hill, 1988.

Pessen, Edward. *The Log Cabin Myth. The Social Backgrounds of Presidents.* New Haven, Connecticut: Yale University Press, 1984.

Phillips, Cabell. *The Truman Presidency. The History of a Triumphant Succession.* New York: Macmillan, 1966.

Pilat, Oliver. *Drew Pearson. An Unauthorized Biography.* New York: Harper's Magazine Press, 1973.

Pitt, Barrie. *1918. The Last Act.* London: Papermac, 1984.

Poen, Monte M., ed. *Strictly Personal and Confidential. The Letters Harry Truman Never Mailed.* Boston: Little, Brown, 1982.

Pogue, Forrest C. *George C. Marshall: Education of a General, 1889–1939.* New York: Viking, 1963.

———. *George C. Marshall: Ordeal and Hope, 1939–1943.* New York: Viking, 1966.

———. *George C. Marshall: Organizer of Victory, 1943–1945.* New York: Viking, 1973.

———. *George C. Marshall: Statesman, 1945–1959.* New York: Viking, 1987.

Polenberg, Richard. *One Nation Divisible. Class, Race, and Ethnicity in the United States Since 1938.* New York: Viking, 1980.

Powell, Eugene J. *Tom's Boy Harry.* Jefferson City, Missouri: Hawthorn, 1948.

Powers, Richard Gid. *Secrecy and Power. The Life of J. Edgar Hoover.* New York: Free Press, 1987.

Prinz, Lucie, and Mary Edith Wilroy. *Inside Blair House.* Garden City, New York: Doubleday, 1952.

Ray, Mrs. Sam. *Postcards from Old Kansas City.* Kansas City, Missouri: Historic Kansas City Foundation, 1980.

Reddig, William M. *Tom's Town. Kansas City and the Pendergast Legend.* Columbia, Missouri: University of Missouri Press, 1986.

Redding, Jack. *Inside the Democratic Party.* New York: Bobbs-Merrill, 1958.

Reeves, Thomas C. *The Life and Times of Joe McCarthy.* Briarcliff Manor, New York: Stein and Day, 1982.

Reston, James. *Deadline.* New York: Random House, 1991.

Rhodes, Richard. *The Inland Ground. An Evocation of the American Middle West.* New York: Atheneum, 1970.

———. *The Making of the Atomic Bomb.* New York: Simon and Schuster, 1986.

Riddle, Donald H. *The Truman Committee: A Study in Congressional Responsibility.* New Brunswick, New Jersey: Rutgers Press, 1964.

Ridgway, Matthew B. *The Memoirs of Matthew B. Ridgway.* New York: 1956.

———. *The Korean War.* New York: Da Capo, 1967.

Riedel, Richard Langham. *Halls of the Mighty.* New York: Luce, 1969.

Rigdon, William M., with James Derieux. *White House Sailor.* Garden City, New York: Doubleday, 1962.

Robbins, Charles. *Last of His Kind. An Informal Portrait of Harry S. Truman.* New York: William Morrow, 1979.

BIBLIOGRAPHY

Roberts, Allen E. *Brother Truman. The Masonic Life and Philosophy of Harry S. Truman.* Highland Springs, Virginia: Anchor Communications, 1985.

Roberts, J. M. *The Pelican History of the World.* Middlesex, England: Penguin, 1980.

Rognow, Arnold R. *James Forrestal. A Study of Personality, Politics and Policy.* New York: Macmillan, 1963.

Roosevelt, James, and Sidney Shalett. *Affectionately, F.D.R. A Son's Story of a Lonely Man.* New York: Harcourt, Brace, 1959.

Rosenman, Samuel S. *Working with Roosevelt.* New York: Harper, 1952.

————, and Dorothy. *Presidential Style: Some Giants and a Pygmy in the White House.* New York: Harper and Row, 1976.

Ross, Irwin. *The Loneliest Campaign. The Truman Victory of 1948.* New York: New American Library, 1968.

Rossiter, Clinton, and James Lare. *The Essential Lippmann.* New York: Random House, 1963.

Rovere, Richard H. *Senator Joe McCarthy.* New York: Harcourt, Brace, 1959.

————. *The American Establishment and Other Reports, Opinions and Speculations.* New York: Harcourt, Brace, 1962.

Rowan, Carl T. *Breaking Barriers.* Boston: Little, Brown, 1991.

Rusk, Dean, as told to Richard Rusk. *As I Saw It.* New York: Norton, 1990.

Safran, Nadav. *The United States and Israel.* Cambridge, Massachusetts: Harvard University Press, 1963.

Salisbury, Harrison E. *A Journey for Our Times. A Memoir.* New York: Harper and Row, 1983.

Salter, J. T., ed. *Public Men In and Out of Office.* Chapel Hill, North Carolina: University of North Carolina Press, 1946.

Samuels, Ernest. *Bernard Berenson. The Making of a Legend.* Cambridge, Massachusetts: Harvard University Press, 1987.

Sann, Paul. *The Lawless Decade, A Pictorial History of a Great American Transition: From the World War I Armistice and Prohibition to Repeal and the New Deal.* New York: Crown, 1967.

Schaller, Michael. *Douglas MacArthur. The Far Eastern General.* New York: Oxford University Press, 1989.

Schirmer, Sherry Lamb, and Richard D. McKinzie. *At the River's Bend. An Illustrated History of Kansas City. Independence and Jackson County.* Woodland Hills, California: Windsor Publications, 1982.

Schlesinger, Arthur M., Jr. *The Crisis of the Old Order.* Boston: Houghton Mifflin, 1957.

————. *Robert Kennedy and His Times.* New York: Ballantine, 1978.

————. *The Almanac of American History.* New York: Perogee, 1983.

————. *The Imperial Presidency.* Boston: Houghton Mifflin, 1973.

————, and Roger Bruns. *Congress Investigates. A Documented History, 1792–1974.* New York: Chelsea, 1975.

Schmidt, Karl M. *Henry A. Wallace: Quixotic Crusade 1948.* Syracuse, New York: Syracuse University Press, 1960.

Seale, William. *The President's House. A History.* Vols. I and II. Washington, D.C.: White House Historical Association with the cooperation of the National Geographic Society, 1986.

Secret Diary of Harold L. Ickes. Vols. 1, 2, and 3. New York: Simon and Schuster, 1953–54.

Sevareid, Eric. *Conversations with Eric Sevareid. Interviews with Notable Americans.* Washington, D.C.: Public Affairs Press, 1976.

————. *Not So Wild a Dream.* New York: Atheneum, 1979.

Shawn, William, ed. *Paris Journal. 1944–1955. Janet Flanner (Genêt).* New York: Harcourt Brace Jovanovich, 1965.

Sherwin, Martin J. *A World Destroyed. Hiroshima and the Origins of the Arms Race.* New York: Vintage, 1987.

Sherwood, Robert E. *Roosevelt and Hopkins: An Intimate History.* New York: Grosset and Dunlap, 1948.

BIBLIOGRAPHY

Simon, James F. *Independent Journey. The Life of William O. Douglas.* New York: Harper and Row, 1980.

Slaughter, Stephen S. *History of a Missouri Farm Family. The O. V. Slaughters 1700–1944.* Harrison, New York: Harbor Hill, 1978.

Smith, Gaddis. *The American Secretaries of State and Their Diplomacy,* Vol. 16, *Dean Acheson.* New York: Cooper Square Publishers, 1972.

Smith, Jean Edward. *Lucius D. Clay. An American Life.* New York: Henry Holt, 1990.

Smith, John. *Alger Hiss. The True Story.* New York: Holt, Rinehart and Winston, 1977.

Smith, Margaret Chase. *Declaration of Conscience,* William C. Lewis, Jr., ed. Garden City, New York: Doubleday, 1972.

Smith, Merriman. *Thank You, Mr. President: A White House Notebook.* New York: Harper, 1946.

Smith, Richard Norton. *Thomas E. Dewey and His Times.* New York: Simon and Schuster, 1982.

Smith, Timothy G., ed. *Merriman Smith's Book of Presidents: A White House Memoir.* New York: Norton, 1972.

Snyder, Louis L. *The War. A Concise History 1939–1945.* New York: Dell, 1960.

Solberg, Carl. *Hubert Humphrey.* New York: Norton, 1984.

Solzhenitsyn, Aleksandr I. *The Gulag Archipelago. 1918–1956: An Experiment in Literary Investigation, I–II.* New York: Harper and Row, 1947.

Spanier, John W. *The Truman-MacArthur Controversy and the Korean War.* New York: Norton, 1965.

Spector, Ronald H. *Eagle Against the Sun. The American War with Japan.* New York: Free Press, 1985.

Spencer, Cornelia. *Straight Furrow.* New York: Day, 1949.

Steel, Ronald. *Walter Lippmann and the American Century.* New York: Vintage, 1981.

Steinberg, Alfred. *The Man from Missouri: The Life and Times of Harry S. Truman.* New York: Putnam's, 1962.

Stimson, Henry L., and McGeorge Bundy. *On Active Service in Peace and War.* New York: Harper, 1948.

Stone, I. F. *The Hidden History of the Korean War 1950–1951.* Boston: Little, Brown, 1952.

————. *The Truman Era 1945–1952. A Nonconformist History of Our Times.* Boston: Little, Brown, 1953.

————. *The War Years 1939–1945. A Nonconformist History of Our Times.* Boston: Houghton Mifflin, 1988.

Strout, Richard L. *TRB. Views and Perspectives on the Presidency.* New York: Macmillan, 1980.

Sullivan, William C., with Bill Brown. *The Bureau. My Thirty Years in Hoover's FBI.* New York: Norton, 1979.

Sulzberger, C. L. *A Long Row of Candles. Memoirs and Diaries (1934–1954).* Toronto, Ontario: Macmillan, 1969.

————. *The American Heritage Picture History of World War II.* Vols. 1 and 2. New York: American Heritage, 1966.

Svobida, Lawrence. *Farming the Dust Bowl. A First-Hand Account from Kansas.* Lawrence, Kansas: University Press of Kansas, 1986.

Swanberg, W. A. *Luce and His Empire.* New York: Scribner's, 1972.

Taft, Senator Robert A. *A Foreign Policy for Americans.* Garden City, New York: Doubleday, 1951.

Tames, George. *Eye on Washington. The Presidents Who've Known Me.* New York: Harper Collins, 1990.

Taylor, A. J. P. *The First World War. An Illustrated History.* New York: Viking, 1985.

Terkel, Studs. *The Good War. An Oral History of World War Two.* New York: Pantheon, 1984.

Theoharis, Athan. *From the Secret Files of J. Edgar Hoover.* Chicago: Dee, 1991.

————, and John Stuart Cox. *The Boss. J. Edgar Hoover and the Great American Inquisition.* Philadelphia: Temple University Press, 1988.

Thomson, Virgil. *Virgil Thomson*. New York: Knopf, 1966.

Time-Life, eds. *This Fabulous Century, 1930–1940*. Vol 4. New York: Time-Life, 1969.

Toland, John. *In Mortal Combat. Korea, 1950–1953*. New York: William Morrow, 1991.

———. *No Man's Land. 1918—The Last Year of the Great War*. Garden City, New York: Doubleday, 1980.

———. *The Last 100 Days*. New York: Random House, 1966.

———. *The Rising Sun. The Decline and Fall of the Japanese Empire*. New York: Bantam, 1971.

Traubel, Helen. *St. Louis Woman*. New York: Duell, Sloan & Pearce, 1959.

Truman, Harry S. *Mr. Citizen*. New York: Geis Associates, 1960.

———. *Truman Speaks*. New York: Columbia University Press, 1960.

———. *Memoirs. Vol. I: Year of Decisions*. Garden City, New York: Doubleday, 1955.

———. *Memoirs. Vol. II: Years of Trial and Hope*. Garden City, New York: Doubleday, 1956.

Truman, Margaret (with Margaret Cousins). *Souvenir. Margaret Truman's Own Story*. New York: McGraw-Hill, 1956.

———. *Bess W. Truman*. New York: Macmillan, 1986.

———. *Harry S. Truman*. New York: William Morrow, 1972.

———. *Letters from Father. The Truman Family's Personal Correspondence*. New York: Arbor House, 1981.

———. *Where the Buck Stops. The Personal and Private Writings of Harry S. Truman*. New York: Warner, 1989.

Tuchman, Barbara. *The Guns of August*. New York: Dell, 1970.

Tugwell, Rexford G. *How They Became President. Thirty-six Ways to the White House*. New York: Simon and Schuster, 1968.

Tully, Grace. *F.D.R. My Boss*. New York: Scribner's, 1949.

Tusa, Ann and John. *The Berlin Airlift*. New York: Atheneum, 1988.

Ulam, Adam B. *Stalin: The Man and His Era*. New York: Viking, 1973.

Underhill, Robert. *The Truman Persuasions*. Ames, Iowa: Iowa State University Press, 1981.

Vandenberg, Arthur H., Jr., ed. *The Private Papers of Senator Vandenberg*. Boston: Houghton Mifflin, 1952.

Vansittart, Peter. *Voices from the Great War*. New York: Franklin Watts, 1984.

Vestal, Stanley. *The Missouri*. New York: Farrar & Rinehart, 1945.

Vidal, Gore. *Washington, D.C.* New York: Ballantine, 1967.

Volkogonov, Dmitri. *Stalin: Triumph and Tragedy*. New York: Grove Weidenfeld, 1991.

Wallace, Henry. *The Price of Vision*. Boston: Houghton Mifflin, 1973.

Walton, Richard J. *Henry Wallace, Harry Truman and the Cold War*. New York: Viking, 1976.

Warren, Earl. *The Memoirs of Earl Warren*. Garden City, New York: Doubleday, 1977.

Wedemeyer, Albert C. *Wedemeyer Reports!* New York: Henry Holt, 1958.

Weinstein, Allen. *Perjury: The Hiss-Chambers Case*. New York: Knopf, 1978.

Weintraub, Stanley. *A Stillness Heard Round the World. The End of the Great War: November, 1918*. New York: Dutton, 1985.

Weisberger, Bernard. *Cold War Peace. The United States and Russia Since 1945*. Boston: Houghton Mifflin, 1984.

Weizmann, Chaim. *Trial and Error: An Autobiography*. New York: Harper, 1949.

West, J. B., with Mary Lynn Kotz. *Upstairs at the White House: My Life with the First Ladies*. New York: Coward, McCann and Geoghegan, 1973.

Whelan, Richard. *Drawing the Line. The Korean War, 1950–1953*. Boston: Little, Brown, 1990.

White, Theodore H. *In Search of History. A Personal Adventure*. New York: Warner, 1978.

White, Walter. *A Man Called White. The Autobiography of Walter White*. New York: Viking, 1948.

———. *How Far the Promised Land*. New York: Viking, 1955.

White, William S. *Citadel. The Story of the U.S. Senate*. New York: Harper, 1957.

———. *The Taft Story*. New York: Harper, 1954.

BIBLIOGRAPHY

Whiting, Allen S. *China Crosses the Yalu. The Decision to Enter the Korean War*. New York: Macmillan, 1960.

Whitney, Major General Courtney. *MacArthur. His Rendezvous with History*. New York: Knopf, 1956.

Wilcox, Pearl. *Independence and 20th Century Pioneers. The Years from 1900 to 1928*. Independence, Missouri, 1979.

———. *Jackson County Pioneers*. Jackson County, Missouri, 1975.

William, Harold A. *The Baltimore Sun*. Baltimore: Johns Hopkins University Press, 1987.

Williams, Robert Chadwell. *Klaus Fuchs, Atom Spy*. Cambridge, Massachusetts: Harvard University Press, 1987.

Williams, T. Harry. *Huey Long*. New York: Vintage, 1981.

Williams, Walter. *The State of Missouri. An Autobiography*. Columbia, Missouri: E. W. Stephens, 1904.

Willis, James F., and Martin L. Primack. *An Economic History of the United States*. 2nd edn. Englewood Cliffs, New Jersey: Prentice-Hall, 1989.

Wyden, Peter. *Day One. Before Hiroshima and After*. New York: Simon and Schuster, 1984.

Yank, The Army Weekly, eds. *Yank. The Story of World War II as Written by the Soldiers*. New York: Greenwich House, 1984.

Yergin, Daniel. *Shattered Peace. The Origins of the Cold War and the National Security State*. Boston: Houghton Mifflin, 1977.

ARTICLES

Acheson, David. "The Truman-Acheson Friendship," *Whistle Stop* (published by the Harry S. Truman Library Institute), Vol. 12, no. 3, 1984.

Acheson, Dean. "The Greatness of Harry Truman," *Esquire*, September 1969.

Alexander, Jack. "Stormy New Boss of the Pentagon," *Saturday Evening Post*, July 30, 1949.

Alsop, Joseph and Stewart. "Candidate Truman's Magic Brew," *Saturday Evening Post*, December 31, 1949.

———. "How Our Foreign Policy Is Made," *Saturday Evening Post*, April 30, 1949.

———. "If Russia Grabs Europe," *Saturday Evening Post*, December 20, 1947.

———. "If War Comes," *Saturday Evening Post*, September 11, 1948.

———. "The Lesson of Korea," *Saturday Evening Post*, September 2, 1950.

———. "What Kind of President Will Dewey Make?" *Saturday Evening Post*, October 16, 1948.

———. "Why Has Washington Gone Crazy?" *Saturday Evening Post*, July 29, 1950.

Alsop, Stewart, and Dr. Ralph Lapp. "The Inside Story of Our First Hydrogen Bomb," *Saturday Evening Post*, October 25, 1952.

"An Interview with Greta Kempton," *Whistle Stop*, Vol. 15, no. 2, 1987.

Armstrong, O. K. "Crusade in Kansas City," *This Week*, March 13, 1938.

Asbury, Edith. "Meet Harry's Boss, Bess," *Collier's*, February 12, 1949.

Aurthur, Robert Alan. "Harry Truman Chuckles Dryly," *Esquire*, September 1971.

———. "The Wit and Sass of Harry S. Truman," *Esquire*, August 1971.

Baldwin, Hanson W. "The Atomic Weapon," *The New York Times*, August 7, 1945.

Bender, James F. "The Truman Voice—'General American,' " *The New York Times Magazine*, April 29, 1945.

Bendiner, Robert. "The Undramatic Man of Drama," *The New York Times Magazine*, March 11, 1951.

Bennett, Charles. "Truman, the Bomb and Today's Peril," *The New York Times*, July 5, 1985.

Berger, Meyer. "Mother Truman's Life Not All Frontier Toil," Kansas City *Times*, June 30, 1946 (reprinted from *The New York Times*).

Bernstein, Barton J. "The Myth of Lives Saved by A-Bombs," Los Angeles *Times*, July 28, 1985.

Blumenthal, Sidney. "The Essential Clark Clifford," *The Washington Post Magazine*, February 5, 1989.

BIBLIOGRAPHY

Boyer, Paul. "The Day You First Heard the News," *The New York Times,* August 4, 1985.

Bradley, Lenore K. "Building Jackson County," *Whistle Stop,* Vol. 13, no. 2, 1985.

Brant, Leroy V. "Music's Significant Place in Modern Life," *Etude,* October 1946.

Brinkley, Alan. "Minister Without Portfolio," *Harper's,* February 1983.

Broad, William J. "40 Years Ago, the Bomb: The Questions Came Later," *The New York Times,* July 16, 1985.

Brooks, Alex. "McCarran's Iron Curtain," *The Nation,* March 29, 1952.

Burrus, Rufus. "Colonel Harry S. Truman as I Knew Him," Speech in Kansas City, Missouri, January 11, 1973.

Busch, Noel. "A Year of Truman," *Life,* April 8, 1946.

Byrd, Senator Robert C. "James F. Byrnes: The 'Insider,' " *Congressional Record,* September 7, 1984. Washington, D.C.: Government Printing Office.

Carlton, John T. "Truman: The Last Real Friend," *The Retired Officer,* June 1984.

Chamberlain, John. "Washington in June," *Life,* June 1, 1945.

Clifford, Clark. "Recognizing Israel," *American Heritage,* Vol. XXVIII, no. 3, April 1977.

Clymer, Floyd. "An Interview with Harry S. Truman," *Floyd Clymer's Historical Motor Scrapbook,* no. 7 (no date).

Cole, David. "McCarran-Walter," *Constitution,* Winter 1990.

Commager, Henry Steele. "A Few Kind Words for Harry Truman," *Look,* August 1951.

Cool, Margaret. "HST'S Dreadful Devil Wagon," *Kansas City.* Vol 1, no. 7, July 1976.

Crawford, Kenneth G. "Everyman in the White House," *American Mercury,* February 1946.

Creel, George. "Independence Makes a President," *Collier's,* August 18, 1945.

Curry, John T. " 'They've Killed the President.' The Attempted Assassination of President Truman," *Whistle Stop,* Vol. 7, no. 4, Fall 1979.

Dains, Mary K. "Fulton's Distinguished Visitors: Truman and Churchill, 1946," *Missouri Historical Review,* April 1984.

Daniel, Margaret Truman. "Bess," *Parade,* March 30, 1986.

Daniels, Jonathan. "How Truman Writes Those Letters," *Collier's,* February 24, 1951.

———. "The Lady from Independence," *McCall's,* April 1949.

Davies, Richard O. "Whistle-Stopping Through Ohio," *Ohio History,* July 1962.

Davis, Elsie Spry. "Forebears of Solomon Young," 1980.

Divine, Robert A. "The Cold War and the Election of 1948," *Journal of American History* (1972).

Donovan, Hedley. "The Presidency: Job Specs for the Oval Office," *Time,* December 13, 1982.

Donovan, Robert. "Truman Seizes Steel," *Constitution,* Fall 1990.

Dorsett, Lyle Wesley. "Alderman Jim Pendergast," *Missouri Historical Bulletin,* October 1964.

Elsey, George M. "Memoir: Some White House Recollections, 1942–1953," *Diplomatic History,* Vol. 12, no. 3, Summer 1988.

Erskine, Helen Worden. "The Riddle of Mrs. Truman," *Collier's,* February 9, 1952.

———. "Truman in Retirement," *Collier's,* February 4, 1955.

Essary, Helen. "Bess Truman: The President's Boss," Vertical File, HSTL.

Everett, Glenn D. "Wow! Did Truman Ever Fool the Farmers!" *Saturday Evening Post,* August 16, 1952.

Farrar, Ronald. "Ross Tops as Newsman; Truman Press Secretary," *Journalism Alumni News,* May 1966.

Ferrell, Robert, ed. "A Visitor to the White House, 1947: The Diary of Vic H. Householder," *Missouri Historical Review.*

Fischer, John. "Mr. Truman Reorganizes," *Harper's,* January 1946.

———. "Mr. Truman's Politico," *Harper's,* June 1951.

Fitzmaurice, Walter. "President Truman's Campaign Special," *Trains,* March 1949.

Fitzsimmons, Tom. "The Nation Talks Back to McCarran," *The New Republic,* January 12, 1953.

Frank, Reuven. "1948: Live . . . From Philadelphia . . . It's the National Conventions," *The New York Times Magazine,* April 17, 1988.

Franklin, Jay. "Inside Strategy of the Campaign," *Life,* November 15, 1948.

BIBLIOGRAPHY

Furman, Bess. "Independent Lady from Independence," *The New York Times Magazine,* June 9, 1946.

Gentry, Sue. "What Was the City Like in '09? A Peek into the Past Reveals an Answer," Independence *Examiner,* July 6, 1971.

Gervasi, Frank. "A President Grows Up," *Collier's,* May 24, 1947.

———. "The Truth About Truman," *Collier's,* January 22, 1949.

Giglio, James. "Harry S. Truman and the Multifarious Ex-Presidency." *Presidential Studies Quarterly,* Spring 1982.

Gilmer, Carol Lynn. "Missouri's One-Family Newspaper," *Harper's,* October 1954.

"The Gold Coast Railroad Museum's Famous U.S. Presidential Car No. 1 *Ferdinand Magellan.* A National Historic Landmark" (brochure).

Grant, Philip A. "The Election of Harry S. Truman to the United States Senate," *Missouri Historical Society Bulletin, 36* (1980).

Graybar, Lloyd J. "The Atomic Bomb Tests: Atomic Diplomacy or Bureaucratic Infighting?" *The Journal of American History,* March 1986.

Griffith, Robert. "Harry S. Truman and the Burden of Modernity," *Reviews in American History,* September 1981.

Grose, Peter. "The Partition of Palestine 35 Years Ago," *The New York Times Magazine,* November 21, 1982.

Grothaus, Larry. "Kansas City Blacks, Harry Truman and the Pendergast Machine," *Missouri Historical Review,* October 1974.

Guard, Samuel R. "From Plowboy to President," *Breeder's Gazette,* June 1945.

Hale, Donald R. "James Chiles—A Missouri Badman," *The West,* October 1968.

Hall, Norman S. "Five Red Days," *Liberty,* May 14, 1927.

Hamburger, Philip. "Profiles: Mr. Secretary" (Dean Acheson), *The New Yorker,* November 12, 1949; November 19, 1949.

Hamby, Alonzo L. "An American Democrat: A Reevaluation of the Personality of Harry S. Truman," *Political Science Quarterly,* Vol. 106, no. 1, 1991.

———. "Harry Truman, Small-Town American," *History Today,* December 1989.

———. "One Hundred Years of Harry Truman," *The American Spectator,* July 1984.

———. "'The Great Drive Has Taken Place and I had a Part in It': Truman, Battery D, and the Meuse-Argonne Campaign," *Whistle Stop,* Vol. 15, no. 4, 1987.

———. "Truman vs. Dewey: The 1948 Election," *The Wilson Quarterly,* Spring 1988.

Hart, Scott. "Truman and Ross: America's No. 1 Team," *Coronet,* January 1946.

Hassett, William D. "The President Was My Boss," *Saturday Evening Post,* October 10, November 28, 1953.

Hatch, Alden. "The New Truman," *Liberty,* July 5, 1947.

Heaster, Brenda L. "Who's on Second: The 1944 Democratic Presidential Nomination," *Missouri Historical Review,* January 1986.

Hehmeyer, Walter. "The President Keeps Himself Fit," *Parade,* May 25, 1947.

Heller, Francis. "The Writing of the Truman Memoirs," *Presidential Studies Quarterly,* Winter 1983.

Henry, Frank. "Artilleryman Truman in the First World War," *The Baltimore Sun Sunday Magazine,* May 13, 1945.

Hoy, P. R. *Journal of an Exploration of Western Missouri in 1854.* Under the Auspices of the Smithsonian Institution.

Hughes, Emmet John. "Our Presidents, Heroes or Nobodies: They All Had Their Own Style," *Smithsonian,* March 1972.

Huie, William Bradford. "How to Think About Truman," *American Mercury,* August 1951.

Hume, Paul. "The Music Critic and the President: The Second Time Around," *Whistle Stop,* Vol. 16, no. 2, 1988.

"I.H.S. Class of '01. Forty-one Boys and Girls Receive High School Diplomas—Commencement Exercises," *Jackson Examiner,* May 31, 1901.

Isaacson, Walter. "Essay: Why Did We Drop the Bomb?" *Time,* August 19, 1985.

Jacobson, Edward. "Two Presidents and a Haberdasher—1948," *American Jewish Archives,* April 1968.

BIBLIOGRAPHY

Jessup, Philip C. "Research Note/The Record of Wake Island—A Correction," *The Journal of American History,* March 1981.

Johns Hopkins Foreign Policy Institute, School of Advanced International Studies. "Dean Acheson and the Making of U.S. Foreign Policy," Washington, D.C., April 6, 1989.

Karp, Walter. "Truman vs. MacArthur," *American Heritage,* April/May 1984.

Kempton, Greta. Interview in *Whistle Stop,* Vol. 15, no. 2, 1987.

————. "Painting the Truman Family," *Missouri Historical Review,* April 1973.

Kirdendall, Richard S. "Harry S. Truman, a Missouri Farmer in the Golden Age," *Agricultural History,* 1974.

————. "Truman and Missouri," *Missouri Historical Review,* LXXXI, January 1987.

Knebel, Fletcher. "We Shall All Miss Him. President, Newspaperman, and Sigs Mourn Passing of Charles G. Ross," *The Sigma Chi,* March 1951.

Kornitzer, Bela. "Harry Truman, Musician and Critic," *Pathfinder,* January 9, 1952.

————. "The Story of Truman and His Father," *Parents Magazine,* March 1951.

La Cossitt, Henry. "He Takes the President on Tour," *Saturday Evening Post,* June 16, 1951.

Lahey, Edwin A. "Good-bye, Mr. Truman!" *Extension,* December 1952.

Larkin, Lew. "The Other Side of Tom Pendergast," *Missouri Life,* April 11, 1978.

Laurence, William L. "The Truth About the Hydrogen Bomb," *Saturday Evening Post,* June 24, 1950.

Lee, R. Alton. "Rebuilding the White House." *American History Illustrated,* February 1978.

Lehman, Milton. "The White House Shudders," *Collier's,* November 13, 1948.

Leuchtenburg, William E. "Give 'Em Harry," *The New Republic,* May 21, 1984.

Leviero, Anthony. "Harry Truman: Musician and Music Lover," *The New York Times Magazine,* June 18, 1950.

Lewis, Anthony. "Shadow on the Stone," *The New York Times,* August 5, 1985.

Littlefield, Dr. Duncan E. "The President Versus the General" (sermon delivered in Grand Rapids, Michigan, on April 15, 1951).

Lubell, Samuel. "What You Don't Know About Truman," *Saturday Evening Post,* March 15, 1952.

————. "Who *Really* Elected Truman?" *Saturday Evening Post,* January 22, 1949.

Macdonald, Rear Admiral Donald J., U.S. Navy (Retired). "President Truman's Yacht," *Naval History,* Winter 1990.

MacKaye, Milton. "He'll Sink or Swim with Harry," *Saturday Evening Post,* May 29, 1948.

————. "Things Are Different in the White House," *Saturday Evening Post,* April 20, 1946.

Markel, Lester. "After Four Years: Portrait of Harry Truman," *The New York Times Magazine,* April 10, 1949.

————. "Truman as the Crucial Third Year Opens," *The New York Times Magazine,* March 16, 1947.

Mayerberg, Samuel S. "Edward Jacobson: President Truman's Buddy." *Liberal Judaism,* August 1945.

McCarthy, Joe. "A Walk Through History with Harry Truman." *Holiday,* November/December 1963.

McCormick, Anne O'Hare. "Abroad: The Promethean Role of the United States," *The New York Times,* August 8, 1945.

McCoy, Donald R. "Harry S. Truman: Personality, Politics and Presidency," *Presidential Studies Quarterly,* Spring 1982.

McCune, Wesley, and John R. Beal. "The Job That Made Truman President," *Harper's,* June 1945.

Means, Marianne. "What Three Presidents Say About Their Wives," *Good Housekeeping,* August 1963.

Michener, James. "A Tough Man for a Tough Job," *Life,* May 12, 1952.

Miles, Rufus E., Jr., "Hiroshima: The Strange Myth of Half a Million American Lives Saved," *International Security,* Fall 1985.

Miller, M. F. "A Century of Missouri Agriculture," *University of Missouri Bulletin,* May 1958.

Miller, Merle. "Mr. Truman's Hometown," *Holiday,* May 1970.

Miner, Paul V. "Boss Tom Pendergast's Wide Open Town," *Kansas City Star Magazine,* July 4, 1976.

BIBLIOGRAPHY

Miscamble, Wilson D. "Anthony Eden and the Truman-Molotov Conversations, April 1945," *Diplomatic History,* Spring 1978.

———. "Harry S Truman, The Berlin Blockade and the 1948 Election," *Presidential Studies Quarterly,* Summer 1980.

———. "The Evolution of an Internationalist: Harry S. Truman and American Foreign Policy," *The Australian Journal of Politics and History,* August 1977.

Mixson, James M., D.M.D. "The Two Crises That Faced President Truman: Korean and Dental," *Bulletin of the History of Dentistry,* October 1988.

Mumford, F. B. "A Century of Missouri Agriculture," *Missouri Historical Review,* January 1921.

Nelson, Anna Kasten. "President Truman and the Evolution of the National Security Council," *The Journal of American History.* September 1985.

Oberdorfer, Don. "Ex-Democrat, Ex-Dixiecrat, Today's Nixiecrat," *The New York Times Magazine.* October 6, 1968.

O'Brien, Pat. "Old Rail Depots in Independence Represent Important Era of History." *Jackson County Historical Society,* April–June 1982.

"Original Landowner Map of the City of Grandview," *Jackson County Advocate,* November 6, 1975.

Osborne, John. "Happy Days for Harry," *Life,* July 7, 1958.

Pearson, Drew. "The Man Who Didn't Want to Be President," April 16, 1945.

Perry, George Sessions. "Independence, Missouri," *Saturday Evening Post,* September 2, 1950.

Phillips, Cabell. "How the President Does His Job." *The New York Times Magazine,* January 4, 1948.

———. "Truman at 75," *The New York Times Magazine,* May 3, 1959.

———. "Truman Likes These," *The New York Times Magazine,* June 17, 1951.

———. "Truman's Home Town Is 'Smalltown, U.S.A.' " *The New York Times Magazine,* July 1, 1945.

Potts, Edward W. "The President's Mother: Martha Ellen Truman," *The Christian Advocate* (n.d.).

Renshaw, Bill. "President Truman. His Missouri Neighbors Tell of His Farm Years," *The Prairie Farmer,* May 12, 1945.

Reston, James. "Dawn of the Atom Era Perplexes Washington," *The New York Times,* August 12, 1945.

Rigdon, Commander William, U.S.N. "We Kept Truman's Big Secret," *Collier's,* July 4, 1953.

Robbins, Jhan and June. "Six Great Turning Points of American History," *This Week,* February 22, 1959.

Roper, Elmo, and Louis Harris. "The Press and the Great Debate," *The Saturday Review of Literature,* July 14, 1951.

Rosenberg, David Alan. "The U.S. Nuclear Stockpile, 1945–1950," *The Bulletin of Atomic Scientists,* May 1982.

Rosenberg, J. Philip. "The Belief System of Harry S. Truman and Its Effect on Foreign Policy Decision-Making During His Administration," *Presidential Studies Quarterly,* Spring 1982.

Ross, Charles G. "How Truman Did It," *Collier's,* December 25, 1948.

Rothe, Albert J., as told to Beverly Smith. "Pst! Truman's Got a Cowlick," *Saturday Evening Post,* November 12, 1949.

Rovere, Richard H. "Letter from the Campaign Train," *The New Yorker,* October 9, 1948.

———. "Letter from the Campaign Train," *The New Yorker,* October 16, 1948.

———. "Letter from Washington," *The New Yorker,* July 28, 1975.

———. "President Harry," *Harper's,* July 1948.

———. "Profiles: Nothing Much to It," *The New Yorker,* September 8, 1945.

———. "The Last Days of Joe McCarthy," *Encounter,* December 1958.

———. "The Most Gifted and Successful Demagogue This Country Has Ever Known," *The New York Times Magazine,* April 1967.

Safly, Elizabeth. "Truman's Books. The Post-Presidential Years," *Whistle Stop,* Winter 1979.

. "Truman's Books. Part II," *Whistle Stop,* Spring 1979.

BIBLIOGRAPHY

Schnell, J. Christopher, Richard J. Collings, and David W. Dillard. "The Political Impact of the Depression on Missouri, 1929–1940," *Missouri Historical Review,* January 1991.

Schumach, Murray. "The Education of Matthew Ridgway," *The New York Times Magazine,* May 4, 1952.

Sevareid, Eric. "A Truly Great Man," *McCall's,* March 1973.

———. "The Human Truman," Vertical file, HSTL

Severo, Richard, and Lewis Milford. "Sweet Wine at Last," *Military History Quarterly,* Winter 1989.

Sheley, O.C. "James Peacock and 'Jim Crow' Chiles," *Frontier Times,* May 1963.

Shogan, Robert. "1948 Election," *American Heritage,* June 1968.

Slichter, Sumner H. "The Past Year and the Next in Our Economy," *The New York Times Magazine,* June 10, 1951.

Slomovitz, Philip. "Harry S. Truman: The Modern Cyrus," *The American Jewish Outlook,* January 23, 1953.

Smith, Beverly. "The Curious Case of the President's Bathtub," *Saturday Evening Post,* August 23, 1952.

———. "Washington's Greatest Storyteller," *Saturday Evening Post,* July 2, 1949.

———. "What a Spanking He Gave Truman!" *Saturday Evening Post,* August 2, 1952.

———. "Why We Went to War in Korea," *Saturday Evening Post,* November 11, 1951.

Smith, Gaddis. "The Acheson Papers," *Whistle Stop,* Spring 1973.

Smith, H. Allen. "A Friend of Ours Named Harry," *This Week,* April 5, 1964.

Snyder, John W. "Unforgettable Harry Truman," *Reader's Digest,* November 1980.

Staley, J. W. "Eyes Across the DMZ," *Army Digest,* October 1969.

Steinberg, Alfred. "How Harry Truman Does His Job," *Saturday Evening Post,* March 3, 10, 1951.

———. "Mr. Truman's Mystery Man," *Saturday Evening Post,* December 24, 1949.

Sutton, Horace. "Key West, The Living End," *Saturday Review,* January 7, 1978.

Tammeus, William D. "He Plowed a Straight Furrow," *Whistle Stop,* Vol. 12, no. 4, 1984.

Thierman, Sue McClelland. "A Church with Roots in History." Louisville *Courier-Journal,* June 3, 1945.

Truman, Harry S. "My First Eighty Years," *Saturday Evening Post,* June 13, 1964.

———. "The Most Mistreated of Presidents," *The North Carolina Historical Review,* April 1959.

Truman, Margaret. "Memories of a Cherished Home," *The New York Times,* April 22, 1984.

Tucker, Captain Frank C. III, USAR. "Reserve Duty Means Adventure for HST," *The Officer,* May 1984.

"Two Presidents and a Haberdasher—1948," *American Jewish Archives,* April 1968.

Vaccaro, Ernest B. "Harry Truman and the Press," *The Quill,* February 1973.

Waugh, Alfred S. "Desultory Wanderings in the Years 1845–46," edited by John Francis McDermott. *Missouri Historical Society,* April and October 1950.

White, Hollis L. "Champ Clark, The 'Leather-Bound' Orator," *Missouri Historical Review,* October 1961–July 1962.

White, Theodore H. " 'Wise Man' in Quest of Security," *The New York Times Magazine,* March 16, 1952.

Whitman, Walter. "Take a Tip from Harry Truman. 'Wake Up and Walk!' " *This Week,* June 4, 1961.

Williams, Herbert Lee. "I Was Truman's Ghost," *Presidential Studies Quarterly,* Spring 1982.

Wills, Garry. "I'm Not Wild About Harry," *Esquire,* January 1976.

Wilson, Richard. "Truman Brings Back Boss Pendergast," *Look,* October 29, 1946.

Wiltz, John Edward. "Truman and MacArthur: The Wake Island Meeting," *Military Affairs,* December 1978.

Woolf, S. J. "President Truman Talks About His Job," *The New York Times Magazine,* July 15, 1945.

Wyden, Peter. "The Sudden Dawn," *The Washingtonian,* July 1985.

Yancey, Noel. "The Day Truman Dropped In," *Spectator,* August 1, 1985.

BIBLIOGRAPHY

Yergin, Daniel. "Harry Truman—Revived and Revised." *The New York Times Magazine,* October 24, 1976. .

REFERENCE SOURCES

American Heritage, eds. *The American Heritage Pictorial History of the Presidents of the United States.* Vols. 1 and 2. New York: American Heritage Publ. Co., 1968.

Bartlett's Quotations. Boston: Little, Brown, 1980.

Boorstin, Daniel J., and Brooks Mather Kelley, with Ruth Frankel Boorstin. *A History of the United States.* Lexington, Massachusetts: Ginn and Co., 1981.
Britannica Book of the Year 1949. Chicago: Encyclopaedia Britannica, 1949.
Britannica Book of the Year 1951. Chicago: Encyclopaedia Britannica, 1951.
Britannica Book of the Year 1952. Chicago: Encyclopaedia Britannica, 1952.
Britannica Book of the Year 1953. Chicago: Encyclopacdia Britannica, 1953.
Cohen, J. M. and M. J. *The Penguin Dictionary of Modern Quotations.* New York: Penguin Books, 1978.
Conrad, Howard L., ed. *Encyclopedia of the History of Missouri. A Compendium of History and Biography for Ready Reference.* Vol. III, Vol. VI. New York: Southern History, 1901.

Current Biography

Daniel, Clifton, ed. *Chronicle of the 20th Century.* Mount Kisco, New York: Chronicle Publications, 1987.
Foner, Eric and John A. Garraty, eds. *The Reader's Companion to American History.* Boston: Houghton Mifflin, 1991.
Gordon, Lois, and Alan Gordon. *American Chronicle. Six Decades in American Life 1920–1980.* New York: Atheneum, 1987.
Information Please Almanac 1949. New York: Farrar, Straus. 1949.
Irvine, E. Eastman, ed. *The World Almanac and Book of Facts for 1945.* New York: New York World-Telegram, 1945.
Morison, Samuel Eliot, Henry Steele Commager, and William E. Leuchtenburg. *Concise History of the American Republic.* New York: Oxford University Press, 1977.
Palmer, Alan. *The Penguin Dictionary of Twentieth Century History 1900–1978.* New York: Penguin Books, 1979.
Presidents. New York: New England Publishing Associates, 1988.
Schoenebaum, Eleanora W., ed. *Political Profiles: The Truman Years.* New York: Facts on File, 1978.
Taylor, Tim. *The Book of Presidents.* New York: Arno Press, 1972.
Time Magazine, eds. *The American Presidents. Special Report.* New York: Time, Inc., 1976.
White House Historical Association. *The White House. An Historic Guide. Revised Edition.* Washington White House Historical Association with the cooperation of the National Geographic Society, 1979.
Young, Brigadier Peter, ed. *The World Almanac Book of World War II.* Englewood Cliffs, New Jersey: Prentice-Hall, 1981.

MAGAZINES AND JOURNALS CONSULTED

American Heritage • American History Illustrated • American Jewish Outlook • American Mercury • American Spectator • Bulletin of Atomic Scientists • Collier's • Coronet • Esquire • Etude • Fortune • Harper's • History Today • Liberty • Life • Look • McCall's • Military History Quarterly • Missouri Life • Nation • New Republic • New Yorker • New York Times Magazine • Newsweek • Parade • Parents Magazine • Reader's Digest • Saturday

BIBLIOGRAPHY

Evening Post • Saturday Review • Smithsonian • This Week • Time • Wallace's Farmer • Washingtonian • Whistle Stop

Newspapers Consulted

Albuquerque (New Mexico) Journal • American Observer • Arizona Republic • Atlanta Journal • Baltimore Sun • Belton (Missouri) Star-Herald • Blue Springs (Missouri) Examiner • Boston Daily Globe • Boston Globe • Boston Post • Catholic Herald Citizen • Charleston (West Virginia) Gazette • Chicago Daily News • Chicago Sun • Chicago Sun-Times • Chicago Tribune • Christian Science Monitor • Cincinnati Enquirer • Cleveland Plain Dealer • Columbus (Ohio) Evening Dispatch • Daily Oklahoman • Dallas Morning News • Denver Post • Deseret News (Utah) • Des Moines Register • Detroit Free Press • Detroit News • Emporia (Kansas) Daily Gazette • Hartford Courant • Idaho Daily Statesman • Illinois State Register • Independence (Missouri) Examiner • Independence (Missouri) Sentinel • Indianapolis Star • Jackson (Mississippi) Daily News • Jackson County (Missouri) Advocate • Jackson County (Missouri) Examiner • Kansas City Jewish Chronicle • Kansas City Business Journal • Kansas City Journal-Post • Kansas City Star • Kansas City Times • Kansas City Weekly Enterprise • Knoxville (Tennessee) News-Sentinel • Lamar (Missouri) Democrat • Lansing (Michigan) Star Journal • Liberty (Missouri) Tribune • Long Island (New York) Press • Louisville Courier-Journal • Memphis Commercial Appeal • Miami Herald • Montana Standard • Morning World Herald (Omaha, Nebraska) • New Bedford (Massachusetts) Standard Times • New York Herald-Tribune • New York Times • New York World-Telegram • Philadelphia Inquirer • Pittsburgh Courier • Pittsburgh Post-Gazette • Portland (Oregon) Journal • Prairie Farmer • Rochester (New York) Democrat and Chronicle • Salt Lake City Tribune • San Antonio Express • San Francisco Chronicle • Seattle Times • Shelby (Kentucky) Sentinel News • Skaneateles (New York) Press • South Bend (Indiana) Tribune • St. Louis (Missouri) Globe-Democrat • St. Louis (Missouri) Post-Dispatch • St. Louis (Missouri) Star-Times • St. Paul Pioneer Press • Syracuse Post Standard • Times (London) • Toledo Blade • Tucson Daily Citizen • Wall Street Journal • Washington (D.C.) Daily News • Washington (D.C.) Post • Washington (D.C.) Star • Washington (D.C.) Times Herald • Willard (Ohio) Times

Photographic Archival Sources

Harry S. Truman Library • Jackson County Historical Society • Joseph C. Pruett • Kansas City *Star* • Library of Congress • National Archives • United States Senate Historical Office • Washington *Star*

Index

INDEX

Battle of Britain, 253–54
Baughman, U. E., 739
Baydur, Huseyin Ragip, 368
Bay of Pigs, 980
Bean, Louis, 710
Beatty, Earl David, 150
Beaverbrook, William Aitken, Lord, 958, 959
Bechtel, Stephen, 279
Belair, Felix, Jr., 496, 505, 526
Bell, Art, 930, 931
Bell, Elliott, 673, 674, 714
Bell, Jasper, 203
Benedict XV, Pope, 953
Bennett, David A., 745
Benny, Jack, 969
Bentley, Elizabeth, 646
Benton, Thomas Hart (artist), 967–69, 986, 989
Benton, Thomas Hart (senator), 18, 967
Berenson, Bernard, 954–55
Berenstein, David, 251
Bergen, Edgar, 724
Berger, Meyer, 701
Bergheim, Myrtle, 826
Bergin, Thomas G., 964
Beria, Lavrenti, 443
Berlin, 413, 414–16, 428–29, 435, 463, 540, 603
Berlin, Irving, 742, 943
Berlin crisis, 622, 633, 646, 655, 772, 820, 837, 853
  airlift in, 630–31, 647–48, 665, 672, 699, 713, 726, 734, 735, 807, 916, 990
  turn of tide in, 734
  Vinson mission and, 686
Bernadotte, Folke, 379
Bernstein, Carl, 552–53
Bernstein, Leonard, 934, 969
Berry, Lucian D., 109
Best Years of Our Lives, The, 482
Bevin, Ernest, 447, 448, 452, 563, 565, 600, 735
Bidault, Georges, 368
Biddle, Francis, 387, 388
Biffle, Les, 224, 252, 299, 346, 353, 505, 704, 843
Bikini, 491, 620
Bingham, George Caleb, 17, 32, 51, 52, 142
Binnagio, Charles, 868
Birdzell, Donald, 809, 810, 811, 812
Black, Hugo L., 216, 900–901
Blackmore, Dwight, 693
blacks, 53–54, 297, 587
  Byrnes and, 297, 302
  murders of, 589
  Roosevelt and, 302–3, 713

as voters, 302, 323, 587–88, 590, 591, 713
  see also civil rights; racial prejudice
Blair, Frank, 78, 99, 100
Blair House, 725, 727, 750, 808, 813
Blandy, William, 491
Blaustein, Jacob, 679
Blitz, Samuel, 42
Block, Herb, 761, 765, 841, 859
Boeing, 469
Boettiger, Anna Roosevelt, 327, 342
Boettiger, John, 342
Bogart, Humphrey, 665
Boggs, Lilburn W., 22, 23
Boggs, Lindy, 575
Bohlen, Charles "Chip," 370, 374, 375, 376, 384, 449, 527, 541, 546, 562–63, 564, 565, 582, 734, 799, 991
  on Marshall, 535
  at Potsdam, 406, 408, 409, 417, 419, 421, 425, 434, 439, 443, 445
Bolich, Daniel A., 871
Bonesteel, Charles, 786
Boone, Daniel, 15
Boone, Daniel Morgan, 15
Borah, William E., 214, 225, 242
Border War, 27–28, 53
Boring, Floyd M., 364, 385, 434–35, 802, 808, 809, 810, 908
Boston *Globe,* 846
Boston *Post,* 697–98
Bourgholtzer, Frank, 821, 826, 886
Bowles, Chester, 632
Bowman, Frederick, 120–21
Boyd, William, 861
Boyle, Clara, 867
Boyle, William, 260, 656, 666, 688–89, 707, 742
  accusations against, 863, 865, 866, 867, 868–70
  background and character of, 867–68
  resignation of, 870, 871
Bradley, John H., 368
Bradley, Omar, 349–50, 400, 428, 498, 580, 603, 737, 742, 749, 797, 813, 838, 938, 991
  atomic bomb and, 761–62
  Berlin crisis and, 631
  Korean War and, 777, 778, 780, 786, 787, 789, 792, 794, 796, 800, 801, 803, 805, 806, 817, 818, 823, 824, 831, 912
  MacArthur and, 792, 796, 800, 801, 803, 805, 806, 823, 824, 834, 835–36, 839, 840, 841, 842, 843, 850, 853, 854, 855
Brandeis, Louis D., 231, 295, 600, 754, 955
Brandeis, Mrs. Louis D., 231
Brandt, Raymond, 514
Brewster, O. C., 391–92

INDEX

Chiang Kai-shek, 447, 460, 508, 534, 742, 743, 744, 798, 838
   MacArthur and, 794, 795, 797, 832
Chiang Kai-shek, Madame, 794
Chicago *Sun,* 520
Chicago *Sun-Times,* 846
Chicago *Tribune,* 330–31, 456, 467, 482, 523, 697, 718, 819, 842, 843, 845
child care, 532
Childs, Marquis, 222, 224, 231, 236, 285, 309, 574, 656, 674, 694, 704
Chiles, Elijah, 34
Chiles, Henry, 171
Chiles, James J. "Jim Crow" (uncle), 29, 31, 33–34, 53, 56
Chiles, Morton, Jr., 367
Chiles, Sarah Ann "Sallie" Young (aunt), 24, 29, 34, 40
Chiles, Sol (cousin), 38, 40
China, 452, 777
   civil war in, 508, 534, 544, 726, 742–44, 759, 764, 798
   Marshall and, 475, 508, 532, 534, 743
   Soviet Union and, 418, 421, 423, 434, 457, 460, 486, 544
   see also Formosa; Manchuria
China, People's Republic of:
   inauguration of, 749
   Korean War and, 794, 795, 799, 802–3, 804–5, 807, 808, 814, 815–18, 820, 821, 823, 824, 825, 831, 835–36, 844, 850, 851, 853, 854
China Lobby, 743, 744
China White Paper, 743–44
Chinese Communists, 508, 534, 544, 734, 742–44
   see also China, People's Republic of
Chinese Nationalists (Kuomintang), 508, 534, 742, 743, 744
   see also Chiang Kai-shek; China; Formosa
"Chorus from Ajax" (Sophocles), 740
Chou En-lai, 799
Christian Science Monitor, 782, 846
Christina's World (Wyeth), 621
Chrysler, 493
Churchill, Clementine, 958
Churchill, Jenny Jerome, 411
Churchill, Mary, 410, 412, 958
Churchill, Sarah, 958
Churchill, Winston, 112, 355, 362, 368, 379–80, 381, 383, 398, 399, 410–12, 562, 583, 600, 715, 718, 790, 916, 918, 958–59
   Acheson and, 874
   background of, 410–11
   Berlin tour of, 415

   death of, 986
   election defeat of, 446
   HST as seen by, 412, 525–26, 632, 874–875
   HST on initial meeting with, 412
   HST's admiration of, 411, 535, 874
   HST's Berlin crisis letter to, 648–49
   "iron curtain" speech of, 383, 486–90, 491, 541, 582, 654
   map room of, 369
   on Marshall, 533
   at Potsdam, 403, 404, 407, 409, 410, 411–412, 415, 420–27, 430, 432–34, 442, 443, 445, 446–47, 918
   in return to office, 874
   Roosevelt and, 333, 371, 373, 379, 410, 411, 412, 434, 459, 619
   Stalin and, 418, 419
   World War II history written by, 936–37, 948
Church of Jesus Christ of Latter-Day Saints, *see* Mormons
CIA (Central Intelligence Agency), 566, 604, 853, 915, 990
Cieplinski, Michel, 683
Cincinnatus, 470, 770, 771, 927
Citizens Security, 172
Civil Aeronautics Act (1938), 246
civil rights, 532, 586–89, 629, 634, 638–40, 672, 677, 915, 990
   anti-lynching legislation and, 234, 570, 587, 639
   black vote and, 323, 587–88, 713
   HST's Harlem speech on, 702
   HST's Lincoln Memorial address on, 569–70
   HST's private vs. public views on, 247, 588, 971, 972
   HST's senatorial reelection campaign and, 247–48
   sit-ins and marches for, 971, 972
   southern Democrats and, 586, 588, 593, 639–40, 645, 675
   "Turnip" congressional session and, 642–43, 651
Civil Rights Commission, 587, 588, 589, 702, 915
civil service, 651, 915
Civil Service Commission, 551, 552
Civil War, U.S., 26–33, 104, 129, 258, 279, 356, 558
   Lincoln's problems with McClellan in, 837–38
Clark, Bennett Champ, 196, 212, 213, 214, 216, 223–24, 226, 235, 236, 241, 242, 245, 247, 249, 250–51, 254, 315, 317, 318, 320, 471, 917

INDEX

INDEX

INDEX

INDEX

Pruden, Edward, 728
Public Utility Holding Company Act (1935), 218–19
Puerto Rico, 810, 812
Pugh, Conley, 940
Pugh, Noah E., 940
Purcell, E. T. "Buck," 633
Pye, John, 497

Quantrill, William, 28–29, 30, 33, 53

Rabaut, Louis C., 877
racial prejudice, 675
  HST and, 54, 83, 86, 110, 247, 569–70, 588, 980
  in military, 587, 639, 651, 667, 915
  see also civil rights
Radford, Arthur, 800, 801
radio, 621, 980
Railway Labor Act (1934), 494
railway strike (1946), 494–95, 497–506, 507, 527, 899
Randall, Clarence, 899
Rash, Bryson, 886
Rayburn, Sam, 291, 340–41, 346, 350, 357, 359, 368, 388, 504, 520, 529, 530, 565, 652, 736, 840, 905, 961, 962, 963, 990
  funeral of, 976
  HST's reelection campaign and, 675, 677–78, 717
  1948 Democratic Convention chaired by, 639–40, 642
  Truman Doctrine supported by, 560
  as vice-presidential candidate, 249, 295, 297, 300
Reagan, Ronald, 665
Reason Why, The (Woodham-Smith), 944
Reconstruction Finance Corporation (RFC), 863, 864, 865–66, 867, 869, 870
Reddig, William, 154, 165, 235
Redding, Jack, 627, 683, 684, 685
Red Legs, 28, 33
Reece, Carroll, 521
Reed, Clyde Martin, 339
Reed, James A. "Fighting Jim," 153, 195, 200, 204
Reed, Nell Donnelly, 200
Reed, Stanley F., 729, 901
Regan, Phil, 728
Remington, Frederic, 142, 402, 787
Reminiscences (MacArthur), 803
rent control, 651
Republican National Committee, 870
Republican National Conventions:
  of 1944, 305
  of 1948, 629–30, 636
  of 1952, 903

Republican Party, 169–70, 585–86, 592, 624, 644
  Jewish votes and, 596
  1946 congressional elections won by, 523–24, 529–31, 627, 660, 813
  1950 congressional elections won by, 813–14
  see also election of 1948; elections; *specific individuals*
Resolution 71, 257, 258–59
Reston, James, 456, 515, 564, 781, 854, 891, 904
Results of County Planning, 177
Reuben James, 268
Reuther, Walter, 633, 781, 845
Reynolds, Frank A., 940
RFC (Reconstruction Finance Corporation), 863, 864, 865–66, 867, 869, 870
Rhee, Syngman, 780, 832
Rice, John, 860
"Richard Cory" (Robinson), 70
Richardson, Seth, 552
Richetti, Adam, 201
Rickenbacker, Eddie, 129, 150
Ricketts, Floyd, 118, 126, 127
Ridge, Albert, 117, 709
Ridgway, Matthew, 79, 786, 787, 794, 795, 815, 823
  in Korean War, 831, 832, 833–35, 843, 848
Riedel, Richard, 270–71, 281
Rigdon, William, 369, 434
Roberts, Roy, 309, 353, 525, 696, 819
Robeson, Paul, 645
Robinson, Edwin Arlington, 70
Robinson, Harold, 260
Robinson, Joseph T., 216, 227
Robinson, S. M., 267
Rockefeller, John D., 178, 705
Rogers, Ginger, 674
Rogers, Will, 214, 220, 691
Romania, 373, 374, 383, 421, 432, 445, 450, 544, 565
Roosevelt, Alice, 567, 672, 886
Roosevelt, Eleanor, 293, 295, 298, 302, 322, 337, 356, 361, 365, 373, 382, 386, 402, 411, 482, 506, 575, 577, 582, 598, 605, 607, 612, 761, 845, 961, 969
  HST endorsed by, 702
  husband's death and, 342, 346, 358
Roosevelt, Elliott, 612
Roosevelt, Franklin, Jr., 612, 781
Roosevelt, Franklin Delano, 148, 169, 193, 195, 196, 201, 202, 203, 206, 207, 220, 224, 225, 241, 244, 252, 314, 347–48, 359, 362, 363, 370, 372, 374, 377, 381, 385, 386, 468, 509–10, 511, 522, 527,

INDEX

Russell, Richard B., Jr., 458, 641, 852, 904, 905

S-1, *see* Manhattan Project
St. Louis *Globe-Democrat,* 208, 281–82
St. Louis *Post-Dispatch,* 209, 212, 215, 240, 242, 248, 249, 285, 310, 313, 321, 363, 456, 502, 514, 574, 697, 846, 866
St. Louis *Star-Times,* 174
Saint-Mihiel, 124–25, 131
Salisbury, Frank O., 522
Salisbury, Spencer, 108, 172
Saltonstall, Leverett, 339, 550, 983
San Antonio *Express,* 676
Sanderson, Julia, 90, 230
San Francisco Conference (1945), 339, 347, 355, 362, 376, 384, 398
San Francisco *Examiner,* 549
Sargent, John Singer, 885
Sato, Naotake, 413, 425, 460
Saturday Evening Post, 482, 492, 714
Saturday Review, 847, 927
Saudi Arabia, 597, 601
Sawyer, Aaron, 50
Sawyer, Charles, 890, 899
Schenectady, 273, 274, 275–76
Scherer, Ray, 930
Schlesinger, Arthur, Jr., 510, 893
Schneider, Edward L., 239
Schoeneman, George J., 871
Schultheiss, Paul, 953
Schwartz, Harry, 252
Schwellenbach, Lewis, 213, 245, 252, 286, 289–90, 387, 388, 494, 495, 497, 566
Scott, Hazel, 576
Scouten, Rex, 808, 881
Seattle *Times,* 846
Sebald, William, 835
Secretary of Defense, creation of office of, 476, 483, 566, 571
Secret Service, U.S., 333, 335, 341, 348, 353, 361, 364, 510, 513, 588, 655, 656, 678, 705–6, 727, 736, 750, 758, 808, 880, 881, 928, 982–83
  assassination attempt and, 809–13
  at Potsdam, 406, 408
Senate, U.S.:
  Appropriations Committee, 217, 229, 254
  Committee to Audit and Control the Contingent Expenses of the Senate, 257
  District of Columbia Committee, 218
  Hoey Committee, 744, 745–46
  HST's career in, 213–332
  Interstate Commerce Committee, 213, 217, 218
  Kefauver Committee, 864–65

Military Affairs Committee, 254, 257
  Nye Committee, 258
  Printing Committee, 217
  Public Buildings and Grounds Committee, 217
  Special Committee to Investigate the National Defense Program, *see* Truman Committee
  Tydings Committee, 766, 769–70, 773–774
  see also Congress, U.S.
Sermon, Roger T., 108, 128, 136, 191, 244, 402, 496, 710, 724
Sevareid, Eric, 192, 253, 271, 754, 921, 992
Seward, William H., 27
Shakespeare, William, 281, 560
Shanghai, 392–93
Shannon, Joseph B., 156–57, 166, 170, 173, 186, 195, 204, 209, 244
Shannon, William V., 502
Shaw, George W., 162, 164
Shaw, Mary, 190
Sherman, Forrest, 777, 778, 796, 862
Sherman, William Tecumseh, 476
Shertok, Moshe, 615
Sherwood, Robert, 331, 482
Short, Dewey, 852
Short, Joe, 820, 842, 843, 858, 862, 866, 899, 902, 910
Shostakovich, Dmitri, 419
Siddeley, Armstrong, 958
Siegel, Benjamin "Bugsy," 864
Silver, Abba Hillel, 598–99, 602
Simpson, Caroline, 45, 46
Simpson, "Letch," 45, 47
Singapore, 271
Slaughter, Elizabeth, 76
Slaughter, O. V., 76, 78, 89, 162
Slaughter, Roger C., 508
Slaughter, Stephen, 78, 86, 89, 95
slavery, 18, 22, 26–28, 29, 53
Sloan, Samuel A., 610
Smith, Alfred E., 169, 609, 701, 713, 970
Smith, Ellison DuRant "Cotton Ed," 216
Smith, Harold D., 369, 473
Smith, Ira, 386
Smith, Jabez, 18
Smith, Joseph, 22
Smith, Margaret Chase, 770
Smith, Merriman, 387, 453, 454, 455, 523–524, 820, 821
Smith, Walter Bedell, 540, 665, 808, 822
Smith-Connally Act (1943), 528
Smyth, James G., 870, 871
Snyder, Drucie, 503
Snyder, John, 229, 244, 245, 308, 309, 351, 357, 388, 451, 471, 497, 502, 503, 507

1106

PHOTO CREDITS

SECTION 1

SECTION 2

SECTION 3

Also available by
DAVID McCULLOUGH

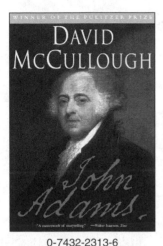

This epic biography unfolds the adventurous life-journey of John Adams, the brilliant, fiercely independent, often irascible, always honest Yankee patriot who spared nothing in his zeal for the American Revolution and who rose to become the second President of the United States.

"**A masterwork** of storytelling." —Walter Isaacson, *Time*

0-7432-2313-6

The Path Between the Seas tells the story of the men and women who fought against all odds to fulfill the 400-year-old dream of constructing an aquatic passageway between the Atlantic and Pacific oceans.

"David McCullough's history of this extraordinary construction job…is everything history ought to be. It is dramatic, accurate… and **altogether gripping**." —*The Washington Star*

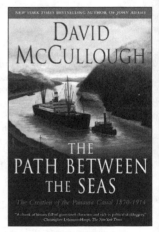

0-671-24409-4

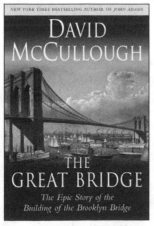

Celebrating the centennial of the opening of the Brooklyn Bridge, The Great Bridge is the classic account of one of the greatest engineering feats of all time.

"*The Great Bridge* is a book so compelling and complete as to be a literary monument, **one of the best books I have read in years**." —Robert Kirsch, *The Los Angeles Times*

0-671-45711-X

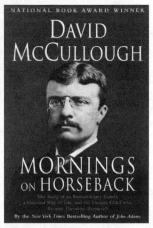

0-671-44754-8

Mornings on Horseback, the brilliant biography of the young Theodore Roosevelt was the winner of the *Los Angeles Times* 1981 Book Prize for Biography and the National Book Award for Biography.

"A **beautifully told** story, filled with fresh detail."
—*The New York Times Book Review*

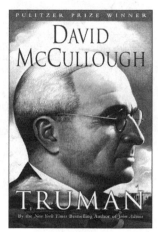

0-671-86920-5

This deeply moving biography of the seemingly ordinary "man from Missouri" who was perhaps the most courageous president in our history was the winner of the 1993 Pulitzer Prize.

"Warm, affectionate and **thoroughly captivating**."
—*The New York Times Book Review*

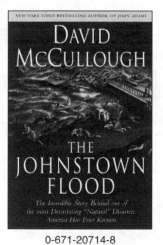

0-671-20714-8

The Johnstown Flood, David McCullough's first book, was praised by *Time* magazine as a "meticulously researched, vivid account of one of the most stunning disasters in U.S. history."

"A suburb job, scholarly, yet **vivid**, balanced yet **incisive**."
—*The New York Times*

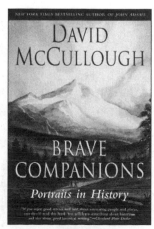

0-671-79276-8

McCullough has collected his favorite pieces —profiles of exceptional men and women past and present who have not only shaped the course of history or changed how we see the world but whose stories express much that is timeless about the human condition.

"**All his subjects come alive**."
—*The Dallas Morning News*

SIMON & SCHUSTER PAPERBACKS
A VIACOM COMPANY